Employment Law

To my parents
(M.R.)

Employment Law

General Editor

MAEVE REGAN

BCL, LLM (NUI), Solicitor

Published by
Tottel Publishing Ltd
Maxwelton House
41–43 Boltro Road
Haywards Heath
West Sussex
RH16 1BJ

Tottel Publishing Ltd
The Fitzwilliam Business Centre
26 Upper Pembroke Street
Dublin 2

ISBN: 978 1 84766 162 3
© Tottel Publishing 2009
Reprinted 2009

British Library Cataloguing-in-Publication Data
A catalogue record for this book is available from the British Library

Typeset by Marlex Editorial Services Ltd., Dublin, Ireland
Printed in the UK by
CPI William Clowes Beccles NR34 7TL

AUTHORS

Marguerite Bolger	Padraic Lyons
Niall Buckley	Cathy Maguire
Gary Byrne	Terence McCrann
Sinead Casey	Cathal McGreal
Ger Connolly	Michelle Ní Longáin
Bryan Dunne	Rory O'Boyle
Marie Griffin	Bairbre O'Neill
Imelda Higgins	Dr Mary Redmond
Conor Hurley	Maeve Regan
Jo Kenny	Des Ryan
Anthony Kerr	Philip Smith
Clíona Kimber	Janice Walshe
Kevin Langford	Emmet Whelan

Notes on the Authors

MAEVE REGAN
BCL, LLM, Dip Employment Law (NUI), Solicitor

Maeve Regan is a solicitor. She trained with Arthur Cox and upon qualification joined the Arthur Cox Employment Law Group, with whom she worked for two years, advising on all aspects of employment law prior to commencing the editorship of Employment Law. She is a consultant to, and examiner on, the Law Society Diploma in Employment Law.

MARGUERITE BOLGER
LLB, M Litt (Dub), Barrister-at-Law (Hon Society of King's Inns)

Marguerite Bolger is a practising barrister specialising in employment law. She is the co-author of *Sex Discrimination Law in Ireland* (Round Hall Sweet & Maxwell, 2000) with Clíona Kimber. She is currently working, with Clíona Kimber, on a new edition of *Sex Discrimination Law in Ireland*. She is a regular contributor to publications and conferences on employment law. She is a member of the Editorial Board of the *Irish Employment Law Review* and is the external examiner in employment law at the Honorable Society of King's Inns.

NIALL F BUCKLEY
BCL (NUI), Barrister-at-Law (Hon Society of King's Inns), LLM (University of London)

Niall Buckley is a practising barrister and works in the area of employment law. He is also a part-time lecturer in contract law in Dublin Institute of Technology.

GARY BYRNE
BCL (NUI), Solicitor, Fellow of the Chartered Institute of Arbitrators

Gary Byrne is a partner with the firm of BCM Hanby Wallace and, prior to that, was a founding partner of Byrne, Collins, Moran (BCM). He joined what was then the Federated Union of Employers, now the Irish Business and Employers Confederation (IBEC) in 1979, where he set up the legal department. He later returned to private practice in which, over the years, he has built up an extensive employment law practice. With BCM Hanby Wallace, he has been head of Employment Law, Managing Partner and was recently appointed head of Commercial Litigation. He is the author of *Transfer of Undertakings: Employment Aspects of Business Transfers in Irish and European Law* (Blackhall Publishing, 1999). He is co-author of the Law Society of Ireland *Employment Law* manual (Oxford University Press), which is currently in its second edition.

SINEAD CASEY
LLB (Dub), Dip Employment Law (Law Society of Ireland), Dip Corporate Governance (Law Society of Ireland), Solicitor

Sinead Casey joined Arthur Cox in September 2006 and recently qualified as an associate in the Employment Law Group specialising in all aspects of employment and industrial relations law, including the management of ongoing employee issues, grievance and disciplinary proceedings and employment disputes such as unfair dismissal, trade disputes, equality and discrimination claims.

GER CONNOLLY
BCL, Dip Employment Law (NUI), Solicitor

Ger Connolly is a senior associate in the Matheson Ormbsy Prentice Employment Pensions and Benefits Group, where he advises on a variety of aspects of employment law, both contentious and non-contentious. Ger has extensive experience of advising on all areas of employment law, employers' liability and health and safety at work. He advises on a broad range of contentious issues such as: discrimination; bullying and harassment; stress at work; wrongful and unfair dismissal and redundancies; both individual and collective; and industrial relations. He also advises clients on the conduct of internal investigations of disciplinary/bullying and harassment complaints. On the non-contentious side, he advises on all employment issues arising in connection with business acquisitions/re-organisations and transfer of undertakings and in the negotiation and drafting of service agreements. He has extensive experience in advising on immigration and is retained by a large number of both US and Asian companies to advise on their business immigration matters in Ireland.

BRYAN DUNNE
BA (University of Limerick), Dip Employment Law (NUI), Dip Commercial Law, Dip European Law (Law Society of Ireland), Solicitor

Bryan Dunne is a partner in the Matheson Ormbsy Prentice Employment Pensions and Benefits Group, where he covers all aspects of employment and labour law and practice, both contentious and non contentious He has extensive experience in advising on employment issues and structuring in commercial transactions, both in the public and private sector. He also regularly advises on international employment issues for both domestic and multi-national employers. He is a tutor and examiner on employment law in the Law Society of Ireland and is a regular speaker on Irish employment law at international conferences in Europe and the US.

MARIE GRIFFIN
BCL (NUI), Barrister-at-Law (Hon Society of Kings Inns), Member of the Institute of Tax of Ireland

Marie Griffin joined Postbank Ireland Limited as Head of Tax/Legal in March 2009. As Head of Tax, Marie is responsible for all aspects of the Bank's taxation policy and planning. Marie is responsible for advising on corporation tax, income tax, VAT, and taxation aspects of employment law. Prior to joining Postbank, she was a senior associate in the Arthur Cox Tax Group where she advised on a wide range of international and domestic tax matters, including taxation aspects of employment law. She also advised on taxation issues in the context of corporate reorganisations, mergers and acquisitions, securitisation transactions, inward investment and doing business in Ireland, tax planning for individuals and capital taxes generally.

IMELDA A HIGGINS
BCL, LLM (NUI), Barrister-at-Law (Hon Society of King's Inns)

Imelda Higgins is a practising barrister. Prior to joining the Bar she worked for a number of years at the Court of Justice of the European Communities in Luxembourg. She has also held several other legal positions, including that of in-house legal consultant. She has considerable practical expertise in employment law gained from her practice at the Bar, her work at the Court of Justice as well as her experience as an in-house legal consultant. In addition to this practical experience, she has published numerous articles on this topic. She was joint co-ordinator of the employment law module in the Barrister-At-Law Degree Course at the Honorable Society of King's Inns for a number of years. She has also lectured in employment law for the King's Inns, the Law Society as well as in the context of a number of academic degree courses and has presented at several employment law conferences both in Ireland and abroad.

CONOR HURLEY
BCL (NUI) Solicitor (Ireland; England and Wales), Associate of the Irish Taxation Institute

Conor Hurley is Head of Tax at Arthur Cox. Prior to joining Arthur Cox, he was a tax partner at international law firm Linklaters for over thirteen years. He advises on the tax aspects of a wide range of international and domestic mergers and acquisitions, employment and employee incentives, financial products, repackagings and structured finance, banking, capital markets, investment funds, corporate recovery, insolvency, restructuring and other areas. He has written numerous articles and spoken at many conferences on various aspects of international and domestic tax.

JO KENNY
MA (Hons) (University of St Andrews), Barrister (Lincoln's Inn)

Jo Kenny is an associate in the Arthur Cox Pensions Group. Jo advises on a wide range of pension matters, including pension aspects of employment law. She also advises on pension issues in the context of mergers and acquisitions and reorganisations. She is a member of the Association of Pension Lawyers in Ireland.

ANTHONY KERR
BA (Mod), (Dub), LLM (London School of Economics), MA (Dub), Barrister-at-Law (Hon Society of King's Inns)

Anthony Kerr is a Statutory Lecturer in the School of Law, University College Dublin where he is the Course Director of the School's Professional Diploma in Employment Law. He has been a Jean Monnet Fellow at the European University Institute and has published extensively as well as editing both the Dublin University Law Journal and the Journal of the Irish Society for Labour Law. He is a member of the Executive

Committee of the International Society for Labour Law and Social Security and is the Irish representative on the European Labour Law Network. He is recognised as a Level One Expert by the European Commission for whom he prepared the 2006 Synthesis Report on *Termination of Employment Relationships: The Legal Situation in the Member States of the European Union*.

CLÍONA KIMBER
LLB, MA (Dub), LLM (University of British Columbia), Barrister-at-Law (Hon Society of King's Inns)

Clíona Kimber is a practising barrister specialising in labour law and equality law. She regularly appears before the High Court, Circuit Court, Employment Appeals Tribunal, Equality Tribunal and Labour Court. She is the author of *Disability Discrimination Law* (Oak Tree Press, 1993) (with Maeve McDonagh and Gerard Quinn) and *Sex Discrimination Law in Ireland* (Round Hall Sweet & Maxwell, 2000) (with Marguerite Bolger). She is currently working, with Marguerite Bolger, on a new edition of *Sex Discrimination Law in Ireland*. She is editor of the *Employment Law Reports* and the *Irish Employment Law Journal*, the leading periodicals in the area of employment law. She is a regular speaker at conferences and seminars on employment and equality law, and advises major Irish companies on labour law and equality issues.

KEVIN LANGFORD
LLB (Dub), Solicitor

Kevin Langford is a partner in the Employment Law Group of Arthur Cox and specialises in all aspects of employment and industrial relations law. His practice includes advisory work as well as representation of employers in employment disputes such as unfair dismissal, trade disputes, equality and discrimination claims. Kevin has published many articles on various topics of employment law and frequently lectures in the area, including to the Law Society of Ireland. Kevin joined Arthur Cox in 2001, having previously held the position of in-house legal advisor with the Irish Business and Employers Confederation (IBEC).

PADRAIC LYONS
LLB (Dub), Barrister-at-Law (Hon. Society of King's Inns)

Padraic Lyons is a barrister practising in the area of employment law.

CATHY MAGUIRE
BCL, LLM (by research) (NUI), Barrister-at-Law (Hon Society of King's Inns)

Cathy Maguire is a barrister practicing in employment and trade union law. She is the author of *Trade Union Membership and the Law* (Round Hall Sweet & Maxwell, 1999) and co-author of *Irish Perspectives on EC Law* (Round Hall, 2003) and *Practical Employment Law* (Thomson Professional Information, Looseleaf, 2000). She was editor of the *Employment Law Reports* (Round Hall Sweet & Maxwell) from 1998 to 2000.

CATHAL MCGREAL
BCL (Eurolegal) (NUI), Barrister-at-Law (Hon Society of King's Inns)

Cathal McGreal is a practising barrister specialising in employment law and criminal law and has appeared on behalf of clients at every level of the Irish judicial and quasi-judicial legal system. He lectures widely throughout the Republic of Ireland and the United Kingdom for continuing professional development. He has, for the past 10 years, lectured post-graduate students at the Smurfit School of Business and the School of Industrial Relations in UCD and contributes annually to the UCD School of Law's Professional Diploma in Employment Law. He is the author of *The Criminal Justice (Theft and Fraud Offences) Act 2001 Annotated* (Round Hall, 2003).

BAIRBRE O'NEILL
BCL (NUI), LLM (Dub), LLM (*O'Reilly Foundation Scholar; Rodney Overend Educational Trust Scholar*) (Yale University), Barrister-at-Law (Hon. Society of King's Inns)

Bairbre O'Neill is a barrister practising in the area of civil litigation, with a particular emphasis on commercial litigation, employment law, medical services and arbitration. Bairbre was called to the Irish Bar in 2001 and to the New York Bar in 2003. Prior to practising in Ireland, Bairbre worked as an attorney in the New York offices of Paul Weiss Rifkind Wharton & Garrison LLP and Cleary Gottlieb Steen & Hamilton LLP.

MICHELLE Ní LONGÁIN
LLB (Hons) (Queens University, Belfast), Solicitor (Ireland; Northern Ireland; England and Wales)

Michelle Ní Longáin is a partner in the BCM Hanby Wallace Employment Law Department. Michelle's main areas of practice are employment, equality and administrative law. She advises and represents many public and private sector clients nationally in all employment fora and courts. She is a member of the Council of the Law Society of Ireland and is the Vice Chair of its Education Committee and its Practice Management Task Force. She is also a member of the Litigation & Labour Law Committee of the Dublin Solicitors Bar Association. She regularly lectures on employment equality and equal status law, freedom of information and data protection legislation, administrative law and employment law generally. She is a co-author of both the Law Society of Ireland *Employment Law* and *Discrimination Law* manuals (Oxford University Press).

RORY O'BOYLE
BA, LLB (NUI), Dip Employment Law (NUI), Solicitor

Rory O'Boyle is a solicitor with the Law Society of Ireland where he is Secretary to the Employment & Equality Law Committee. He coordinates a number of diploma programmes including the Law Society's Diploma in Employment Law.

DR. MARY REDMOND
BCL, LLM (NUI), PhD (Cantab), Solicitor

Mary Redmond is Consultant Solicitor at Arthur Cox. A leading employment lawyer in Ireland with extensive knowledge of employment law and industrial relations, she advises many of Ireland's major companies. Author of several legal articles and of the standard text *Dismissal Law in Ireland* (Tottel, 2007), she was the first Irish woman solicitor to address the European Court of Justice in relation to job sharers in the civil service in 1998. She served during two terms on the Labour Relations Commission. She is an advocate of mediation in employment disputes and is an accredited CEDR mediator. Her non-executive directorships of public and private companies give her particular insight into the employment problems of commercial clients. Before practising law, Dr Redmond, former Winter Williams Commonwealth Scholar and British Council Scholar, lectured in the Law Faculty at University College Dublin and at Cambridge University where she received her PhD. She was a Fellow and Director of Studies in law at Christ's College and before that, at Churchill College Cambridge. In 2004 Dr. Redmond was made an Honorary Fellow of Christ's College, Cambridge.

DES RYAN
LLB (Dub), BCL, MA (Oxon), Barrister-at-Law (Hon Society of King's Inns), Lecturer in Law, Trinity College Dublin.

Des Ryan is a Lecturer in Law at Trinity College Dublin, where he lectures in both Employment Law and Employment Litigation to undergraduate and Masters degree students. His legal education included studying at Osgoode Hall Law School, Toronto and the University of Oxford, and he has been a Visiting Lecturer at the University of San Francisco School of Law. He is the Employment Law Correspondent for the Thomson Round Hall *Annual Review of Irish Law* and is co-editor of the *Employment Law Review* (FirstLaw).

JANICE WALSHE
BCL, LLM (Commercial Law) (NUI), Dip Employment Law (Law Society of Ireland), Solicitor

Janice Walshe is an associate in the BCM Hanby Wallace Employment Law Department. She advises on all aspects of employment law, including contracts of employment, terms and conditions of employment, disciplinary issues, employment equality and atypical work issues, redundancies, restrictive covenants, and transfer of undertakings. She has successfully represented clients before the Rights Commissioner, Labour Court, Employment Appeals Tribunal and Equality Tribunal, as well as before the Civil Courts. She has lectured on many aspects of employment law, and has regularly tutored in the Law Society of Ireland.

EMMET WHELAN
BCL, LLM (Commercial Law) (NUI), Dip Employment Law (Law Society of Ireland), Solicitor

Emmet Whelan is a solicitor in the BCM Hanby Wallace Employment Law Department. He advises on a wide range of statutory rights including payment of wages, minimum notice, terms of employment, working time and redundancy with a specialisation in employment claims before the Rights Commissioner, Employment Appeals Tribunal and Equality Tribunal.

ADVISORY COUNCIL

Marguerite Bolger
Dr Kevin Costello
Marcus Dowling
Anthony Kerr
Clíona Kimber
Peggy O'Rourke
Dr Mary Redmond
Dr Gerry Whyte

The Arthur Cox Foundation

Arthur Cox, solicitor, classical scholar and former president of the Incorporated Law Society of Ireland, was associated with the setting up of many Irish companies, not least the ESB. He was a specialist in company law and was a member of the Company Law Reform Committee which sat from 1951 and reported to the Government in 1958, ultimately giving rise to the Companies Act 1963. When he decided to retire from practice as a solicitor in 1961 a number of his clients, professional colleagues and other friends, in recognition of his outstanding contribution to Ireland and his profession, thought that a fund should be established as a tribute to him which fund would be used to encourage the writing and publication of legal text books. There was a generous response to this appeal.

After his retirement Arthur Cox studied for the priesthood and was ordained in 1963. He went to Zambia to do missionary work. He died there in 1965 as a result of a car accident.

The Foundation was established to honour Arthur Cox and was for many years administered by Mr. Justice John Kenny in conjunction with the Law Society. John Kenny was the encouraging force behind the publication of a number of Irish legal textbooks. Without his quiet drive and enthusiasm there would have been no Foundation. To both Arthur Cox and John Kenny we pay tribute.

The Foundation's funds have been used to assist the writing and publication of Irish legal textbooks and the development of electronic databases of Irish legal materials. The Foundation has recently inaugurated an annual prize for the best overall results in the business and corporate law modules of the Law Society's Professional Practice Courses.

The Law Society, as the continuing trustee of the Foundation, is pleased to have been able to assist in the publication of this book.

John D Shaw
President
Law Society of Ireland

February 2009

Preface

The idea for this book was to create a comprehensive and definitive text on Irish employment law. What began as this idea, in late 2006, has been developed into this book, which brings together the expertise and writing of employment, tax and pensions lawyers. It is our hope that this book will be of use to students, lawyers, those involved in advising and managing working relationships and anyone who simply wishes to have at their fingertips a clear and comprehensive textbook on employment law. It is intended that later editions will build on the foundations that have been laid here in this first edition. In this respect, it is our hope that Employment Law will be a work in progress for years to come.

This book could not have been created without the help and encouragement of a number of people. I am profoundly grateful to Dr Mary Redmond, whose clarity and belief in this work from the moment the idea first appeared through to the final stages of the creation of this book were simply invaluable. I wish to express my deep gratitude to Amy Hayes, Managing Editor at Tottel Publishing. With patience, cheer and tremendous skill, she firmly and steadily guided the idea to realisation. Thanks also to Marian Sullivan, for her meticulous work in typesetting the book, and to Jennifer Lynch in Tottel, whose energy and enthusiasm in marketing Employment Law was infectious. Anthony Kerr's advice, painstaking attention to detail and interest in this work and Marguerite Bolger and Clíona Kimber's concern and vigour helped immensely in keeping focus on the quality of this work. The Arthur Cox Foundation provided fundamental support at the very beginning of this project. I am very grateful to Margaret Byrne, secretary of the Foundation and Law Society Head Librarian, for her help.

I would like to thank Mary Forde for her generosity and for her calm, bright encouragement which gave focus and perspective countless times in this project. Thanks also to Claire Higgins who patiently provided advice and encouragement that grounded the belief in the sense of doing this book. To Freda Mahon for her deeply steadying hand. Thanks to Tina Rowland for her inspiring and enlightening kindness and support. To Emma McHenry, Orlaith Ryan and Mary-Louise O'Loughlin for assuring quite simply that this would be done. To Claire O'Callaghan for care and friendship, regardless of distance. Thanks also to Bríd Jordan, for her constant willingness to help and listen. To Caragh Egan and Simon Egan for laughs and for a burst of fun just when it was really needed. Thanks to Adrian Regan whose voice of wisdom, calmly and kindly, guided me in keeping the decks clear to complete this book. Thanks to Jarlath Regan, for his unrelenting understanding and for his humour, vision and integrity, which were at the heart of this work. Thanks to my parents, Máire and Tady (Adrian) Regan. At a crucial time, they stepped forward and enabled this book to happen. They listened without judgment, supported without question and shone gentle light when at times it seemed to disappear from the journey of this project. My work on this book was done in memory of my grandmother, Mary Regan. It is dedicated to my parents.

Maeve Regan

Kildare, 8 May 2009

Contents

Part I
Employment Law: Sources and Institutions

Chapter 1   Sources and Institutions

Maeve Regan

Part II
The Employment Relationship

Chapter 2   The Contract and Relationship of Employment

Maeve Regan

Chapter 3   The Terms of the Employment Contract

Janice Walshe

Chapter 4   Working Time

Padraic Lyons and Emmet Whelan

Chapter 5   Protective Leave

Rory O'Boyle and Michelle Ní Longáin

Chapter 6   Workplace Privacy and Data Protection

Cathal McGreal

Chapter 7   Bullying, Harassment and Stress at Work

Des Ryan

Chapter 8   Vicarious Liability

Des Ryan

Chapter 9   Part-Time Workers

Des Ryan

Chapter 10   Fixed-Term Workers

Des Ryan

Part III
Pay, Pensions, and Benefits

Chapter 11   Pay, Pensions and Benefits

Jo Kenny and Philip Smith

Part IV
Employers' Insolvency

Chapter 12   Insolvency

Imelda Higgins

Part VI
Termination of Employment

Chapter 14   Dismissal

Dr Mary Redmond

Chapter 15   Redundancy

Imelda Higgins and Terence McCrann

Part VII
Collective Aspects of the Employment Relationship

Chapter 16   Employee Involvement

Sinead Casey, Kevin Langford and Bairbre O'Neill

Chapter 17   Trade Unions

Cathy Maguire

Chapter 18   Industrial Relations Law

Anthony Kerr

Part VIII
Transfer of Undertakings

Chapter 19   Transfer of Undertakings

Gary Byrne

Part IX
Immigration and International Employment

Chapter 20   Immigration and International Employment

Niall Buckley, Ger Connolly and Bryan Dunne

Immigration

Niall Buckley and Ger Connolly

International employment

Bryan Dunne

Part X
Taxation

Chapter 21   Taxation

Marie Griffin and Conor Hurley

Part XI
Practice and Procedure in Employment Law

Chapter 22   Practice and Procedure in Employment Law

Anthony Kerr and Cathal McGreal

Appendices: Codes of Practice

Appendix A: Atypical Employees

Appendix B: Working Time

Appendix C: Bullying and Harassment

Appendix D: Part-Time Workers

Appendix E: Employee Involvement

Appendix F: Dismissal

Appendix G: Trade Unions

Appendix H: Industrial Relations

Table of Cases

C

D

F

G

H

I

J

P

Q

R

S

T

U

V

Table of Legislation

Bunreacht na hÉireann

European Legislation

International Conventions and Treaties

Other Jurisdictions

Statutory Instruments

Part I
Employment Law: Sources and Institutions

Chapter 1

Sources and Institutions

Maeve Regan

SOURCES

[1.01] Employment law is derived from a number of sources: the Constitution, legislation, common law and international law. The balance between these sources is continuously changing. At times common law has been at the cutting edge of the evolution of employment law.[1] At other times, most notably in the 1970s with the enactment of several important employment law statutes,[2] legislation has been the frontrunner in development of the law. This book considers all of these sources of employment law.

Common law

[1.02] Common law is judge-made law. Common law, in the context of employment and labour law, is principally concerned with the law of contract and the law of tort. Claims relating to employment that arise out of the contract of employment, such as dismissal in breach of contract, or from the tortious duty of care of the employer, are within the remit of the courts. The common law has implied terms into the employment contract that are considered to flow from the very nature of the contract. Among the most important are the employer's common law duty of care, the duty to maintain trust and confidence and the duty of good faith and loyalty.[3]

Legislation

[1.03] Since the 1970s, statute has become an increasingly lively source of Irish employment law. In general, the core employment legislation lays down the minimum threshold of employment rights protection. Legislation, in the form of Acts and Statutory Instruments, provides for matters such as working time, minimum wage, health and safety, information and consultation, termination of employment, redundancy, protective leave, the transfer of a business and equality. The legislation imposes terms into the employment contract.

---

[1] See, for example, the discussion of the mutual implied obligation of trust and confidence in Ch 14, Dismissal, paras **[14.24]–[14.33]**.

[2] The Holidays (Employees) Act 1973, the Minimum Notice and Terms of Employment Act 1973, the Anti-Discrimination (Pay) Act 1974, the Employment Equality Act 1977, the Unfair Dismissals Act 1977, the Worker Participation (State Enterprises) Act 1977, the Protection of Young Persons (Employment) Act 1977 and the Protection of Employment Act 1977.

[3] See Ch 3, The Terms of the Employment Contract.

Among the most important employment statutes are the:

(i)   Redundancy Payments Acts 1967–2007;

(ii)   Industrial Relations Acts 1969–2004;

(iii)   Unfair Dismissals Acts 1977–2007;

(iv)   Protection of Employees (Employers' Insolvency) Act 1984;

(v)   Payment of Wages Act 1991;

(vi)   Minimum Notice and Terms of Employment (Information) Acts 1994–2001;

(vii)   Maternity Protection Acts 1994 and 2004;

(viii)   Adoptive Leave Acts 1995 and 2005;

(ix)   Protection of Young Persons (Employment) Act 1996;

(x)   Organisation of Working Time Act 1997;

(xi)   Parental Leave Acts 1998 and 2006;

(xii)   Employment Equality Acts 1998–2008;

(xiii)   National Minimum Wage Act 2000;

(xiv)   Carer's Leave Act 2001;

(xv)   Protection of Employees (Part-Time Work) Act 2001;

(xvi)   Protection of Employees (Fixed-Term Work) Act 2003;

(vii)   EC (Protection of Employees on Transfer of Undertakings) Regulations 2003;

(xviii)   Safety, Health and Welfare at Work Act 2005;

(xix)   Employees (Provision of Information and Consultation) Act 2006; and

(xx)   Employment Permits Act 2006.

The Constitution

[1.04] Articles 40–44 of the Constitution are entitled 'Fundamental Rights'. Among the most important of these rights in the context of employment law are:

Equality

Article 40.1: All citizens shall, as human persons, be held equal before the law. This shall not be held to mean that the State shall not in its enactments have due regard to differences of capacity, physical and moral, and of social function.

Good Name

Article 40.3.2°: The State shall, in particular, by its laws protect as best it may from unjust attack and, in the case of injustice done, vindicate the life, person, good name, and property rights of every citizen.

Freedom of Expression

Article 40.6.1°: The State guarantees liberty for the exercise of the following rights, subject to public order and morality:

(i)   The right of the citizens to express freely their convictions and opinions…

(ii)   The right of the citizens to assemble peaceably and without arms…

(iii)   The right of the citizens to form associations and unions.

Laws, however, may be enacted for the regulation and control in the public interest of the exercise of the foregoing right.

Freedom of Association

Article 40.6.2°: Laws regulating the manner in which the right of forming associations and unions and the right of free assembly may be exercised shall contain no political, religious or class discrimination.

Freedom of Religion

Article 44.2.3°: The State shall not impose any disabilities or make any discrimination on the ground of religious profession, belief or status.

Unenumerated Rights

Article 40.3.1°: The State guarantees by its laws to respect and, as far as practicable, by its laws to defend and vindicate the personal rights of the citizen.

Article 40.3.1°: has been held to provide the basis for the enumeration of other rights, not expressly guaranteed by the Constitution.

The High Court and Supreme Court in *Ryan v the Attorney General*[4] declared clearly for the first time that Article 40.3 contained unspecified personal rights beyond those expressly enumerated.[5] Kenny J held:[6]

> In my opinion, the High Court has jurisdiction to consider whether an Act of the Oireachtas respects and, as far as practicable, defends and vindicates the personal rights of the citizen and to declare the legislation unconstitutional if it does not. I think that the personal rights which may be involved to invalidate legislation are not confined to those specified in Article 40 but include all those rights which result from the Christian and democratic nature of the State ...If it extends to personal rights other than those specified in Article 40, the High Court and Supreme Court have the difficult and responsible duty of ascertaining and declaring what are the personal rights of the citizen which are guaranteed by the Constitution ... the general guarantee in sub-s.1° must extend to rights not specified in Article 40 ... there are many personal rights of the citizen which follow from the Christian and democratic nature of the State which are not mentioned in Article 40 at all – the right to free movement within the State and right to marry are examples of this. This also leads to the conclusion that the general guarantee extends to rights not specified in Article 40.

The Supreme Court agreed with this interpretation:

> The Court agrees with Kenny J that the 'personal rights' mentioned in section 3.1° are not exhausted by the enumeration of 'life, person, good name, and property rights' in section 3.2°, as is shown by the use of the words 'in particular'; nor by the more detached treatment of specific rights in the subsequent sections of the Article. To attempt to make a list of all the rights which may properly fall within the category of 'personal rights' would be difficult ....[7]

---

4   *Ryan v the Attorney General* [1963] IR 294.
5   See further Hogan & Whyte, *Kelly: The Irish Constitution* (4th edn, Tottel Publishing, 2003).
6   *Ryan v the Attorney General* [1963] IR 294 at 312–313.
7   *Ryan v the Attorney General* [1963] IR 294 at 344–345, Ó Dálaigh CJ.

A number of rights of importance to employment law have been found to be encompassed by the guarantee of Art 40.3. The right to work and earn a livelihood was clearly recognised in *Murphy v Stewart*,[8] the right to individual privacy was successfully invoked in *Kennedy v Ireland*,[9] the right to fair procedures was identified in *Re Padraig Haughey*[10] and in *Glover v BLN Ltd*,[11] and the right to strike was recognised in *Brendan Dunne Ltd v Fitzpatrick*[12] and *Educational Co v Fitzpatrick (No 2)*.[13]

The European Convention on Human Rights

[1.05] The European Convention on Human Rights (the Convention) obliges states who are party to the Convention to secure to everyone within their jurisdiction rights and freedoms defined in the Convention. The provisions of most potential influence to employment law are:

Privacy

Article 8.1: Everyone has the right to respect for his private and family life, his home and his correspondence.

Freedom of thought, conscience and religion

Article 9.1: Everyone has the right to freedom of thought, conscience and religion; this right includes freedom to change his religion or belief and freedom, either alone or in the community with others and in public or private, to manifest his religion or belief, in worship, teaching, practice and observance.

Article 9.2: Freedom to manifest one's religion or beliefs shall be subject only to such limitations as are prescribed by law and are necessary in a democratic society in the interests of public safety, for the protection of public order, health or morals, or for the protection of the rights and freedoms of others.

Freedom of Expression

Article 10.1: Everyone has the right to freedom of expression. This right shall include freedom to hold opinions and to receive and impart information and ideas without interference by public authority and regardless of frontiers...

Article 10.2: The exercise of these freedoms, since it carries with it duties and responsibilities, may be subject to such formalities, conditions, restrictions or penalties as are prescribed by law and are necessary in a democratic society, in the interests of national security, territorial integrity or public safety, for the prevention of disorder or crime, for the protection of health or morals, for the protection of the reputation or rights of others, for preventing the disclosure of information received in confidence, or for maintaining the authority and impartiality of the judiciary.

---

8 *Murphy v Stewart* [1973] IR 97.
9 *Kennedy v Ireland* [1987] IR 587.
10 *Re Padraig Haughey* [1971] IR 217.
11 *Glover v BLN Ltd* [1973] IR 388.
12 *Brendan Dunne Ltd v Fitzpatrick* [1958] IR 29.
13 *Educational Co v Fitzpatrick (No 2)* [1961] IR 345.

Freedom of Assembly and Association

Article 11.1: Everyone has the right to peaceful assembly and to freedom of association with others, including the right to form and to join trade unions for the protection of his interests.

Article 11.2: No restrictions shall be placed on the exercise of these rights other than such as are prescribed by law and are necessary in a democratic society in the interests of national security or public safety, for the prevention of disorder or crime, for the protection of health or morals or for the protection of the rights and freedoms of others. This article shall not prevent the imposition of lawful restrictions on the exercise of these rights by members of the armed forces, of the police or of the administration of the State.

Prohibition of Discrimination

Article 14: The enjoyment of the rights and freedoms set forth in this Convention shall be secured without discrimination on any ground such as sex, race, colour, language, religion, political or other opinion, national or social origin, association with a national minority, property, birth or other status.

[1.06] The Convention was incorporated into Irish law by the European Convention on Human Rights Act 2003. The long title to the Act describes the Act as:

An Act to enable further effect to be given, subject to the Constitution, to certain provisions of the Convention for the protection of human rights and fundamental freedoms done at Rome on the 4th day of November 1950 and certain protocols thereto, to amend the Human Rights Commission Act 2000 and to provide for related matter.

The Act provides for interpretative incorporation of the Convention at sub-constitutional level. Section 2(1) of the European Convention on Human Rights Act 2003 provides:

In interpreting and applying any statutory provision or rule of law, a court shall, in so far as possible, subject to the rules of law relating to such interpretation and application, do so in a manner compatible with the State's obligations under the Convention provisions.

Section 3 obliges State organs to perform their functions in a manner which is compatible with the State's obligations under the Convention. This section created a new avenue of redress in the form of an action in tort for breach of statutory duty by an organ of the State. Section 5(1) provides for declarations of incompatibility:

In any proceedings, the High Court, or the Supreme Court when exercising its appellate jurisdiction, may, having regard to the provisions of section 2, on application to it in that behalf by a party or of its own motion, and where no other legal remedy is adequate and available, make a declaration (referred to in this Act as a 'declaration of incompatibility') that a statutory provision or rule of law is incompatible with the State's obligations under the Convention provisions.'

Section 5(2)(a) provides that a declaration of incompatibility:

[s]hall not affect the validity, continued operation or enforcement of the statutory provision or rule of law in respect of which it is made.

Where there is a declaration of incompatibility, the Taoiseach must notify the Houses of the Oireachtas of the declaration and the Government may make an *ex gratia* compensation payment to the party claiming injury due to the incompatibility.[14]

---

[14] European Convention on Human Rights Act 2003, ss 5(3) and 5(4).

The impact of the Convention on employment law has been limited, principally due to the strong protections provided by the Constitution.[15] However, the Convention has potential to influence the interpretation of rights to fair procedures, privacy and freedom of association and expression.[16]

INSTITUTIONS[17]

The Labour Relations Commission

Origin

[1.07] The Labour Relations Commission was established on 21 January 1991 under s 24 of the Industrial Relations Act 1990. The then Minister for Labour, Bertie Ahern, detailed the background to the proposed new Commission:[18]

> The Bill now before the House provides a framework for the improved conduct of industrial relations and for the resolution of trade disputes, with the aim of maintaining a stable and orderly industrial relations climate. The Bill provides for major reform of the law on industrial relations, trade dispute and trade union law and for the establishment of a new Labour Relations Commission....
>
> The changes which the Bill provides for in relation to the dispute resolution machinery have four principal objectives: to give a new general responsibility for the promotion of better industrial relations to an appropriate body; to encourage and facilitate a more active approach to dispute prevention and resolution; to restore the original purpose and status of Labour Court investigation and recommendations; and to make provision for a number of new functions and services.
>
> The major change provided for is the establishment of a new Labour Relations Commission guided by a tripartite council, with employer, trade union and independent representation. In addition to the overall responsibility for the promotion of good industrial relations, the commission will have a wide range of functions including the provision of conciliation and advisory services and the development of codes of practice...

Structure

[1.08] The Labour Relations Commission is headed by a chief executive, appointed by the Minister for Enterprise, Trade and Employment after consultation with the Commission.[19] The Commission consists of a chairman and six ordinary members, two of which are workers' members, two employers' members and two members nominated

---

[15] See Hogan, 'The European Convention on Human Rights Act 2003' (2006) *EPL* 12(3) 331.

[16] See Law Society of Ireland, 'ECHR Act 2003, A Preliminary Assessment' (2006) and Bowers and Lightman, 'Incorporation of the ECHR and its impact on Employment Law' (1998) EHRLR 560–581.

[17] On practice and procedure of the fora involved in the resolution of employment rights disputes, see Ch 22, Practice and Procedure in Employment Law.

[18] Dáil Debates, Seanad Éireann – Volume 125 – 10 July 1990, Industrial Relations Bill 1989: Second Stage, columns 2081–2094.

[19] Industrial Relations Act 1990, s 28.

by the Minister.[20] The workers' members are nominated for appointment by organisations representative of trade unions of workers. The employers' members are nominated by organisations representative of employers. The ordinary members are part-time members of the Commission.[21]

The Minister can, with the consent of the Minister for Finance, appoint such staff as he thinks necessary to assist the Commission in the performance of its functions.[22] The Commission has appointed staff as industrial relations officers.[23] The 1990 Act provides that the officers shall perform any duties assigned to them by the Commission through its chairman or its chief executive officer and, in particular they shall assist in the prevention and settlement of trade disputes.[24] Industrial relations officers assist in the provision of the conciliation services and as chairpersons to a number of Joint Industrial Councils and Joint Labour Committees. From time to time, they also chair working groups of unions and management in various industries. The Commission may also appoint members of its staff, including industrial relations officers, to give advice on matters relating to industrial relations to management and workers or their representatives.[25] Advisory officers assist in the provision of the advisory services of the Commission.

Functions

[1.09] The Commission has general responsibility for promoting the improvement of industrial relations[26] and provides the following services:

   (i)   an industrial relations conciliation service;

   (ii)   an industrial relations advisory service;

   (iii) a Rights Commissioner service. This service is considered below; and the Commission also has particular functions, pursuant to s 202 of the Taxes Consolidation Act 1997, in relation to registered agreements providing for reductions in pay;

   (iv) a workplace mediation service; and

   (v)   assistance to Joint Labour Committees and Joint Industrial Councils.

The Commission also undertakes other activities of a more general kind including:[27]

   (i)   the review and monitoring of developments in the area of industrial relations;

   (ii)   the preparation, in consultation with the Social Partners, of codes of practice relevant to industrial relations;

   (iii) industrial relations research and publications;

---

20 Industrial Relations Act 1990, s 24(3) and Sch 4.
21 Industrial Relations Act 1990, Sch 4.
22 Industrial Relations Act 1990, s 32(1).
23 Industrial Relations Act 1990, s 33(1).
24 Industrial Relations Act 1990, s 33(2).
25 Industrial Relations Act 1990, s 33(3).
26 Industrial Relations Act 1990, s 25(1). This section details the functions of the Commission.
27 Industrial Relations Act 1990, s 25.

(iv)   organisation of seminars and conferences on industrial relations and human resource management issues.

The Rights Commissioner Service

Origin

[1.10] The Industrial Relations Act 1969 provided for the appointment by the Minister for Labour (now the Minister for Enterprise, Trade and Employment) of rights commissioners.[28] The Industrial Relations Act 1990 brought the Rights Commissioner Service under the aegis of the Labour Relations Commission.[29]

Structure

[1.11] Rights commissioners may be appointed for a term of up to three years[30] and can be reappointed for a further term or terms.[31] There are currently 14 rights commissioners.[32] Rights commissioners are appointed by the Minister for Enterprise Trade and Employment from a panel provided by the Commission.[33]

Functions

[1.12] Rights commissioners are empowered to hear claims under a range of Acts and Statutory Instruments:

(i)   Adoptive Leave Acts 1995 and 2005;

(ii)   Carers Leave Act 2001;

(iii)   Competition Acts 2002–2006;

(iv)   Employees (Information & Consultation) Act 2006;

(v)   Employment Permits Act 2006;

(vi)   Industrial Relations Acts 1969–1990;

(vii)   Industrial Relations (Miscellaneous Provisions) Act 2004 (claims of victimisation);

(viii)   Maternity Protection Acts 1994 and 2004;

(ix)   National Minimum Wage Act 2000;

(x)   Organisation of Working Time Act 1997;

(xi)   Parental Leave Acts 1998 and 2006;

(xii)   Payment of Wages Act 1991;

(xiii)   Protection of Employees (Fixed-Term Work) Act 2003;

(xiv)   Protection of Employees (Part-time Work) Act 2001;

(xv)   Protection of Young Persons (Employment) Act 1996;

---

[28]   Industrial Relations Act 1969, s 13(1).
[29]   Industrial Relations Act 1990, s 35(1).
[30]   Industrial Relations Act 1990, s 34(2).
[31]   Industrial Relations Act 1990, s 34(3).
[32]   Labour Relations Commission Annual Report 2007.
[33]   Industrial Relations Act 1969, s 13(1).

(xvi)   Protections for Persons Reporting Child Abuse Act 1998;

(xvii)   Safety, Health and Welfare at Work Act 2005;

(xviii) Terms of Employment (Information) Acts 1994–2001;

(xix)   Unfair Dismissals Acts 1977–2007;

(xx)   European Communities (Protection of Employment) Regulations 2000;

(xxi)   European Communities (Protection of Employees on Transfer of Undertakings) Regulations 2003; and

(xxii)   European Communities (European PLC) (Employee Involvement) Regulations 2006.

According to the 2007 Labour Relations Commission Annual Report, the majority of referrals to the Rights Commissioner Service are under the Payment of Wages Act, the Terms of Employment (Information) Acts, the Unfair Dismissals Acts, the Industrial Relations Acts and the Safety, Health and Welfare at Work Act.[34]

The Labour Court

Origin

[1.13] The Labour Court was established in 1946 under the Industrial Relations Act 1946.[35] It is an industrial relations tribunal and in dealing with industrial relations disputes, except for those heard under the Industrial Relations Acts 2001–2004, the Labour Court's jurisdiction is limited to making recommendations rather than enforceable determinations.

The 1946 Act gave the Labour Court functions in relation to the investigation of disputes and the issuing of recommendations on foot of such investigations,[36] the registration of employment agreements,[37] the establishment of joint labour committees,[38] the making and enforcement of employment regulation orders[39] and the registration of Joint Industrial Councils.[40] The Industrial Relations Act 1990 conferred powers on the Labour Court in relation to interpreting and investigating complaints of breach of codes of practice.[41] The Industrial Relations (Amendment) Act 2001 as amended by the Industrial Relations (Miscellaneous Provisions) Act 2004 provided for the investigation of disputes and binding determinations by the Labour Court where certain preconditions were satisfied in relation to the dispute.[42]

---

[34] On the jurisdiction of, and procedure before, Rights Commissioners, see Ch 22, Practice and Procedure in Employment Law, paras **[22.04]–[22.24]**.

[35] Industrial Relations Act 1946, s 10.

[36] Industrial Relations Act 1946, Part VI.

[37] Industrial Relations Act 1946, s 26.

[38] Industrial Relations Act 1946, s 35.

[39] Industrial Relations Act 1946, s 42.

[40] Industrial Relations Act 1946, s 60.

[41] Industrial Relations Act 1990, s 43.

[42] See further Ch 19, Industrial Relations.

Employment legislation relating to equality,[43] working time,[44] minimum wage,[45] part-time work[46] and fixed-term work[47] conferred jurisdiction on the Labour Court in relation to the enforcement of the legislation.

Structure

[1.14] The Labour Court consists of nine full-time members, composed of a chairman, two deputy chairmen and six ordinary members.[48] Three of the ordinary members are workers' members and three are employers' members.[49] The chairman and the two deputy chairmen are appointed by the Minister for Enterprise, Trade and Employment. The employers' members are appointed by the Minister, on the nomination of IBEC (the Irish Business and Employers' Confederation) and the workers' members are appointed by the by the Minister, on the nomination of ICTU (the Irish Congress of Trade Unions). The court operates in three separate Divisions, of chairman/deputy chairman, employers' member and workers' member, and may also sit as a full court.[50]

Functions

[1.15] The Labour Court's functions are:[51]

1. Industrial Relations:

   To investigate trade disputes under the Industrial Relations Acts 1946–2004 when referred to in the court in any of the following ways:

   (i)   **Appeal of Rights Commissioner Recommendation**
         To hear appeals from Rights Commissioner recommendations under the Industrial Relations Acts;[52]

   (ii) **Advance Acceptance of Recommendation**
         Where workers in a trade dispute or a trade union or all parties agree in advance to accept the Labour Court recommendation, the dispute may be referred directly to the Labour Court;[53]

---

[43]   Employment Equality Acts 1998–2008, s 83 and Pensions Act 1990, s 77.

[44]   Organisation of Working Time Act 1997, s 24, as amended by EC (Organisation of Working Time) (Activities of Doctors in Training) Regulations 2004 (SI 494/2004), Reg 12 and Organisation of Working Time Act 1997, s 28, as amended by Protection of Employees (Fixed-Term) Work Act 2003, s 19(2)(a).

[45]   National Minimum Wage Act 2000, s 41.

[46]   Protection of Employees (Part-Time) Work Act 2001, s 11 and Sch and Protection of Employees (Part-Time Work) Act 2001, s 17.

[47]   Protection of Employees (Fixed-Term Work) Act 2003, s 15.

[48]   Industrial Relations Act 1969, ss 2 and 4.

[49]   Industrial Relations Act 1969, s 2.

[50]   Industrial Relations Act 1969, s 3.

[51]   On the jurisdiction and procedure of the Labour Court, see Ch 22, Practice and Procedure in Employment Law, paras **[22.58]–[22.66]**.

[52]   Industrial Relations Act 1969, s 13(9).

[53]   Industrial Relations Act 1969, s 20(1).

(iii) **Referral by Labour Relations Commission**

The Labour Court may investigate a trade dispute where the parties to the dispute have availed of the services of the Labour Relations Commission but have failed to reach agreement and the Commission refers the dispute to the Labour Court at the request of the parties;[54]

(iv) **Waiver by Labour Relations Commission**

Where the Labour Relations Commission has waived its conciliation function and the parties have requested the Labour Court to investigate the dispute, the Court may hear the dispute;[55]

(v) **Labour Court Intervention**

Where the Court, following consultation with the Commission, is of the opinion that there are exceptional circumstances which warrant it investigating the dispute even though the conditions of hearing from a referral by the Labour Relations Commission are not satisfied, the Court may intervene to hear the dispute;[56]

(vi) **Ministerial Intervention**

Where the Minister for Enterprise, Trade and Employment is of the opinion that a trade dispute, actual or apprehended, affects the public interest, he may refer the matter to the Court and the Court must endeavour to resolve the dispute;[57]

(vii) Industrial Relations (Amendment) Act 2001 as amended by the Industrial Relations (Miscellaneous Provisions) Act 2004;

The court may investigate trade disputes referred to it under the Industrial Relations Acts 2001–2004;[58]

(viii) To establish Joint Labour Committees and decide certain questions as to their operation.[59] Joint Labour Committees are established by order of the Labour Court upon application by the Minister for Enterprise, Trade and Employment, by a trade union or any organisation or group claiming to be representative of workers or employers in a particular sector.[60] The Committee may submit to the Labour Court proposals for fixing the minimum pay and conditions of employment for workers in the sector.[61] The Court may make an employment regulation order giving effect to the proposals;[62]

---

[54] Industrial Relations Act 1990, s 26.

[55] Industrial Relations Act 1990, s 26(3).

[56] Industrial Relations Act 1990, s 26(5).

[57] Industrial Relations Act 1990, s 38(1).

[58] See further Ch 18, Industrial Relations.

[59] Industrial Relations Act 1946, s 35 and Sch 2.

[60] Industrial Relations Act 1946, s 35. At the end of 2007 there were 17 Joint Labour Committees in existence Labour Court Annual Report 2007).

[61] Industrial Relations Act 1946, s 42.

[62] Industrial Relations Act 1946, s 43.

(ix)　To register, vary, and interpret employment agreements;[63]

(x)　To investigate complaints of breaches of registered employment agreements[64];

(xi)　To register Joint Industrial Councils.[65]

Section 59 of the 1946 Act defines 'qualified joint industrial council' as:

an association of persons which complies with the following conditions –

(a)　that it is substantially representative of workers of a particular class, type or group and their employers,

(b)　that its object is the promotion of harmonious relations between such employer and such workers,

(c)　that its rules provide that, if a trade dispute arises between such workers and their employers a lock-out or strike will not be undertaken in support of the dispute until the dispute has been referred to the association and considered by it;

There are currently three registered joint industrial councils. They are the Joint Board of Conciliation and Arbitration for the Boot and Shoe Industry of Ireland, registered on 10 July 1948, the Joint Industrial Council for the Dublin Wholesale Fruit and Vegetable Trade, registered on 27 January 1964, and the Joint Industrial Council for the Construction Industry, registered on 26 July 1965;

(xii)　To investigate complaints of breaches of codes of practice made under the Industrial Relations Act 1990 provided that the complaint has first been considered by the Labour Relations Commission[66];

(xiii)　To give its opinion as to the interpretation of codes of practice made under the Industrial Relations Act 1990.[67]

2.　Employment Equality:

Where a case has been investigated by the Equality Tribunal under the Employment Equality Acts 1998–2008 and the Tribunal has made a decision, either party to the dispute may appeal the decision to the Labour Court.[68] The Court can hear appeals of non-discrimination notices and substantive notices issued by the Equality Authority.[69] The Labour Court may hear appeals of recommendations of equality officers in relation to the equality provisions of the Pensions Act 1990.[70]

---

[63]　Industrial Relations Act 1946, Part III.

[64]　Industrial Relations Act 1946, s 32.

[65]　Industrial Relations Act 1946, Part V.

[66]　Industrial Relations Act 1990, s 43.

[67]　Industrial Relations Act 1990, s 43(1).

[68]　Employment Equality Acts 1998–2008, s 83.

[69]　Employment Equality Acts 1998–2008, ss 63 and 71.

[70]　Pensions Act 1990, s 77.

3. Working Time:

   The Labour Court may, on application on behalf of one of the parties, approve a collective agreement relating to working time.[71] The Court may also hear appeals from Rights Commissioner decisions and complaints of non-implementation of Rights Commissioner decisions.[72]

4. Minimum Wage:

   The Labour Court may, in certain circumstances, exempt an employer from the obligation to pay the national minimum wage under the National Minimum Wage Act 2000.[73] The Court may hear appeals and investigate complaints of non-implementation of Rights Commissioner decisions under the Act.[74] The Court also has powers, in certain circumstances, in relation to determining the minimum wage with the national partners.[75]

5. Part-Time Work:

   The Labour Court may approve collective agreements regarding casual part-time employees under the Protection of Employees (Part-Time Work) Act 2001.[76] It may also hear appeals of Rights Commissioner decisions and complaints of non-implementation of Rights Commissioner decisions under the Act.[77]

6. Fixed-Term Work:

   The Court may hear appeals and investigate complaints of non-implementation of Rights Commissioner decisions under the Protection of Employees (Fixed-Term) Work Act 2003.[78]

The Employment Appeals Tribunal

Origin

[1.16] The Employment Appeals Tribunal (EAT) was established under s 39 of the Redundancy Payments Act 1967 as the Redundancy Appeals Tribunal. The Tribunal's role was initially limited to the adjudication of disputes in relation to redundancy payments. In 1973, the Tribunal's jurisdiction was extended to include claims under the Minimum Notice and Terms of Employment Act 1973. In 1977, s 18 of the Unfair Dismissals Act 1977 changed the name to the Employment Appeals Tribunal. The Act extended the EAT's remit to the hearing of claims of unfair dismissal.

---

[71] Organisation of Working Time Act 1997, s 24, as amended by EC (Organisation of Working Time) (Activities of Doctors in Training) Regulations 2004 (SI 494/2004), Reg 12.

[72] Organisation of Working Time Act 1997, s 28, as amended by Protection of Employees (Fixed-Term) Work Act 2003, s 19(2)(a).

[73] National Minimum Wage Act 2000, s 41.

[74] National Minimum Wage Act 2000, ss 27 and 31.

[75] National Minimum Wage Act 2000, s 13.

[76] Protection of Employees (Part-Time) Work Act 2001, s 11 and Sch.

[77] Protection of Employees (Part-Time) Work Act 2001, s 17.

[78] Protection of Employees (Fixed-Term) Work Act 2003, s 15.

Structure

[1.17] The EAT presently consists of a chairman, 35 vice chairmen and a panel of 80 other members, forty of whom are nominated by the ICTU, and forty of whom are nominated by bodies representative of employers.[79] The Minister for Enterprise, Trade and Employment may appoint additional vice chairmen and members when he is of the opinion that such appointments are necessary for the speedy dispatch of the business of the EAT.[80]

Functions

[1.18] The EAT has jurisdiction to hear claims under the following legislation:[81]

(i)   Redundancy Payments Acts 1967–2007 (appeal of decision of deciding officers);

(ii)   Minimum Notice and Terms of Employment Acts 1973–2001;

(iii)   Unfair Dismissals Acts 1977–2007 (where either party objects to the claim being heard by a Rights Commissioner or on appeal of Rights Commissioner decision);

(iv)   Protection of Employees (Employers' Insolvency) Acts 1984–2001;

(v)   Organisation of Working Time Act 1997 (where the claim is in relation to holidays and made along with other claims that can be made on their own to the Tribunal, such as unfair dismissal);

(vi)   Payment of Wages Act 1991 (appeal of Rights Commissioner decision);

(vii)   Terms of Employment (Information) Acts 1994 and 2001 (appeal of Rights Commissioner decision);

(viii) Maternity Protection Acts 1994 and 2004 (appeal of Rights Commissioner decision);

(ix)   Adoptive Leave Acts 1995 and 2005 (appeal of Rights Commissioner decision);

(x)   Protection of Young Person (Employment) Act 1996 (appeal of Rights Commissioner decision);

(xi)   Parental Leave Act 1998 (appeal of Rights Commissioner decision);

(xii)   Protection for Persons Reporting Child Abuse Act 1998 (appeal of Rights Commissioner decision);

(xiii) EC (Protection of Employees on Transfer of Undertakings) Regulations 2003 (appeal of Rights Commissioner decision);

(xiv)   EC (Protection of Employment) Regulations 2000 (appeal of Rights Commissioner decision);

---

[79] Employment Appeals Tribunal Annual Report 2007.

[80] Redundancy Payments Act 1979, Sch, amending Redundancy Payments Act 1967, s 39(3).

[81] On the jurisdiction and procedure of the Employment Appeals Tribunal, see further Ch 22, Practice and Procedure in Employment Law.

(xv)   Carer's Leave Act 2001 (appeal of Rights Commissioner decision); and

(xvi)   Competition Acts 2002–2006 (appeal of Rights Commissioner decision).

The Equality Tribunal

Origin

[1.19] The Equality Tribunal was established under s 75 of the Employment Equality Act 1998. Under the 1998 Act, the title of the Tribunal was the 'Office of the Director of Equality Investigations'. This title was changed by s 30 of the Equality Act 2004 to 'the Equality Tribunal', and the title of the 'Director of Equality Investigations' was changed to the 'Director of the Equality Tribunal'.

The role of the Tribunal under the 1998 was to mediate and/or investigate complaints of unlawful discrimination under the Act. Under the 1998 Act complaints in relation to dismissal contrary to the Act were referred to the Labour Court.[82] The Equality Act 2004 removed this jurisdiction from the Labour Court.[83] As a result of this change, the Equality Tribunal has jurisdiction to hear all claims of discrimination under the Employment Equality Acts 1998–2008. The Equal Status Act 2000 provided that claims under the Act were referable to the Equality Tribunal[84] and the Social Welfare (Miscellaneous) Provisions Act 2004 amended the Pensions Act 1990 to provide that claims of non-equal treatment in relation to pensions were also to be referred to the Equality Tribunal.[85]

Structure

[1.20] The Equality Tribunal is composed of the Director of the Equality Tribunal, appointed by the Minister for Justice, Equality and Law Reform with the consent of the Minister for Finance, and staff appointed by the Minister for Justice, Equality and Law Reform with the consent of the Minister for Finance to assist the Director in carrying out the Director's functions.[86] The Director may appoint staff to be equality officers and equality mediation officers or both.[87] The Director may delegate to an equality officer or an equality mediation officer any function conferred on her.[88] The Director may also, with the approval of the Minister for Justice, Equality and Law Reform and the consent of the Minister for Finance, appoint others to be equality mediation officers.[89] There are currently 16 equality officers, eight of whom are also equality mediation officers.[90]

---

[82]   Employment Equality Act 1998, s 77(2).

[83]   Equality Act 2004, s 46.

[84]   Equal Status Act 2000, s 21(1).

[85]   Social Welfare (Miscellaneous) Provisions Act 2004, Part VII.

[86]   Employment Equality Acts 1998–2008, s 75(2).

[87]   Employment Equality Acts 1998–2008, s 75(3).

[88]   Employment Equality Acts 1998–2008, s 75(4B).

[89]   The Tribunal has sought and received approval in principle for a pilot programme of outsourcing part of the mediation programme. The Tribunals 2007 Annual Report notes that this proposal is (at page 19) 'partly to deal with inevitable skills gaps during decentralisation and partly to help smooth out peaks in demand for mediation.' The Report notes that final sanction is still outstanding.

[90]   Equality Tribunal Annual Report 2007.

Functions

[1.21] The Equality Tribunal's role is to mediate and/or decide on claims of discrimination made under the Employment Equality Acts 1998–2008, the Equal Status Acts 2000–2008 and the Pensions Acts 1990–2004.[91]

The Equality Authority

Origin

[1.22] The Equality Authority was established on 18 October 1999 under s 38(1) of the Employment Equality Act 1998. The Authority was established as a continuation of the Employment Equality Agency which had been set up under the Employment Equality Act 1977.[92]

Structure

[1.23] The Equality Authority consists of 12 members appointed by the Minister for Justice, Equality and Law Reform, one of whom is the chairperson, and of whom, of the number appointed at any one time, the difference between the number of males appointed and the number of females appointed shall be not more than two.[93] The chairperson may hold office for up to four years and can be re-appointed.[94] The Minister must also appoint a vice-chairperson to act as chairperson in the chairperson's absence.[95]

Of the ordinary members of the Authority, two (one male, one female) must be persons appointed on the nomination of organisations representative of employees as the Minister considers appropriate.[96] A further two ordinary members, again, one male, one female, must be appointed on the nomination of organisations representative of employers as the Minister considers appropriate.[97] The remaining ordinary members must be persons as appear to the Minister to have knowledge of, or experience in:

  (i)   consumer, social affairs or equality issues, including issues related to the experience and circumstances of groups who are disadvantaged by reference to gender, marital status, family status, sexual orientation, religion, age, disability, race, colour, nationality, ethnic or national origin or membership of the Traveller community;

  (ii) issues related to the provision of goods or service; or

---

[91] In 2007, of the 852 referrals to the Tribunal, 659 were under the Employment Equality Acts, 7 were under the Pensions Acts and 185 were under the Equal Status Acts (The Equality Tribunal Annual Report, 2007). On the jurisdiction and procedure of the Equality Tribunal, see Ch 22, Practice and Procedure in Employment Law, paras **[22.52]–[22.59]**.

[92] Employment Equality Act 1977, s 37.

[93] Employment Equality Acts 1998–2008, s 41.

[94] Employment Equality Acts 1998–2008, ss 42 and 45.

[95] Employment Equality Acts 1998–2008, s 46(1).

[96] Employment Equality Acts 1998–2008, s 44(1)(a).

[97] Employment Equality Acts 1998–2008, s 44(1)(b).

(iii)   such other subject-matter (including law, finance, management or administration) as appears to the Minister to be relevant to the issues to which the functions of the Authority relate.[98] Ordinary members are part-time and can hold office for up to four years and can be re-appointed.[99]

The Chief Executive Officer of the Equality Authority is appointed by the Authority. The first Chief Executive Officer was appointed by the Minister.[100] The Chief Executive is responsible for managing and controlling the staff, administration and business of the Authority.

The Authority can appoint advisory committees to advise it on matters relation to its functions.[101] The Minister can, after consultation with the Authority, appoint such number of staff to the Authority as is approved by the Minister for Finance.[102] The Authority operates through five sections, administration, communications, development, legal and research, and currently has 57 staff.[103]

Functions

General functions

[1.24] The Authority has the following general functions:[104]

(a)   to work towards the elimination of discrimination in relation to employment;

(b)   to promote equality of opportunity in relation to the matters to which this Act applies;

(bb)   to provide information to the public on the working of the Parental Leave Act 1998;

(c)   to provide information to the public on and to keep under review the working of this Act, the Maternity Protection Act 1994 and the Adoptive Leave Act 1995 and, whenever it thinks necessary, to make proposals to the Minister [for Justice, Equality and Law Reform] for amending any of those Acts; and

(d)   to keep under review the working of the Pensions Act 1990, as regards the principle of equal treatment and, whenever it thinks necessary, to make proposals to the Minister for Social and Family Affairs for amending that Act.

Section 39 of the Equal Status Act 2000 conferred further functions on the Authority: to work towards the elimination of prohibited conduct; to promote equality of opportunity

---

[98]   Employment Equality Acts 1998–2008, s 44(1)(c).

[99]   Employment Equality Acts 1998–2008, ss 44(2) and 45.

[100]   Employment Equality Acts 1998–2008, s 49(7).

[101]   Employment Equality Acts 1998–2008, s 48(1).

[102]   Employment Equality Acts 1998–2008, s 51(1).

[103]   Equality Authority Annual Report 2007. Under measures to be introduced following Budget 2009, the Equality Authority and Human Rights Commission are to fully integrate their facilities, back office and administrative services and access for citizens. It is not clear what effect this will have on the functioning of the Authority though the proposal has been strongly opposed by the Authority. (*Equality Authority Response to Proposed Amalgamation of State Agencies* Equality Authority Press Release – 14 September 2008).

[104]   Employment Equality Acts 1998–2008, s 39.

in relation to the matters to which the Equal Status Act applies; and to provide information to the public on and to keep under review the workings of the Act and, whenever the Authority thinks it necessary, to make proposals to the Minister for Justice, Equality and Law Reform for its amendment.

Codes of practice

The Authority may, and, if requested to do so by the Minister for Justice, Equality and Law Reform, must, prepare draft codes of practice in furtherance of the aims of the elimination of discrimination in employment and the promotion of equality of opportunity in employment and in relation to the matters to which the Equal Status Acts apply.[105] In 2002, the Authority published the Code of Practice on Sexual Harassment and Harassment at Work.[106]

Research and information

The Authority may undertake or sponsor research or the dissemination of information as it considers necessary and expedient for the purpose of performing any of its functions.[107] The Authority has published a number of information publications on equality legislation, such as the Maternity Protection Acts 1994 and 2004, the Parental Leave Act 1998, the Adoptive Leave Act 1995 and the Equal Status Acts 2000–2004. It has also published policy positions on various aspects of equality, including a report on traveller ethnicity[108] and on building an intercultural society.[109] The Authority has also published a number of good practice guidelines in relation to equality.[110]

Inquiries

The Authority may, and if requested by the Minister, must, for any purpose connected with the performance of its functions, conduct an inquiry[111] for which it may summon witnesses and require the provision of information.[112] Arising from the inquiry the Authority may make recommendations and serve non-discrimination notices.[113]

Assistance in proceedings

The Authority may provide assistance to a person taking proceedings under the Employment Equality Acts and the Equal Status Acts.[114]

Equality reviews

---

[105] Employment Equality Acts 1998–2008, s 56.

[106] Employment Equality Act 1998 (Code of Practice) (Harassment) (Order) 2002 (SI 78/2002).

[107] Employment Equality Act 1998, s 57.

[108] Traveller Ethnicity: An Equality Authority Report (2006, The Equality Authority).

[109] Building an Intercultural Society (2003, The Equality Authority).

[110] Guidelines include 'Guidelines for Equal Status Policies in Enterprises' (2005, The Equality Authority) and 'Delivering Equality of Opportunity in Small and Medium Sized Enterprises (2002, The Equality Authority).

[111] Employment Equality Act 1998, s 58.

[112] Employment Equality Act 1998, s 59.

[113] Employment Equality Act 1998, ss 60 and 61.

[114] Employment Equality Acts 1998–2008, s 67.

The Authority may carry out, or arrange the carrying out of equality reviews in relation to particular businesses or industries and, on foot of the review prepare or arrange the preparation of equality action plans.[115]

Legislation review

The Authority may review any legislation that is likely to affect or impede the elimination of discrimination in relation to employment or the promotion of equality of opportunity in relation to employment and report to the Minister on the review.[116]

Intoxicating Liquor Act 2003

Under s 19 of the Intoxicating Liquor Act 2003, a person who claims that 'prohibited conduct' is being directed against them, which is discrimination contrary to the Equal Status Act 2000 at or on point of entry to a licensed premises, may apply to the District Court for redress. Where it appears to the Authority that prohibited conduct is being directed against persons generally or against a person who has not applied to the District Court for redress and who could not reasonably be expected to do so, the Authority can apply to the Court for redress in respect of that conduct.[117]

Strategic plans

Every three years, the Authority must prepare and submit to the Minister for Justice, Equality and Law Reform a strategic plan containing the key objectives, outputs and related strategies, including the use of resources, by the Authority.[118]

The National Employment Rights Authority

Origin

[1.25] 'Towards 2016', the Ten Year Framework Social Partnership Agreement 2006–2015 contained a strong emphasis on employment law compliance. The Agreement provided:[119]

---

[115] Employment Equality Acts 1998–2008, s 69.

[116] Employment Equality Acts 1998–2008, s 73.

[117] Intoxicating Liquor Act 2003, s 19(6)(a).

[118] Employment Equality Acts 1998–2008, s 40. The current Equality Authority Strategic plan provides for six 'strategic goals': (i) the majority of people in Ireland are aware that they have rights and responsibilities under equality legislation and that they have statutory leave entitlements; (ii) enhanced access to redress under Irish equality legislation and EU Equal Treatment Directives for people experiencing discrimination; (iii) a proactive approach by employers and service providers in key sectors to promote equality and achieve compliance with equality legislation; (iv) continuous enhancement of evidence for and understanding of equality issues; (v) practical responses made to critical priority issues for groups experiencing inequality; and (vi) an effective and efficient Equality Authority. (Equality Authority, Strategic Plan 2009–2011, March 2009).

[119] Section 12.1–12.3, Towards 2016 Ten Year Framework Social Partnership Agreement 2006–2015.

12.1 While recognising the broad level of compliance with employment rights across the economy generally, there is, nevertheless, a significant shared commitment between the parties to securing better compliance with legal requirements, underpinned by adequate enforcement. It is also agreed that an effective employment rights compliance system must cover:

- The active and responsible contribution of employers, employees and trade unions;
- The education of vulnerable workers;
- The promotion of entitlements with a special emphasis on workers from overseas;
- Information provision to all employees and employers;
- Substantially strengthened arrangements for inspection;
- Adjudication by the Rights Commissioners, Employment Appeals Tribunal and Labour Court; and
- Enforcement of adjudication outcomes.

12.2 The overall objective is to secure greatly increased public confidence in the system of compliance on the basis of an informed and empowered working population, who will have simple, independent and workable means of redress, underpinned by the need for fairness and impartiality, with adjudication and if needs be, enforcement available to them, in a reasonable length of time.

12.3 A major package of measures has been agreed by the parties with these aims in mind, including the establishment of a new statutory Office dedicated to employment rights compliance; a trebling in the number of Labour Inspectors; greater coordination among organisations concerned with compliance; new requirements in respect of record keeping; enhanced employment rights awareness activity; the introduction of a new and more user friendly system of employment rights compliance; increased resourcing of the system; and higher penalties for non-compliance with employment law.

Section 13 provided for a new statutory Office of the Director for Employment Rights Compliance, under the aegis of the Department of Enterprise, Trade and Employment. This office was established on an interim basis in February 2007 with the title, 'The National Employment Rights Authority' (NERA). The Employment Law Compliance Bill provides for the establishment of NERA on a statutory basis. The Bill was published by the Department of Enterprise, Trade and Employment on 18 March 2008. The Bill contains detailed provisions on the functions of NERA. It provides that the objective of NERA 'shall be to promote, encourage and secure compliance with employment legislation'.[120]

Structure

[1.26] The interim Director of NERA was appointed by the Minister for Enterprise, Trade and Employment on 12 February 2007. The Employment Rights Compliance Bill provides that the interim Director shall be appointed the Director on commencement of the Act.[121] NERA's interim Advisory Board consists of an independent chairperson, two members appointed by the Minister, three members nominated by organisations

---

[120] Employment Rights Compliance Bill 2008, s 6(2).
[121] Employment Rights Compliance Bill 2008, s 8(2).

representative of employees and three members nominated by organisations representative of employers. The Minister shall make one further appointment also. The Director is supported in carrying out his functions by a management team and staff.

Functions

[1.27] The Employment Law Compliance Bill provides that the Director of NERA shall have functions including: the enforcement of employment legislation; the investigation of instances of suspected offences under employment legislation; and referral of the cases to the Director of Public Prosecutions where the Director has reasonable grounds to believe that an offence under employment legislation has been committed.[122]

The Health and Safety Authority

Origin

[1.28] The National Authority for Occupational Safety and Health was established under the Safety, Health and Welfare at Work Act 1989.[123] The 1989 Act was repealed by the Safety, Health and Welfare at Work Act 2005.[124] The 2005 Act provided for the continuation of that body and for it to be known as the Health and Safety Authority.[125] The Health and Safety Authority operates under the aegis of the Department of Enterprise, Trade and Employment.

Structure

[1.29] The Board of the Authority is composed of a chairperson and eleven ordinary members appointed by the Minister for Enterprise, Trade and Employment.[126] The ordinary members consist of three members nominated by organisations representative of employees, three members nominated by organisations representative of employers and five members that the Minister considers appropriate including one person from the Department of Enterprise, Trade and Employment.[127] The Board may appoint advisory committees from time to time to advise it in relation to its functions.[128] The Chief Executive of the Authority is responsible for the administration and business of the Authority and reports to the Board.[129] The Board can appoint Assistant Chief Executives as assistants to the Chief Executive.[130]

---

[122] Employment Rights Compliance Bill 2008, s 14.
[123] Safety, Health and Welfare at Work Act 1989, s 15(1).
[124] Safety, Health and Welfare at Work Act 2005, s 4.
[125] Safety, Health and Welfare at Work Act 2005, s 32(1)(a).
[126] Safety, Health and Welfare at Work Act 2005, s 37(1).
[127] Safety, Health and Welfare at Work Act 2005, s 37(2).
[128] Safety, Health and Welfare at Work Act 2005, s 38(1).
[129] Safety, Health and Welfare at Work Act 2005, s 39.
[130] Safety, Health and Welfare at Work Act 2005, s 39(3).

Functions

[1.30] The general functions of the Authority are:[131]

(i) to promote, encourage and foster the prevention of accidents, dangerous occurrences and personal injury at work in accordance with the relevant statutory provisions;

(ii) to promote, encourage, foster and provide education and training in the safety, health and welfare of persons at work;

(iii) to encourage and foster measures promoting the safety, health and welfare of persons at work;

(iv) to make adequate arrangements for the enforcement of the relevant statutory provisions;

(v) to monitor, evaluate and make recommendations to the Minister regarding implementation and compliance with –

    (a) the relevant statutory provisions, and

    (b) best practice relating to safety, health and welfare at work, and the review and maintenance of relevant records by employers;

(vi) to promote, encourage and foster cooperation with and between persons or bodies of persons that represent employees and employers and any other persons or bodies of persons, as appropriate, as regards the prevention of risks to safety, health and welfare at work in accordance with the relevant statutory provisions;

(vii) to make any arrangements that it considers appropriate for providing information and advice on matters relating to safety, health and welfare at work;

(viii) to make any arrangements that it considers appropriate to conduct, commission, promote, support and evaluate research, surveys and studies on matters relating to the functions of the Authority and for this purpose –

    (a) to foster and promote contacts and the exchange of information with other persons or bodies of persons involved in safety, health and welfare at work in and outside the State, and

    (b) as it considers appropriate, to publish in the form and manner that the Authority thinks fit, results arising out of such research, studies and surveys;

(ix) to prepare and adopt a strategy statement and to monitor its implementation;

(x) to prepare and adopt a work programme;

(xI) to comply with any directions in writing, whether general or particular, relating to its functions, that the Minister may from time to time give the Authority;

(xii) to give to the Minister any information relating to the performance of the functions that the Minister may from time to time require; and

(xiii) to perform any additional functions conferred on the Authority by order.

---

[131] Safety, Health and Welfare at Work Act 2005, s 34(1) details the functions of the Authority.

The Department of Enterprise, Trade and Employment

[1.31] The Department of Enterprise, Trade and Employment operates in seven divisions:

   (i)   The Labour Force Development Division;

   (ii)   Competitiveness and International Affairs Division;

  (iii)   Employment Rights and Industrial Relations Division;

  (iv)   Science, Technology and Intellectual Property Division;

   (v)   Corporate Services and Economic Policy Division;

  (vi)   Consumers, Competition and Commerce Division; and

 (vii)   Enterprise and Agencies Division.

The Employment Rights and Industrial Relations Division is of particular relevance to employment law. Its role is to establish and protect employment rights and to provide the policy, legislative and institutional framework within which good industrial relations prosper. Its areas of responsibility include licensing of employment agencies, the Employment Appeals Tribunal, employment rights, through the National Employment Rights Authority, liaison between the Health and Safety Authority and the Department, industrial relations, including liaising with the Labour Relations Commission and the Labour Court, administration of the insolvency payments scheme, policy and reporting for the purposes of the International Labour Organisation and the Council of Europe, redundancy payments and preparation of legislation.

Part II
The Employment Relationship

Chapter 2

The Contract and Relationship of Employment

Maeve Regan

INTRODUCTION

[2.01] The employment contract is at the core of employment law. Where there is an employment contract, the following are some of the consequences:

(i) the employer is vicariously liable for the torts committed by the employee in the course of his employment. As a general rule, vicarious liability does not attach for acts done by others;

(ii) duties are implied into the contract. For example, the employer and employee have a duty of cooperation, the employee has a duty not to disclose the trade secrets and confidential information of the employer and there is, between employer and employee, a mutual obligation of trust and confidence;

(iii) duties are imposed by legislation into the contract. Legislation on health and safety, information and consultation, termination of employment, redundancy, protective leave and the transfer of a business create rights and corresponding duties which are imposed into the employment contract; and

(iv) employees are preferential creditors in the event of the winding up or receivership of the incorporated employer.[1]

A contract of employment is distinct from a number of other working arrangements such as a contract with an independent contractor (a 'contract for services'), a partnership or an agency or outsourcing agreement. Increasingly, working arrangements do not fall into the classic relationship of an employee working full time for his employer, under his direction, for a fixed wage, with standard working hours. Working relationships are often individualised with part-time and mobile working, for example, forming part of the picture of working life.

[2.02] The employment contract defines the boundaries of employment law.[2] There is no comprehensive statutory or common law definition of the 'employment contract' or of

---

[1] Companies Act 1963, s 285(2).

[2] In Britain there is great exploration taking place as to how employment law can encompass the individualised nature of working arrangements. In particular, Professor Mark Freedland has proposed a move away from the contract of employment as the core of employment law to a wider concept, the 'personal work nexus'. This core organising category would consist of (i) all contracts personally to execute any work; and (ii) working arrangements which are not necessarily contractual. See Freedland, *The Personal Employment Contract* (Oxford University Press), 2003 and 'Contract of Employment to Personal Work Nexus' [2006] 35 *Industrial Law Journal*, 1.

the 'employee'. Employment legislation commonly defines an 'employee' as a person engaged under a contract of employment and a 'contract of employment' as a contract of service or apprenticeship or a contract with an employment agency to personally provide work to a third party.[3] The courts have had the task of divining when an employment contract, or 'contract of service', as it was traditionally called, exists by formulating tests which track, to some extent, the changing face of working relationships. The High Court in *The Minister for Agriculture and Food v John Barry & Ors* made clear that all of the tests are potential aids to identifying the nature of the working relationship. No single test is definitive. Depending on the circumstances of the particular case, some aids will be more helpful than others.[4]

EMPLOYEES

[2.03] A number of tests have been developed and applied by the courts to ascertain if a person is an employee.

The control test

[2.04] The 'control' test emerged in the 19th and 20th centuries. Under this test, the essence of employment was that the employee was 'subject to the command of the master as to the way in which he shall do his work'.[5] It was adopted by the High Court in *Minister for Industry and Commerce v Elizabeth Healy*[6] and by the Supreme Court in *Lynch v Palgrave Murphy Ltd*[7] and in *Patrick Roche v Patrick Kelly and Co Ltd*.[8] Walsh J, in deciding whether Mr Roche, a builder contracted by the defendant company, was an employee of the defendant, said:[9]

> [w]hile many ingredients may be present in the relationship of master and servant, it is undoubtedly true that the principal one, and almost invariably the determining one, is the fact of the master's right to direct the servant not merely as to what is to be done but how it is to be done. The fact that the master does not exercise that right, as distinct from possessing it, is of no weight if he has the right.

---

[3] Terms of Employment (Information) Acts 1994–2001; Organisation of Working Time Act 1997; Maternity Protection Acts 1994 and 2004; Adoptive Leave Acts 1995 and 2005; Carer's Leave Act 2001; Parental Leave Acts 1998 and 2006; Protection of Young Persons (Employment) Act 1996; Payment of Wages Act 1991; National Minimum Wage Act 2000; Protection of Employees (Part-Time) Work Act 2001; Redundancy Payments Acts 1967–2007; Employment Equality Acts 1998–2008; EC (Protection of Employees on Transfer of Undertakings) Regulations 2003.

[4] *In the matter of the Redundancy Payments Acts, 1967 to 2003 and in the matter of the Minimum Notice and Terms of Employment Acts 1973 to 2001 and in the matter of an appeal by the Minister for Agriculture and Food, Between The Minister for Agriculture and Food v John Barry & Ors* (7 July 2008, unreported) HC.

[5] *Yewens v Noakes* (1880) 6 QBD 530, Bramwell LJ.

[6] *Minister for Industry and Commerce v Elizabeth Healy* [1941] IR 545.

[7] *Palgrave Murphy Ltd* [1962] IR 150.

[8] *Patrick Roche v Patrick Kelly and Co Ltd* [1969] IR 100 (SC).

[9] [1969] IR 100 at 108.

If this test were to be conclusive of the question, only a small category of workers would be classified as employees. Other tests were formulated and, in addition to the control test, applied to ascertain whether a person was an employee.

The integration test

[2.05] The integration test was proposed by Denning LJ in S*tevenson Jordan and Harrison Ltd v MacDonald and Evans*:[10]

> One feature which seems to run through the instances is that, under a contract of service a man is employed as part of the business, whereas under a contract for services, his work, although done for the business is not integrated into it but only accessory to it.

The test was applied by the High Court in *Re Sunday Tribune Ltd*.[11] The liquidator of the Sunday Tribune had applied to the Court to determine if three reporters for the paper were employees of the company. If they were, they would be entitled as preferential creditors to priority in the winding up. Carroll J applied both the control and the integration test. The control test, she held, was not the sole test to be applied. That means of assessment was inappropriate where the employment status of highly skilled professionals was in issue. In such cases, the integration test must also be applied. She referred[12] to the conclusion of Ungoed Thomas J in *Beloff v Pressdram Ltd*:[13]

> ... the greater the skill required for an employee's work, the less significant is control in determining whether the employee is under a contract of service. Control is just one of many factors whose influence varies according to the circumstances. In such highly skilled work as that of the plaintiff [a journalist] it seems of no substantial significance. The test which emerges from the authorities seems to me, as Denning LJ said, whether on the one hand the employee is employed as part of the business and his work is an integral part of the business, or whether his work is not integrated into the business but is only accessory to it.

Carroll J held that, of the three reporters, one was an employee as the relationship satisfied the simple control test, one was an employee on the basis that her employment was an integral part of the business of the newspaper and the third reporter was not an employee as he did not satisfy the control test nor was he an integral part of the business of the newspaper.

The multiple test

[2.06] The 'multiple test' was formulated by McKenna J in *Ready Mixed Concrete (South East) Ltd v Minister of Pensions and National Insurance*:[14]

> A contract of service exists if the following three conditions are fulfilled:
>
> (i)   The servant agrees that in consideration of a wage or other remuneration he will provide his own work and skill in the performance of some service for his master,

---

[10]   *Stevenson Jordan and Harrison Ltd v MacDonald and Evans* [1952] 1 TLR 101 at 111.
[11]   *Re Sunday Tribune Ltd* [1984] IR 505 (HC).
[12]   [1984] IR 505 at 507.
[13]   *Beloff v Pressdram Ltd* [1973] 1 All ER 241 at 250.
[14]   *Ready Mixed Concrete (South East) Ltd v Minister of Pensions and National Insurance* [1968] 1 All ER 433 at 440.

(ii)   he agrees, expressly or impliedly, that in the performance of that service he will be subject to the other's control in a sufficient degree to make that other master,

(iii)   the other provisions of the contract are consistent with its being a contract of service.

The multiple test is not so much a single test as an approach which requires that all of the features of the work relationship, including the extent of control and integration, are examined. This test was applied by the High Court and in *Ó Coindealbháin (Inspector of Taxes) v Mooney.*[15] It has been used most recently by the Labour Court to decipher the nature of more complex working arrangements.[16]

FACTORS INDICATING AN EMPLOYMENT CONTRACT

[2.07] Certain features of a working relationship point towards an employment contract.

Personal service

[2.08] At the heart of the employment contract is the employee's obligation to personally provide services to the employer. The Supreme Court held in *Henry Denny & Sons (Ireland) v Minister for Social Welfare*[17] that the inference that a person is engaged in business on his or her own account can be more readily drawn where he or she employs others to assist in the business. In *Henry Denny*, one of the questions before the Supreme Court was the test to be applied to determine if a shop demonstrator, Sandra Mahon, was an employee of Henry Denny, for whom she carried out demonstrations. The Department of Social Welfare had held that she was an employee and insurable under the Social Welfare Acts. Henry Denny appealed this decision to the High Court. The High Court upheld the Department's finding that Ms Mahon was an employee. This decision was appealed to the Supreme Court. The Supreme Court considered the entire contractual arrangement between Ms Mahon and Henry Denny. Keane J found as a factor pointing toward Ms Mahon being an employee was that she did not as a matter of routine engage other people to assist her in the work. Where she was unable to do the work herself, she had to arrange for it to be done by someone else approved by Henry Denny.[18] This emphasis on personal service as fundamental to the employment relationship is evident in a line of cases: *Minister for Industry and Commerce v Elizabeth Healy,*[19] *Patrick Roche v Patrick Kelly and Company Ltd,*[20] and *Ó Coindealbháin (Inspector of Taxes) v Mooney.*[21]

[2.09] A limitation on a person's ability to engage others to provide the services which he has contracted to provide does not necessarily point to that person being an

---

[15]   *Ó Coindealbháin (Inspector of Taxes) v Mooney* [1990] I IR 422 (HC).

[16]   *Diageo Global Supply v Mary Rooney* [2004] ELR 133 and *Enterprise Ireland v Irene McMahon* EDA 0710.

[17]   *Henry Denny & Sons (Ireland) v Minister for Social Welfare* [1998] 1 IR 34.

[18]   [1998] 1 IR 34 at 50.

[19]   *Minister for Industry and Commerce v Elizabeth Healy* [1941] IR 545 (HC).

[20]   *Patrick Roche v Patrick Kelly and Co Ltd* [1969] IR 100 (SC).

[21]   *Ó Coindealbháin (Inspector of Taxes) v Mooney* [1990] I IR 422 (HC).

employee. Where it is an *individual* that is engaged to provide the services, it would be normal for the engaging party to wish to ensure the competence of those working in place of the particular individual.[22] Similarly, the engaging party may retain a right of approval to comply with industry regulations. Geoghegan J explained the effect of this in *Castleisland Cattle Breeding Society Ltd v Minister for Social and Family Affairs*,[23] where the Supreme Court considered Castleisland's arrangement with cattle inseminators:[24]

> I see no significance whatsoever ... in the inclusion in the contract of terms which required the approval of Castleisland to any substitute inseminator or the ability to assign the contract. Indeed even if there were no statutory regulations [regulating the insemination of cattle] it would obviously be in the interests of Castleisland's business to ensure competence and, therefore, to include such a provision.

[2.10] In *Tierney v An Post*,[25] Keane J, giving the judgment of the court, considered such a clause in the contract in issue between Mr Tierney, a sub-post office master, and An Post. Under the clause, Mr Tierney had to obtain the permission of An Post for the employment of any person in the post office. Keane J held:[26]

> It is not surprising to find that the respondent has, as it were, a right of veto over the appointment of persons who for any reason it might not be appropriate to employ in a post office: the fact remains that it is not normal to find in a contract of service that the employee can hire assistants to perform the work which he or she is employed to do.

[2.11] A strict limitation on the ability to substitute may point to the exercise of strong control exercised by the engaging party, which itself would indicate an employment relationship. In *In the matter of the Social Welfare (Consolidation) Act 1993 ESB v The Minister for Social Community and Family Affairs and Others*,[27] an Appeals Officer in the Department of Social and Family Affairs had found that the respondent meter readers engaged by the ESB had changed over time from being independent contractors to being employees of ESB. The Appeals Officer had based her decision on two factors that she considered had changed the nature of the relationships:

(i) ESB had introduced a new procedure relating to the ability of the metre reader to engage substitutes to perform their work. The meter reader had to obtain the approval of ESB for the substitute and the substitute had to have an ESB identity card; and

---

[22] *McAuliffe v Minister for Social Welfare* [1994] ELR 239 (HC) and *Tierney v An Post* [2000] IR 536 (SC).

[23] *Castleisland Cattle Breeding Society Ltd v Minister for Social and Family Affairs* [2004] 4 IR 150.

[24] [2004] 4 IR 150 at 161–162.

[25] *Tierney v An Post* [2000] I IR 536 (SC).

[26] [2000] I IR 536 at 545 (SC).

[27] *In the matter of the Social Welfare (Consolidation) Act 1993 ESB v The Minister for Social Community and Family Affairs, Eamonn Sheridan, Helen Kiely, Brendan Joyce, Francis Slattery, John McAleer and Aidan Brady* (21 February 2006, unreported) HC.

(ii) ESB had introduced a new system for meters readers for sending the data from the metres to ESB, which involved using a data logger provided by ESB and complying with rules of confidentiality, time and use of the logger.

The High Court held that the Appeals Officer was entitled to draw the inference that these changes resulted in a change in the level of control that was exercised over the readers. This increase in control resulted in their becoming employees of ESB.

[2.12] An employee may, of course, have more than one employer. Freedom to work for others will be a factor to be considered in assessing the relationship. In the EAT decision in *Ryan v Shamrock Marine (Shannon) Ltd,*[28] Mr Ryan, who operated a sludge barge for Shamrock Marine, was held to be an independent contractor. One of the factors that the Tribunal took into consideration in reaching this conclusion was that, while Mr Ryan was carrying out work for Shamrock Marine, he was free to work and indeed did work for others. Freedom to work for others is not a particularly illuminating factor in assessing if an employment contract exists. The Supreme Court made this clear in *Castleisland Cattle Breeding Society Ltd v Minister for Social and Family Affairs.*[29] Geoghegan J said:[30]

> I have not attached great importance one way or the other to the fact that the men were to be allowed carry on other businesses provided they did not interfere with their contractual obligations to Castleisland. I think that could be equally compatible with [an employment contract].

Control

[2.13] The degree of control exercised by the engaging party is always one factor to be taken into account in determining if an employment relationship exists.[31]

[2.14] Control is, however, only one of the factors to be considered. In *Henry Denny*[32] the Supreme Court considered that the fact that the demonstrator engaged by Henry Denny was not continuously supervised in her work could not be regarded as decisive in assessing her employment status. Similarly, the Supreme Court in *Tierney v An Post*[33] concluded that a postmaster was not employed by An Post even though the 'Postmaster's Manual' provided that postmasters were under the control and direction of the regional manager and the immediate direction of the relevant head postmaster. The court pointed to the other factors that had to be taken into account: the fact that the post office business was carried on in the same premises as the postmaster's own business and that he could, even though only to a limited extent, maximise the profit which he derived from the business through his own management. The greater the level of skill

---

[28] *Ryan v Shamrock Marine (Shannon) Ltd* UD 155/90, EAT.

[29] *Castleisland Cattle Breeding Society Ltd v Minister for Social and Family Affairs* [2004] 4 IR 150.

[30] [2004] 4 IR 150 at 163.

[31] *Henry Denny & Sons (Ireland) Ltd v Minister for Social Welfare* [1998] 1 IR 34.

[32] *Henry Denny & Sons (Ireland) Ltd v Minister for Social Welfare* [1998] 1 IR 34. For a summary of the facts of this case, see para **[2.08]**.

[33] *Tierney v An Post* [2000] 1 IR 536.

required for the work in question, the less significant is control in determining whether the person performing the work is an employee.[34]

[2.15] The level of control may have more to do with the nature of the regulation of the industry or the demands of the particular market than with the nature of the relationship. In the Supreme Court decision in *Castleisland Cattle Breeding Society Ltd v Minister for Social and Family Affairs*,[35] Geoghegan J, giving the judgment of the Court, held that in classifying the relationship between Castleisland and cattle inseminators engaged by Castleisland, there was 'no significance whatsoever'[36] in the inclusion in the contract of terms which required the approval of Castleisland to any substitute inseminator and the inability of the inseminator to assign the contract. Such controls were necessary to achieve compliance with the Department of Agriculture regulations. In *Hogan v United Beverages*,[37] the Circuit Court found that the level of control exercised by United Beverages over Mr Hogan, a lorry driver engaged by United Beverages to carry out deliveries, was no more than would be considered normal in a customer driven business where customer requirements must be met if the business is to be retained. Similarly in *McAuliffe v Minister for Social Welfare*,[38] the High Court considered the relevance of strict time requirements to the degree of control as a factor in ascertaining whether Mr McAuliffe, a wholesale distributor of newspaper, engaged newspaper deliverers as employees or independent contractors. Barr J held that for a wholesale distributor of newspapers over a wide area, as Mr McAuliffe was, time and reliability were of the essence in the performance of that service. As a result, whatever the nature of the contract, one would expect stringent terms regarding the time factor. Strict terms as to time, relevant to the element of control exercised, did not in these circumstances shed light one way or the other on the nature of the relationship.[39]

INDEPENDENT CONTRACTORS

The entrepreneurial test

[2.16] The test used to determine if a person is an employee as distinct from self-employed is this: is the person in business on his own account? This test is sometimes referred to as the 'economic reality' or the 'entrepreneurial' test. It was explained by Cooke J in the English High Court in *Market Investigations Ltd v Minister of Social Security*:[40]

>...the fundamental test to be applied is this:

>'is the person who has engaged himself to perform these services performing them as a person in business on his own account?

---

[34] *Re Sunday Tribune Ltd* [1984] IR 505 (HC), see para **[2.05]** above.

[35] *Castleisland Cattle Breeding Society Ltd v Minister for Social and Family Affairs* [2004] 4 IR 150.

[36] [2004] 4 IR 150 at 161.

[37] *Hogan v United Beverages* (14 October 2005) CC [2006] 3 IELJ (note).

[38] *McAuliffe v Minister for Social Welfare* [1994] ELR 239.

[39] [1994] ELR 239 at 242.

[40] *Market Investigations Ltd v Minister of Social Security* [1969] 2 QB 173 at 184–185.

If the answer to that is 'yes', then the contract is a contract for services. If the answer is 'no' then the contract is a contract of service. No exhaustive list has been compiled and perhaps no exhaustive list can be compiled of considerations which are relevant in determining that question, nor can strict rules be laid down as to the relative weight which the various considerations should carry in particular cases. The most that can be said is that control will no doubt always have to be considered, although it can no longer be regarded as the sole determining factor; and that factors, which may be of importance, are such matters as whether the man performing the services provides his own equipment, whether he has his own helpers, what degree of financial risk he takes, what degree of responsibility for investment and management he has, and whether and how far he has an opportunity of profiting from sound management in the performance of his task.

[2.17] This test was applied by the High Court in *McDermott (Inspector of Taxes) v Loy*[41] and in *Ó Coindealbháin (Inspector of Taxes) v Mooney.*[42] It received ringing endorsement by the Supreme Court in *Henry Denny & Sons (Ireland) Ltd v Minister for Social Welfare.*[43] Keane J summarised the development of the tests for distinguishing between an employer and an independent contractor:[44]

The criteria which should be adopted in considering whether a particular employment, in the context of legislation ..., is to be regarded as a contract 'for service' or a contract 'of services' have been the subject of a number of decisions in Ireland and England. In some of the cases, different terminology is used and the distinction is stated as being between a 'servant' and 'independent contractor'. However, there is a consensus to be found in the authorities that each case must be considered in the light of its particular facts and of the general principles which the courts have developed...

At one stage, the extent and degree of the control which was exercised by one party over the other in the performance of the work was regarded as decisive. However, as later authorities demonstrate, that test does not always provide satisfactory guidance. In *Cassidy v Ministry of Health,*[45] it was pointed out that, although the master of a ship is clearly employed under a contract of service, the owners are not entitled to tell him how he should navigate the vessel. Conversely, the fact that one party reserves the right to exercise full control over the method of doing the work may be consistent with the other party being an independent contractor: see *Queensland Stations Property Ltd v Federal Commissioner of Taxation* [1945] 70 CLR 539.

[2.18] Keane J cited Cooke J's formulation of the test in *Market Investigations* and concluded:[46]

It is accordingly clear that, while each case must be determined in light of its particular facts and circumstances, in general a person will be regarded as providing his or her services under a contract of service and not as an independent contractor where the person is performing the services for another person and not for himself. The degree of control exercised over how the work is to be performed, although a factor to be taken into

---

[41] *McDermott (Inspector of Taxes) v Loy* (29 July 1982, unreported) HC.

[42] *Ó Coindealbháin (Inspector of Taxes) v Mooney* [1990] I IR 422.

[43] *Henry Denny & Sons (Ireland) Ltd v Minister for Social Welfare* [1998] 1 IR 34.

[44] [1998] 1 IR 34 at 49.

[45] *Cassidy v Ministry of Health* [1951] 2 KB 343.

[46] [1998] 1 IR 34 at 49–50.

account, is not decisive. The inference that the person is engaged in business on his or her own account can be more readily drawn where he or she provides the necessary premises or equipment or some other form of investment, where he or she employs others to assist in the business and where the profit which he or she derives from the business is dependent on the efficiency with which it is conducted by him or her.

[2.19] The test has since been applied by the High Court and the Supreme Court in a number of cases to ascertain if a person was an employee or an independent contractor: *Tierney v An Post,*[47] *Castleisland Cattle Breeding Society Ltd v Minister for Social and Family Affairs,*[48] *Kirwan v Technical Engineering and Electrical Union,* unreported, 14 January 2005, High Court,[49] *Dower v Radio Ireland Ltd,*[50] and *In the matter of the Social Welfare (Consolidation) Act 1993 ESB v The Minister for Social Community and Family Affairs and Others.*[51]

FACTORS INDICATING A CONTRACT FOR SERVICES

Opportunity for profit and risk of loss

[2.20] An important factor in determining whether a person is an independent contractor is the degree of responsibility and opportunity for investment and management that he has. In *Henry Denny & Sons (Ireland) Ltd v Minister for Social Welfare,*[52] the Supreme Court considered that among the factors pointing to Ms Mahon, a shop demonstrator for Henry Denny, being an employee were that her earnings from Henry Denny were determined exclusively by the extent to which her services were availed of by Denny and that she could not increase her profit by better management and employment of resources. In contrast, in *Ó Coindealbháin (Inspector of Taxes) v Mooney,*[53] Mr Mooney, engaged by the Department of Social Welfare as the manager of an employment office, was able to determine the profit which he made by managing his expenses in running the office. The High Court held that he was in business on his own account. Blayney J concluded, '[Mr Mooney] is clearly in business on his own account as the profit which he makes from the contract depends on how he decides to perform the work which has to be done.'[54]

[2.21] Even if the ability to profit is modest, it points away from an employment relationship. In *Tierney v An Post*[55] the Supreme Court acknowledged that Mr Tierney, a postmaster for An Post, had a modest ability to maximise the profit which he derived

---

47 *Tierney v An Post* [2000] I IR 536 (SC).
48 *Breeding Society Ltd v Minister for Social and Family Affairs* [2004] 4 IR 150 (SC).
49 *Kirwan v Technical Engineering and Electrical Union* (14 January 2005, unreported) HC.
50 *Dower v Radio Ireland Ltd* [2001] ELR 1 (HC).
51 *In the matter of the Social Welfare (Consolidation) Act 1993 ESB v The Minister for Social Community and Family Affairs, Eamonn Sheridan, Helen Kiely, Brendan Joyce, Francis Slattery, John McAleer and Aidan Brady* (21 February 2006, unreported) HC.
52 *Henry Denny & Sons (Ireland) Ltd v Minister for Social Welfare* [1998] 1 IR 34.
53 *Ó Coindealbháin (Inspector of Taxes) v Mooney* [1990] I IR 422.
54 [1990] I IR 422 at 432.
55 *Tierney v An Post* [2000] 1 IR 536.

from the post office. However, the court held that the limited nature of that ability could not affect the legal principles which required that it be a factor pointing to a contract for services.

[2.22] The ability to maximise profit is distinct to the entitlement to commission or other incentive payments. Such incentive payments do not usually indicate a contract for services.[56]

Provision of equipment

[2.23] Where an individual provides the necessary premises or equipment or some other form of investment to perform the work, this points to a contract for services. In *Henry Denny & Sons (Ireland) Ltd v Minister for Social Welfare*,[57] the fact that Denny provided the shop demonstrator, Ms Mahon, with clothing and equipment necessary to carry out the demonstration was one of the factors pointing to her being employed by Denny. In *Hogan v United Beverages*,[58] Smyth J in the Circuit Court held that Mr Hogan was not an employee of United Beverages in carrying out deliveries. Smyth J distinguished Mr Hogan's position to that of Ms. Mahon in *Henry Denny* on this point in that Mr Hogan provided the lorry to carry out the deliveries.

[2.24] In *Tierney v An Post*,[59] Mr Tierney provided the premises necessary for the carrying on of the business of the post office and some of the equipment. The Supreme Court considered this was of great importance in determining that Mr Tierney was engaged by An Post as an independent contractor. Similarly, in *Ó Coindealbháin (Inspector of Taxes) v Mooney*,[60] the High Court held that the fact that Mr Mooney had to provide and furnish the premises from which he was to provide the services was inconsistent with the contract being one of employment.

Code of practice in determining employment status

[2.25] The Employment Status Group set up under the Programme for Prosperity and Fairness produced a code of practice to assist in the task of identifying whether an individual is employed or self-employed. The Code was updated in December 2007 under the Towards 2016 Social Partnership Agreement. It provides practical guidance on how to distinguish between an employee and an independent contractor.[61]

---

[56] In *Byrne v Securispeed* UD 431/2001, EAT, the Tribunal considered that, while Mr Byrne, a motorcycle courier for Securispeed, received a basic payment per week and a payment per job, he did not own, share or determine the profitability of the work. The incentive payment did not, as a result, point to his being an independent contractor.

[57] *Henry Denny & Sons (Ireland) Ltd v Minister for Social Welfare* [1998] 1 IR 34.

[58] *Hogan v United Beverages* (14 October 2005) CC, [2006] 3 IELJ (note).

[59] *Tierney v An Post* [2000] 1 IR 536.

[60] *Ó Coindealbháin (Inspector of Taxes) v Mooney* [1990] 1 IR 422.

[61] The Code is contained in Appendix A.

FURTHER FACTORS TO IDENTIFY NATURE OF THE RELATIONSHIP

Categorisation by the parties

[2.26] The parties may agree that the relationship is one of employment or otherwise. However, any label such as 'independent contractor' or 'employee' is a conclusion as to the nature of the relationship. The label means nothing if the reality of the relationship does not accord with it. As Murphy J held in *Henry Denny & Sons (Ireland) Ltd v Minister for Social Welfare*:[62]

> [The provisions of the contract are] not of decisive importance. In my view their value, if any, is marginal. These terms are included in the contract but they are not contractual terms in the sense of imposing obligations on one party in favour of the other. They purport to express a conclusion of law as to the consequences of the contract between the parties. Whether Ms Mahon [the shop demonstrator engaged by Denny] was retained under a contract of service depends essentially on the totality of the contractual relationship express or implied between her and the appellant and not upon any statement as to the consequence of the bargain.

[2.27] The Supreme Court in *Castleisland Cattle Breeding Society Ltd v Minister for Social and Family Affairs* explained the approach to categorisation by the parties (*per* Geoghegan J):[63]

> There is nothing unlawful or necessarily ineffective about a company deciding to engage people on an independent contractor basis rather than on a 'servant' basis but as this court has pointed out in *Henry Denny* and other cases, in determining whether the new contract is one of service or for services the decider must look at how the contract is worked out in practice as mere wording cannot determine its nature. Nevertheless the wording of a written contract still remains of great importance. It can, however, emerge in evidence that in practice the working arrangements between the parties are consistent only with a different kind of contract or at least are inconsistent with the expressed categorisation of the contract.

Insurance

[2.28] Where an individual providing services is to provide his own insurance cover, for example professional indemnity or public liability insurance, it points to his being an independent contractor. In *Castleisland Cattle Breeding Society Ltd v Minister for Social and Family Affairs*, Geoghegan J considered the fact that the inseminators for Castleisland had to carry their own insurance was 'of huge importance in considering the nature of the contract'.[64]

---

[62] *Henry Denny & Sons (Ireland) Ltd v Minister for Social Welfare* [1998] 1 IR 34 at 53.

[63] *Castleisland Cattle Breeding Society Ltd v Minister for Social and Family Affairs* [2004] 4 IR 150 at 161.

[64] *Castleisland Cattle Breeding Society Ltd v Minister for Social and Family Affairs* [2004] 4 IR 150 at 160.

Taxation

[2.29] Taxation arrangements are a factor to be considered in assessing the working relationship. Where the person is registered as self employed for tax purposes, this will be a factor pointing to an independent contractor arrangement: *Castleisland Cattle Breeding Society Ltd v Minister for Social and Family Affairs*.[65] The taxation arrangement may, however, be due to the type of work involved rather than the working arrangement. In *Re Sunday Tribune*,[66] Carroll J pointed out that, in relation to journalists whose employment status was in question, the fact that income tax was not deducted in accordance with the PAYE system was not the determining factor. She found that the profession was such that a journalist may have income from more than one source under an employment contract or contract for services or both and, as a result, it was a matter of convenience permitted by Revenue to allow payments to be made without deduction of PAYE.

The structure of the industry

[2.30] In assessing the nature of the working arrangement, the structure of the particular industry can cast light on the relative weight to be given to the different elements of the relationship. In *Castleisland Cattle Breeding Society Ltd v Minister for Social and Family Affairs*,[67] the Supreme Court considered that a fundamental factor influencing the decision as to the employment status of cattle inseminators was that the business of artificial insemination of cattle was regulated by the Department of Agriculture. As a result, any contract, whether of employment or on an independent contractor basis, would have to contain such terms as were necessary to achieve strict compliance with the regulations. This had the effect that terms regarding control and the ability to appoint a substitute which would normally have pointed to an employment relationship were considered to be of no significance in assessing the relationship.

[2.31] Similarly, the High Court in *McAuliffe v Minister for Social Welfare*[68] viewed the relationship in the context of how the the haulage industry operated. Barr J considered what the terms of a hypothetical contract for services for a haulage company would be and compared them to the terms of a hypothetical employment contract. He concluded that the terms of the contracts between Mr McAuliffe, a wholesale distributor of newspapers and the individuals delivering newspapers for his company were employment contracts. Barr J based this conclusion on his finding that the contracts contained none of the distinguishing features of the hypothetical contract of service but had much in common with the hypothetical form of employment contract.

---

[65] *Castleisland Cattle Breeding Society Ltd v Minister for Social and Family Affairs* [2004] 4 IR 150.

[66] *Re Sunday Tribune* [1984] IR 505 (HC).

[67] *Castleisland Cattle Breeding Society Ltd v Minister for Social and Family Affairs* [2004] 4 IR 150.

[68] *McAuliffe v Minister for Social Welfare* [1994] ELR 239.

A QUESTION OF FACT AND LAW

[2.32] The question of whether a person is an employee is a mixed question of fact and law. This is important in relation to appeals which are limited to points of law as they are from the Employment Appeals Tribunal to the High Court. As Edwards J held in *The Minister for Agriculture and Food v John Barry & Ors*:[69]

> The test to be applied in identifying whether a contract is one of employment or for services is a pure question of law and so is its application to the facts. But it is for the tribunal of fact not only to find those facts but to assess them qualitatively and within limits, which are indefinable in the abstract, those findings and that assessment will dictate the correct legal answer.

[2.33] As the adjudicator, all elements of the working relationship must be looked at.[70] The Court of Appeal in *Hall (Inspector of Taxes) v Lorimer*[71] approved this explanation provided by Mummery J (whose decision was on appeal to the Court):[72]

> In order to decide whether a person carries on business on his own account it is necessary to consider many different aspects of that person's work activity. This is not a mechanical exercise of running through items on a checklist to see whether they are present in, or absent from, a given situation. The object of the exercise is to paint a picture from the accumulation of detail. The overall effect can only be appreciated by standing back from the detailed picture which has been painted, by viewing it from a distance and by making an informed, considered, qualitative appreciation of the whole. It is a matter of evaluation of the overall effect of the detail, which is not necessarily the same as the sum total of the individual details. Not all details are of equal weight or importance in any given situation. The details may also vary in importance from one situation to another.

[2.34] The adjudicator's role was well illustrated by the Employment Appeals Tribunal decision in *Pringle v Radio Teilifís Éireann*.[73] Mr Pringle worked as a television commercial announcer and radio presenter with RTÉ for almost seven years. He claimed that he had been unfairly dismissed by RTÉ and as a preliminary issue the Tribunal had to determine whether Mr Pringle had been employed by RTÉ. The Tribunal determined that Mr Pringle was not an employee. In reaching that conclusion, it extensively considered the details of the working relationship from the question of control through to the staff structure in RTÉ.

[2.35] The role of the court on appeal on a point of law as explained by Kenny J in *Mara (Inspector of Taxes) v Hummingbird* can be summarised as follows:[74]

---

[69] *In the matter of the Redundancy Payments Acts 1967 to 2003 and in the matter of the Minimum Notice and Terms of Employment Acts 1973 to 2001 and in the matter of an appeal by the Minister for Agriculture and Food, Between The Minister for Agriculture and Food v John Barry & Ors* (7 July 2008, unreported) HC at page 6.

[70] *Henry Denny & Sons (Ireland) v Minister for Social Welfare* [1998] 1 IR 34.

[71] *Hall (Inspector of Taxes) v Lorimer* [1994] IRLR 171.

[72] [1994] IRLR 171 at 174.

[73] *Pringle v Radio Teilifís Éireann* UD108/88.

[74] *Mara (Inspector of Taxes) v Hummingbird* [1982] ILRM 421 at 426 (SC).

- The court cannot set aside findings of primary fact unless there is no evidence to support those findings. The court on appeal will not interfere lightly with those findings. Hamilton CJ explained this in *Henry Denny*:[75]

   [C]ourts should be slow to interfere with the decisions of expert administrative tribunals. Where conclusions are based upon an identifiable error of law or an unsustainable finding of fact by a tribunal such conclusions must be corrected. Otherwise it should be recognised that tribunals which have been given statutory tasks to perform and exercise their functions…with a high degree of expertise and provide coherent and balanced judgments on the evidence and arguments heard by them it should not be necessary for the courts to review their decisions by way of appeal or judicial review.

- As inferences are drawn by applying legal principles to the facts, the court may overturn inferences if (i) they are based on an incorrect interpretation of documents, (ii) it is not reasonable to draw such inferences on the basis that they arise from a misdirection as to the law or a mistake in reasoning, or (iii) they show that a wrong view of the law was adopted.

[2.36] As a result, on appeal on a point of law, the appeal court's role is to assess the relationship in a broader way than the initial adjudicators. Before *Henry Denny*,[76] something of a practice had emerged of the High Court delving deeply into the facts of the relationship to glean employment status.[77]

[2.37] More recently, the courts on appeal have stepped back from wading through the details of the relationship and instead have reviewed the decision of the adjudicator on the basis of whether it was reasonable or not. In *In the matter of the Social Welfare (Consolidation) Act 1993 ESB v The Minister for Social Community and Family Affairs and Others*,[78] Gilligan J explained the approach to the appeal:[79]

   I take the view that this court has to be mindful that its own view of the particular decision arrived at is irrelevant. The court is not retrying the issue but merely considering the primary findings of fact and as to whether there was a basis for such findings and as to whether it was open to the Appeals Officer to arrive at the inferences drawn and adopting a reasonable coherent view, to arrive at her decision…

[2.38] He concluded:[80]

   I am satisfied that there are significant arguments to be made for and against the proposition that the individual respondent meter readers are employed pursuant to a contract of service. There are significant factual situations pertaining to the manner in

---

[75] *Henry Denny & Sons (Ireland) Ltd v Minister for Social Welfare* [1998] 1 IR 34 at 37–38.
[76] *Henry Denny & Sons (Ireland) v Minister for Social Welfare* [1998] 1 IR 34.
[77] See *Ó Coindealbháin (Inspector of Taxes) v Mooney* [1990] I IR 422 and *McAuliffe v Minister for Social Welfare* [1994] ELR 239 and *Re Sunday Tribune Ltd* [1984] IR 505.
[78] *In the matter of the Social Welfare (Consolidation) Act 1993 ESB v The Minister for Social Community and Family Affairs, Eamonn Sheridan, Helen Kiely, Brendan Joyce, Francis Slattery, John McAleer and Aidan Brady* [2006] ITR 63.
[79] [2006] ITR 63 at 77.
[80] [2006] ITR 63 at 79.

which the contract meter reader carried out the prescribed duties which will tend to support the arguments for and against employment pursuant to a contract of service but as previously indicated the situation has probably been finely balanced and I take the view that on the evidence available to her, the Appeals Officer was entitled to draw the inference that there was a change in the level of control that was exercised by the ESB over the individual respondent meter readers which entitled her to come to a conclusion that the individual meter readers were employed by the ESB pursuant to a contract of service.

ATYPICAL RELATIONSHIPS

[2.39] The term 'atypical worker' is often used to describe the working relationship which does not come within the usual arrangement.

Agency workers

[2.40] Agencies may be involved in working arrangements in two distinct ways. The first is where an agency introduces an individual to a client/end-user and the individual is then employed by the client. In this scenario, it is usually clear that the individual is an employee of the client. The second is where an agency assigns an agency worker to an end-user on a temporary basis. Under this arrangement, the agency worker is engaged under contract *sui generis*, a unique kind of contract.[81]

[2.41] The High Court in *The Minister for Labour v PMPA Insurance Company*[82] considered the contractual nature of this kind of agency arrangement. The Minister for Labour had brought proceedings against PMPA under the Holidays (Employees) Act 1973. The prosecution was brought against PMPA as employer of a temporary typist, Ms Nulty, who was engaged by PMPA under a written agreement with a temping agency. Barron J had to determine as a preliminary point if Ms Nulty was an employee of PMPA. He ruled out the possibility of such an employment contract:[83]

> Where, as here, there are three parties, it is necessary to look at the relationship of each of them to the other or others. Undoubtedly the employee worked under the control of *[PMPA]*. As a temporary typist it would probably not have been possible to distinguish the duties performed by her and the manner which they were allocated to her from the duties performed by and allocated to the permanent typists employed by *[PMPA]*. The primary question is not however she did the same work or was subject to the same control as permanent typists, but what rights and duties each had in respect of that work.

He concluded:[84]

> I am satisfied that the rights and duties of [PMPA] and the employee respectively sprang from the two contracts to which I have already referred. So far as [PMPA] was concerned its rights and duties in relation to the employee were enforceable solely under its agreement with the [agency] and against the [agency]. So far as the employee was concerned her rights and duties equally were enforceable solely under the term of her

---

81   *Minister for Labour v PMPA Insurance Company* [1986] JISLW 215.

82   *The Minister for Labour v PMPA Insurance Company* [1986] JISLW 215.

83   [1986] JISLW 215 at 216.

84   [1986] JISLW 215 at 216–217.

agreement with the [agency] and against the [agency]. In such a contractual situation I see no room for any implied contractual relationship between [PMPA] and the employee.

[2.42] Barron J referred to the decision of Cooke J in *Construction Industry Training v Labour Force Ltd*.[85] Cooke J had considered the contractual nature of the agency, end-user, agency worker relationship:[86]

> I think there is much to be said for the view that, where A contracts with B to render services exclusively to C, the contract is not a contract for services, but a contract sui generis, a different type of contract from either of the familiar two [an employment contract or a contract for services.]

Agency worker as employee of the agency

[2.43] It is unlikely that an agency worker will be found to be an employee of the agency. The agency rarely has control over the agency workers day-to-day work and while control is only one factor to be considered in gleaning employment status, it is an important consideration.

[2.44] A series of British cases has made clear that it is highly unlikely that the agency will be found to be the employer of the agency worker due to the lack of control exercised by the agency and insufficient mutuality of obligation between the agency and the agency worker.[87]

Agency worker as employee of the end-user

[2.45] It is more likely that the agency worker could, in certain circumstances, be found to be the employee of the end-user. The approach might be thought to stem from a concern that the agency worker should not stand without the protections of employment law as against the end-user who benefits from his work.

In *Diageo Global Supply v Mary Rooney*[88] the Labour Court held that Ms Rooney, an agency worker placed with Diageo as a part time occupational health nurse, was employed by Diageo. Her wages were paid by an employment agency. She claimed that Diageo was in breach of the Protection of Employees (Part-Time) Work Act 2001 as she was being treated less favourably than a comparable full-time employee of Diageo. To make such a claim, Ms Rooney had to be an employee of Diageo. The Court held that the claimant had entered into a contract with Diageo and had not had any contractual relationship with the agency. She had been interviewed by an employee of Diageo and had agreed her hours of work, rate of pay and other particulars of duties and benefits with Diageo. The Court went on to consider whether the contract was an employment

---

[85] *Construction Industry Training v Labour Force Ltd* [1970] 3 All ER 200.

[86] [1970] 3 All ER 200 at 225.

[87] See the decisions of the Court of Appeal in *McMeechan v Secretary of State for Employment* [1995] IRLR 461; *Montgomery v Johnson Underwood Ltd* [2001] IRLR 269; *Dacas v Brook St Bureau (UK) Ltd* [2004] IRLR 358; *Bunce v Postworth Ltd* [2005] IRLR 557; *Cable & Wireless plc v Muscat* [2006] IRLR 354. On the concept of mutuality of obligation, see para **[2.52]**.

[88] *Diageo Global Supply v Mary Rooney* [2004] ELR 133.

contract and applied the multiple test as set out by MacKenna J in *Ready Mixed Concrete*.[89] In applying the second limb of the test, the Court found that Diageo exercised control over Ms Rooney in the performance of her work to such a degree as to make Diageo her employer.

[2.46] The Court of Appeal in Britain has made clear that an employment contract may be implied between the end-user and the agency worker and that it may come into being over time.[90] However, the Court of Appeal in *James v Greenwich Council*[91] made clear that such a contract will only be implied where it is *necessary* to explain the relationship and not simply where it *looks like* the worker is an employee of the agency. As a result, it would be a rare case where direct employment with the end-user would be found.[92] This decision provided a welcome clarification of the circumstances in which an agency worker could be found to be the employee of the end-user.

The rights of agency workers

[2.47] Certain rights are accorded to agency workers under specific employment legislation. Several employment statutes include within the definition of the 'contract of employment' contracts between an agency and an agency worker. The employer is defined as the person liable to pay the wages of the agency worker, ie the agency. The agency is liable for the protection of the agency worker's rights under the following legislation:

   (i)   Terms of Employment (Information) Acts 1994 and 2001;

   (ii)   Organisation of Working Time Act 1997;

  (iii)   Maternity Protection Acts 1994 and 2004;

  (iv)   Adoptive Leave Acts 1995 and 2005;

   (v)   Carer's Leave Act 2001;

  (vi)   Parental Leave Acts 1998 and 2006;

 (vii)   Protection of Young Persons (Employment) Act 1996;

(viii)   Payment of Wages Act 1991;

  (ix)   National Minimum Wage Act 2000;

   (x)   Protection of Employees (Part-Time) Work Act 2001;

  (xi)   Redundancy Payments Acts 1967–2007;

 (xii)   Employment Equality Acts 1998–2008; and

(xiii)   EC (Protection of Employees on Transfer of Undertakings) Regulations 2003.

---

[89] *Ready Mixed Concrete (South East) Ltd v Minister of Pensions and National Insurance* [1968] 1 All ER 433 at 440.

[90] *Dacas v Brook St Bureau (UK) Ltd* [2004] IRLR 358, *Cable & Wireless plc v Muscat* [2006] IRLR 354 and *Franks v Reuters Ltd* [2003] IRLR 423.

[91] *James v Greenwich Council* [2008] EWCA Civ 35.

[92] *James v Greenwich Council* [2008] EWCA Civ 35.

The Unfair Dismissals Acts 1977–2007 treat the agency worker differently. For the purposes of the Acts, the agency worker is deemed to be the employee of the end-user.[93]

Future regulation
The Directive on Temporary Agency Work

[2.48] On a European level, consensus as to the rights of agency workers has proved difficult to achieve. On 22 October 2008, the European Parliament finally adopted the Temporary Agency Work Directive.[94] The Directive was first proposed in 2002 but the issue of extending equal treatment principles to temporary workers proved contentious, particularly with the UK Government. Key to securing the UK's agreement to the Directive was the provision which allows the UK to implement an agreement reached with the social partners in May 2008 under which agency workers must have 12 weeks' employment to be entitled to equal treatment.

Member States must transpose the Directive within three years of its entry into force. The Directive was published in the Official Journal of the European Union on 5 December 2008. Member States have until 5 December 2011 to implement its provisions.[95]

Main Provisions of the Directive

1. **Aim (Art 2)**

   The aim of the Directive is:
   - to ensure the protection of agency workers and to improve the quality of temporary agency work by ensuring the principle of equal treatment is applied to temporary agency workers and by recognising temporary work agencies as employers; while
   - taking into account the need to establish a suitable framework for the use of temporary agency work to contribute to the creation of jobs and to the development of flexible forms of working.

2. **Definitions (Art 3)**
   - 'temporary-work agency' means any natural or legal person who, in compliance with national law, concludes contracts of employment or employment relationships with temporary agency workers in order to assign them to user undertakings to work there temporarily under their supervision and direction;
   - 'temporary agency worker' means a worker with a contract of employment or an employment relationship with a temporary work agency with a view to being assigned to a user undertaking to work temporarily under its supervision and direction.

     Under this definition a temporary agency worker engaged under a contract *sui generis* would be a 'temporary agency worker' under the Directive.

---

[93] Unfair Dismissals (Amendment) Act 1993, s 13.
[94] Temporary Agency Word Directive 2008/14/EC.
[95] Temporary Agency Work Directive 2008/14/EC, Art 13.

- 'user undertaking' means any natural or legal person for whom and under the supervision and direction of whom a temporary agency worker works temporarily;
- 'basic working and employment conditions' means working and employment conditions laid down by legislation, regulations, administrative provisions, collective agreements and/or other binding general provisions in force in the user undertaking relating to:
  - i. the duration of working time, overtime, breaks, rest periods, night work, holidays and public holidays; and
  - ii. pay.

3. Equal treatment

The core protection provided by the Directive relates to equal treatment of agency workers with comparable permanent employees. Under Art 5 of the Directive:

- The basic working and employment conditions of temporary agency workers shall be, for the duration of their assignment at a user undertaking, at least those that would apply if they had been recruited directly by the undertaking to do the same job (Art 5(1));
- Member States may provide an exemption from this principle in relation to pay for agency workers who have a permanent contract with the agency and who continue to be paid between assignments (Art 5(2)).
- Member States may in collective agreements provide for arrangements which differ to this general equal treatment rule while respecting the overall protection of temporary agency workers (Art 5(3)).
- Member States may also, where there is no system for declaring collective agreements universally applicable or extending them to groups of undertakings establish arrangements for basic working and employment conditions which derogate from the equal treatment principle provided an adequate level of protection is provided (Art 5(4)).

The provision for involvement of the social partners on the detail and implementation of the equal treatment principle was key to finally reaching member state agreement on the Directive.

4. Access to Employment, Collective Facilities and Vocational Training (Art 6)

Temporary agency workers must be informed of any vacant posts in the user undertaking. Member States must take any action required to ensure that any clauses prohibiting or having the effect of preventing the agency worker entering into an employment contract or employment relationship directly with the user undertaking are null and void. Temporary agency workers must be given the same access to amenities as workers employed directly unless the difference in treatment is justified by objective reasons.

5. Representation of Temporary Agency Workers (Art 7)

Temporary agency workers shall count in the calculation of the threshold above which bodies representing workers can be formed at the temporary-work agency or Member States may provide that they count in the calculation for these purposes in the user undertaking.

6.   **Information of Workers' Representatives (Art 8)**

The user undertaking must provide suitable information on the use of temporary agency workers when providing information on the employment situation in that undertaking to bodies representing workers.

Commitments under Towards 2016 – Transitional Agreement

[2.49] Between April and September 2008, the Government and Social Partners reviewed progress under *Towards 2016*, the 10-Year Framework Social Partnership Agreement 2006–2015. The *Towards 2016 – Review and Transitional Agreement* was one of the results of this review. Section 8 of the Transitional Agreement contains provisions on 'Regulating Employment Agencies and Temporary Agency Workers' and provides the following commitments:

•   **The Temporary Agency Work Directive**

The Social Partners committed, arising from Art 5(4) of the Temporary Agency Work Directive, to develop a national framework, to encompass terms and conditions for temporary agency workers, which is appropriate to the Irish economy. The framework will strike the 'appropriate balance between the need to maintain temporary agency work as an instrument of business competitiveness and labour market flexibility, and fairness in the protection to be afforded to temporary agency workers under the Directive.'[96] It will also reflect the particular circumstances of the Irish labour market and take account of the position in other EU Member States. This agreed framework will be provided for in the legislation to transpose the Directive into Irish law[97];

•   **Use of Agency Workers to Replace Employees on Strike**

The Government has agreed to prohibit, save in relation to essential services, the use of agency workers, as defined under Art 3(1) of the Temporary Agency Work Directive, supplied by an agency, as defined in the Employment Agency Regulation Bill to be published before the end of 2008, by an employer for the direct replacement of employees in cases of an official strike or lock-out, where the employees are acting in accordance with a Labour Court recommendation. Until this prohibition is provided in the legislation transposing the Directive, it will apply on an interim basis in legislation to be enacted by the end of 2008, for a period not exceeding the time allowed for transposition of the Directive;[98]

•   **Employment Agency Regulation Bill**

The Government will publish the Employment Agency Regulation Bill before the end of 2008.[99] This legislation relates to the regulation of employment

---

[96]   Transitional Agreement, s 8.3.
[97]   Transitional Agreement, s 8.5.
[98]   Transitional Agreement, s 8.6.

agencies. Employment agencies are currently regulated under the Employment Agency Act 1971. The 1971 Act was enacted mainly to protect young Irish emigrants going to the UK from potential abuses by employment agencies.[100] With the employment market transformed in Ireland, the 1971 Act no longer reflects the labour market and does not, as a result, meet its needs. The Bill is intended to reflect this transformed market.

Mobile workers

[2.50] An increasingly common feature of working relationships is the 'mobile worker' or the 'teleworker' who works outside the normal fixed place of business. Due to the freedom that may be involved in such a working relationship, the question may arise as to whether the worker is an employee at all. As employees, the same rights and obligations arise as for more traditional working arrangements. In particular, the employee has the same entitlement in relation to working hours and health and safety, even though it may be difficult for the employer to monitor these matters. The EU Framework Agreement on Telework, a voluntary agreement negotiated by the European social partners in 2002 was aimed at establishing a general framework at European level to be implemented nationally, as appropriate. The agreement notes in the introduction that telework 'covers a wide and fast evolving spectrum of circumstances and practices' and, for that reason, 'telework' is given a broad definition (section 2):

> TELEWORK is a form of organising and/or performing work, using information technology, in the context of an employment contract/relationship, where work, which could also be performed at the employers premises, is carried out away from those premises on a regular basis.

[2.51] The agreement provides that telework is voluntary, that teleworkers benefit from the same rights as comparable workers at the employer's premises, all questions regarding work equipment are clearly defined before starting telework and, as a general rule, equipment is provided and maintained by the employer, the employer is responsible for the health and safety of the teleworker, the teleworker manages his or her own time within the framework of applicable legislation, collective agreements and company rules. In Ireland, the agreement was implemented by updating the Code of Practice on teleworking agreed by the Irish Congress of Trade Unions and IBEC (the Irish Business and Employers Confederation).

Casual workers

[2.52] Casual workers are those who work on an informal arrangement with no obligation to provide work and no obligation to offer it. The question of whether a casual worker is, in relation to a period of employment, an employee depends on the particular arrangement. Whether a casual worker has what is often referred to as an 'umbrella' or 'overarching' employment contract with the employer during the period

---

[99] Transitional Agreement, s 8.1. As at the time of writing, this has not yet been published.

[100] For further information on the 1971 Act and the need for review, see *Department of Enterprise, Trade and Employment, Review of the Employment Agency Act 1971 Discussion Paper* (May 2004).

between engagements was considered by the House of Lords in *Carmichael v National Power plc*[101] The House of Lords made clear that it considered that there is an irreducible minimum of mutual obligation necessary to create an employment contract (*per* Irvine LJ). The Court cited the judgments of Stephenson LJ in the Court of Appeal decision in *Nethermere (St Neots) Ltd v Gardiner*[102] and that of Sir Christopher Slade in *Clarke v Oxfordshire Health Authority.*[103] Where there is no obligation to accept or offer work during the period between engagements, an umbrella employment contract cannot to exist. The High Court in *The Minister for Agriculture and Food v John Barry & Ors.*[104] described the requirement of mutuality of obligation:[105]

> [t]he requirement of mutuality of obligation is the requirement that there must be mutual obligations on the employer to provide work for the employee and on the employee to perform work for the employer. If such mutuality is not present, then either there is no contract at all or whatever contract there is must be a contract for services or something else, but not a contract of service. It was characterised in *Nethermere (St. Neots) Ltd v Gardiner* [1984] ICR 612 as the 'one sine qua non which can firmly be identified as an essential of the existence of a contract of service'. Moreover, in *Carmichael v National Power PLC* [1999] ICR 1226, at 1230 it was referred to as 'that irreducible minimum of mutual obligation necessary to create a contract of service'. Accordingly the mutuality of obligation test provides an important filter. Where one party to a work relationship contends that the relationship amounts to a contract of service, it is appropriate that the court or tribunal seized of that issue should in the first instance examine the relationship in question to determine if mutuality of obligation is a feature of it. If there is no mutuality of obligation it is not necessary to go further. Whatever the relationship is, it cannot amount to a contract of service. However, if mutuality of obligation is found to exist the mere fact of its existence is not, of itself, determinative of the nature of the relationship and it is necessary to examine the relationship further.

Part-time workers

[2.53] All of the typical and atypical arrangements may be part-time arrangements. The Protection of Employees (Part-Time Work) Act 2001 introduced safeguards that provide that part-time employees are, in general, entitled to the same protections in as comparable full-time employees. Part-time workers are considered in detail in Ch 9, Part-Time Workers.

Fixed-term workers

[2.54] As with part-time workers, this category of relationship is often described as atypical. Fixed-term employees have been given specific protections under the

---

[101] *Carmichael v National Power plc* [1999] 4 All ER 897.

[102] *Nethermere (St Neots) Ltd v Gardiner* [1984] ICR 162.

[103] *Clarke v Oxfordshire Health Authority* [1998] IRLR 125 (CA).

[104] *In the matter of the Redundancy Payments Acts, 1967 to 2003 and in the matter of the Minimum Notice and Terms of Employment Acts 1973 to 2001 and in the matter of an appeal by the Minister for Agriculture and Food, Between The Minister for Agriculture and Food v John Barry & Ors* (7 July 2008, unreported) HC.

[105] (7 July 2008, unreported) HC at 17–18, *per* Edwards J.

Protection of Employees (Fixed-Term Work) Act 2003. Fixed-term workers are considered in Ch 10, Fixed-Term Workers.

OTHER RELATIONSHIPS

[2.55] If a person providing services to another is not an employee and is not an independent contractor, the question arises as to the correct classification of the relationship. The provision of one's work may be provided under as infinite arrangements as contract allows. The most common of these relationships are considered here.

Office holders

[2.56] As an office holder, a person is not an employee. The rights and duties are that of the office. A person may be an office holder and an employee at the same time but the employment relationship arises quite apart from the holding of the office. For example, a statutory director of a company is an office holder and may also be an employee. The characteristic features of an office were stated by the High Court in *Glover v BLN Ltd*:[106]

> ... it is created by Act of the National Parliament, charter, statutory regulation, articles of association of a company or of a body corporate formed under the authority of a statute, deed of trust, grant or by prescription; and that the holder of it may be removed if the instrument creating the office authorises this.

[2.57] A civil servant, a director of a company appointed under the Companies Acts, a member of an Garda Síochána, a secretary of a trade union and members of the clergy are examples of office holders. Administrative, constitutional law and the particular rules of the office may separately confer similar rights of fair procedures as those implicit in the employment relationship.

[2.58] A person may be an employee rather than an office holder if the relationship has moved away from the terms of the office and has taken on the characteristics of the personal employment relationship. This may occur where there has been a clear move away from the terms of the office. In *Kirwan v Technical Engineering and Electrical Union*,[107] Laffoy J considered whether Mr Kirwan a secretary to the defendant union was in fact an employee of the union. She found that the arrangements with Mr Kirwan were not the union rules which established the office but were in fact contractual. Having found that Mr Kirwan was not simply an office holder, the judge found that there was also very little material discernible difference between those arrangements and those in *Henry Denny*[108] and he was, therefore, an employee of the union.

---

[106] *Glover v BLN Ltd* [1973] IR 388 at 414.
[107] *Kirwan v Technical Engineering and Electrical Union* [2005] ELR 177 (HC).
[108] *Henry Denny & Sons (Ireland) Ltd v Minister for Social Welfare* [1998] 1 IR 34.

Apprentices

[2.59] Contracts of apprenticeship are not employment contracts. The difference between an employment contract and a contract of apprenticeship was explained by Widgery LJ in *Dunk v Waller:*[109]

> A contract of apprenticeship is significantly different from an ordinary contract of service if one has to consider damages for breach of contract by an employer. A contract of apprenticeship secures three things for the apprentice: it secures him, first, a money payment during the period of apprenticeship; secondly, that he shall be instructed and trained and thus acquire skills which will be of value to him for the rest of his life; and thirdly, it gives him status, because ... once a young man, as here, completes his apprenticeship and can show by certificate that he has completed his time with a well-known employer, this gets him off to a good start in the labour market and gives him status the loss of which may be of considerable damage to him.

[2.60] The bodies regulating the industry of the particular apprenticeship may provide rules applicable to the terms and conditions of engagement of the apprentice.

The statutory rights that are imposed into the contract of employment are also imposed into the contract of apprenticeship, whether the contract is oral or in writing under the following legislation:

   (i)   the Organisation of Working Time Act 1997;

   (ii)   the Maternity Protection Acts 1994 and 2004;

  (iii)   the Adoptive Leave Acts 1994 and 2005;

  (iv)   the Carer's Leave Act 2001;

   (v)   the Parental Leave Acts 1998 and 2006;

  (vi)   the Protection of Young Persons (Employment) Act 1996;

 (vii)   the Payment of Wages Act 1991;

(viii)   the Protection of Employees (Part-Time Work) Act 2001;

  (ix)   the Redundancy Payments Acts 1967–2007;

   (x)   the Protection of Employment Acts 1977–2007;

  (xi)   the Unfair Dismissals Acts 1977–2007;

 (xii)   the Employment Equality Acts 1998–2008; and

(xiii)   the EC (Protection of Employees on Transfer of Undertakings Regulations 2003.

The National Minimum Wage Act 2000 applies to apprentices and provides for the payment of a reduced minimum wage for certain trainees.[110]

[2.61] Contracts of apprenticeship are not included within the definition of the 'contract of employment' in the Protection of Employees (Fixed-Term Work) Act 2003. The main effect of this exclusion is that apprentices are not entitled under the Act to a permanent contract after four years on two or more successive fixed term contracts.[111]

---

[109] *Dunk v Waller* [1970] 2 All ER 630 at 634.

[110] National Minimum Wage Act 2000, s 16.

[111] *ESB Networks v David Kingham* FTC/05/6 and *ESB Networks v Group of Workers* FTC/06/6.

Workers

[2.62] The term 'worker' is used throughout the Industrial Relations Acts 1946–2004. The Acts provide two definitions. For the purposes of the provisions on trade unions, eg picketing, immunities that apply for acts done in the context of a trade dispute and rules of trade union procedure, s 8 of the Industrial Relations Act 1990 defines a 'worker' as:

> [a]ny person who is or was employed whether or not in the employment of the employer with whom a trade dispute arises, but does not include a member of the Garda Síochána.

[2.63] It is not clear if a person who is not an employee is included in this definition. The best authority on the point is the High Court findings on two occasions that this question is a fair issue to be tried: *Lamb Bros Dublin Ltd v Davidson*[112] and *Daru Blocklaying Ltd v Building and Allied Trades' Union*.[113] 'Employed' does not mean actual present employment but rather refers to the worker's occupation or way of life.[114]

[2.64] For the purposes of industrial relations mechanisms under the Acts, s 23 of the Industrial Relations Act 1990 provides the definition of the term:

> ...'worker' means any person aged 15 years or more who has entered into or works under a contract with an employer, whether the contract be for manual labour, clerical work or otherwise, whether it be expressed or implied, oral or in writing, and whether it be a contract of service or of apprenticeship, or a contract personally to execute any work or labour including, in particular, a psychiatric nurse employed by a health board and any person designated for the time being under subsection (3) [which gives power to the Minister or Finance to designate others as included in this definition those employed under section 30(1)(g) of the Defence Act 1954 or employed by or under the State] but does not include –
>
> (a)   a person who is employed by or under the State,
>
> (b)   a teacher in a secondary school,
>
> (c)   a teacher in a national school,
>
> (d)   [deleted by Industrial Relations Act 1990 (Definition of 'worker' Order 1998, SI No 264 of 1998) so as to include officers of health boards and local authorities],
>
> (e)   an officer of a vocational educational committee, or
>
> (f)   an officer of a school attendance committee.
>
> (4) Any person who stands designated by virtue of section 17(2)(a) of the Industrial Relations Act 1969 at the passing of this Act shall remain designated for the purpose of subsection 1 unless the designation is cancelled under subsection (3)(b) [which gives the Minister for Finance power to cancel such designation. State industrial employees and civilian employees with the Defence Forces were designated under this section on 8 October 1969.

---

[112] *Lamb Bros Dublin Ltd v Davidson* [1978] ILRM 226.

[113] *Daru Blocklaying Ltd v Building and Allied Trades' Union* [2002] 2 IR 619.

[114] *Goulding Chemicals Ltd v Bolger* [1977] IR 211 at 230.

This definition has been held by the Labour Court to include independent contractors.[115]

Agents

[2.65] Where a person is an agent of another, the person is appointed to act as the representative of the other, who is known as the principal. An employee is an agent of the employer but an agent is not necessarily the employee of the principal. The agency relationship is governed by common law principles which recognise particular rights and obligations between the agent and the principal.[116] Commercial agents benefit from specific protections under the EC (Commercial Agents) Regulations 1994[117] and 1997.[118] A 'commercial agent' for the purposes of the Regulations is defined as:

> [a] self-employed intermediary who has continuing authority to negotiate the sale or purchase of goods on behalf of another person, hereinafter called 'the principal', or to negotiate and conclude such transactions on behalf of and in the name of the principal.[119]

Controlling shareholders and directors

[2.66] A person may be both an employee of a company and the controller and owner of the company. This stems directly from the separate legal personality of the company.[120] The Court of Appeal in *Secretary of State for Business, Enterprise and Regulatory Reform v Neufeld and Howe*[121] clarified the approach to be taken in determining if a controlling shareholder is an employee of the company. The Court concluded[122] that whether or not a shareholder or director is an employee of the company is a question of fact for the court or tribunal before which such issue arises. There may be two issues to consider in carrying out that assessment: (i) whether the contract is genuine or a sham; and (ii) if the contract is genuine, is it a contract of employment. As to the first issue, the Court considered that it would probably only arise in relatively exceptional cases.

In relation to the second issue, the Court identified factors that will be of relevance in considering that issue. A director of a company is the holder of an office and will not, merely, by virtue of that office be an employee. It will be relevant to consider how the director has been paid, whether by salary, which points towards employment, or by director's fees, which points away from it. In considering what the putative employee

---

[115] *Mythen Brothers Ltd v Building and Allied Trades Union* [2006] ELR 237 and *McKevitt v Building and Allied Trades Union* REA 95/2005. See Kerr, *The Trade Unions and Industrial Relations Acts* (3rd edn, Round Hall, 2007).

[116] See further *Chitty on Contracts, Specific Contracts* (30th edn, Sweet & Maxwell, 2008). As to when an agency relationship is created, see McDermott, *Contract Law* (Tottel Publishing, 2001).

[117] SI 33/1994.

[118] SI 31/1997.

[119] SI 33/1994, Reg 2(1).

[120] *Salomon v Salomon & Co* [1897] AC 22, *Lee v Lee's Air Farming Ltd* [1961] AC 12, Privy Council, *Sweeney v Duggan* [1991] 2 IR 274.

[121] *Secretary of State for Business, Enterprise and Regulatory Reform v Neufeld and Howe* [2009] EWCA Civ 280.

[122] [2009] EWCA Civ 280 at paras 80–87.

was actually *doing*, it will also be relevant to consider whether he was acting merely in his capacity as a director of the company or whether he was acting as an employee.

The Court also identified factors which will *not* be of particular relevance to the carrying out of the assessment as to whether a contract of employment exists: (i) the fact that the putative employee's shareholding in the company gave him control of the company, even total control; and (ii) the fact that he will have share capital invested in the company or that he may have loan obligations to it or that he has personally guaranteed its obligations or that his personal investment in the company will stand to prosper in line with the company's prosperity or that he has done any of the things that the 'owner' of a business will commonly do on its behalf.

Partners

[2.67] A partnership is the default relationship which exists when parties join together in a business venture without forming a company. A partnership, being a joint venture arrangement, is not a relationship of employer and employee.[123] The consequences of partnership are derived from the Partnership Act 1890 and the common law.

[2.68] To determine if a relationship between parties is one of employment or one of partnership one must have regard to the contract and intention of the parties as appearing from the whole of the arrangement. This is will illustrated by the High Court decision in *DPP and The Collector General v McLoughlin*.[124] Mr McLoughlin was the owner and skipper of a fishing trawler which normally carried a crew of five. The crew were engaged prior to each expedition and tended to turn up regularly for expeditions. He was prosecuted by complainants for failing to make certain returns under social welfare and income tax codes for employees. The question as to whether Mr McLoughlin was the employer of the crew came before the High Court from the District Court. Costello J concluded that the crew were in partnership, and, as such, were not employed by Mr McLoughlin.

[2.69] The factors in favour of the crew being employees were:

(i)   proceeds of the sale of the catch were paid directly to the defendant and then dispersed to the crew;

(ii)   in some instances the defendant made payments to members of the crew by what was known as 'subs'; and

(iii)   when no profit was made, the crew bore no loss.

Costello J held that these factors were outweighed by three other factors which strongly suggested that there was a partnership:

(i)   each weekly voyage was a separate venture and no crew member had a contract which entitled him to take part in any subsequent voyage;

---

[123] *Minister for Social Welfare v Griffiths* [1992] ILRM 44 (HC), where Blayney J held that a share fishing arrangement was a partnership and not a relationship of employer and employee.

[124] *Director of Public Prosecutions and The Collector General v McLoughlin* [1986] IR 355 (HC), Costello J.

(ii)   when he participated in an expedition he was not paid any wages but became entitled to a share in the net profits if any; and

(iii)   most importantly, he held, although McLoughlin engaged each crew member, he did not determine what the rate of remuneration would be.

This was determined partly by custom and partly by agreement between the crew themselves in consultation with him.

Volunteers

[2.70] A volunteer's relationship with the recipient of her services usually lacks the requisite element of control and mutual obligation that would point to an employment contract.[125] However, the title 'volunteer' will not prevent the individual being found to be an employee where the relationship is not simply contained within the parameters of the rules of the volunteering role.[126]

---

[125] *Rogers v Booth* [1937] 2 All ER 751.

[126] *Kirwan v Technical Engineering and Electrical Union* (14 January 2005, unreported) HC, see para **[2.58]** above.

Chapter 3

The Terms of the Employment Contract

Janice Walshe

INTRODUCTION

[3.01] A contract of employment is governed by the common law principles of contract law. Therefore, like any other contract, it must contain the basic elements of:

(i)   offer;

(ii)   acceptance;

(iii)   consideration; and

(iv)   intention to create legal relations

However, over the years, legislation has been enacted to ensure that employees are given certain basic protections within the employment relationship. Thus, certain legislation governing employment rights cannot be contracted out of in the employment contract and, whether or not expressed in written form, these terms will apply to the relationship between the employer and the employee. Similarly, case law over the years has dictated that there are certain terms that are implied into every contract of employment, whether or not the parties to the contract are aware of those terms.

[3.02] The terms of a contract of employment can be express or implied, oral or written. Usually a contract is made up of all four, to a greater or lesser extent. Sometimes, these terms will conflict with each other. In that situation, the traditional approach was to invoke the *parol evidence rule*, ie the rule that no oral evidence could be adduced to vary, contradict or alter the written terms of a contract. However, over time, a less harsh approach has been adopted that has ameliorated the extreme and sometimes unfair consequences of this rule. The modern approach is that while written terms are presumed to have been the intention of the parties, this presumption can be rebutted by other evidence.

EXPRESS TERMS

[3.03] An express term is one which is recorded in a written contract between the parties or openly expressed at the time the contract is entered into.[1]

Written terms

[3.04] Prior to 1973 there was no obligation on an employer to put terms and conditions of employment in writing. The Minimum Notice and Terms of Employment Act 1973 provided that details of certain terms and conditions of employment were to be made

---

[1]   *Chitty on Contracts* (29th edn, Sweet & Maxwell, 2004), Vol I para 13-001.

available to employees on request. However, employees rarely sought these written details. Subsequently, the Unfair Dismissals Act 1977 provided that an employer should make known to an employee, in writing, the procedure that would be adopted in the event of dismissal being proposed or taking place and to do so 'not later than 28 days after (the particular employer) enters into a contract of employment with (the particular employee)'.[2]

It was only in May 1994 with the coming into force of the Terms of the Employment (Information) Act 1994 that employers were required to furnish written notice of certain basic terms of employment to employees.

Terms of Employment (Information) Act 1994

[3.05] Directive 91/533/EEC was adopted by the Council of the European Communites (as it was then known) on 14 October 1991. It obliged employers to inform employees of conditions applicable to the contract of employment or employment relationship. As a result of the Directive, the Oireachtas enacted the Terms of Employment (Information) Act 1994 (the Act) in May 1994. Under s 8 of the Protection of Employees (Part-time Work) Act 2001[3] the protection of the Act was extended to part-time employees.

The Act applies as between employers and employees and also it applies to persons employed through employment agencies who are deemed for the purposes of this legislation to be employed by the party paying the wages.

The legislation does not apply to employees with less than one month's service.

Statements of terms and conditions of employment

[3.06] Under the Act, an employer is obliged to provide an employee with a statement in writing no later than two months after the commencement of employment containing the following particulars:

(i)   the full names of both employer and employee;

(ii)   the address of the employer;

(iii)   the place of work or, alternatively, a statement specifying that the employee is required or permitted to work at various places;

(iv)   the title of the job or nature of the work;

(v)   the date of commencement of the contract of employment;

(vi)   in the case of temporary contracts, the expected duration or in the case of a fixed term contract the date on which the contract expires;

(vii)   the rate or method of calculation of the employee's remuneration and details as to at what intervals the payment of remuneration shall be made;

(viii)   any terms or conditions relating to hours of work including overtime;

(ix)   any terms or conditions relating to paid leave (other than paid sick leave);

(x)   any terms or conditions relating to sick leave or for payment due to incapacity as a result of injury;

---

[2]   Unfair Dismissals Act 1977, s 14.

[3]   The collective citation is the Terms of Employment (Information) Acts 1994 and 2001.

(xi)   details of pensions or pension schemes;

(xii)   the period of notice which the employee is required to give and entitled to receive whether by statute or contract. If a specified period of notice is not provided for then the method or manner by which notice is to be calculated is to be specified;

(xiii)   reference must be made to any collective agreements which directly affect the terms and conditions of the employee's employment including, where the employer is not a party to such agreements, particulars of the bodies or institutions by whom they were made. This requirement only applies to contracts entered into after the commencement of the Act (16 May 1994);

(xiv)   if after the commencement of the Act an employee is required to work outside the State for a minimum period of one month the following details are to be given to the employee or added to the above-mentioned statement:

–   the period of employment outside the State;

–   the currency in which the employee is to be remunerated in respect of that period;

–   any benefits in cash or kind for the employee while working outside the State; and

–   the terms and conditions applying to the employee's repatriation; and

(xv)   employers are obliged to notify employees of any changes in their terms and conditions of employment as soon as possible after the change but no later than one month thereafter.

Any complaints by an employee of contravention of the Act by an employer may be referred to a rights commissioner. The Rights Commissioner may require the employer to provide the particulars and also, if appropriate, may order the payment of compensation to a maximum of four weeks' remuneration.

[3.07] In addition to the Terms of Employment (Information) Act, the Terms of Employment (Information) Act 1994 (Section 3(6)) Order[4] requires employers to provide employees who are under the age of eighteen and who have been in (the employer's) continuous service for at least one month with an 'abstract of the Protection of Young Persons (Employment) Act 1996'; (a 'Summary of Main Rules on Employing People Under 18')[5] and to do so 'not later than one month after the commencement of the…employment'.

The Terms of Employment (Additional Information) Order[6] also requires employers to furnish employees who have been in their (the employers') continuous service for at least one month with statements in writing 'containing particulars of the times and duration of rest periods and breaks referred to in ss 11, 12 and 13 of the Act [Organisation of Working Time Act 1997] that are being allowed to the employee and of

---

4   SI 4/1997.

5   As prescribed by the Protection of Young Persons (Employment) Act 1996, s 12 and in the form specified in the Sch to the Protection of Young Person (Prescribed Abstract) Regulations 1997 (SI 3/1997).

6   SI 49/1998.

any other terms and conditions relating to those periods and breaks' and to do so 'within two months after ... commencement of employment'.

[3.08] It is important to remember that the statement to be furnished to employees under the Terms of Employment (Information) Act 1994 and the additional information required by legislation to be given to employees are not the same as a contract of employment. The Act does not have regard to contract law in a couple of respects. Firstly, it allows that the terms and conditions of employment be furnished after the employment relationship has been entered into; this could well give rise to difficulty if there is subsequently a dispute over the terms because the contract of employment will already have been entered into and any disputed term might be deemed to be an attempted unilateral variation. Secondly, reference is made to amendment and the notification of amendments to employees. No mention is made of the necessity to have consent to contractual amendments or variations. Given that the statement to be furnished to the employee under the Act is not a contract, there is no obligation on the employee to sign or agree the terms as set out in the statement. That said, a prudent employer will seek to have a written and signed contract of employment agreed with the employee that will cover the areas provided for in the Act, and that will also cover additional issues that frequently become contentious between the parties.

Contracts of employment

[3.09] A contract of employment can be as basic or as detailed as the parties choose. Very often, contracts are documents that cover only the most basic terms of the employee's engagement. However, employers frequently seek to have very detailed contracts particularly with senior employees. Employers will that attempt to cover every eventuality that might arise in these contracts.

Contracts of employment often make reference to employment handbooks and state that the contents of the handbook are incorporated into the contract and have binding effect. In such a situation, it is very important to ensure that the handbook is furnished to the employees, and that any amendments to the handbook are notified to the employee. In addition, it is sensible to require an employee to sign for the employment handbook upon receipt of it.

Standard contract terms

[3.10] The following are terms that will generally be found in a well-drafted and comprehensive contract of employment.

Description of contract

[3.11] A contract of employment should expressly state that it is a contract of service, as opposed to a contract for services. While the name or description that parties place on their arrangement will not be conclusive in determining what relationship they have, it may be of persuasive effect and, therefore, if the parties understand that they are 'employer' and 'employee' this should be expressly stated.[7]

---

[7] On the distinction between a contract for services and a contract of service, see Ch 2, The Contract and Relationship of Employment, para **[2.16]**–**[2.19]**.

Parties

[3.12] A contract of employment should expressly state who the parties to the contract are, ie who exactly is the employer and who is the employee. This is particularly important where the employee is employed by one party but paid by another, eg different companies in a group of companies.

Date of commencement

[3.13] A contract should state the date of commencement of the employment. Very often parties agree employment terms a number of weeks or months before the employment starts. Therefore it is very important that the written contract provides a commencement date, in particular because where certain of the employee's statutory entitlements will depend on length of service, eg notice, statutory redundancy payments and the entitlement to take parental leave.

Job title

[3.14] A contract should give a job title for the employee or a description of the duties that the employee will be expected to undertake. While employers often wish to draft a job description as broadly as possible, this can lead to difficulties if a redundancy situation arises for the job that the employee actually carries out.

Probation

[3.15] If the employment is subject to the employee successfully passing a probationary period, this should be expressly stated in the contract. The duration of the probationary period should also be clearly stated.

If an employer wants the employee to have a probationary period, this should be stated to the employee in advance of the employment commencing. In *Doyle v Grangeford Precast Concrete Ltd*[8] the employer sought to impose a probationary period in a written document produced to the employee for his signature after he had commenced employment. The employee refused to sign the contract and was dismissed. The employee obtained an interlocutory injunction pending the outcome of his claim for damages.

The contract should state what provisions apply in respect of notice during the probationary period. Very often, employers will want to ensure that employees, particularly senior executives, are obliged to give relatively lengthy periods of notice but the employer will also want to ensure that it is not obliged to give an employee who does not reach the required standards of performance during the probationary period similarly lengthy notice of termination.

[3.16] While it is generally accepted that the employer has an implied right to terminate during the probationary period on the giving of specified or reasonable notice, a probationary period can sometimes be worded in such a way as to give rise to an argument that the probationary period is in itself a fixed term within the contract. If a contract were to state, for example, 'the first six months of this contract shall be a

---

[8]   *Doyle v Grangeford Precast Concrete Ltd* (1998) ELR 260.

probationary period' this might give rise to a claim on early termination, eg after one month, that the employee is entitled to be paid the balance of five months' salary.

Hours of work

[3.17] The basic hours of work that the employee will be required to undertake should be stated in the contract and in addition, the contract should set out any provisions in respect of rest breaks, payment for Sunday work etc. The contract should expressly state whether or not the employee can be required to work overtime and if so, what provisions apply to the payment of such overtime.

Employers should be aware that under the Organisation of Working Time (Records) (Prescribed Form and Exemptions) Regulations 2001 they are required to keep records of the hours worked by an employee.[9]

Place of work

[3.18] The contract should state where the employee is to carry out his or her work, whether it is in the employer's main place of business or at some other location. Employers should decide whether or not a 'mobility' clause is required in the contract and if so, how broad that clause should be.

In *Rank Xerox Ltd v Churchill*,[10] the appellants were secretaries with a London firm. Their contracts specified a place of work but stated 'the company may require you to transfer to another location'. The company relocated to Marlow and the appellant claimed redundancy. The Industrial Tribunal allowed the claim and held that this was an ambiguous clause and that a degree of reasonableness must therefore be interpreted into the mobility clause. However, the UK EAT allowed the appeal. It held that the clause was not ambiguous and the appellants were contractually obliged to work wherever their employer demanded. There was no scope for introducing the concept of reasonableness in such circumstances.

[3.19] However, it should be noted that in the *Rank Xerox* case, there appeared to be no question that the employer was acting in bad faith or capriciously and the UK EAT took a very different approach in *United Bank v Akhtar*[11] where the contract of employment stated that:

> [t]he bank may from time to time require an employee to be transferred temporarily or permanently to any place of business which the bank may have in the United Kingdom for which a relocation allowance or other allowances may be payable at the discretion of the bank.

In this case, Mr Akhtar received a written notice on Friday, 5 June, from the bank requiring him to move to the bank's Birmingham branch on Monday, 8 June. He was also not offered any financial assistance. Mr Akhtar asked the transfer to be postponed by three months, in view of his wife's ill health and the impending sale of his house. However, the bank refused and Mr Akhtar considered himself constructively dismissed

---

9   SI 473/2001. See further Ch 4, Working Time.
10   *Rank Xerox Ltd v Churchill* (1988) IRLR 280.
11   *United Bank v Akhtar* [1989] IRLR 507.

[3.25] The Pensions (Amendment) Act 2002 provides that all employees must be provided with *access* to a pension or personal retirement savings account where:

(i)   the employer does not provide staff with membership of an occupational pension scheme;

(ii)   all staff are not eligible to join an existing occupational pension scheme;

(iii)   eligibility to join the staff pension scheme exceeds six months;

(iv)   no Additional Voluntary Contribution (AVC) plan exists.

An employer must also give employees time off to allow them to seek access to a pension scheme.

Retirement age

[3.26] Many employers omit to make reference to retirement age because it is provided for in the pension scheme. Employers should specify the actual retirement age. That age may in turn be subject to variation within the terms of the pension scheme. The possibility of such variation should also be referred to by the employer. In *Buckley v Ceimici Teo*,[18] the claimant commenced employment at a time when there was no contractual provision regarding retirement and the normal retirement age was 70 years. His employment was terminated when he reached 65 which was the pension age. The claimant maintained he was entitled to continue working until the normal retirement age of 70. The respondents, however, were in a position to produce documentary evidence that the normal retirement age had changed to 65 years and that the claimant was aware of this. The dismissal was held to be fair.

[3.27] The issues of age, retirement age and fitness to work were considered by the High Court in *Donegal County Council v Porter*.[19] The respondents were employed by the County Council as part-time firemen. When they commenced service the retirement age was 60. Subsequently, the policy of Donegal County Council, in common with other fire authorities in Ireland and Britain, changed in favour of compulsory retirement at age 55. The change was by reason of the fact that it was considered that the work had become more hazardous and stressful and required more agility and flexibility. Firemen employed from the time of the change had a term in their contracts of employment specifying the earlier retirement age. In December 1985 the Department of the Environment issued a Directive recommending the introduction of a retirement age of 55 and compulsory annual medical examination for all operational personnel.

The respondents' contracts provided for retirement at age 60 and they never at any time agreed to an alteration or variation in their contract. The county council subsequently retired them at age 55 which the Court held was an attempt to unilaterally alter the contract and was in breach of contract unless it could be justified in some other lawful way which it was not.

---

[17]   (\...contd) On equal treatment obligations in relation to pensions, see Ch 11, Pay, Pensions and Benefits, para **[11.70]–[11.115]**.

[18]   *Buckley v Ceimici Teo* UD 528/80.

[19]   *Donegal County Council v Porter* [1993] ELR 101.

The council put forward a strong plea with expert evidence that employees should retire at 55 and made reference to the Safety, Health and Welfare Act 1989, s 61. The Court held, in dismissing the claim of the county council to be entitled to compulsorily retire firemen at 55, that there is a statutory duty to observe but it can be observed:

> [b]y a much less draconian measure than dismissal at the age of 55 and one which does not involve a blatant disregard for the Council's contractual obligations ... they can comply with their statutory obligation in requiring ... the respondents to undergo medical examination from such age and at such frequency as they consider necessary to assure all persons concerned of the physical fitness of the men in the fire-fighting services ... this is consistent with the terms implicit in the men's contract of service – while fit and capable they have a contractual expectation of service to age 60 – if not fit and capable there are substantial grounds justifying dismissal.

Grievance and disciplinary procedure

[3.28] A contract of employment or employment handbook should contain a procedure for employees to invoke in the context of any grievance or issue they have at work. Separately, they should also have a clear disciplinary procedure in place to be used when an employee's performance or conduct falls short of the standards reasonably expected. There is no need for either procedure to be overly elaborate but in light of the heavy emphasis given by the courts and tribunals on the need to have such procedures, their importance cannot be over-estimated. The absence of a procedure or the failure to use it correctly will lead to employers being at a serious disadvantage when it comes to defending an unfair dismissal claim.

The presence of a clear grievance procedure will help to reduce any potential industrial relations difficulties at work. The essence of a grievance procedure is that it should allow an employee, however senior they might be, to raise their grievance with the next layer of management and for that grievance to be dealt with in the most appropriate manner, either informally through mediation (if all the parties agree) or formally through an investigation.

[3.29] The Industrial Relations Act 1990 (Code of Practice on Grievance and Disciplinary Procedures) (Declaration) Order 2000[20] contains 'general guidelines on the application of grievance and disciplinary procedures and the promotion of best practice in giving effect to such procedures'.

While the Code of Practice is not legally binding, it certainly represents best practice and it states that 'the principles and procedures of this Code of Practice should apply unless alternative agreed procedures exist in the workplace which conform to its general provisions for dealing with grievance and disciplinary issues'.

The Code states that grievance and disciplinary procedures should be in writing and presented in a format and language that is easily understood, with copies of the procedures given to all employees at the commencement of employment and included in employee programmes of induction and refresher training and trade union programmes of employee representative training.

---

[20] SI 146/2000. This code is contained in the Appendix F.

The Code acknowledges that procedures for dealing with grievance and disciplinary matters will vary according to the particular organisation, but confirms that all procedures must comply with the general principles of natural justice and fair procedures which include:

- That employee grievances are fairly examined and processed;
- That details of any allegations or complaints are put to the employee concerned;
- That the employee concerned is given the opportunity to respond fully to any such allegations or complaints;
- That the employee concerned is given the opportunity to avail of the right to be represented during the procedure;
- That the employee concerned has the right to a fair and impartial determination of the issues concerned, taking into account any representations made by, or on behalf of, the employee and any other relevant or appropriate evidence, factors or circumstances.

Restrictive covenants

[3.30] Restrictive covenants are clauses included in employment contracts which seek to protect an employer's business interests both during and after the termination of an employee's employment. These clauses work so as to restrict employees from competing with their employers after they leave employment or to protect the employer's proprietary interest in trade secrets, confidential information, or customer/ supplier relationships.

Clauses in an employment contract which prohibit an employee from competing with their employer after the termination of their employment amount to a restraint of trade. In the classic exposition of the doctrine of restraint of trade, Lord Macnaghten in *Nordenfelt v Maxim Nordenfelt Guns and Ammuntion Company*[21] stated:

> The public have an interest in every person's carrying on his trade freely: so has the individual. Interference with individual liberty of action in trading, and all restraints of trade themselves, if there is nothing more, are contrary to public policy, and therefore void. That is the general rule. But there are exceptions: restraints of trade and interference with individual liberty of action may be justified by the special circumstances of the particular case. It is a sufficient justification, and indeed it is the only justification, if the restriction is reasonable – reasonable, that is, in reference to the interests of the public, so framed and so guarded as to afford adequate protection to the party in who favour it is imposed while at the same time it is in no way injurious to the public.

There is a clear distinction in law between the enforceability of restrictive covenants during the life of the employment relationship and the enforceability of post-termination restrictive covenants. The restrictive covenants which arise in the course of the employment relationship are essentially bound up in the duty of fidelity, which duty is implied into the contract of employment.[22] This duty encompasses many of the

---

[21] *Nordenfelt v Maxim Nordenfelt Guns and Ammuntion Company* [1894] AC 535 at 565.
[22] See paras **[3.52]**–**[3.53]**, Duty of loyalty and fidelity.

restrictions often sought to be imposed post-termination eg competing with the employer, poaching employees, keeping confidential the employer's confidential information. Even though implied, these restrictions are usually also expressly provided for in the contract of employment. These restrictions, though caught within the restraint of trade doctrine, are rarely found to be unenforceable given the reasonable interest of the employer in the protection of his goodwill and stability of his workforce. However, the implied duty of fidelity comes to an end upon termination of employment. It is at this point that the strength of post-termination restrictive covenants becomes relevant. The courts will uphold a restrictive covenant if it is:

(i)   designed to protect a legitimate interest of an employer.

There are two main interests which an employer is entitled to seek to protect: trade connections and information[23] and the maintenance of a stable workforce;[24] and

(ii)   goes no further than is reasonably necessary to protect that interest. The clause must be reasonable as between the parties and be reasonable in the public interest.

If an employer wishes to protect its business using such a clause then, in order for those clauses to be upheld by the courts, specific criteria must be satisfied.

[3.31] Two cases in particular have come before the Irish courts in recent times which have considered the principles relating to restrictive covenants and have set down guidelines which are helpful in assessing whether or not a restrictive covenant will ultimately be deemed to be reasonable and enforceable by the courts.

In *Murgitroyd & Company v Purdy*[25] the defendant had been employed as a European Patent Attorney to work at the plaintiff's Dublin office. The defendant subsequently left and commenced practicing as 'Purdy & Associates' from premises in Dublin 2. The plaintiffs alleged that in establishing that business and in particular having regard to the fact that two significant clients of the plaintiffs immediately transferred their work to Purdy & Associates, the defendant was in breach of certain covenants in his contract of employment. The defendant's contract of service contained non-compete and non-solicitation clauses as outlined below.

The non-compete clause:

> The Executive will not within the Republic of Ireland during the period of twelve months following determination of his employment hereunder on his account and in competition with the Company carry on any business which competes with the business of the Company or any associated Company having intellectual property work as one of its principal objects existing as of the date of termination of the Executive's employment hereunder and with which the Executive shall have been directly or indirectly concerned PROVIDED THAT nothing contained in this clause shall preclude the Executive from holding at any time any shares or loan capital (not exceeding per centum of the shares or

---

[23]   *Herbert Morris v Saxelby* [1915] 2 Ch 57; *Thomas Marshall (Exporters) Ltd v Guinle* [1979] 1 Ch 227.

[24]   *Dawnay, Day & Company Ltd v de Braconier D'Alphen* [1987] IRLR 442.

[25]   *Murgitroyd & Co v Purdy* [2005] IEUC 110.

loan capital of a class concerned for the time being in issue) in any company whose shares are listed or dealt in on a recognised stock exchange and nothing in this Agreement will affect the Executive's right to accept employment as an employee in another firm of patent attorneys.

The non-solicitation clause provided:

> The Executive, during the period of twelve months during following determination of his employment hereunder shall not either on his account or for any person, firm or company directly or indirectly solicit or interfere with or endeavour to entice away from the Company or any associated company the custom of or provide goods or services of any description to any person, firm or company who or which at the date of the termination as aforesaid or who or which in the period of twelve months immediately prior to such date was a customer or client of or in the habit of dealing with the Company or any associated company or endeavour to prevent any such person, firm or company from continuing so to deal.

Within a short period of time of his departure from the plaintiff company, two major clients of the plaintiff company indicated an intention to move their business to Purdy & Associates. Mr Purdy denied in evidence any solicitation of those clients. In those circumstances, Clarke J was of the view that by virtue of Mr Purdy's denial of any actual solicitation 'it does not appear to me that the imposition of an order restraining solicitation would be likely to cause any significant damage to the defendant'.

[3.32] The question of non-competition was more contentious. Mr Purdy submitted that if he was restrained from competing he would effectively have to put his business on hold for a period of nine months and that by virtue of the difficulty of obtaining alternative employment in the area, he would be forced to emigrate. By virtue of that submission, Clarke J deduced that Mr Purdy had intended to live off the income which he would derive from carrying on the business in competition with the plaintiff. He went on to comment that that was relevant, from the plaintiffs' perspective, in that eventually, the profits attributable to the competing business would be unlikely to remain intact should the plaintiffs ultimately succeed. Accordingly, Clarke J declared that if the plaintiffs failed to obtain the injunction, they would have suffered the potential loss of clients who may or may not return and an intervening financial loss which may, in practice, not be capable of recovery. In all of those circumstances, Clarke J was of the view that damages would not be an adequate remedy.

In relation to the balance of convenience, Clarke J held that the balance of convenience would not favour the grant of an interlocutory injunction in respect of non-competition and ordered instead that the matter be made ready for an early trial. Clarke J proposed that a preliminary issue be tried as to the applicability and enforceability of the non-competition clause.

[3.33] In his judgment in respect of the preliminary issue as to the enforceability of the non-competition clause, Clarke J commented:

> A restraint on a person working or being engaged in one or more lines of business is by definition a restraint of trade. It is well settled that such a term will not be enforceable by the Courts unless it meets a two-fold test:
>
> (a)   it is reasonable as between the parties, and
>
> (b)   it is consistent with the interests of the public.

[3.34] In considering the test of reasonableness, regard should be had to the case of *Stenhouse (Australia) Ltd v Phillips*,[26] where Lord Wilberforce said:

> The proposition that an employer is not entitled to protection from mere competition by a former employee means that the employee is entitled to use to the full any personal skill or experience even if this has been acquired in the service of his employer: It is this freedom to use to the full a man's improving ability and talents which lies at the root of the policy of the law regarding this type of restraint. Leaving aside the case of misuse of trade secrets or confidential information...the employer's claim for protection must be based upon the identification of some advantage or asset inherent in the business which can properly be regarded as, in a general sense, his property, and which would be unjust to allow the employee to appropriate for his own purposes, even though he, the employee, may have contributed to its creation.

The test therefore is whether, in all the circumstances of the case, both the nature of the restriction and its extent is reasonable to protect the goodwill of the employer.

[3.35] In *Murgitroyd*, Clarke J considered the geographical restriction contained in the restrictive covenant to be reasonable in circumstances where there were only 10 patent attorneys operating in Ireland and they all serviced the demands of the Irish business from Dublin. He was equally satisfied that the length of the restrictive covenant was not unreasonable having regard to the specialised nature of the business. However, Clarke J was of the view that the restriction on *all* competition was too wide. He commented:

> Covenants against competition by former employees are never reasonable as such. They may be upheld only where the employee might obtain such personal knowledge of, and influence over, the customers of this employer as would enable him, if competition were allowed, to take advantage of his employer's trade connection.

Clarke J went on to comment that a prohibition on dealing with (in addition to soliciting of) customers of the plaintiff would have been reasonable and sufficient to meet any legitimate requirements of the plaintiff. The wider prohibition which restricted dealing with prospective customers, ie those who might be, but are not, such customers, was excessive. Clarke J acknowledged that there may well be times where it is not practical to distinguish between customers and non-customers but this case was not one of them. He concluded that a prohibition on dealing with those identified customers would be sufficient to protect the defendant taking advantage of the plaintiff's trade connections as the number of customers in this case was small and identifiable.

[3.36] In general terms, in deciding whether or not a restrictive covenant is reasonable, the clause will be considered by reference to the limitation in subject matter, duration and geographical extent.

1. Subject matter

[3.37] The restriction on the conduct or activity must relate to the conduct or activity in which the employee was engaged while working for the employer. It is unlikely to be upheld if it is any wider.

---

[26] *Stenhouse (Australia) Ltd v Phillips* [1974] AC 311.

In *European Paint Importers Ltd v O'Callaghan and Others*[27] the plaintiff sought an interlocutory injunction to restrain the first and second named defendants, formerly its employees, and the third named defendant which was a new company set up by the first and second named defendants and which was in competition directly with the business of the plaintiff, from acting in breach of a restrictive covenant contained in the contracts of employment of the first and second named defendants. The restrictive covenant provided:

> The Employee covenants with the Company that he will not for a period of one year after ceasing to be employed by the Company in connection with the carrying on of any business similar to or in competition with the business of Heavy Duty Coating and Industrial Paint Sales, on its own behalf or on behalf of any person, firm or company, directly or indirectly seek to procure orders from or do business with any persons, firm or company who has at any time during the one year immediately proceeding such cessation of employment done business with the Company.

The parties were in dispute as to the interpretation of the wording 'seek to procure orders from or do business with…'. The plaintiffs contended that the clause meant that the defendants must not (1) seek orders from existing customers of the plaintiff company and (2) do business with customers of the plaintiff company. The defendants, on the other hand, submitted that the clause meant that they must not seek orders and must not seek to do business. This would mean that the defendants would be permitted to respond to business which came their way which they had not sought out or solicited.

[3.38] In this particular case, the interpretation of that clause was, to some extent, academic as the defendants admitted that they had solicited customers of the plaintiff. Accordingly, the damage had already been done. In those circumstances it would be impossible to know if any order received by the defendants from any existing customer of the plaintiff came as a result of the solicitation or came spontaneously from the customer without regard to any approach from the defendants. Peart J was of the opinion that the only way in which the status quo could be maintained was to grant an order that the defendants may not either seek out orders or do any business with existing customers who have already been solicited since to do otherwise would be to permit the defendants to 'reap the harvest of their acknowledged breach of the obligation not to seek orders.'

Having been pressed by both parties to give some determination or guidance on the interpretation of the wording in the restrictive covenant regarding the restriction on seeking to procure orders or to do business with customers of the plaintiff, Peart J stated *obiter* that he would favour the less restrictive interpretation, as contended for by the defendants, provided that the object of the clause could be reasonably achieved. He commented that it appeared to him that the most which ought to be required of the defendants was not to take any positive steps to seek business from existing customers of the plaintiff for a period of twelve months. He made an order based on the more restrictive interpretation of the covenant, as contended for by the plaintiff, purely because there was admitted solicitation of customers by the defendants.

---

[27] *European Paint Importers Ltd v O'Callaghan and Others* (10 August 2005, unreported) HC (Peart J).

Having regard to the fact that the defendant admitted to solicitation of the plaintiff's customers, Peart J was of the view that it would be impossible to calculate the damages because of the impossibility of determining which orders had come as a result of the solicitation and which did not. Peart J was not satisfied that damages would be an adequate remedy. He stated that the balance of convenience lay in favour of the plaintiffs who were innocent at all times.

Accordingly, an interlocutory injunction was granted restraining the defendants from seeking to procure orders from, or doing any business with any person, firm or company who had at any time in the previous year been a customer of the plaintiff, irrespective of whether the business in question was sought out by the said defendants or not.

2. Duration

[3.39] A restrictive covenant is unlikely to be upheld if the restrictions operate for an unduly long period of time. The courts will look to balance the legitimate interests of an employer in protecting their business against the right of an employee to earn a living. A clause which places a restriction which is longer than is necessary to allow the employer to take steps to limit the damage done by the departure of the employee will not be allowed. In general, a restriction on trade for longer than six or twelve months is unlikely to be upheld. In *Murgitroyd*, as discussed above, Clarke J took the view that a period of twelve months was not excessive, having regard to the specialised nature of the business in that case.

3. Geographical limit

[3.40] A restriction is too wide to be enforced if its area is greater than is required to protect the employer's business interests. In the case of *Commercial Plastics Ltd v Vincent*[28] it was held that where an employer had a worldwide restrictive covenant but only operated in the UK, the covenant was geographically too wide and was unenforceable.

In *Murgitroyd*, Clarke J held that the fact that a clause applied to all of Ireland did not of itself make it unreasonable as, in that case, there were only ten patent attorneys operating in Ireland and they all operated from Dublin. Accordingly, the geographical restriction based on the jurisdiction of the Irish State was not unreasonable having regard to the way in which the business operated in Ireland.

Company property

[3.41] Very often employees will receive company property, eg a company car, mobile phone or laptop, as part of their employment. It is very important that there are clear conditions in place regarding their use and regarding their return at the end of the employment relationship. The employer should always ensure that it is a term of the contract that any company equipment is given to the employee entirely at the employer's discretion and that it is open to the employer to either withdraw the entitlement or to change the type, make etc of the equipment given to the employee.

---

[28] *Commercial Plastics Ltd v Vincent* [1965] 1 QB 623.

With respect to company cars, it is important that the employer ensures that it is given to the employee conditional upon the employer driving the car safely and within the strict confines of the law. Employers should be aware that allowing employees use of company property may give rise to vicarious liability, even where use of the property is outside of working hours.[29]

Email and internet use

[3.42] Where employees have use of e-mail, intranet or internet facilities as part of their work, it is very important to ensure that there is a comprehensive policy in place dealing with such use, either in the contract of employment or in an employee handbook. There is a significant risk that where employees use internet and other facilities in an unacceptable or illegal way employers could be held to be vicariously liable in respect of defamation, sexual or racial harassment, copyright infringement, spreading of viruses, accessing of pornography and waste of computer capacity and employer's time.

Bullying and harassment

[3.43] Employers must provide a work environment free of bullying and harassment.[30] They should attempt to do this by putting in place a policy or policies designed to prevent such bullying or harassment occurring in the first place and not just to deal with incidents when they arise. Failure to have such a policy can lead to liability being imposed on the employer the first time such an incident arises. Policies of this sort are rarely included in the text of a letter of appointment or contract but rather are contained in a separate document which is appended to or referred to in the contract.

Notice

[3.44] A well drafted contract of employment will contain an agreed notice period. In the absence of an agreed notice period set out in the contract of employment, an employer must give 'reasonable' notice prior to terminating the employee's contract of employment. This was confirmed in *Doyle v Grangeford Precast Concrete Ltd*[31] where O'Donovan J observed that '[a]n employer may lawfully terminate employment for good or bad reasons or for no reason, provided that the employee is given proper notice of termination'.

What amounts to 'reasonable' notice can give rise to dispute. The most important factor is the status of the employee. Courts tend to look at the following factors:

1. Job function – the more senior an employee, the more likely it is that he or she will be deemed to be entitled to a longer period of notice;

2. Length of service – similarly, the longer the employee has been employed, the longer the period of notice to which he will be entitled. This is reflected in the statutory notice periods to which employees are entitled as set out in s 4 of the Minimum Notice and Terms of Employment Acts 1973–2001;

3. Custom and practice in the organisation in relation to notice, if there is any.

---

[29] On the scope of the employer's vicarious liability, see Ch 8, Vicarious Liability.
[30] See Ch 7, Bullying, Harassment and Stress at Work.
[31] *Doyle v Grangeford Precast Concrete Ltd* (1998) ELR 260.

In the absence of a requirement that notice of termination be given in writing, valid notice may be served orally. The UK EAT has held that when notice is given orally, the period of notice is exclusive of the day on which notice is given.[32]

Variation clause

[3.45] It is wise for an employer to include an express right to vary the employee's terms and conditions of employment, should the need arise. The absence of a variation clause makes it very difficult for an employer to consider altering the employee's terms and conditions of employment, even where the circumstances would seem to make it reasonable for the employer to do so. The variation, where there is a variation clause, must be exercised reasonably.

IMPLIED TERMS

[3.46] Terms can be implied into a contract of employment in a variety of ways – such as by statute, by law, by custom and practice and by the conduct of the parties. Once a term is implied into a contract, it will have the same effect as if it was written down and expressed between the parties. However, if an implied term contradicts or is inconsistent with the express wording of the contract, it may not take effect.[33]

In the classic decision of *The Moorcock*,[34] Bowen LJ stated that an implied term must be 'founded on presumed intention and upon reason'.

Terms can be implied in different ways. Sometimes, the circumstances of the case or the parties' conduct can give rise to a presumption that the parties had a particular intention that could only be implemented through implying a particular term (the officious bystander test). This gives rise to a court or tribunal implying that particular term into the contract. The implication of a term may also be necessary to give business efficacy or commercial sense to a contract and therefore, it is presumed that that is what the parties intended (the business efficacy test).

The officious bystander test

[3.47] According to this test, an implied term 'is something so obvious that it goes without saying; so that, if while the parties were making their bargain, an officious bystander were to suggest some express provision for it in their agreement, they would testily suppress him with a common "oh, of course".'[35]

For a term to be implied it must be obvious and it must be precise. This was emphasised by the Irish Supreme Court in case of *Sweeney v Duggan*.[36] The Court stated that there were at least two situations where the courts would, independently of statutory requirement, imply a term which has not been expressly agreed by the parties to a contract. The Court held that, firstly, a term not expressly agreed upon by the parties

---

[32] *West v Kneels Ltd* [1986] IRLR 430, [1987] ICR 146 (EAT).
[33] *Affreteurs Reunis v Leopold Walford (London)* [1959] AC 801.
[34] *The Moorcock* (1889) 14 PD 64.
[35] *Shirlaw v Southern Foundries* (1926) Ltd (1939) 2 KB 206 at 227.
[36] *Sweeney v Duggan* (1997) 2 ILRM 211.

may be inferred on the basis of the presumed intention of the parties. Secondly, a term may be implied as a matter of law, independently of the intention of the parties, as a necessary legal incident of a definable category of contract.

The Court stated that 'whether a term is implied pursuant to the presumed intention of the parties or as a legal incident of a definable category of contract it must be not merely reasonable but also necessary. Clearly it cannot be implied if it is inconsistent with the express wording of the contract and furthermore it may be difficult to infer a term where it cannot be formulated with reasonable precision.'[37]

The business efficacy test

[3.48] A term will be implied in a contract if it is necessary to make the contract work, from a business or commercial perspective.[38] This is somewhat different to the officious bystander test in that the officious bystander test looks at the presumed intentions of the parties, whereas the business efficacy test looks not just at what the parties intended or did not intend, but what is necessary to give effect to the contract.[39] Of course, even with the application of the business efficacy test, it is likely that the court will deem itself to be giving effect to the parties' intentions in the context that, if the parties intended the contract to make business sense, they must have intended any term necessary to make it work.

Terms implied by law

[3.49] A term is said to be implied into a contract by law if a court or tribunal deems it appropriate or reasonable to hold that a term, albeit never expressed by the parties, should be a binding element of the agreement between them.[40]

The conduct of the parties will be one of the factors to which a court of tribunal will look in deciding whether to imply a term into a contract. Clearly, the parties' conduct prior to or at the commencement of the contract is of the most importance in establishing what their intention was although, on occasion, the courts may look at the subsequent conduct of the parties as well.[41]

The courts may imply whatever term is deemed appropriate in the circumstances of any case. However, there are certain fundamental terms that will be implied into many contracts of employment. These can be seen as duties the employer and the employee have towards each other.

The employer's duties

[3.50] The employer has a number of duties to the employee at common law, eg to pay the wages of the employee, to pay expenses reasonably incurred during the course of work, to provide a safe working environment and to provide work.[42] The employer must

---

[37] *Sweeney v Duggan* (1997) 2 ILRM 211 at 217.
[38] *Reigate v Union Manufacturing Co (Ramsbottom) Ltd* [1918] 1 KB 592, *per* Scrutton LJ.
[39] Friel, *The Law of Contract* (Round Hall Press, 1995) p 162.
[40] *O'Brien v Associated Fire Alarms Ltd* [1969] 1 All ER 93.
[41] *Carmichael v National Power plc* (2000) IRLR 43.
[42] *Langston v Amalgamated Union of Engineering Workers* [1973] 2 All ER 430.

adhere to these common law obligations in a way that also complies with any relevant legislation.

The employee's duties

[3.51] The employee has a personal obligation to serve the employer[43] in a manner that is competent and careful. The employee also has an implied duty to carry out the reasonable instructions of his or her employer. Where the employee fails to comply with these common law duties, the employer could argue that the employee is in breach of the employment contract, thereby entitling the employer to terminate the employment. However, the statutory protections of the Unfair Dismissals Act 1977–2007 will apply to prevent any unfair termination of the employee's contract.

Duty of loyalty and fidelity

[3.52] Employees owe employers an implied duty of loyalty and fidelity.[44] This has developed over time such that it is accepted that a relationship of 'trust and confidence' must exist between the employer and the employee.[45]

In the Supreme Court decision of *Berber v Dunnes Stores*,[46] Finnegan J stated that 'there is implied in a contract of employment a mutual obligation that the employer and employee will not, without reasonable and proper cause, conduct themselves in a manner likely to destroy, or seriously damage the relationship of confidence and trust between them'.

As the judge noted, however:

> The term imposes reciprocal duties on the employer and the employee. What is significant is the impact of the employer's behaviour on the employee rather than what the employer intended ... the impact of an employee's behaviour is also relevant.

[3.53] Within the implied duty of fidelity and loyalty is the obligation of the employee to act honestly. The extent to which this extends to the employee having an obligation to disclose his or her own misdeeds is debatable but in circumstances where the employee is very senior or where the misdeeds are fraudulent, the employee may be so obliged.[47]

Confidential information

[3.54] The duty of fidelity and loyalty encompasses a further obligation on the part of the employee which is an obligation to retain confidential information and trade secrets both during the course of employment and on an ongoing basis thereafter. The obligation of confidentiality will be an express term in many contracts of employment, but regardless of whether it is or not, it has long been accepted as an implied term.[48] This

---

43 *Wallis v Warren* (1849) 4 Exch 361.
44 *Boston Deep Sea Fishing & Ice Co v Ansell* (1888) 39 Ch D 339.
45 On the nature and extent of this duty, in the context of termination of employment, see Ch 14, Dismissals, paras **[14.24]–[14.33]**.
46 *Berber v Dunnes Stores* (12 February 2009, unreported) SC.
47 *Tesco Stores Ltd v Pook* (2003) EWHC 823.
48 *Amber Size and Chemical Co v Menzel* (1913) 2 Ch 239.

duty extends to an obligation not to use information which the employee has obtained in confidence during the course of his employment to the employer's detriment.[49]

The implied duty of confidentiality was examined in the case of *Faccenda Chicken Ltd v Fowler*.[50] Mr Fowler had set up a chicken distribution business in competition with his former employer and had solicited clients using the customer lists and prices he had developed during his previous employment. His contract did not contain any express confidentiality clause or any other term preventing him from using this information or engaging in similar business.

[3.55] The Court held that there were three different types of information that might be obtained during employment and these were:

1. Trivial information, ie information that is easily accessible from public sources and could not be considered to be confidential;

2. Confidential information which may have come to the employee's knowledge expressly or impliedly as confidential information which becomes part of the employee's skills or knowledge. The Court held that the use of this type of information can be protected while the employee is in employment however once the employment has terminated, this type of information can only be protected by an express contractual term;

3. Trade secrets. This type of information, even if only in the employee's memory, can never be used outside of the employment of the original employer. A Court can restrain the disclosure of trade secrets even without an express contractual term.

[3.56] In the circumstances of the *Faccenda Chicken* case, the customer lists fell into the second category of information and the implied duty of fidelity was insufficient to prevent the defendant from using the information to his own benefit. The Court found that when the employment terminated, the obligation on the employee not to use the disclosed information related only to information that was of a sufficiently high degree of confidentiality as to amount to a trade secret. The obligation did not continue to cover all of the information covered prior to termination.

On determining what constitutes a trade secret, the following will be taken into account:[51]

(i) the nature of the employment;

(ii) the nature of the information itself;

(iii) whether the employer impressed on the employee the confidentiality of the information; and

(iv) whether the information can easily be isolated from other information which the employee is free to use or disclose.

[3.57] In the English case of *Cantor Fitzgerald Ltd v Wallace*,[52] the High Court held that an employer could not claim a proprietary interest and protect for itself the customer

---

[49] *Merryweather v Moore* (1892) 2 H 518.
[50] *Faccenda Chicken Ltd v Fowler* [1986] 1 All ER 617.
[51] *Faccenda Chicken Ltd v Fowler* [1986] 1 All ER 617 (Neill LJ).
[52] *Cantor Fitzgerald Ltd v Wallace* [1992] IRLR 215.

connection an employee had built up during the course of employment where that client connection is a function of the employee's qualities such as personality, temperament and ability to get on with people.

Whistleblowing

[3.58] The duty of confidentiality is subject to circumstances where the disclosure is in the public interest. The Irish Supreme Court has said that the:

> [d]isclosure of confidential information will almost always be justified in the public interest where it is a disclosure of information as to the commission or the intended commission of serious crime because the commission of such crime is an attack upon the State and the citizens of the State and such disclosure will always be in the public interest.[53]

Terms implied by statute

[3.59] Legislation implies various terms into a contract of employment, usually for the purpose of providing certain minimum rights to employees out of which parties cannot contract. There terms apply, regardless of whether or not the parties record them in a written agreement.

Unfair dismissal

[3.60] The Unfair Dismissals Acts 1977–2007 imply that an employee has the right not to be unfairly dismissed. The Acts provide that all dismissals will be unfair unless they are on grounds of conduct, competence, capability, redundancy or for some other substantial reason.[54]

Equality

[3.61] The Employment Equality Acts 1998–2008 imply an equality clause into every contract of employment. Thus, every contract of employment has a term that no employee shall be discriminated against on the grounds of age, gender, religion, sexual orientation, family status, race, disability, religion or membership of the Travelling Community.[55]

Organisation of Working Time Act 1997

[3.62] Entitlements in respect of, inter alia, annual leave, rest breaks and working hours are implied by the Organisation of Working Time Act 1997.[56]

---

[53] *National Irish Bank Ltd and National Irish Bank Financial Services Ltd v Radio Telefís Éireann* [1998] 2 IR 465.

[54] See Ch 14, Dismissal.

[55] See Ch 13, Employment Equality.

[56] See Ch 4, Working Time.

Statutory notice

[3.63] The Minimum Notice and Terms of Employment Acts 1973–2001 provide that the following notice periods apply:

An employee in continuous service for less than 2 years	1 week
An employee in continuous service for 2 years or more, but less than 5 years	2 weeks
An employee in continuous service for 5 years or more, but less than 10 years	4 weeks
An employee in continuous service for 10 years or more, but less than 15 years	6 weeks
An employee in continuous service for 15 years or more	8 weeks

Thus, regardless of what notice period parties stipulate in a contract of employment, if the contractual notice period is shorter than the statutory notice period, the statutory notice period will prevail.

The Protection of Employees (Fixed-Term Work) Act 2003 and the Protection of Employees (Part-Time Work) Act 2001

[3.64] Employees engaged under fixed-term or part-time contracts are entitled not to be treated less favourably than comparable permanent or full time employees.

Fixed-term employees must receive a written statement setting out the reason for the temporary nature of their contract and explaining the objective criteria determining the contract, eg arriving at a specific date, or completing a specific project. Furthermore, a fixed-term employee who has been furnished with successive fixed term contracts may ultimately become entitled to a contract of indefinite duration if the conditions set out in s 9 of the Protection of Employees (Fixed-Term) Act 2003 are met.[57]

Health and safety

[3.65] Sections 8(1) and 8(2) of the Safety, Health and Welfare at Work Act 2005 imply certain obligations on the part of the employer into the contract of employment. The Act obliges an employer to ensure, as far as is reasonably practicable, the safety, health and welfare at work of his or her employees.

This duty extends to the following:

(i) managing and conducting work activities in such a way as to ensure the safety, health and welfare at work of employees;

(ii) managing and conducting work activities in such a way as to prevent any improper conduct or behaviour likely to put the safety, health or welfare of employees at risk;

(iii) ensuring that the work place is in a condition that is safe and without risk to health;

(iv) ensuring that there is a safe means of access to and egress from the place of work;

---

[57] See Ch 9, Part-Time Workers and Ch 10, Fixed-Term Workers.

(v)   ensuring that the design, provision and maintenance of plant and machinery or any other articles are safe and without risk to health;

(vi)   ensuring the safety and the prevention of risk to health of employees relating to the use of any article or substance or the exposure to noise, vibration or ionising or other radiations or any other physical agent;

(vii)   providing systems of work that are planned, organised, performed, maintained and revised as appropriate so as to be safe and without risk to health;

(viii) providing and maintaining facilities and arrangements for the welfare of employees at work;

(ix)   providing the information, instruction, training and supervision necessary to ensure the safety, health, and welfare at work of employees;

(x)   determining and implementing the safety, health and welfare measures necessary for the protection of the safety, health and welfare of employees when identifying hazards and carrying out a risk assessment or when preparing a safety statement and ensuring that the measures take account of changing circumstances and the general principles of prevention;

(xi)   providing and maintaining such suitable protective clothing and equipment as is necessary;

(xii)   preparing and revising adequate plans and procedures to be followed and measures to be taken in the case of an emergency or serious and imminent danger;

(xiii) reporting accidents and dangerous occurrences to the Health and Safety Authority, and

(xiv)   obtaining, where necessary, the services of a competent person (whether under a contract of employment or otherwise) for the purpose of ensuring the safety, health and welfare at work of employees.

Protective leave

[3.66] The Maternity Protection Acts 1994 and 2004, the Parental Leave Acts 1998 and 2006, the Carer's Leave Act 2001 and the Adoptive Leave Acts 1995 and 2005 provide for periods of both paid and unpaid leave to an employee, all of which is deemed to be 'protective leave'. Any attempt to terminate an employee's employment during protective leave shall be void.[58]

Custom and practice

[3.67] A term can be implied into a contract of employment by what is known as 'custom and practice'. This arises where a custom or practice is so well known, clear and uninterrupted that it can be implied into the contract. Terms that are more frequently said to be implied by custom or practice relate to paid sick leave, *ex gratia* redundancy payments or leaves of absence.

---

[58]   See Ch 5, Protective Leave.

In *Albion Automotive Ltd v Walker*[59] the Court of Appeal listed the relevant factors as follows:

(a)   whether the policy was drawn to the attention of the employees;

(b)   whether it was followed without exception for a substantial period;

(c)   the number of occasions on which it was followed;

(d)   whether payments were made automatically;

(e)   whether the nature of communication of the policy supported the inference that the employers intended to be contractually bound;

(f)   whether the policy was adopted by agreement;

(g)   whether employees had a reasonable expectation that the enhanced payment would be made;

(h)   whether terms were incorporated in a written agreement;

(i)   whether the terms were consistently applied.

Collective agreements

[3.68] A collective agreement is one made by or on behalf of an employer and a representative trade union which governs pay and/or other conditions of employment. These agreements may form part of the terms and conditions of employment in the organisation. The nature of collective agreements is considered in Ch 18, Industrial Relations.

---

[59]   *Albion Automotive Ltd v Walker* [2002] EWCA Civ 946.

Chapter 4

Working Time

Padraic Lyons and Emmet Whelan

INTRODUCTION

[4.01] The Organisation of Working Time Act 1997 (the 1997 Act) is a far-reaching piece of legislation which implements Council Directive 93/104/EC concerning certain aspects of the organisation of working time (Directive 93/104). With the assistance of a number of supplementary statutory provisions, it regulates the working conditions of the vast majority of workers in Ireland.

Directive 93/104 – The Working Time Directive

[4.02] Directive 93/104/EC proved to be a controversial European initiative, eventually becoming law on 23 November 1993 after a protracted period of negotiation between Member States.[1] Unanimity on the matter of working time was particularly difficult to achieve, resulting in the use of Art 118A of the EC Treaty to allow the passage of Directive 93/104/EC by means of qualified majority voting and confirming that the Directive is a health and safety measure.[2]

The stated purpose of Directive 93/104 is to enhance the safety and welfare of workers and to provide for greater compatibility between work and family life.[3] These concerns derive from a desire to ensure that workers interests should not be subordinated to purely economic considerations, while at the same time ensuring that legitimate business interests are not hindered.[4]

While agreement on regulation of working time was difficult to achieve, the means of achieving these objectives, in particular the idea of the eight-hour working day and the

---

[1] The original Directive 93/104/EC has now been codified with the first amending Directive 2000/34/EC into one consolidated version in Directive 2003/88/EC.

[2] EC Treaty, Art 118A is an alternative procedure, created under the Single European Act of 1986 allowing certain kinds of legislation to be passed by way of qualified majority voting where issues relating to health and safety are involved. This procedure was used despite objection from the United Kingdom which contended that working time was not necessarily a health and safety issue. However, in *United Kingdom v Council of the European Union* [1996] E.C.R. I-5755, para 15, the ECJ interpreted the concepts of 'safety' and 'health' as used in Art 118A widely as embracing 'all factors, physical or otherwise, capable of affecting the health and safety of the worker in his working environment, including in particular certain aspects of the organisation of working time'. See O'Mara, *The Use of Article 118A of the EC Treaty to Achieve Wider Social Goals: United Kingdom v Council* 23 1996 3(11) *CLP* 276 and *Changing Times? Recent European Developments in Working Time Law* (2001) *CLP.* 60.

[3] See Recital 4, 11 and 15. Lavan J in *Royal Liver Assurance Ltd v Macken* [2002] 4 IR 427 refers to the Directive achieving objectives that are both health related and social in nature.

[4] Recital 2.

48-hour working week, can be traced back as far as the Hours of Work (Industry) Convention 1918 of the International Labour Organisation,[5] an organisation of which Ireland has been a member since 1923.

The Organisation of Working Time Act 1997

[4.03] The 1997 Act is the principal working time legislation in Ireland. It deals with the minutiae of the employment relationship and strictly regulates how employees spend their working day.[6] It regulates the hours of work, from the length of the 11 o'clock break to the maximum hours to be worked per day or per week. It deals with the provision of annual leave and payment for bank holidays and also specifies how the employer is to compensate employees for working on Sunday. It deals with atypical work practices, such as shift working, night working, on-call working and zero-hours contracts. It also requires employers to maintain a record of all time worked by each and every employee. In fact, it is difficult to think of another area in which the activities of adults are so carefully and closely monitored by law, with such widespread impact on the lives of so many people.

In line with Directive 93/104,[7] the 1997 Act provides that certain aspects of the Act shall not apply to maritime workers, doctors in training, family workers and persons who determine their own working time. The Minister has also excluded members of the civil protection services and exempted a number of different categories of workers including travelling staff, security staff and activities where the employee's presence is necessary to ensure continuity of production or service.

[4.04] The protections in the 1997 Act have been supplemented by a number of Statutory Instruments dealing with specific sectors of employment such as transport workers, off-shore workers, doctors in training and mobile workers.[8] Specific protections for young persons were already in place prior to the 1997 Act.[9]

---

5 Hours of Work (Industry) Convention 1918 of the International Labour Organisation, Art 2. See www.ilo.org.

6 The 1997 Act became law on 7 May 1997. The commencement order bringing the Act into operation, on a phased basis, was signed on 24 September 1997. Under the commencement order, s 35 of the Act came into operation on 30 September, 1997. The provisions on rest and working hours came into effect on 1 March 1998.

7 Directive 93/104, Arts 18–21.

8 The Organisation of Working Time (Inclusion of Transport Activities) Regulations 2004 (SI 817/2004) and the Organisation of Working Time (Inclusion of Offshore Work) Regulations 2004 (SI 819/2004) extended protection to excluded transport workers, except off-shore and road transport (implementing Directive 2000/34/EC). Directive 99/63/EC then provided alternative protection for off-shore transport workers. The EC (Organisation of Working Time) (Activities of Doctors in Training) Regulations 2004 (SI 494/2004 implementing Directive 2000/34/EC) dealt with 'doctors in training'. The EC (Organisation of Working Time) (Mobile Staff in Civil Aviation) Regulations 2006 (SI 507/2006 implementing Directive 2000/79/EC) regulate the working time of 'mobile staff in civil aviation' and the road transport sector has been regulated by the EC (Organisation of Working Time of Persons Performing Mobile Road Transport Activities) Regulations 2005 (SI 2/2005 implementing Directive 2002/15/EC).

9 The Protection of Young Persons (Employment) Act 1996.

Section 35 of the 1997 Act provides the Labour Relations Commission (LRC) with the power to prepare a Code of Practice to provide 'practical guidance' as to the steps which may be taken for the purposes of complying with any section of the Act. Two such Codes of Practice have been prepared.[10]

THE ORGANISATION OF WORKING TIME ACT 1997: MAIN PROVISIONS

[4.05] The 1997 Act imposes the following minimum standards in the employment relationship:[11]

Section 11:	Daily rest periods of at least 11 consecutive hours' rest every 24 hours[12]
Section 12:	Rests and interval breaks at work of a minimum of 15 minutes break every 4.5 hours or 30 minutes every 6 hours[13]
Section 13:	Weekly rest periods of at least 24 consecutive hours in each period of 7 days or 48 hours in each period of 14 days[14]
Section 14:	Compensation for working on Sundays[15]
Section 15:	Maximum 48 hour working week (subject to averaging provisions)[16]
Section 16:	Regulation of night working[17]
Section 17:	Provision of information on work-schedules[18]
Section 18:	Zero-hour contract worker protections[19]
Section 19:	Entitlement to annual leave[20]
Section 21:	Entitlement in respect of public holidays[21]
Section 23:	Entitlement to compensation on termination of employment[22]
Section 26:	Protection against penalisation

---

[10] See Organisation of Working Time (Code of Practice on Compensatory Rest Periods and Related Matters) (Declaration) Order 1998 (SI 44/1998) and Organisation of Working Time (Code of Practice on Sunday Working in the Retail Trade and Related Matters) (Declaration) Order 1998 (SI 444/1998). While failure on the part of any person to observe the Codes will not, in itself, render that person liable to civil or criminal proceedings, the Codes are admissible in evidence before a Court, the Labour Court or a Rights Commissioner in proceedings under the Organisation of Working Time Act 1997.

[11] The Act repealed the Conditions of Employment Acts 1936–1944, Night Work (Bakeries) Acts, 1936–1981 and the Shops (Conditions of Employment) Acts 1938–1942, the Holidays (Employees) Acts 1973–1991 and those aspects of the Worker Protection (Regular Part-Time Employees) Act 1991 that related to holidays for part-time employees.

[12] Implementing Art 3 of the Directive.

[13] Implementing Art 4 of the Directive.

[14] Implementing Art 5 of the Directive.

[15] Despite an initial reference to Sunday working in the Directive this provision was struck down by the ECJ because the Council had failed to explain why Sunday, as a weekly rest day, was more closely connected with the health and safety of workers than any other day of the week. See Case C-84/94 *UK v Council of EU* [1996] ECR I-575.

[16] Implementing Art 6 of the Directive.

[17] Implementing Art 8 of the Directive.

THE CONCEPT OF 'WORKING TIME'

[4.06] Before going any further, it is important to first consider what is meant by 'work' and 'working time' under the 1997 Act.

'Working time' is defined in Art 2 of the Directive as:

> [a]ny period during which the worker is working, at the employer's disposal and carrying out his activity or duties, in accordance with national laws and/or practice.

The Directive clearly requires that all three factors must be present; that the worker must be; (a) working, (b) at the employer's disposal, and (c) carrying out his activities or duties.

For the purposes of the Directive, there are only two states of being; that of 'working time' and that of rest. A 'rest period' is described in the Directive as 'any period which is not working time', however, there is no specific definition of rest.

[4.07] Section 2 of the 1997 Act implements Art 2 and provides that 'working time' means any time that an employee is:

(i)   at his or her place of work or at his or her employer's disposal; *and*

(ii) carrying on or performing the duties or activities of his or her work.

The section goes on to provide that 'work' shall be construed in accordance with this definition. In keeping with the Directive, it would appear that the the use of the conjunctive 'and' means that an employee must be both carrying on the activity of his work and doing so while in the workplace or while at his employer's disposal.

The distinction between work and rest has been most frequently litigated in the context of 'on call' workers and whether time spent 'on call' will constitute working time. This has been a significant issue for Member States in dealing with the financial implications of providing 'on call' medical services. Equally, it is an important issue for workers who are required to be on call due to its irregular and often unpredictable nature.

[4.08] In *Sindicato de Médicos de Asistencia Publica (SIMAP) v Conselleria de Sanidad y Consumo de la Generalidad Valenciana*,[23] the ECJ was required to consider the status of doctors who were required to be present at specific medical centres and be available for call outs, but were otherwise free to do as they pleased in between calls.

The Court held in the *SIMAP* case that all three components of 'working time' were satisfied; however if the doctors were on call, but not required to be at the medical centre, the requirement of carrying out their duties or activities was not met. Only when called upon would the doctors then be regarded as carrying out their activities or duties.

---

[18]   This provision was not dealt with in the Directive.

[19]   This provision was not dealt with in the Directive.

[20]   Implementing Art 7 of the Directive.

[21]   There was no specific mention of 'public holidays' in the Directive.

[22]   This provision was not dealt with specifically in the Directive, but Art 7 does refer to payments in lieu on termination of employment in relation to annual leave.

[23]   Case C-303/98 *Sindicato de Médicos de Asistencia Publica (SIMAP) v Conselleria de Sanidad y Consumo de la Generalidad Valenciana* [2000] IRLR 845.

On this basis, it would seem that the requirement to attend at a designated location equates to the carrying out of a worker's duties or activities.

[4.09] In the subsequent case of *Landeshauptstadt Kiel v Jaeger*,[24] the ECJ had to consider the case of a doctor who was required to be physically present in a hospital for the purpose of providing emergency medical services. During the time at issue he was provided with sleeping facilities, subject to the requirement that he respond to call-outs where necessary. In the view of the Court, the addition of sleeping facilities did not render Dr Jaeger's case distinguishable from that of *SIMAP*. The fact that the doctor was required to be present at the location specified and available for work led the Court to conclude that time spent in this way could not be a rest period. It was therefore 'working time' for the purposes of the Directive.

[4.10] In reaching this conclusion the Court made the following observation as to the nature of rest:

> It should be pointed out that the purpose of Directive 93/104 is effectively to protect the safety and health of workers. In light of that essential objective each employee must in particular enjoy adequate rest periods which must not only be effective in enabling the persons concerned to recover from the fatigue engendered by their work but are also preventive in nature so as to reduce as much as possible the risk of affecting the safety or health of employees which successive periods of work without the necessary rest are likely to produce.

The issue of on-call employees was further considered in *Dellas v Premier Ministre*[25] where the ECJ emphasised that the Directive does not allow for any intermediate category between working time and rest. In that case the ECJ rejected as incompatible with the Directive the French system of weighting whereby time spent at work was weighted by reference to the intensity of the activity undertaken.[26]

[4.11] It seems reasonably clear, based on these authorities, that time spent on call while at the workplace[27] will be working time, while time spent on call elsewhere will not. Since then, the European Commission has circulated a draft proposal to amend the Directive, which would provide that the inactive part of on-call time would not be regarded as working time unless national law or a collective agreement between the relevant social partners decides otherwise.[28] Under this proposal, the inactive part of on-call time would be calculated taking into account the average industrial experience in the relevant sector and would be excluded from the calculation of daily and weekly rest entitlements. To date there has been no final agreement on this proposal.

---

[24] Case C-151/02 *Landeshauptstadt Kiel v Jaeger* [2003] IRLR 804.

[25] Case C-14/04 *Dellas v Premier Ministre* [2006] IRLR 225.

[26] In that case it was accepted by the French State that this system led to a situation whereby employees were routinely required to be at work for periods of 60 hours per week.

[27] The Commission's proposed draft directive of 31 May 2005 defines 'workplace' as 'the place or places where the worker normally carries out his activities or duties and which is determined in accordance with the terms laid down in the relationship or employment contract applicable to the worker'.

[28] 31 May 2005 COM (2005) 2004/0209 (COD).

The jurisprudence of the ECJ was followed in Ireland in *Feeney v Baquiran*[29] where the Labour Court held that time spent by a person employed as an assistant in a domestic home was working time for so long as she was available to be called on for work. The worker in question was required to be available for 69 hours per week and as a result the employer had breached s 15 of the 1997 Act.

[4.12] Time spent engaged off site by statutory apprentices has been a cause of some difficulty both in determining contractual status[30] and the determination of working time. In *Fitzpatrick v Whelan*[31] the Labour Court described such training as an integral part of the statutory apprenticeship. The Court noted that during this period the apprentice was 'at a place determined by the employer, carrying out the instructions of the employer and fulfilling the employer's obligations under the rules of the scheme'. For this reason the Court found that time spent engaged in 'off-the-job training' was 'working time' for the purposes of the 1997 Act.

[4.13] On call work was considered in the context of rest breaks in the English case of *MacCartney v Oversley House Management.*[32] The claimant was a resident manager of a residence for the elderly. She lived in on-site accommodation which also served as her office. Her responsibilities included scheduled visits to residents, organising communal activities and overseeing visits including visits from medical professionals. A particular duty was to respond to emergencies. Ms MacCartney carried a mobile phone at all times, connected to a residents 'emergency cord', which effectively meant that she was on-call 24 hours per day. The Tribunal determined that a person living in this kind of sheltered accommodation who is required to remain on call and to remain on site or nearby is both working and at work. The Tribunal did not regard the fact that Ms McCartney was, to some extent a live-in employee, sufficient to relieve the employer of its duties under the UK working time regulations.

It should be noted that a specific definition of 'working time' is applied to mobile workers. Please see para **[4.54]**.

EXCLUSIONS AND EXEMPTIONS

Exclusions

[4.14] Directive 93/104 allows certain employees and sectors of work to be excluded from a number of entitlements in the Directive.[33] These consist of work in which the ordinary considerations of working time are such that the employer's traditional discretion or the simple logistics of working time make the imposition of certain entitlements under the Directive unworkable or inappropriate.

In line with Directive 93/104, s 3 of the 1997 Act provides that the protections in relation to daily rest (s 11), rests and interval breaks (s 12), weekly rest (s 13), Sundays

---

[29] *Feeney v Baquiran* [2004] ELR 304.

[30] *Flett v Matheson* [2006] IRLR 277.

[31] *Fitzpatrick v Whelan* DWT36/2005.

[32] *MacCartney v Oversley House Management* [2006] IRLR 514.

[33] Directive 93/104, Art 17.

premium (s 14), 48 hour working week (s 15), night working (s 16), work-schedules (s 17) and zero-hour contracts (s 18) do not apply to the following categories of employees:

   (i)   persons who work in sea fishing or other work at sea;[34]

   (ii)   doctors in training;[35]

   (iii) relatives of the employer who live in the employer's house or on the employer's farm;[36] and

   (iv) those who determine their own working time.[37]

The Minister is empowered to extend this category of excluded workers[38] and has excluded members of the civil protection services such as prison officers, fire-fighters, harbour police and life-boat workers.[39] However, employees subject to the foregoing exclusions are entitled to protection in relation to annual leave, bank holidays and penalisation. Members of An Garda Síochána and the Defence Forces are excluded entirely from the 1997 Act.[40]

Exemptions

Section 4(5): Exemptions by collective agreement

[4.15] Section 4(5) of the 1997 Act provides that an employee may be the subject of an exemption from daily rest periods (s 11), rests and interval breaks at work (s 12) and weekly rest periods (s 13) by way of a registered employment agreement or a collective agreement approved by the Labour Court.[41] Such persons cannot be exempted from the other provisions of the 1997 Act and must be given the benefit of compensatory rest breaks.[42]

---

[34] Organisation of Working Time Act 1997, ss 3(1)(a) (i) and (ii). Directive 99/63/EC now provides alternative protection for certain off-shore workers.

[35] Organisation of Working Time Act 1997, s 3(2)(a). See para [4.68] below in relation to the position of doctor's in training.

[36] Organisation of Working Time Act 1997, s 3(2)(b).

[37] Organisation of Working Time Act 1997, s 3(2)(c). Directive 93/104, Art 17 provides that Member States may derogate from certain protections in the Directive 'when, on account of the specific characteristics of the activity concerned, the duration of the working time is not measured and/or predetermined or can be determined by the workers themselves, and particularly in the case of:

    (a)   managing executives or other persons with autonomous decision-taking powers;

    (b)   family workers; or

    (c)   workers officiating at religious ceremonies in churches and religious communities.'

[38] By s 3(3).

[39] Organisation of Working Time (Exemption of Civil Protection Services) Regulations 1998 (SI 52/1998). Employees specified by schedule are exempt from the application of ss 11, 12, 13, 15 and 16 of the Act.

[40] Organisation of Working Time Act 1997, s 3(1).

[41] Organisation of Working Time Act 1997, s 4(5).

[42] See s 6.

Section 4(3) & (4): Exemptions by ministerial regulation

[4.16] Section 4(3) and (4) of the 1997 Act provide the Minister with a wide power to create exemptions, by way of ministerial regulation, from the requirement for daily rest periods (s 11), rests and interval breaks at work (s 12), weekly rest periods (s 13), regulation of night working (s 16) and provision of information on work-schedules (s 17). However, the Minister cannot provide exemptions from the other protections of the 1997 Act.

The Organisation of Working Time (General Exemptions) Regulations 1998[43] provide for exemptions for persons 'wholly or mainly' employed in the following activities:[44]

(1) those regularly required by the employer to travel significant distances between home and the workplace or between two workplaces, including offshore work[45];

(2) security or surveillance workers required to be continuously present at a particular place or places;

(3) an activity falling within a sector of the economy or in the public service where production or service requirement varies significantly but the employee's presence is necessary to ensure its continuity, in particular those work relating to:

(i) residential care institutions,

(ii) the provision of services at a harbour or airport,[46]

(iii) production in the press, radio, television, cinematographic, postal or telecommunications industries,

(iv) the provision of ambulance, fire and civil protection services,

(v) the production, transmission or distribution of gas, water or electricity,

(vi) the collection of household refuse or the operation of an incineration plant,

(vii) any industrial activity in which work cannot, by reason of considerations of a technical nature, be interrupted,

(viii) research and development,

(ix) agriculture,

(x) tourism.

---

[43] SI 21/1998.

[44] See the SI 21/1998, Sch.

[45] The Regulations were amended by the Organisation of Working Time (Inclusion of Offshore Work) Regulations 2004 (SI 819/2004) to include offshore workers. The 2004 Regulations transpose the provisions of Directive 2000/34/EC of 22 June 2000 amending Council Directive 93/104/EC concerning certain aspects of the organisation of working time to cover sectors and activities excluded from that Directive. Directive 2000/34/EC, Art 1 provides a definition of 'offshore work' as 'work performed mainly on or from offshore installations (including drilling rigs), directly or indirectly in connection with the exploration, extraction or exploitation of mineral resources, including hydrocarbons, and diving in connection with such activities, whether performed from an offshore installation or a vessel.'

[46] See *Coastal Line Container Ltd v Services Industrial Professional Technical Union and the Minister for Enterprise, Trade and Employment* [2000] ELR 1 where 32 crane drivers at Dublin Port involved in loading and unloading vessels claimed were deemed to be 'engaged in the provision of services at a harbour'.

As with the exemptions by registered employment agreement and collective agreement outlined at para **[4.15]** above, these exemptions are also contingent on such persons being afforded the benefit of compensatory rest breaks.[47] These categories of persons are *not* exempted from the other provisions of the 1997 Act.

Section 4(1) & (2): Shift changes and split shift exemptions

[4.17] Directive 93/104 allows for derogations for shift workers and activities involving periods of work split up over the course of a day, such as cleaners.[48] Section 4(1) and (2) of the Act provide that employers of shift workers who change shift, and those whose work is spread out over the day, are exempted from the normal daily rest periods (s 11) and the weekly rest periods (s 13).[49] Such persons are not exempted from the other provisions of the 1997 Act. In addition, the exemptions in s 4 are accompanied by an obligation to provide for equivalent compensatory rest or alternative appropriate protections.[50]

Section 5: Exemptions in emergency situations

[4.18] Section 5 of the 1997 Act provides that an employer shall not be obliged to comply with the requirement for daily rest periods (s 11), rests and interval breaks at work (s 12), weekly rest periods (s 13), regulation of night working (s 16) and the provision of information on work-schedules (s 17) where:

> due to exceptional circumstances or an emergency (including an accident or the imminent risk of an accident), the consequences of which could not have been avoided despite the exercise of all due care, or otherwise to the occurrence of unusual and unforeseeable circumstances beyond the employer's control, it would not be practicable for the employer to comply with the section concerned.

As with the exemptions outlined at paras **[4.15]** and **[4.17]** above, there is an obligation to provide for equivalent compensatory rest or alternative appropriate protections[51] and such exemptions do *not* relate to the other protections in the 1997 Act.

Workers in transportation

[4.19] The Organisation of Working Time (Inclusion of Transport Activities) Regulations 2004 (the 2004 Regulations) applied the full protections of the 1997 Act to general transport workers,[52] with the exception of certain 'mobile workers' as defined below. The 2004 Regulations repealed the Organisation of Working Time (Exemption of Transport Activities) Regulations 1998[53] (the 1998 Regulations) which had provided blanket exemptions for persons involved in 'transport activities'.

---

[47] Organisation of Working Time Act 1997, s 6.
[48] See Art 17(4), which makes particular reference to cleaners.
[49] Organisation of Working Time Act 1997, ss 4(1) and (2) respectively.
[50] See s 6.
[51] See s 6.
[52] SI 817/2004.
[53] SI 20/1998.

The 2004 Regulations provide that 'mobile workers' in general transportation are exempt from the requirement in the 1997 Act for daily rest periods (s 11), rests and interval breaks at work (s 12), weekly rest periods (s 13) and regulation of night working (s 16).[54] The definition of a 'mobile worker' in this regard is limited to 'any worker employed as a member of traveling or flying personnel by an undertaking which operates transport services for passengers or goods by road, air or inland waterway'.[55]

As the 2004 Regulations expressly exclude mobile workers in road transportation and mobile staff in civil aviation[56] this exemption in the 2004 Regulations only applies in practice to workers employed on the inland waterways, while mobile workers on trains or vessels travelling on sea could arguably have the full protections of the 1997 Act.[57] This would seem to be a strange and possibly unintended anomaly in the 2004 Regulations.[58] The law in relation to mobile workers in road transportation and mobile staff in civil aviation is dealt with at paras **[4.50]–[4.67]** below.

Equivalent compensatory rest or alternative compensatory arrangements

Exemptions by collective agreement and by ministerial regulation

[4.20] Section 6(1) of the 1997 Act provides that, where any collective agreement or ministerial regulation exempts an activity from the requirement for daily rest periods (s 11), rests and interval breaks at work (s 12) or weekly rest periods (s 13), it must also require the employer to provide the employee with *equivalent* compensatory rest periods or breaks. Regulations 4 and 5 of Organisation of Working Time (General Exemptions) Regulations 1998[59] provide for this requirement in relation to the specific exemptions contained in those regulations.

Shift changes and split shift exemptions and exemptions in emergency situations

[4.21] The exemptions contained in ss 4(1), 4(2) and 5 of the 1997 Act contain a similar protection for employees. Where an employer intends to rely on such exemptions, the employer must provide the employee with *equivalent* compensatory rest periods or, where this is not possible for objective reasons, appropriate *alternative* compensatory

---

54 SI 817/2004, Reg 6. The 2004 Regulations transpose the provisions of Directive 2000/34/EC of 22 June 2000, amending Council Directive 93/104/EC concerning certain aspects of the organisation of working time to cover sectors and activities excluded from that Directive.

55 Mobile worker is not defined in the 2004 Regulations but the Regulations refer to the definitions to be found in Council Directive 93/104/EC as amended by Directive 2000/34/EC.

56 SI 817/2004, Reg 4: mobile workers in road transportation are covered by Directive 2002/15/EC and mobile staff in civil aviation by Directive 2000/79/EC: see para **[4.50]** below.

57 Unless they would be covered by the general exemptions in the Organisation of Working Time (General Exemptions) Regulations 1998: See para **[4.16]** above.

58 It would seem that they must fall back on the requirement in Reg 7 of the 2004 Regulations for employers to ensure that mobile workers have a rest period and breaks available to them 'that, in all the circumstances, can reasonably be regarded as adequate rest.'

59 SI 121/1998.

arrangements.[60] As a result, the employer has an option to provide such alternative compensatory arrangements where certain rest periods cannot objectively be provided.

Alternative compensatory arrangements

[4.22] There is no specific definition of 'alternative compensatory arrangements', but s 6(3) of the 1997 Act provides that alternative compensatory arrangements cannot be of a monetary or material benefit but may be in the form of 'such a benefit as will improve the physical conditions under which the employee works or the amenities or services available to the employee while he or she is at work.'

The Labour Relations Commission has provided guidance as to what constitutes 'equivalent rest' in the Organisation of Working Time (Code of Practice on Compensatory Rest Periods and Related Matters) (Declaration) Order 1998.[61] The Code includes a timescale for compensatory rest and provides the following non-exhaustive list of suitable measures:

(i)   enhanced environmental conditions to accommodate long periods of attendance at work;

(ii) refreshment facilities and/or recreational and reading material;

(iii) appropriate facilities/amenities such as television, radio and music;

(iv) alleviating monotonous work or isolation;

(v)   transport to and from work where appropriate.

THE WORKING TIME PROTECTIONS

Daily rest periods

[4.23] Section 11 of the 1997 Act implements Art 3 of Directive 93/104 and provides for a daily rest period of 11 consecutive hours in any 24-hour period.[62] It would appear that the intention is to provide for time off at the end of the working day. However, there would seem to be nothing to prevent an employer providing two 11-hour rest breaks back to back in any period of 48 hours. No definition is provided within the 1997 Act or Directive 93/104 as to the meaning of 'rest'. Directive 93/104 has been interpreted in such a way that a person who is not at work is effectively deemed to be 'at rest'.[63]

[4.24] In *Dempsey v Mediaserve (Ireland)*[64] the rostering of a telephonist for 15-hour shifts without a break was found by the EAT to be not only a breach of ss 11 and 12 of the 1997 Act but was also held to be a legitimate basis for claiming constructive dismissal.

---

[60] Organisation of Working Time Act 1997, s 6(2).

[61] SI 44/1998. The Code is available at www.lrc.ie.

[62] But note the exemptions and exclusions as set out at paras **[4.14]**–**[4.22]** above.

[63] C-151/02 *Landeshauptstadt Kiel v Jaeger* Case [2003] IRLR 804.

[64] *Dempsey v Mediaserve (Ireland)* UD 541/2000.

[4.25] In *Commission v United Kingdom*,[65] the ECJ found that there was no strict obligation on the employer to force employees to take their required daily rest periods. Notwithstanding this, the Court held that:

> [i]t is for the employer actively to see to it that an atmosphere is created in the firm in which the minimum rest periods prescribed by Community law are also effectively observed. There is no doubt that this first presupposes that within the organisation of the firm appropriate work and rest periods are actually scheduled. In addition ... no de facto pressure should arise which may deter workers from actually taking their rest periods.[66]

[4.26] In *Doyle and Gilmartin v Midland Tribune*,[67] the claimants were employed by Midland Tribuanal as print technicians and claimed that they were required to work excessive hours without rest breaks. While the Labour Court accepted that the employer was exempted from the provisions of the 1997 Act by virtue of the Organisation of Working Time (General Exemptions) Regulations 1998, the employer was still under a duty to ensure that a rest period or break equivalent to those provided for in ss 11, 12 and 13 was provided.

The employer argued that all workers were free to take their breaks as and when it was practical. This was not satisfactory for the Labour Court. The Court confirmed that the employer was under a duty to ensure that the employee receives his rest periods and breaks, observing that:

> Merely stating that the employee could take rest breaks if they wished and not putting in place proper procedures to ensure that the employee receives these breaks, thus protecting his health and safety, does not discharge that duty.

Rest breaks and intervals at work

[4.27] Section 12 of the 1997 Act implements Art 4 of Directive 93/104 and provides for the following rest breaks during the course of the working day:[68]

(i)   a 15 minute break every 4.5-hours,[69] and

(ii)   30 minutes of break-time every 6-hours.[70]

These breaks can be taken either separately or together,[71] but cannot be taken at the end of the working day.[72] There is no further provision as to where the break is to be taken within the 4.5 hour or 6 hour period and there is no requirement that such breaks are paid

---

[65] Case C-484/04 *Commission v United Kingdom* [2006] IRLR 888.
[66] Opinion of Advocate General Kokott, para 69.
[67] *Doyle and Gilmartin v Midland Tribune* [2004] 15 ELR 255. See also *The Tribune Printing & Publishing Group v GPMU* [2004] 15 ELR 222.
[68] But note the exemptions and exclusions as set out at paras **[4.14]–[4.22]** above.
[69] Organisation of Working Time Act 1997, s 12(1).
[70] Organisation of Working Time Act 1997, s 12(2).
[71] Note the exemptions in the Organisation of Working Time (General Exemptions) Regulations 1998 and Organisation of Working Time (Exemption of Civil Protection Services) Regulations 1998 and SI 817/2004.
[72] Organisation of Working Time Act 1997, s 12(4).

for by the employer. The thirty minute break can be extended to a period of up to one hour by Ministerial regulation for specified classes of employees.[73]

The interval breaks to which an employee is entitled cannot be added up from piece-meal periods of down time and should be an uninterrupted period of free time of which the employee is notified of in advance. The English Court of Appeal found in *Gallagher v Alpha Catering Services Ltd* that:

> [a] period of downtime cannot become a rest break only because it can be seen after it is over that it was an uninterrupted period of 20 minutes. The worker is entitled under Reg 12(1) to a rest break if his working time exceeds six hours, and he must know at the start of a rest break that it is such. To my mind a rest break is an uninterrupted period of at least 20 minutes which is neither a rest period nor working time and which the worker can use as he pleases.[74]

Weekly rest

[4.28] Section 13 of the 1997 Act implements Art 5 of Directive 93/104 and provides that an employee shall be entitled to an uninterrupted rest period of at least 24 hours in any seven-day period.[75] In the alternative, an employer may elect to grant his employee two rest periods of 24-hours duration in the following seven-day period. These periods may be consecutive or non consecutive.

In each case, the employee's 24-hour weekly rest period shall be preceded by a daily rest period of 11 hours.[76] If the two 24-hour periods are allocated together, only the first break of 24 hours must be preceded by an 11-hour daily rest break.[77] The requirement for a weekly rest period to be preceded by a daily rest period will not apply if technical or objective considerations relating to the nature of the work are such as to justify an employer in deciding not to provide an employee with this benefit.[78]

Unless the contract of employment provides otherwise, it shall be presumed that the weekly rest period will fall on a Sunday.[79] The Sunday rest presumption had originally featured in Directive 93/104, however, following the decision in *UK v Council of EU*[80] it has been removed. In that case, the ECJ ruled that no sufficient evidence had been advanced to explain why Sunday rest was more closely connected with the health and safety of employees than rest taken on other days of the week. Notwithstanding this decision, the Sunday rest presumption remains a part of Irish law.

---

[73] See Organisation of Working Time (Breaks at Work for Shop Employees) Regulations 1998 (SI 57/1998) which extends the break for 'shop employees' working between 11.30am and 2.30pm to a minimum duration of one hour.

[74] *Gallagher v Alpha Catering Services Ltd* [2005] IRLR 102, Peter Gibson LJ. See also *MacCartney v Oversley House Management* [2006] IRLR 514.

[75] But note the exemptions and exclusions as set out at paras **[4.14]–[4.22]** above.

[76] Organisation of Working Time Act 1997, s 13(3).

[77] Organisation of Working Time Act 1997, s 13(2)(a)–(b).

[78] Organisation of Working Time Act 1997, s 13(4).

[79] Organisation of Working Time Act 1997, s 13(5).

[80] Case C-84/94 *UK v Council of EU* [1996] ECR I-5755.

Compensation for Sunday working

[4.29] In keeping with the presumption that an employee shall not generally be required to work on a Sunday, s 14 provides that employees who do work on a Sunday will be compensated by way of an allowance, an increase in salary or paid time off in lieu.[81] If the employee's salary already takes account of the requirement for Sunday work no such additional compensation shall be necessary. Where required, the extent of additional compensation shall be a matter for the employer's discretion having regard to what is reasonable in the circumstances.

Where a Rights Commissioner is required to adjudicate on the adequacy of any such compensation the Rights Commissioner shall do so by reference to collective agreements in being for comparable workers. In the case of *Group 4 Securitas v SIPTU*[82] the employee's union attempted to challenge the Sunday premium paid to security staff on the basis that the rate was not reasonable in all of the circumstances. The union argued that the existing agreement between its members and the employer was unreasonable having regard to other comparable collective agreements. However, the Labour Court held that the mechanism under s 14 of the 1997 Act could not be used to secure an increased premium where an agreement already existed in relation to that specific employment.[83]

[4.30] In the case of *Clare County Council v Ensko,*[84] a swimming instructor was offered a Sunday premium of €25 in acknowledgement of the requirement that she work every second Sunday in the Council's swimming pool. The Rights Commissioner deemed this offer to be inadequate and made a backdated award of double time for Sunday hours worked. On appeal to the Labour Court, this award was reduced to time and a half.

For a statement of the principles applicable to Sunday working and compensatory arrangements see the Organisation of Working Time (Code of Practice on Sunday Working in the Retail Trade and Related Matters) (Declaration) Order 1998.[85]

Maximum 48-hour working week

[4.31] Section 15 implements Art 6 of Directive 93/104 and provides that an employee shall not be permitted by his employer to work more than an average of 48-hours during the course of a week.[86] It should be noted that the terms of s 15 are mandatory as far as the employer is concerned, imposing an obligation on the employer to ensure that excessive hours are not worked. As a result, it has been observed that this imposes 'a form of strict liability' on the employer.[87]

---

[81] But note the exemptions as set out at para **[4.15]** above.
[82] *Group 4 Securitas v SIPTU* DWT 06/1999.
[83] See also *Cadbury Ireland v SIPTU* DWT 07/20 where the Labour Court reached a similar conclusion in respect of Sunday premium.
[84] *Clare County Council v Ensko* DWT 073/2007.
[85] SI 444/1998.
[86] But note the exemptions as set out at paras **[4.15]**–**[4.22]** above.
[87] *IBM Ireland v Svoboda* DWT 18/2008.

The reference period over which the 48-working hours shall be averaged varies depending upon the type of work carried out by the employee. In most cases, the reference period is four months.[88] For night workers the reference period is two months.[89] For persons working in the field of agriculture and tourism the reference period is six months. A longer period of up to 12 months may apply in the case of an employee whose conditions are regulated pursuant to a collective agreement approved by the Labour Court.[90]

The reference period used to calculate an employee's average hours may not include periods of annual leave, sick leave, parental leave, maternity leave, adoptive leave or carer's leave.[91] In circumstances where annual leave taken by an employee exceeds the statutory entitlement, the excess period may be reckoned in calculating average hours worked.[92]

For the purposes of computing the hours worked in a week it should be borne in mind that break periods, during which the employee is not liable to be required to work and is not in any sense 'on call', will not count.

In the case of *Svoboda v IBM Ireland*[93] the Labour Court heard an appeal from a determination of the Rights Commissioner concerning breaches of s 15(1) of the 1997 Act. The claimant regularly worked for periods in excess of 48 hours per week, however, the respondent did not require her to work such hours and had instructed the claimant on more than one occasion to confine herself to her contractual hours, which were 39 hours per week. The claimant ignored these instructions and continued to work outside of her contractual hours.

The Labour Court noted that s 15 of the 1997 Act requires than an employer "shall not permit" an employee to work in excess of 48 hours and that the employer's obligations are strict liability in nature. For this reason the Labour Court held that the cimplaint was well founded but went on to find, in view of the respondent's *bona fide* effors to prevent excessive hours being worked, that the breaches were technical and of non-culable type. As a result the Labour Court determined that an award of compensation was not appropriate.

In the UK, the High Court has held[94] that the 48 hour working week enshrined by Art 4(1) of Directive 93/104 is a contractual right which is enforceable at common law. This may be of some significance in proceedings where damages are sought for work related stress.

Regulation of night working

[4.32] Additional working time protections are extended to employees who are classed as night workers as defined by s 16 of the 1997 Act.[95] Section 16 implements Art 8 of

---

[88] Organisation of Working Time Act 1997, s 15(1)(a).
[89] Organisation of Working Time Act 1997, s 16(2)(b)(i).
[90] Pursuant to s 24 of the 1997 Act.
[91] Organisation of Working Time Act 1997, s 15(4).
[92] Organisation of Working Time Act 1997, s 15(4)(a).
[93] *Svoboda v IBM Ireland* DWT 18/2008.
[94] *Barber v RJB Mining UK Ltd* [1999] IRLR 308.
[95] But note the exemptions and exclusions as set out at para **[4.14]** above.

Directive 93/104 and is derived from research to the effect that the human body is more sensitive to environmental disturbances at night time[96] than during daytime. This in turn has lead to a concern that night work is linked to an increase risk to the health and safety of employees and, as a result, limitations on night work are more restrictive than at other times.

For the purposes of the 1997 Act, night time is the period between midnight and 7 am. A night worker is defined as a person who spends 50% or more of their annual hours working at night. In addition to this, the employee must work for three night hours on a normal working day.[97]

In order to prevent or minimise health and safety risks to night workers, an employee shall not be permitted by his employer to work for more than 8 hours on average[98] in any 24-hour period. The reference period against which this average is be calculated shall be two months, or such longer period as may be agreed by collective agreement and approved by the Labour Court.[99]

Section 16(2)(a) of the 1997 Act provides that a 'special category night worker' may only work for eight hours in any 24 hour period, without exception. There are no averaging provisions in respect of these employees.

Under s 19 of the Safety, Health and Welfare at Work Act 2005 employers must carry out a risk assessment in respect of the health and safety of their employee's working conditions. Regulations made pursuant to s 58 of that Act include the Safety Health and Welfare at Work Regulations 2007. Regulation 155 of those Regulations provide that an employer shall carry out a risk assessment of the specific effects and hazards of night work and the risks to the safety and health of the employee concerned so as to determine whether that employee is a special category worker. Where such an assessment determines that an employee is at special risk s 16(2)(a) will apply and the employee will not be permitted to work for more than eight hours at any given time.

Provision of information on work-schedules

[4.33] The Terms Of Employment (Additional Information) Order 1998,[100] provides that an employer must provide an employee with a statement in writing containing particulars of the times and duration of their rest periods and breaks, as referred to in ss 11, 12 and 13 of the 1997 Act, and of any other terms and conditions relating to those periods and breaks, within two months of commencing employment.

Section 17(1) of the 1997 Act provides that if the employee's contract of employment or other relevant agreement does not already specify his starting and finishing time the

---

[96] See Recital 7 of the Directive.

[97] Strangely, Reg 151 of the Safety Health and Welfare at Work Regulations 2007 provides that night work takes place between 11 pm and 6 am. For the purpose of those regulations, a worker must only spend 25% of his time working at night in order to be deemed a night worker. In every other respect, those regulations adopt the definitions set out in the Organisation of Working Time Act 1997.

[98] Organisation of Working Time Act 1997, s 16(2)(b).

[99] Pursuant to s 24 of the 1997 Act.

[100] SI 49/1998.

employee shall be entitled to notice of that starting and finishing time 24 hours before the day or days on which he shall be required to work.[101]

Where the employee is required to work variable additional hours on a particular day or days he is entitled to notice of that requirement 24 hours before the day or days on which he is required to work such additional hours.[102] Section 17(3) provides that if the employee is not working on the day in which the 24-hour notice falls to be given pursuant to s 17(1) or 17(2), that notice must be given on the day prior to the employee's last working day.

In order to comply with the notice requirements referred to, it will suffice for an employer to post such notice in a conspicuous place in the employee's workplace.[103] Where unforeseeable circumstances arise as a result of which the employer needs the services of an employee without giving the requisite notice the employer may require his employee to work as necessary.[104]

Zero hours working practices

[4.34] Section 18 of the 1997 Act grants minimum payment rights to employees who are required to be available for work on the basis of 'zero hours' employment contracts.[105] This is a situation in which the employee's contract requires that (a) the employee be available to work for a certain number of hours in the week without a guarantee that work will be provided, or (b) the employee be available for work as and when the employer requires it.[106]

In either of these situations, or where a combination of the two arises, the employee is entitled to a minimum payment equal to 25% of the hours of which the employee would have been required to work or 15 hours pay, whichever is the lesser.[107] An employee will not be entitled to this minimum payment where a mere previous course of dealing gives the employee reason to expect that he will be required to be available for work on this basis.[108] The requirement to be available for such work must, therefore, be an explicit one on the part of the employer, whether by specific request, or pursuant to the contract of employment.

---

[101] But note the exemptions and exclusions as set out at para **[4.14]** above.

[102] Organisation of Working Time Act 1997, s 17(2). See *Anglo Irish Beef Processors v SIPTU* DWT 19/2000.

[103] Organisation of Working Time Act 1997, s 17(5).

[104] Organisation of Working Time Act 1997, s 17(4).

[105] But note the exemptions as set out at paras **[4.15]–[4.22]** above.

[106] The computation of hours for which the employee must be available in the latter situation shall be the maximum number of such hours worked by another employee of the same employer. See para 18(4).

[107] In *Ocean Manpower Ltd v Marine Port and General Workers Union* [1998] ELR 299 the Labour Court rejected a contention that employees should be entitled to payment for 25% of the hours for which they were required to be available.

[108] Organisation of Working Time Act 1997, s 18(1)(c).

[4.35] In *Ocean Manpower Ltd v Marine Port and General Workers Union*[109] the Labour Court considered a case in which employees were required to be available for a defined period and report for work at a specific location pursuant to an agreement between the employee's union and the employer. The agreement provided that failure to report may result in disciplinary sanction, however, this was not strictly enforced by the employer. Notwithstanding this, the Labour Court held that these terms formed part of the union agreement and were part of the contract of employment. Accordingly, s 18 of the 1997 Act applied.

Entitlement to annual leave

[4.36] Section 19 of the 1997 Act implements Art 7 of Directive 93/104 by setting out the employee's entitlement to annual leave. They are:

(i)   4 working weeks[110] for a leave year in which the employee works 1,365 hours or more; or

(ii)   1/3 of a working week for each month in the leave year in which the employee works 117 hours; or

(iii) 8 per cent of the hours worked by the employee up to a maximum of four working weeks.

Provided the employee qualifies for leave pursuant to one of these criteria, he will be entitled to annual leave up to a maximum of four weeks. Where the employee qualifies under two or more headings he shall be entitled to whichever period of leave is the greater.

It can be expected that s 19 of the 1997 Act will now be amended in light of the recent decision of the ECJ in the joined cases of *Schultz Hoff v Deutsche Rentenversicherung Bund*[111] and *Stringer v Her Majesty's Revenue and Customs*.[112] In interpreting Art 7(1) of Directive 93/104, the ECJ held that the exercise of an employee's right to annual leave under national law cannot be made subject to a requirement to have worked during the relevant leave year. It is difficult to see how s 19 of the 1997 Act can be interpreted in such a way as to conform with this interpretation of Directive, however, it is notable that the ECJ also held that national legislation may lay down conditions for the exercise of the right to paid annual leave which may result in the loss of that right at the end of a leave year.[113]

The reference period for annual leave is the 'leave year' beginning on 1 April.[114] A worker's leave must normally be taken within the allotted leave year unless, by agreement with the employee, the period is extended[115] by a period of six months. In *Royal Liver Assurance Ltd v Macken*,[116] Lavan J noted that this section is designed to

---

[109] *Ocean Manpower Ltd v Marine Port and General Workers Union* [1998] ELR 299.
[110] Unless it is a leave year in which the employee has changed employment.
[111] Case C-350/06 *Schultz Hoff v Deutsche Rentenversicherung Bund* 20 January 2009.
[112] Case C-520/06 *Stringer v Her Majesty's Revenue and Customs* 20 January 2009.
[113] Paragraph 43.
[114] Organisation of Working Time Act 1997, s 2(1).
[115] Pursuant to s 20(1)(c) of the 1997 Act.
[116] *Royal Liver Assurance Ltd v Macken* [2002] 4 IR 427.

provide flexibility in balancing the needs of the employer and the rights of the employee, however, any such extension must be with the prior consent of the employee.

While the meaning of 'working week' is not defined in the 1997 Act the Labour Court has determined that it shall be construed as meaning the number of hours or days ordinarily occuring within the employee's weekly working cycle.[117]

[4.37] The time at which annual leave is taken will, in the first instance, be a matter for the employer.[118] Notwithstanding this, the employer is obliged to take into account the need for the employee to reconcile work and family responsibilities and the opportunity for rest and recreation which is available to the employee.[119] The employer is also obliged to consult the employee, or relevant trade union, no less than one month prior to the commencement of annual leave (or part thereof).[120] Employees who work more than eight months in a given year will be entitled to take two uninterrupted weeks of annual leave together,[121] however, this two week period will include any public holidays or period during which the employee becomes ill.[122]

Payment is made at the normal weekly rate or in proportion to this rate where a lesser period of leave is taken. Where the weekly rate does not vary, the normal weekly rate of pay shall be[123]:

> [t]he sum (including any regular bonus or allowance the amount of which does not vary in relation to the work done by the employee but excluding any pay for overtime) that is paid in respect of the normal weekly working hours last worked by the employee before the annual leave (or the portion thereof concerned) commences.

Where pay varies from week to week the normal weekly rate of pay shall be:

> [t]he sum that is equal to the average weekly pay (excluding any pay for overtime) of the employee calculated over the period of 13 weeks [last worked] before the annual leave (or the portion thereof concerned) commences or, as the case may be, the cesser of employment.

An employer cannot discharge the obligation to provide paid holidays by incorporating a general composite holiday payment into an employee's basic pay. In *Fasercourt Ltd v Shay O'Brien*[124] this argument was made on behalf of an employer before the Labour Court and was unsurprisingly rejected.

---

[117] *Irish Ferries v Seaman's Union of Ireland* DWT35/2001.

[118] Organisation of Working Time Act 1997, s 20.

[119] Organisation of Working Time Act 1997, s 20(1)(a).

[120] In *Bus Éireann v Services Industrial Professional Technical Union* WTC 00/6 a bus driver was required, following consultation between his employer and trade union to take holidays during the summer period. As a result it was determined that holidays taken in contravention of this agreement were to be treated as unpaid leave.

[121] Organisation of Working Time Act 1997, s 19(3).

[122] Organisation of Working Time Act 1997, s 19(4).

[123] Organisation of Working Time (Determination of Pay for Holidays) Regulations 1997 (SI 475/1997).

[124] *Fasercourt Ltd v Shay O'Brien* DWT 743/2007.

[4.38] Maternity leave which coincides with annual leave must not deprive the worker of her entitlement to paid annual leave. The worker will be entitled to take such leave separately.[125]

The entitlement to be paid unconditional annual leave is seen as both a fundamental social entitlement and a matter of health and safety for employees.[126] The fundamental social nature of this right was referred to with apparent approval by Lavan J in *Royal Liver Assurance Ltd v Macken*[127] where he quoted from comments made by Advocate General Tizzano to this effect in *R (BECTU)*.[128]

Leave entitlements for public holidays

[4.39] There are nine public holidays in Ireland, namely Christmas Day, St Stephen's Day, January 1, St Patrick's Day, Easter Monday, the first Monday in May, the first Monday in June, the first Monday in August and the last Monday in October.[129]

Section 21 of the 1997 Act provides that public holidays shall be marked, at the option of the employer, by either a paid day off, a paid day off within one month of the public holiday, a day of annual leave or an additional day's pay. In order to give effect to the employee's public holiday entitlements the employee may, not later than 21 days prior to the public holiday, require his employer to make his election as between modes of compensation. This decision must be notified to the employee no less than 14 days prior to the public holiday. In the event that the employee is not notified within 14 days the employer shall be deemed to have elected to compensate the employee by way of an additional day's pay.

[4.40] In order to qualify, an employee must have worked for 40 hours in the five weeks preceding the public holiday in question.[130] An employee's rights should not be affected by the fact that he is not scheduled to work on a public holiday. In that instance, the employee will be given either a day off within the month, a day of annual leave or an extra day's pay. Where an employee is on certified sick leave the employee will be entitled to an additional day off or pay in lieu.[131]

Section 22 of the 1997 Act provides that the calculation of additional pay for the purposes of s 21 may be determined by Ministerial regulation, namely; the Organisation of Working Time (Determination of Pay for Holidays) Regulations 1997.[132] Where the

---

[125] Case C-342/01 *Maria Paz Merino Gómez v Continental Industrias del Caucho SA* [2004] IRLR 407 ECJ.

[126] See the decision of the Labour Court in *Cementation Skanska v Carroll* DWT 38/2003.

[127] *Royal Liver Assurance Ltd v Macken* [2002] 4 IR 427.

[128] [2002] 4 IR 427 at 436. See Case C-173/99 *R (BECTU) Trade and Industry Secretary* [2001] 1 WLR 2313.

[129] See Sch II of the Act. The Minister for Enterprise, Trade and Employment may vary the public holidays set out in the Sch.

[130] Organisation of Working Time Act 1997, s 21(4).

[131] *Thermo King v Kenny* DWT 06/11. See also *An Post v King* DWT 07/11 where the Labour Court held that an employee who was on sick leave could not lose his public holiday entitlement in respect of a holiday falling during his period of sick leave.

[132] Organisation of Working Time (Determination of Pay for Holidays) Regulations 1997 (SI 475/1997). See Reg 3.

employee's pay is calculated wholly by reference to a time rate or a fixed rate or salary or any other rate that does not vary in relation to the work done, the rate of pay will be the sum that is paid in respect of the normal daily working hours last worked by the employee before the public holiday in question. If not, the rate will be the average daily rate (excluding overtime) paid to the employee calculated over the previous 13 weeks. Those regulations further provide[133] that if a public holiday falls on a day on which the employee normally works the amount payable to him shall be the amount payable in respect of the normal daily hours last worked prior to the public holiday, excluding any overtime. If the public holiday falls on a day on which the employee does not ordinarily work, the appropriate rate is one fifth of a week's pay.

[4.41] In *Cadbury Ireland v SIPTU*[134] employees transferring from a ten-hour shift to an eight-hour shift on the August public holiday claimed that they were entitled to be paid for ten hours on the basis that the last day on which they worked was a ten hour day, even though they did not ordinarily work on a Monday. The Rights Commissioner agreed, but on appeal the Labour Court, applying Reg 5, held that employees who normally work on a Monday were entitled to ten hours pay, but those who did not were only entitled to eight hours' pay.

Compensation upon termination of employment

[4.42] Section 23 of the 1997 Act provides for the compensation of employees where annual leave or public holiday entitlements are outstanding at the date of termination of employment. Where the proportion of leave taken is less than the proportion of the leave year that has expired the employee shall be entitled to payment in recognition of the excess. Where the contract comes to an end in the first half of the employee's leave year the reference period for calculation of the payment is deemed to include the previous leave year.

Calculations under this section are made by reference to the 'appropriate daily rate' or the 'normal weekly rate' as provided for by the Organisation of Working Time (Determination of Pay for Holidays) Regulations 1997[135] discussed above at paragraph **[4.40]**.

Section 23(2) of the 1997 Act provides that employees ceasing to be employed at any time in the week prior to a public holiday are entitled to payment in lieu of the public holiday provided he has worked for the employer for four weeks prior to that public holiday. In *Gazboro Ltd v Building and Allied Trades' Union*,[136] the employees union argued that employees who had ceased work on 18 December 1998 were entitled to pay for public holidays falling on 25 December and 26 December 1998. The Labour Court held that the week ending at midnight on 24 December had commenced on 18 December and therefore the employees were entitled to be paid for 25 December. The Labour Court rejected the argument that the entitlement to be paid for Christmas day meant that the employees should be deemed to have worked on the week commencing on 25

---

[133] See Reg 5.
[134] *Cadbury Ireland v SIPTU* [1999] ELR 202.
[135] SI 475/1997.
[136] *Gazboro Ltd v Building and Allied Trades' Union* DWT 16/1999.

December and therefore no entitlement to be paid for the public holiday on 26 December arose.

In order to provide for entitlements upon the death of an employee, s 23(3) of the 1997 Act makes explicit the entitlement of an employee's legal personal representative to recover on behalf of the estate.

Protection against penalisation

[4.43] Section 26 of the 1997 Act prohibits an employer from penalising an employee for having in good faith opposed by lawful means an act which is unlawful under the Act. Penalisation can take many forms, but s 26 specifies that, if a penalisation constitutes a dismissal relief may not be granted to the employee in respect of that penalisation both under the 1997 Act and the Unfair Dismissals Acts 1977–2007.

WORKING TIME RECORDS

[4.44] Section 25(1) of the 1997 Act provides that employers must keep records to confirm whether the provisions of the Act are being complied with in relation all employees. Such records must be retained by the employer for three years and be available for inspection.[137]

Form of records

[4.45] The Organisation of Working Time (Records) (Prescribed Form and Exemptions) Regulations 2001 (the 2001 Regulations) prescribe the form of working time records. Employers are required to keep:

(i)   The name, address, RSI number and a brief job description;

(ii) A copy of the statement of main terms of employment as required by s 3 of the Terms of Employment (Information) Act 1994;

(iii) a record of the days and number of hours worked by employees (excluding meals and rest breaks) on a weekly basis;

(iv) a record of leave granted to employees in each week by way of annual leave or in respect of a public holiday and any payment made in respect of that leave, and;

(v)   a weekly record of the notification of the starting and finishing time of employees as required by s 17 of the 1997 Act.[138]

---

[137] Records must be kept at the premises or place where the employee works and, if the employee works at two or more premises or places, records must be kept at 'the premises or place from which the activities that the employee is employed to carry on are principally directed or controlled'.

[138] SI 473/2001, Reg 3. Section 17 requires that the employee must, in situations where working hours vary, be given at least 24 hours notice of the times and dates on which the employee will be required to start and finish work. In order to comply with this requirement it is sufficient a notice at a conspicuous place in the employee's work place.

The records must be in such a form 'as will enable an inspector to understand the particulars contained in them without difficulty'.[139] The Schedule to the 2001 Regulations introduces a standard form (Form OWT1) for the recording hours of work. It should be noted that breach of s 25(1) is not a matter in respect of which an employee may make a complaint to the Rights Commissioner pursuant to s 27 of the 1997 Act.

General exemption: clocking in facilities

[4.46] Where an employer has clocking in facilities in place there is no further necessity to record hours in a separate form.[140] However, if no clocking in facilities are in place a Form OWT1, or 'a form substantially to like effect', must be completed in respect of all employees.[141]

Specific exemption: recording rest breaks

[4.47] Section 25(2) of the 1997 Act specifies that the Minister may by regulation exempt certain employers from the requirement to keep working time records. Regulation 5(1) provides for such an exemption in relation to the recording of 'rest breaks'[142] where an employer has:

(i) electronic record-keeping facilities such as flexi-time or clocking-in facilities; or

(ii) manual record-keeping facilities and completes a Form OWT1 or 'a form substantially to like effect' in respect of all employees.[143]

The exemption from recording rest breaks only applies if the employer:

(a) notifies each employee in writing of their statutory rest periods and breaks;[144] and

(b) puts in place procedures whereby an employee may notify the employer in writing of any rest period or break to which such employee is entitled;[145] and

---

[139] SI 473/2001, Reg 3. Similar wording is also contained in Reg 5.

[140] SI 473/2001, Reg 4(1). There is no definition in the Directive, the Act or the Regulations of 'clocking in facilities'.

[141] SI 473/2001, Reg 4(1). There is a requirement that the form is signed by both the employee and the employer. However, the form may be completed by the employee. Regulation 4(2) provides that the employee may complete the form, sign it and submit it to the employer for counter-signature and retention for records purposes.

[142] The 2001 Regulations use the term 'rest breaks', however the Directive and the Act uses the term 'rest periods'. It would, however, seem reasonable to presume that the term 'rest breaks' used here refers to all rest periods provided in the Act ie daily rest period (s 11), rests and intervals at work (s 12) and weekly rest periods (s 13) as such rest periods are referred to specifically in Reg 5(2).

[143] SI 473/2001, Reg 5.

[144] SI 473/2001, Reg 5(2)(a). The relevant rest periods and breaks are those provided for in ss 11, 12 and 13 of the Act and any collective agreement, registered employment agreement and employment regulation order.

[145] SI 473/2001, Reg 5(2)(b).

(c)   notifies each employee in writing of this procedure;

(d)   keeps a record of having notified each employee of the right to rest breaks and the procedures to follow if a rest break is not availed of; and

(e)   records of all such notifications made by any employee under such procedures.[146]

Regulation 5(3) of the 2001 Regulations provides that, in such circumstances, notifications must be made by employees within one week of the rest period in question and the employer must then make an equivalent rest period available. However, failure by the employee to avail of such rest period does not constitute a breach of the Act or Regulations by the employer.

Criminal penalties

[4.48] An employer who fails to keep records is guilty of an offence and may be liable on summary conviction to a fine not exceeding €1,900.[147] Failure to keep appropriate records in respect of any one employee constitutes an offence. Thus, where an employer fails to keep records in respect of a number of employees, that employer could be charged with a number of offences involving multiple fines. While it would appear that these breaches have not been prosecuted with any notable zeal, the increase in the number of inspectors may have an impact on this trend.

Onus of proof

[4.49] Where an employee makes a complaint to a Rights Commissioner that his employer has failed to keep working time records, the onus of proving compliance with the 1997 Act in proceedings before the Rights Commissioner or the Labour Court will lie on the employer.[148] This makes it very difficult for an employer to defend a claim in the absence of such records.

MOBILE WORKERS AND DRIVERS IN ROAD TRANSPORTATION

[4.50] Since the Organisation of Working Time (Inclusion of Transport Activities) Regulations 2004 (the 2004 Regulations) do not apply to mobile workers in road transportation or to non-mobile workers, all workers in road transportation will have the full protection of the 1997 Act.[149] Further protection is provided by the EC (Organisation of Working Time of Persons Performing Mobile Road Transport Activities) Regulations

---

[146] SI 473/2001, Reg 5(2)(c).

[147] SI 473/2001, Reg 7.

[148] Organisation of Working Time Act 1997, s 25(4) of the Act. This was the case in *Goode Concrete v Dermot Munro* DWT051, where the Labour Court awarded €15,000 for various breaches of the Act.

[149] SI 817/2004, Reg 4. See above at para **[4.19]**, unless they would be covered by the general exemptions in the Organisation of Working Time (General Exemptions) Regulations 1998: See para **[4.16]** above.

2005 (the 2005 Regulations)[150] and the EC (Road Transport) (Working Conditions and Road Safety) Regulations 2008 (the 2008 Regulations).[151]

A 'mobile worker' is defined in the 2005 Regulations as 'any worker forming part of the travelling staff, including trainees and apprentices, who is in the service of an undertaking which operates transport services for passengers or goods for hire or reward or on its own account.'[152] The 2008 Regulations provide extra protections specifically for drivers,[153] where 'driver' is defined as 'any person who drives the vehicle even for a short period, or who is carried in a vehicle as part of his duties to be available for driving if necessary'.[154]

Application

[4.51] The 2005 and 2008 Regulations apply generally to drivers and crews of commercial vehicles of more than 3.5 tonnes or transporting more than nine people, including the driver. However, the Regulations specifically exclude certain vehicles such as those working on passenger routes not exceeding 50 kilometres per hour; or with a maximum speed not exceeding 40 kilometres per hour; or providing certain public services.[155]

Self-employed drivers are exempted from the provisions of Directive 2002/15/EC or the 2005 Regulations until March 2009.[156] Their continued exemption after that time will depend on recommendations from the European Commission.

---

[150] SI 2/2005. The 2005 Regulations implement Directive 2002/15/EC which establishes minimum requirements in relation to the organisation of working time of persons performing mobile road transport activities (Directive 2002/15).

[151] SI 62/2008. The 2008 Regulations implement Council Regulation 561/2006/EC of 15 March 2006 on the harmonisation of certain social legislation relating to road transport and give full effect to Council Regulation 3821/85/EC of 20 December 1985 on recording equipment in road transport (as amended by Council Regulation 2135/98/EC of 24 September 1998, Commission Reg (EC) 1360/2002 of 13 June 2002 and Council Regulation 561/2006 of 15 March 2006). The 2008 Regulations also deal with the application of the European Agreement concerning the Work of Crews of Vehicles engaged in International Road Transport, done on 1 July 1970, (the 1970 Agreement) making it an offence to breach that Agreement.

[152] SI 2/2005, Reg 2 implementing Art 3 of Directive 2002/15.

[153] Implementing Council Regulation 561/2006 which applies to all drivers.

[154] Council Regulation 561/2006, Art 4.

[155] A full list of exemptions can be found in Art 4 of Council Regulation 3820/85 and Art 2(2)(b) of the 1970 Agreement.

[156] SI 2/2005, Reg 2 provides that 'self-employed driver' means anyone whose main occupation is to transport passengers or goods by road for hire or reward 'who is entitled to work for himself and who is not tied to an employer by a contract of employment or by any other type of working hierarchical relationship, who is free to organise the relevant working activities, whose income depends directly on the profits made and who has the freedom, individually or through a co-operation between self-employed drivers, to have commercial relations with several customers'.

[4.52] The 2008 Regulations also contain specific exemptions for vehicles used *solely within the State.* [157]

Recording equipment

[4.53] The 2008 Regulations implement the requirement in Council Regulation 3821/85 that recording equipment (tachographs) must be installed and used in all vehicles registered in a Member State which are used for the carriage of passengers or goods by road unless they fall under the categories exempted above.[158]

Working time

[4.54] The 2005 Regulations provide that 'working time' shall, in the case of mobile workers, mean 'the time from the beginning to the end of work, during which the mobile worker is at his workstation, at the disposal of the employer and exercising his functions or activities'.[159] This includes time devoted to all road transport activities including:

(i)   driving;

(ii)   loading and unloading;

(iii)   assisting passengers boarding and disembarking from the vehicle;

(iv)   cleaning and technical maintenance;

(v)   work intended to ensure the safety of the vehicle, its cargo and passengers or administrative formalities linked to legal or regulatory obligations associated with the specific transport operation underway eg customs or police.[160]

For the purposes of the 2008 Regulations, 'driving time' means the duration of driving activity recorded by tachograph or by manual recording. 'Other work' means time devoted to all road transport activities as set out above, except 'driving'. This includes any work for the same or another employer, within or outside of the transport sector.[161]

Maximum weekly working time

[4.55] The 2005 Regulations provide that the working time, including overtime, of a mobile worker must not exceed a maximum of 60 hours in any given week.[162] Also, a mobile worker must not exceed an average of 48 hours working time for each week over

---

[157] For full exemptions, see Reg 5.
[158] SI 2/2005, Reg 21. Drivers will be required to produce such records on the request of enforcement officers: Reg 29.
[159] SI 2/2005, Reg 2.
[160] Council Directive 2002/15/EC, Art 3. It may also include times devoted to other activities, such as time during which the mobile worker cannot dispose freely of his time and is required to be at his/her workstation ready to take up normal work, with certain tasks associated with being on duty or waiting periods where their foreseeable duration is not known in advance either before departure or just before the actual start of the period in question. However, times of breaks, rests and periods of availability will not be included in the calculation of working time.
[161] Council Regulation 561/2006, Art 4.
[162] SI 2/2005, Reg 5 implementing Art 4 of Directive 2002/15/EC.

a four month period and the Regulations set out specific reference periods for such four month periods[163]:

Beginning	End
1 January	1 May
1 May	1 September
1 September	1 January

A mobile worker must advise their employer in writing of any hours worked for another employer and those hours will count towards the average weekly working time of that mobile worker.[164]

By implementing Council Regulation 561/2006, the 2008 Regulations have provided further specific protection for *drivers*. Drivers cannot exceed a maximum weekly driving time of 56 hours.[165] The total accumulated driving time during any two consecutive weeks must not exceed 90 hours.[166] When driving time and other work is added together it must not exceed the maximum weekly working time or 60 hours as set out in the 2005 Regulations as set out above.

Breaks

[4.56] Mobile workers must be provided with a break of at least 30 minutes to be taken when working between six to nine hours and at least 45 minutes when working over nine hours.[167] These breaks may be subdivided into periods of at least 15 minutes each.

Drivers must also take a break of 45 minutes after every 4.5 hours of driving, unless the driver begins a rest period.[168] This may be split into a break of 15 minutes followed by a break of 30 minutes.[169]

Daily and weekly rest

[4.57] As noted above at para **[4.50]**, mobile workers in road transportation are not excluded from the protections in the 1997 Act and have the normal right to a daily rest period of 11 consecutive hours and weekly rest period of 24 consecutive hours. The 2008

---

[163] These reference periods are fall back provisions for situations where there is no collective agreement, employment regulation order or registered employment agreement in place. The employer may also give written notice to the mobile worker in writing that he intends to apply a specific reference period of any period of 17 weeks in the course of the worker's employment.

[164] This period may be extended by a collective agreement or an employment regulation order or a registered employment agreement.

[165] Council Regulation 561/2006, Art 6.

[166] These rules, along with many of the provisions of Council Regulation 561/2006, were originally specified in the 1970 Agreement.

[167] SI 2/2005, Reg 8 implementing Art 5 of Directive 2002/15.

[168] SI 2/2005, Reg 9 implementing Council Regulation 3820/85. However, there is an exception in the case of national carriage of passengers on regular services where the break may be fixed at a minimum of 30 minutes after a driving period not exceeding four hours.

[169] Council Regulation 561/2006, Art 7.

Regulations provide extra protection for drivers with more complicated daily and weekly rest rules.

Within each period of 24 hours after the end of the previous daily rest period or weekly rest period a driver must take a new daily rest period.[170] There is a distinction between regular daily rest periods and reduced daily rest periods for drivers. While the regular daily rest period remains at 11 hours, a reduced daily rest period is between 9 and 11 hours. A driver may have at most three of these reduced daily rest periods between any two weekly rest periods.[171]

[4.58] Alternatively, the daily rest period may be taken in two or three separate periods during the 24-hour period, one of which must be a minimum of nine consecutive hours, but the minimum daily rest period is then increased to 12 hours in total.[172] The daily driving time must not normally exceed nine hours, but may be extended to 10 hours twice during the week.[173] Special rules apply to situations when a vehicle is manned by at least two drivers: During each period of 30 hours, each driver must have a rest period of not less than 9 consecutive hours.[174]

In the course of each week, either the 11-hour rest period or nine hour rest period must be extended, by way of weekly rest, to a weekly rest period of 45 consecutive hours. This 45-hour rest period must be taken at the end of a maximum of 56 hours or six daily driving periods.[175] The weekly rest period may be reduced to a minimum of 36 consecutive hours if taken at the place where the vehicle is normally based or where the driver is based, or to a minimum of 24 consecutive hours, if taken elsewhere.

Drivers' hours are regulated in two-week periods. In any two consecutive weeks a driver must take at least two regular weekly rest periods (45 hours) or one regular weekly rest period and one reduced weekly rest period (minimum 24 hours). However, any reduced period must be compensated by an equivalent period of rest taken en bloc before the end of the third week following the week in question and must be attached to another rest period of at least nine hours.[176]

Daily rest periods and reduced weekly rest periods away from base may be taken in a vehicle, as long as it has suitable sleeping facilities for each driver and the vehicle is stationary.

---

[170] Council Regulation 561/2006, Art 8.

[171] Council Regulation 561/2006, Art 8.

[172] Council Regulation 3820/85, Art 8.

[173] Council Regulation 561/2006, Art 6.

[174] Council Regulation 561/2006, Art 8 and Art 8 of the 1970 Agreement.

[175] A weekly rest period that falls in two weeks may be counted in either week, but not in both. A week is defined in the regulations as the period of time between 00.00 on Monday and 24.00 on Sunday.

[176] Council Regulation 561/2006, Art 8.

Night working

[4.59] The 2005 Regulations provide that the working time of any mobile worker who performs night work shall not exceed 10 hours in any period of 24 hours.[177] 'Night time' means 'in respect of motor vehicles used for carrying goods the period between 00.00 hours and 04.00 hours and in respect of motor vehicles used for carrying passengers the period between 01.00 hours and 05.00 hours'.[178]

Information and records

[4.60] The 2005 Regulations provide that mobile workers must be informed of the working time requirements and the provisions of any applicable collective agreement, employment regulation order or registered employment agreement.[179] Regulation 12 provides that an employer of a mobile worker must:

(i) request from each mobile worker details of any time worked by that worker for another employer;

(ii) include time worked for another employer in the calculation of the mobile worker's working time;

(iii) keep records which are adequate to show whether the requirements of the Regulations are being complied with in the case of each mobile worker employed by him to whom they apply;

(iv) retain such records for at least two years after the end of the period covered by those records;

(v) provide, at the request of the mobile worker, a copy of the record of hours worked by that worker;

(vi) provide to an authorised officer copies of such records relating to mobile workers as the officer may require;

(vii) provide to a mobile worker or authorised officer copies of such documentary evidence in the employer's possession as may be requested by the employer or officer in relation to records provided to him in accordance with paragraph (e) or (f).

Enforcement

[4.61] The maximum fine for a breach of either the 2005 or 2008 Regulations is €5,000, or, alternatively, a court can impose a term of imprisonment not exceeding six months, or both.[180] There is an added sanction for a breach of the 2005 Regulations where, if a contravention in respect of which a person is convicted is continued, the person will be

---

[177] SI 2/2005, Reg 10. This period may be extended for objective or technical reasons or reasons concerning the organisation of work, by a collective agreement or an employment regulation order or a registered employment agreement.

[178] SI 2/2005, Reg 2.

[179] SI 2/2005, Reg 11 implementing Directive 15/2002, Art 9.

[180] SI 2/2005, Reg 18 and Reg 52 of the 2008 Regulations.

guilty of a further offence on every day on which the contravention continues and for each such offence the person may be liable, on summary conviction to a fine not exceeding €1,000.[181] There is no provision for recourse to a Rights Commissioner for a breach of the Regulations.

MOBILE STAFF IN CIVIL AVIATION

[4.62] Since the Organisation of Working Time (Inclusion of Transport Activities) Regulations 2004 (the 2004 Regulations) do not apply to mobile staff in civil aviation (ie crew members on board a civil aircraft), such workers have the full protection of the 1997 Act.[182] Mobile staff in civil aviation are also provided with extra protection by the EC (Organisation of Working Time) (Mobile Staff in Civil Aviation) Regulations 2006.[183]

[4.63] Regulation 2 of the 2006 Regulations provides that 'working time' in this regard means 'any period during which a crew member is working, at the employer's disposal and carrying out the activity or duties of his or her work, including on-call duty performed by a crew member where he or she is required to be physically present at his or her place of work'.

Regulation 11 provides that the maximum annual 'working time' for any crew member must not exceed 2,000 hours, in which the block flying time shall be limited to 900 hours. In this regard, 'block flying time' means the time between an aircraft first moving from its parking place for the purpose of taking off until it comes to rest on the designated parking position and until all engines are stopped. The maximum annual working time for mobile staff in civil aviation must also be spread as evenly as practicable throughout the year.

[4.64] Regulation 5 provides that mobile staff in civil aviation are entitled to at least four weeks' leave per year. Staff must also be given days free of all duty and standby consisting of at least 96 local days in each calendar year, which may include any rest periods required by law, and at least seven local days in each calendar month, which may include rest periods required by law.[184]

[4.65] Regulation 12 provides that an employer of mobile staff in civil aviation must maintain a record of each crew member's working patterns. Such records are to be in the form prescribed by the Minister following consultation with the Irish Aviation Authority. Until such time as the Minister so prescribes, an employer must keep records in such

---

[181] SI 2/2005, Reg 18(4).

[182] SI 817/2004, Reg 4, unless they would be covered by the general exemptions in the Organisation of Working Time (General Exemptions) Regulations 1998. See para **[4.27]** above.

[183] SI 507/2006, implementing Directive 2000/79/EC. The Regulations came into operation on 29 September 2006.

[184] SI 507/2006, Reg 6.

form as will include all the information necessary for the effective monitoring of the Regulations.[185]

[4.66] Regulation 15 provides that a crew member, or their trade union, may present a complaint to a Rights Commissioner in relation to a contravention of the Regulations. The Regulations provide for a possible award in compensation of up to two years' remuneration.

[4.67] Regulation 14 provides a maximum fine of €5,000 for a breach of the Regulations.[186] There is an added sanction that if a contravention in respect of which a person is convicted is continued, the person shall be guilty of a further offence on every day on which the contravention continues and for each such offence the person may be liable, on summary conviction to a fine not exceeding €2,500.[187]

THE ACTIVITIES OF DOCTORS IN TRAINING

[4.68] Pursuant to s 3(1) the 1997 Act the activities of doctors in training were excluded from the Act. Following Directive 2000/34/EC doctors in training were brought within the scope of the Directive. Article 6 of that Directive[188] introduced a transitional period of five years, commencing on 1 August 2004, within which Member States were obliged to reduce the weekly working hours of junior doctors. The transitional period allowed for further extensions of three years in total, within which member states were afforded further time to achieve full compliance with the Directive.

These changes were implemented in Ireland by the European Communities (Organisation of Working Time) (Activities of Doctors in Training) Regulations 2004.[189] Doctors in training are defined as all registered medical practitioners other than hospital consultants, consultant psychiatrists or other registered specialists who may practice without supervision.[190] The provisions of the Doctors in Training Regulations reflect those found in the 1997 Act with the exception of those in respect of the maximum working week found in Reg 9.

[4.69] Regulation 9 provided that between 1 August 2004 and 31 July 2007 the maximum working week for doctors in training was 58 hours averaged over a consecutive 12 month reference period. Between 1 August 2007 and 31 July 2009 the upper limit is 56 hours averaged over a consecutive six-month reference period.[191] From

---

[185] To date, the Minister has not prescribed any particular form of records. The employer must retain the records referred to in this regulation at the premises or place from which the activities that the crew member is employed to carry on are principally directed or controlled and retain them for a period of at least three years from the date of their making.

[186] SI 507/2006, Reg 18.

[187] SI 507/2006, Reg 18(4).

[188] See Council Directive 2003/88/EC, Art 17(5).

[189] SI 494/2004.

[190] SI 494/2004, Reg 2.

[191] Or such other reference period as may be agreed by collective agreement and approved by the Labour Court under s 24 of the 1997 Act.

1 August 2009 onwards, the maximum working week will be 48 hours averaged over a reference period of six consecutive months, unless the employee has worked for his employer for less than six months, in which case it shall be that lesser period. As with s 15 of the 1997 Act, reference periods do not include periods of annual leave, parental leave, *force majeure* leave, carers leave, maternity leave, adoptive leave or sick leave taken by the employee.[192]

The introduction of these employee protections have given rise to considerable debate in the medical community arising from a fear that it may result in junior doctors getting insufficient clinical experience during their training years. On the other hand, it is acknowledged that doctor fatigue may have serious adverse consequences for patients.[193] In view of the background against which these regulations have been introduced, it remains to be seen whether, or to what extent, they are complied with.

WORKING TIME RESTRICTIONS IN THE EMPLOYMENT OF YOUNG PERSONS

[4.70] The Protection of Young Persons (Employment) Act 1996 (the 1996 Act) implements Council Directive 94/33/EC on the protection of young people at work. In doing so it makes specific limitations on the working time of young persons and, where permitted, of children. A young person is defined in the 1996 Act as someone who has reached the age of 16 years but has not reached the age of 18 years. A child is defined as a person under the age of 16 years.

Section 6(1)(a) of the 1996 Act states that an employer may not permit a young person to work for more than 8 hours in a day or 40 hours in any week.[194] It should be noted that, unlike the 1997 Act, there is no reference period over which these hours may be averaged out. A young person may not work between 10 pm and 6 am on the following day. When the following day is not a school day and the Minister has been satisfied that there are particular circumstances affecting the branch of industry in question a young person may work until 11 pm but not before 7 am on the following day.[195] Pursuant to s 8 of the 1996 Act the Minister for Enterprise, Trade and Employment has made regulations which permits a supervised bar apprentice to work until midnight one day per week provided that they do not work before 8 am on the following day.[196]

Young persons must receive at least 12 consecutive hours rest in each 24-hour period.[197] That consecutive period may be broken in respect of young persons who work for less than two hours in a day.[198] Young persons must receive at least two day's rest in

---

[192] (SI 494/2004, Reg 9(6)).

[193] Gaba and Howard 'Patient Safety: Fatigue among Clinicians and the Safety of Patients' *New England Journal of Medicine*, 2002. 347(16): pp 1249–55.

[194] This section does not apply to the employment of close relatives. See Protection of Young Persons (Employment of Close Relatives) Regulations 1997 (SI 2/1997).

[195] Protection of Young Persons (Employment) Act 1996, s 6(1)(b).

[196] Protection of Young Persons (Employment) Act, 1996 (Bar Apprentices) Regulations 2001 (SI 351/2001).

[197] Protection of Young Persons (Employment) Act 1996, s 6(c).

[198] Protection of Young Persons (Employment) Act 1996, s 6(2).

every week which must, as far as practicable, be consecutive.[199] A young person shall not be required or permitted to work for more than 4 hours without a break period of at least 30 minutes.[200] None of these limitations apply to young persons in training or on active service with the Defence Forces, Civil Defence or the Navy.[201]

Children aged between 14 and 16 may be employed in limited circumstances.[202] Children aged 14 years may not be employed whatsoever during term time. Children aged between 14 and 16 may be employed to do light work for a maximum of 35 hours per week during summer holidays and for a maximum period of seven hours in any day provided it is not harmful to the child's health and development and that the child does no work for a period of at least 21 days during the school holidays. Children of 15 years may be employed to do light work for up to eight hours per week during school term. Light work is work which is not industrial in nature and which is not likely to harm the safety, health or development of the child. Pursuant to s 2 of the 1996 Act the Minister may declare any form of work to be industrial in nature.

In certain circumstances, children under 16 years of age may be employed under Ministerial license for sporting, artistic, cultural or advertising purposes.[203]

ENFORCEMENT AND PENALTIES[204]

Complaints to the Rights Commissioner

[4.71] Section 27 of the 1997 Act deals with complaints to the Rights Commissioner. Section 27(2) provides that an employee, or his trade union representative, may present a complaint to a Rights Commissioner in relation to certain breaches of the 1997 Act.[205] In practice, it is not unusual for an employee's solicitor to present such a complaint, acting as agent on behalf of the employee, however, the complaint form must be signed by the employee or a trade union representative. Complaints to the Rights Commissioner should be submitted in the form prescribed.[206] Copy forms in the prescribed format together with notes to assist in the completion of such forms are available at www.lrc.ie/forms.

The 1997 Act allows complaints to be made in relation to breaches of the following provisions of working time legislation:

(i)   ss 11–23 of the 1997 Act, which outline all the main protections of the Act from daily rest up to compensation on termination of employment;

(ii) s 6(2) of the 1997 Act, which deals with compensatory rest periods;

---

[199] Protection of Young Persons (Employment) Act 1996, s 6(d).
[200] Protection of Young Persons (Employment) Act 1996, s 6(e).
[201] Protection of Young Persons (Employment) Act 1996, s 6(5).
[202] See s 3 of the 1996 Act.
[203] Protection of Young Persons (Employment) Act 1996, s 3(2).
[204] On practice and procedure before a Rights Commissioner, the EAT and Labour Court and High Court, on appeal on a point of law, see Ch 22, Practice and Procedure in Employment Law.
[205] Organisation of Working Time Act 1997, s 27(2).
[206] Organisation of Working Time Act 1997, s 27(9).

(iii) the provisions referred to in s 6(1) of any relevant regulations, collective agreement, registered employment agreement or employment regulation order in relation to equivalent rest breaks;

(iv) s 26 of the 1997 Act, which deals with penalisation;

(v) Regs 5–10 of the Doctors in Training Regulations;

The EC (Organisation of Working Time) (Mobile Staff in Civil Aviation) Regulations 2006[207] and the Protection of Young Persons (Employment) Act 1996[208] also allow for complaints to the Rights Commissioner in relation to breaches of the protections in those instruments. However, complaints cannot be made to the Rights Commissioner in relation to breaches of the mobile workers in Road Transportation Regulations.

Any complaint to the Rights Commissioner must be made within six months of the date on which the breach is alleged to have occurred.[209] A Rights Commissioner may, upon 'reasonable cause'[210] shown, hear a complaint made outside the six month time limit, provided that the complaint is made no later than 12 months after the date of the breach alleged.[211] The time limit will run from the date of each alleged breach and not from the date of the latest breach or the date of dismissal.

In some cases the date on which the offence took place will be difficult to pinpoint, for example provision of annual leave and public holidays benefits. These issues were considered by Lavan J in *Royal Liver Assurance v Macken*.[212] In relation to annual leave entitlements, Lavan J held that, in the absence of evidence demonstrating that an employee consented to the extension of his leave year by six months pursuant to s 20(1)(c), the Labour Court had erred in holding that the operative date of the infringement was six months after the end of the leave year in question. While it would appear that the operative date of such an infringement is the last day of the leave year in question this is not entirely clear from the judgment, however, in *Singh & Singh v Guatam*[213] the Labour Court has held that this is the correct interpretation. In relation to a breach of public holiday entitlements, Lavan J held that the operative date of any infringement will be the date of the public holiday. This may be open to some measure of question in light of the fact that an employer may comply with the 1997 Act by providing a day off in lieu within one month of the public holiday in question.

[4.72] The Rights Commissioner will, upon hearing the complaint, determine in writing whether it is well founded or not. The Rights Commissioner may require the employer to comply with the relevant statutory provision and/or require that the employer pay

---

[207] SI 507/2006.

[208] Protection of Young Persons (Employment) Act 1996, s 18.

[209] Organisation of Working Time Act 1997, s 27(4), SI 507/2006, Reg 15(3) and s 18(4) of the 1996 Act.

[210] The term used in the 1997 Act and the 2006 Regulations. However, in The Protection of Young Persons (Employment) Act 1996, the requirement is a higher standard of 'exceptional circumstances'.

[211] Organisation of Working Time Act 1997, s 27(5).

[212] *Royal Liver Assurance v Macken* [2002] 4 IR 428.

[213] *Singh & Singh v Guatam* DWT 44/2005.

such compensation as may be considered just and equitable having regard to the circumstances up to, but not exceeding, the value of two years of the employee's remuneration.[214]

Section 18(3) of the Protection of Young Persons (Employment) Act 1996 does not provide a limit on the level of award merely referring to 'what is just and equitable in all the circumstances'. It also allows the Rights Commissioner to make an order that the employer take a specific course of action.

Appeals

[4.73] A party may appeal in writing from a decision of a Rights Commissioner within six weeks of the date on which the decision is notified to that party.[215] An appeal under the 1997 Act or the 2006 Regulations is made to the Labour Court, but any appeal in relation to the 1996 Act will be made to the Employment Appeals Tribunal. Such appeals are conducted by way of a full *de novo* hearing..

An appeal will lie from the Labour Court or Employment Appeals Tribunal to the High Court on a point of law, which determination shall be final.[216]

Enforcement

[4.74] In the event that an employer fails to comply with a determination of a Rights Commissioner or the Labour Court in relation to the 1997 Act or the 2006 Regulations, an application may be made to the Circuit Court for the purposes of having that decision made an order of the Court.[217] Decisions of the EAT in relation to the 1996 Act may be enforced in a similar manner by means of an application to the District Court.[218] Such applications may be made once six weeks have elapsed from the date of communication of the decision provided that the decision is not under appeal.

Compensation and awards

[4.75] Breaches of working time regulations are increasingly the subject of complaints to the Rights Commissioner Service.[219] While claims for annual leave or public holidays can be quantified quite easily, awards for general breaches of the other working time

---

[214] Organisation of Working Time Act 1997, s 27(3) and Reg 15(2) of the 2006 Regulations.

[215] Organisation of Working Time Act 1997, s 28, Reg 16 of the 2006 Regulations and s 19 of the 1996 Act.

[216] Organisation of Working Time Act 1997, s 28(6).

[217] Organisation of Working Time Act 1997, ss 28(8) and 29(1) of the 1997 Act and Regs 16 and 17 of the 2006 Regulations. See Ch 22, Practice and Procedure in Employment Law, at paras **[22.108]–[22.109]**.

[218] Protection of Young Persons (Employment) Act 1996, s 20. See Ch 22, Practice and Procedure in Employment Law, at paras **[22.94]–[22.95]**.

[219] In 2007, there were 1,541 complaints under this legislation dealt with by Rights Commissioners: See Annual Report of the Rights Commissioner Service for 2007 available on the LRC website, www.lrc.ie. This is an significant increase from the 1,087 received in 2006 and the 665 received in 2005. The Labour Court Annual Report confirms a similar 35% increase in appeals from Rights Commissioner decisions under the 1997 Act in 2007: See Labour Court Annual Report for 2007 available on the Court's website, www.labourcourt.ie.

protections tend to be more difficult estimate. By their nature, such claims tend to involve multiple offences over a period of time. The level of compensation awarded varies and, in many cases, rights commissioners tend to compensate by way of a global figure for all breaches, rather than a sum in respect of individual instances. A review of the most recent decisions of the Rights Commissioner and Labour Court would seem to indicate awards in the region of €1,000 to €5,000 were common for multiple breaches of the 1997 Act.[220]

The maximum value of compensation which may be awarded by the Rights Commissioner for a breach of the 1997 Act is equal to two year's remuneration for the employee concerned.

[4.76] In *Cementation Skanska v Carroll*[221] the Labour Court emphasised the importance of providing real deterrence against future infraction along with financial compensation to the individual employee citing the following European jurisprudence:

> In *Von Colson and Kamann v Land Nordrhein-Westfalen* [1984] ECR 1891 the ECJ has made it clear that where such a right is infringed the judicial redress provided should not only compensate for economic loss sustained but must provide a real deterrent against future infractions.

A case in which this policy was in evidence was *Goode Concrete v Dermot Monroe*[222] in which the employee received an award of €15,000 arising from repeated infractions of the regulations. This case may be seen as the high water mark of compensation levels for cases of this type. In other cases, the Labour Court has significantly increased the level of compensation on appeal from the rights commissioner.[223]

Criminal penalties

[4.77] Offences are created by the 1997 Act for breach of s 8 (impeding an inspector), breach of s 25(1) (failing to keep records), breach of s 32(1) (failing to keep a register of outworkers) and breach of s 33 (double employment) giving rise to breach of working hours protections. Each of these offences may, on summary conviction, give rise to a fine up to €1,904.61.[224] Section 34(5) imposes an additional penalty of €634.87 for every day following conviction for which the employer continues to commit the offence.

The Organisation of Working Time (Records) (Prescribed Form and Exemptions) Regulations 2001, the EC (Organisation of Working Time) (Mobile Staff in Civil Aviation) Regulations 2006 and the EC (Organisation of Working Time of Persons Performing Mobile Road Transport Activities) Regulations 2005 all provide for criminal

---

[220] See Digest of Rights Commissioners Decisions for 2008, available on the LRC website: www.lrc.ie and the Synopsis of Labour Court Determinations for 2007 available on the Labour Court website: www.labourcourt.ie.

[221] *Cementation Skanska v Carroll* Labour Court, WTC 0338, 28 October 2003.

[222] *Goode Concrete v Dermot Monroe* Labour Court, DTW0 51.

[223] See *O'Malley v Liachavicius* DWT 07/4 where an award of €2,000 was increased to €5,000 and *Melbury Developments v Valpeters* DWT 07/19 where an award of €1,000 was increased to €5,000.

[224] Organisation of Working Time Act 1997, s 34(1).

sanctions in the form of imprisonment or fines for breaches of their respective provisions.[225]

THE LABOUR INSPECTORATE: FUNCTIONS AND POWERS

[4.78] Inspectors of the labour inspectorate operate under functions derived from various pieces of employment legislation legislation, such as the Industrial Relations Acts 1946–1990, the Payment of Wages Act 1991, the Protection of Young Persons (Employment) Act 1996 and the National Minimum Wage Act 2000. Section 8 of the 1997 Act allows the Minister for Enterprise, Trade and Employment to appoint inspectors for the purposes of investigating compliance with the provisions of the 1997 Act.

In line with the general increase in public service staffing numbers, recent years have seen an increase in the number of labour inspectors appointed in Ireland. There are currently 90 such inspectors operating from regional centres in Carlow, Cork, Dublin, Shannon and Sligo. These inspectors now operate under the general umbrella of the National Employment Rights Agency (NERA),[226] however, NERA has not yet been put on a formal statutory footing.[227]

Pursuant to s 8(3) of the 1997 Act inspectors are entitled, at all reasonable times, to enter an employee's place of employment. The inspector may, upon reasonable grounds, enter a place from which he or she has reason to suppose that an employee's activities are directed or controlled. An inspector may not enter a dwelling place without the consent of the occupier or a warrant authorising entry from the District Court.[228]

On any premises which the inspector has entered, he or she is entitled to make such examination or inquiry as may be necessary to ascertain whether the provisions of the Act have been complied with. Furthermore, the inspector is entitled to require the employer to produce any records which the employer is required to keep and to inspect or take copies of such records.

The inspector enjoys a general power to require an employer to furnish such information as the inspector may reasonably request.[229] On foot of such requests for information, the inspector may compel the employer to furnish answers to relevant questions and to sign a statutory declaration averring to the truth of those answers.[230] This section is somewhat qualified by the fact that these answers may not include matters which tend to incriminate the employer.

Any person, including a body corporate, who obstructs, impedes, refuses to produce records upon request or otherwise misleads an inspector shall be guilty of an offence[231] and will be liable on summary conviction to a fine not greater than €1,904.61.

---

[225] See paras **[4.62]** and **[4.50]** above.

[226] www.employmentrights.ie

[227] On NERA generally, see Ch 1, Source and Institutions.

[228] Organisation of Working Time Act 1997, ss 8(4) and 8(7).

[229] Organisation of Working Time Act 1997, s 8(3)(d).

[230] Organisation of Working Time Act 1997, s 8(3)(e).

[231] Organisation of Working Time Act 1997, s 8(8).

[4.79] In the case of *Gama v The Minister for Enterprise*[232] the High Court considered the extent of certain implied powers enjoyed by the head of the labour inspectorate pursuant, *inter alia,* to s 8 of the 1997 Act. Finlay Geoghan J considered a report prepared by a labour inspector which purported to be a public report assessing breaches of statutory employment regulations by Gama. Finlay Geoghan J held that an inspector had an implied power to prepare a report on foot of his inquiries and to pass information gathered in his statutory role to the Minister and other enforcement bodies. It was held that the inspector had no statutory power to prepare a report for public consumption and, as a result, the Minister was restrained from publishing the report.

---

[232] *Gama v The Minister for Enterprise* [2007] IR 472.

Chapter 5

Protective Leave

Rory O'Boyle and Michelle Ní Longáin

INTRODUCTION

[5.01] This chapter details the forms of leave to which an employee is entitled under various employment statutes.[1] 'Protective Leave', as the term is used in this chapter, comprises these forms of leave:

1. Maternity leave;
2. Parental leave;
3. *Force Majeure* leave;
4. Adoptive leave; and
5. Carer's leave.

MATERNITY LEAVE

Entitlements

[5.02] The Maternity Protection Acts 1994 and 2004 (the 'Maternity Protection Acts'), along with various regulations which have been made under the Maternity Protection Acts and under health and safety legislation[2] provide the framework of statutory maternity protection entitlements.

---

[1] For detailed annotated commentary on the provisions of the relevant statutes, see Kerr *Consolidated Irish Employment Legislation* (Thomson Roundhall, Release 19, April 2008) Divisions C, D and E. On practice and procedure for enforcing the rights under this legislation, see Ch 22, Practice and Procedure in Employment Law.

[2] Maternity Protection Act 1994; Maternity Protection (Amendment) Act 2004; Safety, Health and Welfare at Work (Pregnant Employees etc) Regulations (SI 218/2000); Maternity Protection (Disputes and Appeals) Regulations (SI 17/1995); Maternity Protection (Time Off for Ante-Natal and Post-Natal Care) Regulations (SI 18/1995); Maternity Protection (Health and Safety Leave Certification) Regulations (SI 20/1995); Maternity Protection (Maximum Compensation) Regulations (SI 134/1999); Maternity Protection (Time Off for Ante-Natal Classes) Regulations (SI 653/2004); Maternity Protection (Protection of Mothers who are Breastfeeding) Regulations (SI 654/ 2004); Maternity Protection (Postponement of Leave) Regulations (SI 655/2004); Maternity Protection Act 1994 (Extension of Periods of Leave) Order (SI 51/2006). For comprehensive annotations on the legislation see Kerr, *Irish Employment Legislation* (Thomson Roundhall, Release 19, April 2008), Division C.

Maternity leave

[5.03] The statutory entitlement to maternity leave for pregnant employees is 26 weeks.[3]

The current 26-week statutory leave entitlement represents the progression of the legislative recognition of the rights of pregnant employees. Section 8 of the Maternity Protection of Employees Act 1981[4] and s 8 of the the Maternity Protection Act 1994[5] provided an entitlement to 14 weeks' maternity leave. The 14 weeks' leave entitlement was extended by the Maternity Protection Act 1994 (Extension of Periods of Leave) Order 2001 to 18 weeks.[6] The 18-week period was extended by the Maternity Protection Act 1994 (Extension of Periods of Leave) Order 2006 to 22 weeks for employees commencing maternity leave after 1 March 2006 and to 26 weeks for employees commencing maternity leave after 1 March 2007.[7]

Additional maternity leave

[5.04] A pregnant employee is entitled to 16 weeks' additional maternity leave beginning immediately after the end of her ordinary maternity leave.

As with ordinary maternity leave, the entitlement to additional maternity leave has developed incrementally. Section 14 of the Maternity Protection of Employees Act 1981 introduced an entitlement to four weeks' additional maternity leave, an entitlement which was extended to eight weeks' additional maternity leave under the Maternity Protection Act 1994 (Extension of Periods of Leave) Order 2001.[8]

If the employee becomes sick during the period of additional maternity leave, the additional leave may be terminated with the consent of her employer and the employee's absence from work must be treated in the same way as any absence due to sickness.[9] The employee is not entitled to resume the additional leave at a later stage.[10]

Qualifications

[5.05] 'Employees' are entitled to the protections provided by the Maternity Protection Acts.[11] An 'employee' is defined by the Acts:[12]

> 'employee', subject to *subsection (2)* [which provides the relevant employer of office holders, civil and public servants and agency workers], means a person who has entered

---

3 Maternity Protection Act 1994 (Extension of Periods of Leave) Order 2006 (SI 51/2006), Art 8.
4 The Maternity Protection of Employees Acts 1981 and 1991 were repealed by the Maternity Protection Act 1994, s 6.
5 Maternity Protection Act 1994, s 8(1).
6 SI 29/2001, Art 4.
7 SI 51/2006, Arts 4 and 8 specify the periods of leave. Arts 2(2), 2(4) and 2(5) of the Regulations provide the effective dates of the periods of leave.
8 SI 29/2001, Art 6.
9 Maternity Protection Acts, s 14A.
10 Maternity Protection Acts, s 14A(4)(b).
11 Maternity Protection Acts, s 2. On the meaning of 'employee' see Ch 2, The Contract and Relationship of Employment, paras **[2.03]–[2.16]**.
12 Maternity Protection Acts, s 2(1).

into or works under (or, where the employment has ceased, entered into or worked under) a contract of employment;

A 'contract of employment' is defined by the Acts as:[13]

(a)   a contract of service or apprenticeship, or

(b)   any other contract whereby an individual agrees with a person who is carrying on the business of an employment agency, within the meaning of the Employment Agency Act 1971, and is acting in the course of that business, to do or perform personally any work or service for another person (whether or not that other person is a party to the contract).

whether the contract is express or implied and if express, whether it is oral or in writing.

Notification requirements

Maternity leave

[5.06] The pregnant employee must notify her employer in writing of her intention to take maternity leave as soon as reasonably practicable, but not later than four weeks before she is due to commence her maternity leave.[14] The employee must also provide her employer with a medical certificate confirming the pregnancy and specifying the expected week of birth (referred to in the Acts as 'confinement').[15] An application for maternity leave may be revoked by a further notification in writing by the employee to her employer.[16]

Additional maternity leave

[5.07] If the employee intends to avail of her entitlement to additional maternity leave, she must notify her employer in writing of this at the same time as notifying her employer of her intention to take ordinary maternity leave or not later than four weeks before her expected date of return to work.[17] An application for additional maternity leave may be revoked by a further notification in writing by the employee to her employer.[18] This notification or revocation by the employee must be made not later than four weeks before the date which would have been the employee's expected date of return to work if she had not taken additional maternity leave.[19]

Timing of leave

[5.08] In general, a pregnant employee may agree with her employer when she will commence and end her maternity leave. This general entitlement is subject to the requirement that at least two weeks' maternity leave must be taken before the expected

---

13 Maternity Protection Acts, s 2(1).
14 Maternity Protection Acts, s 9(1)(a).
15 Maternity Protection Acts, s 9(1)(b).
16 Maternity Protection Acts, s 9(2).
17 Maternity Protection Acts, s 14(4).
18 Maternity Protection Acts, s 14(5).
19 Maternity Protection Acts, s 14(5).

week of birth and at least four weeks' leave must be taken after the end of the expected week of birth.[20]

Early births

[5.09] Where the baby is born four weeks or more before the expected week of birth, the employee is entitled to the full 26 weeks of maternity leave commencing on the date of confinement.[21] The normal notification requirements for taking maternity leave will be deemed to have been complied with if the employee notifies the employer in writing of the intention to take maternity leave within 14 days of the birth.[22]

Late births

[5.10] If, due to the baby's late birth, an employee has less than four weeks' maternity leave remaining after the birth, her maternity leave will be extended for a period of up to a maximum of four weeks (ie the minimum period of maternity leave which an employee must take after the birth).[23] Where an employee wishes to so extend her ordinary maternity leave, she must inform the employer in writing of the proposed extension and, after the birth, confirm in writing to her employer the notification of extension and the duration of the extension.[24]

The employee is also entitled, if she so chooses, to take additional maternity leave commencing at the end of the extended ordinary maternity leave.[25]

Termination of additional maternity leave in the event of the sickness of the mother

[5.11] An employer may agree to terminate a period of additional maternity leave due to the sickness of the child's mother.[26] If an employer agrees to terminate a period of additional maternity leave, the employee's absence will be treated as any absence from work due to sickness.[27]

To apply for such a termination, the employee must submit a request in writing to her employer. The request may be made during the last four weeks of the employee's maternity leave if the employee has notified her employer of an intention to take additional maternity leave or during a period of additional maternity leave.[28] Following

---

[20] Maternity Protection Acts, s 10(1). The Maternity Protection (Amendment) Act 2004 amended the Maternity Protection Act 1994, s 10(1) which had provided that at least four weeks' maternity leave had to be taken before the expected week of confinement.

[21] Maternity Protection Acts, s 13(2).

[22] Maternity Protection Acts, s 13(1).

[23] Maternity Protection Acts, s 12(1).

[24] Maternity Protection Acts, s 12(2).

[25] Maternity Protection Acts, s 14(2).

[26] Maternity Protection Acts, s 14A.

[27] Maternity Protection Acts, s 14A(4).

[28] Maternity Protection Acts, s 14 A(1).

the receipt of such a request, the employer must notify the applicant employee in writing of the decision as soon as reasonably practicable.[29]

If an employer agrees to terminate a period of additional maternity leave, the date of the termination of the period of leave will be agreed between the parties. However, in such circumstances, the agreed date of termination must not be before the date of the commencement of the mother's sickness and must not be after the date on which the period of additional maternity leave would have been due to end.[30]

If an employer agrees to terminate a period of additional maternity leave, the employee is not entitled to take her additional maternity leave or the part of it not taken at a later date following her recovery from her illness.[31]

Postponement of leave due to the hospitalisation of the child

[5.12] If a child in respect of whom a period of leave has been granted is hospitalised, an employer may agree to postpone part or all of the employee's leave entitlement.[32] The maximum period of such postponement is six months.[33]

To apply for such a postponement, the employee must submit a request in writing to her employer.[34] In addition, the employee must submit to her employer a letter or other appropriate documentation from the hospital concerned confirming her child's hospitalisation.[35] At the date of the request for postponement, the employee must have taken at least 14 weeks' maternity leave, at least four weeks of which must have been taken after the birth.[36] Following the receipt of such a request, the employer must notify the employee in writing of the decision as soon as reasonably practicable.[37] Where an employer consents to a request to postpone a period of leave, the employee will return to work on a date agreed between the parties, which will not be later than date on which the leave which is postponed is due to end.[38]

Following the discharge of her child from hospital, an employee is entitled to take the postponed leave, known as 'resumed leave', in one continuous block.[39] The employee must submit to her employer a letter or other appropriate documentation from the hospital confirming her child's discharge.[40] The entitlement to resumed leave is subject to an employee notifying her employer in writing as soon as reasonably practicable but not later than the day on which the leave begins of her intention to commence her

---

[29] Maternity Protection Acts, s 14A(3).

[30] Maternity Protection Acts, s 14(A)(2).

[31] Maternity Protection Acts, s 14(A)(4).

[32] Maternity Protection Acts, s 14B.

[33] Maternity Protection (Postponement of Leave) Regulations (SI 655/2004).

[34] Maternity Protection Acts, s 14B(1).

[35] Maternity Protection (Postponement of Leave) Regulations (SI 655/2004).

[36] Maternity Protection Acts, s 14B(2).

[37] Maternity Protection Acts, s 14B(5).

[38] Maternity Protection Acts, s 14B(4).

[39] Maternity Protection Acts, s 14B(4).

[40] Maternity Protection (Postponement of Leave) Regulations (SI 655/2004).

resumed leave.[41] A period of resumed leave must commence within seven days of the child's discharge from hospital.[42]

If, after the postponement of a period of leave an employee is subsequently absent from work due to her own sickness, the employee will be deemed to commence her resumed leave on the first day of such absence unless she notifies her employer that she does not wish to commence her postponed leave. An absence from work of an employee due to sickness following an employee's notification of an intention not to commence resumed leave is treated as any absence from work due to sickness and the employee is not entitled to the resumed leave.

Father's entitlement to leave

[5.13] Generally, a father has no statutory entitlement to any leave upon the birth of his child. A father of a child is only entitled to statutory leave where the mother of his child dies either before or during her period of maternity leave. In such circumstances, many of the entitlements of the child's mother are assumed the father of the child. Where a mother dies within 32 weeks of her child's birth, the child's father is entitled to leave up until the end of the 32nd week following the birth.[43]

Time off from work for ante-natal or post-natal care

[5.14] Section 15 of the Maternity Protection Acts provides a general entitlement for pregnant employees and employees who have recently given birth to time off work without loss of pay for the purposes of receiving ante-natal and post-natal care. The Maternity Protection (Time Off for Ante-Natal and Post-Natal Care) Regulations[44] set out in detail the entitlements of such employees and the provisions which must be complied with in order to avail of those entitlements. An employee must notify her employer in writing of the date and time of her appointment as soon as reasonably practicable and in any event not later than two weeks before the date of her appointment.[45] The employer may request the employee to produce an appointment card or other appropriate documentation for inspection indicating the time and date of the appointment and confirming the pregnancy or the expected week of confinement.[46] Such notification requirements do not apply to a first appointment.[47]

In the event of an unscheduled ante-natal or post-natal appointment, if non-compliance with applicable notification requirements is not due to the neglect or default

---

[41] Maternity Protection Acts, s 14B(8). Under s 14B(9), an employee may revoke their notification to resume leave under s 14 B(8) provided that such revocation is given in accordance with the time frames set out under s 14B(8). Under s 14B(10) an employer may waive the requirement to receive notification from an employee of an intention to resume leave under s 14B(8).

[42] Maternity Protection (Postponement of Leave) Regulations (SI 655/2004).

[43] Maternity Protection Acts, s 16.

[44] SI 18/1995.

[45] SI 18/1995, Reg 4(1)(a).

[46] SI 18/1995, Reg 4(1)(b).

[47] SI 18/1995, Reg 4(2).

of the employee in relation to the arrangement of the appointment, the employee will be deemed to have complied with the necessary notification requirements if she furnishes to her employer evidence of having kept the appointment and an indication of the circumstances which occasioned non-compliance.[48]

Time off from work to attend ante-natal classes

[5.15] Section 15A(1) of the Maternity Protection Acts provides for a general entitlement for pregnant employees to time off work, without loss of pay, to attend one set of ante-natal classes, other than the last three classes in such a set. Section 15A(2) of the Maternity Protection Acts provides an expectant father with an entitlement once only to time off work, without loss of pay, for the purpose of attending the last two ante-natal classes in a set before the birth of the child.

The Maternity Protection (Time Off for Ante-Natal Classes) Regulations[49] sets out the entitlements of pregnant employees and expectant fathers to such time off and the provisions that must complied with in order to avail of such entitlements. A pregnant employee or an expectant father must notify her or his employer in writing of the date and time of the appointment as soon as reasonably practicable and in any event not later than two weeks before the date of the first class or the class concerned.[50] The employer may request the pregnant employee or expectant father to produce for inspection an appointment card or other appropriate documentation indicating the dates and times of the relevant classes.[51] If non-compliance with applicable notification requirements is not due to the neglect or default of the pregnant employee or expectant father, the employee concerned is deemed to have complied with the necessary notification requirements if they furnish their employer with evidence of having attended the class and provide an indication of the circumstances that occasioned non-compliance.[52]

If a pregnant employee is unable to attend one full set of ante-natal classes, other than the last three in such a set, during a pregnancy due to circumstances beyond her control, including miscarriage, the premature birth of her baby, or her own illness, she will be entitled during one or more subsequent pregnancies to time off work without loss of pay as is necessary for her to attend such classes.[53]

Time off work or reduction of working hours for breastfeeding

[5.16] Section 15B of the Maternity Protection Acts provides a general entitlement for employees who are breastfeeding to either time off from work for the purpose of breastfeeding in the workplace or, alternatively, a reduction in working hours for the purpose of breastfeeding outside the workplace. This entitlement is of limited, if any, practical effect in light of the definition of employee who is breastfeeding, which limits the right to mothers of babies under six months old. If mothers have taken their statutory

---

[48] SI 18/1995, Reg 4(3).

[49] SI 653/2004.

[50] SI 653/2004, Reg 4(1)(a).

[51] SI 653/2004, Reg 4(1)(b).

[52] SI 653/2004, Reg 4(2).

[53] SI 653/2004, Reg 5.

maternity leave, even without additional maternity leave, the protected period is likely to be a period of one or two weeks, depending on how close the birth was to the due date.

An employer is not required to provide facilities for breastfeeding in the workplace if the provision of such facilities would give rise to a cost other than a nominal cost to the employer.[54] The term 'nominal cost' is not defined. The term 'nominal cost' was used in s 16 of the Employment Equality Act 1998. In interpreting the meaning of the term in *An Employee v A Local Authority*,[55] the Equality Officer found that the assessment of whether cost was nominal was a relative test, by reference to factors such as the size and financial resources of the employer.[56]

The Maternity Protection (Protection of Mothers who are Breastfeeding) Regulations[57] set out in detail the entitlements of employees who are breastfeeding. Regulation 3(1) provides that an employee who is breastfeeding at work is entitled to one hour off work each day to breastfeed her child. The break may be taken in one continuous sixty minute break, or two breaks of thirty minutes each or three breaks of twenty minutes each or, alternatively, as agreed between the parties.[58]

Regulation 3(2) provides that an employee who is breastfeeding outside of work is entitled to have her hours of work reduced by one hour per day to breastfeed her child. The reduction in hours of work may be taken in one continuous sixty minute period, or two periods of thirty minutes each or three periods of twenty minutes each or alternatively as agreed between the parties.[59]

Where an employee proposes to take time off work or have her hours of work reduced for the purpose of breastfeeding, she must notify her employer in writing of the proposal as soon as reasonably practicable but, in general, not later than the date on which she is obliged to notify her employer of her intention to return to work after a period of ordinary or additional maternity leave.[60] An employer may request the employee to furnish the birth certificate of the child and any other documentation establishing the date of birth of the child.

Health and Safety leave

Introduction

[5.17] Part III of the Maternity Protection Acts provides that pregnant employees, employees who have recently given birth and employees who are breastfeeding may under certain circumstances be entitled to health and safety leave.

---

[54] Maternity Protection Acts, s 15B(2).

[55] *An Employee v A Local Authority* DEC-E2002-2004.

[56] On the meaning of the term, see further Kerr *Consolidated Irish Employment Legislation* (Thomson Roundhall, Release 19, April 2008) Division C.

[57] SI 654/2004.

[58] SI 653/2004, Reg 3(1). Under Reg 4, time off work for breastfeeding is calculated on a pro rata basis for part time employees.

[59] Under SI 653/2004, Reg 4, a reduction in work for breastfeeding is calculated on a pro rata basis for part-time employees.

[60] SI 654/2001, Reg 5(a).

'Pregnant employee' is defined as 'an employee who is pregnant and who has informed her employer of her condition'.[61] 'Employee who has recently given birth' is defined as 'an employee whose date of confinement was note more than 14 weeks earlier and who has informed her employer of her condition'.[62] 'Employee who is breastfeeding' is defined as 'an employee whose date of confinement was not more than 26 weeks earlier, who is breastfeeding and who has informed her employer of her condition'.[63]

Neither an employee who has recently given birth nor an employee who is breastfeeding are likely to be at work, given the definitions of those terms and the duration of statutory maternity leave.

Risk assessment

[5.18] The Safety, Health and Welfare at Work (General Application) Regulations[64] require employers to assess any risk to the safety or health of pregnant employees, employees who are breastfeeding or post-natal employees.[65] Such an assessment must take into account any possible effect on the pregnancy or the breastfeeding resulting from any activity at the employer's place of work likely to involve a risk of exposure to certain agents, processes or working conditions.[66] The employer must determine the nature, degree and duration of the employee's exposure to such agent, process or working condition.[67] This risk assessment requirement is not met by an employer's general risk assessments or safety statements for its employees. Following the risk assessment, the employer must take the preventative and protective measures necessary to ensure the safety and health of such employees and to avoid any possible effect on the pregnancy or breastfeeding.[68] If it is not practicable to ensure the safety or health of the employee through preventative or protective measures, the employer must adjust temporarily the employee's working conditions and/or the working hours so that exposure to such risk is avoided.[69] If it is not technically or objectively feasible, or it cannot reasonably be required on duly substantiated grounds, to adjust the employee's

---

[61] Maternity Protection Acts, s 2(1).

[62] Maternity Protection Acts, s 2(1).

[63] Maternity Protection Acts, s 2(1).

[64] SI 299/2007.

[65] SI 299/2007, Reg 149.

[66] SI 299/2007, Reg 149(a). Part A of the Regulations lists or makes reference to those agents, processes and working conditions which an employer must take account of when assessing the risk to pregnant, breastfeeding and post natal employees. Part B of Sch 8 of the Regulations makes further reference to additional agents and working conditions which the employer must take account of when assessing the risk to pregnant employees. Part C of the Regulations makes further reference to additional agents and working conditions which the employer must take account of when assessing the risk to employees who are breastfeeding.

[67] SI 299/2007, Reg 149.

[68] SI 299/2007, Reg 149(b).

[69] SI 299/2007, Reg 150(a).

working conditions or working hours, then the employee must be provided with other work which does not present a risk.[70]

Night work

[5.19] Regulation 151 of the Safety, Health and Welfare at Work (General Application) Regulations[71] provides that an employee is not required to perform 'night work' during her pregnancy or for 14 weeks following her child's birth if a registered medical practitioner certifies that it is necessary for the safety or health of the employee.[72] An employee is unlikely to be at work in the 14 weeks following her child's birth. In such circumstances, the employer is obliged to transfer the employee to day-time work or, where such a transfer is not technically or objectively feasible on duly substantiated grounds, grant the employee leave or extend the period of maternity leave.[73]

Health and safety leave

[5.20] If an employer is required to move an employee to other work as a result of a risk assessment or because the employee cannot be required to perform night work but:

(i)   it is not technically or objectively feasible to move the employee; or

(ii)   such a move cannot reasonably be required on duly substantiated grounds; or

(iii)   the work to which the employer proposes to move the employee to is not suitable for her;

the employee concerned will be entitled to leave on health and safety grounds (health and safety leave).[74]

An employee granted health and safety leave is entitled on request to receive a certificate from her employer. The form of such certificate is set out in Maternity Protection (Health and Safety Leave Certification) Regulations[75] and, among other things, requires the employer to:

(i)   identify the risk to the employee;

(ii)   specify why it is not possible to eliminate the risk; and

(iii)   certify the non-feasibility of other work and the granting of the leave.

---

[70] SI 299/2007, Reg 150(b).

[71] SI 299/2007.

[72] 'Night work' is defined in Reg 151(1) of as meaning the period between 11.00 pm and 6 am on the following day where the employee works three hours in that period as a normal course or at least 25 percent of the employee's monthly working time is performed in that period.

[73] SI 299/2007, Reg 151(2)(b).

[74] Maternity Protection Acts, s 18. Section 18(3) defines other work which is suitable for an employee as work which is of a kind which is suitable in relation to employee concerned and appropriate for the employee to do in all the circumstances.

[75] SI 19/1995.

Payment while on health and safety leave

[5.21] The Maternity Protection (Health and Safety Leave Remuneration) Regulations[76] provide that an employee on health and safety leave is entitled to receive her normal weekly wage from her employer for the first 21 days of her health and safety leave.[77] The first 21 days of health and safety leave which attract a normal weekly wage do not have to be consecutive, but can be taken in shorter periods.[78] If a period of health and safety leave extends beyond a 21-day period, s 52 of the Social Welfare (Consolidation) Act 2005 provides that the employee will be entitled to health and safety benefit. Health and safety benefit rates are gradated according to weekly earnings in the relevant tax year.

Termination of health and safety leave

[5.22] Health and safety leave terminates when:

   (i)   the pregnant employee commences maternity leave;

   (ii)   the breastfeeding mother stops breastfeeding; or

   (iii) 26 weeks following the birth even if the mother continues to breastfeed the child.[79]

Health and safety leave will terminate if employer takes whatever measures are necessary to ensure that the employee is not exposed to the risk which gave rise to the leave.

If during a period of health and safety leave an employee who is breastfeeding ceases breastfeeding, she must notify her employer in writing at the earliest practical time.[80] Alternatively, if during the period of health and safety leave the employee becomes aware that her condition is no longer such that she is vulnerable to risk, then she must also notify her employer in writing at the earliest practical time.[81] If an employer who has received such notification has no reason to believe that the employee concerned would be vulnerable to further risk, the employer must take all reasonable measures to enable the employee to return to the job she held immediately before the start of her health and safety leave and must notify her in writing that she can resume that job.[82] Health and safety leave terminates seven days after such notification is received or, if earlier, whenever the employee returns to work.[83]

---

[76] SI 20/1995.

[77] SI 20/1995, Reg 3(1) provides that an employee will be entitled to three times the employee's normal weekly pay during the first 21 days of health and safety leave. 'Normal weekly pay' is defined in Regs 4 and 5 and in general is taken not to include overtime.

[78] SI 20/1995, Reg 3(2) provides further detail on the calculation of remuneration in respect of non-consecutive periods of health and safety leave.

[79] Maternity Protection Acts, s 19(1). Health and safety leave also terminates on the expiration of an employee's fixed term contract.

[80] Maternity Protection Acts, s 20(1).

[81] Maternity Protection Acts, s 20(2).

[82] Maternity Protection Acts, s 20(3)(a).

[83] Maternity Protection Acts, s 20(3)(b).

If during a period of health and safety leave the employer concerned takes whatever measures are necessary to ensure that the employee is no longer exposed to a risk or becomes able to move the employee to other suitable work, the employer must notify the employee concerned in writing that she can return to work. The leave will end seven days after such notification is received or, if earlier, whenever the employee returns to work.[84]

Preservation of rights

[5.23] During a period of absence while on maternity leave, additional maternity leave, father's leave, health and safety leave, leave to attend ante-natal or post-natal care, time off or reduced hours for breastfeeding, or leave to attend ante-natal classes, an employee is deemed to have been in the employment of her/his employer and is treated as not having been absent.[85] Except for the right to remuneration, such an absence does not affect any of the employee's rights, whether conferred by statute, by contract or otherwise. Therefore, a period of absence while on such leave cannot be treated as any other leave, including sick leave or annual leave, to which the employee is entitled. For example, an employee cannot be required to take annual leave to attend ante-natal or post natal appointments and maternity leave cannot be counted as part of an employee's sick leave.

In *North-Western Health Board v McKenna*,[86] the European Court of Justice (ECJ) held that a sick leave scheme that treats pregnancy related illness in the same way as other illness does not breach EU discrimination law. Ms McKenna, an employee of the North Western Health Board, was absent on sick leave for almost the entire period of her pregnancy due to a pregnancy-related illness. The Health Board's sick-leave scheme provided staff with an entitlement to 365 days of paid sick leave over any period of four years. Staff were entitled to full pay for a maximum of 183 days incapacity over any period of 12 months, with any additional days of sick leave taken within the same 12-month period attracting half pay only, up to a maximum total of 365 days' paid sick leave within that four-year period. Ms McKenna exhausted her entitlement to full pay and was receiving half pay when her maternity leave began. During her maternity leave, McKenna received her full pay in accordance with the regulations that applied to the Health Boards by the Department of Health and Children. On the expiry of her maternity leave, Ms McKenna was still unfit for work on medical grounds and her salary was once again reduced to half pay under the terms of the sick-leave scheme. Ms McKenna challenged the application of the sick-leave scheme to her situation before an Equality Officer. She contended that she had been the victim of discrimination contrary to the Equal Treatment Directive[87] inasmuch as her pregnancy-related illness had been treated

---

[84]   Maternity Protection Acts, s 20(4).

[85]   Maternity Protection Acts, s 22.

[86]   Case C-191/03 *North-Western Health Board v McKenna* [2005] ECR I-7631. This case is considered in detail, in relation to its implications for employment equality law, in Ch 13, Employment Equality.

[87]   Council Directive EC/76/207 ([1976] OJ L39/40). The Equal Treatment Directive has been recently re-cast as Council Directive 2006/54/EC ([2006] OJ L204/23).

in the same way as a 'normal' illness and her period of absence offset against her overall sick-leave entitlement. She also argued that placing her on half pay after the 183-day period during which she had been entitled to full pay constituted unfavorable treatment in respect of pay contrary to Art 141 of the EC Treaty and the Equal Pay Directive.[88]

The Equality Officer upheld Ms McKenna's argument and ordered that the arrears of pay be paid, together with compensation for the discrimination that she had suffered. On appeal, the Labour Court referred the case to the ECJ. The ECJ held that the continued payment of wages to a worker in the event of illness falls within the concept of 'pay', and therefore such a sick-leave scheme is covered by Art 141 of the EC Treaty and the Equal Pay Directive, but not by the Equal Treatment Directive. The Court ruled that it does not breach EU discrimination law for a pregnant worker who is absent due to a pregnancy-related illness to suffer a reduction in her pay, provided that she is treated in the same way as a male worker who is absent on the grounds of illness, and provided that the amount of sick pay is not so low as to undermine the objective of protecting pregnant workers. The ECJ also ruled that it is not a breach of EU law for a sick-leave scheme to offset absence through illness, pregnancy-related or not, against a maximum period of paid sick leave to which a worker is entitled. However, the ECJ went on to caution that offsetting absence on the grounds of pregnancy-related illness should not have the effect that, during later periods of absence, the female worker receives pay that is lower than the minimum amount to which she was entitled during her earlier illness which arose while she was pregnant.

Payment during maternity leave

[5.24] Section 22 of the Maternity Protection Acts exempts from the rights preserved by the employee, the right to remuneration.

Maternity benefit

[5.25] Although there is no statutory entitlement to remuneration during a period of maternity leave, an employee will usually be entitled to maternity benefit for the first 26 weeks of her maternity leave, payable by the Department of Social and Family Affairs, subject to the employee having made the requisite PRSI contributions and having complied with applicable procedural requirements.

Maternity benefit is currently paid at the rate of 80 per cent of reckonable weekly earnings up to a maximum of €280, or €230.30, whichever is the greater.[89] Section 48 of the Social Welfare Act 2005 details the requisite PRSI contribution requirements to qualify for maternity benefit. A claim for maternity benefit must be made within the prescribed time or the claimant runs the risk of being disqualified from part of the benefit.[90]

---

[88] Council Directive EC/75/117/EEC ([1975] OJ L45/19).

[89] Social Welfare (Consolidation) Act 2005, s 47, as amended by Social Welfare Act 2005, s 7.

[90] See the Social Welfare (Consolidation Payment Provisions) Regulations 1994 (SI 417/1994) as amended.

Contractual entitlement to payment

[5.26] It is quite common for employees to have contractual entitlements to payment during maternity leave. A common contractual arrangement is for an employee to be entitled to be paid as normal during their maternity leave less the maternity benefit to which they are entitled to during that period. Alternatively, the arrangement may be that the employee receives full payment during a period of maternity leave with maternity benefit cheques being remitted to their employer.

It is also common for an entitlement to payment during a period of maternity leave to be subject to a service requirement, such as a 12-month period of employment, before the employee may avail of the scheme. Furthermore, the scheme may also include a 'claw-back' provision whereby the employee will be required to pay back payment received while on maternity leave if they do not return to work for a stipulated period following their leave entitlements.

Protection against dismissal

[5.27] Any purported termination, notice of termination or suspension of employment while an employee is on a period of maternity leave, additional maternity leave, father's leave, health and safety leave, leave to attend ante-natal classes, leave to attend ante-natal or post-natal care or for breastfeeding will be void.[91] Any notice of termination or notice of suspension which is given before the employer receives notification from the employee as to an entitlement to leave which is due to expire during that period of leave is extended by the period of the leave.[92]

The dismissal of an employee is automatically unfair if it results wholly or mainly from:[93]

(i)   the employee's pregnancy, giving birth, breastfeeding or any connected matter; or

(ii)   as a result of the employee exercising or proposing to exercise rights under the Maternity Protection Acts; or

(iii)   from the employee taking time off from work to attend ante-natal classes or time off from work or a reduction in hours for breastfeeding.

The one-year service requirement, which is required in most circumstances to bring a claim a under the Unfair Dismissals Acts, does not apply to employees dismissed for pregnancy, giving birth or breastfeeding or any connected matters.

An employee dismissed on grounds relating to pregnancy may, alternatively, make a claim of discriminatory dismissal before the Equality Tribunal under the Employment Equality Acts 1998–2008, on the basis that such action constituted discrimination on the gender or family status ground.[94]

---

[91]   Maternity Protection Acts, s 23.

[92]   Maternity Protection Acts, s 24.

[93]   Unfair Dismissals Acts 1977–2007, s 6(2)(g).

[94]   See further Ch 13, Employment Equality.

Right to return to work

[5.28] On the expiry of a period of maternity leave, additional maternity leave or health and safety leave, an employee is entitled to:[95]

(i)   return to work with the same employer, or if there has been a change of owner, with the new owner;

(ii)   the same job and the same contract of employment held immediately before the start of the period of leave;

(iii)   terms and conditions not less favourable than those that would have been applicable if they had not been absent from work, which also incorporate any improvements to which the employee would have been entitled.

Suitable alternative work

[5.29] Where it is not reasonably practicable for the employer to permit an employee to return to the job held before commencing protective leave, the employee is entitled to be offered suitable alternative work under a new contract of employment.[96]

Section 27(2) of the Maternity Protection Acts provides that work under a new contract of employment constitutes suitable work for the purposes of that Act if the work is of a kind which is suitable in relation to the employee concerned and appropriate for the employee to do in the circumstances; and the terms and conditions of the contract relating to the place where the work is to be done, the capacity in which the employee is to be employed and any other terms and conditions of employment are not less favourable to the employee than those of her or his contract of employment immediately before the start of the leave, and incorporate any improvement to the terms and conditions to which the employee would have been entitled if she or he had not been so absent from work during that period.

Notification of intention to return to work

[5.30] In order to be entitled to return to work following an absence due to a period of protective leave, an employee must notify their employer in writing of their intention to return to work not later than four weeks before the date on which they are expected to resume work.[97]

ADOPTIVE LEAVE

Entitlements

[5.31] The scheme of adoptive leave introduced pursuant to the Adoptive Leave Act 1995 replicated to a large extent the statutory maternity leave entitlements. Under the 1995 Act, an adopting mother or a sole male adopting father was entitled to 14

---

[95] Maternity Protection Acts, s 26.

[96] Maternity Protection Acts, s 27.

[97] Maternity Protection Acts, s 28(1).

consecutive weeks' adoptive leave beginning on the day of the placement of the child and up to eight weeks' additional adoptive leave.

The Adoptive Leave Act 1995 was amended by the Adoptive Leave Act 2005. The 2005 Act supplemented the entitlements of employees in relation to adoptive leave. The collective citation for the Acts is the Adoptive Leave Acts 1995 and 2005 (the 'Adoptive Leave Acts'). The current entitlement to adoptive leave is set out in the Adoptive Leave Act 1995 (Extension of Periods of Leave) Order.[98] An adopting mother or a sole male adopting father is entitled to:

(i)   a minimum of 24 consecutive weeks of adoptive leave beginning on the day of the placement of the child; and

(ii)   up to 16 weeks' additional adoptive leave.

In general, a period of additional adoptive leave will commence immediately after the period of ordinary adoptive leave. In the case of a foreign adoption, some or all of the period of additional adoptive leave may be taken before the date of the placement for the purpose of familiarisation with the child.[99]

The 24-week period of adoptive leave attracts social welfare benefit if the adopting parent has made the requisite PRSI contributions.

Qualifications

[5.32] The entitlements under the Adoptive Leave Acts apply to adopting mothers and sole male adopters. These terms are defined in s 2(1) of the Adoptive Leave Acts.

(i)   'adopting mother' means a woman, including an employed adopting mother, in whose care a child (of whom she is not the natural mother) has been placed or is to be placed with a view to the making of an adoption order, or to the effecting of a foreign adoption or following any such adoption;

(ii)   'sole male adopter' means a male employee who is not an adopting father within the meaning of the Act in whose sole care a child has been placed or is to be placed with a view to the making of an adoption order, or to the effecting of a foreign adoption or following any such adoption.

In certain circumstances, an 'adopting father' is entitled to adoptive leave where the adopting mother dies either before or during her period of adoptive leave. Section 2(1) of the Adoptive Leave Acts defines 'adopting father' as 'a male employee in whose care a child has been placed or is to be placed with a view to the making of an adoption order, or to the effecting of a foreign adoption or following any such adoption'.

'Employee' is defined in s 2(1) of the Adoptive Leave Acts as 'a person who has entered into or work under (or where the employment has ceased, entered into or worked under) a contract of employment'. 'Contract of employment' is defined in s 2(1) as:

(a)   a contract of service or apprenticeship, or

(b)   any other contract whereby an individual agrees with a person, who is carrying on the business of an employment agency within the meaning of the Employment

---

[98]   SI 52/2006.

[99]   Adoptive Leave Acts, s 8.

Agency Act, 1971, and is acting in the course of that business, to do or perform personally any work or service for another person (whether or not that other person is a party to the contract,

whether the contract is express or implied and if express, whether it is oral or in writing.

Notification requirements

[5.33] An adopting parent must notify their employer in writing of their intention to take adoptive leave as soon as reasonably practicable, but not later than four weeks before the expected date of placement of the child. In addition, the employee must notify their employer in writing as soon as reasonably practicable of the expected day of the placement of the child. An employee must supply their employer with the certificate of placement, as soon as reasonable practicable, but not later than four weeks after the date of placement.[100]

In the case of a foreign adoption, an adopting parent must provide the employer with a declaration of suitability made pursuant to s 5(1)(iii)(II) of the Adoption Act 1991 as soon as reasonably practicable before the expected day of placement and, following the placement, supply their employer with the particulars of placement as soon as reasonably practicable.[101]

If it is the intention of the adopting parent to avail of their entitlement to additional adoptive leave, the parent must notify their employer in writing of their intention not later than four weeks before their expected date of return to work.[102]

In general, an adopting parent must notify their employer in writing of their intention to return to work not later than four weeks before the date on which they are expected to return to work.[103]

Time off to attend pre-adoption classes

[5.34] An adopting parent is entitled to take time off work without loss of pay for the purposes of attending any pre-adoption classes and meetings that the employee is obliged to attend.[104]

Termination of additional adoptive leave due to sickness of the adopting parent

[5.35] An employer may agree to terminate a period of additional adoptive leave due to the sickness of the adopting parent. An employee's absence from work due to sickness following the termination of a period of additional adoptive leave shall be treated as any absence from work due to sickness. If an employer so agrees to terminate a period of additional adoptive leave, the employee concerned shall not be entitled to resume the additional adoptive leave.[105]

---

[100] Adoptive Leave Acts, s 7.
[101] Adoptive Leave Acts, s 7(2).
[102] Adoptive Leave Acts, s 8(3).
[103] Adoptive Leave Acts, s 20.
[104] Adoptive Leave Acts, s 11A.
[105] Adoptive Leave Acts, s 11B.

Postponement of leave due to hospitalisation of the child

[5.36] If an adopted child is hospitalised, the employer may agree to postpone part of the adoptive leave and/or the additional adoptive leave. Following the discharge of the child from hospital, the employee shall then be entitled to take the postponed leave in one continuous block, commencing not less than seven days after the discharge of the child from hospital.[106]

Placements of less than 20 weeks

[5.37] Where the placement of an adoptive child terminates (other than as a result of the death of the child) before the expiration of the period of leave to which the employee is entitled, then the employee concerned shall be required to return to work. The employee must notify their employer of the date of termination as soon as reasonably practicable but not later than seven days after that date.[107]

Preservation of rights

[5.38] During a period of absence from work on adoptive leave and/or additional adoptive leave, an employee is deemed to have been in the employment of the employer and is to be treated as if the employee had not been so absent. Except for the right to remuneration or superannuation benefits or any obligations to pay contributions in or in respect of the employment during the absence, such an absence due to adoptive leave/ additional adoptive leave does not affect the employee's employment rights, whether conferred by statute, contract or otherwise. A period of absence while on such leave cannot be treated as any other leave, including sick leave or annual leave, to which an employee is entitled.[108]

Payment during adoptive leave and adoptive benefit

[5.39] Section 15(1) of the Adoptive Leave Acts makes clear that a period of adoptive leave is unpaid. However an employee will generally be entitled to 'adoptive benefit' during such leave, subject to the requirement of having made the requisite PRSI contributions. Section 59 of the Social Welfare (Consolidation) Act 2005 (as amended) details the requisite PRSI contribution requirements in order to qualify for adoptive benefit. Adoptive benefit is currently paid at the rate of 80 per cent of reckonable weekly earning up to a maximum of €280 or €230.70, whichever is the greater.

Right to return to work

[5.40] On the expiry of a period of adoptive leave and/or additional adoptive leave, an employee is entitled to return to work with the same employer, or if there has been a change of ownership of the undertaking in which the employee was employed, with the new owner. An employee is entitled to return to the same job under the same contract of employment as held immediately before the start of the leave. The employee is entitled to terms and conditions not less favourable than those which would have been

---

[106] Adoptive Leave Acts, s 11C.

[107] Adoptive Leave Acts, s 12.

[108] Adoptive Leave Acts, s 15.

applicable, which also incorporate any improvements to which the employee would have been entitled if they had not been absent from work.[109]

Where it is not reasonably practicable for an employer to permit the employee concerned to return to the job as held before commencing leave, the employee is entitled to be offered suitable alternative work under a new contract of employment.[110] The work to be done under such a new contract must be work of a kind which is suitable in relation to the employee concerned and appropriate for her to do; and the terms and conditions of the contract relating to the place where the work is to be done, the capacity in which the employee is to be employed and any other terms and conditions of employment are not less favourable to the employee than those of her or his contract of employment immediately before the start of the leave, and incorporate any improvement to the terms and conditions to which the employee would have been entitled if she or he had not been so absent from work during that period.[111]

PARENTAL LEAVE AND *FORCE MAJEURE* LEAVE

Entitlements

[5.41] The Parental Leave Act 1998 transposed the Parental Leave Directive[112] into Irish law. The Act introduced entitlements to parental leave and *force majeure* leave into Irish law. The 1998 Act was amended by the Parental Leave (Amendment) Act 2006. The collective citation for the Acts is the Parental Leave Acts 1998 and 2006 (the 'Parental Leave Acts'). Under the Parental Leave Acts, an employee who is a 'relevant parent' is entitled to 14 weeks' unpaid leave to enable him or her to take care of his or her child (parental leave)[113] and an employee is entitled to limited paid leave to deal with family emergencies (*force majeure* leave).[114]

Qualifications

[5.42] An employee who is a 'relevant parent' is entitled to parental leave. The term 'relevant parent' is defined as a person who is the natural parent, the adoptive parent or the adopting parent in respect of the child or who is acting *in loco parentis* to the child.[115] 'Employee' is defined in s 2(1) of the Parental Leave Acts as 'a person of any age who has entered into or works under (or where the employment has ceased, entered into or worked under) a contract of employment...'. 'Contract of employment' is defined in s 2(1) as:

(a)   a contract of service or apprenticeship, or

(b)   any other contract whereby an individual agrees with a person, who is carrying on the business of an employment agency within the meaning of the Employment

---

[109] Adoptive Leave Acts, s 18.

[110] Adoptive Leave Acts, s 19.

[111] Adoptive Leave Acts, s 19(2).

[112] Council Directive 96/34/EC of 3 June 1996 on the framework agreement on parental leave concluded by UNICE, CEEP and the ETUC.

[113] Parental Leave Acts, s 6(1).

[114] Parental Leave Acts, s 13(1).

[115] Parental Leave Acts, s 6(9).

> Agency Act, 1971, and is acting in the course of that business, to do or perform personally any work or service for another person (whether or not that other person is a party to the contract,

whether the contract is express or implied and if express, whether it is oral or in writing.

The leave must be taken before the child concerned attains the age of eight years of age.[116] Different rules apply in respect of children adopted between the ages of six and eight years of age, in which case the employee must take the parental leave within two years of the adoption order.[117] If the child has a disability, the employee is entitled to parental leave in respect of the child until the child attains 16 years of age or until the disability, or any other disability, ceases.[118]

[5.43] In general, a parent must have completed one year's continuous service with the employer before the leave is taken.[119] However, if a parent has at least three months' continuous employment with their employer the employee shall be entitled to parental leave for a period of one week for each month of continuous employment that he or she has completed with the employer at the time of commencement of the leave.[120]

Noticification requirements

[5.44] An employee who proposes to take parental leave must notify their employer in writing as soon as reasonably practicable but not later than six weeks before the commencement of the leave.[121] Such notification must specify the date of the commencement of the leave, the duration of the leave and the manner in which it is proposed that the leave is to be taken and must be signed by the employee.[122] The employer must retain a copy of such notification and must give a copy of it to the employee concerned.[123] An employer may request further information from the employee in relation to the date of birth of the child, evidence of the employee's status as a 'relevant parent' or, where relevant, evidence as to the child's disability.[124]

An application for parental leave may be revoked by a further notification in writing from the employee to their employer before the commencement of the leave.[125]

Transfer of leave

[5.45] The entitlement to parental leave is not transferable between parents unless they are employed by the same employer and the employer consents to the transfer.[126]

---

[116] Parental Leave Acts, s 6(2)(a).
[117] Parental Leave Acts, s 6(2)(b).
[118] Parental Leave Acts, s 6(2)(c).
[119] Parental Leave Acts, s 6(3).
[120] Parental Leave Acts, s 6(8).
[121] Parental Leave Acts, s 8(1). Under s 8(4), an employer may waive the requirement to receive such notification.
[122] Parental Leave Acts, s 8(2).
[123] Parental Leave Acts, s 8(5).
[124] Parental Leave Acts, s 6(6).
[125] Parental Leave Acts, s 8(3).
[126] Parental Leave Acts, s 6(6) and s 6A, as inserted by Civil Law (Miscellaneous Provisions) Act 2008, s 72.

Manner in which leave may be taken

[5.46] Parental leave may be taken in one continuous period of 14 weeks or two separate periods each consisting of not less than six weeks and/or in another manner agreed by the employer and the employee.[127]

In determining the 14-week period to which an employee is entitled, absences from work due to sick leave, maternity leave, adoptive leave or *force majeure* leave are excluded from the calculation and a corresponding number of days immediately before the commencement of the relevant period shall be included.[128]

Confirmation of parental leave

[5.47] Not less than four weeks before the leave is due to commence, a 'confirmation document' must be prepared and signed by the employer and the employee specifying:[129]

   (i)   the date of the commencement of the leave;

   (ii)   the duration of the leave; and

   (iii) the manner in which the leave is to be taken.

An employer must retain a copy of the confirmation document and also give a copy of the document to the employee.[130]

The parties may agree to postpone the taking of the leave, even after the signing of the confirmation document, and, in such circumstances, the leave may be taken at such other times as the parties agree.[131]

Postponement due the sickness of the parent

[5.48] A period of parental leave may be postponed or suspended if the employee concerned becomes sick and is unable to care for their child.[132] The employee must notify the employer in writing as soon as reasonably practicable and provide relevant evidence in respect of the sickness.[133] If the leave is postponed and because of this fact the child exceeds the relevant age within which time the leave must be taken (ie generally eight years of age or sixteen years of age in respect of a disabled child), the parent concerned is entitled to take the postponed parental leave at a later stage notwithstanding the fact that the child has exceeded the threshold age.[134]

Postponement by the employer

[5.49] An employer may decide to postpone a period of parental leave for a maximum period of six months if satisfied that the granting of the leave would have a 'substantial

---

[127] Parental Leave Acts, s 7(1).

[128] Parental Leave Acts, s 7(2)(b).

[129] Parental Leave Acts, ss 9(1) and 9(2).

[130] Parental Leave Acts, s 9(3).

[131] Parental Leave Acts, ss 10(2) and 10(3).

[132] Parental Leave Acts, s 10(2)(b).

[133] Parental Leave Acts, s 10(2)(b).

[134] Parental Leave Acts, s 10(4).

adverse effect on the operation of his or her business, profession or occupation'.[135] In deciding whether to postpone the leave, the employer may have reference to:[136]

(i)   the seasonal variations in the volume of the work concerned;

(ii)   the unavailability of a person to carry out the duties of the employee;

(iii)   the nature of the duties;

(iv)   the number of employees;

(v)   the number of employees on parental leave during the period of leave requested; or

(vi)   any other relevant matters.

An employer must notify the employee concerned in writing of the decision to postpone the leave not later than four weeks before the intended commencement of the leave. This notice must contain a statement in summary form of the grounds for the postponement.[137] Before giving such notice the employer must consult with the employee in relation to the proposed postponement.[138] In any event, the parental leave cannot be postponed by the employer more than once unless the ground for the postponement is the seasonal variation of the volume of work concerned, in which case the leave cannot be postponed more than twice.[139]

If parental leave is postponed by the employer and because of this fact the child exceeds the relevant age within which time the leave must be taken (ie generally eight years of age or 16 years of age in respect of a disabled child), the parent concerned is entitled to take the postponed leave at a later stage, notwithstanding the fact that the child has exceeded the threshold age.[140]

Abuse of parental leave

[5.50] An entitlement to parental leave is subject to the condition that the employee uses the leave 'to take care of the child concerned'.[141] If an employer has reasonable grounds to believe that the leave is being used for a purpose other than this, the employer may terminate the leave.[142]

Before terminating the leave, the employer must notify the parent in writing of the proposal containing a summary of the grounds for terminating the leave. The notification of the proposal must state that the employee may, within seven days of receiving the notice, make representation to the employer regarding the matter, and any

---

[135] Parental Leave Acts, s 11(1). Under s 11(5), the employer's entitlement to postpone leave under s 11(1) does not apply if both parties have already signed the confirmation document.

[136] Parental Leave Acts, s 11(1).

[137] Parental Leave Acts, s 11(3).

[138] Parental Leave Acts, s 11(2).

[139] Parental Leave Acts, s 11(4).

[140] Parental Leave Acts, s 11(6).

[141] Parental Leave Acts, s 12(1).

[142] Parental Leave Acts, s 12(2).

such representation must be considered by the employer before reaching their decision.[143]

If following such consultation the employer has reasonable grounds to believe that the employee is not using the leave to take care of the child, the employer may terminate the leave by notice in writing. Such notice must contain a statement in summary form of the grounds for terminating the leave. The notice must also specify the day on which the leave is to terminate, which day must not be earlier than seven days after the date of the receipt of the notice by the employee.[144]

An employer may refuse to grant parental leave if they believe that the proposed leave will be used for a purpose other than to take care of the child concerned.[145] Before doing so, an employer must also engage in a similar notification and consultation process.[146]

Force Majeure leave

[5.51] An employee is entitled to leave with pay from their employment where for urgent family reasons, owing to an injury or the illness of a dependent person, the immediate presence of the employee at the place where a person specified in s 13(2) of the Acts is, whether at home or elsewhere, is indispensable.[147] This is known as '*force majeure* leave'. The maximum amount of paid time off allowed in respect of *force majeure* leave is three days in any 12 consecutive months or five days in any 36-month period.[148]

The persons specified in s 13(2) are:

(i)   a person of whom the employee is the parent or adoptive parent;

(ii)   the spouse of the employee or a person with whom the employee is living as a husband or wife;

(iii)   a person to whom the employee is *in loco parentis;*

(iv)   a brother or sister of the employee;

(v)   a parent or grandparent of the employee; and

(vii)   a person who otherwise resides with the employee in a relationship of domestic dependency.

When an employee takes *force majeure* leave, he or she must, as soon as reasonably practicable, by notice in a prescribed form to his employer, confirm that he or she has taken the leave. The notice must specify the dates on which the leave was taken and contain a statement of the facts which entitled the employee to the leave. The 'prescribed form' for such notification is set out in the Parental Leave (Notice of Force Majeure Leave) Regulations.[149]

---

[143] Parental Leave Acts, s 12(7).

[144] Parental Leave Acts, s 12(2).

[145] Parental Leave Acts, s 12(4).

[146] Parental Leave Acts, ss 12(4) and 12(6).

[147] Parental Leave Acts, s 13(1).

[148] Parental Leave Acts, s 13(4). Section 13(5) provides that absence for part of one-day *force majeure* leave is deemed as one day of *force majeure* leave.

[149] SI 454/1998.

During a period of absence while on *force majeure* leave, an employee is regarded for all purposes relating to their employment as still working and none of their employment rights is affected by the leave.[150] Absence while on *force majeure* leave is not to be treated as any other leave, including sick leave or annual leave, adoptive leave, maternity leave and parental leave, to which the employee is entitled.[151]

Preservation of rights

[5.52] During a period of absence while on parental leave, an employee is regarded for all purposes relating to their employment as not being absent from work and none of their rights, except for the right to remuneration, superannuation benefits and/or any obligation to pay contributions in or in respect of the employment during the absence, is affected by the leave.[152]

Absence while on parental leave is not to be treated as any other leave, including sick leave or annual leave, adoptive leave, maternity leave and *force majeure* leave, to which the employee is entitled.[153]

Where an employee is on probation in the employment or is undergoing training or is employed under a contract of apprenticeship and takes parental leave, if the employer considers that a period of parental leave would not be consistent with the continuance of the probation, training or apprenticeship the employer may require that the period of probation, training or apprenticeship be suspended during the period of parental leave and be completed at the end of the leave.[154]

Return to work

[5.53] On the expiry of a period of parental leave, an employee is entitled to return to work with the same employer, or if there has been a change of ownership of the undertaking in which the employee was employed, with the new owner.[155] The employee is entitled to return to the same job under the same contract of employment as held immediately before the start of the parental leave. The employee is entitled to terms and conditions not less favourable than those which would have been applicable to the employee, which also incorporate any improvements to which the employee would have been entitled if the employee had not been absent from work.[156]

Suitable alternative work

[5.54] Where it is not reasonably practicable for an employer to permit an employee to return to the job that they had held before commencing a period of parental leave, the employee is entitled to be offered suitable alternative work under a new contract of employment. Work under a new contract of employment constitutes 'suitable alternative

---

[150] Parental Leave Acts, s 14(4).
[151] Parental Leave Acts, s 14(5).
[152] Parental Leave Acts, s 14(1).
[153] Parental Leave Acts, s 14(2).
[154] Parental Leave Acts, s 14(3).
[155] Parental Leave Acts, s 15(1).
[156] Parental Leave Acts, s 15(1).

work' if the work to be done under such a new contract is of a kind that is suitable in relation to the employee concerned and appropriate for the employee to do in the circumstances; and the terms and conditions of the contract relating to the place where the work is to be done, the capacity in which the employee is to be employed and any other terms and conditions of employment are not less favourable to the employee than those of her or his contract of employment immediately before the start of the leave, and incorporate any improvement to the terms and conditions to which the employee would have been entitled if she or he had not been so absent from work on parental leave.[157]

Protection from penalisation

[5.55] An employer is prohibited from penalising an employee for exercising or proposing to exercise their entitlement to parental leave or *force majeure* leave.[158] Penalisation of an employee includes:[159]

(i)   dismissal of the employee;

(ii)   unfair treatment of the employee, including selection for redundancy; and

(iii)   an unfavourable change in the conditions of employment of the employee.

If the act of penalisation is the dismissal of the employee, the employee may institute proceedings under the Unfair Dismissals Acts 1977–2007 in respect of the dismissal.[160]

An employee who is entitled to return to work after a period of parental leave but who is not permitted to do so:

(i)   is deemed to have been dismissed and such dismissal is deemed, for the purposes of the Unfair Dismissals Acts 1977–2007, to have been to be an unfair dismissal unless, having regard to all the circumstances, there were substantial grounds justifying the dismissal;

(ii)   is deemed for the purposes of the Redundancy Payments Acts 1967 to 2007, to have had their employment terminated as at the date they were due to return to work.

Records

[5.56] An employer must keep a record of the parental leave and *force majeure* leave taken by employees, showing the period of employment of each employee and the dates and times upon which each employee was on parental leave or *force majeure* leave.[161] Such records must be maintained for eight years.[162]

---

[157] Parental Leave Acts, s 16(2).
[158] Parental Leave Acts, s 16(A)(1).
[159] Parental Leave Acts, s 16A(2).
[160] Parental Leave Acts, s 16A(3).
[161] Parental Leave Acts, s 27(1).
[162] Parental Leave Acts, s 27(2).

CARER'S LEAVE

Entitlements

[5.57] Under the Carer's Leave Act 2001 (the 'Carer's Leave Act'), employees are entitled to unpaid leave of up to 104 weeks to provide full time care and attention for a 'relevant person'.[163] The definition of 'relevant person' is provided in s 99 of the Social Welfare (Consolidation) Act 2005 as meaning 'a person who has such a disability that he or she requires full-time care and attention'. An employee who wishes to avail of carer's leave must apply to the Minister for Social and Family Affairs for a decision by a deciding officer.[164] The employee must give a copy of this decision to the employer and shall not be entitled to carer's leave until he or she does so.[165]

[5.58] Carer's leave may be taken in the form of:[166]

(a)   one continuous period of 104 weeks for each relevant person; or

(b)   a number of periods, the aggregate duration of which does not exceed 104 weeks.[167]

An employer may refuse on reasonable grounds to permit an employee to take a period of carer's leave which is less than 13 weeks' duration, in which case the employer must specify in writing the grounds for such refusal.[168] Six weeks must elapse between the end of one period of carer's leave and the commencement of another period of carer's leave in respect of the same relevant person.[169] If a period of carer's leave has terminated the employee concerned is not entitled to commence carer's leave in respect of another relevant person for a period of six months.[170]

Qualifications

[5.59] Employees who have been employed for a period of 12 months' continuous employment with the employer are entitled to carer's leave. 'Employee' is defined in s 2(1) of the Carer's Leave Act as 'a person of any age who has entered into or works under (or where the employment has ceased, entered into or worked under) a contract of employment...'. 'Contract of employment' is defined in s 2(1) as:

(a)   a contract of service or apprenticeship, or

(b)   any other contract whereby an individual agrees with a person, who is carrying on the business of an employment agency within the meaning of the Employment Agency Act, 1971, and is acting in the course of that business, to do or perform

---

[163] Parental Leave Acts, 6(1).
[164] Carer's Leave Act 2001, s 6(1).
[165] Carer's Leave Act 2001, s 6(2).
[166] Carer's Leave Act 2001, s 8(1).
[167] Carer's Leave Act 2001, s 8(4).
[168] Carer's Leave Act 2001, s 8(2).
[169] Carer's Leave Act 2001, s 8(3).
[170] Carer's Leave Act 2001, s 8(4).

personally any work or service for another person (whether or not that other person is a party to the contract,

whether the contract is express or implied and if express, whether it is oral or in writing.

An employee who is on carer's leave must notify their employer as soon as possible of any change of circumstances that affects their entitlement to carer's leave.[171]

On one occasion only, an employee who is on carer's leave may apply for carer's leave for another person if that other person resides with the person in respect of whose care the original carer's leave was granted.[172] In such circumstances, the total amount of carer's leave shall not exceed 208 weeks, ie 104 weeks in respect of each person.[173]

Notification requirements

[5.60] Where an employee proposes to take carer's leave, the employee must, within six weeks of the proposed commencement of the leave, provide the employer with a notice in writing of:[174]

(a)   the proposal to take carer's leave;

(b)   the decision of the Minister for Social and Family Affairs as to whether or not the person in respect of whose care the leave is requested constitutes a 'relevant person';

(c)   the proposed date of commencement of the leave and the form in which the proposed leave is to be taken.

Not less than two weeks before the leave is due to commence, a 'confirmation document' must be prepared and signed by the parties specifying:[175]

(i)   the date of the commencement of the leave;

(ii)   the duration of the leave; and

(iii) the form in which the leave is to be taken.

An application for carer's leave may be revoked by the employee by notice in writing to the employer before the date of the confirmation document.[176] If after the date of the confirmation document, whether or not carer's leave has commenced, the employer and employee agree to postpone all or part of the leave, to curtail it or vary the form of the leave, the confirmation document must be amended to reflect this.[177]

---

[171] Carer's Leave Act 2001, s 7(1).

[172] Carer's Leave Act 2001, s 7(2).

[173] Carer's Leave Act 2001, s 7(4).

[174] Carer's Leave Act 2001, s 9(1).

[175] Carer's Leave Act 2001, s 10(1).

[176] Carer's Leave Act 2001, s 9(3).

[177] Carer's Leave Act 2001, s 12(1).

An employee on carer's leave must, not less than four weeks before he or she is due to return to work, give notice in writing to the employer of the intention to return to work.[178]

Preservation of rights

[5.61] During a period of absence while on carer's leave an employee is regarded as not being absent from work for all purposes relating to their employment. None of the employee's rights or obligations related to the employment shall be affected by availing of carer's leave other than the right to:[179]

    (i)   remuneration;

    (ii)   annual leave, save in relation to the first 13 weeks of carer's leave, during which time, annual leave will accrue in accordance with the Organisation of Working Time Act 1997;

    (iii) public holidays, save in relation to the first 13 weeks of carer's leave, during which time, entitlements in relation to public holidays will accrue in accordance with the Organisation of Working Time Act 1997;

    (iv) superannuation benefits; and

    (v)   any obligation to pay contributions in, or in respect of, the employment.

Absence from work on carer's leave shall not be treated as part of any other leave, including sick leave, annual leave, adoptive leave, maternity leave, parental leave and *force majeure* leave, to which the employee is entitled.[180]

Where an employee who is on probation in the employment or is undergoing training or is undertaking an apprenticeship takes carer's leave, if the employer considers that the absence on carer's leave would not be consistent with the continuance of the probation, training or apprenticeship, the employer can require that the probation, training or apprenticeship be suspended during the carer's leave and be completed by the employee at the end of the leave.[181]

Return to work

[5.62] On the expiry of a period of carer's leave, an employee is entitled to return to work with the same employer, or if there has been a change of ownership of the undertaking in which the employee was employed, with the new owner.[182] The employee is entitled to return to the same job under the same contract of employment held immediately before the start of carer's leave and is entitled to terms and conditions not less favourable than those that would have been applicable to the employee if he or she had not been so absent from work.[183]

---

[178] Carer's Leave Act 2001, s 9(6).
[179] Carer's Leave Act 2001, s 13(1).
[180] Carer's Leave Act 2001, s 13(4).
[181] Carer's Leave Act 2001, s 13(5).
[182] Carer's Leave Act 2001, s 14(1)(a).
[183] Carer's Leave Act 2001, ss 14(1)(b) and (c).

Sustainable alernative work

[5.63] Where it is not reasonably practicable for the employer to permit the employee to return to the job held before commencing carer's leave, the employee is entitled to be offered suitable alternative work under a new contract of employment.[184] Work under a new contract of employment constitutes 'suitable alternative work' if the work to be done under such a new contract is of a kind that is suitable in relation to the employee concerned and appropriate for the employee to do in the circumstances; and the terms and conditions of the contract relating to the place where the work is to be done, the capacity in which the employee is to be employed and any other terms and conditions of employment are not less favourable to the employee than those of her or his contract of employment immediately before the start of the leave, and incorporate any improvement to the terms and conditions to which the employee would have been entitled if she or he had not been so absent from work on carer's leave.[185]

Protection from penalisation

[5.64] An employer is prohibited from penalising an employee for exercising or proposing to exercise their entitlement to carer's leave.[186] Penalisation of an employee includes:[187]

   (i)   dismissal of the employee;

   (ii)   unfair treatment of the employee, including selection for redundancy; and

   (iii) an unfavourable change in the conditions of employment of the employee.

If the act of penalisation is the dismissal of the employee, the employee may institute proceedings under the Unfair Dismissals Acts 1977–2007 in respect of the dismissal.[188]

An employee who is not permitted to return to work following a period of carer's leave:[189]

   (i)   is deemed to have been dismissed and such dismissal is deemed for the purposes of the Unfair Dismissals Acts 1977–2007 to have been an unfair dismissal unless having regard to all the circumstances there were substantial grounds justifying the dismissal;

   (ii)   is deemed for the purposes of the Redundancy Payments Acts 1967 to 2007 to have had their employment terminated as at the date they were due to return to work.

---

[184] Carer's Leave Act 2001, s 15(1).
[185] Carer's Leave Act 2001, s 15(2).
[186] Carer's Leave Act 2001, s 16(1).
[187] Carer's Leave Act 2001, s 16(2).
[188] Carer's Leave Act 2001, s 16(3).
[189] Carer's Leave Act 2001, s 16(4).

Reference by an employer to the Minister for Social, Community and Family Affairs

[5.65] If an employer is of the opinion that:

(a)   the person in respect of whose care an employee either proposes or is currently taking carer's leave to care for ceases to be a 'relevant person'; or

(b)   the person in respect of whose care an employee either proposes or is currently taking carer's leave ceases to require full time care and attention; or

(c)   the employee on carer's leave has engaged in employment;

the employer must notify the Minister of Social and Family Affairs.[190] If the deciding officer or the appeals officer agrees with the employer's contention the employee is not entitled to the leave.[191]

Records

[5.66] An employer must keep a record of carer's leave taken by employees, showing the period of employment of each employee and the dates and times upon which each employee was on carer's leave.[192] Such records must be maintained for eight years.[193]

---

[190] Carer's Leave Act 2001, s 18.
[191] Carer's Leave Act 2001, s 18(4).
[192] Carer's Leave Act 2001, s 31(1).
[193] Carer's Leave Act 2001, s 31(2).

Chapter 6

Workplace Privacy and Data Protection

Cathal McGreal

PART I – SOURCES OF WORKPLACE PRIVACY LAW

[6.01] There is not yet any single unified Irish jurisprudence of privacy law. There are however a number of legal sources from which the right to privacy has gained acceptance and legal authority. While it is true that this acceptance is relatively recent[1] and that there remains doubt about the proper constitution of the law,[2] there is little doubt that taken together, these sources now comprise a formidable body of authority supporting a right to privacy. The practical application of these sources is examined below, but in order to dispel remaining doubts about the origin and content of these sources we examine these briefly now.

(I) THE COMMON LAW CONTRACT OF EMPLOYMENT

[6.02] From the preponderance of authorities discussed in the following pages, there is a discernable acceptance of an implied right of a reasonable expectation of privacy in employment. The contract of employment, in any event, contains an implied term of mutual trust and confidence which must logically include a duty to respect privacy. The question is not whether the trust and confidence formula is capable of encapsulating a right to privacy but rather: '... whether the conduct in question is likely, on an objective assessment, to seriously damage the employment relationship.'[3] There should be little doubt from the authorities discussed below that failure to afford a reasonable expectation of privacy is capable of seriously damaging the employment relationship.

[6.03] It is now 20 years since the United States Supreme Court considered what has come to be referred to as a worker's 'reasonable expectation of privacy'. In *National Treasury Employees Union v Von Raab,*[4] the Court was asked to consider the petition of customs workers who complained of being subject to searches and more particularly to

---

[1]   A good starting place is the seminal essay by Warren and Brandeis, 'The right to privacy' (1890) 4 Harvard LR, 193.

[2]   For instance, see the comment that the approach in US jurisprudence (with acute development since '9/11') differs in its individual approach to a European approach which contains an aspect of community integration: Jay, *Data Protection, Law and Practice* (3rd edn, London: Sweet & Maxwell, 2007) para 1–04.

[3]   *Mahmud and Malik v BCCI* [1997] ICR 606 at 623, *per* Lord Steyn. This formula was endorsed by Laffoy J in *Berber v Dunnes Stores Ltd* [2007] ELR 1 at 15. See, also, *Cronin v Eircom Ltd* [2007] ELR 84.

[4]   *National Treasury Employees Union et al v Von Raab, Commissioner, United States Customs Service* 489 US 656 (1989).

urine testing for illicit drug use. While the Court approved of the practice of searches and testing, it also clearly recognised that there is an expectation of privacy in employment and that the extent of this expectation depends on the type of employment concerned. The Court said:

> We have recognized ... that the "operational realities of the workplace" may render entirely reasonable certain work-related intrusions by supervisors and co-workers that might be viewed as unreasonable in other contexts...[5]. While these operational realities will rarely affect an employee's expectations of privacy with respect to searches of his person, or of personal effects that the employee may bring to the workplace, id, at 716, 725, it is plain that certain forms of public employment[6] may diminish privacy expectations even with respect to such personal searches.[7]

It has not been seriously contended that workers retain the same level of privacy that they would have, for example, in their private homes.[8] The question in many cases is whether workers surrender part of their normal entitlement to privacy when they enter the workplace. Allen, Crasnow and Beale put the matter as follows:

> '[I]n taking up employment a person decides to engage with the world beyond the home. He or she makes a decision to accept rules and constraints which apply specifically within the workplace. Normally there is a choice whether to accept or refuse any employment. Likewise, when terms or conditions or employment are changed there is a fresh opportunity to choose whether to accept or refuse such changes.'[9]

---

5   The quotation cites *O'Connor v Ortega* 480 US 709, 717 (1987) (plurality opinion); see also at 731 (Scalia J, concurring in judgment).

6   As with the various other sources of privacy law there has been progressive development from the 'public' sphere to private enterprise employment. The European Convention on Human Rights, for example, refers to a right of privacy in Art 8 apparently limiting the right to the public sphere. As we see below, the distinction is increasingly immaterial for the purpose of the application of the privacy right.

7   *National Treasury Employees Union and Others v Von Raab and Others* 489 US 656, 671 (1989), *per* Kennedy J. The privacy entitlement in *Von Raab* derives from the protection against unreasonable search provided by the Fourth Amendment of the US Constitution. Constitutional privacy and the relevance of the Irish Constitution are dealt with separately below as *Von Raab* is unconcerned with the 'private dwelling' aspect of Irish constitutional privacy and is peculiarly specific to worker rights. In this respect, US case law differs from our own constitutional development. See also *Luck v Southern Pacific Transportation Co*, 267 Cal Rep 618 (1990).

8   See generally Oliver, 'Email and Internet Monitoring in the Workplace: Information Privacy and Contracting-Out' (2002) 31(4) Industrial LJ 321; Ford, 'Two Conceptions of Worker Privacy' (2002) 31(2) Industrial LJ 135. Interestingly the Data Protection Commissioner refers on his website to the use of CCTV systems in the domestic context, advising that while the processing of this personal data which is concerned solely with the management of personal, family or household affairs is exempt from the provisions of the Data Protection Act, this exemption might not apply if the occupant works from home: www.dataprotection.ie, 'Data Protection & CCTV', 'Domestic use of CCTV systems'.

9   Allen, Crasnow and Beale, *Employment Law and Human Rights* (2nd edn, Oxford University Press, 2007) para 8.53.

[6.04] In a similar vein, the Data Protection Working Party concluded in their Working Document on the Surveillance of Electronic Communications in the Workplace:

> Workers do not abandon their right to privacy and data protection every morning at the doors of the workplace. They do have a legitimate expectation of a certain degree of privacy in the workplace as they develop a significant part of their relationships with other human beings within the workplace. However, this right must be balanced with other legitimate rights and interests of the employer, in particular the employer's right to run his business efficiently to a certain extent, and above all, the right to protect himself from the liability or the harm that workers' actions may create. These rights and interests constitute legitimate grounds that may justify appropriate measures to limit the worker's right to privacy. The clearest example of this would be those cases where the employer is victim of a worker's criminal offence.[10]

While these statements reflect the contractual nature of employment law, it is important to remember that employment law is not an orthodox species of commercial contract law.[11] It is often the case that the employee has no real choices when entering employment.[12] In addition to the unequal bargaining power typical upon entering the contractual agreement itself, once the worker enters the workplace he or she inevitably loses a great deal of control as regards the physical work environment. Compromise is inevitable and workers have to tolerate a degree of restriction in respect of freedom of movement, communication or the right to work in competition with an employer. There may equally be limitations of the worker's freedom of expression, freedom of thought or conscience and the right to spend quality time with family.[13] However, even where the employee signs a general waiver of rights and entitlements, this will not necessarily permit the employer to exercise a wide power of search and surveillance.[14] The consensus, as we shall see, recognises the right to a reasonable expectation of workplace privacy.

---

[10] Article 29 – Data Protection Working Party, *Working Document on the Surveillance of Electronic Communications in the Workplace* (5401/01/EN/Final WP 55), 4. The Working Document was adopted on 29 May 2002. The Working Party was established under Article 29 of Directive 95/46/EC. Similar language is used at para 9.1 of the Article 29 – Data Protection Working Party, *Opinion 8/2001 on the Processing of Personal Data in the Employment Context* (5062/01/EN/Final WP 48).

[11] There are many authorities for this view but perhaps the best of these is the superb treatise of Freedland, *The Personal Employment Contract* (Oxford University Press, 2003) at 75.

[12] This is acknowledged by Allen, Crasnow and Beale *Employment Law and Human Rights* (2nd edn, Oxford University Press 2007) paragraph 8.53. See, further below, on the concept of consent and waiver under the title 'Processing of personal data – consent or necessity?' at para **[6.31]**.

[13] In *Knudsen v Norway* (1985) 42 DR 247, a clergyman who had been outspoken regarding his views on abortion failed to show that this was an unlawful basis to remove him from office. Neither is it a violation of the right to private family life to be required to work on Sundays: *Stedman v UK* (1997) 23 EHRR CD 168.

[14] The relevance and reliability of consent is discussed in detail below under the title 'Processing of personal data – consent or necessity?' at para **[6.32]**.

(II) The Irish Constitution

[6.05] The word 'privacy' does not appear in the Irish Constitution. Nevertheless, the concept forms a fundamental basis for rights which are now recognised as constitutional rights. In the case of *McGee v The Attorney General*,[15] the Supreme Court was prepared to accept that Art 40.3 (which is an open-ended 'personal rights' guarantee) could be interpreted to include the right to marital privacy. In the case of *Kennedy v Ireland*,[16] the High Court recognised that interference with private telephone communications could not, without appropriate safeguards, be permitted without violating the constitutional right to privacy of the home and of private communication. As we can see, the Irish courts have been primarily concerned with privacy of the family, the home and private dwelling.[17]

The constitutional right to privacy has been confirmed in several cases since *McGee* and *Kennedy* albeit without any real assessment of its scope or direct relevance to the workplace.[18] It is true that in *Hanahoe v Hussey*,[19] equivalent protections to those applied to private dwellings were applied to a search of a solicitor's office. Speaking generally, Kinlen J said of the right to privacy protecting the solicitor's workplace, that '[t]he courts must protect this privacy and only allow invasion of that right under strict interpretation of any constitutional law which seeks to demean it.'[20]

While not a case dealing with employment, we do have the general guidance of cases like *Kennedy* which holds that the right to privacy is not an absolute right and is subject to general considerations such as public order, public morality and the common good.[21] However, the precise constitutional parameters of the law of privacy appear to remain as imprecise as they were in *Desmond v Glackin (No 2)*[22] in which Hanlon J examined the authorities and noted that:

> No precise definition was given of the qualifications which circumscribe that right to privacy, nor perhaps, is it possible to do so. Essentially, when the right is asserted and is

---

[15] *McGee v The Attorney General* [1974] IR 284.

[16] *Kennedy and Arnold v Ireland and The Attorney General* [1987] IR 587.

[17] On the limitations of this approach see the classification of privacy claims of La Forest J of the Canadian Supreme Court in *R v Dyment* [1988] 2 SCR 417 discussed at para **[6.07]**.

[18] See *Re a Ward of Court* [1996] 2 IR 79 and *Haughey v Moriarty* [1999] 3 IR 1.

[19] *Hanahoe v Hussey* [1998] 3 IR 69.

[20] [1998] 3 IR 69 at 108. This protection is given practical meaning (which employer's should note) in this case by way of vicarious liability of the State for actions of the Gardaí, the High Court indicated that 'disclosure emanating from some careless conduct on the part of one or more Gardaí would amount to negligence under the principle set out in *Ward v McMaster* [1988] IR 337 [ie the duty of care owed by public bodies to members of the public].' Following Hanahoe, Quirke J held in *Gray v Minister for Justice* [2007] IR 654 at 668, that the negligence of gardaí in 'leaking' the fact that a sex offender was living in Ballybunion, thereby causing distress and injury to the family with whom he was staying, was a violation of their constitutionally protected right to privacy and peaceful enjoyment of their home.

[21] See, also, *Haughey v Moriarty* [1999] 3 IR 1 at 59.

[22] *Desmond v Glackin, The Minister for Industry and Commerce, Ireland and The Attorney General (No 2)* [1993] 3 IR 67.

alleged to have been breached, the circumstances of each particular case remain to be considered.[23]

[6.06] In his minority decision in *Norris v The Attorney General*,[24] McCarthy J made it clear that it is one thing to recognise a right, but that defining its scope is another. He said:

> How then, to identify the nature of the personal right of privacy? The right to privacy has been called by Brandeis J of the United States Federal Supreme Court "the right to be let alone"…By way of definition it has brevity and clarity and I would respectfully adopt it as accurate and adequate for my purpose but, to a degree, the very definition begs the question. The right to privacy is not in issue; the issue is the extent of that right or the extent of the right to let alone.[25]

It should be noted that Art 40.5 also provides for the protection of privacy, providing as it does for the 'inviolability' of the dwelling. The Law Reform Commission (the 'LRC'), in its *Report on Privacy: Surveillance and the Interception of Communications* refers to '…a very strong protection of privacy within the confines of a "private dwelling".'[26] The report makes it clear that this protection or 'shield' against invasion of privacy is bolstered by the right to private property, and the right to exclude others from one's private property provided in Art 40.3.1°. The LRC explains that the right or prerogative to exclude others from the home is bound up with the concept of property and is therefore effectively, one more way of protecting privacy.[27]

[6.07] And yet this kind of legal protection, based as it is on the notion of private property and the right to exclude others from that private property, would not appear to cater for workers unless they work from home. The LRC states in its report, however, that the right to privacy thus formulated:

> …points to, and further augments, the protection of the inviolability of the dwelling and arguably extends it to cover other real property including a garden, curtilage *or office*.[28] (Emphasis added)

While the right to privacy, then is not necessarily restricted to the home, it is in the home that the right is closest to being absolute.[29] The relevance therefore of a privacy right focused principally on the home and on private property is of limited value to most workers. Employment is generally an activity taking place in public or on the property of the employer. There is a view, however, that privacy is a right which inheres principally in the individual and that it has manifested itself in terms of property only because of historical circumstance.

---

23 [1993] 3 IR 67 at 98.

24 *Norris v The Attorney General* [1984] IR 36.

25 [1984] IR 36 at 101.

26 Law Reform Commission of Ireland, *Report on Privacy: Surveillance and the Interception of Communications* (LRC 57-1998) para 3.27.

27 LRC 57-1998 at para 3.28.

28 LRC 57-1998 at para 3.28

29 LRC 57-1998 at para 2.13.

In *R v Dyment*[30] La Forest J said that:

> ... it may be confusing means with ends to view [the privacy right] as essentially aimed at the protection of property. The lives of people in earlier times centred around the home and the significant obstacles built by the law against governmental intrusions on property were clearly seen by Coke to be for its occupant's "defence" and "repose".[31]... Though rationalized in terms of property in the great case of *Entick v Carrington*,[32] the effect of the common law right against unreasonable searches and seizures was the protection of individual privacy. Viewed in this light, it should not be cause for surprise that a constitutionally enshrined right against unreasonable search and seizure should be construed in terms of that underlying purpose unrestrained now by the technical tools originally devised for securing that purpose. However that may be, this Court...[held that it]... "is ... to protect individuals from unjustified state intrusions upon their privacy"...and that it should be interpreted broadly to achieve that end, uninhibited by the historical accoutrements that gave it birth.[33]

(III) IRISH STATUTORY LAW AND STATUTORY DATA PROTECTION

[6.08] There is no Irish statute dedicated to the concept of privacy.[34] This contrasts, for example, with the position in the United States which has long made such provision in the form of the US Privacy Act 1974. The Irish Law Reform Commission, as we have seen, has made extensive recommendations on privacy and the issues of surveillance and interception of communications.[35] However, with the exception of specific legislation to deal with interception of correspondence and telecommunications,[36] little action appears to have been taken to address the Commission's concerns. One area, however, which has attracted extensive legislative protection, albeit indirectly, is in respect of information held by an employer concerning workers. The following is an examination of those protections from the moment an employer invites or asks for information about a prospective to the many ways in which the employer may thereafter deal with, or 'process' those private items of information which have come to be known in modern legislative parlance as an employee's 'personal data'.

Inquiry, information processing and discrimination

[6.09] An employer inevitably becomes involved in handling the personal information of workers. Before considering the employer's statutory duty with respect to handling or 'processing' the personal data of workers, it should be noted that an employer owes a

---

30 *R v Dyment* [1988] 2 SCR 417.

31 La Forest J gives the following citation: *Semayne's Case* (1604), 5 Co Rep 91 a, 77 ER 194 at 91 b and 195 respectively.

32 *Entick v Carrington* (1765) 19 St Tr 1029, 2 Wils KB 275, 95 ER 807.

33 The case of *Hunter v Southam Inc* [1984] 2 SCR 145 is cited.

34 On the need for a devoted statute see Kelleher, *Privacy and Data Protection Law in Ireland* (Tottel Publishing, 2006) paras 1.02–1.04.

35 Law Reform Commission of Ireland, *Report on Privacy: Surveillance and the Interception of Communications* (LRC 57-1998).

36 The Postal and Telecommunications Services Act 1983, s 98(1). Even this measure, as will be noted, pre-dates the Law Reform Commission's report.

particular duty from the moment of inquiry in terms of equal treatment on certain statutorily protected grounds. It was inappropriate, for example, in the US case of *Soroka v Dayton Hudson Corporation*[37] for applicants to the job of security guard to be asked questions about religious convictions and sexual orientation. Such questions may give rise to a claim of discrimination which is prohibited in Ireland by the Employment Equality Acts 1998–2008. Classic discrimination occurs, for example, where a female job applicant is asked at interview whether she intends to marry and have children.[38] Where this question is not asked of male candidates this amounts to discrimination on the gender ground.[39] The employer must now consider the equality implications of data on nine separate grounds recognised under the Employment Equality Acts, namely: gender, marital status, family status, race, age, religion, disability, sexual orientation or membership of the Traveller Community. Furthermore this duty applies whether the information is used in recruitment or when dealing with grievances, discipline and promotion. It is also important to note that, pursuant to provisions of the Data Protection Acts 1988 and 2003 (considered in detail below) employers may *obtain* data only in as far as it:

(i)   shall be obtained [solely] for one or more specified and lawful purposes;

(ii)   shall not be further processed in a manner incompatible with that purpose or those purposes;

(iii)   shall be adequate, relevant and not excessive in relation to that purpose or those purposes; and

(iv)   shall not be kept for longer than is necessary for that purpose or those purposes.[40]

Domestic workers

[6.10] While the issue of an employer's entitlement to interfere with the privacy rights of an employee who works from their own home has not been addressed by our legislation, a significant legislative step has been taken for those more vulnerable workers who work and live in their employer's home. The Industrial Relations Act 1990 (Code of Practice for Protecting Persons Employed in Other People's Homes)[41] was introduced *inter alia* to provide certain guidance on the safeguarding of the privacy of home workers. Paragraph 5.2.1 of the code provides that an employee may conduct surveillance of the workplace in the home only where there is a statement to this effect in the employee's written statement of terms and conditions of employment.[42] Neither

---

[37] *Soroka v Dayton Hudson Corporation* 1 Cal Rep 2d 77 (1991).

[38] See for example *Prima (Primark) Ltd v Gibson* EE 8/91.

[39] See the Employment Equality Acts 1998–2008, s 6(2)(a).

[40] Data Protection Act 1988, s 2(1)(c) as substituted by Data Protection (Amendment) Act 2003, s (3)(a). It is worth emphasising that the verbs 'obtain' in subparagraphs (i), (ii) and (iii) and 'keep' in subparagraph (iv) have been inserted by way of an amendment in 2003 in place of the original simple use of the word 'kept'. Clearly, the duty is now broader and focuses not only upon the retention of data, but also upon the purpose for which it was sought in the first place.

[41] SI 239/2007. This Code is contained in Appendix A, p 880.

[42] As required by the Terms of Employment (Information) Acts 1994–2001, s 3.

may an employer search a worker's personal belongings without prior written consent. Notably such consent extends to the reading of an employee's personal mail or listening to personal phone calls. Importantly, the code provides that an employer shall not withhold personal documentation such as the employee's passport or bank account documents. An employer is required to take all reasonable steps to ensure that workers are aware of their legal rights and shall not prevent them from access to trade union membership.

Information privacy

[6.11] It will come as no surprise to the modern lawyer that personal information is subject to restricted access. Most of us will have at least some knowledge of the Freedom of Information Act 1997 and the Data Protection Acts 1988 and 2003 (collectively 'the DPA 1988–2003')[43] and the concern expressed in those statutes in relation to access to, and privacy of, personal information. This relatively recent concern for information privacy is principally a reaction to the increasingly transferable nature of records and data due to computerisation.[44] But we examine below the marked shift from the protection of computer data to the wider concern of manual records which now makes these laws very significant indeed.

The discussion here will relate to Data Protection, but it should be noted that the Freedom of Information Act 1997 provides a qualified right to access to information held by public bodies which does not necessarily have to be 'personal data' as with the Data Protection legislation. While s 1(5)(a) of the Data Protection Act 1988 provides that a right conferred by those Acts will not prejudice any right conferred by the Freedom of Information Act, the Data Protection Commissioner (the Commissioner) has issued a notice that underlines that public bodies are now encouraged where a request is made to them under the Freedom of Information Act, that this request should also be taken as a request under the Data Protection Acts without the need for the person to have to make a separate request.[45]

Data protection law is complex and very technical. For these reasons, together with the central importance anticipated for this area of law in the field of employment, a considerable amount of this chapter is dedicated to the origins and concepts as well as the exceptions and duties attached to data protection.

---

[43] See the Data Protection (Amendment) Act 2003, s 23(2) for collective citation of the Acts. The date of commencement of the 2003 Act is 1July 2003 save as to ss 5(a), 16 and 22. The 2003 Act applies to all manual data containing personal data from 24 October 2007: the Data Protection (Amendment) Act 2003, s 23(4).

[44] It is doubtful, however, whether computer files were involved in cases such as *Murphy v PMPA* [1978] ILRM 25 which concerned a Garda request for information relating to an insurance claim pursuant to the Road Traffic (Confidential Information) Regulations 1962. The High Court expressed the view that these regulations were to be construed narrowly according to recognized constitutional privacy rights.

[45] www.dataprotection.ie, 'Data Protection and Freedom of Information in the Public Sector.'

The Data Protection Act

[6.12] Data privacy law is based not upon any indigenous initiative but upon a number of European measures, principally the Council of Europe Convention on the Protection of Individuals with Regard to Automatic Processing of Personal Data 1981 (the 'Council of Europe Convention')[46] and more recently the European Union Directive 95/46/EC (the Data Protection Directive or the DPD). The Data Protection Act 1988 (or 'the DPA 1988') implements the 1981 Convention and the Data Protection (Amendment) Act 2003 (the DPAA 2003) implements the Data Protection Directive.[47] The most immediate distinction to be made between the two Acts and their European instruments is that the first of the Acts was concerned with 'automatic processing' whereas the second measure extends the application of the law to 'manual data'.[48] In other words, we were first concerned to ensure fairness in the access and processing of computer held information but now the duty extends to traditional means of filing and storage of information.

Object and purpose of data protection

[6.13] The Data Protection Directive expressly concerns itself with '… the protection of individuals with regard to the processing of personal data and on the free movement of such data.'[49] Interestingly the 'object and purpose' clause of the Council of Europe Convention states:

> The purpose of this convention is to secure in the territory of each Party for every individual, whatever his nationality or residence, respect for his rights and fundamental freedoms, and in particular his right to privacy, with regard to automatic processing of personal data relating to him.

We can see that while the foremost concern of the Council of Europe Convention is for the human rights of privacy, the Directive does not expressly refer to this right and refers somewhat awkwardly to what might be termed the more European Union oriented

---

[46] Done at Strasbourg on 28 January 1981. Guidelines were generated also during this period by the Organisation for Economic Co-operation and Development (OECD) on the protection of privacy and trans-border flows of personal data (23 September 1980).

[47] The long title of the DPA 1988 states: 'An Act to give effect to the Convention for the Protection of Individuals with regard to Automatic Processing of Personal Data done at Strasbourg on the 28 January 1981, and for that purpose to regulate in accordance with its provisions the collection, processing, keeping, use and disclosure of certain information relating to individuals that that is processed automatically.' The long title of the DPAA 2003 states: 'An Act to give effect to Directive 95/46/EC of the European Parliament and of the Council of 24 October 1995 on the protection of individuals with regard to the processing of personal data and on the free movement of such data, for that purpose to amend the Data Protection Act 1988 and to provide for related matters.'

[48] The DPAA 2003, s 2(a)(ii) of amends the definition in the DPA 1988, s 1 of the term 'data' to include manual data. See, however, the transition provision in the DPAA 2003, s 23(4) which, *inter alia,* delays the implementation of the amendments to the DPA 1988, s 2 as amended, until 24 October 2007.

[49] See long title of the DPD.

objective of 'free movement of data'. On the other hand, the Council of Europe document refers to automated processing of personal data whereas the Directive is not so restricted. The Convention emphasises that a worker is to be treated as an individual and not as a number or statistic.[50]

[6.14] One of the primary purposes of the Data Protection Directive was highlighted in the English case of *Durant v Financial Services Authority*[51] in which Auld LJ said:

> 'The intention of the Directive…is to enable an individual to obtain from a data controller's filing system, whether computerised or manual, his personal data, that is, information about himself. It is not an entitlement to be provided with original or copy documents as such, but…with information constituting personal data in intelligible and permanent form. This may be in documentary form prepared for the purpose and/or where it is convenient in the form of copies of original documents redacted if necessary to remove matters that do not constitute personal data (and/or to protect the interests of other individuals…).'[52]

We return to the right of access (and its exceptions) below but the implications for employers are writ large in this passage. An employee is entitled to know by way of facilitated access not only what information is being processed by the employer but also how it is processed.

Data protection terminology

[6.15] The data protection legislation is very technical and term-specific with many definitions that will probably be new to both the lawyer and non-lawyer. 'Data' means automated data and manual data.[53] 'Automated data' means information that—

(a)   is being processed by means of equipment operating automatically in response to instructions given for that purpose, or

(b)   is recorded with the intention that it should be processed by means of such equipment.[54]

'Manual data' is defined as 'information that is recorded as part of a relevant filing system or with the intention that it should form part of a relevant filing system'.[55]

[6.16] The employer is invariably a 'data controller' who must carefully process, and also provide access to, personal data held in respect of an employee – the 'data

---

[50]   This is a criteria particularly well outlined at the Industrial Relations Act 1990 (Code of Practice for Protecting Persons Employed in Other People's Homes) (SI 239/2007), para 5. This Code is contained in Appendix A, p 880.

[51]   *Durant v Financial Services Authority* [2004] FSR 573, [2003] EWCA Civ 1746 CA.

[52]   *Durant v Financial Services Authority* [2004] FSR 573 at 586, [2003] EWCA Civ 1746 CA at para 26. See further comment on this case at para **[6.17]**.

[53]   DPA 1988, s 1 as amended by DPAA 2003, s 2(a)(ii).

[54]   DPA 1988, s 1(1) as amended by DPAA 2003, s 2(a)(i).

[55]   DPA 1988, s 1 as amended by DPAA 2003, s 2(a)(i). See further 'From protection of computer data to manual data' at para **[6.19]**.

subject'.[56] While the data subject must be a 'natural person', the controller may be a legal personality such as a company or a statutory body.[57] 'Data controller' is defined as 'a person who, either alone or with others, controls the contents and use of personal data.'[58] This is clearly the role of responsibility and contrasts with the more functional role of 'data processor' defined as 'a person who processes personal data on behalf of a data controller …'.[59] Thus where an employer is able to manipulate personal employee data rather than merely act on instructions in relation to it, the employer will be a data controller.[60] Another term which needs to be understood from the outset is the word 'processing'. The entire Act is concerned with those who process personal data and the duty to do so fairly:

> 'processing', of or in relation to information or data means, performing any operation or set of operations on the information or data, whether or not by automatic means, including –
>
> (a) obtaining, recording or keeping the information or data,
>
> (b) collecting, organizing, sorting, altering or adapting the information or data,
>
> (c) retrieving, consulting or using the information or data,
>
> (d) disclosing the information or data by transmitting, disseminating or otherwise making it available, or
>
> (e) aligning, combining, blocking,[[61]] erasing or destroying the information or data.[62]

---

56 See Article 29 – Data Protection Working Party, *Opinion 8/2001 on the Processing of Personal Data in the Employment Context* (5062/01/EN/Final WP 48), 4.

57 DPD, Art 2(d) of the DPD. See also Recital 28 of the DPD where the employers are a partnership, it is astutely noted by Kelleher that the data controller is one or several of the partners but not the firm itself, for want of legal personality: Kelleher, *Privacy and Data Protection Law in Ireland* (Tottel Publishing, 2006) para 8.17 citing *Re a Debtor* [1929] IR 129.

58 DPA 1988, s 1(1). Art 2(d) of the DPD refers to the controller as 'alone or jointly with others determine[ing] the purposes and means of the processing of personal data.'

59 DPA 1988, s 1(1).

60 In *Data Protection Commission v Francis Joseph Griffin* (22 February 1993, unreported), (1993) Times, 5 March, the issue of joint control of data was considered by the English High Court in the context of an accountant who was given personal data by clients which were held on his personal computer. As he was able to manipulate the data in the application of his professional skill, judgement and discretion he was held to be going beyond merely acting on instructions given to him and should therefore be said to control the data (Cited by Kelleher, *Privacy and Data Protection Law in Ireland* (Tottel Publishing, 2006) para 8.11).

61 DPA 1988, s 1(1) as amended by DPAA 2003, s 2(i), states that: '"Blocking", in relation to data, means so marking the data that it is not possible to process it for purposes in relation to which it is marked.'

62 DPA 1988, s 1(1) as amended by DPAA 2003, s 2(a)(v). Article 2(b) of the DPD provides as follows: '"processing of personal data" ("processing") shall mean any operation or set of operations which is performed upon personal data, whether or not by automatic means, such as collection, recording, organization, storage, adaptation or alteration, retrieval, consultation, use, disclosure by transmission, dissemination or otherwise making available, alignment or combination, blocking, erasure or destruction.'

This is clearly an attempt by the legislature to be almost exhaustive, and it is probably fair to say that almost anything you might conceivably do with information would constitute 'processing'.[63]

[6.17] Perhaps the most fundamental concept of all is that of 'personal data' which means data relating to a living individual[64] who can be identified from the data or from the data in conjunction with other information within the possession of the data controller.[65] This concept will be crucial in any response by an employer where there is a suggestion of unfair data processing or where an employer seeks to withhold data from a data subject. It is therefore worthy of detailed consideration.

The definition of personal data provided in the Act is clearly an interpretation of what is meant by 'directly or indirectly identifiable', the wording used in the Directive which defines the concept as 'any information relating to an identified or identifiable natural person (data subject); an identifiable person is one who can be identified, directly or indirectly, in particular by reference to an identification number or to one or more factors specific to his physical, physiological, mental, economic, cultural or social identity.'[66] In *Bodil Lindqvist v Aklagarkammaren I Jonkoping*,[67] the European Court of Justice (ECJ) construed the terms of the Directive broadly, stating that the term encompasses 'any information relating to an identified or identifiable natural person.'[68] The Court of Appeal in England for its part, took a more restrictive view in *Durant v The Financial Services Authority*.[69] The Court chose to limit the meaning of personal data for the purpose of the right of access of the data subject, giving two criteria by which the concept may be gauged. First, one should ask 'whether the information is biographical in a significant sense, that is, going beyond the recording of the putative data subject's involvement in a matter or an event that has no personal connotations, a life event in respect of which his privacy could not be said to be compromised....'[70] The second criterion is '... one of focus. The information should have the putative data subject as its focus rather than some other person with whom he may have been involved or some transaction or event in which he may have figured or have had an interest, for example,

---

63 A&L Goodbody Solicitors, *A Practical Guide to Data Protection Law in Ireland*, (Dublin, Round Hall, 2003) 6.) The ECJ addressed the concept of processing in Case C-101/01 *Bodil Lindqvist* [2003] ECR I-1297 at para 13 saying: '... the act of referring, on an Internet page, to various persons and identifying them by name or by other means, for instance by giving their telephone number or information regarding their working conditions and hobbies, constitutes the processing of personal data ...'

64 Meaning 'natural persons' as opposed to 'legal persons' such as companies which are excluded from the DPD: Recital 28.

65 DPA 1988, s 1 as amended by DPAA 2003, s 2(a)(iv). Information in the possession of the data controller expressly includes data that is likely to come into the possession of the data controller.

66 DPD, Art 2(a).

67 Case C-101/01 *Bodil Lindqvist v Aklagarkammaren I Jonkoping*.

68 [2003] ECR I-1297 at para 24.

69 *Durant v The Financial Services Authority* [2004] FSR 573, [2003] EWCA Civ 1746.

70 *Durant v The Financial Services Authority* [2004] FSR 573 at 587, [2003] EWCA Civ 1746 at para 28.

as in this case, an investigation into some other person's or body's conduct that he may have instigated. In short, it is information that affects his privacy, whether in his personal or family life, business or professional capacity...'[71]

[6.18] With respect it is difficult to find any mandate in the Directive for the use of such language as 'significantly biographical' of 'data subject focus'.[72] The core language used in the Directive and the Act is simply the phrase 'relate to' which does not carry any condition of focus or biographical significance. The Data Protection Commissioner at one point adopted the various points of guidance in *Durant* as direct guidance at www.dataprotection.ie, but has since deleted previous references to the concepts elicited in *Durant*.

The Commissioner now advises that the definition is a very broad one covering any information that relates to an identifiable, living individual but bearing in mind that data may become personal from information that could likely come into the possession of a data controller.[73] The Commissioner defers to the Opinion published by the Article 29 Working Party on the concept of personal data,[74] which gives a broad definition. The Working Party notes firstly that the protection of privacy as a fundamental right is a primary principle of guidance.[75] It then takes the general view in assessing the scope of personal data that the Directive is on the one hand self-limiting, setting out in detail the

---

[71] *Durant v The Financial Services Authority* [2004] FSR 573 at 587, [2003] EWCA Civ 1746 at para 28.

[72] Neither does the Directive say anything of the relevance and proximity of the data subject referred to in *Durant*, nor whether the data concerned is sought for the purpose of ascertaining whether a breach of privacy is occurring nor finally that the data concerned identifies the subject in a manner going beyond his involvement in matter or event with no personal connotations. The House of Lords in England has recently considered the concept of personal data, albeit from a different angle. Lord Hope of Craighead gave the leading judgement in *Common Services Agency v Scottish Information Commissioner* [2008] 1 WLR 1550, a case concerned with a Freedom of Information application by a local parliamentary representative for certain statistical information relating to incidents of childhood leukaemia in the area of Dumfries and Galloway which are adjacent to various nuclear facilities in Scotland. The request was refused on the ground that there was a significant risk of the indirect identification of living individuals due to the low numbers resulting from the combination of the rare diagnosis, the specified age group and the small geographic area. It was argued that as personal data, this information was exempt from disclosure. Lord Hope noted that the Court below had relied upon *Durant* and the two criteria by which Auld LJ defined personal data, but found that the criteria used did not resolve the issue. Indeed he went as far as to say that it had no relevance to the issue before him. Rather, the answer to the problem was to be found in the definition of personal data in English Data Protection Act, s 1(1) read in the light of Council Directive 95/46/EC and in particular recital 26 of the preamble which concerns anonymisation of data by the controller.

[73] www.dataprotection.ie, 'What is personal data?' A similar tension is evident in the guidelines supplied by the Commissioner's UK counterpart, on which see discussion of Jay, *Data Protection, Law and Practice* (3rd edn, London: Sweet and Maxwell, 2007) 123.

[74] Article 29 – Data Protection Working Party, *Opinion 4/2007 – on the Concept of Personal Data* (01248/07/EN WP 136). Adopted 20 June 2007.

[75] *Opinion 4/2007 – on the Concept of Personal Data* (01248/07/EN WP 136) at 4.

areas which are excluded from application, and on the other hand intends a certain flexibility.[76] The Working Party analysed the words and phrases of the definition: 'any information', 'relating to', 'identified or identifiable' 'natural person(s)'. For an employee (a natural person) seeking specific information by which he is identifiable, the crucial issue will be whether the information 'relates to' him her or her.[77] Certainly it will be personal data if it refers to the identity or characteristics or behaviour of an individual.[78] While the words 'relate to' generally mean that data is 'about' the data subject, the Working Party avoid any undue limitation of the concept saying that personal data may concern objects (or processes or events) in the first instances not individuals.[79] Importantly the data need not 'focus' on the putative data subject in order for it to be personal data and thus contradicts a fundamental tenet of the *Durant* analysis.[80] The Working Party however uses a rather abstract and difficult analysis of the phrase 'relating to' which refers disjunctively to the 'content', 'purpose' and 'result' of the data concerned. By this analysis, the data will relate to a data subject, regardless of the purpose of the processing, where there is 'content' which falls within the definition.[81] The 'purpose' of the processing will be relevant having regard to how the data is used or likely to be used which may ultimately relate to the data subject.[82] Finally the Working Party place emphasis on the 'result', that is to say where the use of the data is likely as a result to impact (even in a minor way) on the data subject's rights or interests even where there appear to be no content or purpose implications for the data subject.[83] It would be sufficient to show that the data subject would be treated differently as a result of the processing.

The Irish High Court has given a similarly broad ruling on a comparable provision of the Freedom of Information Act which provides for access to records which 'relate to personal information'. In this specific context the phrase 'relates to' was interpreted in *H(E) v Information Commissioner*[84] to mean that the document in question did not itself

---

[76] Article 29 – Data Protection Working Party, *Opinion 4/2007 on the Concept of Personal Data* (01248/07/EN WP 136), at 5.

[77] Indeed the Working Party appears to take the view generally that this element is the crucial building block of the definition: *Opinion 4/2007 – on the Concept of Personal Data* (01248/07/EN WP 136) at 9.

[78] *Opinion 4/2007 – on the Concept of Personal Data* (01248/07/EN WP 136) at 10. Note also that the Commissioner advises that among the different ways in which an individual can be considered 'identifiable' is obviously the use of a person's full name. He advises that a person can also be identifiable from other information, including a combination of identification elements such as physical characteristics, pseudonyms occupation, address etc. See www.dataprotection.ie, 'What is personal data?'

[79] Article 29 – Data Protection Working Party, *Opinion 4/2007 on the Concept of Personal Data* (01248/07/EN WP 136), 9.

[80] *Opinion 4/2007 on the Concept of Personal Data* (01248/07/EN WP 136) at 11.

[81] *Opinion 4/2007 on the Concept of Personal Data* (01248/07/EN WP 136) at 10.

[82] *Opinion 4/2007 on the Concept of Personal Data* (01248/07/EN WP 136) at 10.

[83] Article 29 – Data Protection Working Party, *Opinion 4/2007 on the Concept of Personal Data* (01248/07/EN WP 136) 11.

[84] *H(E) v Information Commissioner* [2001] IEHC 182.

have to contain personal information to attract an obligation of access. What appears to be required rather is a reference, be it a trivial or insubstantial (but nevertheless direct) reference to the person seeking access.[85]

From protection of computer data to manual data

[6.19] Give the broad implications of data protection it is surprising the courts have not had more work do in terms of interpreting its parameters. It was perhaps the initial restriction of the measures to 'automated processing' (normally meaning computer held data) which lead many to simply ignore the new data protection law as a concern for those who held information on computers. Automatically processed information, for example, for a plumber and his helper might be limited to having a contact number on a mobile phone. However this is an area of the law which now applies in a very real way to those who hold personal information in paper or tangible form and this inevitably includes employers and work providers of every conceivable kind.

[6.20] The Data Protection (Amendment) Act 2003 came into operation on 1 July 2003.[86] Not every provision of the Act, however, was brought into effect on that date.[87] Of particular significance was the transitional provision providing for a delayed deadline in respect of 'manual data'. Section 23(4) of the DPAA 2003 provides as follows:

(4) This Act, in so far as it—

(a)   amends section 2 of the Principal Act [Collection, processing, keeping, use and disclosure of personal data] and applies it to manual data, and

(b)   inserts sections 2A and 2B [processing of personal data and sensitive personal data respectively] into that Act,

comes into operation on 24 October 2007 in respect of manual data held in relevant filing systems on the passing of this Act.'

Therefore, the amendments made by the DPAA 2003 to s 2 of the DPA 1988 were commenced in respect of manual data on 24 October 2007.[88] The provision refers to manual data held in *relevant filing systems* on the passing of this Act.' (Emphasis

---

[85] [2001] IEHC 182 at para 7.

[86] Data Protection (Amendment) Act 2003 (Commencement) Order 2003 (SI 207/2003).

[87] The following three areas were left over until the Minister sees fit to make a commencement order:

    (i)   enforced data access requests in connection with employment and recruitment (s 5(d), in so far as it inserts DPA 1988, s 13(4));

    (ii)   exception from registration obligation of data controllers and data processors concerned with making data available to the public and those solely concerned with manual data (s 16);

    (iii)   certain repeals and revocations (s 22 in so far as it repeals DPA 1988, Sch 3, *ie* public bodies exceptions etc.).

[88] DPAA 2003, s 23(5) permitted measures to be taken at the request of the subject of the data from an earlier date to rectify, erase, block or destroy any data relating to him or her which are incomplete or inaccurate, or cease holding manual data relating to him or her in a way incompatible with the legitimate purposes pursued by the data controller. (contd.../)

added). Presumably there is no duty in respect of manual data which no longer formed part of a filing system on that date.[89]

[6.21] A question which arises is precisely how structured or formal must a filing operation be to qualify as a 'system' and therefore activate the duties under these Acts? The relevant filing system must be a set of information which is structured in such a way that information relating to a particular individual is readily accessible.[90] It is arguably the case that computer-held information is structured, locatable and systematised by the very manner in which it is held whereas a drawer or a shoe box full of bits of paper containing employee personal details is not. Such an interpretation, discouraging as it does the development of coherent filing, and placing in doubt any meaningfully secure and accessible data processing, does not sit easily with the central purposes of the Directive.[91] A conscientious regard for the privacy implications of misplacing personal data surely presupposes knowledge of (and controller-access to) any obtained data to ensure an awareness of the nature and content of the data and the security measures required. The self-defeating potential of an interpretation of the application of the Act to manual records 'only if they are of sufficient sophistication to provide the same or similar ready accessibility as a computerized filing system'[92] is self-evident. Those with control over data need only throw the manual data in a pile and disregard them until the need arises to sort through them not knowing who, when or whether someone else has done so. To this extent the application of the fair processing to personal data under the

---

[88] (\...contd) The Directive provides for general implementation at the latest at the end of a period of three years from the date of its adoption, (25 October 1995) and for the processing of data already held in manual filing systems be brought into conformity with Arts 6, 7 and 8 (provisions as to fair processing and special categories of data processing) of this Directive within 12 years of the date on which it is adopted (Art 32 of the DPD).

[89] See further, DPAA 2003, s 23(5) which permits certain rectification of prior manual data upon written request of the data subject.

[90] DPA 1988, s 1 as amended by DPAA 2003, s 2(a)(i). It should be noted that the definition provided in the Directive does not use the word '"readily", referring rather to 'any structured set of personal data which are accessible according to specific criteria ...': Art 2(c) of the DPD.

[91] See however, Recital 27 of the DPD which is unequivocal in its closing phrase that in the absence of specific criteria laid down by the Member State, files '...which are not structured according to specific criteria, shall under no circumstances fall within the scope of this Directive.'

[92] *Durant v Financial Services Authority* [2004] FSR 573 at 577, [2003] EWCA 1746 at para 48 *per* Auld LJ. It should be noted, however, that it is expressly stated by the Court of Appeal that this dictum must be read '...alongside the narrow meaning of personal data' which narrow meaning appears to be inconsistent with the Directive and does not appear to form part of the data protection regime in this jurisdiction: [2004] FSR 573 at 594, [2003] EWCA at para 46. Auld LJ also spoke of the statutory scheme only having any sensible and practical effect in a context of accessibility ensuring a minimum of time and cost: [2004] FSR 573 at 594, [2003] EWCA at para 46. The Directive and the DPA 1988–2003 only go as far as to use the conditional words: 'impossibility' or 'disproportionate effort': Art 12(c) and DPA 1988, s 4(9)(a), as inserted by DPAA 2003, s 5(d), respectively.

Act is a chicken and egg scenario: it is only fairly processed if it can be easily located but if it cannot be easily located it does not have to be fairly processed.

The following guidance has been given by the Data Protection Commissioner to help identify manual data which forms part of a 'relevant filing system':[93]

(a)   the personal data must be part of a set ie a regular filing system within a particular organisation which the organisation maintains for conducting its business. If the organisation maintains different Departments in different locations, the data subject should specify the subject matter and, if known to him/her, the department/office where he/she believes the file/data is located;[94]

(b)   the set must be structured by reference to individuals or by reference to criteria relating to individuals. If a file exists with a person's name or ID number on it this meets the criterion. If the file does not have a name on it but has sub-divisions with a name or ID, and the file title indicates that it contains personal data eg record of sick absences then this would also meet the criterion. If the file has a subject matter on its title, rather than a person's name, and it is known that the subject matter relates to individuals, then it meets the criterion – eg a file concerning a competition for promotion within a workplace;[95]

(c)   the data must be readily accessible. If files are archived and are not used for decision–making as part of the day-to-day operations of the organisation, and retrieval involves disproportionate effort (or perhaps even cost where a storage company is used), then the data could be said to be not readily accessible. In such a circumstance, the data subject would need to be able to identify particular data by file reference or date so that on a reasonable view of things the data could be said to be readily accessible;[96]

(d)   electronically created documents are usually stored on computer databases. Frequently such documents are copied on to manual files. If, in searching for electronically stored documents by reference to an individual, a data controller

---

[93]   www.dataprotection.ie, 'What is Manual Data and what is a Relevant Filing System?'

[94]   As noted by Kelleher, the phrase 'for conducting its business' is misleading. Kelleher, *Privacy and Data Protection Law in Ireland* (Tottel Publishing, 2006) para 8.56. That author quite rightly takes issue with the suggestion that it is for the data subject to specify the location of the data (paras 8.57-8.58). See the first subparagraph of Art 12(a) of the DPD.

[95]   Lest it be thought that a full data-subject name index is required, the reader's attention is drawn once again to the definition of personal data in DPA 1988, s 1(1) as amended by DPAA 2003, s 2(a)(iv), as 'data relating to a living individual identified either from the data *or* from the data in conjunction with other information that is in, or is likely to come into, the possession of the data controller.' (Emphasis added).

[96]   Pending a judicial consideration in Ireland of the scope of application of the Act to manual data, caution should be exercised in light of the fact that the legislation is self-limiting with regard to back-up data (DPA 1988, ss 2(4) and 5(1)(i)) and yet, the definition of processing in both Directive and Act includes reference to storage (Art 2(b) of the DPD and DPA 1988, s 1(1) as amended by DPAA 2003, s 2(a)(v), respectively).

finds a reference number for a manual file, that manual file should be considered to form part of a relevant filing system.[97]

The Act applies to employers but not employees

[6.22] In the employment context it is the employer who holds the responsibilities under this Act. While the employee may actually execute the processing of data this does not mean he or she is the data controller. It is an express provision of the Act that an employee cannot even be a data processor under the Act.[98] The data controller is clearly more influential than a mere data processor, having control of the content and use of personal data.[99] Not only is the employer a data controller, it seems that *all* employers and direct work providers (and those undertakings which directly service the work relationship) are data controllers as they will retain or control at least some limited information of a personal nature concerning workers. This will include employment agencies and extends to functions which are sub-contracted by the data controller (for example payroll). The employer will control and process data from recruitment throughout the period of employment and will usually continue to be a data controller, through the retention of data, after the relationship has terminated.[100] The defining criteria are that the data can be processed upon the employer's instruction and, more importantly, that the data can be protected from intrusion by a responsible employer.

Exclusions from the Act

[6.23] While the Act excludes employees from being data processors, it should be remembered that other persons undertaking the processing of data on behalf of the employer who are not employees (again, outsourced payroll companies is an example) may well fall under the provisions of the Act as data processors. It should be noted also that the exclusion of employees applies only in so far as they are acting in the course of their employment. It will be a defence for employers where unfair processing occurs

---

[97] This guideline appears to be a more limited restatement of an earlier guideline expressly based on 'specific access criteria' which was in turn a paraphrasing of Art 2(b) of the DPD defining 'personal data filing system' (filing system) to mean 'any structured set of personal data which are accessible *according to specific criteria*, whether centralized, decentralized or dispersed on a functional or geographical basis.' (Emphasis added). The existence of a cross-reference number from electronic to manual fail is an obvious example of specific criteria.

[98] 'Data processor' means a person who processes personal data on behalf of a data controller but does not include an employee of a data controller who processes such data in the course of his employment', DPA 1988, s 1(1). It is conceivable that an employee controls data outside of his or her employment just as it is possible that an employer is a data subject but only if he or she enters an employment relationship in his or her personal capacity. The DPD does not apply to data relating to legal persons (Recital 14). On the meaning of 'employee' which is unfortunately not defined by the Act, see Ch 2, The Contract and Relationship of Employment.

[99] DPA 1988, s 1(1).

[100] A fact which is emphasised in the Working Party. See Article 29 – Data Protection Working Party, *Opinion 8/2001 on the Processing of Personal Data in the Employment Context* (5062/01/EN/Final WP 48), 6–7.

where it was the fault of an employee who was acting outside of the course of employment.

The Act does not apply to data:

- which, in the opinion of the Minister for Justice, Equality and Law Reform or the Minister for Defence, is kept for the purpose of safeguarding the security of the State;[101]
- which must, as a matter of law, be made public;[102]
- which is kept only for the purpose of managing personal, family or household affairs or which is kept for recreational purposes.[103]

Neither does the Act apply in significant respects to data kept solely for the purpose of historical research, or consisting of archives or departmental records.[104] There are various further exclusions to the right of a data subject to access his or her data which are discussed below.[105] Restrictions on data 'processing' (as opposed to data 'access') imposed by the Act do not apply to processing which is:

- required for the purpose of preventing, detecting or investigating 'offences' or apprehending or prosecuting purported 'offenders';[106]
- required for the purpose of assessing or collecting tax;[107]

---

[101] DPA, s 1(4)(a), Art 3(2) of the DPD. This exemption recurs in the Act at DPA 1988, s 8(a), as amended by DPAA 2003, s 9(a), which exempts such data from the restrictions on processing imposed by the Act, subject to certification by a ranking member of the Defence Forces or An Garda Síochána.

[102] DPA, s 1(4)(b). This provision is not required by the Directive and would appear to be at odds with the views taken by the Working Party established pursuant to Art 29 of the Directive (*Opinion 3/99*).

[103] DPA 1988, s 1(4)(c), Art 3(2) of the DPD.

[104] DPA 1988, s 1(3B)(c), as inserted by DPAA 2003, s 2(b). On the meaning of 'archives' and 'departmental records' see ss 2(1)–2(2) of the National Archives Act 1986 respectively. DPA 1988, ss 2, 2A and 2B, as amended by DPAA 2003, ss 3–4 do not apply.

[105] DPA 1988, s 5, as amended by DPAA 2003, s 6. See paras **[6.44]–[6.45]**.

[106] DPA 1988, s 8(b), as amended by DPAA 2003, s 9(a). The Data Protection Commissioner has taken the view that this refers to criminal offences. See guidance given at http://www.dataprivacy.ie/viewdoc.asp?m=m&fn=/documents/guidance/3gm1.htm. It is some small comfort to the data subject that data which is subject to a restriction under the Act or direction of a Court. pursuant to the provisions of the Act, may not be used against the data subject or his or her spouse in criminal proceedings: DPA 1988, s 27(2).

[107] DPA 1988, s 8(b), as amended by DPAA 2003, s 9(a). Tax includes 'any tax' including monies owed or payable to the State, a local authority or a health board. This exemption was considered by the ECJ in the case of Case C-465/00 *Rechnungshof, Neukomm and Lauermann v Österreichischer Rundfunk (Örf)* [2003] ECR I-4989, which concerned an Austrian law obliging employers to submit accounts for audit where payment of salaries and pensions exceeded a given threshold. The employer Örf refused to disclose to the Austrian Court of Audit certain personal information bearing the identity of its employees. The Court of Justice held that the required processing was legitimate in the context of auditing public funds and the economic well-being of the country provided, however, that it was shown that the disclosure is necessary and appropriate. (contd.../)

- required to protect the interests of international relations of the State;[108]
- required urgently for the prevention of injury or other damage to the health of a person or serious loss of or damage to property;[109]
- required pursuant to any law or rule of court;[110]
- necessarily giving rise to legal professional privilege;[111]

Logically, the processing of data which is done because the data subject requested it or unambiguously consented[112] is not subject to the Act's data processing restrictions.[113] It must be emphasised that these exemptions are premised on the relevant processing being 'required' in these various circumstances, a condition presumably for the processor to establish.

Duty to process data fairly

[6.24] The opening substantive provision of the Act requires that the data controller comply with a number of principles in the manner of obtaining and processing personal data.[114] The data shall:

(a) be processed fairly,

(b) be accurate and complete and, where necessary, kept up to date,

---

107 (\...contd) See, also, *Guyer v Walton (Her Majesty's Inspector of Taxes)* [2001] STC (SCD) 75 where disclosure of such information is discussed below in the context of legal professional privilege, considered at para [6.54].

108 DPA 1988, s 8(c), as amended by DPAA 2003, s 9(a).

109 DPA 1988, s 8(d), as amended by DPAA 2003, s 9(a).

110 DPA 1988, s 8(e), as amended by DPAA 2003, s 9(a).

111 DPA 1988, s 8(f), as amended by DPAA 2003, s 9(a). The phrase is 'necessarily giving rise' is used because the wording of the provision rather awkwardly refers to data '*required* for the purpose of obtaining legal advice or for the purposes of, or in the course of, legal proceedings in which the person making the disclosure is a party or a witness.' (Emphasis added). In *Guyer v Walton (Her Majesty's Inspector of Taxes)* [2001] STC (SCD) 75, a solicitor was required to disclose his client's ledger and cash book. The solicitor argued that this would infringe Art 8 of the Convention, legal professional privilege and the English Data Protection Act 1998. The Tribunal was satisfied that the employer was properly obliged by a statutory duty of disclosure under English Taxes Management Act 1970, s 19A. In *Case Study 2/2007* the Data Protection Commissioner considered the use of two medical reports procured as part of personal injury proceedings brought by an employee, not only for the purpose of dismissing the employee but also produced at the hearing of an unfair dismissal hearing brought by the same employee. The Commissioner considered the exemption in s 8(f) and found that this exemption cannot apply to sensitive personal data which has already been improperly processed to support the decision (dismissal) which was the subject matter of the legal process.

112 See Art 7(a) of the DPD. See also DPA 1988, s 2B, as inserted by DPAA 2003, s 4.

113 Strangely s 8(g) which provided as much was deleted by DPAA, s 9(b). See, further, Recital 30 of the DPD. See, also, the exemption of processing subject to the certified requirement of State Security in DPA 1988, s 8(a), as amended by DPAA 2003, s 9(a), mentioned above in the context of DPA 1988, s 1(4)(a), Art 3(2) of the DPD. See footnote 100 above.

114 DPA 1988, s 2(1), as substituted by DPAA 2003, s 3(a).

(c)   (i)   have been obtained only for one or more specified, explicit and legitimate purposes,[115]

     (ii)   not be further processed in a manner incompatible with that purpose or those purposes,[116]

     (iii)   be adequate, relevant and not excessive in relation to the purpose or purposes for which they were collected or are further processed, and

     (iv)   not be kept for longer than is necessary for that purpose or those purposes, and

(d)   appropriate security measures shall be taken against unauthorised access to, or unauthorised alteration, disclosure or destruction of, the data, in particular where the processing involves the transmission of data over a network, and against all other unlawful forms of processing.

Whereas data *controllers* must comply with all of these principles, data *processors* need comply only with the final principle. The first, and most general, of these principles is a duty to obtain and process data fairly.[117] The Act deals with data processing differently depending on the manner in which it was obtained by the data controller. A data controller typically obtains data in two ways: either when the data subject provides the data (direct data) or alternatively, where the data are obtained indirectly by other means (indirectly obtained data).

(i) Fairness in the processing of directly obtained data

[6.25] Where the data are obtained from the data subject directly the controller must, as far as is practicable, make the following information (as a minimum) readily available to the subject.[118]

---

[115] The need to specify purpose is highlighted in *Case Study 2/2007*. There, the controller had used medical reports obtained in the course of personal injury proceedings as a basis both to dismiss the subject (an employee) and to defend the subsequent unfair dismissal action. In response to a Data Protection Commissioner investigation, the controller relied on the purported legitimate purposes of defending personal injury and unfair dismissal proceedings brought by the data subject (their employee), and that s 2(1)(c)(i) specifically envisages that the data may be obtained and used for more than one purpose, provided that both purposes are legitimate. The Commissioner however found there had been a breach of the Act as there had been consent only to the first of these purposes. Consent is considered below under Processing of personal data – consent or necessity?

[116] The Commissioner considered the concept of further processing in *Case Study 2/2007* (on which see preceding footnote). The employer argued that DPA 1988, s 2(1)(c)(ii), as amended by DPAA 2003, s 2(a), only prohibits 'further processing' in so far as that processing is incompatible with the original purpose or purposes and that the use of the reports to defend legal proceedings against the controller under the Unfair Dismissals Act could not be said to be incompatible with the original purpose. The Commissioner rejected the argument, as there was consent only to the first purpose. Consent is considered below under Processing of personal data – consent or necessity?

[117] This requirement is given substance under DPA 1988, s 2D, as inserted by DPAA 2003, s 4.

[118] DPA 1988, s 2D(2), as inserted by DPAA 2003, s 4. On the differing ways various Member States have implemented the Directive's access obligations see *Analysis and Impact Study on the Implementation of Directive 95/46 in Member States* page 19. Available at: http://www.europa.eu.int/comm/privacy.

(a)   the identity of the data controller,

(b)   if the data controller has nominated a representative for the purposes of the Act, the identity of the representative,

(c)   the purpose or purposes for which the data are intended to be processed, and

(d)   any other information which is necessary, having regard to the specific circumstances in which the data are or are to be processed, to enable processing in respect of the data to be fair to the data subject, such as:-

   •   information as to the recipients or categories of recipients of the data,

   •   whether replies to questions asked for the purpose of the collection of the data are obligatory,

   •   the possible consequences of failure to give such replies, and

   •   the existence of the right of access to, and the right to rectify, the data concerning him or her.

(ii) Fairness in the processing of indirectly obtained data

[6.26] Where data is not obtained from the data subject, but indirectly from another data controller, the requirement of transparency goes further. Each of the above conditions must be complied with, but in addition the controller must be in a position to provide the categories of data concerned and the identity of the original data controller.[119] This must be done at the time, and no later, than when the data is first processed or disclosed to a third party.[120] There is provision in the Act that, upon the making of regulations by the Minister, the 'indirect data controller' will not be subject to these conditions.[121] Where the controller complies with the (as yet unknown) conditions of such regulations, the controller will not be required to satisfy the 'fairness' test in s 2D where:

(i)   it would be impossible or would involve a disproportionate effort,[122] or

(ii)   the processing of data by the controller is necessary because the provision of information is required by way of legal obligation (other than a contractual obligation).[123]

These two circumstances seem quite odd when placed together – the first, seemingly a question of convenience, and the second being a strict obligation. The disproportionate effort exception is unfortunately undefined – the provision only goes so far as to say that this would be particularly the case where the processing is for the purpose of historical research or the compiling of statistics. In *Case Study 3/97* the Commissioner has confirmed that a data access request must be complied with however 'inconvenient or disagreeable'. If these are the specific examples contemplated, this suggests that indirect data processing should still be the subject of the strict duty of fairness where the processing is for a more particularised purpose.

---

[119] DPA 1988, s 2D(3), as inserted by DPAA 2003, s 4.

[120] DPA 1988, s 2D(1)(b)(i)\&\(ii), as inserted by DPAA 2003, s 4.

[121] DPA 1988, s 2D(4), as inserted by DPAA 2003, s 4.

[122] DPA 1988, s 2D(4)(a), as inserted by DPAA 2003, s 4.

[123] DPA 1988, s 2D(4)(b), as inserted by DPAA 2003, s 4.

Duty to be accurate, complete and up-to-date

[6.27] Section 2(1)(b) of the DPA 1988[124] provides that data controllers must ensure that data is accurate, complete and, where necessary, kept up-to-date. This principle is also expressed in the International Labour Organisation code of practice and reflects the concern for misrepresentation or misleading information based on the data subject.[125] The duty is not an overwhelming one; it is not a duty to keep all data up-to-date at all times.[126]

Restrictions on disclosure of data and on purpose, extent and duration of data processing

[6.28] There is a detailed requirement in s 2(1)(c)(i) of the DPA 1988–2003 that the keeping of data by data controllers must be for a specified, explicit and legitimate purpose. The time at which the purpose must be determined is the time of collecting it.[127] The use of the word 'keep' (necessarily apposite once the data is obtained), suggests passive holding or storage but does not limit the duties of the data controller because it is further provided that the data shall not be 'further processed' (*eg* disclosed) in a manner incompatible with that purpose or those purposes.[128] Importantly a specified database of an employer may not be used for a purpose which is not expressly contemplated or specified. This point is illustrated in *Case Study 2/2000* where a group of teachers had been engaged in an industrial dispute with the Department of Education. An employer is entitled to withhold payment in such circumstances[129] but the teachers complained about the manner in which the Department had ascertained the identity of employees who were members of a trade union. The method by which a trade union is funded is by a

---

[124] As amended by DPAA 2003, s 3(a).

[125] ILO, *Code of Practice on the Protection of Workers' Personal Data* (International Labour Organisation Geneva, 1997).

[126] It does not apply, for example, to back-up data: DPA 1988, s 2(4).

[127] Recital 28 of the DPD. See also DPA 1988, s 2D(2)(c), as inserted by DPAA 2003, s 4, as to readily available access as to purpose which is a prerequisite (and therefore, practically speaking, an immediate requirement) for fair processing.

[128] DPA 1988–2003, s 2(1)(c)(ii), as amended by DPAA 2003, s 3(a). Clearly there may be one or more purposes. The phrase 'further processed in a manner' was substituted for 'used or disclosed in any manner': DPAA 2003, s 3(a). The result is to restate in a phrase the duty of fair processing but retains the prohibition on incompatible disclosure. Importantly incompatible disclosure does not include a disclosure made '...directly or indirectly by a data controller or a data processor to an employee or agent of his for the purpose of enabling the employee or agent to carry out his duties...': DPA 1988, s 1(1). Employers will clearly be obliged to make personal data of employees available to other employees in order to process pay, scheduling, annual leave, domestic leave and so on. The access must, however, be linked with his or her 'duties'. Thus, the staff of a Human Resource Department will have a work-related interest in accessing personal data held by employers: see *Case Study 1/1998*. Note that disclosure does not take place where identification of the subject depends on further data which is not disclosed: DPA 1988, s 1(1).

[129] Payment of Wages Act 1991, s 5(5)(e).

salary deduction consent form commonly known as a 'check-off' form. The Department accessed their payroll database and confirmed by the use of these forms which staff members were unionised and withheld pay accordingly. The Commissioner could not countenance the 'purpose' contended by the Department being for a specified and lawful purpose.[130] The access process had been vaguely described as 'payment matters' (the description given in the Departments' register entry) but the Commissioner noted that the check-off form said nothing of any purpose for use in confirming salary deduction for participating in industrial action.

Some degree of measured control and arguably an audit as to the extent and necessity of data processing are required as there is an express limitation in the Act that data 'shall be adequate, relevant and not excessive in relation to the purpose or purposes for which they were collected or are further processed'.[131] An example of this would be excessive or irrelevant questions at interview during the recruitment process.[132] Importantly, the data must not be kept for longer than is necessary for those purposes.[133] The only exception to this duty is that it does not apply to data kept for statistical or research or other scientific purposes.[134] The key to these criteria is 'purpose'. It appears to have been satisfactory in *Johnson v The Medical Defence Union*[135] to have retained data in anticipation of claims, complaints and for the purpose of risk management.[136] This is a very wide criterion and may involve retention of data for up to (and in excess of) the 6 year statutory limitation period in a relationship fundamentally based on contract.[137] Where a breach of contract can arise from almost any aspect of employment[138] one

---

[130] DPA 1988, s 2(1)(c)(i) originally provided for a requirement, *inter alia,* that data be kept only for 'specified and lawful purposes'. This was amended by DPAA 2003, s 3(a) to 'specified, explicit and legitimate purposes'.

[131] DPA 1988, s 2(1)(c)(iii), as amended by DPAA 2003, s 3(a).

[132] Although not an employment case, in *Case Study 1/2002,* a motor insurance company asked a motorist if he was married in assessing his insurance application. In response to his complaint, the Garage indicated to the Commissioner that marital status was not taken into account in the insurance process itself. The question was asked for reasons of ensuring equal treatment and non-discrimination. The Commissioner saw no relevance in the question to the complainant's case.

[133] DPA 1988, s 2(1)(c)(iv), as amended by DPAA 2003, s 3(a). See www.dataprotection.ie FAQ 7.2 How long should personal data be held to meet the obligations imposed by the Acts?

[134] DPA 1988, s 2(5)(a), as amended by DPAA 2003, s 3(b). This exception is in turn subject to the proviso that the keeping of such personal data complies with such requirements (if any) as may be prescribed for the purpose of safeguarding the fundamental rights and freedoms of data subjects. It will be important for the effect of this section that it be interpreted as part of the exception in s 2(5) rather than a general provision in respect of s 2.

[135] *Johnson v The Medical Defence Union* [2006] EWHC 321 (Ch).

[136] *Johnson v The Medical Defence Union* [2006] EWHC 321 (Ch) at para 206.

[137] Statute of Limitations 1957, s 11(1)(a). See, also, The Data Protection Commissioner, *The Sixteenth Annual Report of the Data Protection Commissioner 2004,* 32. at

[138] See *Mahmud and Malik v Bank of Credit and Commerce International* [1997] ICR 606 at 623 *per* Lord Steyn.

wonders at the wisdom of limiting the retention, for example, of work performance assessment for two to three years.[139]

Security measures and cost of processing data

[6.29] The onus on the data controllers to ensure that no unlawful data processing occurs includes a duty to take appropriate security measures against unauthorised access, alteration, disclosure or destruction of the data.[140] There is a particularly high security onus where data is transmitted over a network.[141] This onus applies to data processors as well as data controllers.[142] While the implications are clearly inconvenient and will probably involve significant cost to a data controller, the Act expressly includes 'cost' as a factor which the employer may have regard to, in addition to the state of technological development and the cost of implementation.[143] There is also an incremental duty depending on the nature of the data concerned and the possible harm resulting from failure to protect the data.[144] Again, these provisions apply 'in particular' to situations where processing involves transmission of data over a network.[145]

The Act also makes specific reference to employee duties. In an odd formula which appears to place a further burden on employers and (only as a consequence) on their employees, the Act provides that employers are under a duty to ensure that employees and 'other persons at the place of work concerned' are both made aware of *and comply* with the employer's security measures.[146] Codes of practice and public notices will no doubt be a feature of practical compliance with this provision.[147]

Employers who have personal data processed on their behalf (except by employees acting in the course of employment) will have to ensure that this is done in a formal manner (eg a written contract) making it clear that the processing is to be done in compliance with the duty to take appropriate security measures.[148] The controller is under the seemingly onerous obligation to secure guarantees from the processor in terms of technical security and organization measures. Presumably this means that the controller must have recourse to respectable and reliable processors who can give the

---

[139] On which see Article 29 – Data Protection Working Party, *Opinion 8/2001 on the Processing of Personal Data in the Employment Context* (5062/01/EN/Final WP 48), 22.

[140] DPA 1988, s 2(1)(d), as amended by DPAA 2003, s 3(a).

[141] DPA 1988, s 2(1)(d), as amended by DPAA 2003, s 3(a). See European Communities (Electronic Communications Networks and Services) Regulations 2003 (SI 535/2003).

[142] DPA 1988, s 2(2), as amended by DPAA 2003, s 3(a).

[143] DPA 1988, s 2C(1)(a), as inserted by DPAA 2003, s 4.

[144] DPA 1988, s 2C(1)(b), as inserted by DPAA 2003, s 4.

[145] DPA 1988, s 2C(1), as inserted by DPAA 2003, s 4.

[146] DPA 1988, s 2C(2), as inserted by DPAA 2003, s 4.

[147] While the Commissioner advises, that '[n]o matter what technical or physical controls are placed on a system, the most important security measure is to ensure that staff are aware of their responsibilities' he goes on to suggest however that the requirement 'is purely intended as an indication of issues which data controllers and data processors may wish to consider when developing security policies: www.dataprotection.ie, 'Security Guidelines'.

[148] DPA 1988, s 2C(3)(a), as inserted by DPAA 2003, s 4.

appropriate guarantees in this regard.[149] The Act therefore ensures that the controller does not sit back once the matter is handed over to an alternate controller/processor and imposes a further duty on the controller to ensure the security measures guaranteed by the other controller/processor are complied with.[150] The Commissioner gives various advices on his website which include the use of standard certification of information security management systems.[151] At the simplest level, passwords should be placed onto a computer and the password should be kept secure.[152] Smart cards, encryption and biometrics are suggested where more sophisticated measures are appropriate.[153] A controller should also regularly review the nature of access allowed to an individual, in order to ensure that he or she only has access to the data required to perform his or her duties.[154] The Commissioner promotes the use of a logging and reporting systems (with and availability of Logs and Audit trails) to identify abuses and develop appropriate responses, as well as practical measures such as firewalls and automatic screensavers.[155] Where a security breach occurs, the data controller is advised to take steps to prevent further unauthorised access and then to contact the Commissioner's office for investigation and advice.[156]

Exception of data kept for statistical research or other scientific purposes

[6.30] In respect of personal data kept for statistical or research or other scientific purposes, the controller is exempt from the duty both to keep data for no longer than is necessary[157] and to ensure that kept data is not further processed in a manner incompatible with the purposes for which they are kept.[158] It is left open to the Minister to prescribe rules for the purpose of safeguarding the fundamental rights and freedoms of data subject.[159] The obtaining of data for statistical or other scientific purposes will

---

[149] DPA 1988, s 2C(3)(b), as inserted by DPAA 2003, s 4. The Commissioner refers on his website to the use of standard certification of information security management systems. Go to www.dataprotection.ie, 'Security Guidelines', 'IS17799 Certification' where the Commissioner refers with approval to the standards certified by the National Standards Authority of Ireland. Further information on IS 17799 may be found on the NSAI website.

[150] DPA 1988, s 2C(3)(b), as inserted by DPAA 2003, s 4.

[151] See footnote 148 above referring to the Commissioner's approval of standard certification of information security management systems.

[152] www.dataprotection.ie, 'Security Guidelines', 'Access'.

[153] www.dataprotection.ie, 'Security Guidelines', 'Access'.

[154] www.dataprotection.ie, 'Security Guidelines', 'Access'.

[155] www.dataprotection.ie, 'Security Guidelines', 'Access'.

[156] www.dataprotection.ie, FAQ 7.7 'What do I do if there is a security breach?'

[157] DPA 1988, s 2(5)(a), as amended by DPAA 2003, s 3(b). The exception is from the duty set out in DPA 1988, s 2(1)(c)(iv), as amended by DPAA 2003, s 3(a).

[158] DPA 1988, s 2(5)(a), as amended by DPAA 2003, s 3(b). The exception is from the duty set out in DPA 1988, s 2(1)(c)(ii), as amended by DPAA 2003, s 3(b).

[159] DPA 1988, s 2(5)(a), as amended by DPAA 2003, s 3(b). Note that there is an exclusion from the right of access, discussed below, to data held for the purpose of preparing statistics or carrying out research where the subject cannot be identified from the results DPA 1988, s 5(1)(h).

not be unfair merely by reason of the fact that the purpose for which it was obtained was not disclosed at the time.[160] A condition precedent to the application of the exception in respect of statistical and scientific data is that the use of the data will not cause damage or distress to any data subject.[161]

Exception of data processed for journalistic, artistic or literary purposes

[6.31] Section 22A exempts data processed for journalistic, artistic or literary purposes from many of the central protective provisions of the Act.[162] The data controller must *inter alia* hold the reasonable belief that, having regard in particular to the special importance of the public interest in freedom of expression, such publication would be in the public interest. The meaning given to the word publication seems to contemplate even the release or 'leaking' of information.[163]

Processing of personal data – consent or necessity?

[6.32] The Data Protection Directive and the Data Protection (Amendment) Act 2003 Act added further conditions (or specified exemptions) to the Data Protection Act 1988 on the processing of personal data. These are based generally on either *consent* of the data subject or the *necessity* of the data processing (s 2A). It should be noted that there is also a new category of data introduced by that Act which is called 'sensitive personal data' which is subject to even tighter controls still (s 2B, dealt with below).

Where the conditions outlined above are satisfied, the data controller may proceed to process personal data upon satisfying one of four conditions set out in s 2A:[164]

1. Processing of personal data with 'consent or waiver'

[6.33] The first criterion by which s 2A may be satisfied is by the giving of consent by the data subject to the processing of his or her personal data.[165] While it might be argued that in the light of subsequent provision in the Act, that this consent would appear to be sufficient if it is indirect or implied,[166] the giving of consent by a data subject in the employment context attracts the distinct potential of being an imposition rather than a free and voluntary permission. There are not only indications that consent or 'waiver'

---

[160] DPA 1988, s 2(5)(b).

[161] DPA 1988, s 2(5).

[162] Inserted by DPAA 2003, s 21. The protective provisions of the DPA 1988–2003 exempted are (a) DPA 1988, s 2, as amended by DPAA 2003, s 3, other than s 2(1)(d), as amended by DPAA 2003, s 3(a); (b) ss 2A, 2B and 2D, as inserted by DPAA 2003, s 4; (c) DPA 1988, s 3; (d) s 4, as amended by DPAA 2003, s 5; (e) DPA 1988, s 6, as amended by DPAA 2003, s 7; and (f) ss 6A and 6B, as inserted by DPAA 2003, s 8.

[163] See DPA 1988, s 22A(4), as inserted by DPAA 2003, s 21. See generally on competing rights, *Cogley v RTE* [2005] 4 IR 79.

[164] As inserted by DPAA 2003, s 4.

[165] DPA 1988, s 2A(1)(a), as inserted by DPAA 2003, s 4. Art 7(a) of the DPD.

[166] Contrast DPA 1988, s 2A(1)(a), as inserted by DPAA 2003, s 4, with DPA 1988, s 2B(1)(b)(i), as inserted by DPAA 2003, s 4, discussed below at **[6.40]**.

clauses will be strictly scrutinised by the courts,[167] the International Labour Organisation Code of Practice on the Protection of Worker's Personal Data specifically states that the worker's right to data privacy should not be subject to waiver.[168] A significant distinction moreover may be drawn between new employees entering employment and those who are effectively forced to accept such a waiver as a new term of their contracts.[169]

The Data Protection Working Party expressed concerns, in the context of surveillance, about the abuse of consent in the processing of personal data. It observed that employers may seek to legitimise processing through consent and reliance on consent, and that waiver clauses should therefore be confined to cases where the worker has a genuine free choice and is subsequently able to withdraw the consent without detriment.[170] The Data Protection Commissioner has acknowledged the potential of waiver clauses to be imposed rather than freely entered into in the employment context. He advises (in the context of use by employers of biometric data as validation or identification systems at work) that consent is generally not a satisfactory 'legitimiser' in an employment context, as it can be argued that consent is not freely given.[171] The Article 29 Working Party, in its Opinion on the processing of personal data in the employment context, repeatedly refer with open circumspection to reliance solely on the consent of the worker as a basis for departure from worker privacy rights.[172]

While consent is not defined in the Data Protection Act the Directive gives some guidance: Article 2(h) of the DPA 1988–2003 provides that '"the data subject's consent" shall mean any freely given specific and informed indication of his wishes by which the data subject signifies his agreement to personal data relating to him being processed.' It is clear therefore that the consent must not only be freely given but must also be given in circumstances where the employee is fully informed of the specific circumstances of the data processing. This provision is illustrated in *Case Study 2/2000*, discussed above,[173] where the Commissioner found that the accessing by the employer of the complainants' payroll information to ascertain whether they were paid-up members of a trade union constituted unfair data processing. The Commissioner noted that forms used to make the

---

[167] *Rommelfanger v Germany* (1989) 62 DR 151.

[168] At para 5(13).

[169] See *Glasenapp v Germany* (1986) 9 EHRR 25. Ford makes interesting reference to the French legal system which relies less on the contractual agreement and therefore the waiver of rights is less of a focus: Ford 'Two Conceptions of Worker Privacy' (2002) 31(2) Industrial LJ 135, 142–3. It remains to be seen whether a worker can enter a valid agreement which contemplates an element of compensation for abandoned privacy rights: see *O'Keefe v Ryanair* [2002] 3 IR 228 at 231.

[170] Article 29 – Data Protection Working Party, *Working Document on the Surveillance of Electronic Communications in the Workplace* (5401/01/EN/Final WP 55), 21.

[171] www.dataprotection.ie, 'Biometrics in the workplace', 'Fair obtaining and processing'.

[172] Article 29 – Data Protection Working Party, *Opinion 8/2001 on the Processing of Personal Data in the Employment Context* (5062/01/EN/Final WP 48), 4, 23 and 28. See, further, Jay, *Data Protection Law and Practice*, (3rd edn, London: Sweet and Maxwell, 2007) para 2–27.

[173] See para **[6.28]**.

payment did not refer to any such purpose. In these circumstances there could not have been a valid consent.

[6.34] Consent was the central focus in the important *Case Study 2/2007* in which the employer used personal data in the form of two medical reports relating to the employee complainant for three separate purposes, where consent was given in relation to only one of these. The complainant had been involved in an accident at work resulting in a prolonged absence from work. She had attended a consultant neurologist at the request of her employer, in response to personal injury proceedings that against her employer. The complainant made a data access request for copies of the medical reports, but was advised that she should address her request to the company's insurers. In the meantime the complainant was dismissed, presumably for long-term incapability, but her dismissal was expressly stated to be on the basis of the medical evidence available to the company. In the course of a subsequent unfair dismissal hearing, copies of the medical reports were furnished by the employer to a Rights Commissioner and to all persons present at the hearing. These medical reports had not been previously provided to her in response to her access request. The Commissioner's primary finding in *Case Study 2/ 2007* was that the medical reports constituted 'sensitive personal data' obtained for the purpose of defending the High Court personal injury claim. However, the reports were used for two further purposes: the decision to terminate the data subject's employment and to defend the unfair dismissal proceedings. While no data protection issue arose in relation to the use of the medical reports in relation to the decision to terminate employment, the use of the medical reports to defend the unfair dismissal proceedings was done without the data subject's consent. The Act requires that the data shall have been obtained only for one or more specified, explicit and legitimate purposes, and that the data subject is informed of the purposes or purposes for which the data are intended to be processed. The Commissioner stated that the consent of the data subject is the default position for the fair processing and obtaining of personal data. And where it was absent, the data controller may not process personal data unless it can find another basis in the Acts.

The issue of consent also arises as a central concern where an employer or owner transfers or merges the undertaking, and employees continue to be employed in the acquired business. The traditional rule in relation to contracts is that they are bi-lateral, and therefore a contract of employment cannot be assigned to a new employer without the consent of all parties.[174] A business transfer, being an agreement between the buyer and seller of the undertaking, does not involve any input from workers and the buyer does not automatically enter individual contracts with each pre-transfer employee. Community law on the transfer of undertakings has fundamentally altered this common law rule. The European Communities (Protection of Employees on Transfer of Undertakings) Regulations 2003 implement the mandatory requirements of Council Directive 2001/23/EC,[175] which provides that in the transfer of undertakings the

---

[174] *Nokes v Doncaster Amalgamated Collieries Ltd* [1940] AC 1014.

[175] Council Directive 2001/23/EC [2001] OJ L82/16 on the approximation of the laws of the Member States relating to the safeguarding of employees' rights in the event of transfers of undertakings, businesses or parts of undertakings or businesses.

employment of the existing workers is preserved.[176] A very serious issue arises however as to the extent to which data should be protected both in the negotiation process and in the process of preserving and transferring individual employees with the business. Effectively, the body of personal data controlled may be transferred to a new owner without the consent of the data subject.

[6.35] While disclosure to the prospective buyer of non-sensitive personal data may be based on the legitimate interests of the employer,[177] sensitive data should not be disclosed without first ascertaining whether it is possible to satisfy the conditions set out in s 2B of the DPA 1988–2003[178] and then ensuring that that data subjects are informed of disclosures of their personal data pursuant to s 2D of the DPA 1988–2003.[179] To paraphrase the steps which the Data Protection has advised:[180] the data controller proposing to transfer the undertaking should ensure that, where practicable, the data which is initially supplied (as necessary) to the prospective transferee or its agent is anonymised. Even at this stage, it should only disclose personal data after securing formal assurances in respect of confidentiality; the controller should be assured that the data will only be used for the evaluation of assets and liabilities and will be destroyed or returned once this is done; workers should be advised that their employment records are to be disclosed to another organisation before an acquisition or merger takes place and if it is intended to disclose sensitive personal data, the controller should ensure that one of the necessary sensitive personal data conditions is satisfied.[181]

2. Data processing in pursuit of 'vital interest'

[6.36] The second possible way of satisfying s 2A of the DPA 1988–2003[182] is to comply with s 2A(1)(b)[183] which is stated as a list of 'vital interests'. While this list, as expressed in the Act, is a combination of contractual and statutory necessity as well as the prevention of possible damage to health or property of the data subject,[184] the Directive is much more confined in the manner in which it sets out the 'vital interest' condition. Article 7(d) of the DPD provides for the condition as a stand-alone provision and in terms of the vital interests of the data subject only.[185] The Article 29 Working

---

[176] See Ch 19, Transfer of Undertakings.

[177] DPA 1988, s 2A(1)(d) as inserted by DPAA 2003, s 4.

[178] As inserted by DPAA 2003, s 4.

[179] As inserted by DPAA 2003, s 4.

[180] www.dataprotection.ie, go to 'Transfer of ownership of Business' and then to 'Arrangements in relation to Employees'.

[181] The Commissioner goes on to advise in relation to transfers of data outside the Member States to which the Directive is applicable and advise the transferee to ensure it conducts a compliance audit of personal data.

[182] As inserted by DPAA 2003, s 4.

[183] As inserted by DPAA 2003, s 4.

[184] DPA 1988, s 2A (1)(b), as inserted by DPAA 2003, s 4.

[185] Art 7(d) of the DPD provides that '...data may be process but only if ... (d) processing is necessary in order to protect the vital interests of the data subject.'

Party has stated that the relevance of Art 7(d) may be limited to safety issues.[186] It would perhaps be wise to view the Act's conflation of 'vital interest' together with obligations relating to contractual and statutory obligation and prevention of harm to the data subject as a case of cumbersome over-inclusive drafting.

Nonetheless, the phrase 'vital interests' does appear to take on certain meaning, albeit a less onerous and certainly wider meaning, in the DPA 1988–2003. The provisions of the Directive from which the most closely co-relevant exceptions are taken are Arts 7(b) and (c), which provide that personal data may be processed only if the:

- – processing is necessary for the performance of a contract to which the data subject is party or in order to take steps at the request of the data subject prior to entering into a contract; or

- – processing is necessary for compliance with a legal obligation to which the controller is subject.

These criteria appear to be directly implemented by s 2A(1)(b)(i) and s 2A(1)(b)(iii).[187] Notably, the Article 29 Working Party specifically point to these obligations as relevant exceptions in the employment field.[188] The processing and payment of wages is an example of personal data processing which is necessary for the performance of the employment contract.[189] The payment of tax and compliance with social welfare obligations is an example of personal data processing which is necessary for compliance with a legal obligation.[190]

The Act however goes beyond the circumstances anticipated by Article 7(b)–(c) of the DPD to include steps taken at the request of the data subject prior to entering a contract.[191] This would appear to be applicable to consensual medical checks and vetting at recruitment stage. It would also include the placing of an employee on the various voluntary schemes and policies requiring personal data such as pension, health insurance and voluntary training. Finally, the exception extends to processing for the purpose of preventing damage or harm to the data subject. This provision might have been in anticipation of the various health and safety measures now provided for in the Safety Health and Welfare at Work Act 2005[192] but it does not appear to be a direct product of the Directive.[193] The only reference in the Directive to harm is an indirect one, referring to the processing of data which is essential for the data subject's life.[194]

---

[186] Article 29 – Data Protection Working Party, *Opinion 8/2001 on the Processing of Personal Data in the Employment Context* (5062/01/EN/Final WP 48), 15.

[187] As inserted by DPAA 2003, s 4.

[188] As inserted by DPAA 2003, s 4.

[189] As inserted by DPAA 2003, s 4.

[190] As inserted by DPAA 2003, s 4.

[191] DPA 1988, s 2A(1)(b)(ii), as inserted by DPAA 2003, s 4.

[192] See, in particular, Safety Health and Welfare at Work Act 2005, ss 22 and 23.

[193] See, further, Kelleher, *Privacy and Data Protection Law in Ireland* (Tottel Publishing, 2006) para 11.39.

[194] Recital 31 of the DPD.

3. Processing of personal data in the 'public interest'

[6.37] The third alternative way of satisfying s 2A of the DPA 1988–2003 concerns the processing of personal data which may be necessary for a reason which is based on statute or regulation or for the performance of a public function – in other words, for a specific governmental administrative reason or, simply put, in the 'public interest'.[195] While it may be necessary, for example, for a Tribunal to process the personal data of a claimant as necessary in the administration of justice,[196] the Article 29 Working Party in its *Opinion 8/2001* felt that the circumstances in which this criterion will be relevant in employment are likely to be very limited.[197]

4. Processing of personal data for purpose of 'legitimate interest'

[6.38] The fourth and final alternative condition under s 2A is an undefined and potentially wide category. It is provided that personal data processing may be necessary for the purpose of a 'legitimate interest' pursued by the data controller. Again, 'legitimate interest' is unfortunately undefined but extend to legitimate interests pursued not just by the data controller but also by any third party to whom the data is disclosed.[198] The saver placed on this last condition is that the processing must not be unwarranted by reason of prejudice to the fundamental rights and freedoms or legitimate interests of the data subject.[199] We await elaboration of case law and case-studies to give some indication of the parameters of this criterion. There is every indication, however, to suggest that the rights and freedoms saver does nothing to favour the unconditional pursuit of business interests.[200] The Article 29 Working Party was emphatic in its view in the context of employee personal data:

> The legitimate interests of the employer justify certain limitations to the privacy of individuals at the workplace. Sometimes it is the law or the interests of others which impose these limitations. However, no business interest may ever prevail on the principles of transparency, lawful processing, legitimisation, proportionality, necessity and others

---

[195] DPA 1988, s 2A(1)(c), as inserted by DPAA 2003, s 4.

[196] See, for example, *McGowan v Scottish Water* [2005] IRLR 167 where an intrusion upon rights under Art 8 of the Convention was deemed necessary to ensure a fair trial.

[197] Article 29 – Data Protection Working Party, *Opinion 8/2001 on the Processing of Personal Data in the Employment Context* (5062/01/EN/Final WP 48), 16 referring to Art 7(e) of the DPD which provides for processing '…necessary for the performance of a task carried out in the public interest or in the exercise of official authority vested in the controller or in a third party to whom the data are disclosed.'

[198] The Minister for Justice Equality and Law Reform, after consulting with the Commissioner, is given power to make regulations specifying particular circumstances in which this condition may be satisfied: DPA 1988, s 2A(2), as inserted by DPAA 2003, s 4.

[199] DPA 1988, s 2A(1)(d), as inserted by DPAA 2003, s 4.

[200] It is clear from *Case Study 7/2007,* where Aer Lingus was found to be in breach of the Act for having supplied the names and addresses of its staff to HSA Ireland for the purpose of a medical expenses assistance scheme, that a more self-interested or corporate agenda will not impress the Commissioner.

contained in Directive 95/46/EC. Workers can always object to the processing when it is susceptible of unjustifiably overriding his/her fundamental rights and freedoms.[201]

The Working Party clearly seem to think that the legitimate interest exception has a direct application to employment,[202] but it advises that this criterion requires a balance to be struck between the interests of the employer and the interests of workers. Finally, it should be observed that the employee may, at any time on legitimate compelling grounds, file a notice of objection to the processing of data which is sought to be justified on the basis of legitimate interest.[203] Where there is a justified objection, the processing instigated by the controller may no longer involve those data.

Processing of sensitive personal data

[6.39] Where it is clear that the relatively inoffensive use of a person's name and address is now subject to restrictions and conditions,[204] the use of such potentially discriminatory or sensitive information as a person's race, medical status or religion attract even greater precaution. Where all the above conditions are satisfied[205] there is yet one more criteria to be satisfied if the data in question is 'sensitive personal data'. Section 2B of the DPA 1988[206] sets out a list of 13 conditions, one of which must be met to validly process what is referred to as 'sensitive personal data'. Thus, there is a particularly high duty to maintain privacy in respect of 'sensitive personal data' which are defined as data as to:

(a)   the racial or ethnic origin, the political opinions or the religious or philosophical beliefs of the data subject,

(b)   whether the data subject is a member of a trade union,

(c)   the physical or mental health or condition or sexual life of the data subject,

(d)   the commission or alleged commission of any offence by the data subject,[207] or

---

[201] Article 29 – Data Protection Working Party, *Opinion 8/2001 on the Processing of Personal Data in the Employment Context* (5062/01/EN/Final WP 48), 28.

[202] In Article 29 – Data Protection Working Party, *Opinion 8/2001 on the Processing of Personal Data in the Employment Context* (5062/01/EN/Final WP 48), 15-16, the Working Party reviews the criterion and refers with direct relevance to paragraphs (b), (c) and (f) only.

[203] Art 14(a) of the DPD as implemented by DPA 1988, s 6A, as inserted by DPAA 2003, s 8.

[204] This is undoubtedly personal data. It should be noted, however, that an employee may object if his or person data is kept for the purpose of junk-mail advertising or direct marketing of this kind. DPA 1988–2003, ss 2(7)-(8), as amended by DPAA 2003, s 3(d). The right to object does not, however, extend to direct marketing of a political party or a member of such party or by a body established under statute. See definition of 'direct marketing' in DPA 1988, s 1(1).

[205] DPA 1988, s 2B(1)(a), as inserted by of the DPAA 2003, s 4.

[206] As inserted by DPAA 2003, s 4.

[207] DPA 1988, s 2B, as inserted by DPAA 2003, s 4, concludes with what might loosely be called a reference to 'previous convictions / legal proceedings' data.

(e)   any proceedings for an offence committed or alleged to have been committed by the data subject, the disposal of such proceedings or the sentence of any court in such proceedings.[208]

The employer, then, (and because of the complexity of the Act it is worth repeating) must first satisfy ss 2 (fair processing) and 2A (consent or necessity) and in the case of sensitive data also comply with at least one of the conditions contained in s 2B. Some of these options repeat or echo some of the criteria above. They are as follows:

[6.40] The first option is that the consent of the data subject already referred to above[209] must in the case of s 2B be given 'explicitly'.[210] The second alternative under s 2B is related to legal rights or obligations of the controller in connection with employment:[211] sensitive personal data may be processed if it is necessary to do so in order to 'perform' (*sic*) a right or obligation conferred by law on a data controller in connection with employment.[212] Employers are obliged to disclose a whole host of details pertaining, for example, to worker health status discernible from details which they must furnish under the Tax Acts and the Social Welfare (Consolidation) Act 2005. It might also be necessary, for example, to process information in relation to a worker's ethnicity if the employer is to prevent a worker being the subject of racial harassment. There is an obligation placed on the employer by s 14A of the Employment Equality Acts 1998–2008, to take such steps as are reasonably practicable to prevent such harassment. It will also be necessary for employers to disclose personalised information concerning health and fitness[213] information relevant to the granting of work permits, visas and

---

[207] The Minister is empowered to make regulations in respect of the offences committed (or proceedings in respect thereof) by data subjects. This includes acts or omissions (even where only alleged) leading to administrative sanction and any civil proceedings to which the data subject is not just a party held liable but who merely stands as a party thereto: DPA 1988, s 2B(3), as inserted by DPAA 2003, s 4. See generally Thomas 'Employment Screening and the Criminal Records Bureau' (2002) 31(1) Industrial LJ 55.

[208] DPA 1988, s 1(1), as amended by DPAA 2003, s 2(a)(i).

[209] See para **[6.32]**.

[210] DPA 1988, s 2B(1)(b)(i), as inserted by DPAA 2003, s 4. This unusual phraseology does cast a somewhat vague light on the consent provision in s 2A for if the consent must now be explicit what kind of consent is contemplated in the earlier provision? Presumably the consent cannot be indirect or implicit. Does this mean that persons who are unable to appreciate the nature and effect of consent by reason of physical or mental incapacity or age cannot give (as they can under s 2B) consent through a guardian?

[211] It is noted at Article 29 – Data Protection Working Party, *Opinion 8/2001 on the Processing of Personal Data in the Employment Context* (5062/01/EN/Final WP 48), 17, that this is clearly directed at the employment context and 'can have wide effect' depending on the content of Member State domestic law and/or custom an practice.

[212] DPA 1988, s 2B(1)(b)(ii), as inserted by DPAA 2003, s 4. The Minister is empowered to make regulations giving this nebulous provision greater specificity (DPA 1988, s 2B(2), as inserted by DPPA 2003, s 4).

[213] Pursuant to the Safety Health and Welfare at Work Act 2005, or for the purposes of any health insurance agreement in employment.

authorisations,[214] the payment of trade union check-off[215] in addition to ethos related information for schools and institutions availing of ethos exemptions.[216]

The third means by which an employer can satisfy s 2B is by showing that the processing of sensitive personal data is necessary to prevent damage to health or serious damage to property or otherwise to protect the vital interests of either the data subject or another person. This provision states that while it applies in a general way to 'injury' or 'damage to health', where the damage concerned is damage to property it must be 'serious' damage. This provision is also conditional upon the controller being unable to secure consent under s 2A whether through a guardian or where the controller 'cannot reasonably be expected to obtain consent' or finally, where consent is unreasonably withheld.[217] While the provision draft in open ended language (otherwise...protect the vital interest) it is anticipated that the physical and mental health of the data subject (or of another person with whom the data subject's data protection rights conflict) will be the most common factual issue here.[218]

The fourth possibility in satisfying s 2B is by establishing that the processing is carried out in the course of the legitimate activities of a non-profit organisation.[219] The organisation need not be incorporated and the kind of organisation contemplated by the Act is listed as follows: those which exist for political, philosophical, religious or trade union purposes. The provision is confined to persons who are either members of, or who 'have regular contact'[220] with, the organisation concerned in connection with those purposes. This provision will be important for trade unions which in the first instance obviously have to process data concerning 'whether the data subject is a member of a trade union.' However the exemption is not limited to that category of sensitive data. As with other provisions under the Act, there is a precautionary saver to the effect that there must be appropriate safeguards for the fundamental rights and freedoms of data subjects. Finally, the data may not be disclosed to third parties without the consent of the data subject.

[6.41] The list of alternative conditions to satisfy s 2B goes on to include circumstances where: the data subject deliberately makes the data public;[221] where processing is necessary for public administration or administration of justice;[222] where the processing

---

[214] Employment Permits Act 2006.

[215] See *Case Study 2/2000* at www.dataprotection.ie

[216] See Employment Equality Act 1998, ss 12(4) and 37(1), as amended.

[217] DPA 1988, s 2B(1)(b)(iii), as inserted by DPAA 2003, s 4. The difficult process of compliance would appear to be unnecessary given the provision in DPA, s 8(d).

[218] Jay, *Data Protection Law and Practice* (3rd edn, London: Sweet and Maxwell, 2007) 279.

[219] DPA 1988, s 2B(1)(b)(iv), as inserted by DPAA 2003, s 4.

[220] 'Regular conduct' is undefined by the DPA 1988–2003.

[221] DPA 1988, s 2B(1)(b)(v), as inserted by DPAA 2003, s 4.

[222] DPA 1988, s 2B(1)(b)(vi), as inserted by DPAA 2003, s 4. In *Stone v SE Coast Strategic Health Authority* [2006] EWCA 1668 (Admin) the Court of Appeal in England held that the publication of a report of inquiry made pursuant to English National Health Service Act 1977, s 2 was justified under the equivalent sensitive data provision in that jurisdiction: ie the Data Protection Act 1998, Sch 3, para. 7.

of data becomes necessary in contemplation of legal proceedings;[223] where the processing is necessary for medical purposes and the processor operates normal health professional confidentiality;[224] where the information is sought for the purposes contemplated under the provisions of the Statistics Act 1993;[225] where data relating to political opinion is sought on behalf of candidates for elective political office – subject to safeguarding fundamental rights;[226] where the Minister makes regulations by reason of substantial public interest;[227] where the data subject provides information solely for the purpose of monies owed to the State;[228] and finally, where the processing of data is required to administer certain schemes under the auspices of the Department of Social, Community and Family Affairs.[229]

---

[223] DPA 1988, s 2B(1)(b)(vii), as inserted by DPAA 2003, s 4. See *Case Study 2/2007* at www.dataprotection.ie set out in more detail in para **[6.34]**. There, the Commissioner examined the sensitive data provision in s 2B (b)(vii) providing for processing required for the purpose of obtaining legal advice in connection with legal proceedings. The Commissioner found on the facts that the purpose for which the data were originally obtained (a personal injury claim) was not compatible with their production at a hearing of an unfair dismissal claim. In the absence of the data subject's consent, this processing of the data subject's sensitive personal data constituted a breach of the Acts. See, further, *Case Study 1/2004* and *R (on the application of B) v Stafford Combined Court* [2006] EWHC 1645.

[224] DPA 1988, s 2B(1)(b)(viii), as inserted by DPAA 2003, s 4. The provisions speak in terms of the confidentiality usually associated with a 'medical professional'. This is defined as including a registered medical practitioner, within the meaning of the Medical Practitioners Act 1978, a registered dentist, within the meaning of the Dentists Act 1985 or a member of any other class of health worker or social worker standing specified by regulations made by the Minister after consultation with the Minister for Health and Children and any other Minister of the Government who, having regard to his or her functions, ought, in the opinion of the Minister, to be consulted. 'Medical purposes' is defined in s 2B(4) as including the purposes of preventive medicine, medical diagnosis, medical research, the provision of care and treatment and the management of healthcare services. See, also, *Stone v SE Coast Strategic Health Authority* [2006] EWCA 1668 (Admin) mentioned above at footnote 221. *Stone* passed muster on the public administration of justice exception but the Court went on to say that publication of the report of inquiry in that case could have been justified on the basis of medical purposes as it was for the management of healthcare services and was concerned with the care, treatment and supervision of the data subject and had been carried out by relevant professionals.

[225] DPA 1988, s 2B(1)(b)(ix), as inserted by DPAA 2003, s 4.

[226] DPA 1988, s 2B(1)(b)(x), as inserted by DPAA 2003, s 4.

[227] DPA 1988, s 2B(1)(b)(xi), as inserted by DPAA 2003, s 4. See *Stone v SE Coast Strategic Health Authority* [2006] EWCA 1668 (Admin), mentioned at footnote 221, which might be of relevance. See, also, National Treasury Employees Union and Others v Von Raab and Others 489 US 656 (1989) where urine testing of customs employees was justified in the interest of the prevention of crime.

[228] DPA 1988, s 2B(1)(b)(xii), as inserted by DPAA 2003, s 4.

[229] DPA 1988, s 2B(1)(b)(xiii), as inserted by DPAA 2003, s 4.

Right of access of the data subject

[6.42] Perhaps the foremost practical implication of the Act for many employees will be the right of access to personal information held by the employer.[230] This may be a most useful facility for employees and a most inconvenient one for employers where a dispute has arisen and the employee seeks to obtain the contents of his or her personnel file. While the documents contained therein should clarify the issue and resolve the matter, the reality is quite often that access serves the opposite purpose.[231] Data access is a personal right and it appears a request for data access cannot be made on behalf of the data subject.[232] A data subject is entitled on making a written request pursuant to s 4 of the DPA 1988–2003 to be provided with a copy, clearly explained, of any information relating to him or her which is kept on computer or in a structured manual filing system or intended for such a system.[233]

---

[230] 'Access' to data by the data subject is not of itself included in the very broad meaning of the concept of 'processing' and therefore the exemptions set out in DPA 1988, s 8, as amended by DPAA 2003, s 9(a) from the rule against disclosure of personal data do not affect or relate to the right of access (which would, in any event, be made a nonsense of by DPA 1988, s 8(h), as amended by DPAA 2003, s 9(a)).

[231] See, for example, the Data Protection Commissioner's *Case Study 12/06*, where the rather weak excuse that the employer had likely been confused between data protection obligations and duties under employment legislation is referred to. The Commissioner states that he intends 'to use these powers on a routine basis where the right of access to personal data is not granted promptly': www.dataprotection.ie, 'Case Studies'. On the practical parameters drawn on the right to access see *Durant v Financial Services Authority* [2004] FSR 573, [2003] EWCA Civ 1746 in which the English Court of Appeal was not prepared to accept that the data controller is obliged to give full access to every document which happened to mention Mr Durant's name. A clear distinction was made between manual documents and computerised records. Only those manual documents filed in a systemised manner equivalent to (or as accessible as) computer records were deemed to be covered by the duty to give access. See, also, *Johnson v Medical Defence Union* [2007] 1 All ER 464, [2004] EWHC 347 (Ch) and [2006] EWHC 321 which affirmed *Durant* and took a similarly narrow view of the disclosure obligation, holding that it was designed to impose on the data controller an obligation of disclosure only where the data is retained in a form allowing searches which can be undertaken quickly and cheaply. There must therefore be ready access in order for the data to be discoverable. Neither will the data subject necessarily have a right to participate in data control decisions: see comments of Rimer J *at* para 202). This interpretation appears to discourage coherent filing and data processing and does not sit easily with the central purposes of the DPD: but see further, Recital 27 of the DPD. See also section above entitled 'From protection of computer data to manual data'. It should be noted furthermore that the narrow construction placed in *Durant* on the concept of 'personal data' has (ultimately) not been followed by the Data Protection Commissioner and is not consistent with Community jurisprudence. See footnote 71.

[232] The Data Protection Commissioner has expressed clear doubt even in respect of access by parents of guardians to a child's personal data, www.dataprotection.ie, FAQ 'Can anyone else make an access request on my behalf?'

[233] DPA 1988, s 4(1), as amended by DPAA 2003, s 5. See www.dataprotection.ie, 'Accessing your personal information.'

While there is no prescribed format for requests in the legislation, the formula suggested by the Commissioner is the following:

> Dear ...
> I wish to make an access request under the Data Protection Acts 1988 and 2003 for a copy of any information you keep about me, on computer or in manual form. I am making this request under section 4 of the Data Protection Acts.

The access process is not simply the provision of a copy of the documents on a personnel file but an implicit disclosure of how the data is being controlled.[234] It should be noted that a data access request is separate and distinct from a request for confirmation that data is being kept. Such a request is made under s 3 of the DPA 1988–2003 and seeks merely to confirm the keeping of data together with a description of the data and the person for which it is kept.[235] A data access request, on the other hand is, in effect, a request for a copy together with a description of whatever categories of data are being processed whether by the controller or on the controller's behalf. The right of access refers to details of, access to and the form of the personal data being processed. Therefore the subject may insist on being informed of the purpose of the processing, the categories of data being processed as well as the recipients or categories of recipients to whom the data may be disclosed. The controller is obliged to send an 'intelligible' copy or explanation of the information held by the controller and also the source of this information (where revealing the source is not contrary to the public interest).[236] The subject is entitled to a copy of the information in 'permanent form' unless this is not possible, this would involve a disproportionate effort or unless the subject is simply agreeable not to receive one.[237]

[6.43] The employee will be required, if requested, to cover the nominal cost of any such request except in the case of automated procedures which lead to any significant decision being made in relation to him or her.[238] The Act peculiarly provides that in such cases the data subject is entitled to be informed free of charge of the 'logic involved in

---

[234] DPD, Art 12(a) provides that 'Member States shall guarantee every data subject the right to obtain from the controller...confirmation as to whether or not data relating to him are being processed and information at least as to the purposes of the processing, the categories of data concerned, and the recipients or categories of recipients to whom the data are disclosed...'

[235] DPA 1988, s 3. The time limit for responding to such a request is 21 days as opposed to 40 days under a s 4 access request.

[236] DPA 1988, s 3.

[237] DPA 1988, s 4(9), as inserted by DPAA 2003, s 5(d). The Directive, however does not appear to support this saver. Art 12 of the DPD requires Member States to 'guarantee' access 'without restraint'. See Art 13 of the DPD. on the exceptions to the right of access which does not make mention of disproportionate effort.

[238] The nominal cost is currently set at €6.35 pursuant to DPA 1988, s 4(1)(c). This fee must be returned if the request is not complied with. The question of whether a controller can ask for a separate fee in respect of separate categories of data is dealt with somewhat obliquely in DPA 1988, s 4(2). The employer must be given enough information in the request to satisfy himself of the identity of the individual concerned: DPA 1988, s 4(3).

the processing'.[239] This is perhaps an instance where the Act's provision for an explanation wherever information is expressed in terms that are not intelligible to the average person may be of particular importance. The time limit for compliance with data access requests is 40 days after which a complaint may be made in a prescribed form to the Data Commissioner.[240] Delay may not be used as a means of avoiding disclosure of items of information recently obtained.[241] Limitation on the right of access will occur where the information sought concerns other individuals who may not necessarily consent to such access.[242] This limitation does not cover opinions (unless expressly confidential) expressed by another person about the data subject.[243] Work references, for example, which are marked 'confidential' between an ex-employer and a prospective employer are not subject to data access by the data subject.[244] It is clear, however, that

---

[239] The only limitation on this would seem to be in DPA 1988, s 4(12), as inserted by DPAA 2003, s 5(d), where the logic behind a process or decision would adversely affect trade secrets or intellectual property (in particular any copyright protecting computer software).

[240] DPA 1988, s 4(1), as amended by DPAA 2003, s 5(a). The one exception to this is in relation to examination (which is widely defined to include any assessment of the employee) where the time limit is 60 days: DPA 1988, s 4(6).

[241] DPA 1988, s 4(5) refers to 'taking account' of changes made to the data after the request has been received.

[242] DPA 1988, s 4(4). It is implicit that the employer must attempt to comply with the request by editing references to third parties whose consent would otherwise be required. Fair procedures may require that the identity of witnesses and the source of complaints against an employee be disclosed. Para 4(6-7) of the Statutory Code of Conduct on Grievance and Disciplinary Procedures requires that an employer disclose the source of allegations or complaints be given. For example, it was an error which received the criticism of the Employment Appeals Tribunal in *Redmond v Ryanair Ltd* UD123/05 to 'blank out' the names on statements which were crucial to her defence against disciplinary proceedings for misconduct. See, further, *Asda Stores v Thompson* [2002] IRLR 245 where the EAT in the UK ordered that the identity of certain 'whistleblowers' of misconduct remain confidential and anonymous, stating that the Claimants did not need to know the identity of those making statements leading to the misconduct investigation.

[243] DPA 1988, s 4(4A)(a), as inserted by of the DPAA 2003, s 5(b). This is subject to the exception of confidential opinions and also to personal data held by or on behalf of the person in charge of an institution referred to in DPA 1988, s 5(1)(c) and consisting of an expression of opinion by another person about the data subject if the data subject is being or was detained in such an institution.

[244] DPA 1988, s 4(4A)(b)(ii), as inserted by DPAA 2003, s 5(b). Disclosure of work-references would appear then to fall within one of the few exceptions to the general principle that personal information about a person (or 'data subject') must be disclosed to that person under the Data Protection Acts 1988–2003. DPA 1988, s 4(4A)(a), as inserted by DPAA 2003, s 5(b) provides that expressions of opinion about the data subject 'may' be disclosed to the data subject without the consent of the person expressing the opinion. This provision, which is discretionary in any event, is subject to DPA 1988, s 4(4A)(b)(ii), as inserted by DPAA 2003, s 5(b), which provides that s 4(4A)(a) does not apply if the opinion was given in confidence. It is also a provision focusing on the reference giver. The Data Protection Commissioner will construe very strictly an applicant's wishes in respect of the contacting of referees and it is generally advisable that prospective employers consider carefully any reservations expressed by applicants in respect of referees. (contd.../)

the Commissioner takes a restrictive view of the confidential opinion exemption.[245] He has also expressed the view that confidentiality cannot reasonably be applied to appraisals of employees.[246] Transparency is required both in a positive response to a request and also refusals – the Act requires a refusal of a request to be in writing and to include a statement of the reasons for the refusal plus an indication that the subject may complain to the Commissioner about the refusal.[247] An employee cannot make with repeated data access applications of identical or similar nature. The employer can decide if a reasonable interval has elapsed since the last similar request.[248] The Act makes it clear on pain of criminal liability that data access requests cannot be used as a means of obtaining information about a person in connection with their employment by requiring that person to make a request or handing over the results of a request.[249]

An employee's personnel file is, by definition, personal data protected by the Act[250] but data by which the data subject is identifiable is likely to go beyond any designated file to feature in very many aspects of employment administration. Employees are in theory entitled to any of these data falling within the definitions (and outside the

---

[244] (\...contd) Referees should only be contacted if the applicant has been short-listed: *Case Study 3/2004*, www.dataprivacy.ie. Where recruitment agencies become involved in the dissemination of reference data, the Commissioner has expressed concern: see The Data Protection Commissioner, *The Sixteenth Annual Report of the Data Protection Commissioner 2004*, 22. Finally, it should be noted that references may be withheld where they would prejudice proceedings currently in train: see *Chief Constable of West Yorkshire Police v Khan* [2001] IRLR 830.

[245] Available at: www.dataprotection.ie, 'Data Protection Access Requests for Personnel Records'.

[246] Available at: www.dataprotection.ie, 'Data Protection Access Requests for Personnel Records'. On confidentiality see DPA 1988, s 4(4A)(b)(ii), as inserted by DPAA 2003, s 5(b). On appraisals and evaluation materials generally see Article 29 – Data Protection Working Party, *Recommendation 1/2001 on Employee Evaluation Data*, (5008/01/EN/Final WP 42).

[247] DPA 1988, s 4(7).

[248] DPA 1988, s 4(10), as inserted by DPAA 2003, s 5(d). This discretion will, however, be subject to the nature of the data, the purpose for which the data are processed and the frequency with which the data are altered: DPA 1988, s 4(11) as inserted by DPAA 2003, s 5(d)). The Report from the Commission, *First Report on the Implementation of the Data Protection Directive (95/46/EC)*, (COM (2003) 265 Final), indicates a general rule of 12 months save in cases of reasoned justification.

[249] DPA 1988, s 4(13), as inserted by DPAA 2003, s 5(d).

[250] If it is described as a 'file' and dedicated to the specific purpose of employee personnel it is 'part of a set' or at least part of a 'system for conducting business' and it is likely to be 'structured by reference' to the individual employees and thus sufficiently accessible and structured even in the case of manual data. See para **[6.19]**. From protecting computer data to manual data' above. See, further, www.dataprotection.ie, 'Data Protection Access Requests for Personnel Records', where the Commissioner states that personnel 'records' will 'normally' be personal data. However, see, Article 29 – Data Protection Working Party, *Opinion 8/2001 on the Processing of Personal Data in the Employment Context* (5062/01/EN/Final WP 48), 13 which clarifies the Working Party's view that manual documents held outside of the 'file' may very well be included within the term 'personal data'.

exceptions) relevant to data access. Flashpoints concerning employer duties of data protection are likely to come in the form of disclosure to third parties (eg employment references, outsourced pay-roll companies, transfer of undertakings) and withholding of documents on request where disputes arise such as those concerning grievance, discipline and dismissal. The Commissioner has expressly stated that the right of access to personal data supports fair procedures and natural justice which provide that an individual be made aware of the case he or she has to answer.[251] An employee has a right of access to personal data in connection with discipline, grievance and dismissal procedures, even if the disciplinary procedure is ongoing or the subject of legal proceedings such as a tribunal claim or court application.[252]

Exceptions to the right of access

[6.44] While various matters may be exempt from the restrictions placed by the DPA 1988–2003 on 'processing',[253] s 5 sets out a number of exceptions to the separate and free standing right of 'data access'.[254] The exceptions to data which must be disclosed in the context of disputes include opinions given in confidence,[255] data covered by legal professional privilege[256] and data which must be withheld because it may prejudice the investigation of an offence.[257] A further exception to the access obligation which may be relevant is data which would prejudice the data controller's interests in relation to a claim for damages or compensation.[258] While an employer may try to argue that many documents relevant to the dispute could conceivably be classified in this way, the exception is limited to data amounting to 'an estimate' or which is 'kept for the purpose of estimating' the amount of liability of the data controller.[259] The data controller may

---

[251] www.dataprotection.ie, 'Data Protection Access Requests for Personnel Records', 'Discipline, grievance and dismissal'.

[252] www.dataprotection.ie. See below, para **[6.44]** concerning documents are prepared in contemplation of legal proceedings.

[253] DPA 1988, s 8, as amended by DPAA 2003, s 9.

[254] Although the process of providing access might conceivably be seen as processing, the right of access is a separate issue. This would appear to be the only sensible reading of an act which provides exemptions to data access on the one hand (DPA 1988, s 5, as amended by DPAA 2003, s 6) and to processing (DPA 1988, s 8, as amended by DPAA 2003, s 9). See also Kelleher, *Privacy and Data Protection Law in Ireland* (Tottel Publishing, 2006) para 7.18.

[255] DPA 1988, s 4(4A), as inserted by DPAA 2003, s 5(b). An issue arises, however, concerning the expression of opinions given in confidence which are permissible exceptions to data access: see footnote 243. On the giving of opinion evidence as part of investigation see: "Vetting and investigation' below at para **[6.75]**.

[256] DPA 1988, s 5(1)(g).

[257] DPA 1988, s 5(1)(a). The Data Protection Commissioner has taken the view that this refers to criminal offences. See guidance given at:http://www.dataprivacy.ie/viewdoc.asp?m=m&fn=/documents/guidance/3gm1.htm.

[258] DPA 1988, s 5(1)(f).

[259] That this provision is limited to real or actually prospective legal action is underlined by Article 29 – Data Protection Working Party, *Opinion 8/2001 on the Processing of Personal Data in the Employment Context* (5062/01/EN/Final WP 48), 17.

attempt to use this objection in conjunction with legal professional privilege. An insight into the 'increasing tendency' (according to the Commissioner) of parties to refuse to give access to such documents is provided by *Case Study 13/2007* concerning an employee access request to Dairygold Co-Operative Society Ltd/REOX. The company refused to grant access to an Internal Accident Report and a Consulting Engineer's Report stating that both documents were prepared in contemplation of a personal injury claim and were therefore privileged. The Accident Report Form had been created just days immediately following the workplace accident, however, the Consulting Engineers Report was created some nineteen months later. The Commissioner indicated that the claim of legal privilege related only to communications between a client and his professional legal advisers or between those advisers, and that this provision could not be applied to the internal accident report created shortly after the incident (this applying to the Engineer's report only). The data controller continued, through its solicitor, to claim legal privilege on both documents necessitating the serving of an Information Notice by the Commissioner leading ultimately to the release of the Accident Report.

[6.45] An employer is exempt from giving access to data kept for the purpose of assessing or collecting tax or duties,[260] or for the maintenance of order in a place of incarceration.[261] Access does not have to be given to data kept for the purpose of protecting the public against loss occasioned by the dishonesty, malpractice or incompetence of persons in the financial services or persons who have been made bankrupt.[262] Information may be kept undisclosed if this is for the purpose of protecting the interests of international relations of the State,[263] or if it is required by a post-DPA enactment.[264] However, even if the information is kept for one of the foregoing purposes, the subject may still be entitled to the information unless disclosure of this information would impede that purpose.[265] This would seem especially important in terms of investigating an offence where disclosure of the fact of the investigation would lead to destruction of further evidence or frustrating the investigation.

The functions and processing of the Data Commissioner, for example, are not subject to data access.[266] We have already seen that the compilation of data for research or for statistical analysis is considered an activity deserving of exception where the data is not

---

[260] DPA 1988, s 5(1)(a). Tax includes 'any tax' including monies owed or payable to the State, a local authority or a health board.

[261] DPA 1988, s 5(1)(c).

[262] DPA 1988, s 5(1)(d).

[263] DPA 1988, s 5(1)(e).

[264] DPA 1988, s 5(1). Note that this extends to a pre-existing rule of law. However, DPA 1988, s 5(3)(a) permits the Minister to make regulations negating the exceptions set out in s 5(1). For example, see, Adoption Act 1952, s 22(5) and Ombudsman Act 1980, s 9. See, further, Data Protection Act 1988 (Restriction of Section 4) Regulations 1989, SI 81 of 1989.

[265] Note, however, that opinions given in confidence are not excluded by reference to whether such data is kept for that purpose but whether simply they 'consists of an expression of opinion ...etc': DPA 1988, s 4(4A)(a) as inserted by DPAA 2003, s 5(b).

[266] DPA 1988, s 5(1)(g). This is an exemption which also extends to the Information Commissioner: DPA 1988, s 5(1)(gg), as inserted by DPAA 2003, s 6.

made available in a manner which discloses the identity of the subject.[267] For reasons, no doubt associated with administrative cost and convenience, the employer need not disclose data which is genuinely only back-up data.[268] The Act also provides for specific provisions in respect of health care data[269] and social work data.[270]

(IV) EUROPEAN CONVENTION ON HUMAN RIGHTS

[6.46] The European Convention on Human Rights (the Convention/ECHR) is a source of privacy law which offers on the one hand a very flexible and adaptable instrument of protection while at the same time (being expressly a 'qualified right') provides perhaps the most developed system of balancing interests of the individual and of the community.[271]

Article 8 provides as follows:

> (1) Everyone has the right to respect for his private and family life, his home and his correspondence.

> (2) There shall be no interference by a public authority with the exercise of this right except such as is in accordance with the law and is necessary in a democratic society in the interests of national security, public safety or the economic well-being of the country, for the prevention of disorder or crime, for the protection of health or morals, or for the protection of the rights and freedom of others.

---

[267] DPA 1988, s 5(1)(h).

[268] DPA 1988, s 5(1)(i) provides that s 4 does not apply to back-up data. DPA 1988, s 2(4) provides that a data controller is not obliged to ensure that back-up data is accurate and complete and kept up to date as would normally be required under of the DPA 1988, s 2(1)(b), as amended by DPAA 2003, s 3(a).

[269] Pursuant to the Data Protection (Access Modification) (Health) Regulations 1989 (SI 82/1989), data relating to an individual should not be made available to an individual in response to a DPA access request if it would be likely to case serious harm to the physical or mental health of the data subject. Therefore, a person who is not a health professional should not disclose health data to an individual without first consulting the individual's own doctor, or some other suitably qualified health professional.

[270] See Data Protection (Access Modification) (Social Work) Regulations, 1989 (SI 83/1989). These regulations provide that social work data (*ie* referring to work carried on by publicly funded body) should not be made available in response to a s 4 request if it would be likely to cause serious harm to the mental or physical health of the data subject.

[271] It has been said that ECHR law and, in particular, the law deriving from Art 8, may resolve the traditional antagonism in the common law between the property rights of employers and the competing privacy rights of workers: see *R v Dyment* [1988] 2 SCR 417. This is because Art 8(2) offers a framework by which competing rights may be taken account of – and they clearly do not focus on property rights. See generally Feldman, 'The Developing Scope of Article 8 of the ECHR' [1997] EHRLR 265. Ford takes the view that Art 8 jurisprudence will bring the matter to a head: Ford, 'Two Conceptions of Worker Privacy' (2002) 31(2) Industrial LJ 135, 138.

A flexible and adaptable source of law

[6.47] The flexibility and adaptability of Art 8 is undeniable given that it has applied (as we shall see below) to workers and to non-governmental workplaces notwithstanding the express language which appears to render it irrelevant to private as opposed to public sector employers and says nothing at all about the workplace. While the Convention was clearly drafted, by its reference in Art 8(2) to public authorities, to deal with public law rights (ie employers which are state or semi-state bodies or delegates), Allen, Crasnow and Beale observe as follows:

> Although the [Convention][272] has its most immediate effect on public authorities (which include employment tribunals), it undoubtedly has an indirect effect on the way in which we relate to one another; whether employer or employee, trade union official or officer of an employer's organisation, lawmaker, judge, or tribunal member…
>
> …The [Convention] affects employment law at almost every level: from decisions about what is reasonable in an unfair dismissal context to the procedure in the employment tribunal; from decisions about e-mail policies at work to discrimination against persons of different religious faiths…[273]

A further apparent difficulty is that the Art 8 entitlement appears to refer, as does the constitutional protection above, to the home. It may look then to be of some use only to those who work from home.[274] The distinction, first of all, between the workplace and the home has proven increasingly difficult to clearly define.[275] The Data Protection Working Party in its *Working Document on the Surveillance of Electronic Communications in the Workplace* put the matter as follows:

---

[272] The text in fact refers to the English domestic implementing legislation of the ECHR: Human Rights Act 1998.

[273] Allen, Crasnow and Beale, *Employment Law and Human Rights* (2nd edn, Oxford University Press, 2007) paras 1.08 and 1.10. See further below, 'Scope and application of the ECHR' para [6.51].

[274] Even those working from home may find they are not entirely immune from intrusion, for instance, where the equipment used (certainly electronic equipment) belongs to the employer. See *Coleman v ARUP Consulting Engineers* [2004] ELR 11 where the EAT determined that Internet facilities used by a worker are the property of the employer and should not be abused. See, further, *Lambert v France* (2000) 30 EHRR 346 where the employer argued unsuccessfully that its interception of phone communications was valid because the complainant was using a phone belonging to the employers.

[275] Ford comments that: 'Temporal dichotomies such as work/leisure and spatial ones such as workplace/home, which underpin even conservative visions of privacy, may have some use in a world in which workers leave home, go to a factory, work for set periods and clock off. If that worldview was always at best an incomplete vision of work in the past, it is increasingly inadequate to capture the slippery distinctions between work and life outside in modern working arrangements. Home workers, workers on call, workers using employers' computers at home to send private emails, contracts placing restrictions on what workers may do in their spare time – all these illustrate the difficulty of drawing sharp spatial or temporal boundaries between work and life outside.' Ford, 'Two Conceptions of Worker Privacy' (2002) 31(2) Industrial LJ 135, 138.

...conditions of work have evolved in a way that it becomes more difficult today to clearly separate work hours from private life. In particular, as "home office" is developing, many workers continue their work at home using their computer infrastructure provided by the employer...[276]

The law of sexual harassment, for example, provides for protections against mistreatment which occurs 'in the course of employment' which includes circumstances ranging from Christmas parties to taking a lift home in a colleague's car.[277] Many workers mix work and home life seamlessly. Relationships at work certainly, can become more than working relationships. But the distinction between home-workers and non-home-workers notwithstanding, ultimately every person needs some private space during the working day[278] and others simply need to communicate with their family and private associates during normal working hours.[279]

[6.48] ECHR jurisprudence met this somewhat blurred distinction head on in *Niemietz v Germany* where a lawyer's offices were considered to come within the protection of Art 8.[280] The reasoning was as follows:

> The Court does not consider it possible or necessary to attempt an exhaustive definition of the notion of 'private life'. However, it would be too restrictive to limit the notion of an 'inner circle' in which the individual may live his own personal life as he chooses and to exclude therefrom entirely the outside world not encompassed with that circle. Respect for private life must also comprise to a certain degree the right to establish and develop relationships with other human beings. There appears, furthermore, to be no reason of principle why this understanding of the notion of 'private life' should be taken to exclude activities of a professional or business nature since it is, after all, in the course of their working lives that the majority of people have a significant, if not the greatest opportunity of developing relationships with the outside world...especially in the case of a person exercising a liberal profession, his work in that context may form part and parcel of his life to such a degree that it becomes impossible to know in what capacity he is acting at a given time.[281]

---

[276] Article 29 – Data Protection Working Party, *Working Document on the Surveillance of Electronic Communications in the Workplace*, (5401/01/En/Final WP 55), 6.

[277] See Employment Equality Acts 1998–2008, s 14A. For an example of non-statutory assessment of incidents occurring in the course of employment outside of normal work activities see: *Cassidy v Shannon Castle Banquets* [2000] ELR 248.

[278] Allen, Crasnow and Beale, *Employment Law and Human Rights* (2nd edn, Oxford University Press, 2007) paragraph 8.04.

[279] A French court struck down a ban on political or religious discussions conversations 'having nothing to do with work.': *Ministre du Travail v SITA*, Conseil d'Etat 25 January 1989. In another French decision, a rule preventing cashiers in a shop from serving family members was similarly struck down: *Ministre du Travail v Société Obi-France*, Conseil d'Etat, 9 December 1994.

[280] *Niemietz v Germany* (1993) 16 EHRR 97. In the case of *Chappell v UK* (1990) 12 EHRR 1, Art 8 was first interpreted as applying not just to the private home but also professional premises.

[281] *Niemietz v Germany* (1993) 16 EHRR 97 at para 29.

The ECJ was persuaded that the word 'domicile' in the French version of the Convention meant more than simply the 'home'. The Court saw no clear distinction between home and office for some kinds of work. In particular the Court felt that 'to interpret the words "private life" and "home" as excluding certain professional or business activities or premises would not be consonant with the essential object and purpose of Art 8.'[282]

[6.49] The applicability of Art 8 to the workplace was placed beyond question in *Halford v United Kingdom*.[283] In this case it was held that telephone calls made from the workplace are capable of coming within the protection afforded to private life by Art 8 of the Convention. The claimant was an Assistant Chief Constable with Merseyside police who had brought a discrimination claim against her employer, alleging that she had not been promoted because of her gender. In proceedings before the ECJ, she claimed that her right to privacy had been breached when telephone calls from her home and from her office telephones were intercepted by her employer for the purpose of obtaining information with which to defend the discrimination claim. The Court did not accept the employer's argument that calls made from work fell outside the protection of Art 8 or that an employee should have no reasonable expectation of privacy while at work. The Court held that telephone calls made from business premises as well as from home may be covered by the notions of 'private life' and 'correspondence' within the meaning of Art 8. The Court pointed to the fact that no warning had been given to the claimant that calls made on the Merseyside police telephone system would or might be intercepted. A positive finding was made that she did in fact have a reasonable expectation of privacy for such calls.[284]

A qualified right

[6.50] The right to privacy under the Convention is a qualified right.[285] The express considerations which must be observed in Art 8(2) are that any interference with Art 8(1) will be legitimate only if is in accordance with law, if it is necessary in a democratic society and in the various common-good interests which are set out as follows: national security,[286] public safety or the economic well-being of the country, the

---

[282] (1993) 16 EHRR 97 at para 31. See also *Peck v United Kingdom* [2003] ECHR 44 at para 57.

[283] *Halford v United Kingdom* [1997] IRLR 471. See, further, the curious case of *R v Law Society, ex p Pamplin* [2001] EWHC Admin 300. There, a solicitor's clerk was accused of altering an attendance note which gave rise to disciplinary proceedings by the English Law Society. The privacy issue revolved around whether the file of evidence of the public prosecutor (the Chief Constable of Lancashire) should have been disclosed to the Law Society. It was held, on this issue, that Art 8 was not relevant because the matter being considered was concerned with the applicant's employment. This, the Court said, was part of the clerk's public life and not his private life.

[284] *Halford v United Kingdom* [1997] IRLR 471 at paras 12, 17 and 43–46.

[285] 'Absolute' rights in the Convention are limited to Articles 3,4,7,12 and 17 of the ECHR and Article 1 of Protocol 6.

[286] The retention and use of personal data gathered in the employment context carries with it a positive obligation to inform the data subject of the extent and content of the data being held: *Leander v Sweden* (1987) EHRR 433. *Leander* is authority, however, for the permissible exception to that rule where the information is sensitive in the context of national security.

prevention of disorder or crime, the protection of health or morals, and the protection of the rights and freedom of others.

Additionally, criteria has developed to supplement these qualifiers to include a consideration of proportionality,[287] legitimacy, effectiveness,[288] necessity (or reasonable suspicion)[289] and consistency.[290] There is therefore what is referred to as a 'margin of appreciation' in the application of the privacy provision.[291] The test however, of justification of infringements of Art 8(1) would appear in practice to be a test strongly in favour of privacy. The suggestion that the test should be the well-known administrative law test of irrationality, for example, was rejected by the ECJ in *Smith v UK*.[292] In that case the ECJ ruled that a ban on homosexuals serving in the British armed forces was an incursion of Art 8 privacy which is *not* justifiable under Art 8(2). The Court held that restrictions referring to a person's sexual orientation or sexual life concerns one of the most intimate aspects of the person's life and therefore required justification of a particularly strong kind.

Another relevant example of justified incursion is *Guyer v Walton (Her Majesty's Inspector of Taxes)*,[293] a case concerning a solicitor who was required to disclose details in relation to a client's ledger and cash book (one can imagine such a scenario easily arising in respect of an employee). The solicitor argued that this would infringe Art 8 of the Convention. The Special Commissioners, the appellate body deciding the matter, were satisfied, however, that there was ample justification – especially under the disclosure requirements contemplated under s 19A of the English Taxes Management Act 1970 – justifying infringement of Art 8(1).

Scope and application of the ECHR

[6.51] Article 8 is, in strict theory, restricted to the protection against interferences by public authorities. The protections in Art 8 do however have application in the private

---

[287] See *R (on the application of Daly) v Secretary of State for the Home Department* [2001] 2 WLR 1622 (HL).

[288] A measure taken which compromises privacy may not be permissible if it is ineffective in securing its objective, see *Saroka v Dayton Hudson Corporation* 1 Cal Rep 2d 77 (1991).

[289] See *McDonnell v Hunter* (809) F 2d 1302 (1989) holding that strip-searching of prison officers was only justified where it was based upon reasonable suspicion. Cited by Kevin Costello in notes accompanying the Diploma in Employment Law Course, UCD 2003.

[290] In *Anchorage Police Department v Municipality of Anchorage* 24 P 3d 547 (2001), the employer was required to reach a higher burden of justification for subjecting employees to drugs testing where the testing was random rather than a pre-requisite to appointment. Cited by Kevin Costello in notes accompanying the Diploma in Employment Law Course, UCD 2003.

[291] The margin of appreciation is a concept used in the interpretation of the qualified rights under the ECHR. 'The scope of the margin of appreciation will vary according to the circumstances, the subject-matter and its background...For example, the Court has allowed a wide margin of appreciation as regards the framing and implementation of policies in the area of taxation.' Council of Europe, *Explanatory Memorandum to Protocol 12*.

[292] *Smith v UK* [1999] IRLR 734 at para 89.

[293] *Guyer v Walton (Her Majesty's Inspector of Taxes)* [2001] STC (SCD) 75.

sphere and may have a horizontal or vertical application. This means that there is a positive obligation on citizens who are employers to respect the privacy of their fellow citizen employees (horizontal effect) while in addition the State must respect the privacy of all of its citizens (vertical effect).[294] These positive obligations arising from Art 8 have the effect of informing common law and contractual duties involving semi-public and private actors in employment.[295] In a recent English case involving the publication of details of the marriage of Michael Douglas and Catherine Zeta-Jones, Brooke LJ quoted from the case of *X v The Netherlands:*

> [T]hese [positive] obligations may involve the adoption of measures designed to secure respect for private life even in the sphere of the relations of individuals between themselves.[296]

The Court went further in *Von Hannover v Germany*[297] to say as follows:

> ...although the object of Article 8 is essentially that of protecting the individual against arbitrary interference by the public authorities, it does not merely compel the State to abstain from such interference: in addition to this primarily negative undertaking, there may be positive obligations inherent in an effective respect for private or family life. These obligations may involve the adoption of measures designed to secure respect for private life even in the sphere of the relations of individuals between themselves...[298]

Furthermore, where a public body, a Court or a Tribunal, is placed under the scrutiny of Art 8 it will be necessary to consider whether that body has acted in pursuance of a legitimate aim, in accordance with law and in a manner necessary in a democratic society. In the current climate of innovation in respect of the ECHR, it is likely that as regards the requirement to act 'in accordance with law' any such body, the Employment Appeals Tribunal for example, will require clear and established guidelines in dealing with issues of privacy.[299]

Other relevant Convention rights in employment law

[6.52] It is to be noted that the application of the Convention to employment is not confined to the rights provided in Art 8. The Convention also provides for such rights as the prohibition of slavery and forced labour (Art 5), the right to have accusations dealt by way of fair trial (Art 6), freedom of thought, conscience and religion (Art 9), freedom

---

[294] See for example, assessment by Jay of the implications of the Copland decision (discussed in detail below under *"Realms" or "zones" of privacy at work*), Jay, *Data Protection Law and Practice*, (3rd edn, London: Sweet and Maxwell, 2007) para 23–08.

[295] Ford, 'Two Conceptions of Worker Privacy' (2002) 31(2) Industrial LJ 135, 135.

[296] *Douglas v Hello!* [2001] 2 All ER 289 at paras 2–45 *ff* citing *X v The Netherlands* (1986) 8 EHRR 235, at paras 83-86. See, also, Jay, *Data Protection, Law and Practice* (3rd edn, London: Sweet and Maxwell, 2007) paras 2–22 *ff.* A similar conclusion has been reached in the context of the constitutional right to privacy: settled as a general principle in *Tierney v An Post* [2000] 1 IR 536 at 547.

[297] *Von Hannover v Germany* (24 June 2004) ECtHR.

[298] (24 June 2004) ECtHR at para 57.

[299] See the manner in which the English Employment Appeals Tribunal ultimately dealt with *De Keyser Ltd v Wilson* [2001] IRLR 324 examined below at para **[6.58]**.

of expression (Art 10),[300] freedom of assembly and association (Art 11),[301] peaceful enjoyment of property (Art 1, Protocol 1) and finally, the prohibition of discrimination (Art 14).[302] The very fact that these varied and seemingly unrelated rights and freedoms have been considered in an employment context suggests that the Convention is a source of unenumerated rights with a wide potential for further expansion and development. It is clear, for example, that Art 8 does not consist merely of a right to 'private life' but extends this core right to issues of personal safety[303] and even personal autonomy and development.[304] This can range from the right of an employee to freedom in relation to his or her appearance[305] to the right not to be embarrassed in an employment hearing with the use of evidence collected by intrusive means[306] as well as the right not to have medical data used for purposes other than those authorised by the employee providing it.[307] There is an over-lap too from the section above dealing with data protection. The collection of personnel-file information such as sick-notes and medical information as well as information relating to family circumstances has been held to fall within the protection of private life under Art 8.[308]

PART II – APPLYING PRIVACY LAW IN PRACTICE

CONVERGENCE OF SOURCES OF PRIVACY LAW

[6.53] Where once it was difficult to identify a law of privacy, or indeed any practical application for the notion,[309] we are now seeing a convergence of practical application the different sources of privacy law in Ireland. The High Court for instance in *Cogley and Others v RTÉ*,[310] relied on both Irish constitutional case law as well as cases brought before the European Court of Human Rights under Art 8 of the Convention. The High Court approved of the approach taken in *Douglas v Hello! Ltd*,[311] in which the English

---

[300] See *Vogt v Germany* (1996) 21 EHRR 205 (dismissal of teachers maintaining communist beliefs).

[301] *Wilson and Palmer v United Kingdom* [2003] IRLR 128 (trade unions must be free in one way or another to seek to persuade the employer to listen to what it has to say on behalf of its members.)

[302] For an excellent analysis of these and other issues see Allen, Crasnow and Beale, *Employment Law and Human Rights* (2nd edn, Oxford University Press, 2007).

[303] Failure of the State to protect the applicant from pollution was held to be a breach of Art 8 in *Lopez Ostra v Spain* (1994) Application No 303, (1994) 20 EHRR 277 at para 51.

[304] See Grosz, Beatson, and Duffy, *Human Rights: The 1998 Act and the European Convention* (London: Sweet & Maxwell, 2000) 268 *ff*.

[305] Allen, Crasnow and Beale, *Employment Law and Human Rights* (2nd edn, Oxford University Press, 2007) paras 8.158–8.162.

[306] See *Nassé v Science Research Council* [1979] ICR 921.

[307] *MS v Sweden* (1997) 3 BHRC 248.

[308] *Chave née Julien v France* No 14461/88 DR 141.

[309] See Warren and Brandeis, 'The Right to Privacy' (1890) 4 *Harvard LR* 193.

[310] *Cogley and Others v RTÉ* [2005] 4 IR 79.

[311] *Douglas v Hello! Ltd* [2001] QB 967, [2001] 2 WLR 992.

Court of Appeal relied on the jurisprudence of the Convention,[312] notwithstanding the fact that the defendant was a private, and not a public body (once seen as a pre-requisite for the application of the ECHR[313]). Clarke J in *Cogley* acknowledged that privacy is a qualified right using an ECHR analysis, but clearly regarded the right as a dynamic one capable of application in his own analysis which he described as 'degrees of privacy'.[314]

[6.54] The Data Protection Acts 1988–2003, a measure based essentially in European Union law, are now equally referable to Art 8 of the Convention given the obligation within the EU to respect the fundamental rights guaranteed by the Convention.[315] In *Rechnungshof, Neukomm and Lauermann v Österreichischer Rundfunk ('Örf')*[316] the ECJ considered the compliance with the Data Protection Directive of an Austrian law obliging employers to submit accounts for audit where payment of salaries and pensions exceeded a given threshold. Örf, found itself in the position of having to disclose to the Austrian Court of Audit certain personal information bearing the identity of its employees. They refused to do so, relying on the DPD. The ECJ held that the processing involved was 'processing of personal data' under the DPA. Significantly, the Court

---

[312] See also *Brian Robertson Reid v Secretary of State for the Home Department* [2001] EWCA Admin 915 where Art 8 appears to be relied upon directly.

[313] See, further: *X v The Netherlands* (1986) 8 EHRR 235 and *Von Hannover v Germany* (24 June 2004) ECtHR at para 57.

[314] *Cogley and Others v RTÉ* [2005] 4 IR 79 at 91. The case itself concerned an interlocutory application for an application to restrain the defendant from showing certain covertly recorded images as part of a controversial report of the treatment of residents of Leas Cross nursing home. In the course of his judgement, Clarke J expressed the view that the right to privacy, weighed against competing rights such as public interest, varies depending on the individual concerned and their capacity. Thus he separated the rights of patients, care-workers and the owners of the nursing home. The Court was prepared therefore to protect the privacy rights of the residents of the nursing home but found that their privacy could, by appropriate editing, be preserved. The clear implication is that the owners and care-workers are not protected to the same degree.

[315] The Treaty on European Union, Art 6(2). The Data Protection Directive (the DPD) expressly refers in its first recital to Community objectives based on the fundamental rights recognised in the constitution and laws of Member States *and* in the Convention. It should be noted however, that the European Union is not a signatory to the Convention which does give rise to jurisdictional issues: *Opinion 2/94 (Accession to the ECHR)*, [1996] ECR I-1759 at paras 34–35). Nevertheless, the long-standing commitment of the Union to respect fundamental rights inspired by the constitutional traditions of Member States and to have recourse to international human rights treaties of which Member States are signatories should place the application of the privacy right beyond any practical doubt: *Internationale Handelsgesellschaft Case* 11/70 [1970] ECR 1125 at para 4; *Nold Case* 4/73 [1974] ECR 491 at para 13). Note also the language of Lord Hope of Craighead in *Common Services Agency v Scottish Information Commissioner* [2008] 1 WLR 1550 at para 7, where he said of the legislative purpose of the English Data Protection Act that: 'The guiding principle is the protection of the fundamental rights and freedoms of persons, and in particular their right to privacy with respect to the processing of personal data: see recital 2 of the preamble to, and Art 1(1) of the Directive.'

[316] *Rechnungshof, Neukomm and Lauermann v Österreichischer Rundfunk (Örf)* C-465/00 [2003] ECR I-4989.

considered the application of the DPD in the context of Art 8 of the European Convention on Human Rights.[317] It considered the right a qualified one, capable of justification.[318] Thus the Court went on to consider whether the processing was in accordance with law, which it was satisfied it was, but left the proper application of this law to the Member State. The application of this law was deemed to be for a legitimate aim in auditing public funds which was consistent essentially with the 'economic well-being of the country'. Also significant was the finding that the DPD was directly applicable in the Member State.[319] Thus, the Convention is now a means by which a privacy argument can be made in Community law. The Community right to privacy may also be premised on the constitutional recognition in Ireland of a privacy right.[320] If the UK had, as we do in Ireland, recourse to a written Constitution this would have undoubtedly been added to the numerous legal sources relied upon in *Guyer v Walton (Her Majesty's Inspector of Taxes)*.[321] There, a solicitor was required to disclose his client's ledger and cash book. The solicitor argued that this would infringe Art 8 of the Convention, legal professional privilege and the English Data Protection Act 1998. The Tribunal did not find that any of these legal sources were applicable, but was satisfied only after a broad ranging legal analysis that the employer was properly obliged by a statutory duty of disclosure.[322]

The law of privacy is developing apace at almost every level and avenue of legal recourse. The obligations arising from Art 8 appear to have the effect of informing common law and contractual duties involving semi-public and private actors in employment.[323] The Data Protection Acts 1988–2003 now expressly provide for a public and private civil wrong or 'tort' of unfair data processing.[324] Kelleher notes an instance of equitable injunctive action taken by a musician against a newspaper who also relied on the Data Protection (Amendment) Act 2003.[325] The Article 29 Working Party repeatedly refers in its *Opinion 8/2001* to the 'interaction between data protection law and labour law and practice.'[326]

Notwithstanding the clear convergence of law on privacy (and indiscriminate use of sources), it is anticipated that courts and tribunals, certainly at quasi-judicial level, may

---

[317] *Rechnungshof, Neukomm and Lauermann v Österreichischer Rundfunk (Örf)* C-465/00 [2003] ECR I-4989 at paras 72–74.

[318] Pursuant to the normal Art 8(2) analysis, para 84 *ff.*

[319] Art 8(2).

[320] As can be seen above the reception of the right to privacy is both from constitutional traditions of Member States and human rights Convention law. Albeit in this context, the DPD does seem to refer to a free standing 'right to privacy': recitals 2 and 10.

[321] *Guyer v Walton (Her Majesty's Inspector of Taxes)* [2001] STC (SCD) 75.

[322] English Taxes Management Act 1970, s 19A.

[323] See Ford, 'Two Conceptions of Worker Privacy' (2002) 31(2) Industrial LJ 135, 135.

[324] DPA 1988, s 7 as set out below at para **[6.57]**.

[325] Kelleher, *Privacy and Data Protection Law in Ireland* (Tottel Publishing, 2006) para 2.01 citing Burns and McDonald 'Tabloid fights edge on privacy' (2005) The Sunday Times, 23 January.

[326] Article 29 – Data Protection Working Party, *Opinion 8/2001 on the Processing of Personal Data in the Employment Context* (5062/01/EN/Final WP 48), 28.

yet query the practical application of principles that have until recently been recognized in the abstract only. The following therefore is a brief commentary on the issue of the practical application of the different sources before our courts and tribunals.

The common law right to reasonable expectation of privacy applied

[6.55] The reception by a given tribunal to an argument based on privacy will depend largely upon the tribunal before which the argument is made and the source of law relied upon. Common law authorities will always be received as persuasive (depending on the jurisdiction) as they are principally concerned with construing the terms of the employment contract. The common law offers a basis in the implied contractual term of mutual trust and confidence as well as a reasonable expectation of privacy in the workplace, and the contract of employment is generally the platform from which most legal entitlements derive. This source is therefore universally applicable in Ireland. The remedy available in the ordinary course is damages with the possibility of apportionment of contribution.[327]

The Constitutional right to privacy applied

[6.56] The Constitution takes pride of place in the hierarchy of domestic sources of Irish law. However it may be seen as a somewhat abstract and declaratory source of privacy law when cited before a quasi-judicial tribunal presided over by a non-lawyer. Nevertheless it must be said that these same tribunals are asked to apply the abstract principles of natural and constitutional justice on a daily basis in questions of fair procedures.[328] The Constitution provides expressly for the exercise of limited functions and powers of a judicial nature notwithstanding the absence of the status of judge or constitutional court (quasi-judicial employment tribunals).[329] The Constitution also provides for courts of local and limited jurisdiction, namely the District and Circuit courts.[330] While there may be doubt concerning the constitutional status (and therefore jurisdiction) of quasi-judicial tribunals,[331] the role of the District and Circuit courts is clearer: they have no jurisdiction to consider the constitutionality of laws. They have an obligation nonetheless to uphold the Constitution.[332] The superior courts, comprising the High Court and the Supreme Court, are specifically constituted by the instrument itself and must enforce as well as interpret the Constitution.[333] The practical remedy for breach

---

[327] It is submitted that contribution will be an area of relevance for those defendants who argue that claimants did not act to ensure their own privacy. See, for example, the comments of Keane J in *Nason v Cork Corporation* (Unreported HC, 12 April 1991).

[328] The Supreme Court in *Glover v BLN Ltd (No 2)* [1973] IR 388 put paid to the idea that only office holders were entitled the protection of natural and constitutional justice (comprising among other concepts, *audi alteram partem* and *nemo iudex in causa sua*).

[329] Bunreacht na hÉireann, Art 37.1.

[330] Bunreacht na hÉireann, Art 34.3.4°.

[331] See *Government of Canada v Employment Appeals Tribunal* [1991] ELR 57.

[332] *The State (Byrne) v Frawley* [1978] IR 326; *DPP (Stratford) v O'Neill* [1998] 1 ILRM 221 (not applicable to pre-1937 statutes); *DPP v Delaney* [1997] 3 IR 453. Art 34.5.1° requires that judges take an oath to uphold the Constitution.

[333] Bunreacht na hÉireann, Art 34.3.

of Constitutional rights in the ordinary course is damages.[334] There is no question but that the right to privacy under the Constitution consists of positive obligations, not just upon State bodies but also in the sphere of the relations of individuals between themselves.[335] It will be recalled, finally, that even where it is demonstrated that there is a right to privacy in a given context, it is not an absolute right but one which must be weighted against or balanced with the exigencies of the common good.[336]

European and statutory law on privacy applied

[6.57] It is trite to say that statutory employment protections in Ireland owe a substantial debt to European Community law[337] and that Community law enjoys supremacy over conflicting national law.[338] Thus, the various sources of statutory entitlement which concern privacy in the workplace may be relied upon as of course,[339] but where such statutes derive from Community law the question arises not whether the Community law takes precedence but whether the supremacy of the Community law may be argued directly before the domestic court or tribunal. This question has been answered in part by the Grand Chamber decision of the ECJ in *Impact v Minister for Agriculture and Food*.[340] The ECJ now recognises that statutory employment tribunals are 'national courts' for the purpose of Community law and may therefore in the first instance interpret that law and in the second instance must enforce it.[341] The Court went further on the question of forum to observe that the enforcement of Community law entitlements must not be complicated or made difficult by an unwieldy system of separate fora or tribunals.[342] Where the Data Protection Acts 1988–2003 which implement the directly effective Data Protection Directive are of such an important part of privacy protection in employment, the enforcement of those rights will no doubt be raised not just before the superior courts but at local and quasi-judicial levels of the system. The dedicated officer charged with data protection complaints is the Data

---

[334] In *Kennedy and Arnold v Ireland and The Attorney General* [1987] IR 587, notwithstanding that the High Court was satisfied that the plaintiffs had not suffered any loss, and that the reputations of the plaintiffs were vindicated, it held that the injury done to the plaintiffs' right to privacy was serious and awarded £20,000.00 to each of the principal plaintiffs and ordered that the transcripts of recorded telephone conversation be given over to them.

[335] Settled as a general principle in *Tierney v An Post* [2000] 1 IR 536 at 547.

[336] *Haughey v Moriarty* [1999] 3 IR 1 at 58. The implications of this in the employment context remains to be explored by the Courts but see generally Kelleher, *Privacy and Data Protection Law in Ireland* (Tottel Publishing, 2006) paras 2.09 *ff*.

[337] Just some examples are the Protection of Employees (Part Time Work) Act 2001, Protection of Employees (Fixed Term Work) Act 2003, Organisation of Working Time Act 1997, Maternity Protection Act 1994 and 2004, Employment Equality Acts 1998–2008 and the Terms of Employment (Information) Acts 1994–2001.

[338] Bunreacht na hÉireann, Art 29.4.3°.

[339] Subject to specified jurisdiction, time limits and forum within the statute concerned.

[340] Case C-268/06 *Impact v Minister for Agriculture and Food* [2008] EU ECJ.

[341] Case C-268/06 *Impact v Minister for Agriculture and Food* [2008] EU ECJ at para 55.

[342] Case C-268/06 *Impact v Minister for Agriculture and Food* [2008] EU ECJ at para 51.

Protection Commissioner and it is unclear, how far that officer's power of interpretation and enforcement extend[343] and, more importantly, it is unclear how a data protection issue is to be resolved where it arises before a tribunal hearing an employment claim.

The Data Protection Commissioner for his own part performs an enforcement and compliance function ultimately with potential of criminal sanction at his instigation.[344] There is an appellate jurisdiction to the Circuit Court[345] with an appeal on a point of law to the High Court.[346] Perhaps most significant in terms of actionable remedies, certainly in the context of converging sources of law, is s 7 of the DPA 1988 which provides as follows:

> For the purposes of the law of torts and to the extent that that law does not so provide, a person, being a data controller or a data processor, shall, so far as regards the collection by him of personal data or information intended for inclusion in such data or his dealing with such data, owe a duty of care to the data subject concerned.[347]

The European Convention on Human Rights applied

[6.58] The European Convention on Human Rights Act 2003 (the ECHRA 2003) came into force in Ireland on the 31 December 2003. The Act gives the ECHR domestic effect in so far as quasi-judicial bodies which deal with employment claims must 'act in a manner compatible with the Convention' and the Irish courts must 'interpret and apply

---

[343] DPA 1988, s 9(1C-1D), as inserted by DPAA 2003, s 10, and DPA, s 10(1A), as inserted by DPAA 2003, s 11(b), have not yet been the subject of judicial analysis but give the officer a role which extends from the monitoring and supervision and dissemination of information to the investigation and enforcement of data protection. Neither is it clear what standard of proof is applied or how the burden of proof is apportioned. DPA 1988, s 10(1)(a), as inserted by DPAA 2003, s 11(a), provides that the Commissioner may investigate upon complaint or if he is 'otherwise of the opinion' that there may be a contravention. In the former case he needs only to be satisfied that the complaint is not 'frivolous or vexatious': DPA 1988, s 10(1)(b)(i). In terms of defences, it is clear that mistake is no defence: *Case Study 3/2003*.

[344] DPA 1988, s 22, and DPA 1988, s 31, as amended by DPAA 2003, s 19.

[345] DPA 1988, s 26. The first such appeal was brought before Cork Circuit Court by Don O'Connor, a solicitor who obtained and used a former Client's conviction order for perjury as evidence before the Law Society when that client lodged a complaint against him. The appeal successfully overturned the Data Protection Commissioner's decision that this was unfair data processing. (2008) The Sunday Times, 3 August.

[346] DPA 1988, s 26(3)(b).

[347] The Irish courts have been express in their pronouncements of how breaches of tort or constitutional right concerning privacy may be measured: *Conway v Irish National Teachers Organisation* [1991] 2 IR 305 at 317. In the absence of any Court determination on the matter of DPA 1988, s 7 or data privacy breaches, it should be noted that there is a distinctly resistant attitude in the Courts for actions seeking damages for distress and reputation pursuant to the wrongful data processing in our neighbouring jurisdiction of England and Wales: *Colman v General Medical Council* [2005] EWCA 433 and *Johnson v The Medical Defence Union* [2006] EWHC 321. Breach of the Data Protection Acts would not appear in that jurisdiction to be a separate and independent cause of action: *Ogle v Chief Constable of the Thames Valley Police* [2001] EWCA Civ 598.

[provisions applicable to the claim] in a manner consistent with the Convention.'[348] It remains to be seen how the parties or their representatives will be received when they complain on the basis of Art 8 of the Convention. Given how limited the position is in relation to damages for breach of the Convention,[349] it is an area of law more relevant in principle, parameters and proper procedure than it is in terms of remedy in the breach. Certainly the entitlement to receive a fair trial will be a considerable priority for tribunals. In *McGowan v Scottish Water* it was held that a court or tribunal may properly adduce evidence, notwithstanding the fact that it has been gathered in breach of Art 8, where to do so is adjudged to be necessary in order to secure a fair hearing as required both by common law and by Art 6 of the Convention. In *Chairman and Governors of Amwell View School v Doghery*,[350] the English EAT was unimpressed by the argument that the family or private lives of a disciplinary board were affected by evidence consisting of covert recordings obtained by an employee before a disciplinary hearing. For reasons based on fair procedures (and not the law of privacy or Art 8), the Tribunal deemed admissible that part of the evidence recorded when the claimant was present before the Board whereas the part consisting of the Board's private deliberations was not admitted.

Employment tribunals may be prevented from using or publicising matters which impinge upon the privacy of the parties before them.[351] Tribunals must find a balance between the interests of the opposing parties and also, where relevant, between the interests of the claimant and public policy.[352] Some quasi-judicial bodies, for example, Rights Commissioners, conduct hearings in private.[353] Their concern for privacy rights will extend to issues, for example, of the relevance (or presence) of witnesses during

---

[348] See ECHRA 2003, ss 2 and 3 respectively. The definition section of the Act defines "organ of the State" as including a tribunal or any other body which is established by law or through which any of the legislative, executive or judicial powers of the State are exercised (Except the President, the Oireachtas, either House of the Oireachtas, a Committee of either such House or Joint Committee of both such Houses or a court: see ECHRA 2003, s 1(1). There is a clear role in the Act for the Courts in *interpreting and applying* rules of law to do so in a manner compatible with the State's obligations under the Convention. There is a second distinct function assigned to 'organs of the State' (which includes the many tribunals and mediators which deal with employment disputes) – these must *perform their functions* in a compatible matter.

[349] ECHRA 2003, s 3.

[350] *Chairman and Governors of Amwell View School v Doghery* [2007] IRLR 198.

[351] See, for example: *Chief Constable of West Yorkshire Police v A* [2002] ICR 128 (the equivalent domestic legislation in England and Wales is the Human Rights Act 1998).

[352] In *Woolgar v Chief Constable of Sussex Police* [2001] 1 WLR 25, the English Court of Appeal found that a statement given by a nurse to the police during an investigation of the suspicious death of a patient should be disclosed to the regulatory body – the United Kingdom Central Council. An interesting, if distinct, comparison can be made with the duty under Unfair Dismissals Act 1977-07, ss 8(11) & 8(12), whereby the EAT is obliged to inform the revenue or the Department of Social, Community and Family Affairs of any fraud relevant on the public revenue.

[353] An exception to this rule is the provision for unlawful deduction claims under the Payment of Wages Act 1991.

hearings, indirect publication of their decisions,[354] the opening of private correspondence or matters which either party argues should not be disclosed to the other side. Where hearings are held in public, however, there will always be the competing freedom of expression or the freedom to report on proceedings, under the Convention. While freedom of expression may be a formidable opposing interest to privacy interests, it clear that freedom of expression may be less compelling than the right to privacy.[355] The Convention should not be viewed as a sequential list of rights obeying any kind of strict hierarchy (though it is true some rights are always more compelling than others – Art 2, for example, the right to life). Indeed, as Allen, Crasnow and Beale comment, '[i]t is fundamental to human rights jurisprudence that the rights are indivisible, so that there can be no automatic hierarchy of rights.'[356]

Competing rights were a consideration in the English Tribunal decision in *De Keyser Ltd v Wilson*[357] The claimant, Miss Wilson, had claimed that she had been subjected to stress at work culminating in her constructive dismissal. The employer instructed a doctor to examine her and furnished to the doctor personal information it considered relevant to her claim of stress. The employer had not taken the precaution of seeking an authority from Miss Wilson for the release of such details. She objected to the evidence being given from this examination and sought a fresh 'untainted' examination. The Industrial Tribunal, hearing the dismissal claim at first instance, perhaps took its duty under the Convention somewhat too far. The Tribunal, not content with acceding to Miss Wilson's request for a fresh examination, refused to hear the employer on the basis of the employer's 'scandalous' breach of the right to respect for private and family life in Art 8. On appeal, the English Employment Appeal Tribunal took a very different view of the letter. Lindsay J for the EAT was satisfied that the letter was admissible.[358] One of the grounds for overturning the first instance finding was the failure of the first instance

---

[354] Rights Commissioner *ex tempore* decisions are delivered in written form (various statutes are relevant but see the requirement to 'set forth' in the establishment provision, Industrial Relations Act 1969, s 13(3)(a)). They are not published, as for example, are those of the Equality Tribunal, the Labour Court and more recently the Employment Appeals Tribunal, each of which publish their decisions on-line (see for example the obligation to publish decision of the Labour Court, Employment Equality Act 1998, s 89(1)). The decisions at first instance are, however, synopsised and reviewed in the journals and anecdotal evidence suggests they have been relied upon before other rights commissioners and appellate tribunals. The Rights Commissioner service notably (and probably because their decisions are not published on any website) do not anonymise the identities of the parties in the decision as do the Equality Tribunal and the Labour Court.

[355] See *Douglas v Hello Ltd* [2001] QB 967.

[356] Allen, Crasnow and Beale, *Employment Law and Human Rights* (2nd edn, Oxford University Press, 2002) para 8.5.3.

[357] *De Keyser Ltd v Wilson* [2001] IRLR 324.

[358] Among the more significant facts were that: the letter was written before the English Human Rights Act 1998 came into effect: it was the complainant who actually initiated the proceedings giving rise to the revelations in the letter; there was no 'public body' concerned as envisaged by the 1998 Act; and the information contained in the letter was not obtained surreptitiously nor was it given in confidence.

forum to consider what practical prejudice the letter would have in the context of its function, namely to fairly try the issue of dismissal. The question the original tribunal should have asked was whether the letter presented an obstacle to a fair trial. Lindsay J concluded that the right to respect for one's privacy is qualified by the right of both parties to have a fair trial.[359]

The more practical implications of this case may be that the EAT was satisfied that a doctor specifically assigned to examine a case already operates under confidentiality rules.[360] Most significant, however, was the Tribunal's appreciation of a tribunal's function in assessing admissibility of private information. The Tribunal seemed quite satisfied that Miss Wilson would be given advance sight of the letter for the purpose of a tribunal hearing and would therefore have adequate opportunity to object to the letter, as she had done.[361] In the various quasi-judicial bodies dealing with employment claims there will certainly have to be an increased awareness of privacy law. However, in the light of the above, it would seem that privacy will simply add a new aspect to the admissibility rules of evidence. Where such bodies strive for a more flexible and less legalistic approach to the formalities of presenting a case, there will no doubt be an informal approach taken with regard to privacy issues.

Damages may be awarded for breach of the ECHRA 2003[362] in circumstances where an organ of the State does not perform its functions in a manner compatible with the State's obligations under the Convention.[363] Such a remedy however, would be very much a last resort as it is a pre-condition upon any recourse to such remedy that no other remedy in damages is available.[364]

'Realms' or 'zones' of privacy at work

[6.59] There have been many attempts to formulate specific fields of application of the right to privacy. It is probably true to say that it has defied a clear legal conceptualisation. Lord Woolf commented that 'an interference with privacy is not even

---

[359] A similar scenario was dealt with by the Data Protection Commissioner in *Case Study 2/2007* which emphasises the principle of consent to the specific purpose for which personal data is being used and the sensitive nature of medical information. See further above section entitled 'Processing of personal data – consent or necessity?' para **[6.32]**.

[360] It should be noted that under the Data Protection (Access Modification) (Health) Regulations 1989 (SI 82 of 1989), data relating to an individual should not be made available to an individual in response to a Data Protection Act access request if it would be likely to cause serious harm to the physical or mental health of the data subject. Therefore, a person who is not a health professional should not disclose health data to an individual without first consulting the individual's own doctor or some other suitably qualified health professional. Hospitals and doctors are also subject to the scrutiny of Art 8 of the European Convention on Human Rights. The disclosure of medical records must be subject to effective and adequate safeguards against abuse: *A Health Authority v X and Others* (2001) 2 Family Law Reports 673, CA 21 Dec 2001.

[361] Also relevant is the settled principle that a litigant who complains of injury accepts that his or her medical privacy must necessarily be compromised in pursuit of that claim: *McGrory v ESB* [2003] 3 IR 407.

[362] ECHRA 2003, s 3.

[363] ECHRA 2003, s 3(1).

[364] ECHRA 2003, s 3(2).

like an elephant, of which it can be said it is at least easy to recognise if not define.'[365] La Forest J, however, in the Canadian Supreme Court decision in *R v Dyment,*[366] refers to three 'zones' or 'realms' of privacy:[367]

- those involving territorial or spatial aspects,
- those related to the person, and
- those arising in the information context.

Territorial claims were originally, according to La Forest J, legally and conceptually tied to property, which in effect confined this kind of claim of privacy to the home.[368] He referred however to Stewart J in *Katz v United States,*[369] who had commented that people, and not places are protected.[370] La Forest J then proceeded to consider the concept of personal privacy, quoting from a Canadian Task Force report on computers and privacy:

> ...this sense of privacy transcends the physical and is aimed essentially at protecting the dignity of the human person. Our persons are protected not so much against the physical search (the law gives physical protection in other ways) as against the indignity of the search, its invasion of the person in a moral sense.[371]

La Forest J turned finally to information privacy, stating that this is also based on the notion of the dignity and integrity of the individual. He quoted the same source as follows:

> This notion of privacy derives from the assumption that all information about a person is in a fundamental way his own, for him to communicate or retain for himself as he sees fit.[372]

---

[365] *R v Broadcasting Standards Commission ex parte BBC* [2000] 3 WLR 1327 at 1332 *per* Lord Woolf.

[366] *R v Dyment* [1988] 2 SCR 417.

[367] He relies in fact on the analysis in Report of the Task Force Established by the Department of Communications/Department of Justice, *Privacy and Computers*, (Ottawa: Information Canada, 1972), especially at 12–14.

[368] It is perhaps ironic that the right to privacy (of employees) encounters a particular conceptual difficulty when it conflicts with the right to property (of employers) which is the very right to which privacy owes its origin. Ford comments that: 'On one conception of privacy, property rights simply trump privacy rights; on another, privacy rights cannot be waived and are resistant to what is 'agreed' in the contract. Nor is there, I think, an actual or emerging consensus which will resolve this question; the concept is simply a contest one.' Ford, 'Two Conceptions of Worker Privacy' (2002) 31(2) Industrial LJ 135, 138.

[369] *Katz v United States* 389 US 347 (1967).

[370] 389 US 347 (1967) at 351. The decision in *Katz* adopts a view taken by Brandeis J in what was a dissenting view in *Olmstead v US* 277 US 438, 478 (1928) that the Fourth Amendment of the US Constitution should be interpreted as a right to left alone.

[371] *R v Dyment* [1988] 2 SCR 417 at para 21 citing the Report of the Task Force established by the Department of Communications/Department of Justice, *Privacy and Computers*, (Ottawa: Information Canada, 1972), 13.

[372] [1988] 2 SCR 417 at para 22.

[6.60] It is this last dictum which fits most easily with the current body of laws protecting work-place privacy in Ireland. It is proposed to deal with the major areas of concern in work-place privacy as set out below, while accepting that there is a considerable degree of overlap between them. An attempt is made here to include the physical aspect of privacy but to acknowledge that it is only in cases of spontaneous physical searches or perhaps 'live' surveillance that privacy does not concern a process, in one form or another, of 'data gathering'. The issues examined are the following:

- Physical or psychological privacy, including:
  - (i)   searches
  - (ii)   medical questions, testing or analysis
- Information privacy, including:
  - (iii) monitoring of e-mails, internet abuse and misuse of computer data
  - (iv)   ordinary telephone and correspondence interception
  - (v)   vetting and investigation
  - (vi)   video or CCTV surveillance

It should be noted that the *recording* of information gathered in categories (i) and (ii) inevitably become 'data' and therefore, as we come to grips with the concept of 'data protection' it is probable that data protection will, in time, come to form the mainstay of workplace privacy protections. Equally, the basic technology involved in categories (iii) and (iv) and the nature of the surveillance mean that often cases concern both kinds of surveillance.[373] An example can be seen in the case of *Copland v The United Kingdom*,[374] which provides a good illustration of the variety of privacy abuses which can occur in a single case in the workplace where a manager takes on the role, effectively, of a covert intelligence agent.

[6.61] Lynette Copland ('the applicant') was a personal assistant to a third-level College Principal. The Applicant became aware she had been the subject of extensive surveillance by the College Deputy Principal over a period of several months (for example, her movements throughout the campus were being tracked). The discovery came when the applicant's stepdaughter told her that she had been contacted by the college in relation to certain e-mails originating from a home computer she shared with the applicant. The applicant spoke with a number of her colleagues who confirmed that the Deputy Principal had subjected them to similar inquiry. The applicant submitted that the Deputy Principal suspected that she was having an affair with the Principal. The College claimed that the Deputy Principal merely suspected she was abusing college property, including Internet facilities. There was no privacy policy or contractual search or surveillance consent clause in place for staff at the College.

The College argued that the monitoring of telephone usage consisted merely of analysis of the college telephone bills showing telephone numbers called, the dates and times of the calls and their length and cost. The applicant believed, however, that there

---

[373] On the use of Global Positioning Technology in the employment context see the Labour Court recommendation in *Mac Rental Ltd v AGEMOU* LCR 18460 (Labour Court).

[374] *Copland v The United Kingdom* (2007) 45 EHRR 37.

had been detailed and comprehensive logging of the length of calls, the number of calls received and made and the telephone numbers of individuals calling her. The applicant's Internet usage was monitored by analysing the web sites she visited, the times and dates of the visits and their duration.

[6.62] The Court made reference to the apparent apprehension on the part of the College that a law was soon to come into effect in the UK which meant that the practices described above would no longer be lawful.[375] It was clear, however, for the purpose of Art 8(2), that this law was not in place at the time. The Court addressed the argument that this was not a case of phone-tapping but legitimate access to College phone bills as follows:

> The mere fact that these data may have been legitimately obtained by the College, in the form of telephone bills, is no bar to finding an interference with rights guaranteed under Article 8.[376]

The Court went on to state unequivocally that the mere *storage* of personal data can give rise to a breach and it is not necessary for such data to be used against the applicant,

> Moreover, storing of personal data relating to the private life of an individual also falls within the application of Article 8 §1.[377] Thus, it is irrelevant that the data held by the college were not disclosed or used against the applicant in disciplinary or other proceedings.[378]

Significantly, while, the Court did not preclude the possibility that the monitoring of an employee's use of a telephone, e-mail or internet at the place of work may in certain circumstances be considered 'necessary in a democratic society' in pursuit of a legitimate aim, as there had been no domestic law regulating monitoring at the relevant time, the interference could not have been 'in accordance with the law' as required by Art 8(2) of the Convention.[379]

(i) Searches

[6.63] In *O'Connor v Ortega*[380] the United States Supreme Court was prepared to accept there was a 'reasonable expectation' of workers to the privacy of their office desk or filing cabinet. While searches of desk drawers and lockers should generally be conducted on the basis of express consent there is little doubt that physical contact with

---

[375] Telecommunications (Lawful Business Practice) Regulations (SI 2699/2000).

[376] *Copland v The United Kingdom* (2007) 45 EHRR 37 at 43. The Court said that '...the use of information relating to the date and length of telephone conversations and in particular the numbers dialled can give rise to an issue under Art 8 as such information constitutes an "integral element of the communications made by telephone" (see *Malone v the United Kingdom*, judgment of 2 August 1984, Series A no. 82, § 84).'

[377] Citing *Amann v Switzerland* (2000) 30 EHRR 843 at para 65.

[378] *Copland v The United Kingdom* (2007) 45 EHRR 37 at para 43.

[379] (2007) 45 EHRR 37 at para 48. In accordance with the modest compensatory jurisdiction of the ECJ, the Applicant was awarded a sum of €3,000.00 non-pecuniary compensation for breach of Art 8 of the Convention and €6,000.00 costs (para 59).

[380] *O'Connor v Ortega* 480 US 709 (1987).

the employee will be subject to the consent of the employee. Physical contact with the worker may arise where it is proposed to conduct medical examination or testing of the worker or to search the body or personal affects (including clothing) of the worker. A prudent employer will seek the consent of the worker in the form of an express term of the contract of employment or at the very least give a clear warning that searches may take place.[381] In *Sharon Donohue v Professional Contract Services Ltd,*[382] the Employment Appeals Tribunal was satisfied that it was unreasonable for a contract cleaner to refuse to submit to a search of a handbag, and the dismissal that followed was consequently held to be a justified dismissal. Although she did not recall doing so, the claimant, who was a cleaner in a hospital, had signed a contract which expressly permitted searches. A security guard asked the claimant if he could search her handbag when she was leaving the hospital. No evidence was given of any particular suspicion or basis for the search. By contrast, a French Court found that an employer did not have an implied power to search an employee's car parked on a public street. The dismissal of the worker for refusal to allow the search was therefore unjustified.[383]

The employer may expressly reserve the right to search or to enter what might otherwise be regarded as private places. Such a term will have to be clearly stated (preferably in writing) and must come as no surprise to the employee whose person, personal belongings or private workspace is being searched. Where so many other areas of employment and the treatment of workers are now referable to codes of practice with guidelines on transparency and warnings, it is expected that courts and Tribunals will decide cases on the basis of clear communication of the employer's privacy policy and the adequacy of search warnings.[384]

It may be a civil wrong to search the person or property of a worker. Although there is no known common law tort of breach of privacy,[385] unwarranted or unjustified search may constitute a form of trespass to the person, an unlawful imprisonment or even an assault. In all of the above cases consent will be a defence. And as with all matters of

---

[381] In a French decision a policy of searching lockers was deemed only permissible where adequate warning had been given, *Société Gantois*, Conseil d'Etat, 12 June 1987.

[382] *Sharon Donohue v Professional Contract Services Ltd* [1997] ELR 35.

[383] *Begat v Prisunic*, Cour de Cassation, 9 April 1987.

[384] See, further, *Chenkin v Bellevue Hospital* 479 F Supp 207 (1979) in which the searching of an employee's bag was based upon a warning by the employer that packages could be searched. The American Court rejected that a worker's expectation of privacy is reduced by such warnings, basing its decision on the Constitutional provision for privacy.

[385] In *Wainright v Home Office* [2002] QB 1334 and on appeal [2003] WLR 1137, Scott LJ said 1152 that '... whatever remedies may have been developed for misuse of confidential information, for certain types of trespass, for certain types of nuisance and for various other situations in which claimants may find themselves aggrieved by an invasion of what they conceive to be their privacy, the common law has not developed an overall remedy for the invasion of privacy.' There is certainly a tort of breach of confidence which applies in any relationship where one party holds confidential information of a significant kind in circumstances where the information is not otherwise made public: *National Irish Bank v RTE* [1998] 2 IR 465. There is also a tort of unfair data processing provided in DPA 1988–2003, s 7.

contract, a consent clause may possibly be implied, for instance, where there is a custom and practice of searching the property of employees.[386]

(ii) Medical questions, testing and assessment

[6.64] An employer will frequently be concerned with selecting the right physical or psychological profile for a given job. Thereafter, the employer will be concerned that no issues or risks arise with respect to an employee's health or substance dependence or abuse. The employer may wish (or be required) to ask questions or perform various tests to confirm whether candidates are suitable for engagement or whether they would pose a risk to health or security in the workplace during the currency of their employment. The question then arises whether these questions, tests or assessments are unnecessary or overly intrusive. It will be recalled from the preceding pages that the DPA 1988–2003 requires the giving of explicit consent before sensitive data of this nature can be processed.[387] Where questions of a medical nature are, more often than not, very personal and intrusive, the focus will inevitably be upon the necessity or justification for such intrusions where they occur. Furthermore, it is clear that the holding of medical data by an employer activates the protection of 'private life' provided for in Art 8 of the European Convention on Human Rights.[388] Equal treatment is also relevant. A worker suffering from HIV/AIDS for example is likely to fall under the protection of the disability ground of the Employment Equality Act 1998–2008.

Information in the nature of medical or 'biometric' data are now commonly used by employers as part of security systems based on the identification of an employee's fingerprints, iris/retina, face, hand or ear outline, to voice patterns, DNA or body odour. Less obvious examples of biometric data are hand-writing or keystroke analysis. The implications for the invasion of privacy and data abuse are self-evident. The Data Protection Commissioner advises that employers should fully consider whether there is a need for a biometric system at all, and if so, proceed to assess the privacy impact of different systems.[389] In *Case Study 12/2007*, the Commissioner responded to a complaint by workers in a logistics company that they were to be subject to a fingerprinting system to log attendances at work. The Commissioner acknowledged the fact that employees had been notified in advance of the proposals and that the company had invited any queries or objections. Nonetheless, it was agreed with the company that the system was unnecessary and that a pin code system should be used.[390] Where such systems are deemed necessary, certain provisions of the Act must be borne in mind: the use of such systems must be 'adequate, relevant and not excessive in relation to the purpose or purposes for which they were collected or are further processed.'[391] This presupposes an assessment of the necessity of the measure taking account of the specific context of the security measures and the alternatives available. The Commissioner makes the point that

---

[386] *Corcoran v Jacob* [1945] IR 446.

[387] DPA 1988, s 2B(1)(b)(i), as inserted by DPAA 2003, s 4.

[388] *Chave née Jullien v France* (1991) 71 DR 141.

[389] www.dataprotection.ie, 'Biometrics in the workplace'.

[390] www.dataprotection.ie, 'Case Studies', Case Study 12/2007.

[391] DPA 1988, s 2(1)(c)(iii), as amended by DPAA 2003, s 3(a).

for the purpose of satisfying s 2(1)(a) of the DPA 1988–2003 and in particular the preconditions set out in s 2A, that consent in the employment context be given as one of several options rather than an empty consent formula.[392] Nor will the Commissioner be easily impressed with the 'legitimate interest' defence.[393] Where the biometric data reveal or contain sensitive data such as the existence of an illness or disability, the Employer will have to comply with the extra precautions which sensitive data attract.[394] In short, the use of biometric data is clearly seen as personal data for the purpose of the Act and will attract the rigorous protections which that legislation affords.

Medical questions and analysis may be required to protect against hazards at work. The protection of health and safety at work has now been specifically addressed, and various duties and powers now provide for medical questions, testing and assessments. The Safety Health and Welfare at Work Act 2005 (the SHWWA 2005) provides in s 23 that:

(1)   An employer may require an employee of a class or classes, as may be prescribed, to undergo an assessment by a registered medical practitioner, nominated by the employer, of his or her fitness to perform work activities referred to in subsection 2 and the employee shall co-operate with such a medical assessment.

(2)   An employer shall ensure that employees undergo assessment by a registered medical practitioner of their fitness to perform work activities, as may be prescribed, which, when performed, give rise to serious risks to the safety, health and welfare of persons at work.

It remains to be seen how the courts will interpret the concepts of 'fitness to perform' and 'co-operate' in s 23(1) and of 'serious risk' in s 23(2). Psychological screening of applicants to establish sound judgment and emotional stability was not acceptable, for example, to the US courts for the position of security personnel.[395] Such tests should be based on accepted and sound methodology and specifically linked to transparent objectives and the requirements of a particular job.

The SHWWA 2005 provides further in s 13 for a specific duty in respect of intoxicants which, in the first instance, is placed squarely on the shoulders of employees. Their duty is to ensure that they are not under the influence of an intoxicant to the extent that they are a danger to their own safety, health or welfare at work or that of any other person.[396] However, the duty extends to the employer in so far as employees, if reasonably required to do so, must submit to any appropriate, reasonable and

---

[392] www.dataprotection.ie, 'Biometrics in the workplace', 'Fair obtaining and processing'. Consent is not generally a satisfactory legitimiser in an employment context, as it can be argued that consent is not freely given. See further Article 29 – Data Protection Working Party, *Opinion 8/2001 on the Processing of Personal Data in the Employment Context* (5062/01/EN/ Final WP 48), 4.

[393] See www.dataprotection.ie, 'Biometrics in the workplace', 'Fair obtaining and processing' where it seems a balance will be required to be struck and case-by-case analysis is preferred.

[394] See DPA 1988, s 2B, as inserted by DPAA 2003, s 4.

[395] *Soroka v Dayton Hudson Corporation* 1 Cal Rep 2d 77 (1991).

[396] SHWWA 2005, s 13(b).

proportionate tests for intoxicants under the supervision of a registered and competent medical practitioner."[397] The necessary implication is that employers are under a duty to monitor employees so that they may know when such tests are 'reasonably required'.

[6.65] This duty is confirmed in s 22 of the SHWWA 2005 which provides that,

> Every employer shall ensure that health surveillance appropriate to the risks to safety health and welfare that may be incurred at the place of work identified by a risk assessment...is made available to his or her employees.[398]

'Health surveillance' is defined as the periodic review for the purpose of protecting health and preventing occupation-related disease, so that any adverse variations in their health that may be related to working conditions are identified as early as possible.[399] Thus it is clear, at least in so far as the prevention of accidents is concerned, that the employer is under a duty to assess the necessity of periodic surveillance of variations in the health of employees in the particular workplace of which it has charge.

It is clear that much will depend on the nature of the work undertaken. In *National Treasury Employees Union v Von Raab*,[400] Kennedy J of the US Supreme Court said,

> It is plain that certain forms of public employment may diminish privacy expectations even with respect to personal searches. Employees of the United States Mint, for example, should expect to be subject to certain routine personal searches when they leave their work everyday. Similarly, those who join our military or intelligence services may not only be required to give what in other contexts might be regarded as extraordinary assurances of trustworthiness and probity, but may also expect intrusive inquiries into their physical fitness.

In this case it was held to be a legitimate practice to subject customs workers to urinalysis. Interestingly, the Supreme Court, in applying this finding, went beyond the front line officers (who were actually conducting searches and therefore handling contraband drugs) to all those who carried guns. In *Luck v Southern Pacific Transportation Co*,[401] the Californian Court was not satisfied that a computer programmer should have to undergo similar drugs testing. While she worked for a railway company, she was not involved in the operation of trains.

The testing concerned may not necessarily be of a medical or psychological nature to fall foul of the privacy principle. In the case of *Ministre du Travail v Sociétés Peintures Corona*,[402] a French appeal court restricted the use of an alcohol test to those actually involved in work where there was a potential health and safety hazard. The Court made it clear that alcohol testing of workers who did not fall within this category, office workers for example, were being subject to unwarranted interference with their bodily integrity and suffered an affront to their human dignity.

---

[397] SHWWA 2005, s 13(c).
[398] On Risk Assessments see SHWWA 2005, s 19.
[399] Safety Health and Welfare at Work Act 2005, s 2.
[400] *National Treasury Employees Union v Von Raab* 489 US 656 (1989).
[401] *Luck v Southern Pacific Transportation Co* 267 Cal Rptr 618 (1990).
[402] *Ministre du Travail v Sociétés Peintures Corona* (1980) 6 Dr Soc 317.

(iii) Monitoring of e-mails, Internet abuse and misuse of computer data

[6.66] One topical concern in the workplace has been the monitoring of e-mails and Internet abuse. The idea that Internet facilities are the property of the employer is central (if not necessarily helpful) to employee monitoring, internet abuse and misuse of computer data. The idea was a decisive consideration, for example, in the case of *PennWell Publishing (UK) Ltd v Ornstien and others.*[403] *PennWell* is not a case about privacy *per se*, but rather an application to restrain an ex-employee from using a list of e-mail addresses he had downloaded from his employer's 'Outlook' database for use in his subsequent employment for a direct competitor. It highlights the persistent notion that an employer retains pre-ordinate proprietary rights in workplace property and even data. The English High Court granted the injunction finding that the list was the property of the employer as it was held on the employer's e-mail system. The Court said as follows:

> [T]he ownership in this database has at all material times been with PennWell, since it was created in the Outlook system of PennWell and [the employee] is not entitled either to exclusive or shared use of it.

It follows that, in principle, the claimant is entitled to retain the database as delivered up and to a permanent injunction preventing use of it, but not of individual parts of its content which may be known to [the employee] by other means.'[404]

While no real consideration is given to the question of precisely where an employer's system ends and a private access entitlements begin, the Court gave careful consideration to certain dilemmas which might arise. The Court emphasised the importance of a clearly communicated policy in the maintenance of such systems and then went on to consider the difficult issues which arise in the absence of such a policy:

> On one view, these lists plainly consist of confidential information of the employer. They include details of the individuals with whom the employee is expected to and will have made contact during his employment for his employer's purpose. They are backed up, generally, on a system maintained or at least paid for by the employer.

> On the other hand, in the new electronic age, electronic address books, whether on mobile telephones, communicators or e-mail systems, are inevitably used by individuals, whether employees or executives, for the convenient storage of those that they wish to contact. In the absence of a declared e-mail policy, it may well be that such employees will use such systems, including on mobile telephones provided for their use, for retaining the records of all sorts of contacts, from personal friends and family, through friendships that they have developed in work…through to the normal business contacts of their employer.

> It may well be the case that many employees do not think of the implications of using their mobile telephones or computers to record their own personal contacts and simply use them for convenience. In the case of mobile telephones, modern technology permits the transfer of contact details either one by one or as a block from one telephone or SIM card to another telephone or SIM card. Thus employees may routinely take copies of those

---

[403] *PennWell Publishing (UK) Ltd v Ornstien and others* [2007] EWHC 1570 (QB), [2007] IRLR 700.

[404] *PennWell Publishing (UK) Ltd v Ornstien and others* [2007] EWHC 1570 (QB), [2007] IRLR 700 at paras 145–6.

contacts at the end of their employment before handing over the telephone to their employer. Similarly, they may well choose to use their employer's e-mail system or even be required not to use their employer's e-mail system or even be required not to use a personal e-mail system such as hotmail on their work computers, so that the only means of communicating during working hours by e-mail is by using their employer's computer.

I am satisfied that where an address list is contained on Outlook or some similar program which is part of the employer's e-mail system and backed up by the employer [it] will belong to the employer. I do not consider that the position will change where the database is accessed not from the employer's computer but from the employee's home computer by "dialling up" or otherwise "logging on" to the employer's e-mail system by some form of remote access.[405]

The helpful analysis in PenWell notwithstanding, what is interesting about the decided cases is the absence (to date) of any penetrative substantive discussion of the privacy issue. The cases focus instead on the conduct issue of abusing employer property and facilities. In *Coleman v ARUP Consulting Engineers*,[406] a graphic designer was found to have been using his employer's Internet facilities to advertise and market a private business enterprise (he was designing and launching a website). He had signed a company policy on Internet, e-mail and computer use, and 'Misuse of Company's Computer System' was listed under the heading 'Gross Misconduct' in the company disciplinary procedures. The Tribunal unanimously found the employee to be 100% contributory to his own (unfair) dismissal. Notably the Tribunal did not consider the employer's entitlement to read or monitor an employee's communications (the matter does not appear to have been raised) but simply whether the employee may use an employer's computer facilities to set up a non-work-related website.[407] This is perhaps surprising given that the Tribunal appear to have relied on the results of an investigation (if not a lengthy one) which established a connection between the claimant's work facilities and the commercial website he had set up and launched. It is clear from the decision of the Tribunal, rather, that the computer system and Internet facilities were viewed as the property of the employer and that these are not to be abused.[408]

[6.67] In *O'Leary v Eagle Star Life Assurance Co*[409] the Tribunal were not satisfied that harassment and threats communicated to colleagues by e-mail constituted 'gross-misconduct' as defined in the respondent's procedures. A sizeable award was made in the claimant's favour based upon the employer's failure to follow procedure but again,

---

[405] *PennWell Publishing (UK) Ltd v Ornstien and others* [2007] EWHC 1570 (QB), [2007] IRLR 700 at paras 124–127.

[406] *Coleman v ARUP Consulting Engineers* [2004] ELR 11.

[407] The worker in question refused to co-operate when the employer requested that any connection his website had with the employer's website be removed. A Technician gave evidence confirming the connection.

[408] See also *Mehigan v Dyflin Publications Ltd* UD 582/01.

[409] *O'Leary v Eagle Star Life Assurance Co* [2003] ELR 223.

the Tribunal did not appear to be concerned with the privacy issue.[410] The Tribunal gave the following details of the steps taken by the Respondent:

> To investigate [the employer] contacted their IT unit, and asked them to look at their internal e-mail system. They found a lot of material regarding a group called "The Legends". The witness said he was shocked when he saw the material. The group were harassing staff and forming hit-lists of people within the company that they identified as "company men". The witness got a print-off of the material and a list of those strongly involved with the group...The respondent found an e-mail that referred to [an] incident where the claimant had told another member of the group, who was also involved in the incident, to make up some story about the incident...There was an e-mail on October 26, 2001 saying that a group member had been kicked out of the group. The witness said that the claimant did not deny this, he said that a group member was expelled for showing e-mails to non-group members. [411]

No concern whatever was mentioned (or apparently submitted) on the basis of privacy despite what appears to be 'the Legend's" own concern for group secrecy.[412]

[6.68] While neither the Tribunal, parties nor their representatives in the foregoing cases seemed concerned with the issues of privacy, there can be little doubt that this position will change with increasing awareness of the right to a reasonable expectation of privacy at work. In *Bodil Lindqvist v Aklagarkammaren I Jonkoping*[413] the ECJ considered the application of the Data Protection Directive to a Swedish criminal prosecution of a woman who posted personal and work-related information about her co-workers on the Internet. While the technical matter of having to access the data posted on the webpage from a third country ultimately disposed of the case, it should be noted that the Court made an express finding that the activity involved did not fall outside of any exception

---

[410] The award was in excess of €20,000. In the case of *Linda Dunne v Peak Performance Ltd* UD385/04 the Tribunal found that the claimant had been constructively dismissed through various incidents including an accusation that she abused the company computer facilities by sending personal e-mails. The employer gave open evidence of having decided to look at her computer and of removing her files from her computer. There is no mention of the issue of privacy and no particular attention is drawn to the interception aspect of the case. The privacy issue did not arise either in *Fogarty v IBM* UD771/00, albeit for quite a different but equally interesting reason. The Tribunal deemed a dismissal fair which was based upon the claimant's participating in the on-line commentary facility provided by a website called 'Virtual Vengeance'. The Tribunal was satisfied that an investigation had taken place which established that the claimant had made offensive comments in the employment context, even if (and this was perhaps decisive) the website was in the public domain. See further *Kiernan v A Wear Ltd* UD 643/2007.

[411] *O'Leary v Eagle Star Assurance Co* [2003] ELR 223 at 229–230.

[412] The concern of the Claimant in *Kiernan v A Wear Ltd* UD 643/2007 was somewhat less well-founded given that the derogatory comments she had made on the 'Bebo' social networking website were seen by the employer to have been in the public domain.

[413] Case C-101/01 *Bodil Lindqvist v Aklagarkammaren I Jonkoping* [2003] ECR I-1297.

to Community law nor was it permissible as exclusively a matter of private or family life.[414]

One area which is likely to emerge at the forefront of the privacy debate, is the potential liability arising from s 14A of the Employment Equality Acts 1998–2008 in the form of harassment or the possibility that pornography may be found on the company system. In *Mehigan v Dyflin Publications Ltd,*[415] the Employment Appeals Tribunal referred to English case law in pointing out the dangers of incidental exposure of employees of inappropriate materials such as pornography imported into the workplace by a colleague. The Tribunal said that the exposure of co-employees to such material, if left unchecked could be seen as a hostile working environment. The Tribunal referred to the case of *Morse and Future Reality* in which the company was held liable in a case of constructive dismissal (using the phrase 'hostile work environment'). Ms Morse shared a room with four male colleagues who regularly downloaded pornographic material from the Internet.

[6.69] Clearly much will depend in this area, like any other, on the employer's policies and how they are enforced.[416] It is quite clear from the Data Protection Commissioner's guidelines that access to e-mails or Internet usage should be in response to a specific and reasonable suspicion of inappropriate use of the facilities provided.[417] In anticipation of such a necessity arising, computer facilities provided by an employer should provide an on-screen notice, on entry into the relevant facility, that use of the facility will be monitored. Where this monitoring or 'surveillance' establishes that the worker is accessing inappropriate material through the facility, the employer would appear to be entitled to discipline the worker on the basis of such surveillance.[418] The more cautious employer will use firewall software to screen communications *via* the Internet. In *Simons v United States,*[419] the employer was able to trace access to pornographic web sources by adopting this approach, and then proceeded to locate items of child pornography downloaded by an employee. The warning that had been given, namely, that users would be periodically monitored, was sufficient to satisfy the Court that this was a permissible intrusion into the private communications of the worker.

---

[414] DPD, Art 3.2 excludes from the application of the Directive processing of personal data 'by a natural person in the course for purely personal or household activity.'

[415] *Mehigan v Dyflin Publications Ltd* UD 582/01.

[416] See www.dataprotection.ie, FAQ 4.1 'Can my employer access my email or internet usage? / Can I access my employees' email or internet usage?' In *Mehigan v Dyflin Publications Ltd* UD 582/01, the Tribunal suggested that while unauthorised use of the internet in the absence of prior notice that this is a dismissable offence will not generally justify dismissal, that the downloading of pornographic material may however be an exception to this.

[417] See www.dataprotection.ie.

[418] In *US v Monroe* 52 MJ 326 (2000), when the worker logged on, the following warning appeared on the screen: 'Users logging on to the system consent to monitoring by the host administrator.' See further, *McLaren v Microsoft Corporation* (1999) WL 339015 (Tex App Dallas).

[419] *Simons v United States* (2000) F 2d 392.

It is clearly now the case that the employer may utilise the reasonable expectation to privacy with regard to the communications.[420] Equally there can be little doubt that the right to privacy is reduced (though not altogether effaced) by warnings and policies. That is not to say that a traditional proprietarian attidue does not still sometimes prevail. In *Smyth v Spilsbury*,[421] the employer argued he had been justified in its suspicion that the plaintiff was making inappropriate and provocative comments deliberately to create friction between his colleagues. The employer felt that he had a duty to act to prevent inappropriate use of e-mail facilities to this end. This argument was upheld without the usual saver that warnings must be given and procedures must be followed.

[6.70] The foregoing authority notwithstanding, it is normally the case that an appropriate policy followed by an appropriate procedure will result in the desirable result for an employer. In the case of *Burtchell v Premier Recruitment Ltd*,[422] a recruitment consultant was dismissed for what the employer called 'a complete break down of trust' when it found that the claimant had been using her internet facilities at work to send defamatory and harassing e-mails to co-workers and managers. Although the discovery was made while Ms Burtchell was absent from work due to illness, the employee handbook contained a policy stating that e-mails of employees were not private and the right to monitor e-mail traffic was reserved. When the abuse was put to Ms Burtchell, she did not attempt to explain the e-mails nor was any apology forthcoming. In considering her unfair dismissal claim, the Tribunal examined the policy and the investigation and the opportunity which was given to the claimant to respond to the allegation of abuse. The Tribunal went on to find that the claimant's use of the employer's internet facilities was unrelated to her work. Only after making these determinations, the Tribunal ultimately found as follows:

> [T]he nature of the emails were at the very least offensive and resulted in creating a tense and unpleasant atmosphere in the place of employment affecting in particular four employees at senior level...the trust and confidence which has been long established to be fundamental to proper working conditions necessary for the correct administration of any reputable business to be virtually destroyed to such an extent that the claimant could no longer be retained by the respondent.

The courts are likely to expect employers to be disciplined in their investigation and restrict searches to the specific allegations, whether they concern sexual harassment, bullying or downloading inappropriate material. The Data Protection Working Party has expressed the following view on the surveillance of emails:

> Given that e-mails contain person data of both the sender and the recipient, and employers can only generally obtain the consent of one of these parties without major difficulty (unless the e-mails comprise inter-staff correspondence), the possibility of legitimizing the monitoring of e-mails on the basis of such consent is very limited.... Where a worker is given an e-mail account for purely personal use or is allowed access to a web-mail account, opening of e-mails in this account by his employer (apart from scanning viruses)

---

[420] For an example of where no warning was given and the search fell foul of the entitlement to privacy see: *United States v Slanina* 283 F 2d 670 (2002).

[421] *Smyth v Spilsbury* 914 F Supp 97 (1996).

[422] *Burtchell v Premier Recruitment Ltd* UD 1290/02.

can only be justified in very limited circumstances [criminal or employer liability] and cannot under normal circumstances be justified...because it is not in the legitimate interests of the employer to have access to such data. Instead, the fundamental right to secrecy of correspondent prevails.[423]

The Commissioner has included on his website a 'Template for Acceptable Usage Policy – Email and Internet'.[424] The guidelines are mostly of a technical nature including advice on the opening of potentially dangerous material. The controller is reminded that systems (mail, Internet etc.) should to be used for downloading or distributing offensive material. While there should be automatic screening of all mail for known viruses, attachments etc, mail intended for individuals should not normally be read or mailboxes opened. The Commissioner mentions the following exceptions:

(i)   where the screening software or a complaint from an individual indicates that a particular mailbox contains material which is dangerous or offensive.

(ii)   where a legitimate work reason exists to open the e-mail.

[6.71] The Commissioner advises that the opening of mail for the purpose of investigation requires senior management authorisation on a case-by-case basis. There is a suggestion that it is only where investigation proves that a problem exists that it needs to be reported to the sender, their organisation, the staff member concerned, Head of Division and HR Manager for appropriate action.[425] While these advices appear sound, caution is advised on covert or surreptitious monitoring as the evidence procured in this manner may be characterised as unnecessary, disproportionate or otherwise dubious surveillance.[426]

(iv) Telephone and correspondence interception

[6.72] Interception of a telecommunicated message can amount to a grave violation of personal privacy and can even give rise to criminal prosecution.[427] The case of *Kennedy v Ireland*[428] was concerned with what was ultimately held to be unconstitutional use of listening devices or 'phone-tapping' of telephone communications. With the developing case law under Art 8 of the Convention there is ample basis for the courts to scrutinize very closely any attempt to listen in or intercept a worker's communications. It will not

---

[423] Article 29 – Data Protection Working Party, *Working Document on the Surveillance of Electronic Communications in the Workplace* (5401/01/EN/Final WP 55), 21.

[424] www.dataprotection.ie, 'Template for Acceptable Usage Policy – Email and Internet.'

[425] www.dataprotection.ie, 'Template for Acceptable Usage Policy – Email and Internet', 'Screening Procedure'.

[426] See Data Protection Commissioner Case study 6/2007 discussed below in section 'Video surveillance and recording'; *Tytex v SIPTU* CD/97/132 Recommendation No LCR 15502; Article 29 – Data Protection Working Party, *Opinion 8/2001 on the Processing of Personal Data in the Employment Context* (5062/01/EN/Final WP 48), 3; and; Article 29 – Data Protection Working Party, *Working Document on the Surveillance of Electronic Communications in the Workplace* (5401/01/EN/Final WP 55), para 3.1.5 and see further at 4; *Chairman and Governors of Amwell View School v Doghery* [2007] IRLR 198; and *Law Debenture Trust Group v Terence Malley and The Pensions Ombudsman* [1992] OPLR 167.

[427] Postal and Telecommunications Services Act 1983, s 98(1).

[428] *Kennedy and Arnold v Ireland and The Attorney General* [1987] IR 587.

avail the employer to say that the worker was using the employer's phone and therefore has no standing to complain under Art 8.[429]

Article 8 refers expressly to privacy of 'correspondence' which may mean either a written or spoken communication. Not only is it a breach of an express protection of the Convention to open someone's private letter, it is also a criminal offence.[430] As early as 1985 the ECJ was not prepared to allow even State-sponsored surveillance of telephone conversations in the absence of clear legal guidelines giving an adequate indication of the circumstances allowing such intrusion. In *Malone v UK,*[431] the UK Government was unable to show a sufficient legal basis for the interception of telephone conversations.[432] There is no reason to assume that where a private citizen seeks to undertake surveillance the requirements will be any less. Indeed, there are indications that the requirements should be of a higher order.[433]

[6.73] In the case of *Halford v United Kingdom,*[434] we see the interesting combination of a State-sponsored body operating surveillance as an employer (Ms Halford was an officer of the English police service). The Court found that telephone calls made from the workplace are capable of coming within the protection of private life in Art 8 of the Convention. The Court said:

> [T]here was a reasonable likelihood that calls made by Ms Halford from her office were intercepted by the Merseyside police with the primary aim of gathering material to assist in the defence of the sex discrimination proceedings brought against them. This interception constituted an [interference] within the meaning of Article 8(2), with the exercise of Ms Halford's right to respect for her private life and correspondence...[435]

The Court went on to say:

> There is no evidence of any warning having been given to Ms Halford, as a use of the internal telecommunications system operated at Merseyside police headquarters, that calls made on that system would be liable to interception. She would, the Court considers, have had a reasonable expectation of privacy for such calls, which expectation was moreover reinforced by a number of factors. As Assistant Chief Constable she had sole use of her office where there were two telephones, one of which was specifically designated for her private use. Furthermore, she had been given the assurance, in response to a memorandum, that she could use her office telephones for the purpose of her sex discrimination case.[436]

---

[429] *Lambert v France* (2000) 30 EHRR 346.

[430] The offence is contained in Postal and Telecommunications Services Act 1983, s 98. For an example of a breach of Art 8 of the ECHR. See *Petra v Romania* (2001) 33 EHRR 5.

[431] *Malone v UK* (1985) 7 EHRR 14.

[432] This led to the introduction, in the UK, of the Interception of Communications Act 1985. In Ireland, we have the Interception of Postal Packets and Telecommunications Messages (Regulations) Act 1993.

[433] Certainly where private individuals undertake surveillance on their own behalf. Contrast the LRC's position in respect of surveillance conducted by (1) An Garda Síochána and of (2) private individuals: Law Reform Commission of Ireland, *Report on Privacy: Surveillance and the Interception of Communications* (LRC 57-1998), 20 and 116 respectively.

[434] *Halford v United Kingdom* [1997] IRLR 471.

[435] *Halford v United Kingdom* [1997] IRLR 471 at para 48.

[436] *Halford v United Kingdom* [1997] IRLR 471 at para 45.

Again we see the consideration of warnings as a prerequisite to surveillance. We also see the concept of 'reasonable expectation'. Allen, Crasnow and Beale comment:

> In some workplaces the employers make it explicit that telephone conversations may be monitored. The principles could equally apply to the use of email or the Internet, or even post from the office. However, employers need to recognize that even a general warning of the kind discussed may not be enough. The Court did not give a general licence to employers to invade employees' privacy.[437]

We are all familiar with routine warnings given on call helplines that the conversation will be recorded for training purpose. It should be noted that employees involved in taking such calls have the right to be informed that phone calls will be recorded, as the recordings will also constitute their personal data.[438]

[6.74] Factors which will be taken into account as to whether an employer is justified in conducting surveillance will therefore start with whether a warning was given. Examples at one end of the scale are circumstances of investigations of harassment or explicitly inappropriate content – on the other end of the scale are communications in a clearly private context such as emergency family calls or communications with doctors. The Data Protection Working Party has put the matter (in the context of electronic communications surveillance) in the following terms:

> [B]alancing different rights and interests requires taking a number of principles into account, in particular proportionality. It should be clear that the simple fact that a monitoring activity or surveillance is considered convenient to serve the employer's interest would not solely justify any intrusion in worker's privacy. Before implementing in the work place, any monitoring measure it must pass a list of tests.[439]

These tests are set out by the Working Party as follows:

1. Is the monitoring activity transparent to the worker?
2. Is it necessary? Could the employer not obtain the same result with traditional methods of supervision?
3. Is the proposed processing of personal data fair to the workers?
4. Is it proportionate to the concerns that it tries to allay?[440]

---

[437] Allen, Crasnow and Beale, *Employment Law and Human Rights* (2nd edn, Oxford University Press, 2007) para 8.83. As a result of the finding against the UK in *Halford*, the UK now has the benefit of the Regulation of Investigators Powers Act 2000. The Act makes provision for criminal and civil liability in respect of unlawful interception of a private telecommunications system. Such systems are defined to include telephones, beepers, text messaging and email – the definition makes reference to a system existing 'for the purpose of facilitating the transmission of communications by any means involving the use of electrical or electro-magnetic energy: Regulation of Investigators Powers Act 2000, s 2(1).

[438] See www.dataprotection.ie, FAQ 4.6 'What are the requirements if I wish to record phone calls for training purposes?' The Commissioner advises, however, that listening in or monitoring of phone calls, without any actual recording taking place, for training purposes does not need to be made known to customers.

[439] Article 29 – Data Protection Working Party, *Working Document on the Surveillance of Electronic Communications in the Workplace* (5401/01/EN/Final WP 55), at p 4.

Automatic recording of telephone calls can be unnerving and may be said to go to the trust inherent in the employment relationship. However, the recoding of calls does seem to have taken root as standard practice in certain service industries. In *Irish Life v Amicus*,[441] the Labour Court determined that while a call recording system was not objectionable in principle, facilities were to be put in place by which first, required use of the system reflected length of service (and therefore a reduced requirement for training) and secondly, private unrecorded staff phone calls could be made.[442]

(v) Vetting and investigation

[6.75] There are several scenarios which arise in employment where discretion, confidence and even surreptitious behaviour is required. Investigation or surveillance or 'fact-finding' may be undertaken in the work-context arising out of allegations or suspicions of misconduct. Preliminary monitoring will inevitably take place prompting performance issues. Inqueries may be undertaken at recruitment stage (sometimes called 'vetting') or they may simply be undertaken as a preventative measure to avoid future difficulties. Indeed, investigations have been assessed by the courts which were undertaken simply as vetting measures to assure the employer as to who they were contracting with, and whether they are trustworthy or appropriate for the role with which they have been entrusted.[443]

The Data Protection Commissioner advises that employer should inform potential employees in advance of any potential checks that may be undertaken and seek their specific consent. Whereas some information in the public domain can be openly accessed in certain sectors, for example where employees have contact with children or vulnerable adults, an employer is permitted to make use of Garda vetting checks. But again, these should be carried out with the consent of the potential employee.[444] The Commissioner is at pains to point out that employers seeking to ascertain the background of potential employees, for whatever purpose, should not require those persons to submit access requests to the Gardaí. It is noted that this would be an abuse of a person's rights under data protection and that it is envisaged to be an offence in s 4(13) of the DPA 1988,[445] albeit this provision has not yet been enacted.[446]

[6.76] While it might be said that more is at stake in the course of a pre-disciplinary investigation, similar concerns arise to those of vetting. When examining the privacy implications of investigations, a distinction must be drawn between the investigation stage of any proceeding or process and an active disciplinary process. The first stage is a

---

[440] Article 29 – Data Protection Working Party, *Working Document on the Surveillance of Electronic Communications in the Workplace* (5401/01/EN/Final WP 55), at p 4.

[441] *Irish Life v Amicus* CD/05/627.

[442] See also *United Airlines v A Worker* Dec 18643 issued 10 July 2006 (reviewed in (2006/07) 3 Employment Law Review Ireland, 14).

[443] *Leander v Sweden* (1987) 9 EHRR 433; *Rocha v Portugal* [2005] ECHR 335.

[444] See www.dataprotection.ie, FAQ 4.2 'What type of background checks can I carry out on potential employees?'

[445] As amended by DPAA 2003, s 5(d).

[446] See www.dataprotection.ie, FAQ 4.3 'How can I seek Garda vetting of a potential employee?'

fact-gathering exercise, whereas the second is concerned with accusation, response and drawing of conclusions. As such, the rules of fair procedure do not always apply to the first stage.[447] An employee may not know that an investigation has been undertaken and indeed to place the employee on notice that there is an investigation may defeat its legitimate purpose. However employees do have certain privacy rights in these circumstances. In *Leander v Sweden*[448] the plaintiff applied for a permanent post as a museum employee. The Swedish authorities reviewed a secret police file which held information about his private life. On the facts the ECtHR found that as a civil servant working in a job with national security sensitivity, there was not therefore, in the Court's view, the same positive obligation to allow the applicant to know the content of those files.[449] However it is implicit in the Court's finding that for ordinary employees, the storing and release of such information to the employer as well as the refusal to allow the employee to refute it, was an interference with his right to private life.[450]

An opinion given in confidence is one of the few exceptions to the duty of transparency under the Data Protection Act 1988.[451] Opinions however, may not as might be thought, consist simply of work references to potential future employers. The Data Protection Commissioner supports the view that it may be necessary to withhold data consisting of an opinion given as part of an internal investigative/disciplinary process. He advises that '…a colleague who reports a matter relating to an individual in confidence to a supervisor could be expected to be protected by the confidentiality provision.'[452] The Act however, refers expressly to 'opinions' only and not to the reporting of facts.[453] The Commissioner does not appear to take account of this distinction nor the general rule that opinion as evidence is inadmissible.[454] That said, an opinion is sometimes very difficult to separate from permissible inferences based on primary facts.[455] Keeping such matters confidential might be necessary for the protection of a witness or the integrity of an investigation. S 4(1)(a)(iii)(II) of the DPA 1988–2003

---

[447] *Minnock v Irish Casing Company Ltd and Stewart* 11 June, Irish Times (2007).

[448] *Leander v Sweden* (1987) 9 EHRR 433.

[449] *Leander v Sweden* (1987) 9 EHRR 433 at para 48.

[450] In *Antunes Rocha v Portugal* [2005] ECHR 335 in a similar finding, the surveillance of the home and questioning of close acquaintants of a civil emergency planning worker as part of her job was held to be an interference with Art 8. The ECJ went on, however, to find that the security-sensitive nature of her job and the fact that security checks were part of the job might have made these measures legitimate. The measures in question, however, fell foul of Art 8(2) for want of clarity parameters and notification to the surveillance subject.

[451] DPA 1988, s 4(4A), as inserted by DPAA 2003, s 5(b). See 'Right of access to data of the data subject' above on opinions given in confidence.

[452] www.dataprotection.ie, 'Data Protection Access Requests for Personnel Records', 'Discipline, grievance and dismissal'.

[453] Contrast the English provision in the Data Protection Act 1998, Sch 7, para. 1 which provides specifically for confidential 'references' setting out the parameters of such to include employment, appointment but without any objective reference to disciplinary or investigative proceedings.

[454] *AG (Ruddy) v Kenny* (1960) 94 ILTR 185. See generally McGrath, *Evidence* (Thomson Round Hall, 2005) Ch 6.

[455] *Sherrard v Jaco*b [1965] NI 151 at 156.

for example, may prove to be a relevant 'public interest' exception where revealing the source of the information would be a disincentive to others providing similar information in the future.[456] However, it is submitted that any departure from transparency should be very much an exception and the principles applicable to the right to confront one's accuser (a derivative of the fair procedures principle known as 'audi alteram partem') are closely relevant. While evidence in confidence was not mentioned, Henchy J was emphatic in *Kiely v Minister for Social Welfare*[457] where he stated that:

> Audi alteram partem means that both sides must be fairly heard. That is not done if one party is allowed to send in his evidence in writing, free from the truth eliciting process of a confrontation which is inherent in an oral hearing, while his opponent is compelled to run the gauntlet of oral examination and cross-examination. The dispensation of justice, in order to achieve its ends, must be even handed in form as well as content.[458]

Whistle-blowing is not currently a generally applied device in Irish employment law.[459] The only available guidance (which does however offer some insights) comes in the very narrow context of where an Irish data processor may become concerned with the US Sarbanes-Oxley Act 2002 on confidential, anonymous submissions regarding corporate accounting and auditing. The Article 29 Working Party has issued various cautionary self-assessment questions on the issue.[460] These include whether anonymity is necessary or whether it can be limited to certain individuals.[461] An assessment should be made as to quantity of data, how long the complaint is (or needs to be) stored and in what circumstances.[462] Importantly the data controller should assess not only whether

---

[456] See the view expressed in Article 29 – Data Protection Working Party, *Opinion 8/2001 on the Processing of Personal Data in the Employment Context* (5062/01/EN/Final WP 48), 15-16, that the public interest exception is likely to have very limited relevance in employment.

[457] *Kiely v Minister for Social Welfare* [1977] IR 267.

[458] [1977] IR 267 at 281.

[459] See, further, Health Act 2007, Part XIV. There are however, a number of significant provisions protecting those employees who make complaints (without specific provision for confidential complaint): Safety, Health and Welfare at Work Act 2005, s 27; Employment Equality Act 1998 (as amended), Part VII. The Unfair Dismissals Act 1977 (as amended) protects against the dismissal of an employee because he or she has participated in legal proceedings against the employer: s 6(2)(c)–(d).

[460] Article 29 – Data Protection Working Party, *Opinion 1/2006 on the Application of EU Data Protection Rules to Internal Whistleblowing Schemes in the Fields of Accounting, Internal Accounting Controls, Auditing Matters, Fight against Bribery, Banking and Financial Crime* (00195/06/EN WP 117). See, also, www.dataprotection.ie, "Whistleblower' schemes and Compliance with the US Sarbanes-Oxley Act', 'Whistleblowing Compliance where Personal Data are involved'.

[461] Article 29 – Data Protection Working Party, *Opinion 1/2006 on the Application of EU Data Protection Rules to Internal Whistleblowing Schemes in the Fields of Accounting, Internal Accounting Controls, Auditing Matters, Fight against Bribery, Banking and Financial Crime* (00195/06/EN WP 117), 10.

[462] *Opinion 1/2006 on the Application of EU Data Protection Rules to Internal Whistleblowing Schemes in the Fields of Accounting, Internal Accounting Controls, Auditing Matters, Fight against Bribery, Banking and Financial Crime* (00195/06/EN WP 117) at 12.

the interests of accuser are protected but also the accused.[463] Unlike most procedural entitlements in employment (and this gives the entire proposition some considerable context) the Working Party advises against data controllers encouraging potential whistle-blowers by advertising the availability of the process.[464]

(vi) Visual surveillance and recording

[6.77] Monitoring of a worker for every minute of every day spent at work is clearly contrary to public policy and to the development of a healthy work environment. One particularly vivid description of the evils of constant surveillance was given in the American case of *Re Electronics Instrument Company and the International Union of Electrical Workers*[465] where it was said to be:

> ...not only personally repugnant to employees but it has such an inhibiting effect as to prevent the employees from performing their work with confidence and ease. Every employee has occasion to cause in the course of their work, to take a breather, to scratch his head, to yawn or otherwise be himself without affecting his work. An employee, with reason would hesitate at all times to so behave, if his every action is being recorded on TV. To have workers constantly televised is...reminiscent of the era depicted by Charlie Chaplin in 'Modern Times' and constitutes an affront to the dignity of man.[466]

Surveillance is not merely the watching of persons but may also consist of monitoring of communications. Thus we are not concerned simply with video cameras surveying the activities of workers to record incidents of pilfering or damage to the employer's property.[467] Employers are increasingly capable, through the wider range (and decreasing cost) of surveillance devices, to monitor their workers. Employers can now afford the expense of placing cameras, even in rest areas as well as high risk or sensitive zones, and by these means can monitor discrete activities such as keyboard use previously beyond the reaches of technology.

Again, there is nothing wrong in principle with having an electronically monitored place of work where warnings are given and the structure of the work and the workplace

---

[463] *Opinion 1/2006 on the Application of EU Data Protection Rules to Internal Whistleblowing Schemes in the Fields of Accounting, Internal Accounting Controls, Auditing Matters, Fight against Bribery, Banking and Financial Crime* (00195/06/EN WP 117) at 13.

[464] *Opinion 1/2006 on the Application of EU Data Protection Rules to Internal Whistleblowing Schemes in the Fields of Accounting, Internal Accounting Controls, Auditing Matters, Fight against Bribery, Banking and Financial Crime* (00195/06/EN WP 117) at 11, para 4.

[465] *Re Electronics Instrument Company and the International Union of Electrical Workers* (1965) LA 563.

[466] The limited circumstances in which constant monitoring are perhaps permissible are outlined in ILO *Code of Practice on the Protection of Workers' Personal Data* (International Labour Office Geneva, 1997), para 5(4).

[467] Allen, Crasnow and Beale, *Employment Law and Human Rights* (2nd edn, Oxford University Press 2007), at para 8.06, cite an example in England where cleaners and a security officer were arrested and their work suspended when an alleged drugs transaction was caught on camera at their workplace. Taken from Clarke, 'The monitoring of staff needs regulations', (1999) Times, 6 April. It should be noted that a video recording is no different from a statement of accusation and should be shown to an employee before he or she is asked to comment upon it: *McCollum v Dunnes Stores (Oakville) Ltd* UD424/03.

clearly suggest that work activities are not private.[468] It would appear that an interview or disciplinary meeting, which is conducted in circumstances where all parties are aware of the recording device, cannot give rise to a claim of privacy.[469] Furthermore it has recently been held that evidence covertly recorded of a disciplinary meeting can be admitted in evidence before a tribunal. In *Chairman and Governors of Amwell View School v Doghery*,[470] the English EAT drew a distinction between evidence obtained while the employee was *present* during a disciplinary hearing which was deemed admissible, whereas evidence of the private deliberation of the board when the employee was absent was inadmissible. Questions arise, however, where the recording is covert or where the worker is subject to surveillance when he or she is not working. It may well be impermissible, for example, to conduct video surveillance of a worker taking his break away from the work floor in the coffee area even where it is suspected of illicit gambling on the work premises.[471] It is certainly impermissible and probably criminal to conduct surveillance of lavatories.[472]

[6.78] We saw in *Halford* above in the context of interception of telephone calls that the ECJ will be more tolerant of intrusions upon the privacy of workers where clear warnings are given. It is the essence, however, of certain kinds of surveillance that it be conducted secretly. While the Law Reform Commission has issued recommendations which contain detailed reservations and conditions on the issue of covert surveillance,[473] there is authority for the acceptance of the use of covert surveillance techniques at work. In *Law Debenture Trust Group v Terence Malley and The Pensions Ombudsman*,[474] Alliott J saw nothing wrong with the use of covert surveillance and allowed evidence to be submitted in the appeal of the Respondent's refusal to grant early retirement based on ill-health. This is consistent with the Data Protection Working Party's acceptance as legitimate that an employer may have to resort to covert surveillance to deal with possible fraudulent or criminal behaviour in the workplace.[475]

[6.79] The Irish Data Protection Commissioner has considered, in at least two cases, the use of closed circuit television at work. The repeated advice is that the use of covert monitoring should not be excessive and must have a clearly defined purpose with

---

[468] *Vega Rodriguez v Puerto Rico Telephone Co* 110 F 3d 174.

[469] *Devoy v Dublin Corporation* (18 October 1995, unreported) HC.

[470] *Chairman and Governors of Amwell View School v Doghery* [2007] IRLR 198.

[471] *State of Hawaii v Bonnell* 75 Haw 124 (1993).

[472] See *R v Choi* [1999] 8 Archbold News 3, CA 7 May 1999. This case concerned a successful prosecution for offences against public decency consisting in secretly recording women in a supermarket toilet. See, however, www.dataprotection.ie, 'Data Protection & CCTV', 'Use of CCTV on a business premises, including toilet areas'.

[473] Law Reform Commission of Ireland, *Report on Privacy: Surveillance and the Interception of Communications* (LRC 57-1998).

[474] *Law Debenture Trust Group v Terence Malley and The Pensions Ombudsman* [1992] OPLR 167.

[475] Article 29 – Data Protection Working Party, *Working Document on the Surveillance of Electronic Communications in the Workplace* (5401/01/EN/Final WP 55), 4. The approach taken in *Jones v Warwick* [2003] EWCA 151 was to allow covert video footage to be used as evidence but to penalise the Defendant on costs.

appropriate regard for the relevance of information collected.[476] The Commissioner underlines the importance of considering necessity and proportionality.[477] This refers not only to the question of whether surveillance is necessary in the first place, but also to where it is conducted and how long recordings should be kept.[478] Even where the Gardaí seek access to recordings, the controller should ask whether there is a genuine necessity and require, where appropriate, a request in writing.[479]

The Commissioner provides a good illustration of how he will deal with the use of covert CCTV footage at work in *Case Study 6/2007*. The complainant, a supervisor in the Gresham Hotel, was called to a meeting with management and confronted with compromising footage from covert cameras installed on foot of cash handling complaints. The complainant had never been made aware of the investigation nor the covert CCTV but was required to explain her actions from the footage and was ultimately dismissed based on her replies. The Commissioner indicated that such covert surveillance is normally only permitted on a case by case basis where the data is gathered for the purposes of preventing, detecting or investigating offences, or apprehending or prosecuting offenders. It implies an actual involvement of An Garda Síochána or an intention to involve An Garda Síochána which had never been the case here. The employer relied on the 'legitimate and specified purpose' of investigating a complaint regarding cash handling. The employer also maintained, somewhat dubiously, that the cameras were not hidden or actually covert and it presumed that all employees would have seen them. The Commissioner was unimpressed by the employer and found that a breach of the DPA 1988–2003 amounting to unfair processing had occurred.[480]

[6.80] Employers should ensure that those people whose images are likely to be captured on camera are informed, for example, by publishing or mounting an appropriate notice.[481] Where an employer intends to use cameras to identify disciplinary (or other) issues relating to staff, the Commissioner advises that employees must be

---

[476] *Case Study 14/1996* and *Case Study 6/2007*.

[477] See www.dataprotection.ie, FAQ 6.1 'What issues surround the use of CCTV?' A point which illustrates this is the use of CCTC in toilets. An employer would need strong justification for such measures for example repeated security breaches in a toilet area and should never be focussed into the private spaces of toilets such as cubicles or the urinal areas: ww.dataprotection.ie, 'Data Protection & CCTV', 'Use of CCTV on a business premises, including toilet areas'.

[478] See www.dataprotection.ie, FAQ 6.1. The Commissioner advises that images captured should be retained for a maximum of 28 days, except where the image identifies an issue and is retained specifically in the context of an investigation of that issue.

[479] See www.dataprotection.ie, FAQ 6.2 'What if I am asked by a law enforcement authority for access to the recordings?'

[480] The Case Study indicates that an undisclosed settlement was reached between the parties. See also *Tytex v SIPTU* CD/97/132 Recommendation No LCR 15502; *Meadow Meats v SIPTU* CD/98/72 Recommendation No LCR 15878.

[481] See www.dataprotection.ie, 'Data Protection & CCTV', 'Fair obtaining'.

informed of this before the cameras are used for these purposes.[482] He advises that covert surveillance is normally only permitted on a case by case basis where the data are kept for the purposes of preventing, detecting or investigating offences, or for apprehending or prosecuting offenders. This provision automatically implies an involvement of An Garda Síochána and should be used sparingly.[483] The Article 29 Working Party has published its views on the processing of personal data by means of video surveillance[484] highlighting, as with the areas of privacy concerns we have seen above, the need for an assessment of legitimacy, and transparency[485] and of course the ever present caution of proportionality[486] which is expressed unusually as a principle of 'moderation'.[487]

GUIDANCE AND CODES OF PRACTICE[488]

[6.81] A search of the Internet provides a surprising amount of guidance on data protection and monitoring at work. These largely consist of private enterprise interpretations of the codes prepared by the UK Information Commissioner (formerly entitled the Data Protection Commissioner like his current equivalent in Ireland).

A visit to the UK Commissioner's website is worthwhile.[489] In Ireland, we have a similar facility to the Information Commissioner known as the Data Protection Commissioner. A visit to www.dataprivacy.ie is also recommended. While the scope of the UK website is helpful it is important to treat the guidelines found there as instructive only. Ultimately both the UK and Ireland operate under the same Directive and it is the Directive which is binding. However, the UK operates under Regulations which do not have an equivalent in this jurisdiction.[490]

[6.82] We await an effective statutory code of practice in Ireland but it is anticipated that the UK code of practice will be closely followed and there is considerable guidance in the compilation of privacy statements and also in privacy policies available from www.dataprivacy.ie.[491] In any comprehensive code, there will undoubtedly be a duty to take preventative steps to ensure data is not unlawfully or inappropriately handled.

---

[482] See www.dataprotection.ie, 'Data Protection & CCTV', 'Fair obtaining'.

[483] See www.dataprotection.ie, 'Data Protection & CCTV', 'Covert Surveillance'.

[484] Article 29 – Data Protection Working Party, *Opinion 4/2004 on the Processing of Personal Data by means of Video Surveillance* (11750/02/EN WP 89).

[485] *Opinion 4/2004 on the Processing of Personal Data by means of Video Surveillance* (11750/02/EN WP 89) at 6–7.

[486] *Opinion 4/2004 on the Processing of Personal Data by means of Video Surveillance* (11750/02/EN WP 89) at 18.

[487] *Opinion 4/2004 on the Processing of Personal Data by means of Video Surveillance* (11750/02/EN WP 89) at 21.

[488] The Data Protection Commissioner is empowered, albeit indirectly, to engage in the process of promulgating codes of conduct pursuant to DPA 1988, s 13, as amended by DPAA 2003, s 14.

[489] www.informationcommissioner.gov.uk and click on 'Data Protection'. Click on Codes of Practice and you will find the various instalments of the code of practice which is currently nearing completion.

[490] Regulation of Investigators Powers Act 2000 discussed at para **[6.72]**.

[491] See 'Guidelines for the content and use of privacy statements on websites', August 2004, at www.dataprivacy.ie.

Training will be recommended.[492] Prevention will be prioritized over cure.[493] There will be a requirement for transparency and the duty to keep data subjects informed whether directly or through their representatives.[494] There will be a requirement to ensure security,[495] accuracy,[496] proportionality[497] and legitimacy.[498] Codes should be kept up to date and apace with technology.[499]

---

[492] See, for example, ILO, *Code of Practice on the Protection of Workers' Personal Data* (International Labour Office Geneva, 1997), para 5(13).

[493] See Article 29 – Data Protection Working Party, *Working Document on the Suveillance of Electronic Communications in the Workplace* (5401/01/EN/Final WP 55), 4. The French approach is apposite: There is a right to privacy in Art 9 of the Code Civile which is more specifically dealt with in the Labour Code L 122–35 where the internal disciplinary rules of the enterprise must not infringe the personal right to privacy unless the employer can provide justification by reference (according to the principle of proportionality) to the nature of the job and the purpose to be achieved by any restriction or infringement. See, also, Act No 82-689 of 4 August 1982. These rules are obligatory (L 122–33) and are enforced by the labour inspectorate having the power to scrutinise them *before* implementation.

[494] See for example, ILO, *Code of Practice on the Protection of Workers' Personal Data* (International Labour Organisation, Geneva 1997), para 5(8). DPA 1988, s 4, as amended by DPAA 2003, s 5, requires the data controller to respond in writing even where there is a refusal of a data access request citing reasons for the refusal. See Article 29 – Data Protection Working Party, *Working Document on the Suveillance of Electronic Communications in the Workplace* (5401/01/EN/Final WP 55), 14-15. See also Article 29 – Data Protection Working Party, *Opinion 8/2001 on the Processing of Personal Data in the Employment Context* (5062/01/EN/Final WP 48), 3.

[495] See Article 29 – Data Protection Working Party, *Working Document on the Suveillance of Electronic Communications in the Workplace* (5401/01/EN/Final WP 55), 18. DPA 1988, s 2C, as inserted by DPAA 2003, s 4, provides specifically for this concern. Article 29 – Data Protection Working Party, *Opinion 8/2001 on the Processing of Personal Data in the Employment Context* (5062/01/EN/Final WP 48), 3.

[496] See Article 29 – Data Protection Working Party, *Working Document on the Suveillance of Electronic Communications in the Workplace* (5401/01/EN/Final WP 55), 18. DPA 1988, s 2D, as inserted by DPAA 2003, s 4 makes specific provision.

[497] Article 29 – Data Protection Working Party, *Working Document on the Suveillance of Electronic Communications in the Workplace* (5401/01/EN/Final WP 55), 17–18. Article 29 – Data Protection Working Party, *Opinion 8/2001 on the Processing of Personal Data in the Employment Context* (5062/01/EN/Final WP 48), 3.

[498] Article 29 – Data Protection Working Party, *Working Document on the Suveillance of Electronic Communications in the Workplace* (5401/01/EN/Final WP 55), 16–17. Article 29 – Data Protection Working Party, *Opinion 8/2001 on the Processing of Personal Data in the Employment Context* (5062/01/EN/Final WP 48), 3.

[499] See DPA 1988, s 2D, as inserted by DPAA 2003, s 4 and para 5(7) ILO Code of Practice on the Protection of Workers' Personal Data (1997).

Chapter 7

Bullying, Harassment and Stress at Work

Des Ryan

INTRODUCTION: THE NATURE OF CLAIMS RELATING TO BULLYING, HARASSMENT AND STRESS AT WORK

Growth area in Irish employment law

[7.01] The issue of employers' liability at common law for workplace bullying, harassment and stress is one that has exercised the Irish and English courts in a significant number of high-profile cases in recent years: this has undoubtedly been one of the great growth areas of Irish employment law in the past decade. In this chapter, the focus is on common law proceedings brought by employees against their employers on the basis of workplace bullying, harassment and stress. Because of the significant impact it has exerted on the Irish case law, the flow of judicial developments in England and Wales is analysed in some detail in this chapter. So too is consideration given to jurisprudence from other jurisdictions, including Australia. A comprehensive analysis is provided of the most significant judicial developments in Irish law, up to and including the Supreme Court's decision in 2009 in *Berber v Dunnes Stores Ltd*.[1] Consideration is also given to the latest Code of Practice published by the Health and Safety Authority concerning bullying at work.

Multiplicity of potential legal sources of claims

[7.02] It is important to emphasise at the outset that, in addition to this emerging common law framework, the statutory backdrop of both the Employment Equality legislation and the Unfair Dismissals legislation may well present avenues of redress for employees who suffer bullying, harassment and stress at work.[2] So too does the Safety, Health and Welfare at Work Act 2005 present important new avenues of legal recourse for bullying, harassment and stress.[3] As these topics are the subject of separate chapters in the present work, they will not be considered in this chapter which instead concerns itself with identifying and analysing the growing line of case law concerning common law actions against employers in this context, primarily in negligence but also in breach

---

[1] *Berber v Dunnes Stores Ltd* [2009] IESC 10.

[2] For an overview of the various different jurisdictional features of the different fora in this context see for example Neligan, 'Jurisdictions and causes of action: Commercial considerations in dealing with bullying, stress and harassment cases' (2008) 15(1) *CLP* 3 (Part I) and (2008) 15(2) CLP 38 (Part II).

[3] Amongst the most important of these may be the potential for vicarious liability to be imposed on an employer for an employee's breach of his or her duty to fellow employees under s 13 of the 2005 Act: see the chapter on Vicarious Liability in this work.

of contract. Another important point to be made at the outset is the relevance of the potential imposition of vicarious liability upon employers in cases of this nature: reference should also be made to the separate chapter on vicarious liability in this work. The most prominent of the Irish cases requiring analysis in this chapter include the decisions of the Supreme Court in *Quigley v Complex Tooling and Moulding,*[4] and *Berber v Dunnes Stores Ltd*[5] and the High Court judgments in *Quigley* and *Berber*[6] and those in *Maher v Jabil Global Services Ltd,*[7] *Pickering v Microsoft Ireland Operations Ltd,*[8] and *Shortt v Royal Liver Insurance Ltd.*[9] In this chapter, analysis is given to the nature and extent of liability for workplace bullying, harassment and stress at work. Focus is also placed upon practical difficulties that attend bringing and defending such claims.

Relationship between negligence principles and the contract of employment

[7.03] It is well established that the basis for the application of negligence principles in the employment context is an implied term in the contract of employment that the employer will provide a safe working environment for the employee.[10] The potential for inconsistencies between the contract of employment and common law negligence principles can, however, give rise to difficulties. Consider the English Court of Appeal ruling in *Johnstone v Bloomsbury Health Authority*[11] where the plaintiff, a junior hospital doctor, argued that he had been required by his employers to work such excessively long hours as foreseeably to damage his health. His employers argued that his contention, even if it were correct, gave rise to no cause of action in negligence since his contract expressly obliged him to work long hours. This express contractual provision, they argued, took priority over any duty in tort, or any implied term of the contract, to safeguard the health of the plaintiff as an employee. The Court of Appeal accepted that the express terms of the contract superseded any tortious or implied contractual duty, but a majority[12] refused to strike out the claim, holding that on the proper construction of the contract of employment, the express and implied duties were not inherently in conflict. Accordingly, the defendants had not established beyond argument that they had in fact secured by means of the contract the right to insist that the plaintiff work so hard as to endanger his health and well being. It should be noted in this regard that in *Johnstone*, no cause of action premised on tort was apparently pleaded; rather, the focus of the case rested on the contractual sphere.

---

[4]   *Quigley v Complex Tooling and Moulding* [2008] ELR 297 (appeal from the judgment of Lavan J reported at [2005] ELR 305).

[5]   *Berber v Dunnes Stores Ltd* [2009] IESC 10 (appeal from the judgment of Laffoy J reported at [2007] ELR 1).

[6]   *Berber v Dunnes Stores Ltd* [2007] ELR 1.

[7]   *Maher v Jabil Global Services Ltd* [2008] IR 25.

[8]   *Pickering v Microsoft Ireland Operations Ltd* [2006] ELR 65.

[9]   *Shortt v Royal Liver Insurance Ltd* [2008] IEHC 332 (21 October 2008).

[10]   See, for example, *Bernadone v Pall Mall Services Group* [1999] IRLR 617.

[11]   *Johnstone v Bloomsbury Health Authority* [1992] QB 333.

[12]   Sir Nicolas Browne-Wilkinson VC and Stuart-Smith LJ; Leggatt LJ dissenting.

[7.04] Notwithstanding the fact that the majority in *Johnstone* declined to strike out the plaintiff's case, the implications of the approach taken in that case will be regarded by some as troubling. As Buckley has remarked, 'the implication ... that if the contract unambiguously so provides an employer can at common law acquire the right foreseeably to injure the health of his employees seems, to say the least, unattractive'.[13] Subsequent developments, however, may give still greater cause for unease at the prospect of the protection of the tort of negligence being emasculated by express contractual clauses. Thus, in the leading House of Lords judgment in *Barber v Somerset County Council*,[14] *Johnstone* was referred to with approval, with Lord Rodger observing that a tortious duty of reasonable care to protect employees from stress may 'not sit easily with ... contractual arrangements'. This tension between negligence principles and the terms of the contract of employment will be returned to later in this chapter.

Relationship between common law duties and statutory obligations

[7.05] There is a close overlap between the common law duty of care in negligence and statutory obligations placed on employers under workplace health and safety legislation.[15] Whilst it is of course the case that a court must assess an employer's liability in negligence separately from any statutory obligations owed to the employee, the reality is that the negligence inquiry is increasingly being informed and influenced by a consideration of statutory obligations. McMahon and Binchy suggest that the statutory code sends three messages to guide the courts in cases in which employers are sued in negligence: first, the statutory regime underlines the overall social support that exists for employees and what the authors refer to as 'paternalistic protective values'; secondly, the specificity of its provisions provides guidance as to what an employer might be expected to do in specific situations; and finally, 'the procedures prescribed by statutes may easily translate into useful models for what constitutes a 'safe system of work' for the purposes of employers' liability litigation at common law'.[16] If the latter two functions are considered together, a number of high-profile examples from the recent Irish jurisprudence are apparent. Let us consider briefly some examples in the context of bullying, harassment and stress in which the courts have clearly had regard to this interplay between statutory and common law duties: the High Court judgments in *McGrath v Trintech Technologies*[17] and *Quigley v Complex Tooling and Moulding Ltd*.[18]

---

[13] Richard A. Buckley, *The Law of Negligence* (4th edn, LexisNexis Butterworths, 2005), 360. See also Dr John PM White, 'The Employer's Duty and his Servant's Work-Load' (1991) 9 *ILT* 240.

[14] *Barber v Somerset County Council* [2004] UKHL 13; [2004] 1 WLR 1089 at [34].

[15] For detailed treatment of the action in breach of statutory duty in health and safety law, see Neil Foster (2006) 14 *TLR* 79.

[16] McMahon and Binchy, *Law of Torts* (3rd edn, Tottel Publishing, 2000) p 488.

[17] *McGrath v Trintech Technologies* [2005] 4 IR 382, [2005] ELR 49.

[18] *Quigley v Complex Tooling and Moulding Ltd* [2005] ELR 305. Although the High Court judgment was reversed by the Supreme Court, this did not affect the correctness of the approach taken by Lavan J on the law.

[7.06] In the leading case of *McGrath v Trintech Technologies*[19] the relevance of the health and safety legislation to a claim for occupational stress was considered by the High Court. The plaintiff claimed, *inter alia,* damages for personal injuries which he alleged he suffered as a result of occupational stress. He argued that the defendant employer was in breach of its obligations pursuant to the Safety, Health and Welfare at Work Act 1989 and the 1993 Regulations made thereunder. Although the High Court (Laffoy J) ultimately found against the plaintiff on this point, in principle the Court had no difficulty with the argument that the 1989 Act and the 1993 Regulations covered psychiatric health and psychiatric injuries. Laffoy J stated:

> It is undoubtedly the case that the general duties imposed by the Act of 1989 extend to the protection of the psychiatric health of employees and comprehend the obligation to provide assistance and measures which safeguard the employee against psychiatric injury induced by the stress and pressures of the employees working conditions and work load. As is pointed out in McMahon & Binchy at p.605 (footnote 93), almost without exception, the 1993 Regulations provide 'for strict and even absolute duties'. However, in a civil action the plaintiff must establish that the injury was caused by the breach. The question which arises in this case is whether the plaintiff has established a breach of a statutory duty in consequence of which he has suffered the injury and loss of which he complains.[20]

[7.07] Health and safety law was also expressly referred to by the High Court in the case of *Quigley v Complex Tooling and Moulding,*[21] where Lavan J stated:

> It has been a fairly recent movement towards the thinking that an employer must take care not only of the physical health of their employees, for example by providing safe equipment, but also must take reasonable care to protect them against mental injury, such as is complained of by the plaintiff in this case. It follows on from this that employers now have an obligation to prevent their employees from such that would cause mental injury, ie stress, harassment and bullying in the workplace.[22]

[7.08] The most important recent legislative initiative in this area is now the Safety, Health and Welfare at Work Act 2005.[23] In cases of bullying, harassment and stress, breach of statutory duty with specific reference to the 2005 Act is almost invariably pleaded in addition to negligence. There are important differences between the two claims, however, not least of which is that breaching a statutory duty does not in and of itself mean that liability in negligence will result, unless the existence of the statutory duty gives rise to (or, of course, mirrors) the existence of a common law duty of care. Healy has noted that:

> [t]he fact that a defendant is found to have breached a statutory duty enacted for the benefit of persons such as the plaintiff itself encourages the court to locate a corresponding duty under the common law.[24]

---

[19] *McGrath v Trintech Technologies* [2005] 4 IR 382, [2005] ELR 49.

[20] *McGrath v Trintech Technologies* [2005] 4 IR 382, at 418–419.

[21] *Quigley v Complex Tooling and Moulding* [2005] ELR 305.

[22] *Quigley v Complex Tooling and Moulding* [2005] ELR 305 at 317.

[23] For detailed analysis see Byrne, *Safety, Health and Welfare at Work Act 2005* (Thomson Round Hall, 2006), Shannon, *Health and Safety: Law and Practice* (Thomson Round Hall, 2007).

[24] Healy, *Principles of Irish Torts* (Clarus Press, 2006), p 233.

[7.09] Developments under the 2005 legislation are awaited with interest when its potential to inform the contours of the negligence action can be witnessed. To date, however, the principal source of judicial comment on the relevance of health and safety legislation remains the case law emanating from the previous health and safety regime, the Safety, Health and Welfare at Work Act 1989. This legislation was primarily designed at ensuring regulation rather than at enhancing civil liability – so much so that s 60(1) of the Act expressly provided that the core duties owed by an employer under the statute (those laid down in ss 6–11) were not to be taken independently to ground a civil cause of action but were instead enforceable by criminal prosecution. Section 28 of the 1989 Act enabled the Minister to pass regulations applicable to all work activities, however, and s 60(2) provided that the breach of a duty imposed by the regulations 'shall, so far as it causes damage, be actionable except in so far as the regulations provide otherwise'.

[7.10] The General Application Regulations adopted pursuant to this section did not preclude civil enforcement, and in fact created broad and open-textured duties capable of tempering the harshness of the s 60(1) denial of actionability. These regulations have been preserved in force under the 2005 Act,[25] unless and until repealed by further regulations adopted under s 58 of the new Act. The stringency of the obligations placed on employers through these regulations is to be viewed from the decided cases of the courts considering physical injuries in the context of the 1989 Act. Perhaps the most significant of these is the High Court decision in *Everitt v Thorsman Ireland Ltd*,[26] a case which illustrates the capacity of the regulations to fill the lacunae in the tort of negligence with which a plaintiff will frequently be confronted. The plaintiff sustained an injury when a lever with which he was supplied by his employers snapped and broke causing him to fall backwards onto the ground and sustain an injury. The evidence established that a latent defect within the metal lever caused it to snap and break. This was not known to the employer, who had bought the lever in good faith and who blamed the supplier of the bin (and who in turn blamed the manufacturer). The High Court (Kearns J) dismissed the employee's common law claim in negligence on the basis that the employer had not been unreasonable. Kearns J asked:

> What further steps could the employer have taken ... Short of having the lever assessed by an expert in metallurgy or breaking the lever with a view to determining its maximum stress resistance, it is difficult to see what could have been done. It was a newly purchased tool which appeared strong enough for the job and had been purchased from a reputable supplier and there is no suggestion to the contrary.[27]

[7.11] However, Kearns J regarded as of key relevance to the litigation s 19 of the General Application Regulations, which provided:

> It shall be the duty of every employer, to ensure that ... the necessary measures are taken so that the work equipment is suitable for the work to be carried out or is properly adapted for that purpose and may be used by employees without risk to their safety and health.

---

[25] Safety, Health and Welfare at Work Act 2005, s 4(4).
[26] *Everitt v Thorsman Ireland Ltd* [2000] 1 IR 256.
[27] *Everitt v Thorsman Ireland Ltd* [2000] 1 IR 256 at 262.

Kearns J expressed in very clear terms his view that this section imposed a positive obligation on the employer, describing it as placing 'virtually an absolute duty on employers in respect of the safety of equipment provided for the use of their employees'.[28] The aim of this statutory provision was inferred as being 'to ensure that an employee who suffers an injury at work through no fault of his own by using defective equipment should not be left without remedy'.[29]

[7.12] *Everitt* was considered by the High Court in 2008 in *Doyle v ESB*[30] where Quirke J similarly held that the employer had not breached its common law duty of care, but that recourse to the 1993 Regulations did enable the plaintiff to recover.

[7.13] Cases such as *Everitt* and *Doyle* illustrate the capacity for statutory obligations to provide routes to the imposition of liability upon employers where exclusive reliance on the tort of negligence would not permit such a result. It is further submitted, however, that the inverse is also true: an employer might be found to have fulfilled its statutory obligations, but nevertheless to have breached its common law duty of care in negligence. Statutory obligations may exceed the common law duty, may equal it, or may fall some way short of it.[31] There is, however, authority for the proposition that where an employer has discharged its statutory obligation it will be difficult to establish negligence,[32] and this may prove accurate in a great many cases.

Stress, bullying and harassment now clearly risks within scope of employer's duty of care

[7.14] Notwithstanding the 'comparative novelty of the cause of action',[33] it is now well established that stress, bullying and harassment are incidents of working life against which an employer must take steps to safeguard employees. As Cox has observed:

> It is now abundantly clear that employers owe a duty of care to employees in this regard and that failure to fulfil such duty of care can either justify an employee resigning and then claiming constructive dismissal, or alternatively can lead to an employee bringing a personal injuries action against the employer.[34]

In one leading High Court judgment in the area, Lavan J observed:

> It has been a fairly recent movement towards the thinking that an employer must take care not only of the physical health of their employees, for example, by providing safe equipment, but also take reasonable care to protect them against mental injury, such as is

---

[28] *Everitt v Thorsman Ireland Ltd* [2000] 1 IR 256 at 263.

[29] *Everitt v Thorsman Ireland Ltd* [2000] 1 IR 256 at 263. Kearns J noted, however, the lack of blameworthiness on the employer's part but, referring to *Connolly v Dundalk Urban District Council* (18 November 1992, unreported) SC, laid emphasis on the employer's ability to seek indemnity against the supplier.

[30] *Doyle v ESB* [2008] IEHC 88 (4 April 2008) Quirke J.

[31] *Bux v Slough Metals Ltd* [1973] 1 WLR 1358.

[32] *Roberts v Dorman Long & Co* [1953] 1 WLR 942 at 947 *per* Lord Goddard CJ.

[33] *Per* Fennelly J in *Quigley v Complex Tooling and Moulding* [2008] ELR 297.

[34] Cox, 'Employers' Liability for Workplace Stress: New Legal Developments' (2006) 1(2) *QRTL* 10, 10.

complained of by the plaintiff in this case. It follows on from this that employers now have an obligation to prevent their employees from such that would cause mental injury, *ie* stress, harassment and bullying in the workplace.[35]

Regarding the basis upon which the court should approach these cases Lavan J noted that '[the fundamental question is whether the defendant fell below the standard to be properly expected of a reasonable and prudent employer'.[36]

It is now proposed to consider in some detail the seminal decisions of the Irish courts and of the courts in other common law jurisdictions in this growing area.

Ordinary negligence principles apply in cases of workplace stress, bullying and harassment

[7.15] The case law thus far has been consistent in recognising that ordinary principles of negligence apply in cases of occupational stress. As was stated in one of the leading judgments:

> There is an argument that stress is so prevalent in some employments, of which teaching is one, and employees so reluctant to disclose it, that all employers should have in place systems to detect it and prevent its developing into actual harm.... [T]his raises some difficult issues of policy and practice which are unsuitable for resolution in individual cases before the courts. If knowledge advances to such an extent as to justify the imposition of obligations upon some or all employers to take particular steps to protect their employees from stress-related harm this is better done by way of regulations imposing specific statutory duties. In the meantime the ordinary law of negligence governs the matter.[37]

Of the familiar inquiries embarked upon by a court in any negligence inquiry, the question of foreseeability in terms of breach of duty has emerged as the most pressing in this area of employment law. It is examined in detail below. So too, however, do the other aspects of the negligence inquiry apply in workplace stress claims. An example of a key constituent ingredient of the negligence action which must be satisfied by plaintiffs and which may pose difficulty in stress, bullying and harassment cases is that the damage requirement of the negligence action must be established. As the Supreme Court has recently confirmed in the context of claims for workplace bullying and harassment, the damage complained of 'must amount to an identifiable psychiatric injury'.[38]

[7.16] The classic starting point in the case law in this area is the decision of the Queen's Bench Division of the English High Court in *Walker v Northumberland County Council*.[39] There the plaintiff worked as a social worker dealing with child abuse cases. His workload increased significantly over the years, without any increase in resources.

---

[35] *Quigley v Complex Tooling and Moulding* [2005] ELR 305.
[36] For further examples in an Irish context see, *inter alia*, *Saehan Media Ireland Ltd v A Worker* [1999] ELR 41, where the Labour Court acknowledged work-related stress as a health and safety issue and held that 'employers have an obligation to deal with instances of its occurrence which are brought to their attention'.
[37] *Per* Hale LJ in *Hatton v Sutherland* [2002] 1 All ER 1 at 16.
[38] *Per* Fennelly J in *Quigley v Complex Tooling and Moulding* [2008] ELR 297 at [17].
[39] *Walker v Northumberland County Council* [1995] ICR 702.

In 1987 he suffered a nervous breakdown which was found to have been caused by his workload. On his return to work he was promised support which did not materialise. Some months later he suffered another breakdown and was eventually dismissed on grounds of ill-health.

[7.17] Colman J found that although the first breakdown had been caused by the plaintiff's excessive workload, it was not reasonably foreseeable at that stage that his work would give rise to a risk of a nervous breakdown. However, on his return to work the employer should have foreseen that there was a risk that he would suffer further mental illness if again exposed to the same workload as before given that the plaintiff was vulnerable to psychiatric damage. Colman J[40] held that, at the point of the plaintiff's return to the same workload, it was 'quite likely, if not inevitable'[41] that he would suffer another breakdown and that he had not been afforded the 'measure of additional assistance'[42] with his work that he ought to have been given so as to avoid a recurrence of the illness. Colman J described the issue involved in the case as 'work-engendered psychiatric injury'.

ANALYSIS OF THE *HATTON* PRACTICAL PROPOSITIONS

'Practical Propositions' laid down in *Hatton v Sutherland*

[7.18] The issue came before the Court of Appeal in *Hatton v Sutherland*.[43] *Hatton* is now the leading English case and, owing to its frequent invocation in Irish case law, merits detailed analysis. In *Hatton*, the Court of Appeal attempted, in the course of four conjoined appeals, to provide guidelines for the resolution of claims being made in relation to workplace stress. In her judgment in that case Hale LJ (as she then was) set out a number of 'practical propositions' to be considered by a court in dealing with a case of occupational stress. It is worth setting out this list of propositions in full as the list summarises – albeit in only a general way – many of the chief concerns and questions which guide the courts in this area. Moreover, the practical propositions have been approved as providing helpful guidance in the Irish courts.[44] The propositions will then be analysed as a composite whole before turning to assess the manner in which they have subsequently been applied (and, in some cases, nuanced) by the courts both in this jurisdiction and in England.

> (1) There are no special control mechanisms applying to claims for psychiatric (or physical) illness or injury arising from the stress of doing the work the employee is required to do The ordinary principles of employer's liability apply.
>
> (2) The threshold question is whether this kind of harm to this particular employee was reasonably foreseeable: this has two components (a) an injury to health (as distinct from

---

[40]   Citing the earlier Court of Appeal judgment in *Petch v Customs and Excise Commissioners* [1993] ICR 789.

[41]   *Walker v Northumberland County Council* [1995] ICR 702 at 718.

[42]   *Walker v Northumberland County Council* [1995] ICR 702 at 721.

[43]   *Hatton v Sutherland* [2002] 2 All ER 1.

[44]   This is discussed more fully below; para **[7.32]** *et seq.*

occupational stress) which (b) is attributable to stress at work (as distinct from other factors).

(3) Foreseeability depends upon what the employer knows (or ought reasonably to know) about the individual employee. Because of the nature of mental disorder, it is harder to foresee than physical injury, but may be easier to foresee in a known individual than in the population at large. An employer is usually entitled to assume that the employee can withstand the normal pressures of the job unless he knows of some particular problem or vulnerability.

(4) The test is the same whatever the employment: there are no occupations which should be regarded as intrinsically dangerous to mental health.

(5) Factors likely to be relevant in answering the threshold question include: (a) The nature and extent of the work done by the employee. Is the workload much more than is normal for the particular job? Is the work particularly intellectually or emotionally demanding for this employee? Are demands being made of this employee unreasonable when compared with the demands made of others in the same or comparable jobs? Or are there signs that others doing this job are suffering harmful levels of stress? Is there an abnormal level of sickness or absenteeism in the same job or the same department? (b) Signs from the employee of impending harm to health Has he a particular problem or vulnerability? Has he already suffered from illness attributable to stress at work? Have there recently been frequent or prolonged absences which are uncharacteristic of him? Is there reason to think that these are attributable to stress at work, for example because of complaints or warnings from him or others?

(6) The employer is generally entitled to take what he is told by his employee at face value, unless he has good reason to think to the contrary. He does not generally have to make searching inquiries of the employee or seek permission to make further inquiries of his medical advisers.

(7) To trigger a duty to take steps, the indications of impending harm to health arising from stress at work must be plain enough for any reasonable employer to realise that he should do something about it.

(8) The employer is only in breach of duty if he has failed to take the steps which are reasonable in the circumstances, bearing in mind the magnitude of the risk of harm occurring, the gravity of the harm which may occur, the costs and practicability of preventing it, and the justifications for running the risk.

(9) The size and scope of the employer's operation, its resources and the demands it faces are relevant in deciding what is reasonable; these include the interests of other employees and the need to treat them fairly, for example, in any redistribution of duties.

(10) An employer can only reasonably be expected to take steps which are likely to do some good: the court is likely to need expert evidence on this.

(11) An employer who offers a confidential advice service, with referral to appropriate counselling or treatment services, is unlikely to be found in breach of duty.

(12) If the only reasonable and effective step would have been to dismiss or demote the employee, the employer will not be in breach of duty in allowing a willing employee to continue in the job.

(13) In all cases, therefore, it is necessary to identify the steps which the employer both could and should have taken before finding him in breach of his duty of care.

(14) The claimant must show that that breach of duty has caused or materially contributed to the harm suffered. It is not enough to show that occupational stress has caused the harm.

(15) Where the harm suffered has more than one cause, the employer should only pay for that proportion of the harm suffered which is attributable to his wrongdoing, unless the harm is truly indivisible. It is for the defendant to raise the question of apportionment.

(16) The assessment of damages will take account of any pre-existing disorder or vulnerability and of the chance that the claimant would have succumbed to a stress-related disorder in any event.[45]

[7.19] Due to the importance of the 16 practical propositions and the frequency with which they have been cited, it is instructive to reflect on their content and scope.

Propositions clarifying ingredients in the cause of action

[7.20] The first and most fundamental of the practical propositions confirms that special control mechanisms do not apply in this area of tort law and that, moreover, as discussed above, such claims might be brought in either tort or contract. Many of the remaining propositions are concerned with illuminating the nature and scope of the constituent ingredients that plaintiffs must satisfy and the various factors that will determine whether the employer had been negligent in the circumstances. Thus the second proposition, for example, underlines the nature of the plaintiff's task when alleging personal injury in these cases, identifying as the threshold question that of whether this kind of harm to this particular employee was reasonably foreseeable. Significant here is the explicit bifurcation of the two separate components: first, an injury to health which was, secondly, attributable to the workplace. This distinction sounds a warning note in terms not only of causation but also of foreseeability.

[7.21] Experience in both the Irish and English courts indicates that it is in relation to the question of foreseeability that plaintiffs will frequently face their most problematic hurdle. The importance of foreseeability was, for example, again emphasised in the later case of *Hartman v South Essex Mental Health and Community Care NHS Trust*.[46] In that case, Scott Baker LJ said that liability for psychiatric injury suffered due to stress at work was in principle no different from liability for physical injury, but added:

> It is foreseeable injury flowing from the employer's breach of duty that gives rise to the liability. It does not follow that because a claimant suffers stress at work and that the employer is in some way in breach of duty in allowing that to occur that the claimant is able to establish a claim in negligence.[47]

[7.22] According to the third *Hatton* proposition, foreseeability depends upon what the employer either knows or ought reasonably to know about the individual employee. In this regard, it is noteworthy that Hale LJ endorsed the familiar and well-established principle that in the context of employers' liability the content of the employer's duty may be higher in situations where the employer knows of the vulnerability of the

---

[45] *Hatton v Sutherland* [2002] 2 All ER 1 at [43].
[46] *Hartman v South Essex Mental Health and Community Care NHS Trust* [2005] ICR 782.
[47] *Hartman v South Essex Mental Health and Community Care NHS Trust* [2005] ICR 782 at 788.

employee. Recognising that it is harder to foresee mental disorder than physical injury, she said that an employer is usually entitled to assume that the employee can withstand the normal pressures of the post unless the employer is on notice of some particular problem or vulnerability. An important point here is Hale LJ's acknowledgement in the fourth proposition that there are no occupations which should be regarded as intrinsically dangerous to mental health. This proposition has more recently been affirmed by the High Court of Australia in the case of *New South Wales v Fahy*.[48]

[7.23] Hale LJ expanded on proposition 2 in propositions 14–16, where the causal requirements of the claim were amplified. Emphasising that the employee must establish that the employer's breach of duty caused or materially contributed to the harm suffered, Hale LJ furthermore stressed that the assessment of damages should take account of any pre-existing disorder or vulnerability and of the possibility that the plaintiff would have sustained a stress-related disorder in any event.

[7.24] The fifth proposition addresses factors that will be relevant in answering the crucial threshold question of foreseeability. They include not only the 'nature and extent of the work done by the employee', but also refer to 'signs from the employee of impending harm to health'. Again, this bifurcation is important, since the foreseeability inquiry is one that addresses both the particular and the general: was this particular employee at a special risk of which the employer knew or ought to have known? Was the plaintiff evidencing a problem shared by employees generally, so that the employer ought reasonably to have appreciated the problem? Such questions are at the heart of the foreseeability analysis in these cases.

Propositions qualifying the employer's duty

[7.25] It is important to note that propositions 6–13 qualify the employer's duty. Proposition 6 provides that an employer is generally entitled to accept at face value what it is told by an employee: there is generally no obligation on employers to make probing inquiries, medical or otherwise. In terms of what the courts will deem to be a catalyst requiring subsequent steps to be taken by the employer, Hale LJ stressed that the indications of impending damage to the employee's health must be sufficiently obvious that any reasonable employer would appreciate that action was required. And even in these extreme circumstances, the employer will only be held liable if it failed to take steps which are reasonable in the circumstances, having regard to the magnitude of the risk of harm occurring, the gravity of the harm which may occur, the costs and practicability of preventing it, and the justifications for running the risk. In this reasonableness inquiry, the nature, size and resources of the employer's enterprise are all relevant in determining what is reasonable; so too are the interests of other employees and the need to treat them fairly (as, for example, in any distribution of duties) to be considered in this regard. In what can be described as a general point of qualification of duty, the Court of Appeal stressed that in all cases, it is necessary to identify the steps which the employer both could and should have taken before determining that the employer has breached its duty of care (proposition 13).

---

[48] *New South Wales v Fahy* [2007] HCA 20 (22 May 2007).

[7.26] A further point of qualification in relation to the employer's duty of care is that an employer will not be penalised for having avoided action that would either have been ineffective or inimical to the employee's own interests. One of the most-discussed aspects of *Hatton* in this regard is the emphasis placed on the practical effectiveness of the provision of a confidential advice service: according to proposition 11, an employer who has put such a service in place is unlikely to be held to have been negligent. In relation to this eleventh *Hatton* proposition concerning the value to an employer of having a confidential advice service, a number of subsequent cases have thrown doubt upon the capacity of such a service to save an employer from exposure in negligence. The judgment of the Irish High Court in *Maher v Jabil Global Services Ltd*,[49] for example, provides strong support for the proposition that policies and procedures in place must have a practical value and relevance to the employment environment: mere paper compliance is not sufficient.

[7.27] A number of more recent English cases have further shown how the provision of a confidential support service may not necessarily save employers. In *Hartman*,[50] for example, the Court of Appeal held that confidential information held by the employer's occupational health department could not be deemed to be within the employer's knowledge for the purposes of determining what was foreseeable – although in this particular case the confidentiality of the service was a fact that assisted the employer.

[7.28] More recently in delivering his judgment in *Daw v Intel Corp (UK) Ltd*[51] Pill LJ afforded detailed consideration to this question. The key point considered in *Daw* was whether the High Court had erred in finding that the psychiatric injury suffered by an employee as a result of an excessive workload had been reasonably foreseeable by the employer. This was the first judicial consideration of the relevance of a confidential counselling service since *Hatton*. Importantly, it was held that the reference to counselling services in *Hatton* did not mean that this factor would be determinative in any given case. As Pill LJ explained in the course of his judgment:

> A very considerable amount of helpful guidance is given in *Hatton*. That does not preclude or excuse the trial judge either from conducting a vigorous fact-finding exercise, as the trial judge in this case did, or deciding which parts of the guidance are relevant to the particular circumstances. The reference to counselling services in *Hatton* does not make such services a panacea by which employers can discharge their duty of care in all cases.[52]

As Moore has observed:

> It is now abundantly clear that employers cannot assume that provision of a counselling service is akin to a before the event insurance policy behind which refuge can be taken when things go wrong.[53]

---

49 *Maher v Jabil Global Services Ltd* [2008] 1 IR 25.
50 *Hartman v South Essex Mental Health and Community Care NHS Trust* [2005] ICR 782.
51 *Daw v Intel Corp (UK) Ltd* [2007] EWCA Civ 70.
52 *Daw v Intel Corp (UK) Ltd* [2007] EWCA Civ 70, *per* Pill LJ at [45].
53 (2007) 151 *Solicitors' Journal* 383.

[7.29] Difficulties arise where it may be that the appropriate step to manage the situation is to dismiss or to demote the employee. As seen above, in *Hatton*, Hale LJ held that the employer will not be in breach of duty in permitting a willing employee to continue in his or her role (proposition 12). It has, however, been pointed out that there may be a conflict between this and Hale LJ's ninth proposition.[54] In the ninth proposition Hale LJ observed that the employer has to take into account the interests of other employees; she gave as an example the need to treat them fairly in respect of any distribution of work. What of a situation in which the interests of other employees require that the individual employee not continue at work? As Barrett has observed:

> These propositions can only be reconciled provided the employee who is at risk is working effectively and not placing extra burdens on colleagues. There is, however, a question whether the employer should dismiss the employee who, being stressed, is imposing burdens on the rest of the workforce. In some cases the conduct of the employee (harassing or otherwise disturbing colleagues) may require at least suspension; but whether in even this situation an employer could proceed to a disciplinary hearing and dismissal as opposed to requiring the employee to take sick leave is controversial.[55]

[7.30] Hale LJ rooted her twelfth proposition in the authority of *Withers v Perry Chain Co Ltd*[56] where an unsuccessful claim for damages for personal injury had been brought by an employee who chose to work in a situation where there was known to be an exceptional risk to her personally. In that case Devlin LJ expressed the view that, '[t]he employee is free to decide for herself what risks she will run...'.[57] The rationale given for this approach in *Withers* was the undesirability of imposing any restriction on the freedom of the individual – since the relationship between employer and employee is not akin to that between schoolmaster and pupil[58] –- or of causing oppression to the employee by limiting his or her ability to find work.[59] It has, however, been questioned whether this approach has survived developments in European legislation.[60] By contrast with *Withers*, in *Coxall v Goodyear Great Britain Ltd*[61] liability was imposed where an employee's asthma condition worsened because, given the magnitude of the risk, it would have been proper to move him to other work or to dismiss him. A fundamental point to be made in this regard is that both of these authorities concerned physical as opposed to psychiatric injury; in *Hatton*, Hale LJ emphasised that she was dealing only with psychiatric injury, and that in this regard it has to be for the employee to decide whether he or she wishes to run the risk of psychiatric injury by continuing in employment.

---

[54] See Barrett, 'Psychiatric Stress: An Unacceptable Cost to Employers' [2008] *JBL* 64, 76.

[55] Barrett, 'Psychiatric Stress: An Unacceptable Cost to Employers' [2008] *JBL* 64, 76.

[56] *Withers v Perry Chain Co Ltd* [1961] 1 WLR 1314.

[57] *Withers v Perry Chain Co Ltd* [1961] 1 WLR 1314 at 1320.

[58] *Withers v Perry Chain Co Ltd* [1961] 1 WLR 1314 at 1320.

[59] *Withers v Perry Chain Co Ltd* [1961] 1 WLR 1314.

[60] Cotter and Bennett eds, *Munkman on Employers' Liability* (14th edn, LexisNexis Butterworths, 2006), p 134.

[61] *Coxall v Goodyear Great Britain Ltd* [2003] 1 WLR 536.

[7.31] Having analysed the sixteen propositions both from the point of view of their framing the content of an employee's cause of action and of qualifying the employer's duty, the application of these propositions in English and Irish law will now be analysed.

The application of the practical propositions in English and Irish case law

[7.32] The *Hatton* propositions were implicitly accepted by the House of Lords in *Barber v Somerset CC*.[62] Thereafter, several cases were appealed to the Court of Appeal – with the appeals being received with some surprise, and perhaps even a degree of judicial exasperation.[63] Thus in *Hartman v South Essex Mental Health and Community Care NHS Trust,* in which six cases were appealed, Scott Baker LJ in delivering the judgment noted that despite the decisions of the Court of Appeal in *Hatton* and the House of Lords in *Barber*, judges were finding difficulty in applying the appropriate principles in claims arising from stress at work. It was noted that litigation was being fought at a cost of time and money out of all proportion to the value of the claims. Scott Baker LJ also emphasised that in *Barber* Lord Walker warned that while Hale LJ's judgment gave useful practical guidance: '[Iit must be read as that, and not as having anything like statutory force. Every case will depend on its own facts.'

[7.33] Similarly, in *Vahidi v Fairstead House School Trust Ltd*[64] the Court of Appeal regretted that mediation had not taken place since the courts had settled many of the principles in stress at work cases.

'Practical Propositions' in *Hatton* not to be read as if worded in a statute – but have been afforded considerable recognition by Irish courts

[7.34] While the above guidelines represent a valuable contribution to the development of the law and comprise highly useful practical guidance, it should be emphasised, as courts have emphasised, that they must not be read 'as having anything like statutory force'.[65] Equally, it has been remarked that 'the 16 propositions in *Sutherland* do not necessarily offer an employer a scheme for avoiding civil liability for stress-related psychiatric injury.'[66] That having been said, the Irish courts have consistently demonstrated a willingness to have regard to these propositions. Thus in the course of his judgment in *Maher v Jabil Global Services Ltd*,[67] one of the leading cases in this area, Clarke J stated as follows:

> In *McGrath v Trintech Technologies Ltd*, Laffoy J reviewed the authorities in relation to an employer's liability for psychiatric illness induced by stress and pressures at work. In the

---

[62] *Barber v Somerset CC* [2004] UKHL 13; [2004] 1 WLR 1089, analysed below at para [7.34] *et seq.*

[63] Barrett, 'Psychiatric Stress: An Unacceptable Cost to Employers' [2008] *JBL* 64, 73.

[64] *Vahidi v Fairstead House School Trust Ltd* [2005] EWCA Civ 765.

[65] *Per* Lord Walker in *Barber v Somerset County Council* [2004] UKHL 13, [2004] 1 WLR 1089, [65].

[66] Barrett, 'Psychiatric Stress: An Unacceptable Cost to Employers' [2008] *JBL* 64, 77.

[67] *Maher v Jabil Global Services Ltd* [2008] 1 IR 25 at 38. The Supreme court judgment in *Berber v Dunnes Stores Ltd* [2009] IESC 10 also places emphasis on the relevance of the *Hatton* propositions.

course of her judgment Laffoy J cited with approval 16 'practical propositions' set out in the judgment of Hale LJ in *Hatton v Sunderland* which are designed to assist in the assessment of such cases. While not all of those practical propositions will be relevant in each case, it was accepted by both sides that the principles identified by Laffoy J represent the law in this jurisdiction.

[7.35] The Court of Appeal in *Hatton* placed a considerable onus on the employee to inform the employer of the nature of his or her difficulties and that those difficulties were having an adverse effect on his or her health. The apparently onerous nature of that requirement was lessened by the House of Lords in dealing with one of the four cases on appeal, *Barber v Somerset County Council*.[68]

Difference of approach between Court of Appeal and House of Lords in *Barber*

[7.36] In *Barber v Somerset County Council*[69] the plaintiff was a teacher whose post as head of department had been eliminated in a restructuring arrangement. In order to maintain his salary, he had applied to take on, in addition to his regular teaching duties, the position of school project manager for public and media relations. This resulted in his working long hours which led to stress and to what he described as 'work overload'. He informed management of this situation and, following a period off work, he returned with sick notes from his doctor recording that he was overstressed and suffered from depression (information he also supplied on his employer's form of sickness declaration). He also discussed his problems with the senior management team, but no steps were taken to remedy or investigate this situation. However, for some five months between July and November he gave no indication to his employers that his problems were continuing. In November, he suffered a serious breakdown and became permanently incapable of engaging in anything more than part-time work. He sued the council for personal injuries in the form of a serious depressive illness.

[7.37] His claim was upheld by Trigger J at first instance but was rejected by the Court of Appeal. The Court of Appeal found that the injuries sustained by the employee were not reasonably foreseeable and that it was 'expecting far too much' to expect the employer to pick up the fact that problems of which they had been made aware previously were continuing without some such indication being made by the employee.

[7.38] The House of Lords allowed the employee's appeal – though it should be noted that the House of Lords considered the case to be 'fairly close to the borderline'[70] and the decision was not unanimous.[71]

[7.39] As to the correct legal test to be applied in cases of this kind, Lord Walker agreed[72] that Hale LJ's analysis of the issue provided 'useful practical guidance', but

---

[68] *Barber v Somerset County Council* [2004] UKHL 13, [2004] 1 WLR 1089.

[69] *Barber v Somerset County Council* [2004] UKHL 13, [2004] 1 WLR 1089.

[70] *Barber v Somerset County Council* [2004] UKHL 13, [2004] 1 WLR 1089 *per* Lord Walker at [67].

[71] The dissenting judgment of Lord Scott is discussed further at para **[7.41]**.

[72] *Barber v Somerset County Council* [2004] UKHL 13, [2004] 1 WLR 1089 at [65].

said that the following well-known statement of Swanwick J in *Stokes v Guest, Keen and Nettlefold (Bolts and Nuts) Ltd*[73] remained 'the best statement of general principle':

> [T]he overall test is still the conduct of the reasonable and prudent employer, taking positive thought for the safety of his workers in the light of what he knows or ought to know; where there is a recognised and general practice which has been followed for a substantial period in similar circumstances without mishap, he is entitled to follow it, unless in the light of common sense or newer knowledge it is clearly bad; but, where there is developing knowledge, he must keep reasonably abreast of it and not be too slow to apply it; and where he has in fact greater than average knowledge of the risks, he may be thereby obliged to take more than the average or standard precautions. He must weigh up the risk in terms of the likelihood of injury occurring and the potential consequences if it does; and he must balance against this the probably effectiveness of the precautions that can be taken to meet it and the expense and inconvenience they involve. If he is found to have fallen below the standard to be properly expected of a reasonable and prudent employer in these respects, he is negligent.[74]

[7.40] The majority found that a three-week period of certified stress leave should have led to enquiries from management about what they could do to ease the plaintiff's problems. The Law Lords held that management should have, at the least, made 'sympathetic inquiries' in this respect on the plaintiff's return to work; attempted to reduce his workload and monitored his condition. The employer's failure to carry out these steps had caused the employee's ill health. It should be noted that the Law Lords accepted that the factual conclusion in this case involved a delicately balanced value judgment – providing a further reason why the findings of the trial judge ought not to be upset on appeal.

Strong dissenting judgment in House of Lords in *Barber*

[7.41] It should be noted that Lord Scott, in a strong dissenting judgment, took the view that the question on the appeal was one of law as opposed to fact: namely, what standard of care should be imposed upon the employer in these circumstances. Lord Scott considered that the appeal should be dismissed on the basis that Mr Barber had failed to bring his difficulties to the attention of his employer. The tone of his dissenting judgment is perhaps best captured in the following passage:

> Schools operate under considerable difficulties. I do not suppose there are many, if any, teachers whose workload does not place them under considerable continuous pressure apt to cause stress and sometimes depression. The same, I suspect, would apply to many professional employees. Nurses and doctors working in the NHS are an obvious example. Employed lawyers working in busy city firms are probably another. Pressure and stress are part of the system of work under which they carry out their daily duties. But they are all adults. They choose their profession. They can and sometimes do complain about it to their employers. In under funded institutions, providing vital social services there is often very little that the employers can do about stress problems. Colleagues in he school or hospital are likely to be carrying an equally heavy workload. Is it fair to ask them to

---

[73] *Stokes v Guest, Keen and Nettlefold (Bolts and Nuts) Ltd* [1968] 1 WLR 1776 at 1783.

[74] The test originally propounded by Swanwick J in *Stokes v Guest, Keen and Nettlefold (Bolts and Nuts) Ltd* [1968] 1 WLR 1776 at 1783.

assume a greater burden in order to relieve the stress on a particular teacher? Can the school afford to ask for a supply teacher? As a last resort the school may have to do so. But the school is entitled to expect, first, to be kept fully informed by the teacher of his or her problems.[75]

Whether *Hatton* imposes 'heightened scrutiny' threshold

[7.42] The four appeals considered by the Court of Appeal in *Hatton* were all appeals by employers on whom liability had been imposed at first instance: in three of the four cases their appeals succeeded. Although the House of Lords did reverse the decision of the Court of Appeal in one case (*Barber*), as seen above, it did so whilst expressing the view that the case was a borderline one and the majority judgment was accompanied by a strong dissent from Lord Scott. This may provoke the conclusion that after *Hatton*, the bar has been raised for plaintiffs instituting proceedings in bullying, harassment and stress cases. This conclusion may, however, be over-pessimistic from a plaintiff's point of view. Given that these cases are quintessentially evidence-based cases, their outcome will frequently be unpredictable.

[7.43] Whilst it is indeed possible to point to a number of English cases decided post-*Hatton* in which claimants have been unsuccessful,[76] so too have there been recent cases in which plaintiffs have successfully invoked the principles in *Hatton* to recover damages for injuries caused by workplace stress.[77]

[7.44] Nevertheless, the recent Court of Appeal judgment in *Deadman v Bristol City Council*[78] provides further evidence of the tendency to limit the scope of stress at work claims since the decision in *Hatton*. The plaintiff was employed as a manager of the defendant's mechanical and Electrical Services Team. After an encounter in June 1998, he was accused by a female colleague of sexual harassment. In due course the employer carried out an investigation, but failed to follow its own procedures correctly. Contrary to the employer's policy entitled 'Procedure for stopping harassment in the workplace', the panel convened to consider the complaint composed only two, rather than three, members. The panel found against Mr Deadman, but its decision was set aside when Mr Deadman challenged it pursuant to the defendant's grievance procedure. Following his successful appeal, a decision was taken to convene a new panel to carry out a fresh investigation. This decision was communicated to Mr Deadman in a letter which was left on his desk for him to find when he next came into work. After receipt of this letter, Mr Deadman ceased work permanently as a result of depression. He sued the defendant for breach of contract and for breach of the common law duty of care.

[7.45] At first instance, the claim was upheld. The judge found that the defendant had acted in breach of contract in the way it conducted the initial investigation and in the insensitive manner in which it had informed Mr Deadman of the renewal of the investigation after the original panel's decision was overturned, and that those breaches

---

[75] *Barber v Somerset County Council* [2004] UKHL 13, [2004] 1 WLR 1089 at [14].

[76] See for example *Deadman v Bristol City Council* [2007] EWCA Civ 822, [2007] IRLR 888.

[77] See for example *Daw v Intel Group* [2007] EWCA Civ 70.

[78] *Deadman v Bristol City Council* [2007] EWCA Civ 822, [2007] IRLR 888.

had caused Mr Deadman's illness. The judge did not however hold that the defendant breached its common law duty of care.

[7.46] The defendant appealed, arguing that the terms upon which the decision at first instance was based did not form part of the contract of employment, and that there was an inconsistency in the judge's finding that the defendant had not breached its duty of care and his finding that the defendant was in breach of contract. Although the Court of Appeal did not accept that there was necessarily an inconsistency between the judge's rejection of the claim in tort and his finding that the defendant was in breach of contract, the defendant's appeal was successful.

[7.47] Whilst the Court of Appeal accepted that the defendant was guilty of breach of contract, it held that the plaintiff was not entitled to damages. This was because it was not reasonably foreseeable that the council's failure to comply with its investigation procedure would cause Mr Deadman to suffer psychiatric harm. The Court of Appeal also rejected the plaintiff's cross-appeal that there was a breach of duty of care in this case. Citing *Hatton*, the Court of Appeal noted that the threshold question was whether this kind of harm to this particular employee was reasonably foreseeable, the Court of Appeal noted that to all appearances Mr Deadman was a person of robust good health. (The plaintiff had worked for the defendant for almost thirty years and had been absent from work for only five days during that period.) Leave to appeal to the House of Lords was refused.

[7.48] *Deadman* is thus a significant development in the ever-growing line of case law relating to stress and bullying at work: it further illustrates the problems of foreseeability that plaintiffs in such cases will face. From the Irish standpoint, this is of course highly pertinent in light of the third limb of the test laid down by Clarke J in the important case of *Maher v Jabil Global Services Ltd*.[79]

BULLYING, HARASSMENT AND STRESS AT WORK: THE IRISH CASE LAW

[7.49] It is now proposed to conduct an analysis of the key Irish cases in this growing and difficult area. By way of introductory comment, and in light of the foregoing analysis of the English authorities, it would appear that the dissenting approach of Lord Scott in the House of Lords in *Barber* is more consistent with the approach that has been seen from the Irish courts in recent cases. It will thus be important to consider the treatment in the preceding paragraphs of the difference between the majority and minority opinions in *Barber* when reflecting on the approaches taken by the Irish courts.

Analysis of 16 Practical Propositions in *McGrath v Trintech*

[7.50] In the leading case of *McGrath v Trintech Technologies Ltd*[80] Laffoy J set out a detailed analysis of the relevant legal principles relying significantly on the decision of the Court of Appeal in *Hatton*. She concluded as follows:

---

[79] *Maher v Jabil Global Services Ltd* [2008] 1 IR 25.
[80] *McGrath v Trintech Technologies Ltd* [2005] 4 IR 382.

The effect of the decisions of the Court of Appeal and the House of Lords in the *Hatton/Barber* case is to assimilate the principles governing an employer's liability at common law for physical injury and for psychiatric injury where an employee claims that the psychiatric injury has resulted from the stress and pressures of his/her working conditions and work load. In my view, there is no reason in law or in principle why a similar approach should not be adopted in this jurisdiction. I consider that the practical propositions summarised in the judgment of the Court of Appeal in the *Hatton* case are helpful in the application of legal principle in an area which is characterised by difficulty and complexity, subject, to the caveat of Lord Walker in the *Barber* case – but one must be mindful that every case will depend on its own facts.[81]

[7.51] The plaintiff in *McGrath* was a senior project manager in a multinational information technology company. He claimed that he had suffered from stress as a result of the manner in which he had been treated by his employer during his time on a placement in Uruguay. The plaintiff claimed that during his time in Uruguay he was subjected to serious work related stress and pressure which he claimed resulted in psychological injury. The evidence included a number of crises having occurred during the material time which the plaintiff had had to manage, as well as an acrimonious relationship between him and his immediate boss. On his return to Ireland the plaintiff was on certified sick leave until he was made redundant.

[7.52] Laffoy J in her judgment undertook an extensive review of the Irish and English case law in the area. She accepted that the plaintiff had established that he suffered from what she termed 'a recognisable psychiatric illness'. Nevertheless, the plaintiff's case failed in relation to foreseeability.

[7.53] The Court in *McGrath* concluded that the defendant did not have any actual knowledge of the plaintiff's vulnerability to psychological injury or harm, having had him medically assessed before the commencement of his employment. It should be noted that in taking this approach in relation to foreseeability Laffoy J placed particular emphasis upon the fact that the plaintiff had been an employee in a workplace environment that embodied a robust corporate culture. She explained:

> It clearly emerged from the evidence that the corporate culture in the defendant's companies is competitive and demanding of their employees. [It was described as] the American model where employees work hard and play hard against the background of 'economic ups and downs'. It was not a place where one would admit weakness...On the evidence I conclude that there was no reason why the... defendant should not assume that the plaintiff could withstand the stresses and pressures of this type of work environment and of the workload which he was required to undertake.[82]

[7.54] On the evidence Laffoy J found that the defendant had adequately addressed any signs of vulnerability on the part of the plaintiff or possible harm to his health. She referred specifically to the fact that the plaintiff had not informed the defendant of his medial problems while in Uruguay and that he was not absent on sick leave. This echoes the emphasis placed in *Hatton*, seen above, on the proposition that an employer can in

---

[81] *McGrath v Trintech Technologies Ltd* [2005] 4 IR 382 at 416.
[82] *McGrath v Trintech Technologies Ltd* [2005] 4 IR 382 at 433–434.

the ordinary course, accept at face value what it is told by its employees. In an attempt to satisfy this criterion, the plaintiff in *McGrath* sought to point to a conversation which he had had with his manager as amounting to evidence of placing the defendant on notice of his particular vulnerability. Laffoy J concluded, however, that this conversation was a casual conversation which did not put the individual in question on any further enquiry as to the plaintiff's psychological condition. She found that to the extent that the defendant had been put on notice in relation to the plaintiff's health problems, the defendant had discharged its duty of care by procuring medical advice.[83]

[7.55] In concluding that the plaintiff had failed to establish foreseeability, Laffoy J stated that the fundamental test was whether the defendant fell below the standard to be properly expected of a reasonable and prudent employer and concluded that this defendant did not, having done what was reasonable in the circumstances. Laffoy J, in *McGrath,* accepted that the plaintiff undoubtedly held a 'subjective perception' that he was not being properly supported. However, she concluded that, viewed objectively in the light of what the defendant knew about the plaintiff, what his role was, and what was expected of him, the manner in which the plaintiff was treated by the defendant did not give rise to a breach of the defendant's duty of care to the plaintiff. Accordingly, it seems that the courts in this context will require an objective analysis of the treatment complained of. As Bolger observes, this is 'in stark contrast to the statutory law on harassment including sexual harassment at work which seems to permit a very subjective analysis.'[84]

The *Maher v Jabil* test

[7.56] The later judgment of the High Court in *Maher v Jabil Global Services Ltd*[85] is now arguably the leading Irish authority on point since the High Court (Clarke J) articulated a three-stage inquiry or test for assessing whether recovery lies in a case of workplace stress which has since been applied in subsequent cases.[86] This judgment of the High Court in 2005 provides another prominent example of a case where the plaintiff failed to establish reasonable foreseeability on the part of the employer.

---

[83] *McGrath v Trintech Technologies Ltd* [2005] 4 IR 382 at 435.

[84] Bolger, 'Claiming for occupational stress, bullying and harassment' (2006) 3(4) *IELJ* 108, points out that this approach has been supported by the High Court in the case of *Cronin v Kostler* (1 December 2005) HC *(ex tempore* judgment of Haugh J, reported in The Irish Times Law Report 27 February 2006) and in the Circuit Court in the case of *Hickey v Health Insurance Authority* (3 February 2006, unreported) CC, (2006) The Irish Times 4 February, Smyth J) where the plaintiffs' subjective perceptions of their treatment were found not to constitute actionable bullying and harassment. In both cases the plaintiffs complained of treatment which the defendant maintained was reasonable management of their employees. Ultimately the courts in both cases relieved the defendants of liability.

[85] *Maher v Jabil Global Services Ltd* [2008] 1 IR 25.

[86] See in particular the 2006 judgment of the High Court (Laffoy J) in *Berber v Dunnes Stores Ltd* [2007] ELR 1, analysed below at para **[7.68]** *et seq*. Although the High Court judgment was reversed on appeal to the Supreme Court ([2009] IESC 10) this does not affect the correctness of the legal principles identified by the HIgh Court in *Berber*.

[7.57] The plaintiff in *Maher* had claimed damages for stress arising from one period of alleged over work and one period of alleged under work. The Court was satisfied that he had suffered personal injury which was caused by his work environment. In relation to the period of overwork, Clarke J concluded:

> [I]t does not seem to me that, having regard to such factors as those identified in item 5 of the practical propositions specified in *Hatton*, that the objective threshold for foreseeability is met. There is no evidence from which I could conclude that the work load was more than is normal in the particular job. While it may be that the work turned out to be more demanding for the plaintiff I am not satisfied that there was any evidence upon which it is reasonable to infer that the employer should have known this. It does not appear that there is any real evidence that the demands made of the plaintiff were unreasonable when compared with the demands made on others in the same or comparable jobs. Nor were there any signs that others doing the job had suffered harmful levels of stress or that there was an abnormal level of sickness or absenteeism in the same job or in the same department.

[7.58] As in its earlier judgment in *McGrath*, the High Court in *Maher* again emphasised the importance of an objective analysis of the treatment complained of, as opposed to the plaintiff's subjective views of that treatment. As in *Hatton*, Clarke J's foreseeability covers not only employee-specific but also general inquiries: the reference in the above passage to general 'sickness or absenteeism in the same job or in the same department' is highly significant in suggesting that same can be used by plaintiffs to establish foreseeability in relation to their *individuated* situation.

[7.59] In relation to the period of under work, the Court concluded:

> I am not satisfied that there was any concerted plan on the part of the employer to seek to exclude the plaintiff from his employment. As also appears above I am satisfied that the plaintiff did make some complaint about the inadequacy of the work which he was been given but not as frequently or in the terms which he claims. In those circumstances I am not satisfied that the plaintiff has established a breach on the part of his employer of a duty of care during this period either.

[7.60] Clarke J was satisfied that 'the starting point for any consideration of liability in a case such as this' was the consideration of three questions:

(a) has the plaintiff suffered an injury to his or her health as opposed to what might be described as ordinary occupational stress;

(b) if so is that injury attributable to the workplace; and

(c) if so was the harm suffered to the particular employee concerned reasonably foreseeable in all the circumstances.

The formulation here sets out very clearly the separate thresholds of injury, causation and foreseeability and underlines the autonomous status of each threshold in the negligence inquiry in these cases. Of these three criteria, *Maher* itself demonstrates the difficulties facing plaintiffs in terms of the foreseeability inquiry. The point was again emphasised by the later High Court judgment in *Shortt v Royal Liver Insurance Ltd*.[87] In

---

[87] *Shortt v Royal Liver Insurance Ltd* [2008] IEHC 332 (21 October 2008, unreported) HC (Laffoy J).

Shortt, the plaintiff claimed, *inter alia*, damages for stress arising from a disciplinary inquiry which he alleged was unfairly conducted. Rejecting the claim, Laffoy J emphasised that stress in such circumstances is an ordinary consequence not amounting to an injury over and above regular occupational stress. Significantly, however, Laffoy J went on to state that even if the plaintiff's stress had constituted a recognised psychological injury, this was not reasonably foreseeable. She continued:

> While it is reasonable to assume that being subjected to a disciplinary process in the workplace and being transferred to a different position in the workplace against one's will are events which are accompanied by a certain degree of stress, they are events which are encountered in the normal course of the management of a business or organisation. In the absence of any reason for a contrary conclusion, an employer is entitled to assume that an employee is able to withstand such stress. On the basis of the evidence in this case, the management of the defendant did not know, and there was no reason why the management personnel ought to have known, that the plaintiff was vulnerable or likely to succumb to psychiatric or psychological injury because of the implementation of the disciplinary process ...

The Supreme Court appeal in *Quigley v Complex Tooling and Moulding*[88]

[7.61] *Quigley*, in which the Supreme Court gave its judgment in July 2008, is one of the leading Irish cases. Whereas the High Court ruling in *Maher v Jabil* is of central importance for an illustration of the difficulties facing plaintiffs in terms of the third stage of Clarke J's test – foreseeability – the judgment in the Supreme Court appeal in *Quigley* emphasises the problems plaintiffs can encounter in the second stage of that test: causation. The case is striking in that whilst the plaintiff's complaints of bullying and harassment were upheld, and the employer found to have been in breach of its duty of care to him, the plaintiff failed to establish this crucial causal link.

[7.62] The plaintiff was a factory operative who had been subjected to harassment, bullying and victimisation at work which the company had taken no reasonable steps to prevent or stop. He gave evidence of having been subjected to excessive scrutiny and unfair and humiliating treatment by management, which was not challenged by the defendant. (Indeed, one of the most striking features of the case was the availability and willingness of fellow employees to testify on behalf of the plaintiff. At the time of the trial of the action, the defendant had ceased trading; none of the witnesses were still employed by the defendant.) The High Court found, as a matter of fact, that the plaintiff had been a successful worker prior to the arrival of the current defendant, that he had an exemplary work record and never missed a day's work, that the defendant, through their servants or agents, had adopted a particularly unfair approach towards him by singling him out for unacceptable treatment and attempting to force his departure from the work force and that his treatment resulted in him suffering illness and depression. Lavan J relied on health and safety legislation and the Code of Practice made thereunder in finding that the plaintiff had been subjected to 'a campaign of bullying which had

---

[88] *Quigley v Complex Tooling and Moulding* [2008] ELR 297, on appeal from the High Court judgment of Lavan J reported at [2005] ELR 305.

repercussions on the mental health of the plaintiff' for which the defendant was liable in damages.

[7.63] The defendant appealed to the Supreme Court, arguing that the evidence, though uncontradicted, did not bear out the plaintiff's complaints of bullying and that, secondly, there was not sufficient evidence of a causal link between the bullying that the High Court judge found that the plaintiff had been subjected to and the depression his doctor found him to have suffered. Fennelly J (with whom Denham and Geoghegan JJ concurred) allowed the appeal on the basis that the medical evidence presented was consistent only with the plaintiff's depression having been caused by his dismissal and the subsequent unfair dismissal proceedings, and there was no medical evidence of a link with the harassment. That was consistent with the plaintiff's own evidence. Consequently, the plaintiff failed to discharge the burden of proving that his depression was caused by his treatment during his employment.

[7.64] Before the Supreme Court, both parties accepted the definition of workplace bullying' in the Industrial Relations Act 1990 (Code of Practice detailing Procedures for Addressing Bullying in the Workplace) (Declaration) Order 2002, para 5[89] as an accurate definition of bullying to be referred to when considering the employer's duty. This definition is as follows:

> Workplace Bullying is repeated inappropriate behaviour, direct or indirect, whether verbal, physical or otherwise, conducted by one or more persons against another or others, at the place of work and/or in the course of employment, which could reasonably be regarded as undermining the individual's right to dignity at work. An isolated incident of the behaviour described in this definition may be an affront to dignity at work but, as a once off incident, is not considered to be bullying.

[7.65] Having regard to the above definition, Fennelly J accepted the submission that bullying must bear the following characteristics: it must be repeated; it must be inappropriate, and it must undermine the dignity of the employee at work. Fennelly J was satisfied that the bullying complained of by the plaintiff in *Quigley* 'amply meets the criteria of being repeated, inappropriate and undermining of the dignity of the plaintiff at work.' He so found on the basis that the 'treatment of the plaintiff represented a unique amalgam of excessive and selective supervision and scrutiny of the plaintiff, unfair criticism, inconsistency, lack of response to complaint and insidious silence.' Based on this finding, the employer's first ground of appeal was rejected.

[7.66] On the second ground of appeal – causation – the employer was successful. In its judgment, the Supreme Court parsed closely the medical reports in *Quigley*. The first of these reports revealed that the plaintiff had told his general practitioner in January 2001 that he had been dismissed from his job in October 1999 and that he had been suffering from depression for six months before his visit to her. He said that he had won his case before the Rights Commissioner but that the company were appealing the decision and the uncertainty of waiting for a date was adding to his anxiety. The medical report stated that the plaintiff 'had become increasingly anxious about his impending case' and that

---

[89] SI 17/2002.

'his symptoms of depression had intensified.' It concluded that the plaintiff had 'suffered from a moderately severe depressive episode arising directly from his industrial relations problems.' Very significantly, the report did not record that the plaintiff had had been bullied or harassed at work.

[7.67] The Supreme Court concluded that '[t]he picture presented by the medical evidence ... is consistent only with the plaintiff's depression having been caused by his dismissal and subsequent unfair dismissal proceedings and there is no medical evidence of a link with the harassment.' Accordingly, the Court held that the plaintiff had not discharged the burden of proving that his depression was caused by his treatment during his employment.

[7.68] The analysis above illustrates the formidable hurdles facing plaintiffs under the *Maher v Jabil* test. These hurdles are futher illustrated by the subsequent decision of the Supreme Court in *Berber v Dunnes Stores Ltd*.[90] The plaintiff commenced his employment with the defendant as a trainee manager in April, 1980 and was thereafter employed as a store manager at various locations. He moved from store management to buying in 1988 and remained in buying until late 2000, when he was requested by management to transfer back to store management in the defendant's Blanchardstown store. The plaintiff agreed to this transfer on the basis of assurances that he said had been given to him by the defendant to the effect that he would be 'fast-tracked' through the store management department so that he could be appointed store manager or regional manager within six to 12 months.

[7.69] A disagreement subsequently arose in relation to the transfer, the terms of which the plaintiff considered to be inconsistent with the assurances he had been given; this resulted in his refusing to move which in turn gave rise to his being suspended from work by the defendant. At this juncture the plaintiff's solicitors wrote to the defendant setting out the plaintiff's understanding of the assurances he was given by the defendant, and further alleging that the defendant's conduct towards the plaintiff and the stress which it had caused had resulted in his becoming ill. Although the plaintiff did subsequently report for work in the Blanchardstown store at the end of December 2000, he ultimately spent very little time there due to various periods of sick leave and annual leave. The plaintiff wrote to the defendant on 30 May 2001 claiming that the defendant had repudiated his contract of employment and that his contract was at an end. He specifically referred to a disagreement with the store manager in the course of a discussion on 15 May 2001 and to his medical advice that, in the interests of his health, he should cease working in the environment immediately. The plaintiff sought, *inter alia*, a declaration that the defendant had unlawfully repudiated his contract of employment and further sought damages for, *inter alia*, personal injuries. Laffoy J upheld the plaintiff's claim, but the employer appealed successfully to the Supreme Court.

[7.70] It is significant that in *Berber* the High Court was satisfied that the plaintiff had fulfilled all the criteria of the *Maher v Jabil* three-step test discussed above. This

---

[90] *Berber v Dunnes Stores Ltd* [2009] IESC 10, (12 February 2009) SC.

included the damage requirement: the plaintiff had suffered an injury to his health, as opposed to mere ordinary occupational stress, a disorder that exacerbated the plaintiff's Crohn's disease symptoms and hampered the treatment of those symptoms. By contrast, the Supreme Court held that the claim failed on the basis of lack of foreseeability. The contrast between the approach of the High Court and that of the Supreme Court reveals the great difficulties involved in predicting the outcome in such cases as these.

Employer's duty of care includes duty to enable employee to overcome stress

[7.71] The employer's duty of care includes a duty to enable employees to attempt to overcome stress when it is clear to the employer that the employee is suffering from same. This was well illustrated in the judgment of the High Court in July 2008 in *Murtagh v Minister for Defence*.[91] The plaintiff, a former soldier, successfully took a negligence claim against the Army for failing to diagnose and treat him for post-traumatic stress arising from his experiences in Lebanon. Budd J found that the plaintiff was 'obviously stricken' with post-traumatic stress disorder (PTSD) following the deaths of colleagues while in Lebanon in 1986-1987 and that culpable negligence by senior staff in failing, despite his 'strange and abnormal behaviour', to refer him for diagnosis and treatment led to his contracting chronic PTSD. The court was particularly critical of the fact that the plaintiff had not received any counselling or treatment from the Army for severe anxiety attacks and stress-related illness sustained from his experiences in Lebanon. When he was sent for treatment to a medical centre in Lebanon on three occasions, warning bells should have sounded about his condition.

[7.72] Budd J emphasised that an employer's duty of care for the safety of his employees includes a duty to keep abreast of contemporary knowledge in relation to reducing 'potential afflictions' which soldiers are likely to be exposed to. The perils of PTSD had been well known for many years prior to 1986.

[7.73] In *Murtagh*, Budd J, in addition to referring to, *inter alia*, *Maher v Jabil* and *Quigley*, also drew on his earlier judgment in *McHugh v Minister for Defence*,[92] another important Irish precedent in this area. There the plaintiff sought damages for post-traumatic stress disorder sustained during the course of service with United Nations peace-keeping forces in Lebanon. The plaintiff was exposed to a series of stressful events including a near miss when another soldier negligently fired his rifle and the bullet flew past the plaintiff's head. Whilst involved in high risk search and recovery work, the plaintiff had to deal with badly mutilated bodies. The negligence claim was that these events had a cumulative effect on the plaintiff and that the defendant employers failed properly to observe the early symptoms of post-traumatic stress disorder and to take appropriate action. Budd J imposed liability, concluding that the defendant was under a duty of care to be aware of developments in relation to psychiatric medicine relevant to stressors to which employees were likely to be exposed. Budd J stated:

---

[91] *Murtagh v Minister for Defence* [2008] IEHC 292 (22 July 2008).
[92] *McHugh v Minister for Defence* [2001] 1 IR 424.

The plaintiff was employed by the defendants as a member of the defence forces and as such the first defendant owed to the plaintiff a duty to take reasonable care for the health and safety of the plaintiff. In my view there was a negligent failure to take appropriate care for the health of the plaintiff in that once he became subject to stress, as was likely to happen and eminently foreseeable in the dangerous and macabre situations in the Lebanon, the defendants failed to spot the obvious manifestations of post traumatic stress disorder or else negligently failed to recognise the significance of the symptoms, and also negligently failed to obtain remedial therapy for the plaintiff[93].

Failure to monitor return to work after stress-related sick leave

[7.74] An emerging issue in the case law is the potential for the imposition of liability for failure to monitor an employee's return to work where that employee has taken time off owing to stress. Indeed, it will be recalled that in the foundational English case in this area, *Walker v Northumberland County Council*,[94] analysed above, it was held that the council was in breach of its duty to Mr Walker in relation to the second of two nervous breakdowns that he suffered as a result of work-related stress in circumstances where the second breakdown occurred after his return to work having sustained the first.

[7.75] Another instructive English authority is the later decision in *Young v The Post Office*.[95] The plaintiff began his work at the Post Office in 1978 as a technician. In 1993 he became the manager of the workshop and remained in that post until 1998 when he took voluntary early retirement because of a nervous breakdown. He had no managerial training and found the position of manager a stressful one, particularly after computer systems were introduced. From 1994 he began to show signs of stress and was prescribed anti-depressants. In appraisals he complained that he could not achieve certain targets owing to his extended workload. At one stage, the plaintiff wrote on a memorandum in capital letters 'I NEED SOME HELP'.

[7.76] After four months of sick leave, the plaintiff returned to work. During his sick leave, he had been visited by representatives of the Post Office who promised to assess any changes that were needed, and to spend more time with him when he returned to work. It was agreed that the plaintiff would return on a flexible basis; he could work the hours he wanted to work. Just seven weeks after his return, the plaintiff was off sick again. The depressive illness had recurred, and he did not return to work. The trial judge found that although he was visited during his first two weeks back, there was no attempt to assess what changes needed to be made, as had been promised. Moreover, the plaintiff was required to attend a stressful two week training course and when he returned, he was left alone to run the workshop. The trial judge imposed liability, and the Court of Appeal affirmed.

[7.77] Significantly, in the Court of Appeal, the Post Office argued that steps had been taken to enable the plaintiff to return to work at his own pace, and that the plaintiff had been free to come and go as he pleased. The Post Office claimed that they had taken

---

[93] *McHugh v Minister for Defence* [2001] 1 IR 424 at 426–427.
[94] *Walker v Northumberland County Council* [1995] ICR 702.
[95] *Young v The Post Office* [2002] IRLR 660.

reasonable steps and had no means of knowing that those steps had not been successful. Liability was nonetheless imposed, and the essence of the holding was that the employer had failed to ensure that the arrangements made during the period of absence were adhered to.

[7.78] It is important to note that the Court of Appeal in *Young* rejected the argument that the onus was on the plaintiff employee to alert his employer to the fact that the risk of further psychiatric injury was continuing or had not been eliminated. Notably, this proposition was also rejected by the House of Lords in *Barber v Somerset County Council*,[96] analysed above.

Employers' liability for third party harassment

[7.79] The failure of an employer to introduce steps and procedures to combat harassment by third parties suffered by their employees may give rise to a cause of action against them. Indeed, a significant English Employment Appeals Tribunal ruling, *Gravell v London Borough of Bexley*,[97] opens up the possibility that employers can be held liable for the harassment of their employees by the actions of third parties, be they customers in a shop or schoolchildren. Whilst it should be noted that the case was decided on the basis of a distinct statutory framework and not in negligence, the approach taken in such contexts may well have implications for negligence actions.

[7.80] The claimant was employed in the respondent's housekeeping department. She complained *inter alia* that customers of the respondent used racist language and that the respondents had a policy of not preventing such conduct. The UK Employment Appeals Tribunal took the view that there was 'considerable scope' for arguing that the employer's alleged policy of not allowing its staff to challenge racist comments had had the effect of creating an offensive environment for the claimant which could, if established on the facts, constitute racial harassment under the relevant statutory scheme.[98] It therefore reinstated her claim and referred the matter to a different tribunal to consider whether on full investigation the facts supported the existence of a no-challenge policy. Once again, the statutory basis of this claim – and its distinctiveness from the negligence action – should be emphasised; nevertheless, it is submitted that the case is of relevance in illustrating the circumstances in which relief may lie in the context of harassment by third parties.

Embarrassment and humiliation caused to employee

[7.81] Whilst it is hornbook law to say that the courts will award damages for stress but not for distress, the courts have in certain instances been prepared to assess the level of distress caused to plaintiffs in the specific context of bullying and to factor this into the remedy awarded. A good illustration of this in the context of a breach of contract claim is the decision of the High Court in *O'Byrne v Dunnes Stores*.[99] The plaintiff in *O'Byrne*

---

[96]   *Barber v Somerset County Council* [2004] UKHL 13, [2004] 1 WLR 1089.

[97]   *Gravell v London Borough of Bexley* [2007] All ER (D) 220.

[98]   Race Relations Act 1976 (as amended).

[99]   *O'Byrne v Dunnes Stores Ltd* [2003] ELR 297.

was awarded damages where the Court found that it must have been in the contemplation of the defendants that the plaintiff would suffer mental distress from the breach of his contract, which arose from the plaintiff being forced to move location without any notice or opportunity to make representations. The plaintiff had also been subjected to an incident of bullying which Smyth J described as 'absolutely outrageous', 'inexcusably offensive' and 'reprehensible, to say the least'. Awarding general damages for the stress and distress sustained, Smyth J also criticised the employer for having made no effort to apologise. He concluded that the plaintiff, as an employee of 25 years, was entitled to 'no more or no less than a civilised treatment, which he did not receive'.

[7.82] More recently, the question of humiliating treatment causing distress grounding a cause of action against an employer was raised in *Larkin v Dublin City Council*,[100] where the plaintiff advanced what Clark J described as 'an unusual case'. He sought damages for the humiliation and disappointment he suffered when, owing to an administrative error concerning examination results, he was wrongly advised that he had been successful in applying for promotion, only to have this good news withdrawn days later when the error was discovered. Although he had not sustained any psychiatric illness and as such did not seek damages for nervous shock, the plaintiff contended that the negligence of the employer had occasioned him considerable upset and disappointment.

[7.83] It is interesting that Clark J accepted that a duty of care was owed by the employer in these circumstances, and had been breached. She observed that:

> [I]t seems to me, in all the circumstances of the case that there was a duty to ensure that the results were not presented to candidates until their accuracy had been checked. This was not a case of a moment of momentary inadvertence where someone accidentally hit the wrong button. The mistake which occurred was multifaceted and required the omission of an entire set of written exam results from inclusion in the spread sheet in the final calculation of marks.[101]

However, because the plaintiff in *Larkin* could show no recognised psychiatric injury, his claim was dismissed as disclosing no actionable damage. The significant point to note here is that the expansive approach taken to the questions of duty and breach may very well avail a future claimant who can show such psychiatric injuries.

RELATIONSHIP BETWEEN NEGLIGENCE AND BREACH OF CONTRACT CLAIMS

[7.84] It *Berber v Dunnes Stores*,[102] where the plaintiff's personal injury claim was founded both in contract and in tort, the High Court held that it was not necessary to distinguish between the two causes of action because the scope of the duty of care owed to an employee to take reasonable care to provide a safe system of work was co-extensive with the scope of the implied term as to the employee's safety in the contract of

---

[100] *Larkin v Dublin City Council* [2008] 1 IR 391.
[101] *Larkin v Dublin City Council* [2008] 1 IR 391 at 396–397.
[102] *Berber v Dunnes Stores Ltd* [2007] ELR 1.

employment. Reliance for this proposition was placed upon the decision in *Walker*[103] discussed above. This position was confirmed as the correct approach on appeal to the Supreme Court.[104]

[7.85] In this regard, it is significant to consider the approach of the High Court in *Pickering v Microsoft Ireland Operations Ltd,*[105] where Judge Esmond Smyth, sitting as a judge of the High Court, imposed liability via breach of contract as distinct from negligence. The court found that it was an express term of the plaintiff's contract of employment with the defendant that she would be party to the resolution of difficulties arising out of the implementation of an organisational plan in so far as a result of specific representations made to her. The defendant had breached this term in failing to adequately address certain concerns that she had raised with management, which breach was found to have given rise to a psychological injury to the plaintiff's health. Smyth J expressly applied the *Hatton* principles to the case before him and found that the plaintiff had suffered a psychological injury to her health which exceeded mere ordinary occupational stress and that the harm was attributable to a breach of contract. He found that the harm was reasonably foreseeable from the time when the defendant became aware that the plaintiff was suffering from stress which was when the company doctor and nurse consulted with her. The court also relied on evidence of a clinical psychologist that it would have been useful and good practice if the plaintiff was contacted by a manager while on stress leave in an effort to resolve her situation.

[7.86] Two points may be noted in relation to the approach in *Pickering*. First, notwithstanding that breach of contract was the route adopted by the Court in sourcing the imposition of liability for workplace stress, the analysis of the questions of foreseeability and breach is identical to that already examined in the context of the imposition or withholding of negligence liability. That this is undoubtedly the case is shown by the express recourse in *Pickering* to the *Hatton* principles. The second point to be made here flows the first: given that the courts have evinced their readiness to apply the breach of contract claim interchangeably with the negligence claim in these cases, there may well be strategic incentives for plaintiffs to pursue the former cause of action, in light of, for example, a wider latitude in terms of limitation periods.

More restrictive contractual approach taken by High Court of Australia

[7.87] In relation to this breach of contract point, the High Court of Australia delivered an important judgment in this area in the case of *Koehler v Cerebos (Australia) Ltd.*[106] This approach is striking for the emphasis placed on the employee's contract of employment. It has been said that the decision in *Koehler* 'means that it is now going to

---

[103] *Walker v Northumberland County Council* [1995] ICR 702. Reference was also made to *Gogay v Hertfordshire County Council* [2000] IRLR 703.

[104] *Berber v Dunnes Stores Ltd* [2009] IESC 10.

[105] *Pickering v Microsoft Ireland Operations Ltd* [2006] ELR 65. It is understood at the time of writing that this judgment is under appeal to the Supreme Court.

[106] *Koehler v Cerebos (Australia) Ltd* (2005) 79 ALJR 845. For analysis see Hor, 'Psychiatric Injury in the Workplace: The Implications of *Koehler*' (2005) 27 *Syd L Rev* 557.

be very difficult for Australian workers to claim for psychiatric injury caused by stress at work, at least in cases…where the stress was caused by being given too much work to do.'[107]

[7.88] The plaintiff in *Koehler* was a sales representative negotiating sales of the defendant's products to independent supermarkets. She was made redundant, but was offered a substitute job setting up displays in supermarkets, working three days a week. When she saw the list of stores she was required to visit she immediately complained to her superiors that there was too much territory to cover in the three days a week for which she was paid, and that she would have to have help, or more time to do the work. She made these complaints on a number of different occasions. After five months, she resigned. She went to see her doctor, complaining of aches and pains and difficulty in moving as a result of lifting heavy cartons, but the doctor said that she was suffering from a stress related illness. Over the next few months, this developed into a relatively severe depressive illness.

[7.89] In the High Court of Australia, the defendant was relieved of liability on the basis that a reasonable employer would not have foreseen the risk of psychiatric injury to the employee. Since the complaints made had related to the physical problem of getting the work done in the available time, and did not reveal that any difficulties she was encountering were affecting her health, the defendant employers could not reasonably be expected to work out for themselves that her health might be at risk.

[7.90] The court reasoned that given the nature of Mrs Koehler's complaints, which related solely to the physical problem of getting her work done in the time available, the employers could not reasonably be expected to work out for themselves that she was at risk. The anomalous result of such an approach, as Mullany and Handford have noted, is that 'the employee who stoically battles on, or who makes some sort of reference to his or her workload but is hesitant to disclose personal medical details, will be in a poorer position than someone who pours out a litany of problems at the earliest opportunity.'[108]

[7.91] Interestingly, the High Court of Australia in *Koehler* expressly endorsed the judgment of Lord Rodger in *Barber v Somerset County Council*.[109] In that case, Lord Rodger referred to the contract between the plaintiff and the defendant, and concluded that the demands placed on the plaintiff were not excessive in themselves, but only because of some factor in the plaintiff's personality which made him more vulnerable to developing a mental illness as a result of work stress.

[7.92] The High Court of Australia in *Koehler* was convinced, as Lord Rodger appears to have been in *Barber*, that the introduction of a tortious duty of care did not sit easily with contractual arrangements between the parties. The court in *Koehler* held that not only was the psychiatric injury not foreseeable, but Mrs Koehler had agreed to perform the

---

[107] Mullany & Handford's *Tort Liability for Psychiatric Damage* (Sydney Law Book Company, 2006) p 560.

[108] Mullany & Handford's *Tort Liability for Psychiatric Damage* (Sydney Law Book Company, 2006) p 561.

[109] *Barber v Somerset County Council* [2004] ICR 457.

duties which were the cause of her injury. Insistence by an employer that an employee perform his or her contractual obligations cannot amount to a breach of a duty of care in negligence. The court stated that developing the law of negligence in a way that undermined or inhibited freedom of contract would be a big, and perhaps unwelcome, step to take.

[7.93] If the *Koehler*/Lord Rodger type of approach is to gain currency, it is clear that many plaintiffs will be unable to successfully argue that a duty of care is consistent with the terms of their contract of employment.

ORDERS FOR DISCOVERY IN STRESS, BULLYING AND HARASSMENT CASES

[7.94] The decision of Master Honohan in *Foley v County Waterford Vocational Education Committee*[110] provides guidance as to the principles to be adopted in applications for discovery in cases of workplace stress, bullying and harassment. The plaintiff in *Foley* began to feel stress at work in the first half of 2000. He worked as an adult education teacher who brought a case of bullying and harassment against his former employer, with which he had worked in its Vocational Training and Opportunities Scheme in Dungarvan. His case against his employer was that his experiences in the workplace since January 2000 had caused him to suffer illness. The plaintiff sought discovery of, *inter alia*, the following categories of documents: 'documentation regarding all complaints made by the plaintiff'; and 'documentation regarding all investigations made by the defendant as a result of complaints made by the plaintiff'.

[7.95] Considering the request for documentation regarding all complaints made by the plaintiff, Master Honohan observed as follows:

> I would normally make an order for [this category] or some more focussed category along these lines. I find, however, in this case that the pleadings are wholly imprecise. Discovery *'regarding all complaints'* really encompasses discovery regarding all conversations about the plaintiff's treatment at the hands of his fellow workers. The plaintiff should be required to further particularise his 'complaints' (date, to whom, content etc.) before he is permitted to trawl the defendant's documents for what, after all, is merely evidence confirmatory of his own evidence of the making of a complaint.

[7.96] Further, Master Honohan declined to order discovery of the documentation regarding all investigations made by the defendant as a result of complaints made by the plaintiff. He explained his reasoning for this decision in the following way:

> What I have to decide at this stage is what evidence the plaintiff needs to prove the employer's negligence. Although he is alleging that the complaints were not processed, 'expeditiously and fairly', it is his perception of the events (to that effect) which is the corner stone of the case, rather than the actuality of the employer's complaint solving process. Of course, his perception may very well correspond to the actuality, but if it is at

---

[110] *Foley v County Waterford Vocational Education Committee* (17 June 2005, unreported) HC, Master Honohan.

variance with it, it is surely the employer's fault that the plaintiff was not, at the appropriate time, properly and fully appraised of the facts, or was not able to judge the outcome for himself by deduction from the cessation of the behaviour complained of, or from the removal of the offending co-worker from the work place. Either way, the facts *as then known to the plaintiff* were the immediate cause of his stress. Accordingly, it is logically and necessarily the plaintiff's *own* evidence of that state of knowledge (at the material times) which is the only basis on which he can prosecute the case. He cannot now, some five or six years later, be permitted to 'feed' that recollection by accessing the defendant's file and perhaps learning more than he knew at that time. Curious and all though he may be, he has no 'need' to see the defendant's files. He has his own evidence as to his state of knowledge back in 2000. That is all he needs to make his case.

HEALTH AND SAFETY AUTHORITY CODE OF PRACTICE 2007

Introduction of New Code of Practice in 2007

[7.97] The Health and Safety Authority's *Code of Practice for Employers and Employees on the Prevention and Resolution of Bullying at Work*[111] came into effect on 1 May 2007. This latest new Code of Practice is aimed at both employers and employees and refers, in particular, to the duties in the Safety, Health and Welfare at Work Act 2005 (the 2005 Act). The new Code provides practical guidance for employers on identifying and preventing bullying at work arising from their duties under s 8(2)(b) of the 2005 Act as regards 'managing and conducting work activities in such a way as to prevent, so far as is reasonably practicable, any improper conduct or behaviour likely to put the safety, health and welfare at work of his or her employees at risk'. It also applies to employees in relation to their duties under s 13(1)(e) of the 2005 Act to 'not engage in improper conduct or behaviour that is likely to endanger his or her own safety, health and welfare at work or that of any other person'.

Definition of bullying

[7.98] The Code recognises (in s 3.1) the established definition of bullying at work as 'repeated inappropriate behaviour, direct or indirect, whether verbal, physical or otherwise, conducted by one or more persons against another or others, at the place of work and/or in the course of employment, which could reasonably be regarded as undermining the individual's right to dignity at work' (Report of the Task Force on the prevention of workplace bullying, 2001; also used in the 2005 Report of the Expert Advisory Group on Workplace Bullying and in the Surveys conducted by the ESRI to determine the incidence of workplace bullying.) It confirms that an isolated incident of the behaviour in this definition may be an affront to dignity but as a once-off incident is not considered to be bullying. The Code thus articulates a vision of bullying that coheres with that accepted by the courts – most recently, by the Supreme Court in *Quigley v Complex Tooling and Moulding*.[112]

---

[111] Available at www.hsa.ie. The Code is reproduced in Appendix C.
[112] *Quigley v Complex Tooling and Moulding* [2008] ELR 297.

Key procedural changes in new Code

[7.99] Although the new Code does not differ very markedly from its 2002 predecessor, the most significant changes relate to the procedures for resolution of complaints and the proposed involvement of the Labour Relations Commission.

In terms of the procedure for resolution of complaints, a 'contact person' remains the first port of call for an employee who feels they have been bullied, although the role of this 'contact person' has been altered slightly in that, under the new Code, the contact person has no involvement in the complaints procedure and does not act as an advocate for either party. He or she is simply required to listen and give guidance to a complainant in relation to the procedures available under internal policies. The complainant may then use an informal procedure and, in the absence of a successful conclusion, proceed to the formal stage.

[7.100] The Code recommends that the employer should first decide if the facts constitute 'bullying' and put in place a monitoring system to the satisfaction of the parties. The purpose of this informal procedure is to establish if agreement can be reached between the parties to bring to an end the behaviour complained of. Naturally, the importance of retaining records of the procedure as it progresses is emphasised in the Code.

[7.101] Where the complaint is made against a senior member of the organisation, it may be necessary to have recourse to external services such as the mediation services of the Labour Relations Commission.

[7.102] The formal procedure requires the complaint to be made in writing and to be signed and dated by the complainant. The person against whom the complaint is made should also be notified, in writing, of the complaint and thereafter a formal investigation will take place pursuant to the employer's internal bullying policy, which should reflect the new Code. The Code stipulates that there must be an appeals procedure available to the parties following the outcome.

[7.103] Where internal procedures fail to resolve the complaint, the Code provides that the Rights Commissioner Service should be accessible to the persons involved in the complaint. The Rights Commissioner may look at the internal procedures applied and may opt to carry out a new investigation.

Status of Code in criminal and civil proceedings

[7.104] Although failure to adhere to the Code is not an offence, the Code is admissible in evidence in criminal proceedings under s 61 of the 2005 Act. In practice, it is highly likely to be taken into account in civil cases alleging bullying and harassment at work, in light of the judicial instances of its being cited which were analysed above, the most prominent example of which to date is the judgment of the High Court is the case of *Quigley v Complex Tooling and Moulding*[113] where Lavan J referred to the definition of

---

[113] *Quigley v Complex Tooling and Moulding* [2005] ELR 305.

bullying as contained in the Code of Practice detailing procedures for addressing bullying in the workplace made under the Industrial Relations Act 1990 (SI 17/2002) and expressly applied it to the plaintiff's evidence. On appeal to the Supreme Court, the parties were agreed that this was appropriate and it was on this basis that the Supreme Court analysed the factual matrix of the plaintiff's claim.[114]

---

[114] Para **[7.61]** *et seq.*

Chapter 8

Vicarious Liability

Des Ryan

INTRODUCTION: MEANING OF AND RATIONALE BEHIND VICARIOUS LIABILITY

[8.01] As was explained in the context of Ch 2 of the present work,[1] one of the most fundamental consequences of the coming into being of the employment relationship is the potential for vicarious liability to be imposed upon an employer for wrongs committed by an employee in the course of his or her employment. It is this fundamental principle that is the subject of scrutiny in this chapter: an attempt is made to explain the operation of the principle of vicarious liability both in common law and statutory contexts, with particular emphasis being placed on recent and potential changes to the conventional application of vicarious liability doctrine in both contexts.

Meaning and rationale of vicarious liability

[8.02] Put plainly, the principle of employers' vicarious liability means that a defendant employer can be held liable for the wrongdoing of its employee. In this respect, the principle is a species of strict liability, in that it is not necessary at all to prove any fault or any moral blameworthiness on the part of the defendant employer. The concept is a loss-distribution device which is based on judicial views on social or economic policy. It is a principle of strict or no-fault liability whereby an employer is liable for a wrong committed by his employee acting in the course of his employment.

[8.03] In order to establish vicarious liability, a plaintiff must show that wrong was committed by an agent of the defendant who was under the control of the defendant and whose actions were within the scope of that control. To put this formulation in the context of the employment relationship, a plaintiff seeking to establish vicarious liability for negligence, for example, must show that negligence was committed by an employee of the defendant who at the time of the negligence complained of was acting within the course of his employment with the defendant. The rationale for the principle of vicarious liability was summarised in a prominent 2006 case in the following terms:

> [A]ll forms of economic activity carry a risk of harm to others, and fairness requires that those responsible for such activities should be liable to persons suffering loss from wrongs committed in the conduct of the enterprise. This is 'fair', because it means injured persons can look for recompense to a source better placed financially than individual wrongdoing employees. It means also that the financial loss arising from the wrongs can be spread more widely, by liability insurance and higher prices. In addition, and importantly, imposing strict liability on employers encourages them to maintain standards of 'good

---

[1] See Ch 2, The Contract and Relationship of Employment, para **[2.01]**.

practice' by their employees. For these reasons employers are to be held liable for wrongs committed by their employees in the course of their employment.[2]

[8.04] It will be recalled that in Ch 2 of this work, extensive analysis was conducted of the distinction between a contract of service (where the person providing the service is an employee) and a contract for services (where the person providing the service is an independent contractor). Given that vicarious liability is concerned with (and is a consequence of) the employment relationship, in an individual case the question of whether an employer has engaged someone on a contract of service or contract for services may well be in issue in determining whether vicarious liability can arise. There are authorities, however, that suggest that even where wrongdoing is committed by an independent contractor, vicarious liability will arise if the employer had control over the independent contractor. In *Phelan v Coilte Teoranta Ireland Attorney General and Minister for Fisheries and Forestry*,[3] Barr J held that whether the particular contract of full-time employment is one for services, or of service is irrelevant to the issue of vicarious liability once the evidence establishes on the balance of probabilities that the employer exercises control over the other party.

Cases on vicarious liability very fact specific

[8.05] Individual cases in the area of vicarious liability are very fact specific and clear rules and guidance are not all that readily discernible. As is stated in one leading textbook:

> The decided cases are not very amenable to any scientific classification and the issue tends to be 'fact sensitive'; the best that can be done is to select and illustrate a few of the more common factual situations to see if one can discern broad trends. [4]

As O'Higgins J observed in one of the most important High Court cases on vicarious liability, '[t]he application of the doctrine of vicarious liability to the facts of a particular case can often be a matter of great difficulty'.[5]

Whether more than one defendant can be held vicariously liable?

[8.06] This question as yet does not appear to have been considered in Ireland. It arose in England in a recent Court of Appeal case, *Viasystems (Tyneside) Ltd v Thermal Transfer (Northern) Ltd*.[6] It was held that where the employee was so much a part of the work, business or organisation of both defendants that it was just to make them both liable 'dual responsibility' could be imposed.

---

2 *Per* Lord Nicholls in *Majrowski v Guy's and St Thomas' NHS Trust* [2006] UKHL 34, [2006] 3 WLR 125, [9]. On enterprise theory see further Douglas Brodie, 'Justifying Vicarious liability' (2007) 27 *OJLS* 493.
3 *Phelan v Coilte Teoranta Ireland Attorney General and Minister for Fisheries and Forestry* [1993] ELR 56.
4 Rogers, *Winfield and Jolowicz on Tort* (17th edn, London, Sweet & Maxwell, 2006), at p 894.
5 *Delahunty v South Eastern Health Board* [2003] 4 IR 361 at 373 *per* O'Higgins J.
6 *Viasystems (Tyneside) Ltd v Thermal Transfer (Northern) Ltd* [2006] 2 WLR 428.

Whether wrongdoing committed within scope of employment

[8.07] This question of whether the acts amounting to negligence were 'within the scope of the employment' is the 'infelicitous but time-honoured phrase'[7] in cases of alleged vicarious liability.[8] Perhaps more than any other aspect of vicarious liability doctrine, it has come under intense judicial scrutiny in recent years. The key changes which have taken place in recent years to this test will now be analysed.

VICARIOUS LIABILITY AT COMMON LAW: THE COURSE OF EMPLOYMENT TEST

[8.08] Under the traditional interpretation of the 'course of employment' test – which was first articulated in a student tort text just over one hundred years ago[9] and was rapidly to become the most frequently cited touchstone for determining vicarious liability[10] – an employer could be held vicariously liable both for employee acts authorised by the employer and for unauthorised acts so connected with authorised acts that they could be regarded as modes (albeit improper modes) of performing authorised acts.[11]

The limits of the practical utility of the Salmond test – 'an apparently simple test whose simplicity is largely deceptive'[12] – have long been acknowledged in the context of intentional wrongdoing, particularly when compared with its attractiveness in the context of the tort of negligence. Thus, in his still leading work on the subject of vicarious liability published over forty years ago,[13] Patrick Atiyah rightly emphasised the attractiveness of the test in the negligence sphere, observing '[t]here can be no question but that [the Salmond] test works best when applied to acts of negligence because in many circumstances negligence is a way of doing something rather than an act in itself.'[14] By contrast, Atiyah accepted that the test gave rise to much greater

---

[7] *Morris v C W Martin & Sons Ltd* [1966] 1 QB 716 *per* Diplock LJ, 737.

[8] *Per* Lord Nicholls in *Majrowski v Guy's and St Thomas' NHS Trust* [2006] UKHL 34, [2006] 3 WLR 125.

[9] Sir John Salmond, *Salmond on Torts* (1st edn, Sweet & Maxwell, 1907), 83–84.

[10] Lord Millett in *Lister v Hesley Hall Ltd* [2001] UKHL 22, [2002] 1 AC 215, [2001] 2 WLR 1311, said of the Salmond test that it 'has probably been cited more often than any other single passage in a legal textbook' ([67]). Early examples of its approval in the English courts include the judgment of Bankes LJ in *Poland v Parr (John) & Sons* [1927] 1 KB 236 at 240 and that of Lord Thankerton in *Canadian Pacific Railway v Lockhart* [1942] AC 591 (PC), at 599. Express judicial endorsements of the Salmond test in an Irish context include the judgment of Blayney J in *Reilly v Ryan* [1991] 2 IR 247 at 249, discussed at para **[8.14]**.

[11] As has frequently been observed, the first branch of the Salmond test in reality amounts to primary as opposed to vicarious liability. See CA Hopkins, 'What is the Course of Employment?' [2001] *CLJ* 458 at 458; see also the judgment of Lord Millett in *Lister v Hesley Hall Ltd* [2001] UKHL 22, [2002] 1 AC 215, [2001] 2 WLR 1311 [67].

[12] Atiyah, *Vicarious Liability in the Law of Torts* (Butterworths, 1967), p 172.

[13] Atiyah, *Vicarious Liability in the Law of Torts* (Butterworths, 1967), p 257.

[14] On this point see further *Kooragang Investments Pty Ltd v Richardson & Wrench Ltd* [1982] AC 462 at 472 *per* Lord Wilberforce.

difficulty in the case of a wilful act than in the case of a negligent act, going so far as to declare '[i]n dealing with such wilful acts there is no doubt that the Salmond test really ceases to be of much help.'[15] In the last decade, the courts in many common law jurisdictions have been called upon to acknowledge this limitation of the Salmond test as traditionally applied and to shift the emphasis to the reference in Salmond's classic formulation to unauthorised acts *connected* with authorised acts. In the recent cases under consideration here, this 'connection' aspect of the Salmond test has now been brought sharply into focus.[16]

[8.09] The leading authority in England and Wales on the reformulation of the Salmond test is the decision of the House of Lords in *Lister v Hesley Hall Ltd.*[17] The wrongful acts of the employee in *Lister* consisted of sexual abuse of schoolboys residing in a boarding house annexed to their school, which catered for maladjusted boys. The employee was a person employed by the school as a warden to care for the boys. His responsibilities included disciplining the boys, supervision duties and intimate daily tasks such as putting the boys to bed and getting them up for school. In particular, emphasis was placed upon the fact that the warden had capitalised on the opportunities for committing his transgressions by implementing what appeared to be a very relaxed system of discipline that included the use of gifts and undeserved leniency.

[8.10] At both the first instance and Court of Appeal level, an earlier Court of Appeal ruling[18] was regarded as precluding the imposition of vicarious liability. On appeal by the plaintiffs, the House of Lords overruled this earlier decision and unanimously held that the acts were sufficiently connected with the work that the warden was employed to do such that they could be described as being done in the course of employment. In the same way that the Supreme Court of Canada had done in a groundbreaking judgment in that jurisdiction[19] the House of Lords emphasised that component of the Salmond test which was traditionally often overlooked, that is, the emphasis on closeness of connection.

[8.11] A number of distinct strands can be discerned from the judgments of the Law Lords in *Lister*. First, the 'nature of the employment' was regarded as so closely connected with the wrongful acts as to make it just to hold the employer liable. Lord Steyn[20] isolated the relevant question as being 'whether the warden's torts were so closely connected with his employment that it would be fair and just to hold the employers vicariously liable'.[21] Lord Steyn cautioned against an unduly narrow or

---

15 Atiyah, *Vicarious Liability in the Law of Torts* (Butterworths, 1967), p 263.
16 For detailed analysis in a comparative context see Ryan, 'Making Connections: New Approaches to Vicarious Liability in Comparative Perspective' (2008) 30 *DULJ* 41.
17 *Lister v Hesley Hall Ltd* [2001] UKHL 22, [2002] 1 AC 215, [2001] 2 WLR 1311, [67]. See Giliker, 'Rough Justice in an Unjust World' (2002) 65 *MLR* 269.
18 *Trotman v North Yorkshire County Council* [1998] EWCA Civ 1208, [1999] LGR 584.
19 *Bazley v Curry* [1999] 2 SCR 534. For analysis see Ryan, 'Making Connections: New Approaches to Vicarious Liability in Comparative Perspective' (2008) 30 *DULJ* 41.
20 With whose judgment Lords Hutton and Hobhouse agreed.
21 *Lister v Hesley Hall Ltd* [2001] UKHL 22, [2002] 1 AC 215, [2001] 2 WLR 1311, [28].

restrictive approach to the Salmond test on the basis that it can lead to artificial conceptions of what an employee is employed to do. Instead, Lord Steyn preferred a broad approach that concentrated on the 'relative closeness of the connection between the nature of the employment and the particular tort.'[22] He found the wrongdoing in *Lister* to be 'inextricably interwoven' with the warden's employment duties.[23] Lord Clyde also identified as the key question the closeness of the connection between the employee's act and the employment.[24]

[8.12] In *Lister*, both Lord Hobhouse and Lord Millett placed chief emphasis on the employer's duty to the child being to care for and protect the child. The employer delegated performance of that duty to the employee who, in breach of his contractual duties to his employer, assaulted the child entrusted to his care. In this regard, however, analysis might have been expected to focus more heavily on the existence of a non-delegable duty of care rather than vicarious liability and criticism of *Lister* has included the contention that the non-delegable duty analysis was conflated with vicarious liability analysis.[25] In an important closing observation, Lord Hobhouse was of the view that vicarious liability would also attach if the warden had not been the perpetrator but had discovered the fact of abuse by a fellow employee and had negligently failed to report it – here again, there would have existed a sufficiently close connection between the tort and the employment status of the wrongdoer.[26] It is submitted that the choice of example is significant – the tort of negligence as distinct from the intentional torts which were in fact at issue in *Lister*. This would suggest that, at least according to Lord Hobhouse, the *Lister* approach is of equal application to the non-intentional torts as it is to the intentional torts, an issue which remains unsettled across the common law world.[27]

[8.13] Considering the significance of *Lister* generally, it has recently been observed in the House of Lords that as a result of that decision the law in the United Kingdom was 'radically changed'.[28] As Lord Hoffmann said in January 2008 of the *Lister* decision, '[a]fter that, claims against the operators of schools, detention centres and similar institutions for sexual abuse by employees came thick and fast.'[29] The influence of *Lister* on the law relating to vicarious liability in the United Kingdom has extended far beyond the question of vicarious liability for employee sexual abuse.[30]

---

[22] *Lister v Hesley Hall Ltd* [2001] UKHL 22, [2002] 1 AC 215, [2001] 2 WLR 1311, [24].

[23] *Lister v Hesley Hall Ltd* [2001] UKHL 22, [2002] 1 AC 215, [2001] 2 WLR 1311, [28].

[24] *Lister v Hesley Hall Ltd* [2001] UKHL 22, [2002] 1 AC 215, [2001] 2 WLR 1311, [50].

[25] See for example Robert Stevens, *Torts and Rights* (OUP, 2007), 273; Claire McIvor, 'The Use and Abuse of the Doctrine of Vicarious Liability' (2006) 35 *Comm L World Rev* 268, 295.

[26] By contrast, vicarious liability would not have attached for acts of abuse by a groundsman whose duties had nothing to do with the tortious conduct.

[27] See Ryan, 'Making Connections: New Approaches to Vicarious Liability in Comparative Perspective' (2008) 30 *DULJ* 41.

[28] *A v Hoare* [2008] UKHL 6; [2008] 2 WLR 311, [22].

[29] *A v Hoare* [2008] UKHL 6; [2008] 2 WLR 311, [22].

[30] The ramifications of *Lister* continue to be explored: see *A v Hoare* [2008] UKHL 6; [2008] 2 WLR 311, and *A v Hoare* [2008] EWHC 1573 (QB). (contd.../)

One difficulty arising from the approach adopted in *Lister* is that the 'sufficiently close connection' test is extremely vague and open-ended. Consequently, it is now very difficult to tell when precisely an employee will be deemed to have committed a tort *in the course of his employment*. As Lord Nicholls observed in *Dubai Aluminium Co Ltd v Salaam*,[31] the close connection test 'affords no guidance on the type or degree of connection which will normally be regarded as sufficiently close…Essentially the court makes an evaluative judgment in each case, having regard to all the circumstances'.[32]

Comparison of House of Lords approach in *Lister* with that of Irish High Court in *Reilly v Ryan*

[8.14] It is submitted that the reasoning in *Lister* may usefully be compared with the decision of the Irish High Court some 15 years ago in *Reilly v Ryan*.[33] In that case, an intruder armed with a knife entered a pub on Parnell Street, Dublin, and demanded money from the till. The barman, in an effort to protect himself, grabbed an unsuspecting customer who was sitting at the bar, and used that person as a human shield. The customer was stabbed by the intruder, and suffered severe personal injury, loss and damage. He alleged in the High Court that the employer was vicariously liable for the acts of the barman. Blayney J disagreed, and relieved the employer of liability. Blayney J reasoned that the barman's principal duty was to serve the defendant's customers, including looking after their comfort and safety. Instead of looking after the plaintiff's safety, however, the barman was the cause of his being injured. Such a divergence from the duties of his employment took the employee's actions outside the scope of cases in which vicarious liability could be imposed upon the employer.

Doubtful whether *Reilly v Ryan* still good law

[8.15] It has been suggested that *Reilly v Ryan* might be decided differently today.[34] Blayney J's conclusion that the conduct of the barman was so excessive as to take it outside 'the class of acts impliedly authorised' is based on the 'implied authority' argument as opposed to the 'close connection' argument. As seen above in this chapter, it is the latter argument that has recently found favour in both *Lister*, discussed above, and in jurisprudence in Canada and elsewhere.[35] Thus, the emphasis in *Reilly v Ryan*

---

[30] (\…contd) See also *Robertson v The Scottish Ministers* [2007] CSOH 186 where Lord Emslie remarked at [11]: 'Given the breadth of the test affirmed in *Lister* and followed in various circumstances since then … I do not consider that the possibility of a finding of vicarious liability here can at this stage be excluded.' See further *McE (AP) v The Reverend Joseph Hendron and Others* [2007] CSIH 27.

[31] *Dubai Aluminium Co Ltd v Salaam* [2003] 2 AC 366.

[32] [2003] 2 AC 366, [25]–[26].

[33] *Reilly v Ryan* [1991] 2 IR 247, [1991] ILRM 449.

[34] Ryan and Ryan, 'Vicarious Liability: Emerging Themes and Trends and their Potential Implications for Irish law' (2007) 4 *IELJ* 1.

[35] Indeed, the trend in England and Wales post-*Lister* has been to impose liability on defendants for outrageous, violent acts by employees. Perhaps the clearest example of this is to be found in the Court of Appeal case of *Mattis v Pollock (t/a Flamingos Nightclub)* [2003] 1 WLR 2158, discussed Ryan and Ryan, 'Vicarious Liability: Emerging Themes and Trends and their Potential Implications for Irish law' (2007) 4 *IELJ* 1.

upon the fact that the barman's conduct was so far removed from the carrying out of his duties in the course of his employment – that is, endangering the plaintiff rather than serving or protecting him – may now require to be reassessed in light of more recent judicial approaches in other jurisdictions; were this approach to be strictly followed, persons such as the schoolboys in *Lister* could *never* establish vicarious liability since in that case the warden abused the boys whom he was employed to care for.

Lister in an Irish context

[8.16] It is at present unclear whether the approach taken in other common law jurisdictions to the 'close connection' test in vicarious liability will be applied in Ireland. In particular, the recent Supreme Court decision in *O'Keeffe v Hickey*[36] reveals significant disagreement amongst the judges of the Court as to whether this modification to vicarious liability should be applied. Before analysing this decision, it is necessary to consider earlier judgments in which *Lister* was referred to in the Irish courts.

[8.17] The starting point in this context is the significant decision of the Irish High Court, in which the approach in *Lister* was first considered. *Delahunty v South Eastern Health Board*[37] involved, *inter alia*, a claim that vicarious liability be imposed upon an industrial school and upon the Minister for Education and Science for a sexual assault perpetrated upon a visitor to the school by a member of staff at the school. Significantly, counsel for the defendants submitted that *Lister* constituted 'a departure in the law which had not been adopted in this country' – a proposition that O'Higgins J said 'might perhaps be open to question'.[38] Referring to *Lister* as 'the leading United Kingdom [a]uthority', O'Higgins J did not regard it necessary to consider whether *Lister* was good law in Ireland, since the 'strong connection' argument could not assist the plaintiff in *Delahunty*, who was only a visitor at the school. Accordingly, the Court held that, even if *Lister* were applicable in Ireland – a point not determined in *Delahunty* – this would not have availed the plaintiff. Having determined that the defendant school could not be held vicariously liable for the acts of the employee, O'Higgins J went on to note that, *a fortiori*, the Minister for Education and Science could not be held vicariously liable either since its connection was 'quite remote'.[39]

[8.18] Despite the reference to *Lister* in *Delahunty*, the judgment of O'Higgins J cannot be construed as either rejecting or accepting the *Lister* approach. O'Higgins J merely found that the requisite degree of connection, necessary under *Lister* to establish vicarious liability, was not satisfied in *Delahunty*. This was because there:

> [w]as not such a connection between the employment of [the housemaster responsible for the assault] and the assault on the plaintiff as to fix liability on his employers. The plaintiff in this case was a visitor in respect of whom [the housemaster] had no particular duties.... This is in contrast to *Lister* ... where the abuser was a warden and the close contact with the pupils and inherent risks that it involved were important factors in the decision.[40]

---

[36] *O'Keeffe v Hickey* [2008] IESC 71 (19 December 2008) SC.
[37] *Delahunty v South Eastern Health Board* [2003] 4 IR 361.
[38] [2003] 4 IR 361 at 377.
[39] [2003] 4 IR 361 at 377.
[40] [2003] 4 IR 361 at 377.

[8.19] It is at present unclear whether the approach taken in other common law jurisdictions to the 'close connection' test in vicarious liability will be applied in Ireland. In particular, the recent Supreme Court decision in *O'Keeffe v Hickey*[41] reveals significant disagreement amongst the judges of the Court as to whether this modification to vicarious liability should be applied. Before analysing this decision, it is necessary to consider earlier judgments in which Lister was referred to in the Irish courts.

The first occasion on which the Supreme Court considered this question was in its judgment in late December 2008 in *O'Keeffe v Hickey*,[42] an appeal from a judgment of de Valera J. The central issue was whether the Department of Education could be held vicariously liable for torts committed by a teacher, in circumstances where the Board of Management of the school was, in fact, the employer. It was on the basis of this 'triangular' relationship that the majority of the Supreme Court held that vicarious liability could not be imposed. Significantly, however, the judges afforded consideration to whether *Lister* and *Bazley* represented the law in this jurisdiction.

[8.20] In their judgments in *O'Keeffe*, members of the Supreme Court expressed differing opinions as to whether these innovations should be adopted in Ireland. Of the *Bazley* decision, for example, Hardiman J described the formulations of law by the Supreme Court of Canada as 'vague in the extreme and quite unhelpful'. More fundamentally, Hardiman J described as 'firmly rooted in principle and precedent' the earlier decision of the English Court of Appeal in *Trotman* referred to above to the effect that vicarious liability could not be imposed on an employer for independent criminal acts of sexual assault committed by an employee. Hardiman J indicated that legislative reform would be a more desireable route to altering the law on vicarious liability rather than judicial decision.

Fennelly J – although also rejecting Ms O'Keeffe's claim – delivered a separate judgment in which he expressed greater support for the international innovations in vicarious liability, in particular the 'close connection' test as adopted in House of Lords in *Lister*.

Finally, Geoghegan J, in his dissenting judgment, described the Canadian Supreme Court's innovation in *Bazley* as 'the leading modern case' and went on to conclude that he would have allowed Ms O'Keeffe's appeal on the basis of an application of 'the general modern principles underlying vicarious liability'.

[8.21] The judgments in *O'Keeffe* therefore indicate not only that there is a lack of consensus amongst the judiciary as to the law in Ireland on vicarious liability principles generally, but also that Irish law may differ markedly from that in other countries. If this ultimately proves to be the case, then individuals seeking damages in the courts for child sexual abuse may stand in a far weaker position than persons seeking the same redress in, for example, England, Canada and Australia. Given that the core issue in *O'Keeffe* concerned this 'triangular relationship' between the school, the Board of Management and the employer, however, the various comments made on these issues could strictly be described as *obiter*. In light of the pace at which developments in vicarious liability have

---

[41] *O'Keeffe v Hickey* [2008] IESC 71 (19 December 2008) SC.
[42] *O'Keeffe v Hickey* [2008] IESC 71 (19 December 2008) SC.

been emerging, however, it seems fair to predict that the cases will be further considered by the superior courts in the near future.[43]

SPECIFIC DIFICULTIES ARISING IN THE 'COURSE OF EMPLOYMENT' ANALYSIS

[8.22] In this section, consideration is given to a number of peculiar difficulties that can arise when engaging in an analysis of whether an employee has acted 'in the course of employment'.

Where employee wrongfully performs function he is employed to carry out

[8.23] Vicarious liability will generally arise where an employee wrongfully performs a function he is employed to carry out. In *Century Insurance Ltd v Northern Ireland Road Transport Board*,[44] vicarious liability was made out where the employee lit a cigarette while unloading a petrol tanker and fire resulted.

Where employee wrongfully permits another person to do his job

[8.24] In circumstances where an employee permits another person to discharge a duty which the employee should be performing, the employer may be vicariously liable on the ground that the employee was negligent in so permitting that other person to do his job. Thus in *ILKIW v Samuels*[45] a lorry driver in the employment of the defendants permitted a stranger to drive his lorry, which resulted in an accident. As the stranger was not an employee of the defendants, they could not be held liable for his negligence,[46] but could be and were held liable for the negligence of the employee in permitting the stranger to take charge of the function of driving without having made an inquiry of whether he was competent to do so.[47]

[8.25] A related situation arises in cases where the employee has usurped the role of another person. In such cases, vicarious liability may be imposed as long as the employee's acts are sufficiently connected with the employer's enterprise. The question arose for determination in the difficult case of *Kay v ITW Ltd*.[48] There a storekeeper who was employed by the defendants needed to return a fork-lift truck to a warehouse but found that his path was blocked by a large lorry belonging to a third party. Even though the situation was not particularly urgent – and without seeking to approach or inquire about the driver of the lorry – the employee attempted to move the lorry himself. In doing so, he negligently caused injury to the plaintiff. The Court of Appeal considered the case to be a difficult one, since it cannot be for every conceivable act of an

---

[43] A yet more recent example is the Supreme Court decision in *Reilly v Devereux* [2009] IESC 22, (24 March 2009) SC in which Kearns J referred to *Bazley* without analysing its status in this jurisdiction.

[44] *Century Insurance Ltd v Northern Ireland Road Transport Board* [1942] AC 509.

[45] *ILKIW v Samuels* [1963] 1 WLR 991.

[46] *ILKIW v Samuels* [1963] 1 WLR 991, *per* Willmer LJ at 996.

[47] Although see the more difficult reasoning of Diplock LJ at 1003–1006.

[48] *Kay v ITW Ltd* [1968] 1 QB 140.

employee, no matter how extreme, that an employer will be liable if that act is performed in furtherance of the employer's enterprise.[49] Nonetheless, having regard to the fact that it was clearly within the terms of the storekeeper's contract of employment to move certain obstacles out of the way if they obstructed the entrance to the warehouse, and given that it was part of his normal employment to drive both trucks and smaller vans, the Court of Appeal held that the employee's act of attempting to move the lorry was not so extreme so as to take it outside the scope of his employment. Vicarious liability was accordingly imposed.

Where employee engages in a frolic of his own

[8.26] Traditionally it was said that there could be no liability for a tort committed by an employee who was engaging in a frolic of his own.[50] However, the sweeping nature of this 'rule' obscures the difficulty involved in actually applying it to the facts of an individual case. For instance, the extremely serious criminal actions of the warden in *Lister v Hesley Hall*,[51] on one view, clearly amounted to the employee acting on a 'frolic' of his own, and yet, as seen above in this chapter, vicarious liability was held to exist on the facts of that case.

Where employee breaches express prohibition

[8.27] Although it might be thought unfair that an employer can be held liable even where his employee acts contrary to clear instructions and engages in forbidden behaviour, the better view on the authorities is that an employer may still be liable in these circumstances. The mere fact that the employee does something which he is expressly forbidden from doing does not necessarily mean that the employee was acting outside the scope or course of his employment. In an old English case, the defendant's bus driver was forbidden from racing competitors to bus stops. When an accident happened, the defendant was liable, even though the driver had been racing.[52]

Vicarious liability of employer for employee 'pranks'

[8.28] In considering the question of vicarious liability of employers for employee pranks, it is instructive to have regard to two recent decisions of the courts in Northern Ireland.

[8.29] *McCready v Securicor Ltd*[53] concerned a plaintiff and a fellow employee who were fooling about together playing on trolleys used at their work place when the plaintiff's hand was crushed. The Court of Appeal, applying the Salmond test, held that

---

[49] *Kay v ITW Ltd* [1968] 1 QB 140 *per* Sellers LJ at 151–152.

[50] This celebrated phrase was coined by Parke B in *Joel v Morrison* (1834) 6 C & P 501 at 503.

[51] *Lister v Hesley Hall* [2001] UKHL 22, [2002] 1 AC 215, [2001] 2 WLR 1311.

[52] *Limpus v General Omnibus Co* (1862) 1 H & C 526. Difficulties have arisen in this context in cases where employees have given a lift in the employer's vehicle to unauthorised passengers: compare *Twine v Bean's Express Ltd* [1946] 1 All ER 202 with *Rose v Plenty* [1976] 1 WLR 141.

[53] *McCready v Securicor Ltd* [1991] NI 229.

the wrongful act on the plaintiff's fellow employee was an independent act for which the employer was not vicariously liable.

Where 'prank' committed outside workplace but at work-related event

[8.30] More difficult issues may arise in the context of conduct committed outside the workplace but where the event is nevertheless work-related. Perhaps the most common instance is the work Christmas party. The recent case of *Hunter v Department for Regional Development for Northern Ireland*[54] arose from a Christmas party prank by one employee resulting in personal injury to another. The latter sued her employer, seeking to have vicarious liability imposed in these circumstances. During the course of their office Christmas party in a hotel in County Down, the plaintiff had been dancing with a fellow employee. Following this dancing, as the plaintiff was about to sit down the same fellow employee pulled away her chair, causing her to fall to the ground and to fracture her right wrist.

[8.31] Stephens J declined to impose vicarious liability on the employer in these circumstances. Distinguishing the case from one where a prank is perpetrated by an employee during working hours on the employer's premises, he stressed that the wrongdoing employee was employed as a road surfaces foreman; the particular act which he committed was to pull a chair away from underneath the plaintiff at an office Christmas party being held in a hotel. Having referred to the close connection test in *Lister v Hesley Hall*, Stephens J considered that the act of the wrongdoer was 'an independent act and was not so closely connected to his employment as to make it fair and just to hold the defendant vicariously liable.' Although the tort was committed at an event that did have connections to the employment of all staff members in attendance, a number of factors persuaded the Court that vicarious liability could not be imposed. These included the fact that attendance at the party was entirely voluntary; that it was held outside working hours; that the location was a hotel which was open to the public; that the employer made no financial contribution towards it; and that it was organised principally as an opportunity for work colleagues to enjoy a night out together. While the Court accepted that the event 'undoubtedly had a benefit to the employer in so far as it encouraged good working relationships and boosted office morale', those benefits were found to be 'incidental to the main motivation behind the organisation and holding of this party.'[55]

VICARIOUS LIABILITY IN STATUTORY CONTEXTS

[8.32] In this section, two specific examples are given of significant statutory embodiments of the vicarious liability principle of particular relevance for employment lawyers: vicarious liability in the employment equality context, and in the health and safety context, with comments being offered as to salient features of vicarious liability doctrine in each of these areas.

---

[54] *Hunter v Department for Regional Development for Northern Ireland* [2008] NIQB 88 (5 September 2008).

[55] *Hunter v Department for Regional Development for Northern Ireland* [2008] NIQB 88, [14].

Employment Equality Act 1998

[8.33] Perhaps the most significant statutory example of the potential for vicarious liability to be imposed upon an employer is s 15 of the Employment Equality Act 1998.

Section 15 of the Employment Equality Act 1998, which is entitled *'Vicarious Liability etc'* provides in subs (1) as follows:

> (1) Anything done by a person in the course of his or her employment shall, in any proceedings brought under this Act, be treated for the purposes of this Act as done also by that person's employer, whether or not it was done with the employer's knowledge or approval.

[8.34] This provision is subject to s 15(3) which provides that it shall be a defence for the employer to prove that the employer took such steps as were reasonably practicable to prevent the employee from doing the particular act or from doing, in the course of his or her employment, acts of that description.

[8.35] It has been said that the 1998 Act, by making express provision for vicarious liability and by providing for a defence for employers, 'has brought some certainty to this confusing area of the law'.[56] Much of the 'confusion' referred to arguably grew out of the High Court decision in *The Health Board v BC*[57] In that case, the High Court rejected the contention made by an employee that her employer could be vicariously liable for acts of sexual harassment perpetrated by her fellow employees. The relevant statutory framework was then the Employment Equality Act 1977, which made no reference to the possible vicarious liability of an employer when such conduct was committed by an employee. Costello J (as he then was) in that case had stated that:

> The law in this country in relation to the liability of an employer for a tortious act, (including statutory torts) of his employee is perfectly clear — an employer is vicariously liable where the act is committed by his employee within the scope of his employment.

Costello J then went on to observe, however, that:

> An employer may, of course, be vicariously liable when his employee is acting negligently or even criminally ... [b]ut I cannot envisage any employment in which they were engaged in respect of which a sexual assault could be regarded as so connected with it as to amount to an act within its scope.[58]

[8.36] It is suggested that, while the first passage set out above from the judgment of Costello J is uncontroversial, the second might not withstand scrutiny in a fully argued common law claim today. Indeed, in the context of a claim for sexual harassment or discrimination of an employee at work, the landscape in this jurisdiction was, as noted above, significantly altered by the coming into force of s 15 of the Employment Equality Act 1998. This Act repealed the Act of 1977, and expressly sought to deal with, *inter alia*, the question of whether vicarious liability could be imposed in a situation such as that which had presented itself in *The Health Board v BC*. The provision thus constitutes an extremely significant alteration of a hitherto strict rule precluding vicarious liability,

---

[56] Marguerite Bolger and Clíona Kimber, *Sex Discrimination Law* (Round Hall, 2000), p 278.
[57] *The Health Board v BC* [1994] ELR 27.
[58] [1994] ELR 27 at 34.

and expands the parameters of vicarious liability considerably in the discrimination context.

Safety, Health and Welfare at Work Act 2005

Vicarious liability of employer for bullying, harassment and stress

[8.37] The second statutory regime of particular note in relation to vicarious liability it the Safety, Health and Welfare at Work Act 2005. In particular, it is possible to argue that this Act may well generate the possibility of vicarious – as distinct from primary – liability being imposed on employers in the context of bullying, harassment and stress in the workplace. This issue of employers' liability for workplace harassment, bullying and stress is, of course, one that has exercised the Irish courts in a number of high-profile cases in recent years and is the subject of a detailed chapter in the present work, to which the reader is referred.[59] To date, however, the core issue in the Irish jurisprudence has been whether the employers had themselves been negligent regarding the treatment inflicted upon the plaintiff, ie. whether primary liability could be imposed upon the employers. For present purposes, it is necessary to consider whether *vicarious* liability could be imposed upon an employer —even in the absence of a finding of wrongdoing on the part of the employer— for the wrongdoing of employees in the context of a bullying and harassment claim. In this context, it is submitted that it may be possible to argue that by virtue of s 13 of the Safety, Health and Welfare at Work Act 2005, it could be possible for vicarious liability to be imposed upon an employer for bullying committed by one employee against one another in breach of employees' individual duties to safeguard their colleagues' welfare pursuant to that section. In considering this question, it is instructive to have regard to two recent English cases, decided in 2006, which it is suggested may have implications for the potential of this Irish statutory provision to give rise to vicarious liability.

[8.38] The first case to be considered in this regard is *Majrowski v Guy's and St Thomas's NHS Trust.*[60] For present purposes, it is a case of particular interest as the decision of the House of Lords involves an extension of the vicarious liability principle to a situation in which an employee had breached a statutory duty, owed exclusively by himself, as opposed to a common law duty such as the duty of care in negligence. Such statutory duties have two distinct characteristics: first, the duty, a creature of statute, does not arise by operation of common law principles; secondly, the statute imposes the duty upon the employee personally and makes no reference to the employer. What is the effect of these distinct characteristics on attempts to impose vicarious liability on an employer for breach of a statutory duty by an employee?

[8.39] In *Majrowski,* it was held that an employer could be held vicariously responsible for the breach of a statutory duty by an employee even where that statutory duty was only owed by the employee. The case arose from the harassment of one employee by another, contrary to the UK's Protection from Harassment Act 1997. The employee

---

[59] Ch 7, Bullying, Harassment and Stress at Work.
[60] *Majrowski v Guy's and St Thomas's NHS Trust* [2006] UKHL 34, [2006] 3 WLR 125.

alleged that he was bullied, intimidated and harassed by his departmental manager over a period of time. He pointed to excessive criticism, ostracism, abusive conduct and the setting of unreasonable work targets, and alleged that this treatment was motivated by homophobia on the part of his departmental manager. When Mr Majrowski complained, the departmental manager was suspended and, after an internal investigation which found that Mr Majrowski had been subjected to homophobic harassment, she resigned.

[8.40] In instituting legal proceedings, Mr Majrowski elected not to sue the departmental manager herself, but rather the employer, whom he alleged was vicariously liable. He claimed damages for distress and anxiety and consequential losses caused by the harassment he suffered while employed by the defendants. The departmental manager, Mr Majrowski claimed, was at all times acting in the course of her employment. Significantly, Mr Majrowski did not make any claim against the employer for negligence or breach of his contract of employment. His claim was based exclusively on the employer's vicarious liability for the departmental manager's alleged breach of the statutory prohibition of harassment.

[8.41] At first instance, the proceedings were struck out summarily. The judge held that the statutory framework to combat harassment was not designed to create another level of liability in employment law, since employees were already adequately protected by the common law. On appeal, the Court of Appeal ruled by a majority (Auld and May LJJ, Scott Baker LJ dissenting in part) that the employer could be vicariously liable for the employee's breach of statutory duty. Accordingly, the Court of Appeal held that the case should be permitted to go to trial. On appeal to the House of Lords, it was acknowledged that there was little judicial authority for the proposition that vicarious liability could (in the absence of express statutory guidance) be imposed upon an employer for an employee's breach of statutory duty. Notwithstanding this, all of the judges in the House of Lords were in agreement about the correctness of the result reached in the Court of Appeal. The judgments raise a number of interesting points that are worth mentioning briefly in the context of considering whether the Irish courts may adopt the approach taken in *Majrowski*.

[8.42] The first point of note is that the House of Lords in *Majrowski* held, as a matter of law, that vicarious liability could arise in a situation where an employee had breached a statutory duty. According to Lord Nicholls, the basic policy reasons underlying the common law principle of vicarious liability were equally applicable to both equitable wrongs and breaches of statutory duty. Lord Nicholls expressly rejected the so-called 'master's tort' theory of vicarious liability – involving a conception of vicarious liability as based on the wrongdoing of the employer – in favour of an approach focusing upon the wrongdoing of the employee, or the 'servant's tort' theory.

[8.43] Having accepted that an employee's breach of statutory duty could give rise to vicarious liability of the employer, the court had to consider whether vicarious liability arises *unless* the statutory provision expressly or impliedly *excludes* such liability, or whether vicarious liability arises only *if* the statutory provision expressly or impliedly *envisages* such liability? The first of these options was favoured by the House of Lords. Lord Nicholls explained that this was 'more consistent with the general rule that employers are liable for wrongs committed by employees in the course of their employment. The general rule should apply in respect of wrongs having a statutory source unless the statute displaces the ordinary rule'.[61]

[8.44] In *Majrowski,* emphasis was placed on the conclusion that the legislature, in enacting the Protection from Harassment Act 1997, had intended that vicarious liability could attach to an employer. Although the relevant section of the statute was silent on this point, Lord Hope drew attention to another subsection in the Act which clearly envisaged that vicarious liability could operate in the context of proceedings in Scotland. Because the legislature would have had no reason to introduce different regimes as between Scotland and England and Wales, the court was satisfied that the relevant statutory intent to permit the imposition of vicarious liability had been identified. This is an important point to take from the judgment in *Majrowski,* since otherwise, the appeal may very well have been decided differently.[62]

[8.45] It is submitted that the approach taken in *Majrowski* represents an important development in the law relating to vicarious liability. From an Irish perspective, it will be of interest to note whether the courts in this jurisdiction follow the approach to vicarious liability for breach of statutory duty taken in *Majrowski.* Perhaps the area in which such an approach would most likely be adopted is that concerning the statutory framework governing health and safety at work. In a recent article considering the implications of the Safety, Health and Welfare at Work Act 2005, Professor Binchy has noted the potential significance of the Court of Appeal decision in *Majrowski* in the context of s 13 of the Act, which imposes a duty upon employees not to act in a manner that undermines the safety, health or welfare of their fellow employees.[63]

Developments post-Majrowski: the judgment in Green

[8.46] The case *of Green v DB Group Services (UK) Ltd,*[64] is the second of the two English decisions concerning vicarious liability handed down in the summer of 2006. It too is worthy of analysis in an Irish context. The case attracted considerable media attention when judgment was delivered in August 2006, not least because of the size of the award for bullying and harassment in the workplace, which was in excess of £800,000. The claimant sued her former employer, Deutsche Bank, after persistent bullying by colleagues at the bank caused her to suffer two nervous breakdowns. The judge concluded that Ms Green had been 'subjected to a relentless campaign of mean and spiteful behaviour designed to cause her distress'.[65]

[8.47] Of particular interest for present purposes is the approach taken by Owen J in finding the employer vicariously liable for the bullying suffered by the claimant at the

---

[61] *Majrowski v Guy's and St Thomas's NHS Trust* [2006] UKHL 34, [2006] 3 WLR 125 at [16].

[62] See, for example, the comments of Lord Brown in *Majrowski,v Guy's and St Thomas's NHS Trust* [2006] UKHL 34, [2006] 3 WLR 125 at [81].

[63] Binchy, 'Torts claims against schools: the implications of the Safety, Health and Welfare at Work Act 2005' (2006) 1(2) *QRTL* 28, at 30.

[64] *Green v DB Group Services (UK) Ltd* [2006] EWHC 1898, [2006] IRLR 764.

[65] *Green v DB Group Services (UK) Ltd* [2006] EWHC 1898, [2006] IRLR 764, [99].

hands of some of her colleagues. The claimant asserted that her psychiatric injury, and consequential loss and damage, were the result of bullying and harassment on the part of a number of the defendant's employees for whom the defendant was vicariously liable; and also that there was a negligent failure on the part of the management and of the defendant's Human Resources department to take any or any adequate steps to protect her from such conduct.

[8.48] The claimant in *Green* succeeded on both grounds. Interestingly, Owen J cited the House of Lords' decision in *Majrowksi,* then just days old. He also referred to the decision in *Lister.* Owen J noted that the defendant in no sense condoned the bullying carried out by its employee; it genuinely was appalled that this should have taken place, and was sorry that the claimant was subjected to it. Equally, however, the defendant argued that it could not fairly be held vicariously liable. The bullying had nothing to do with the work of either the bullies or the claimant. All that could be said was that the fact that they were employed by the defendant gave the bullies the opportunity to behave as they did. Owen J rejected this argument and imposed vicarious liability. He identified a close connection between the wrongdoers' employment and the behaviour in issue. The bullying directly affected the working environment in which the claimant worked; and some aspects of the wrongful behaviour involved work that one or other of the wrongdoing employees were required to undertake in the course of their employment. By way of example on this latter point, Owen J noted that one of the bullies was responsible for distributing post, and had deliberately withheld the claimant's post and then would fill her in-tray with what seemed like a week's internal post. A further example given was that a colleague of the claimant's, when asked to compile a list of all staff to give to security, had deliberately omitted the claimant's name and details. Owen J applied the test set out by Lord Steyn in the Privy Council case of *Bernard v Attorney General of Jamaica,*[66] where Lord Steyn explained the correct approach to the issue of vicarious liability in the following terms: 'The correct approach is to concentrate on the relative closeness of the connection between the nature of the employment and the particular tort, and to ask whether in looking at the matter in the round, it is just and reasonable to hold the employer vicariously liable'.[67]

[8.49] It is to be noted that in *Green* the court also held the employer negligent in failing to have put in place any or any adequate system of protecting Ms Green from bullying or harassment. The court gave a more detailed analysis of the negligence of the employer as opposed to its vicarious liability. However, it is still important that vicarious liability was found on the facts of this case: if Ms Green had failed to establish breach of duty by her employer she would still have won her case by virtue of vicarious liability having been imputed to the employer for bullying by its employees.

[8.50] It is submitted that each of the two cases analysed above may very well exert significant implications on vicarious liability analysis in this jurisdiction both in the context of s 13 of the 2005 Act and in relation to bullying, harassment and stress claims generally.

---

[66] *Bernard v Attorney General of Jamaica* [2005] IRLR 398.
[67] *Bernard v Attorney General of Jamaica* [2005] IRLR 398, [18].

Chapter 9

Part-Time Workers

Des Ryan

INTRODUCTION

[9.01] In this chapter, a detailed analysis is conducted of the provisions of the Protection of Employees (Part-Time Work) Act 2001 (the 2001 Act)[1] and of the relevant case law affecting part-time workers. In terms of subject-matter, there are a number of parallels between the content of this chapter and that of other chapters of the present work, and the reader is encouraged to refer to other specialist chapters as necessary. Perhaps the most important cross-reference directions which should be explicitly stated at this point, however, are the relationship between the law on part-time workers and employment equality law generally, owing to the relevance of the concept of indirect discrimination in the context of part-time workers,[2] and the strong similarities in statutory construction between the 2001 Act and the Protection of Employees (Fixed-Term Work) Act 2003. In relation to the connection between these two pieces of protective legislation, it has been held that the 2003 Act should be construed *in pari materia* with the 2001 Act.[3] For this reason, the reader is also invited to consult Ch 10 of the present work, relating to fixed-term workers, and to refer to that chapter in conjunction with the material in the present chapter.

Background to the Protection of Employees (Part-Time Work) Act 2001

[9.02] The law relating to part-time workers in Ireland was radically changed by the introduction of the 2001 Act,[4] which seeks to provide for the removal of discrimination against part-time workers. The purpose of the 2001 Act was to effect the transposition into Irish law of Council Directive 97/81/EC of 15 December 1997 concerning the Framework Agreement on part-time work concluded by the general cross-industry organisations at European level. This Framework Agreement between the Union of Industrial and Employers' Confederations of Europe (UNICE), the European Trade Union Confederation (ETUC) and the European Centre of Enterprises with Public Participation (CEEP) was concluded on 6 June 1997 and the agreement was adopted as Directive 97/81/EC on 15 December 1997.

---

[1] For detailed annotated commentary on the provisions of the 2001 Act, see Anthony Kerr, *Consolidated Irish Employment Legislation* (Thomson Round Hall, Release 19, April 2008), Division H.

[2] See Ch 13, Employment Equality.

[3] *ESB v McDonnell* PTD 081 (6 March 2008).

[4] The Act came into operation on 20 December 2001: see SI 636/2001. The 2001 Act repeals in its entirety the Worker Protection (Regular Part-Time Employees) Act 1991.

[9.03] At the outset, it is critical to gain an understanding of the Framework Agreement in relation to fixed-term workers, given the requirement that transposing legislation must be interpreted and applied in light of the purpose and wording of the directive so as to achieve the objectives pursued by the directive.[5] The first and second paragraphs of the preamble to the Framework Agreement state:

> This Framework Agreement is a contribution to the overall European strategy on employment. Part-time work has had an important impact on employment in recent years. For this reason, the parties to this agreement have given priority attention to this form of work. It is the intention of the parties to consider the need for similar agreements relating to other forms of flexible work.

> Recognising the diversity of situations in Member States and acknowledging that part-time work is a feature of employment in certain sectors and activities, this Agreement sets out the general principles and minimum requirements relating to part-time work. It illustrates the willingness of the social partners to establish a general framework for the elimination of discrimination against part-time workers and to assist the development of opportunities for part-time working on a basis acceptable to employers and workers.

[9.04] The objective of the Framework Agreement on part-time work is two-fold. First, it seeks to prevent discrimination against part-time workers and to improve the quality of part-time work. Furthermore, it aims to facilitate the development of part-time work on a voluntary basis and to contribute to the flexible organisation of working time in a manner that takes into account the needs of both employers and workers.[6] Clause 4 of the Agreement lays down the principle of non-discrimination, namely that, in respect of employment and conditions, part-time workers should not be treated in a less favourable manner than comparable full-time workers solely because they work part-time, save where the difference in treatment can be justified on objective grounds. Clause 5(2) states that an employee's refusal to transfer from full-time to part-time status or *vice versa* should not constitute a valid reason for termination of employment (without prejudice to termination for other reasons such as may arise from the operational requirements of the establishment concerned). In light of these objectives and provisions of the Framework Agreement, an overview of the 2001 Act can now be offered.

OVERVIEW OF THE 2001 ACT

[9.05] The introduction of the 2001 Act was long overdue in Irish employment law. Long before it was introduced, part-time workers had not only come to represent a considerable proportion of the workforce: they were also denied access to crucial protective legislation (such as the Unfair Dismissals Act 1977, with its stipulated threshold of 18 hours a week) and, indeed, to the social welfare system.[7] While piecemeal legislative measures were introduced to improve the lot of the part-time

---

[5] Case C-14/83 *Von Colson and Kamann v Land Nordrhein-Westfalen* [1984] ECR 1891.

[6] Framework Agreement on Part-Time Work (OJ No L14, 20.1.1998, p 9), clause 1.

[7] For a detailed discussion of these points see Anthony Kerr, *Consolidated Irish Employment Legislation* (Thomson Round Hall, Release 19, April 2008), Division H.

worker on both fronts in the early 1990s,[8] a unified legislative framework protecting part-time workers remained lacking.

[9.06] In general terms, the 2001 Act pursues the objective in the Framework Agreement of ensuring that part-time employees will not be treated less favourably than comparable full-time employees unless there are objective grounds for the less favourable treatment: where a benefit is determined by the number of hours an employee works, it shall be on a *pro rata* or proportionate basis to part-time employees.

At this juncture, some fundamental points in relation to the influence of the 2001 Act on litigation involving part-time workers should be made. First, there is no provision in the 2001 Act, or elsewhere in Irish employment law, for a statutory entitlement to part-time work. Rather, the Act is concerned with preventing unfavourable treatment of part-time workers where such treatment cannot be objectively justified on a ground that is unrelated to the employee's part-time status. Another obvious[9] point to clarify at the outset is that a part-time worker's grievance must relate to his or her status as a part-time worker in that it must be capable of being characterised in such a way as to bring the grievance within the scope of the scheme of redress laid down in this legislation.

[9.07] The Act also makes provision for the Labour Relations Commission (the LRC) to carry out studies for the purposes of identifying obstacles that may exist in particular industries or sectors to access to part-time work, and for the Commission, in consultation with the social partners, to prepare a Code of Practice which would be of practical benefit to employers and employees in addressing such obstacles.[10]

[9.08] Section 3 of the 2001 Act provides definitions of many key terms, a large proportion of which are common to the protective legislation generally in this jurisdiction. Thus, the definition of 'collective agreement', for example, is identical to that in s 2(1) of the Organisation of Working Time Act 1997; so too does the definition of 'contract of employment'[11] raise the perennial question, discussed at length in Ch 2 of

---

[8]   For a detailed discussion of these points see Anthony Kerr, *Consolidated Irish Employment Legislation* (Thomson Round Hall, Release 19, April 2008), Division H.

[9]   Though still one that recently required to be stated by the Labour Court in *Top Security Ltd v Jun Yu Wang* PTD 061 (27 February 2006). The point can also become difficult where a person claims that a portion of their employment duties require to be characterised as representing a discrete part-time employment, a claim which was unsuccessfully made by the employee in *Eileen Peters v Wesley College* PTD 054 (4 October 2005).

[10] For analysis of the LRC Code, see below para **[9.31]** *et seq.*

[11] Defined as meaning:
   (a)   a contract of service or apprenticeship, and
   (b)   any other contract whereby an individual agrees with another person, who is carrying on the business of an employment agency within the meaning of the Employment Agency Act 1971, and is acting in the course of that business, to do or perform personally any work or service for a third person (whether or not the third person is a party to the contract),
   whether the contract is express or implied and, if express, whether it is oral or in writing.

this work[12] of whether a person is employed under a contract of service or a contract for services.[13]

PART-TIME WORK AND THE RIGHTS OF PART-TIME EMPLOYEES

Who is a part-time worker?

[9.09] The 2001 Act straightforwardly defines a 'part-time employee' as 'an employee whose normal hours of work are less than the normal hours of work of an employee who is a comparable employee in relation to him or her'.[14] In the same section of the 2001 Act, the concept of 'normal hours of work' is defined as meaning the average number of hours worked by the employee each day during a reference period; the reference period, in turn, is defined as a period which complies with the following conditions:

(a)   the period is of not less than seven days nor more than 12 months' duration;

(b)   the period is the same period by reference to which the normal hours of work of the other employee referred to in the definition of 'part-time employee' in this section is determined; and

(c)   the number of hours worked by the employee concerned in the period constitutes the normal number of hours worked by the employee in a period of that duration.

In terms of the definition of part-time employee, the 2001 Act can be regarded as relatively generous to persons seeking to come within its ambit. Thus, there is recent Labour Court authority to the effect that seasonal workers are included within the meaning of part-time employees, that is, the contract of employment does not have to extend over the entire reference period in order for the employee to be considered a part-time employee under the 2001 Act.[15]

The 2001 Act does, too, envisage a broader definition being given to the phrase 'contract of employment' than, for example, that used in the context of the Protection of Employees (Fixed-Term Work) Act 2003. The 2001 Act provides, for example, that apprentices are included within its ambit, which is not the case under the 2003 Act.[16] It should also be noted that the Labour Court has been prepared to regard agency workers as being part-time employees of the organisation to whom the employee is referred by the agency where that organisation exercises sufficient control over the agency worker.[17]

---

[12]   See Ch 2, The Contract and Relationship of Employment.

[13]   For a fuller discussion of the overlap in nomenclature between the definitions in s 3 of the 2001 Act and other pieces of employment legislation see Anthony Kerr, *Consolidated Irish Employment Legislation* (Thomson Round Hall, Release 19, April 2008), Division H.

[14]   Protection of Employees (Part-Time Work) Act 2001, s 7(1).

[15]   *ESB v McDonnell* PTD 081 (6 March 2008).

[16]   In the context of apprenticeships, the decision of the Labour Court in *ESB Networks v Kingham* [2006] ELR 181 reversed a decision of the Rights Commissioner that an apprenticeship scheme could come within the scope of protection of the 2003 Act.

[17]   *Diageo Global Supply v Rooney* [2004] ELR 133.

Meaning of comparable employee

[9.10] Of fundamental importance in the context of part-time employment is the notion of the comparator. Pursuant to s 7(3) of the 2001 Act, an employee will be a comparator for the purposes of a claim by a part-time employee if one of the following circumstances obtains:

(a) the employee and the relevant part-time employee are employed by the same employer or associated employers and one of a number of conditions (set out below) is satisfied in respect of those employees;

(b) in case (a) does not apply (including a case where the relevant part-time employee is the sole employee of the employer), the employee is specified in a collective agreement applying to the relevant part-time employee, to be a type of employee who is to be regarded for the purposes of the 2001 Act as a comparable employee in relation to the relevant part-time employee;

(c) in case neither (a) nor (b) applies, the employee is employed in the same industry or sector of employment as the relevant part-time employee is employed in and one of the conditions referred to below is satisfied in respect of those employees.

The conditions to be satisfied if a comparator is to be established

[9.11] Section 7(3) continues by setting out the conditions to be satisfied for establishing a comparator. It should be noted that only one of the following conditions must be fulfilled in order to establish the comparator. The conditions are:

(i) both of the employees concerned perform the same work under the same or similar conditions or each is interchangeable with the other in relation to the work;

(ii) the work performed by one of the employees concerned is of the same or a similar nature to that performed by the other and any differences between the work performed or the conditions under which it is performed by each, either are of small importance in relation to the work as a whole or occur with such irregularity as not to be significant;

(iii) the work performed by the relevant part-time employee is equal or greater in value to the work performed by the other employee concerned, having regard to such matters as skill, physical or mental requirements, responsibility and working conditions.

It should be noted that the Act states that, for the avoidance of any doubt, a comparable full-time employee refers to such an employee either of the opposite sex to the part-time employee concerned or of the same sex as him or her.[18] It is, moreover, noteworthy that s 7(3) of the 2001 Act is drafted in terms similar to the definition of 'like work' in s 7 of the Employment Equality Act 1998.[19] In at least one important respect, however, the

---

[18] Protection of Employees (Part-Time Work) Act 2001, s 9(5).
[19] See Ch 13, Employment Equality.

2001 Act is more generous to claimants in this respect: unlike the position under the 1998 Act, in the absence of a comparable full-time employee in the employment where the part-time employee is employed, the comparator may be drawn from the same industry or sector of employment.

[9.12] In relation to the assessment of like work as between part-time workers and their chosen comparators, the approaches of both the Rights Commissioner Service and the Labour Court display extremely detailed assessments of the value of ostensibly similar work, with one of the most helpful determinations of the Labour Court on this point being its recent determination in *Bus Éireann v Group of Workers,*[20] where part-time bus drivers were held not to come within the scope of the s 7 'like work' requirement when compared with full-time drivers. The Court's assessment included an exhaustive analysis of the skills, physical and mental requirements and responsibilities on each employee and relied on the differences it identified in these categories to reject the part-time workers' claim. Another consideration that may be relevant to be taken into account is the existence of any formal title distinguishing the complainant from the desired comparator in terms of employment function[21]; though the comparator's length of service is, it seems, irrelevant.[22] It should be emphasised, however, that the inquiry of whether the comparator is engaged in 'like work' with the claimant is a question to be resolved on a case by case basis, with courts and tribunals being reluctant to articulate any binding criteria that must govern the inquiry.

CONDITIONS OF EMPLOYMENT FOR PART-TIME EMPLOYEES

[9.13] The relevant law on conditions of employment for part-time employees is set out in s 9 of the 2001 Act. Its key provisions are as follows:

(i) a part-time employee shall not, in respect of his or her conditions of employment, be treated in a less favourable manner than a comparable full-time employee, unless that less favourable treatment can be justified on objective grounds.[23]

(ii) in so far – but only in so far – as it relates to any pension scheme or arrangement, the prohibition of less favourable treatment does not apply to a part-time employee whose normal hours of work constitute less than 20 per cent of the normal hours of work of a comparable full-time employee.[24]

This section thus gives effect in Irish law to clause 4(1) of the Framework Agreement. As noted, a key feature of the section is the provision in s 9(2) that a part-time employee may, in respect of a particular condition of employment – which includes, *inter alia,*

---

[20] *Bus Éireann v Group of Workers* PTD 071 (18 May 2007).

[21] *O'Leary v Cahill May Roberts* PTD 044 (4 May 2004) (claim upheld on basis of a work inspection which revealed no comparator had any formal title that would distinguish the selected comparator from her fellow workers).

[22] *Dunnes Stores Letterkenny v A Group of Workers* PTD 046 (12 May 2004).

[23] Subject to s 9(4) and s 11(2) of the 2001 Act.

[24] Protection of Employees (Part-Time Work) Act 2001, s 9(4).

access to employee ownership schemes;[25] entitlements to sick pay;[26] and service pay[27] – be treated less favourably than a comparable full-time employee if that treatment can be justified on 'objective grounds'. The objective grounds must be based on considerations other than the status of the employee as a part-time worker and the less favourable treatment must be for the purpose of achieving a legitimate objective of the employer and must be necessary for that purpose. This is explicitly set out in s 12 of the 2001 Act, which provides as follows:

> A ground shall not be regarded as an objective ground for the purposes of any provision of this Part unless it is based on considerations other than the status of the employee concerned as a part-time employee and the less favourable treatment which it involves for that employee is for the purpose of achieving a legitimate objective of the employer and such treatment is appropriate and necessary for that purpose.

[9.14] The concept of objective justification thus coheres with the classic European Court of Justice (ECJ) formulation in *Bilka-Kaufhaus*.[28] As is well known, in that case the ECJ set out a three-stage test by which an indirectly discriminatory measure may be justified. The Court held that the measure must first meet a 'real need' of the employer; secondly, the measure must be 'appropriate' to meet the objective which it pursues; lastly, the measure must be 'necessary' in order to achieve that objective.

Requirement to consider alternative options less detrimental to employee

[9.15] In considering a claim under the 2001 Act, the Labour Court in *Diageo Global Supply v Rooney*[29] held that in order to satisfy the requirement of objective justification, an employer is obliged to give consideration to alternative options whose effects would be less serious for the employee affected:

> In the normal course, an employer would be expected to have considered alternative means of achieving the objective being pursued which might have a less detrimental effect on the part-time worker concerned. It is only if it can be demonstrated that there are no viable, less discriminatory means of achieving the objective being pursued can the defence of objective justification succeed.

Requirement that objective grounds not be based on part-time status

[9.16] As to the requirement that the objective grounds must not be based on the status of the employee as a part-time worker, it is instructive to consider the interesting case of *Mullaney Brothers v Two Workers*,[30] concerning the granting by the employer of so-called 'Christmas shopping leave' to full-time, but not part-time, employees in a drapery and travel business. The half-day paid shopping leave had applied to the claimant workers since they commenced employment until November 2004 when it was removed

---

[25] *ESB v McDonnell* PTD 081 (6 March 2008).

[26] *Dunnes Stores Letterkenny v SIPTU* PTD 052 (26 January 2005); *Dunnes Stores Cavan v A Group of Workers* PTD 045 (12 May 2004).

[27] *Dunnes Stores Cavan v A Group of Workers* PTD 045 (12 May 2004).

[28] Case C-170/84 *Bilka-Kaufhaus v Weber von Hartz* [1986] ECR 1607.

[29] *Diageo Global Supply v Rooney* [2004] ELR 133.

[30] *Mullaney Brothers v Two Workers* PTD 066 (22 September 2006).

from part-time staff on the basis that it had been given on a concessionary basis and applied only to full-time workers who were working six days per week in the two weeks prior to Christmas. (It was found as a fact, however, that the concession was also restored to full-time staff in the travel business, who did not work a six-day week.) The Labour Court, upholding the Rights Commissioner's determination on this point,[31] held that the employer had contravened the 2001 Act, since the only basis upon which the benefit was withdrawn from the claimants was that they were part-time employees. This clearly could not, the Court noted, constitute objective grounds within the meaning of s 12 of the Act.

By contrast, the Labour Court in *Louth VEC v Martin*[32] accepted that the requirement for teachers to be fully qualified before proceeding upon the incremental scale corresponded to a real need on the part of the employer to ensure that all persons teaching in its schools had the appropriate academic qualifications. It further accepted the employer's contention that it was appropriate and necessary to have such a financial sanction in order to encourage employees to obtain the necessary qualifications, and that there was no alternative means by which this objective could be achieved.

Objective grounds must justify less favourable treatment of part-time workers as distinct from more favourable treatment of full-timers

[9.17] In *Abbott Ireland Ltd v SIPTU*[33] the union claimed that part-time workers were entitled to rest breaks on a *pro rata* basis with full-time employees and that part-time employees working between 4 pm and midnight were entitled to shift premium payments on a *pro rata* basis with comparable full-time employees. Both claims were successful, with the Labour Court emphasising in its determination that in relation to objective justification there is a distinction between less favourable treatment of part-time workers and more favourable treatment of full-time workers being capable of justification:

> The purpose of this Act is to prevent part-time employees being less favourably treated than comparable full-time employees. In this case, the full-time employees receive a thirty minute break during their four hour shift. The fact that the break given to full-time employees is in line with their entitlements under the Organisation of Working Time Act cannot be used as objective justification for the less favourable treatment of part-time employees. Indeed the Act is quite clear in what must be justified is not the more favourable treatment of full-time employees, but the less favourable treatment of part-time employees...
>
> If the part-time employee works the same hours as a full-time employee and the full-time employee receives an unsocial shift premium for those hours then the part-time employee is also entitled to that premium unless there are objective grounds for its non-payment.

---

[31] But not on the question of *pro rata* allocation of the benefit: see para **[9.21]** *et seq.*

[32] *Louth VEC v Martin* PTD 051 (13 January 2005).

[33] *Abbott Ireland Ltd v SIPTU* PTD 043 (28 January 2004).

Temporal considerations relevant to pleas of objective justification

[9.18] In the context of an employer attempting to advance an objective justification, it is important to stress that treatment which was objectively justifiable in the past may subsequently become unjustifiable, with the Labour Court having indicated that it will scrutinise justifications valid at one period of time to assess whether they remained valid at the time of the impugned treatment.[34]

Part-time workers and overtime

[9.19] A significant body of jurisprudence has now built up concerning the rights of part-time workers to payment for overtime and their position in this regard vis-à-vis their full-time comparators.

In *Stadt Lengerich v Angelika Helmig*[35] the ECJ decided that a provision (whether in a collective agreement or in terms and conditions of employment) whereby part-time workers do not receive overtime until they have completed the standard number of hours under which a comparable full-time worker would be entitled to claim overtime is not unfavourable treatment and is not discriminatory. Subsequent case law both in this jurisdiction and before the ECJ has, however, raised more difficult points for determination.

An example of these more difficult situations arose in an Irish context in the case of *Curry v Boxmore Plastics Ltd.*[36] In *Curry*, part-time workers who were contracted to work weekend shifts were on occasions requested to work during the normal Monday to Friday week. They claimed that they should be entitled to overtime payment for any hours worked outside their normal contract hours. The employer's response was that weekend workers were not entitled to receive any overtime payments until they had completed 40 hours in any one week. Significantly, the union representing the part-time employees claimed that although the standard working week for full-time production operatives was 40 hours per week, these full-time workers did not in fact have to complete 40 hours prior to receiving overtime payments. The union accordingly argued that weekend shift workers were treated in a less favourable manner by virtue of the fact that the company insisted that they must complete 40 hours' service before they could receive any overtime payments. It claimed that the company insisted that only the part-time workers had to work a minimum of 40 hours per week prior to receiving overtime.

An important factual feature of this case was the lack of any documentary evidence to support the union's claim that comparable full-time workers did not have to work the 40 hours before being eligible for overtime. Finding for the employer, the Labour Court held that a condition of employment whereby part-time employees do not receive overtime until they have completed the standard number of hours under which a comparable full-time employee would be entitled to claim overtime is not unfavourable treatment and is thus not discriminatory.

---

[34] *O'Leary v Cahill May Roberts* PTD 044 (4 May 2004).
[35] Case C-399/92 *Stadt Lengerich v Angelika Helmig* [1994] ECR I-5727.
[36] *Curry v Boxmore Plastics Ltd* PTD 035 (31 December 2003).

[9.20] The approach taken in *Curry* should now be viewed in the light of the more recent ruling of the ECJ concerning part-time workers and overtime in *Voß v Land Berlin*,[37] a ruling which again demonstrates the degree of overlap between the law relating to part-time workers and that concerning employment equality. The case concerned the remuneration of a part-time teacher who worked overtime, but whose total working hours were not sufficient to bring the hours worked to the level of a full-time civil servant. National legislation provided that remuneration for additional work which took place outside normal working hours was paid at the same rate with regard to full-time as well as part-time public servants, and that rate was lower than the *pro rata* remuneration allotted to full-time public servants as regards a period of equal length within normal working hours. The ECJ held that Art 141 EC was to be interpreted as precluding national legislation on the remuneration of civil servants which defines overtime, for both full and part-time civil servants, as hours worked over and above their normal working hours and which remunerates those additional hours at a rate lower than the hourly rate applied to their normal working hours. The result of such an arrangement, the Court held, was that part-time civil servants were less well paid than full-time civil servants in respect of hours worked over and above their normal working hours, but which amounted to fewer hours than the normal working hours of a full-time civil servant. The ECJ held that in the group subject to that legislation a considerably higher percentage of women was affected than men and the difference in treatment was not justified by objective factors wholly unrelated to gender.

THE *PRO RATA* PRINCIPLE UNDER THE 2001 ACT

[9.21] In securing the provision of equal treatment in conditions of employment for part-time workers, the 2001 Act operates on the principle of proportionate provision or *pro rata temporis*. This is explained in s 10 of the Act which provides:

> (1) The extent to which any condition of employment... is provided to a part-time employee for the purposes of complying with section 9(1) shall be related to the proportion which the normal hours of work of that employee bears to the normal hours of work of the comparable full-time employee concerned.

> (2) The condition of employment mentioned in subsection (1) is a condition of employment the amount of the benefit of which (in case the condition is of a monetary nature) or the scope of the benefit of which (in any other case) is dependent on the number of hours worked by the employee.

[9.22] To date, the jurisprudence in relation to proportionate provision has been characterised by a rigorous assessment of whether *pro rata* approaches are strictly necessary: if the benefits in question do not have a sufficiently strong connection with the actual number of hours worked by the employee, then the employer's *pro rata* approach may be impugned. Thus, in *Department of Education and Science v Gallagher*,[38] the Labour Court said that s 10(2) must be construed in harmony with clause 4(2) of the Framework Agreement which provides that the principle of non-

---

[37] Case C-300/06 6*Voß v Land Berlin* December 2007.

[38] *Department of Education and Science v Gallagher* PTD 047 (21 May 2004).

discrimination could be satisfied by applying conditions of employment *pro rata* where appropriate. This, the Court said, recognised that the *pro rata* principle was not of universal application. Accordingly, the Court felt that the type of benefits contemplated by s 10(2) were 'connected to those which by their nature are appropriately dependent on the number of hours worked by the employee'.

Evidence of this strict necessity approach is further in evidence in a number of later decisions of the Labour Court. A good example is the Court's decision in *Mullaney Brothers v Two Workers*,[39] a case discussed above involving the granting of a half-day's leave to full-time but not part-time workers for the purposes of Christmas shopping, where the Court held the scope of the benefit at issue was not dependent on the hours worked by employees to whom it applied since it applied equally to full-time staff who worked a five-day week or a six-day week. Consequently, it would be inappropriate that the benefit be pro rated having regard to the provision of s 10(2) of the Act.

[9.23] Another instructive authority in this context is the Labour Court's decision in *Department of Justice, Equality and Law Reform v Ennis*.[40] There, the claimant was employed as a part-time traffic warden. In 2002 the claimant was redeployed from Dublin City to Dun Laoghaire. She claimed that she and fourteen other part-time workers received a lower rate of travel allowance than full-time colleagues in contravention of the 2001 Act. The allowance was not contingent on the number of hours worked but was dependent on the distance travelled to work. She claimed that her treatment was based on her part-time status and that there was no objective ground for less favourable treatment. The employer claimed that the travel allowance was an intrinsic part of the basic pay of the complainant and it was therefore consistent with the provisions of the Act to pay the allowance on a *pro rata* basis. The Rights Commissioner found that the travel allowance was not dependent on the number of hours worked but on the distance to the employee's place of work. The Commissioner found that the claim was well founded and ordered the respondent to treat the claimant no less favourably than a full-time warden. This finding was upheld by the Labour Court. The Court found that the allowance could not be regarded as part of the claimant's pay, but was compensation for the time and expense involved in travelling to work. It held that no objective grounds were put forward to justify paying the claimant on a *pro rata* basis.

[9.24] So too did an employer's attempt at making *pro rata* payments attract the criticism of the Labour Court in *Department of Education and Science v Gallagher*,[41] an important authority demonstrating that an employer's *bona fide* view that the part-time employee was fairly entitled to a *pro rata* payment is irrelevant for the purposes of determining whether the payment meets the strict necessity test being applied to s 10 of the 2001 Act. In that case the employee worked as a home economics teacher in a secondary school under a job-sharing contract, working half of the class contact hours done by her full time counterparts. In April 2003 the Department of Education

---

[39] *Mullaney Brothers v Two Workers* PTD 066 (22 September 2006).
[40] *Department of Justice, Equality and Law Reform v Ennis* PTD 041 (14 January 2004).
[41] *Department of Education and Science v Gallagher* PTD 047 (21 May 2004).

authorised a retrospective payment of €1,000 for supervision and substitution duties between September 2001 and March 2002. The claimant received €499 although she had done the same amount of supervision and substitution as her full-time colleagues. She claimed that the only reason she was paid half the amount paid to her comparator was her status as a part-time teacher. The Department claimed that because the level of substitution and supervision undertaken by teachers differed in individual schools and between schools, it had decided that the only practical way of rewarding teachers for having undertaken these duties was by way of an *ex gratia* payment. It was not intended to reflect the quantum of hours worked by individual teachers. The payment was agreed with the teacher unions: the agreement was not designed to discriminate against part-time teachers and did not discriminate as the payment was not based on hours worked. The Labour Court, upholding the decision of the Rights Commissioner, found that while the payment was based on the *bona fide* understanding of the parties that teachers would have undertaken substitution and supervision duties in proportion to their contract hours, this did not happen in the instant case. The claimant was rostered for the same amount of duty as the comparator and in those circumstances the Court was satisfied that the claimant was treated less favourably because she was a part-time employee which could not constitute an objectively justifiable reason.

PART-TIME EMPLOYEES WORKING ON A CASUAL BASIS

[9.25] The 2001 Act also makes provision for part-time employees working on a casual basis. Section 11(2) provides that a part-time employee may, if such less favourable treatment can be justified on objective grounds, be treated, in respect of a particular condition of employment, in a less favourable manner than a comparable full-time employee. By virtue of s 12(2), however, what may not be considered as an objective ground in relation to a part-time employee may be considered an objective ground in relation to a casual part-time employee.

Who is a casual part-time employee?

[9.26] Who, then, is a casual part-time employee under the 2001 Act? Section 11(4) goes on to provide that a part-time employee shall, at a particular time, be regarded as working on a casual basis if:

(i)   at that time he or she has been in the continuous service of the employer for a period of less than 13 weeks, and that period of service and any previous period of service by him or her with the employer are not of such a nature as could reasonably be regarded as regular or seasonal employment;

or

(ii)   by virtue of his or her fulfilling, at that time, conditions specified in an approved collective agreement[42] that has effect in relation to him or her, he or she is regarded for the purposes of that agreement as working on such a basis.

---

[42]   That is, a collective agreement approved by the Labour Court under the Sch to the 2001 Act.

The Act states that the service of an employee in his or her employment shall be deemed to be continuous unless that service is terminated either by the dismissal of him or her by the employer, or by the employee voluntarily leaving his or her employment.

[9.27] Sections 11(7)–11(9) set out a framework for review whereby the Minister shall from time to time cause to be reviewed, in such manner as he/she determines, the operation of this section in relation to part-time employees. In determining the manner in which such a review shall be carried out, the Minister shall consult with such organisations representative of employers, such organisations representative of employees, and such other bodies as the Minister considers appropriate and, before making regulations under this section, the Minister shall consult with such organisations and bodies in relation to the terms of the proposed regulations. The Minister may, following such a review, prescribe a class or classes of such employee to be a class or classes of employee to whom this section shall not apply. This can only be done, however, where the Minister forms the opinion that there cannot, in ordinary circumstances, be objective grounds for treating the class or classes of employees to whom the regulations relate in a less favourable manner than a comparable full-time employee.

OBSTACLES TO THE PERFORMANCE OF PART-TIME WORK

[9.28] An important feature of the 2001 Act – inspired by the Framework Agreement – is the commitment it embodies to the need to keep performance of part-time work under review. In considering this commitment, it is helpful to focus on two distinct questions: first, what are examples of obstacles to part-time work; and, second, what steps have to date been taken in Ireland in relation to this commitment to monitor such potential obstacles?

Obstacles to part-time work

[9.29] An interesting example of an obstacle to part-time work contained in domestic law was the measure at issue in the preliminary reference recently before the ECJ in the joint cases *Michaeler and Subito GmbH*.[43] The relevant national legislation in Italy imposed an obligation on employers to send a copy of a part-time employment contract to the provincial office of the Labour and Social Security Inspectorate, within 30 days of signature of the part-time contract. Failure to comply with this obligation resulted in the imposition of administrative fines. The ECJ held that such a measure comprised an obstacle to the objective of promoting part-time work. The Court noted that there had been no indication given to it that a similar procedure was in place in relation to full-time employment contracts.[44] The Italian government contended that the obligation to give notice was justified 'by the need to combat undeclared work and to keep the authorities informed of employers' practices', a contention that the court rejected as being 'unconvincing'. This was on the basis of its inherently disproportionate reach: there were other less restrictive measures which would have enabled the Italian

---

[43] Cases C-55/07 and C-56/07 *Michaeler and Subito GmbH* (24 April 2008).

[44] Cases C-55/07 and C-56/07 (24 April 2008) at [24].

government to achieve its stated objectives of combating fraud and undeclared work. When looked at in its totality, both the administrative burden on employers and the potential threat of a fine combined to set up a system that the Court felt would discourage employers from making use of part-time work. The Court further noted[45] that, owing to the cost and the penalties, the obligation to notify the authorities of part-time contracts risked particularly affecting small and medium-sized undertakings which, because they would not have the same resources as larger undertakings, may 'consequently be inclined to avoid that form of organisation of work, namely part-time work, which it is the aim of Directive 97/81 to promote.'[46]

Analysis of LRC Code of Practice on Access to Part-Time Working

[9.30] As explained above, the 2001 Act enshrines a commitment to monitor obstacles to the performance of part-time work. To this end, s 13 provides a mechanism whereby the LRC may (and, at the request of the Minister, shall) study every industry and sector of employment for the purposes of identifying obstacles that may exist in that industry or sector to persons being able to perform part-time work and make recommendations as to how any such obstacles so identified could be eliminated. The section provides, *inter alia*, for the possibility of the LRC's preparing and publishing Codes of Practice with respect to the steps that could be taken by employers for the purposes of Clause 5.3 of the Framework Agreement. Acting under this section, the LRC has prepared a code of practice on access to part-time working which has been implemented by the Industrial Relations Act 1990 (Code of Practice on Access to Part- Time Working) (Declaration) Order 2006.[47] This Code of Practice will now be analysed.

[9.31] The stated objectives of the Code of Practice are:

(i) to encourage best practice and conformity with the provisions of both the Employment Equality Acts 1998–2004 and the 2001 Act;

(ii) to promote the development of policies and procedures to assist employers, employees and their representatives, as appropriate, to improve access to part-time work for those employees who wish to work on a part-time basis;

(iii) to promote discussion and encourage employers, employees and their representatives, as appropriate, to consider part-time work and to address any barriers that may exist;

(iv) to stimulate employers – where consistent with business requirements – to provide wider access to part-time work options;

(v) to provide a framework and practical guidance on procedures for accessing part-time work; and to inform those who are interested in part-time work.

---

[45] Cases C-55/07 and C-56/07 (24 April 2008) at [29].

[46] Cases C-55/07 and C-56/07 (24 April 2008) at [29]. A separate feature of the case of interest was the *Bilka* argument to the effect that because the majority of part-time workers are women, such an administrative rule constituted indirect discrimination. In light of its finding above, however, the Court did not consider it necessary to rule on this interpretation of the principle of equal treatment of men and women.

[47] SI 8/2006.

[9.32] While space does not permit a full rehearsal of the content of the Code,[48] it is arguably s 6 of the Code that sets out the most significant steps to be taken by employers in ensuring that employment practices give effect to the principle of promoting part-time work and guarding against the existence of obstacles to that work. Entitled 'Reviewing and Developing Company/Organisational Policies and Practices', the section can be summarised as setting out the following principles of best practice:

1. Requirement of general overview by employers

    Providing for access to part-time work should be considered in the context of developing company/organisational policies and practices to respond to modern work environments, including mechanisms to promote flexible work organisation, equal opportunity and work life balance.

2. Requirement of introduction of new policies/ review of existing policies

    As best practice it is recommended that companies/organisations introduce, in consultation with their employees and representatives, as appropriate, new policies or review existing policies to facilitate effective access to and performance of part-time work and specify how part-time working arrangements will operate in the company or organisation.

3. Requirement of assessing and/or expanding scope of part-time working opportunities

    In terms of assessing and/or expanding scope of part-time working opportunities, best practice recommends that employers should explore, in consultation with their employees and representatives, as appropriate, the possibility of introducing part-time work opportunities and/or maximise the range of posts as suitable for part-time working at all levels in the organisation, including skilled and managerial positions. A range of objective criteria should be developed to determine the suitability or otherwise of positions for part-time working. Barriers to the introduction of part-time work, at all levels in the organisation, should be identified and considered when an application for part-time work is made or when a vacancy arises. In this regard possible measures on how best to overcome such barriers should be considered.

4. Specific factors for employers to take into account in terms of removing obstacles to part-time work

    The Code specifically sets out factors to be taken into account by employers in assessing how obstacles to part-time work may be removed. These include posing the following questions:

    •   What demand is there, if any, for part-time working in the organisation?

    •   Where a demand is identified, can work be organised differently to facilitate part-time working?

    •   How does the organisation deal with/process a request for part-time working?

---

48   The text of which is available at www.lrc.ie. The Code is reproduced in Appendix D.

- What are the business implications of introducing or expanding part-time working, for example in terms of service delivery, covering absence, business continuity, administration and costs generally?
- Can part-time working – to a greater or limited extent – be accommodated having regard to both the business needs of the organisation and the needs of the employee(s)?
- Are there business benefits and opportunities to the organisation in widening access to part-time work?
- What posts – including managerial and skilled posts – are suitable (or unsuitable) for part-time working?
- Are there regulatory or licensing implications?
- Does an employee need to be present in a particular post during all hours of work and, if not, can
- the necessary work be done by a part-time worker?
- Implications of seniority/service as appropriate
- If a request from an employee to work part-time is refused what are the implications? For example would the employee leave and, if so, what are the recruitment and training implications/costs of a replacement?
- Are there issues around demotivation/poor morale in not providing part-time working opportunities?
- Are there opportunities in the organisation for existing part-time workers to move around the organisation in the interests of job/career development?
- Are there Employment Equality Act implications? An application for part-time working should be considered on non-discrimination grounds in accordance with the legislation. What do the policies of the organisation provide for in terms of promoting equal opportunities and work life balance?
- What will be the impact of part-time working, if any, on existing employees and their workloads?
- Are there increased time demands on management?

Outcome of employer's assessment

- The Code states that the outcome of any assessment of part-time working possibilities should indicate the following:
- The relevant factors to be taken into account in evaluating/determining part-time working options for the organisation;
- The actual potential for part-time working to contribute to the success of the organisation;
- The barriers, where they exist, and what reasonable steps may be necessary to overcome such barriers.

[9.33] The Code further advises that policies should, where possible, be adapted, stressing that a key element to be considered in introducing a successful part-time working policy (particularly in large organisations) is the necessity for the support and commitment of members of management at all levels of the organisation to such policies.

Status of the Code of Practice on Part-Time Work

[9.34] As to the status of Codes of Practice introduced pursuant to s 13 of the 2001 Act such as the 2006 LRC Code, s 42(4) of the Industrial Relations Act 1990 provides that such codes shall be admissible in evidence in any proceedings before a court, the Labour Court, the LRC, the Employment Apeals Tribunal (the EAT) or the Equality Tribunal and any provision of the Code which appears to the body concerned to be relevant to any question arising in the proceedings shall be taken into account in determining that question. The LRC Code of Practice was declared to be a code of practice for the purpose of the Industrial Relations Act 1990 by the Industrial Relations Act 1990 (Code of Practice on Access to Part-Time Working) (Declaration) Order 2006 (SI 8/2006). A failure on the part of any person to observe any provision of a code of practice does not of itself render him or her liable to any proceedings.

SETTLEMENT AGREEMENTS IN THE CONTEXT OF THE **2001** ACT

[9.35] Section 14 of the 2001 Act provides that, save as expressly provided otherwise in the Act, a provision in an agreement (whether a contract of employment or not and whether made before or after the commencement of the provision concerned of this Act) shall be void in so far as it purports to exclude or limit the application of, or is inconsistent with, any provision of the Act. The section thus ensures that a person cannot agree to waive or exclude the application of the 2001 Act.[49]

Test to be applied to voidance rule in 2001 Act

[9.36] The Labour Court has identified the test to be applied under s 14 of the 2001 as whether 'the factual result of a contractual term is to frustrate or defeat the achievement of the result envisaged by the Directive and the Act': if so, then the term shall be void.[50]

Settlement agreements in relation to claims under the 2001 Act

[9.37] In relation to employees entering settlement agreements in relation to their rights under the 2001 Act, the important 2007 High Court judgment in *Sunday Newspapers Ltd v Kinsella*[51] should be noted. Given that this case arose in the context of the fixed-term rather than the part-time work legislation, it is dealt with more fully in the fixed-term work chapter.[52] The case is, however, significant in the context of the other protective legislation including the 2001 Act. In *Kinsella*, starting from the proposition that an employee can lawfully enter into an agreement in relation to his or her statutory rights, Smyth J emphasised that the question of whether or not such rights have been compromised is a matter for the proper construction of the agreement itself. Informed

---

[49] The section is worded in terms similar to those of the Unfair Dismissals Act 1977, s 13 and the Payment of Wages Act 1991, s 11.

[50] *ESB v McDonnell* PTD 081 (6 March 2008).

[51] *Sunday Newspapers Ltd v Kinsella* [2008] ELR 53.

[52] See Ch 10, Fixed-Term Workers.

consent is crucial if the compromise is to be upheld, as the Circuit Court identified in *Hurley v Royal Yacht Club*.[53] Where an employee is being offered a severance package, he or she is entitled to be advised of his entitlements under the employment protection legislation and any agreement or compromise should list the various applicable statutes or at least make it clear that same had been taken into account by the employee. In the absence of such advice, a severance agreement waiving the statutory rights of the employee would be void. In the instant case, Smyth J held that, given that the employees received appropriate advice and the agreement they signed was expressly stated to be in full and final settlement of any claims or potential claims under several statutes and 'all or any employment legislation', their statutory rights had been compromised. Thus, it is possible under both the 2001 and the 2003 Acts for an employee to settle claims under the legislation provided there is informed consent.[54]

PROHIBITION ON PENALISATION OF PART-TIME WORKERS

[9.38] The 2001 Act contains a strong prohibition on penalisation of employees. The wording of the relevant section, s 15, is as follows:

(1) An employer shall not penalise an employee—

(a)   for invoking any right of the employee to be treated, in respect of the employee's conditions of employment…, or

(b)   for having in good faith opposed by lawful means an act which is unlawful under this Act, or

(c)   for refusing to accede to a request by the employer to transfer from performing—

   (i)   full-time work to performing part-time work, or

   (ii)   part-time work to performing full-time work,

   or

(d)   for giving evidence in any proceedings under this Act or giving notice of his or her intention to do so or to do any other thing referred to in paragraph (a), (b) or (c).

What amounts to penalisation under the 2001 Act

[9.39] Section 15(2) provides that an employee is penalised if he or she is dismissed,[55] suffers any unfavourable change in his or her conditions of employment or any unfair treatment (including selection for redundancy), or is the subject of any other action

---

[53] *Hurley v Royal Yacht Club* [1997] ELR 225.

[54] See further the determination of the Labour Court in *ESB v English* PTD 065 (28 August 2006), where the Court said that it could 'find no evidence that the complainant acted under a misapprehension' on the basis that the claimant 'was specifically aware of his rights… as a part time worker and acted upon that knowledge.' Accordingly the Court was satisfied that the claimant gave a free and informed consent to settle all and any claims which he may have had under the 2001 Act.

[55] Protection of Employees (Part-Time Work) Act 2001, s 15(3) specifically provides that if a penalisation of an employee constitutes a dismissal of the employee within the meaning of the Unfair Dismissals legislation, relief may not be granted to the employee in respect of that penalisation under both legislative schemes.

prejudicial to his or her employment. The penalisation prohibition in the 2001 Act contains an important exception: where the prejudicial action is in respect of an employee's refusal to transfer status (from part-time to full-time or vice versa), this shall not amount to penalisation as long as *both* of the following conditions are complied with:

(i) having regard to all the circumstances, there were substantial grounds both to justify the employer's making the request concerned and the employer's taking that action consequent on the employee's refusal: and

(ii) the taking of that action is in accordance with the employee's contract of employment and the provisions of the protective legislation generally.

[9.40] A part-time worker's claim for penalisation under s 15 was upheld in *Beacon Automotive v A Worker.*[56] The employer, having recently taken over the company in which the claimant worked, had asked her to work full time; when she had declined this offer, it had altered her work pattern to Monday to Friday. The Labour Court found as a fact that the employer had decided to dismiss the employee when she refused to switch from part-time to full-time work. Upon returning to work from a week's holiday, the employee found someone else in her place; she was allowed to remain at work all day without any explanation being offered; and was dismissed that evening. Unsurprisingly, the Labour Court identified all three occurrences as manifest breaches of s 15(2)(a) of the 2001 Act.

COMPLAINTS UNDER THE 2001 ACT: SOME KEY POINTS OF PRACTICE AND PROCEDURE[57]

[9.41] The 2001 Act provides that complaints under the Act may be referred in the first instance to a Rights Commissioner whose decision shall do one or more of the following: (i) declare that the complaint was or was not well founded; (ii) require the employer to comply with the relevant provision; (iii) require the employer to pay to the employee compensation of such amount (if any) as is just and equitable having regard to all the circumstances, but not exceeding two years' remuneration.[58] A significant point to note here is that, in awarding compensation, the Rights Commissioner (and the Labour Court on appeal[59]) must specify whether the award is or is not an award 'in respect of remuneration including arrears of remuneration', as the distinction has significant income tax implications.[60]

---

[56] *Beacon Automotive v A Worker* PTD 072 (17 July 2007).

[57] For an overview of practice and procedure, see Ch 22, Paractice and Procedure in Employment Law.

[58] Protection of Employees (Part-Time Work) Act 2001, s 16(2).

[59] See para **[9.43]**.

[60] The Taxes Consolidation Act 1997, s 192A (inserted by the Finance Act 2004, s 7). For general comment on this area see Farrelly, 'Taxation of Employment Awards: A Basic Understanding' (2006) 3(4) *IELJ* 113.

[9.42] Complaints must be made within six months of the date of contravention of the Act, although this period may be extended by a further 12 months if the failure to refer the case within six months was due to 'reasonable cause'.[61] This power to extend the time limit was considered by the Labour Court in *Cementation Skanska v Carroll*,[62] where the Court held that, in considering if 'reasonable cause' existed, it was for the claimant to establish that there were reasons which both explain the delay and afford an excuse for it. The Court continued:

> The explanation must be reasonable, that is to say it must make sense, be agreeable to reason and not be irrational or absurd. In the context in which the expression 'reasonable cause' appears in statute it suggests an objective standard but it must be applied to the facts and circumstances known to the claimant at the material time.

Related considerations in this context will include the length of the delay as well as possible prejudice to the opposing party.[63]

Appeals from and enforcement of decisions of Rights Commissioner

[9.43] Section 17 of the 2001 Act provides for an appeal mechanism to the Labour Court by either party. A notice of appeal must be furnished in writing to the Labour Court within six weeks of the date of the decision to which the appeal relates. A copy of this notice is then given by the Labour Court to the other party concerned 'as soon as may be after the receipt of the notice by the Labour Court'. A party to proceedings before the Labour Court under s 17 may appeal to the High Court from a determination of the Labour Court on a point of law and the determination of the High Court shall be final and conclusive.

[9.44] Where a decision of a Rights Commissioner in relation to a complaint under this Act has not been carried out by the employer concerned in accordance with its terms, the time for bringing an appeal against the decision has expired and no such appeal has been brought, the employee concerned may bring the complaint before the Labour Court and the Labour Court shall, without hearing the employer concerned or any evidence (other than in relation to the matters aforesaid) make a determination to the like effect as the decision.[64]

What constitutes a decision for the purposes of appeal?

[9.45] It was noted above that a decision of a Rights Commissioner may be appealed to the Labour Court within six weeks of the date of the decision. But what constitutes a decision for this purpose? In *Bus Éireann v SIPTU*,[65] the Labour Court held that the reference in that section to a decision of a Rights Commissioner could only be a reference to 'a complete or final decision which determines whether or not there has

---

[61] Protection of Employees (Part-Time Work) Act 2001, s 14(4).

[62] *Cementation Skanska v Carroll* DWT0338 (31 October 2003).

[63] See further the judgment of Laffoy J in *Minister for Finance v Civil and Public Service Union* [2007] ELR 36.

[64] Protection of Employees (Part-Time Work) Act 2001, s 17(8).

[65] *Bus Éireann v SIPTU* PTD 048 (13 October 2004).

been an infringement of the Act'. In that case, the Labour Court was satisfied that the decision which the company sought to appeal was merely a preliminary ruling on a single issue in the case and consequently did not have the character of a 'decision' under the section. Nevertheless, the Court did recognise that there would be 'limited circumstances in which a preliminary point should be determined separately from other issues arising in a case'. The Court indicated that this would only normally be permitted 'where it could lead to considerable savings in both time and expense' and where the point was 'a question of pure law where no evidence is needed and where no further information is required'.

Right of appeal to High Court on point of law

[9.46] Under the 2001 Act, it is possible to institute a further appeal on a point of law only to the High Court.[66] The rarity of the circumstances in which the High Court will overturn a decision of a specialist tribunal such as the Labour Court has been emphasised by the superior courts in many cases, of which the best-known example is *Henry Denny & Sons (Ireland) Ltd v Minister for Social Welfare*.[67] In that case Hamilton CJ warned that:

> [...] the courts should be slow to interfere with the decisions of expert administrative tribunals. Where conclusions are based upon an identifiable error of law or an unsustainable finding of fact by a tribunal such conclusions must be corrected. Otherwise it should be recognised that tribunals which have been given statutory tasks to perform and exercise their functions, as is now usually the case, with a high degree of expertise and provide coherent and balanced judgments on the evidence and arguments heard by them it should not be necessary for the courts to review their decisions by way of appeal or judicial review [...][68]

Mixed questions of fact and law

[9.47] This passage invites consideration of another fundamental question: when will a determination of the Labour Court properly be characterised as amounting to a matter of law, and when one of fact? On this point, it is instructive to have regard to the more recent Supreme Court decision in *National University of Ireland Cork v Ahern*[69] where the Court considered what was meant by a 'question of law' in the context of an appeal from the Labour Court (in that case, under s 8(3) of the Anti-Discrimination (Pay) Act 1974).

---

[66] As to the procedural requirements for this appeal, see r 2 of Order 84C, inserted by the Rules of the Superior Courts (Statutory Applications and Appeals) 2007 (SI 14/2007), and the commentary by Anthony Kerr in his annotation to the 2003 Act: Anthony Kerr, *Consolidated Irish Employment Legislation* (Thomson Round Hall, Release 19, April 2008), Division H. See also Ch 22, Practice and Procedure in Employment Law, at paras **[22.112]–[22.116]**.

[67] *Henry Denny & Sons (Ireland) Ltd v Minister for Social Welfare* [1998] 1 IR 34. More recently, see *Minister for Agriculture & Food v Barry & Ors* [2008] ELR 245.

[68] *Henry Denny & Sons (Ireland) Ltd v Minister for Social Welfare* [1998] 1 IR 34 at 37.

[69] *National University of Ireland Cork v Ahern* [2005] 2 IR 577.

McCracken J, with whom the other members of the Supreme Court agreed, stated:

> The respondents submit that the matters determined by the Labour Court were largely questions of fact and that matters of fact as found by the Labour Court must be accepted by the High Court in any appeal from its findings. As a statement of principle, this is certainly correct. However, this is not to say that the High Court or this court cannot examine the basis upon which the Labour Court found certain facts. The relevance, or indeed admissibility, of the matters relied on by the Labour Court in determining the facts is a question of law. In particular, the question of whether certain matters ought or ought not to have been considered by the Labour Court and ought or ought not to have been taken into account by it in determining the facts, is clearly a question of law, and can be considered on an appeal....[70]

In considering whether to allow an appeal against a decision of the Labour Court, the High Court must consider whether that court based its decision on an identifiable error of law or on a finding of fact that is not sustainable.

Whether arguments not pursued below can be advanced on High Court Appeal

[9.48] An important point for consideration concerning High Court appeals on points of law under the 2001 Act is whether legal arguments not pursued in the Labour Court can be advanced on appeal to the High Court. In the recent High Court case of *Minister for Finance v McArdle*,[71] which concerned the Protection of Employees (Fixed-Term Work) Act 2003, this issue arose in circumstances where the employer sought to advance legal arguments as to the jurisdiction of the fora below. Laffoy J described as 'correct in point of principle' the proposition that such legal arguments not presented before the Labour Court could not properly be canvassed on appeal to the High Court. She further emphasised the necessity for 'precision as to the points of law for determination by this Court ... and the grounds on which it [is] asserted the Labour Court erred' in the special summons.

Enforcement of determinations of Rights Commissioner

[9.49] Where a decision of a Rights Commissioner has not been carried out by the employer, and an appeal has not been brought, the employee may refer the complaint to the Labour Court and the Court, without hearing any evidence, shall make a determination to the like effect as the decision of the Rights Commissioner.

Enforcement of determinations of Labour Court

[9.50] Section 18 of the 2001 Act provides that the Labour Court's determination can be enforced by the employee, the employee's trade union or the Minister in the Circuit Court without the employer or any evidence, other than in relation to non-implementation, being heard. The procedures governing applications for enforcement are set out in Order 57 Rule 7 of the Circuit Court Rules 2001 as inserted by SI 721/2004.

---

[70] *National University of Ireland Cork v Ahern* [2005] 2 IR 577 at 580.

[71] *Minister for Finance v McArdle* [2007] 2 ILRM 438.

Interaction between 2001 Act and Employment Equality Legislation

[9.51] Section 101 of the Employment Equality Act 1998 provides that, where an employer's conduct constitutes both a contravention of Part III or IV of that Act and a contravention of the 2001 Act, relief may not be granted to the employee in respect of the conduct under both Acts. As discussed in a separate chapter in the context of fixed-term workers, however, this does not prevent the *processing* of separate claims, but merely double recovery in those claims.[72]

---

[72] See the similar discussion in the relevant section of Ch 10, Fixed-Term Workers.

Chapter 10

Fixed-Term Workers

Des Ryan

INTRODUCTION

[10.01] The adoption of the Protection of Employees (Fixed-Term Work) Act 2003[1] (the 2003 Act) in order to implement Directive 99/70/EC has introduced an entirely new legal regime in Ireland in relation to fixed-term workers.[2] Although relatively recently introduced, the 2003 Act has provoked a considerable amount of litigation both before the Rights Commissioner and Labour Court, and there is indeed by now significant case law from the High Court concerning the interpretation of the 2003 Act. Moreover, owing to the failure of the Irish government to implement Directive 99/70/EC by 10 July 2001 as required,[3] complex questions of the direct effect of Community law in light of a State failure to transpose timeously the Directive have arisen. Most recently, the consequences of this failure have been illustrated by the preliminary ruling from the European Court of Justice (ECJ) in April 2008 in *Impact v Minister for Agriculture and Food & Others*.[4] There is thus much legal complexity to be grappled with in attempting to analyse the current state of employment law concerning fixed-term workers. As one commentator has recently observed, '[t]he huge changes in the law, the ambiguity of certain aspects of the legislation pertaining to fixed-term workers, as well as the uncertainty surrounding the issue of direct effects of the Directive, has made the treatment of fixed-term workers by employers a complex one, both for employers and their legal advisers'.[5] In this chapter, a comprehensive analysis is conducted both of the key legislative provisions introduced by the 2003 Act and of the now considerable body of case law of both the ECJ and the Irish courts and tribunals concerning fixed-term workers.

Background to the 2003 Act

[10.02] The background to Council Directive 1999/70 of June 28 1999 is the Framework Agreement on fixed-term work concluded by ETUC, UNICE and CEEP.[6] At the outset,

---

[1] For detailed annotated commentary on the provisions of the 2003 Act, see Kerr, *Consolidated Irish Employment Legislation* (Thomson Round Hall, Release 19, April 2008), Division H.

[2] Prior to the introduction of the 2003 Act, there existed some minimal, piecemeal protection for fixed-term workers via the avenues of both gender equality and unfair dismissal legislation. For discussion see Imelda Higgins, 'Protection of Fixed-Term Workers' (2004) 1 *IELJ* 12.

[3] The 2003 Act came into force on 14 July 2003.

[4] Case C-268/06 *Impact v Minister for Agriculture and Food & Others* [2008] ELR 181, Grand Chamber, 15 April 2008.

[5] Kimber, 'Fixed-term workers – Where are we now?' (2007) 4 *IELJ* 103.

[6] [1999] OJ L175/43.

it is critical to gain an understanding of the Framework Agreement in relation to fixed-term workers, given the requirement that transposing legislation must be interpreted and applied in light of the purpose and wording of the directive so as to achieve the objectives pursued by the directive.[7]

[10.03] An important initial point to make about the Framework Agreement is that it proceeds on the premise[8] that employment contracts of indefinite duration are the general form of employment relationship, while recognising that fixed-term employment contracts are a feature of employment in certain sectors or in respect of certain occupations and activities. In essence, the Framework Agreement and the Directive (and consequently the transposing Irish legislation) embody two specific purposes, set out in clause 1 of the Framework Agreement. These are:

(i) to improve the quality of fixed-term work by ensuring the application of the principle of non-discrimination;

(ii) to establish a framework to prevent abuse arising from the use of successive fixed-term employment contracts or relationships.

[10.04] Clause 4 of the Framework Agreement, which is entitled 'Principle of non-discrimination', attempts to flesh out the first aim of non-discrimination. It provides:

(i) in respect of employment conditions, fixed-term workers shall not be treated in a less favourable manner than comparable permanent workers solely because they have a fixed-term contract or relation unless different treatment is justified on objective grounds;

(ii) where appropriate, the principle of *pro rata temporis* shall apply;

(iii) the arrangements for the application of this clause shall be defined by the Member States after consultation with the social partners and/or the social partners, having regard to Community law and national law, collective agreements and practice;

(iv) period-of-service qualifications relating to particular conditions of employment shall be the same for fixed-term workers as for permanent workers except where different length-of-service qualifications are justified on objective grounds.

[10.05] The second of the twin aims – that of the prevention of abuse – is dealt with in clause 5(1) of the Framework Agreement, which obliges Member States to introduce (in a manner which takes account of the needs of specific sectors and/or categories of workers) one or more of the following measures:

(i) a requirement of objective reasons justifying the renewal of such contracts or relationships;

---

[7] Case C-4/83 *Von Colson and Kamann v Land Nordrhein-Westfalen* [1984] ECR 1891, recently referred to by the Labour Court in the context of the 2003 Act in *Our Lady's Children Hospital Crumlin v Khan* FTD 0813 (28 July 2008).

[8] Framework Agreement, 'General Considerations', paras 6 and 8.

(ii) a specification of the maximum total duration of successive fixed-term employment contracts or relationships;

(iii) a limit on the number of renewals of such contracts or relationships.

Although more will be said in the context of clause 5 presently,[9] suffice it to note that the language here is conditional and open-ended. The clause requires Member States to introduce measures to guard against the abuse of fixed-term contracts, but leaves open to Member States a number of options as to how that objective is to be achieved, which include defining those circumstances regarded as constituting abuse. Ireland has chosen to implement clause 5 by prohibiting the placing of employees on fixed-term contracts for more than four years, unless the use of such a contract is capable of being objectively justified. If an employee's contract exceeds the four year threshold, and there is no objective justification for this, the 2003 Act deems the employee to have what is termed a 'contract of indefinite duration'. Analysis now turns to the 2003 Act and to a consideration of how the Framework Objective is reflected in that Act.

Twin objectives of the 2003 Act

[10.06] The twin objectives of the Framework Agreement find direct expression in the 2003 Act. Thus, s 6 of the 2003 Act confers an entitlement on a fixed-term employee not, in respect of his or her conditions of employment, to be treated in a less favourable manner than a comparable permanent employee, unless the less favourable treatment can be justified on objective grounds.

[10.07] Secondly, the prevention of the abuse of successive fixed-term contracts is provided for in s 9 of the 2003 Act which states that an employer may not renew a fixed-term contract so as to bring the aggregate period for such a contract to more than four years, except where there are objective grounds justifying such renewal. Section 9(3) of the 2003 Act provides that, where a provision in a fixed-term contract purports to contravene the prohibition on renewing the contract over the four year limit, that provision 'shall have no effect and the contract concerned shall be deemed to be a contract of indefinite duration' unless there is an objective ground justifying such renewal.

[10.08] It can therefore be seen that this twin approach of the 2003 Act confers two separate and distinct entitlements upon fixed-term workers: the entitlement to equal treatment vis-à-vis permanent workers and an entitlement to the recognition of a change in status for fixed-term workers once the fixed-term worker can satisfy certain conditions. Each of these separate and distinct conditions will be analysed later in this chapter.[10]

---

9   See below, in particular discussion of the 2008 ECJ preliminary ruling in Case C-268/06 *Impact v Minister for Agriculture and Food & Others* [2008] ELR 181, Grand Chamber, 15 April 2008.

10   See below, sections entitled 'Fixed-Term Work and the Rights of Fixed-Term Workers' and 'Successive Fixed-Term Contracts'.

Who is a fixed-term employee?

[10.09] Pursuant to s 2 of the 2003 Act, a fixed-term employee is defined as a person having a contract of employment entered into directly with an employer where the end of that contract is determined by an objective condition, such as arrival at a specific date, completion of a specific task or the occurrence of a specific event.

[10.10] A number of employees are specifically excluded from the scope of the Act. Thus, s 2 of the 2003 Act provides that it does not apply to agency workers placed by a temporary work agency at the disposition of a user enterprise. Section 2 also excludes from the definition of fixed-term employees, employees in initial vocational training relationships or apprenticeship schemes or employees with a contract of employment which has been concluded within the framework of a specific public or publicly-supported training, integration or vocational retraining programme. Other employees excluded from the scope of the Act are set out in s 17. Pursuant to s 17, the Act does not apply to a contract where the employee is: (a) a member of the Defence Forces; (b) a trainee garda; or (c) a trainee nurse.

[10.11] Notwithstanding the relative clarity of these exclusions, litigation under the 2003 Act has sought to test their parameters. Thus, in the context of apprenticeships, the decision of the Labour Court in *ESB Networks v Kingham*[11] reversed a decision of the Rights Commissioner that an apprenticeship scheme could come within the scope of protection of the 2003 Act. An interesting example of a case in which an employee's status as a fixed-term worker was in dispute is the Labour Court determination in *Irish Prison Service v Donal Morris*.[12] There the complainant, a Catholic priest, was appointed prison chaplain in Castlerea prison. At the time of his appointment in September 1998 there were no agreed terms or conditions of appointment. Agreement was reached on this matter in 2004 and the claimant signed a contract in June 2005, the terms of which were retrospective to July 2002. This contract provided for the termination of his employment by the Minister upon revocation of his nomination by the bishop. In August 2005, the bishop informed the Minister that he was revoking the claimant's nomination. His employment as chaplain ended the following month. The claimant claimed that he was a fixed-term worker for the purposes of the 2003 Act and that his employment had terminated as a result of the occurrence of a specific event, as provided for in the Act. He submitted that he was employed continuously for seven years and for the last four years and nine months on a temporary contract. He thus claimed that he was entitled to a contract of indefinite duration. Rejecting the claimant's argument, both the Rights Commissioner and the Labour Court held that the procedure to terminate the employment relationship and the potential to utilise this procedure, did not constitute a 'specific event' determining the contract for the purpose of the Act and therefore the claimant was not a fixed-term worker within the meaning of the Act. The rationale for this approach was that if the revocation of the bishop's nomination and the claimant's recall by the bishop and his consequent reassignment were to be taken as 'the

---

[11] *ESB Networks v Kingham* [2006] ELR 181. See also the determination of the Labour Court in *ESB Networks v Group of Workers* FTD 074 (7 March 2007).

[12] *Irish Prison Service v Donal Morris* FTD 073 (7 March 2007).

occurrence of a specific event' within the meaning of the Act, then so could the occurrence, for example, of a redundancy situation which is a normal occurrence within employment relationships. Accordingly the Labour Court found that the claimant was not a fixed-term worker within the meaning of the Act and the Court had no jurisdiction to hear the matter.

[10.12] A more recent determination of the Labour Court has focused attention on the question of whether the 2003 Act definition of 'fixed-term' worker will apply in the relatively unusual situation of workers being engaged on a month-to-month basis.[13] Here, the Labour Court answered this question in the affirmative, giving its reason for so doing in the following passage:

> If it were to be held that the protection of the Act does not extend to the use of contractual arrangements under which the continuation of an employment relationship could be opened to reconsideration on a month-to month basis (as an alternative to providing a fixed termination date) the purpose of the Framework Agreement would be subverted and the attainment of its object would be seriously compromised.'[14]

[10.13] In *Doyle v National College of Ireland*,[15] the High Court confirmed that the ability of the parties to bring a fixed-term contract to an end at an earlier date by the giving of notice did not alter the status of that contract as a fixed-term contract.

DIRECT EFFECT: THE ECJ'S 2008 *RULING* IN IMPACT

[10.14] Ireland's delay in transposing the Directive resulted in many litigants claiming that the Directive gave rise to directly enforceable rights in the period between 10 July 2001 and 14 July 2003, relying on the EC law doctrine of direct effect.[16] As is well known, this doctrine enables litigants in domestic courts in the Member States to invoke a piece of European law directly, as long as the law meets certain conditions of precision and unconditionality. In the fixed-term work context, this question of direct effect has been particularly pressing given the frequency with which fixed-term contracts are utilised by large public sector employers. Owing to this frequency of use, a great number of state and public sector employers have sought to rely on the protection of the Directive in an attempt to realise the vindication of the rights contained in the Directive in the period between July 2001 to July 2003, before the 2003 Act was in force. This issue was recently the subject of a high-profile preliminary reference ruling by the ECJ in *Impact v Minister for Agriculture and Food & Others*.[17]

[10.15] The complainants in the Irish proceedings the subject of the preliminary reference were all unestablished civil servants working in various civil service

---

13 *Dublin Port Authority – Shannon Airport v Keehan and Flannery* [2008] ELR 281.

14 *Dublin Port Authority – Shannon Airport v Keehan and Flannery* [2008] ELR 281.

15 *Doyle v National College of Ireland* [2006] ELR 267.

16 For detailed treatment of this doctrine in the context of the 2003 Act see Kimber, 'Fixed-term workers – Where are we now?' (2007) 4 *IELJ* 103.

17 Case C-268/06 *Impact v Minister for Agriculture and Food & Others* [2008] ELR 181, Grand Chamber, 15 April 2008.

departments under fixed-term contracts which had commenced at various times prior to the date of Ireland's transposition of the Directive on 14 July, 2003. A number of complainants had more than three years' continuous service and were claiming, in addition to equality of employment conditions vis-à-vis permanent employees, contracts of indefinite duration. (Indeed, in the period immediately before the 2003 Act came into force, a certain number of the complainants had their contracts renewed for a fixed term of up to eight years.) Some of the complainants had less than three continuous years' service as fixed-term employees and those complainants were thus claiming employment conditions equal to those of comparable permanent employees.

[10.16] The complainants brought proceedings before the Rights Commissioner seeking redress for alleged abuse of fixed-term contracts by the government departments. Their complaints were based on clauses 4 and 5 of the Framework Agreement as regards the period between 10 July 2001, the deadline for transposing Directive 1999/70, and 14 July 2003, the date on which the provisions transposing the Directive into Irish law entered into force. As regards the period after 14 July 2003, the complaints were based on s 6 of the 2003 Act.

[10.17] The government departments challenged the jurisdiction of the Rights Commissioner to entertain the complaints to the extent that they were grounded on the Directive. They contended that the Rights Commissioner's jurisdiction was confined to adjudicating on complaints alleging a contravention of the relevant domestic law. Furthermore, the government departments contended that clauses 4 and 5 were neither unconditional nor sufficiently precise and thus could not be relied upon by individuals before their national court. The Rights Commissioner found that she did enjoy jurisdiction to entertain the totality of the complaints and that clause 4 was directly effective but that clause 5 was not. This was appealed to the Labour Court (with the Union also cross-appealing on the Rights Commissioner's determination in respect of clause 5); the Labour Court then referred five questions by way of the Art 234 of the EC Treaty preliminary reference procedure to the ECJ. For ease of analysis, it will be convenient to deal immediately below with each question followed by the Court of Justice's answer to that question, in turn.

[10.18] The first question referred to the Court of Justice in *Impact* was as follows:

1. Do the Rights Commissioner and Labour Court have jurisdiction to apply a directly effective provision of the Directive where they have not been given express jurisdiction to do so under domestic law and individuals can pursue alternate claims?

Answering this question in the affirmative, the Court of Justice held that Community law, and in particular the principle of effectiveness, requires that a specialised court which is called upon under the (albeit optional) jurisdiction conferred on it by the 2003 Act to hear and determine a claim based on an infringement of that legislation, must also have jurisdiction to hear and determine an applicant's claims arising directly from the Directive itself in respect of the period between the deadline for transposing the Directive and the date on which the transposing legislation entered into force if it is established that the obligation on that applicant to bring, at the same time, a separate claim based directly on the Directive before an ordinary court would involve procedural disadvantages liable to render excessively difficult the exercise of the rights conferred on him by Community law. The ECJ held that it was for the Labour Court to undertake the necessary checks in that regard.[18]

[10.19] The second question referred to the ECJ in *Impact* was as follows:

> 2. If the answer to question 1 is in the affirmative, are clauses 4 and 5 of the Framework Agreement unconditional and sufficiently precise to be relied upon by individuals before their national courts?

The Court of Justice, as had the Rights Commissioner, found that clause 4 was sufficiently unconditional and precise, but that clause 5 was not.

In relation to clause 4, the ECJ noted that the prohibition of discrimination was worded 'in a general manner and in unequivocal terms': its subject-matter was thus sufficiently precise to be relied upon by an individual and to be applied by the national court. Significantly, the ECJ rejected Ireland's submission that the fact that there was no definition of 'employment conditions' in clause 4 rendered that provision incapable of being applied by a national court to the facts of a dispute. In rejecting that argument, the ECJ invoked its previous case law to the effect that the provisions of a directive can be said to be sufficiently precise notwithstanding the absence of a Community definition of the social law terms included in those provisions[19]; that the fact that directives do not require the adoption of any further measure of the Community institutions militates in favour of a finding of direct effect[20]; and that the application of a qualification (here the objective grounds qualification to the prohibition on less favourable treatment) is subject to judicial control.[21] Taken together, these principles led the Court towards a finding of direct effect in relation to clause 4.

By contrast, clause 5 was again found not to enjoy direct effect, principally on the basis that it was not possible to determine sufficiently the minimum protection which should, on any view, be implemented pursuant to clause 5(1) of the Framework Agreement.

[10.20] The third question referred to the Court of Justice in *Impact* was as follows:

> 3. Does clause 5 prohibit an employer from renewing a fixed-term contract for up to eight years after the Directive came into force but before it was enacted in domestic law?

The ECJ answered this third question in the affirmative – a conclusion which may initially seem surprising in light of its finding concerning clause 5(1). When analysed closely, however, the Court's response here is readily understandable. Emphasising the second of the twin objectives of the Directive – the prevention of abuse of fixed term contracts – and drawing on both Art 10 of the EC Treaty, and the third paragraph of Art 249 of the EC Treaty, the ECJ held that Directive 1999/70 must be interpreted as

---

18 [2008] ELR 181 (Case C-268/06), Grand Chamber, 15 April 2008, [55].
19 Joined Cases C-6/90 and C-9/90 *Francovich v Italy* [1991] ECR I-5357.
20 Case C-41/74 *Van Duyn v Home Office* [1974] ECR 1337.
21 Case C-212/04 *Adeneler v Ellinikos Organismos Galaktos* [2006] ECR I-6057.

meaning that an authority of a Member State acting in its capacity as a public employer may not adopt measures contrary to the objective pursued by that Directive and the Framework Agreement as regards the prevention of the abusive use of fixed-term contracts. This was the case in *Impact* because of the renewal of the employees' contracts for an unusually long term in the period – as noted, eight years in some cases – between the deadline for transposing Directive 1999/70 and the date on which the transposing legislation entered into force.

[10.21] The fourth question referred to the Court of Justice in *Impact* was as follows:

> 4.   If the answer to question 1 or 2 is in the negative, are the Rights Commissioner and Labour Court required to interpret domestic law in accordance with the wording and purpose of a Directive and if so are they required to interpret the provisions of the 2003 Act as having retrospective effect to the date on which the Directive should have been transposed?

The Court replied that the answer to this question must be that, in so far as Irish law contains a rule that precludes the retrospective application of legislation unless there is a clear and unambiguous indication to the contrary, a national court hearing a claim based on an infringement of a provision of national legislation transposing Directive 1999/70 is required, under Community law, to give that provision retrospective effect to the date by which that directive should have been transposed only if that national legislation includes an indication of that nature capable of giving that provision retrospective effect. This, the ECJ held, was a matter for the Labour Court to determine.[22]

[10.22] The fifth and final question referred to the Court of Justice in *Impact* was as follows:

> 5.   If the answer to question 1 or 4 is in the affirmative, are remuneration and pensions included in the meaning of 'employment conditions' referred to in clause 4 of the framework agreement?'

The ECJ held that Clause 4 of the Framework Agreement must be interpreted as meaning that employment conditions within the meaning of that clause encompass conditions relating to pay and to pensions which depend on the employment relationship, excluding conditions relating to pensions arising under a statutory social-security scheme. Because the Framework Agreement was associated with the improvement of living and working conditions and the existence of proper social protection for fixed-term workers, in the light of those objectives, clause 4 of the Framework Agreement must be interpreted as articulating a principle of Community social law which cannot be interpreted restrictively. The Court held that to interpret clause 4 of the Framework Agreement as categorically excluding from the term 'employment conditions' for the purposes of that clause financial conditions such as those relating to remuneration and pensions, would be effectively to reduce — contrary to the very objective of that clause — the scope of the protection against discrimination

---

[22]   Case C-268/06 *Impact v Minister for Agriculture and Food & Others* [2008] ELR 181, Grand Chamber, 15 April 2008 at [104].

for the workers concerned by introducing a distinction based on the nature of the employment conditions, which the wording of that clause did not in any way suggest.

The Court placed further emphasis on the fact that, as the Advocate General had noted in her Opinion,[23] such an interpretation would render the reference in clause 4(2) of the Framework Agreement to the principle of *pro rata temporis* meaningless, that principle being intended by definition only to apply to divisible performance, such as that deriving from financial employment conditions linked, for example, to remuneration and pensions.

Broader implications of *Impact* ruling

[10.23] The ruling of the ECJ in *Impact* will clearly have significant implications for many other cases currently at various stages of progression in the domestic fora in Ireland. Perhaps the most-discussed example of another such case is that of *Scoil Íosagáin v Martin Henderson*.[24] The complainant was a teacher employed on a fixed-term contract between August 2002 and August 2003. In May 2003, the employer placed an advertisement in a national newspaper seeking applications for permanent teaching posts. The claimant was not informed of the vacancy and did not see the advertisement. He claimed that the failure of the employer to inform him of the vacancy contravened the 2003 Act when it came into force in July 2003 and/or in the alternative contravened clause 6.1 of the Directive. He argued that through the application of the doctrine of direct effect he was entitled to rely on the Directive in proceedings against the employer prior to the coming into force of the domestic legislation. Before the Rights Commissioner, the employer submitted that the Rights Commissioner had no jurisdiction to hear the complaint as the Act was not in force at the time of the alleged contravention. The employer further argued that the claimant could not rely on the doctrine of direct effect, as one of the conditions necessary before a provision of a directive can have direct effect is that the action must be taken against the state and that the claimant's contract was not with the state but with the board of management of the school in which he was employed. The Rights Commissioner declined jurisdiction to hear the complaint as the matters complained of occurred prior the enactment of the 2003 Act in July 2003. On appeal to the Labour Court, the Labour Court did not directly address the matter of the jurisdiction or direct effects. The Court determined that the provision of primary education was a public service performed under the control of the state, and that the employer was an emanation of the state. It concluded therefore that the Directive was directly effective in an action taken against the board of management, and that the school was in breach of the requirement of the Directive and of the 2003 Act. This decision had been under appeal to the High Court; it is of interest to note that this High Court appeal in *Henderson* was withdrawn following the *Impact* ruling.

---

[23] Opinion of Advocate General Kokott delivered on 9 January 2008, [161].
[24] *Scoil Íosagáin v Martin Henderson* [2005] ELR 211.

FIXED-TERM WORK AND THE RIGHTS OF FIXED-TERM WORKERS UNDER THE 2003 ACT

[10.24] The focus of this Chapter now moves from the question of the direct effect of the 2003 Act to a detailed consideration of the scope of the legislation and the considerable body of litigation that has resulted from it in the domestic context.[25] Part II of the 2003 Act sets out the rights of fixed-term workers. It is convenient to identify each of the rights owed to fixed-term workers under the 2003 Act at this point. The rights are:

   (i)   the right not to be treated, in respect of his or her conditions of employment, in a less favourable manner than a comparable permanent employee;

   (ii) the right to receive written statements at engagement and renewal;

   (iii) the right, in certain circumstances, to be deemed to be employed on a contract of indefinite duration;

   (iv) the right to be informed by the employer of vacancies which become available to ensure that the fixed-term employee shall have the same opportunity to secure a permanent position as other employees;

   (v)   the right to have the employer facilitate, as far as practicable, access by a fixed-term employee to appropriate training opportunities to enhance his or her skills, career development and occupational mobility;

   (vi) the right to be taken into account for the purposes of calculating the threshold above which employees' representative bodies may be constituted in an undertaking in accordance with s 4 of the Transnational Information and Consultation of Employees Act 1996;

   (vii) the right not to be penalised for, *inter alia*, invoking the protections of the 2003 Act.

Less favourable treatment regarding conditions of employment for fixed-term workers

[10.25] The term 'employment conditions' is defined in s 2 of the 2003 Act as including conditions in respect of remuneration, which in turn is defined as including pensions. However, in relation to pensions, s 6(5) provides that the requirement of equal treatment does not apply where the normal hours of work of the fixed-term employee constitute less than 20 per cent of the normal hours of work of a comparable permanent employee. Moreover, pursuant to ss 6(6) and 6(7) of the Act, the *pro rata* principle applies in relation to any benefit the amount or scope of which is dependent on the number of hours worked by the employee. Thus, the entitlement of the fixed-term employee to a given benefit is limited to the proportion of hours worked by that employee as compared to those worked by the comparable permanent employee. One of the most significant judicial authorities interpreting 'conditions of employment' in the context of the 2003 Act is the judgment of Laffoy J in *Minister for Finance v McArdle*,[26] to be analysed later

---

[25] For a detailed overview of earlier case law see Meenan, 'Protection of Employees (Fixed-Term Work) Act 2003' (2006) 3 *IELJ* 39; Kimber, 'Fixed-term workers – Where are we now?' (2007) 4 *IELJ* 103.

[26] *Minister for Finance v McArdle* [2007] 2 ILRM 438.

in this Chapter. There Laffoy J held that this term does not include conditions as to duration or tenure of employment.[27]

Meaning of 'comparable permanent employee'

[10.26] In order to establish the existence of a difference in treatment in the employment conditions applicable to fixed-term and permanent employees, it is necessary to identify a comparable permanent employee. Section 5 of the 2003 Act sets out three situations in which fixed-term and permanent employees can be considered comparable. First, where the permanent employee and the fixed-term employee are employed by the same employer or by an associated employer; secondly, where the first situation is not applicable, where the comparable permanent employee is specified in a collective agreement; thirdly, where neither of the above situations applies, where the comparable permanent employee is employed in the same industry or section of employment as the fixed-term employee. In relation to the first and third of these situations, one of the following conditions must be met under s 5(2) in order for the permanent employee to be a valid comparator:

(i) both of the employees concerned perform the same work under the same or similar conditions or each is inter-changeable with the other in relation to the work;

(ii) the work performed by one of the employees concerned is of the same or a similar nature to that performed by the other and any differences between the work performed or the conditions under which it is performed by each, either are of small importance in relation to the work as a whole or occur with such irregularity as not to be significant;

(iii) the work performed by the relevant fixed-term employee is equal or greater in value to the work performed by the other employee concerned, having regard to such matters as skill, physical or mental requirements, responsibility and working conditions.

CLAIMS OF LESS FAVOURABLE TREATMENT OF FIXED-TERM WORKERS AND THE CONCEPT OF OBJECTIVE JUSTIFICATION

Less favourable treatment not simply different treatment

[10.27] An important, if elementary, point to be noted here is that simply establishing a difference in treatment will not necessarily amount to establishing that that treatment is less favourable. That the need to show less favourable treatment may involve complex issues of proof is well illustrated in the Labour Court's determination in *Eircom v McDermott*,[28] where the Labour Court considered that it was not possible to determine whether a fixed-term worker's being afforded access to one type of pension scheme was less favourable than another.

---

[27] The case is discussed below in this chapter.
[28] *Eircom v McDermott* FTD 051 (16 February 2005).

Non-renewal of fixed term contract not in itself capable of amounting to less favourable treatment

[10.28] The Labour Court has held on a number of occasions that the non-renewal of a fixed-term contract is not in itself capable of constituting less favourable treatment for the purposes of this section. So, in *Prasad v Health Service Executive*,[29] the Court held that, except in the circumstances envisaged by s 9 of the 2003 Act, a fixed-term employee does not have an automatic right to have his or her fixed-term contract renewed on its expiry. In so deciding the Court adopted the reasoning of the English Court of Appeal in *Department for Work and Pensions v Webley*,[30] in particular the following passage in the judgment of Wall LJ:

> Once it is accepted, as it must be, that fixed-term contracts are not only lawful, but are recognised in the Preamble to Directive 99/70 as responding, 'in certain circumstances, to the needs of both employers and workers', it seems to me inexorably to follow that the termination of such a contract by the simple effluxion of time cannot, of itself, constitute less favourable treatment by comparison with a permanent employee. It is of the essence of a fixed-term contract that it comes to an end at the expiry of the fixed-term. Thus unless it can be said that entering into a fixed-term contract is *of itself* less favourable treatment, the expiry of a fixed-term contract resulting in the dismissal of the fixed-term employee cannot, in my judgment, be said to fall within regulation 3(1).[31]

[10.29] The Labour Court had taken a similar view in the earlier case of *Aer Lingus v A Group of Workers*.[32] More recently, in *Dublin Port Company v McKraith and Kieran*[33] the Labour Court held that as far as the 2003 Act was concerned, the employer 'would have been perfectly entitled' to terminate the employment of the claimants if they had not been appointed to permanent vacancies. The rationale for this approach by the Labour Court is explained by its statement in another determination that '[i]f the conclusion of a fixed-term contract was to be regarded as less favourable treatment within the meaning of clause 4 of the Directive and s 6 of the Act, all fixed-term contracts would be *prima facie* unlawful. This could not have been intended.'[34] The Court in *Prasad* concluded that neither the Directive nor the 2003 Act required 'that a fixed-term contract of employment must be renewed unless the employer can show that the requirement for the work being performed by the fixed-term employee [has] ceased'.

---

[29] *Prasad v Health Service Executive* FTD 062 (7 April 2006).
[30] *Department for Work and Pensions v Webley* [2005] ICR 577.
[31] [2005] ICR 577 at 585, *per* Wall LJ (with whom Jacob and Ward LJJ agreed) (emphasis in original). The reference to Reg 3(1) is to the Fixed-Term (Prevention of Less Favourable Treatment) Regulations 2002.
[32] *Aer Lingus v A Group of Workers* [2005] ELR 261.
[33] *Dublin Port Company v McKraith and Kieran* FTD 0814 (12 August 2008).
[34] *Our Lady's Children Hospital Crumlin v Khan* [2008] ELR 314.

Whether renewal of a fixed-term contract can amount to less favourable treatment?

[10.30] As analysed above, the position adopted by the courts in relation to non-renewal of a fixed-term contract is that same cannot in and of itself amount to less favourable treatment. But what of the corollary situation: can the *renewal* of a fixed-term contract amount to less favourable treatment within the meaning of that term in the 2003 Act? As a matter of statutory construction, the answer to this question appears plainly to be in the affirmative: s 7(1) of the 2003 Act states (albeit parenthetically) that less favourable treatment 'may include the renewal of a fixed-term employee's contract for a further fixed term'. It would appear to follow that the 2003 Act does envisage that the fact of renewal of a fixed-term contract can in and of itself amount to less favourable treatment. In the recent case of *Our Lady's Children Hospital Crumlin v Khan,*[35] however, the Labour Court has rejected this construction, preferring instead to explain the wording used in brackets in s 7 as relating to s 9(4) of the 2003 Act[36] rather than to s 6. Section 9(4) expressly requires objective justification for the renewal for a further fixed term of a contract which would otherwise become one of indefinite duration by operation of s 9(1) or s 9(2) of the Act. The Court observed:

> A reading of the Act as a whole suggests that the reference in s 7 … is intended to convey that the standard of objective justification required for the purpose of derogating from the requirements of s 9 are [*sic*] the same as those required to derogate from s 6. However, these words do not imply that a person who cannot avail of s 9 of the Act to obtain a contract of indefinite duration, because he or she does not meet the requirements of that section, could achieve the same result by relying upon s 6.

With respect, it is submitted that this interpretation places a somewhat strained construction on the clear wording of s 6, which appears plainly to countenance the further renewal of a fixed-term contact as being capable of comprising less favourable treatment.

The meaning of objective justification

[10.31] The issue of what constitutes objective justification of less favourable treatment is one which requires detailed analysis. Section 7(1) of the 2003 Act, which lays down the requirement of objective justification of less favourable treatment, provides as follows:

> A ground shall not be regarded as an objective ground for the purposes of any provision of this Part unless it is based on considerations other than the status of the employee concerned as a fixed-term employee and the less favourable treatment which it involves for that employee (which treatment may include the renewal of a fixed-term employee's contract for a further fixed term) is for the purpose of achieving a legitimate objective of the employer and such treatment is appropriate and necessary for that purpose.

---

[35] *Our Lady's Children Hospital Crumlin v Khan* [2008] ELR 314.
[36] See below in this chapter.

[10.32] In *Health Service Executive v Prasad*,[37] the Labour Court observed that the second limb of s 7(1) – that the grounds relied upon must be justified as being for the purpose of achieving a legitimate objective of the employer and that such treatment must be appropriate and necessary for that purpose – amounted to a restatement of the 'three tier test for objective justification in indirect discrimination cases' formulated by the ECJ in its celebrated ruling in *Bilka- Kaufhaus*.[38] As is well known, in that case the ECJ set out a three-stage test by which an indirectly discriminatory measure may be justified. The Court held that the measure must firstly meet a 'real need' of the employer; secondly, the measure must be 'appropriate' to meet the objective which it pursues; lastly, the measure must be 'necessary' in order to achieve that objective.

[10.33] Employment lawyers will be well aware that the *Bilka* test is effectively now set out in s 22(1)(a) of the Employment Equality Act 1998.[39] Although there is a difference in wording between s 7 of the 2003 Act and the *Bilka* formulation, the Labour Court recently confirmed that s 7 comprises 'essentially the same test' as that laid down in *Bilka*.[40] In reaching this conclusion, the Labour Court placed emphasis on the recent ruling of the Court of Justice in *Adeneler and Others v Ellinikos Organismos Galakto*.[41] In its ruling in *Adeneler* the ECJ referred to the need to show that the ground relied upon 'responds to a genuine need, is appropriate for achieving the objective pursued and is necessary for that purpose'.[42] The Court stressed that the concept of 'objective reasons' within the meaning of clause 5 of the Framework Agreement could only be understood as referring to 'precise and concrete circumstances characterising a given activity' which might result from the specific nature of the inherent characteristics of the tasks or from pursuit of a legitimate social policy objective of a Member State. This builds on previously well-established principles in relation to objective justification, which include that the employer bears the burden of proof of establishing the objective reasons and that monetary considerations cannot in and of themselves be sufficient to discharge that burden.

Examples of pleas of objective justification in defence of less favourable treatment which have been accepted as amounting to objective justification include public pay policies;[43] those in which the defence has been rejected have included arguments as to industrial relations issues,[44] and differences in collective bargaining processes.[45] It is important to emphasise, however, that the inquiry into the existence of objective

---

[37] *Health Service Executive v Prasad* FTD 062 (7 April 2006).

[38] Case C-170/84 *Bilka-Kaufhaus v Weber von Hartz* [1986] ECR 1607.

[39] For detailed analysis of the various elements of the test see the determination of the Labour Court in *Inoue v NBK Designs Ltd* [2003] ELR 98.

[40] *HSE v Ghulam* [2008] ELR 325.

[41] Case C-212/04 *Adeneler and Others v Ellinikos Organismos Galakto* [2006] ECR I-6057.

[42] Case C-212/04 *Adeneler and Others v Ellinikos Organismos Galakto* [2006] ECR I-6057 at [74].

[43] *28 Workers v Courts Service* [2007] ELR 212.

[44] *McGarr v Department of Finance* E 2003/036.

[45] Case C–127/92 *Enderby v Frenchay Health Authority* [1993] ECR I-5535.

justification is one that will be conducted against the backdrop of the full context of the working environment.[46]

[10.34] Section 7(2) of the 2003 Act provides that less favourable treatment may be justified if the terms of the fixed-term employee's contract of employment are, when considered in their totality, at least as favourable as the terms of the comparable permanent employee's contract of employment. This was well captured by Laffoy J in the course of her judgment in *Minister for Finance v McArdle*[47] when she observed of s 7(2) that:

> In essence, sub-s (2) provides that what would otherwise be a discriminatory contractual term shall be regarded as justified on objective grounds if the overall 'package' of terms of the fixed-term employee is at least as favourable as the overall 'package' of the comparable permanent employee.

[10.35] It is thus important to stress the distinction between this provision in the fixed-term workers legislative scheme and the position obtaining under the Employment Equality Acts 1998–2008, since under the latter regime this broad, totality approach is not permissible: there, each individual element of the contract of employment must be compared *vis à vis* the claimant and a comparator.

Requirement to consider alternative options less detrimental to employee

[10.36] In the context of the equivalent section in the Protection of Employees (Part-Time Work) Act 2001, the Labour Court in *Diageo Global Supply v Mary Rooney*[48] held that in order to satisfy the requirement of objective justification, an employer is obliged to give consideration to alternative options whose effects would be less serious for the employee affected. The Court explained:

> In the normal course, an employer would be expected to have considered alternative means of achieving the objective being pursued which might have a less detrimental effect on the part-time worker concerned. It is only if it can be demonstrated that there are no viable, less discriminatory means of achieving the objective being pursued can the defence of objective justification succeed.

Fixed-term workers' rights to receive written statements at recruitment and on renewal

[10.37] Section 8 of the 2003 Act confers an entitlement upon fixed-term employees to be informed in writing as soon as practicable by the employer of the objective condition determining the contract, whether that condition is the arrival at a specific date, completion of a specific task, or the occurrence of a specific event. Furthermore, s 8(2) provides that where an employer proposes to renew a fixed-term contract, the fixed-term employee shall be informed in writing by the employer of the objective grounds justifying the renewal of the fixed-term contract and the failure to offer a contract of indefinite duration, at the latest by the date of the renewal. The Labour Court has

---

[46] *28 Workers v Courts Service* [2007] 18 ELR 212.
[47] *Minister for Finance v McArdle* [2007] 2 ILRM 438.
[48] *Diageo Global Supply v Mary Rooney* [2004] ELR 133.

observed that the requirement to give the information in writing is imposed so as to avoid 'the type of uncertainty or misunderstanding that can occur with verbal communications'.[49]

[10.38] The written statements referred to in s 8 are expressly deemed to be admissible as evidence in any proceedings under the 2003 Act.[50] Very significantly, if either the Rights Commissioner or the Labour Court in such proceedings takes the view that an employer omitted to provide a written statement or has provided one that is evasive or equivocal, then the Rights Commissioner or the Labour Court may 'draw any inference he or she or it consider just and equitable in the circumstances.'[51] These provisions thus demonstrate that the requirements under s 8 are capable of being used so as to effect robust protection of fixed-term workers. Employers will make light of their statements obligations under s.8 at their peril. This conclusion is, indeed, supported by case law. Thus, the Labour Court has characterised s 8(2) as 'a mandatory provision admitting of no exceptions'.[52] As a result, a failure to provide the written notice before the renewal of the contract, even where this is due to inadvertence rather than wilful non-compliance, 'can neither be overlooked nor excused'.[53] Thus the employer's contention in *Clare County Council v Power*[54] that its breach of s 8 was 'a technical breach and was not motivated by any bad faith' did not avail the employer in that case.[55] More recently, the Labour Court has used more trenchant language still in relation to the s 8(4) obligation, stating that:

> There is no doubt that the failure to provide such a statement is a breach of the provisions of the Act. The failure to provide a written statement of these grounds is to be deplored and in normal circumstances would put the Respondent in a position of considerable difficulty.[56]

[10.39] In *Khan v HSE, North Eastern Area*[57] the Labour Court took the view that the requirement to provide a written statement of objective grounds is designed, in part, to ensure that a ground subsequently relied upon for renewing a fixed-term contract beyond the period normally permitted by s 9 is the real or operative reason justifying a derogation from the provisions of that section. The Labour Court went on to observe:

> Moreover, a purposive interpretation of section 9 indicates that a Respondent must establish that the reason relied upon as constituting objective grounds was the operative

---

49   *Management of North Dublin Muslim School v Naughton* FTD 0811 (21 May 2008).
50   Protection of Employees (Fixed-Term Work) Act 2003, s 8(3).
51   Protection of Employees (Fixed-Term Work) Act 2003, s 8(4). For an example of the Labour Court drawing such an inference see eg *Irish Rail v Stead* FTD 052 (1 March 2005).
52   *Galway City Council v Mackey* FTD 065 (23 June 2006).
53   A phrase that the Labour Court repeated in *HSE v Ghulam* FTD 089 (12 May 2008).
54   *Clare County Council v Power* FTD 0812 (4 June 2008).
55   Although it should be noted that the Labour Court did expressly find that the breach here was culpable. It is submitted that, however, that the emphasis placed upon this culpability was merely to illustrate the seriousness of the breach and its impact on the employee rather than to suggest that inadvertent breaches are to be regarded with leniency under the 2003 Act.
56   *HSE v Ghulam* [2008] ELR 325.
57   *Khan v HSE, North Eastern Area* [2006] ELR 313.

reason for the failure to offer a contract of indefinite duration at the time the fixed-term contract was renewed. This suggests that the Respondent must at least have considered offering the Claimant a contract of indefinite duration before renewing his or her fixed-term contract and decided against doing so for the reason relied upon.

Section 8(2) is also of considerable significance on this point. It seems to the Court that the purpose of Section 8 is not just to ensure that a fixed-term employee is informed of the reason why his or her contract is being renewed. On a reading of the Section as a whole it is clear that it is intended to ensure that the employer definitively commits itself, at the point at which the contract is being renewed, to the grounds upon which it will rely if subsequently pleading a defence under Section 9(4). Thus where an employer fails to provide a fixed-term employee with a statement in writing, in accordance with Section 8(2), it is apt to infer, in accordance with Section 8(4) of the Act, that the grounds subsequently relied upon were not the operative grounds for the impugned decision and it would be for the employer to prove the contrary.

[10.40] More recently, the Labour Court in *Clare County Council v Power*[58] helpfully provided a description of the type of conduct which will trigger censure under s 8:

The Court has taken the view that the Respondents decided to, as it were, leave the gate open. They could not make up their minds whether to employ the Complainant on a full time basis and decided to have the best of both worlds by renewing her contract for another year. This is exactly the type of conduct which this Act was enacted to prevent and, in the view of this Court, represents more than a technical breach of Section 8.

Information must be made available in writing 'as soon as practicable'

[10.41] Section 8(1) of the 2003 Act requires that an employer inform a fixed-term employee in writing 'as soon as practicable' of the objective condition determining the contract. The meaning of this phrase 'as soon as practicable' was recently considered by the Labour Court in *Board of Management of North Dublin Muslim School v Naughton*,[59] where the Court referred in detail to the decision of the Supreme Court in *McC and McD v Eastern Health Board*.[60] There the Supreme Court approved an earlier decision of Costello J (as he then was) on the meaning of the expression in *Hobbs v Hurley*.[61] In *McC and McD v Eastern Health Board* it was held that in construing the phrase, regard must be paid to the context in which the words were used and all the surrounding circumstances and, in particular, the nature and purpose of the statutory obligation on the respondent. It was held that the phrase was not synonymous with 'as soon as possible'. Relying on this authority, the Labour Court concluded as follows:

It seems to the Court that the nature of the obligation imposed by the Section is to inform a fixed-term employee of the duration of his or her employment or, where this is indeterminable, of the circumstances in which it will expire. At least one purpose of the obligation is to ensure that the fixed-term employee knows the duration the employment so as to be in a position to arrange his or her affairs accordingly. This suggests that the information should be given in close proximity to the commencement of the employment.

---

[58] *Clare County Council v Power* FTD 0812 (4 June 2008).
[59] *Board of Management of North Dublin Muslim School v Naughton* FTD 0811 (21 May 2008).
[60] *McC and McD v Eastern Health Board* [1997] 1 ILRM 349.
[61] *Hobbs v Hurley* (10 June 1980, unreported) HC.

The authorities also suggest that regard should also be had to any practical difficulties which might impede the [employer] in providing the information. Since the existence of any such difficulties are necessarily within the particular knowledge of the [employer] it is for it to explain any delay in providing the information.

SUCCESSIVE FIXED-TERM CONTRACTS

[10.42] As noted at the outset of this Chapter, in addition to ensuring equal treatment for fixed-term workers, the Framework Agreement and thus the 2003 Act also seek to guard against the potential abuse of successive fixed-term contracts. Section 9(1) provides that where a fixed-term employee completes or has completed his or her third year of continuous employment then his or her fixed-term contract may be renewed by that employer on only one occasion and any such renewal shall be for a fixed term of no longer than one year.[62] Section 9(2) provides that where a fixed-term employee is employed on two or more continuous fixed-term contracts and the date of the first such contract is subsequent to the date on which the 2003 Act was passed, the aggregate duration of such contracts shall not exceed four years.

Once again, this section comprises a vigorous pursuit of the aims of the Framework Agreement: here, to guard against the abusive deployment of successive fixed-term contracts by employers. The strength of the provision is seen in s 9(3), which provides that where any term of a fixed-term contract purports to contravene s 9(1) or s 9(2) that term shall have no effect and the contract concerned shall be deemed to be a contract of indefinite duration.

However, the strength of the section is perhaps diluted somewhat by the fact that the provisions of s 9(1) and 9(2) do not apply where there are objective grounds justifying the renewal.

The meaning of contract of indefinite duration

[10.43] A number of questions arise from the provisions in the 2003 Act concerned with avoiding contracts of indefinite duration. First, the term itself requires consideration. The term 'contract of indefinite duration' is not defined in the 2003 Act but it has been judicially defined outside the context of the 2003 Act as meaning no more than a contract terminable upon the giving of reasonable notice. The most prominent recent example of this judicial definition is the judgment of the Supreme Court in *Sheehy v Ryan*,[63] where the Supreme Court affirmed the approach taken by Carroll J to the effect that a 'contract of indefinite duration' was essentially a contract terminable upon the giving of reasonable notice.[64]

---

[62] It is thus important to note that a fixed-term employee could be employed on a number of successive contracts which cumulatively amount to less than four years and could thereby become entitled to a contract of indefinite duration, a point noted, with reference to Rights Commissioner authority, by Ennis and O'Sullivan, 'Fixed Term Workers, Contract Renewals and Less Favourable Treatment: Recent Developments' (2007) 6 *Emp Law Rev – Ireland* 2, p 9.

[63] *Sheehy v Ryan* [2008] IESC 14 (9 April 2008, unreported) SC.

[64] [2004] ELR 87.

From the standpoint of the 2003 legislation and the meaning to be accorded to the term 'contract of indefinite duration', a number of authorities now assist in understanding the term.

[10.44] In *Health Service Executive (North Eastern Area) v Khan*,[65] the Labour Court ruled that the contract of indefinite duration to which a fixed term employee might become entitled by operation of s 9(3) 'is identical in its terms, including any express or implied terms as to training and qualifications, as the fixed term contract from which it was derived'. The effect of s 9(3), then, is to transform a contract of definite duration into one of indefinite duration: no more and no less. This interpretation has recently been confirmed in the important recent case of *Minister for Finance v McArdle*,[66] where Laffoy J held that the Labour Court had erred in law in accepting that the employee's conditions as to duration or tenure of her employment must not be less favourable than that of her chosen comparator.[67] This judgment will now be analysed.

The High Court approach in *McArdle*

[10.45] The leading authority to date on the meaning of the term 'contract of indefinite duration' in the 2003 Act is the decision of the High Court in *Minister for Finance v McArdle*.[68] The kernel of the High Court ruling is perhaps best encapsulated in Laffoy J's observation in respect of s 9(3) that it 'only impacts on one aspect of a contract of employment when it comes into play: its duration'.[69]

The background to this case was that Ms McArdle commenced employment in the State Laboratory in her capacity as a laboratory technician in March 2000, on a fixed-term contract for one year. Her contract was renewed on an annual basis thereafter until 21 March, 2004. From that point onwards her contract was not managed appropriately, such that it was not until 31 May, 2005, that she was furnished with a renewed contract which purported to be in respect of the period from 22 March, 2004 until 21 March, 2005. The Minister for Finance accepted that the contract furnished did not comply with the 2003 Act and that as a result Ms McArdle became entitled to a contract of indefinite duration with effect from 22 March, 2004. However, the issue still to be decided was what precisely was meant by a 'contract of indefinite duration'.

[10.46] The Rights Commissioner defined the contract of indefinite duration as being one that should be 'no less favourable than an established civil servant', that is, that the claimant should enjoy the same tenure on the same basis and subject to the same procedure as an established civil servant. The Labour Court adopted the finding of the Rights Commissioner on this point; the employer appealed to the High Court.

[10.47] In the High Court, Laffoy J found that the Labour Court had erred in law in concluding that the defendant acquired security of tenure similar to the security of tenure enjoyed by the comparator, namely an established civil servant. Laffoy J found that the

---

[65] *Health Service Executive (North Eastern Area) v Khan* [2006] ELR 313.
[66] *Minister for Finance v McArdle* [2007] 2 ILRM 438.
[67] See also *HSE v Arefi* FTD 081 (21 February 2008).
[68] *Minister for Finance v McArdle* [2007] 18 ELR 165.
[69] *Per* Laffoy J in *Minister for Finance v McArdle* [2007] 2 ILRM 438 at 453.

effect of s 9(3) of the 2003 Act was that where an employee is given a renewed fixed-term contract in contravention of s 9(1) or (2), then s 9(3) operates to render void *ab initio* the term of the contract which purports to provide for its expiry by passing of time or the occurrence of event. Accordingly, by operation of law the offending term is severed from the contract, 'transmuting' its character from one of definite duration or fixed-term to one of indefinite duration. Crucially, the remaining terms of the contract are unaffected – including terms as to pensionability and termination. Laffoy J held that the terms and conditions of a contract of indefinite duration which comes into operation under s 9(3) must therefore be the same as those pertaining to the fixed-term contract from which it is derived in all respects other than its definite duration.

Objective justification for offering further fixed-term contracts or not offering a contract of indefinite duration

[10.48] As already noted, s 9(3) of the 2003 Act provides, in essence, that once the four year threshold has expired then the fixed-term contract is transmuted into a contract of indefinite duration by operation of law, unless there is objective justification for not altering the status of the contract in this way. Section 9 of the 2003 Act also prevents the renewal of a fixed-term contract such as to bring the aggregate period to more than four years, except where there are objective grounds for renewal. However, as with objective justification for less favourable treatment, there is no further detail in the legislation as to what amounts to an objective justification contravening the four year threshold in the 2003 Act. There now exists, however, a considerable body of case law providing guidance on the question of when successive contracts will be objectively justified. From this case law it is possible to indentify a number of key principles. First, significant restructuring that the employer is obliged to undertake for the purposes of economic viability will likely pass muster as an objective justification for repeated recourse to fixed-term contracts. This is well illustrated by the case of *Aer Lingus v Group of Workers,*[70] where the Labour Court found that there were objective grounds for the non-renewal by Aer Lingus of fixed-term contracts of employees. The complainants were cabin crew members whose contracts had expired and were renewed; nevertheless, the employer had advertised vacancies internally for temporary cabin crew positions. The complainants had only been employed on contracts of nine months' duration; candidates for the new temporary cabin crew positions were required to have at least twelve months' service with the employer. At the material time the company was undertaking a major re-organisation of its operation and an increasing number of staff posts were being made redundant.

[10.49] The claimants contended that the employer was in breach of the 2003 Act by not renewing the contracts when there was a continuing requirement for the work which they performed. They claimed that the existence of such work *required* that their contracts be renewed. Both the Rights Commissioner and the Labour Court rejected the claim, holding that there was no obligation on the company under the 2003 Act to renew a contract even where there was an ongoing requirement for work of that kind. They further accepted that the claimants were treated the same as permanent workers in that

---

[70]   *Aer Lingus v Group of Workers* [2005] ELR 261.

permanent workers were also subject to the 12 months' service requirement. In light of the fact that the airline was engaged in the process of seeking to redeploy long-serving staff in circumstances of redundancy and engaging in reorganisation, the Court concluded that the imposition of a service qualification was objectively justified.

[10.50] In *University College Hospital Galway v Awan*[71] the complainant was employed as a consultant anaesthetist between January 1999 and June 2004 on a succession of fixed-term contracts. He claimed that he became entitled to a contract of indefinite duration with effect from January 2004. He further complained that the employer failed to provide him with a written statement of the objective reasons relied upon in renewing his fixed-term contracts, and submitted that he was treated less favourably than a comparable permanent employee when the employer advertised the post which he held and required him to apply for that post in open competition. The claimant did not participate in the competition: he believed that he was already legally entitled to hold the post permanently.

The employer contended that the appointment of consultant doctors in the public health sector is governed by the Local Authority (Officers and Employees) Act 1926 and the Health Act 1970 and accordingly the Health Board was precluded from making appointments to permanent positions other than by way of public competition. It submitted that the constraints imposed under those Acts constituted objective reasons for the continued renewal of his employment for a fixed term. Strongly rejecting this argument, the Labour Court held that the post which the claimant held since 1999 on a succession of fixed-term contracts became one of indefinite duration by law on 1 January 2004. The Court held that national legislative measures could not be relied upon as objective reasons for derogating from the obligations imposed by the EU Directive on fixed-term work.

The meaning of 'continuous employment' in the context of successive fixed-term contracts

[10.51] A key issue in relation to fixed-term workers litigation is the question of how the courts are likely to characterise 'successive fixed-term contract'. In particular, what is the position when the fixed-term contracts have been renewed, but only following a break in service? What length of a break will destroy the element of continuity such that the contract will be deemed not to be successive? This question was considered in *Department of Foreign Affairs v Group of Workers*[72] where the claim was brought by a group of temporary clerical workers employment by the Department of Foreign Affairs on a number of fixed-term contracts between 2001 and 2006. The breaks between the various fixed-term contracts amounted to a number of weeks or months in each case. Their claim turned on the interpretation of 'continuous employment' within s 9 of the 2003 Act, for the employer argued that each employee's continuity of employment was broken by virtue of the expiry of each fixed-term contract. Thus, the employer argued,

---

[71] *University College Hospital Galway v Awan* [2008] ELR 64.
[72] *Department of Foreign Affairs v Group of Workers* [2007] ELR 332. See also *ESB v McDonnell* PTD 081 (6 March 2008).

none of the claimants had completed his or her third year of continuous employment, the condition required to open the door to the operation of s 9(1) of the 2003 Act.

[10.52] In a determination that marks a generous approach to the question of continuity of service from the perspective of employees, the Labour Court held that an employee is continuously employed for the purposes of the 2003 Act even where there are breaks of weeks or months between successive contracts and that such breaks are to be considered as periods of 'lay-off' provided that the employee has a reasonable belief that he or she will be re-employed and this does in fact occur. In considering whether there was a break in contracts and if so what break would lead litigants to fall outside s 9, the Labour Court noted that:

> ...there appears, at first sight, to be a conflict between s 9 of the Act and Clause 5 of the Framework Agreement. This arises from the fact that Clause 5 of the Framework Agreement applies to fixed-term contracts which are successive thus giving it a considerably wider scope than if its application was confined to employment relationships which were continuous. It seems to the Court that there is a significant qualitative difference between the concept of a continuous employment relationship and one which is successive. The former connotes an employment relationship without interruption whereas the latter indicates a series of relationships which follow each other but can be separated in time.

> It will be noted that clause 5.2(a) of the Framework Agreement permits Member States to define, *inter alia,* the conditions under which fixed-term contracts will be regarded as successive. This provision, however, could hardly authorise a Member States to define the concept of successive employment as meaning something which is qualitatively different and narrower in scope than that term would normally bear.

In so holding, the Labour Court placed heavy reliance on the determination of the ECJ, discussed above, in *Adeneler and Others v Ellinikos Organismos Galaktos,*[73] where the Court ruled that clause 5 of the Framework Agreement was to be interpreted as 'precluding a national rule under which only fixed term employment contracts that are not separated from one another by a period of time longer than 20 working days are to be regarded as "successive".'

[10.53] It is instructive to quote a passage from the judgment of the ECJ in *Adeneler* in its entirety:

> It is clear that a national provision under which only fixed-term contracts that are separated by a period of time shorter than or equal to 20 working days are regarded as successive must be considered to be such as to compromise the object, the aim and the practical effect of the Framework Agreement.

> As observed by the referring court and the Commission, and by the Advocate General in points 67 to 69 of her Opinion, so inflexible and restrictive a definition of when a number of subsequent employment contracts are successive would allow insecure employment of a worker for years since, in practice, the worker would as often as not have no choice but to accept breaks in the order of 20 working days in the course of a series of contracts with his employer.

---

[73] Case C-212/04 *Adeneler and Others v Ellinikos Organismos Galaktos* [2006] ECR I-6057.

Furthermore, a national rule of the type at issue in the main proceedings could well have the effect not only of in fact excluding a large number of fixed-term employment relationships from the benefit of the protection of workers sought by Directive 1999/70 and the Framework Agreement, largely negating the objective pursued by them, but also of permitting the misuse of such relationships by employers.[74]

[10.54] Having referred to the above passage in *Adeneler*, the Labour Court in *Department of Foreign Affairs* thus upheld the finding of the Rights Commissioner that the claimants were employed on continuous contracts for the purpose of s 9 of the 2003 Act. The decision thus constitutes the conferral of an extremely broad latitude to fixed-term employees seeking to characterise as continuous several contracts which may have been interspersed by not insubstantial break periods. Furthermore, it is important to note that the Labour Court rejected the employer's argument that 'seasonal' or 'fluctuating' need could be capable of constituting objective justification in the circumstances for the continued use of fixed-term contracts, thus once again illustrating how high the bar will be set in relation to employers' attempts at establishing objective justification. In the subsequent case of *Vassilikas*,[75] however, the ECJ held that Clause 5 of the Framework Agreement is to be interpreted as not precluding, as a general rule, a national provision according to which only fixed-term employment contracts or employment relationships that are separated by a period of time shorter than three months can be regarded as 'successive' for the purposes of that clause.

RIGHTS OF FIXED-TERM WORKERS TO INFORMATION ON EMPLOYMENT AND TRAINING OPPORTUNITIES

[10.55] Section 10 of the 2003 Act enshrines fixed-term employees' rights to information on employment and training opportunities. Section 10(1) obliges an employer to inform a fixed-term employee in relation to vacancies which become available, so as to ensure that the fixed-term employee has the same opportunity to secure a permanent position as other employees. This information may be provided by means of a general announcement at a suitable place in the undertaking or establishment.[76] The High Court has held that the section carries 'a concomitant obligation to allow the employees to apply for such vacancies'.[77] Section 10(3) states that an employer shall, as far as practicable, facilitate access by a fixed-term employee to appropriate training opportunities to enhance his or her skills, career development and occupational mobility.

[10.56] The scope of the employer's obligation to inform of vacancies was considered by the Labour Court in *Aer Lingus v IMPACT*.[78] There the Labour Court concluded that, while fixed-term employees had the right to receive information concerning vacancies

---

[74] Case C-212/04 *Adeneler and Others v Ellinikos Organismos Galaktos* [2006] ECR I-6057, [84]–[86].

[75] Case-364/07 *Vassilikas*.

[76] Protection of Employees (Fixed-Term Work) Act 2003, s 10(2).

[77] *Minister for Finance v McArdle* [2007] 2 ILRM 438 at 454.

[78] *Aer Lingus v IMPACT* [2005] ELR 261.

for which they were qualified to apply, this provision did not restrict the right of an employer to determine the content of those qualifications.

[10.57] The obligation imposed on employers by s 10 of the 2003 Act is to inform fixed-term employees of permanent vacancies so as to provide them with an opportunity to secure a permanent post. The nature of the obligation was considered by the Labour Court in *Henderson v Scoil Íosagáin*.[79] Here it was held that the mere placing of an advertisement in a newspaper was insufficient: the Court found that notification must be delivered to the fixed-term employee in person or a notice must be placed in a prominent position in the workplace.

[10.58] The Labour Court further considered this provision in *Board of Management of North Dublin Muslim School v Naughton*,[80] where a notice concerning vacancies for permanent posts which were to be filled in September was posted in the complainant teacher's school in July. This was during the school holidays when the claimant was not at work. It was conceded ('rightly', according to the Labour Court), on behalf of the employer that this could not have discharged the obligation under this section. In *Naughton*, however, there was evidence that the employer also instructed its solicitors to write to the claimant informing him of the vacancies and enclosing a copy of the advertisement which had been placed in the public press. The Labour Court stated that it was satisfied that 'in causing the notification to be sent to the Claimant by post the Respondent did all that it could to fulfil its obligation under the Section'.

[10.59] The High Court has held that subs (1) is not limited to vacancies for posts at the same level as a post occupied by a fixed-term employee: it also includes promotions.[81]

SETTLEMENT AGREEMENTS IN THE CONTEXT OF THE 2003 ACT

[10.60] Section 12 of the 2003 Act provides that:

> Save as expressly provided otherwise in this Act, a provision in an agreement (whether a contract of employment or not and whether made before or after the commencement of the provision concerned of this Act) shall be void in so far as it purports to exclude or limit the application of, or is inconsistent with, any provision of the Act.

A very significant recent High Court ruling concerning this section is that of Smyth J in *Sunday Newspapers Ltd v Kinsella*.[82] The High Court found that the Labour Court had erred in law in allowing the claimants to consider as void a severance agreement because they mistakenly believed that they had been advised that the severance agreements would not preclude them from bringing claims pursuant to the 2003 Act. More generally, the judgment of Smyth J helpfully lays out a number of key principles to be followed in the context of severance agreements purporting to compromise entitlements under the 2003 Act (and indeed protective legislation generally).

---

[79] *Henderson v Scoil Íosagáin* [2005] ELR 271.
[80] *Board of Management of North Dublin Muslim School v Naughton* FTD 0811 (21 May 2008).
[81] *Minister for Finance v McArdle* [2007] 2 ILRM 438.
[82] *Board of Management of North Dublin Muslim School v Naughton* [2008] ELR 53.

[10.61] The respondents (the employees) were employed by the appellant (the employer) on fixed-term contracts. They were offered severance packages by the employer, based on the earnings they would have received up to the expiration of their contracts in less than a year. Permanent employees were offered a minimum of one year's salary. A clause in the general conditions of the severance packages provided that no employee was entitled to be paid more than 'the normal expected gross amount that otherwise may have been earned to age 65'.

[10.62] Following some discussion and negotiation and appropriate professional advice, the employees signed a severance agreement which was stated to be 'in full and final settlement of any and all outstanding entitlements whether statutory or otherwise'. The agreement also further stated that it was 'based on any/all claims in relation to [the employees'] employment with [the employer], stated or as yet un-stated, being fully resolved (including, but not limited to all claims under … the Protection of Employment Acts … and all or any employment legislation)'. The employees brought complaints under the 2003 Act to a Rights Commissioner, claiming, *inter alia*, that the waiver of their rights under the Act was void. The Rights Commissioner found against the employees on the basis that they had voluntarily, and with the benefit of the representation of their union, accepted a severance package and signed a waiver that confirmed their acceptance of the terms in full and final settlement.

[10.63] The employees had then successfully appealed to the Labour Court. The Labour Court found, *inter alia*, that the employees believed, as a result of advice they had received, that they could not contract out of their rights and that any document which they signed would not prevent them from pursuing a claim under the 2003 Act. The employer successfully appealed to the High Court. Smyth J in allowing the appeal clarified a number of key principles which should be followed in all severance agreement situations, not only in the context of the fixed term workers legislation but in the context of all protective legislation. Starting from the proposition that an employee can lawfully enter into an agreement in relation to his or her statutory rights, Smyth J emphasised that the question of whether or not such rights have been compromised is a matter for the proper construction of the agreement itself. Informed consent is crucial if the compromise is to be upheld, as the Circuit Court identified in *Hurley v Royal Yacht Club*.[83] Where an employee is being offered a severance package, he or she is entitled to be advised of his entitlements under the employment protection legislation and any agreement or compromise should list the various applicable statutes or at least make it clear that same had been taken into account by the employee. In the absence of such advice, a severance agreement waiving the statutory rights of the employee would be void. In the instant case, Smyth J held that, given that the employees received appropriate advice and the agreement they signed was expressly stated to be in full and final settlement of any claims or potential claims under several statutes and 'all or any employment legislation', their statutory rights had been compromised: s 12 of the 2003 Act is thus no exception to the principle that a properly-informed employee can compromise protective legislation entitlements in this manner.

---

[83] *Hurley v Royal Yacht Club* [1997] ELR 225.

PROHIBITION ON PENALISATION OF FIXED-TERM WORKERS

[10.64] Just as the Protection of Employees (Part-Time Work) Act 2001 contains a strong prohibition on penalisation of employees,[84] so to does the 2003 Act prohibit the penalisation of fixed-term employees by their employer. The wording of the relevant section, s 13, is as follows:

(1) An employer shall not penalise an employee—

(a)   for invoking any right of the employee to be treated, in respect of the employee's conditions of employment, in the manner provided for by this Part,

(b)   for having in good faith opposed by lawful means an act which is unlawful under this Act,

(c)   for giving evidence in any proceeding under this Act or for giving notice of his or her intention to do so or to do any other thing referred to in paragraph (a) or (b), or

(d)   by dismissing the employee from his or her employment if the dismissal is wholly or partly for or connected with the purpose of the avoidance of a fixed-term contract being deemed to be a contract of indefinite duration under section 9(3).

(2) For the purposes of this section, an employee is penalised if he or she—

(a)   is dismissed or suffers any unfavourable change in his or her conditions of employment or any unfair treatment (including selection for redundancy), or

(b)   is the subject of any other action prejudicial to his or her employment.

[10.65] In *Clare County Council v Power*[85] the Labour Court held that there were 'compelling reasons' for construing section 13(1)(d) as applicable to both the non-renewal of fixed-term contracts as well as dismissals at common law. The Court took the view that where a decision is made not to renew a fixed term contract when no objective grounds for its extension have been given, this falls 'squarely within the ambit of cases which might be heard under Section 13(1)(d).' In so holding, the Court was fortified by the judgment of the ECJ in *Adeneler & Others v Ellinikos Organismos Galaktos*[86] which dealt with the thwarting of an employee's rights when the needs of the job are not of limited duration but fixed and permanent. In those circumstances, the Court ruled 'the protection of workers against the misuse of fixed-term employment contracts or relationships, which constitutes the aim of clause 5 of the Framework Agreement, is called into question'. The Labour Court, in *Power*, relied on this passage to arrive at its conclusion that 'real and effective judicial protection against abuse of fixed-term contracts can only be guaranteed if the non-renewal of a fixed-term contract, when used as an instrument of abuse, is rendered unlawful.'

---

[84] Protection of Employees (Fixed-Term Work) Act 2003, s 15. For discussion see, Ch 9, Part-Time Workers.

[85] *Clare County Council v Power* FTD 0812 (3 June 2008).

[86] Case C-212/04 *Adeneler & Others v Ellinikos Organismos Galaktos* [2006] ECR I-6057.

COMPLAINTS UNDER THE 2003 ACT: SOME KEY POINTS OF PRACTICE AND PROCEDURE[87]

[10.66] The 2003 Act provides that complaints under the Act may be referred in the first instance to a Rights Commissioner whose decision shall do one or more of the following: (i) declare that the complaint was or was not well founded; (ii) require the employer to comply with the relevant provision; (iii) require the employer to re-instate or re-engage the employee (including on a contract of indefinite duration); (iv) require the employer to pay to the employee compensation of such amount (if any) as is just and equitable having regard to all the circumstances, but not exceeding two years' remuneration.[88] A significant point to note here is that, in awarding compensation, the Rights Commissioner (and the Labour Court on appeal[89]) must specify whether the award is or is not an award 'in respect of remuneration including arrears of remuneration', as the distinction has significant income tax implications.[90]

[10.67] Complaints must be made within six months of the date of contravention of the Act, although this period may be extended by a further 12 months if the failure to refer the case within six months was due to 'reasonable cause'.[91] This power to extend the time limit was considered by the Labour Court in *Cementation Skanska v Carroll*,[92] where the Court held that, in considering if 'reasonable cause' existed, it was for the claimant to establish that there were reasons which both explain the delay and afford an excuse for it. The Court continued:

> The explanation must be reasonable, that is to say it must make sense, be agreeable to reason and not be irrational or absurd. In the context in which the expression 'reasonable cause' appears in statute it suggests an objective standard but it must be applied to the facts and circumstances known to the claimant at the material time.

Related considerations in this context will include the length of the delay as well as possible prejudice to the opposing party.[93]

Appeals from and enforcement of decisions of Rights Commissioner

[10.68] Section 15 of the 2003 Act provides for an appeal mechanism to the Labour Court by either party. A notice of appeal must be furnished in writing to the Labour Court within six weeks of the date of the decision to which the appeal relates. A copy of this notice is then given by the Labour Court to the other party concerned 'as soon as may be after the receipt of the notice by the Labour Court'. As noted below, a party to proceedings before the Labour Court under s 15 may appeal to the High Court from a

---

87 On practice and procedure generally, see Ch 22, Practice and Procedure in Employment Law.
88 Protection of Employees (Fixed-Term Work) Act 2003, s 14(2).
89 See below in this chapter.
90 Taxes Consolidation Act 1997, s 192A (inserted by s 7 of the Finance Act 2004). For general comment on this area see Farrelly, 'Taxation of Employment Awards: A Basic Understanding' (2006) 3(4) *IELJ* 113.
91 Protection of Employees (Fixed-Term Work) Act 2003, s 14(4).
92 *Cementation Skanska v Carroll* DWT0338 (31 October 2003).
93 See further the judgment of Laffoy J in *Minister for Finance v Civil and Public Service Union* [2007] ELR 36.

determination of the Labour Court on a point of law; the determination of the High Court shall be final and conclusive.

[10.69] Pursuant to s 15(8) of the 2003 Act, where a decision of a Rights Commissioner has not been carried out by the employer and an appeal has not been brought, the employee may refer the complaint to the Labour Court and the Court, without hearing any evidence, shall make a determination to the like effect as the decision of the Rights Commissioner.

What constitutes a decision for the purposes of appeal?

[10.70] It was noted above that a decision of a Rights Commissioner may be appealed to the Labour Court within six weeks of the date of the decision. But what constitutes a decision for this purpose? In *Bus Éireann v SIPTU*,[94] a case concerning the equivalent provision under the Protection of Employees (Part-Time Work) Act 2001, the Labour Court held that the reference in that section to a decision of a Rights Commissioner could only be a reference to 'a complete or final decision which determines whether or not there has been an infringement of the Act'. In that case, the Labour Court was satisfied that the decision which the company sought to appeal was merely a preliminary ruling on a single issue in the case and consequently did not have the character of a 'decision' under the section. Nevertheless, the Court did recognise that there would be 'limited circumstances in which a preliminary point should be determined separately from other issues arising in a case'. The Court indicated that this would only normally be permitted 'where it could lead to considerable savings in both time and expense' and where the point was 'a question of pure law where no evidence is needed and where no further information is required'.

Enforcement of determinations of Labour Court

[10.71] Section 16 of the 2003 Act provides that that the Labour Court's determination can be enforced by the employee, the employee's trade union or the Minister, in the Circuit Court without the employer or any evidence, other than in relation to non-implementation of the determination, being heard. The procedures governing applications for enforcement are set out in Ord 57, r 9 of the Circuit Court Rules 2001, as amended.[95]

Right of appeal to High Court on point of law

[10.72] Under the 2003 Act, it is possible to institute a further appeal on a point of law only to the High Court.[96] The rarity of the circumstances in which the High Court will

---

[94] *Bus Éireann v SIPTU* PTD 048 (13 October 2004).

[95] SI 510/2001 as amended by Circuit Court Rules (Protection of Employees (Fixed-Term Work)) 2006 (SI 532/2006).

[96] As to the procedural requirements for this appeal, see r 2 of Order 84C, inserted by the Rules of the Superior Courts (Statutory Applications and Appeals) 2007 (SI 14/2007), and the commentary by Anthony Kerr in his annotation to the 2003 Act: Kerr, *Consolidated Irish Employment Legislation* (Thomson Round Hall, Release 19, April 2008), Division H. See aalso Ch 22, Practice and Procedure in Employment Law, paras **[22.112]**–**[22.116]**.

overturn a decision of a specialist tribunal such as the Labour Court has been emphasised by the superior courts in many cases, of which the best-known example is *Henry Denny & Sons (Ireland) Ltd v Minister for Social Welfare*.[97] In that case Hamilton CJ warned that:

> ... the courts should be slow to interfere with the decisions of expert administrative tribunals. Where conclusions are based upon an identifiable error of law or an unsustainable finding of fact by a tribunal such conclusions must be corrected. Otherwise it should be recognised that tribunals which have been given statutory tasks to perform and exercise their functions, as is now usually the case, with a high degree of expertise and provide coherent and balanced judgments on the evidence and arguments heard by them it should not be necessary for the courts to review their decisions by way of appeal or judicial review.[98]

Mixed questions of fact and law

[10.73] This passage invites consideration of another fundamental question: when will a determination of the Labour Court properly be characterised as amounting to a matter of law, and when one of fact? On this point, it is instructive to have regard to the more recent Supreme Court decision in *National University of Ireland Cork v Ahern*[99] where the Supreme Court considered what was meant by a 'question of law' in the context of an appeal from the Labour Court (in that case, under s 8(3) of the Anti-Discrimination (Pay) Act 1974). McCracken J, with whom the other members of the Supreme Court agreed, stated:

> The respondents submit that the matters determined by the Labour Court were largely questions of fact and that matters of fact as found by the Labour Court must be accepted by the High Court in any appeal from its findings. As a statement of principle, this is certainly correct. However, this is not to say that the High Court or this court cannot examine the basis upon which the Labour Court found certain facts. The relevance, or indeed admissibility, of the matters relied on by the Labour Court in determining the facts is a question of law. In particular, the question of whether certain matters ought or ought not to have been considered by the Labour Court and ought or ought not to have been taken into account by it in determining the facts, is clearly a question of law, and can be considered on an appeal....[100]

[10.74] In considering whether to allow an appeal against a decision of the Labour Court, the High Court must consider whether that court based its decision on an identifiable error of law or on a finding of fact that is not sustainable.

Whether arguments not pursued below can be advanced on High Court Appeal

[10.75] An important point for consideration concerning High Court appeals on points of law under the 2003 Act is whether legal arguments not pursued in the Labour Court

---

[97] *Henry Denny & Sons (Ireland) Ltd v Minister for Social Welfare* [1998] 1 IR 34.
[98] *Henry Denny & Sons (Ireland) Ltd v Minister for Social Welfare* [1998] 1 IR 34 at 37.
[99] *National University of Ireland Cork v Ahern* [2005] 2 IR 577.
[100] [2005] 2 IR 577 at 580.

can be advanced on appeal to the High Court. In the recent High Court case of *Minister for Finance v McArdle*,[101] this issue arose in circumstances where the employer sought to advance legal arguments as to the jurisdiction of the fora below. Laffoy J described as 'correct in point of principle' the proposition that such legal arguments not presented before the Labour Court could not properly be canvassed on appeal to the High Court. She further emphasised the necessity for 'precision as to the points of law for determination by this Court ... and the grounds on which it [is] asserted the Labour Court erred' in the special summons.

The position relating to parallel claims under the 2003 Act

[10.76] The question of parallel claims raises a number of distinct issues in the context of a consideration of the 2003 Act. In s 18 of the 2003 Act, for example, it is provided that in the event that penalisation constitutes a dismissal of the employee within the meaning of the Unfair Dismissals legislation, relief may not be granted to the employee in respect of that penalisation both under the 2003 Act and under the unfair dismissals legislation. The section goes on to provide that an individual who is a fixed-term employee under the 2003 Act and a part-time employee under the 2001 Act may obtain relief[102] arising from the same circumstances under either, but not both, of the Acts.

[10.77] Another point to be noted here is that s 18 of the 2003 Act, unlike s 15 of the Unfair Dismissals Act 1977, does not limit an employee's right of access to the High Court to enforce his or her common law rights.[103]

[10.78] In relation to employment equality claims, s 101A of the Employment Equality Act 1998 provides that where an employer's conduct constitutes both a contravention of Pts III or IV of that Act and a contravention of this Act, relief may not be granted to the employee concerned in respect of the conduct under both the 1998 Act and the 2003 Act. This section thus provides that a party may not obtain 'double relief', but does not preclude the *processing* of more than one claim. Accordingly, where an application under the unfair dismissals or the employment equality legislation has been unsuccessful, a claimant is not precluded by this section from pursuing a claim under the 2003 Act.[104]

---

[101] *Minister for Finance v McArdle* [2007] 2 ILRM 438 at 448.

[102] Though this does not prevent two separate claims from being processed, as was confirmed by the Labour Court in *Galway City Council v Mackey* FTD 065 (23 June 2006).

[103] *Ahmed v Health Service Executive* [2008] ELR 117.

[104] *Galway City Council v Mackey* FTD 065 (23 June 2006).

Part III
Pay, Pensions, and Benefits

Chapter 11

Pay, Pensions and Benefits

Jo Kenny and Philip Smith

Introduction[1]

[11.01] In Ch 2, the role that remuneration plays in determining the employment contract was explored and it was noted that whether wages/salary or a commission based remuneration is involved is just one factor in determining whether an employment contract exists.[2] For the purposes of this chapter, it is assumed that an employment relationship exists. This chapter explores the main forms of remuneration customarily used with particular focus on pensions.

[11.02] There are a number of expressions used to refer to the monetary consideration under an employment contract such as: pay; salary; wages; remuneration; emoluments; fees; expenses; commission; overtime; bonus; allowance; and gratuity. Notwithstanding these different terms, remuneration (used here to mean the entirety of an employee's monetary consideration) is essentially comprised of three parts:

(i) regular payments (which need not necessarily be of the same amount at each payment);

(ii) irregular payments (eg annual bonuses, seasonal overtime, commission repayments); and

(iii) deferred payments (pensions and insurances).

In addition, an employee may receive one or more forms of non-monetary consideration (eg the provision and use of a mobile phone/car/laptop/accommodation etc). This chapter first considers regular monetary payments – pay; then deferred pay in the form of pensions; and finally, related insurances such as PHI cover. Other irregular payments and non-monetary consideration (benefits in kind) are primarily dealt with in Ch 21, Taxation.

Pay

[11.03] Pay is a fundamental element of the employment contract. As has already been explored in Ch 2, the way in which an employee is remunerated provides a vital indication as to whether there is an employment contract or whether, on the other hand, the extent of entrepreneurship is such as to suggest a contract for services.[3] The

---

[1] We wish to acknowledge the considerable assistance and contribution of our colleagues, Olivia Mullooly and Louise O'Byrne, to the preparation of this chapter.

[2] See eg para **[2.25]**.

[3] See para **[2.05]**.

fundamental nature of pay is recognised in that it is one of the terms of employment required to be covered in the written terms to be provided to an employee within two months of commencement of employment.[4]

[11.04] Pay is always an express term. This is usually not an issue for regular payments but can cause difficulty in determining entitlements to, for example, irregular bonuses.

European approach to 'pay'

[11.05] The European Court of Justice (ECJ) has formulated a well recognised definition of the term 'pay' which is largely repeated in the definition of 'remuneration' contained in the legislation relating to part-time and fixed term workers.[5]

[11.06] In the case of *Garland v British Rail Engineering*[6] the Court stated that:

> [t]he concept of pay contained in the second paragraph of Article 119 comprises any other consideration whether in cash or in kind, whether immediate or future, provided that the worker receives it, albeit indirectly, in respect of his employment from his employer.

This has been adopted in many subsequent cases including *Barber v Guardian Royal Exchange Assurance.*[7] In this case, the Court held that compensation was a form of pay when it is granted in connection with redundancy in that 'such compensation constitutes a form of pay to which the worker is entitled in respect of his employment, which is paid to him upon termination of the employment relationship'.

[11.07] It is clear from the decision in *Garland* that the *ex gratia* nature of the payments is irrelevant to their classification as remuneration. In *Alabaster v Woolwich plc and Secretary of State for Social Security,*[8] the Court made clear that benefits paid to a pregnant woman during maternity leave are to be treated as pay. The definition of pay does not however include social security schemes and benefits (including state social welfare pension benefits)[9] but does, for ECJ law purposes, include occupational benefit schemes.[10]

Irish approach to 'pay'

[11.08] There is no legislative definition of pay in Ireland. While there have yet to be higher court decisions on the point it appears that the Irish courts will adopt the European-style reasoning in respect of pay. The Labour Court has recently held that severance payments being made to employees were pay, as there was a causal

---

[4] Terms of Employment (Information) Acts 1994 and 2001, s 3 following EU Directive 91/533/ EEC.

[5] Protection of Employees (Fixed-Term Work) Act 2003, s 2 and the Protection of Employees (Part-Time Work) Act 2001, s 2.

[6] Case 12/81 *Garland v British Rail Engineering* [1982] ECR 359.

[7] Case C 262/88 *Barber v Guardian Royal Exchange Assurance* [1990] ECR I-1889.

[8] Case C-147/02 *Alabaster v Woolwich plc and Secretary of State for Social Security* [2004] ECR Page I-03101.

[9] Case C-149/77 *Defrenne v Société anonyme belge de navigation aérienne Sabena* [1978] ECR 1365.

[10] Case C-109/91 *Ten Oever v Stichting Bedrijfspensioenfonds voor het Glazenwassers- en Schoonmaakbedrijf* [1993] ECR I-4879.

connection between the employment and the payment.[11] The Labour Court adopted *Garland* in making the pronouncement that these payments amounted to remuneration within the meaning of legislation protecting fixed-term workers.

Irish law definitions of 'remuneration'

[11.09] The Employment Appeals Tribunal in *McGivern v Irish National Insurance Co Ltd*[12] stated that 'remuneration is not mere payment for work done but is what the doer expects to get as a result of the work he does in so far as what he expects to get is quantified in terms of money'.

[11.10] The term remuneration is defined in various statutory provisions in a manner consistent with the ECJ definition of 'pay'. The Protection of Employees (Part-Time Work) Act 2001 and the Protection of Employees (Fixed-Term Work) Act 2003 define remuneration in relation to an employee as:

(a) any consideration, whether in cash or in kind, which the employee receives, directly or indirectly, from the employer in respect of the employment, and

(b) any amounts the employee will be entitled to receive on foot of any pension scheme or arrangement.

[11.11] For historic reasons (it predates European law on pay) the Unfair Dismissals Act 1977 contains a slightly different definition of 'remuneration' in the context of an employee who has been unfairly dismissed.[13] However, the definition is again all-encompassing and is in effect the same as the ECJ definition.

[11.12] At first it might appear unusual in the face of this series of all-encompassing definitions that the Employment Equality Acts 1998–2008 define 'remuneration' in relation to an employee as *not* including pension rights 'but, subject to that, includes any consideration, whether in cash or in kind, which the employee receives, directly or indirectly, from the employer in respect of the employment'.[14] The reason for the exclusion of pension rights is that equal treatment in respect of rights under occupational benefit schemes (including occupational pension schemes) is provided for under the principle of equal pension treatment contained in Part VII of the Pensions Acts 1990–2008.[15] For redress involving occupational benefit schemes, the Pensions Act incorporates an amended version of parts of the Employment Equality Acts.[16]

[11.13] It should also be noted that there are different definitions of 'pay' and/or 'remuneration' for the purposes of tax law, discretionary revenue limits for pension schemes, family law and social welfare law. For example Sch E of the Taxes Consolidation Act 1997 dealing with income taxation defines 'remuneration' as

---

[11] *Sunday World Newspapers Ltd v Steven Kinsella & Luke Bradley* Labour Court Recommendation 18 July 2006.

[12] *McGivern v Irish National Insurance Co Ltd* PS/1982 (EAT).

[13] Unfair Dismissals Act 1977, s 7(3).

[14] Employment Equality Acts 1998–2008, s 2.

[15] Pensions Act 1990, s 69 and Part VII generally.

[16] See Pensions Act 1990, s 81J and the fourth schedule.

meaning 'emoluments including pay during illness, holiday pay, arrears of pay, pension, bonuses, overtime, commission, any non cash benefits, any non cash emoluments and any other like emoluments and payments'.

Wages

[11.14] Wages are a sub-set of 'pay' when given the wide ECJ meaning. The meaning of wages is defined[17] in Irish law as:

> ... any sums payable to the employee by the employer in connection with his employment.

The use of the phrase 'in connection with' is very wide. This is expressed to include:

(i)   any fee, bonus or commission, or any holiday, sick or maternity pay, or any other emolument, referable to his employment, whether payable under his contract of employment or otherwise; and

(ii)   any sum payable to the employee upon the termination by the employer of his contract of employment without his having given to the employee the appropriate prior notice of the termination, being a sum paid in lieu of the giving of such notice.

The section goes on to exclude the following payments from the definition:

(i)   any payment in respect of expenses incurred by the employee in carrying out his employment;

(ii)   any payment by way of a pension, allowance or gratuity in connection with the death, or the retirement or resignation from his employment, of the employee or as compensation for loss of office;

(iii)   any payment referable to the employee's redundancy;

(iv)   any payment to the employee otherwise than in his capacity as an employee;

(v)   any payment in kind or benefit in kind.

[11.15] From the definition it can be seen that elements which are 'pay' in European terms (or 'remuneration' in Irish terms) are not wages – the obvious exclusions are pensions and benefits in kind. Broadly speaking, 'wages' are immediate monetary payments.

[11.16] The Payment of Wages Act governs the method of payment of wages. In particular, it is not permitted to make deductions from an employee's wages unless the deduction is authorised under the contract, required by statute or is made with the prior written consent of the employee agreeing to the deduction and its purpose.[18] This consideration is sometimes overlooked when making later changes to the employment relationship – eg amending a pension scheme to provide for member contributions for the first time.

---

[17]   In the Payment of Wages Act 1991, s 1.
[18]   Payment of Wages Act,1991, s 5(1).

Minimum wage

[11.17] Most employees are entitled to a minimum wage, which is governed by the terms of the National Minimum Wage Act 2000. The National Minimum Wage was increased on 1 July 2007 following a Labour Court recommendation, in accordance with s 13 of the Act, to €8.65 per hour. In accordance with s 14(a) of the Act, an employee who has attained the age of 18 years shall be remunerated by his or her employer in respect of the employee's working hours in any pay reference period, at an hourly rate of pay that on average is not less than the national minimum hourly rate of pay. Different rates apply to employees under 18 years of age (s 14(b)), those over 18 for their first two years in employment (s 15) and employees categorised as trainees in accordance with s 16 of the Act.

[11.18] An employer may be exempted from paying the minimum wage under s 41 of the Act where they can show to the Labour Court that they cannot afford to pay minimum wage due to financial difficulty.

[11.19] There are other minimum rates of pay for employees in certain sectors. In some sectors such as contract cleaning, hairdressing and tailoring they are set out in Employment Regulation Orders made by Joint Labour Committees. In other sectors such as the construction industry, drapery and printing they are set out in Registered Employment Agreements made by collective agreements.

Pay for piece-work

[11.20] A piece rate worker is a worker whose pay fluctuates according to the work he does, eg a person paid solely by bonuses, commissions etc, in contrast to a person with a rate of pay fixed by reference to a period of time, as is the situation with most people.

[11.21] The National Minimum Wage Act applies to piece rate workers. Sch 1 of the Act cites piece and incentive rates as reckonable components in calculating the average hourly rate of pay. As the national minimum wage is expressed as an hourly rate of pay (not a piece or productivity rate), pay at the end of a reference period must be such that an employee's reckonable pay when divided by the employee's hours of work is not less than the employee's statutory minimum hourly rate of pay entitlement under the Act.

[11.22] The ECJ, in its decision in *Special arbejderforbundet i Danmark v Dansk Industri*,[19] held that Art 119 (now Art 141) of the Treaty and Directive 75/117 EC (Equal Treatment for Men and Women) apply to piece-work pay schemes. This conclusion was based on the fact that piece-work is specifically mentioned in the third paragraph of Art 119 and having regard for the liberal manner in which the notion of pay has been interpreted by the ECJ.

Taxation of pay

[11.23] The taxation of pay is dealt with in Ch 21, Taxation.

---

[19]   Case C-400/93 *Special arbejderforbundet i Danmark v Dansk Industri* [1995] ECR I-1275.

Salary sacrifice/bonus sacrifice

[11.24] Sometimes employers will suggest (usually for tax reasons) that employees should agree to 'sacrifice' salary or bonus in order to take advantage of a more tax-beneficial means of receiving the same remuneration. As a general rule, the Revenue prohibits salary sacrifice arrangements and treats sacrificed salary as having been received by the employee prior to the sacrifice.

Having said that, the Revenue has officially sanctioned the sacrifice of bonus to participate in tax-approved share option schemes. It also does not appear to be concerned about arrangements with little materiality such as the sacrifice of bonus to receive gift tokens of up to €250 tax free. On the other hand, it does not encourage the sacrifice of significant portions of salary or bonus into pension arrangements. This means that so-called 'bonus sacrifice' arrangements linked to pension schemes must be carefully structured and accurately documented so as not to result in a salary sacrifice of the type prohibited by the Revenue.[20]

PENSIONS

Introduction

[11.25] A pension may be defined simply as an income payable from the date of an employee's retirement until the date of his/her death.

[11.26] The provision of pensions is complicated in practice by the different benefit designs and additional benefits (such as life cover and pensions for dependants) and the different vehicles available through which to provide these benefits. Because pension schemes run for a long time,[21] they tend to involve documentation that is unique to each scheme having been amended by various advisers along the way. Of necessity, there are also a number of defined terms which makes pension schemes less accessible to those outside the industry.

[11.27] It is beyond the scope of this text to provide a complete guide to pension law, not least as such texts are already available.[22] The aim of this section is to provide a guide to pension law for the employment practitioner with signposts to further information for those interested in more detailed study of the subject.

Nature of pension promise

[11.28] The interaction between pension law and employment law is ill-defined. The grey area exists because the significant majority of funded pension arrangements are created under trust – primarily for tax reasons. The benefit is therefore an equitable

---

[20] For salary sacrifice in the context of share options schemes see Ch 21, Taxation.

[21] A model member might join a scheme aged 25, work for 40 years before retiring aged 65. Such a member could be receiving pension payments from the scheme for a further 30 years. This means the lifetime of an open pension scheme today (or at least the duration of its liabilities) is of the order of 70+ years.

[22] Finucane and Buggy with Tighe, *Pensions Law and Practice* (2nd edn, Thomson Round Hall, 2006).

entitlement under a trust at the same time as it is an important part of the overall remuneration under the employment contract. The situation is similarly vague in unfunded public sector 'pay-as-you-go' schemes.[23] In these cases, the benefits are described and set out in statutory instruments which are not themselves necessarily part of the employment contract.

[11.29] The use of trusts for pension schemes has a number of advantages over and above the Revenue requirement. The main advantages are: (i) it separates the pension fund assets from the assets of the company; and (ii) it provides beneficiaries[24] who have no relationship with the employing company with enforceable rights which they would not have under an employment contract due to a lack of privity of contract in their relationship with the employer of the person on whom they are dependent.

[11.30] In general, therefore, while acknowledging that pension benefits form a significant part of the employment promise, there is an as yet unresolved tension as to whether the pension scheme trust documentation is definitive on questions such as the ability to amend and terminate the pension promise in the absence of express wording to the contrary in the employment contract.

[11.31] The view of the ECJ is clear on one aspect. In a series of rulings, it has stated its conclusion that a pension amounts to deferred pay. As such, certain employment rights apply to pensions the main one being the right to equal treatment.[25]

Pension promises in the employment contract

[11.32] Difficulties can arise where the pension promise under a scheme is summarised in the employment contract without reference to the terms and conditions of the scheme itself. Pension scheme trust documents tend to be lengthy and detailed extending to 100+ pages of technical legal provisions. These are summarised for the benefit of members, employers and administrators in explanatory booklets which are customarily expressed to be subject to the legal documentation from which they are derived. Those booklets may themselves be summarised further in announcements or benefit statements, which should ideally again defer to the formal scheme documents in the event of conflict.

[11.33] Where benefits are summarised in the employment contract without reference to any of the pension scheme materials, there is a risk that a separate and distinct commitment is being made to provide a type, amount or level of pension irrespective of the vehicle or scheme used to provide it. As a promise in the employment contract is scheme-independent, it may be unconstrained by Revenue or other restrictions resulting in a pension benefit which is greater than that which would apply under the scheme rules (with correspondingly greater expense for the employer). Additional complications may include the fact that scheme trustees are unwilling or unable to pay the benefit promised

---

[23] NB. These schemes are not set up under trust as there are no funds invested. The pension payments are met from a combination of contribution income and central government funding.

[24] Eg an employee's spouse or children.

[25] Pensions Act 1990, s 69 and Part VII.

under the employment contract. 'Target benefit' schemes have proved to be problematic in this regard.[26]

Typical contract wording

[11.34] Given that pension schemes last a long time, that the eventual liability is uncertain and that they may be amended more than once during that period, it is essential that reference be made to the variability of the pension terms and to the power to terminate the scheme.

Precedence of deeds and rules over booklets and announcements

[11.35] The pension case law referred to in this section is primarily based on English cases as there is a dearth of decided Irish cases relating to pensions. Having said that, the two main Irish decisions are helpful in considering how to interpret pension documentation and provide the starting point for consideration of questions of precedence in attempting to resolve discrepancies in wording between various pension scheme documents.

[11.36] *Irish Pensions Trust v Central Remedial Clinic*[27] provides some helpful guidance on the interpretation of pension scheme documentation (ie that it is generally practical and purposive rather than literal). It also noted *obiter* that on the facts (which were quite specific) precedence would be given to a member's notification rather than the rules. The deed specifically stated that benefits were to be as described in the members' notifications so the case is likely to be of restricted 'application'.

[11.37] More generally *Irish Pensions Trust v First National Bank of Chicago*[28] is the starting point in Irish law for considering whether announcements and booklets override trust deeds and rules. The case upheld exclusion wording in an explanatory booklet and rejected the proposal that a sentence in the booklet constituted a contractual promise. Since that case there have been several attempts in the English courts to override trust deeds using general communications and estoppel arguments and as yet these attempts have failed.[29] The precise wording of the deeds and the communications is vital in determining the outcome of any such claim and the reality is that general principles in this area beyond those set out above have yet to emerge.

---

[26] A 'target benefit' scheme is a defined contribution scheme under which an intention is expressed that contributions will be made at a level necessary to 'target' a particular benefit. Difficulties arise where the employer's intention is understood by the employee to be a commitment and/or where either an inadequate or no effort is made to adjust the contributions to attempt to attain the target.

[27] *Irish Pensions Trust v Central Remedial Clinic* [2005] IEHC 87 (18 March 2005, unreported) HC (Kelly J).

[28] *Irish Pensions Trust v First National Bank of Chicago* (15 February 1989, unreported) HC (Murphy J).

COMMON TERMS DEFINED

[11.38] Pension schemes have a jargon all of their own and a glossary is set out below to assist in understanding this section.

Active Member – A pension scheme member who is still in **Reckonable Service**.

ARF – Approved Retirement Fund: a fund managed by an investment manager which allows the individual in retirement to choose when he draws an income from it, in contrast to an **Annuity**. **ARF/AMRFs** are available to certain proprietary directors and in respect of moneys transferred from **AVCs** and **PRSAs**.

AMRF – Approved Minimum Retirement Fund: similar to an **ARF** except that payments cannot be drawn down until age 75.

Annuity – A guaranteed annual income payable on retirement by a life office in return for a capital payment. The amount of capital required to purchase the annuity will be based on the 'annuity rate', which takes into consideration factors likely to influence the duration of payment, namely mortality and factors affecting the cost of funding the annuity namely long term interest rates.

AVC – Additional Voluntary Contribution: contributions which a scheme member can make in addition to any mandatory employee contributions payable under the terms of the pension scheme.

Commutation – The facility to take part of a pension as a tax-free lump sum at retirement. This facility is always subject to **Revenue Limits**.

Deferred Member – A pension scheme member who has left the employer's service and whose pension payment is deferred until attainment of **Normal Retirement Age**.

Defined Benefit Scheme (Final Salary) – A pension scheme which promises members a specific amount of pension. This is typically a percentage of the member's final salary multiplied by their years of membership in the pension scheme. For example, 1/60th x Final Pensionable Salary x Pensionable Service will give a member who serves 40 years 40/60ths (2/3rds) of their Final Pensionable Salary on an annual basis from retirement until death.

Defined Contribution Scheme (Money Purchase) – A pension scheme which, instead of promising members a specific amount of pension, invests a fund on behalf of the member over the course of the member's service. The fund typically consists of employer and employee contributions which are set at a defined percentage of basic

---

[29] See for example, *Hoover Ltd v Hetherington* [2002] EWHC 1052 and *Lansing Linde v Alber* [2000] PLR 15 and most recently *Steria & Others v Hutchinson* [2006] EWCA Civ 1551, in which the Court of Appeal held on the facts that the notice in the booklet expressly stating that the trust deed and scheme rules were to prevail made it impossible for the employee to establish reliance on the other statements and that the employee was unable to show that he had suffered a detriment either to satisfy the requirements of estoppel by representation or to show that the administration of benefits in line with the trust deed and rules was inequitable and unconscionable.

salary. On retirement the fund is used to purchase an **Annuity** (and **AVCs** can be used to purchase an **AMRF/ARF**) for the member.

Early Retirement – The option available under a pension scheme to take retirement before **Normal Retirement Age**. In a **Defined Benefit Scheme** this usually requires employer and/or trustee consent, in view of the potentially significant cost implications for scheme funding and therefore other scheme members. Pensions payable to members who take **Early Retirement** are usually subject to an actuarial reduction, in consideration of the facts that (a) they are in payment for a longer period; and (b) the funds used to secure the pension have enjoyed a shorter period of investment return.

Exempt Approved – One of the most attractive aspects of using a pension scheme as a savings vehicle for a future income stream is the available tax relief on employee and employer contributions as well as on investment return. In order to ensure that a pension scheme benefits from this tax relief, it is necessary to establish it by way of an irrevocable trust[30] and register it with the Revenue to obtain 'exempt approved' status and thereby obtain tax reliefs. Income tax is chargeable at the other end, on pensions in payment. Public sector schemes established under statute (which are usually **Pay as You Go** schemes) automatically enjoy tax relief on employee contributions and are not required to obtain exempt approval. Since they are generally **Pay as You Go** schemes they do not require tax relief on employer contributions and investment gains.

Hybrid Scheme – A pension scheme with characteristics of a **Defined Benefit** and **Defined Contribution** scheme, for example a defined contribution scheme with a minimum benefit underpin.

Life Assurance Scheme – A policy set up with an insurance company (life office) which provides death benefits in respect of employees, usually a multiple of salary payable to the employee's spouse and/or dependants. Some employers who do not offer a pension scheme offer this to employees, while other employers who do offer a pension scheme offer it to employees who are not (yet) eligible for membership.

Occupational Pension Scheme – An **Exempt Approved** pension scheme.

Normal Pensionable Age A Pensions Act definition for **Preservation** purposes, meaning **Normal Retirement Age** unless a member can receive benefits before that point without employer or trustee consent, in which case such earlier date is treated as **Normal Pensionable Age**.

Normal Retirement Age (Normal Retirement Date) – The date specified in the pension scheme rules at which members will normally retire.

Pay as You Go (Unfunded) – A scheme which does not fund in advance for payment of pensions promised to members, eg public sector schemes which pay out of contribution income and central government funds.

Pension – An annual stream of income payable on retirement.

---

30   In that the trust over the assets cannot be revoked by the employer. This does not mean that the employer cannot terminate or amend the scheme under the terms of the trust deed and rules, rather, if he does, the assets must still be applied to provide pensions for scheme members.

Pension Adjustment Order – An order made by the court following judicial separation or divorce which adjusts spouses' entitlements under a pension scheme. It is binding on pension scheme trustees.

Pensioner – A member of a pension scheme who has reached **Normal Retirement Age** or who has taken **Early Retirement** and to whom pension is payable.

Preservation – Under the Pensions Act, where a member completes two years of service,[31] the benefits he has accrued under the scheme are 'preserved' and enjoy a degree of statutory protection from that point on. If the member leaves service at some point thereafter, he can choose whether to transfer the preserved benefit to (for example) a new employer's scheme or whether to leave it as a deferred benefit to be taken at retirement. In recognition of the eroding effect of inflation on the real value of preserved benefit, it is revalued annually until retirement in accordance with the annual increase in the Consumer Price Index to a maximum of 4%. Where a member leaves service and chooses to leave his preserved benefits as a deferred benefit his consent is required for those benefits to be transferred (other than in the case of a scheme wind up). This requirement for member consent may have implications for pension scheme reorganisations, depending on the timing and nature of the reorganisation, see para **[11.187]**.

PRSA – Personal Retirement Savings Account: established by way of contract between the account-holder and the PRSA provider to provide a vehicle by which the employee can save for a pension and enjoy tax reliefs, see Employer's Statutory Duties below at para **[11.39]**. Currently, the proceeds of a **PRSA** can be used to purchase an **Annuity** or transferred to an **ARF**. The account-holder can commute 25% of the proceeds into a tax free lump sum at retirement.

Reckonable Service – Service in a pension scheme in respect of which the member is accruing pension benefits.

Retirement Annuity Contract – A pension policy taken out usually by a self-employed individual with a life office, which enjoys tax reliefs.

Revenue Limits – Limits set out in the Revenue Pensions Manual applicable to employee and employer contributions and maximum benefits payable on retirement, eg the aggregate benefits payable to an employee who retires at Normal Retirement Age after 40 or more years' service should not exceed 2/3rds of his final remuneration when expressed as an annual amount.

Transfer Value – The amount of benefit attributable to a member who leaves a pension scheme before **Normal Retirement Age** and transfers their benefit to, for example, another pension scheme.

---

[31] Between 1 January 1991 and 2 June 2002 the requisite period was five years.

EMPLOYER'S STATUTORY DUTIES

Provision of Pension Schemes or PRSA

[11.39] Under Irish legislation, an employer is not obliged to provide employees with a pension scheme (but see next paragraph regarding PRSA obligations). Where an employer does provide an exempt approved pension scheme, Revenue guidance requires the employer to make 'meaningful contributions'. The employer can meet this requirement by covering the running costs of the pension scheme and death benefit costs.

[11.40] With effect from 15 September 2003, where an employer does not provide an occupational pension scheme, or where the employer's occupational pension scheme imposes a waiting period which exceeds six months or membership criteria which limit eligibility, the employer is obliged to facilitate access to a PRSA to 'excluded employees'. Excluded employees are either all employees (where there is no occupational pension scheme) or employees who are not eligible to join the scheme (where the occupational pension scheme limits eligibility). Employers are permitted to impose a waiting period of up to six months.

[11.41] An employer is also required to facilitate access to a PRSA where their occupational pension scheme does not permit members to make AVCs.

[11.42] Breach of the statutory obligation to facilitate access to a PRSA is a criminal offence, which can attract fines from €5,000–€25,000 and/or imprisonment. The Pensions Board has the power to issue on-the-spot fines. It is a statutory offence for an employer not to provide information on their PRSA facilitation on request and the Pensions Board has exercised its power to prosecute employers who do not provide such information.

[11.43] Facilitating access to a PRSA entails that the employer takes the following steps:

  (i)   entering into an arrangement with a PRSA provider to enable employees to participate in a PRSA;

  (ii)   notifying the employees of their right to participate in a PRSA;

  (iii) allowing the PRSA provider reasonable access to the workplace to assist the employees in entering into a PRSA;

  (iv)   making the appropriate payroll deductions for the contributions agreed; and

  (v)   remitting the contributions to the PRSA provider within the statutory timeframe (21 days).

[11.44] Employers are not obliged to contribute to PRSAs on employees' behalf, although they may do so.

Deduction of wages

[11.45] Employers are obliged[32] to ensure that pension scheme members and PRSA contributors have authorised employee contributions to the scheme through deductions from their wages.

---

[32] Payment of Wages Act 1991, s 5(1).

Duty to deduct and hand over contributions and notify employees

[11.46] Employers who deduct member contributions from wages for pension purposes are obliged to remit the contributions to the trustees/PRSA provider within 21 days following the end of the month in which the deductions was made.[33] Similarly, employer contributions to a defined contribution scheme calculated as a specified cash/percentage amount must also be handed over with in 21 days.[34] Employees must be provided with details of deductions and the running totals not less frequently than once a month and provision of such information on payslips satisfies this requirement.[35]

Duty to provide information on scheme

[11.47] Employers are obliged to provide such information to the trustees of a pension scheme (and the actuary, the auditor and the Pensions Board) as they reasonably require for the purpose of their functions under the scheme and the Pensions Act.[36] The employer is also jointly responsible with the Trustees for compliance with certain of the disclosure requirements in providing information to members and others under the Pensions Act.[37]

[11.48] For a very brief outline of the information obligations of trustees and rights of members see para **[11.66]** onwards.

Equal treatment

[11.49] Employers are obliged[38] to ensure that access to any pension scheme they provide complies with equal treatment requirements, see below at para **[11.77]** onwards.

EMPLOYER'S COMMON LAW DUTIES

Imperial duty of good faith

[11.50] Employers are required to exercise any powers in relation to a pension scheme in good faith and in such a way that would not undermine the basis of mutual trust and confidence which is supposed to underlie the employer/employee relationship.

[11.51] This duty stems from what the English High Court termed the 'implied obligation of good faith' in *Imperial Group Pension Trust Ltd v Imperial Tobacco Ltd.*[39] The principle is based on the finding that:

> ...employers will not, without reasonable and proper cause, conduct themselves in a manner calculated or likely to destroy or seriously damage the relationship of confidence

---

[33] Pensions Act 1990, s 58A(1).

[34] Pensions Act 1990, s 58A(2).

[35] Pensions Act 1990, ss 58A(3) and (5).

[36] Pensions Act 1990, s 54(4).

[37] Pensions Act 1990, s 54(1).

[38] Pensions Act 1990, s 78.

[39] *Imperial Group Pension Trust Ltd v Imperial Tobacco Ltd* [1991] 2 All ER 597.

and trust between employer and employee...' (*Woods v WM Car Services (Peterborough) Ltd*).[40]

It applies no less to an employer's exercise of rights and powers under a pension scheme. In *Imperial* the Court considered the exercise of the employer's right to give or withhold consent to a scheme amendment to increase pensions in payment. It was suggested that the employer was withholding consent for the purpose of inducing members to transfer their pension rights to a separate employer pension fund, with a view to controlling a surplus which would arise on the transfer.

[11.52] On those facts Sir Michael Browne-Wilkinson VC was keen to emphasise that while it is open to the employer look after its own interests, where a pension scheme is in place the

> ...duty of good faith requires the company to preserve its employees' rights and pensions fund, not to destroy them. If there are financial and other considerations which require the fund to be determined, so be it. But if the sole purpose of refusing to consent to an amendment increasing benefits is the collateral purpose of putting pressure on members to abandon their existing rights, including the right to the surplus on determination, in my judgment the company would not be acting good faith....

[11.53] While the *Imperial* duty does not prevent the employer from taking into account financial interests in exercising its powers in relation to a pension scheme, it does oblige him to act reasonably and properly. An employer who attempts to exercise a power of amendment in pursuit of returning a surplus to himself would find it difficult to show that he had acted in good faith.

No general duty to advise

[11.54] The courts have been careful to distinguish between, on the one hand the *Imperial* duty to exercise powers in good faith, and on the other hand a general duty of care to advise employees, which they have stopped short of finding. The current position is that if a contract of employment does not impose on the employer (whether implicitly or explicitly) a duty of care to advise, no such duty arises independently in tort.

[11.55] In *Outram v Academy Plastics Ltd*[41] a pension scheme member resigned from his employment and returned to service the following year but did not rejoin the pension scheme. Nor did his employer advise him to do so. He resigned again due to ill-health and died before his pension came into payment. The Court of Appeal rejected the widow's claim that his employer should have advised him to apply to rejoin the pension scheme (in which case he would have been entitled to an early retirement pension) on the basis that no contractual duty to so advise was identified and accordingly, no co-extensive duty arose in tort.

[11.56] Nevertheless, where an employee has to take positive action to benefit from a valuable pension right and he simply could not be aware of the existence of that right without the employer drawing his attention to it, the courts may find it necessary to read

---

[40] *Woods v WM Car Services (Peterborough) Ltd* [1981] ICR 666 at 670.
[41] *Outram v Academy Plastics Ltd* [2001] ICR 367.

a duty to advise into the employment contract. In *Scally v Southern Health and Social Services Board*[42] the House of Lords implied into the contract of employment a duty to inform pension scheme members of the option to buy pensionable years. It is worth noting that *Scally* appears to have turned very much on its own facts. Although claimants have since sought to rely on it, the courts have distinguished it in various instances.

[11.57] In *Crossley v Faithful & Gould Holdings Ltd*[43] an employee resigned because of ill-health and was granted benefits at the discretion of the insurer, who stopped payment after a period. He argued that his employer should have advised him that were he to remain in employment he would automatically be paid disability benefit for so long as he was 'unable by reason of sickness to follow his occupation'. The Court of Appeal noted the development in the common law and in particular the *Imperial* duty of good faith, but rejected the proposition that the common law should go so far as to imply a term that the employer should take reasonable care for the economic well-being of his employee. Dyson LJ reasoned that such a term would impose an unfair and unreasonable burden on employers.

[11.58] In *Nortel Networks UK Pension Plan Lewis v Pensions Ombudsman & Ors*,[44] the English High Court found *obiter* that the employee's settlement agreement did not need to be interpreted as subject to an implied term that the employer should have informed the employee of a new tax régime which may have affected the pension payable under the settlement agreement.

[11.59] In *Crossley* and in *Nortel*, the courts have considered relevant the fact that the employee had access to independent advice and could reasonably be expected to have established the position vis-à-vis their rights.

[11.60] One final note of caution should be sounded in relation to the provision of advice. In *Crossley,* Dyson LJ accepted that where an employer assumes responsibility for giving financial advice to an employee, he falls under a duty to take reasonable care in doing so. So where an employer (whether through human resources or otherwise) assumes an advisory role in relation to an employee and his pension rights and options which goes further than the mere provision of information, a duty of care may arise.

[11.61] This caveat is illustrated in the Court of Appeal case of *Lennon v Commissioner of Police of the Metropolis*.[45] A personnel executive officer who managed a police officer's transfer assured the officer that she had handled a lot of transfers and that taking time off between posts would not affect his continuity of service. In fact, taking leave marked a break in service and adversely affected the police officer's entitlement to housing allowance. The employer was found to have voluntarily assumed a duty of care which it breached in failing to advise the claimant of the requirement to apply for unpaid leave. Mummery LJ distinguished *Outram*, noting that whereas the employer in *Outram*

---

[42] *Scally v Southern Health and Social Services Board* [1991] ICR 77.
[43] *Crossley v Faithful & Gould Holdings Ltd* [2004] EWCA Civ 293.
[44] *Nortel Networks UK Pension Plan Lewis v Pensions Ombudsman & Ors* [2005] PLR 195.
[45] *Lennon v Commissioner of Police of the Metropolis* [2004] EWCA Civ 130.

had neither expressly nor impliedly assumed responsibility to give pension advice on which the employee would rely, the employer in *Lennon* had expressly assumed responsibility in relation to the claimant's transfer.

Fiduciary nature of employer's powers

[11.62] When considering the exercise of an employer's power under a pension scheme, it is important to bear in mind that not all powers under a pension scheme are regarded in the same way. The employer's duty to employees does not necessarily stop with the *Imperial* implied duty of good faith. English cases have held that while an employer is free to exercise some powers under a pension scheme without regard to the interests of any other party, in other cases the employer is constrained by fiduciary considerations.

[11.63] Unfortunately there is no definitive list of which powers are fiduciary and which are not. The power to appoint new trustees has been held to be fiduciary;[46] the power to distribute surplus is not.[47] Cases have been decided on their particular facts and the absence of clear principles is exemplified in the cases concerning the investment power.

[11.64] In many defined benefit schemes, the employer bears a substantially greater part of the cost. By taking greater risks with the scheme's investments the employer can (if the investments are successful) use the growth in the investments to offset the future costs of the scheme. It can be in the interests of the employer therefore to adopt a riskier investment strategy. On the other hand, the members' interests and therefore the trustees' may dictate a closer link between the behaviour of the assets and the liabilities – usually achieved by adopting a more conservative investment strategy. As yet there is still significant debate as to the extent to which the employer is entitled to take into account its own financial considerations in adopting or approving the investment strategy for a scheme.[48]

[11.65] Depending on the exact terms of the scheme documentation, the employer can also be considered as a potential beneficiary of the scheme. The main ways in which this analysis applies are where the employer is an indirect beneficiary (eg benefiting from the reduced costs resulting from improved investment returns), or as a direct ultimate beneficiary – many schemes provide that any residual assets on scheme wind-up are to be refunded to the employer.

---

[46] *Re Skeats' Settlement* (1889) 42 Ch D 522; *Mettoy Pension Trustees Ltd v Evans* [1991] 2 All ER 513. *Mettoy* contains a helpful categorisation of duties and powers by reference to pension schemes.

[47] *National Grid Company plc v Mayes* [2001] UKHL 20 – although in deciding on a distribution of surplus an employer is entitled to take its own interests into account and the power is not fiduciary, the exercise of the power was held to be subject to the *Imperial* duty of good faith.

[48] Contrast the position in the Canadian case of *Lock v Westpac Banking Corporation* (1991) 25 NSWLR 593, [1991] PLR 167 (trustees taking employer considerations into account) with the narrower view regarding trustees as mainly being concerned with looking after the interests of the members *per* Beach J in the Australian case *Asea Brown Boveri* [1999] 1 VR 144. More recently in England *in the case of Alexander Forbes Trustee Service Ltd* v *Halliwell* [2003] EWHC 1685, [2003] PLR 269 Hart J accepted the argument that the trustees are required to consider the interests of the employer.

MEMBERS' RIGHTS TO INFORMATION

Terms of Employment (Information) Act 1994

[11.66] Under s 3 of the Terms of Employment (Information) Act 1994, employers are required to issue employees with a statement of the terms of their employment, including terms and conditions relating to pension schemes. The employer can discharge this duty by referring the employee to the administrative provisions setting out the particular terms, for example a pension scheme booklet. Under s 5(1) employers are required to notify employees of amendments to statements of terms and conditions no later than one month after the change. Accordingly, where amendments are made to terms set out in the written statement issued to employees, the employee must be notified. In practice, the written employment contract will often refer to the pension scheme booklet, material amendments to which must be notified to the employee under the disclosure regulations referred to at para **[11.70]** in any event.

Pensions Act

[11.67] All pension scheme members (actives, deferreds and pensioners) enjoy certain rights to information under the Pensions Act, some of which are automatic and others of which are on request. Third parties such as members' relatives (potential beneficiaries under the scheme) and 'authorised trade union' representatives also enjoy certain rights. An 'authorised trade union' is defined in the Pensions Act as a body to whom a negotiation licence is issued under the Trade Union Act 1941.

[11.68] Disclosure rights are triggered at various stages: eg pre-employment; during service; leaving service; or a member's death.

[11.69] The corollary of the right to information is a duty imposed on pension scheme trustees to provide the information. Employers should bear in mind that notwithstanding that the primary duty to disclose lies on the trustees, the employer is jointly obliged to provide some of this information.

[11.70] The disclosure of information to members and trade unions is governed primarily by the Occupational Pension Scheme (Disclosure of Information) Regulations 2006, particularly Sch C.[49] Members of a pension scheme have an automatic right to be supplied with what is termed 'basic information' within two months of joining the scheme. Prospective members, trade unions, spouses and other beneficiaries have the right to be provided with this information on request, within four weeks of the request. 'Basic information' broadly comprises information on benefits, contribution rates, insured benefits and should provide contact details, often a human resources manager. This information is typically provided in the pension scheme booklet. The trustees must notify members of any material alteration to the 'basic information' within four weeks of the alteration.

---

[49] SI 301/2006.

[11.71] Active Members[50] are automatically entitled to receive to annual benefit statements (which detail current and prospective benefits at Normal Retirement Age, membership data, death-in-service benefits, AVC details, trustee details, and details of whether a pensions adjustment order applies).

[11.72] Where a member leaves service,[51] he is automatically entitled to details of options within two months of leaving. The extent of detail will depend upon whether he has more than two years' service, in which case he will have preserved rights. Having left deferred members continue to be entitled on request to receive details of transfer options and accrued benefits on request, within two months of the request.

[11.73] Other information to which members are entitled to on request:

(i)   the most recent annual report (within four weeks of the request);

(ii)   earlier annual reports and accounts (on payment of a reasonable charge within four weeks of the request);

(iii)   in the case of a defined benefit scheme, the actuarial valuation report (on payment of a reasonable charge within four weeks of the request);

(iv)   trust deed and rules (within four weeks of the request);

(v)   transfer-in options (within two months of the request); and

(vi)   leaving service options (within two months of the request).

Investment choices in defined contribution schemes

[11.74] Where a defined contribution scheme (or the AVC option under a defined benefit scheme) provides that trustees shall invest resources in accordance with member directions, the trustees must take such steps as are reasonable to ensure that the members have 'any further information necessary to enable the members to make informed decision with regard to the giving of direction in relation to the different types of investment available'.[52] While Sch I of the Disclosure of Information Regulations[53] sets out certain information to be provided on request to such members, it is not clear that the provision of that information necessarily meets what is likely (with the application of hindsight) to prove to be a difficult standard for trustees to prove that they have satisfied.

Employees (Provision of Information and Consultation) Act 2006

[11.75] With effect from 23 March 2008, employers with at least 50 employees (determined as an average over the previous year) are required to inform and consult employees on developments affecting employment, particularly on decisions likely to lead to changes. This obligation is triggered by a request of at least 10% of employees (minimum 15). Where the obligation to consult arises, the employee must enter into negotiations with employees to make arrangements for consultation on, for example,

---

[50] See SI 301/2006, Art 13 and Sch D.

[51] See SI 301/2006, Art 14 and Sch E.

[52] Pensions Act 1990, s 59(2)(a)(iv).

[53] SI 301/2006.

pension scheme changes. The effect of this could be to delay implementation of changes to pension arrangements where these provisions are invoked.

Trust law

[11.76] Trust beneficiaries have a proprietary interest in certain aspects of the trust documentation and are entitled to be given access to it by the Trustees.[54]

EQUAL TREATMENT

[11.77] European law has impacted fundamentally on domestic legislation in this area. The principle of equal treatment prohibits unlawful discrimination. Unlawful discrimination does not simply refer to different treatment as between any given groups. It means **less favourable** treatment based on an **identifiable ground** as between **comparable** persons/groups without **objective justification**.

[11.78] Even where a rule is apparently neutral, if it can be shown to make it more difficult for a certain group to gain access to the scheme or accrue benefits, it may give rise to a claim of indirect discrimination. Indirect discrimination can in principle be objectively justified in relation to all identifiable grounds whereas direct discrimination can only be objectively justified in relation to certain identifiable grounds eg age and disability. What is meant by 'less favourable treatment' and 'objective justification' is considered below.

Less favourable treatment

[11.79] In *Barry v Midland Bank Plc*[55] the House of Lords advocated a nuanced approach towards assessing whether treatment was 'less favourable', finding:

> ...it is not sufficient merely to ask whether one gets more or less money than the other. It is necessary to consider whether, taking account of the purpose of the payments, there is a difference in treatment...

In *Barry,* the House of Lords considered a severance payment which was based on a multiple of years of service by final salary. The appellant was a part-timer who had previously worked full-time. She argued that the calculation disregarded her years of full-time service and indirectly discriminated against women, who constituted the majority of the part-time workforce. The House of Lords found that the purpose of the severance payment was to compensate for the immediate loss of salary on being made redundant and to cushion the employee against unemployment and job loss. Its purpose was not to remunerate for past service. There was no discriminatory treatment as between part-time and full-time workers or women and men.

[11.80] The English High Court followed this approach in *The Trustees of Uppingham School Retirement Benefits Scheme for Non-Teaching Staff and the Trustees of Uppingham School v Shillcock*.[56] They rejected the argument that the fact that the

---

[54] *Londonderry's Settlement Re Peat v Walsh* [1964] 3 All ER 855.

[55] *Barry v Midland Bank plc* [1999] WLR 1465.

[56] *The Trustees of Uppingham School Retirement Benefits Scheme for Non-Teaching Staff and the Trustees of Uppingham School v Shillcock* [2002] EWHC 641.

pension scheme rules excluded lower earners, who were for the most part women, was 'less favourable' treatment. The policy underlying the pension scheme structure was to integrate the employer's pension with the State Pension, which lower earners could access by paying voluntary National Insurance Contributions.

[11.81] In *Eircom v Orla McDermott*,[57] the Labour Court rejected a fixed-term employee's argument that membership of the defined contribution scheme constituted less favourable treatment than her permanent comparator's membership of the defined benefit scheme. Having considered actuarial evidence from both sides the Labour Court concluded:

> ...any potential loss of benefit will only crystallise when her employment terminates or she retires, therefore, any contingent detriment can only be measured when benefit becomes payable at retirement. In reaching its conclusion, the Court accepts that it is generally accepted that membership of a defined benefit scheme is more beneficial than membership of a defined contribution scheme...however the level of both employer and employee contributions under eircom's defined contribution scheme is more beneficial than the norm and indeed equals the levels of contributions under eircom's defined benefit scheme....

This case may, at first blush, contradict the popular impression that defined benefit schemes are more beneficial to members than defined contribution schemes. It is nevertheless instructive to note that the Labour Court found that the relevant question was whether in retrospect the treatment would be shown to have been less favourable. On the facts it found that it could not assess this issue with any certainty.

Objective justification

[11.82] An employer can show objective justification by evidencing that in differentiating between one group and another, to the detriment of the other, he had a legitimate aim which he pursued proportionately. Proportionality requires that the impugned rule does not exceed what is reasonably necessary to achieve its objective.

[11.83] The usual approach to objective justification is the step-by-step approach identified in *Bilka Kaufhaus v Karin Weber Von Hertz*,[58] which requires one to show:

(i)   a real need on the part of the undertaking – a 'legitimate aim';

(ii)   that the means chosen correspond to that legitimate aim; and

(iii)   that the measure in issue is appropriate and necessary to achieve the objective.

The courts have also accepted the compendious approach found in subsequent ECJ case law eg *Nolte*,[59] which considers the totality of factors and asks a single question – whether the measure in question was necessary to achieve the social policy aim.

[11.84] Sound and orderly management of public finances and a grading structure which rewards increased responsibility and status have been considered relevant factors in

---

[57] *Eircom v Orla McDermott* FTD 051.

[58] Case C-170/84 *Bilka Kaufhaus v Karin Weber von Hertz* [1986] ECR 1607.

[59] Case C-317/93 *Nolte* [1995] ECR I-4625.

identifying a legitimate objective justifying differential treatment, for example in a case concerning the civil service *28 Named Employees v Courts Service*.[60]

[11.85] In the context of a pension scheme, equal treatment issues can arise in a number of ways, including on foot of applying different eligibility criteria, contribution rates, dependants' benefits and retirement ages.

[11.86] In considering pension scheme design, employers should bear in mind three pieces of Irish legislation governing equal treatment: the Pensions Act (with effect from 18 July 2004), the Protection of Employees (Part-Time Work) Act 2001 (with effect from 20 December 2001) and the Protection of Employees (Fixed-Term Work) Act 2003 (with effect from 14 July 2003).

Pensions Act

[11.87] The Pensions Act sets out nine identifiable grounds on which it is prohibited to discriminate: gender; marriage; family status; sexual orientation; religious belief; age; disability; race; traveller. It includes several savers which permit what would otherwise be unlawful discrimination.

Gender

[11.88] On the gender ground, a saver applies in relation to:

   (i)   levels of employer contributions for the purpose of removing/limiting differences between men and women in defined contribution schemes or ensuring adequate funding in defined benefit schemes;

   (ii)   benefits in defined contribution schemes where it is actuarially justified; and

   (iii) benefits in defined benefit schemes if the difference results from the application of different actuarial factors for funding eg commutation factors, transfer values and early retirement benefits.

[11.89] Historically, in funding for pension schemes the actuarial practice has been to differentiate between men and women in view of the fact that women live longer. In *Neath*[61] the ECJ found that an employer's 'funding arrangements' for a defined benefit scheme (which extend to commutation factors and transfer values) fell outside the scope of EC Treaty, Art 141, the equal pay article. EC Directive 2006/54 expressly exempts funding for defined benefit schemes from the equal treatment rules. To the extent that the Pensions Act saver referred to above deals with an employer's funding arrangements for a funded defined benefit scheme, it is consistent with European case law and legislation.

[11.90] However, the ECJ has not considered or pronounced on defined contribution schemes or unfunded defined benefit schemes. There may be exposure on the European front should such pension schemes be challenged for applying gender-based actuarial factors to commutation factors and/or transfer values.

---

[60] *28 Named Employees v Courts Service* [2007] 18 ELR 212.
[61] Case C-152/91 *Neath*.

Age

[11.91] On the age ground the Pensions Act provides savers for:

(i) fixing age or qualifying service or both as a criterion for admission to a scheme or entitlement to benefits;

(ii) fixing age or qualifying service or both in relation to the accrual of benefits where to do so is objectively justified; and

(iii) actuarial valuations so long as they do not offend the gender ground (see above).

[11.92] Age discrimination covers relative as well as absolute ages and catches so-called 'age gap clauses', eg scheme provisions which provide that lesser benefits will be payable to 'spouses more than 10 years younger than the scheme member'.[62] The facts of *Bartsch* predated the time for transposition of age discrimination provisions into domestic law and so the ECJ did not need to consider the substantive facts. Nevertheless Advocate General Sharpston made comments in passing which may indicate the kind of approach the ECJ would take. On the facts before her, widowers more than 15 years younger than the deceased scheme member were provided with no spouse's pension. Advocate General Sharpston commented that she would have found this provision to be disproportionate, pointing out that the scheme could have provided younger surviving spouses with reduced benefits.

Difference between scheme and contractual retirement ages

[11.93] A saver in EC Directive 2000/78 provides that the fixing of ages for entitlement to benefit under occupational benefit schemes shall not constitute age discrimination, provided it does not discriminate on the gender ground. It is therefore permitted to specify a set normal retirement age in occupational pension schemes

[11.94] In *Palacios de la Villa*,[63] the ECJ made clear that the Member State's competence to impose a mandatory retirement age in an employment contract is subject to an EU yardstick of objective justification. In reaching its conclusion on the facts of *Palacios*, the ECJ considered whether 'reasonable pension provision' had been made before the worker in question was compelled by law to retire. It would seem at odds with this approach to justification if the effect of a pension scheme's Normal Retirement Age were to hinder a member from building up reasonable pension provision.

[11.95] The Employment Equality Act 1998 exempts the setting of a default retirement age in an employment contract from the equal treatment requirement.[64] In *R (on the application of the Incorporated Trustees of the National Council for Ageing (Age Concern England) v Secretary of State for Business, Enterprise and Regulatory*

---

[62] Case C-427/06 *Bartsch*.

[63] Case C-411/05 *Palacios de la Villa v Cortefiel Servicios SA*.

[64] NB – while the equal treatment provisions for contractual rights are set out in the Employment Equality Acts 1998–2008, the equal treatment provisions for pension (and occupational benefit scheme) rights are set out in the Pensions Act 1990, Pt VII.

Reform,[65] the ECJ found that the UK default retirement age of 65 could in principle be justified if (i) it were justified by a legitimate social policy aim and (ii) the means chosen to pursue that aim were appropriate and necessary. In contrast to the Advocate General's approach in this matter, the ECJ places the burden of proof in demonstrating proportionality on the respondent and states that Art 6(1) of Directive 2000/78 imposes on Member States a '... burden of establishing to a high standard of proof the legitimacy of the aim relied on as a justification ...'. In these times of dwindling pension funds and flexible working, it will be interesting to monitor the extent to which the English High Court scrutinises the legitimacy of the social policy underlying a default retirement age of 65.

Marital, family status and sexual orientation

[11.96] The Pensions Act currently provides a saver in relation to death benefits which permits employers to have in place pension schemes rules which provide death benefits for widows but not for same sex or unmarried opposite sex partners.

[11.97] In *Maruko*[66] a same-sex partner was refused entitlement to a widower's pension under his deceased partner's pension scheme. The ECJ noted that Germany had:

> ...altered its legal system to allow persons of the same sex to live in a union of mutual support and assistance which is formally constituted for life. Having chosen not to permit those persons to enter into marriage, which remains reserved solely to persons of different sex, that Member State created for persons of the same sex a separate régime, the life partnership, the conditions of which have been gradually made equivalent to those applicable to marriage....

The ECJ went on to find that although it was for the domestic court to determine whether a surviving 'life partner' was in a comparable situation to a spouse entitled to a survivor's benefit, if he was comparable, legislation which discriminated in respect of survivors' benefits between the two classes was in breach of EC Directive 2000/78.

[11.98] Accordingly, if Ireland were to establish a legislative framework which effectively put civil partners on an analogous footing to married couples, it would be discriminatory under European legislation for pension schemes to treat same-sex partners less favourably in respect of death benefits and other benefits under the scheme provisions. The current Pensions Act saver for death benefits would need to be amended.

[11.99] The heads of the 'Civil Partnership Bill' were published on 24 June 2008, under which same-sex and opposite sex couples may (depending on whether they are eligible) may enter into a civil partnership. If this Bill enters into force as proposed, contingent or survivors' benefits or pensions provided under pension schemes are to be provided for

---

[65] C-388/07 *R (on the application of the Incorporated Trustees of the National Council for Ageing (Age Concern England) v Secretary of State for Business, Enterprise and Regulatory Reform* (5 March 2009).

[66] Case C-267/06 *Maruko*.

registered civil partners. Provision will also be made for pension adjustment orders in respect of dissolved civil partners.

Disability

[11.100] On the disability ground, the Pensions Act provides a saver for a pension scheme rule which provides more favourable benefits in relation to the amount of work done.

[11.101] In *Coleman*[67] the ECJ found that the prohibition on discrimination contained in Directive 2000/78 extends not only to people who are themselves disabled, but also to employees who are carers of disabled people and who are treated less favourably on the basis of the disability of their child. Accordingly, employees who are carers of disabled children who are granted less favourable benefits because of having taken carer's leave may raise a claim under disability discrimination which will require objective justification.

[11.102] Employers should ensure that any pension scheme communications are made readily available to disabled employees, such as deaf and blind employees.

Association

[11.103] Under the Pensions Act, unlawful discrimination can take place by association. For example, if an employee is treated less favourably in the workplace because they are associated with a person of a particular religion, and to treat the religious person that way would be found to be unlawful discrimination, this will be in breach of the equal treatment provision. Given that this legislative protection is already in place, *Coleman* may not add much to the current position under Irish law.

Victimisation

[11.104] An employee who complains to their employer about an alleged breach of the equal treatment rule or assists another employee in the making of such a complaint or intends to do either of these things must not be adversely treated or dismissed on this basis.

Protection of Employees (Part-Time Work) Act 2001

[11.105] Part-time employees are defined as employees whose normal hours of work are less than the normal hours of work of an employee who is a comparable employee, excluding those employees who work less than 20% of the normal hours of the full-time comparator. They enjoy the right to equal treatment in relation to access to and benefits under a pension scheme.

[11.106] A complainant can draw on comparators from an associated employer (in a group pension scheme) or even within the same industry or sector of employment. Benefits payable under a pension scheme can be provided on a pro rata basis. An

---

[67] Case C-303/06 *Coleman*.

employer can seek to objectively justify less favourable treatment of part-time employees on the usual basis, see para **[11.82]** above.

[11.107] It is permissible to treat part-time employees who work on a 'casual basis', ie for less than 13 weeks and such that it cannot be deemed seasonal or regular, in a less favourable manner if it can be objectively justified. A ground which does not constitute objective justification for non casual part-time employees may nonetheless objectively justify less favourable treatment of casual part-time employees.

[11.108] Where part-time employees are concerned, including those who work less than 20% of the full-time comparator's hours, there may arise indirect discrimination if it can be shown that the impugned rule has a disparate impact on one sex.

Protection of Employees (Fixed-Term Work) Act 2003

[11.109] Fixed-term employees are defined as employees with a contract whose end is determined by a specific date or occurrence and excluding those employees who work less than 20% of the hours of the permanent comparator. They enjoy the right to equal treatment in relation to access to and benefits under a pension scheme.

[11.110] A notable difference between the definition of equal treatment under the fixed term legislation and the part-timer legislation is that in establishing whether less favourable treatment in respect of a pension scheme benefit is objectively justified, the fixed-term employee's contract of employment can be viewed as a whole, ie pension benefits do not have to be considered in isolation. So if an employer excluded fixed-term workers from access to the pension scheme but provided an overall employment package which, when taken in the round, was no less favourable than that provided to other employees, he could show objective justification.

[11.111] The Labour Court has found that an employer's failure to offer fixed-term employees access to their pension scheme (where those employees can identify permanent comparators) will constitute less favourable treatment which must be objectively justified. This was not withstanding that the employer offered the fixed-term employees access to a PRSA.[68]

Agency workers

[11.112] The Directive on Temporary Agency Workers,[69] agreed by Member States on 10 June 2008, provides for equal treatment in terms of pay, with the possibility of derogation through collective agreements. Member States have until 5 December 2011 to implement the Directive.

---

[68] *Irish Rail v Malcom Stead* FTD 052. In *Irish Rail* the Labour Court noted that the employer had not put forward an objective justification for the exclusion of fixed-term workers from the pension scheme.

[69] 2008/104/EC.

Gender reassigned persons

[11.113] It is in breach of the European Convention on Human Rights (ECHR) to treat gender reassigned persons any less favourably. The High Court has found that Irish legislation is incompatible with ECHR law for failing to recognise a transsexual in her new gender, see *Foy v An t-Ard Chláráitheoir & Ors*.[70] The ECJ has found less favourable treatment of transsexuals in relation to employment and pensions to breach equal treatment legislation.[71] There is as yet no Irish legislation under which a person can obtain recognition of their new gender for all purposes, although under the Passports Act 2008 a gender-reassigned person may apply for their passport to be reissued.

Remedies

[11.114] An employee who alleges discrimination or victimisation under the Pensions Act is entitled to bring a complaint to the Equality Tribunal while in employment or within six months of termination of employment.

[11.115] If successful, the Tribunal may order that the employee receives the favourable treatment from the date of breach. If this is in relation to wrongly denied access to a contributory pension scheme, the employer is entitled to require the employee to pay backdated contributions. In *Fisscher*[72] the ECJ found that the fact that a worker could claim retroactively to join a pension scheme should not mean that that they did not have to pay contributions relating to the period of membership concerned. The Tribunal may also order the employer to implement the equal treatment for the future. Where the Tribunal finds victimisation to have occurred, it may order compensation for the successful complainant.

EMPLOYEE ABSENCES

[11.116] The governing trust deed and rules for a pension scheme will often include a provision on temporary absence. The main issues arising are: preservation requirements, Revenue rules and (with particular regard to defined benefit schemes) continuity of service.

[11.117] The Revenue permits scheme members who are temporarily absent or seconded and remain resident in Ireland to remain in full membership of an approved scheme, even where no remuneration is paid, on the condition that there is a definite expectation that the member will return to service and the member does not join another approved pension scheme (other than in respect of concurrent employment). No such conditions apply where the scheme member does not continue to accrue benefits throughout the period of absence, where the benefit of being a member flows from

---

[70] *Foy v An t-Ard Chláráitheoir & Ors* [2007] IEHC 470 (on appeal to the Supreme Court at the time of writing).

[71] Case C-13/94 *P v S*; Case C-117/01 *KB*; Case C-423/04 *Richards v Secretary of State for Work and Pensions*.

[72] Case C-128/93 *Fisscher* [1994] ECR I-4583.

aggregation of two periods of service or where the member is only covered for life assurance.

Maternity leave

EU Law

[11.118] EU law does not require employees on maternity leave to be paid as they would be were they at work. Directive 92/85/EEC (the Pregnant Workers Directive) requires that employees on maternity leave are paid an 'adequate allowance' in accordance with national legislation. However it does require that other 'rights connected to the employment contract' are ensured for employees on maternity leave. The ECJ has expressed the view that the accrual of pension rights in an employer's pension scheme must be maintained during the period of maternity leave of at least 14 weeks to which workers are entitled.[73]

Maternity Protection Act 1994

[11.119] The Pregnant Workers Directive was transposed into Irish legislation by the Maternity Protection Act 1994 (as amended) (the 1994 Act), s 22 of which which requires that:

   (i)   the period of absence due to 'maternity leave' shall not affect any right (other than remuneration) whether conferred by statute, contract or otherwise and related to the employee's employment; and

   (ii) the period of absence due to 'additional maternity leave' shall not affect any right or obligation (other than remuneration or superannuation benefits or any obligation to pay contributions in or in respect of the employment during such absence), whether conferred by statute, contract or otherwise and related to the employee's employment.

[11.120] 'Maternity leave' refers to the statutory period of leave to which the pregnant employee is entitled (26 weeks at the time of writing). Thereafter the pregnant employee is statutorily entitled to a further period of 'additional maternity leave' (16 weeks at the time of writing).

Pensions Act

[11.121] The Pensions Act requires members who are absent from work due to pregnancy or childbirth and being paid remuneration by their employer to be treated equally throughout that period in respect of continued scheme membership, the accrual of rights and the amount of benefits relating to that period. The Pensions Act specifically obliges employers to take such measures as are necessary to ensure that such a member is treated no less favourably in this regard.

Consequences for defined benefit schemes

[11.122] Taking account of the above the position for defined benefit schemes is that:

---

[73] Case C-411/96 *Boyle & Ors v Equal Opportunities Commission* [1998] ECR I-6401.

(i) paid maternity leave and paid additional maternity leave count as pensionable service;

(ii) the position with regard to unpaid maternity leave is uncertain[74] but is probably best treated as pensionable service, particularly where the employee returns to work;

(iii) unpaid additional maternity leave need not be treated as pensionable service.

These rights are of course subject to the provisions of the scheme rules, which may provide greater benefits.

Consequences for defined contribution schemes and death benefit arrangements

[11.123] The position for defined contribution schemes appears at first sight to be less complicated. Paid maternity leave counts as pensionable service and contributions are payable by reference to the remuneration received. Death benefits are likely to be insured by reference to the last notified salary, which is likely to be greater than or equal to the maternity pay and therefore the insurance proceeds will equal or exceed the death benefit payable.

[11.124] The most straightforward analysis in respect of all unpaid maternity leave is that contributions are payable at a nil rate and the death benefits are nil (as the salary both these benefits are based on is zero). The position appears to be clear in relation to unpaid additional maternity leave as there is no statutory obligation to maintain superannuation benefits throughout this period. The position is less clear in relation to unpaid maternity leave bearing in mind on the one hand the finding in *Boyle* (see para **[11.118]**) and on the other hand the fact that paid salary is a fundamental reference point for defined contribution schemes and death benefits and the practical difficulties which arise. There is no judicial pronouncement on this point to date. As with defined benefit schemes, these minimum statutory rights are subject to the provision of more generous pension scheme rules.

Adoptive leave

[11.125] Employees may be entitled to adoptive leave and additional adoptive leave under the Adoptive Leave Acts 1995 and 2005, 24 weeks and 16 weeks respectively at the time of writing. Adoptive leave does not affect any rights related to employment other than the right to remuneration. Additional adoptive leave does not affect any right or obligation relating to employment other than the right to remuneration or superannuation benefits or obligations to pay contributions in or in respect of employment.

---

[74] On the one hand the ECJ clearly envisages pension rights continuing – on the other hand the remuneration (which is generally a factor in valuing benefits) during the period in question is zero.

[11.126] Employees enjoy statutory protection in respect of their pension rights throughout the initial period of adoptive leave, however continued accrual of pension benefits throughout additional adoptive leave will depend on the pension scheme rules.

Carer's leave and parental leave

[11.127] Both the Carer's Leave Act 2001 and the Parental Leave Acts 1998 and 2006 exclude superannuation benefits and obligations to pay contributions to or in respect of employment from those employment rights and obligations which are protected throughout the period of leave. However the employee is to be regarded as working for all other purposes. Once more, the continued accrual of pension benefits will depend on the scheme rules.

Pensions Act

[11.128] Under s 81B of the Pensions Act, where an employee is absent from work for family reasons and continues to be paid throughout that period his pension rights must not be adversely affected by the absence. The scheme trustees (or where appropriate the employer) is under a positive duty to take measures to ensure equal treatment in this regard.

[11.129] If an employer chooses to continue to pay employees who have taken leave under the Carer's Leave Act or the Parental Leave Act he may be obliged to honour pension commitments in respect of such employees if their leave can be said to have been taken 'for family reasons'.

DIVORCE AND SEPARATION PENSIONS ADJUSTMENT ORDERS

[11.130] Under the Family Law Act 1995 and the Family Law (Divorce) Act 1996, benefits arising out of membership of a pension scheme (pension and death benefits) are assets which are factored into settlements between spouses on judicial separation/divorce.

[11.131] The non-member spouse may wish to agree to a non pension asset such as savings or property and leave the member spouse's pension benefits intact. Alternatively he may seek a 'pensions adjustment order', by which a designated benefit is payable when the member spouse dies or retires. This order is binding on the trustees of a pension scheme and overrides the pension scheme trust deed and rules.

[11.132] A spouse who has remarried is not permitted to apply for a pensions adjustment order. Pension adjustment orders cannot be granted in relation to consensual separation agreements (as opposed to judicial separation orders).

[11.133] If a non-member spouse wishes for a clean break in relation to pension benefits, he may apply to have the pension benefits 'split' at the time of the judicial separation/divorce. The potential disadvantage of this course of action would be in relation to a defined benefit scheme, since the amount of benefit will be fixed by reference to the member spouse's current salary and so the non-member spouse risks losing out on the benefit of the member's future salary increases.

PUBLIC SECTOR PENSIONS

Introduction

[11.134] Public sector pensions fall into two main types – those which are funded and those which are not. Generally speaking, funded public sector pension arrangements operate in essentially the same way as private sector funded pension schemes and many of the comments elsewhere in this chapter apply. This section deals with some of the peculiarities that apply solely to public sector pension schemes whether funded or unfunded and the more common issues which arise in connection with unfunded arrangements.

Power to establish scheme

[11.135] The power of almost all state and semi-state entities to establish a pension scheme (or 'superannuation arrangement') is expressly provided for in the governing legislation for the entity in question. It is important to refer to this legislation as it may contain specific restrictions or requirements. Such requirements will typically include:

(i) where a new body is established which will take a transfer of staff from an existing body, a provision requiring that terms and conditions relating to superannuation arrangements for transferring staff should be no less favourable than those prior to transfer;

(ii) provision that new arrangements may be established subject to the consent of the relevant Minister and the Minister for Finance (so as to control costs at the new entity); and

(iii) provision that arrangements may not be amended without the consent of the relevant Minister and the Minister for Finance (so as to control the costs associated with any change to benefits).

[11.136] In addition to the above provisions there may be specific provisions relating to the rate of contribution to the arrangements or relating to the establishment of pension arrangements for the chief executive (amongst other common provisions).

Operating on an 'administrative' basis

[11.137] In practice the requirement to obtain two Ministerial consents can lead to significant delays in obtaining formal approval to establish schemes but employees' pension rights require to be provided. In order to manage this difficulty the practice of operating on an 'administrative basis' has arisen. This involves obtaining consent in principle from the relevant Government Department to the new arrangements on the premise that Ministerial consent will follow in due course. This process relies on the fact that the new arrangements replicate the existing arrangements either entirely or substantively and are therefore not controversial (not least because the existing arrangements themselves will usually be the model scheme terms used for the public sector). Where changes are proposed to the standard terms it may be difficult to obtain consent for those terms.

Usual features of public sector superannuation arrangements

[11.138] Unfunded public sector pension arrangements almost always have the same benefit structure known as the 'model scheme'. Some of the basic features of these schemes are:

(i)   a normal retirement age of 65 (although for new entrants from 1 April 2004 this is a minimum retirement age rather than a compulsory one);[75]

(ii)   contributions of 3.5% of pensionable remuneration less twice the State social welfare contributory pension plus 1.5% of full pensionable remuneration;

(iii)   a defined benefit pension promise based on 1/80th of pensionable remuneration which is integrated (or 'co-ordinated' – ie twice the State social welfare pension is deducted) (sometimes called 'superannuation allowance');

(iv)   a compulsory tax free lump sum of 3/80ths of pensionable earnings ('gratuity');

(v)   a death gratuity of the deceased's pensionable remuneration or if greater the ill-health gratuity that would have been payable on ill-health grounds had death not occurred;

(vi)   the 'pay parity' system of guaranteed pension increases which links pension increases to the increases in salaries of current employees. This system, introduced in 1986, is significantly more generous than the nearest equivalent in the private sector;

(vii)   alternative pension benefits (of 1/200th of full as opposed to co-ordinated pensionable remuneration) for full Class A PRSI contributors to the extent that pensionable remuneration is less than 3 and 1/3rd times the State pension; and

(viii)   separate spouse's and children's schemes with contribution rates of 1.5% of full pensionable remuneration for established civil servants (the contribution is based on coordinated remuneration for non-established civil servants) providing a pension of 50% of the member's actual pension in retirement or 50% of the prospective pension in the event of death in service.

[11.139] As with private sector schemes not all public sector arrangements are the same. Although some of the differences are touched on in the list of common features above, a full exposition is beyond the scope of this text.[76] It is also important to bear in mind that some but by no means all such schemes are exempted from the funding and preservation requirement of the Pensions Act. Similarly some are exempted from the provisions of the Public Service Superannuation (Miscellaneous Provisions) Act 2004 for technical reasons.

[11.140] Further complications can arise in dealing with funded semi-state schemes which are similar to but not exactly the same as the public sector model. These often have a trust deed which governs the funds but regulations prescribed by statutory instrument which describe the benefits. Delays in production of the statutory

---

[75] Public Service Superannuation (Miscellaneous Provisions) Act 2004.

[76] For a more detailed examination see Finucane & Buggy with Tighe, *Irish Pension Law and Practice* (2nd edn, 2006) Ch 8.

instruments may mean that the governing documents do not accurately describe the scheme.

[11.141] Disputes are often dealt with by means of referral to the relevant Minister as part of the Internal Dispute Resolution Procedure (IDRP) (see para **[11.142]** for more on disputes). This system often results in delay in breach of prescribed timescales. Following criticism from the Pensions Ombudsman it appears that there may be a policy shift to a more practical approach to dispute resolution in public sector schemes.

DISPUTE RESOLUTION AND THE PENSIONS OMBUDSMAN

[11.142] Under the Pensions Act all pension schemes are required to have in place an internal dispute resolution procedure by way of which scheme members can raise complaints. The obligation to establish this procedure rests on the pension scheme trustees. Where the member exhausts this procedure and wishes to take the matter further, he can take the complaint to the Pensions Ombudsman.

[11.143] The complaint should relate to an act done by or on behalf of a 'person responsible for the management of the scheme', which includes employers.

[11.144] The Ombudsman has jurisdiction over disputes of fact and law relating to pension schemes[77] and over maladministration which causes financial loss. His jurisdiction is generally restricted to matters where the claim is made within six years of the act concerned and generally within three years of when the member became or ought to have become aware of the act.[78] Generally the Pensions Ombudsman will not investigate until a pension scheme's IDRP[79] has been exhausted. He may not investigate where proceedings have been initiated.

[11.145] Where an employer is named as a respondent to a complaint to the Pensions Ombudsman, he should bear in mind that a written response is due within 21 days of receipt of the complaint. It should include a full response to the allegations, details of the matters on which the respondent relies and a statement as to whether any other party has a direct interest in the complaint. The employer can request further particulars/clarification of the complaint, in which case the time-frame for response can be extended to 14 days after receipt of the further particulars/clarification.

TAXATION OF PENSIONS

[11.146] The vast majority of pension arrangements benefit from favourable tax treatment. There are three main different types of arrangement benefiting from

---

[77] Complaints in relation to personal pensions and related products (eg ARFs) are more properly the remit of the Financial Services Ombudsman with whom the Pensions Ombudsman has a memorandum of understanding as to the responsibility for dealing with complaints. The Ombudsman also does not have any jurisdiction over social welfare pensions.

[78] Pensions Act 1990, s 131.

[79] The details for IDRPs are prescribed in the Pensions Ombudsman Regulations 2003 (SI 397/2003), Art 5.

preferential tax treatment in the accumulation of pension benefit. These are: tax approved occupational pension schemes (including pay-as-you-go unfunded public sector pension schemes); retirement annuity contracts and PRSAs. The payment of benefits out of these arrangements following retirement or death also receives preferential tax treatment.

[11.147] Since 1999, there has been a tax preferential alternative to annuity purchase to provide post-retirement benefit – the ARF and its corollary the AMRF. These are vehicles for managing the draw-down of pension funds in retirement (as opposed to pension schemes which are vehicles for the accumulation of those pension funds during employment).

[11.148] Pension arrangements which do not benefit from preferential tax treatment are possible but rare in practice. They are often called 'unapproved' arrangements and arise because either the benefits either exceed the Revenue limits on tax approved pension arrangements or are of a different type to those the Revenue allows to be paid from approved arrangements. The most common unapproved arrangements are top-up schemes for senior executives which provide benefits in excess of those permitted under approved arrangements. Another example would be an *ex-gratia* pension paid directly from company revenue to a relative of an employee or a person who is not an employee (and who cannot therefore receive an approved pension as they do not have any earnings in respect of which contributions and benefits can be paid).

Relevant provisions

[11.149] The tax treatment of pension arrangements, the limits on contributions and benefits and treatment of investment returns on invested funds, are set out in Part 30 of the Taxes Consolidation Act 1997. While these provisions outline the basic structure of the tax regime they are supplemented in the case of occupational pension schemes by discretionary rules published by the Revenue from time to time known as the Revenue Pensions Manual. This Manual deals with the detail of permissible practices regarding contributions and benefits for 'exempt approved' schemes. A detailed discussion of Revenue limits and the content of the Manual is beyond the scope of this text. Some of the basic provisions are summarised below. Further detail is contained in the Manual itself and also in other practitioners' texts.[80]

Benefit limits

[11.150] Revenue limits are complex and individual calculations are best carried out by experienced pensions administrators. The basic structure of tax approved pension schemes is that a member of such a scheme can accrue a pension amount (in per annum terms and payable at normal retirement age) of 1/60th of 'final remuneration'[81] for each

---

[80] See the 2007 Revenue Pensions Manual available at www.revenue.ie; Finucane & Buggy with Tighe, *Irish Pensions Law & Practice* (2nd edn, 2006 Thomson Round Hall); Dolan, Murray & Reynolds, *Pensions: Revenue Law and Practice* (9th edn, 2007).

[81] This is a specifically defined term – see the Revenue Pensions Manual and the Taxes Consolidation Act 1997, s 770.

year of service as a member of a scheme. At the point of retirement if the rules of the scheme allow, part of this pension amount can currently be converted ('commuted') into a tax free lump sum of up to 3/80ths of final remuneration for each year of service as a member of the scheme.

[11.151] This structure is designed so that after 40 years' service (from age 25 to at age 65) the maximum pension is 40/60ths (or 2/3rds) of final remuneration. The 1/60th accrual tax regime is equivalent to the public sector 1/80th of pensionable salary accrual rate and compulsory lump sum (also known as a 'gratuity') of 3/80ths of pensionable salary for each year of pensionable service.[82]

[11.152] When looking at a particular individual's case complicating factors may include:

(i)   the inclusion of benefits attributable to additional voluntary contributions;

(ii)   faster rates of accrual (ie more generous fractions such as 1/50ths) which result in attainment of a maximum 2/3rds benefit after less than 40 years' service;

(iii) benefits from other schemes (which must be taken into account if the benefit for each year of service is more generous than 1/60th);

(iv)   part-time status;

(v)   the effect of early retirement;

(vi)   whether the member is a shareholder (ie proprietary) director;

(vii) ill-health;

(viii) periods of absence/reduced earnings such as carer's and maternity leave;

(ix)   reductions in earnings or fluctuating emoluments such as bonuses meaning that indexed earnings from previous years may be relevant; and

(x)   variations due to particular rules of the scheme.

[11.153] Detailed rules on how these various factors must be taken into account in calculating Revenue limits are contained in the Revenue Pensions Manual. In many cases the Revenue limits are in excess of scheme benefits and need not be considered. They will fall to be considered where augmentations to benefits are proposed, for example on severance or early retirement.

[11.154] The benefit limits outlined above apply to both defined contribution and defined benefit schemes. The structure of the limits coincides with the design of most defined benefit schemes but does not tally with the design of defined contribution schemes. In practice this is rarely an issue as the level of contribution to most defined contribution schemes means that the benefits which the scheme generates are unlikely to breach the Revenue limits.

[11.155] There are three main exceptions where it is important to obtain advice as to whether benefit limits are likely to be breached in a defined contribution scheme. These

---

[82]   The equivalence is based on the fact that the Revenue approved conversion rate from pension to cash is 9 to 1. Using that conversion rate 1/60th accrual without a lump sum converts to 1/80 once 3/80ths has been converted to cash.

are: where substantial contributions are being made to a defined contribution scheme on severance, redundancy or as part of a settlement; where a member has throughout her working life made maximum AVC contributions; and, where a senior executive or owner/director is involved who has ensured significant employer/employee contributions to maintain scheme funding close to Revenue limit maxima.

Contribution limits

[11.156] There are limits on the maximum amount an employer and an employee can pay to a pension scheme and claim tax relief for.

[11.157] The limits are complicated but the basic principle is that the employer can pay ordinary contributions which are required to fund the benefits in accordance with actuarial advice. A special contribution is permitted which does not exceed the normal ordinary annual contribution. If contributions are required in excess of such a special contribution, such excess contributions will not receive tax relief in the year in which they are made (but it may be possible to claim tax relief in future years).

[11.158] There are two sets of limits on the maximum amount of member contributions: the first governs the contributions (including AVCs) which can count for tax relief. These limits are set out in s 774 Taxes Consolidation Act 1997. The second limit is an overall maximum limit on tax relieved pension funds. This limit is unlikely to be relevant except for high earners and senior executives as the maximum tax-relieved fund was set at €5,000,000 in 2006 and is indexed thereafter in line with an earnings factor.[83]

Taxation on payment of pensions

[11.159] In general, pension funds must be received in the form of a pension (ie an annual amount received usually in a series of monthly payments). This is taxed in the same way as an employee's salary and the tax is usually deducted under the PAYE system as is PRSI.

[11.160] At the point of retirement there are several options which an employee can choose regarding the application of his benefits. Whether all of these options are available will depend on the terms of the pension scheme's governing documentation. The basic options are:

(i)   to surrender some of the pension and receive in its place a lump sum which is currently free of tax – the amount of the lump sum is subject to a Revenue limit which depends on the employee's final remuneration and length of service (this option is very common);

(ii)   to surrender some of the pension in exchange for an increase in benefits for a spouse or dependant in the event of the pensioner's death (this option is often available in larger defined benefit schemes).

---

[83]   Taxes Consolidation Act 1997, Ch 2C of Pt 30 and Sch 23B. Allowing for the current conversion factor of 20 to 1 applicable for these purposes this becomes an issue for persons entitled to an annual pension in excess of €250,000.

Approved Retirement Funds (ARFs) and AMRFs

[11.161] In place of receiving a pension an employee may transfer the proceeds of a PRSA or AVCs[84] to an ARF. At present, main scheme benefits may not generally be transferred to an ARF. An ARF is an investment vehicle which is used to manage the pension fund and from which an income can be drawn down by the individual. It is essentially a savings account. The risk for the individual is that the money in the ARF account is exhausted before death leaving the individual with limited resources in retirement. In theory the individual will still receive some form of regular income as it is a requirement before using an ARF that either:

   (i)   the employee has a separate guaranteed annual income in retirement of €12,700; or

   (ii)   the first €75,000 of his pension fund must be used to secure an AMRF – this is a vehicle which has restricted drawdown facilities, the proceeds of which must be used to provide a pension annuity at age 75 if not before. The theory is that the restrictions on an AMRF mean that a person cannot overspend their entire pension fund and run out of money.

[11.162] In the event of death the proceeds of an ARF can be passed on through testamentary dispositions (unlike any residual funds in an annuity, which revert to the insurance company to the extent that they are not used to fund death benefits).

[11.163] To avoid ARFs being used as wealth transfer vehicles, tax legislation deems that 3% of the ARF funds have been paid out in each year and that tax must be paid on this deemed distribution (to the extent that tax has not already been paid on actual distributions).[85] This assumes that a person with an ARF will live for 33 years' post retirement, which is at present relatively conservative given the current actuarial data.

No mixed benefits

[11.164] In general, all pension funds relating to a given employment must be treated in the same way at the same time. So where a transfer is being made of a main scheme benefit any additional voluntary contributions in an accompanying scheme must be transferred at the same time. Similarly if a refund of member contributions on leaving service is being paid to a member with less than two years' service, Revenue would not allow AVCs in respect of that employment to be transferred to another scheme.

Retirement and consultancy arrangements

[11.165] The retirement which results in pension payment must be genuine. It is permitted to progress to retirement by means of a consultancy arrangement provided that the consultancy represents a genuine change in status. Revenue does not permit a

---

[84] However a proprietary director who has within three years of the date of retirement controlled more than 5% of the voting rights of a company may transfer his entire proceeds to an ARF/AMRF. See Taxes Consolidation Act 1997, s 770 for the precise terms of this definition.

[85] Taxes Consolidation Act 1997, s 784A.

retirement on pension to be accompanied by a re-engagement on consultancy terms which result in the provision of identical (or near identical) services and performance.

CONSIDERATIONS IN COMMERCIAL TRANSACTIONS

Introduction

[11.166] In the lifetime of an employer, it is likely that it will acquire employees from another employer or it will take over, merge with or be taken over by another employer. In any of these events the employer will be faced with dealing with more than one pension scheme. Unlike most aspects of employment law, pension schemes can be a complication on a share sale just as much as on a TUPE business transfer. This is because group pension schemes often have more than one participating employer. The result is that although a company is being sold, the group pension scheme does not necessarily transfer with the company being sold. Negotiations are therefore required to determine what replacement pension arrangements will apply.

[11.167] Conversely, on a TUPE transfer it is not always the case that a transfer out of the previous company's pension arrangement is necessary. It may be that for structural reasons the part of the business being sold has a stand-alone pension scheme which is transferred to the purchaser along with the employees – resulting in a relatively straightforward pension situation with no change in provision.

[11.168] It can be seen therefore that the main consideration in a sale and purchase of a business or company is:

  (i) is there to be a transfer of pension rights from a company or group pension scheme; or

  (ii) is there a stand-alone scheme to be transferred with the employees/company affected by the transaction?

Stand-alone scheme

Stand-alone scheme transfers to purchaser

[11.169] Where there is a stand-alone scheme which is being acquired (as a result of either a share or asset transfer), the main pension consideration will revolve around the due diligence exercise in relation to the scheme and its past administration. The main pension provisions in the agreement will concern warranties in relation to the pension scheme and indemnities or price adjustments in relation to any specific issues arising from the due diligence exercise. The employees will be largely unaffected as they will remain in the scheme. However, it may be necessary to negotiate a 'pensions schedule' to the agreement to deal with the transfer back to the seller of any employees who participate in the scheme but who are to remain with the seller.

Scheme remains with seller

[11.170] Where the pension scheme is to remain with the seller, the due diligence exercise will be primarily focused on identifying the current entitlements of the affected employees in order to determine the nature (and value) of replacement arrangements required to be put in place.

[11.171] In the case of a share sale, the extent to which the purchaser may be required to provide a replacement arrangement will depend on the extent to which the pension promise forms part of the employment contract and/or collective agreements and/or because of the industrial relations issues which would otherwise arise.

[11.172] In the case of an asset sale/TUPE transfer, the purchaser is not required to replace occupational pension schemes unless there is a contractual agreement to the contrary in the sale agreement.[86] There is no contractual protection for the employees as they will be engaged by the purchasing entity on new contracts. However, it is important to note that PRSAs are not occupational pension schemes and obligations in relation to PRSAs do pass to the purchaser including any contractual employer contribution obligations. Similarly life insurance obligations which are contractual under the employment contract (as opposed to being provided under the terms of an occupational pension scheme) also pass to the purchaser.

[11.173] Obligations under other arrangements which are not occupational pension schemes do pass to the purchaser. These include:

(i)   contractual arrangements for early retirement or redundancy enhancements to pension benefits;[87]

(ii)   life assurance benefits not established as an occupational pension scheme;

(iii) contractual obligations to contribute to a personal retirement savings account (PRSAs are contractual arrangements between the employee and the PRSA provider and as such are neither occupational pension schemes nor 'supplementary schemes' for the purposes of the TUPE regulations); and

(iv)   other insured arrangements such as PHI.

Typical pension provisions in sale and purchase agreement

[11.174] A sale and purchase agreement for a commercial transaction will almost always contain pension warranties. The other pension provisions which will be present if necessary depending on the circumstances are pensions indemnities and a pensions schedule. These provisions will always be tailored to the specific circumstances of the transaction and unusual transactions (such as reversible outsourcings, IPOs, etc) may require particular wording beyond the scope of this text. The aim of this section is to provide an introduction to the basic issues and provisions applicable to some illustrative situations.

---

[86] EC (Protection of Employees on Transfer of Undertakings) Regulations 2003 (SI 131/2003), Art 4(3). NB: This is different to the corresponding position in the UK where a degree of replacement benefit may be required if the transferee's pension arrangements do not meet certain minimum standards of benefit or contribution.

[87] By virtue of the ECJ decisions in Case C-164/00 *Beckmann v Dynamco Whicheloe MacFarlane* [2002] ECR I-4873, [2002] All ER 865 and Case C-4/01 *Martin v South Bank University* [2003] PLR 329.

Pension warranties

[11.175] Although there are frequently a large number of pension warranties in standard sale and purchase precedents many of these are relevant solely to the transfer of a funded defined benefit occupational pension scheme. As these arrangements are decreasing in number so the majority of the often extensive standard warranties are in many cases inapplicable.

[11.176] Asset sale – no transfer of scheme: As there are no past service pension liabilities transferred by the sale and there is no obligation to provide pensions for future service under TUPE there is arguably no need for any pension warranties on an asset sale where no scheme transfers.[88] In practice the following minimal warranties are reasonable in order to give the purchaser comfort that they understand the pension position prior to acquisition and, if there is to be a bulk transfer of the past service rights, that they have sufficient detail to ensure that the transfer is correct:

   (i)   that the pension scheme(s) disclosed are the sole pension arrangements;

   (ii)   that all material details of the applicable arrangements have been disclosed;

   (iii) that all death in service and risk benefits are fully insured; and

   (iv) that there are no disputes or claims.

The remainder of most standard sets of warranties concern issues which give rise to liability for the previous employer. As that entity is not being acquired in an asset sale, that information, while no doubt interesting to a purchaser, is not strictly relevant to the transaction.

[11.177] Share/asset sale – scheme transfers: In this case more extensive warranties are appropriate to identify the pension liabilities which exist either in the company or in the Scheme or both. Typical additional warranties will include:

   (i)   that there are no equal treatment issues (including in relation to part-timers and fixed term workers);

   (ii)   that all contributions have been paid when due;

   (iii) that the terms of the Scheme and all pension legislation has been complied with;

   (iv) that up-to-date member details including as to member contribution rates have been disclosed;

   (v)   that all members have been admitted to a scheme when first eligible; and

   (vi) that in the case of a defined contribution pension scheme it has not been converted from or preceded by a defined benefit pension scheme.

---

[88] It is often argued that the purchaser has an obligation under TUPE to ensure that the past service rights of transferees are protected but in practice this is a statutory requirement as a result of the preservation requirements under the Pensions Act 1990.

[11.178] The rationale for all these additional warranties is that a breach of any of them would result in an additional and almost certainly unfunded liability which a purchaser may be obliged to meet.

Funding warranties

[11.179] A funding warranty is often sought by a purchaser where a defined benefit scheme is involved. Such warranties should be avoided by a seller where possible as they can be very difficult to control even if they can be drafted meaningfully (which can be challenging in itself). The difficulties with such warranties include:

   (i)   setting a date by which to calculate the pension liabilities and to fix a value for the assets;

  (ii)   the basis for the calculation: pension scheme liabilities (and assets) can be valued on a number of actuarial and accounting bases, each of which will produce a different measure of funding; and

 (iii)   whatever date is chosen and whatever basis, it is inevitably the case that the funding position as at that date will be historic by the time the deal is done.

The reality is that an underfunded scheme will result in additional future contribution costs for the purchaser but that is a matter usually better addressed (in terms of certainty) for both the purchaser and the seller in a price adjustment than by means of a funding warranty.

[11.180] Having said that, it may be a requirement for a multi-national purchaser to achieve a degree of certainty over the international/group accounting consequences of the transaction. In these circumstances, the agreement may contain drafting which refers to the state of funding of the relevant scheme on an accounting basis. Such drafting will then provide for the consequences in the event that at completion the scheme is over/under-funded by reference to this standard. It is important to note that this is simply an accounting position and does not necessarily result in the same over/under-funding position when considering the scheme as an ongoing entity. This may present difficulties for the trustees in making payments at the level envisaged in the commercial agreement. It is always prudent to ensure that the scheme's actuarial advisers are aware of and have commented on significant transfer payments.

Pensions schedule

[11.181] A pensions schedule is used where there is either a transfer of past service rights being made between defined benefit schemes and/or there is to be an interim period of participation in a seller's scheme (defined benefit or defined contribution) by a purchaser pending the establishment of a replacement arrangement by the purchaser.

[11.182] Typically a pensions schedule will contain provisions which deal with the following matters:

   (i)   definitions;

  (ii)   terms relating to the interim period of participation by the purchaser in the seller's scheme (eg the rate of contributions to be paid by the purchaser);

    (iii)   details of how a transfer payment in respect of past service rights is to be calculated;

    (iv)   details of how and when the transfer payment is to be made;

    (v)   provisions dealing with any additional voluntary contributions; and

    (vi)   details of how any disputes over the transfer payments are to be resolved.

SOME CONSIDERATIONS WHEN AMENDING, REORGANISING AND TERMINATING PENSION SCHEMES

Scheme amendment

[11.183] Almost all pension schemes have an express amendment power.[89] Such a power must be exercised in accordance with its terms, which are often very widely drawn and may permit amendment without member consent, without notice and even retrospective amendment.

[11.184] The extent to which the scope of a pensions trust amendment power is constrained by the terms of the employment contract has yet to be tested in the courts but the pensions industry currently operates on the basis of a number of working assumptions as follows:

    (i)   the amendment power is likely to be constrained by the presence of unqualified benefit promises in the employment contract that do not refer to the scheme terms, the booklet or the amendment power;

    (ii)   retrospective amendments may be possible but are exposed to challenge particularly if they act to reduce benefits and are implemented without consent or consultation; and

    (iii)   entitlements which have crystallised (eg preserved benefits on leaving service or pensions in payment) may not be reduced without member consent except where permitted or required by statute.[90]

In any event as a general principle a pension in payment cannot be reduced below the amount payable in the previous year.[91]

[11.185] Case law has provided guidance in this area and confirmed unsurprisingly that scheme amendments which are implemented to give effect to a 'collateral purpose' are not a valid exercise of the power and will be held to have been made in breach of the *Imperial* duty of good faith.[92]

---

[89]   Where there is no amendment power any trust provisions can only be amended in accordance with the Variation of Trusts Act 1958 or with the agreement of all the members (and contingent beneficiaries) under the principle in *Saunders v Vautier* (1841) 4 Beav 115.

[90]   Either under the Pensions Act 1990, s 50 where the Pensions Board orders a reduction in benefit or under the Pensions Act 1990, s 48 where benefits may be abated where there are insufficient assets to meet all the liabilities in a particular category under the priority of benefit categories applicable to schemes being wound-up.

[91]   Pension Act 1990, s 59B(1).

[92]   *Imperial Group Pension Trust Ltd v Imperial Tobacco Ltd* [1991] 2 All ER 597.

[11.186] Where a benefit reduction (or employee contribution increase) is proposed in general the following steps are advisable to minimise the risk of successful challenge from an aggrieved member:

(i)   audit the employment contracts to identify any express promises which would operate to restrict the amendment power or confer contractual promises outside the scope of the pension scheme;

(ii)   endeavour to ensure that the amendment is made prospectively rather than retrospectively;

(iii)   if practicable consider seeking written member consents to the amendment;

(v)   if consent is not possible, ensure that meaningful consultation with the members has been conducted in accordance with any procedures in place under collective agreements and/or arrangements made under the Employees (Provision of Information and Consultation) Act 2006;

(vi)   where the amendment power is jointly vested in the employer and trustees, ensure the trustees of the pension scheme have access to independent advice and that they are given adequate time to obtain and consider the independent advice in relation to the proposed amendments;

(vii)   prepare detailed member communication materials which document the amendments; and

(viii) ideally, have the necessary technical deeds of amendment prepared for execution prior to the implementation date (to avoid a period during which the administration is relying on a summary announcement in place of detailed amended scheme rules).

Reorganisation

[11.187] The reorganisation of pension arrangements is a highly technical area which is beyond the scope of this text save for some summary observations. In preparing for a reorganisation the following considerations will need to be borne in mind amongst others:

(i)   before the company gets too far down the line in considering a reorganisation it is prudent to give some thought to potential conflicts of interest in the composition of the trustee boards which will also be required to implement the proposals;

(ii)   where schemes are to be merged a detailed review of the provisions of both schemes is essential to check for the absence of particular powers (eg is there a power to make bulk transfers – often there is not);

(iii)   it is prudent to assess the balance of power in each scheme – the employer may wish to end up with the assets in the scheme over which it has most control;

(iv)   the funding impact of a merger is crucial and may impact on the trustees' ability to agree to the merger (trustees will be reluctant to sacrifice a surplus which provides funding comfort and security for their members to fund a transferred in deficit without some incentive by way of benefit improvements for the members of the receiving scheme);

(v)   it is important to involve all affected parties (employers, trustees, members and trade unions) and their respective advisers at an early stage to ensure that timetables are not derailed by unanticipated considerations;

(vi)   if it is necessary to establish a brand new scheme the time required to do this will need to be factored in;

(vii)   the requirements of any external consent parties (eg overseas parents, Government Departments) will need to be taken into account;

(viii) the final composition of the trustees in the merged scheme may be a matter which requires negotiation with different employee constituencies;

(ix)   the transferring trustees are likely to require indemnity protection (as they have transferred all their assets to a new arrangement) – this will be a matter for negotiation but is likely to be an important consideration;

(x)   actuarial and accounting advice will be required not least as the merger of scheme assets may result in an adverse accounting impact for one or more group companies;

(xi)   one or more sets of trustees are likely to require independent legal advice;

(xii)   consideration should be given as to whether any scheme amendments (and associated deeds of amendment) are required;

(xiii) it is customary to record details of the assets and liabilities being reorganised and the various undertakings in relation to the reorganisation in a formal transfer agreement; and

(xiv)   following completion of the transfer it may be necessary to complete the formal winding up of residual arrangements.

[11.188] The list of issues above is not comprehensive or exhaustive but provides in indication of the steps involved and an explanation as to why pension scheme reorganisations can take some time to organise.

Termination/winding up

[11.189] Almost all pension schemes have express termination provisions. These usually provide that the principal employer has the power to trigger a full termination or winding up of the scheme. Again, a detailed consideration of pension scheme winding up is beyond the scope of this text but the following summary observations may be helpful.

[11.190] In addition to the employer's power to trigger a winding up, the power is occasionally reserved to the trustees in limited circumstances. It may also be triggered by a liquidation or receivership event or by the dissolution of the company.

[11.191] The Protection of Employees (Employers' Insolvency) Act 1984 provides that a limited amount, usually the unpaid employer contributions during the 12 months preceding an insolvency, can be claimed out of the Social Insurance Fund.[93] There may

---

[93] Protection of Employees (Employers' Insolvency) Act 1984, s 7.

also be other claims on moneys remaining in a solvent employer and trusts arising in respect of moneys deducted from members and not handed over to the scheme.

[11.192] EU law[94] requires Member States to have necessary measures to protect employees of insolvent employers in respect of their entitlements under occupational pension schemes. The ECJ has accepted[95] that this does not require a full guarantee of accrued pension rights, however it found that a system which guarantees less than 50% of full entitlement falls short of the degree of protection required. It is as yet impossible to pinpoint what level of protection is required.

[11.193] Once a scheme has commenced winding up, the significant majority of the powers under it are effectively disabled. The role of the trustees is then to gather in the assets and to apply them in meeting the liabilities of the scheme in accordance with its provisions and the requirements of the Pensions Act 1990.

[11.194] The Pensions Act provides a statutory priority order for the application of assets, which in broad terms runs in the following order in respect of a winding up which commences after 2 June 2002: expenses of winding up; AVCS/Transfers-in; pensions in payment; preserved benefits for active and deferred members; and other non-preserved benefits.[96] Assets are applied to meet the liability in full for each such priority category before moving to the next category. There may be other considerations to take into account under the trust deeds once the statutory priorities have been met. In certain circumstances involving potential abatements of benefit or refunds to employers, it may be necessary to consult with members.[97]

[11.195] As with a reorganisation, there are a significant number of steps to winding up a pension scheme. The process begins with realising the assets and confirming the liabilities for the benefits (which in the case of a defined benefit scheme crystallize at the date of commencement of winding up). However, there are likely to be data cleansing issues involving clarifying dates of birth, dates of employment, dates of leaving service, addresses for deferred members and indeed confirming if all members are still alive. Actuarial and legal advice are likely to be required on certain aspects of regulatory and scheme interpretation. Administrators will be instructed to obtain annuity quotes to secure benefits. Communications must be drafted and sent to members and responses considered. Eventually after the application of the assets, final accounts are prepared and it is customary for the termination of the scheme to be recorded in a deed of termination and discharge. All of this is likely to take at least 18 months in a scheme of any significance.

---

[94] Directive 80/987/EEC, Art 8.

[95] Case C-278/05 *Robins and Others v Secretary of State for Work and Pensions*.

[96] Pensions Act 1990, s 48.

[97] Pensions Act 1990, s 59D and the Occupational Pension Scheme (Disclsoure of Information) Regulations 2006 (SI 302/2006), Art 16(2A).

CROSS-BORDER PENSIONS

Introduction

[11.196] There are a large variety of methods of providing for pensions internationally which means that arrangements in different countries can be very different in form, tax treatment and compatibility with other countries. While membership of the EU has brought a degree of harmonisation to some aspects (either voluntarily or as a result of EU directives – eg equal treatment) pension provision is still very varied largely because of the significant financial consequences for governments and the significant tax implications involved in altering either the systems of provision or the tax treatment of funded pensions. It is beyond the scope of this section to address cross-border pensions in depth. This section highlights some of the main international combinations which an Irish-based practitioner may come across with a signpost to the relevant tax provisions. In each case expert advice from international benefit specialists is likely to be advisable.

[11.197] Within the EU, some broad principles regarding minimum standards for pensions arrangements have been addressed in the provisions of the IORPS Directive.[98] An 'Institution for Occupational Retirement Provision' is not necessarily a cross-border arrangement – it is simply the European term for an occupational pension scheme. The IORPS directive did however specify certain minimum requirements for an IORP to operate on a cross-border basis within the EU. These are contained in Art 20 of the Directive.

[11.198] Ironically the Directive which was intended to promote pan-European pension schemes has led to the dissolution of the substantial majority of the main body of cross-border EU schemes then in existence (dual approved UK-Irish schemes). Most such schemes were separated into two single country arrangements by 29 March 2006 in order to avoid the risk of having to be become 'fully funded at all times'.

[11.199] The main cross-border options considered in this section below are:

  (i)   Irish employer/overseas employees in Irish scheme;

  (ii)   Irish employer/overseas employees in overseas scheme;

  (iii) Overseas employer/Irish employees in Irish Scheme;

  (iv)   Overseas employer/Irish employees in overseas scheme;

  (v)   International mobile employees scheme in low tax jurisdiction

Having briefly summarised the issues arising in each case, some of the main issues arising in secondment arrangements are considered.

Irish employer/overseas employees in Irish scheme

[11.200] The first issue to consider in this case is whether the overseas employees are Irish based and on secondment or whether they are likely to remain overseas. If there is a secondment, see below at para **[11.209]**.

---

[98]   EC Directive 2003/41/EC.

[11.201] If there is no secondment the next question is whether the overseas employees are in an EU Member State. If so and contributions are being received from an undertaking in that member state then the pension scheme is a cross-border pension scheme for the purposes of the IORPS directive and must comply with that Directive and the provisions of Part XII of the Pensions Act. Very broadly speaking, the main requirements are that local overseas social, labour and tax law must be complied with at the employee level as well as the scheme complying with Irish tax and pension law. The requirements vary from state to state but are likely to include provisions regarding disclosure of information, local social security law and may include local family law.

[11.202] If the overseas employee is not employed in an EU Member State, then the main issues will concern at the employee level local tax and social security law and at the scheme level compliance with the requirements of the Revenue Commissioners regarding overseas membership. These requirements are set out in Chapter 17 of the Revenue Practice Manual for approved schemes.[99]

Irish employer/overseas employees in overseas scheme

[11.203] This situation is less complicated as from an Irish perspective there are likely to be fewer Irish tax complications. In this case, there is unlikely to be a secondment (as if so the overseas employee would by implication be likely to return to Ireland in which case they could remain in the Irish scheme see secondment at para **[11.209]**). The simplest solution will usually be to set up a local arrangement consistent with local tax, pension and employment law. Another option is for the Irish employer to set up a tax-approved scheme in Ireland solely for overseas employees and employments.[100]

[11.204] A related situation involves an overseas employee coming to work in Ireland and wishing to remain in the overseas scheme to which they were contributing prior to coming to Ireland. Within the EU, such employees are known as 'migrant members' for the purposes of the Taxes Act and contributions paid to the overseas scheme are capable of being eligible for tax relief (subject to meeting the qualifying requirements) under the migrant member relief regime set out in Chapter 2B of Part 30 of the Taxes Consolidation Act 1997.

Overseas employer/Irish employees in Irish scheme

[11.205] This situation is the inverse of that in the preceding paragraph. Again the simplest and most common approach is for the Irish branch or subsidiary to establish a stand-alone Irish approved occupational pension scheme which relates solely to the Irish employees. In this case it is important that any employees posted or seconded to the Irish branch do not remain in the overseas scheme (otherwise than by secondment) or else there may be consequences for the status of the overseas scheme and it may (at least within the EU) become a cross-border scheme. Similarly if employees of the Irish operation are seconded to the overseas parent and remain in the Irish scheme this may create a risk of the Irish scheme becoming a cross-border pension scheme. As above, if

---

[99] 2007 Revenue Pensions Manual available at www.revenue.ie.
[100] 2007 Revenue Pensions Manual, paragraph 17.7.

the Irish employees move overseas within the EU, they may continue contributing to the Irish scheme under the migrant members regime.

Overseas employer/Irish employees in overseas scheme

[11.206] If Irish-resident employees are included in an overseas scheme established within the EU then that scheme is a cross-border IORPS. The scheme will have to comply with the IORPS Directive in accordance with the national legislation implementing the Directive in that overseas member state. The scheme must also comply with the social and labour laws of Ireland identified by the Pensions Board for the purposes of the Directive. Failure to comply with those requirements is a matter for the overseas regulator failing which the Pensions Board may intervene.[101]

[11.207] If an Irish resident employee is transferred overseas and the Irish scheme is not a cross-border IORPs (or the employee is transferred outside the EU) then accrual of benefit in the Irish scheme must cease.[102]

'International scheme' for mobile employees

[11.208] International schemes are usually established in an off-shore, low-tax jurisdiction such as Bermuda. These are used to provide either a top-up benefit or a total pension promise usually for senior employees who are required to move between international jurisdictions during their career. Such schemes benefit from tax free compounding of the investment fund and are usually designed so as not to create any tax liability for the employee during the accrual of benefit. Communications regarding such schemes should be prepared carefully as the benefits are not restricted by any Revenue limits, which may lead to the inadvertent creation of larger than anticipated benefits.

Secondment

[11.209] The law relating to secondment is complicated not least by the fact that there are by definition two jurisdictions to take into account – that from which the employee is being sent, and that in which the employee is currently working. The potential for cross-border jurisdictional conflict is significant in a number of areas, not just pensions. A very high level summary follows but detailed consideration of tax and legislative provisions is likely to be required in every case.

Employees seconded into Ireland from overseas

[11.210] Contributions will usually continue to be made to a foreign pension fund in this case. A contribution by an employer is a taxable emolument.[103] There are exceptions where the charge to tax is relieved by a double tax treaty or where s 778 of the Taxes Consolidation Act 1997 applies.

---

[101] Pensions Act 1990, s 153(5).

[102] 2007 Revenue Pensions Manual, paragraph 17.6.

[103] Taxes Consolidation Act 1997, s 777 and 2007 Revenue Pensions Manual, paragraphs 17.3 and 4.

[11.211] Outside these general provisions relief may also be available under general Revenue discretions where the secondment is for less than ten years; the scheme benefits are within Revenue Limits; and the scheme is set up under trust.[104]

Employees seconded overseas from Ireland

[11.212] Employees seconded from Ireland to an overseas entity may remain in an Irish pension scheme provided that the secondment is for a limited period, the employee intends to return to and retire in Ireland and the employee is deemed to remain on the Irish employer's payroll. In addition to this last Revenue condition, it is important to consider the cross-border IORPS impact of secondments. A scheme is cross-border for the purposes of the IORPS directive if it receives contributions from an 'undertaking' in another EU Member State. The precise treatment of secondees is far from clear and given the law on secondment (and the local implementation of the IORPS Directive in the other Member State) is possible for a particular arrangement to be regarded as a secondment in one jurisdiction but not the other and similarly for the pensions scheme to be cross-border in one jurisdiction but not in the other. Care should be taken in relation to the cross-border implications arising from the pensions aspects of secondments.

OCCUPATIONAL BENEFIT SCHEMES (OTHER THAN PENSIONS)

Death benefits

[11.213] Pension Schemes will normally include provision for death-in-service benefits and death-in-retirement benefits. Death-in-service benefits are usually a multiple of the member's salary at the time of death and are more often than not payable to the member's 'spouse' and 'dependants' (as defined in the scheme rules). These are insured with a life office. Some employers have in place separate life assurance cover (see above at para **[11.38]**) with an insurer for some or all of their employees. In such a case the death benefits fall outside the definition of a pension scheme for TUPE purposes and accordingly transfer on a TUPE transfer, see para **[11.173]** above.

PHI

[11.214] Permanent Health Insurance (PHI) is an insured benefit payable to employees which covers the employee who is absent from work due to sickness/incapacity. It is also referred to as income continuance. Although details as to entitlement and payment are often set out in the pension scheme booklet, strictly speaking PHI does not form part of the pension scheme established by way of trust deed and rules. This is because it is not an asset being held on trust by the trustees for the benefit of the pension scheme members and is not governed by the trust deed and rules.

[11.215] PHI provides the employer with a benefit which is passed on to the employee. The benefit acts as a replacement level of income for the employee in the event of illness/incapacity. The level of income provided by PHI is capped at a specified percentage (usually in the range 50%–75%) of the employee's salary before the illness.

---

[104] 2007 Revenue Pensions Manual, paragraph 17.5.

Benefit usually starts after an initial waiting period of 13, 26 or 52 weeks (which is selected to fit in with the employer's sick pay arrangements) and is payable until the employee returns to work, dies, or is dismissed, whichever happens first. PHI usually also provides payment to enable the continuation of the employer and employee contributions.

[11.216] While an employee is a beneficiary under a PHI arrangement they remain in employment. Insurers offer rehabilitation programmes and back to work programmes to employees in receipt of payment. The aim of these programmes is to keep the period of benefit payments to a minimum. The corollary of this is that premiums are kept low for employers and the insurance provider's exposure is reduced.

[11.217] PHI is not within the definition of a pension scheme for TUPE purposes and PHI obligations therefore transfer to a Purchaser in the event of a TUPE transfer, see para **[11.173]** above.

SHARE SCHEMES

[11.218] See Ch 21, Taxation.

TAXABLE AND EXEMPT BENEFITS IN KIND

[11.219] See Ch 21, Taxation.

Part IV
Employers' Insolvency

Chapter 12

Insolvency

Imelda Higgins

INTRODUCTION

[12.01] Generally, an employer becomes insolvent when its liabilities exceed its assets.[1] While the impact of insolvency on the employment contract depends both on the nature of the insolvency proceedings and the terms of the employment contract, insolvency clearly has grave consequences for an employee. In particular, an employee may not be able to usefully avail of traditional contractual or employment remedies and risks losing all his/her employment protection in the financial wreck of the company, partnership or individual.[2] There are, however, two mechanisms through which employees are offered a degree of protection in the event of their employer's insolvency. Firstly, employees have preferential creditor status in the assets of an insolvent employer under the Bankruptcy Act 1988 and the Companies Act 1963, as amended (the 'Companies Acts'). Secondly, the Protection of Employees (Employers' Insolvency) Act 1984, as amended[3] (the 'Insolvency Act') entitles employees falling within the terms of that Act to recover debts against insolvent employers from the general Social Insurance Fund where those debts arise out of their contracts of employment or from the employment relationship. That Act also provides for the recovery of certain contributions to occupational pension schemes and Personal Retirement Savings Accounts (PRSA) from the Social Insurance Fund.

INSOLVENCY AND THE EMPLOYMENT CONTRACT

[12.02] When faced with an employer's insolvency, a key issue for employees is the effect of that insolvency on the employment relationship and rights arising from that relationship such as: the right to payment of wages; the right to minimum notice; and the right to consultation in redundancy situations. In this respect, much depends on the type of insolvency. An employer's insolvency can come about in a variety of ways, and in particular by virtue of bankruptcy or liquidation proceedings. However, the appointment of a receiver or an examiner may also indicate that an employer has serious financial problems and impact on the employment relationship.

---

[1] Pursuant to Companies Act 1963, s 214, a company may be deemed insolvent in certain circumstances.

[2] Bowers, *Employment Law* (7th edn, Oxford University Press).

[3] Protection of Employees (Employers' Insolvency) Act 1984 (Amendment Order) Order 1988 (SI 48/1988); European Communities (Protection of Employees) (Employers' Insolvency) Regulations 2005.

Bankruptcy

[12.03] Bankruptcy is a process whereby the property or assets of an individual, who is unable or unwilling to pay their debts, is transferred by court order to a trustee to be sold. A person must be declared bankrupt by the High Court pursuant to a petition made either by or on behalf of the person him or herself or of a creditor. A debtor may bring a petition for his/her own bankruptcy where he or she is unable to pay debts to creditors and where his/her available estate is sufficient to produce at least €1,900. A creditor may petition the court where the debtor has committed an act of bankruptcy within the previous three months.[4] The most common acts of bankruptcy are:[5] a failure by the debtor to comply with a bankruptcy summons requesting payment of a specific sum due, within 14 days from service of the summons on the debtor; and the making of a return of no goods in respect of the debtor, by the sheriff or county registrar.

[12.04] Upon being adjudicated bankrupt, an individual's property automatically vests in the Official Assignee,[6] whose obligations are similar to those of a liquidator of a company. However, rights arising under the employment contract are not regarded as proprietary for these purposes and are not transferred.[7] Employment contracts often provide that the employment will terminate without notice if the employer is adjudicated bankrupt or makes a composition or arrangement with his creditors.[8] However, where the contract is silent on this point, the effect of such an adjudication on the employment contract is not entirely clear. Depending on the facts of the case, the adjudication of bankruptcy may frustrate the contract, bring it to end by operation of law, lawfully terminate it, or constitute an unfair dismissal. In addition, the employee may be entitled to treat any of the successive steps in the process of bankruptcy as 'evidence of the uncreditworthiness of the employer', and accordingly as entitling the employee to treat the employment contract as wrongfully repudiated.[9]

Liquidation

[12.05] The legal death of a company can come about either through a compulsory or voluntary winding up. A compulsory winding up is made at first instance by the High Court. In *Donnelly v Gleeson*, Hamilton J held that in the ordinary case, 'an order for the winding up of a company is notice of discharge to all persons in the employment of the company'.[10] It is not entirely clear whether the date of dismissal is the date of publication of the order or the date when the petition is presented. Pursuant to the terms of the Companies Act 1963, where a winding up order is made against a company, it applies retrospectively from the date of the presentation of the petition.[11] While this would

---

4   The creditor must also fulfil the requirements set out in the Bankruptcy Act 1988, s 11.
5   The various acts of bankruptcy are listed in the Bankruptcy Act 1988, s 7.
6   Bankruptcy Act 1988, s 44(1).
7   *Re Collins* [1925] Ch 536.
8   Redmond, *Dismissal Law in Ireland* (2nd edn, Tottel Publishing, 2007).
9   Freedland, *The Contract of Employment* (Oxford University Press, 1976).
10   *Donnelly v Gleeson* (1985) 4 JISLL 109; See also *Re Evanhenry Ltd* (1986) 5 JISLL 161; *Re General Rolling Stock Co* (1866) 1 LR Eq 346.
11   Companies Act 1963, s 220.

appear to support the proposition that the date of dismissal should also be backdated to the date of the petition[12] there are strong arguments against that view. In particular, it would undermine the employee's entitlement to a proper notice period. In this respect the better view appears to be that the notice of dismissal is not backdated and this view appears to have been accepted by the courts.[13] Specifically, in *Donnelly v Gleeson*,[14] Hamilton J refused to make an order declaring the employment contracts of certain employees to have been determined on the date on which the petition for the winding up was presented, despite the fact that the relevant section of the Companies Act was brought to his attention.[15]

[12.06] An employee dismissed by virtue of a compulsory winding up order and whose employment ceases at that time may be entitled to damages for wrongful dismissal, breach of his or her contractual rights and/or statutory rights.[16] In particular, if the employee has the right to a period of notice under the Minimum Notice and Terms of Employment Act 1973, this right will be infringed by the immediate termination of the employment contract.

[12.07] The position of employees who continue working after the date of the order depends on the circumstances of the case. Normally, as mentioned, there is a presumption that the winding up order is notice of discharge to employees and tantamount to the giving of proper contractual notice. This means that employees who continue working may be simply working out their contractual or statutory notice period.[17] However, this notice of discharge can be waived by the liquidator so that the original contract is deemed to subsist.[18] A third possibility is that an employee's original contract is terminated by the winding up order but a new contract of employment has come into existence.

[12.08] Clearly, when employees are expressly told that the winding up does not constitute notice of discharge there is no discharge. However, it is also possible for the notice to be waived by implication. An example of an implied waiver arose in *Dodd v Local Stores (Trading) Ltd*.[19] In that case, the court-appointed liquidator did not initially communicate with the trade union or the employees after his appointment but subsequently terminated the employees' employment contracts without notice. The employees responded by claiming compensation under the Minimum Notice and Terms of Employment Act 1973, however the liquidator claimed that they had suffered no loss.

---

[12] Forde, *Employment Law*, (2nd edn, Thomson Round Hall, 2002).

[13] See Pollard, *Corporate Insolvency: Employment and Pension Rights* (3rd edn, Tottel Publishing, 2007).

[14] *Re Evanhenry* (1986) 5 JISLL 161; *Donnelly v Gleeson* (1985) 4 JISLL 109.

[15] See also *Re General Rolling Stock Co Chapman's Case* (1866) LR 1 Eq 346, *Fowler v Commercial Timber Co Ltd* [1930] 2 KB 1; *Commercial Finance Co Ltd v Ramsingh Mahahir* [1994] 1 WLR 1297.

[16] See eg *Re RS Newman Ltd (Raphael's claim)* [1916] 2 CH 309.

[17] *McDowall's case* (1886) 32 Ch D 366; *Re Forster & Co Ltd Ex Parte Schumann* (1887) 19 LR Ir 240.

[18] *Re Collins* [1925] Ch 536.

[19] *Dodd v Local Stores (Trading) Ltd* [1992] ELR 61. Contrast this with *Irish Shipping Ltd v Byrne and the Minister for Labour* [1987] IR 468.

The EAT rejected this argument, and, in an apparent reference to the failure of the liquidator to make contact with the union and the employees, held that the notice of discharge normally implicit in the making of the winding up order had been waived by the liquidator. A waiver of notice may also be implied where the employee is retained beyond the period of his legal notice entitlement.[20] However, the mere fact that a short delay occurs between the making of the winding up order and the subsequent appointment of the official liquidator will normally not be sufficient to waive the notice.[21]

[12.09] Even where the original employment contract is deemed to have been terminated pursuant to the notice of discharge, circumstances may be such that a new contract of employment between the employee and the company comes into existence. In *Donnelly v Gleeson*,[22] Hamilton J indicated that a specfic request by the liquidator was necessary to form such a contract. Initially, however, the EAT took a different view. In *Re Evanhenry Ltd*,[23] the employees were retained for more than three months after the making of the winding up order. Murphy J observed that:

> In the circumstances it seems to me reasonable to infer that either expressly or by implication some new arrangement or agreement was entered into between the official liquidator and the two employees concerned.

However, in *Irish Shipping Ltd v Byrne and the Minister for Labour*,[24] the court refused to imply new contracts of employment in circumstances where the official liquidator had retained the employees for a full four months after having been dismissed. In that case, the liquidator successfully argued that although it had failed to give the notice required pursuant to the Minimum Notice and Terms of Employment Act 1973, the employees had not suffered any loss as they had been re-employed on a daily basis for longer than the notice period. In this respect, Lardner J considered that the sole significance to be attached to the fact that the respondent's re-employment lasted for a longer period than the relevant employee's notice period was that they suffered no loss by reason of the termination of their contracts of employment and were thus entitled to no compensation under the 1973 Act.

[12.10] In some cases the court may appoint a provisional liquidator to safeguard the assets of the company before ordering a winding up. Where such a liquidator is authorised to carry on the business of the company, the employment contract is not discharged.[25]

Voluntary liquidation

[12.11] There are two types of voluntary liquidation: creditor's voluntary winding up and members' voluntary winding up. In the former, the creditors play a dominant role,

---

[20] *Re Forster & Co Ltd Ex Parte Schumann* (1887) 19 LR Ir 240.
[21] *Re Evanhenry Ltd* (1986) 5 JISLL 161.
[22] *Donnelly v Gleeson* (1985) 4 JISLL 109.
[23] *Re Evanhenry Ltd* (1986) 5 JISLL 161.
[24] *Irish Shipping Ltd v Byrne and the Minister for Labour* [1987] IR 468.
[25] *Donnelly v Gleeson* (1985) 4 JISLL 109.

while in the latter the liquidation is conducted largely by the liquidator and the members of the company. In both cases, the company will normally be deemed to be dissolved on the expiration of three months after the Registrar of Companies registers the account of the winding up which is submitted to him by the liquidator.

[12.12] Where a resolution for voluntary winding up is accompanied by the immediate cessation of an employee's employment, that employee will have been wrongfully dismissed and the employer will have committed a repudiatory breach of the employment contract.[26] The legal position is more complicated where the employee continues to work after the resolution is passed. In *Re Forster & Co, ex parte Schumann*,[27] Chatterton V-C considered that the passing of the resolution has the same effect as the making of a winding up order, stating:

> I take it to be settled law, since Chapman's case, that the resolution or order for winding up operates in law as notice of discharge to the company's servants. The liquidator is in the same position as any other employer of labour, who is bound to give notice of dismissal, or compensation in lieu of such notice. The resolution operates as notice, and takes effect from the expiration of the period corresponding with the length to which the person is entitled.[28]

However, it is not always clear that this is the case. According to Forde, the test in this respect is 'whether in all the circumstances the employee is justified as regarding the winding up as indicating an intention by the company to repudiate its obligations under the contract'.[29] In England it appears that where employment continues after a resolution of voluntary winding up, the resolution does not automatically terminate the employment contract.[30] Moreover, academic opinion has argued forcefully that:

> A more satisfactory approach from the employees' point of view to the problem of determining the legal significance to be attached to a resolution for voluntary winding up would be to regard it as a repudiatory breach of the contract of employment. Such an approach would enable the employee to choose between accepting the breach, and thus regarding himself as dismissed for the purposes of his statutory employment rights, and as free to leave for other employment on the one hand and affirming the contract on the other.[31]

---

[26] *Reigate v Union Manufacturing Co Ltd* [1918] 1 KB 592 at 606; See also Barrett, 'The Effect of Insolvency on the Contract of Employment' (1996) 3(1) *DULJ* 15.

[27] *Re Forster & Co Ltd ex parte Schumann* (1887) 19 LR Ir 240; see also *Midland Counties Bank v Attwood* [1905] 1 Ch. 357; *Reigate v Union Manufacturing Co* [1918] 1 KB 592.

[28] *Re Forster & Co Ltd ex parte Schumann* (1887) 19 LR Ir 240, p 244.

[29] Forde, *Employment Law*, (2nd edn, Thomson Round Hall, 2002), p 242.

[30] *Midland Countries District Bank Ltd v Attwod* [1905] 1 Ch 357; *Gerard v Worth of Paris* [1936] 2 All ER 905; See generally, Pollard, *Corporate Insolvency: Employment and Pension Rights* (3rd edn, Tottel Publishing, 2007) and Freedland, *The Contract of Employment* (Oxford University Press, 1976).

[31] Barrett, 'The Effect of Insolvency on the Contract of Employment' (1996) 3(1) *DULJ* 15 at p 27.

Receivership

[12.13] Normally where a substantial loan is made to a company, the lender will take a charge over the company's assets, so as to create for himself a degree of priority if the company subsequently becomes insolvent. The loan agreement/debenture will typically provide that on default the receiver may be appointed to enforce the security. The functions of a receiver have been described as being 'to get in the assets charged, to collect the rents and profits, to exercise the debenture holders powers of realisation and to pay the net proceeds to the holders in reduction of their charge'.[32] While a receiver is not faced with the same task as a liquidator upon the winding up of a company as the receiver's only task is to ensure the discharge of the company's liability to the debenture holder who appointed him,[33] receiverships often lead to liquidations. As has been observed:

> In practice, however, lenders are unlikely to appoint receivers until the company's commercial future is in considerable doubt, and the enforcement of the lenders security will then be the death-knell of the company. Consequently, receiverships often lead to liquidations, at least if it seems likely that there will be anything left over for the general (unsecured) creditors or the shareholders after the receiver has finished.[34]

[12.14] In cases where the receiver is appointed by the debenture holder, the debenture will normally provide that that receiver is an agent of company which is affected by the receivership. Accordingly, there is no change in the identity of the employer. Consequently, in those cases the appointment of the receiver does not operate to terminate existing contracts of employments between the company and its employees.[35] There are exceptions to this rule. In particular, there will of course be a dismissal if the company ceases to carry on business.[36] Moreover, where the continued employment of a particular individual is inconsistent with the appointment of a receiver manager, for example the managing director, the appointment will terminate that employment. Whether or not there is the requisite inconsistency will depend on the facts of the case and in particular, upon the degree of board control over the manager before the commencement of the receivership, and on whether the receiver is intended to conduct all the company's business or to merely exercise general supervision and control.[37] While the English courts appear to have taken the position that the employment is automatically terminated in such cases, it has been argued that a fairer and more legally sound view would be to regard the appointment of a receiver as a repudiatory breach of

---

[32] Gower, *Principles of Modern Company Law* (4th edn, Sweet & Maxwell, 1979) pp 468 – 472.

[33] See *Re B. Johnson & Co (Builders) Ltd* [1955] Ch. 634.

[34] Davies and Freedland, 'The Effects of Receivership upon Employees of Companies' (1980) 9 *ILJ* 95 at 97.

[35] *Griffiths v Secretary of State for Social Services* [1974] QB 468; *Re Mack Trucks (Britain) Ltd* [1967] 1 WLR 780; *Deaway Trading Ltd v Calverley* [1973] 3 ALL ER 776; *Nicoll v Cutts* [1985] BCLC 322.

[36] *Re Foster Clark Ltd's Indenture Trusts* [1966] 1 All ER 43.

[37] *Re Foster Clark Ltd's Indenture Trusts* [1966] 1 All ER 43 at 486.

such an employee's employment contract which the employee can choose to accept or reject.[38]

[12.15] Where a receiver is appointed by the court, the position is different as such a receiver is not an agent of the company.[39] The traditional view is that the appointment automatically terminates the employees' contracts of employments.[40] However, the courts in Australia have recently refused to follow this approach.[41]

Examinerships

[12.16] Pursuant to the Companies (Amendment) Act 1990, the High Court has the power to appoint, on petition, an examiner to any company which appears to the Court unable or unlikely to be able to pay its debts and in relation to which no winding up resolution subsists or winding up order has been made.[42] The immediate effect of an examiner's appointment is that, for a maximum initial period of 70 days beginning with the presentation of a petition, the company is deemed to be 'under the protection of the court' from its creditors.[43] There appears to be no reason in principle why the appointment of an examiner into a company's affairs under the 1990 Act should bring an end to the employment contracts of the company's employees.[44] In particular, the entire purpose of the mechanism is to allow a company a period of protection from its creditors, within which time the examiner seeks to rescue the company and return it to health. This purpose would be ill served if the mere appointment of an examiner resulted in the immediate dismissal of the company's employees without whom, in many cases, a rescue package would be unlikely to succeed.

Employees as preferential creditors

[12.17] Preferential creditors are essentially creditors who gain priority in a distribution of an estate, not because of any particular agreement between them and the debtor, but because of some priority conferred on them as a result of the operation of law. Preferential creditor status offers considerable advantages to a creditor as it is more likely that the debts owed to a preferential creditor by a company will be discharged either entirely or on a pro rata basis. Pursuant to the Bankruptcy Act 1988[45] and the Companies Acts,[46] employees[47] have preferential creditor status in the assets of the

---

[38] Barrett, 'The Effect of Insolvency on the Contract of Employment' (1996) 3(1) *DULJ* 15.
[39] See *Burt, Bolton & Haywood v Bull* [1895] 1 QB 276; *Moss Steamship Company Ltd v Whinney* [1912] AC 254.
[40] *Reid v Explosives Co Ltd* (1887) 19 QBD 264.
[41] *Sipad Holding DDPO v Popovic* (1996) 12 ACLC 307.
[42] Companies Act 1990, s 2.
[43] Companies Act 1990, s 5.
[44] Forde, *Employment Law*, p 244, but see also Barrett, 'The Effect of Insolvency on the Contract of Employment' (1996) 3(1) *DULJ* 15, at p 33.
[45] See Bankruptcy Act 1988, s 81.

insolvent employer in respect of specified debts. Employees are not the only ones with preferential creditor status, which is also accorded to, *inter alia*, the Revenue Commissioners in respect of certain back taxes. The traditional justification for including employees as preferential creditors has been their almost complete financial dependence on the income provided by their work and their relatively weak bargaining power when it comes to obtaining payment from their employer firm when it is in financial difficulties.[48]

[12.18] Employees' preferential debts include:[49]

(i) wages earned during the four months prior to winding up subject to a maximum of €3,174;

(ii) all accrued holiday pay; all sickness pay;

(iii) all compensation payable to an employee on termination of employment where the statutory minimum notice of termination has not been given;

(iv) statutory redundancy lump sums;

(v) compensation awarded by the EAT in respect of unfair dismissals; company contributions and contributions deducted from employees in respect of any pension schemes.

[12.19] However, while providing an employee with a certain degree of protection, preferential creditor status suffers from a number of disadvantages. Specifically, preferential creditor status only provides protection in the case of insolvency where the insolvent employer owns assets of sufficient value to discharge debts owed to its preferential creditors. In addition, where a valuable asset comprises real or intangible property, it is likely to be already subject to a fixed charge, which trumps preferential creditor status. Moreover, arrears of wages are only covered to a maximum of €3,174. Finally, even if there are enough assets to cover all the debts owed to an employee he or she may have to wait years for the liquidator or Official Assignee to make a distribution.

[12.20] Nevertheless, preferential creditor status is still important, in particular for those who do not fall within the scope of the Insolvency Act. For example in *Kelly v Vigilant Security Ltd*,[50] the claimant was owed eight weeks' pay for his minimum notice period from a company which had gone into liquidation. The claimant was ineligible for payments from the Social Insurance Fund, however, he successfully sought an award under the Minimum Notice and Terms of Employment Acts 1973–2001, so that he could become a preferential creditor of the company for the recovery of compensation for the lack of a minimum notice payment.[51]

---

46 Companies Act 1963, s 285, as amended.

47 See *Re Sunday Tribune Ltd* [1984] IR 505 where several journalists from the Sunday Tribune were not able to claim preferential creditor status as they were independent contractors.

48 Barrett, 'The Effect of Insolvency on the Contract of Employment' (1996) 3(1) *DULJ* 15; for general arguments against preferential creditor status see Lynch, 'The Bankruptcy Act 1988' (1989) 7 *ILT* 300, pg 304.

49 Companies Act 1963, s 285, as amended; Bankruptcy Act 1988, s 86.

50 *Kelly v Vigilant Security Ltd* MN646/2006.

The Insolvency Act

[12.21] Employees are in a somewhat better position under the Insolvency Act which sets up an Insolvency Payments Scheme, the purpose of which is to protect pay-related entitlements owed to employees who lose their employment because of the insolvency of an employer. That Act has its origins in the Insolvency Directive 80/987,[52] which was the third in the trilogy of European Community measures designed to confer some protection on employees in the event of their employer's insolvency due to increased competition caused by the advent of the Common Market.[53] The Insolvency Directive has two central objectives, namely: to promote the approximation of laws and to improve the living and working conditions by protecting employees in the event of the insolvency of their employer.[54] The Directive seeks to achieve these objectives, in particular by requiring Member States to put in place an institution guaranteeing employees the payment of their outstanding claims to remuneration for a specified period. That Directive was amended by Directive 2002/74,[55] which adapted the original Directive to reflect changes in the insolvency law in the Member States. However, both of these Directives have now been repealed and replaced by Directive 2008/94[56] which codifies the previous Directives.

The material and personal scope of the Insolvency Act

[12.22] The Insolvency Act applies to employees' claims arising from their contract of employment or employment relationship against insolvent employers. This raises three questions. Firstly, what is meant by 'insolvency', secondly, who are 'employees' and thirdly who are 'employers'.

The definition of insolvency

[12.23] While generally, as mentioned, insolvency arises where a person's liabilities exceed their liabilities, the Act defines insolvency in specific terms. In particular, it deems the employer to be insolvent, for the purposes of the rights conferred on employees, in some situations in which the employer would not be deemed insolvent commercially or for the purpose of other legal rules. In this respect, the intention was to

---

[51] See also *Hughes v Hitachi Imaging Solutions Europe* [2006] IEHC 233, in which the plaintiff sought a mareva injunction against an insolvent defendant to require that sufficient sums be retained to meet her eventual claim in relation to a wrongfully terminated disability benefit payment. Clarke J recognised that it was open in principle to the plaintiff to seek this form of relief but did not think the conditions necessary for the grant of such an injunction had been met in that case.

[52] Council Directive 80/987/EEC (OJ [1980] L283/23) on the approximation of the laws of the Member States relating to the protection of employees in the event of the insolvency of their employer, as amended by Directive 87/164 (OJ [1987] L66/11). See COM(96) 696 on the implementation of the Directive.

[53] Barnard *EC Employment Law* (OUP, 2006).

[54] See Preamble, paras 5 and 6. See also Case 22/87 *Commission v Italy* [1989] ECR 143.

[55] OJ [2002] L270/10.

[56] OJ [2008] L 283/36.

define insolvency as broadly as possible to ensure that the maximum number of workers fall within the scope of the Act.[57] A person is insolvent for the purposes of the Insolvency Act, where he or she falls within one of the five categories identified in that Act, namely:

(i)   bankruptcy;

(ii)   where an employer has died insolvent;

(iii)   liquidation or receivership;

(iv)   the employer falls within regulations under s 4(2) of the Act; or

(v)   the employer is an undertaking insolvent under the laws of another EU Member State.

The Act does not cover circumstances where the employer shuts down without becoming legally insolvent. In such a case the employer remains responsible for the payment of the employee's pay and other entitlements and the employees are unable to claim these from the Social Insurance Fund.[58] The Act's failure to deal with informal insolvency is probably its greatest defect and certainly its most controversial one.

Bankruptcy

[12.24] The first category covers three situations, namely where the employer:

(i)   has been adjudicated bankrupt; or

(ii)   has petitioned for arrangement; or

(iii)   has executed a deed of arrangement.

The circumstances in which an employer may be adjudicated bankrupt have been considered above. The second and third situations apply where the employer has petitioned for or executed a deed of arrangement within the meaning of s 4 of the Deeds of Arrangement Act 1887. An employer may file a petition for a deed of arrangement under the Bankruptcy Act 1988 or the Companies Act 1990. In contrast, a debtor may execute a deed of arrangement without any court involvement, by obtaining the approval of a simple majority of creditors. The term 'deed of arrangement' includes any of the following instruments whether under seal or not, made by, for, or in respect of the affairs of a debtor, for the benefit of his or her creditors generally:

(i)   an assignment of property;

(ii)   a deed of agreement for a composition and in cases where a debtor's creditors obtain control over his property or business;

(iii)   a deed of inspectorship entered into for the purpose of carrying on or winding up a business;

(iv)   a letter of licence authorising the debtor or any other person to manage, carry on, realise, or dispose of a business, with a view to the payment of debts; and

---

[57]   354 Dáil Debates Cols 270–271.

[58]   See *Referral by Minister for Enterprise in PSK Construction Ltd, in liquidation* EAT, 15 June 2007.

(v)   any agreement or instrument entered into for the purpose of carrying on or winding up the debtor's business, or authorising the debtor or any other person to manage, carry on, realise, or dispose of the debtor's business, with a view to the payment of his or her debts.

Insolvent deceased

[12.25] The second category applies where the employer has died insolvent and his estate is being administered in accordance with the rules set out in Succession Act 1965, Sch 1, Pt 1. Pursuant to these rules, funeral, testamentary and administration expenses have priority. Otherwise bankruptcy rules apply with the date of death being substituted for the date of adjudication in bankruptcy.

Liquidation

[12.26] The third category applies specifically to cases where the employer is a company and sets out a number of situations where a company will be insolvent. Specifically, a company will be deemed insolvent where a winding up order is made[59] or a resolution for voluntary winding up is passed with respect to it. In *Reference by the Minister for Labour in re Keyes and Others*[60] the EAT interpreted the latter requirement broadly, observing:

> It seems to us that the lawmakers contemplated the situation where winding up procedures do not comply with the provisions of the Companies Acts and pronounced themselves satisfied that an insolvency had occurred in a situation in where there [was] no doubt that a resolution was passed by some people in [the employer company]. That resolution expressed an intention to wind up the company. It was about winding up in a general way.

[12.27] A company will also be insolvent where a receiver or manager of its undertaking is duly appointed or if possession is taken, by or on behalf of the holders of any debentures secured by any floating charge, of any property of the company comprised in or subject to the charge.

Regulations

[12.28] The fourth category applies where the employer is deemed insolvent pursuant to circumstances specified in regulations by the Minister for Enterprise, Trade and Employment (The Minister). This could be of importance to an employee where no steps have been taken to declare an employer insolvent.

EU-based insolvency

[12.29] The fifth situation provides that employers who are insolvent under the rules of another Member State are also insolvent in this jurisdiction once the employees concerned are employed or habitually employed in this State.

---

[59]   Companies Act 1963, as amended, s 213(e).
[60]   *Reference by the Minister for Labour in re Keyes and Others* I 1/90.

Employees

[12.30] Entitlements under the Act are confined to employees who fulfil certain requirements. Anyone who has entered into or works under a contract with an employer is an employee.[61] The relevant requirements are that the employee must either be: in employment which is insurable for all benefits under the Social Welfare (Consolidation) Act 2005; in employment which would be so insurable but for that fact that the employment concerned is an excepted employment by virtue of the First Sch, Pt 2, paras 2, 4, or 5 of that Act; or be over 65.[62] In *Kenny v Minister for Trade and Employment*,[63] the applicant, who had worked abroad on behalf of his employer for four years was unable to make a claim under the Act in respect of an award for wrongful dismissal because he did not fall within the definition of 'employee'. Pursuant to the terms of the Social Welfare (Consolidation) Act 2005, in order to be in insurable employment, a person must be employed within the State. While there is an exception for those who are temporarily employed abroad, employees cease to be treated as temporarily employed outside the State after 52 weeks. Consequently, Kenny J held that the applicant could not make a claim under the Act.

[12.31] The employee must also be employed by an employer who becomes insolvent. This requirement was considered in *Referral by Minister for Enterprise in matter of PSK Construction Ltd, in liquidation*.[64] The applicants in that case had been employed by PSK Construction Ltd up to 20 February 2006, on which date they were transferred to another company PLK, run by the same management. PSK Construction Ltd ceased trading on 18 February and was subsequently wound up voluntarily by resolution passed on 16 March 2006, at which point it became insolvent under the terms of the Act. PSK had used monies deducted from workers' wages ie pension contributions, tax and PRSI and union contributions in order to continue in operation and they were owed at least one week's wages. However, as the applicants had been transferred to PLK by the date of insolvency, the Tribunal held that their claims for payment from the Social Insurance Fund were not allowable.

Employers

[12.32] In order to make an application to the Social Insurance Fund, the employee must be employed by an employer who is either established in Ireland or who carries out activities here. Otherwise the competent guarantee institution is that of the Member State in which the employer is established.[65] For example, in *Everson v Barrass*,[66] the

---

61 Protection of Employees (Employers' Insolvency) Act (1984), s 1.
62 Protection of Employees (Employers' Insolvency) Act 1984, s 3.
63 *Kenny v Minister for Enterprise, Trade and Employment* [1999] ELR 163.
64 *Referral by Minister for Enterprise in matter of PSK Construction Ltd, in liquidation* EAT 16/06/2007.
65 Case C-117/96, *Danmarks Aktive Handelsrejsende v Lonmondtagernes Garantifond* [1997] ECR I-5017.
66 Case C-198/98, *Everson and Barrass v Secretary of State for Trade and Industry* [1999] ECR I-8903.

claimants were employed by the English establishment of the Irish company Bell in Avonmouth. In 1997, the Irish holding company was declared insolvent and a liquidator appointed. Subsequently, the English High Court appointed a special manager for the winding up of Bell's affairs in the UK. After being made redundant, Bell's UK staff applied to the Secretary of State for payment of arrears of pay, unpaid holiday pay and compensation pay in lieu of notice. The Secretary refused on the ground that, although Bell's UK establishment was a registered company in the UK, it did not have legal personality and consequently the employees should apply to the Irish guarantee institution instead. On a referral to the ECJ, the Court held that it was for the UK authorities to settle the applicants' claim.

[12.33] In *Svenska Staten v Anders Holmqvist*,[67] the ECJ was asked to interpret whether the term 'activities' as used in the Insolvency Directive, requires that the undertaking have a branch or permanent place of business in another Member State. That case concerned a lorry driver for a Swedish company whose only place of business was Sweden. However, the applicant's work consisted of delivering goods from Sweden to Italy and from Italy to Sweden. The Swedish authority refused the applicant's claim for benefits under the Swedish guarantee fund on the basis that the employer had carried out activities in other Member States and he performed his work primarily in those Member States. However, the applicant contested this refusal on the basis that his employer did not have a place of business or commercial presence outside Sweden. In its judgment, the ECJ observed that the concept of 'activities' must be interpreted broadly and held that there is no requirement that the undertaking have a branch or fixed establishment in another Member State but it must have a stable economic presence featuring human resources which enable it to perform activities there. According to the ECJ:

> In the case of a transport undertaking established in a Member State, the mere fact that a worker employed by the undertaking in that State delivers goods between that State and another Member State by crossing other Member States cannot demonstrate compliance with the criterion set out in the previous paragraph of this judgment and is therefore not sufficient for the undertaking to be regarded, for the purposes of Article 8a of Directive 80/987, as carrying out activities elsewhere than in the Member State in which it is established.

Employees' rights

[12.34] Where an employer is insolvent, an employee is entitled to have certain debts arising out of the employment relationship which are in existence on the 'relevant date' and have arisen in the 'relevant period', paid to him or her out of the Social Insurance Fund.[68] The Act covers three main categories of debts, namely: (1) those relating to payment of wages, sick pay, holiday pay and minimum notice; (2) those arising out of an award made pursuant to specified employment protection legislation or equivalent common law provisions; and (3) payments into occupational pension schemes or Personal Retirement Savings Scheme. However, in the case of all three, the Act places

---

[67] Case C-310/07 *Svenska Staten v Anders Holmquist*.
[68] Protection of Employees (Employers' Insolvency) Act 1984, s 6.

certain limits on the maximum amount which may be recovered from or paid out of the Social Insurance Fund.

Relevant date

[12.35] In each of the three cases, the employee must be entitled to all or part of the debt on the 'relevant date'. However, this date varies depending on the type of debt owed to the employee and the type of insolvency involved.[69] Where the debt is for arrears of pay, the relevant date depends on whether the applicant's employment was terminated by his or her employer's insolvency or not. If the employment is terminated as a result of the insolvency, it is for the employee to choose whether the relevant date is to be the date of the insolvency or the date his or her employment terminated.[70] Where the employee's employment is not terminated by the insolvency, then the date is the date of termination of employment.[71] In the case of debts resulting from claims arising out of legislation governing unfair dismissal, pay discrimination or employment equality, the relevant date is the date on which the employer becomes insolvent or the date the relevant body granted the claim, whichever is the later.[72]

[12.36] The date of insolvency depends on the type of insolvency involved. In the case of bankruptcy, it is the date on which the employer has been adjudicated bankrupt.[73] Where the employer has petitioned for arrangement, it is the date on which the petition is filed.[74] Where the employer has executed a deed of arrangement, then it is the date of such execution.[75] In cases where the employer has died, the relevant date is the date of his death.[76] If the insolvency results from the appointment of a receiver, the employer is regarded as having become insolvent on the date of his or her appointment.[77] Similarly, where the holder of a debenture secured by a floating charge takes possession of that charge, then the relevant date is the date of the possession.[78] In the case of a company wound up by court order, the date is the date of the appointment of a provisional liquidator or, if none is appointed, the date of the order.[79] In the case of a company voluntarily wound up, the date is the date of the passing of the resolution to wind up the company.[80] The Minister may also specify the date on which an employer is to be

---

[69] Protection of Employees (Employers' Insolvency) Act 1984, s 6(9).
[70] Protection of Employees (Employers' Insolvency) Act 1984, s 6(9)(b)(i).
[71] Protection of Employees (Employers' Insolvency) Act 1984, s 6(9)(b)(ii).
[72] Protection of Employees (Employers' Insolvency) Act 1984, s 6(9)(a).
[73] Protection of Employees (Employers' Insolvency) Act 1984, s 4(1)(a).
[74] Protection of Employees (Employers' Insolvency) Act 1984, s 4(1)(b).
[75] Protection of Employees (Employers' Insolvency) Act 1984, s 4(1)(c).
[76] Protection of Employees (Employers' Insolvency) Act 1984, s 4(1)(d).
[77] Protection of Employees (Employers' Insolvency) Act 1984, s 4(1)(e)(i).
[78] Protection of Employees (Employers' Insolvency) Act 1984, s 4(1)(e)(i).
[79] Protection of Employees (Employers' Insolvency) Act 1984, s 4(1)(e) and Companies Acts, 1963, s 285(1)(i).
[80] Protection of Employees (Employers' Insolvency) Act 1984, s 4(1)(e) and Companies Acts, 1963, s 285(1)(ii); see *Referral by Minister for Enterprise in PSK Construction Ltd, in liquidation* EAT, 15 June 2007.

regarded as having become insolvent for the purposes of the Act.[81] Where the employer is an undertaking which is insolvent under the laws, regulations and administrative procedure of another Member State, the date is that on which the insolvency was established under those laws, regulations or administrative procedures.[82]

The relevant period

[12.37] Claims in respect of debts such as arrears of pay, sick leave, holiday entitlements etc can only be made where those debts have accrued during the 'relevant period' which is 18 months immediately preceding the relevant date.[83] Similarly a claim can only be made in respect of awards arising under employment protection legislation, including the Minimum Notice and Terms of Employment Act 1973, the Unfair Dismissals Act 1977, the Anti-Discrimination (Pay) Act 1974 and the Employment Equality Act 1998, where such awards were made during or after the 18 months immediately preceding the 'relevant date'.[84] In *Meade v Irish Ispat Ltd*,[85] the Tribunal held that it was not permitted 'to look further back than to 18 months prior to the liquidation'. However, in *Sheedy v Minister for Labour*,[86] the EAT permitted the claimant to recover in respect of holidays initially accrued outside the relevant period in circumstances where the employer had induced the claimant to believe that her holiday entitlement would be preserved. In that case the EAT appeared to view the fact that the claimant and the employer had agreed to transfer her holiday entitlement from one year to the next meant that the entitlement did in fact arise during the relevant period.[87]

[12.38] Establishing that a claim arises in the relevant period may give rise to difficulties where there is a long delay between the employer company ceasing to trade and the date of the insolvency. For example, in *Kennedy v Minister for Labour*,[88] the employer ceased operations 29 months before the appointment of a liquidator. An employee's claim in respect of outstanding debts owed to him by his employer was dismissed by the EAT because the debts in respect of which he had made the claim had arisen earlier than the commencement of the 18-month relevant period.

---

[81] Protection of Employees (Employers' Insolvency) Act 1984, s 4(1)(f). The Minister exercised this power in two cases. The Protection of Employees (Employers' Insolvency) (Specification of Date) Regulations 1985 (SI 322/1985 specify the date on which an insolvency is deemed to arise in the case of bodies corporate under the Industrial and Provident Societies Act 1893; The Protection of Employees (Employers' Insolvency) (Specification of Date) Regulations 1986 (SI 50/1986) specify the date in which an insolvency is deemed to arise in the case of bodies corporate under the Industrial and Provident Societies Acts 1893 – 1978).

[82] Protection of Employees (Employers' Insolvency) Act 1984, s 4(1)(g).

[83] Protection of Employees (Employers' Insolvency) Act 1984, s 6(9).

[84] Protection of Employees (Employers' Insolvency) Act 1984, s 6(2)(b).

[85] *Meade v Irish Ispat Ltd* I 1/2002.

[86] *Sheedy v Minister for Labour* I 169/1989.

[87] See also *Barron and Others v Minister for Labour* I 861/1986; *Lynam, O'Reilly and Curley v Minister for Labour* I 163/1989.

[88] *Kenny v Minister for Labour* I 160/1989.

Arrears of wages, sick pay, holiday pay and minimum notice

[12.39] An employee may claim payment of arrears of: normal weekly remuneration;[89] sick pay;[90] holiday pay;[91] and pay in lieu of notice[92] from the Social Insurance Fund. Where an employee has been paid less than the statutory minimum remuneration, that employee may also claim a sum representing the difference between the statutory minimum remuneration and the remuneration actually paid, in cases where proceedings have been instituted against the employer for an offence under s 45(1) of the Industrial Relations Act 1946.[93]

[12.40] The term 'normal weekly remuneration' has the same meaning under this Act as in the Redundancy Payments Acts 1967–2007, Sch 3.[94] It covers an employee's earnings for a normal working week, including any regular bonus or allowance that does not vary in relation to the amount of work done. Also any payment in kind normally received by an employee, eg free accommodation, free meals, etc, must be taken into account. Wage increases due to an employee but never actually paid to him come within the definition of arrears of normal weekly remuneration. For example, in *Cruise and Others v Minister for Labour*,[95] the second phase of a 5% increase was taken into account in calculating entitlements in the 1984 Act although the claimant employee had received only the first phase from his employer. In *Re Solus Teoranta Minister for Labour v O'Toole*,[96] Murphy J held that sums deducted from the weekly wages of an employee by an employer in respect of the employee's trade union membership but which were not paid over for their designated purpose, fell within normal weekly remuneration. Murphy J was of the view that the 'deduction' notice signed by the employee did not operate as an assignment and the employee had not divested herself of the right to recover the money.

[12.41] As mentioned, an employee is only entitled to claim debts which arise in the 18 months preceding the termination of his or her employment. However, where an employer makes periodic payments to an employee during this period and has outstanding liabilities to the employee from before this period, any amounts paid are first set against those liabilities. For example, in *Regeling*,[97] an employee had been paid sporadically by his employer during the relevant period but subsequently claimed the entire amount of his wages for that period from the relevant guarantee fund. His claim was upheld on the basis that the sums paid during the period had first to be set against

---

89 Protection of Employees (Employers' Insolvency) Act 1984, s 6(2)(a)(i).
90 Protection of Employees (Employers' Insolvency) Act 1984, s 6(2)(a)(ii).
91 Protection of Employees (Employers' Insolvency) Act 1984, s 6(2)(a)(iv).
92 Protection of Employees (Employers' Insolvency) Act 1984, s 6(2)(a)(iii).
93 Protection of Employees (Employers' Insolvency) Act 1984, s 6(2)(a)(vii).
94 Protection of Employees (Employers' Insolvency) Act 1984, s 6(9).
95 *Cruise and Others v Minister for Labour* I 321/1986; but see *Power v Minister for Labour* I 159/1989.
96 *Re Solus Teoranta Minister for Labour v O'Toole* [1990] ILRM 180.
97 Case C-125/97 *Regeling v Bestuur van de Bedrijfsvereniging voor de Metaalnijverheid* [1998] ECR 4493.

the employer's liabilities to him which had arisen before that period rather than being considered as payment of his wages during that period.

[12.42] There is an eight-week limit for arrears of pay,[98] sick pay, holiday pay and pay in lieu of statutory notice. Moreover, all entitlements based on pay are limited to a maximum weekly rate, which is currently €600 per week for insolvencies which occurred on or after 1 January 2005.[99] This maximum rate relates to the amount of debt, not to the amount of weekly pay.[100] In other words, the fact that the employee earned more than €600 and/or has been paid more than that amount is not a bar to recovering other outstanding arrears: what matters is the size of the debt still owed to the employee.[101]

[12.43] The amount recoverable in relation to any sick-pay scheme is also limited to the difference between normal weekly remuneration and the sum of any disability or injury benefit and any pay-related benefit payable for the period.[102]

Awards

[12.44] The second category covers amounts which an employer is required to pay pursuant to an award made under the following legislation:

   (i)   Unfair Dismissals Act 1977[103] or damages at common law for wrongful dismissal;[104]

  (ii)   Employment Equality Act 1998;[105]

 (iii)   Maternity Protection Act 1994;[106]

 (iv)   Adoptive Leave Act 1995;

  (v)   Parental Leave Act 1998;

 (vi)   National Minimum Wage Act 2000;[107]

 (vii)   Carer's Leave Act 2001;[108]

(xiii)   Payment of Wages Act 1991;[109]

 (ix)   Terms of Employment (Information) Act 1994;[110]

---

[98] See eg *Freeney v Ardiff Securities Ltd* UD 149/1987.

[99] Protection of Employees (Employers' Insolvency) Act 1984, s 6(4)(a): see Protection of Employees (Employers' Insolvency) (Variation of Limit) Regulations 2004 (SI 696/2004).

[100] *Minister for Labour v Monaghan* I 24/1990; see also *Cronin v Red Abbey Garage (PMPA) Ltd* UD871/1984.

[101] *Lynch and Tighe v Minister for Labour* I 9/1988.

[102] Protection of Employees (Employers' Insolvency) Act 1984, s 6(4)(b).

[103] Protection of Employees (Employers' Insolvency) Act 1984, s 6(2)(a)(v)(I); see eg *Woodgate v Jason Davies Security Management Services* UD 764/2006.

[104] Protection of Employees (Employers' Insolvency) Act 1984, s 6(3).

[105] Protection of Employees (Employers' Insolvency) Act 1984, s 6(2)(a)(viii)(III).

[106] Protection of Employees (Employers' Insolvency) Act 1984, s 6(2)(a)(v)(II).

[107] Protection of Employees (Employers' Insolvency) Act 1984, s 6(2)(a)(xii), (xiii).

[108] Protection of Employees (Employers' Insolvency) Act 1984, s 6(2)(a)(v)(II).

[109] Protection of Employees (Employers' Insolvency) Act 1984, s 6(2)(a)(xiv).

    (x)   Protection of Young Persons (Employment) Act 1996;[111]

    (xi)   Organisation of Working Time Act 1997;[112]

    (xii)   Protection for Persons Reporting Child Abuse Act 1998;[113]

    (xiii) European Communities (Protection of Employment) Regulations 2000;[114]

    (xiv) Protection of Employees (Part-Time Work) Act 2001;[115]

    (xv)   Competition Act 2002;[116]

    (xvi) Protection of Employees (Fixed-Term Work) Act 2003;[117]

    (xvii) European Communities (Protection of Employees on Transfer of Undertakings) Regulations (2003);[118]

    (xviii) Industrial Relations (Miscellaneous Provisions) Act 2004;[119]

    (xix) Employment Permits Act 2006.[120]

[12.45] Generally, no payments can be made from the Fund in respect of entitlements arising under the above-mentioned employment protection legislation where those entitlements are subject to an appeal unless any appeal brought has been withdrawn or determined or the time limit for lodging an appeal has expired.[121] Moreover, where the award is calculated by reference to the employee's remuneration, it may not exceed €600 in respect of any one week.[122]

Pensions

[12.46] The Insolvency Payments Scheme also covers contributions falling to be paid by an employer in accordance with an occupational pension scheme or PRSA either on his own account or on behalf of an employee.[123] The Act defines an occupational scheme broadly as:

> Any scheme or arrangement which, forming part of a contract of employment, provides or is capable of providing, in relation to employees in any description of employment, benefits (in the form of pensions or otherwise) payable to or in respect of any such employees on the termination of their employment or on their death or retirement.[124]

---

[110] Protection of Employees (Employers' Insolvency) Act 1984, s 6(2)(a)(xv).

[111] Protection of Employees (Employers' Insolvency) Act 1984, s 6(2)(a)(xvi).

[112] Protection of Employees (Employers' Insolvency) Act 1984, s 6(2)(a)(xvii).

[113] Protection of Employees (Employers' Insolvency) Act 1984, s 6(2)(a)(xviii).

[114] Protection of Employees (Employers' Insolvency) Act 1984, s 6(2)(a)(xxi).

[115] Protection of Employees (Employers' Insolvency) Act 1984, s 6(2)(a)(xix).

[116] Protection of Employees (Employers' Insolvency) Act 1984, s 6(2)(a)(xxiii).

[117] Protection of Employees (Employers' Insolvency) Act 1984, s 6(2)(a)(xx).

[118] Protection of Employees (Employers' Insolvency) Act 1984, s 6(2)(a)(xxii).

[119] Protection of Employees (Employers' Insolvency) Act 1984, s 6(2)(a)(xxv).

[120] Protection of Employees (Employers' Insolvency) Act 1984, s 6(2)(a)(xxvi).

[121] Protection of Employees (Employers' Insolvency) Act 1984, s 6(2)(c); s 6(3); s 6(4)(c).

[122] Protection of Employees (Employers' Insolvency) Act 1984, s 6(4).

[123] Protection of Employees (Employers' Insolvency) Act 1984, s 7(1).

[124] Protection of Employees (Employers' Insolvency) Act 1984, s 1.

The EAT has also taken a broad approach in determining what constitutes an occupational pension. In *Re Caven Rubber Ltd (in voluntary liquidation)*,[125] the liquidator of the insolvent company submitted a claim for payment of both the employer's and employees' unpaid pension contributions to the retirement benefit scheme although the trust deed accompanying the claim was not signed, the rules of the scheme had never been adopted, the scheme had not been approved by the Revenue Commissioner, and the only documents which had been completed in respect of the scheme were respectively, membership application forms, a proposal form by the employer as trustee of the scheme and the letter issued to the employees setting out the details of the scheme.

[12.47] In the case of contributions payable on the part of the employer, the Fund pays the lower of the following amounts:[126]

(a) the balance of the employer's contributions remaining unpaid in respect of the period of 12 months immediately preceding the date of the employer's insolvency;[127]

(b) the amount certified to be necessary by an actuary for the purpose of meeting the liability of a pension scheme on dissolution to pay the benefits provided by the scheme or in respect of the employees concerned. This only applies, where the pension scheme provides for such a liability.

[12.48] In the case of contributions payable on behalf of an employee, payment can only be made where the amount of the contributions was deducted from the pay of the employee but was not paid into the pension scheme.[128]

Application procedure

[12.49] Applications in respect of outstanding debts under the Scheme should be made to the Insolvency Payments Section of the Department of Enterprise, Trade and Employment. Such an application must normally be made via the 'relevant officer' and be accompanied by a statement in the prescribed form made by that officer'.[129] The 'relevant officer' is essentially the insolvent employer's representative and may be an executor, administrator, liquidator, receiver etc depending on the nature of the insolvency.[130] The Minister may also appoint a relevant officer where there is no such person existing in relation to an insolvency.[131] The statement sets out the amount of unpaid debt which appears to be owed to the employee on the relevant date. However, the Minister may make a payment absent such a statement in cases where no statement

---

[125] *Re Cavan Rubber Ltd* [1992] ELR 79.

[126] Protection of Employees (Employers' Insolvency) Act 1984, s 7(3).

[127] Protection of Employees (Employers' Insolvency) Act 1984, s 7(4).

[128] Protection of Employees (Employers' Insolvency) Act 1984, s 7(2).

[129] Protection of Employees (Employer's Insolvency) Act 1984, ss 6(6) and 7(6), 7(7); see Protection of Employees (Employers' Insolvency) (Forms and Procedure) Regulations 2005 (SI 682/2005), reg 4(1).

[130] Protection of Employees (Employers' Insolvency) Act, 1984, s 1(1).

[131] Protection of Employees (Employers' Insolvency) Act, 1984, s 5.

has been received by the Minister within six months of receipt of the application for payment and further delay is likely.[132]

[12.50] Once processed, the payments are made to that relevant officer who makes the appropriate statutory deductions including income tax and PRSI from these payments before paying the employees.[133] The employer's representative must notify the Insolvency Payments Section of the Department of Enterprise Trade and Employment when the payments have been made to employees.[134] The notification should set out any deductions made.

[12.51] In processing a claim, the Minister may require the employer concerned or the relevant officer to provide him with such information that he may reasonably consider to be relevant to an application.[135] In addition, the Minister may require any person having custody of control of relevant records or documents to produce them for examination.[136] Any such requirement must be notified in writing to the person on whom the requirement is imposed.[137] Where the Minister is not sure as to whether a claim is allowable in whole or in part, he has a discretion to refer any matter arising in connection with the claim to the EAT for a decision by it.[138]

[12.52] If in processing a claim, the Department becomes aware that the employer had the means to pay all or part of the debt, but there was an agreement between the employee and the employer concerned that the whole or any part of the debt would be claimed under the Scheme, no payment will be made.[139]

Transfer of employees' rights and remedies to the Minister

[12.53] Where a payment is made from the Social Insurance Fund under the terms of the Act, the rights and remedies of the employees concerned, or the persons competent to act in respect of an occupational pension scheme or PRSA, in respect of the amounts paid are transferred to the Minister.[140] In other words, the insolvent employer's liability is not eliminated by the Insolvency Act but merely transfers from the employee to the Social Insurance Fund to the extent to which that institution pays the employee the outstanding debt. Consequently, the Minister becomes a preferential creditor under the Bankruptcy Act 1988 and the Companies Acts.[141] In addition, the Minister takes priority over any

---

[132] Protection of Employees (Employers' Insolvency) Act, 1984, ss. 6(7) and 7(8).
[133] Protection of Employees (Employers' Insolvency) (Forms and Procedure) Regulations 2005, reg 4(3).
[134] Protection of Employees (Employers' Insolvency) (Forms and Procedure) Regulations 2005, reg 4(4).
[135] Protection of Employees (Employers' Insolvency) Act 1984, s 8(1)(a).
[136] Protection of Employees (Employers' Insolvency) Act 1984, s 8(1)(b).
[137] Protection of Employees (Employers' Insolvency) Act 1984, s 8(2).
[138] Protection of Employees (Employers' Insolvency) Act 1984, s 9(3); see eg *Referral by Minister for Enterprise in PSK Construction Ltd, in liquidation* (15 June 2007) EAT; see also *Kenny v Minister for Enterprise, Trade and Employment* [1999] ELR 163.
[139] Protection of Employees (Employers' Insolvency) Act 1984, s 6(8).
[140] Protection of Employees (Employers' Insolvency) Act 1984, s 10.

other outstanding claims of the employee in respect of which the employee is a preferential creditor.[142]

Appeals to the Employment Appeals Tribunal

[12.54] The Minister's decision on claims relating to arrears of remuneration, sick pay and holiday pay may be appealed to the EAT either on the grounds that:

(1) the Minister has failed to make a payment under the Act to which an employee is entitled; or

(2) the payment made is less than the amount outstanding.[143]

Normally, the appeal must be made to the Tribunal within six weeks of the communication of the minister's decision on the application to the applicant. However, the Tribunal has a discretion to extend that six-week period in certain circumstances.

Offences

[12.55] The Act provides for a number of offences.[144] In particular it is an offence to knowingly make a false statement or false representation or knowingly conceal a material fact. Offences under the Act are punishable on summary conviction to a fine not exceeding €634.87.

Conclusion

[12.56] An employer's insolvency has possibly the most drastic effect of all on the employment relationship. As set out above, in some cases, the appointment of an insolvency practitioner such as a liquidator or receiver will operate to terminate the employment contract in and of itself. Moreover, in those situations where such an appointment does not automatically terminate the employment contract, that practitioner may still decide to terminate the contract. While redundancy, by definition, also involves the termination of the employment relationship, insolvency tends to be significantly more serious than redundancy both from the employer's and from the employee's perspective. Specifically, it not only results in the termination of the employment relationship but it is very likely that there will be no possibility of the employee receiving any compensation from the employer in respect of its liabilities arising out of breaches of the employee's contractual or statutory rights.

[12.57] The potentially catastrophic effect of an employer's insolvency on an employee is attenuated to some degree by the fact that the employee becomes a preferential creditor of the employer with regard to certain debts and by his or her right to have certain debts paid out of the Social Insurance Fund. Nevertheless there are significant limits on the employee's right of recourse under both these options. Neither deals with cases of informal insolvency which arises where a company simply ceases trading without any voluntary winding up. While in theory it is open to an employee to whom a

---

[141] Protection of Employees (Employers' Insolvency) Act 1984, s 10(2).
[142] Protection of Employees (Employers' Insolvency) Act 1984, s 10(2).
[143] Protection of Employees (Employers' Insolvency) Act 1984, s 9.
[144] Protection of Employees (Employers' Insolvency) Act 1984, s 15.

debt is owed to put such a company to liquidation, the costs of such proceedings are likely to be prohibitive for an employee who has just lost his or her job. Moreover, in cases where the company has few valuable assets it will not be worth the employee's while to make such a petition for liquidation in the first place.

[12.58] Even in cases where there is a formal insolvency situation, an employee's rights to recover outstanding debts from his former employer are somewhat limited. For example, in respect of arrears of wages or holiday pay, the amount outstanding may be significantly more than the amount which the employee can obtain from either the Social Insurance Fund or as a preferential creditor. In addition, not all awards arising from breaches of contractual or statutory obligations arising from the employment relationship are covered by the relevant sections of the Bankruptcy Act, the Companies Acts or the Insolvency Act. In respect of those awards, the employee will have to take his place behind preferential creditors and hope for the best.

Part V
Employment Equality

Chapter 13

Employment Equality

Marguerite Bolger and Clíona Kimber

INTRODUCTION[1]

Background to Irish employment equality law

[13.01] From the outset, European Community law has been the engine that has driven Irish equality law. The first Irish legislation outlawing discrimination in the workplace was the Anti-Discrimination (Pay) Act 1974 (the 1974 Act), passed to ensure implementation of Ireland's obligations pursuant to the Equal Pay Directive.[2] Later, the Employment Equality Act 1977 (the 1977 Act) was passed in order to ensure implementation of the Equal Treatment Directive.[3] Those Directives had their legislative basis in Art 119 of the Treaty of Rome which recognised the principle of equal pay between men and women for equal work. Article 119, which permitted the European Court of Justice (ECJ) to view gender equality as a fundamental principle of European law,[4] was significantly developed and expanded by the Treaty of Amsterdam which provided for equality between men and women as one of its tasks under Art 2 and, in Art 13,[5] extended the principle of equality to race and ethnic origin, sexual orientation, religion and belief, age and disability. This led to the introduction of the Race Directive,[6]

---

[1] We wish to acknowledge the considerable assistance and contribution of Claire Bruton BL to the preparation of this chapter.

[2] Council Directive 75/117/EEC [1975] OJ L45/19. For further detail on the background to the Equal Treatment Directive see Curtin, *Irish Employment Equality Law* (Round Hall Press, 1989) at Ch 2.

[3] Council Directive 76/207/EEC [1976] OJ L39/40. The Equal Treatment Directive has been recently re-cast as Council Directive 2006/54/EC ([2006] OJ L204/23).

[4] For further detail on Art 119 see Curtin, *Irish Employment Equality Law* (Round Hall Press, 1989) at Ch 2.

[5] For more detail on Art 13 see Waddington, 'Article 13 EC: Setting Priorities in the Proposal for a Horizontal Employment Directive' (2000) *ILJ* 176.

[6] Council Directive 2000/43/EC [2000] OJ L180/22 on Race Discrimination. See Connolly, 'The Race Directive and the Framework Directive: An Analysis of Their Effect on Irish Employment-Part I' [2001] 13 *ILT* 206 and Connolly, 'The Race Directive and the Framework Directive: An Analysis of Their Effect on Irish Employment-Part I' [2001] 14 *ILT* 219, Guild, 'The EC Directive on Race Discrimination: Surprises, Possibilities and Limitations' (2000) *ILJ* 416 and Jones, 'Race Directive Redefining Protection from Discrimination in EU Law' (2003) 5 *EHRLR* 515.

the Framework Directive covering the grounds of sexual orientation, religion and belief, age and disability[7] and the Recast Equal Treatment Directive.[8]

[13.02] While the 1974 and 1977 Acts were introduced directly as a result of European Directives, more recent employment equality legislation in Ireland went beyond the obligations of our membership of the European Union. In 1998, the Employment Equality Act 1998 (the 1998 Act) was enacted which extended the then European principles of non-discrimination on grounds of gender and marital status to what where known as the 'new grounds' of family status, sexual orientation, religion, age, disability, race and membership of the traveller community. The extension of the principles of gender equality protection to these new grounds took place two years later in European law.[9] The new European Directives[10] necessitated some further changes to the 1998 Act. These changes were implemented by the Equality Act 2004.[11]

[13.03] National employment equality law is now therefore contained in the Employment Equality Acts 1998–2008 (the Employment Equality Act). This chapter will consider that law, and the community legal principles and jurisprudence which underlies it. Due to the fact that employment equality law, for the first twenty years or so, consisted of the law on equal pay and equal treatment on grounds of gender as well as discrimination against pregnant women, these grounds will be looked at first. The principles developed by the ECJ and the Irish courts and tribunals were then extended, broadly speaking, to the 'new' grounds. This chapter will therefore then turn to consider the new grounds which have given rise to the greatest amount of litigation, namely, age, disability, race. Finally, harassment and sexual harassment, victimisation and the level of awards will be considered. The remaining grounds of religion or belief, membership

---

[7] Council Directive 2000/78/EC [2000] L303/16 establishing a general framework for equal treatment in employment and occupation. It is worth noting that this Directive has been followed by a recent Proposed Directive on Implementing the Principle of Equal Treatment which seeks to extend the principle of equal treatment for persons irrespective of religion or belief, disability, age or sexual orientation beyond the sphere of employment and occupation. See COM(08) 436 final. For more detail on Council Directive 2000/78/EC see Skidmore, 'EC Framework Directive on Equal Treatment in Employment: Towards a Comprehensive Community Anti-Discrimination Policy' (2001) *ILJ* 126 and Waddington and Bell, 'More Equal Than Others: Distinguishing European Equality Directives' (2001) *CML Rev* 587.

[8] Council Directive 2006/54/EC ([2006] OJ L204/23).

[9] See the Race Directive, Council Directive 2000/43/EC [2000] OJ L180/22 on Race Discrimination and the Framework Directive, Council Directive 2000/78/EC ([2000] L303/16) establishing a general framework for equal treatment in employment and occupation.

[10] Race Directive, Council Directive 2000/43/EC [2000] OJ L180/22 on Race Discrimination and Council Directive 2000/78/EC ([2000] L303/16) establishing a general framework for equal treatment in employment and occupation. See also Connolly, 'The Race Directive and the Framework Directive: An Analysis of Their Effect on Irish Employment-Part I' [2001] 13 *ILT* 206 and Connolly, 'The Race Directive and the Framework Directive: An Analysis of Their Effect on Irish Employment-Part I' [2001] 14 *ILT* 219.

[11] The Equality Act 2004 came into force on 19 July 2004. For the consolidated version of the Acts, see Kerr, *Consolidated Irish Employment Legislation* (Thomson Round Hall, Release 19, April 2008), Division L.

of the Traveller community and sexual orientation will not be neglected. The legal principles discussed are also applicable to these grounds, and important cases on these grounds will be referred to at appropriate junctures in the chapter.

Basic concepts

[13.04] A consideration of employment equality law must commence with a setting out of the basic concepts. These are applicable through all the grounds.

Discrimination

[13.05] Section 8(1) of the Employment Equality Act outlaws discrimination in relation to:

(i)   access to employment;

(ii)   conditions of employment;

(iii)   training or experience for or in relation to employment;

(iv)   promotion or re-grading; or

(v)   classification of posts.

Discriminatory grounds

[13.06] Section 6(2) of the Employment Equality Act provides the 'discriminatory grounds':

As between any two persons, the discriminatory grounds (and the descriptions of those grounds) for the purposes of this Act) are –

(a)   that one is a woman one the other is a man (in this Act referred to as 'the gender ground'),

(b)   that one has marital status and the other does not (in this Act referred to as 'the marital status ground'),

(c)   that one has family status and the other does not (in this Act referred to as 'the family status ground'),

(d)   that they are of different sexual orientation (in this Act referred to as 'the sexual orientation ground'),

(e)   that one has a different religious belief from the other, or that one has a religious belief and the other has not (in this Act referred to as 'the religion ground'),

(f)   that they are of different ages, but subject to subsection (3) (in this Act referred to as 'the age ground'),

(g)   that one is a person with a disability and the other either is not or is a person with a different disability (in this Act referred to as 'the disability ground'),

(h)   that they are of different race, colour, nationality or ethnic or national origins (in this Act referred to as 'the ground of race'),

(i)   that one is a member of the Traveller community and the other is not (in this Act referred to as 'the Traveller community ground').

[13.07] An 'employee' for the purposes of the Employment Equality Act means[12]:

> subject to subsection (3), a person who has entered into or works under (or where the employment has ceased, entered into or worked under) a contract of employment and, where the context so admits, includes a member or former member of a regulatory body, but, so far as regards access to employment, does not include a person employed in another person's home for the provision of personal services for person residing in that home where the services affect the private or family life of those persons;

Section 2(3) of the Employment Equality Act, referred to in that definition, stipulates that the relevant employer under the Act of a person holding office under or in the service of the State, including a member of the Gardaí or the Defence Forces, is the State or Government; of an officer or servant of a local authority, harbour authority, HSE or VEC, is the authority, HSE or committee; and of an agency worker, is the person liable to pay the agency worker.

[13.08] 'Contract of employment' means a contract of service[13] or apprenticeship or any other contract whereby an individual agrees with another person to personally execute any work or service for that person, or an whereby an individual agrees with an employment agency to personally perform work for another person, whether the contract in question is express or implied, and, if express, whether oral or in writing.[14]

Discrimination – definition

[13.09] The Employment Equality Act[15] has a broad scope of application. Discrimination is defined as occurring where:[16]

(a) a person is treated less favourably than another person is, has been or would be treated in a comparable situation on any of the grounds specified in subsection (2) (in this Act referred to as 'discriminatory grounds') which –

   (i)   exists,
   (ii) existed but no longer exists;
   (iii) may exist in the future, or
   (iv) is imputed to the person concerned,

'Less favourable treatment' is more commonly known as 'direct discrimination' although that particular phrase is not used in the Employment Equality Act.

'Discrimination' includes discrimination by association, indirect discrimination and harassment.[17] Victimisation is also prohibited by the Act.

---

[12] Employment Equality Acts 1998–2008, s 2(1).

[13] On the meaning of this common law concept, see Ch 2, The Contract and Relationship of Employment.

[14] Employment Equality Acts 1998–2008, s 2(1).

[15] Employment Equality Acts 1998–2008, s 17, in relation to age discrimination, was amended by the Protection of Employment (Exceptional Collective Redundancies and Related Matters) Act 2007, s 27.

[16] Employment Equality Acts 1998–2008, s 6(1).

[17] For an excellent analysis of the models of discrimination in use in the EU anti discrimination legislative landscape see Doyle, 'Direct Discrimination and Indirect Discrimination and Autonomy' (2007) 27 *OJLS* 537.

Discrimination by association

[13.10] 'Discrimination' includes discrimination by association:[18]

(b)   a person who is associated with another person—

      (i)   is treated by virtue of that association, less favourably than a person who is not so associated is, has been or would be treated in a comparable situation, and

      (ii)   similar treatment of that other person on any of the discriminatory grounds would, by virtue of paragraph (a), constitute discrimination.

While not provided for in the Framework Directive,[19] the concept of unlawful discrimination by association was recognised by the ECJ in a recent decision[20] which makes it clear that the principle of non-discrimination in the Framework Directive[21] applies equally to employees who are treated less favourably or subjected to harassment by their employer on the grounds of their association with an individual protected by the Directive.

Indirect discrimination

[13.11] Indirect discrimination is defined in a number of sections in this lengthy Act, although the broad concept remains the same.[22] The definitions are all essentially similar

---

18 Employment Equality Acts 1998–2008, s 6(1)(b).

19 Council Directive 2000/78/EC [2000] L303/16 establishing a general framework for equal treatment in employment and occupation. It is worth noting that this Directive has been followed by a recent Proposed Directive on Implementing the Principle of Equal Treatment which seeks to extend the principle of equal treatment for persons irrespective of religion or belief, disability, age or sexual orientation beyond the sphere of employment and occupation. See COM(08) 436 final. For more detail on Council Directive 2000/78/EC see Skidmore, 'EC Framework Directive on Equal Treatment in Employment: Towards a Comprehensive Community Anti-Discrimination Policy' (2001) *ILJ* 126 and Waddington and Bell, 'More Equal Than Others: Distinguishing European Equality Directives' (2001) *CML Rev* 587.

20 Case C-303/06 *Coleman v Attridge Law* [2008] ICR 1128 and see also Pilgerstorfer, 'Transferred Discrimination in European Law' [2008] *ILJ* 384. Note also the case of *Six Complainants v A Public House* DEC-S2004-009-14 in which claims of discrimination by association were allowed is a claim heard under the Equal Status Act 2000. This case concerned admittance to a public house where only one of the six complainants was disabled.

21 Council Directive 2000/78/EC [2000] L303/16 establishing a general framework for equal treatment in employment and occupation. It is worth noting that this Directive has been followed by a recent Proposed Directive on Implementing the Principle of Equal Treatment which seeks to extend the principle of equal treatment for persons irrespective of religion or belief, disability, age or sexual orientation beyond the sphere of employment and occupation. See COM(08) 436 final. For more detail on Council Directive 2000/78/EC see Skidmore, 'EC Framework Directive on Equal Treatment in Employment: Towards a Comprehensive Community Anti-Discrimination Policy' (2001) *ILJ* 126 and Waddington and Bell, 'More Equal Than Others: Distinguishing European Equality Directives' (2001) I 587.

22 See Employment Equality Acts 1998–2008, ss 19(4), 22 and 31.

and can be illustrated by reference to the first one that appears in the Act at s 19(4),[23] which provides for the principle of indirect discrimination on grounds of gender in relation to pay:

(4)(a) Indirect discrimination occurs where an apparently neutral provision puts a person of a particular gender (being As or Bs) at a particular disadvantage in respect of remuneration compared with other employees of their employer.

(b) Where paragraph (a) applies, the persons referred to in that paragraph shall each be for the purposes of sub-section (1) as complying, or as the case may be, not complying with the provision concerned, whichever results in the higher remuneration, unless the provision is objectively justified by a legitimate aim and the means of achieving the aim are appropriate and necessary.

(c) In any proceedings statistics are admissible for the purpose of determining whether the sub-section applies in relation to A or B.

There is a significant distinction between less favourable treatment (direct discrimination) and indirect discrimination in that indirect discrimination can be justified by objective justification, whereas direct discrimination cannot be justified and therefore seems to attract strict liability.

Objective justification is not given a detailed definition in the Act, although the remit of the concept can be seen for example in s 19(4)(b) where indirectly discriminatory rates of pay are prohibited 'unless the provision is objectively justified by a legitimate aim and the aims of achieving the aim are appropriate and necessary.'

[13.12] The Labour Court has expressed some doubt as to whether the definition of indirect discrimination contained in s 19(4) fully comported with the definition of that concept as set out in the Framework Directive.[24] In *Department of Justice, Equality & Law Reform v The Civil Public and Services Union*[25] the Court adopted the test for objective justification utilised in the case of *Barton v Investec PC Henderson Crosthwaite Securities Ltd*[26] as follows:

(1) that there were objective reasons for the difference;

(2) unrelated to sex;

(3) corresponding to a real need on the part of the undertaking;

(4) appropriate to achieving the objective pursued;

(5) it was necessary to that end;

(6) that the difference conformed to the principle of proportionality;

(7) that was the case throughout the period during which the differential existed.

---

[23] This section was amended by the Equality Act 2004 to reflect the new definitions of indirect discrimination in the European Directives.

[24] Council Directive 2000/78/EC ([2000] L303/16) establishing a general framework for equal treatment in employment and occupation.

[25] *Department of Justice, Equality & Law Reform v The Civil Public and Services Union* EDA 13/2007 (Labour Court).

[26] *Barton v Investec PC Henderson Crosthwaite Securities Ltd* [2003] IRLR 332.

[13.13] The case of *O'Donnell and Others v The HSE*[27] shows an interesting application by the Equality Tribunal of the concept of indirect discrimination and whether such discrimination can be objectively justified on the facts. A complaint of indirect discrimination on grounds of marital status and family status was brought by a number of nurses who were required to work a roster of seven consecutive days in a row and on occasion thirteen out of sixteen days which meant that they were away from home for thirteen and a half hours per day for continuous periods. The Equality Officer found that the roster indirectly discriminated against the complainants on gender and family status grounds and found that the maintenance of the roster was not objectively justified. She awarded compensation of €5,000 to each of the complainants. Even more significantly in terms of the remedies available to the Equality Officer and their willingness to apply them, the Equality Officer in this case directed the employer to immediately implement a new roster.

Harassment on a protected ground

[13.14] 'Discrimination' includes 'harassment', which is defined in s 14A(7):

(a) In this section—

    (i) references to harassment are to any form of unwanted conduct related to any of the discriminatory grounds, and

    (ii) references to sexual harassment or to any form of unwanted verbal, non-verbal or physical conduct of a sexual nature,

(b) being conduct which in either case has the purpose or effect of violating a person's dignity and creating an intimidating, hostile, degrading, humiliating or offensive environment for the person.

    (i) Without prejudice to the generality of paragraph (a) such unwanted conduct may consist of acts, requests, spoken word or gestures or the production, display or circulation of written words, pictures or other material.

[13.15] Harassment is considered in para **[13.19]** *et seq* of this chapter. It is important to remember that the scope of harassment on a protected ground is an act which subjects a person to unwanted conduct on any of the protected discriminatory grounds, for example, sexual harassment, religious harassment or racial harassment. The Employment Equality Act does not apply to a generalised bullying or harassment claim which has no link to the discriminatory grounds.

Victimisation

[13.16] 'Victimisation' is also prohibited by the Employment Equality Act. Section 74(2) provides:

(2) For the purposes of this Part victimisation occurs where dismissal or other adverse treatment of an employee by his or her employer occurs as a reaction to—

(a) a complaint of discrimination made by the employee to the employer,

(b) any proceedings by a complainant,

---

[27] *O'Donnell and Others v The HSE* DEC-E2006-023 (Equality Tribunal).

(c)   an employee having represented or otherwise supported a complainant,

(d)   the work of an employee having been compared with that of another employee for any of the purposes of this Act or any enactment repealed by this Act,

(e)   an employee having been a witness in any proceedings under this Act or the Equal Status Act 2000 or any such repealed enactment,

(f)   an employee having opposed by lawful means an act which is unlawful under this Act or the said Act of 2000 or which was unlawful under any such repealed enactment, or

(g)   an employee having given notice of an intention to take any of the actions mentioned in the preceding paragraphs.

Punishing a person for complaining about or opposing unlawful discrimination, bringing proceedings or assisting another person in bringing proceedings is outlawed under this section. What constitutes unlawful victimisation is defined in broad terms. Even though it may not involve actual discrimination, the concept of victimisation has been the subject of very effective litigation with high levels of awards. Victimisation is considered in paras **[13.50]** *et seq* of this chapter.

Vicarious liability

[13.17] Vicarious liability is expressly provided for by s 15(1) of the Employment Equality Act:

> anything done by a person in the course of his or her employment shall, in any proceedings brought under this Act, be treated for the purpose of this Act as done also by that person's employer, whether or not it was done with the employer's knowledge or approval.

That is subject to a defence under s 15(3) available where the employer can prove that they took such steps as were 'reasonably practicable' to prevent the employee from doing the act or from doing in the course of his or her employment, acts of that description.

Burden of proof

[13.18] The burden of proof on a claimant under the Employment Equality Act reflects the provisions of the European Directives[28] and the jurisprudence developed by the ECJ. Due to the difficulties encountered by litigants in proving discrimination against employers who tend to have all of the information and documentation, the burden of proof of discrimination has been partly shifted to the employer. Section 85A of the Employment Equality Act provides:

---

[28] See Council Directive 1997/80/EC on the burden of proof in cases of discrimination based on sex, Art 19 of the Recast Equal Treatment Directive, Council Directive 2006/54/EC on the implementation of the principle of equal opportunities and equal treatment of men and women in matters of employment and occupation [2006] OJ L204/23, Art 9 of the Race Directive, Council Directive 2000/43/EC [2000] OJ L180/22 on race discrimination and Art 10 of the Framework Directive, Council Directive 2000/78/EC [2000] L303/16 establishing a general framework for equal treatment in employment and occupation.

(1) Where in any proceedings facts are established by or on behalf of a complainant from which it may be presumed that there has been discrimination in relation to him or her, it is for the respondent to prove the contrary.....

(4) In this section 'discrimination' includes –

(a)   indirect discrimination,

(b)   victimisation,

(c)   harassment or sexual harassment,

(d)   the inclusion in a collective agreement to which section 9 applies of a provision which, by virtue of that section, is null and void.

Thus in an employment equality claim the claimant must only establish a *prima facie* case of discrimination. Once this has been established, the burden shifts to the respondent to rebut the claim on the balance of probabilities.

HARASSMENT

[13.19] Harassment, including sexual harassment, was prohibited by the Employment Equality Act 1998 even before the European Community began to legislate in the area.[29] The European Directives, including the Recast Equal Treatment Directive,[30] the Race Directive[31] and the Framework Directive,[32] all now specifically include a prohibition on harassment discrimination.

Defining harassment

[13.20] The Recast Equal Treatment Directive[33] defines harassment in relation to gender in Art 2(1)(c):

> where unwanted conduct related to the sex of a person occurs with the purpose or effect of violating the dignity of a person, and of creating an intimidating, hostile, degrading, humiliating or offensive environment.

Article 2(1)(d) defines sexual harassment as occurring:

> where any form of unwanted verbal, non-verbal or physical conduct of a sexual nature occurs, with the purpose or effect of violating the dignity of a person, in particular when creating an intimidating, hostile, degrading, humiliating or offensive environment.

---

[29] For a discussion of the development of sexual harassment in Irish law see Bolger and Kimber, *Sex Discrimination Law* (Round Hall, 2000), Ch 8. For a discussion of developments in harassment and sexual harassment in the United Kingdom see Barmes, 'Constitution, Conceptual Complexities in UK Implementation of EU Harassment Provisions' [2007] *ILJ* 446 and Clarke, 'Harassment, Sexual Harassment and the Employment Equality (Sex Discrimination) Regulations 2005' (2006) *ILJ* 161.

[30] Council Directive 2006/54/EC [2006] OJ L204/23.

[31] Council Directive 2000/43/EC [2000] OJ L180/22 on race discrimination.

[32] Council Directive 2000/78/EC [2000] L303/16 establishing a general framework for equal treatment in employment and occupation.

[33] Council Directive 2006/54/EC [2006] OJ L204/23.

[13.21] The Race Directive[34] provides at Art 2(3) that harassment:

> shall be deemed to be discriminative within the meaning of paragraph 1, when an unwanted conduct related to racial or ethnic origin takes place with the purpose or effect of violating the dignity of a person and/or creating an intimidating, hostile, degrading, humiliating or offensive environment.

The Framework Directive makes similar provision in relation to harassment on grounds of religion or belief, disability, age or sexual orientation.[35]

[13.22] Each of the three Directives uses the phrase 'related to' the outlawed grounds in defining harassment. That phrase was found to have significance in the UK EAT decision of *English v Thomas Sanderson Blinds Ltd*[36] where the Tribunal found that there was a material difference between the wording contained in the relevant Regulations and the wording in Art 2(3) of the Framework Directive.[37] It held that the phrase used in the Regulations, 'on grounds of' sexual orientation, imported the concept of causation; asking why the alleged discriminator acted as he did, which the Tribunal found was not the same issue as that raised by Art 2(3) of the Directive. The Tribunal held that the phrase 'on the grounds of' in the UK Regulations did not properly implement the Directive.[38]

[13.23] By contrast, s 14(A)(7) of the Employment Equality Act provides that references to harassment are to 'any form of unwanted conduct relating to any of the discriminatory grounds'. So while s 6, which outlaws discrimination in general, refers to discrimination occurring where a person is treated less favourably 'on any of the [discriminatory] grounds', s 14A(7) ensures compliance with the Directives by using the phrase 'related to' rather than the potentially more narrow 'on grounds of' in setting out the scope of unlawful harassment.

Section 14A was inserted into the Employment Equality Act 1998 by the Equality Act 2004 and was designed to ensure implementation of the new definitions of harassment and sexual harassment contained in the European Directives. The previous definitions of harassment were far more objective in that there was express reference to what a 'reasonable person' may have viewed as offensive and intimidatory. These definitions were replaced with a new one in s 14A(7) which is significantly more subjective in providing:

(a)   In this section –

    (i)   references to harassment are to any form of unwanted conduct related to any of the discriminatory grounds, and

    (ii)   references to sexual harassment or to any form of unwanted verbal, non-verbal or physical conduct of a sexual nature,

---

[34] Council Directive 2000/43/EC [2000] OJ L180/22 on race discrimination.

[35] Framework Directive, Council Directive 2000/78/EC [2000] L303/16 establishing a general framework for equal treatment in employment and occupation, Art 2.

[36] *English v Thomas Sanderson Blinds Ltd* [2008] ICR 607.

[37] Council Directive 2000/78/EC ([2000] L303/16) establishing a general framework for equal treatment in employment and occupation.

[38] For a discussion of this case, see Banton, 'Sexual Anomalies' [2008] *NLJ* 47.

(b)   being conduct which in either case has the purpose or effect of violating a person's dignity and creating an intimidating, hostile, degrading, humiliating or offensive environment for the person.

(c)   Without prejudice to the generality of paragraph (a) such unwanted conduct may consist of acts, requests, spoken word or gestures or the production, display or circulation of written words, pictures or other material.

[13.24] Harassment and sexual harassment are clearly defined as 'unwanted' conduct which inevitably and necessarily involves an analysis of the conduct from the point of view of the recipient rather than the perpetrator. While s 14A(7)(b) refers to conduct which has the 'purpose' of violating a person's dignity etc, it also refers to conduct which has the 'effect' of doing so. By referring to 'effect', the purpose or intention of the perpetrator is largely irrelevant particularly when the conduct in question is defined as unwanted conduct. The net result is that conduct which is viewed by the recipient as unwanted and as having the effect of violating their dignity etc, could be deemed to be harassment regardless of the intention of the perpetrator and of the reasonableness of the recipient's inevitably subjective views of the conduct or the effect which the conduct has on them. There is no requirement in these definitions that the conduct in itself be reasonably capable of being viewed as harassment.

The subjective definition of sexual harassment gives rise to the very real possibility that a person could be found guilty of harassment simply because the recipient of their innocent conduct perceives that conduct as harassment, in spite of there being no reasonable basis for that perception. It is difficult in practice to see a court or tribunal taking such an approach but in theory, the definition as contained in the Employment Equality Act and as required by the European Directives, does seem to require and permit that approach.

[13.25] In practice, a less rigid approach has been adopted by the Equality Tribunal and the Labour Court, although they have on a number of occasions pointed out that it is the effect that the conduct has on the recipient rather than the intention of the perpetrator which matters. The Equality Tribunal has repeatedly stated that the person alleging harassment must establish, on the balance of probabilities, that the harassment did in fact take place. If this is established, the Tribunal will consider whether the employer was vicariously responsible for the harassment and whether the employer took reasonable steps to prevent it from taking place. Therefore even where a claimant alleges harassment on what is clearly a subjective standpoint, it does not absolve them of the burden of proving a *prima facie* case that the conduct did in fact occur.

[13.26] An example of this approach can be seen in the case of *Scanlon v St Vincent's Hospital*[39] where the claimant claimed to have been subjected to discriminatory treatment and harassment on grounds of his race after his supervisor became aware that he was born in England. The claimant relied in particular on comments made by his supervisor about England having lost a soccer match. While the Equality Officer accepted that a comment had been made about England losing the match because the team was over confident, he went on to conclude:

---

[39]   *Scanlon v St Vincent's Hospital* DEC-EE2004/284 (Equality Tribunal).

I am therefore satisfied that the comment was made in that context and was not directed at the complainant personally in a manner that could be construed as harassment under the Act. I am supporting my decision in this regard by the fact that the complainant's colleagues, including Mr X were unaware until that time that he was born in England... and that on two occasions in June 2004 when the complainant had an opportunity to raise his concerns about Mr X's senior management in the hospital, he did not do so. In the light of the foregoing, I find that the complainant has failed to establish any primary facts from which it could be inferred he was harassed on grounds of his race.

While the approach adopted by the Equality Officer is a sensible one, it does not necessarily fit in with the subjective definition of harassment as contained in s 14A. The Equality Officer found that the comment about the soccer match had occurred. The claimant claimed that this conduct had the effect of violating his dignity and/or created an intimidating, hostile, degrading, humiliating or offensive environment for him. The claimant also presumably took the view that the conduct in question was unwanted. Therefore the conduct seems to come within the definition of harassment as set out in s 14A(7). On the other hand, it is still up to the claimant to establish a *prima facie* case that the conduct was related to his race although the level of evidence to establish such a *prima facie* case does seem to be quite low. On the facts, the Equality Officer found that such a *prima facie* case had not been raised. While the outcome is sensible, it is questionable whether the approach is entirely consistent with the relevant provisions of the Act.

[13.27] In ascertaining the intention of the perpetrators in *Scanlon*,[40] the fact that they were unaware at the time of the comments that the claimant was even born in England clearly influenced the Equality Officer's decision. However innocent intent of itself does not prevent conduct from constituting harassment. In the case of *Gabrielle Piazza v The Clarion Hotel*[41] the claimant claimed that he was harassed on grounds of his sexual orientation in the form of emails sent from his manager to the Human Resources manager and verbal comments made by his fellow employees. He reported each incident to the general manager who investigated the matter under the hotel's grievance procedure and advised him that there had been no 'intent, desire or deliberate attempt to offend you or the nature of your sexual orientation'. During the hearing, the Equality Officer inquired as to the operation of the grievance procedure and the types of issues that would be dealt with by way of the grievance procedure. The respondent indicated that the procedure would be utilised for general grievances such as work practice issues and employees having inter-personal problems. The Equality Officer did not consider that a serious issue such as an allegation of harassment should be dealt with by way of the grievance procedure. The respondent had no policy on the prevention of harassment in the workplace at the relevant time. Furthermore, she felt that the grievance procedure referred to in the handbook was not sufficiently detailed and would leave the employee uncertain as to how the matter would proceed. The Equality Officer found that the investigation had been totally unsatisfactory and that the claimant had been

---

[40] *Scanlon* DEC-E2007-011 (Equality Tribunal).
[41] *Gabrielle Piazza v The Clarion Hotel* DEC-E2004-033 (Equality Tribunal).

discriminated against on the sexual orientation ground. Compensation of €10,000 was awarded.

[13.28] It is clear in relation to sexual harassment that the conduct itself must be 'of a sexual nature' as set out in s14A(7)(a)(ii). The significance of that can be seen in *A Government Department v Complainant*[42] where the claimant made a claim of sexual harassment arising from a written comment made by a male colleague who suggested that the claimant wished to have a sexual relationship with a named female colleague. The colleague admitted to making comments which the investigator found could have caused offence and ought not to have been used. However the Court found that 'a single comment made regarding the interest of one person in another of the opposite sex could not really be regarded as sexual harassment'. The Court pointed out that there were no particular or out of the ordinary circumstances which could come within the definition of same-sex harassment. The Court looked to the definition of sexual harassment in the Act and to the Employment Equality Act 1998 (Code of Practice) (Harassment) Order 2002[43] and held:

> The Court does not accept that even if it was made as the complainant describes, that it could reasonably be regarded as *sexually* offensive to the complainant, or humiliating to him on the *gender* ground. Neither can it be regarded as a sexual advance, proposition or as pressure for sexual activity. The Court does accept that it may have been offensive, humiliating and even intimidating but it does not accept the complainant's contention that it constitutes discrimination/sexual harassment within the meaning of the 1977 Act.

The nature of the conduct

[13.29] While it is clear from the definitions of harassment and sexual harassment that even relatively minor conduct may constitute unlawful harassment, it is also clear from the case law that the Equality Tribunal and the Labour Court will take a very different view of the remedies to be awarded depending on the severity of the conduct involved. The various different ways in which harassment and sexual harassment can occur are considered here.

Assault

[13.30] Cases of harassment and sexual harassment can range from relatively minor incidents of verbal harassment to very serious incidents of actual or attempted sexual assault. There are many examples of the maximum level of compensation being awarded where a claimant has been found to have been the victim of serious harassment such as a sexual assault. For example, in *A Complainant v A Contract Cleaning Company*[44] the claimant alleged that crude and sexually offensive remarks had been made to her by a security guard at a shopping centre where she was employed to provide cleaning services. This behaviour culminated in the security guard striking her on her bottom. The company accepted that a witness had seen the security guard strike the claimant on her bottom but suggested that these actions were not intended as an act of

---

[42] *A Government Department v Complainant* EDA 0515/2005 (Labour Court).

[43] SI 78/2002. This Code is reproduced in Appendix C.

[44] *A Complainant v A Contract Cleaning Company* DEC-E2004-068 (Equality Tribunal).

any intimacy and that the claimant appeared amused by the security guard's actions. The Equality Officer decided, on the balance of probabilities, that the claimant's evidence was more compelling particularly as she had reported the matter to the Gardaí early the following morning. However the Equality Officer also pointed out that:

> even a single slap on the bottom is sufficient to constitute an act of sexual harassment... I note the respondent's comment, whilst accepting Mr B struck the complainant on the bottom that his actions were in no way intended as an act of any intimacy. The question of intent on Mr B's part is not relevant as section 23(3) of the Act[45] clearly leaves the decision as to whether or not the behaviour is unwelcome with the complainant. I am satisfied that she found the behaviour unwelcome and she spoke with her husband about it on her return home (he confirmed this at the hearing), she reported the incident to the Gardaí later that night (19 December) and also reported the matter to both her employer and Mr B's employer the next morning (the first opportunity for her to do so).

Having found that the steps taken by the respondent after the claimant made her complaint did not entitle them to a defence under s 15, the Equality Officer awarded the maximum compensation available of €21,000. He stated that had the constraint of the statute not been placed upon him, he would have ordered a significantly higher award given the severity of the treatment to which the claimant was subjected.

[13.31] It is possible that a physical assault might not constitute unlawful sexual harassment if it is not considered to constitute conduct of a sexual nature. In the case of *A Female Employee v A Printing Company*[46] the claimant alleged non consensual acts of physical intimacy by her male co-employees and mangers including slapping and pinching her bottom and pinching her arms. She also referred to an incident during which a male colleague kicked her and told her to 'shut up'. While the Equality Officer was satisfied that some of the conduct to which the complainant was subjected amounted to sexual harassment, in relation to the kick he was:

> not satisfied that it could be regarded on the gender ground to be offensive, humiliating or intimidating to the complainant in accordance with section 23(3) of the Act.[47]

While a physical assault is clearly at the upper end of the scale of what may constitute harassment and sexual harassment, there have been cases where non-physical conduct has also been found to constitute very serious harassment. In *BH v Named Company trading as a Cab Company*,[48] the female claimant described a number of non-physical incidents including the display of highly offensive material in her workplace, an incident where dead fish had been thrown on to the internal roof of the office and another incident where laxative tablets and steroids were placed in the office kettle that she had

---

[45] Employment Equality 1998, s 23(3) provided the definition of sexual harassment. Section 23 was repealed by the Equality Act 2004 and the new definition is contained inserted as s 14A of the Employment Equality Acts 1998–2008. The definition is noted above in para **[13.20]** *et seq.*

[46] *A Female Employee v a Printing Company* DEC-E2008-022 (Equality Tribunal).

[47] Employment Equality 1998, s 23(3) provided the definition of sexual harassment. Section 23 was repealed by the Equality Act 2004 and the new definition is contained inserted as s 14A of the Employment Equality Acts 1998–2008. The definition is noted above in para **[13.20]** *et seq.*

[48] *BH v Named Company trading as a Cab Company* DEC-E2006-026 (Equality Tribunal).

used which she believed was intended to refer to her gender and her weight. She made a complaint to her manager even though the employer had no policy in place but nothing was done. The Director of Equality Investigations had no difficulty whatsoever in finding the company liable for the sexual harassment that had been perpetrated and in the light of its 'grossly offensive nature' and the complete failure of the employer to address it, the Director considered it appropriate to make the maximum award possible under the Act of two years' remuneration along with interest from the date of the reference of the complaint. She also directed the employer to put a sexual harassment and harassment policy in place.

Text messages

[13.32] A number of cases have found the use of offensive text messages to constitute harassment and/or sexual harassment. In the case of *A Female Employee v A Recruitment Company*[49] the claimant received a number of sexually explicit text messages from a male colleague's phone during an after-work drinks evening. The claimant was very shocked and upset and concerned about going to work the following day. She was later told that the text messages had been sent by someone else on her colleague's telephone. The claimant sought an investigation and this was rejected by the employer. The claimant was dismissed because of her refusal to return to work. The Equality Officer had no difficulty in find that the text messages from the phone constituted sexual harassment which had been carried out in the course of the claimant's colleague's employment, whether or not it was carried out without the employer's knowledge or approval.

[13.33] Text messages also arose in the case of *CL v CRM*[50] and again the conduct was found to constitute sexual harassment. However in the light of what the Equality Officer referred to as 'compelling evidence that the complainant herself instigated some of the incidents in the respondent organisation', a relatively low award of compensation of €1,000 was made which suggested some form of contribution to the sexual harassment by the claimant.

That is not to say that evidence of a claimant contributing to or participating in a certain level of banter, including sexual banter, in the workplace will in itself deprive the claimant of an entitlement to claim that they have been sexually harassed. The weight to be attached to the evidence of such participation will be seen in the level of award made rather than a refusal to make a finding of harassment. In *A Female Employee v A Recruitment Company*,[51] the respondent sought to make the case that the claimant was someone who had engaged in explicit sexual banter with other employees in the respondent company and had had a casual sexual relationship with at least one employee during her time there. Therefore they suggested that her reaction to the text was entirely inconsistent with her character and demeanour. The Equality Officer found that whether the claimant was engaged in sexual banter was 'irrelevant in deciding whether she was

---

[49]   *A Female Employee v A Recruitment Company* DEC-E2008-15 (Equality Tribunal), referred to also in para **[13.38]**.
[50]   *CL v CRM* [2004] 15 ELR 265.
[51]   *A Female Employee v A Recruitment Company* DEC-E2008-15 (Equality Tribunal).

sexually harassed'. In coming to that conclusion, the Equality Officer referred to a determination of the Labour Court in *A Company v a Worker*[52] where the Labour Court accepted that there was some element of the complainant being a willing participant in sexual banter, but found that the treatment she had received and the atmosphere directed towards her was 'totally unacceptable'. The Equality Officer in the *Recruitment Company*[53] stated that that case:

> should not be interpreted as a finding that sexual banter is permissible in any workplace and I consider that in certain circumstances, it could in itself constitute sexual harassment within the meaning of Section 14A of the Employment Equality Acts 1998 and 2008.

Verbal harassment

[13.34] Even where harassment involves verbal abuse only, it can have serious effects on the victim. In *Odion v Techniform (Waterford) Ltd*[54] the claimant was a Nigerian national who had been subjected to ongoing negative remarks referring to his nationality and colour. He made a formal complaint of harassment. An external investigation found that no bullying or harassment had occurred, but considered that cultural differences had arisen which required tolerance and acceptance by both sides. By that time the claimant was on sick leave due to his experiences at work. The Equality Officer found that the claimant had been subjected to harassment on grounds of his race and while the employer had acted promptly in dealing with the complaint, the Equality Officer was not satisfied that the outcome of the investigation adequately described the circumstances between the workers. She found the employer's failure to deal with the situation left the claimant feeling isolated in the workplace, which constituted discrimination on grounds of race. Compensation of €7,500 was awarded.

[13.35] In *A Worker v An Engineering Company*[55] the claimant was a British national who claimed to have been subjected to constant harassing remarks because of his nationality including name calling, laughing and sniggering. He also claimed that the crew would gather around him, jump like a football crowd and sing anti-British rebel songs. As a result of his experiences, the complainant started to have lunch in his car. While he did not make any complaints to anyone during his employment, the Equality Officer found that this was justified in circumstances where his own supervisor had participated in the treatment of which he complained. That supervisor at the hearing described the treatment as 'banter'. In spite of that view, the Equality Officer had no difficulty in finding that the treatment constituted harassment on grounds of the claimant's nationality and awarded significant compensation of €20,000 for the harassment. In awarding this sum, the Equality Officer expressly took account of the fact that the harassment had persisted for nearly the entire time of his employment, that some of the acts committed were of a blatant and intimidatory nature and that the supervisor was aware of the situation and failed to take any action in respect of same.

---

[52] *A Company v a Worker* DEC-2001-018 (Equality Tribunal).
[53] *Recruitment Company* DEC-E2008-15 (Equality Tribunal).
[54] *Odion v Techniform (Waterford) Ltd* DEC-E2007-018 (Equality Tribunal).
[55] *A Worker v An Engineering Company* DEC-2008-38 (Equality Tribunal).

Harassment by non-employees

[13.36] The Equality Tribunal and the Labour Court have long held the view that an employer can be liable for harassment and sexual harassment perpetrated by non-employees, where the employer has some control over the individuals who perpetrated the harassment. In a case under the 1977 Act, *A Boys' Secondary School v Two Female Teachers*,[56] the Labour Court upheld the Equality Tribunal decision which found that a school was responsible for the sexual harassment of two teachers by the pupils. In coming to its conclusion, the Labour Court relied on two English decisions, *Bennett v Essex County Council*[57] and *Burton and Rhule v DeVere Hotels*[58] and concluded that:

> if an employer controls the situation in which harassment occurs and fails to exercise that control so as to prevent the harassment from occurring or in reducing the extent of it, he/she will be directly liable for having subjected the employee to the harassment. As the Court understands the principle, liability arises not from the existence of control but from the failure to properly exercise that control so as to protect the employee against harassment. To hold otherwise would be to confuse vicarious liability, which is strict, with direct liability, which depends on a causal link between the harassment complained of and some fault on the part of the employer.

Section 14A(1)(a)(iii) now provides for liability where an employee is harassed by:

> a client, customer or other business contact of the victim's employer and the circumstances of the harassment are such that the employer ought reasonably to have taken steps to prevent it.

[13.37] In *Atkinson v Carty & Others*[59] the Circuit Court found the employer liable for the sexual harassment perpetrated by its accountant, who was not an employee, but who regularly attended at the employer's premises and had dealings with the plaintiff in private in the course of the plaintiff's employment during which the plaintiff was subjected to conduct which clearly constituted sexual harassment.

In the more recent case of *BH v A Named Company Trading as a Cab*,[60] the claimant had been sexually harassed by a number of drivers who provided services for the company. The company argued it could not be vicariously liable for the actions of its drivers. The Tribunal held that the drivers clearly came within the scope of the Act either as employees or as business contacts with whom the employer might reasonably expect the complainant to come into contact in the workplace or otherwise in the course of her employment.

Harassment outside of the workplace

[13.38] The Employment Equality Act 1998 (Code of Practice) (Harassment) Order 2002[61] confirms the possibility of harassment and sexual harassment occurring outside the workplace:

---

[56] *A Boys' Secondary School v Two Female Teachers* DEE 021 (Labour Court).
[57] *Bennett v Essex County Council* EAT-1447-98.
[58] *Burton and Rhule v DeVere Hotels* [1996] IRLR 596.
[59] *Atkinson v Carty & Others* [2005] 16 ELR 1.
[60] *BH v A Named Company Trading as a Cab* DEC-E2006-026 (Equality Tribunal).
[61] SI 78/2002. This Code is reproduced in Appendix C.

The scope of the sexual harassment and harassment provisions extends beyond the workplace for example, to conferences and training that occur outside the workplace. It may also extend to work-related social events.

Section 14A of the Employment Equality Act also recognises that harassment may take place outside of the workplace in providing for liability where it occurs other than at the workplace 'in the course of his or her employment'.[62]

The Equality Tribunal and the Labour Court have had little difficulty in establishing liability where a person is harassed at what is clearly a work related event such as a conference or a Christmas party. A situation which gives rise to more difficulty is a social event over which the employer has no control such as post work drinks on a Friday night. Liability clearly arises in relation to the former and may or may not arise in relation to the latter, depending on the circumstances.

In *A Female Employee v A Recruitment Company*[63] the claimant was subjected to sexually offensive text messages during and after a night out with work colleagues. It was not an event organised by her employer. In finding that the employer was liable for what took place, the Equality Officer referred to the case of *Maguire v North Western Health Board*[64] where the employer was held to be liable for discrimination which occurred at a Christmas party. The Equality Officer pointed out, in relying on that case, that the employee would not have been present had she not been employed by the employer and therefore found that the actions of her colleagues were carried out in the course of their employment and 'notwithstanding that the actions may have been carried out without the employer's knowledge or approval, the respondent is vicariously liable.'.

[13.39] However, the analogy with the Christmas party is not necessarily one which can be made given that the Christmas party in *Maguire*[65] was clearly an event organised by the employer whereas the drinks evening in *A Recruitment Company*[66] was one which was organised by the employees themselves. While it would appear that the Equality Tribunal was correct in finding the employer liable given the inadequate manner in which they responded to the complaint made, it would perhaps have been more correct to have found that liability on the basis of the inadequacy of the response rather than on the basis of the responsibilty of the employer for conduct which took place at an event in which it had absolutely no input and over which it had no control.

[13.40] In the case of *O'N v An Insurance Company*[67] the sexual harassment occurred while the claimant was on a night out with the employee's sports and social club which in turn was sponsored by the employer. The Equality Officer found that financial sponsorship by an employer of a social event where sexual harassment occurs is sufficient in itself to establish liability. In the case of *Z v An Hotel*,[68] the Equality Officer

---

[62] Employment Equality Acts 1998–2008, s 14A(1)(a).

[63] *A Female Employee v A Recruitment Company* DEC-E2008-015 (Equality Tribunal).

[64] *Maguire v North Western Health Board* [2003] 14 ELR 340.

[65] [2003] 14 ELR 340.

[66] *A Recruitment Company* DEC-E2008-015 (Equality Tribunal).

[67] *O'N v An Insurance Company* DEC-E2004-052 (Equality Tribunal).

[68] *Z v An Hotel* DEC-E2007-014 (Equality Tribunal).

had no great difficulty in finding the employer responsible for verbal harassment by the employer's manager which took place at the employer's Christmas party.

Harassment arising from discrimination by association

[13.41] As noted in para **[13.10]** above, the Employment Equality Act includes discrimination by association within the definition of discrimination.[69] It follows that harassment of a person as a result of their association with a person who falls into a protected ground constitutes unlawful harassment and is actionable pursuant to s 14A. While there is no decided case in Irish employment equality law where a person has successfully claimed harassment arising from such an association, a recent decision of the ECJ gives clear appraisal to this concept of harassment on grounds of association.[70]

In *Coleman v Attridge Law*[71] the plaintiff claimed that she had been treated less favourably than other employees because she was the primary carer of a disabled child. She claimed that she had been discriminated against and harassed. In relation to the harassment claim, she alleged abusive and insulting comments were made both about her and her child whereas no such comments were made when other employees asked for time off or a degree of flexibility in order to look after non-disabled children. The ECJ found that the Framework Directive[72] outlawed not only direct discrimination of people who are themselves disabled but also less favourable treatment of a person where that treatment is based on the disability of their child. The Court held:

> Where it is established that the unwanted conduct amounting to harassment which is suffered by an employee who is not himself disabled is related to the disability of his child, whose care is provided primarily by that employee, such conduct is contrary to the principle of equal treatment enshrined in Directive 2000/78 and, in particular to the prohibition of harassment laid down by Article 2(3) thereof.[73]

A defence to a claim of harassment

[13.42] Sections 14(2) and 15(3) of the Employment Equality Act allow an employer a defence to a claim of harassment and/or sexual harassment where the employer can show that it took such steps as were reasonably practicable to prevent the employee from doing the act which is found to have constituted harassment or from doing in the course of his employment acts of that description.

---

[69] Employment Equality Acts 1998–2008, s 6(1)(b).

[70] Case C-303/06 *Coleman v Attridge Law* [2008] ICR 1128. This case is considered in para **[13.198]** above in relation to discrimination on the disability ground. However, a case in which claims of discrimination by association were allowed is that of *Six Complainants v A Public House* DEC-S2004-009-14 heard under the Equal Status Act 2000. This case concerned admittance to a public house where only one of the six complainants was disabled.

[71] Case C-303/06 *Coleman v Attridge Law* [2008] ICR 1128 and see also Pilgerstorfer, 'Transferred Discrimination in European Law' [2008] *ILJ* 384.

[72] Council Directive 2000/78/EC [2000] L303/16 establishing a general framework for equal treatment in employment and occupation.

[73] In his opinion, the Advocate General considered the rationale for providing such protection from discrimination in more detail than the ECJ. See his Opinion of 31 January 2008.

The Employment Equality Act 1998 (Code of Practice) (Harassment) Order 2002[74] places a significant emphasis on having a policy in place and gives practical assistance to an employer on how the policy should be drawn up, implemented and communicated to employees and any other persons such as clients or business contacts who may be affected by it. The Code emphasises that the purpose of a policy is to prevent harassment:

> Prevention is the best way to minimise sexual harassment and harassment in the workplace. An effective policy and a strong commitment to implementing it is required. The purpose of an effective policy is not simply to prevent unlawful behaviour but to encourage best practice and a safe and harmonious work place where such behaviour is unlikely to occur. This policy is likely to be more effective when it is linked to a broader policy of promoting equality of opportunity.
>
> Employers should adopt, implement and monitor a comprehensive, effective and accessible policy on sexual harassment and harassment.

The case law illustrates in very stark terms how the existence of a policy which has been effectively communicated to employees can provide a defence to an employer, even where an employee has been found guilty of harassment or sexual harassment. The absence of a policy can make it difficult if not impossible for an employer to avoid liability for harassment or sexual harassment perpetrated by an employee or business contact.

[13.43] In *SC v A Named Organisation*,[75] the Equality Officer rejected the claimant's claim of sexual harassment and found that the employer had responded properly to the complaints made by her. The decision sets out a good summary of what the law requires from an employer once a complaint has been made to it:

> I am satisfied that the internal investigation carried out by the investigator appointed by the respondent was conducted in an appropriate manner. The formal process was agreed by the parties to the complaint and the investigator conducted his investigation to the best of his ability thereafter. In terms of a complaint of this nature the respondent organisation should have personnel who are trained in the Employment Equality legislation and in the processes to be followed in carrying out such an investigation. Ideally two persons should conduct the investigation. There should be a formally agreed procedure for the investigation and a timeframe by which the investigation should be completed. Where possible witnesses should be consulted but the onus should be on the parties to the complaint to have these witnesses make a written statement and/or be available for questioning by the Investigators at an agreed time and venue. This would form part of the agreed process.... There should also be a mechanism for appealing the findings of an internal investigation to a more senior level appeal body in the respondent organisation.

A similar approach can be seen in the case of *A Manager of an English Language School v An Institute of Technology*.[76] While the Equality Officer found that the claimant had been subjected to verbal harassment on grounds of race, the employer had a good

---

[74] SI 2002/78. This Code is contained in Appendix, Codes of Practice.
[75] *S v A Named Organisation* DEC-E2006-025 (Equality Tribunal).
[76] *A Manager of an English Language School v An Institute of Technology* DEC-E2007-019 (Equality Tribunal).

defence because of its equal opportunities policy which was regularly updated and regularly communicated to staff. In *A Worker v A Named Organisation*,[77] the Equality Officer determined that the fact that a prompt investigation had been conducted which made findings based on evidence and which had offered mediation to improve the relationship gave the employer a good defence to the employee's claim.

[13.44] Even where a policy is in place and is invoked by an employee, there are ongoing obligations on the employer to ensure that the investigation is conducted properly and fairly. In *A v A Contract Cleaning Company*,[78] the investigation was conducted by a supervisor who was present at the time the incident occurred and had stated that it was merely 'a joke'. The Equality Officer had little difficulty in finding that the investigation failed to deal with the serious allegation and that the employer was therefore liable for the harassment.

For an employer to avail of the defence, an investigation must be conducted whether or not the person against whom the allegations have been made is still in employment. In the case of *G v A Hotel Reservation Company*[79] allegations of sexual harassment were made against an employee who had left the organisation prior to the commencement of the investigation. The employer argued that even though a finding of sexual harassment had been made out, it could take no further action as no sanction could be imposed on the perpetrator. In spite of this, the Equality Officer stated:

> [...] the least it could have done was to acknowledge the distress suffered by the complainant and apologise for the behaviour of Mr Z – given that it is liable for his actions under the Act and it was responsible for the delay in the investigation process. It could also have used the situation to heighten staff awareness on the issue of sexual harassment within the organisation and reiterate its policy on the matter. However, it took no action at all, instead deciding that it could not take the matter further as Mr Z had left his employment. In the circumstances I am not satisfied that the respondent did all that was reasonably practicable to reverse the effects of the treatment of the complainant and it cannot therefore rely on the defence at section 23(5) of the Act.

The Equality Tribunal and the Labour Court have repeatedly criticised employers for not having a policy in place and have highlighted the implications this has for a victim of harassment or sexual harassment ie the employee does not know how they can complain about their situation or attempt to bring the treatment to an end. However it does seem to be implicitly suggested in the case of *A Female Employee v A Printing Company*[80] that while the employer was at fault in not having a policy in place, a claimant who is aware of how other types of complaints are dealt with may have some level of responsibility if they choose not to make any complaint. In that case, while there was no such policy in place, the Equality Officer referred in her decision to the fact that the complainant was a shop steward during the last year of her employment and was involved in bringing issues concerning other employees to the attention of management.

---

[77] *A Worker v A Named Organisation* DEC-E2006-006 (Equality Tribunal).
[78] *A v A Contract Cleaning Company* DEC-E2004-068 (Equality Tribunal).
[79] *G v A Hotel Reservation Company* DEC-E2005-053 (Equality Tribunal).
[80] *A Female Employee v A Printing Company* DEC-E2008-022 (Equality Tribunal).

[13.45] There are many examples of where the absence of a policy deprives the employer of any defence under s 15(3). In *Atkinson v Carty*[81] the employer argued that, although there was no policy in place, he operated an open door policy and that any of his employees, including the plaintiff, were welcome to approach him at any time. This did not particularly impress Delahunt J who held:

> It is not sufficient for the Defendants to plead that no amount of paper compliance would have helped in the case of the Plaintiff. The failure of the Defendants to have in place adequate procedures renders them liable and by reason of their failure to fulfil their statutory obligations they are responsible and cannot plead immunity from same simply because the Plaintiff failed to make a complaint.

Very substantial compensation of €137,000 (which was reduced by 25% for contributory negligence due to delay on the part of the plaintiff in making a complaint) was awarded.

[13.46] In the case of *BH v A Named Company t/a a Cab Company*[82] the employer had no policy in place. In spite of this, the claimant made a complaint to a manager but nothing was done. The Tribunal had no difficulty in finding the company liable and the maximum compensation of two years' salary was awarded.

The case law also makes it clear that even where an employer has a policy in place, they are obliged to show that it has been effectively communicated before they can use it to invoke the defence under the Act. In *A Worker v An Engineering Company*[83] the claimant had not made any complaints, whether pursuant to the policy that was in place or otherwise. However this was in circumstances where his supervisor had participated in the harassment. In his evidence, the supervisor accepted that certain statements had been made to the claimant but described it as 'banter'. The Equality Officer in finding the employer liable pointed out that the employer was unable to show how the policy on bullying and harassment had been disseminated amongst staff and also pointed out that the complainant had 'credibly asserted' that he did not know who to approach about the matter in circumstances where his own supervisor had condoned the harassment. Substantial compensation of €20,000 was awarded.

[13.47] It is also clear that a mere grievance procedure will not suffice. In *Gabriele Piazza v The Clarion Hotel*[84] a complaint had been made about verbal and written harassment which had been investigated under the grievance procedure. The Equality Officer found that an issue as serious as an allegation of harassment should not be dealt with by way of the grievance procedure which in itself, was not sufficiently detailed and, in her view, would leave the employee uncertain as to how the matter would proceed. She found that the entire manner in which the investigation had been concluded was totally unsatisfactory. She reiterated that the existence of a policy on harassment is not sufficient to prevent harassment and what was essential was effective communication of that policy.

---

[81] *Atkinson v Carty* [2005] ELR 1.

[82] *BH v A Named Company t/a a Cab Company* DEC-E2006-026 (Equality Tribunal).

[83] *A Worker v An Engineering Company* DEC-E2008-038 (Equality Tribunal).

[84] *Gabriele Piazza v The Clarion Hotel* DEC-E2004-033 (Equality Tribunal).

As well as a requirement to implement a policy, it is clearly at least good practice – if not obligatory – for an employer to comply with recommendations made by an investigation. In the case of *An Employer v A Worker*[85] the Labour Court was highly critical of the company's decision to ignore the advice of its own doctor to whom the complainant had been referred. The doctor found that the claimant was suffering from stress at work due to an incident of harassment and the manner in which it was handled by the company and advised that an outside intermediary be brought in to deal with the matter. This was not done. The Court concluded that the respondent's conduct amounted to an undermining of the relationship of trust and confidence between the parties, was unreasonable in the circumstances and entitled her to claim that she was constructively dismissed.

[13.48] A decision by an employer to bring in an outside investigator is usually one which will be commended by the Equality Tribunal or the Labour Court but it is important to remember that that in itself is not sufficient. In *Odion v Tecnhiform (Waterford) Ltd*,[86] the company had brought in an independent investigator who found that there was no case of bullying and harassment but found that cultural differences had arisen which required tolerance and acceptance by both sides. Following the investigation, the employer was involved in written and verbal communications with the claimant urging him not to resign and committing to supporting him on his return. They invited the claimant to meet an independent expert on bullying and harassment who had been engaged by the company to review their policy. The Equality Officer commended the company for acting promptly in dealing with the formal and informal complaints made but was not satisfied that the outcome of the independent investigation adequately described the circumstances between the workers or that the appointment of an independent investigator absolved the respondent of further responsibility. While she accepted that the employer was genuinely committed to the claimant's return to work, she felt that 'some form of support' should have been made available to facilitate this. She found that the employer's failure to deal with the claimant feeling isolated in the workplace after the complaints were investigated constituted discrimination on grounds of race. Compensation of €7,500 was awarded for the effects of that discrimination.

[13.49] While it is clear that an employer is obliged to investigate any complaints made by an employee, it is difficult to see how a complaint could be fairly investigated where an employee declines to furnish the name of the alleged perpetrator. Bearing in mind the constitutional rights which a person against whom allegations have been made has to fair procedures and natural justice, at the very least an employer is entitled to assume that it cannot be expected to investigate a compliant where the complainant either refuses to furnish the name of the alleged perpetrator or refuses to allow the allegation to be furnished to the alleged perpetrator. However arising from the decision of the Labour Court in *A Complainant v A Hospital*,[87] there does seem to be some obligation on an employer to progress its procedures even where a complainant declines to identify the

[85] *An Employer v A Worker* EED 053/2005 (Labour Court).
[86] *Odion v Tecnhiform (Waterford) Ltd* DEC-E2007-018 (Equality Tribunal).
[87] *A Complainant v A Hospital* DEE 029/2002 (Labour Court).

person against whom allegations are being made. The employee in that case made very serious allegations of sexual abuse but refused at that time to name the alleged abuser as she had a history of sexual abuse as a child and wished to receive counselling before naming the alleged abuser. She did subsequently provide his name to the employer. The Labour Court held that during the period before the alleged abuser was named, the employer had a duty, on being informed of the harassment, to put in place such procedures as would enable the appellant to avail of working conditions free from discrimination.

The Court set out its view that the employer, in the circumstances of this particular case, should have taken proactive measures including the following. The employer should have (i) contacted the Gardaí; (ii) contacted the appellant's union official; (iii) spoken to co-workers to seek to establish the truth or otherwise of the allegations; (iv) transferred the appellant to another working area; (v) explained the bullying/harassment policy to her and provide her with a copy of the policy.

The Court concluded that:

> By its failure to take these steps, the employer failed to provide the employee with working conditions free from discrimination and accordingly was in breach of its duty to the appellant under section 8(1) of the Act.

> The Court wishes to emphasise that it is not suggesting that any or all of these steps should be taken in every case of sexual harassment. The appropriate response to each case must be studied by the employer who should then put in place procedures proportionate with the gravity of the offence.

It is very difficult to see how at least some of the proactive measures which the Court stated should have been taken, could have been taken at a time when the complainant was not prepared to identify her alleged abuser. In particular, it is difficult to see how the employer could have spoken to co-workers to seek to establish the truth or otherwise of the allegations without causing not only serious industrial relations issues within the organisation but also acting in a manner which would ultimately have been unfair to the person against whom allegations were eventually made. It is also questionable whether it would be appropriate to contact the union official of an employee who had made a complaint particularly if there were issues around confidentiality or a clear reluctance on the part of the employee to progress the matter any further. The suggestion that a copy of the employer's harassment policy should be furnished as soon as any allegation is made even where the identity of the alleged perpetrator is not provided, is sensible. However to find a failure to do so as establishing actionable discrimination under the Act is questionable.

VICTIMISATION

[13.50] The Employment Equality Act, in furtherance of their protection of the rights of workers to challenge discriminatory treatment, provide protection against victimisation. Victimisation is defined in quite broad terms under the Employment Equality Act. Section 74(2) provides:

> (2) For the purposes of this Part victimisation occurs where dismissal or other adverse treatment of an employee by his or her employer occurs as a reaction to—

(a)   a complaint of discrimination made by the employee to the employer,

(b)   any proceedings by a complainant,

(c)   an employee having represented or otherwise supported a complainant,

(d)   the work of an employee having been compared with that of another employee for any of the purposes of this Act or any enactment repealed by this Act,

(e)   an employee having been a witness in any proceedings under this Act or the Equal Status Act 2000 or any such repealed enactment,

(f)   an employee having opposed by lawful means an act which is unlawful under this Act or the said Act of 2000 or which was unlawful under any such repealed enactment, or

(g)   an employee having given notice of an intention to take any of the actions mentioned in the preceding paragraphs.

It is important to note that this definition permits persons other than the victim of discrimination, such as representatives, witnesses and comparators, to bring complaints of victimisation. It is also important to realise that the complainant need only show the adverse treatment is a 'reaction to' a complaint. Prior to the Equality Act 2004, the phrase used was that the treatment was 'solely or mainly occasioned by' which is a narrower requirement.[88] Following the 2004 amendments, it is clear that the complainant need not actually have made a complaint. It is sufficient that an employee gives notice of an intention to bring a complaint.[89] The Equality Act 2004 also removed the requirement that a complaint must be taken in good faith.[90] In summary, the law as it stands is designed to give maximum protection to anyone seeking to rely on, or use, employment equality rights in the workplace from adverse treatment by the employer as a result.

What constitutes victimisation?

[13.51] A perusal of the case law shows that a wide variety of actions have been found to be victimisation, for example a notice put up by a respondent thanking 'the vast majority of staff' for supporting him during the investigation into allegations of sexual harassment;[91] moving a complainant to another branch for three months against her wishes on the insistence of her manager following a complaint of sexual harassment against that manager;[92] and disclosing personal information about a Roman Catholic priest to his peers which was directly responsible for the deterioration of his relationship with his fellow chaplains and bishop.[93]

---

[88]   Employment Equality Act 1998, s 74(2).

[89]   Employment Equality Acts 1998–2008, s 74(2)(g).

[90]   The requirement that the action of the employee was taken in good faith was provided in s 74(2) of the Employment Equality Act 1998.

[91]   *Beardmore v (1) South West Trains (2) WE Hamilton* ET/2305257/00 (Employment Tribunal, UK).

[92]   *A Complainant v A Financial Institution* DEC-E2003-053 (Equality Tribunal).

[93]   *Mr M v A State Authority* DEC-E2006-015 (Equality Tribunal).

[13.52] On occasion, the mishandling of a discrimination complaint can give rise to a finding of victimisation. In *A Company v A Worker* [94] the complainant alleged that she was subjected to sexual harassment at work and complained to her immediate superiors. The respondent regarded the complaints as vexatious and took them into account in deciding to terminate the complainant's employment. The Labour Court stated:

> In the Court's view a person who is dismissed wholly or mainly for having reported in good faith incidents which they believe to constitute sexual harassment, or for having made complaints in that belief, or for otherwise seeking to prevent its occurrence or reoccurrence, is victimised within the meaning of [the Act].

[13.53] As well as being treated badly while in employment, or being dismissed, victimisation can also occur through the actions of an employer after the employment has terminated. In *Catherine Connerty v Caffrey Transport Ltd*[95] the complainant contended that she was treated less favourably on the grounds of her gender, marital status and family status by her employer, Caffrey Transport, when her son was ill in hospital. Following her departure from the employer company, the complainant alleged that two prospective employers received bad references about her from Caffrey Transport with specific mention being made to the equality case she had brought against the respondent and, as a result, one of these prospective employers refused to offer her a job.

The Equality Officer found that the complainant had failed to establish a *prima facie* claim of discriminatory treatment on the grounds of gender, marital status and family status. However, the Equality Officer did determine that the complainant had been victimised by her former employer when it made reference to her equality claim and to other employment claims she had brought against the respondent. In this regard, the Equality Officer ordered the respondent to pay to the complainant the sum of €15,000 in compensation for the stress suffered as a result of the victimisation.

[13.54] A similar situation occurred in *Coote v Granada Hospitality Ltd*,[96] where a claimant, after settling a sex discrimination case against her former employer, began looking for a new job. Two employment agencies she approached were unable to obtain references from Granada and this was found to be discriminatory.

The employer can be guilty of victimisation even if they have not have discriminated against an employee in the first place if they treat the employee badly when a complaint, even one without foundation, is made. In *Byrne v Association of Irish Racehorses Ltd*,[97] the claimant was casually employed by the respondent as a security system operator on various racecourses around the country. She claimed that after another casual employee, who was a male, was taken on, she had not been offered further work by the respondent after March 2005. She lodged her complaint of discriminatory dismissal with the Tribunal in March 2006. Her claim of discriminatory dismissal failed as the Equality Officer accepted that she was still on the panel and could be offered work. The Equality

---

[94] *A Company v A Worker* EED 035/2003 (Labour Court).
[95] *Catherine Connerty v Caffrey Transport Ltd* DEC-E2008-018 (Equality Tribunal).
[96] *Coote v Granada Hospitality Ltd* [1999] IRLR 452 (EAT, UK).
[97] *Byrne v Association of Irish Racehorses Ltd* DEC–E2008-008 (Equality Tribunal).

Officer took the view that the facts suggested that victimisation might be an issue, and requested the parties to put in submissions on the point. He concluded that Ms Byrne had been victimised on not being offered any more work after the submission of her claim. The Equality Officer determined that:

> In a case like this one, where casual employment at an extremely low level is at issue, it will be difficult to determine which level of not offering the casual worker work raises an inference of adverse treatment. However, I find that the fact that the complainant was not offered any work by the respondent for 30 months, after she had previously worked between one and two days in any twelve month period, does raise an inference of adverse treatment.

He awarded:

> [t]he complainant €500—for the effects of the victimisation. This award is not in respect of lost pay, and is therefore not subject to tax. The small size of the award is determined by the low income the complainant derives in an average year from her low level of casual work for the respondent, pursuant to s 84(2) of the Acts.

[13.55] Similarly, in *A Complainant v A Department Store*,[98] an employer was found to have victimised a complainant who had sought advice from the Equality Authority on an allegation of discrimination on the disability ground following several unsuccessful applications for employment, even though the employer was not found to have discriminated against the complainant. The respondent wrote to her saying 'in view of the untrue and unfounded allegations you have made to the Employment Equality Authority … we are not for the foreseeable future going to accept any application from you for employment in our store, or indeed any other branch'. An award of €12,700 was made.

Where the claimant refuses to participate in the investigation, this does not absolve a respondent of the duty to investigate or allow the employer to infer that the complaint is unfounded and vexatious. In *Icon Clinical Research v Tsourova*,[99] the complainant made a number of complaints to her employer alleging various forms of harassment. Two members of the management team were appointed to investigate but the complainant said that they were not independent. The complainant declined to answer questions in regard to this assertion. The Vice-President of HR issued a report on the independence of the investigators and directed them to proceed and they did so without the co-operation of the complainant. They concluded that none of the complaints made by the complainant were well founded. The investigation further found that a number of the complaints were malicious and/or vexatious and the complainant was dismissed.

[13.56] The complainant had not been given a copy of the report before the decision to terminate her employment was taken nor was she given any opportunity to respond to the allegations against her contained in the report. The Labour Court found that at no stage was the complainant told that the investigation would inquire into her own conduct or that she was in danger of being found guilty of a dismissible offence. The complainant was not informed of the contents of the report that were adverse to her or

---

98 *A Complainant v A Department Store* DEC-E2002-017 (Equality Tribunal).
99 *Icon Clinical Research v Tsourova* EDA 071/2007 (Labour Court).

provided with any opportunity to address the charges against her contained in the findings. The investigation was not established to inquire into the complainant's conduct. As a result, it was not subsequently open to the company to determine that the complainant was actuated by malice or vexation without conducting the most basic form of inquiry in which the complainant would be told what was alleged against her and given a fair opportunity to respond. The dismissal was found to be victimisation and an award of €15,000 was made. In a follow-on case reported in January 2007, which enquired into the allegations of discrimination, the Court found that these were unproven but that the complainant had a valid cause of complaint regarding the manner in which her complaints had been investigated. The Court however was satisfied that any claim which the complainant may have had in respect of victimisation arising from the investigation into her complaints of discrimination was merged with her claim of victimisation relating to her dismissal, which was the subject of the previous proceedings, and no further award was given.

Claims of victimisation generally attract large awards as victimisation is seen as an attempt by and employer to flout the applicability of the legislation. This is apparent from *Dublin City Council v McCarthy*[100] where an employee who had succeeded in an equality case against her employer was subsequently marginalised by her manager who refused to speak to her for three years. Meanwhile the in-house magazine persistently refused to correct a misleading report to the effect that her case had been won by the employer. The Equality Officer commented:

> ... the victimisation of a person for having in good faith taken a claim under the Equality Legislation is very serious as it could have the impact of undermining the effectiveness of the legislation and is completely unacceptable.

The Labour Court on appeal reduced the award from €50,790 to €25,000.[101]

[13.57] Similarly, in *McGinn v Board of Management St Anthony's Boys National School*[102] the Equality Officer awarded the maximum amount of two years' salary (€117,362) for victimisation and €10,000 for stress. This case was ultimately appealed to the Labour Court and settled on appeal for a fraction of the award, but the decision of the Equality Tribunal nevertheless stands. It is a reminder of the seriousness with which a Tribunal will view victimisation. In some cases, the award of compensation for victimisation can be higher than the amount given for the initial act of discrimination.

Victimisation must have a nexus with assertion of equality rights

[13.58] In *Moriarty v Dúchas*,[103] the Equality Tribunal emphasised that the act which results in victimisation must be connected to a reliance on rights in the Employment Equality Act. The complainant alleged that she was victimised for discovering an anomaly in the rostering arrangements which resulted in certain staff being due arrears

---

[100] *Dublin City Council v McCarthy* DEC-EE2001-15 (Equality Tribunal).
[101] EDA 022/2002 (Labour Court).
[102] *McGinn v Board of Management St Anthony's Boys National School* DEC-E2004-032 (Equality Tribunal).
[103] *Moriarty v Dúchas* DEC-E2003-013 (Equality Tribunal).

of pay. The Tribunal found that victimisation had not occurred as the issue was not one of equality. It determined that the Employment Equality Act required the complainant 'to demonstrate the connection between his or her actions in relation to defending entitlements under the Act and the treatment complained of'.

Employers could be vulnerable to collective victimisation claims. In *St Helens Borough Council v Derbyshire and Others*[104] the 39 applicants were among 510 catering staff that made equal pay claims in 1998. The majority of the claims were settled out of court, but 39 of the women did not accept the Borough Council's offer of a lump sum. They objected to a letter sent to them which they complained pressurised them by threatening adverse consequences if they did not accept the lump sum and claimed that the letter constituted victimisation. The Employment Tribunal, the Employment Appeals Tribunal and the Court of Appeal upheld the claims. However, an aspect of the Court of Appeal decision was overturned by the House of Lords on appeal.[105] The House of Lords upheld the Court of Appeal's finding that the letters sent by the employer would not have been sent by a reasonable employer and in the circumstances the employees had suffered detriment.

EQUAL TREATMENT ON GROUNDS OF GENDER

Gender discrimination

[13.59] The law has required equal treatment on grounds of gender since 1977. Where a prospective employer imposes a requirement that a person must be of a particular gender in order to get a job, or an employer imposes a gender requirement to obtain a promotion, this is unlawful discrimination, unless the employer can avail of one of the exceptions in the legislation. Given the length of time which equal treatment legislation has been in place and the broad acceptance in society of the principle of equal treatment, it is rare to see litigation where an employer has engaged in blatant gender discrimination. Most complaints of gender discrimination currently being taken relate to areas such as pregnancy discrimination or claims which overlap with claims of discrimination on grounds of family status, for example where flexible working hours are sought or where issues arise on a woman's return to work after maternity leave. The more traditional claims that a person was less favourably treated simply by virtue of the fact of their gender are becoming less common.

Exceptions

[13.60] The most important exception to direct gender discrimination is that set out in s 25 of the Employment Equality Act, namely that gender is a *bona fide* occupational qualification. To be precise, s 25 provides that it will not be unlawful to confine a post to a man or woman where gender is a *bona fide* occupational requirement.[106] As this is an

---

[104] *St Helens Borough Council v Derbyshire and Others* [2005] EWCA Civ 977 (EAT, UK).

[105] [2007] ICR 841.

[106] Such a provision is permitted by Art 14(2) of the Recast Equal Treatment Directive, Council Directive 2006/54/EC ([2006] OJ L204/23) which allows the sex of a worker to be a determining factor as regards access to employment where such a characteristic constitutes a 'genuine and determining occupational requirement'. For case law on this derogation see Barnard, *EC Employment Law* (3rd edn, Oxford University Press, 2006) at pp 507–412.

exception to general principles on equality, it will be strictly construed. For example, in *M v A Language School*[107] in strictly construing s 25, the Equality Officer rejected the employer's contention that a position which involved visiting the homes of host families and coping with homesick or emotional Italian students made the position unsuitable for a man. The Equality Officer held that the exclusion of a person from employment on gender grounds must be reasonable in all the circumstances for it to be lawful. The Equality Officer found that the respondent had acted under the mistaken belief that only women were capable of carrying out the duties required for the position and therefore discriminated against the complainant in an unlawful manner.

[13.61] Other exceptions to gender discrimination are contained in s 26 of the Act (relating to the provision of family and personal services) and s 27 (relating to Gardaí and the Prison Services) which permit direct discrimination in circumstances set out in those sections. These sections will also be construed strictly as can be seen in the case of *Hunt and Doherty v Irish Prison Service.*[108] In that case, the Equality Officer confirmed that any deviation from the principle of equal treatment, such as that under s 27 of the Act, must be construed strictly. Section 27 excludes from the scope of the Act certain posts in the Garda Síochána and the prison service. It allows for the assignment of a man or a woman to a particular post where the assignment is considered necessary in the interests of privacy or decency or from a security point of view. Ultimately the employer's argument that maintaining an adequate female officer presence in a women's prison required a certain number of female prison offcers was accepted by the Equality Officer and the requirement was deemed essential by the Equality Officer in terms of privacy and decency.

Apart from these exceptions, it must be remembered that indirect discrimination can be permissible if it is objectively justifiable, as defined in Bilka Kaufhaus discussed in para **[13.94]** below.

Burden of proof

[13.62] In practice, it is most unusual to have clear evidence of gender discrimination. It is highly significant that the Act permits the burden of proof to be shifted from the claimant to the respondent upon the establishment of *prime facie* evidence. Once a person can establish *prima facie* evidence of discrimination on grounds of gender, it is then a matter for the respondent employer to prove that the treatment being challenged was not in fact on grounds of the gender but on other non-discriminatory grounds. The case law consistently shows that evidence of less favourable treatment which a respondent employer does not succeed in attributing to objective, non-discriminatory grounds is sufficient to establish discrimination.[109]

---

[107] *M v A Language School* [2005] 16 ELR 35.

[108] *Hunt and Doherty v Irish Prison Service* [2006] 17 ELR 354.

[109] A rare example of where objective, non-discriminatory grounds were upheld is *Burke v NUI Galway* [2001] ELR 181.

While the Act would not on its face appear to require any sort of connection between the gender and the less favourable treatment, the lack of a nexus was deeply problematic for the complainant in the Labour Court case of *Rescon Ltd v Scanlan*:[110]

> In this case the Complainant has adduced no evidence to establish a nexus between his gender and the Respondent's failure to offer him the disputed post other than that a woman was appointed and he was not. In the Court's view a mere difference in gender and a difference in treatment (in the sense that the Comparator was appointed and the Complainant was not) could never in itself provide a sufficient evidential basis upon which to raise a presumption of discrimination.

An area where claims of gender discrimination still continue to be seen is that of access to employment and/or promotion where a complainant challenges an interview or a selection process.[111] Due to the frequency of claims of this type it is worth considering some of the case law in detail, and examining the role which the shifting burden of proof plays in allowing a claimant to establish discrimination.

[13.63] It is clear from the case law that a badly conducted interview or a selection process which does not conform to good practice can be vulnerable to a claim of gender discrimination even where there is no evidence of the person's gender having been the reason for their non selection.[112] While the Equality Tribunal and the Labour Court have recognised that the purpose of an oral interview is to assess a candidate's performance on the day, there are many cases where the Tribunal and the Court have found *prima facie* evidence of discrimination from their view that the claimant's qualifications or experience were deemed to be superior. Such findings by the Tribunal or the Court will likely establish *prima facie* evidence of discrimination that will shift the burden of proof to the respondent employer. Unless the respondent can establish non-discriminatory, objective reasons for preferring the successful candidate, a finding of discrimination may be made. Where an interview has been conducted in a way that might be viewed as contrary to good interview practice, such as not retaining interview notes, not establishing clear criteria or allocating marks well in advance of the interview and not having a clear mechanism whereby marks will be allocated under different and clear headings, it will be very difficult if not impossible for a respondent employer to stand over an interview and/or selection process where *prima facie* evidence of discrimination has been established.[113]

[13.64] In the case of *South Eastern Health Board v Brigid Burke*,[114] the complainant, who was an assistant director of nursing and stand-in director of nursing, applied for the position of director of nursing. She was one of two candidates interviewed and the male candidate was appointed. The complainant submitted that the level of marking did not reflect the reality of her situation and was indicative of bias against her as a female. She also relied on what she maintained was evidence of discrimination in the profession in

---

[110] *Rescon Ltd v Scanlan* EDA 085/2008 (Labour Court).

[111] For a more detailed analysis of the earlier and more commonly occurring claims of this type, see Bolger and Kimber, *Sex Discrimination Law* (Round Hall, 2000), Ch 11.

[112] See for example *Gleeson v Rotunda Hospital* [2000] ELR 206.

[113] See for example *Gleeson v Rotunda Hospital* [2000] ELR 206.

[114] *South Eastern Health Board v Brigid Burke* EDA 041/2004 (Labour Court).

that male nurses occupy 2% of general nursing posts but 15% of nursing director positions. It was accepted that the respondent, rather than using a formal marking procedure, allowed the interview board to deliberate on the marking system and the types of questions to be asked as the respondent felt it was preferable to allow sufficient flexibility in the interview in order to allow considerations such as experience to emerge. The claim was unsuccessful before the Equality Officer. On appeal to the Labour Court, the Court found that there was an inference of discrimination and the onus therefore shifted to the respondent to prove that no infringement of equal treatment had taken place. The Court found that the respondent did not discharge that onus as it failed to give a reasonable explanation for the remarkably generous marks awarded to the successful male candidate in comparison to the female complainant. It also noted that the interview board had failed to keep notes. The Court said that it was 'sustained' in its findings by the fact that no objective justification was presented for the statistical imbalance between the number of male and female nurses occupying management positions. Substantial compensation of €45,000 was awarded.

By contrast, the Labour Court's decision in *Ballinrobe Community School v Walsh*[115] illustrates how the burden of proof can be discharged by the respondent even where there is *prima facie* evidence of discrimination shifting the burden of proof to the respondent. The Court accepted the evidence that the successful candidate was appointed because a selection board considered his qualities and attributes were the most suitable for the post. Significantly, the Court found that the statistical analysis did not disclose any pattern of bias against women in the making of appointments. The claim of discrimination, which had been upheld by the Equality Officer, was overturned by the Labour Court.

In comparing the two determinations, it can be seen that a statistical gender imbalance within a particular profession is relevant in establishing whether a respondent employer has discharged a burden of proof. That is not to say that a profession such as general nursing where there is such a statistical imbalance places an employer at risk but simply that an employer in any interview situation needs to be very careful to ensure that the manner in which its interviews are conducted complies with best practice and that they can show clearly how a person was assessed as compared to another person of a different gender.

[13.65] Another significant case in which the selection process for promotion was challenged was *Dublin City University v Horgan*.[116] In this case, the Labour Court found on the facts that the evidential burden should shift to the University given that they found the complainant was better qualified on paper than her male comparators, all of whom were appointed and she was not. The Court set out a number of factors that should have been taken into account in deciding if the burden, shifted to the respondent, had in fact been discharged:

> Firstly, since the facts necessary to prove an explanation can only be in possession of the respondent, the Court should expect cogent evidence to discharge the burden of proof (*See Barton v Investec Henderson Crosthwaithe Securities* [2003] IRLR 332 and the decision

---

[115] *Ballinrobe Community School v Walsh* EDA 065/2006 (Labour Court).
[116] *Dublin City University v Horgan* EDA 0715/2007 (Labour Court).

of the Court of Appeal for England and Wales in *Wang v Igen Ltd and Others* [2005] ICR 931).

Secondly, the requirement to establish that there was no discrimination whatsoever means that the Court must always be alert to the possibility of unconscious or inadvertent discrimination and real denials of a discriminatory motive, in the absence of independent corroboration, must be approached with caution (See *Nevins Murphy Flood v Portroe Stevedores* [2005] 16 ELR 282).

Finally in *Wang v Igen Limited and Others* Peter Gibson L J considered the scope which should be ascribed to the notion of 'no discrimination whatsoever'. He found that if the protective factor or characteristic was more than a 'trivial inference' in the impugned decision, a claim of discrimination will have been made out. That is a highly persuasive authority which the Court readily adopts.

[13.66] A good example of what can render an interview process vulnerable to a finding of discrimination is the failure to retain interview notes. In *South Eastern Health Board v Bridget Burke*[117] the failure to retain interview notes rendered it, in the view of the Equality Officer, 'extremely difficult' for the respondent to discharge the onus of proof placed upon them. On the other hand, a failure to retain interview notes is not automatically indicative of a strong case. In *Tesco Ireland v Kirwan*[118] the Labour Court found that the failure on the part of the respondent to retain interview notes constituted what they considered was a departure from best practice and, combined with other elements in the case, found that it supported the conclusion that a *prima facie* case of discrimination had been made out. However, ultimately, the Court accepted that the reason for appointing the successful candidate was because she was regarded as a better candidate by the store manager. The Court also noted that the previous occupant of the post was a man and that the complainant was later appointed to a similar post. On that evidence, the Court found that the respondent had discharged the onus of proof transferred to it.

[13.67] As with any interview case, the consequences of a finding of discrimination in any access to employment and/or promotions case can be very significant for an employer. In the case of *Horgan v DCU*[119] the claimant successfully established that the university's failure to appoint her to the post of Associate Professor within an internal promotion process was discriminatory. The Labour Court awarded back pay from the time that it found she should have been promoted to the position, together with damages of €10,000 for stress. The university was directed to appoint the complainant to the position of Associate Professor with effect from the date on which she interviewed for the position, almost five years before the Court's determination and directed them to pay full retrospective salary and benefits from that date. In addition the University was directed to set out clearly the minimum requirement in respect of the gender composition of interview panels and to introduce a policy obliging all members of interview panels to make contemporaneous notes of interviews with those notes to be retained by the university for a minimum of 12 months.

---

[117] *South Eastern Health Board v Bridget Burke* EDA 041/2004 (Labour Court).
[118] *Tesco Ireland v Kirwan* DEE 041/2004 (Labour Court).
[119] *Horgan v DCU* EDA 0715/2007 (Labour Court).

[13.68] In conclusion, gender discrimination claims, where direct discrimination is alleged, are less frequent now than in the early years following the adoption of the equal treatment legislation. The bulk of litigation which now takes place is in relation to interviews and promotions where it is alleged that indirect discrimination has taken place in some shape or form. Nevertheless, the principles of equality law worked out in the earlier cases, such as objective justification and shifting burdens of proof, have suffused employment equality law and been applied to the newer grounds. Jurisprudence on equal treatment therefore continues to be relevant and applicable.

Gender discrimination claims

[13.69] Claims for gender discrimination are brought to the Equality Tribunal. However, a claim for gender discrimination can, in the alternative, be commenced directly in the Circuit Court. No other claim for discrimination can be commenced in that forum. This anomaly follows on from the jurisprudence of the ECJ which has held that in relation to the remedy provided for in national law for a breach of gender discrimination, legislation must also enable that breach to be penalised under conditions, both procedural and substantive, which are analogous to those applicable to infringements of domestic law.[120] At the time of these judgments of the ECJ, the only form of discrimination which was prohibited at EU level was gender discrimination. Thus the judgments of the ECJ had no application in relation to other grounds of discrimination. It remains open to question, however, whether the prohibition on commencing discrimination claims on non-gender grounds in the Circuit Court is compatible with Community law.

Pregnancy discrimination

Pregnancy discrimination in European law

[13.70] In the early years, equality law found it difficult to conceptualise and compensate for pregnancy discrimination due to the fact that the fundamental paradigm of equality law is equal treatment to a similarly situated comparator. The lack of an obvious comparator for a pregnant women gave rise to conceptual difficulties within gender discrimination law, sometimes leading to the illogical approach of comparing a pregnant woman to a hypothetical sick male in order to establish whether a woman treated less favourably on grounds of her pregnancy was in fact a victim of unlawful discrimination on grounds of her sex.[121] In the landmark decision of the ECJ in *Dekker v Stichting Vormingscrentrum voor Jong Volwassen,*[122] the Court recognised that since employment could not be refused because of the pregnancy of a woman, refusal to appoint a woman on the grounds of her pregnancy constituted direct discrimination on the grounds of her sex contrary to the Equal Treatment Directive.[123] The labelling of

---

[120] See, for example, Case C-14/83, *Von Colson v Land Nordrhein-Westfalen* [1984] ECR 1891 and Case C-271/91, *Marshall v Southampton & SW Hants AHA* [1993] ECR I-4367.

[121] For a more detailed discussion see Bolger and Kimber, *Sex Discrimination Law* (Round Hall, 2000) pp 293–4 and Fenwick and Hervey, 'Sex Equality in the Single Market: New Directions for the ECJ' (1995) 32 *CML Rev* 443.

[122] Case C-77/88 *Dekker v Stichting Vormingscrentrum voor Jong Volwassen* [1990] ECR I-3941.

pregnancy discrimination as direct discrimination on grounds of gender without the need to establish a comparator was an important step forward in conceptualising pregnancy discrimination. The decision was a highly significant landmark in outlawing pregnancy discrimination in the workplace, the implications of which still regularly arise before the courts as pregnancy discrimination continues to be a very real issue in the lives of working women.

[13.71] On the same day as the ECJ handed down its decision in *Dekker*,[124] the Court in *Hertz v Aldi*[125] placed some limitations on the scope of pregnancy discrimination as direct discrimination contrary to the Equal Treatment Directive.[126] The Court limited the period of protection from dismissal on grounds of pregnancy and/or a pregnancy related illness to the period of the statutory maternity leave. However, the protection to be afforded to women with pregnancy related illness and the fact that this is different to other forms of illness was recognised by the ECJ in *Brown v Rentokil*.[127] The employer had a policy of dismissing any employee after 26 weeks' sick leave but the Court held that the employer was not entitled to commence calculation of that twenty six week period until after the end of the employee's maternity leave where the illness was related to her pregnancy.[128]

Thus the ECJ had given a high level of protection to equal treatment rights during pregnancy and maternity, but only in the specific time period from the beginning of pregnancy to the end of maternity leave. This high level of protection of the pregnant women's job can be seen in recent case law. A recent decision of the ECJ has extended the protection of the Equal Treatment Directive to women who are at an advanced stage in the in vitro fertilisation (IVF) process.[129] This case is discussed further below at para **[13.77]**.

[13.72] The treatment of a pregnant employee can be seen in *CNAVTS v Thibault*.[130] In that case, the Court found that to deny a female employee the right to have her performance assessed annually discriminated against her because had she not been pregnant and on maternity leave, she would have been assessed during the year she took the leave and could therefore have qualified for promotion. Similarly in *Lewan v Lothar Denda*[131] the Court held that Art 141 precluded an employer from taking periods of

---

[123] Council Directive 76/207/EEC Equal Treatment Directive ([1976] OJ L39/40). For further reading on EU law in the realm of maternity protection see Barnard, *EC Employment Law*, (3rd edn, Oxford University Press, 2006), chapters 8 and 9.

[124] Case C-77/88 *Dekker* [1990] ECR I-3941. See also Bolger and Kimber, *Sex Discrimination Law* (Round Hall, 2000) at pp. 296-298, Ellis, 'Discrimination on the Grounds of Pregnancy in EEC Law' (1991) *Public Law* 159 and Shaw, 'Pregnancy Discrimination in Sex Discrimination' (1991) *EL Rev* 313.

[125] Case C-179/88 *Hertz v Aldi* [1990] ECR I-3979.

[126] Council Directive EC/76/207 ([1976] OJ L39/40).

[127] Case C-394/96 *Brown v Rentokil* [1998] ECR I-4185. See also Boch, 'Official: During Pregnancy, Females are Pregnant' (1998) 23 *EL Rev* 488.

[128] For criticism of this approach see Ellis, 'Case Note on Brown v Rentokil' [1999] *CML Rev* 625.

[129] Case C-506/06 *Mayr v Backerei und Konditorei Gerhard Flockner Ohg Case* [2008] IRLR 387.

[130] Case C-136/95 *CNAVTS v Thibault* [1998] ECR I-2011.

maternity leave into account when granting a Christmas bonus so as to reduce the benefit *pro rata*.[132]

Just how far the ECJ has been prepared to go in protecting employees from discrimination on grounds of pregnancy is well illustrated by its decision in *Busch v Klinikum Neustadt GmbH & Co Betriebs-KG*.[133] Ms. Busch had a baby in June 2000 and took parental leave which was due to be for a period of three years. In October 2000 she became pregnant again and in January 2001 she requested permission to terminate her parental leave early and to return to full time work in April 2001 at which stage she was seven months pregnant. The nature of her work as a nurse meant that she was prohibited from working at that stage in her pregnancy. Her employer sought to rescind its consent to her return to work on grounds of fraudulent misrepresentation and mistake. The ECJ found they were not entitled to do so as they were taking Ms Busch's pregnancy into consideration when refusing to allow her to return to work before the end of her parental leave and that constituted unlawful direct discrimination on grounds of sex. The Court found that Ms Bush was not under any obligation to inform her employer that she was pregnant given that the employer could not take her pregnancy into account in deciding whether she could return to work early or not. Neither the financial loss to the employer nor the legislative prohibition on her performing all of her duties because of her pregnancy nor the fact that her return to work meant that she would receive a maternity allowance higher than her parental leave allowance could justify that discrimination.

[13.73] The high level of protection does not however extend to providing a right to sick pay due to pregnancy and childbirth, nor to maternity pay. The approach of treating pregnancy-related illness differently to other forms of illness and/or sick leave does not extend to preserving a woman's pay during an extended sick leave necessitated by a pregnancy related illness. In the Irish case of *McKenna v North Western Health Board*,[134] the ECJ was asked to consider the situation of a woman who was on long term sick leave throughout her pregnancy due to a pregnancy-related illness.[135] During the pregnancy she exhausted her right to full pay and was moved to half pay in accordance with her employer's sick pay provisions. She argued that placing her on half pay constituted unfavourable treatment in respect of her pay and was therefore unlawful in terms of her right to equal pay. She also argued that taking account of her pregnancy-related illness in terms of her future right to sick pay, as she was limited to taking a total of one year's sick pay over a four year period, constituted less favourable treatment on grounds of her pregnancy and was therefore unlawful. Ms McKenna had succeeded before the Equality Tribunal. When the Health Board appealed to the Labour Court, the Court referred a

---

[131] Case C-333/97 *Lewan v Lothar Denda* [1999] ECR I-7243.

[132] See Bruning and Plontenga, 'Parental Leave and Equal Opportunities' (1999) 9 *JESP* 195.

[133] Case C-320/01 *Busch v Klinikum Neustadt GmbH & Co Betriebs-KG* [2003] ECR I-2041.

[134] Case C-191/03 *McKenna v North Western Health Board* [2005] IRLR 895. The Directives under consideration by the ECJ in this decision were the Equal Pay Directive, Council Directive EC/75/117/EEC [1975] OJ L45/19 and the Equal Treatment Directive, Council Directive EC/76/207 [1976] OJ L39/40.

[135] See Ennis, '*McKenna v North Western Health Board* – The recent decision of the ECJ regarding pregnancy-related illness and conditions of employment – A missed opportunity or a sound policy-based decision' [2006] 3 *ELRev* 63.

number of questions to the ECJ. To some extent, the decision of the ECJ arose from their conclusion that the Equal Treatment Directive[136] did not apply as it was an equal pay rather than an equal treatment case. That preliminary finding effectively limited the Court's approach as, historically, the Court has always tended to take more a liberal approach to the treatment of pregnant employees than to the issue of pay in relation to pregnancy and maternity leave.

In its decision in *McKenna*, the ECJ followed the approach taken in *Gillespie v The Northern Health and Social Services Board*[137] where the Court rejected the argument that an employee on maternity leave was entitled to her full rate of pay. In *McKenna* the Court applied the same clearly economically motivated reasoning to sick pay during pregnancy.

[13.74] The Court stated:[138]

> If a rule providing, within certain limits, for a reduction in pay to a female worker during her maternity leave does not constitute discrimination based on sex, a rule providing, within the same limits, for a reduction in pay to that female worker who is absent during her pregnancy by reason of an illness related to that pregnancy also cannot be regarded as constituting discrimination of that kind.

While the Court acknowledged the special nature of pregnancy-related illness, it held that this could be accommodated by denying an employer the right to dismiss a female worker suffering from such an illness. This was in spite of the fact that, as acknowledged by the Advocate General, the application of the sick leave scheme constituted a disadvantage that could only affect women as they alone could be subject to incapacity to work due to pregnancy related illness.

[13.75] Interestingly, the Directives which were in place at the time of the Court's decision in *McKenna*[139] have since been replaced by the Recast Equal Treatment Directive[140] which specifically brings pay within the concept of working conditions. This may result in the ECJ being able to apply its more liberal approach to the treatment of pregnant workers even in relation to issues of pay. At the same time, given the clear underlying economic motivation behind the Court's decision in *McKenna*, realistically it is unlikely that the Court is going to take any fundamentally different approach in applying the new Directive in spite of the clear logic of what is required by a law which purports to protect women from discrimination on grounds of their pregnancy.

A more liberal view of the ECJ can perhaps be seen in the case of *Sarkatzis Herrero v Instituto Madrileño de la Salud (Imsalud)*[141] where an employee who was appointed to a promotional position was entitled to have her seniority dated from the time of her appointment, even though she was not in a position to take up her post at that time as she

---

[136] Council Directive EC/76/207 [1976] OJ L39/40.

[137] Case C-342/93 *Gillespie v The Northern Health and Social Services Board* [1996] ECR I-475.

[138] Case C-191/03 [2005] IRLR 895 at para 60.

[139] Case C-191/03 [2005] IRLR 895.

[140] Council Directive 2006/54/EC ([2006] OJ L204/23).

[141] Case C-294/04 *Sarkatzis Herrero v Instituto Madrileño de la Salud (Imsalud)* [2006] IRLR 296.

was on maternity leave.[142] In *Alabaster v Woolwich plc, Secretary for State for Social Security*,[143] the Court found that a pay rise awarded during maternity leave must be included in the calculation of maternity pay. The Court held[144]:

> To deny such an increase to a woman on maternity leave would discriminate against her, since, had she not been pregnant, she would have received the pay rise.

[13.76] The ECJ has also relied on the Pregnancy Directive[145] in protecting female workers from pregnancy discrimination. Article 10 provides that pregnant workers cannot be dismissed during the period from the beginning of their pregnancy to the end of their maternity leave, save in exceptional circumstances not connected with their condition which are permitted under national law or practice. If such a worker is dismissed in that period, they must be provided with 'duly substantiated' grounds in writing and Member States must provide a remedy for pregnant workers who are dismissed. In *Jiménez Melgar v Ayuntamiento De Los Barrios*[146] the ECJ held that Art 10 enjoys direct effect. Interestingly the Court also found that the prohibition of dismissal, as set down in Art 10, applies both to fixed-term contracts of employment and permanent contracts, thereby finally dispelling the ambiguity left by the Court's decision in *Webb v EMO Air Cargo*[147] about the dismissal of a pregnant worker on a fixed-term contract.

[13.77] Finally, a recent decision of the ECJ considered whether women who are undergoing IVF are protected by the Pregnancy Directive[148] and the Equal Treatment Directive. In *Mayr v Backerei und Konditorei Gerhard Flockner Ohg*[149] Ms Mayr was employed by the respondent as a waitress. During periods of her employment she was undergoing IVF treatment. After a course of hormone treatment, she went on sick leave for a week. During this period of sick leave, she was notified of her dismissal by her employer. At the time of the notice of dismissal, she was at an advanced stage in the IVF process, but the fertilised ova had not been transferred to her womb. The question posed by the Austrian Court was whether Ms Mayr was protected by the Pregnancy Directive and Equal Treatment Directive. The ECJ was of the view that Ms Mayr could not come within the definition of pregnancy in the Pregnancy Directive as implantation had not yet occurred. The ECJ was of the view that if it allowed for in-vitro fertilised ova not yet planted in the womb to come within the definition of pregnancy, the benefit of the

---

[142] See EU Focus, 'Case Comment Maternity Leave Delaying Start of Post Should not Affect Seniority' [2006] *EU Focus* 18.

[143] Case C-147/02 *Alabaster v Woolwich plc, Secretary for State for Social Security* [2004] ECR I-3101.

[144] Case C-147/02 [2004] ECR I-3101 at para 47.

[145] Council Directive 92/85/EEC Pregnancy Directive [1992] OJ L348/1. For more detail on the Pregnancy Directive, see Barnard, *EC Employment Law* (3rd edn, OUP, 2006) at pp 454–459.

[146] Case C-438/99 *Jiménez Melgar v Ayuntamiento De Los Barrios* [2001] ECR I-6915. See also EU Focus, 'Case Note: Non-Renewal of Fixed Term Contract because of Pregnancy may be Direct Discrimination' (2001) *EU Focus* 14.

[147] Case C-32/93 *Webb v EMO Air Cargo* [1994] ECR I-3567.

[148] Council Directive 92/85/EEC Pregnancy Directive [1992] OJ L348/1.

[149] Case C-506/06 *Mayr v Backerei und Konditorei Gerhard Flockner Ohg* [2008] IRLR 387.

Pregnancy Directive could be extended to situations even where the transfer of the fertilised ova into the uterus was postponed, for whatever reason, for a number of years, or even where such a transfer was definitively abandoned. The ECJ took a broad view of the Equal Treatment Directive and found that as the treatment Ms Mayr underwent only affects women and as her dismissal from employment essentially was because she was undergoing IVF treatment, her employer had directly discriminated against her on grounds of her sex. Accordingly, the ECJ held that the Equal Treatment Directive precludes the dismissal of a female employee who was at an advanced stage of IVF treatment where the dismissal was essentially based on the fact the woman was undergoing such treatment. This decision is hugely significant as it has extended the protection of the Equal Treatment Directive to women who are at an advanced stage in the IVF process. It also establishes that women are protected under the Equal Treatment Directive in the period prior to when the fertilised ova have been implanted. It remains to be seen what exactly the ECJ meant when it referred to 'an advanced stage in the IVF process', as it appears from its decision that the protection of the Equal Treatment Directive only applies to women at this stage in the IVF process.

Pregnancy discrimination in Irish law

[13.78] The Equality Tribunal and the Labour Court have taken a proactive approach to protection of pregnant employees. The jurisprudence of the ECJ plays an important part in their decisions, due to the supremacy of Community law. In many of the determinations of the Equality Tribunal and Labour Court, these tribunals have found in favour of employees who were dismissed during their pregnancy or who suffered unfavourable treatment which they claimed was on grounds of their pregnancy and/or maternity leave.

It would appear from determinations of the Equality Tribunal and the Labour Court that the existence of the pregnancy itself is sufficient to shift the burden of proof to the employer to prove that a dismissal or other less favourable treatment of a pregnant employee was not on grounds of the pregnancy. Even though the requirement of Art 10 of the Pregnancy Directive[150] to cite duly substantiated grounds in writing where a pregnant worker is dismissed has never been implemented in national law and no such requirement exists either in the Employment Equality Act or the Maternity Protection Acts 1994 and 2004, the Equality Tribunal and the Labour Court have regularly referred to the legal requirement that a woman who is dismissed during her pregnancy regardless of the reason for that dismissal must have duly substantiated reasons for the dismissal furnished to them in writing. Where an employer fails to do that, it is likely that the dismissal will be found to have been unlawful even though no such requirement exists in relation to any other dismissal outside of the pregnancy situation. For example in the case of *Assico Assembly Ltd v Corcoran*[151] the Labour Court held:

> Where the employee is dismissed while pregnant or on maternity leave, both legislation and case law state that the employer must show that the dismissal was on exceptional

---

[150] Council Directive 92/85/EEC Pregnancy Directive [1992] OJ L348/1. For more detail on the Pregnancy Directive, see Barnard, *EC Employment Law* (3rd edn, OUP, 2006) at pp 454–459.

[151] *Assico Assembly Ltd v Corcoran* EED 033/2003 (Labour Court).

grounds not associated with her pregnancy and such grounds, in the case of dismissal, as a matter of law and in the case of discrimination as a matter of good practice should be set out in writing.

On the facts of the case, the Court found that the claimant had informed the company of her pregnancy before she was advised that she was being dismissed. While the Court was prepared to accept that the company was unhappy with her work performance, it found no evidence that a firm decision had been taken to dismiss her 'or more importantly that a particular day had been nominated for her dismissal'. The Court concluded that the company had not made a firm decision on a day to implement her dismissal and ultimately found that the company had not discharged the burden on it to show that the claimant's dismissal was for exceptional reasons unconnected with her pregnancy.

[13.79] In the case of *Herco Investments Ltd v O'Sullivan*,[152] the claimant was dismissed on stated grounds of unpunctuality and unreliability some two months after she advised her employer that she was in the early stages of pregnancy, following which she was required to take sick leave due to the pregnancy. She claimed that the dismissal was, in reality, on grounds of her pregnancy. The Labour Court referred to the respondent's inability to produce any records to show when the complainant was late for work or the extent of the alleged lateness. The Court pointed out that she had never received any written warnings in relation to her conduct and that there was no record to substantiate the claim that she had received a series of verbal warnings. In those circumstances the Court found that it was for the respondent to prove on the balance of probabilities that the dismissal was unrelated to the pregnancy. The Court found that the burden of proof had not been discharged in circumstances where there was a complete absence of any documentary records.

[13.80] Similarly in *Bermingham v Colour's Hair Team*[153] the Equality Officer pointed out that the employer had not used any form of disciplinary procedure other than one verbal warning and had put nothing in writing to the complainant before dismissing her. In those circumstances the Equality Officer found that the respondent had failed to demonstrate that there were exceptional circumstances not associated with the complainant's pregnancy for her dismissal.

[13.81] Interestingly, the decision of the High Court in *Mulcahy v Minister for Justice, Equality and Law Reform and Waterford Leader Partnership Ltd*[154] suggests that where the Labour Court accepts the respondent's explanation for the dismissal as not due to the pregnancy, the High Court will not interfere with the Labour Court's findings even where the employer's explanations are not found to be particularly credible. The employer in that case had dismissed the employee during her maternity leave and claimed that the dismissal had been on grounds of allegations which O'Sullivan J in the

---

[152] *Herco Investments Ltd v O'Sullivan* EED 0316/2003 (Labour Court).

[153] *Bermingham v Colour's Hair Team* DEC-E2008-040 (Equality Tribunal).

[154] *Mulcahy v Minister for Justice, Equality and Law Reform and Waterford Leader Partnership Ltd* [2002] 13 ELR 12.

High Court found were 'so tenuous as to be virtually non-existent'. Nevertheless, O'Sullivan J stated:

> I do not, in fact, agree that it is erroneous either in law or in logic to state that because a person offers a bad reason this necessarily means that the bad reason is not the real one.

The Court accepted:

> [...] that the mere coincidence of the date of dismissal with the ending of the employee's pregnancy leave is not in itself sufficient to raise an inference (as distinct from a suspicion) that the reason for the dismissal was related to the pregnancy so as to shift the onus to establish that it was not on to the defendant. I agree that something else is required.

That would certainly suggest, according to the High Court, that the mere existence of pregnancy or maternity leave is not in itself sufficient to shift the burden of proof to an employer where a woman is dismissed or treated less favourably during her pregnancy or maternity leave. Nevertheless, in practice, the Equality Tribunal and the Labour Court require very little else to shift the burden of proof to the employer to prove less favourable treatment was unrelated to the pregnancy or the employee's gender.

[13.82] An example of a lawful dismissal that took place during the employee's pregnancy occurred in the case of *McGuirk v Irish Guardian Publishers*.[155] The employer argued that the dismissal had been on grounds of continued poor performance for a number of months prior to the dismissal which had been raised with the complainant through appraisals and disciplinary processes. The Equality Officer accepted that a number of meetings had been held and the possible consequences of a failure to improve were explained to the complainant. While the Equality Officer accepted that the complainant had informed her employer of her pregnancy before she was advised of their decision to terminate her employment, he was satisfied that the decision to dismiss her had already been taken prior to when she advised them of her pregnancy and that it was therefore unconnected with her pregnancy.

While the evidence in that case did establish a dismissal for recorded poor performance, it surely cannot be said that an employer is not entitled to decide to dismiss an employee once they have been advised of the employee's pregnancy. Certainly a pregnant employee is entitled to special protection, as is recognised by the law, but where there are recorded and substantiated reasons for the dismissal, the timing of when the employer is advised of the pregnancy should not in itself be indicative of the legality of that dismissal, although it may go to the employer's credibility in citing non-pregnancy related reasons for the less favourable treatment.

Indeed, this special form of treatment during pregnancy has been extended by the Labour Court to mean that pregnant employees are not, in particular, to be subjected to conduct which could expose them to physical or psychiatric illness or injury. In *Shinkwin v Millett*[156] the Labour Court stated:

> [...] in a modern employment relationship, employees are entitled to expect that they will be treated with respect during the course of their employment. Employees generally, and

---

[155] *McGuirk v Irish Guardian Publishers* DEC-2007-031 (Equality Tribunal).
[156] *Shinkwin v Millett* EED 044/2004 (Labour Court).

pregnant employees in particular, are also entitled to expect that they will not subjected to conduct which exposes them to physical or psychiatric injury including stress related *sequelae.*

Dismissal due to non-availability during maternity leave

[13.83] A number of cases have arisen where an employer has sought to justify the dismissal of an employee who was recruited to cover another employee's leave and then announced that they would be on maternity leave during the crucial period. Those facts arose in *Webb v EMO Air Cargo*,[157] although it was suggested during the case that Ms. Webb had in fact been taken on as a long term employee, even though the immediate reason for her recruitment was to cover during another employee's maternity leave. Similar facts arose in the case of *Fox v National Council for the Blind*.[158] The decision of the ECJ in *Webb* was distinguished on the basis that Ms. Webb's contract was one of indefinite duration whereas Ms. Fox's contract was a fixed term contract where she was required to be available during a crucial training period, which coincided with the period of time she was due to be on maternity leave. In an unconvincing decision which was upheld by the Labour Court, the Equality Officer found that there was no unlawful discrimination on grounds of sex.

[13.84] A more recent decision of the Equality Tribunal emphatically rejected the employer's argument that they were entitled to dismiss an employee who would be unable to cover the full period of maternity leave for which she was originally engaged due to her own pregnancy and pending maternity leave. In *Rabbitte v EEC Direct*[159] the complainant commenced employment on 21 November 2005 in order to cover a period of another's employee's leave. On 28 November she informed the respondent that she was pregnant. The employer almost immediately terminated her employment and sought to justify this on the basis that she was engaged to cover another employee's maternity leave and would not be available for that specific purpose. The Equality Officer pointed out that such a scenario was specifically held to be discriminatory by the ECJ in *Webb*[160] and therefore found that the respondent had failed to discharge their burden to prove that the dismissal was not on grounds of pregnancy. Compensation of €18,000 was awarded of which only €2,000 represented loss of earnings.

Less favourable conditions of employment on grounds of maternity leave

[13.85] The Equality Tribunal and the Labour Court have also been robust in dealing with claims of unfavourable treatment other than pay, to which employees claim they were subjected due to pregnancy or maternity leave.[161] In the case of *Gardiner v Mercer*

---

[157] Case C-32/93 *Webb v EMO Air Cargo* [1994] ECR I-3567. See also Carocciolo di Torella and Maslot, 'Pregnancy, maternity and the organisation of family life: an attempt to classify the case law of the Court of Justice' (2001) 26 *EL Rev* 239, Fredman, 'Parenthood and the Right to Work' (1995) 111 *LQR* 220 and More, 'Sex, Pregnancy and Dismissal' (1994) 18 *EL Rev* 553.

[158] *Fox v National Council for the Blind* [1995] ELR 74.

[159] *Rabbitte v EEC Direct* DEC-E2008-07 (Equality Tribunal).

[160] Case C-32/93 *Webb* [1994] ECR I-3567.

[161] This is in spite of the potential overlap between this type of claim and a claim under the Maternity Protection Acts 1994 and 2004.

Human Resource Consulting,[162] the Tribunal found that an employee who returned to work after maternity leave and suffered a dimunition in the level of responsibility and range of work she had enjoyed prior to going on leave, had been discriminated against within the meaning of the Employment Equality Act. The Equality Officer also rejected the suggestion that a matter which is covered by the Maternity Protection Act 1994 is therefore outside the scope of the Employment Equality Act.

[13.86] In the case of *Devereux v Bausch and Lomb*[163] the complainant applied for promotion shortly after returning from maternity leave. She was unsuccessful and when she queried this, she was informed that she had 'been out so long on maternity leave'. The Equality Officer noted that no criteria had been drawn up for the process, no marking system was used and only one person made the decision in relation to the candidates. The Equality Officer found that this fell short of transparency, objectivity and the fairness that must be expected in the circumstances, as a result of which, the burden of proof shifted to the employer. The Equality Officer noted that the manager who made the decision had taken account of the fact that he had worked closely with the successful candidate in the previous 12 months. The Equality Officer found that, 'the complainant was at a disadvantage as she had not been in employment for a period in the previous 12 months which was primarily due to maternity leave'. As a result, the Equality Officer found that the respondent had failed to rebut the claim of discrimination and awarded compensation of €5,000.

[13.87] In *Harrington v Board of Management Scoil Chríost Rí*[164] a teacher alleged discrimination on grounds of gender when she was not permitted to withdraw her application for a career break when she became pregnant. The Equality officer found evidence of discrimination and ordered compensation of €10,000 and directed the employer to restore one year's career break entitlements.

However, it is clear that an employee will not be permitted to take an entirely subjective view of different treatment during their pregnancy in making a case that they have been subjected to unlawful discrimination on grounds of that pregnancy. In the case of *Limerick County Council v Carroll*[165] the Labour Court considered the obligations of an employer pursuant to the (now revoked) Safety, Health and Welfare at Work (Pregnant Employees etc) Regulations 2000[166] which required the employer to conduct a risk assessment in relation to its pregnant employees. On foot of the assessment that was carried out, the employer proposed to transfer the employee to clerical duties but retaining her existing pay, allowances etc. The employee was unhappy with this and wanted to remain within the fire service. There were no clerical or administrative positions available there but she put forward a proposal whereby she would undertake non-operational duties for the duration of her pregnancy. The Court found that:

---

[162] *Gardiner v Mercers Human Resource Consulting* DEC-E2006-007 (Equality Tribunal).

[163] *Devereux v Bausch and Lomb* DEC-E2005-020 (Equality Tribunal).

[164] *Harrington v Board of Management Scoil Chríost Rí* DEC-E2005-022 (Equality Tribunal).

[165] *Limerick County Council v Carroll* EDA 0816/2008 (Labour Court).

[166] The Regulations were repealed and replaced by the Safety, Health and Welfare at Work (General Applications) Regulations 2007 (SI 299/2007).

[i]t could not be held that the respondent was reasonably required to make the adjustments which the complainant had sought in her working conditions. The situation may be different in a case in which there is no other suitable work available or whether the pregnant worker may lose financially.

Equality rights after maternity leave

[13.88] While there is no right of an employee returning to work after a period of maternity leave to work reduced hours, the Labour Court and Equality Tribunal have tended to require that an employer treat any applications for family-friendly hours reasonably. This can be seen in the case of *Tesco Ireland v Walsh*.[167] The complainant had sought to work part-time on her return from maternity leave which was refused by the company over the summer because of staff shortages and holidays. They did, however, allow her every Friday and every second Saturday off. She was eventually transferred to part-time work some months after her return from maternity leave. She claimed that she had been discriminated against on grounds of gender in not being allowed to return to part-time work immediately on her return from maternity leave and also argued that a requirement by her employer to work full time indirectly discriminated against her on grounds of gender. The Labour Court held that the company had acted reasonably, having regard to the needs of the business and found no evidence of discrimination on grounds of gender. However it does appear, in principle, that the Equality Tribunal and the Labour Court in cases such as this will require an employer to establish evidence of having acted reasonably in relation to any request for reduced working hours and, in particular, a refusal to grant an employee a job share request must be based on objective reasons relating to the proper operation of its services and not relating to the employee's sex or marital status.[168]

Similarly, a delay in dealing with a request for job sharing was found in *Morgan v Bank of Ireland*[169] to constitute indirect discrimination on grounds of gender. In awarding compensation of €30,000, the Equality Officer stated:

> It is accepted that flexible working arrangements are not an entitlement and are subject to the needs of the organisation. It is also accepted that the significant majority of people taking up flexible working arrangements are female. It is therefore incumbent upon the organisation to operate these arrangements according to fair procedures otherwise there could be a *prima facie* case of indirect discrimination on gender grounds. In this complaint I find that the respondent was discriminatory in that it failed in its duties to operate its procedures fairly and this led to an unacceptable delay before the complainant was offered a job sharing position.

[13.89] In the case of *O'Brien v Cork University Hospital*[170] even though a policy of requesting staff to take up promotional positions on a full-time basis was found to raise a

---

[167] *Tesco Ireland v Walsh* DEE 062.

[168] *Burke v NUI Galway* [2001] ELR 181 and *Tesco Ireland v Swift* EDA 0514/2005 (Labour Court).

[169] *Morgan v Bank of Ireland* DEC-E2008-29 (Equality Tribunal).

[170] *O'Brien v Cork University Hospital* DEC-E2008-021 (Equality Tribunal).

prima facie case of discrimination on grounds of gender and family status, on the facts of the case the policy was found to be objectively justified.

EQUAL PAY

The European background to equal pay[171]

[13.90] Equal pay is provided for in Art 141 (formerly Art 119) of the Treaty of Rome, as amended by the Treaty of Amsterdam. Article 141 is located amongst the social provisions of the Treaty in Title II of Part 3 and provides:

> Each Member State shall ensure that the principle of equal pay for male and female workers for equal work or work of equal value shall be applied.

Although the general view is to see Art 141 as the source of the community principle of sex equality, it has also been argued that the principle of sex equality exists independently of Art 141 and is a fundamental principle of the community legal order.[172] This is not just a technical legal distinction, but has direct practical application when looking at whether the right to equal pay has horizontal as well as vertical direct effects. In other words, if it is a fundamental principle of the community legal order, then the right to equal pay has both horizontal as well as vertical direct effects, ie in the absence of national legislation; the rights apply horizontally between private individuals and vertically between the state and its citizens.

[13.91] At first it was thought that Art 119 did not give rise to any legal effects at all. This understanding was changed by the landmark decision of *Defrenne v Sabena*[173] which established that the right to equal pay was legally binding. Ms Defrenne, a Belgian air hostess, felt that she was entitled to a similar salary as male air stewards. Although there was no equal pay legislation in Belgian law, she argued that her entitlement was derived *directly* from Art 119. The ECJ agreed with this interpretation of the article. This decision opened the door to the development of the protection of equal pay by the ECJ. Directives have since been adopted which provide for equal pay, namely the Recast Equal Treatment Directive,[174] the Race Directive[175] and the Framework Directive.[176]

---

[171] See generally Ellis, *EC Sex Equality Law* (1998); see also Craig and de Búrca, *EC Equality Law*, (1998), pp 805–841; Fredman, *Women and the Law* (1997) pp 226–263. Barnard, *EC Employment Law* (2006).

[172] Docksy, 'The Principle of Equality between Women and Men as a Fundamental Right under Community Law' (1991) 20 *ILJ* 258.

[173] Case 149/77 *Defrenne v Sabena* [1978] ECR 1365.

[174] Council Directive 2006/54/EC on the implementation of the principle of equal opportunities and equal treatment of men and women in matters of employment and occupation ([2006] OJ L204/23)

[175] Council Directive 2000/43/EC ([2000] OJ L180/22) on race discrimination.

[176] Council Directive 2000/78/EC ([2000] L303/16) establishing a general framework for equal treatment in employment and occupation.

[13.92] Community law on equal pay is firmly based on comparing the work of a woman with the work of a comparable man, and similarly for the other grounds. If like work or work of equal value is found to exist, and there is no applicable defence, then the worker is awarded the same pay as the comparator. This is one of the main limitations of the law on equal pay as it exists at present. Many writers have argued that there should be a concept of 'proportionate pay' whereby if for example a worker is doing work which is 90% of the value of the work of comparator, but is only getting 40% of the pay, that there should be a remedy. At present there is no recognition of any entitlement to 'proportionate pay'.[177]

Indirect discrimination and equal pay

[13.93] Indirect discrimination is an important concept with regard to equal pay. It is defined in Art 2 of the Recast Equal Treatment Directive[178] along with direct discrimination:

Definitions

1. For the purposes of this Directive, the following definitions shall apply:

   (a) 'direct discrimination': where one person is treated less favourably on grounds of sex than another is, has been or would be treated in a comparable situation;

   (b) 'indirect discrimination': where an apparently neutral provision, criterion or practice would put persons of one sex at a particular disadvantage compared with persons of the other sex, unless that provision, criterion or practice is objectively justified by a legitimate aim, and the means of achieving that aim are appropriate and necessary;

[13.94] The test for indirect discrimination was set out in detail in the now leading case of *Bilka-Kaufhaus v Weber von Hartz.*[179] In this case the issue which arose was the differential treatment of part-time and full-time staff relating to pension rights. The employers justified their refusal to pay pensions to part-time workers on the basis that it was necessary, for economic reasons, to discourage staff from working part-time. The relevant part of the Court's judgment merits extensive quotation as it sets out the classic test for objective justification:[180]

> Article 119 of the EEC Treaty is infringed by a department store company which excludes part-time employees from its occupational pension scheme, where that exclusion affects a far greater number of women than men, unless the undertaking shows that the exclusion is based on objectively justified factors unrelated to any discrimination on grounds of sex...
> It is for the national court, which has sole jurisdiction to make findings of fact, to determine whether and to what extent the grounds put forward by an employer to explain

---

[177] See Barnard, *EC Employment Law* (3rd edn, Oxford University Press, 2006), pp 380–381.

[178] Council Directive 2006/54/EC on the implementation of the principle of equal opportunities and equal treatment of men and women in matters of employment and occupation [2006] OJ L204/23.

[179] Case 170/84 *Bilka-Kaufhaus v Weber von Hartz* [1986] ECR 1607.

[180] At paras 31 and 36.

the adoption of a pay practice which applies independently of a worker's sex but in fact affects more women than men may be regarded as objectively justified economic grounds. If the national court finds that the measures chosen by Bilka correspond to a real need on the part of the undertaking, are appropriate with a view to achieving the objectives pursued and are necessary to that end, the fact that the measures affect a far greater number of women than men is not sufficient to show that they constitute an infringement of Art 119.'

On the facts in *Bilka*, the question was whether the requirement to work full-time in order to have access to the employer's pension scheme was one which could be objectively justified. In that case the argument of the employers that exclusion of part-time workers from the company pension plan was necessary, for economic reasons, to discourage staff from working part-time, was rejected by the Court. Since *Bilka,* the Court has held that mere generalisations and assumptions will not be allowed to objectively justify indirect discrimination.[181]

The meaning of 'pay'

[13.95] 'Pay' is a concept which is defined widely both a Community level and in Irish legislation and jurisprudence. Article 141, which is the starting point, has the following definition:

> For the purpose of this Article, 'pay' means the ordinary basic or minimum wage or salary and any other consideration, whether in cash or in kind, which the worker receives, directly or indirectly, in respect of his employment from his employer.

The ECJ has taken this broad definition on board and has generally found that all employer based payments are pay. National courts have followed suit. The following matters have been held to be pay:[182] sick pay;[183] travel concessions;[184] grading systems;[185] inconvenient hours supplement;[186] termination/redundancy payments;[187] maternity benefits[188]; bonus payments;[189] and share allocations.[190]

---

[181] Case C-184/89 *Nimz* [1991] ECR I-297.

[182] For a full list see Barnard, *EC Employment Law* (3rd edn, Oxford University Press, 2006), pp 342–343.

[183] Case 171/88 *Rinner Kühn v FWW Special Gebäudereinigung Gmbh & Co KG* [1989] ECR 2743.

[184] Case 12/81 *Garland v British Rail* [1982] ECR 359.

[185] Case C-243/95 *Hill and Stapleton v The Revenue Commissioners* [1998] ECR I-03739.

[186] Case C-236/98 *Jämställdhetsombudsmannen v Örebro läns landsting* [2000] ECR I-2189.

[187] Case C-220/02, *Österreichische Gewerkschaftsbund v Wirtschafts Kammer Österreich* 8 June 2004.

[188] Case C342/93 *Gillespie v Northern Health and Social Services Board* [1996] ECR I-475.

[189] Case 109/88 *Handel-Og Kontorfunkionaerernes Forbund I Danmark v Dansk Arbejdsgiverforesing* [1989] ECR 3199; Case C-184/89, *Nimz v Freie und Hansestadt Hamburg* [1991] ECR I-297; Case C-281/97, Andrea Krüger v Kreiskrankenhaus Ebersberg [1999] ECR I-05127 and Case C-333/97 *Lewen v Lothar Denda* [1999] ECR I-7243.

[190] *Brady and McGivern v TSB ESOP Trustees* (2005) 16 ELR 356.

[13.96] In fact, the scope of pay is so broad that in *Arbeiterwohlfahrt der Stadt Berlin v Bötel*[191] the Court held that it includes:[192]

> [...] all consideration, whether in cash or in kind, whether immediate or future, provided that the worker receives it, albeit indirectly, in respect of his employment from his employer, whether under a contract of employment, by virtue of legislation or on a voluntary basis.

However, the payment received must be a 'consideration' or benefit. The repayment of an expense incurred by an employee for travel or subsistence does not amount to 'pay'.[193]

Social security and pensions

[13.97] The broadness of the definition of pay has made it difficult to draw a boundary between pay and social security. The boundary is significant as equal treatment in social security is not covered by Art 141[194] but primarily by Directive 79/7 on the progressive implementation of the principle of equal treatment for men and women in matters of social security[195] (the Occupational Social Security Directive). This Directive has limitations that do not apply to the principle of equal pay. The Recast Equal Treatment Directive[196] has attempted to codify the case law in this area in Art 7(2) although an understanding of the case law which it consolidates is required.

The ECJ has stated that, in general, social security payments, such as retirement pensions or sick pay which are directly governed by statute and are obligatory for general categories of workers, are not covered by Art 141. In *Schönheit v Stadt Frankfurt am Main*,[197] the Court set out at three-tier test. A scheme fell within Art 141 even if established by law if: (1) it concerned a particular category of workers; (2) it was directly related to the period of service completed; and (3) its amount was calculated by reference to the individual's final salary.

[13.98] Similarly after *Barber v Guardian Royal Exchange Assurance*[198] and *Bilka Kaufhaus v Weber von Hartz*[199] it is clear that all forms of occupational pensions constitute an element of pay within the meaning of Art 141.[200] Furthermore, it appears

---

[191] Case C-360/90 *Arbeiterwohlfahrt der Stadt Berlin v Bötel* [1992] ECR I-03589.

[192] [1992] ECR I-03589 at para 12.

[193] *Fleury v Minister for Education and Science* DEC-E2009-28.

[194] For the wording of Art 141, see para **[13.95]**.

[195] Council Directive 79/7/EEC of 19 December 1978 on the progressive implementation of the principle of equal treatment for men and women in matters of social security.

[196] Council Directive 2006/54/EC on the implementation of the principle of equal opportunities and equal treatment of men and women in matters of employment and occupation ([2006] OJ L204/23).

[197] Joined Cases C-4/02 and C-5/02 *Schönheit v Stadt Frankfurt am Main* [2003] ECR I-12575.

[198] Case C-262/88, *Barber v Guardian Royal Exchange Assurance Group* [1990] ECR I-1889.

[199] Case 170/84 *Bilka Kaufhaus v Weber von Hartz* [1986] ECR 1607.

[200] Implicitly it also includes all forms of benefit deriving from occupational social security schemes. See Hervey, 'Sex Equality in Social Provision' (1998) 4 *European Law Review* 196 at p 216.

that the only statutory social security schemes which fall outside Art 141 and under the Occupational Social Security Directive, are statutory social security pensions provided for workers in general as a matter of social policy and funded from the public purse. The fact that equal treatment rights with regard to pensions are protected by a Treaty article rather than simply by a Directive has important consequences. Due to the doctrine of horizontal direct effects, the ruling in *Barber* and *Bilka* can be relied on between individuals and not just against the State.

Part-time workers and overtime

[13.99] The ECJ has held, from an early time, that less favourable treatment of part-time workers[201] constitutes indirect discrimination on the gender ground.[202] In *Bilka Kaufhaus v Weber von Hartz*[203] the ECJ extended protection from equal pay to equal access to pension rights and established the standard by which such indirect discrimination may be justified – that the justification is objective, that it is based on genuine business needs and that the discriminatory means are necessary and suitable to achieving the aims.

Thus, where a part-time employee earns less pay for doing the same work as a full-time employee, that may constitute indirect discrimination on grounds of sex as the vast majority of part-time employees are women. However, where overtime is paid at a premium when employees work in excess of a full week's hours, a part-time employee can claim an entitlement to such a premium as soon as they work in excess of their normal part-time hours.[204] On the other hand, if overtime is paid at a lower rate, then a part-time employee does not go onto the lower rate until they have reached the basic hours of a full-time worker.[205] Similarly a refusal to pay a part-time employee for hours spent on a course beyond their normal working hours could constitute indirect discrimination.[206]

Pay and pregnancy/maternity

[13.100] In spite of the Court's broad approach to what constitutes 'pay', they have drawn some limits. For example, the allowances paid to a woman on maternity leave have been held not to constitute pay. In *Gillespie & ors v Northern Health and Social Services Board*[207] the complainants failed in an ambitious and logical claim in arguing that their employer was infringing Art 141 (then Art 119) by paying them less than their full salary during maternity leave.[208]

---

[201] On part-time workers generally, see Ch 9, Part-time Workers.

[202] The first case was Case 96/80 *Jenkins v Kingsgate Clothing* [1981] ECR 911. This case is considered below at para **[13.119]**.

[203] Case 170/84 *Bilka Kaufhaus v Weber von Hartz* [1986] ECR 1607.

[204] Cases C-399/92, C-409/92, C-34/93, C-50/93, C-79/93 *Stadt Lengerich v Helmig* [1995] IRLR 216.

[205] Case C-300/06 *Voß v Land Berlin*.

[206] Case C-360/90 *Arbeiterwohlfahrt der Stadt Berlin v Botel* [1992] 3 CMLR 446.

[207] Case C-342/93 *Gillespie & ors v Northern Health and Social Services Board* [1996] ECR I-475.

[208] *Gillespie* is discussed at para **[13.73]**.

Similarly in *North-Western Health Board v McKenna*[209] the ECJ held that a female worker who is absent by reason of a pregnancy related illness is not entitled to maintenance of full pay, provided that the amount of remuneration payable is not so low as to undermine the Community law objective of protecting female workers.[210]

Equal pay versus equal treatment

[13.101] The ECJ has steadily emphasised that there is a clear distinction between what is equal pay and what is equal treatment – something cannot be both. *Wippel v Peek & Cloppenberg Gmbh*[211] concerned a complex challenge by a part-time worker to her contract of employment which failed to provide her with hours of work and, therefore, pay, up to the maximum of full-time hours, whereas a worker on a full-time contract was paid for the maximum of full-time hours whether they worked them or not. The Court, in considering the question, set out very clearly that its first task was to determine whether the issue was one of equal pay or equal treatment. It stated that the fact that a contract of employment has financial consequences is not sufficient to bring it within the scope of equal pay as the law governing equal pay is based on the close connection between the nature of the work done and the amount of the worker's pay. In *McKenna* the Court stated that[212] 'pay within the terms of Art 141 and Directive 75/117 [the Equal Pay Directive] cannot also come within the scope of Directive 76/207 [the Equal Treatment Directive]'. The distinction between the two is important as somewhat different legal principles apply to claims for equal pay and those for equal treatment. The six-month time limit for bringing claims under the Employment Equality Act, for example, does not apply to claims for equal pay.[213] Claims for equal pay would have to show like work, which again would not apply to claims for equal treatment. The first step therefore in practical terms in bringing a claim for equal pay, is to ensure that it is a claim for equal pay and not one for equal treatment.

The meaning of worker

[13.102] At common law, there is a clear split between those employed on a contract of service and a contract for services.[214] However, the common law definitions do not necessarily apply in Community law. In *Allonby v Accrington & Rosendale College*,[215] the ECJ made clear that the definition of worker in Community law is independent of definitions of worker in domestic legal systems and thus of common law definitions.[216] The term 'worker' used in Art 141 must be considered as a person 'who for a certain

---

[209] Case C-191/03 *North-Western Health Board v McKenna* [2005] ECR I-7631.

[210] The specific application of the principle of equal pay to women during pregnancy and maternity is considered in para **[13.73]**.

[211] Case C-313/02 *Wippel v Peek & Cloppenberg Gmbh* [2004] ECR I-9483.

[212] Case C-191/03 *McKenna* [2005] ECR I-7631 at para 30.

[213] See *Power v Blackrock College* DEC E2008-72 where a claim for discriminatory treatment on grounds of age in non-payment of redundancy was held to be in time as it was an equal pay claim. The case failed however due to a lack of a comparator.

[214] On the distinction, see Ch 2, The Contract and Relationship of Employment.

[215] Case C-256/01 *Allonby v Accrington & Rosendale College* [2002] ECR I-7325.

[216] Case C-256/01, [2002] ECR I-7325 at para 66.

period of time, performs services for and under the direction of another person in return for which he receives remuneration'.[217] This definition gives a wider application to equal pay law than a narrow common law-based definition of contract of service. The Employment Equality Act is not out of step with this EU approach as the definition of 'contract of employment' under the Act includes a contract where an individual agrees personally to execute any work or service for another person.[218]

Employment Equality Act and equal pay

[13.103] In relation to the entitlement to equal pay as between women and men, s 19(1) of the Employment Equality Act provides:

> It shall be a term of the contract under which A is employed that subject to this Act, A shall at any time be entitled to the same rate of remuneration for the work which A is employed to do as B who, at that or any other relevant time, is employed to do like work by the same or an associated employer.

In relation to the entitlement to equal pay as between employees who differ in respect of any of the other eight prohibited grounds of discrimination, s 29(1) of the Act similarly provides:

> It shall be a term of the contract under which C is employed that subject to this Act, C shall at any time be entitled to the same rate of remuneration for the work which C is employed to do as D who, at that or any other relevant time, is employed to do like work by the same or an associated employer.

The entire basis of equal pay is that they are doing like work with an identified comparator. 'Like work' is defined in s 7 of the Employment Equality Act:

> Subject to subsection (2), for the purposes of this Act, in relation to the work which one person is employed to do, another person shall be regarded as employed to do like work if—
>
> (a)   both perform the same work under the same or similar conditions, or each is interchangeable with the other in relation to the work,
>
> (b)   the work performed by one is of a similar nature to that performed by the other and any differences between the work performed or the conditions under which it is performed by each either are of small importance in relation to the work as a whole or occur with such irregularity as not to be significant to the work as a whole, or
>
> (c)   the work performed by one is equal in value to the work performed by the other, having regard to such matters as skill, physical or mental requirements, responsibility and working conditions.

[13.104] The definition of like work is almost identical to that under the 1974 Act.[219] Any person therefore who wishes to succeed in a claim for equal pay must identify a comparator who is similarly situated but is treated differently on the basis of a

---

[217] Case C-256/01, [2002] ECR I-7325 at para 67. See further Fredman, *European Developments-Marginalising Equal Pay Laws* [2004] 33 *ILJ* 281.

[218] Employment Equality Acts 1998–2008, s 2(1). The full wording of the provision is noted in para **[13.08]**.

[219] Anti Discrimination (Equal Pay) Act 1974, s 3.

discriminatory ground. So, for example, a woman must show that she is paid less than a man engaged in like work, a person with a disability must show that he or she is paid less than a person without a disability engaged in like work, and so on with the other discriminatory grounds. There are, therefore, two hurdles for a plaintiff to cross: he or she must establish like work and he or she must identify a comparator engaged in like work who is paid a greater amount.

Like work

[13.105] As set out at para **[13.103]**, like work is defined as work that is:[220]

(i) Identical or interchangeable;

(ii) Similar in nature where the differences are infrequent or of small importance in relation to the work as a whole; or

(iii) Equal in value in terms of the demands made in relation to matters such as skill, physical or mental requirements, responsibility and working conditions.

It is useful to examine each category in detail.

(i) Identical or interchangeable

[13.106] Work that is identical is self-explanatory. The idea of work being interchangeable suggests that the claimant would be able to take over from the comparator without any notice. In the early decision of *Department of Posts and Telegraphs v Kennefick*[221] a comparison was made between two post and telegraph clerks. The employer claimed that the man's job carried additional duties, but he was seldom called upon to actually perform those duties. The Labour Court refused to be guided by the job description. The Court found that the nature of the two jobs were substantially the same and awarded equal pay.

However, where a claimant might be capable of doing most of the duties performed by the comparator on a day to day basis, but does not hold the qualifications for the comparator's job, the higher qualifications have been held to justify a higher level of pay.[222]

(ii) Similar in nature

[13.107] Work that is described as being similar in nature suggests that the work is not identical or even interchangeable, but the work is alike in many respects and whatever differences exist are not significant. Thus differences between the jobs are permitted, even where those differences are somewhat frequent, so long as the differences are of small importance in relation to the job as a whole. In *Dowdall O'Mahony v 9 Female Employees*[223] for example both jobs were general factory operatives. Equal pay was

---

[220] Employment Equality Acts 1998–2008, s 7(1).

[221] *Department of Posts and Telegraphs v Kennefick* EP9/1979; DEP 2/1980.

[222] See *O'Leary v The Minister for Transport and Communications* [1998] ELR 113 and *Angestelltenbetriebsrat der Wiener Gebietskrankenkasse v Wiener Gebietskrankenkasse* C-309/97 [1999] 2 CMLR 1173.

[223] *Dowdall O'Mahony v 9 Female Employees* EP2/1987 (Labour Court).

awarded as the differences were found to be infrequent and of little importance in the context of the work as a whole.[224]

(iii) Equal in value

[13.108] More difficult to establish is a claim which involves an assertion that although different, both jobs are equal in value. An assessment of a claim for equal pay on this basis involves adopting a comparison of both jobs across a series of criteria such as skill, physical and mental effort, responsibility, working conditions and any other relevant heading that allows two substantially different jobs to be compared as equally demanding. This task is undertaken through a complex and time consuming process of work inspections, where an Equality Officer, quite literally, visits the workplace and inspects the work.

The case of *24 Female Employees v Spring Grove Services*[225] remains one of the most useful in understanding how an evaluation of the value of two different jobs is done. In this case a number of the claimants were employed in the finishing area of a linen services supply factory and sought to compare themselves with eight named male comparators who worked in the wash house area. The Equality Officer chose one claimant of the twenty four and compared her with one of the eight comparators under the headings of skill, physical effort, mental effort, responsibility and working conditions. On the basis of an extensive comparative exercise the Equality Officer concluded that the claimants were not doing work of equal value to that of the comparators.

The need for a comparator

[13.109] The definition of like work and the basic principle of equal pay for equal work, requires that the person seeking equal pay must compare their work to someone else. The need for comparators has always been fraught with difficulties. It inhibits the law in attacking, for example, occupational sex segregation where large numbers of women are clustered in work that is thereby lesser valued on the basis of its being perceived as 'women's work'.

The ECJ has consistently stated that with regard to equal pay, there is a need for a real identifiable comparator and not a hypothetical one.[226] The comparator must also be in an identical situation with the claimant. Thus in *Österreichische Gewerkschaftsbund v*

---

[224] See also *O'Leary v Minister for Transport* [1998] ELR 113 where differences that occurred between radio operators at Dublin airport were found to be more than of small importance in that the comparators required additional qualifications and skills in order to ensure the Department complied with certain UN conventions on broadcasting on aeronautical and maritime frequencies

[225] *24 Female Employees v Spring Grove Services* [1996] ELR 147. See also *14 Named Female Employees v Department of Justice, Equality and Law Reform* DEC-E2005-57 (Equality Tribunal).

[226] Case C-129/79 *MacCarthys Ltd v Smith* [1980] ECR 1275. See also *Power v Blackrock College* DEC E2008-72 where a claim for discriminatory treatment on grounds of age in non-payment of redundancy failed however due to failure to identify a comparator.

Wirtschafts Kammer Österreich[227] a woman absent from the workplace on parental leave was not in a similar situation to a man absent from the workplace on military service and thus could not have that time counted for length of service in calculating redundancy type payments. A part-time worker on a contract to work hours as required was not in a similar situation to a full-time worker contracted to work for a predefined number of hours on an ongoing basis.[228]

[13.110] In an interesting twist, the Labour Court in *Irish Ale Breweries Ltd v O'Sullivan*[229] determined that while the comparator has to be a real person, it does not necessarily have to be a person known to the claimant. The claimant who was a cleaner for Irish Ale Breweries at their premises in Ballyfermot, Dublin, sought to compare herself with a yardman in Waterford who was known to the company but not to her. She claimed that she was the only woman in the depot and her job was excluded from a grading structure. The company would not provide her with information on the pay and conditions which she requested under s 76 of the Employment Equality Act. The Labour Court, relying on the decision of the ECJ in *Brünnhofer v Bank der Österreichische Postsparkasse AG*,[230] determined that while as a general rule it is for the claimant to identify the comparator and to prove that they are receiving lower pay, the rigid application of this rule could impair the effectiveness of equal pay guarantees where a claimant is obstructed by an employer from obtaining evidence which is in the employers power of procurement.

The Labour Court therefore stated that it would proceed on the basis of a rebuttable inference that the claimant, Ms O'Sullivan, was engaged in like work with the yardman.[231] The respondent offered no evidence to the contrary. Thus, the Labour Court awarded €25,000 in compensation.

While a claimant is entitled to choose its comparator,[232] the context in which they are employed must be considered and taken into account.[233] However, the ECJ has rejected attempts to cherry pick a comparator group for the purpose of an equal value claim. In *Dansk Industri*, a claim for equal pay between piece-rate workers, the Court held that the claimant and comparator groups had to:[234]

---

[227] Case C-220/02 *Österreichische Gewerkschaftsbund v Wirtschafts Kammer Österreich* 8 June 2004.

[228] Case 313/02 *Wippel v Peek & Cloppenberg Gmbh* [2004] ECR I-9483.

[229] *Irish Ale Breweries Ltd v O'Sullivan* [2007] 18 ELR 150.

[230] Case C-381/99 *Brünnhofer v Bank der Österreichische Postsparkasse* AG [2001] ECR I-4961.

[231] Employment Equality Acts 1998–2008, s 81 provides that it is open to a court or tribunal to draw such inferences as are appropriate from the failure of an employer to provide information under s 76.

[232] *Wilton v Irish Steel* [1999] ELR1 and *National University of Ireland v Aherne* [2005] 2 IR 577 at para 13.

[233] *National University of Ireland v Aherne* [2005] 2 IR 577; *Department of Justice, Equality and Law Reform v CPSU* [2008] ELR 140 (Labour Court).

[234] Case C-400/93 *Specialarbejderforbundet i Danmark v Dansk Industri, formerly Industriens Arbejdsgivere, acting for Royal Copenhagen* [1995] ECR I-1275 at para 38.

[e]ncompass all the workers who, taking account of a set of factors such as the nature of the work, the training requirements and the working conditions, can be considered to be in a comparable situation and that they cover a relatively large number of workers ensuring that the differences are not due to purely fortuitous or short-term factors or to differences in the individual output of the workers concerned.

Same establishment or service

[13.111] The ECJ confirmed in *Lawrence v Regent Officer Care Ltd*[235] that a cross-employer comparison is permitted where a difference in pay is attributable to a single source of funding. This was not the case in *Lawrence* where catering workers formerly working for a local council whose work had been contracted out sought to compare themselves to a gardeners and caretakers for the purposes of an equal pay claim. A similar conclusion was reached in the much criticised decision in *Allonby*.[236]

Section 19(1) of the Employment Equality Act directs that the claimant and the comparator must be employed to do like work by the same or an associated employer at that or at any other relevant time. 'Relevant time' is defined in s 19(2)(b) as any time during the three years preceding or following the particular time. Employers are defined as associated in s 2(2) if:

> [...]one is a body corporate of which the other (whether directly or indirectly) has control or if both are bodies corporate of which a third person (whether directly or indirectly) has control.

A further condition is imposed by ss 19(3) and 29(3), which provide that a claimant and the comparator employed by associated employers cannot be regarded as employed to do like work 'unless they both have the same or reasonably comparable terms and conditions of employment'.

[13.112] One of the most important cases in an Irish context is *Brides v The Minister for Agriculture*[237] which examines the applicable legal principles in this area. Employees of Teagasc sought unsuccessfully to compare themselves with employees of the Department of Agriculture. The High Court held that Teagasc was an independent government unit which was not controlled by the Department of Agriculture such as to make them associated employers. In the High Court, Budd J found that the requirement of 'associated employer was inserted in the Irish legislation in order to keep the necessary identification of discrimination'. Otherwise, he said:

> a prospective claimant could pick a comparator from anywhere, having no connection with the employer of the claimant and rely simply on the fact that they perform like work. The ramifications of such a wide application of the principle of equal pay are far reaching and would go far beyond the scope of the principle as envisaged in *Defrenne*[238] and *MacCarthys*.[239]

[235] Case C-320/00 *Lawrence v Regent Officer Care Ltd* [2002] ECR I-7325.
[236] Case C-256/01 *Allonby v Accrington & Rosendale College* [2004] ECR I-2002. See Fredman, *European Developments-Marginalising Equal Pay Laws* [2004] 33 *ILJ* 281.
[237] *Brides v The Minister for Agriculture* [1998] 4 IR 250.
[238] Case C-149/77 *Defrenne v Sabena Case* 149/77 [1978] ECR 1365.
[239] Case C-129/79 *MacCarthys Ltd v Smith* [1980] ECR 1275.

With respect to Budd J, the limitation with the 'single source' test is that inequality of pay is frequently a consequence of institutional arrangements for which no single factor is to blame.[240] It is often the case also, that an employer will manipulate the employment situation in order to save money, as in *Allonby*[241] and *Lawrence*[242] which involved two groups of workers working side by side in the same establishment but some of whose work had been contracted out to service providers.

The burden of proof

[13.113] Having found an appropriate comparator, the next hurdle for a complainant to overcome is to discharge the burden which the law places on him or her to show that the difference in pay is due to discrimination on one of the prohibited grounds. This is always a difficult burden, but has been made even more so in recent times by the changing nature of paid work. The increased deregulation of the workplace facilitates pay systems which may be lacking in transparency by enhancing pay with extras such as commission, flexibility payments, performance increments and other such bonuses. This makes it difficult for the complainant to show that their lower wage is on prohibited grounds.

The ECJ has made very significant decisions in this area which can ease the complainant's burden of proof, by shifting the burden of proof to the employer to justify a difference in pay if the complainant establishes that he or she is engaged in like work with an appropriate comparator.[243] The rationale for shifting the burden of proof is set out in *Jämställdhetsombudsmannen v Örebro läns landsting*[244] a case in which two female midwives sought to compare themselves to a group of male lab technicians. The Court concluded:[245]

> [W]here there is a *prima facie* case of discrimination; it is for the employer to show that there are objective reasons for the difference in pay. Workers would be deprived of the means of securing compliance with the principle of equal pay before national courts if evidence establishing a *prima facie* case of discrimination did not have the effect of imposing on the employer the onus of proving that the difference in pay is not in fact discriminatory.[246]

[13.114] The accumulated law on the burden of proof is now set out in Art 19 of the Recast Equal Treatment Directive[247] which provides:

---

[240] See Barnard, *EC Employment Law* (3rd edn, Oxford University Press, 2006) p 354, Fredman, *European Developments-Marginalising Equal Pay Laws* [2004] 33 *ILJ* 281 at 281.

[241] Case C-256/01 *Allonby v Accrington & Rosendale College* [2004] ECR I-2002.

[242] Case C-320/00 *Lawrence v Regent Officer Care Ltd* [2002] ECR I-7325.

[243] See Case C-127/92 *Enderby v Frenchay Health Authority* [1993] ECR I-5535, described by Ellis as 'a victory for the forces of common sense and realism on the embattled field of equal pay law', Casenote [1994] CMLR 387 at 387.

[244] Case C-236/98 *Jämställdhetsombudsmannen v Örebro läns landsting* [2000] ECR I-02189.

[245] Case C-236/98, [2000] ECR I-02189 at para 53.

[246] See Case C-127/92 *Enderby v Frenchay Health Authority* [1993] ECR I-5535 at para 18.

Burden of proof

1. Member States shall take such measures as are necessary, in accordance with their national judicial systems, to ensure that, when persons who consider themselves wronged because the principle of equal treatment has not been applied to them establish, before a court or other competent authority, facts from which it may be presumed that there has been direct or indirect discrimination, it shall be for the respondent to prove that there has been no breach of the principle of equal treatment.

For grounds of discrimination other than gender, Art 8 of the Race Directive[248] and Art 10 of the Framework Directive[249] contain similar provisions shifting the burden of proof.

The ECJ has also held that if a pay system is completely lacking in transparency, where a female employee shows by comparison with a relatively large group of employees that the pay of female employees is lower than that of male employees, the burden of proof shifts to the employer to show that the pay system is not discriminatory.[250]

The justification of unequal pay

[13.115] In terms of establishing an entitlement to equal pay for equal work, once the claimant has identified a similarly situated comparator and established the comparator is in receipt of greater pay, it is still open to the employer to justify the difference in treatment. It is essential to realise that the prohibition is of difference of treatment on grounds of sex, or another discriminatory ground. It is therefore open to an employer to show that the difference of treatment is not on the discriminatory ground, but for some other valid non-discriminatory reason. This 'defence' if it can be called such, is set out in s 19(5) (for the gender ground) and s 29(5) (for the other grounds) of the Employment Equality Act. In reality, there is some difficulty in calling it a defence, as, if there is no difference of treatment on a discriminatory ground, then the prohibition has not been breached.[251]

If there is difference of treatment on a discriminatory ground, and this difference of treatment amounts to indirect discrimination, the employer may be able to objectively justify the discrimination. It is important that an employer has the possibility of justifying unequal pay. This was first recognised in *Bilka Kaufhaus v Weber von Hartz*,[252] discussed above at para **[13.94]**.

[13.116] This test is now wrapped up in what is known as 'objective justification' and the *Bilka* test is codified throughout employment legislation at community and national

---

[247] Council Directive 2006/54/EC on the implementation of the principle of equal opportunities and equal treatment of men and women in matters of employment and occupation ([2006] OJ L204/23)

[248] Council Directive 2000/43/EC ([2000] OJ L180/22) on race discrimination.

[249] Council Directive 2000/78/EC ([2000] L303/16) establishing a general framework for equal treatment in employment and occupation.

[250] *Danfoss* [1989] ECR 3199.

[251] For a discussion of the issues, see Barnard, *EC Employment Law* (3rd edn, Oxford University Press, 2006) pp 354–357.

[252] Case 170/84 *Bilka Kaufhaus v Weber von Hartz* [1986] ECR 1607.

level.[253] The decision establishes an ends and means test, with the requirement of proportionality. The means must lead to the objective, the objective must be necessary and the means chosen must be proportionate to the objective. The employer must be able to show how and why the decision to discriminate was taken at that time and retrospective justification is unacceptable. Grounds such as the worker's flexibility, adaptability to hours and places of work, training or length of service may be objective grounds if they can be attributed to the needs and objectives of the employer.

Requirements which have been held to satisfy the test of objectively justifying indirect discrimination in pay include a salary based on mobility, training and length of service, a job classification system based on criteria of muscle demand or effort and lower social security benefits on account of the marital status or family situation of the claimant.[254] However an attempt by an employer to justify indirect discrimination in pay will not necessarily be accepted by the ECJ. For example in *Hill and Stapleton v The Revenue Commissioners*[255] the Court refused to allow the discrimination inherent in treating job sharing employees less favourably than full time employees[256] 'solely on the ground that avoidance of such discrimination would involve increased costs'.

The strict test of objective justification laid down in *Bilka-Kaufhaus*[257] may not be applicable in all circumstances. Barnard states:[258]

> There seem now to be at least three tests for objective justification: the strict *Bilka* test for indirectly discriminatory conduct by employers, recently affirmed in *Hill*,[259], the weaker *Seymour-Smith*[260] test for indirectly discriminatory employment legislation, and the very dilute test for social security legislation in *Nolte/Megner*[261].

The application of a lesser test seems to be apparent when the State puts forward justifications in relation to budgetary policy. This is discussed in para **[13.120]**.

General justifications are considered in the following paragraphs.

---

[253] In the Employment Equality Act s 19(4) (for the gender ground) and s 29(4) (for the other grounds), in Art 2(1)b of the Recast Equal Treatment Directive, Council Directive 2006/54/EC ([2006] OJ L204/23) and in common Art 2 of the Race Directive, Council Directive 2000/43/EC ([2000] OJ L180/22) on race discrimination, and the Framework Directive, Council Directive 2000/78/EC ([2000] L303/16) establishing a general framework for equal treatment in employment and occupation.

[254] See Case 237/85 *Rummler* [1986] ECR 2101; Case 30/85 *Teuling v Bedrijfsvereniging voor de Chemische Industrie*; Case C-171/88 *Rinner-Kuhn v FWW Spezial-gebaudereinigung GmbH & Co KG* [1989] ECR 2743; Case C-33/89 *Kowalska* [1990] ECR I-2591; Case 109/88 Danfoss [1997] ECR I-2757; and Case C-184/89 *Nimz v Freie und Hansestadt Hamburg* [1991] ECR I-297.

[255] Case C-243/95 *Hill and Stapleton v The Revenue Commissioners* [1998] ECR I-03739.

[256] [1998] ECR I-03739 at para 40.

[257] Case 170/84 *Bilka-Kaufhaus* [1986] ECR 1607.

[258] Barnard, *EC Employment Law* (3rd edn, Oxford University Press, 2006) p 368.

[259] Case C-243/95 *Hill and Stapleton v The Revenue Commissioners* Case C-243/95 [1998] ECR I-03739.

[260] Case C-167/97 *R v SSE, ex parte Nicole Seymour-Smith & Anor* [1999] ECR I-623.

[261] Case C-317/93 *Inge Nolte v Landesversicherungsanstalt Hannover* [1995] ECR I-4625; Case C-444/93 *Ursula Megner and Hildegard Scheffel v Innungskrankenkasse Vorderpfalz, now Innungskrankenkasse Rheinhessen-Pfalz* [1995] ECR I-4741.

Grounds other than a discriminatory ground

[13.117] *National University of Ireland v Aherne*[262] and *Wilton v Irish Steel*[263] clarify the application of this justification. These cases were decided under the Anti-Discrimination (Pay) Act 1974, which provided:[264]

> Nothing in this Act shall prevent an employer from paying to his employees who are employed in like work in the same place different rates of remuneration on grounds other than sex.

In *Aherne*[265] the issue was whether security operatives who were performing like work to telephone operatives but receiving less pay were entitled to be paid the same as the telephone operatives. The Supreme Court found that the security operative could choose the comparators. However it then went on to consider the question as to why the telephone operatives were being paid more money and found that this was due to matters other than their sex. The telephone operatives were getting more pay because they had initially been doing more work but, because of family responsibilities, had been facilitated in that they did less work while retaining the higher amount of pay. It was on this basis the Supreme Court held that there was no discrimination because there were grounds other than sex for paying the telephone operatives more money.[266]

Similarly in *Wilton*,[267] the female complainant was permitted to choose a comparator who was doing the same work as her but was being paid more money. The High Court then went on to find that there was no discrimination in this particular case because the comparator was actually being paid more money due to his greater length of service and that this was a ground other than sex under the 1974 Pay Act.[268]

[13.118] More recently in *Department of Justice, Equality and Law Reform v CPSU*,[269] the Labour Court determined that the Department had had grounds other than gender for paying higher rates of pay to members of An Garda Síochána performing clerical duties as compared with female clerical workers. The force had legitimate reasons for reserving certain clerical posts for Gardaí and paying a higher wage to the Gardaí doing that work, even though the non-Garda clerical workers were performing like-work.[270]

The defence of market forces

[13.119] From an early time the ECJ was also willing to consider a market forces defence. *Jenkins v Kingsgate Clothing*[271] was one of the first cases to recognise that

---

[262] *National University of Ireland v Aherne* [2005] 2 IR 577.

[263] *Wilton v Irish Steel* [1999] ELR 1.

[264] Anti-Discrimination (Pay) Act, s 2(3).

[265] *National University of Ireland v Aherne* [2005] 2 IR 577.

[266] See also *Department of Justice v CPSU (the Garda Clericals case)* [2008] 19 ELR 140.

[267] *Wilton v Irish Steel* [1999] ELR 1.

[268] For a recent case on the age ground where a difference in pay based on a structured performance assessment process was held to be lawful in accordance with Employment Equality Acts 1998–2008, s 29(5), see *Cassidy v Citibank* DEC E2005-35 (Equality Tribunal).

[269] *Department of Justice, Equality and Law Reform v CPSU* [2008] ELR 140 (Labour Court).

[270] As at time of writing, this case is under appeal.

[271] Case 96/80 *Jenkins v Kingsgate Clothing* [1981] ECR 911.

lower pay rates for part-time employees was indirect discrimination. The Court also held that the employer would have a defence if they could show that lower pay for part-time workers was genuinely part of its business strategy on economic grounds that could be objectively justified. This justification was extended from external market forces to internal forces in *Bilka-Kaufhaus*[272] where the employer persuaded the Court that non-payment of pension contributions for part-time employees was justified by the necessity for the business of a department store to encourage its employees to work full-time.

The issue of a market forces defence has been developed further by the Court in *Enderby.*[273] The case involved a comparison between speech therapists, the majority of whom were women, and pharmacists, the majority of whom were men. The employer argued that the differential pay levels was not due to sex discrimination but rather was due to a shortage of candidates for pharmacist positions, which obliged the employer to offer higher salaries in order to attract suitable candidates. The argument did find some favour with the Court, although the degree to which a market forces defence can be used was limited by the application of the principle of proportionality.

[13.120] The ECJ will not usually accept an argument by employers or even the State that it simply costs too much to secure equal pay. In *Hill and Stapleton v The Revenue Commissioners*[274] the Court refused to allow the discrimination inherent in treating job sharing employees less favourably than full time employees[275] 'solely on the ground that avoidance of such discrimination would involve increased costs'. If so, the ECJ has stated, the protection for equality could vary in time and place according to the state of public finances of the Member States.[276] However, States have been successful in putting forward budgetary arguments for policies which indirectly discriminated on grounds of sex. In *Jorgenson*,[277] the ECJ accepted that the need to ensure sound management of public expenditure on medical care to ensure access to such care was a legitimate objective.

The Irish courts have considered the justification of unequal pay on economic grounds in a series of Labour Court determinations and High Court judgments in the case of *550 Sales and Clercial Assistants (Mandate) v Penneys*[278] where the courts seemed to accept to a certain extent economic justifications, although the decisions are somewhat unclear. The decision of the High Court in *Mandate v Penneys* also rests uneasily with the judgment of the ECJ in *Hill and Stapleton v The Revenue Commissioners.*[279] The better view is perhaps that simply trying to save money is not a

---

[272] Case 170/84 *Bilka-Kaufhaus* [1986] ECR 160.

[273] Case C-127/92 *Enderby v Frenchay Health Authority* [1993] ECR I-5535.

[274] Case C-243/95 *Hill and Stapleton v The Revenue Commissioners* [1998] ECR I-03739.

[275] [1998] ECR I-03739 at para 40.

[276] See Case C-187/00 *Kutz-Bauer v Freie und Hansestadt Hamburg* [2003] ECR I-02741, a case in which a collective argument with different eligibility rules for a scheme of part-time work for older persons applied to part-time versus full-time workers.

[277] Case C-226/98 *Jorgenson* [2000] ECR I-2247.

[278] *550 Sales and Clercial Assistants (Mandate) v Penneys* EP 06/1994, DEP1/1996, [1997] ELR 218; [1998] ELR 94; [1999] ELR 89.

[279] Case C-243/95 *Hill and Stapleton v The Revenue Commissioners* [1998] ECR I-03739.

legitimate aim in itself, but there may be a legitimate aim which can only be achieved by paying more money to one group rather than another, such as attracting the necessary workers as in *Enderby*,[280] or securing access to medical care for as many people as possible, as in *Jorgenson*.[281]

The defence of collective bargaining

[13.121] There has been some inconsistency in the approach of the ECJ to the defence of collective bargaining to a claim of pay discrimination. In *Enderby*,[282] the comparison was between speech therapists and pharmacists, both of whom had their own collective agreement with the employer. The employer sought unsuccessfully to rely on this as a defence to the claim for equal pay. The Court held:[283]

> The fact that the rates of pay at issue are decided by collective bargaining processes conducted separately for each of the two professional groups concerned, without any discriminatory effect within each group, does not preclude a finding of *prima facie* discrimination where the results of those processes show that two groups with the same employer and the same trade union are treated differently. If the employer could rely on the absence of discrimination within each of the collective bargaining processes taken separately as sufficient justification for the difference in pay, he could, as the German Government pointed out, easily circumvent the principle of equal pay by using separate bargaining processes.

Once again, the Court was clearly influenced by the need to ensure the effectiveness of the equality principle. If this could be circumvented by historical factors without a willingness on the part of the court to examine that history, the entire basis of a legal prohibition on unequal pay on grounds of sex could be undermined. The significance of this aspect of *Enderby* cannot be overstated. Wynn[284] suggests that that the decision will allow equal pay claims to be mounted which transcend traditional bargaining structures and expose neutral pay practices.[285] Ellis describes the decision as being of enormous theoretical and practical importance with 'huge potential significance for countless other cases'.[286]

[13.122] Unfortunately that potential may not be realised as a result of the Court's decision in *Dansk Industri*[287] where the Court held that:[288]

> the fact that the rates of pay have been determined by collective bargaining or by negotiation at local level may be taken into account by the national Court as a factor in its

---

[280] Case C-127/92 *Enderby v Frenchay Health Authority* [1993] ECR I-5535.

[281] Case C-226/98 *Jorgenson* [2000] ECR I-2247.

[282] Case C-127/92 *Enderby v Frenchay Health Authority* [1993] ECR I-5535.

[283] [1993] ECR I-5535 at para 22.

[284] Wynn, 'Equal Pay and Gender Segregation' [1994] LQR 556.

[285] Wynn, 'Equal Pay and Gender Segregation' [1994] LQR 556 at 560.

[286] Ellis, Casenote [1994] CMLR 387 at 392–393.

[287] Case C-400/93 *Specialarbejderforbundet i Danmark v Dansk Industri, formerly Industriens Arbejdsgivere, acting for Royal Copenhagen* [1995] ECR I-1275.

[288] Case C-400/93 *Specialarbejderforbundet i Danmark v Dansk Industri*, formerly Industriens Arbejdsgivere, acting for *Royal Copenhagen* [1995] ECR I-1275 at para 46.

assessment of whether differences between the average pay of two groups of workers are due to objective factors unrelated to any discrimination on grounds of sex.

It is arguable that *Dansk* is not as strong an authority as *Enderby* on the issue of collective bargaining as a defence, on the basis that the claim of unequal pay had already been rejected by the Court in *Dansk* before they reached the issue of different collective bargaining processes. In any event, the issue is bound to arise again before the Court when hopefully it will be definitively decided upon. If the Court wishes to continue in their approach of emphasising the effectiveness of equality law, the only logical analysis would be to prevent historical issues such as collective bargaining to perpetrate inequality between men and women doing like work.

[13.123] In *550 Sales and Clerical Assistants (Mandate) v Penneys*[289] the employer relied on the fact that the difference in pay was based on a productivity agreement negotiated by the comparators's trade union during the 1970s when the union had considerable collective bargaining power. The Labour Court distinguished the decision of the ECJ in *Enderby* on the basis that this case involved two separate collective bargaining processes whereas the one trade union represented both the claimants' and the comparators' group in *Enderby*. The Labour Court found that the bargaining processes in both cases were 'so different from each other as to make any analogy with the rationale of the *Enderby* judgment quite unjustified'.[290] In relation to the standing of social partnership agreements, in *Department of Finance v 7 Named Complainants*,[291] the Labour Court determined that PPF and Benchmarking were not collective agreements.[292]

The defence of red-circling

[13.124] Circumstances may arise in the workplace which merit an employee being moved from doing one job to doing a different job. For example a person may have been doing a job involving a significant level of intellectual effort where the introduction of computers reduces the demands of their job and leaves them doing little more than data entry. Clearly it would be very unfair to pay them a wage reflecting the work they are actually doing where they were originally employed, and are qualified, to perform more demanding duties. To get over this difficulty their job may be 'red-circled' whereby their work is of one level or grade while their wages are of a higher level or grade. Another possibility may be where a person is moved from one job to another due to illness or other personal circumstances. Again, they may be left on the rate of pay of their original job. In those situations the employer could rely on the red-circling process to justify what would otherwise be unequal pay for like work. However the claim will be carefully examined to see if there is a genuine red-circling arrangement in place or

---

[289] *550 Sales and Clerical Assistants (Mandate) v Penneys* EP 06/1994; DEP1/1996; [1997] ELR 218; [1998] ELR 94; [1999] ELR 89.

[290] [1998] ELR 94 at 97–98.

[291] *Department of Finance v 7 Named Complainants* EDA 068/2006 (Labour Court).

[292] Collective bargaining as evidenced by the social partnership process and the benchmarking process was successfully put forward as one justification recently before the Equality Tribunal in *Courts Service v 28 Named Employees* DEC-2007/07.

whether this is simply an artificial device of the employer to avoid the allegation of discrimination on grounds of sex.

In *Snoxell and Davies v Vauxhall Motors Ltd*[293] the UK EAT explained that red-circling occurs where:

> it is necessary to protect the wages of an employee, or a group of employees, moved from a better paid type of work to a worse paid type of work, perhaps because the first type is no longer undertaken.

To be added to that explanation are situations where for health reasons, or compassionate reasons, the wages are preserved even though the full range of duties are not being undertaken.

[13.125] The justification of red circling has been accepted and the case of *Campbell v Minister for Transport*[294] is instructive in explaining how the test is applied. In that case the applicants were employed as communications assistants responsible for processing the charges levied on international users of air or ground communications and the data relating to flights departing from Ireland. They sought to compare themselves with male radio officers. The defence was put forward that the comparators, due to ill-health, had been assigned to posts less onerous than their previous positions and that that was the reason for the differential in wages. The Labour Court treated the employer's case as a defence of red circling which it defined as applying to situations:

> where for specific reasons an individual or group may not be required to perform what would normally be considered the full list of the duties of their grade and an arrangement is made whereby those concerned retain their grade while being reassigned to duties, which, in the normal course, would attract a lower rate of pay.

This is the very essence of red circling: whereby the employees retain their previous rate of pay but perform less onerous duties as employees. On appeal to the High Court, Keane J agreed that the Labour Court had misdirected itself in law in holding that the onus rested on the employer to prove not just that this was a genuine case of red-circling but also that a recognised, factual and acknowledged position of red-circling existed. The matter was returned to the Labour Court[295] where, on the facts, the Court found:[296]

> that the differential in pay between the claimants and the comparators is not genuinely based on grounds other than sex. It finds that the defence of 'red-circling' on grounds of unsuitability for shift work was put forward in an attempt to justify the position of the particular comparators in this case, but that the real reason for the differential in pay is that the radio officers are male and the communications assistants are female.

The award ultimately made to the four claimants was in excess of £100,000 each and constituted one of the largest ever equal pay awards made in this jurisdiction.[297]

---

[293] *Snoxell and Davies v Vauxhall Motors Ltd* [1977] ICR 700.

[294] *Campbell v Minister for Transport* [1996] ELR 106.

[295] [1998] ELR 1.

[296] [1998] ELR 1 at 3–4.

[297] See another determination of the Labour Court in *Irish Crown Cork Co. Ltd v SIPTU* DEP 1/1994 in which red-circling was not accepted on the facts of the case.

More recently, in *McManus v Diageo Ltd*,[298] a case on gender discrimination, and *58 Complainants v Goode Concrete*,[299] a case on race discrimination, the defence of 'red-circling' was accepted on the basis of regrading and injury to an employee respectively.

Seniority/length of service

[13.126] The extent to which seniority or length of service can justify a difference in pay is fraught with difficulties. This is because rewarding seniority or length of service with greater pay can have the effect of privileging two groups, males and older persons in comparison with females and younger persons. Women as a group tend to accrue service and seniority more slowly as they tend to take time off work for family and caring reasons. Older persons naturally tend to have greater length of service than younger.

Section 34(7) of the Employment Equality Act provides that it shall not constitute discrimination on grounds of age to use length of service or seniority as a criterion for awarding different rates of remuneration.

[13.127] At present length of service and equal pay have only been dealt with by the ECJ in the context of gender discrimination. At first the ECJ accepted a length of service criterion on the basis that since length of service and experience went hand in hand, an employer was free to reward length of service.[300] It seemed to take a different view in *Nimz*,[301] *Gerster*,[302] *Kording*[303] and *Hill and Stapleton v The Revenue Commissioners*.[304] In *Hill and Stapleton*, the purpose of the system of job-sharing, which was introduced into the Irish Civil Service in 1984, was to permit two civil servants to share one full-time job equally in such a way that both workers benefited equally while the costs of the post for the national administration remained the same. Job-sharers work half the number of hours of full-time workers and are paid the same hourly rate. The scale of annual incremental salary increases for job-sharers was parallel to that for full-time workers with each point on the job-sharers scale representing 50% of the corresponding point on the full-time scale. 98% of job-sharers in the Irish Civil Service are women. According to the national referring tribunal a job-sharer could acquire the same experience as a full-time worker.

When Mrs Hill and Mrs Stapleton transferred from job-sharing to full-time work they were initially assimilated to the same point on the full-time incremental scale as that which they had occupied on the job-sharers' scale. They were both subsequently reclassified at a lower point on the full-time scale on the grounds that two years on the job-sharers' scale represented one year on the full-time scale. The ECJ held that this practice was discriminatory as it failed to take into account:[305]

---

[298] *McManus v Diageo Ltd* DEC E2007-21 (Equality Tribunal).

[299] *58 Complainants v Goode Concrete* DEC E2008-020 (Equality Tribunal).

[300] Case C-400/95 *Danfoss* [1990] ECR I-2757.

[301] Case C-184/89 *Nimz v Freie und Hansestadt Hamburg* [1991] ECR I-297 at para 14.

[302] Case C-1/95 *Gerster v Freistaat Bayern* 2 October 1997 at para 39.

[303] Case C-100/95 *Kording v Senator für Finanzen* 2 October 1997 at para 24.

[304] Case C-243/95 *Hill and Stapleton v The Revenue Commissioners* [1998] ECR I-03739 at para 32.

[305] Case C-243/95 *Hill and Stapleton v The Revenue Commissioners* [1998] ECR I-03739 at para 32.

either of the fact that job-sharing, as pointed out in paragraph 26 of the present judgment, is in a unique category as it does not involve a break in service, or of the fact, stated in paragraph 27 of the present judgment, that a job-sharer can acquire the same experience as a full-time worker. Furthermore, a disparity is retroactively introduced into the overall pay of employees performing the same functions so far as concerns both the quality and the quantity of the work performed. The result of this disparity is that employees working full time but who previously job-shared are treated differently from those who have always worked on a full-time basis.

[13.128] In *Gerster*[306] the ECJ would not automatically accept the link between length of service and greater experience:[307]

> In *Nimz*, moreover, the Court took the view that it is impossible to identify objective criteria unrelated to any discrimination on the basis of an alleged special link between length of service and acquisition of a certain level of knowledge or experience, since such a claim amounts to no more than a generalization concerning certain categories of worker. Although experience goes hand in hand with length of service, and experience enables the worker in principle to improve performance of the tasks allotted to him, the objectivity of such a criterion depends on all the circumstances in each individual case, and in particular on the relationship between the nature of the work performed and the experience gained from the performance of that work upon completion of a certain number of working hours.

[13.129] The recent decision in *Cadman*[308] therefore came as a surprise in light of these earlier decisions. This case involved the rather straightforward claim of Ms Cadman that the lower pay she was receiving for doing the same job as four male comparators was discriminatory. The employer put forward the justification that the male comparators had greater length of service. Ms Cadman countered that this was indirectly discriminatory against women. The ECJ rejected her claim, accepting without much analysis or question that the criterion of length of service is appropriate to attain the legitimate objective of rewarding experience acquired which enables an employee to do their job better.

The decision has been much criticised.[309] Uncritically accepting that length of service goes hand in hand with experience seems to go against previous decisions in which mere generalisation were not allowed and employers were required to provide specific evidence showing that the particular measure chosen was suitable for achieving a legitimate aim. Furthermore, Beck points out that the Court does not address whether length of service pursues a legitimate objective at all, and if so, which one, followed by a properly reasoned argument designed to establish the economic or other benefits of that objective.[310] Instead the Court seems to oscillate between the appropriate objective being the reward of experience and that of achieving better performance. Ultimately it is not

---

[306] Case C-1/95 *Gerster v Freistaat Bayern* 2 October 1997.

[307] Case C-1/95 *Gerster v Freistaat Bayern*, 2 October 1997 at para 39.

[308] Case C-17/05 *Cadman v HSE* [2006] ECR I-09583.

[309] See Beck, 'The State of EC Anti-Sex Discrimination Law and the Judgment in Cadman' [2007] 32(4) *European Law Review* 549.

[310] Beck, 'The State of EC Anti-Sex Discrimination Law and the Judgment in Cadman' [2007] 32(4) *European Law Review* 549.

clear whether there is in fact a direct causal link between greater experience and superior performance, or that that link is evident in all workplaces or professions. It may simply be, as Beck suggests, that the ECJ, faced with the factual reality that many Member States have public services which pay higher wages to employees as they move up a seniority/length of service continuum, decided not to upset the applecart.[311]

Redress

[13.130] The redress for a breach of the prohibition on unequal pay is an order for equal pay, together with an order for payment of arrears. The Employment Equality Act places a time limit of three years retrospectively from the date of reference of the claim on equal pay claims.[312] The EU permits the imposition of time limits on the basis that these are necessary for legal certainty.[313]

The only difficulty is with pensions cases. The ECJ has held that national rules placing restrictions on back-dating are permissible as long as they do not make it impossible to exercise the right. Thus employees have been held to be allowed retrospectively to join pension schemes and to require an employer to pay the arrears. However, the ECJ has said that it is permissible to require employees to pay arrears of the employee contribution.[314] Most recently in *Jonkman*,[315] the Court ruled that a Member State cannot require interest to be paid on arrears other than that required to compensate for inflation nor can it require that the arrears be paid as a single sum.

DISCRIMINATION ON THE RACE GROUND

[13.131] In recent years, there has been a large increase in the number of cases coming before the Equality Tribunal and the Labour Court alleging discrimination on grounds of race.[316] This is unsurprising given the increasing diversification in nationality of the Irish workplace. The Employment Equality Act prohibits less favourable treatment of an employee on the ground 'that they are of different race, colour, nationality or ethnic or national origins'.[317]

---

[311] Beck, 'The State of EC Anti-Sex Discrimination Law and the Judgment in Cadman' [2007] 32(4) *European Law Review* 549.

[312] Employment Equality Acts 1998–2008, s 82(1)(a).

[313] See Case C-246/96 *Magorrian & Cunningham v Eastern Health and Social Services Board & Department of Health and Social Services* 11 December 1997 and Case C-326/96 *BS Levez v TH Jennings (Harlow Pools) Ltd* [1998] ECR I-07835.

[314] See Case C-57/93 *Vroege v NCIV Institut voor Volkshuisvesting BV & Stichting Pensioenfonds NCIV* [1004] ECR I-4541 and Case C-128/93 *Fisscher v Voorhuis Hengelo BV & Stichting Bedrijfspensioenfonds voor de Detailhandel* [1994] ECR I-4583.

[315] Case C 232/06 *Office National des Pensions v Emilienne Jonkman* [2007] ECR I-05149.

[316] In its Annual Report for 2007, the Equality Tribunal notes a 106% increase in the number of race claims coming before it and states that discrimination on grounds of race is the most cited ground in relation to employment equality claims. It is also interesting to note that a 2006 study found that harassment on grounds of race was the second most reported form of discrimination (after harassment on the street) reported by migrants in Ireland. See McGinnity, O'Connell, Quinn and Williams, 'Migrants' Experience of Racism and Discrimination in Ireland: Survey Report' (ERSI, 2006).

[317] Employment Equality Acts 1998–2008, s 6(2)(h).

This broad approach to discrimination on the grounds of race has avoided much of the difficulties that have arisen in other jurisdictions in establishing whether discrimination on grounds of ethnic background is covered by the concept of 'race' or whether a particular nationality can come within the concept of a distinct ethnic group.

The statutory protection goes significantly beyond the scope of the Race Directive[318] where the concept of discrimination at Art 2 is limited to 'direct or indirect discrimination based on racial or ethnic origin'. Article 3(2) expressly provides that the Directive does not cover difference of treatment based on nationality. While that could lead to some discussion as to whether discrimination based on ethnic origin could equate to discrimination on grounds of nationality where a particular nationality comprises of a specific ethnic group, all of that debate is rendered irrelevant in the Irish context as a result of the clear prohibition in the Act of all less favourable treatment whether on grounds of race, skin colour, ethnic origin or nationality. As a result a vast number of claims have been brought before the Equality Tribunal and the Labour Court in recent times by non-Irish workers, many of whom might find it difficult to fit within the narrow confines of the Race Directive where their race and/or ethnic origin is arguably no different to that of their Irish counterparts but where their nationality is clearly different.

[13.132] An example of the evidence which established different treatment and therefore discrimination on grounds of race arose in the case of *A Complainant v The Health Board*[319] where a British social worker argued that his nationality was a factor in his failure to be appointed to a permanent position and that his contract was prematurely terminated because of bias against him. The Equality Officer found:

> From the written communications of both the Team Leader and the Senior Social Worker, it is clear that issues of assimilation, integration and cultural differences were raised by both men as problems for the complainant to address. Contrary to the respondent's assertions, the comments do not appear to be solely job related. If the complainant had been advised that he required more experience, this would have been understandable. The constant references to difference in culture, however, appear designed to mark the complainant as 'different'. I can find no other reason for the ongoing comments made by the two supervisors than discrimination on the grounds of race.

Statutory exceptions

[13.133] Exceptions to what would be considered discrimination the race ground are provided in s 36 of the Employment Equality Act. Section 36(2) permits requirements of residency and/or citizenship in relation to employees who are to hold office in the service of the State including the Gardaí and the Defence Forces. Section 36(3) permits the imposition of a requirement on teachers to have a proficiency in the Irish language.[320] Section 36(4) allows an employer to require, in relation to a particular post,

---

[318] Council Directive 2000/43/EC ([2000] OJ L180/22) on race discrimination and see Guild, 'The EC Directive on Race Discrimination: Surprises, Possibilities and Limitations' (2000) *ILJ* 416 and Jones, 'Race Directive Redefining Protection from Discrimination in EU Law' (2003) 5 *EHRLR* 515.

[319] *A Complainant v The Health Board* DEC-E2004-010 (Equality Tribunal).

[320] See *NUI Galway v McBrierty* EDA 091 (Labour Court).

a specified education, technical or professional qualification which is a generally accepted qualification in the State for posts of that description.

The Equality Tribunal and the Labour Court have traditionally adopted a very strict approach to any suggestion of less favourable treatment on grounds of a person's race, ethnic origin or nationality. For example in one of the first cases on unequal pay on grounds of race, *St James's Hospital v Eng*,[321] the Labour Court found that the claimant, who was a Malaysian doctor, had been discriminated against in relation to his pay on grounds of his race. The Court accepted that the hospital had acted at all times without any discriminatory intent but they refused to allow their bona fides to give them any defence to the claim of unequal pay. The fact of unequal pay between the claimant and his comparators of a different nationality and/or race in the absence of any evidence of the discrimination having been on grounds other than race, gave the claimant a right to equal pay regardless of the intentions of the employer.

[13.134] In *Irish Society of Chartered Physiotherapists v Venera Ilieda Tsvetko Mitov*,[322] the respondent had sought to rely on s 12(7) of the Employment Equality Act which allows a training body to apply different treatment in relation to fees charged to citizens of the European Union and any other citizens. The Labour Court found that:

> As the section provides an exception to the general prohibition of discrimination on grounds of age or race it must be construed strictly and should be given no wider scope than the word used actually suggests.

The Court pointed out that what was issue in the case was not the allocation of cases on a course of training but a practice which allowed for augmentation of qualifications in the case of EU nationals but denied non-EU nationals a similar facility. The Court refused to allow the rule to be saved by s 12(7) of the Act and found that the respondent had discriminated against the complainant when they rejected their applications for membership without offering them an opportunity to undergo the period of adaptation that was allowed to a national of an EU Member State.

Section 36(4) exception

[13.135] In the case of *Gji-Youn Henning v An Bord Altranais*,[323] the employer successfully relied upon the s 36(4) exception. The complainant had trained as a general nurse in the Republic of Korea and later moved to Germany where she worked as a nurse for a number of years. She applied to An Bord Altranais for registration to enable her to work as a nurse in Ireland. The Bord refused to register her until it had received original documentary evidence from the relevant registration authorities in Korea and Germany on her current registration status. The complainant unsuccessfully argued that she had been unfavourably treated by the Bord because of her Korean nationality as she argued that there was no requirement for her to be registered in Germany. The Equality Tribunal found that the respondent was acting in accordance with its statutory functions under the

---

[321] *St James's Hospital v Eng* EDA 023/2002 (Labour Court).

[322] *Irish Society of Chartered Physiotherapists v Venera Ilieda Tsvetko Mitov* EDA 0519/2005 (Labour Court).

[323] *Gji-Youn Henning v An Bord Altranais* DEC-E2004-001 (Equality Tribunal).

Nurses Act 1985 and referred to s 36(4) of the Act. In finding no evidence that the complainant was treated less favourably on grounds of her nationality, the Equality Officer noted that some 35% of nurses registered by the respondent board during 1998 to 2003 were non-Irish.

Proving discrimination on grounds of race

[13.136] Section 85A(1) of the Employment Equality Act shifts the burden of proof to the respondent where facts are established by a complainant 'from which it may be presumed that there has been discrimination in relation to him or her'. This is particularly significant for victims of discrimination on grounds of race, many of whom may find it difficult to establish overt evidence of such discrimination. Even prior to the implementation of this section by virtue of the Equality Act 2004,[324] the Equality Tribunal and the Labour Court had developed a similar approach to shifting the burden of proof to the respondent once *prima facie* evidence of discrimination had been established. For example in *Massinde Ntoko v Citibank*[325] the Labour Court set out the rationale for the approach:

> A person who discriminates unlawfully will rarely do so overtly and will not leave evidence of the discrimination within the complainant's power of procurement. Hence, the normal rules of evidence must be adapted in such cases so as to avoid the protection of anti-discrimination laws being rendered nugatory by obliging complainants to prove something which is beyond their reach and which may only be in the respondent's capacity of proof.

Since the enactment of s 85A, the jurisprudence of the Labour Court on shifting the burden of proof and its recognition of the subtleties of race discrimination is less significant. However what is also clear from the same line of authorities is the Court's view that non-Irish workers may encounter special difficulties in their employment arising from matters such as a lack of knowledge of their legal rights, differences in language and in culture. The Court also seems sensitive to the fact that employers may not treat foreign workers as well as Irish workers because the employer believes that a non-Irish worker may not be able to assert their legal rights and/or may not be in a position to obtain support in doing so.

[13.137] The Labour Court has clearly applied the principle of the ECJ in *Finanzamt Köln-Altstadt Schumacker*,[326] that discrimination can arise not only through the application of different rules in comparable situations but also by the application of the same rule to different situations. A good example of this approach can be seen in *Rasaq v Campbell Catering Ltd.*[327] The claimant, who was Nigerian, commenced employment as a catering assistant in April 2002. During her induction she was informed that employees were allowed to take food for consumption on the premises but that taking food off the premises was a serious disciplinary matter. On 8 May the claimant, who

---

[324] This section was inserted into the Employment Equality Act 1998 by the Equality Act 2004, s 36.

[325] *Massinde Ntoko v Citibank* [2004] 15 ELR 116.

[326] Case-279/93 *Finanzamt Köln-Altstadt Schumacker v Roland Schumacker* [1995] ECR 1225.

[327] *Rasaq v Campbell Catering Ltd* [2004] ELR 310.

was pregnant at the time, had not eaten during the course of her working day due to nausea. At the end of her shift she took three bananas from the kitchen which she intended to eat in the locker room before leaving. On the following day she was summarily dismissed for having stolen the bananas. She did not get any written reasons for her dismissal. In denying her claim of discrimination on grounds of race, the employer contended that other employees had also been dismissed in similar circumstances for taking food off the premises, regardless of their race or nationality.

[13.138] The Court referred to its own determination in *Ntoko v Citibank*[328] and found on the evidence that the normal practice was to afford employees accused of serious misconduct fair procedures in the investigation of the allegations against them. The claimant was not afforded fair procedures in the investigation of misconduct of which she was accused and was therefore treated less favourably by the respondent than other employees facing allegations of serious misconduct were or would have been treated. Therefore, the probative burden of proof was shifted to the employer to show that the claimant was not discriminated against on grounds of her race. On the evidence, the Court found that this burden had not been discharged. The Court, in citing the *Schumacker*[329] principle that discrimination can arise not only through the application of different rules to comparable situations but by the application of the same rule for different situations, stated:

> It is clear that many non-national workers encounter special difficulties in employment arising from a lack of knowledge concerning statutory and contractual employment rights together with differences of language and culture. In the case of disciplinary proceedings, employers have a positive duty to ensure that all workers fully understand what is alleged against them, the gravity of the alleged misconduct and their right to mount a full defence, including the right to representation. Special measures may be necessary in the case of non-national workers to ensure that this obligation is fulfilled and that the accused worker fully appreciates the gravity of the situation and is given appropriate facilities and guidance in making a defence. In such cases, applying the same procedural standards to a non-national worker as would be applied to an Irish national could amount to the application of the same rules to different situations and could in itself amount to discrimination.

[13.139] The Equality Officer relied on this decision in *Ning Ning Zhang v Towner Trading*.[330] The complainant had received a mobile phone text message from her employer accusing her of stealing bus tickets. The employer claimed to have this act on camera. The text message threatened her with the police. The complainant met her employer that evening and denied the allegations of theft. Later that day she was advised that her name had been taken off the roster. On the next day she was due to work, she sent a text to her employer asking if she was working and was advised by text message that she was not working there anymore. Another meeting took place at which the complainant repeated that she had not stolen the bus tickets and at the end of that meeting, her understanding was that a further meeting would be arranged for her to view

---

[328] *Ntoko v Citibank* [2004] 15 ELR 116.

[329] Case-279/93 *Schumacker* [1995] ECR 1225.

[330] *Ning Ning Zhang v Towner Trading* DEC-E2008-001 (Equality Tribunal).

clearer CCTV footage. She then received a further text from the employer telling her that there was no job for her anymore. That was the final contact she received from them. The Equality Officer found that the respondent did not follow fair procedures, did not carry out an investigation and denied the complainant the opportunity to seek representation, prepare a defence and attend a disciplinary hearing as a result of which she was treated less favourably by the respondent than another employee facing similar charges would have been treated. The Equality Officer accepted that the complainant had established a *prima facie* case of discriminatory treatment on grounds of her race, and that the burden of rebutting that case on the balance of probabilities had not been discharged by the respondent. Compensation of €15,000 was awarded.

[13.140] In the decision of *A Company v A Worker*,[331] the Labour Court gave more guidance as to the circumstances in which less favourable treatment might be viewed by the Court as having been on grounds of a person's race or nationality. The claimant had come to Ireland to take up a job in a nursing home but on her arrival, found that this position was not available. She was left with no alternative but to take a job as an assembly worker in a factory owned by the same employer. She claimed to have been subjected to sexual harassment, distressing rumours amongst her colleagues and false allegations of theft. She was suspended from her employment for allegedly harassing her employer's mother. When she tried to respond to the allegations and sought her suspension terms to be put in writing to her, she was ordered off the premises and was told that she was sacked.

The Court pointed out that the employer had done nothing to reassure the complainant or ease her worries in relation to her concerns about her work permit. The Court held that the complainant was treated differently by her employer than an Irish national would have been treated in similar circumstances:

> The Court is satisfied on the balance of probabilities, that the correct inference to be drawn from this difference in treatment is that it arose from the complainant's nationality.... On the balance of probabilities the treatment of the worker by the manager, and the almost non-implementation of relevant legislation, was due to the fact that it regarded the worker as someone of a different nationality, who would not have the capability to stand on their legal rights and that by its actions up to and including its constructive dismissal of the worker, it discriminated against her on grounds of her nationality.

The Court pointed out its concern about the duty of care that is associated with recruitment of foreign nationals and referred to the 'very difficult position' that the complainant was forced to react to when she discovered the post in the nursing home was not available. The Court pointed out that in a 'normal' recruitment situation:

> the indigenous prospective employee would have far greater confidence about the situation. It would be possible to seek support in making their decision from advisory services, family, understanding of the structure and the interactions of the labour market, financial support of the State, to name but a few. In this situation these options did not exist. It was either return to her country of origin (bearing in mind that she had sought to leave her country and committed substantial resources to bring it into effect) or take up the job offer. It was not a situation which would relate to an Irish employee.

---

[331] *A Company v A Worker* EED 024/2002 (Labour Court).

That determination is a good illustration of what the Labour Court is concerned about in dealing with a non-Irish worker and in particular its apparent intention to ensure special protection of such workers given the vulnerability which the Court feels they may be facing in an Irish workplace. The Court is clearly minded to deal with the particular consequences which such discrimination may have for a non-Irish worker, such as making the employee 'invisible' by retaining their passport.[332]

[13.141] That is not to say that it will be easy for every non-Irish worker to establish *prima facie* evidence of discrimination on grounds of their race. For example in the case of *Client Logic Trading as UCA+L v Kulwant Gill*[333] the complainant's claim of discrimination on grounds of race arising from the respondent's failure to appoint her to a promotional position was unsuccessful.[334] The complainant contended that she was the best-qualified candidate and had more relevant experience than the successful candidate. She sought to rely on statistical evidence which showed that some 50% of the workforce were not Irish whereas only 33% of those in management were which she claimed was indicative of a racial bias against non-Irish workers. She also relied on the fact that she was interviewed by two persons of Irish background and nationality.

The Court stated that it would not normally look behind a decision unless there is clear evidence of unfairness in the selection process or manifest irrationality in the result. The Court was not satisfied that the complainant's experience could be superior to that of the successful candidate.

The Court accepted that statistics can be of a:

> probative value in raising an inference of covert discrimination or the presence of inbuilt or unrecognised bias. However, it is always a matter for the Court, having regard to all the circumstances of the case, to determine if the statistical evidence is used to provide a sufficient basis upon which such an inference should properly be drawn.

The Court accepted the respondent's submission that the average length of service of those employees from countries other than Ireland is relatively short and that this explained the apparent disparity in racial mix as between management and other grades. It therefore did not accept the statistical evidence relied upon by the complainant to have been of sufficient significance to raise an inference of discrimination.

In relation to the lack of racial balance among the interviewers, the Court stated:

> While the maintenance of an appropriate balance in the make-up of interview groups is always desirable the Court is not satisfied, in the circumstances of this case, that the absence of balance complained of is a fact from which discrimination may be inferred.

[13.142] A further example of where the evidence did not establish discrimination was the case of *Ice Group Business Services Ltd v Czerski*.[335] The complainant was a Polish applicant to an employment agency who claimed discrimination on grounds of her race

---

[332] *Golovan v Portulin Shellfish Ltd* DEC-E2008-032 (Equality Tribunal).

[333] *Client Logic Trading as UCA+L v Kulwant Gill* EDA 0817/2008 (Labour Court).

[334] For a case where an applicant for a job as a professor was successful in establishing a prima facie case on the basis of a requirement to have a research record with an Irish relevance, see *Munck v NUI Maynooth* DEC-E2005-030 (Equality Tribunal).

[335] EDA 0812/2008 (Labour Court).

arising from the agency's requirement that she furnish two Irish references. The Equality Tribunal upheld her claim that she was indirectly discriminated against on grounds of her race in that the requirement of two Irish employment related references operated to the disadvantage of a non-Irish national as compared with an Irish national and could be complied with by a substantially smaller number of non-Irish employees. The Labour Court upheld the agency's appeal and expressly accepted their evidence that they did inform the complainant that a character reference would be acceptable as one of the references. The Court stated that it could not see how, in those circumstances, a non-Irish person would be placed at a greater disadvantage than an Irish person:

> While the Court accepts that there are inherent difficulties in applying any policy without regard to individual circumstances, the Court is of the view that the requirement to provide two references one of which might be a character reference, does not constitute indirect discrimination on the race ground. Furthermore, the Court accepts that in the circumstances of the Respondent's business as an employment agency, where it is dependant on its reputation for clients, the requirement to seek two named referees in order to recommend a person for employment with its clients, is a reasonable requirement in the circumstances.

[13.143] In July 2008, the ECJ handed down its first decision under the Race Directive.[336] In *Feryn* the ECJ had to consider whether a discriminatory recruitment policy publically acknowledged by an employer could amount to discrimination for the purposes of the Race Directive in the absence of any actual identifiable complainant. The employer in this case was a company specialising in the installation of garage doors. The Centre for Equal Opportunities commenced an action before the Belgian courts seeking a declaration that the employer had applied a discriminatory recruitment policy. To this end, it relied on statements made publicly by a director of the employer where he stated that although his company was recruiting installers, it would not take on employees of a particular ethnic origin ('immigrants') owing to a reluctance of its customers to give access to their homes during installation work. The ECJ expressed the view that as the objective of the Race Directive was to implement the principle of equal treatment between persons irrespective of racial or ethnic origin. this principle would be undermined if the Directive only applied to circumstances where an unsuccessful candidate for employment instituted proceedings against a discriminatory employer. The ECJ was also mindful of the dissuasive effect such discriminatory statements would have on potential applicants. Therefore it held that the statements constituted direct discrimination in respect of recruitment within the Directive.[337]

The ECJ then considered the relevant burdens of proof in such cases. It ruled that public statements whereby an employer acknowledges that its recruitment policy is not to recruit employees of a certain ethnic or racial origin are sufficient for a presumption

---

[336] Case C-54/07 *Centrum voor gelijkheid van kansen en voor racismebestrijding v Firma Feryn NV.*

[337] Council Directive 2000/43/EC, Art 2(2)(a) ([2000] OJ L180/22) on race discrimination provides for the concept of direct discrimination which is the same as that in all of the Equal Treatment Directives: less favourable treatment than another person is, has, would be treated in a comparable situation on any of the respective grounds.

of the existence of a recruitment policy which is directly discriminatory.[338] In order for the employer to rebut the burden of proof in such cases, it must be able to demonstrate that there was no breach of the principle of equal treatment, for example by showing that its recruitment policy did not correspond with the statements made.

Finally, the ECJ stated that appropriate sanctions for discrimination at the recruitment stage must be effective, proportionate and dissuasive even where there is no identifiable complainant. For example, the ECJ indicated that a suitable sanction in the instant case may be a finding of discrimination in conjunction with adequate level of publicity, an order that the employer cease the discriminatory practice and an award of damages to the body bringing the proceedings. This decision clearly paves the way for interest groups to institute proceedings alleging discrimination even in the absence of an individual complainant. This may allow for an equality agenda to be pursued by such interest groups. Further, given the recognition by the ECJ that sanctions are to be effective, proportionate and dissuasive for discrimination at the recruitment stage, it appears that the Employment Equality Act may be out of line with this sentiment. The Act provides for a cap of €12,697.38 on the level of compensation which may be awarded to an unsuccessful job applicant at the access or recruitment to employment stage.[339] It is arguable that this low level of compensation may not be sufficiently effective, proportionate and dissuasive.

Breach of other employment legislation as evidence of race discrimination

[13.144] There have been a number of decisions where evidence of non-compliance with other employment legislation has in itself been permitted to establish *prima facie* evidence of discrimination on grounds of race. For example in the case of *Five Complainants v Hennon's Poultry Export Ltd*[340] a number of allegations were made by five Brazilian workers that they had been harassed, victimised, subjected to unequal pay and discriminated against, all on grounds of their race. The claims in relation to overtime, accommodation, pay, harassment, dismissal and victimisation were all rejected. However their claim that they had been subjected to unlawful discrimination on grounds of their race because unlawful deductions had been made from their wages was upheld. The claimants had each made a separate claim to a Rights Commissioner pursuant to the Payment of Wages Act 1991 relating to the unlawful deductions from their wages which had been upheld by the Rights Commissioner. The employer argued that the deductions would also have been made from the wages of an Irish employee but the Equality Officer was not satisfied that this would be the case. She stated:

> I consider it more likely that an existing Irish employee approaching management for a loan would be required to sign an undertaking of repayment, or at the very least would have been very clear about the necessity for repayment. It seems to me to be possible that the complainants may not have understood this clearly. I note that the translated contract of employment specifies that cost of flights and accommodation will be deducted from

---

[338] Council Directive 2000/43/EC, Art 8 ([2000] OJ L180/22) on race discrimination provides for the burden of proof.

[339] Employment Equality Acts 1998–2008, s 82(4).

[340] *Five Complainants v Hennon's Poultry Export Ltd* DEC-E2006-050 (Equality Tribunal).

wages, but at the time the complainants were engaged no such translation was available. On balance, I consider that the complainants were discriminated against on the grounds of race by virtue of having unlawful deductions made from their wages.

Interestingly, in the same decision the claim by the complainants that they were forced to do overtime did not establish discrimination on grounds of race even though the Rights Commissioner had made a finding in their favour under the Organisation of Working Time Act. The Rights Commissioner looked at the figures that showed that the Irish employees worked between 48.9 and 56.3 hours while the complainants worked between 50.6 and 59.5 hours and found that the figures did not appear to demonstrate 'a significant difference'.

Compensation of €5,000 was awarded to each of the complainants 'for the effects of the discrimination'. This was in addition to whatever monies had been awarded to the complainants in relation to their claims under the Payment of Wages Act 1991 which had been upheld by the Rights Commissioner. It would appear in that case that the complainant's status as non-national employees gave them a race discrimination claim in addition to their Payment of Wages Act claim. An Irish employee who had the same unlawful deductions from their wages would be limited to a claim under the Payment of Wages Act alone.

[13.145] A similar approach can be seen in the decision of the Equality Officer in *58 Complainants v Goode Concrete Ltd*[341] where compensation of €5,000 was awarded to each of the fifty eight complainants arising from the respondent's failure to give them a copy of their contract of employment and certain safety documentation:

> in a language which was understandable to each of them or where there is no evidence that these terms and conditions of employment were explained to each of them by a person speaking a language they understood who was appointed by Goode Concrete Limited for this specific purpose.

These findings were made by the Equality Officer without evidence of their individual capacity to understand English. The Equality Officer held that each of the complainants were discriminated against on grounds of their race when their terms and conditions of employment and safety documentation were not set out in a language which was understandable to each of them or where there was no evidence that those terms and conditions of employment were explained to each of them by a person speaking a language they understood. The findings of the Equality Officer seem to have been on the basis of assumptions made about the complainants' comprehension of English given their non-Irish nationalities. The decision has been appealed to the Labour Court. However for the moment and on the basis of the Equality Officer's decision, it would appear that any employee whose mother tongue is not English is entitled to be furnished with a contract of employment and other essential documentation such as safety documentation, in a language other than English. The precise parameters of this requirement are unclear as the Equality Officer was not suggesting that they were automatically entitled to the documentation in their own language but rather in a

---

[341] *58 Complainants v Goode Concrete Ltd* DEC-2008-020 (Equality Tribunal).

language which they understood, albeit in circumstances where there does not seem to have been any clear evidence of what languages they did or did not understand.

[13.146] On the other hand, it would appear that where an employer fails to provide any contracts of employment at all, albeit that it is clearly in breach of their obligations pursuant to the Terms of Employment (Information) Acts 1994 and 2001, their actions do not constitute discrimination on grounds of race as they will have treated all of their employees equally even though that treatment is in itself unlawful. In *Gorys v Igor Kurakin*[342] an employer who did not give any of his employees written contracts was found not to have discriminated on grounds of race as he treated all of the employees the same. The logic of these two decisions, handed down by the same Equality Officer within the same month is difficult to reconcile. It would certainly seem to be contrary to the spirit of the legislation to suggest that the employer who does not even attempt to comply with their statutory obligations will be found not to have discriminated against their employees whereas the employer who makes some attempt to comply may, in doing so, be found guilty of race discrimination.

AGE DISCRIMINATION

[13.147] Age is one of the new grounds of discrimination and a ground which has given rise to a significant amount of litigation at both national and Community level. One of the most difficult issues currently being worked out in employment equality jurisprudence is in the area of age discrimination, namely the legitimacy of mandatory retirement ages, In *Heyday*, the ECJ delivered its somewhat inconclusive judgment on this issue (which will be considered below).[343] As the Advocate General[344] has pointed out, classification of individuals on the basis of age alone is no longer acceptable, but age discrimination is somewhat different to other forms of discrimination. The reasons for that difference are a useful place to begin to consider age discrimination in employment equality law.

[13.148] Swift[345] points out that there are three typical justifications for anti-discrimination legislation. First that the discrimination is irrational, second, that it is unjust and, third, that it is inefficient. Making decisions on who to hire, for example, on the basis of race or sex can be irrational if there is no difference between the two candidates, unjust in that if fails to respect the human rights of the candidates and inefficient in that persons are being assessed on the basis of an irrelevant characteristic rather than the most efficient use of their resources. Swift however points out that age discrimination does not fit very neatly into these justifications as somebody's young or old age may indeed bring with it characteristics which an employer would be acting

---

[342] *Gorys v Igor Kurakin* DEC-E2008-014 (Equality Tribunal).

[343] Case C-388/07 *The Incorporated Trustees of the National Council on Ageing (Age Concern England) the Secretary of State for Business, Enterprise and Regulatory Reform* 5 March 2009.

[344] Case C-388/07 *The Incorporated Trustees of the National Council on Ageing (Age Concern England) the Secretary of State for Business, Enterprise and Regulatory Reform* 23 September, 2008.

[345] Swift, 'Justifying Age Discrimination' (2006) *ILJ* 35 at 228.

rationally and/or efficiently to take into account. Nor would such differentiation in all cases be unjust. Age, therefore, to some extent, is in a similar category to disability in that age related characteristics may affect the person's ability to do the job. The value which is unacceptable to society therefore is not that age should never be looked at, but that making blind assumptions and ascribing stereotypical characteristics to persons simply because of their age is or can be irrational, unjust or inefficient.

The legal working out of this difference can be seen in the fact that there are many explicit exceptions to the prohibition on discrimination on grounds of age contained in both European and Irish legislation. The Framework Directive[346] and the Employment Equality Act permit direct discrimination on the grounds of age. This difference in the treatment of age discrimination must be borne in mind when considering this area of law. Indeed in *Heyday*,[347] the ECJ had been asked to decide whether the test for objective justification of direct discrimination on grounds of age is the same as that for objective justification of indirect discrimination on grounds of age. The Advocate General was of the opinion that the tests are the same,[348] and the ECJ held likewise.[349]

[13.149] Prior to the enactment of the Employment Equality Act 1998, Irish law provided only very limited protection against age discrimination. The Unfair Dismissals Act 1977 was amended in 1993 to prohibit unfair dismissal on the grounds of age alone. Age discrimination which was direct or indirect discrimination on grounds of gender was prohibited by EC sex discrimination law. Article 40.1 of the Constitution, although it provides a general guarantee of equal treatment, was not relied upon by persons seeking to prohibit age discrimination. It was only with the enactment of the Employment Equality Act 1998 that discrimination in employment on the grounds of age, along with the other nine grounds, was prohibited. As noted in the introduction to this chapter, the 1998 Act was amended by the Equality Act 2004.[350]

---

[346] Council Directive 2000/78/EC ([2000] L303/16) establishing a general framework for equal treatment in employment and occupation. It is worth noting that this Directive has been followed by a recent Proposed Directive on Implementing the Principle of Equal Treatment which seeks to extend the principle of equal treatment for persons irrespective of religion or belief, disability, age or sexual orientation beyond the sphere of employment and occupation. See COM(08) 436 final. For more detail on Council Directive 2000/78/EC see Skidmore, 'EC Framework Directive on Equal Treatment in Employment: Towards a Comprehensive Community Anti-Discrimination Policy' (2001) *ILJ* 126 and Waddington and Bell, 'More Equal Than Others: Distinguishing European Equality Directives' (2001) CML Rev 587.

[347] Case C-388/07 *The Incorporated Trustees of the National Council on Ageing (Age Concern England) the Secretary of State for Business, Enterprise and Regulatory Reform* (5 March 2009).

[348] Case C-388/07 *The Incorporated Trustees of the National Council on Ageing (Age Concern England) the Secretary of State for Business, Enterprise and Regulatory Reform* (23 September 2008), at para 65.

[349] Case C-388/07 (5 March 2009) at para 66.

[350] See para **[13.102]** and see also O'Cinnéide 'Age Discrimination and Irish Equality Law' in O'Dell (Ed) *Older People in Modern Ireland: Essays on Law and Policy* (Firstlaw, 2005) pp 293–326.

It is open to question whether the Irish legislation is indeed fully in line with the Directive as there are a number of issues which appear problematic, in particular the exception for retirement ages. The difficulties are discussed below.

The Framework Directive

[13.150] The source of age discrimination protection in European law is the Framework Directive.[351] The purpose of the Directive is set out in Art 1 as being to lay down a general framework for combating discrimination and putting into effect the principle of equal treatment. The Directive has specific provisions in relation to age.

[13.151] The 14th and 25th recitals in the preamble to the Directive provide:

(14) this Directive shall be without prejudice to national provisions laying down retirement ages....

(25) the prohibition of age discrimination is an essential part of meeting the aims set out in the Employment Guidelines and encouraging diversity the work force. However, differences in treatment in connection with age may be justified under certain circumstances and therefore require specific provisions which may vary in accordance with the situation in Member States. It is therefore essential to distinguish between differences in treatment which are justified, in particular by legitimate employment policy, labour market and vocational training objectives, and discrimination which must be prohibited.

[13.152] Article 6 of the Directive provides justifications for differences of treatment on grounds of age:

1. Notwithstanding Article 2(2) [prohibition of direct and indirect discrimination], Member States may provide that differences of treatment on grounds of age shall not constitute discrimination, if, within the context of national law, they are objectively and reasonably justified by a legitimate aim, including legitimate employment policy, labour market and vocational training objectives, and if the means of achieving that aim are appropriate and necessary.

   Such differences of treatment may include, among others:

   (a) the setting of special conditions and access to employment and vocational training, employment and occupation, including dismissal and remuneration conditions, for young people, older workers and persons with caring responsibilities in order to promote their vocational integration or ensure their protection;

   (b) the fixing of minimum conditions of age, professional experience or seniority in service for access to employment or to certain advantages linked to employment;

   (c) the fixing of a maximum wage for recruitment which is based on the training requirements of the post in question or the need for a reasonable period of employment before retirement.

---

[351] Council Directive 2000/78/EC ([2000] L303/16) establishing a general framework for equal treatment in employment and occupation.

2.   Notwithstanding Article 2(2), Member States may provide that the fixing for occupational social security schemes of ages for admission or entitlement to retirement or invalidity benefits, including the fixing under those schemes of different ages for employees or groups or categories of employees, and the use, in the context of such schemes, of age criteria in actuarial calculations, does not constitute discrimination on the grounds of age, provided this does not result in discrimination on the grounds of sex.

The Employment Equality Act and age discrimination

[13.153] As noted in the introduction to this chapter, the Framework Directive[352] is transposed into Irish law by the Employment Equality Act. The scheme of the Act in relation to discrimination.on the grounds of age is similar to those in relation to the other grounds of discrimination. However there are a number of specific exceptions for age.

[13.154] In essence, there are four sets of exceptions. The first is in relation to occupational benefit schemes which allow employers to fix different ages for admission to the scheme for entitlement to benefits under it and to use age criteria and actuarial calculations. This exception is subject to the significant proviso that the age discrimination shall not constitute discrimination on the grounds of gender. The second exception allows, although it is not completely clear, for employers to fix mandatory retirement ages. The third exception allows an employer to set a maximum age of recruitment where it would not be worthwhile for the employer to take the person on because training is required and because there is not enough time left between the time the person is taken on and the time the person retires for the employer to claw back the cost of the training. The fourth exception permits different treatment of employees to the extent that a collective agreement allows seniority in a particular post or employment to be determined by reference to the relative ages of employees on their entry to the post for the purpose of calculating length of service.

The exceptions are set out in ss 34(3), 34(4) and 34(5) and 34(7A). These provide:

(3) In an occupational benefits scheme it shall not constitute discrimination on the age ground for an employer—

(a)   to fix ages for admission to such a scheme or for entitlement to benefits under it,

(b)   to fix different such ages for all employees or a category of employees

(c)   to use, in the context of such a scheme, age criteria in actuarial calculations, or

(d)   to provide different rates of severance payment for different employees or groups or categories of employees, being rates based on or taking into account the period between the age of an employee on leaving the employment and his or her compulsory retirement age

provided that that does not constitute discrimination on the gender ground....

(4) Without prejudice to subsection (3), it shall not constitute discrimination on the age ground to fix different ages for the retirement (whether voluntarily or compulsorily) of employees or any class or description of employees.

---

[352] Council Directive 2000/78/EC ([2000] L303/16) establishing a general framework for equal treatment in employment and occupation.

(5) Without prejudice to the generality of subsection (3), it shall not constitute discrimination on the age ground to set, in relation to any job, a maximum age for recruitment which takes account of—

(a) any cost or period of time involved in training a recruit to a standard at which the recruit will be effective in that job, and

(b) the need for there to be a reasonable period of time prior to retirement age during which the recruit will be effective in that job.

(7A) Nothing in this Act invalidates any term in a collective agreement, whenever made, to the effect that in particular circumstances, where length of service would otherwise be regarded as equal, seniority in a particular post or employment may be determined by reference to the relative ages of employees on their entry to that post or employment.

There is a serious question as to whether the blanket fixing of mandatory retirement ages by individual employers is permissible under Community law. In this respect it is possible that Ireland may have failed to correctly transpose the Framework Directive.[353] It would seem, following the ECJ decision in *Palacios de la Villa*,[354] that Community law requires a different approach to fixing of retirement ages In other words, national measures providing for fixed retirement ages must be capable of justification having regard to public policy considerations. The setting of a mandatory retirement age may only be permissible if it is objectively justified. This is particularly evident from the ECJ decision in *Heyday*, which held that a derogation from the principle of age discrimination could only be permitted in respect of measures permitted by legitimate social policy objectives, such as those related to employment policy, the labour market or social policy training.[355]

Scope of the prohibition

[13.155] The Employment Equality Act prohibits direct and indirect discrimination on the grounds of age. However, unlike the other grounds, direct discrimination on grounds of age may be permitted.

The question arises whether there must be a minimum difference in age for discrimination on the age ground to apply. This question affects what is sufficient to prove the *prima facie* case of discrimination on the grounds of age.[356] It is clear that a difference of twenty to thirty years for example can be relevant. However a difference in age of a day or two days could be irrelevant. If the argument is that one candidate was preferred over another because one was two days older than the other, clearly there would appear to be room for a *de minimis* argument. On the other hand, a very small difference in age may be relevant in schemes where, for example, enhanced redundancy benefits are payable to those who become of certain age on a certain date. The issue of

---

[353] Council Directive 2000/78/EC ([2000] L303/16) establishing a general framework for equal treatment in employment and occupation.

[354] Case C-411/05 *Félix Palacios de la Villa v Cortefiel Servicios SA* 16 October 2007.

[355] Case C – 388/07 *The Incorporated Trustees of the National Council on Ageing (Age Concern England) the Secretary of State for Business, Enterprise and Regulatory Reform* 5 March 2009.

[356] On the burden of proof in cases under the Employment Equality Acts 1998–2008, see para **[13.18]**.

the difference in age came up for examination in three cases – *Freeman v Sean Quinn,*[357] *County Louth VEC v Johnson*[358] and *Reynolds v Limerick City Council.*[359]

[13.156] In *Johnson*, the argument was made that it was age brackets which were important, ie when people were grouped by age, eg 40 to 45, 50 to 55 etc. The defence put forward by the respondent employer that age discrimination cannot arise where the complainant and successful candidate are in the same age bracket (in this case the successful candidate was 50 and the complainant was 56) was rejected by the Director as 'an entirely arbitrary construct, adopted usually for convenience'[360] and the Labour Court agreed with this view. However, this may be relevant where an employer themselves uses age brackets. In those circumstances it could be argued that if the employees are in the same age bracket then they are not of different ages for the purposes of the Employment Equality Act.

[13.157] In *Freeman*,[361] the Labour Court rejected the argument that a difference in age of three years (the complainant was 31 years of age and the successful candidate was 28 years of age) was sufficient to establish a presumption of discrimination in the absence of any other facts indicating less favourable treatment on grounds of age. It may be that a relatively small difference in age may be an overall factor which may lead a Tribunal to believe that age was not a material factor in making a decision. On the other hand a relatively small difference in age may in certain circumstances provide evidence of discrimination on grounds of age. For example, in *Reynolds*,[362] the Labour Court accepted that an age difference of eight years, (the complainant was 45 years of age and the successful candidate was 37) was 'significant' in the context of promotion in the fire service. Given that it is common for those employed in active service in the fire service to retire at a relatively early age, it is unsurprising that this minor age difference was emphasised by the Labour Court as being a factor in the raising of an inference of discrimination on grounds of age.

[13.158] Another issue under the heading of direct discrimination is how, what some commentators term, 'age proxies'[363] are to be treated as direct or indirect discrimination. An argument can be made that factors which are essentially what might be termed a euphemism for age such as 'young and dynamic' might in fact be seen as direct discrimination whereas other items such as experience or seniority or post qualification experience might be seen as indirect discrimination. The *Ryanair v The Equality*

---

[357] *Freeman v Sean Quinn* DEE 02/1 (Labour Court).

[358] *County Louth VEC v Johnson* EDA 0712 (Labour Court).

[359] *Reynolds v Limerick City Council* EDA 048 (Labour Court).

[360] *Johnson* DEC-E2006-052 (Equality Tribunal).

[361] *Freeman* DEE 02/1 (Labour Court).

[362] *Reynolds* EDA 048 (Labour Court).

[363] O'Cinnéide 'Age Discrimination and Irish Equality Law' in O'Dell (Ed) *Older People in Modern Ireland: Essays on Law and Policy* (Firstlaw, 2005) at 308 fn 71, citing Hepple, 'Age Discrimination in Employment: Implementing the Framework Directive 2000/78/EC' in Fredman and Spencer Eds, *Age as an Equality Issue* (Hart, 2003), pp 71–115.

Authority[364] case is in point here. The Equality Authority challenged a Ryanair advertisement looking for young and dynamic people. Ryanair sought to argue that this was not an ageist advertisement in that what they meant was young at heart and that people could be dynamic at any age. However the Equality Tribunal found that the advertisement was directly discriminatory on the age ground.

[13.159] More recent cases have arisen as a result of requests for dates of birth. In *Cunningham v CMS Sales Ltd*,[365] the Equality Tribunal considered whether an inference of age discrimination arose in respect of a prospective employee who was asked for his date of birth at interview. The Equality Officer had very little difficulty in finding that the complainant had established a *prima facie* case of direct discrimination on grounds of age in relation to access to employment in that it had sought the complainant's age and date of birth on the registration form and subsequently pursued the matter with him. Compensation of €5,000 was awarded which was expressly for distress and breach of rights under the Act and did not contain any element of lost income.

[13.160] In *MacGahainn v Salesforce.com*[366] the complainant claimed that he had been discriminated on grounds of age when he was asked for his date of birth in German at his job interview. The respondent argued that the question was asked to ascertain the complainant's proficiency in the German language, which was a requirement for the position. Interestingly, the Equality Officer found that the complainant had suffered discrimination on grounds of age, but that he would not have been successful at interview even if he had not been asked for his age. Therefore a distinction was drawn between the discriminatory effect of the question and the decision not to employ the complainant. He was awarded €1,000 for the effects of the discrimination. Although the Tribunal found that the complainant would not have been successful in obtaining the position, the fact that a discriminatory question was asked at interview was sufficient to justify an award, albeit of a modest amount, of compensation.

Indirect discrimination

[13.161] The Framework Directive[367] and the Employment Equality Act prohibit indirect discrimination on the age ground but this is permissible where the provision, practice or criteria in question is objectively justified. The act which is indirectly discriminatory will be examined very closely by the tribunal or court to see whether the requirement which has the adverse impact on the person or woman particularly age over another is required by a legitimate aim of the employer and if so, if the requirement imposed by the employer is the appropriate and necessary.

Claims of indirect discrimination on grounds of age, have arisen in a wide variety of contexts and will now be discussed under selected categories below.

---

[364] *Ryanair v The Equality Authority* DEC E2000/14.

[365] *Cunningham v CMS Sales Ltd* [2008] ELR 165.

[366] *MacGahainn v Salesforce.com* DEC-E2007-048.

[367] Council Directive 2000/78/EC ([2000] L303/16) establishing a general framework for equal treatment in employment and occupation.

Promotions

[13.162] Just as with gender discrimination discussed at para **[13.69]** above, indirect discrimination has arisen in situations in which employers have imposed on applicants for jobs or promotions requirements of seniority, experience, qualifications or experience. Traditionally, promotion was often linked to age or length of service. The prohibiton on age discrimination has now had an impact on this practice. Automatic assumptions and linkages between age and length of service can no longer be made. If a certain number of years is required either for promotion or re-grading or moving up a scale it must be shown very clearly by the employer that this is objectively justifiable.

[13.163] In *McGarr v The Department of Finance*,[368] the claimant brought a complaint against his employer that the imposition of a five-year service requirement for a promotional post was indirectly discriminatory on the grounds of age. The complainant had been provided with figures that confirmed that the bar to promotion to Higher Executive Officer until five years' service had been achieved resulted in age discrimination, in that the requirement resulted in a significant under-representation of candidates under the age of 30 years and consequently an under-representation of Higher Executive Officers under that age. The complainant contended that the five-year service requirement had a more negative impact on people under 30 than on those over that age. The Equality Officer found that the five years' service requirement could not be justified as being reasonable under the circumstances and therefore did not justify indirect discrimination.

[13.164] In *Dun Laoghaire/Rathdown v Richard Morrissey*,[369] the complainant claimed that following the upward re-grading of his post and his assimilation on a new scale using the promotional rules agreed between trade unions and the respondent, his service had been reduced to the equivalent of seven years for salary purposes. This affected the complainant personally, as he was less than three years from retirement, this prevented him from reaching the second long service increment on his new salary scale despite him being in the post for 23 years. He submitted that the use of the promotional rules in re-grading discriminated against persons with long service in their old grade. The Labour Court found that long service increments reflect service not age and that the appellant had been treated no differently to the other employees who were re-graded at that time. It stated that the fact that the complainant was unable to fulfil the necessary service requirements before retirement did not constitute discrimination on grounds of age.

Limitations on years of post-qualification experience

[13.165] *O'Connor v Lidl Ireland*[370] concerned a challenge to an advertisement which set out a specified number of years of post-qualification experience. The respondent's advertisement stated that, 'the ideal candidate should be highly motivated and flexible, be ambitious and mobile, have a high interest in retail, be results orientated and work

---

[368] *McGarr v The Department of Finance* DEC E2003-36 (Equality Tribunal).

[369] *Dun Laoghaire/Rathdown v Richard Morrissey* EDA 0410 (Labour Court).

[370] *O'Connor v Lidl Ireland* DEC-E 2005-012 (Equality Tribunal).

well under pressure, have excellent communication, interpersonal and leadership skills, be a graduate, ideally with not more than two–three years' experience in a commercial environment, no retail experience required.' Mr O'Connor responded to the advertisement and applied for the position in an application in which he outlined his 5½ years sales experience in his own business and his significant and job-relevant educational background. As part of his application he included a copy of his Curriculum Vitae which outlined his work experience of 31 years. Mr O'Connor, at the time of the hearing of the claim, was 51 years old. He received a letter from the respondent informing him that they had decided not to proceed with his application and he was not, therefore, called for interview. Mr O'Connor's claim was on two grounds – that the advertisement was indirectly discriminatory on the age ground and that he had been discriminated against on the age ground in relation to access to employment. The Equality Tribunal held that the claim in relation to the advertisement could only be made by the Equality Authority under the relevant statutory provision[371] but that Mr O'Connor had indirectly discriminated against on the grounds of age in relation to the selection process when he was not invited for interview.

Ethos and approach

[13.166] The failure of a person to be selected for retention in employment because of her old fashioned approach to teaching and ethos was found to be indirectly discriminatory on grounds of age in the case of *Mary Immaculate College v Sister Loye*[372] In this interesting case which pushes the boundaries on what constitutes age discrimination, the complainant, a member of a Religious Order, was employed on successive fixed-term contracts as an Assistant Lecturer with the respondent from 1995 until 2002, when she received a 5 year contract to the date of her retirement in 2007.

[13.167] In 2001, a competition was held whereby a number of academics on long-term 'back to back' fixed-term contracts were given the opportunity to attain permanency in their respective positions, subject to success in a confined assessment process. The candidates competed against criteria tailored to their own areas/departments. They were not competing against one another. The complainant was not, however, successful. She was the oldest applicant by 11 years and was 27 years older than the average age of the other applicants for permanency. She was the only applicant out of seven across five departments not to succeed. The Labour Court in finding that the complainant had been discriminated against made the following comments, which are worth quoting at length:

> During the course of the hearing, it became clear to the Court that the thrust and ethos of the interview process was to change and modernise the institution, and to appoint to permanency younger and more dynamic people who would be able to meet the requirements of a younger and more dynamic head of Department.

> At the time of the interview the complainant was 59 years of age, and was a long serving member of a religious order, schooled in a different ethos, and guided strongly by the virtue of obedience, both to those above and below. It is the view of the Court that, unfortunately, her employers regarded her as a person from another era who was 'out of

---

[371] Employment Equality Act 1998–2008, s 85.

[372] *Mary Immaculate College v Sister Loye* EDA 082/2008 (Labour Court).

her time' and would not fit into the idea of a modern 21st Century institution which the College wished to establish.

The Court finds that the respondents have not satisfactorily discharged the burden placed upon them. The Court finds that while the complainant would have undoubtedly lost marks for not having completed her PhD, and for her lack of research and publication, nevertheless the difference in marking between her and the other candidates in an interview for permanency, coupled with the fact that, having found her completely unsuitable, without any effort to provide retraining, the College then re-appointed her to that position until retirement, can only lead the Court to conclude that the Respondents, while not specifically taking the plaintiff's age into account, decided that because her approach and ethos were those of someone from a different era, accordingly she would simply not 'fit in'. Since the complainant's approach to teaching and her ethos were inextricably linked to her age and the era in which she grew up, the respondents did discriminate against the complainant on the grounds of her age in breach of Section (2) & 8 (1) of the Act.

The complainant was awarded €3,500 for loss of earnings and €5,000 for the effects of the Act of discrimination.

Costs

[13.168] In terms of objective justification of indirect age discrimination, the Equality Tribunal made clear in *McGarr v The Department of Finance*[373] that the fact that it is expensive not to discriminate will not be sufficient justification for the discrimination.

Burden of proof

[13.169] The burden of proof which must be satisfied by a comparator in order to raise an inference of discrimination on grounds of age has been considered in a number of decisions. As with gender discrimination, there is a shifting burden of proof applied in age discrimination complaints. Thus a *prima facie* case only must be established, at which point the burden shifts to the employer to justify any difference in treatment.

The application of this approach to the nature of the evidence which constitutes a *prima facie* case can be seen in a number of recent cases. In *Meehan v Leitrim City Council*,[374] the complainant, who was employed as a firefighter, alleged that he had been treated less favourably that younger colleagues in relation to promotion and access to training by his respondent employer. In relation to the role of the Equality Tribunal in the area of interviews or selection process, the Director stated that it was 'not of course the Tribunal's function to identify the most suitable candidate but to examine whether the selection process was tainted by age discrimination.' She stated that the bare fact that that a successful candidate is younger than the complainant is not sufficiently probative to shift the evidential burden required to establish a *prima facie* case. On the facts, she noted that the complainant's qualifications and experience were greater than the successful candidate and this was sufficient for the complainant to discharge the evidential burden required of him.

---

[373] *McGarr v The Department of Finance* DEC E2003-36 (Equality Tribunal).
[374] *Meehan v Leitrim City Council* DEC-2006-014 (Equality Tribunal).

[13.170] The mere fact that the complainant alleges that he or she has greater experience or skills than their comparator is not of itself sufficient to raise an inference of discrimination. This is evident from the decision of the Labour Court in *O'Halloran v Galway City Partnership*.[375] The Labour Court stated that it is only where an individual with better qualifications related to the position at issue is passed over in favour of a less qualified candidate, that an inference of discrimination can arise. The Labour Court also made useful comments on when it is appropriate for it to interfere with the employer's qualification or criteria set for a particular position. It stated:

> Where a better qualified candidate is passed over in favour of a less qualified candidate an inference of discrimination can arise (see *Wallace v South Eastern Education and Library Board* [1980] NI 38; [1980] IRLR 193). However the qualifications or criteria which is to be expected of candidates is a matter for the employer in every case. Provided the chosen criteria are not indirectly discriminatory on any of the proscribed grounds, it is not for the Court to express a view as to their appropriateness. It is only if the chosen criteria are applied inconsistently as between candidates or an unsuccessful candidate is clearly better qualified against the chosen criteria that an inference of discrimination could arise.

[13.171] The complainant in *Moate Community School v Moriarty*[376] alleged that he had been discriminated against on grounds of age when he had been unsuccessful in his application for promotion to Assistant Principal. The Labour Court acknowledged that in many cases it can prove difficult to prove age discrimination and commented on the type of evidence which will satisfy the burden of proof in this area:

> Evidence of discrimination on the age ground will generally be found in the surrounding circumstances and facts of the particular case. Evidence of it can be found where job applications from candidates of a particular age are treated less seriously than those from candidates of a different age. It can also be manifest from a conclusion that candidates in a particular age group are unsuitable or might not fit in, where an adequate appraisal or a fair assessment of their attributes has not been undertaken. Discrimination can also be inferred from questions asked at interview which suggest that age is a relevant consideration.

Interview process

[13.172] The transparency or otherwise of the interview process plays an important part in whether or not an employer can establish that discrimination did not take place. The Labour Court and particularly the Equality Tribunal have placed an overwhelming emphasis on a transparent interview process with full-record keeping as a necessary requirement to rebut any inference of discrimination. This is true for all the grounds of discrimination, not just age discrimination. In fact, it is arguable that some determinations have gone too far in this regard and have inferred discrimination solely from a failure to keep adequate records of an interview process.

There are two age discrimination cases which set out perhaps the most useful guidelines with regard to the interview process. The first of these is *Johnson v Louth VEC*.[377] In this case the complainant alleged that he had been discriminated against on

---

[375] *O'Halloran v Galway City Partnership* EDA 077/2007 (Labour Court).
[376] *Moate Community School v Moriarty* EDA 0718/2007 (Labour Court).

the grounds of age when he was not appointed to the position of Assistant Principal and a younger, less experienced candidate was appointed. The Labour Court expressed approval of the following factors which were put in place by the respondent for its interview process:

- the interview and selection procedure were fully in compliance with the relevant Department of Education and Science circular;

- the procedures were clear and transparent;

- the members of the interview board were independent of the employer, had extensive experience and were trained in the requirements of ant-discrimination law;

- a pre-interview meeting was held at which the panel drew up questions relating to key areas;

- marks were allocated for critical attributes required for the duties of the position based on objective pre-determined criteria.

The Labour Court upheld the decision of the Equality Tribunal that the complainant had failed to raise a presumption of discrimination. It noted that although the complainant had superior qualifications, the successful candidate was awarded higher marks by the interview board as she was regarded as a better candidate. The Labour Court re-iterated its role when dealing with claims of discrimination in the selection process that it not the function of the Court to decide who the most meritorious candidate for the position was. Rather the Labour Court opined that its function is to determine whether the age of the complainant influenced the decision of the employer. On the facts, it found no basis for such a finding and rejected the complainant's appeal.

[13.173] While the employer in *Johnson* had an exemplary interview process, in *Fagan v The Revenue Commissioners*[378] there were significant difficulties. Mr Fagan claimed that he was discriminated against by the Office of the Revenue Commissioners on grounds of age when it (i) failed to appoint him to an acting position of Assistant Principal Officer in April, 2003 and (ii) failed to consider him suitable for promotion to the substantive grade of Assistant Principal Officer on the basis of seniority/suitability in August, 2003. The Equality Officer awarded a high level of compensation for the discrimination suffered by the complainant and also made useful comments in relation to the interview process.

The Equality Officer noted that no minutes or other formal record of the Promotion Conference meeting was maintained, nor was the basis on which candidates were deemed suitable/unsuitable reduced to writing. The respondent was unable to furnish a single document to demonstrate that the complainant's failure to be appointed to the acting post in February 2003 and his exclusion from the promotion panel in September 2003 were due to factors unconnected with the complainant's age. He held therefore that the respondent had failed to rebut the inference of discrimination raised and that the complainant's claim was entitled to succeed. He awarded the complainant €60,000 by

---

[377] *Johnson v Louth VEC* EDA 0712/2007 (Labour Court).
[378] *Fagan v The Revenue Commissioners* DEC-E2008-004.

way of compensation and ordered the respondent to take immediate steps to ensure that the process of promotion was conducted in an open an transparent fashion and that adequate records of how decision were arrived at were retained. Significantly, the Equality Officer noted that the Framework Directive[379] requires that sanctions for infringement of the principle of equal treatment be effective, proportionate and dissuasive and it was for that reason that such a high award of compensation was awarded.

Redundancy and severance packages

[13.174] Age discrimination challenges have also been mounted to the packages offered to employees in voluntary redundancy or severance. Traditionally employers have adopted the approach of applying different packages to different age brackets. Depending on the plan, the approach could be seen as incentivising older employees to leave or younger employees to stay. There have been a number of cases in this regard.

[13.175] In *Ruddy v An Post*,[380] the claimant was refused access to an owner-driver scheme which was part of a restructuring programme that the respondent undertook in an effort to address its poor financial position. The respondent also offered voluntary redundancy. The claimant expressed an interest in the owner-driver scheme as it offered a more generous financial package than the redundancy package and would have allowed him to commence working as a self-employed driver. The claimant was told by a representative of his trade union, the Communication Workers Union, that he 'could not avail of the scheme because he was over 60'. The respondent accepted that an age restriction had been placed on the scheme, but argued that without this restriction 'it would have incurred significant costs'. This was an attempt to come within s 34(3) of the Employment Equality Act which allows discrimination in circumstances where it can be demonstrated that significantly increased costs would be caused if the discrimination was not permitted. However, the evidence submitted was only prepared for the hearing. The respondent also argued that as the claimant had not actually made an official application for the scheme, he lacked *locus standi* in respect of his claim. The Equality Officer was 'satisfied that had the complainant submitted an application it would have been rejected by the respondent on the basis that he was over 60 years of age'. She found that the respondent discriminated against the complainant on grounds of age. She awarded the complainant €70,316 which was the difference in the amount the complainant would have been permitted to had he been allowed to avail of the owner-driver scheme in 2003 of €92,442 and the amount he received on retirement, €22,126.

[13.176] In *Calor Teoranta v McCarthy*,[381] along with providing important comments concerning s 34(4) of the Employment Equality Act, the Labour Court considered assurances made to the complainant during his negotiations surrounding a voluntary redundancy package. The facts were that in 1987, the complainant had signed a

---

[379] Council Directive 2000/78/EC establishing a general framework for equal treatment in employment and occupation.
[380] *Ruddy v An Post* DEC-E2007-020 (Equality Tribunal).
[381] *Calor Teoranta v McCarthy* [2008] 19 ELR 269.

document regarding pension contributions, which acknowledged that from 1 April 1991, the normal retirement age was age 60. However, Mr McCarthy said that he elected for the voluntary redundancy scheme in 1994 and was advised and given to understand that the retirement age would remain at 65 and that he had 'relied on this promise and inducement.' He then took voluntary redundancy in 1994 and he submitted that he was given to 'understand that he could continue to work to age 65 in 1994 and in 2002'.

The Labour Court accepted Mr McCarthy's evidence that he had been told that he could work until he was 65 and thus that the contractual retirement age was 65 and not age 60. The Court concluded that when the respondent terminated the complainant's employment on 1 January 2005, it did so on grounds of his age. He was thus treated differently than a person in a comparable position who had not attained the age of 60 would have been treated. An award of compensation in the amount of €46,000 was granted.

As a result of these decisions, companies have had to alter their voluntary redundancy packages and think very seriously about how these are offered. Further, large awards of compensation were awarded in these cases which demonstrate the Equality Tribunal and Labour Court's disapproval of any actions which unnecessarily adversely affect older employee's access to voluntary redundancy schemes.

Retirement and age discrimination

[13.177] As noted in para **[13.154]**, the issue of whether the imposition of a mandatory retirement age is permitted under Community law is the subject of much litigation. The Framework Directive lacks clarity on this point. While the recitals to the Directive state that the Directive is 'without prejudice to national provisions laying down retirement ages', the text of the Directive does not contain any specific exception for retirement ages. Rather the Directive only permits discrimination which is objectively justifiable. The legality of retirement ages has been at issue in three cases before the ECJ: *Mangold*,[382] *Palacios de la Villa*[383] and *Heyday*.[384]

[13.178] The ECJ decision in *Mangold* concerned the legality of a provision of domestic German law which authorised the entering into fixed-term contracts of employment once the worker had reached the age of 52. Thus it was not specifically a retirement case but rather concerned the forced change in the status of the worker once they had reached the age of 52.

Mr Mangold challenged the lawfulness of the fixed-term nature of his contract. The German Labour Court made a reference to the ECJ. The main issue before the ECJ was whether Art 6(1) of Directive 2000/78, the directive establishing a general framework for equal treatment in employment and occupation, precluded a provision of domestic law which authorised, without restriction, the conclusion of fixed-term contracts of employment once the worker had reached the age of 52.

---

[382] Case C-144/04 *Mangold v Helm* [2005] ECR 19981.
[383] Case C-411/05 *Palacios de la Villa v Cortefiel* [2007] ECR I-8531.
[384] Case C-388/07 *Incorporated Trustees of the National Council on Ageing v Secretary of State for Business, Enterprise and Regulatory Reform* 5 March 2009.

The ECJ held that Community law, and 'more particularly' Art 6(1) of Directive 2000/78, precluded a provision of domestic law that authorised the conclusion of fixed-term contracts of employment once the worker has reached the age of 52.

In its reasoning, the ECJ first addressed the question whether allowing fixed term contracts without justification in respect of all workers over the age of 52 constituted age discrimination. It noted that under Art 6(1) of the Directive, differences in treatment on grounds of age would not amount to discrimination if they were objectively and reasonably justified by a legitimate aim and if the means of achieving that aim are appropriate and necessary. The ECJ was satisfied that the German legislation had a legitimate purpose, which was to promote the vocational integration of unemployed workers above a certain age. However, the Court was not satisfied that setting the age at 52 was the appropriate and necessary means of achieving that legitimate purpose.

Although the ECJ recognised that Member States enjoyed a broad discretion in the field of social and employment policy, it considered that by this measure the German legislature had exceeded that discretion. By setting the age at 52, there was a significant body of workers (determined solely on the basis of age) who were in danger, during a substantial part of their working life, of being excluded from the benefit of stable employment. It had not been shown that fixing the age threshold was objectively necessary to the attainment of the objective of vocational integration of unemployed older workers. Since the measure did not respect the principle of proportionality in this way, it could not be justified under Art 6(1) of the Directive.

[13.179] The legality of retirement ages was addressed more squarely in *Palacios de la Villa v Cortefiel Servicios SA*. A Spanish Court referred the questions to the ECJ in the course of proceedings between an employee and his employer concerning the automatic termination of his contract of employment by reason of his reaching the age-limit set by Spanish law for compulsory retirement at age 65. The ECJ concluded that, although the Directive was without prejudice to national provisions laying down retirement ages, this in no way precluded the application of the Directive to national measures governing the conditions for termination of employment contracts where the retirement age, thus established, had been reached:[385]

> It is true that, according to recital 14 in its preamble, Directive 2000/78 is to be without prejudice to national provisions laying down retirement ages. However, that recital merely states that the Directive does not affect the competence of the Member States to determine retirement age and does not in any way preclude the application of that Directive to national measures governing the conditions for termination of employment contracts where the retirement age, thus established, has been reached.
>
> The legislation at issue in the main proceedings, which permits the automatic termination of an employment relationship concluded between an employer and a worker once the latter has reached the age of 65, affects the duration of the employment relationship between the parties and, more generally, the engagement of the worker concerned in an occupation, by preventing his future participation in the labour force.

---

[385] Case C-411/05 *Palacios de la Villa v Cortefiel* [2007] ECR I-8531 at paras 44–47.

Consequently, legislation of that kind must be regarded as establishing rules relating to 'employment and working conditions, including dismissals and pay' within the meaning of Article 3(1)(c) of Directive 2000/78.

In those circumstances, Directive 2000/78 is applicable to a situation such as that giving rise to the dispute before the national court.

The Court went on to hold that the retirement age in issue in the main proceedings was lawful where, in accordance with Article 6 of the Directive:

- [T]he measure, although based on age, is objectively and reasonably justified in the context of national law by a legitimate aim relating to employment policy and the labour market, and

- the means put in place to achieve that aim of public interest do not appear to be inappropriate and unnecessary for the purpose.

[13.180] The issue was addressed most recently in *The Incorporated Trustees of the National Council on Ageing (Age Concern England) v Secretary for State for Business, Enterprise and Regulatory Reform*, known as the *Heyday* case. At issue in these proceedings was the legality of UK regulations which provided, subject to certain conditions, that it was not unlawful for an employer to dismiss an employee who had reached the age of 65 when the reason for the dismissal was retirement. This provision is implied into every contract of employment unless the employer provided for a different retirement age.

On an consideration of the applicable legal principles, the ECJ held that it is lawful to impose mandatory retirement ages in national legislation (which was an expansion from collective agreements, as in *Palacios de la Villa*) but that such provisions must be objectively and reasonably justified based on employment policies, labour market or vocational training objectives and the means of achieving those aims must be appropriate and necessary. The ECJ made it clear that aims which may be considered legitimate to provide for derogation from the general principle prohibiting discrimination on grounds of age are those which are social policy objectives, such as those related to employment policy as distinct from purely individual reasons such as cost reduction or improving competitiveness.[386] It is significant that the ECJ held that Art 6 of the Framework Directive imposes on Member States the burden of establishing 'to a high standard of proof the legitimacy of the aim relied upon as a justification'. It is not clear what is meant by 'a high standard of proof' and whether that is different or more onerous than the standard required to prove other discrimination claims. The scope of the questions referred by the UK High Court and the fact that it did not ask the ECJ to rule on the compatibility of the UK regulations with the Directive, means that the judgment of the ECJ in this issue is necessarily limited. As regards the *Heyday* challenge, the matter was returned to the UK High Court for its determination on this issue.

The consequences of this trio of cases for Irish law is unclear as we do not have a national retirement age set out in legislation. It is not certain if individual employers can

---

[386] [2007] ECR I-8531 at para 46.

avail of the possibility of objectively justifying the impostion of a retirement age or whether it is only a State which can do so.

Section 34(4) defence

[13.181] The position is complicated by the fact that Irish employment equality law contains a specific exception at s 34(4) of the Employment Equality Act which provides that it shall not constitute a breach of the Employment Equality Act to fix different ages for retirement. It is open to question whether this is compatible with Community law as interpreted by the ECJ in *Heyday*.

The reservations which the Labour Court has in relation to s 34(4) can be seen in *Calor Teoranta v McCarthy*.[387] Mr McCarthy's complaint arose from his compulsory retirement on reaching age 60. The Equality Officer found that age 60 was the retirement age fixed by Calor Teoranta. She went on to hold that Mr McCarthy was required to retire on reaching that age and that the fixing of a retirement age was saved by s 34(4) of the Act and did not constitute discrimination on the age ground.

Mr McCarthy appealed to the Labour Court. In 1987, the complainant signed a document regarding pension contributions, which acknowledged that from 1 April 1991, the normal retirement age was age 60. Mr McCarthy submitted that while he accepted that he signed the document in 1987, he signed it with the intention of working until 60 and retiring on full pension at that stage. However, because he took redundancy in 1994 and returned to work as a 'casual worker', he believed that he could work until 65 years of age. The complainant submitted that at the time that he elected for the voluntary redundancy scheme, he was advised and given to understand that retirement age would remain at 65 and that he had 'relied on this promise and inducement.' He then took voluntary redundancy in 1994 and he submitted that he was given to 'understand that he could continue to work to age 65 in 1994 and in 2002.'

[13.182] The Labour Court accepted the complainant's evidence that he was informed that he could work until he was 65 and accepted that it had acted as an inducement to the complainant to take the voluntary redundancy. It then concluded as follows:

> It follows that when the Respondent terminated the Complainant's employment on 1st January, 2005, it did so on grounds of his age. He was thus treated differently than a person in a comparable position who had not attained the age of 60 would have been treated. That constituted discrimination within the meaning of Section 6(1) of the Act. Accordingly the Complainant is entitled to succeed in this appeal.

> For the sake of completeness and for the avoidance of doubt the Court wishes to point out that this case was decided on the factual circumstances of the complaint herein as disclosed in evidence. It has no application beyond this case. Secondly, the Court has not reached any concluded view on the submissions made to it in relation to the compatibility of Section 34(4) of the Act with the provisions of Directive 2000/78/EC. The Court wishes to expressly reserve its position on that question to another case in which it is a determinative issue.

---

[387] *Calor Teoranta v McCarthy* EDA 089/2008 (Labour Court).

Calor was appealed to the High Court on a point of law, and the High Court found in favour of the plantiff.[388]

[13.183] In other cases the imposition of a mandatory retirement age has been upheld. In *Vickers v Daughters of Charity of St Vincent de Paul*,[389] the complainant was employed as supervisor at the respondent's Knockmaroon facility under a Fás Sponsored Social Employment Scheme. She stated that her contract of employment with the respondent did not contain any clause regarding compulsory retirement age and she was unaware of any such conditions on her post until she received a letter shortly before her 66th birthday wishing her well in her retirement. She wrote to the respondent stating that she wished to continue working there as she still had the capacity and capability to do so. She asserted that her compulsory retirement, being based solely on age, was discriminatory. The respondent denied that any discrimination had taken place. In line with government policy, employees cease to be funded by Fás upon reaching their 66th birthday, as this is the time at which they will be entitled to receive a State pension. Without funding for her employment, the respondent was not in a position to retain Ms Vickers, and this was the sole reason behind her mandatory retirement.

The Equality Officer found that the respondent was not enforcing a discriminatory policy of another organisation under the Act, and the complainant's claim for discriminatory dismissal therefore failed.

[13.184] As we have seen above, the ECJ in its recent judgment in *Heyday*[390] has firmly placed objective and reasonable justification for mandatory retirement ages in the realm of social policy and not those of a purely individual employment nature. Further, given the recognition by the ECJ in Heyday of the onerous burden which must be overcome to justify mandatory retirement ages as being non-discriminatory, it is likely that s 34(4) in its blanket coverage in the absence of any justification will be found to be incompatible with the Framework Directive.

It is worth noting that the Unfair Dismissals Acts 1977–2007 exclude certain categories of employee from protection under the Acts. One of the categories excluded is:[391]

> Employees who on or before the date of dismissal have reached the normal retiring age for employees with the same employer in similar employment or who on that date had not attained the age of 16 years.

The practical effect of this is that the ending of the contract of employment simply by virtue of the employee reaching normal retiring age for that employer will not constitute an unfair dismissal for the purpose of the Unfair Dismissals Acts.[392]

---

[388] (19 March 2009) HC.

[389] *Vickers v Daughters of Charity of St Vincent de Paul* DEC-E2007-017 (Equality Tribunal).

[390] Case C-388/07 *The Incorporated Trustees of the National Council on Ageing (Age Concern England) v Secretary of Sate for Business, Enterprise and Regulatory Reform* (5 March 2009).

[391] Unfair Dismissals Act 1977, s 2(1)(b) as amended by Unfair Dismissals (Amendment) Act 1993, s 14.

[392] On retirement age and unfair dismissal, see Ch 14, Dismissal at paras **[14.77]**–**[14.79]** and Bruton, 'Retirement Age and the Unfair Dismissals Act' [2008] 5(4) *IELJ* 121.

Age discrimination and pensions[393]

[13.185] The rules about equality in pensions follow those existing under the Employment Equality Act. However, due to many exceptions in these Act, occupational pension schemes can still contain many provisions which might otherwise appear to violate principles of non-discrimination. On equal treatment in relation to pensions, see Ch 11, Pay, Pensions and Benefits.

Case law on the age ground

[13.186] To date there has been little case law on pensions and age discrimination. This is partly due to the fact that the Act contains a wide number of exceptions. The following cases have some relevance in this area.

[13.187] In *Coillte Teoranta v Peter O'Dwyer*,[394] the employer made an appeal to the Labour Court from a determination of the Equality Tribunal with regard to a severance package disparity based solely upon the age ground. The appellant employer was unable to rely upon the exemption contained in s 34(3) of the Employment Equality Act, which provided an exemption if it could be established that significantly increased costs would result if the discrimination was not permitted to continue. The Court held that the sum of €43,792 was not considered a significant cost when set against the company's profits.

[13.188] The case of *Maura Perry v Garda Commissioners*[395] concerned a voluntary early retirement scheme for traffic wardens. There was a discrepancy in the severance package offered to those in different age brackets. The respondent sought to argue that this discrepancy was based on an incentive to encourage early retirement and was structured to reflect the differences in income forgone. The Equality Officer concluded that the disparity in the severance gratuity was based exclusively on the ages of the employees and that the disparity was therefore discriminatory. The respondent was found not to be in breach despite the existence of discrimination as they were entitled to rely upon the three year transitional period provided for under the Employment Equality Act 1998 Act, for achieving compliance with the 1998 Act.

[13.189] It is not clear why there has not been further litigation in relation to pensions and age discrimination. Perhaps the area of law is not well understood by tribunals or there is a feeling that it will not be understood. There may also be a difficulty in proving discrimination without obtaining the use of the services of an actuary, which might be too costly for the ordinary complainant. However, pension equality in the UK has come very much into focus since 2007 due to changes in the law there under the Employment Equality (Age) Regulations 2001, Sch 2 of which applies to pensions, and which came into force on the 1 October 2006. This has lead companies and pension lawyers in Ireland to question the Irish experience. This may lead to an increased request for advices and perhaps to litigation. Lawyers are therefore well advised to be aware of the existence of, and the pitfalls pursuant to, pensions equality law.

---

[393] On equal treatment in relation to pensions, see also Ch 11, Pay, Pensions and Benefits.
[394] *Coillte Teoranta v Peter O'Dwyer* [2006] 17 ELR 291.
[395] *Maura Perry v Garda Commissioners* [2002] 13 ELR 18.

DISABILITY[396]

[13.190] The Employment Equality Act prohibits discrimination on the grounds of disability.[397] The Act contains an extremely wide definition of disability. Section 2(1) of the Act provides:

'disability' means—

(a) the total or partial absence of a person's bodily or mental functions, including the absence of a part of a person's body,

(b) the presence in the body of organisms causing, or likely to cause, chronic disease or illness,

(c) the malfunction, malformation or disfigurement of a part of a person's body,

(d) a condition or malfunction which results in a person learning differently from a person without the condition or malfunction, or

(e) a condition, illness or disease which affects a person's thought processes, perception of reality, emotions or judgement or which results in disturbed behaviour

and shall be taken to include a disability which exists at present, or which previously existed but no longer exists, or which may exist in the future or which is imputed to a person.

[13.191] This definition of disability is probably wider than that required by the Framework Directive.[398] In *Chacón Navas v Eurest Colectividades SA*,[399] the ECJ ruled that disability referred to a limitation that resulted in particular from 'physical, mental or psychological impairments'[400] which hinders the person's participation in professional life and would probably last for a long time.[401] The Court also made clear that sickness and disability were different in that a person dismissed for sickness was unprotected by the disability provisions of the Framework Directive.[402] The Irish courts and tribunals

---

[396] On the subject of discrimination on the grounds of disability, see Fredman 'Disability Equality: A Challenge to the Existing Anti-Discrimination Paradigm?' in Lawson (Ed) *Disability Rights in Europe: From Theory to Practice* (Hart Publishing, Oxford & Portland Oregon, 2005), O'Cinnéide, 'A New Generation of Equality Legislation? Positive duties and Disability Rights' in Lawson (Ed), *Disability Rights in Europe: From Theory to Practice* (Hart Publishing, Oxford & Portland Oregon, 2005); Muchrane and Kelleher, 'Disability Discrimination under the Employment Equality Act, 1998 and the Equality Bill 2004' [2004] 2 *IELJ* 42; Gallagher, 'When the Employee becomes a Legal Dilemma' [2008] *ELRI* 2, Quinn, 'Disability discrimination law in the European Union', in Meenan (Ed) *Equality Law in An Enlarged European Union*, (Cambridge University Press, 2007).

[397] Employment Equality Acts 1998–2008, s 6(2)(g).

[398] Council Directive 2000/78/EC ([2000] L303/16) establishing a general framework for equal treatment in employment and occupation.

[399] Case C-13/05 *Chacón Navas v Eurest Colectividades* SA [2006] ECR I-000.

[400] Case C-13/05 [2006] ECR I-000, para 43.

[401] Case C-13/05 [2006] ECR I-000, para 45.

[402] Council Directive 2000/78/EC ([2000] L303/16) establishing a general framework for equal treatment in employment and occupation.

have diverged very strongly from this and in a number of decisions have included many types of sickness as well as conditions, such as alcoholism or drug addiction, as coming within the term 'disability'. The condition of being disabled is also materially different for the purposes of equality law than most of the other nine grounds, apart perhaps from age discrimination. This is the case for a number of reasons as set out by Barnard:[403]

> First it may or not be immutable (in the case of some disabilities, individuals are born with them or a condition develops later in life may or never improve; in respect of others the individuals may well recover). The second ... the disability may be visible (eg a wheelchair user) or it may not (eg a person suffering from a mental disability). The third ... the disability may extend an individual's ability to do a job (eg a person with a learning disability would not be able to become a surgeon) or it may not (eg a wheelchair user could perform an office based job), or it may affect an individual's ability to do a job with a certain amount of assistance to overcome their difficulty (eg a person with arthritis may work perfectly well as a secretary with the help of an adapted keyboard). The key issue with disability is that there are all kinds of disabilities and one rule does not fit all situations.

The other issue with disability is that it can affect a person's ability to do a job. This is materially different from, for example, the grounds of sex or race which should have no impact on a person's ability to do the job. How to prevent discrimination on grounds of disability while acknowledging that the employer should not be required to employ somebody who is not up to the job presents a challenge for the law.

[13.192] This legal challenge is dealt with by use of the legal concept of 'reasonable accommodation'. Article 5 of the Framework Directive[404] refers to the duty to provide reasonable accommodation:

> In order to guarantee compliance with the principle of equal treatment in relation to persons with disabilities, reasonable accommodation shall be provided. This means that employers shall take appropriate measures, where needed in a particular case, to enable a person with a disability to have access to, participate in, or advance in employment or to undergo training, unless such measures would impose a disproportionate burden on the employer. This burden shall not be disproportionate when it is sufficiently remedied by measures existing within the framework of the disability policy of the Member State concerned.

[13.193] The Employment Equality Act contains detailed provisions in s 16 as to what is required by 'reasonable accommodation'. The section commences with an affirmation that nothing in the Act will be construed as requiring any person to recruit or promote an individual to a position or to retain them in a position if they are not or are no longer fully competent and able to undertake the duties attached to the position.[405] The section then goes on to provide the definition of 'fully competent':

> (3)(a)   For the purpose of this Act a person with a disability is fully competent to undertake and fully capable of undertaking, any duties if the person would be so

---

[403] Barnard, *EC Employment Law* (3rd edn, Oxford University Press, 2006) p 393.

[404] Council Directive 2000/78/EC ([2000] L303/16) establishing a general framework for equal treatment in employment and occupation.

[405] Employment Equality Acts 1998–2008, s 16(1).

fully competent and capable on reasonable accommodation (in this subsection referred to as 'appropriate measures') being provided by the person's employer.

Section 16(3)(b) provides the circumstances in relation to which the employer must take appropriate measures:

> The employer shall take appropriate measures, where needed in a particular case, to enable a person who has a disability–
>
> (i)   to have access to employment, or
>
> (ii)   to participate or advance in employment, or
>
> (iii)   to undergo training,
>
> unless the measures would impose a disproportionate burden on the employer.

The question of what is a 'disproportionate burden' is assessed taking into account financial and other costs, the scale and financial resources of an employer's business and the possibility of obtaining public funding or assistance.[406]

[13.194] Section 16(4) defines 'appropriate measures':

> 'appropriate measures' in relation to a person with a disability–
>
> (a)   means effective and practical measures, where needed in a particular case, to adapt the employer's place of business to the disability concerned,
>
> (b)   without prejudice to the generality of paragraph (a), includes, the adaptation of premises and equipment, patterns of working time, distribution of tasks or the provision of training or integration resources, but
>
> (c)   does not include any treatment, facility or thing that the person might ordinarily or reasonably provide for himself or herself;

'Appropriate measures' are not simply physical adaptation of the premises but also may involve changes in working patterns. The provision of appropriate rest breaks might be required in certain circumstances.

[13.195] Section 35(1) permits an employer to provide, for an employee with a disability, a particular rate of remuneration for work of a particular description if, by reason of the disability, the amount of that work done by the employee is less than the amount of similar work done, or which could reasonably be expected to be done, by a person without the disability.

Scope of 'disability'

[13.196] The ECJ as well as the Irish courts and tribunals have taken a very broad view of disability. It has been held to include a temporary malfunction due to physical injury in the shoulder, back and neck after a road traffic accident;[407] a period of hospitalisation

---

[406] Employment Equality Acts 1998–2008, s 16(3)(c).

[407] *Customer Perception v Leydon* [2004] 15 ELR 101.

after a kidney infection;[408] alcoholism;[409] acute anxiety and stress attributed to work related stress and depression[410] and diabetes.[411]

[13.197] Disability includes a condition which is imputed to a person which they don't necessarily have. This can be seen in *HSE Employee v HSE*[412] where a nurse complained that she was discriminated against in being denied access to a post of staff nurse on the grounds that she had not satisfied the standards necessary relative to the functional requirements of the post because of her weight. The HSE stated that it had not discriminated against the complainant and that it was acting on specialist medical advice that the nurse had an increased risk of illness because of her weight. The Equality Tribunal found that the HSE had imputed a disability to the complainant without carrying out a risk assessment and without communicating directly with the complainant about the situation and had discriminated against the employee based on this imputed disability.[413] A finding of discrimination was made and compensation of €3,000 was awarded. In addition, the Equality Officer ordered that the complainant's appointment be backdated to the date on which the health clearance was deferred and also that she be paid back salary from this date. The remedy awarded was of far greater value to the employee than the compensation awarded.

[13.198] The scope of disability has recently been extended by the ECJ to include workers with disabled dependants. In the recent decision in *Coleman v Attridge Law*,[414] the ECJ held that the Framework Directive[415] and, in particular Arts 1, 2(1) and (2)(a) of the Directive, must be interpreted as meaning that the prohibition of direct discrimination in these provisions is not limited to people who are themselves disabled. Where an employer treats an employee who is not disabled less favourably than another employee is, has been or would be treated in a comparable situation, and it is established that the less favourable treatment of that employee is based on the disability of his child whose care is provided primarily by that employee, such treatment is contrary to the prohibition on direct discrimination laid down by Art 2(2)(a).

The case involved the allegation by Ms Coleman that she had been treated less favourably than other employees because she was the primary carer of a disabled child. She claimed that that treatment had caused her to stop working for her former employer.

---

408 *Fernandez v Cable & Wireless* DEC-E2002-052 (Equality Tribunal).

409 *Government Department v An Employee* EDA 062/2006 (Labour Court).

410 *A Prison Officer v The Minister for Justice, Equality & Law Reform* DEC-2007-025 (Equality Tribunal).

411 *Cascella & Anor t/a Donatellos v A Worker* [2005] 16 ELR 282.

412 *HSE Employee v HSE* DEC-E2006-013 (Equality Tribunal).

413 Hedigan J in *Eagle Star Life Assurance Company of Ireland Ltd v The Director of the Equality Tribunal and others* (18 March 2009, unreported) HC remarked, after examining the medical definition of disability, rather than whether it is an imputed disability that there 'can be no doubt but that it is questionable whether a particularly high body mass index falls within any of the categories listed in that section'.

414 Case C-303/06 *Coleman v Attridge Law* [2008] ICR 1128.

415 Council Directive 2000/78/EC ([2000] L303/16) establishing a general framework for equal treatment in employment and occupation.

of disadvantageous treatment of her due to her taking time off because of her disabled child, such that she felt she had to leave her employment. This was essentially a constructive dismissal case under UK law. The evidence that Ms Coleman gave was that she had been treated consistently worse than other employees who had taken similar amounts of time off and in refusing to allow her the same flexibility as regards her working hours and working conditions as those of her colleagues who were parents of non-disabled children. She claimed that abusive and insulting comments had been made about both her and her and her child. The ECJ was careful to limit discrimination by association to direct discrimination and harassment.[416] It pointed out that the obligation to take appropriate measures is confined to the employee who is disabled. Nevertheless the decision is of great significance as it will prevent employers from treating those with disabled dependants less favourably than those with non-disabled dependents.[417]

The appropriate comparator

[13.199] The issue of the appropriate comparator may be a difficult one. It is for the complainant to compare themselves to an able-bodied person or somebody with a different type of disability or to an able-bodied person with some other impediment which prevents them from doing the particular task or job required. The difficulties can be seen in the case of *Minister for Education and Science v A Worker*.[418] The complainant, a teacher, was suffering from a serious illness requiring transplant surgery. The illness, both parties agreed, constituted a disability under the Employment Equality Act. During the entire school year from August 2001 until May 2002 the complainant was suffering from the disability and was absent and was, therefore, unable to perform her voluntary supervisory or indeed any duties. A lump sum payment was to be paid to employees certified as having carried out voluntary supervision and substitution. The complainant did not receive payment of the supervisory allowance for the period, although she did receive her salary and other allowances in full in accordance with the Department's sick pay policy. The complainant claimed that the failure to pay her the supervisory allowance while other able-bodied teachers got the allowance constituted discrimination. The Equality Officer found against her and the Labour Court upheld this, stating:

---

[416] Case C-303/06 [2008] ICR 1128 at paras 56 and 63.

[417] Some commentators have pointed out that this affirmation of at least a partial role for discrimination by association should apply to other newer grounds of discrimination such as age discrimination to address the issue of the ever increasing number of employees caring for elderly parents. See Smith, *Harvey on Industrial Relations and Employment Law* (August, 2008) at L(1301-03. See Pilgerstorfer, 'Transferred Discrimination in European Law' [2008] *ILJ* 384 where the author argues that some of the language used both by the Advocate General and the Court indicates that where discrimination is on the basis of one of the grounds within the Framework Directive being attributed to an individual when in fact they are not covered by that ground (for example treated less favourably on the grounds of sexual orientation where the individual is assumed to be gay when in fact they are not), this may amount to discrimination for the purposes of the Framework Directive.

[418] *Minister for Education and Science v A Worker* EDA 087/2008 (Labour Court).

The Complainant has picked as her comparator an able-bodied teacher who was in a position to perform the work and got paid for it. However the requirement is quite clear. To receive payment not alone must the able-bodied teacher be willing to perform the duty, they must be certified as having performed the duty. In the Court's view therefore the only appropriate comparator having the same relevant characteristic as the Complainant is an able-bodied teacher who was willing to do the work but for one reason or another did not do so. Such a person would equally not have been paid, because they did not perform the work in question.

Pre-employment medical

[13.200] In some circumstances it is necessary for an employer to determine the capability of a prospective employee to perform certain duties or to identify what needs to be done to accommodate someone with a disability. A pre-employment medical may facilitate this. In a practical sense it can be advisable to defer pre-employment medicals until the person has actually been offered the job and make such offer subject to satisfactory completion of a pre-employment medical. Otherwise an employer will run the practical risk of being accused of using a pre-employment medical as a screening process. In *Ms X v An Electronic Component Company*[419] the Equality Officer had to consider the appropriateness of pre-employment medicals in the employment arena. The Equality Officer determined that the operation of pre-employment medical examinations or questionnaires is not *per se* unlawful. The Equality Officer did acknowledge that in some circumstances a medical examination is hugely necessary for an employer as it allows them to determine the capability of a prospective employee to perform certain duties or to examine what needs to be done to accommodate someone with a disability and those mechanisms facilitate this determination. However, the Equality Officer did warn that employers should exercise caution when using the information obtained from such medical assessments so as not to fall foul of employment equality legislation.

Reasonable accommodation[420]

[13.201] Despite the detailed provisions in s 16 of the Employment Equality Act, it is not easy to assess in advance what 'reasonable accommodation' is required and what is meant by 'disproportionate burden'. Case law provides some guidance on the interpretation of these terms. Ultimately, the courts and tribunals will be guided by a general sense of what is reasonable. The ECJ has held that the obligation to take 'appropriate measures' applies only to the disabled person and does not cover imputed disabilities.[421]

[13.202] In the Labour Court decision in *A Government Department v An Employee*,[422] the complainant was employed as a clerical officer in the civil service. She suffered

---

[419] *Ms X v An Electronic Component Company* DEC-E2006-042 (Equality Tribunal).
[420] See generally Waddington and Hendricks, 'The Expanding Concept of Employment Discrimination in Europe: From Direct and Discrimination to Reasonable Accommodation Discrimination', (2002) *International Journal of Comparative Labour Law and Industrial Relations* 403, and Waddingon, 'Reasonable Accommodation' in Schiek, Waddington and Bell, *Cases, Materials and Text on National, Supranational and International Non-Discrimination Law* (Hart Publishing, 2007).
[421] Case C-303/06 *Coleman v Attridge Law* [2008] ICR 1128 at para 42.

from a serious eye condition, which constituted a disability under the Employment Equality Act. Because of the disability, the complainant was unable to use a VDU on a computer and she performed non-computerised manual work only. From 1994 onwards the work of the Department became computerised and the complainant became confined to a limited range of functions which could be undertaken manually. This in turn progressively restricted the range of experience available to the complainant in the different duties and tasks involved in running the local office. The amount of manual work available to the complainant continued to diminish over time. In 2002, a vacancy arose for a staff officer which was to be filled by the most senior suitable candidate. The complainant was the most senior candidate. However in the selection process the complainant's manager decided that the complainant did not have the necessary qualities or experience to be promoted. The complainant was not appointed to the post. An agreement was in place between the trade unions representing civil servants and the civil service management which provided that where it was apprehended that an officer's performance might be such as to render them unsuitable for promotion, the officer would be notified not later than 12 months before the officer would ordinarily be considered for promotion. The complainant was not so informed.

The Labour Court, in finding that the complainant had been discriminated against on the disability ground held:

> The difficulties in finding useful work for the Complainant and her resulting failure to accrue experience commensurate with her length of service were a consequence which were noted from her disability. The Respondent should have anticipated the likely impact which those consequences would have on the Complainant's promotional prospects. Against that background the Respondent had a duty under Section 16(3)(b) of the Act to assess the Complainant's position and to at least consider, in consultation with her, what if any alleviating measures could be put in place. The Respondent's failure to do so negates any direct or indirect reliance which it can now place on her lack of capacity to justify the decision not to recommend her for promotion.

The obligation to provide reasonable accommodation can only be properly satisfied where an employer has done some sort of an assessment, whether that is medical, ergonomic or occupational, in order to see whether reasonable accommodation can be made. Assumptions that there is nothing to be done or a failure to take any action will more than likely lead to a finding that reasonable accommodation has not been made. On the other hand, an employer who actually engages in the process of the medical or ergonomic assessment and then finds that there is nothing which can be done or there is nothing which can be done at a reasonable cost is more likely to be able to avail of the defences in s16(3).

[13.203] The obligation to make reasonable accommodation was very clear in one of the few cases to reach the Circuit Court, *Humphries v Westwood Fitness Club*.[423] The claimant suffered from anorexia and/or an eating disorder and was employed as a child-care worker in a crèche run by Westwood Fitness Club. It appeared that initially the employer had been reasonably accommodating in keeping her job open when she was

---

[422] *A Government Department v An Employee* EDA 061/2006 (Labour Court).

[423] *Humphries v Westwood Fitness Club* [2004] 15 ELR 296.

hospitalised from time to time and in allowing her time off to meet medical appointments. Ultimately the employer dismissed her on the basis that she was not fit for work due to her condition. In finding that Westwood Fitness Club had discriminated against Ms Humphreys on grounds of disability, the Labour Court examined the nature and extent of the enquiries which an employer should take prior to the dismissal of an employee on this ground. It stated:

> At a minimum … an employer, should ensure that he or she is in full possession of all the material facts concerning the employee's condition and that the employee is given fair notice that the question of his or her dismissal for the incapacity is being considered. The employee must also be allowed an opportunity to influence the employer's decision.
>
> In practical terms this will normally require a two stage enquiry which looks firstly at the factual position concerning the employee's capability including a degree of impairment arising from the disability and its likely duration. This would involve looking at the medical evidence available to the employer from either the employee's doctors or obtained independently.
>
> Secondly if it is apparent that the employee is not fully capable, Section 16 (3) of the Act requires the employer to consider what if any special treatment or facilities may be available whereby the employee can become fully capable. The section requires that the cost of such special treatment or facilities must also be considered. Here, what constitutes nominal cost will depend on the size of the organisation and its financial resources.[424]

The determination of the Labour Court was confirmed on appeal to the Circuit Court by Dunne J who took the view that an employer has a legal obligation under the Employment Equality Act to take appropriate medical advice before taking a decision to dismiss an employee or in deciding whether reasonable accommodation could be made whereby the employee could be kept on.[425]

[13.204] Reasonable accommodation was considered briefly by the ECJ in *Chacon Navas v Eurest Colectividades SA*.[426] In October 2003 the applicant was certified as unfit for work on medical grounds and began receiving temporary incapacity benefits. In May 2004, she was given notice of her dismissal without any reasons. Spanish law distinguishes between 'unlawful dismissal' and 'void dismissal'. Dismissal because of disability is a void dismissal and the worker is entitled to a immediate reinstatement and back pay. By contrast, in cases of unlawful dismissal the worker is only entitled to compensation for the loss of employment. The applicant was offered compensation for her dismissal. She challenged her dismissal as discriminatory as she had been on leave of absence and temporarily unfit for work for eight months. The Spanish Court asked the ECJ for its view on the relationship between sickness and disability and whether sickness was subsumed into disability for the purposes of the Framework Directive. In addressing this issue, the ECJ considered the role which the obligation of reasonable

---

[424] [2004] 15 ELR 296 at 300–3001.

[425] See also *A Government Department v An Employee* EDA 061/2006 (Labour Court); McCrory *Scaffolding (NI) Ltd v A Worker* EED 055/2005 (Labour Court); *An Employee v A Worker* [2005] ELR 159; *Mr A v A Government Department* DEC-E2008/23 (Equality Tribunal); and *A Worker (Mr O) v An Employer (No 1)* [2005] 16 ELR 113.

[426] Case C-13/05 *Navas v Eurest Colectividades SA*.

accommodation has in protecting an individual with a disability from dismissal. The ECJ held that the Framework Directive prohibits dismissal of a disabled employee where following the making of reasonable accommodation they are competent and capable of performing the essential functions of the job.[427]

[13.205] Reasonable accommodation is also required at the interview stage.[428] The duty to provide reasonable accommodation is a proactive duty. This was clear in the case of *Mr A v A Government Department*.[429] This case involved a civil servant who had fractured his spine in an accident. This resulted in a disability that prevented him from sitting uninterruptedly for more than an hour or undertaking long journeys by car or aeroplane. Following a long period of absence, he had been certified as fit to return to work full-time provided his work did not entail car travel on a more than intermittent basis. The difficulty was that Mr A's role required a significant amount of car travel, in particular by way of a commute from his home to his place of work. Despite his being certified as fit to work on 7 February 2007, it was not until three and a half months later, approximately six weeks after Mr A had lodged his complaint of discrimination with the Equality Tribunal, that a meeting took place between Mr A and his supervisor to consider the options for him. The Equality Tribunal emphasised that the duty to provide special treatment or facilities is proactive and that the respondent Government Department had failed to fulfil this duty.

Disability and dismissal

[13.206] Section 16(1) of the Employment Equality Act provides:

> Nothing in this Act shall be construed as requiring any person to recruit, or promote an individual to a position, to retain an individual in a position or to provide training or experience to an individual in relation to a position, if the individual-...
>
> (b)   Is not (or, as the case may be, is no longer) fully competent and available to undertake, and fully capable of undertaking, the duties attached to that position, having regard to the conditions under which those duties are, or may be required to be, performed.

This provision carries with it as its logical conclusion the right of an employer to dismiss somebody if they are not capable of doing the job. This is a potentially very broad and complicated area as most ordinary illnesses falling within the scope of disability will come under the provisions of the Employment Equality Act. The Employment Equality Act also provides for an independent cause of action of discriminatory dismissal.[430] What is clear, as follows on from the statements in *Humphreys v Westwood Fitness Club*,[431] is that if an employer wishes to dismiss an employee on the basis they are not fully capable of performing the duties, the employer must get the full facts and a medical opinion in order to ascertain the employee's capability, including the degree of

---

[427] Case C-13/05 at para 52.
[428] *Harrington v East Coast Area Health Board* DEC-E2002-001 (Equality Tribunal).
[429] *Mr A v A Government Department* DEC-E2008-23 (Equality Tribunal).
[430] Employment Equality Acts 1998–2008, s 77.
[431] *Humphreys v Westwood Fitness Club* [2004] 15 ELR 296.

impairment and its likely duration and whether any specialist treatment or facilities would overcome any such impairment.[432]

[13.207] Section 35(1) of the Employment Equality Act provides:

Nothing in this Part or Part II shall make it unlawful for an employer to provide, for an employee with a disability, a particular rate or remuneration for work of a particular description if, by reason of the disability, the amount of that work done by the employee during a particular period is less than the amount of a similar work done, or which could reasonably be expected to be done, during that period by an employee without the disability.

Section 35(4) provides that references in this section to rates of remuneration are to rates which are not be below the national minimum wage. Nevertheless, section 35(1) clearly allows an employer to pay a disabled employee less on the basis that he or she is not doing the same amount of work as an able bodied employee. It is hard to know on balance whether or not this is a provision which is of benefit or detriment to those with a disability. Clearly an employer will argue that it does merit the employment of people with disabilities to be paid an economic wage. This may ultimately result in more people with disabilities being employed. On the other hand there is a possibility that this provision may be used to exploit those with disabilities.

Section 35(2) allows for positive treatment of those with disabilities. However this positive treatment is limited to the provision of special treatment or facilities to allow a person to undertake vocational training of a particular kind to allow an employer to provide a person with a disability with training or a working environment due to their disability or for an employer to assist a person with a disability in relation to vocational training or work. This is a narrow permission to provide positive discrimination and is tied into special treatment related in particular to facilitating training or selection processes. If any special treatment is provided to a person with a disability then that special treatment cannot be alleged to be discriminatory by somebody who has not got that disability.

[13.208] Section 35(3) provides that where, by virtue of s 35(1) or s 35(2), a person with a disability receives a particular rate of remuneration or special treatment, a person with a different disability or without a disability shall not be entitled to that special rate or facility. This section copper fastens the idea that such special treatment is permissible different treatment as a person with a disability may not be able to perform the same job or perform it in the same way without either being paid differently or being given special treatment or facilities.

Exceptions

[13.209] There are a number of additional exceptions to the prohibition of discrimination on the disability ground. These are contained in ss 35 and 36 of the Employment Equality Act. Section 36(4) of the Employment Equality Act provides:

---

[432] See also *An Employee v A Third Level Educational Institution* DEC-E2006-009 (Equality Tribunal).

Nothing in this Part or Part II shall make it unlawful to require, in relation to a particular post –

(a)   the holding of a specified educational, technical or professional qualification which is a generally accepted qualification in the State for posts of that description, or

(b)   the production and evaluation of information about any qualification other than such a specified qualification.'

Similarly s 36(5) provides:

Nothing in this Part or Part II shall make it unlawful for a body controlling the entry to, or carrying on of, a profession, vocation or occupation to require a person carrying on or wishing to enter that profession, vocation or occupation to hold a specified educational, technical or other qualification which is appropriate in the circumstances.

[13.210] The exception at s 36(4) was successfully relied upon by the employer in *Office of the Civil Service and Local Appointments Commissioners v Gorry*,[433] Mr Gorry, a tax official in the office of the Revenue Commissioners, claimed that the respondent's application of an educational requirement to him constituted indirect discrimination on the disability ground. The respondent had excluded Mr Gorry from consideration for appointment to the grade of Executive Officer in the civil service because he had not passed English in his Leaving Certificate. The eligibility criteria for the post included a requirement that candidates obtained a pass in English or Irish in the Leaving Certificate examination (or its equivalent). Mr Gorry had not met this requirement. Mr Gorry suffered from dyslexia and contended that his failure to pass the English exam was due to that condition. His claim was investigated by the Equality Tribunal which found against him. Mr Gorry appealed to the Labour Court. Mr Gorry argued that the educational recruitment was indirectly discriminatory on the disability ground as it was one which could be complied with by a substantially smaller proportion of persons with dyslexia than those who did not have dyslexia.

The Labour Court held that even assuming that the disability of dyslexia would mean that fewer persons could meet that educational requirement, s 36(4) provided a complete defence to a claim of indirect discrimination grounded on the imposition of the educational requirement provided that the educational requirement was one which was generally accepted for posts of that description within the State. It noted that the stipulation of educational qualifications is an established feature of recruitment practice in Ireland and elsewhere and is a generally accepted means of providing a basic objective indicator of suitability for a large range of positions and occupations. In s 36(4), the Court considered, the Oireachtas must have intended to remove from the purview of the Employment Equality Act criteria in the nature of educational, technical or professional qualifications generally regarded as necessary for posts of a particular category.[434]

---

[433]   *Office of the Civil Service and Local Appointments Commissioners v Gorry* EDA 0614/2006 (Labour Court).

[434]   For a more detailed examination of *Gorry* and the s 36 exception see Smith, 'Side-Stepping Equality: Disability Discrimination and 'Generally Accepted Qualifications' [2008] 15(1) *DULJ* 279.

Section 36(5) has not yet been litigated but one could see that similar considerations could be applicable to bodies regulating or controlling entry into professions. For example, if a disability impacted on the ability of a person to pass exams or training requirements, following *Office of the Civil Service on Local Appointments Commissioners v Gorry*[435] a court may have some sympathy for the regulatory body and give an exemption from the prohibition against discrimination on the disability ground and allow the body insist upon the passing of the exam.

REDRESS UNDER THE EMPLOYMENT EQUALITY ACT

[13.211] Section 82(1) of the Employment Equality Act provides for the redress which may be ordered by the Equality Tribunal:

> Subject to this section, the types of redress for which a decision of the Director under section 79 [investigation of case by Equality Tribunal] may provide are such one or more of the following as may be appropriate in the circumstances of the particular case:
>
> (a) an order for compensation in the form of arrears of remuneration (attributable to a failure to provide equal remuneration) in respect of so much of the period of employment as begins not more than 3 years before the date of the referral under section 77(1) [claim of discrimination, discriminatory dismissal, victimisation or equal pay] which led to the decision;
>
> (b) an order for equal remuneration from the date referred to in paragraph (a);
>
> (c) an order for compensation for the effects of acts of discrimination or victimisation which occurred not earlier than 6 years before the date of the referral of the case under section 77;
>
> (d) an order for equal treatment in whatever respect is relevant to the case;
>
> (e) an order that a person or persons specified in the order take a course of action which is so specified;
>
> (f) an order for re-instatement or re-engagement with or without an order for compensation.

The level of awards and the permissibility of parallel claims are considered here. On practice and procedure before the Equality Tribunal, Labour Court and Circuit Court, see Ch 22, Practice and Procedure in Employment Law.

Level of awards

Equality Tribunal

[13.212] Where the Tribunal finds that there has been discrimination, the Tribunal may require that a particular course of action be taken[436] and/or make an award:[437]

---

[435] *Office of the Civil Service on Local Appointments Commissioners v Gorry* EDA 40614/2004 (Labour Court).
[436] Employment Equality Acts 1998–2008, s 82 (1)(e).
[437] Employment Equality Acts 1998–2008, s 82.

- In an equal pay case, it can award equal pay and up to three years' arrears of pay from the date of the claim;[438]

- In other cases, equal treatment and compensation of up to a maximum of two years' pay (or €12,697 where the person was not in receipt of remuneration at the time of referral of the claim).[439]

In gender equality cases the Tribunal may award interest on any compensation awarded.[440]

In practice, awards are not commonly made of two years' pay. Awards are not linked to loss of wages but can taken into account distress suffered.[441] In its jurisprudence the ECJ has repeatedly stated that the remedy decided upon by a Member States to penalise discrimination between men and women, where it is compensation, that compensation must be such as to guarantee real and effective judicial protection, have a real deterrent effect on the employer and must in any event be adequate to the damage claimed.[442] By implication, these principles would appear to apply to other forms of discrimination as well. In *Fagan v The Revenue Commissioners*[443] the Equality Officer noted that the Framework Directive[444] requires that sanctions for infringement of the principle of equal treatment are to be effective, proportionate and dissuasive and on that basis a high level of compensation was awarded. A similar view on sanctions was expressed by the Equality Officer in *Kavanagh v Aviance UK Ltd*.[445]

[13.213] A perusal of the case law shows that the levels of awards have been in the following range:

- on average €3,000–€5,000 for discrimination in access to employment or promotion, sometimes accompanied by appointment to the position or promotion to the position;

- for discrimination, €15,000–€20,000;

- for more serious cases of discrimination €30,000 upwards;

- discriminatory dismissal: in the range of €7,000–€60,000 depending on salary; and

- where victimisation is involved, awards are higher, between €40,000 and €120,000 as this is seen as a deliberate attempt by employers to prevent the operation of the equality legislation.

---

[438] Employment Equality Acts 1998–2008, s 82(1)(a).

[439] Employment Equality Acts 1998–2008, ss 82(1)(b), 82(1)(c), 82(1)(d) and 82(4).

[440] Employment Equality Acts 1998–2008, s 82(5).

[441] Employment Equality Acts 1998–2008, s 82(1)(c).

[442] See, for example, Case C-14/83 *Von Colson v Land Nordrhein-Westfalen* [1984] ECR 1891 and Case C-271/91 *Marshall v Southampton & SW Hants AHA* [1993] ECR I-4367.

[443] *Fagan v The Revenue Commissioners* DEC-E2008-004.

[444] Council Directive 2000/78/EC establishing a general framework for equal treatment in employment and occupation.

[445] *Kavanagh v Aviance UK Ltd* DEC E2007-039 (Equality Tribunal).

One of the highest awards ever was made in *McGinn v Board of Management St Anthony's Boys National School*[446] where €10,000 for discrimination and €117,000 plus interest was awarded for victimisation. The Equality Officer stated that it was the worst case of victimisation she had seen.

[13.214] Amounts for discriminatory dismissal can be based on loss of salary, but not necessarily so. This is apparent from *Kavanagh v Aviance UK Ltd.*[447] In that case, which involved both discrimination and discriminatory dismissal, the Equality Tribunal decided as follows:

> In the circumstances of the above and in accordance with Section 82 of the Employment Equality Acts 1998–2004 I hereby order that
>
> – Aviance Limited pay Mr Kavanagh the sum of €65,000 in respect of loss of earnings due to the discriminatory dismissal. Mr Kavanagh's annual salary (including shift pay) was in excess of €33,000.
>
> – Aviance Limited pay Mr Kavanagh the sum of €60,000 by way of compensation for the stress suffered as a result of the discrimination and the failure to provide reasonable accommodation. The amount of this award is to reflect the fact that Mr Kavanagh had every expectation of continuing in this employment and the difficulty he has since encountered in obtaining alternative employment. It is also in accordance with Article 17 of the Framework Directive, which states 'sanctions must be effective, proportionate and dissuasive'.

On the other hand, as little as €7,000 was awarded for discriminatory dismissal in *Wynne v Irish Crane & Lifting Ltd.*[448] The award seemed to have little relation to loss of earnings. The complainant was laid off due to a downturn in business, which appears to have been a genuine reason on the part of the employer, but was done on a discriminatory basis due to the age of the complainant, in circumstances where the complainant had only been working a short time. The complainant was on a wage of €15.50 per hour.

The Equality Tribunal can make separate awards for discriminatory dismissal and discrimination, even where this arises out of the same set of facts.[449] Thus in *Kavanagh v Aviance UK Ltd,*[450] the complainant got the maximum of two years' salary for *both* heads of the complaint.

Circuit Court

[13.215] When a gender equality case is commenced in the Circuit Court, that Court is not constrained by the normal jurisdictional limits, and may order any of the forms of redress set out above in para **[13.211]** in relation to the Equality Tribunal. The only limitation is a six-year limit on backdating of compensation or arrears of

---

[446] *McGinn v Board of Management St Anthony's Boys National School* DEC-E2004-032 (Equality Tribunal).

[447] *Kavanagh v Aviance UK Ltd* DEC E2007-039 (Equality Tribunal).

[448] *Wynne v Irish Crane & Lifting Ltd* DEC E2007-42 (Equality Tribunal).

[449] See the reasoning of the Equality Tribunal on this point in *Kavanagh v Aviance UK Ltd* DEC E2007-039.

[450] *Kavanagh v Aviance UK Ltd* DEC E2007-039.

remuneration.[451] Gender equality cases are the only ones which can be commenced directly before the Circuit Court.

The Circuit Court has made high awards under the Acts. For example, in *Atkinson v Carty*,[452] which was a serious case of sexual harassment, Delahunt J made an award of €137,000 less 25% for contributory negligence.

Labour Court

[13.216] The Labour Court, on appeal, has the power to vary the determination of the Equality Officer as to the level of award.[453] The Labour Court has also confirmed that in measuring the quantum of damages, regard must be had to all of the effects of discrimination, and not just for financial loss but also for distress and indignity suffered.[454]

In *Ntoko v Citibank*,[455] a case of race discrimination and dismissal, in considering the level of award, the Labour Court stated:

> The Court is satisfied that the appropriate redress is an award of compensation. The Court notes that the complainant was employed in a temporary capacity at approximately €270 per week. The Court estimates that the economic loss suffered by the complainant is unlikely to have exceeded €2,000. However, it is now well settled that an award of compensation for the effects of discrimination must be proportionate, effective and dissuasive. Apart from economic loss the complainant was humiliated, deprived of his fundamental right to equal treatment and freedom from racial prejudice. In all the circumstances the Court determines that an award which is fair and equitable should be measured at €15,000, €2,000 of which should be regarded as compensation for loss of earnings. The respondent herein is ordered to pay compensation to the complainant in that amount.

Orders made by Equality Tribunal and Labour Court

[13.217] The Employment Equality Act empowers the Equality Tribunal, Labour Court and Circuit Court to make an order that a person or persons specified in the order take a specific course of action.[456] In some instances, this order can be more beneficial than an award of compensation. For example, an employer can be ordered to pay back pay to an employee, appoint an employee to a particular position from a specified date or put a particular policy in place in its workplace. It is common for both the Equality Tribunal and the Labour Court to make orders which can be burdensome for employers to implement. For example, it is particularly common for an employer to be ordered to implement a particular policy in order to prevent similar discrimination from occurring in the future. The respondent employer in *A Manager of an English Language School v*

---

[451] Employment Equality Acts 1998–2008, s 82(c).
[452] *Atkinson v Carty* [2005] ELR 1.
[453] Employment Equality Acts 1998–2008, s 83(4).
[454] *Fox v Lee* DEE 6/2003, *Citibank v Ntoko* [2004] ELR 116 referred to in Kerr, *Consolidated Irish Employment Legislation* (Thomson Round Hall, Release 19, April 2008), Division L, para LB.257.
[455] *Ntoko v Citibank* [2004] ELR 116.
[456] Employment Equality Acts 1998–2008, ss 82(1)(e) and 82(3)(c).

An Institute of Technology[457] was ordered to draft a policy on the prevention of harassment and sexual harassment in the workplace and to take appropriate measures to communicate this to all employees.

[13.218] The burdensome and costly nature of an order of an Equality Officer was appealed by the employer to the Labour Court in *A Distribution Company v A Worker*.[458] At first instance, the Equality Officer found that the complainant had been discriminated against on the disability ground and awarded him €4,000 in compensation. The Equality Officer further ordered the respondent to arrange training seminars for all staff, within six months, to brief them on the provisions of the Employment Equality Act. The respondent appealed this aspect of the decision only.

The respondent told the Labour Court that it had arrangements in place by which information concerning the rights and responsibilities of employers and employees under the Employment Equality Act was disseminated and provided details to the Labour Court. However, it told the Labour Court that the cost of arranging seminars for all staff within six months to inform them of the provisions of the Employment Equality Act would be €153,600 at a time when it was incurring serious trading losses.

The Labour Court held that it was satisfied that adequate arrangements were already in place within the employment whereby management and staff of the respondent were made aware of their rights and responsibilities under equality legislation. It determined that in light of:

> these circumstances, and having regard to the costs involved, the Court is satisfied that the training requirement ordered by the Equality Officer would place an unnecessary and disproportionate burden on the respondent. Accordingly, the Court is satisfied that the respondent is entitled to succeed in its appeal.

Therefore it ordered that the decision of the Equality Officer be amended so that the requirement for the respondent employer to arrange seminars for all staff within six months in order that they be briefed on the provisions of the Employment Equality Act be deleted.

[13.219] Although the Circuit Court decision in *Dublin City Council v Deans*[459] relates to an appeal under the Equal Status Act 2000, it is still interesting as it demonstrates clearly that far reaching and unduly burdensome orders made by Equality Officers are likely to be overturned by Judges. In this case Judge Hunt in the Circuit Court overturned the decision of the Equality Officer that ordered Dublin City Council to revise the provisions of its scheme of priority in relation to disabled persons and to broaden the allocation criteria for housing units to take account of applicant's disability. Judge Hunt stated that he was:

> not happy with the broad spread of the order made in this particular case. It is for the City Council to maintain and operate its housing plan, to exercise its discretion in that regard and to provide reasonable accommodation on a case by case basis on an application made by a person to it for reasonable accommodation.

---

[457] *A Manager of an English Language School v An Institute of Technology* DEC-E2007-019.
[458] *A Distribution Company v A Worker* EDA 0414.
[459] *Dublin City Council v Deans* (15 April 2008) Circuit Court (Hunt J).

PARALLEL CLAIMS

Part-time workers' and fixed-term workers' legislation

[13.220] A litigant may not obtain relief in respect of discrimination under both the Employment Equality Act and the Protection of Employees (Part-Time Work) Act 2001 or the Protection of Employees (Fixed-Term Work) Act 2003.[460] There does not however appear to be anything to prevent two separate claims being processed. This is considered further in Ch, 9, Part-Time Workders, at para **[9.51]** and in Ch 10, Fixed-Term Workders at paras **[10.76]–[10.78]**.

Unfair dismissal and common law claims

[13.221] The interaction between unfair dismissal and discriminatory dismissal claims on the one hand, and discrimination and personal injuries on the other is unclear. Section 101 of the Employment Equality Act attempts to provide for the situation where parallel claims are brought, but the section is far from clear. It provides as follows:

(1) If an individual has instituted proceedings for damages at common law in respect of a failure, by an employer or any other person, to comply with an equal remuneration term or an equality clause, then, if the hearing of the case has begun, the individual may not seek redress (or exercise any other power) under this Part in respect of the failure to comply with the equal remuneration term or the equality clause, as the case may be.

(2) Where an individual has referred a case to the Director under section 77(1) and either a settlement has been reached by mediation or the Director has begun an investigation under section 79, the individual—

(a)   shall not be entitled to recover damages at common law in respect of the case, and

(b)   if he or she was dismissed before so referring the case, shall not be entitled to seek redress (or to exercise, or continue to exercise, any other power) under the Unfair Dismissals Acts 1977–2001 in respect of the dismissal, unless the Director, having completed the investigation and in an appropriate case, directs otherwise and so notifies the complainant and respondent.

(3) If an individual has referred a case to the Circuit Court under section 77(3) in respect of such a failure as is mentioned in subsection (1), the individual shall not be entitled to recover damages at common law in respect of that failure.

(4) An employee who has been dismissed shall not be entitled to seek redress under this Part if—

(a)   the employee has instituted proceedings for damages at common law for wrongful dismissal and the hearing of the case has begun,

(b)   in the exercise of powers under the Unfair Dismissals Acts 1977–2001, a Rights Commissioner has issued a recommendation in respect of the dismissal, or

(c)   the Employment Appeals Tribunal has begun a hearing into the matter of the dismissal.

---

[460] Employment Equality Acts 1998–2008, s 101A.

The effect of these provisions is that, while a litigant would not appear to be prevented from commencing claims at both common law and before the tribunal, once a hearing has commenced in one, any action to seek relief in the other must come to a halt, and relief cannot be granted in the other. It is open to question what the position would be where an employee seeks to obtain damages for personal injuries arising out of a breach of an equality provision in a contract of employment. Breach of contract is increasingly pleaded in personal injuries action either in addition to or instead of negligence.

[13.222] The position is similar where the employee has been dismissed for a discriminatory reason which might also constitute an unfair dismissal.[461] There is a discretionary power to permit the claimant to proceed under the unfair dismissals legislation even though the Tribunal investigation has been completed.[462] This may be to allow for the situation where the Tribunal is of the opinion that the respondent may have unfairly dismissed a complainant but has not been found to have dismissed the claimant for a discriminatory reason.

In *Cullen v Connaught Gold Ltd*,[463] the Employment Appeals Tribunal was asked to determine whether the claimant could proceed before the Employment Appeals Tribunal in her claim for unfair dismissal where she had also lodged a claim with the Equality Tribunal. No hearing had commenced before the Equality Tribunal although written submissions had been lodged. The Employment Appeals Tribunal declined jurisdiction and forced the claimant to continue her case before the Equality Tribunal as it found that the investigation before the Equality Tribunal had begun by virtue of the lodging of written submissions. The decision of the Employment Appeals Tribunal was successfully judicially reviewed by Mr Cullen.[464]

CONCLUSIONS

[13.223] It will be clear from the above chapter that employment equality is a complex area of law with its own particular concepts, such as objective justification and indirect discrimination, and its own practices, such as the shifting burden of proof. Many of the concepts and practices have their origin in the first attempts of the ECJ to work out a jurisprudence in the area of equal pay and equal treatment for women. The success of the legal concepts has lead to their extension to the new grounds of discrimination, but also to other types of employment equality not covered in this chapter, such as the protection of fixed-term workers and part-time workers.

Employment equality jurisprudence still has its conceptual challenges and limitations however, of which two are worth highlighting, both in the area of equal pay. First, there is a lack of a right to proportionate pay if an employee is doing work which is proportionate in value to that of a comparator but is grossly underpaid due to the membership of a protected ground. Second, there is a difficulty caused by the firmness

---

[461] Employment Equality Acts 1998–2008, s 101(4).
[462] Employment Equality Acts 1998–2008, s 101(2)(b).
[463] *Cullen v Connaught Gold Ltd* UD787/2006 (EAT).
[464] *Cullen v Employment Appeals Tribunal* (14 April 2008, unreported), HC (O'Neill J).

with which the ECJ has applied the single source test when it comes to ascertaining whether an employee has picked a comparator working for the same or an associated employer. It is worth noting that for fixed term workers, Irish law has hugely extended the range of employers from which a comparator can be chosen from 'an associated employer' to an employee 'working in the same industry or sector'.

In substantive terms there remains a mismatch between Irish law and Community law in two important areas: retirement ages and the definition of disability. In relation to the first, it is likely that s 34(4) of the Employment Equality Act is not in conformity with Community law as the exception permitting the fixing of retirement ages is probably over-generous. In relation to the definition of disability, Irish law is more generous than Community law, and in particular covers illness, whereas the ECJ has attempted to draw a line between ordinary illness and a disability. These conflicts will no doubt be worked out in the future.

[13.224] There is also the issue of adequacy of the grounds of discrimination outlawed by the law. It has been suggested[465] that the legislation should be extended to cover discrimination on four new grounds, namely socio-economic status, trade union membership, a criminal conviction or political opinion. There has been very little political interest shown in extending the grounds in this or any other way. Nevertheless, employment equality law still has the potential for further legislative intervention in the future.

---

[465] 'Extending the Scope of Employment Equality Legislation. Comparative Perspectives on the Prohibited Grounds of Discrimination' (Department of Justice, Equality and Law Reform 2004).

Part VI
Termination of Employment

Chapter 14

Dismissal[1]

Dr Mary Redmond

GENERAL

[14.01] Unfair dismissal is a statutory concept and is to be distinguished from wrongful dismissal at common law. Under the Unfair Dismissals Acts 1977–2007, a dismissing employer must prove the reason or reasons for dismissal and must satisfy a Rights Commissioner or the Employment Appeals Tribunal (EAT) that it had good cause and acted reasonably in all the circumstances. Wrongful dismissal, on the other hand, is dismissal in breach of the contract of employment. If an employer has terminated the contract of employment in accordance with its terms, express or implied, and is not guilty of an unconstitutionality, then irrespective of its motives or of the arbitrary nature of its action, an employee's claim for wrongful dismissal will not succeed.

[14.02] Dismissal of a person whose employment is regulated by statute,[2] to be valid, will depend on the *vires* of the employer in regard to dismissal and/or any limitations upon termination of employment imposed by statute or by regulation. Dismissal in breach of statute will be null and void.

WRONGFUL DISMISSAL

Termination with notice

[14.03] The contract of employment is subject to an implied term allowing it to be terminated by the unilateral act of giving notice. The right to terminate with reasonable notice is separate from the right to terminate the contract summarily in the case of breach by the other side. The principle of termination by reasonable notice was first accepted in *Beeston v Collyer*,[3] but the basic concept was of a contract impliedly for a year. With time, examples of an implied yearly hiring declined and the notion of an implied term as to notice to terminate gained ground. Early Irish cases took the view that whatever reason an employer might have for dismissal, he could always secure his

---

[1] See Redmond, *Dismissal Law in Ireland* (2nd edn, Tottel Publishing, 2007).

[2] Established civil servants hold office under statute: *Gilheaney and Meehan v Revenue Commissioners* [1996] ELR 265; some office-holders may hold office in accordance with terms set out in a contract : *Glover v BLN Ltd* [1973] IR 388. And see *Cahill v Dublin City University* [2007] IEHC 20.

[3] *Beeston v Collyer* (1827) 2 C & P 607, 4 Bing 30.

position by giving reasonable notice.[4] Common law, however, is no longer the sole determinant of the lawfulness of dismissal in Ireland.

[14.04] If an employer gives notice of the length which the contract requires, or the minimum statutory notice, if that is greater, the contract is lawfully terminated. Generally, in the absence of an express term in the contract, or a statutory provision concerning dismissal or custom or practice or where there is no written contract, the law requires that reasonable notice is given. Notice is not required where the contract is frustrated although it is sometimes erroneously thought to be necessary.

[14.05] The question, what is reasonable notice, depends upon a number of things. Most important however, is the status of the employee. For instance, a year's notice has been held appropriate for the managing director of a company. Similarly the Group Credit Controller of an international company has been held entitled to six months' notice as appropriate and reasonable.

Contracts apparently incapable of termination by notice

[14.06] Parties to a contract of employment may make a contract which is apparently incapable of termination by notice. Employment may be described as 'permanent'. If employment is so described by statute, it will generally be possible from the legislation to determine the various incidents attaching to the status. In the case of an ordinary contract of service, a person may be said to be 'permanently' employed when he is employed for an indefinite period on the regular staff of a particular employer, as distinct from persons taken on casually for a temporary or defined period. This does not necessarily mean that such a person has a contract of employment for life. On the other hand a person may be given 'permanent and pensionable' employment where, under his contract, he holds employment for life or for life subject to the right of the employer to dismiss him for misconduct, neglect of duty or unfitness. A particular contract must be construed in the light of the surrounding circumstances and all relevant matters.[5]

Termination by mutual consent

[14.07] Parties may end the contract of employment by mutual consent. For example, when a fixed-term contract expires, the contract automatically comes to an end in accordance with its terms.

Statutory notice

[14.08] In manual and blue-collar employment, the implied period of an employer's notice was not regarded as reasonable by social or economic standards. In 1973 the Minimum Notice and Terms of Employment Act (the 1973 Act) was passed laying down minimum periods of notice for every employee defined therein. The definition of 'employee' excludes self-employed persons and ex-employees. Section 4 provides that where the employee has been employed for at least 13 weeks' continuous service the

---

4   *Carvill v Irish Industrial Bank Ltd* [1986] IR 325; *Riordan v Butler* [1950] IR 347; *Cooper v Millea* [1938] IR 749.

5   *Walsh v The Dublin Health Board* (1964) 98 ILTR 82 following *McClelland v Northern Ireland General Health Services Board* [1957] 2 All ER 129. See similarly *Dooley v Great Southern Hotel* [2001] ELR 340, *Sheehy v Ryan and Moriarty* [2004] 15 ELR 87, [2008] IESC 14.

employer is required to give notice of dismissal which satisfies certain minimum requirements.

Period of Continuous Service	Notice Required
13 weeks to 2 years	Not less than one week
2 years to 5 years	2 weeks
5 years to 10 years	4 weeks
10 years to 15 years	6 weeks
15 years and over	8 weeks

[14.09] According to s 4 of the 1973 Act, the minimum period of notice required of an employee to terminate his contract of employment is, in all cases, not less than one week, provided the employee has been in continuous service for not less than 13 weeks. This statutory period replaces any shorter one specified in the contract but may be displaced by an express contractual requirement of a longer period of notice. Equally custom and practice or any other method of implying better terms may suffice. Withdrawal of an employee's resignation can be done only with the employer's consent.

On termination of employment and provided the parties are in agreement, an employer or an employee may waive their right to notice or an employee may accept payment in lieu of notice.

[14.10] Under s 8, if an employee is dismissed for 'misconduct' he is not entitled to notice or pay in lieu. In *Brewster v Burke and the Minister for Labour*[6] the High Court accepted a UK definition of 'misconduct':

> It has long been part of our law that a person repudiates the contract of service if he wilfully disobeys the lawful and reasonable orders of his master. Such a refusal fully justifies an employer in dismissing an employee summarily.

Dismissal without notice

[14.11] The right to terminate the contract of employment with reasonable notice is separate from the right to terminate the contract summarily, ie without notice in the case of breach by the other side where the 'grounds for dismissal during the term contracted for must be such that they amounted to a repudiation of a contract on the part of the employee': *Power v Binchy.*[7]

[14.12] Termination of employment without notice will constitute a lawful dismissal only where there are grounds which the law regards as sufficient to justify the dismissal. If these grounds do not exist, an employer will be held to be in breach of contract and liable to pay damages for wrongful dismissal. It is not possible to define the reason or reasons which will be regarded as sufficient to justify summary dismissal. The High Court, in *Carvill v Irish Industrial Bank Ltd,*[8] expressed the view that the grounds relied on to justify a dismissal without notice of an employee must be actions or omissions by

---

[6]   *Brewster v Burke and the Minister for Labour* [1985] 4 JISLL 1998.
[7]   *Power v Binchy* (1929) 64 ILTR 35 at 39, *per* Meredith J.
[8]   *Carvill v Irish Industrial Bank Ltd* [1986] IR 325.

the employee which are inconsistent with the performance of the express or implied terms of its contract of service.

> One of these implied terms is that the employee will have that degree of competence which he has represented himself as having at the time when he was originally employed; another term is that the employee will conduct his employer's business with reasonable competence. The incompetence relied on to justify summary dismissal must, however, be judged by reasonable standards, and the employer must establish that an error was caused by incompetence and not by mistaken judgement or human error. An error relied on to justify summary dismissal must be judged by the standards which prevail among people in Ireland who are engaged in business...

> Another implied term of the contract of service between an employer and an employee is that the employee will act honestly towards his employer and that the employee will not take or misuse the employer's property or divert to himself profits or property which belong to the employer.

[14.13] Misconduct is generally recognised as one such ground, although it is impossible to define the misconduct which justifies summary dismissal: *Glover v BLN Ltd.*[9] The burden of establishing misconduct rests on the defendant and a *prima facie* case only will not suffice.

Contractual limitations on the employer's power to dismiss

[14.14] A contract of employment may have express or implied terms which are capable of limiting the employer's power of termination. These terms may be procedural or substantive.

Breach of procedural limitations

[14.15] The parties to a contract may have expressly incorporated procedural safeguards into the agreement. If so, breach will give rise to an action at common law. In *Gunton v London Borough of Richmond-Upon-Thames*[10] the employee college registrar had a contract terminable by one month's notice in writing on either side. He was also subject to a disciplinary procedure which allowed for appeals and which, if followed properly, would take over one month to run its course. The Court of Appeal held by a majority that the effect of the disciplinary code was to render it wrongful to dismiss the plaintiff on disciplinary grounds without following the agreed procedure but that it would not have affected a dismissal for other reasons such as redundancy.

[14.16] The Unfair Dismissals Act 1977, s 14(1), requires an employer, whether requested to or not, to give to an employee not later than 28 days after he enters into a contract of employment a notice in writing setting out the procedure to be observed before and for the purpose of dismissing the employee. These terms will be binding on the employer if they have been expressly incorporated into an individual employee's contract of employment.

---

9   *Glover v BLN Ltd* [1973] IR 388.
10 *Gunton v London Borough of Richmond-Upon-Thames* [1970] IRLR 321.

[14.17] Guided by the Constitution, the courts are willing to imply a term of procedural fairness into contracts of employment and have done so where the employer was subject both to express procedural and substantive limitations in relation to dismissal. In *Glover v BLN Ltd*[11] clause 12 (c) of the service agreement provided that the employee could not be validly dismissed for misconduct unless it was serious misconduct and was of a kind, which, in the unanimous opinion of the Board of Directors of the holding company present and voting at the meeting, injuriously affected the reputation, business or property either of that company or of the subsidiary companies. The Supreme Court based its decision on contractual considerations and held that it was necessarily an implied term of the contract in question that the enquiry and determination should be fairly conducted. It derived support from its earlier decision in *Re Haughey*[12] that a guarantee of fair procedures was among a citizen's personal rights under Art 40.3 of the Constitution. Walsh J declared that

> … public policy and the dictates of constitutional justice required that statutes, regulations or agreements setting up machinery for the taking of decisions which may affect rights or impose liabilities should be construed as providing for fair procedures.

[14.18] In the case of express procedural limitations, the purpose and effect of implying a term of fairness will be to inject a greater degree of efficacy into these stipulations. Where the limitations are substantive, the implied term will ensure that constitutional justice is observed.

[14.19] Ordinary employees whose dismissal is limited by express contract terms are entitled to the same procedural safeguards as office holders. The overriding principle of fairness applies to both categories of worker. In *Gunn v Bord An Choláiste Náisiúnta Ealaíne Is Deartha*[13] McCarthy J said in the Supreme Court:

> I share the view of Walsh J that, in the absence of any particular prescribed procedure the principles of natural justice or constitutional justice would govern the relationship between the Plaintiff and An Bord. These principles are not the monopoly of any particular class.

Breach of substantive limitations

[14.20] A contract of employment may contain substantive limitations on an employer's power to dismiss. For example, dismissal may be restricted to specified grounds having a defined effect as in *Glover v BLN Ltd*.[14] The Supreme Court there endorsed the opinion of the High Court that because of the express provisions in clause 12 (c) of Glover's service agreement, no implied term could be read into the contract that the plaintiff might be summarily dismissed for misconduct. On the contrary, the clause expressly provided that the plaintiff could not be validly dismissed for misconduct unless it was 'serious misconduct' of the kind set out.

---

[11] *Glover v BLN Ltd* [1973] IR 388.

[12] *Re Haughey* [1971] IR 217.

[13] *Gunn v Bord An Choláiste Náisiúnta Ealaíne Is Deartha* [1990] 2 IR 168. See similarly the Supreme Court in *Mooney v An Post* [1998] ELR 238.

[14] *Glover v BLN Ltd* [1973] IR 388.

[14.21] If an employee is appointed for life, for example, with dismissal only for misconduct, there will be a presumption against his dismissal for any other reason. But whatever substantive limitations are found in the contract of employment, if an employee behaves in a way that is seriously inconsistent with the contract, if he is guilty for example of gross misconduct, he should not be able to complain if his employer reacts by summarily dismissing him.

Breach of implied terms

[14.22] Implied terms have developed mainly in the context of the employer's right to dismiss an employee without notice and in the context of constructive dismissal. The courts imply terms in order to make the contract workable. Terms can be implied in fact or as a legal incident of the relationship, ie by operation of law. Where terms are implied in fact, it is either where it is necessary 'to give business efficacy to the transaction as must have been intended'[15] or the term is implied as:

> [S]omething so obvious that it goes without saying that if, while the parties were making their bargain, an officious bystander were to suggest some express provision for it in their agreement they would testily suppress him with a cry of "Oh, of course".[16]

[14.23] Terms implied by operation of law relate to the status of the parties as employer and employee. The most important terms implied by law in the contract of employment include:

   (i)   The employer's duty to exercise reasonable care;

   (ii)   The employer's duty to provide work;

  (iii)   The reciprocal duty of cooperation;

  (iv)   The employee's duty of faithful service;

   (v)   The employee's duty not to disclose trade secrets or confidential information;

  (vi)   The employee's duty to obey instructions;

 (vii)   The mutual obligation of trust and confidence.

The last mentioned has assumed considerable significance in recent times.

Breach of mutual implied obligation of trust and confidence

[14.24] In *Courtaulds Northern Textiles Ltd v Andrew,*[17] a case of constructive dismissal the EAT in Britain, Arnold J described the implied term as follows

> The employer will not, without proper reason and cause, conduct themselves in a manner calculated or likely to destroy or seriously damage the relationship of confidence and trust between the parties.

[14.25] The obligation may have positive as well as negative effects on the behaviour of the parties to the contract of employment. In *Imperial Group Pension Trust Ltd v Imperial Tobacco Ltd*[18] the High Court held that the employer was obliged to exercise

---

15 *The Moorcock* (1889) 14 PD 64.

16 *Shirlaw v Southern Foundaries Ltd* [1939] 2 KB 206.

17 *Courtaulds Northern Textiles Ltd v Andrew* [1979] IRLR 84.

18 *Imperial Group Pension Trust Ltd v Imperial Tobacco Ltd* [1991] ICR 524.

rights and powers under a pension scheme so as to preserve the employee's trust. The implied obligation has also been invoked to prohibit conduct on the employer's part as in the constructive dismissal case of *Pickering v Microsoft Ireland Operations Ltd.*[19] The implied obligation has also been applied to the exercise of discretionary powers under the contract of employment eg in relation to suspension: *Gogay v Hertfordshire CC.*[20]

[14.26] The potential significance of the implied obligation in relation to termination of a contract of employment is as yet uncertain. In *Malik and Mahmood v Bank of Credit and Commerce International SA*[21] two employees were summarily dismissed on grounds of redundancy and failed to find employment thereafter. Subsequently, it became public knowledge that the Bank had been operating in a dishonest manner. The plaintiffs successfully relied on the term implied by law of mutual trust and confidence and were awarded so-called 'stigma damages'. The Law Lords held that there is no bar to recovery of damages for breach of the implied term if the breach is discovered only after the employee leaves. Nor need the conduct complained of be targeted at a particular employee or group of employees. The scope of the implied obligation concerns conduct which either deliberately destroys the relationship of trust and confidence or has the effect of seriously damaging it.

[14.27] In *Johnson v Unisys*[22] the applicant alleged his dismissal was in breach of the implied obligation of mutual trust and confidence thus bringing the question of compatibility between an employer's express term as to dismissal and the implied terms in the contract of employment to the fore. Johnson claimed the company had been negligent and/or that it had acted in breach of the implied term of trust and confidence in dismissing him without a proper hearing and in breach of the contractual disciplinary procedure. The House of Lords held that *Malik* did not justify a breach of contract claim regarding the manner of dismissal and that a common law right embracing the manner of dismissal could not co-exist with the statutory right of unfair dismissal. Parliament had limited the damages recoverable in an action for unfair dismissal and the House of Lords took the view that it would be an improper exercise of the judicial function to develop a common law remedy which was contrary to Parliament's intended limitations. *Johnson* has been severely criticised.[23] In Ireland, unlike in Britain, there is a prohibition on double redress for dismissal at common law and under the statute: Unfair Dismissals Act 1977, s 15.

[14.28] The High Court in *McGrath v Trintech*[24] followed *Johnson*. The plaintiff claimed that a term should be implied into his contract that mere compliance with the express notice provision would not validly and effectively terminate the contractual relationship at common law. The Court correctly noted that there was no authority for such a

---

[19] *Pickering v Microsoft Ireland Operations Ltd* [2006] 17 ELR 55 (under appeal).
[20] *Gogay v Hertfordshire CC* [2000] IRLR 703 see in relation to discretionary bonus power *Horkulak v Cantor Fitzgerald International* [2004] IRLR 492.
[21] *Malik and Mahmood v Bank of Credit and Commerce International SA* [1997] 2 WLR 95.
[22] *Johnson v Unisys* [2001] ICR 480.
[23] See Redmond, *Dismissal Law in Ireland* (2nd edn, Tottel Publishing, 2007), p 79.
[24] *McGrath v Trintech* [2005] 16 ELR 49.

provision. It seemed to rule out any development of the law regarding remedies for the manner in which the express power of termination was exercised.

> Such protection and remedies as are afforded by statute law to the Plaintiff... cannot be pursued at first instance in a plenary action in the High Court.

[14.29] That the implied obligation is one implied by law is apparent from *obiter dicta* of Laffoy J in *Cronin v Eircom Ltd*:[25]

> I do consider that as a matter of principle a contractual term of mutual trust and confidence which was recognised by the House of Lords in the *Malik and Mahmood* case should be implied into each contract of employment in this jurisdiction by operation of law.

[14.30] The most damning indictments of *Johnson* have been delivered by Lord Steyn in the House of Lords in *Eastwood v Magnox Engineering Plc* and *McCabe v Cornwall County Council*.[26] The employees claimed damages for breach of the duty of trust and confidence in respect of their employers' campaign to humiliate and undermine them and procure false evidence in order to dismiss them. The Court of Appeal held that since this pattern of events formed part of the manner and circumstances of dismissal, compensation could be sought only in a statutory claim. The House of Lords felt obliged to follow *Johnson* but their reluctance was self-evident. Not least of the difficulties effected by *Johnson* was the type of demarcation disputes which would be generated:

> The dichotomy will often give rise to questions whether earlier events do or do not form part of the dismissal process. After all such problems in relationships between an employer and an employee will often arise because of a continuing course of conduct.

[14.31] Lord Steyn concluded that *Johnson* could be justified if and only if it could be shown that the co-existence of a statutory scheme and the development of a common law remedy would be unworkable.

[14.32] In the last few years the so-called '*Johnson* exclusion area' has implicitly influenced the drafting of pleadings as plaintiffs seek to avoid contamination of their claims emphasising, instead alleged wrongs prior to termination of the contract.

[14.33] In *Maha Lingam v Health Service Executive*[27] the plaintiff argued that there had developed in parallel with the statutory claim for dismissal 'the tendency of the Courts' to imply a term of good faith and mutual trust into contracts of employment. According to the Fennelly J in the Supreme Court:

> This is a development which is perhaps at its early stages and it is not contested in the present case.

No doubt there will be an opportunity before long for the Supreme Court to analyse the application of the implied mutual obligation of trust and confidence to the manner and circumstances of dismissal. There are already ample incidents where implied and

---

[25] *Cronin v Eircom Ltd* [2006] IEHC 380.

[26] *Eastwood v Magnox Engineering Plc and McCabe v Cornwall County Council* [2004] IRLR 733.

[27] *Maha Lingam v Health Service Executive* [2006] ELR 137.

express terms co-exist. The implied term does not disapply the express term but requires good faith in the manner of its exercise.

REMEDIES FOR WRONGFUL DISMISSAL

Damages

[14.34] A breach of contract by one party confers upon the other party a right to sue for damages. Where an employer wrongfully dismisses an employee and thereby discharges the contract by its breach, a number of alternatives are open to the employee. The remedy of damages for wrongful dismissal is by far the most important remedy given by the common law or by the rules of equity for the protection of an employee's job security. A claim for damages for wrongful dismissal must be brought within six years under the Statute of Limitations Act 1957, s 11(1). If an employee has completed his part of the contract, he can sue for wages under the terms of the contract. If he is dismissed during the period of notice covered by the contract of service he cannot sue for wages under its terms unless the contract is divisible, but he can sue either quasi-contractually on a *quantum meruit* for service already rendered or he may bring an action for damages for breach of contract.

Judicial review

[14.35] Order 84 of the Rules of the Superior Courts 1986 created a single comprehensive procedure known as 'an application for judicial review'. It enables a person to challenge the legality of administrative action in the High Court and aims to reduce the likelihood that a good case will be lost solely because the wrong remedy is sought.

[14.36] Much difficulty has been caused by the issue as to whether employment decisions are susceptible to judicial review. The Supreme Court's preference that judicial review is not applicable in respect of decisions made in the course of disciplinary proceedings forming part of a private contract of employment was evident in *O'Neill v Iarnród Éireann*.[28] The traditional test of considering whether a person or body in its decision-making process is subject to judicial review is to look at both the source of the power being exercised and at the nature of that power. Where the power on which the decision depends is derived from statute, the courts have almost invariably regarded the decision-maker as a subject for review. In *Eogan v University College Dublin*[29] Shanley J (High Court) reviewed the jurisprudence on whether a decision is subject to judicial review.

[14.37] The most effective, and in Ireland the most frequently sought, remedies by way of judicial review for wrongfully dismissed workers in special categories of employment are a declaration that dismissal is null and void or an order of *certiorari* quashing a purported decision to dismiss. An injunction may also be sought to restrain dismissal.

---

[28] *O'Neill v Iarnród Éireann* [1991] 2 ELR 1.
[29] *Eogan v University College Dublin* [1996] 2 ILRM 302. See also *Rafferty v Bus Éireann* [1997] 2 IR 424 and *Bane v Garda Representative Association* [1997] 2 IR 449.

[14.38] The important doctrine of 'legitimate expectation' enables employees governed by public law principles to seek protection which ordinary employees cannot.[30]

Injunctions to restrain dismissal

[14.39] In recent years, plaintiffs have increasingly sought injunctions to restrain dismissal in the High Court. In the main they have been senior executives for whom High Court proceedings are strategically important against their employer (not least because of bad publicity and high legal costs for the employer) and for whom the prospect of delays before the EAT are not acceptable. There are several injunction applications every year.

[14.40] Following UK authorities in the wake of what was described as a 'highly exceptional case' – *Hill v CA Parsons Ltd*[31] – the first case in Ireland to mark a departure from the traditional approach of the courts not to grant injunctions in employment disputes was *Fennelly v Assicurazioni Generali SpA*.[32] The plaintiff had given up a permanent pensionable post in the Garda Síochána at the instance of the defendant company in return for what he argued was an unusual contract of employment of 12 years' duration. The defendant contended that it had been forced to terminate his employment by reason of a downturn in business, although both parties continued to have high regard for each other. Costello J, delivering his judgment *ex tempore*, granted an interlocutory injunction on terms not of reinstatement, but that the defendant would continue to pay the plaintiff his salary and bonus until the trial of the action, and that the plaintiff should be prepared to carry out such duties as were requested of him, recognising, however, that the defendant might prefer not to give him any duties but to put him on leave of absence (this has become known as 'the *Fennelly* order').

[14.41] An injunction is sought to protect the rights of a plaintiff whether at common law, under statute, the Constitution or in equity. Within each of these the legal rules relevant to the particular context apply. The granting of an injunction to restrain dismissal is at the court's discretion.

[14.42] An injunction to restrain disciplinary or dismissal procedures is prohibitory, that is, it restrains the performance or continuance of an allegedly wrongful act. The courts are far less inclined to grant mandatory injunctions which would have the effect of specific performance of the contract. Most employment injunctions are interim or interlocutory, sought and granted prior to the trial. Whereas an interim injunction will endure until the next hearing, an interlocutory injunction will be effective until the final hearing of the action, maintaining the parties' *status quo* as far as possible until the court decides the issues in dispute. If at trial a plaintiff is successful, a perpetual injunction may be granted. Where breach is threatened or feared, a plaintiff may seek a *quia timet*

---

[30] See *Webb v Ireland and AG* [1988] ILRM 565 and *Eogan v University College Dublin* [1996] 2 ILRM 302 and *O'Leary v Minister for Finance* (3 July 1998 unreported), HC.

[31] *Hill v CA Parsons Ltd* [1972] Ch 305 (CA).

[32] *Fennelly v Assicurazioni Generali SpA* (1985) 3 ILT 73.

injunction. In *Clane Hospital Ltd v Voluntary Health Insurance Board*[33] the High Court (Quirke J) provided a useful summary of the issues required to be considered.

1. Whether or not the applicant has raised a fair, substantial, *bona fide* question for determination;

2. Whether if the applicant were to succeed at the trial in establishing his right to a permanent injunction, he could be adequately compensated by an award of damages;

3. Whether, if the respondent were to be successful at the trial he could be adequately compensated under the applicant's undertaking as to damages for any loss which he would have sustained by reason of a grant of interlocutory relief;

4. If either party or both have, by way of evidence, raised a real and substantial doubt as to the adequacy of the respective remedies in damages available to either party, then where does the 'balance of convenience' lie?

[14.43] Authorities in Ireland illustrate that there is no one single unifying principle in employment injunction cases. However, common characteristics have emerged in this jurisdiction over the last 20 years. It goes without saying that where interlocutory injunctions have been granted, damages were found not to have been an adequate remedy and/or the balance of convenience did not favour the plaintiff.

[14.44] Irish cases where interlocutory injunctions have been granted against employing entities share one or more of the following characteristics:

(i)   The employer was a public body and/or the employee was an office-holder[34] and/or;

(ii) There were alleged contractual limitations on discipline and/or dismissal, procedural or substantive, express or implied.[35]

[14.45] Issues in such applications have concerned matters as diverse as: alleged breach of a substantive limitation regarding termination in the contract; dismissal of office

---

[33] *Clane Hospital Ltd v Voluntary Health Insurance Board* [1998] IEHC 78. See *American Cyanamid v Ethicon Ltd* [1975] AC 396.

[34] *Shortt v Data Packaging* [1994] ELR 251, *Phelan v BIC (Ireland) Ltd* [1997] ELR 208, *Harte v Kelly Anderson and HKC Ltd* [1997] ELR 125, *Cahill v Dublin City University* [2007] IEHC 20.

[35] *Cassidy v Shannon Heritage & Others* [2000] ELR 198, *Courtenay v Radio 2000 Ltd t/a Classic Hits 98FM* [1997] ELR 198, *O'Malley v Aravon School Ltd* (13 August 1997, unreported) HC, *Maher v Irish Permanent plc (No 1)* [1998] ELR 77, *Martin v The Nationwide Building Society* [1999] ELR 241, *Carroll v Dublin Bus* [2005] ELR 192 and [2006] ELR 149. A higher threshold is required where an application is made for a mandatory injunction: *Stoskus v Goode Concrete Ltd* [2007] IEHC 432, *Kurt Naujoks v National Institute of Bioprocessing Research and Training Ltd* [2007] 18 ELR 25, *Coffey v William Connolly & Sons Ltd* [2007] IEHC 319. Note that the courts will not generally intervene in an uncompleted disciplinary process even where the proposition put forward by the plaintiff is arguable unless a step(s) or an act has been taken in the process which cannot be cured and which is manifestly at variance with fair procedures and the entitlement to them: *Bergin v Galway Clinic Doughiska Ltd* (2 November 2007, unreported) HC, *Turner v O Reilly* [2008] IEHC 92.

holders with contracts of employment; alleged breach of procedural limitations in the contract; and/or of the implied term of fairness.

[14.46] Common characteristics in which interlocutory injunctions have generally been refused have included applications where the injunction was sought at a stage where no allegations had been made against an employee.[36] Injunctions were also refused when they were sought to restrain dismissal whether with or without notice, where no allegations of misconduct or otherwise had been made.[37] Regarding this latter category the rationale has in part been based on the general principle that damages are an adequate remedy, reinforced by the fact that an aggrieved employee may also pursue a statutory remedy.

THE CONSTITUTION AND DISMISSAL

[14.47] The High Court or the Supreme Court may declare a purported dismissal invalid or unconstitutional if it can be established that the dismissal contravened the Constitution or any of its provisions. The exercise of a common law or statutory right of dismissal is regarded as an abuse of that right if it is also an infringement and an abuse of the Constitution. In *Meskell v CIE*[38] Walsh J in the Supreme Court pointed out that if an employer dismisses a worker because of the latter's insistence upon exercising his constitutional right, the fact that the form or notice of dismissal is good at common law does not in any way lessen the infringement of the right involved or mitigate the damage which the worker may suffer by reason of his insistence upon exercising his constitutional rights. Constitutional rights must not be exercised in such a way as to frustrate, infringe or destroy the constitutional rights of others. In *Meskell*, the Supreme Court held that Meskell was entitled to a declaration that his dismissal for refusing to be party to a closed shop arrangement was a denial and a violation of, and an unlawful interference with, his constitutional right of disociation, that an agreement between CIE and four unions to procure or cause that dismissal was an actionable conspiracy because the means employed constituted a breach or infringement of the plaintiff's constitutional rights and that the plaintiff was entitled to damages.

[14.48] Constitutional rights may be expressed or 'unspecified'. The former are set out in Arts 40–44 and cover inviolability of the dwelling, freedom of association, of expression and of assembly, property rights and freedom of religion. The importance of unspecified constitutional rights derives from *Ryan v AG*[39] in which the High Court was called upon to interpret Art 40.3.1° under which the State guarantees to protect the

---

[36] *Foley v Aer Lingus* [2001] ELR 193, *Conway v An Taoiseach* (12 April 2006 unreported) HC, *Morgan v The Provost, Fellows and Scholars of the College of the Most Holy and Undivided Trinity of Queen Elizabeth, Smyth and Buchanan* [2003] 3 IR 157, *O'Brien v Aon Insurance Managers (Dublin) Ltd* (14 January 2005, unreported) HC.

[37] *Orr v Zomax Ltd* [2004] ELR 161, *McGrath v Trintech Technologies Ltd* [2005] 16 ELR 49 and *Nolan v EMO Oil Service Ltd* [2008] IEHC 15.

[38] *Meskell v CIE* [1973] IR 121.

[39] *Ryan v AG* [1963] IR 294.

'personal rights' of the citizen. In the course of his judgement which was upheld by the Supreme Court, Kenny J held that:

> The personal rights which may be invoked to invalidate legislation are not confined to those specified in Article 40 but include all those rights which result from the Christian and democratic nature of the State.

[14.49] Acknowledgement of implied or undisclosed human or personal rights in Art 40.3.1° has encouraged a great deal of judicial creativity not least in the area of employment law. Of most significance perhaps is a right central also to statutory unfair dismissals namely the right to basic fairness of procedures. Art 40.3 of the Constitution was described in the Supreme Court as a guarantee to the citizen of basic fairness of procedures in *Re Haughey*:[40]

> ... in proceedings before any tribunal where a person to the proceedings is on risk of having his good name or his person or property, or any of his personal rights jeopardised, the proceedings may be correctly classed as proceedings which may affect his rights, and the State, either by its enactments or through the courts, must, in compliance with the Constitution, outlaw any procedures which will restrict or prevent the party concerned from vindicating these rights.

[14.50] The constitutionally-inspired term of fairness was implied by the Supreme Court in the contract of employment of a company director in *Glover v BLN Ltd*[41] Irish courts are willing to graft an implied term of fairness onto terms already in an employee's contract of employment.

Remedies

[14.51] In *Meskell,* damages were settled out of court by agreement between the Board of CIE and Meskell. In *W v Ireland (No 2)*[42] the High Court considered the circumstances in which the courts will award damages for breach of constitutional rights. The crucial issue to decide is whether a constitutional action for breach of a right may be taken in addition to or as an alternative to an action for damages for personal injuries in negligence. The High Court considered it was unnecessary to interpret the Constitution as conferring a discrete cause of action for damages in circumstances where damages are available at common law.[43] The European Convention on Human Rights Act 2003 came into effect on the 31 December 2003. In a comprehensive *Preliminary Assessment of Impact of the ECHR Act 2003* jointly sponsored by the Law Society's Human Rights Committee and the Dublin Solicitors Bar Association and published in 2006, it was concluded that while there is no comprehensive study on the significant congruity in terms of substantive rights protection between the Irish Constitution and the ECHR:

---

[40] *Re Haughey* [1971] IR 217.
[41] *Glover v BLN Ltd* [1973] IR 388.
[42] *W v Ireland (No 2)* [1997] 2 IR 141.
[43] See also such cases as *Cotter v Aherne* [1976–77] ILRM 248, *Kearney v Minister for Justice* [1986] IR 116 and *Conway v INTO* [1991] IR 305.

[i]t is hardly disputed that such congruity exists and that the areas of direct or clear conflict between the requirements of the Constitution and the Convention are minimal. This can lead to a certain lowering of expectations in terms of the added-value to be gained from invocation of the Convention and the jurisprudence of the European Court of Human Rights before the Irish Courts…but there is established and anticipated scope for cross-fertilisation between the Convention and constitutional standards applicable in each area mentioned [in the Convention]…

THE UNFAIR DISMISSALS ACTS 1977–2007

[14.52] The Unfair Dismissals Act 1977 restricted the hitherto largely unlimited authority of an employer to dismiss his employees for whatever reason he thought fit. The introduction of the Act was influenced by ILO Recommendation No 119 on the Termination of Employment (Geneva 1963). To be a qualified 'employee' to claim under the Act, an individual must:

(i)   be an employee as defined in s 1 of the Act, and

(ii) have the requisite continuous service of not less than 1 year with the employer, except where dismissal is related to pregnancy, maternity or matters concerned therewith or is connected with trade union membership or activity.

Under s 1 an 'employee' means:

an individual who entered into or works under (or, where the employment has ceased, worked under) a contract of employment and, in relation to redress for dismissal under this Act, includes, in the case of the death of an employee concerned at any time following the dismissal, his personal representatives.

The legal meaning of 'employee' is considered in the context of the common law in Ch 2, The Contract and Relationship of Employment.

[14.53] An individual supplied by an employment agency within the meaning of the Employment Agency Act 1971 and acting in the course of that business is deemed to be an employee employed under a contract of employment by the third party user of the labour for the purposes of the 1977 Act and any redress under the Act is awarded against the third party: Unfair Dismissals (Amendment) Act 1993, s 13.

[14.54] A person working under a Fás Scheme is not regarded as an employee[44] and an independent contractor is self-evidently not an employee.

[14.55] An office-holder will be eligible to claim but only if he works also under a contract of employment.

[14.56] The definition of 'employer' is as follows:

An employer in relation to an employee means the person by whom the employee is (or in the case where the employment has ceased was) employed under a contract of employment and an individual in the service of a local authority for the purposes of the Local Government Act 1941 shall be deemed to be employed by the local authority.

---

[44] *Dempsey v Grant Shopfitting Ltd* [1990] ELR 43.

[14.57] A receiver's obligations have been held to be the same as an employer's: *Lynch v Jim Dwyer Motors Ltd (in receivership)*[45] likewise a company under administration: *McCarthy v Du Buisson and Sykes*.[46] A liquidation on the other hand may mean redundancy: *Farrell v Donabates Steelworks Ltd.*[47]

Continuity of service

[14.58] With stated exceptions, an employee must have at least 52 weeks' continuous service with the employer before he can claim unfair dismissal: s 2(a) of the 1977 Act as amended. Continuous service is calculated by reference to the First Sch to the Minimum Notice and Terms of Employment Act 1973 (the 1973 Act) as amended. Continuity involves both length of service and the number of hours normally worked per week. Fifty-two weeks means that if, say, the year begins on 1 January it ends on 31 December the following year, not on the anniversary of the first day.

[14.59] There are four exceptions to the requirement to have continuous service with the dismissing employer. They arise where an employee is dismissed for

   (i)   trade union membership or activity;

   (ii)   pregnancy, maternity or matters connected therewith;

   (iii) exercising his rights under the National Minimum Wage Act 2000; or

   (iv) exercising his rights under the Safety, Health & Welfare at Work Act 2005, s 27(a).

[14.60] Under para 8 of the Sch to the 1973 Act, an employee must have been normally expected to work at least 18 hours a week. This must be read in light of the Protection of Employees (Part-Time Work) Act 2001 (the 2001 Act) which is considered in Ch 9, Part-Time Workers. In that Act, a part-time employee is defined in s 7 to mean:

> An employee whose normal hours of work are less than the normal hours of an employee who is a comparable employee in relation to him or her.

[14.61] Under s 8 of the Act of 2001, the Unfair Dismissals Act applies to a part-time employee in the same manner as it does to an employee to whom the Act relates. The basic principle is set out in s 9:

> The part-time employee shall not, in respect of his or her conditions of employment, be treated in a less favourable manner than a comparable full-time employee.

[14.62] The exceptions to the requirement of continuity in the 1977 Act apply irrespective of the number of hours worked per week.

[14.63] An employee's holiday entitlement cannot be added to a period of service in order to qualify for a statutory unfair dismissal claim: *Maher v B & I Line*.[48]

---

[45] *Lynch v Jim Dwyer Motors Ltd (in receivership)* UD1025/1984.

[46] *McCarthy v Du Buisson and Sykes* UD325/1990.

[47] *Farrell v Donabates Steelworks Ltd* UD273/1987.

[48] *Maher v B& I Line* UD271/1978.

[14.64] The First Sch to the 1973 Act provides that service shall be deemed to be continuous unless it is terminated either by the dismissal of the employee by his employer or by the employee voluntarily leaving his employment.[49] A lock-out does not constitute a dismissal nor does a lay-off amount to a termination by an employer of an employee's service.[50] A strike does not amount to an employee's voluntarily leaving employment[51] but if in any week or part of a week an employee is absent from employment because he was taking part in a strike in relation to the trade or business 'in which he is employed', that week does not count as a period of service.[52] The contrary applies to absence on account of lock-out[53] or on account of strike or lock-out in a trade or business other than that in which the person is employed.[54] Continuity is preserved.

[14.65] An employee who claims and receives redundancy payment in respect of lay-off or short-time shall be deemed to have voluntarily left his employment.[55]

[14.66] The continuous service of an employee is not broken by his dismissal 'followed by the immediate re-employment of the employee'.[56] The word 'immediate' is not literally construed. It has been found to apply to a space of one week, but not four months, between employment and re-employment. If an employee is absent from his employment for not more than 26 weeks between consecutive periods of employment because of lay-off, sickness or injury or by agreement, the period concerned counts as a period of service.[57]

[14.67] Temporary employees are protected against unfair dismissal[58] unless they fall within the category of employees whose contracts are terminated under s 2 (b) of the 1977 Act and who have signed a waiver of rights. Where a fixed-term or specified purpose contract is in writing, signed by or on behalf of the employer and by the employee and provides that the 1977 Act shall not apply to a dismissal consisting only of the expiry of the term or cesser of the purpose, the Act will not apply to dismissal.

Temporary employees on successive fixed-term contracts

[14.68] Regarding temporary fixed-term contracts an important amendment to s 2 of the 1977 Act was introduced by s 3 of the Unfair Dismissals (Amendment) Act 1993. The amendment was intended to deal with temporary contracts entered into for less than 52 weeks followed by a second or subsequent contract (generally after a short absence) also for a term which fell short of 52 weeks. If the entry by the employer into the subsequent

---

49 Sch 1, para 1 eg *Oakes v Lynch* UD 214/1978.
50 Sch 1, paras 2 and 3, see *Kilgannan and Hegarty v Peamount Hospital* UD 722 and 733/1987.
51 Sch 1, para 4.
52 Sch 1, para 11.
53 Sch 1, para 12.
54 Sch 1, para 13.
55 Sch 1, para 5.
56 Sch 1, para 6.
57 Sch 1, para 10.
58 *Sinclair v City of Dublin Vocational Education Committee* UD 349/1986. See Protection of Workers (Fixed Term Work) Act 2003.

contract was wholly or partly to avoid liability for unfair dismissal, in the opinion of the Rights Commissioner, EAT or Circuit Court, as the case may be, then the term of the prior contract and of any antecedent contracts can be added to that of the subsequent contract and the period so ascertained is deemed to be one of continuous service.

[14.69] The amended s 2 of the 1977 Act requires that: the re-employment must take place within three months of the expiry of the prior contract; the nature of the employment must be the same or similar; the employer must be the same; and the dismissal complained of must consist only of the expiry of the term of the subsequent contract. The amendment is a proviso to s 2(b) of the 1977 Act. The proviso was recast in sub-sections 2(a) and 2(b) inserted by s 25(2) of the Protection of Employment Exceptional Collective Redundancies and Related Matters) Act 2007.

Dismissal followed by re-employment within 26 weeks

[14.70] Dismissal, other than dismissal covered by the proviso, noted in paragraph [14.69], of an employee followed by his re-employment by the same employer not later than 26 weeks afterwards will not break continuity of service if the dismissal was wholly or partly for or was connected with the purpose of avoiding liability under the 1977 Act: s 2(5) of the 1977 Act.

[14.71] The 'dismissal' here relates to termination of the prior contract and, if it was for a period in excess of 52 weeks or was open-ended and had lasted in excess of such a period, it will be difficult to establish a motive of avoidance. In contrast to the proviso the test here seems to be more demanding.

Transfer of undertaking

[14.72] An important amendment to the First Sch to the Minimum Notice and Terms of Employment Act 1973 was added by the Unfair Dismissals (Amendment) Act 1993 whereby the transfer of a whole or part of a trade, business or undertaking to another person will not operate to break the continuity of service of the employee and his service before the transfer in the trade, business or undertaking would be reckoned as part of his service with the transferee. However, the amendment provides an exception where the employee received and retained redundancy payment from the transferor at the time of and by reason of the transfer.

The amendment ceases to have effect if an employee hands back the redundancy payment to his employer and it is a moot question whether the phrase 'redundancy payment' covers an *ex gratia* payment paid by the employer on the occasion of a termination described as a redundancy. 'Redundancy payment' is a statutory phrase, first used in the Redundancy Payments Act 1967. Moreover there will strictly speaking be no redundancy on the facts.[59] The whole purpose of the European Communities (Protection of Employees on Transfer of Undertakings) Regulations 2003 is to preserve employment rights, including continuity. Where jobs continue with the transferee it is difficult to see how redundancy could have any place in the scheme of things.

---

[59] See EAT's comments in *Brett v Niall Collins Ltd* [1995] ELR 69.

Illegality

[14.73] A contract tainted with illegality is unenforceable at common law. Most cases involving illegality are about non-payment of tax and PRSI. Suppose an employee receives bonuses from time to time knowing them to be untaxed. Whatever about unenforceability of the contract at common law, s 8 para 11 of the Unfair Dismissals Act 1977 as amended in 1993 provides:

> Where ... a term or condition of the contract of employment concerned contravened any provision of or made under the Income Tax Acts or the Social Welfare (Consolidation) Act 2005 to 1993, the employee shall, notwithstanding the contravention, be entitled to redress under this Act, in respect of the dismissal.

It is also mandatory under para 12 for the rights commissioner, the EAT or the Circuit Court as appropriate to refer a matter of illegality to the Revenue Commissioners or the Department of Social and Family Affairs where it is shown that a term or condition of a contract of employment contravened the Acts aforesaid.

[14.74] It would appear from decisions of the EAT that employees without valid work permits and who have not had such permits in previous employment can claim under the Act of 1977. Under the Employment Permits Act 2003 s 2(2) as amended 'a person shall not employ a foreign national in the state except in accordance with an employment permit granted by the Minister...'

EXCLUSIONS

Types of employee

[14.75] An employee qualified in terms of 'continuous service' may be excluded if he falls into any one of the categories set out in s 2 (1) of the 1977 Act as amended by the 1993 Act. The list of employees not eligible comprises:

(i) employees who on or before the date of dismissal have reached the normal retiring age for employees of the same employer in similar employment or who on that date, had not attained the age of 16 years;

(ii) persons employed by a close relative in a private house or on a farm where both reside;

(iii) members of the Defence Forces and of the Garda Síochána;

(iv) FÁS trainees and apprentices;

(v) persons employed by or under the State who are dismissed by the Government;

(vi) managers of a local authority for purposes of the Local Government Act 2001, s144;

(vii) officers of a vocational education committee established by the Vocational Education Act 1930;

(viii) the Chief Executive Officer of the Health Service Executive for purposes of the Health Act 2004, s 17.

[14.76] Civil servants were excluded from the scope of the Act but since 4 July 2006 are eligible to claim (other than, as described above, civil servants who are dismissed by the Government). The Civil Service Regulation (Amendment) Act 2005, Pt 6, has applied the statutory code of unfair dismissal to thousands of officers whose remedies were theretofore exclusively in public law. While preserving the principle that civil servants hold office at the will and pleasure of the Government, the said Act provides for the delegation of power in matters of discipline and dismissal of most civil servants from the Government to Ministers and to Secretaries General. Specifically for civil servants, definitions of 'employer', 'employee' and 'contract of employment' are provided in a new s 2A to the Act of 1977.

Normal retiring age

[14.77] There is no single fixed retirement age for employees in Ireland. Some contracts have a mandatory retirement age and they may also allow for earlier retirement. The usual retirement age in contracts of employment is 65. Many contracts have provision for early retirement from age 60 or in some cases from age 55 years. There may also be a statutory retirement age. The retirement age in the public sector for those who joined before 1 April 2004 is 65 years. New entrants to the public service will not have to retire at 65 but can continue working, subject to suitability and health requirements. It is possible since 6 October 2006 to appoint persons who have attained the age of 65 years to the Civil Service provided they are new entrants. In accordance with the Public Service Superannuation (Miscellaneous Provisions) Act 2004 they have no mandatory retiring age.

[14.78] If a contract contains a 'normal retiring age' that will be the relevant age for the exclusion. If a contract contains no 'normal retiring age' for employees, the Rights Commissioner and the EAT will look at the normal retiring age of employees of the same employer in similar employment. In *Donegal County Council v Porter and Others*[60] all four employees were employed as part-time retained firemen. They were dismissed on the date each one of them respectively attained the age of 55 years. They challenged their dismissal under the 1977 Act. The case eventually went to the High Court where both sides agreed on one central fact, namely that when the employees joined, beginning in 1960, there had been no formal written contract and no reference to a specific date of retirement. The Court was satisfied that each employee was employed on the basis of an expectation that, all things being equal, he would continue in the fire brigade service until 60 years. Hence it found that was the 'normal retirement age'.

[14.79] The Unfair Dismissals (Amendment) Act 1993, s 14 provides that the exclusion as to normal retirement age does not apply where dismissal is for trade union membership or activity.

---

[60] *Donegal County Council v Porter and Others* [1993] ELR 101. See too *Reilly and Drogheda Borough Council* [2008] IEHC 357.

TYPES OF CONTRACT

Fixed-term/specified purpose

[14.80] A contract is for a fixed term where, at the time it is entered into, the date of commencement and of termination respectively are capable of being ascertained. A contract is for a specified purpose where, at the time of its making, the duration of the contract is limited but incapable of precise ascertainment. An example of a specified purpose contract would be to fill in for a named employee while he is absent on sick leave. Where such contracts expire either because the term expires and the contract is not renewed in the case of a fixed-term contract, or the specified purpose is not completed, under s 2(2)(b) the Unfair Dismissals Acts shall not apply if:

(i) the contract is in writing;

(ii) it was signed by both parties and;

(iii) it contains a statement that the Act shall not apply to a dismissal consisting only of the expiry or cesser as aforesaid.

[14.81] A waiver only excludes liability that would otherwise attach to termination upon expiry of the term or cesser of the purpose. Thus, an employee whose fixed-term contract is unfixed within the term or whose specified purpose contract is terminated before the completion of the purpose, eg for poor performance or misconduct, will be eligible to challenge dismissal provided the other requirements of the legislation are satisfied. The proviso introduced by the Unfair Dismissals (Amendment) Act 1993 is now restated in the Protection of Employment (Exceptional Collective Redundancies and Related Matters) Act 2007.

Covering for employees on protective leave or natal care absence

[14.82] A particular type of specified purpose contract, covering for an employee on protective leave or natal care absence, is named in s 2(2)(c) of the 1977 Act as amended. Whether or not a waiver is added, the expiry of this form of temporary contract lies outside unfair dismissals law. The employer must inform the employee (who is covering for an employee on leave or natal care absence) at the commencement of the employment in writing that the employment will terminate on the return to work with it of the other employee who was absent from work while on protective leave or natal care absence within Part IV of the Maternity Protection Act 1994 (the 1994 Act). 'Protective leave' is defined in the 1994 Act, s 21 as maternity leave, additional maternity leave, leave to which a father is entitled under the Act, and leave granted thereunder on health and safety grounds.

Covering for employees on adoptive leave

[14.83] A further exclusion relates to an employee taken on for the specified purpose of covering for someone on adoptive leave. Again, the employer must inform the employee in writing at the commencement of the employment that employment will terminate on the return to work with that employer of an adopting parent who is absent from work while on adoptive leave or additional adoptive leave under the Adoptive Leave Act

1995. The dismissal must occur for the purposes of facilitating the return to work of the adopting parent.

Employees ordinarily working outside the State

[14.84] The 1977 Act endorses the generally recognised principle that an employee cannot seek the protection of the laws of a state as regards a contract of employment performed outside it. In the world of e-commerce, perhaps, this principle is becoming more and more outdated.

[14.85] Under s 2(3) of the 1977 Act an employee who 'ordinarily worked' outside the State cannot challenge a dismissal unless:

   (a)   he was ordinarily resident in the State during the term of the contract; or

   (b)   he was domiciled in the State during the term of the contract and the employer;

   (i)   was ordinarily resident in the State (if an individual), or

   (ii)   had its principal place of business in the State during the term of the contract (if a body corporate or an unincorporated body of persons).

The 'term of the contract' means the whole of the period from the time of the commencement of work under the contract to the time of the relevant dismissal.

[14.86] The most contentious application of s 2(3) of the 1977 Act has concerned employees in cross-channel employment. See, for example, *Roche and Others v Sealink Stena Line Ltd*[61] where the evidence given satisfied the EAT that the employees were 'ordinarily resident' in the State during the period of their contracts.

FACT AND DATE OF DISMISSAL

[14.87] An employee must have been 'dismissed' within the meaning of the Act. Once that is established, the 'date of dismissal' needs to be ascertained. This can be critical for employees when computing continuous service as almost all challenges to dismissal require a claimant to have at least 52 weeks' continuous service.

The fact of dismissal

[14.88] Before the fairness or unfairness of a dismissal will be examined, the enforcing authorities must be satisfied an employee has been dismissed. Dismissal is defined in s 1 of the Unfair Dismissals Act 1977 to mean:

   (a)   the termination by his employer of the employee's contract of employment with the employer, whether prior notice of the termination was or was not given to the employee;

   (b)   the termination by the employee of his contract of employment with his employer, whether notice of the termination was or was not given to the employer, in circumstances in which, because of the conduct of the employer, the employee was or would have been entitled, or it was or would have been

---

[61] *Roche and Others v Sealink Stena Line Ltd* [1993] ELR 89. Contrast *Davis v Sealink Stena Line Ltd* UD874/1993.

reasonable for the employee, to terminate the contract of employment without giving prior notice of the termination to the employer; or

(c) the expiration of a contract of employment for a fixed term without it being renewed under the same contract, or, in the case of a contract for a specified purpose (being a purpose of such a kind that the duration of the contract was limited but was, at the time of its making, incapable of precise ascertainment), the cesser of the purpose.

The definition of dismissal in paras (a) and (b) constitute the conceptual core of the legislation. Unfair dismissal is an artificial creature, not easy to be understood by lay persons, Philips J once described it as 'dismissal contrary to the statute': *W Devis & Sons Ltd v Atkins*.[62]

[14.89] A termination of employment will not always constitute 'dismissal'. For instance there is no dismissal where the parties agree to part thus making termination consensual as for example in a voluntary redundancy scheme,[63] where the employer retained discretion to accept or reject an employee's application to go.

[14.90] If an employee resigns because the employer has threatened that if he does not resign he will be dismissed, the mechanics for the resignation do not cause it to be other than a dismissal: *Sheffield v Oxford Controls Company Ltd*.[64]

[14.91] A contract of employment may end as a result of the legal doctrine of frustration, that is, where performance of the employee's duties now or in the future have or would become radically different from that undertaken by him. Frustration mainly arises in the context of illness or incapacity. A party who is at fault cannot rely on frustration as to their own act. The imposition of a custodial sentence on an employee is capable in law of frustrating a contract of employment: *FC Shepherd & Co Ltd v Jerrom*.[65]

[14.92] The death of either party to the contract of employment will terminate it. An employer in this situation would be an individual. The Unfair Dismissals Act allows a claim for unfair dismissal to be brought by the personal representative of a deceased employee: s 1(1).

[14.93] The retirement or death of an existing partner, where the employer is a partnership, generally terminates the contracts of employment of its then employees at least in the absence of an express or implied contractual provision to the contrary.[66]

[14.94] An employer's insolvency is rarely dealt with in the written contract of employment but if not, common law principles or the European Communities (Protection of Employees on Transfer of Undertakings Regulations) 2003 generally

---

62 *W Devis & Sons Ltd v Atkins* [1977] AC 931.
63 *Griffin v Telecom Éireann* UD148/1994, (3 March 1992, unreported) CC.
64 *Sheffield v Oxford Controls Company Ltd* [1979] IRLR 133.
65 *FC Shepherd & Co Ltd v Jerrom* [1986] IRLR 358.
66 *Bruce v Calder* [1895] 2 QB 253.

provide the answers. In many circumstances, the latter negates what would otherwise be a harsh result for employees at common law.

[14.95] It is often provided in a contract that it will terminate if the employee is adjudicated bankrupt or makes an arrangement or composition with his creditors. If the employer is adjudicated bankrupt, all depends on the facts and the terms of the contract, if any, as to whether the bankruptcy is a frustrating event or brings the contract to an end by operation of law or lawfully terminates it.

[14.96] The winding up of a company can be compulsory by the court, voluntary by the members or voluntary by the creditors.[67] In general, an order for compulsory winding up will operate as a matter of law to terminate the contracts of employment of the employees concerned. If the liquidator wishes to carry on the business of the company he may waive the deemed notice of dismissal and continue to employ some or all of the employees.[68] Similarly, if a provisional liquidator is authorised to carry on the business of the company the employment contracts are not discharged.

[14.97] The appointment of a receiver out of court by the debenture holders does not, as such, terminate contracts of employment.[69]

Date of dismissal

[14.98] The 'date of dismissal' establishes the end of an employee's length of continuous service and hence the qualifying period of service for a complaint and the period for the calculation of an award of compensation. The date is also important to establish the time when an employee is entitled to written statement of reasons, his age at the time of dismissal, the particular version of the statutory enactment that is applicable and whether an employee's claim has been presented within the six-month time limit.

[14.99] Under s 1 of the Unfair Dismissals Act 1977 the 'date of dismissal' is defined as the date on which a notice of termination expires or would have expired where the notice is, or would have been, in accordance with the contract of employment or with the Minimum Notice and Terms of Employment Act 1973 whichever is the greater. For fixed-term or specified purpose contracts the date of dismissal is the date of the expiry or cesser. Special provisions in relation to the 'date of dismissal' apply under the Maternity Protection Act 1994, s 40(4), the Adoptive Leave Act 1995, s 26(2), the Parental Leave Act 1998, s 25(3)(a) and the Carers Leave Act 2001, s 16(4).

[14.100] The claimant's remaining annual leave entitlement will not be taken into account when determining the date of dismissal : *Twomey v O'Leary Office Supplies Ltd*.[70] In relation to internal appeals, where an internal or external appeal is provided, there should be no doubt in the contract drawn up between the parties as to whether a contract is saved in all the circumstances pending conclusion of the appeal. This issue arose in *O'Neill v Bank of Ireland*[71] where the EAT was influenced by the statement in

---

67   Companies Act 1963, Pt IV, ss 206–313.
68   *Re Collins* [1925] Ch 536.
69   See *Mythen v Buttercrust Ltd* [1990] 1 IR 98.
70   *Twomey v O'Leary Office Supplies Ltd* [1997] ELR 42.
71   *O'Neill v Bank of Ireland* [1993] ERL 145.

the employer's agreed procedures that following the decision to dismiss disciplinary action would not be taken pending the outcome of the hearing of an appeal (presuming the right to appeal was exercised). In the absence of such a provision or practice the effective date of dismissal will be the date on which termination is communicated to the employee and not the date on which he is informed that his appeal against dismissal has failed: *Savage v J Sainsbury Ltd.*[72]

Reason for dismissal

[14.101] The adjudicating body must determine whether dismissal was fair or unfair in the circumstances. First of all, an employer's reason for dismissal must be identified. Secondly, whether the reason was one which is deemed fair or unfair or whether there were other substantial grounds for the dismissal, an employer must be able to justify his decision to dismiss. The test of reasonableness is applied to determine the fairness or unfairness of his actions. Section 6(7) of the Act of 1977 further emphasises the importance of reasonableness. In determining if a dismissal is unfair regard may be had 'to the reasonableness or otherwise of the conduct (whether by act of omission) of the employer in relation to the dismissal'. In *Hennessy v Read & Write Shop Ltd*[73] the EAT described 'the test of reasonableness', as applied to:

(i) the nature and extent of the enquiry carried out by the employer prior to the decision to dismiss the claimant; and

(ii) the employer's conclusion following such enquiry that the claimant should be dismissed.

[14.102] In *Dunne v Harrington*[74] the EAT declared that an employer may investigate either

(a) personally in a fair and reasonable manner ie as fully as is reasonably possible, confronting the 'suspected' employee with 'evidence', checking on and giving fair value to the employee's explanation or comments and allowing the employee to be represented at all such meetings/confrontations if the employee requests it or a union/management agreement requires it and to produce 'counter evidence'; or

(b) he may rely on the reports of others. If he does so without confronting the accused employee with the contents of the same, without hearing, investigating and giving value to his replies, giving him reasonable opportunity to produce rebutting 'evidence', and to be represented if the employee feels this to be desirable, then such employer breaches a fundamental rule of natural justice viz that the other party (ie the employee in these circumstances) should be heard. In short, an employer acting on the reports of third parties and not acquainting the employee with same does so at his peril if it results in the dismissal of that employee.

---

[72] *Savage v J Sainsbury Ltd* [1980] IRLR 109.
[73] *Hennessy v Read & Write Shop Ltd* UD 192/1978.
[74] *Dunne v Harrington* UD 166/1979.

The burden of proof lies with an employer to establish his reason or reasons for dismissal. Great care should be taken in drafting disciplinary and dismissal procedures to ensure that constitutional fairness is provided to employees. Such procedures, guided by the Code of Practice on Grievance and Disciplinary Procedures[75] may be progressive (providing for a series of stages from oral warnings to dismissal which may be chosen in that order or passed over depending on the circumstances) or constructive (placing the onus fairly on the employee).

A considerable jurisprudence has developed in relation to the reasons which under the 1977 Act deem dismissals either not unfair or unfair.

Dismissals deemed not to be unfair

[14.103] Certain reasons are deemed not to be unfair by the Act, namely:

(a) the capability, competence or qualifications of the employee for performing work of the kind he was employed to do;

(b)   the conduct of the employee;

(c) the redundancy of the employee;

(d) that the employer was prohibited by statute (affecting hime of the employee) from continuing to employ the individual in the job; and/or

(e) that there were other substantial grounds which justify the dismissal.

Dismissals deemed to be unfair

[14.104] Certain reasons for dismissal are deemed unfair under ss 5 and 6 of the 1977 Act. Section 5 concerns dismissal for participation in strike or other industrial action although union bargaining power will generally ensure there is no discrimination where workers are dismissed for participating in strike or other industrial action. Section 5 of the Act provides that:

The dismissal of an employee for taking part in a strike or other industrial action shall be deemed for the purposes of this Act, to be an unfair dismissal if:

(a)   one or more employees of the same employer who took part in the strike or other industrial action were not dismissed for taking part; or

(b)   one or more of such employees dismissed for so taking part were subsequently permitted to resume their employment on terms and conditions at least as favourable to the employees as those specified in paragraph (a) or (b) [of s 7(1) of the Act which deals with reinstatement and reengagement respectively] and the employee was not.

[14.105] This default option protecting workers against loss of their jobs protects the freedom to strike and is consonant with the theory that Ireland recognises a positive right to strike in domestic and international law. Section 6(1) of the Act applies to non-selective dismissals. Sub-section 2(A) inserted by s 26 of the Protection of Employment (Exceptional Collective Redundancies and Related Matters) Act 2007 effects a conclusive presumption that selective dismissals for taking part in a strike or other

---

[75] SI 146/2000.

industrial action are unfair but does not deem non-selective dismissals to be fair. Such dismissals are subject to the general presumption of unfairness under s 6(1) of the 1977 Act.

[14.106] Sub-sections 2 and 3 of s 6 as amended deem the following grounds unfair:

(a) trade union membership or activities;

(b) religious or political opinions;

(c) involvement by an employee in civil proceedings against or involving an employer;

(d) involvement by an employee in criminal proceedings against or involving an employer;

(e) the exercise or proposed exercise by the employer of the right to parental leave or *force majeure* leave, leave under and in accordance with the Parental Leave Act 1998 or carer's leave under the Carers Leave Act 2001;

(f) race, colour or sexual orientation;

(g) age;

(h) membership of the travelling community;

(i) pregnancy, attendance at ante-natal classes, giving birth or breast feeding or matters connected therewith;

(j) the exercise or proposed exercise of a right under the Maternity Protection Act 1994 to any form of protective leave or natal care absence; or to time-off from work or a reduction of working hours for breast feeding under the said Act as amended;

(k) the exercise or contemplated exercise by an adoptive parent of her right under the Adoptive Leave Acts 1995 and 2005 to adoptive leave or additional adoptive leave or to a period of time off to attend certain pre-adoption classes or meetings; and/or

(l) unfair selection for redundancy.

These reasons do not automatically constitute unfair grounds for dismissal, because s-ss 2 and 3 of s 6 begin 'without prejudice to the generality of sub-section (1) of this Section' and sub-section (1) deems every dismissal unfair for purposes of the Act 'unless, having regard to all the circumstances, there are substantive grounds justifying the dismissal'. Fairness enters dismissals law at every point.

[14.107] Employment statutes in recent years have included protection against unfair dismissal for penalisation of an employee in connection with the exercise of rights thereunder. For example, the National Minimum Wage Act 2000, s 36(2) provides that the dismissal of an employee for exercising his rights under that Act shall be deemed to be an unfair dismissal. There are similar provisions in each of the Safety Health and Welfare Work Act 2005 and the Employees (Provision of Information and Consultation) Act 2006.

[14.108] The EAT does not assume the mantle of an employer regarding the facts in any case before it. Its function is to decide whether an employer's decision is not unfair. It is possible for different responses to be made by an employer in a given set of circumstances. Each of the responses may in its own way be reasonable. Because of the fact that there are a number of possible responses the EAT does not and should not substitute its view for that of the employer. In *Bunyan v United Dominions Trust*[76] the EAT endorsed the view that:

> The fairness or unfairness of dismissal is to be judged by the objective standard of the way in which a reasonable employer in those circumstances in that line of business would have behaved.

> The Tribunal therefore does not decide the question whether or not, on the evidence before it, the employee should be dismissed. That decision has been taken, and our function is to test such decision against what we consider the reasonable employer would have done and/ or concluded.

Constructive dismissal

[14.109] In constructive dismissal claims, because the employee has terminated his contract of employment, the fact of dismissal is in dispute. In cases of alleged constructive dismissal, the employee goes into evidence first as he bears the burden of proof as to dismissal. He must persuade the Rights Commissioner or the EAT that his resignation was not voluntary. There are two tests for constructive dismissal in the statutory definition, either or both of which may be invoked by an employee. The first is the contract test where the employee argues 'entitlement' to terminate the contract because of a fundamental breach of contract on the part of the employer. Secondly, the employee may allege that he satisfies the Act's 'reasonableness' test, that is, that the conduct of the employer was such that it was reasonable for him to resign. In some circumstances, the employer may have acted within the terms laid down in the contract of employment as to mobility or flexibility clauses but his conduct may nonetheless be unreasonable.

[14.110] The breach of contract being alleged must be either a significant breach going to the root of the contract or one which shows that the employer no longer intends to be bound by one or more of the essential terms of the contract.[77] The breach may not be actual but anticipatory. Where an employer relies on the contract test, it will be essential to ascertain the precise scope of the contract. Express terms present little difficulty. Thus, constructive dismissal may arise where an employer unjustifiably reduces an employee's remuneration. But difficulties can arise where constructive dismissal is alleged in the face of breach of an implied term. An employee may encounter problems identifying such terms although the process has been facilitated by a change in judicial attitude to the status of the employment relationship. Examples of such terms have been given earlier.[78]

---

[76] *Bunyan v United Dominions Trust* [1982] ILRM 404.

[77] *Cosgrave v Kavanagh Meat Products* UD 6/1988, *Harrison v National Engineering and Electrical Trade Union* UD 406/1987, *Higgins v Donnelly Mirrors Ltd* UD 104/1979.

[78] See para **[14.23]**.

[14.111] An employee should invoke the employer's grievance procedures in an effort to resolve his grievance before initiating a claim for unfair dismissal. This duty is an imperative almost always in employee resignations: *Conway v Ulster Bank Ltd*.[79]

[14.112] It is a matter for advice as to whether an employee who feels forced to resign because of alleged sexual harassment or discrimination on any of the prescribed grounds should proceed under the 1977 Act or the Employment Equality Acts 1998–2008. There may be advantages in choosing the former route in particular circumstances.

The Industrial Relations Act 1990 and dismissal

[14.113] Workers engaged in strike or industrial action are granted immunity from civil suit for civil and criminal conspiracy, picketing, inducing breaches of employment contracts, intimidation or interference with trade, business or employment. These immunities are provided under the Industrial Relations Act 1990 (the 1990 Act) but only if workers are acting 'in contemplation or furtherance of a trade dispute'. Outside the 1990 Act, the workers' action must not be inconsistent with the Constitution. Under s 9 of the 1990 Act, strike or industrial action arising out of one-worker disputes (highly relevant to dismissal) no longer enjoys statutory immunity where agreed procedures have not been resorted to and exhausted. The section removes the protection from individuals taking wildcat action eg in relation to dismissal and from those supporting them.

Remedies for unfair dismissal

[14.114] The 1977 Act provides for a choice of remedies for the adjudicating authorities. Depending on the circumstances, they may award redress consisting of reinstatement, re-engagement or compensation. Reinstatement and re-engagement are regarded as primary remedies under the Act. An employee unfairly dismissed is entitled to whichever of the remedies the rights commissioner, the EAT or the Circuit Court as the case may be considers appropriate having regard to all the circumstances. The primary remedy of reinstatement is described as follows:[80]

> Reinstatement by the employer of the employee in the position which he held immediately before his dismissal on the terms and conditions on which he was employed immediately before his dismissal together with the term that the reinstatement shall be deemed to have commenced on the day of the dismissal.

[14.115] Re-engagement[81] is defined as:

> Re-engagement by the employer of the employee either in the position which he held immediately before the dismissal or in a different position which would be reasonably suitable for him on such terms and conditions as are reasonable having regard to all the circumstances.

---

[79] *Conway v Ulster Bank Ltd* UD474/198.
[80] UDA 1977, s 7(1)(a).
[81] UDA 1977, s 7(1)(b).

[14.116] The remedy of compensation[82] means:

> ...if the employee incurred any financial loss attributable to the dismissal, payment to him by the employer of such compensation in respect of the loss (not exceeding in amount 104 weeks' remuneration in respect of the employment from which he was dismissed calculated in accordance with regulations under s 17 of this Act) as is just and equitable having regard to all the circumstances; or

> if the employee incurred no such financial loss, payment to the employee by the employer of such compensation (if any, but not exceeding in amount four weeks' remuneration in respect of the employment from which he was dismissed calculated as aforesaid) as is just and equitable having regard to all the circumstances.

[14.117] The statute gives no power to award exemplary damages. 'Financial loss' is defined by s 7(3) of the 1977 Act to include:

(i)   any actual loss; and

(ii)   any estimated prospective loss of income attributable to the dismissal; and

(iii)   the value of any loss or diminution, attributable to the dismissal, of the rights of the employee under the Redundancy Payments Acts 1967–2007 or in relation to superannuation.

'Remuneration' includes allowances in the nature of pay and benefits in lieu of or in addition to pay.

[14.118] Sub-section 2 of s 7 provides clarification regarding the calculation of compensation. Regard is to be had to:

(a)   the extent (if any) to which the financial loss was attributable to an act, omission or conduct by or on behalf of the employer;

(b)   the extent (if any) to which the said financial loss was attributable to an action, omission or conduct by or on behalf of the employee;

(c)   the measures (if any) adopted by the employer, or, as the case may be, his failure to adopt measures, to mitigate the loss aforesaid; and

(d)   the extent (if any) of the compliance or failure to comply by the employer, in relation to the employee, with the procedure referred to in sub-section 1 of s 14 of this Act [regarding procedures in relation to disciplinary and dismissal] or with the provisions of any code of practice relating to procedures regarding dismissal approved of by the Minister;

(e)   the extent (if any) of the compliance or failure to comply by the employer, in relation to the employee, with the said s 14; and

---

[82]   UDA 1977, s 7(1)(c) as amended. See the exceptional levels of compensation of 208 and 260 weeks' remuneration provided for in the case of exceptional collective redundancies: Protection of Employment (Exceptional Collective Redundancies and Related Matters) Act 2007, s 9.

(f)   the extent (if any) to which the conduct of the employee (whether by act or omission) contributed to the dismissal.

[14.119] In brief, the EAT computes an employee's net loss from dismissal to the date of the hearing, taking into account basic pay, average bonuses and average overtime pay. If an employee has sustained no loss by reason of the dismissal as, for example, by obtaining immediate employment without injury, pension or otherwise he will be entitled to compensation of not greater than four weeks' remuneration. An employee's prospective loss of income also has to be estimated which involves computing any reduction he is likely to suffer in future net earnings and fringe benefits. Loss of protection in respect of statutory rights under unfair dismissals, redundancy and minimum notice will also be computed and an assessment made as to any expenses, pre-requisites or pension rights lost by an employee as a result of dismissal.

Procedural aspects of statutory claims

[14.120] If requested, an employer must provide a dismissed employee within 14 days of the request of a written statement of particulars of the grounds for dismissal: s 14 of the 1977 Act. An employer is not estopped from denying the accuracy of the particulars contained in the statement. An employee has no grievance or right of redress if an employer unreasonably refuses to provide a written statement or if the written statement is inaccurate or untrue but failure to comply with s 14 may have financial implications for an employer as default is likely to be taken into account in determining the appropriate redress to which an aggrieved employee may be entitled.

[14.121] The adjudicatory service for statutory unfair dismissal comprises the Rights Commissioner and the EAT. Appeal lies to the ordinary courts from the decisions of the EAT.

Proceedings before a Rights Commissioner are held 'otherwise than in public'[83] and their recommendations are not available to members of the public.

[14.122] The EAT, along with the rights commissioners and the Circuit Court, is obliged when awarding redress to an employee to state the reasons why either of the other forms of redress specified in s 7(1) of the 1997 Act was not awarded.

[14.123] Although a claim for unfair dismissal may be brought before either a Rights Commissioner or the EAT in the first place, the choice is not unrestricted. The 1977 Act as amended stipulates that the Rights Commissioner may not hear a claim for redress where:

(a)   the Tribunal has made a determination in relation to the claim; or

(b)   any party concerned notifies the Rights Commissioner in writing within 21 days of the giving to the employer pursuant to sub-section 2 of s 8 of the Act copy of the notice concerned referred to in that subsection and relating to the claim, that he objects to the claim being heard by a rights commissioner.

---

[83]   UDA 1977, s 8 (6).

Regulations have been made regarding applications to the EAT. The relevant application forms are Form T1-A for direct claims to the EAT and Form T1-B for appeals of a rights commissioner's recommendation to the EAT.

[14.124] Under s 8(5) the EAT may not hear a claim for redress under the Act except by way of appeal from a recommendation of a rights commissioner:

    (a)   if the Rights Commissioner has made a recommendation in relation to the claim, or

    (b)   unless, before the commencement of the hearing of the claim, one of the parties concerned notifies in writing:

        (i)   In a case where the claim has been initiated before a rights commissioner, or

        (ii)   In any other case, the Tribunal,

    that he objects to the claim being heard by a rights commissioner.

[14.125] A dismissed employee must initiate his claim in writing to a Rights Commissioner or to the EAT as the case may be within six months, beginning on the date of the relevant dismissal: s 8(2). If the Rights Commissioner or the EAT is satisfied that 'exceptional circumstances' prevented the giving of notice within this period then notice must be given within such period not exceeding 12 months from the date of dismissal as the Rights Commissioner or the EAT considers reasonable. These words are regarded as meaning 'something out of the ordinary'. The circumstances must be unusual. In order to extend the time limit. the adjudicating body must be satisfied that the exceptional circumstances prevented the lodging of the claim within the general time limit.

[14.126] There is a right of appeal in relation to the recommendation of a Rights Commissioner to the EAT within six weeks of the date on which the recommendation of the Rights Commissioner was given to the parties concerned: s 9.

[14.127] Similarly, a party may appeal to the Circuit Court from a determination of the EAT within six weeks from the date on which the determination is communicated to the parties: s 11 of the Unfair Dismissals (Amendment) Act 1993. The Circuit Court may order the employer concerned to make 'the appropriate redress' to the employee concerned. The six-week time limit for appealing is crucial and cannot be extended by the Circuit Court. In general, in civil cases, appeal lies to the High Court from decisions in cases originating in the Circuit Court. There have been several appeals to that Court from Circuit Court decisions and a right of appeal in relation to cases under the Unfair Dismissals Acts was confirmed by the High Court in *The Commissioners of Irish Lights v Noel Sugg*.[84]

---

[84] *The Commissioners of Irish Lights v Noel Sugg* [1994] ELR 97. See *McKernan v EAT* [2008] IEHC 40 wherein the applicant failed in judicial review proceedings to obtain an order of *certiorari* quashing a determination of the EAT.

Chapter 15

Redundancy

Imelda Higgins and Terence McCrann

INTRODUCTION[1]

[15.01] No organisation can afford to stay the same for long. Competitiveness and the need to react to a range of changing economic circumstances mean that employers must constantly reorganise their resources. Such reorganisation may result in a change in the deployment of resources including rationalisation and/or redundancy. Redundancy can include one individual, part of a workforce or the entire workforce in a complete closure situation. Employers, depending on the circumstances, may seek to achieve their objectives by first offering voluntary redundancies followed by compulsory redundancies.

[15.02] An employer is entitled to dismiss one or all of its employees where the employee's position becomes redundant.[2] However, an employee with more than two years' service who is made redundant is entitled to the payment of a lump sum, the amount of which increases with the employee's salary and seniority. This entitlement was first introduced by the Redundancy Payments Act 1967 and, while that Act has been amended on a number of occasions, principally in 1971, 1979, 2003 and 2007 (collectively, the Redundancy Payments Acts), the employee's entitlement to a lump sum payment remains.[3]

[15.03] The Redundancy Payments Act 1967 was adopted against a background of considerable industrial malaise arising out of the impact of new technological innovations on employment. By the early to mid-1960s, it was clear that almost all

---

[1] We wish to acknowledge the considerable assistance and contribution of Ailbhe Dennehy to the preparation of this chapter.

[2] See *Kaur v MG* [2004] EWCA Civ 1507.

[3] The Redundancy Payments Act 1971 provided for a new definition of redundancy and improvements in the rates of redundancy payments as well as making a number of technical amendments to the Redundancy Payments Act 1967. The principal changes introduced by the Redundancy Payments Act 1979 were the discontinuance of weekly payments provided for under the 1967 Act, the simplification of the rebate system, the abolition of workers' contributions and the provision of time off to look for new employment. The Redundancy Payments Act 2003 enhanced redundancy payments limits, modified the method for calculating the lump sum and introduced a simpler method for calculating service. Finally, the Protection of Employment (Exceptional Collective Redundancies and Related Matters) Act 2007, while essentially concerned with collective redundancies, also, *inter alia*, removed the upper age limit for entitlement to a redundancy payment and updated the penalties in the redundancy payments legislation.

industries had excessive numbers of employees. The purpose of the Act was to make it easier for employers to respond to economic, organisational and technological change by reducing employee resistance to any resulting job losses.[4] The Act sought to achieve this objective by guaranteeing lump sum payments to employees who lost their jobs. Crucially, the Act did not seek to enhance job security, prevent dismissal on redundancy grounds or otherwise create a disincentive to the dismissal of employees. While it did impose a requirement on employers to pay an employee a sum of money when terminating his or her employment contract, it spared employers the far greater costs associated with strong collective resistance to the declaration of redundancies.[5]

[15.04] The Unfair Dismissals Acts 1977–2007 (the Unfair Dismissals Acts) also have a bearing on redundancy-based dismissals. While those Acts recognise an employer's entitlement to dismiss an employee if the dismissal is due wholly or mainly to redundancy,[6] for such a dismissal to be fair a number of requirements must be fulfilled. Specifically, the redundancy selection process must be fair[7] and in particular must not breach any of the statutory prohibitions or an agreed or customary procedure within the particular employment. In addition the employer's conduct must be reasonable. Most challenges to redundancy-based dismissals are brought under the Unfair Dismissals Acts.[8]

[15.05] The combined effect of the Redundancy Payments Acts and the Unfair Dismissals Acts is that an employer, when contemplating a dismissal on grounds of redundancy, must first ensure that the relevant circumstances fall within the definition of redundancy set out in the Redundancy Payments Acts. Once this is the case, that employer must then ensure that the procedures whereby an employee is selected for redundancy are transparent, objective and fair. In all cases, the employer must ensure that he conducts himself reasonably. Any employee dismissed following the redundancy process must then be provided with his or her statutory redundancy entitlements.

[15.06] Other legislation may also impact on redundancy-based dismissals. In particular, specific procedural requirements applicable in the case of large-scale collective redundancies are set out in the Protection of Employment Acts 1977–2007 (the Protection of Employment Acts) and related regulations. Further requirements relating to so-called exceptional collective redundancies are set out in the Protection of Employment (Exceptional Collective Redundancies and Related Matters) Act 2007.

---

[4]   Fryer, 'Redundancy, Values and Public Policy' (1973) 4 *IRJ* 2; Fryer, 'The Myths of the Redundancy Payments Act' (1975) 2 *ILJ* 1.

[5]   Barrett, 'The Law on 'Downsizing' – Some Reflections on the Experience of Redundancy Payments Legislation in Ireland 4 (1998) 5(1) *DULJ* 1; see also Grunfeld, *Law of Redundancy* (3rd edn, London: Sweet & Maxwell, 1989) who states, at pg 2–3 that the purpose of the UK Redundancy Payments Act 1965 was 'to mitigate the resistance of individual employees (and their unions) to the extensive changes which have accompanied and will continue to accompany the response of British industry, commerce and finance to the searching demands of world trade and competition…'.

[6]   Unfair Dismissals Act, s 6(4)(c).

[7]   Unfair Dismissals Act, s 6(3).

[8]   See Compton and Doyle, 'Practice and Procedure' (2005) 2(2) *IELJ* 58.

MEANING OF REDUNDANCY

[15.07] For the purposes of the Redundancy Payments Acts and the Unfair Dismissal Acts an employee is dismissed by reason of redundancy if, 'for one or more reasons not related to the employee concerned', his dismissal is attributable 'wholly or mainly' to one of the five situations outlined in s 7(2) of the Redundancy Payments Acts.

[15.08] The phrases 'for one or more reasons not related to the employee concerned' and 'wholly or mainly' both emphasise one of the essential characteristics of a redundancy situation, namely its 'impersonality'.[9] Specifically, in order for a dismissal to be due to redundancy, it must be unrelated to the employee who is to be made redundant. In practical terms, it means that a redundancy situation must not be contrived so as to enable the employer to dismiss a specific employee or be otherwise mainly attributable to the individual employee rather than the objective needs of the undertaking. For example, in *Daly v Hanson Industries Ltd*[10] an employee was dismissed on the morning she had given evidence before the Employment Appeals Tribunal (the EAT) in the hearing of a claim by the former general manager of the company. While the respondent claimed that she had been made redundant and the EAT accepted that there was a redundancy element to her dismissal, it held that the dismissal was not due to redundancy but rather to the fact that she had testified before the EAT. Similarly, in *Edwards v Aerials and Electronics (Ireland) Ltd*,[11] the EAT accepted that there was an overall situation of redundancy in the work place, but considered that the claimant's dismissal from the role of managing director of the Irish subsidiary of the company was attributable to personal difficulties between the director and various board members. Again in *O Driscoll v Siebel Systems Emea Ltd*[12] the EAT found that a genuine redundancy situation did not exist, despite the fact that the respondent company had experienced a significant downturn in its business and had made a significant number of employees redundant. In this case, the claimant had successfully argued that while a number of redundancies had taken place, her selection for redundancy was due to a deterioration in her working relationship with her manager.[13]

[15.09] As mentioned, a dismissal will be due to redundancy where it is wholly or mainly attributable to one or more of the five situations outlined in the Redundancy Payments Acts. These situations are each characterised by changes in the workplace and cover: (1) change in the purpose or place of the business;[14] (2) reduction in the

---

9   *St Ledger v Frontline Distributors Ireland Ltd* [1995] ELR 160.
10 *Daly v Hanson Industries Ltd* UD 719/1986; see also *Foley v Castle Timber Frame Homes Ltd* UD 743/2007.
11 *Edwards v Aerials and Electronics (Ireland) Ltd* UD 236/1985; See also *Hurley v Royal Cork Yacht Club* [1999] ELR 7; *Moloney v Deacon and Sons Ltd* [1996] ELR 230; *Elbay v Iona National Airways* UD 873/1991.
12 *O'Driscoll v Siebel Systems Emea Ltd* UD1257/2003.
13 See also *Moloney v Deacon* [1996] ELR 230.
14 Redundancy Payments Act 1967, s 7(2)(a).

requirements of the business;[15] (3) a diminution in the number of employees required by the business;[16] (4) change in work methods;[17] and/or (5) change in work.[18]

(i) Change in purpose or place of the business

[15.10] The first situation covers an employee's dismissal where that dismissal is attributable wholly or mainly to:

> [t]he fact that his employer has ceased, or intends to cease, to carry on the business for the purposes of which the employee was employed by him, or has ceased or intends to cease, to carry on that business in the place where the employee was so employed.[19]

[15.11] This situation essentially covers dismissals resulting from: changes in the business's purpose; closure of the business and/or closure of the particular part of the business where the employee was employed. The crucial question is whether there has been the requisite change or closure and not the reasons for it. In particular, the Tribunal will not consider arguments that the change or closure was not necessary because there were alternative options open to the employer, or that it was motivated by malice rather than economic necessity.[20]

[15.12] An example of redundancy resulting from the closure of a business arose in *Ajai and Ajai v Anne Byrne*[21] In that case, the respondent business supplied emergency services to the Immigration Service at the Department of Justice, Equality and Law Reform, Dublin City Council and the North Eastern Health Board. The claimants were employed as supervisors to manage the respondent's hostel but were dismissed after the number of clients arriving at the hostel began to decrease dramatically and the hostel had to close. The EAT held that there was a genuine redundancy situation. In *O'Connor v Power Securities Ltd,*[22] the employer company closed the place in which the employee was employed but continued carrying on business elsewhere. In that case, the respondent had three employees who worked as security guards, one (the claimant) who worked in the Grafton Court Arcade, one at the Powerscourt Town Centre and one at the William Elliot Centre. The respondent sold its interest in the Grafton Court Arcade and the claimant was made redundant. The EAT was satisfied that a redundancy situation existed once the respondent sold his interest in the Grafton Court Arcade.

---

[15] Redundancy Payments Act 1967, s 7(2)(b).

[16] Redundancy Payments Act 1967, s 7(2)(c).

[17] Redundancy Payments Act 1967, s 7(2)(d).

[18] Redundancy Payments Act 1967, s 7(2)(e).

[19] Redundancy Payments Act 1967, s 7(2)(a).

[20] See *Moon v Homeworthy Furniture (Northern) Ltd* [1977] ICR 177.

[21] *Ajai and Ajai v Anne Byrne* UD 449/2004 and UD 335/2004; *Campbell v Dunoon & Cowal Housing Association Ltd* [1993] IRLR 496; See also *Flanagan v MW Wallpaper Specialists Ltd* UD 153, 154, 155, 156/1989 in which the EAT accepted that there was some evidence that the claimants' dismissal was by reason of joining a trade union but was obliged to acknowledge that there was a redundancy situation in view of the fact that the particular branch of the respondent had been totally closed down. See also *O'Connor v Zero Four Ltd* RP 187/2008.

[22] *O'Connor v Power Securities Ltd* UD 344/89; see also *Brady v Donegan* UD 280/1980.

[15.13] In some cases, where an employer ceases to carry on business in one place but continues in other places, the question may arise as to where the employee was actually employed. Specifically, is the place of employment the place where the employee actually worked, or is it any place where he or she could have been contractually required to work? The answer to this question is important because many employment contracts both specify an employee's normal place of work and contain a mobility clause to the effect that the employee may be required to work in another location or at any location within a specified radius. This question has been considered by the English EAT on a number of occasions. While initially, that Tribunal took the view that the employee's place of employment was wherever the employee could be contractually required to work,[23] this approach has not been followed in subsequent cases. In *Bass Leisure Ltd v Thomas*,[24] the English EAT held that the claimant was entitled to a redundancy payment when she resigned after being relocated to a depot some 20 miles away, despite the existence of a mobility clause in her employment contract providing that the company reserved the right to transfer her to a suitable alternative place of work. This case was subsequently upheld by the Court of Appeal in *High Table Ltd v Horst*.[25] In the latter case, Mrs Horst was employed as a silver-service waitress by the appellant company which provided catering services for companies and firms in the City of London and elsewhere. While her letter of appointment specified that she was appointed as waitress to one particular client, Hill Samuel, her contractual terms of employment included a mobility clause. Cuts in Hill Samuel's catering budget necessitated a reorganisation of services provided by the appellants which resulted in the need for fewer waitresses working longer hours. Consequently, Mrs Horst and two other applicants were dismissed as redundant. The employees presented complaints for unfair dismissal. One of the questions which arose in determining this issue was how to determine where the employee was employed. The Court of Appeal held that this was a factual test. According to Peter Gibson LJ:

> The question it poses – where was the employee employed by the employer for the purpose of the business? – is one to be answered primarily by a consideration of the factual circumstances which obtained until the dismissal. If an employee has worked in only one location under his contract of employment for the purposes of the employer's business, it defies common sense to widen the extent of the place where he was employed, merely because of the existence of a mobility clause. Of course, the refusal by the employee to obey a lawful requirement under the contract of employment for the employee to move may constitute a valid reason for dismissal, but the issues of dismissal, redundancy and reasonableness in the actions of an employer should be kept distinct. It would be

---

[23] *United Kingdom Atomic Energy Authority v Claydon* [1974] ICR 128. According to Donaldson J in that case '[m]any men and women are employed under contracts of employment which provide for transfers over a wide area. If work is short in one place but available elsewhere within the area, there will be no redundancy situation and the employer can dismiss without being liable to make any redundancy payment. If, however, he does so without offering to transfer the employee to a place where work is available, he will risk being liable to pay compensation for unfair dismissal.

[24] *Bass Leisure Ltd v Thomas* [1994] IRLR 104.

[25] *High Table Ltd v Horst* [1997] IRLR 513.

unfortunate if the law were to encourage the inclusion of mobility clauses in contracts of employment to defeat genuine redundancy claims. Parliament has recognised the importance of the employee's right to a redundancy payment. If the work of the employee for his employer has involved a change of location, as would be the case where the nature of the work required the employee to go from place to place, then the contract of employment may be helpful to determine the extent of the place where the employee was employed. But it cannot be right to let the contract be the sole determinant, regardless of where the employee actually worked for the employer.

[15.14] This approach potentially allows the employer the best of both worlds in so far as mobility clauses are concerned. Specifically, if there is such a clause in the contract and the employee refuses an order to move pursuant to it, there could well be a fair dismissal.[26] If however, the employer does not activate the clause when work ceases or diminishes in the existing location, the employer can still rely on a redundancy in spite of the clause.[27]

(ii) Reduction in requirements of the business

[15.15] The second situation arises where the dismissal is attributable wholly or mainly to:

> the fact that the requirements of that business for employees to carry out work of a particular kind in the place where he was so employed have ceased or diminished or are expected to cease or diminish.[28]

[15.16] This second situation is essentially concerned with dismissals resulting from a downward change in the business's requirements for employees to carry out work of a particular kind.[29] The most obvious case in which such a situation arises is where the volume of work of an employer has fallen off either partially or completely. In such cases, some or all of the employees engaged in the work are surplus to the requirements of the business and so are redundant.

[15.17] However, before an employee is redundant for this reason, the downward change must impact on the particular kind of work the employee was contracted to perform. According to the English National Industrial Relations Court, the same phrase in the English legislation means 'work which is distinguished from other work of the same general kind by requiring special aptitudes, skills or knowledge'.[30] In this jurisdiction, in *Dinworth v Southern Hotel Board*,[31] the EAT held that day work was a different kind of work than night work. In *Kelleher v St James Hospital Board*,[32] the EAT considered that work of a part-time nature was of a different kind from on-call work.[33] In *Shine v SKS*

---

26 *Rowbothan v Arthur Lee & Sons Ltd* [1974] IRLR 377.
27 *Harvey on Industrial Relations and Employment Law* (Bulletin No 229, August 1997) p 3.
28 Redundancy Payments Acts, s 7(2)(b).
29 However an upward change in the volume or work will not imply redundancy under the statutory definition, see *St Ledger v Frontline Distributors Ireland Ltd* [1995] ELR 160.
30 *Amos v Max-Arc Ltd* [1973] IRLR 285; *O'Neill v Merseyside Plumbing Ltd* [1973] ICR 96.
31 *Dinworth v Southern Hotel Board* UD 284/1977.
32 *Kelleher v St James Hospital Board* UD 59/1977.

Communications Ltd[34] the EAT held that work consisting of repairing machines off-site as opposed to on the employer's premises constituted work of a different kind within the meaning of this section.

[15.18] By way of contrast, in *Vaux and Associated Breweries Ltd v Ward,*[35] the employers decided to re-launch one of their hotels by employing young 'bunny girls' in place of older barmaids, and the vital question in deciding whether one of the dismissed middle-aged barmaids was entitled to a redundancy payment concerned whether 'the work that the barmaid in the altered premises was going to do was work of a different kind to what the barmaid in the unaltered premises had been doing'. The Divisional Court found that the work was not different, even though the type of person required to fill the position was, and therefore the applicant was not entitled to a redundancy payment.

[15.19] An employer is not required to wait for the downward change to occur before making employees redundant and it is sufficient if such a change is anticipated in the near future.[36] In this respect, the Tribunal held, in *Keenan v the Gresham Hotel*, that where the redundancy is due to an expected diminution in the requirements of the business, such diminution:

> [m]ust be expected to occur at or within a very short time after the time of the alleged redundancy as otherwise an employer who merely expects that his requirements for employees to do work of a particular kind may diminish at some distant time in the future could greatly reduce the redundancy entitlements of such employees by serving R21 forms on them prematurely.[37]

(iii) Diminution in required number of employees

[15.20] The third situation covers dismissals due wholly or mainly to the fact that:

> [h]is employer has decided to carry on the business with fewer or no employees, whether by requiring the work for which the employee had been employed (or had been doing before his dismissal) to be done by other employees or otherwise.[38]

[15.21] Unlike the second situation, this third situation is not concerned with a diminution in the volume of work *per se*, but with the diminution in the number of employees required to carry out such work. Thus while the work in question remains to be done or has even increased, the employer has so organised his affairs that fewer employees[39] are required to do that work. Such a situation could arise because of improved mechanisation, automation or other technical advance. It could also arise by

---

[33] See also *Farren v Lee* UD 496/1979.
[34] *Shine v SKS Communications Ltd* UD 975/2007.
[35] *Vaux and Associated Breweries Ltd v Ward* (1968) 3 ITR 385.
[36] Redundancy Payments Acts, s 7(2)(b).
[37] *Keenan v The Gresham Hotel Ltd* UD 478/1988.
[38] Redundancy Payments Acts, s 7(2)(c).
[39] In determining whether an employer has decided to carry out his business with fewer or no employees no account is taken of the employer's mother, father, brothers, sisters, sons, daughters and/or grandchildren. See Redundancy Payments Acts, s 4A.

virtue of a reorganisation of the work force pursuant to which two or more jobs are combined with each other. For example, in *Lillis v Kiernan*,[40] the claimant who was a former general manager of the respondent's pig farming business was made redundant after the respondent decided to redistribute his functions among the regular managers of the business. The EAT accepted that this was a redundancy situation. In *Dennehy v Millstreet Country Park Ltd*,[41] the EAT found that a genuine redundancy situation existed.

[15.22] Where an employer reorganises its business so as to involve a switch for its employees from employment to self-employment this may also constitute redundancy as the requirements of the business for 'employees' to carry out work of a particular kind will have ceased or diminished.[42] However, it should be noted that in *Scully v Laragan Developments Ltd*,[43] the EAT held that the claimant was unfairly selected for redundancy in circumstances where agency workers with less service than him were retained to perform duties which he was able and willing to perform.

(iv) Change in work methods

[15.23] The fourth situation covers the dismissal of an employee which is wholly or mainly attributable to:

> [t]he fact that his employer has decided that the work for which the employee had been employed (or had been doing before his dismissal) should henceforward be done in a different manner for which the employee is not sufficiently qualified or trained.[44]

[15.24] This covers situations where an employee is dismissed because of a change in the manner in which the work is done or some other form of qualitative change in the nature of the job and the employee is not sufficiently qualified or trained to do the job in the new manner.[45] In *Byrne v Trackline Crane Hire Ltd*,[46] the employer made the employee redundant because the crane he was hired to operate was no longer profitable and it would take an excessive amount of time to retrain him to operate the other cranes. The EAT accepted that there was a redundancy situation. It considered that the employee's position no longer existed as the greater part of his employment with the company had been driving one particular type of crane, which had to be sold.[47] In *Daniels v County Wexford Community Workshop (New Ross) Ltd*,[48] the company was advised to appoint a manager with a third level qualification by an independent

---

40 *Lillis v Kiernan* EAT, 22/06/2004.
41 *Dennehy v Millstreet Country Park Ltd* UD1384/2005.
42 Redmond, *Dismissal Law in Ireland* (2nd edn, Tottel Publishing, 2007); However, see *Scully v Largan Development Ltd* UD 10/2007.
43 *Scully v Laragan Developments Ltd* UD 10/2007.
44 Redundancy Payments Acts, s 7(2)(d).
45 *St Ledger v Frontline Distribution Ltd* [1995] ELR 160.
46 *Byrne v Trackline Crane Hire Ltd* EAT, 02/05/2003.
47 There was evidence to the effect that re-training the claimant in the use of a more profitable crane would take an excessively long time.
48 *Daniels v County Wexford Community Workshop (New Ross) Ltd* [1996] ELR 213.

consultant which it had engaged to improve its operation. The existing manager did not have such a qualification and the company offered her a new position under the same conditions of employment, which she refused as she was unhappy with one aspect of the new job. She was then made redundant and replaced with a new person with third level qualifications. The EAT held that this was a valid redundancy on the qualification ground. In contrast, in *Moore v Custom House Dining Club*,[49] an employee claimed redundancy on the basis that the introduction of a new operated process meant that he was being asked to undertake work for which he was not sufficiently well trained. The EAT held that there was no redundancy situation on the basis that employees are expected to adapt to new technological techniques and the change was not sufficiently radical to fall within this category.

[15.25] To fall within this fourth situation, the redundancy must relate to either the employee's qualification or training. In *Lefever v The Trustees of the Irish Wheelchair Association*,[50] the EAT held that the issue is whether the employee is sufficiently qualified or trained to carry out the job in the future and not the employee's personal qualities. In that case, the claimant was a supervisor for an annual scheme run by the respondent employer and funded by FÁS. The claimant was awarded the job for the first year, following which her appointment was rolled over for the second scheme. The position was then advertised for the third scheme but the claimant did not get the job. The EAT considered that the important issue in determining whether or not there was a redundancy situation was whether there was a qualitative change in the nature of the scheme and therefore in the nature of the supervisor's role.

[15.26] The EAT has distinguished between training and ability. Specifically, employees replaced by a more able employee are not redundant pursuant to this category. For example, in *St Ledger v Frontline Distributors Ireland Ltd*,[51] the EAT rejected the employer's claim that the employee had been dismissed by reason of redundancy, in a situation where the employee had been replaced with another employee based on ability rather than training. The EAT held that ability was not the same as training and it was irrelevant that the replacement was better able to do the work previously done by the employee.

(v) Change in work

[15.27] The fifth situation arises where the employee's dismissal stems from:

> [t]he fact that his employer has decided that the work for which the employee had been employed (or had been doing before his dismissal) should henceforward be done by a person who is also capable of doing other work for which the employee is not sufficiently qualified or trained.[52]

---

[49] *Moore v Custom House Dining Club* UD 237/1977.
[50] *Lefever v The Trustees of the Irish Wheelchair Association* [1996] ELR 220; see also *Hurley v Royal Yacht Club* [1997] ELR 225.
[51] *St Ledger v Frontline Distributors Ireland Ltd* [1995] ELR 160.
[52] Redundancy Payments Acts, s 7(2)(e).

[15.28] As in the case of the fourth situation, this fifth situation is concerned with a change in the nature of the job. According to the EAT in *St Ledger v Frontline Distribution Ltd*,[53] in order to fall within this category, the reference to *'other work'* means work of a different kind. In this respect, the EAT observed that:

> Definition (e) must involve, partly at least, work of a different kind, and that is the only meaning we can put on the words 'other work'. More work or less work of the same kind does not mean 'other work' and is only a quantitative change.

[15.29] In the case of *O'Brien v Hays Specialist Recruitment (Ireland) Ltd*,[54] the claimant had been employed as a credit controller, but was made redundant following a reorganisation of his employer's credit control and billing department, pursuant to which the claimant's credit controller position was amalgamated with the customer relationship manager position. The EAT rejected the claimant's unfair dismissal claim on the basis that a genuine redundancy situation existed. In contrast, in *Gammell v Pall Ireland*,[55] the EAT held that a genuine redundancy situation did not exist, despite the fact that the claimant's role of Production Shift Supervisor had been amalgamated into a new position of Module Manager, following restructuring. In reaching this conclusion, the EAT observed that the restructuring occurred because the company was expanding its product line and turnover, and that it should have been able to redeploy the claimant to a suitable position.

SELECTION

[15.30] The manner in which employees are selected for redundancy is of crucial importance. An area where employers sometimes fall foul of the Unfair Dismissals Acts is in deciding upon appropriate selection criteria and determining the pool of employees to whom those criteria should be applied. Pursuant to the Unfair Dismissals Acts, even in circumstances where there is a genuine redundancy situation, an employee who is unfairly selected for redundancy will be able to bring a successful unfair dismissal action.[56] Moreover, subjective, non-transparent or unfair selection procedures may influence the EAT's assessment as to whether a genuine redundancy situation exists in the first place, whether a dismissal was for one or more reasons not related to the employee concerned and/or was wholly or mainly the result of the redundancy situation. For example, in *Shanley v IT Allliance Ltd*[57] one of the reasons the Tribunal concluded that there was no genuine redundancy was that the process and selection criteria used to justify the claimant's redundancy were very subjective and there was an unnecessary element of secrecy connected with the dismissal.

[15.31] This raises the question as to what constitutes a fair selection procedure. In essence, what is required of the employer in this respect is that it be able to objectively

---

[53] *St Ledger v Frontline Distribution Ltd* [1995] ELR 160; See also *Tarah Jenkins v Esat Telecommunications Ltd and Murphy v Epsom College* [1984] IRLR 271.

[54] *O'Brien v Hays Specialist Recruitment (Ireland) Ltd* UD 1172/2006.

[55] *Gammell v Pall Ireland* UD 1057/2007.

[56] Unfair Dismissals Act 1977, s 6(3).

[57] *Shanley v IT Allliance Ltd* UD467/2002.

justify why a particular employee was selected for redundancy as opposed to another employee.[58] Specifically, the employer must be able to demonstrate that a particular employee has been compared to others who might have been made redundant and has been selected fairly on the basis of independent, objective and verifiable criteria. In assessing whether selection criteria meet this standard much depends on the facts of the case and what is fair in one instance will not necessarily be fair in another.

[15.32] Generally, if there is an agreed or customary procedure for redundancy, the employer should follow that procedure. Pursuant to the Unfair Dismissals Acts, there can be a finding of unfair dismissal if an employee is dismissed due to redundancy but his selection was in contravention of an agreed or customary procedure relating to redundancy and there were no special reasons justifying departure from that procedure. Moreover, in certain cases an agreed or customary procedure will form part of an employee's contract of employment, in which case a failure to follow such a procedure will also constitute a breach of contract.

[15.33] In *Devlin and Leahy v McInerney Construction Ltd*,[59] the EAT upheld a selection based on a 'last in first out' (LIFO) policy which the employer applied objectively on a site-by-site basis for which there was a precedent in the construction industry. The fact that the policy was not applied universally within the industry did not make its use in a particular case unfair. In *Cullen v Masterlift*,[60] the EAT found that the claimant had been unfairly selected for redundancy because of his employer's failure to show a good reason for not implementing the company's policy of LIFO. Similarly in *Hartnett v Kit-Fab*,[61] the EAT upheld an unfair dismissal claim in a case where the respondent company had a policy of LIFO, but in a choice between two company drivers, the respondent had based its decision on purely 'humanitarian grounds', namely that the claimant had a farm and therefore an alternative source of income, whereas the second driver had four children and no other means of supporting them.

[15.34] While an employer may depart from an agreed or customary redundancy procedure where there are special reasons to do so, this requirement will only be met in exceptional cases. One case in which the employer did succeed in establishing such a justification was *Bradley v Kilsheelan Technology International Ltd*.[62] In that case the company had entered into a collective agreement with the union providing for the application of a LIFO policy in the event of redundancies. However, the majority of staff agreed to new selection criteria by way of a secret ballot and the EAT upheld the new selection process.

[15.35] Where there is no agreed procedure or custom, the EAT will normally focus on the reasonableness of the selection criteria, which tend to be assessed 'by the objective standard of the way in which a reasonable employer in these circumstances, in that line

---

[58] See Redmond, *Dismissal Law in Ireland* (2nd edn, Tottel Publishing 2007).

[59] *Devlin and Leahy v McInerney Construction Ltd* UD 726 and UD727/2004.

[60] *Cullen v Masterlift Ltd* UD 753/2003.

[61] *Hartnett v Kit-Fab* UD 959/2007.

[62] *Bradley v Kilsheelan Technology International Ltd* 6 June 2005.

of business, at that time would have behaved'.[63] In this respect, the question is whether the selection is one which a reasonable employer could have made, not whether the EAT would itself have made that selection.[64] As observed by the Court of Appeal in *British Aerospace Ltd v Green*[65]:

> ... In general the employer who sets up a system of selection which can reasonably be described as fair and applies it without any overt sign of conduct which mars its fairness will have done all that the law requires of him.... The tribunal is not entitled to embark upon a re-assessment exercise..... it is sufficient for the employer to show that he set up a good system of selection and that it was fairly administered, and that ordinarily there is no need for the employer to justify all the assessments on which the selection for redundancy was based.

[15.36] Normally, in a redundancy situation, an employer will wish to retain its best staff and the question inevitably arises as to the extent to which an employer is entitled to take the personal characteristics of his individual staff members into account when selecting for redundancy. From the case law it appears that while an employer may take account of such characteristics, the assessment must be done in an objective manner. Elements of selection criteria include but are not limited to:

(i)   Qualifications and Training / Relevant Educational Qualifications[66];

(ii)   Relevant Experience;

(iii)   Punctuality;

(iv)   Job Technical/Skill Requirements;[67]

(v)   Criticality to Organisation;

(vi)   Quality of Work;

(vii)   Length of Service.[68]

For example, in *Dean Cassidy v LM Ericsson,*[69] the Tribunal upheld selection criterion based on technical competence. In that case, the claimant was employed as a business development manager in the respondent's fraud office, a position for which technical knowledge was needed. Following his employment the parent company decided that the services organisation would become more technically focused and directed the fraud office to focus on the delivery of technical support. This meant that one of the then two positions for business development managers became redundant. The respondent's general manager consulted with the manager of the fraud office who assessed the technical competence of both managers and found the claimant to be much weaker

---

[63]   *Boucher v Irish Productivity Centre* UD 882, 99, 1005/1992. See also *Watling & Co Ltd v Richardson* (1978) EAT 774/777; *Kelly v Langarth Properties Ltd* UD 742/1993; *Clancy v Productivity Centre* UD 882/1992.

[64]   See eg *BL Cars v Lewis* [1983] IRLR 58.

[65]   *British Aerospace Ltd v Green* [1995] IRLR 433.

[66]   See *Kelly v Weller Ltd* UD 657/2006; *Harrington v Carrigaline Joinery Ltd* UD 741/2006.

[67]   See *Balmer v E Casey Bonding Co Ltd* UD 550/2006.

[68]   *Duffy v John Sisk & Sons Ltd* UD 870/2002.

[69]   *Dean Cassidy v LM Ericsson* UD 934/2004.

technically. The claimant was then selected for redundancy on this basis. The Tribunal found that the selection on the basis of the level of technical competence and experience was fair having regard to the direction from the parent company. Similarly, in *Dawson v Eir Imports Ltd*,[70] the EAT upheld selection based on competence, observing that:

> Following an assessment of the comparative performance of all similar staff the claimant was selected. The respondent retained the employees who he thought could best contribute to the company. The claimant's performance was judged to be weakest. The criteria used in the absence of any other procedures were appropriate in the circumstances. The respondent was competent to make the assessment having regard to the small number of staff and his close contact with them. The principles of natural justice did not require the respondent to give the claimant (employee) details of this assessment and his not doing so resulted in no injustice.

[15.37] However, in *Kirwan v Iona National Airways Ltd*,[71] the claimant was selected for redundancy due to alleged slow productivity. The Tribunal deemed the selection to be unfair because his low productivity was never addressed with him and he was not advised that such productivity might impact on his future with the company.

[15.38] Where attendance figures are used as a basis for selection for redundancy,[72] it is unlikely to be sufficient for the employer to establish the simple fact of an employee's absence. Rather, the employer must go further and ascertain the reason for that absence. Failure to carry out such an investigation may well render the dismissal unfair.[73] Also if an employee's attendance record is poor due to certified sick leave, the employer should bear in mind his obligations in respect of the Employment Equality Acts 1998–2008 (the Equality Acts) and in particular principles of disability discrimination. Leave periods may also be impacted on by maternity leave, or other forms of statutory leave.

[15.39] Selection criteria based on an employee's personal characteristics, but which are overly subjective are likely to be struck down. For example in *Graham v ABF Ltd*,[74] 'attitude to work' was considered to be a highly relative term involving personal and subjective judgments and to the dangerously ambiguous and vague. Similarly, in *Williams v CompAir Maxam Ltd*[75] the employees selected were those 'who in the opinion of the managers concerned would be able to keep the company viable'. This failed to meet the objectivity requirement as it depended solely on the opinion of the person making the selection and was not capable of independent verification.

[15.40] Criteria such as misconduct, strike action, LIFO and an employee's temporary or part-time status are more controversial bases for selection. Where misconduct forms part

---

[70] *Dawson v Eir Imports Ltd* UD 616/93.

[71] *Kirwan v Iona National Airways Ltd* UD 156/87.

[72] See eg *Balmer v E Casey Bonding Co Ltd* UD 550/2006.

[73] *Paine and Moore v Grundy (Teddington) Ltd* [1981] IRLR 267; However, see also *Gray v Shetland Norse Preserving Co Ltd* [1985] IRLR 53 from which it appears that an employer is not required to warn an employee that his poor attendance may lead to his being selected for redundancy.

[74] *Graham v ABF Ltd* [1986] IRLR 90.

[75] *Williams v CompAir Maxam Ltd* [1982] IRLR 83.

of the redundancy criteria, the employer runs the risk that the dismissed employee will argue that there was no genuine redundancy situation and that it is merely a pretext for dismissing him. In so far as selection based on industrial action is concerned, the Tribunals have taken a mixed view. In *Cruikshank v Hobbs*,[76] a redundancy arose after a dispute at the employer's Newmarket racing stables. The employer chose five out of the six stable lads that had gone on strike and the English EAT thought that this was a fair reaction, having regard to the loyalty of the other 24 lads during the dispute. Similarly, in the Irish case of *Jordan v McKenna Ltd*[77] the EAT upheld the dismissal of all employees involved in a strike as it accepted that management were faced with industrial action by employees who had not joined the strike if the strikers were re-employed. On the other hand, in *Laffin and Callaghan v Fashion Industries (Hartlepool) Ltd*,[78] the English EAT deemed the claimant's selection for dismissal based on her involvement in strike action to be unfair in circumstances where the employer had failed to consult anyone and two employees retained had shorter service than the claimant.

[15.41] While LIFO is a time-honoured basis for redundancy selection and continues to be applied,[79] it should be approached with caution as it may be discriminatory under the Equality Acts on grounds of age discrimination. Also, in seeking to retain certain skill sets with fewer employees, organisations may wish to have more flexibility in order to objectively achieve the best selection, and this may not be in accordance with a LIFO policy.

[15.42] Selecting temporary or part-time workers for redundancy may also be indirectly discriminatory on gender or family status grounds.[80] In addition, any such selection could be in breach of the Protection of Employees (Part Time Work) Act 2001 and the Protection of Employees (Fixed-Term Work) Act 2003.

[15.43] Selection based wholly or mainly on the following grounds is discriminatory and will be automatically unfair[81]: trade union membership[82] or activities; religious or political opinions of the employee; actual or threatened participation in civil or criminal proceedings against the employer; age, gender, religion, disability, race, sexual orientation, marital status, family status, membership of the Traveller community; and exercising a right to maternity leave, parental leave, adoptive leave or carer's leave. For instance, failing to include employees who are on maternity leave in the selection pool

---

[76] *Cruikshank v Hobbs* [1977] ICR 725.

[77] *Jordan v McKenna Ltd* UD 577/1982.

[78] *Laffin and Callaghan v Fashion Industries (Hartlepool) Ltd* [1978] IRLR 488.

[79] See, for example, *Hackett v Banberry Trading Company Ltd* (25 July 2006); *Bessenden Properties Ltd v Corness* [1977] ICR 821.

[80] Contrast *Clarke v Eley (IMI) Kynoch Ltd* [1982] IRLR 482 (in which dismissing part-time workers first was indirectly discriminatory) with *Kidd v DRG (UK) Ltd* [1985] IRLR 90 in which it was held not to be discriminatory and if it was discriminatory, to be justifiable because of the marginal advantages in cost and efficiency.

[81] Unfair Dismissals Act 1977, s 6(2).

[82] *Butler v John Spicer & Co Ltd* UD 642/99 in which the claimant's non-union status was held against him when he was selected for redundancy.

for consideration could convert other redundancies into unfair dismissals. On the other hand, selecting someone for redundancy who is on or taking maternity leave solely for that reason will make their dismissal automatically unfair and will almost inevitably amount to discrimination on grounds of gender.

(i) Pools and selection

[15.44] For a redundancy selection to be fair, objective selection criteria must be applied to the correct pool of employees. In particular, the pool of selection must be reasonably defined and the selection criteria employed by the employer must be applied to all employees 'in similar employment'. What constitutes 'similar employment' is seldom considered by the EAT. In *Kennedy v J&L Goodbody Ltd*[83] the EAT accepted that a supervisor, who was dismissed by reason of redundancy, having 'worked in a different plant from the four supervisors who were retained, and it was the plant in which the Appellant worked that was closed down, while the other plant in which the other four worked was retained', had not been in 'similar employment' to the other four supervisors. In *McCormick v DA Ellison Apaseal Ireland Ltd*,[84] the Tribunal found that, although there was 'some overlapping' between the two jobs, they were not 'equal'.

In the absence of any customary or contractual arrangement, the employer will have some flexibility in deciding what the redundancy pool should be, provided that they have actively considered the issue and acted genuinely and reasonably. Factors that may be relevant in identifying the correct pool are whether other groups of employees are doing similar work to the group, whether they have similar qualifications and training as the pool of employees from which selections were made and whether the selection pool was agreed with the union or employees' representatives.

[15.45] Where employees' positions are interchangeable, the employer should give consideration to whether a wider pool of selection might be appropriate.[85] In particular, the courts have taken the view that a dismissal will be due to redundancy even where the dismissed employee's position is not actually redundant once another position is redundant. As a result, when selecting employees for redundancy, the employer should consider whether the selection criteria should be applied not only to those who are actually working in the area that is most directly affected by the circumstances giving rise to the redundancy, but also to those carrying out tasks which workers in that area are also capable of performing. In *Crawford v Modern Plant*,[86] the claimant was product controller in the motor control section. The EAT held that the employer's failure to offer him work as a product controller of the electronics division in place of the existing product controller, who had less service than him, was unreasonable, as the claimant was also competent to work in that section. Similarly, in *Dowling v Whole Foods Wholesale Ltd*,[87] the EAT found that the claimant had been unfairly dismissed because he was the only employee considered for redundancy and was considered 'against no

---

[83] *Kennedy v J&L Goodbody Ltd* UD 8/1978. See also *O'Doherty v System Dynamics Ltd* UD 803/1995.

[84] *McCormick v DA Ellison Apaseal Ireland Ltd* [1990] ELR 170.

[85] *Blundell Permoglaze Ltd v O'Hagen* EAT 540/84.

[86] *Crawford v Modern Plant* UD 123/1998.

other employee in the same class of employment'. In that case, the claimant was a general operative who worked in the department which was being closed down but he had frequently worked in other sections of the warehouse. In *Cullen v Masterlift*,[88] the claimant had initially been employed as a Crown service engineer and, after about 14 months, became the service manager of the Crown products, which were narrow aisle forklift trucks. Two other engineers were then employed to do the claimant's previous work. The claimant was subsequently dismissed, due to a downturn in the business relating to Crown products. One of the reasons the EAT found the dismissal to be unfair was that the company had failed to conduct a real analysis as between the claimant and his natural competitors, namely the two service engineers both of whom had less seniority than the claimant, and who had also worked partially on Crown products.

[15.46] By way of contrast, in *Green v Fraser*,[89] the employee was a lorry driver who was dismissed when the employer decided to reduce the size of its fleet. The dismissed employee argued that he was a competent mechanic and that an existing employee with shorter service should have been dismissed. The Tribunal rejected the claim observing that the employer's decision was a legitimate operational decision within a band of reasonable responses.

(ii) Employer's conduct

[15.47] When dismissing an employee on grounds of redundancy, employers are also required to conduct themselves reasonably.[90] This requirement arises by virtue of the Unfair Dismissals Acts which provide that when determining if a dismissal is unfair regard may be had to, *inter alia*, the reasonableness or otherwise of the conduct (whether by act or omission) of the employer in relation to the dismissal.[91] The UK Tribunal has elaborated on this standard of reasonableness, finding in *Williams v CompAir Maxam Ltd*[92] that 'the fairness or unfairness of dismissal is to be judged by the objective standard of the way in which a reasonable employer in those circumstances in that line of business would have behaved'.

However, the EAT may also take the employer's conduct into consideration when determining whether or not there was a genuine redundancy situation and whether or not an employee was fairly selected for redundancy. For example, in *Hart v Zed Candy Ltd*,[93] the EAT held that the claimant had been unfairly selected for redundancy because of the lack of explanation of the selection process and a lack of fair procedure. Similarly, in *Clohissy v Control Equipment (Dublin) Ltd*,[94] the EAT held that the employer's conduct made the redundancy unfair. However, by way of contrast, in *Dennehy v Millstreet*

---

[87] *Dowling v Whole Foods Wholesale Ltd* UD 95/2006 and *Sheehan and O'Brien v Vintners Federation of Ireland* UD 787/2007.

[88] *Cullen v Masterlift Ltd* UD 753/2003.

[89] *Green v Fraser* [1985] IRLR 55.

[90] *Dowling v Harbour Technology Ltd* UD500/2002.

[91] Unfair Dismissals Act 1977, s 6(7).

[92] *Williams v CompAir Maxam Ltd* [1982] IRLR 83.

[93] *Hart v Zed Candy Ltd* UD 9/2003.

[94] *Clohissey v Control Equipment (Dublin) Ltd* UD 601/2003.

Country Park Ltd,[95] the EAT did not uphold the claimant's unfair dismissal case, despite finding that the manner in which the employer communicated the redundancy to the claimant was seriously deficient. Conversely, in *Pencov v John Mowlam Construction Ltd*[96] the EAT found that the employer had failed to notify the employee in advance of the alleged redundancy. Additionally, the EAT held that notification through a payslip was an unacceptable practice. Any assessment of the reasonableness or otherwise of an employer's conduct will mainly depend on the facts of the case. However, issues such as the extent to which the employer has consulted with those affected by the dismissal and/ or considered the question of alternative employment are generally relevant to any such assessment, as is the manner in which the employee is treated.[97]

[15.48] In so far as consultation is concerned, in *Beaumont v Muintir na Tíre,*[98] the Tribunal stated, in holding against the existence of a genuine redundancy situation:

> Further as a basic principle of natural justice and fairness items as important as redundancy should be clearly discussed with the employee. In this case the evidence was clear that this was not done.

In *Mulvihill v Castlebar Social Services Ltd,*[99] the failure to discuss the proposed redundancy with the employee at any stage, was one of the factors which led the Tribunal to reject the respondent's claim that there was a genuine redundancy situation. Similarly, in *O Driscoll v Siebel Systems Emea Ltd,* failure to consult with the employee who was made redundant was one of the factors which the Tribunal took into consideration in determining that no genuine redundancy situation existed.[100]

[15.49] In so far as alternative employment is concerned, the EAT frequently takes into consideration whether or not the employer has attempted to find alternative employment for the employee in determining whether it has acted reasonably.[101] For example, in *O'Brien v Smurfit (Ireland) Ltd,*[102] the claimant was an area manager for the respondent company and was dismissed on redundancy grounds. At the time of his dismissal a vacancy arose for a sales representative which the company did not offer the claimant as they claimed that he was not suitable for it. The EAT held that there was no genuine redundancy situation within the company. The EAT considered that the company had merely assumed that the claimant did not satisfy the requirements for the sales job and had not discussed it with him. The EAT observed that if further training was required, it would not have been too onerous for the employer to provide such training.

---

[95] *Dennehy v Millstreet Country Park Ltd* UD 1384/2005.

[96] *Pencov v John Mowlam Construction Ltd* (25 June 2007) EAT.

[97] See *Williams v CompAir Maxam Ltd* [1982] IRLR 83 (EAT) and *Polkey v A E Dayton Services Ltd* [1987] IRLR 503.

[98] *Beaumont v Muintir na Tíre* UD 688/2004. See also *Crosby and Rooney v Fuss Door Systems Ltd* UD 294/2007.

[99] *Mulvihill v Castlebar Social Services Ltd* UD 298/2004.

[100] *O'Driscoll v Siebel Systems Emea Ltd*; see also *Roche v Richmon Earthworks Ltd* UD 329/97.

[101] See eg *Fortune v Zed Candy Ltd* UD 18/2003 and *Farrell v Lechtina Ltd* UD 908/2007.

[102] *O'Brien v Smurfit (Ireland) Ltd* UD 640/92.

[15.50] The fairness of a redundancy dismissal will be judged not simply at the date on which notice is given, but also with regard to events up to the date on which it takes effect. So if an alternative position becomes available in that period, the employer should offer it to the redundant employee or at least make them aware of its existence. In *O'Connor v Power Securities Ltd*,[103] the Tribunal, while satisfied that a genuine redundancy situation existed, held that the claimant had been unfairly selected for redundancy because the respondent had failed to look for an alternative. In particular, the respondent had employed another security guard three months prior to the claimant's dismissal for redundancy and the Tribunal observed that:

> There is an obligation on an employer to look for an alternative to redundancy. We are satisfied, in this case, that the respondent in the person of Mr McElearney did not look around before he selected the claimant; if he had he would have found that there was a position, that of Mr Foley's for him.

[15.51] The onus is on the employer to put forward proposals for redeployment. However, an employee should pursue any proposals made. In *Donohoe v Smith*,[104] a claim of unfair dismissal failed, based on the fact that the employee was offered alternative employment with the employer but failed to pursue it. Here the employee was employed in a shop attached to a hospital and although the employer's shop lease was expiring, the hospital had asked it to remain trading until a new franchisee was hired. The employer offered the employee alternative employment which she failed to pursue. The EAT was satisfied that a transfer of undertakings had not taken place and it was further satisfied that the offer of alternative employment by the employer negated the employee's claim of unfair dismissal.

[15.52] In *Paisley v McCormack Dental Ltd*,[105] the EAT held that the worker must be aware that he or she is being considered for redundancy when offered alternative employment. In that case, the appellant was a purchasing manager. His employer informed the employees that there was a need for redundancies. However, the appellant was informed that the company was anxious to retain his services as he was one of the most experienced of the company's employees. The appellant was subsequently offered a position in customer service. However, as he considered that the job involved substantially more work than the one in which he was engaged, the appellant sought an increase in salary from his employer, among other things. Subsequently, he was informed that his job was being combined with that of the other purchasing manager and he was offered that job at a salary of €7,000 lower than that which he was being paid. The appellant refused that offer and was subsequently made redundant. The Tribunal held that the appellant had been unfairly dismissed, observing that it was satisfied that when he refused the offer he had not been made aware that his own redundancy was being contemplated. According to the Tribunal:

> The Respondent acted unreasonably in that the Appellant was not told that he was being considered for redundancy until late in the day, a fact that might have coloured his attitude

---

[103] *O'Connor v Power Securities Ltd* UD 344/89.
[104] *Paddy Donohoe v Bede Smith* RP 665/2006.
[105] *Paisley v McCormack Dental Ltd* UD 1257/2002.

to the earlier job offer and his negotiation of terms and that the earlier job offer was not made again once it became clear that its refusal was leading to redundancy.

Employers are not obliged to create alternative employment for redundant employees where none already exists. Moreover an employer need not offer an equivalent job; if employees are prepared to accept jobs of lower status, a failure to offer such a job may render the dismissal unfair.[106] Furthermore, where an employer is part of a group of companies it should consider whether or not there is alternative employment not only in the employing company but in associated companies. In *Vokes v Bear*,[107] one of the factors which led the Tribunal to hold the dismissal to be unfair was the fact that no attempt had been made to find alternative employment for the applicant in any of the other 299 companies forming part of the employer's group of companies. Moreover, there was evidence that several vacancies existed in the type of senior management positions which the applicant had held before his redundancy in the group at that time. In contrast, in *Fay v CR2 Ltd*,[108] the claimant was made redundant following a restructuring which resulted in the employer's marketing function being relocated to Dubai. The EAT held that there was no obligation on the Dubai company to offer the claimant a position in Dubai as that company was a separate legal entity to the respondent.

[15.53] An employer must also give the employee enough information to enable him or her to make a realistic decision as to whether to accept the alernative job. The English EAT in the case of *Fisher v Hoopoe*[109] found that the employer's reasonable obligation to consider alternative employment does not necessarily end with drawing the employee's attention to job vacancies that may be suitable. The employer should also provide information about the financial prospects of any vacant alternative positions to enable the employee to make an informed decision. A failure to do so may lead to a redundancy dismissal being found to be unfair. In *Modern Injections Moulds Ltd v Price*,[110] a redundancy situation arose and the company proposed to offer Mr Price a position as shop foreman with fewer shifts, as opposed to dismissing him. The company did not give Mr Price any information about the overtime prospects of the new job and after due consideration he rejected the offer and claimed he had been unfairly dismissed. The court observed that:

> ... In as much as there is this obligation on the part of the employers to try and find suitable alternative employment within the firm, it must follow that if they are in a position pursuant to their obligation to make an offer to the employee of suitable alternative employment they must give him sufficient information on the basis of which the employee can make a realistic decision whether to take the new job.

---

[106] *Barrat Construction Ltd v Dalrymple* [1984] IRLR 385.
[107] *Vokes v Bear* [1974] ICR 1; however, see *MDH Ltd v Sussex* [1986] ILRL 123; *British United Shoe Machinery Co Ltd v Clarke* [1977] IRLR 297; *Barratt Construction Ltd v Dalrymple* [1984] IRLR 385.
[108] *Fay v CR2 Ltd* UD 1233/2005.
[109] *Fisher v Hoopoe Finance Ltd* EAT 0043/05.
[110] *Modern Injections Moulds Ltd v Price* [1976] ICR 370.

[15.54] Another factor which may be relevant in determining the reasonableness of the employer's conduct is its approach to the redundancy settlement offered, be it a negotiated settlement or a unilateral offer. In the case of *Higgins v Texoil Ltd*[111] the claimant argued that he had negotiated a redundancy settlement with the respondent on the basis that this was a redundancy situation. The claimant then claimed that, as he had not known about the takeover of another company (Campus Oil), by his then employer, the offer of an alternative job at a much lower salary was in reality a 'sham' and the settlement should be declared void. The EAT found that there was not enough evidence to establish a connection between the redundancy and the takeover of Campus Oil. Thus, the redundancy settlement stood and could not be set aside. Noteworthy considerations for employers in this context, were that the claimant had received independent legal advice and the settlement had been of a negotiated nature.

[15.55] Aside from the above instances, employers are generally required to treat employees with consideration and respect in the context of redundancy. For example, in the above mentioned case of *O' Driscoll v Siebel Systems Emea Ltd*, the claimant was informed of her redundancy the day before her scheduled return from maternity leave. In finding that a genuine redundancy situation did not exist, one of the factors referred to by the EAT was that the manner in which the respondent had terminated the claimant's employment was 'tantamount to summary dismissal'. Similarly, in *Sinnott v Wrights of Howth Export Kilmore Quay Ltd*,[112] the EAT upheld an unfair dismissal claim because the employer had failed to act reasonably. In that case, the claimant was a director of the company who had initially been headhunted as the company wanted his specialist knowledge. In holding in favour of the claimant the EAT observed:

> ... Although the claimant was aware of the trading difficulties and, indeed, had made some suggestions as to how these might be addressed and although some months beforehand he and other managers did feel that their jobs were under threat, his selection as the sole person to go was made suddenly and without warning at a board meeting which he did not attend. The sudden nature of his dismissal was underlined in the letter itself in which his name was removed from the list of directors, although of course the end of his employment did not remove him from the board in company law. We attach weight to these points in assessing whether "the conduct of the employer in relation to the 'dismissal' was reasonable", and we rule that it was not.

[15.56] Reasonableness also dictates that the employer should consider all possible options and should not immediately opt for redundancies, without first addressing possible alternatives.

[15.57] An employer should record the decision making process which gives rise to the possibility of redundancies in order to be able to demonstrate that it has acted reasonably. For example, if the company is experiencing financial problems, discussions or meetings regarding the problems should be minuted and proposals with regard to dealing with the problem should be recorded. Similarly, the employer should minute or note any consideration given to alternative employment to those employees who will be

---

[111] *Higgins v Texoil Ltd* UD 359/2006.

[112] *Sinnott v Wrights of Howth Export Kilmore Quay Ltd* UD 723/2004.

affected by the redundancy. In *O'Kelly v Xsil Ltd*,[113] the EAT, in holding that the employer had failed to act fairly and reasonably, referred to the fact that the respondent was unable to supply any documentation to support its claim that the company was in a '*perilous financial position*'. The EAT further found that the respondent was not in a position to furnish the template used for the redundancy criteria or the minutes of the meetings in coming to the decision to make the claimant redundant. The EAT ordered reinstatement of the claimant. In circumstances where the redundancy is based on the qualifications or training of the individual, the employer should consider whether the employee might be re-trained so as to meet the required standard or acquire the relevant skills and record those considerations.

Disputes

[15.58] The majority of challenges to redundancy come before the EAT under the Unfair Dismissals Acts questioning the legitimacy of the redundancy and claiming unfair dismissal. Such challenges can centre not solely on whether the redundancy situation is genuine, but also whether fair and proper procedures were followed by the employer. In *Alex Campbell v Qumas Ltd*[114] the Tribunal accepted that there was a genuine redundancy situation, but found that the company fell far off the mark in relation to its procedures. Here the employee was approached by human resources and offered a 'separation package' to leave his employment. Subsequently the employee was offered a choice to either accept that package offered or to leave. The Tribunal found that the company had failed to show how their selection process resulted in the loss of employment for the claimant. Moreover, the Tribunal was highly critical of the company presenting the claimant with a choice of either leaving on its terms or having his employment terminated.

[15.59] In *Shortt v Data Packaging Ltd*[115] Keane J granted an injunction restraining the defendant from appointing any person other than the plaintiff to the plaintiff's position as Managing Director, pending the trial of the action. For some time this judgment has been regarded as authority for the proposition that injunctions can be granted by the courts in order to restrain redundancy dismissals. However, more recently, the judgments of the Supreme Court in *Maha Lingham v Health Service Executive*[116] and *Sheehy v Ryan*,[117] have cast doubt upon that suggestion. Ultimately it has been resolved in *Nolan v EMO Oil Services Ltd*[118] that Shortt is not authority for the proposition that injunctions should be granted to restrain redundancy dismissals. Here Laffoy J considered an application for a interlocutory injunction restraining an employer from giving effect to a dismissal by reason of redundancy. The court determined that the correct forum for such a challenge is before the Rights Commissioner or the EAT.

---

[113] *O'Kelly v Xsil Ltd* RP 630/2007.

[114] *Alex Campbell v Qumas Ltd* UD 48/2007. See also *Power v House of Donohoe Ltd* UD 1210/2003.

[115] *Shortt v Data Packaging Ltd* [1994] ELR 251.

[116] *Maha Lingham v Health Service Executive* [2006] 17 ELR 137.

[117] *Sheehy v Ryan* [2008] IESC 14.

[118] *Paul Nolan v EMO Oil Services Ltd* [2009] IEHC 15.

CONSULTATION

[15.60] As set out above, while there is no statutory obligation for an employer to consult with individual employees when contemplating individual redundancy-based dismissals, such an obligation arises by virtue of the requirement for the employer to act reasonably. In contrast, when contemplating collective redundancies, an employer is under a statutory obligation to consult pursuant to the Protection of Employment Acts. When conducting consultations on either an individual or collective basis, the employer should remember to include employees on maternity leave or on long-term sick leave, to reduce the risk of discrimination claims on the basis of gender or disability and/or unfair dismissals.

Individual consultation

[15.61] With regard to an employer's obligation to consult in the context of individual redundancies, the principles are well summarised by the English EAT in the case of *Mugford v Midland Bank plc*[119] as follows:

(a)   where no consultation of any kind has taken place, the dismissal will normally be unfair, unless the tribunal finds that a reasonable employer would have concluded that consultation would be an utterly futile exercise in that particular case.

(b)   consultation with the trade union over selection criteria does not of itself release the employer from consulting with the employee individually, who is identified for redundancy.

(c)   it will be a question of fact and degree for the tribunal to consider whether consultation with the individual and/or his union was so inadequate as to render his dismissal unfair, viewing the overall picture up to the date of termination.

[15.62] The principle that an employer is not under a duty to consult with employees where such consultation can serve no useful purpose was recognised by the EAT in *Saul & Others v Mahony Manufactured Signs Ltd*.[120] In that case, the respondent had terminated the claimant's employment because he could not get insurance against accidents in the workplace and, therefore, was unable to employ people. The issue for the Tribunal was whether or not in a redundancy situation there is an obligation on the employer to notify his employees of the difficulties being experienced and to consult with them on the best way forward. While the Tribunal recognised that there was some obligation on the employer to notify and discuss a possible redundancy situation with its employees, it held that such an obligation does not exist where such consultation would be futile. In the circumstances of the case, the Tribunal found that no amount of consultation with the employees would have put a valid insurance policy in place and it did not consider that the employer had acted unreasonably such that the redundancies amounted to unfair dismissals.

---

[119] *Mugford v Midland Bank plc* [1977] IRLR 209.
[120] *Saul & Others v Mahony Manufactured Signs Ltd* UD 37/2003.

[15.63] However, much will depend on the circumstances of the case. In *Heron v Citylink Nottingham*[121] the English EAT overturned the findings of the Industrial Relations Tribunal that failure to consult did not render the dismissal of an employee on the grounds of redundancy unfair because of exceptional circumstances. The EAT observed as follows:

> The fact that an employer, on the facts known to him, reasonably believes that he has no alternative but to make his employee redundant does not *per se* obviate the need for consultation. There may be circumstances known to the employee but unknown to the employer which might cause the latter to change his mind. The employee might be prepared to accept a more junior post or a significantly reduced salary in order to remain in work. Unless the employer consults, the employee will have no opportunity to put forward any such suggestions. Furthermore, even if redundancy is inevitable, there are other areas in which consultation will be of benefit to the employee. It would at the very least provide an opportunity for the parties to discuss what help an employer can provide for the employee's alternative employment.

While the form and the timing of individual consultation will vary depending on the circumstances, the employer should, at a minimum, inform the employee in advance of the proposal to make the position redundant, giving the reasons for the changes and the proposed process for effecting it.[122] The employer should also seek the employee's feedback on the proposals, particularly as to any alternatives to redundancy and/or options for redeployment. In *Cahill v SDL Global Solutions Ireland Ltd*,[123] the EAT found that the employer did not give the claimant an opportunity to suggest ways to improve the situation and thereby avoid the necessity for redundancies. Where the redundancy involves a selection process, the employer should also discuss the selection criteria with employees likely to be affected by it.[124] For example, in *Fortune v Zed Candy Ltd*,[125] one of the reasons the EAT found the dismissal to be unfair was that 'there was a complete lack of explanation of the selection process for redundancy'.[126] The employee should also be given an opportunity to comment on their redundancy selection assessment.[127]

[15.64] Other issues which should be addressed include:

(i)   would the candidate be willing to work in another department (and have they to date)?

---

[121] *Heron v Citylink Nottingham* [1993] IRLR; see also *Polkey v AE Dayton Services* (1987) IRLR 503; *Duffy v Yeomans & Partners*.

[122] *Air 2000 Ltd v Mallam* EAT 0773/03 and 0058/04.

[123] *Cahill v SDL Global Solutions Ireland Ltd* UD 292/2003.

[124] See *O'Kelly v Xsil Ltd* UD 1086/2007. See also *Boucher v Irish Productivity Centre* [1990] ELR 205.

[125] *Fortune v Zed Candy Ltd* UD 18/2003.

[126] *Fortune v Zed Candy Ltd* UD 18/2003; *Hart v Zed Candy Ltd* UD 9/2003.

[127] *Mugford v Midland Bank plc* [1977] ICR 399. It appears that consultation with the trade union over selection criteria does not of itself release the employer from consulting with the employee individually about their selection for redundancy. See *Alstom Traction Ltd v Birkenhead and Ors* EAT 1131/00.

(ii)   would the candidate be willing to relocate?[128]

(iii)   would the candidate be willing to work in another position? and/or

(iv)   would the candidate be suitable/qualified to work in another position?[129]

Collective consultation

[15.65] The Protection of Employment Acts set down specific notification and consultation requirements with regard to collective redundancies. The impetus for this Act was the need to transpose the Collective Redundancies Directive 75/129.[130] At the time that directive was adopted, there was diversity among the Member States in relation to the labour costs of restructuring and this was seen as a threat to continued economic integration.[131] Concerns about social dumping were raised when Akzo, a Dutch-German multinational enterprise which wanted to make 5,000 workers redundant as part of a programme of restructuring, compared the costs of dismissing workers in the various states where it had subsidiaries and dismissed workers in the country where costs were the lowest.[132] This led to calls for action at European level to ensure that this did not happen again. Consequently the directive seeks 'to ensure comparable protection for workers' rights in different Member States and to harmonise the costs which such protective rules entail for Community undertakings'.[133]

[15.66] The Protection of Employment Acts define 'collective redundancies' as dismissals which are effected for redundancy where in any period of thirty consecutive days the number of such dismissals is:[134]

(i)   at least five in an establishment[135] normally employing more than 20 and less than 50 employees;

---

[128] See eg *Kelly v Weller Ltd* UD 657/2006.

[129] *O'Kelly v Xsil Ltd* UD 1086/2006.

[130] Council Directive 75/129/EEC of 17 February 1975 on the Approximation of the Laws of the Member States Relating to Collective Redundancies (OJ [1975] L48/29). This directive was amended by Directive 92/56/EEC OJ [1992] L245/3 which was drafted to cater for the increasing transnationalisation of companies, with decisions affecting employees in a subsidiary company in one Member State being take by the parent company in another Member State. Directive 75/129 and Directive 92/56 were later consolidated and repealed by Council Directive 98/59/EC OJ [1988] L255/16.

[131] See Burrows and Mair, *European Social Law* (Wiley, 1996).

[132] Blanpain, *Labour Law and Industrial Relations of the European Community* (Kluwer, 1991) p 153.

[133] *Commission of the European Communities v UK* [1994] ECR Kenner, Jeff, *EU Employment Law* (Hart Publishing, 2003).

[134] Protection of Employment Act 1977, as amended, s 6(1): In calculating the number of dismissals, it appears that it is not necessary to include termination of employment by the employees themselves – see AG Tizzano's opinion in Case C-188/03 *Wolfgang Kuhnel v Junk* (2005) 2(2) IELJ 68.

[135] For the definition of "establishment" see Case C-449/93 *Rockfon* [1995] ECR I-4291 in which the ECJ held that the term must be given a community meaning and interpreted it as the unit to which the workers made redundant were assigned to carry out their duties.

(ii)   at least ten in an establishment normally employing at least 50 but less than 100 employees;

(iii)   at least 10% of the number of employees in an establishment normally employing at least 100 but less than 200 employees; and

(iv)   at least 30 in an establishment normally employing 300 or more employees.

[15.67] When calculating the number of employees for the purpose of the collective redundancy consultation requirements it is necessary to count all employees falling within the definition of that term under the Protection of Employment Acts. In this respect, the Protection of Employment Acts define an employee as a person who has entered into or works under a contract of employment with an employer.[136] However, the Protection of Employment Acts specifically exclude certain employees.[137] In particular, those employed by or under the State, with the exception of 'industrial' civil servants, officers of a local authority, and merchant seamen employed under a prescribed agreement do not fall within the scope of the Protection of Employment Acts. In addition, the Protection of Employment Acts do not apply to dismissals resulting from the due expiry of a fixed-term contract or, where the employee was employed to do a specific task, a dismissal resulting from the completion of that task.

[15.68] Pursuant to the relevant requirements, when proposing to create collective redundancies, employers must consult with the appropriate employee representatives 'in good time' and in any event at least 30 days before giving the notice to dismiss.[138] The objective of such consultation is to investigate the possibility of avoiding the proposed redundancies, reduce the numbers of employees affected and to mitigate the consequences of dismissal. In addition, the employees' representatives should be consulted on the redundancy selection criteria.

[15.69] The employees' representatives can be a trade union, a staff association or an excepted body[139] with which it has been the practice of the employer to conduct collective bargaining negotiations.[140] Where no such body exists, the employees are entitled to choose their representatives from among their fellow employees.[141] The Protection of Employment Acts do not provide for the situation where employees fail to choose their representatives. In such a situation, it is suggested that it is best practice for the employer to consult with each affected employee directly regarding the need for redundancies, the process for implementing the redundancies and the redundancy package.

---

[136] Protection of Employment Act 1977, as amended, s 2(1).

[137] Protection of Employment Act 1977, as amended, s 7(2). See *Griffin v South West Water Services Ltd* [1995] IRLR 15.

[138] Protection of Employment Act 1977, as amended, s 9.

[139] Trade Union Act 1941, s 6(3), as amended.

[140] Protection of Employment Act 1977, as amended, s 2.

[141] Protection of Employment Act 1977, as amended, s 2d. European Communities (Protection of Employment) Regulations 2000 (SI 488/2000) sets out the position in relation to the selection of employee representatives where there is no recognised trade union.

[15.70] For the purposes of consultation under the Protection of Employment Acts, the employer must supply the employees' representatives with all relevant information in writing relating to the proposed redundancies. This information must include:[142]

(i) the reasons for the proposed redundancies;

(ii) the number and descriptions or categories of employees whom it is proposed to make redundant;

(iii) the number of employees, and descriptions of categories, normally employed;

(iv) the period in which it is proposed to effect the redundancies;

(v) the criteria proposed for the selection of the workers to be made redundant; and

(vi) the method of calculating any redundancy payments other than those methods set out in the Redundancy Payments Acts or any other relevant enactment.

The employer must supply the Minister for Enterprise, Trade and Employment (the 'Minister') with copies of all information supplied to employees as soon as possible. The consultations must be conducted with a view to reaching agreement. It is clear from the ECJ's decision in *Junk v Kuhnel*,[143] that in this context, what is required goes beyond what is classically understood as consultation and the employer is required to negotiate with the employee representatives.

[15.71] An employer is not entitled to implement redundancies during the course of the consultation period and must wait until its conclusion. According to the ECJ in the case of *Junk v Kuhnel*:[144]

> [t]he effectiveness of such an obligation would be compromised if an employer was entitled to terminate contracts of employment during the course of the procedure or even at the beginning thereof. It would be significantly more difficult for workers' representatives to achieve the withdrawal of a decision that has been taken than to secure the abandonment of a decision that is being contemplated.

[15.72] While the ECJ has not explicitly pronounced on whether this is also the case where an early agreement has been reached between the employer and the employee representatives in the context of the consultations, it is advisable for an employer to wait until the conclusion of the thirty-day period even in this context. In particular, issues may come to light after the conclusion of the negotiations, but prior to the elapse of the thirty day period, which necessitate the re-opening of consultation.

[15.73] An employer is also obliged to notify the Minister of the proposed redundancies at the earliest opportunity, but at least 30 days before the first dismissal is effected.[145] The purpose of this is to allow the Minister to seek solutions to the problems raised by

---

[142] Protection of Employment Act 1977, as amended, s 10(2).

[143] *Case C-188/03 Wolfgang Kuhnel v Junk* (2005) 2(2) IELJ 68; see also *Stonearch Branch Randstone Ltd v O'Brien and Others* PEI/2003 – PE44/2003.

[144] Case C-188/03 *Wolfgang Kuhnel v Junk* (2005) 2(2) IELJ 68.

[145] Protection of Employment Act 1977, as amended, s 12.

the projected collective redundancies.[146] The employer must include the following information in the notification to the Minister:[147]

(i) the name and address of the employer indicating that the employer is a company;

(ii) the address of the premises where the collective redundancies are proposed;

(iii) the total number of persons normally employed at that premises;

(iv) the numbers and descriptions or categories of employees whom it is proposed to make redundant;

(v) the period within which the collective redundancies are proposed to be effected, starting from the dates on which the first and final dismissals are expected to take effect;

(vi) the reasons for the proposed collective redundancies;

(vii) the names and address of the trade unions or staff associations representing employees affected by the proposed redundancies and with which it has been the practice of the employer to conduct collective bargaining negotiations;

(viii) the dates on which consultations with each trade union or staff association commenced and the progress achieved at those consultations to the date of the notification;

(ix) the criteria for selection of redundancy; and

(x) the method of calculating redundancy payments other than a statutory redundancy payment.

The notification made to the Minister must be copied to the employees' representatives affected, who may make written observations to the Minister relating to the notification.

[15.74] The Minister may request the employer to enter consultations with the Minister, or an officer authorised by the Minister, in order to seek solutions to the problems caused by the proposed redundancies. Authorised officers are usually civil servants of the Department of Enterprise, Trade and Employment. Such officers have the power to enter an employer's premises and make enquiries for the purpose of ensuring that the employer has complied with the statutory requirements. The employer is obliged to keep all necessary records to show that the requirements applicable to collective redundancies have been complied with. The records must be retained for at least three years.

[15.75] An employee, trade union, staff association or excepted body may refer a complaint to a Rights Commissioner arising out of a failure to inform or consult.[148] The Rights Commissioner may order the employer to comply with its obligations and/or award compensation of up to four weeks' remuneration to the employee concerned.

---

[146] Case C-188/03 *Wolfgang Kuhnel v Junk* (2005) 2(2) IELJ 68.

[147] Protection of Employment Act 1977 (Notification of Proposed Collective Redundancies) Regulations 1977.

[148] European Communities (Protection of Employment) Regulations 2000 (SI 488/2000).

Failure to inform or consult may also form the basis of a successful unfair dismissal action on the part of an employee. Failure to provide information to and/or consult with the employee's representatives and failure to notify the Minister are both offences. Upon conviction, the employer may be fined up to €5,000 per offence. Moreover, if the employer proceeds to effect the collective redundancies before the expiration of the timescales prescribed for notification of the Minister, the employer will be guilty of an offence and liable to a fine up to €250,000.

[15.76] The consultation requirements imposed on employers under the Protection of Employments Acts do not obviate the need for employers to comply with consultation requirements imposed by the Redundancy Payments Acts and/or any other Acts. The Employees (Provision of Information and Consultation) Act 2006 (the 2006 Act), may be of particular relevance in this respect.[149] The 2006 Act requires all employers with more than 50 employees to inform and consult employees on developments affecting employment in the workplace, when a written request is made by 10% of employees (meaning the lesser of (a) 10% of the employees in the undertaking concerned (but not less than 15 employees) or (b) 100 employees) to the employer or the Labour Court. Developments affecting employment in the workplace include: any threats to employment; decisions likely to lead to substantial changes in the organisation of work or in contractual relations, including those covered by legislation dealing with transfer of undertakings; and collective redundancies.

LEGAL ENTITLEMENTS UNDER THE REDUNDANCY PAYMENTS ACTS

[15.77] Pursuant to the Redundancy Payments Acts, where employees falling within the scope of these Acts are dismissed on the basis of redundancy or are placed on short time or laid off for a period that is in excess of a temporary period, they are entitled to a redundancy certificate and a lump sum payment from their employer. Employees are also entitled to time off work to look for alternative work. In addition, employees dismissed on redundancy grounds are entitled to notice of their dismissal.

EMPLOYEES

[15.78] The Redundancy Payments Acts cover all private and public sector employees employed for at least 104 weeks in continuous employment which is insurable for all

---

[149] The Transnational Information and Consultation of Employees Act 1996 and the European Communities (Transnational Information and Consultation of Employees Act 1996) (Amendment) Regulations 1999 require multinationals, if requested by the required number of employees to set up European Works Councils, to inform and consult with their employees on a range of management issues relating to transnational developments within the organisation. Moreover, the European Communities (Protection of Employees on Transfer of Undertakings) Regulations 2003 impose information and consultation obligations on both selling and purchasing parties in a business acquisition. These matters are considered in Ch 16, Employee Involvement, and Ch 19, Transfer of Undertakings.

benefits under social welfare legislation.[150] An employee is any person of 16 years or older who has entered into or works under an employment contact.[151] An employer is normally the person with whom the employee has entered that contract. However, in the case of agency workers, for the purposes of the Redundancy Payment Acts, the employer is whoever is responsible for paying the employee's remuneration.[152]

[15.79] In order to be entitled to a redundancy payment, an employee must ordinarily work in the State or be working in the State on the date of dismissal.[153] Employees ordinarily working abroad will not be entitled to a redundancy payment unless they fulfil two conditions. Firstly, they must have been domiciled in Ireland before starting work abroad. Secondly, they must have been back within Ireland on the date of the dismissal or their employer must not have given them a reasonable opportunity of returning home before that date.

[15.80] The requirement that the person seeking a redundancy payment be, in actuality, employed by the employer in question is an important consideration. In the case of *Buggle v Magna Donnelly Electronics*[154] the EAT found that an employee who had been on certified sick leave for 15 years prior to returning to work in 2000 could not include that period of absence as reckonable for the purpose of calculating the sum payable when being made redundant in 2007. Here the EAT found that it was up to the claimant to prove that she had remained an employee during the period in question, a burden of proof which, in the EAT's point of view, she could not discharge.

[15.81] In calculating whether the employee has been in continuous employment for 104 weeks, a week is taken to be a working week of five days rather than a calendar week of seven days.[155] Periods of employment with an employer prior to the employee reaching the age of 16 years are excluded.[156] A person's employment is presumed to be continuous[157] unless terminated by dismissal or by the employee voluntarily leaving the employment.[158] In particular, continuity is not affected by interruptions in service of not more than 26 consecutive weeks by reason of holidays, lay-offs or any cause authorised

---

[150] Redundancy Payments Act 1967, s 4(1); See *Leen v Henry Denny & Sons Ireland Ltd* UD 1169/2006, as an example of a case where the claimant did not have the requisite service to lodge a redundancy appeal. See *Coyle v Hanley Developments Ltd* RP 389/2006 for an example of a case where there was a break in the claimant's continuity of service.

[151] Redundancy Payments Act 1967, s 2(1).

[152] Redundancy Payments Act 1967, s 2(4).

[153] Redundancy Payments Act 1967, s 25(1).

[154] *Buggle v Magna Donnelly Electronics* RP358/2007; see also *Quinn v GN Resound Ireland Ltd* UD 457/2006.

[155] *Gormley v McCartin Bros (Engineering) Ltd* [1982] ILRM 215; The Redundancy Payments Acts, s 2 defines 'week' in relation to an employee whose remuneration is calculated weekly by a week ending on a day other then Saturday, as a week ending on that other day and, in relation to any other employee, as ending on a Saturday.

[156] Redundancy Payments Act 1967, as amended, s 7(5).

[157] Redundancy Payments Act 1971 s 10.

[158] Redundancy Payments Act 1967, as amended, Sch 3.

by the employer. Nor is continuity affected by strikes.[159] In *Irish Shipping Ltd v Adams*,[160] the claimants were seamen who had served on the appellant's ships prior to its being wound up. Each of the seamen had served for varying periods of engagements on different ships with periods elapsing between engagements. The EAT took the view that the periods between engagements were merely lay-offs and did not affect continuity. On appeal to the High Court, Murphy J held, on the basis of the evidence, that the EAT was entitled to conclude that the periods spent ashore by the claimants constituted for the first part holidays and, to the extent that the employee was not re-engaged when he sought to resume his service, lay-off, and that the balance of the period was another similar period of leave authorised by the employer.

REDUNDANCY-BASED DISMISSALS

[15.82] In order to be entitled to a lump sum payment, an employee must normally be dismissed by his employer by reason of redundancy. The definition of redundancy has already been considered. However, the question remains as to what constitutes a dismissal in this context. Pursuant to the Redundancy Payments Acts, an employee is taken to be dismissed by his employer where his employment contract is terminated with or without notice.[161] Fixed-term employees and those employed for a specified purpose are dismissed where the term expires or the purpose ceases without being renewed under the same or a similar contract.[162] A dismissal may also occur where the employee terminates the contract in circumstances where he or she is entitled to do so by reason of the employer's conduct.[163] An employee who volunteers for redundancy will still be considered to have been dismissed by his employer.[164] There is a rebuttable presumption that an employee who has been dismissed by his employer has been so dismissed by reason of redundancy.[165]

[15.83] An employee will not be taken to be dismissed by his employer where he or she continues in employment with his employer or an associated company,[166] either because his employment contract is renewed or because he is re-engaged by that employer under a new employment contract.[167] Where the employee continues his employment in the same capacity and place and under the same or substantially similar terms or conditions, the renewal or re-engagement must either take effect on or before the day of the

---

[159] See eg *Mlynarczyk v Andrew Mannion Structural Engineers Ltd* UD 1089/2006.
[160] *Irish Shipping Ltd v Adams* (1987) 6 JISLL 186.
[161] Redundancy Payments Act 1967, s 9(1)(a).
[162] Redundancy Payments Act 1967, s 9(1)(b).
[163] Redundancy Payments Act 1967, s 9(1)(c).
[164] *Optare Group Ltd v Transport and General Workers Union* UKEAT/0143/07; *Burton Allton & Johnson v Peck* [1975] ICR 193.
[165] Redundancy Payments Act 1971, s 10(2).
[166] Redundancy Payments Acts, s 16; Pursuant to that section, two companies are taken to be associated companies if one is a subsidiary of the other, or both are subsidiaries of a third company.
[167] Redundancy Payments Acts, s 9(2).

proposed redundancy.[168] Otherwise, the employee's renewal or re-engagement must be pursuant to a written offer from his employer made before the ending of his employment under his previous contract and take effect either immediately on the ending of that employment or after an interval of not more than four weeks.[169] In *Caulfield v Dunnes Stores,*[170] the claimant was a security guard in his employer's head office. The head office was relocated and the new office came with its own security provided by the landlord. The claimant was offered an alternative position in another location which was in or about the same distance as his old position, which he refused. The Tribunal held that he was not entitled to a redundancy payment.

[15.84] Similarly, an employee will not be taken to have been dismissed by his employer where he is re-engaged by a new employer immediately on the termination of his previous employment and that re-engagement takes place with the agreement of the employee, the previous employer and the new employer.[171] The employee must receive a written statement on behalf of his previous employer and new employer, before the commencement of the period of employment, setting out his or her new terms and conditions and providing for continuity of service between the old and new employment.[172]

[15.85] Where an employee is dismissed due to redundancy, he or she is not necessarily obliged to wait for the expiration of the obligatory period in the redundancy notice in order to benefit from the protection of the Redundancy Payments Acts.[173] Once the employer has given notice to an employee to terminate his employment contract, the employee may give counter-notice to the employer terminating that contract on an earlier date than that specified in the employer's notice. Where the employer agrees in writing to alter the date of dismissal so as to ensure that the employee's notice is within the obligatory period of the notice of dismissal, the employee is taken to be dismissed by the employer and his entitlement to redundancy payment is unaffected.[174] However, where the employer gives the employee written notice requiring him or her to continue in employment until the date on which the employer's notice terminates, the employee cannot terminate his employment contract if he wishes to retain his entitlement to a redundancy payment.[175]

LAY-OFF AND SHORT-TIME

[15.86] Generally, under the Redundancy Payments Acts, a right to a redundancy payment arises not only where an employee is dismissed by reason of redundancy but

---

[168] Redundancy Payments Acts, s 9(2)(a).

[169] Redundancy Payments Acts, s 9(2)(b).

[170] *Caulfield v Dunnes Stores* RP663/2003.

[171] Redundancy Payments Acts, s 9(3).

[172] Redundancy Payments Acts, s 9(3); see *Cahill v Knight's Cleaning Services Ltd* EAT 10 April 2003.

[173] Redundancy Payments Act, s 10.

[174] Redundancy Payments Act, s 10(3A).

[175] Redundancy Payments Act, s 10(3).

also where he or she is laid off or kept on short-time for a period of four or more consecutive weeks or for a period of six or more weeks within a period of thirteen consecutive weeks.[176] At common law, a lay-off with pay is normally lawful since an employer is under no duty to provide work, however the employer will be in breach of contract if he lays off an employee without pay, unless there is an express or implied term permitting the lay-off.[177]

[15.87] An employee is deemed to have been laid off where his or her employment ceases because the employer is unable to provide him or her with work, it is reasonable for the employer to believe that the cessation is temporary and the employer gives notice to that effect to the employee prior to cessation.[178] An employee is deemed to be on short-time where his or her hours of work or remuneration are less than half of their normal weekly amount by reason of a diminution in the work provided for the employee by the employer.[179] As in the case of lay-offs, it must be reasonable in the circumstances for the employer to believe that the diminution will be temporary and he must give notice to that effect to the employee prior to the reduction.

[15.88] While Part A of Form RP9 may be used to notify an employee of a temporary lay-off or short time, verbal notice is also sufficient.[180] In the case of both lay-offs and short-time, the issue as to whether it is reasonable for the employer to believe the diminution to be temporary is determined by reference to the 'reasonable man'. Even if an employer has a bona fide belief that business difficulties are temporary, this is not sufficient if that belief is not also one which fulfils the 'reasonable man' test.[181]

[15.89] Where an employee has been laid off or placed on short-time for the requisite periods, he or she may give his employer written notice of his intention to claim a redundancy payment on the expiry of that period or in any event not later than four weeks after the cessation of the lay-off or short-time.[182] Alternatively an employee may choose to terminate his employment contract by giving the employer the required contractual notice period, or where no such period is specified, at least one week's

---

[176] Redundancy Payments Act, ss. 7(1) and 7(3). This right is qualified in respect of employees who, during the period of 4 years immediately preceding the date of dismissal or lay off, have been laid off for an average annual period of more than 12 weeks. See Redundancy Payments Acts, s 8. Furthermore, it should be noted that an employee who is not available for work anyway, for example, because of illness, will not be treated as laid off: See *Johnson v Knowsley Caravans Ltd* ET Case No 5071/74.

[177] See *Law v Irish Country Meats (Pig Meats) Ltd* [1988] ELR 266; *Warburton v Taff Vale Railway Co* (1902) 18 TLR 429, *Turner v Sawdon* [1901] 2 KB 653. According to Bowers, *Employment Law* (7th edn, OUP, 2005) at p 69 'at common law, the employer is in breach of contract if he lays off an employee without pay unless there is an express or implied term permitting the lay-off'. See also, Rideout, *Principles of Labour Law* (4th edn, Sweet & Maxwell,) at p 267.

[178] Redundancy Payments Act, s 11(1).

[179] Redundancy Payments Acts, s 11(2).

[180] *Ferrick v Monaghan Poultry Products* MN2795/2001.

[181] See *Ferrick v Monaghan Poultry Products Ltd* MN2795/2001; *Hayes v O'Kelly Bros Civil Engineering Ltd* UD268/2001.

written notice of his intention to terminate. That notice is then deemed to be notice of an intention to claim redundancy payments.[183]

[15.90] An employee is not entitled to a redundancy payment in pursuance of a notice of intention to claim if, on the date that notice was served, it was reasonably expected that the employee would, not later than four weeks after that date, enter into a period of full employment for not less than thirteen weeks.[184] For this to apply, the employer must serve a counter-notice,[185] informing the employee that he will contest any liability to pay to him a redundancy payment in pursuance of the notice of intention to claim. This counter-notice must be served within seven days of the service of the notice of intention to claim.[186]

NOTICE OF PROPOSED DISMISSAL FOR REDUNDANCY

[15.91] An employer who proposes to dismiss an employee by reason of redundancy must give that employee notice in writing of the proposed dismissal on the requisite form – Part A of Form RP50. This statutory notice must be given at least two weeks before the date of dismissal.[187] This notice period cannot be abridged by means of a payment in lieu of notice but can run concurrently with any contractual or statutory minimum notice entitlement. Requirements as to the particulars which must be contained in the notice and the method of service of the notice are set out in the Redundancy (Notice of Dismissal) Regulations.[188] It is an offence for an employer to fail to give the requisite notice or to furnish false information. Such an offence is punishable on summary conviction to a fine not exceeding €5,000.[189]

REDUNDANCY CERTIFICATE

[15.92] The employer must also give the employee a redundancy certificate (in the form of Part B of the RP50) not later than the date of the dismissal.[190] Where the employee has served the employer with a notice of intention to claim a redundancy payment, the employer must give him the certificate not later than seven days after the service of that

---

[182] Redundancy Payments Acts, s 12. In *Donnelly v DD O'Brien Ltd* RP524/2005, the EAT held that it was a 'fundamental requirement' of s 12 to render the notice valid that the claimant be on short-time or lay-off for a continuous period of four weeks prior to the service of the notice.

[183] Redundancy Payments Acts, s 12(2).

[184] Redundancy Payments Acts, s 13(1).

[185] An employer may use Part C of Form RP9 to give the requisite counter-notice; see *Bolger v O'Neill* UD 831/2006.

[186] Redundancy Payments Acts, s 13(2).

[187] Redundancy Payment Act, s 17; Employees may be entitled to longer notice periods under the Minimum Notice and Terms of Employment Act, 1973 or pursuant to their employment contract.

[188] SI 348/1991.

[189] Redundancy Payment Act, s 17(3).

[190] Redundancy Payment Act, s 18.

notice.[191] One of the purposes of such a certificate is to enable the employee to see how his or her entitlement to a statutory lump sum is calculated.[192]

[15.93] Another purpose of the Redundancy Certificate is that it establishes that the lump sum has been paid so that the employer can claim a payment of the rebate from the Social Insurance Fund. The particulars to be stated on a redundancy certificate are set out in the Redundancy Certificate Regulations 1991.[193] A failure to provide an employee with a redundancy certificate is an offence punishable on summary conviction by a fine not exceeding €5,000.

LUMP SUM PAYMENT

[15.94] The crux of the Redundancy Payments Acts is that the employee is entitled to a lump sum payment upon dismissal.[194] This lump sum comprises a sum equal to two weeks' normal remuneration for every year of service regardless of age in addition to one bonus week payment.[195] Where shift premium, overtime, bonus or commission are a feature of employment they must be included in the calculation of a week's pay.[196] The remuneration is capped at €600 per week or €31,200 per annum[197] and earnings in excess of this figure are disregarded for the purposes of calculating the redundancy payment.

[15.95] Schedule 3 of the Redundancy Payments Acts contains provisions regulating the manner in which years of service are to be calculated for the purposes of the lump sum payment. That Schedule provides that none of the following absences from work during the three year period ending with the date of termination of employment are to be included in the calculation:

(a) absence in excess of 52 consecutive weeks by reason of an occupational accident or disease within the meaning of the Social Welfare (Consolidation) Act 1993;

(b) absence in excess of 26 consecutive weeks by reason of any illness not referred to in paragraph (a); and/or

(c) absence by reason of lay-off by the employer.

[15.96] The employer is primarily responsible for paying the lump sum to the employee. The employer is then entitled to claim 60% of that sum from the Social Insurance Fund.[198] In order to claim the rebate, the employer must submit the completed form

---

[191] Redundancy Payment Act, s 18(2).
[192] *Minister for Labour v O'Connor* (1985) 4 JISLL 72.
[193] SI 347/1991, as amended by Redundancy Payment Act 2003, s 7.
[194] Redundancy Payment Act, s 19.
[195] Redundancy Payment Act 1967, Sch 3 as amended. Pursuant to the Redundancy Payments Act 1967, s 23 this sum is modified where a previous redundancy payment has been made once certain requirements are fulfilled.
[196] Redundancy Payments Act, 1967, s 23.
[197] Redundancy Payments (Lump Sum) Regulations 2004 (SI 695/2004).

RP50 to the Department within six months of the payment of the lump sum to the employee.

[15.97] In cases where the employer refuses or is unable to pay a lump sum due to an employee under the Redundancy Payments Acts, the Minister will pay the sum or whatever part of the sum the employer has refused to pay to the employee.[199] The employee must have taken all reasonable steps to obtain the payment of the lump sum from the employer except where the failure to pay is due to the employer's insolvency or death.[200] Where the Minister pays the lump sum, he will then seek to claim the amount of the payment made to the employee from the employer.[201] The amount claimed may be less the amount of the rebate from the Social Insurance Fund to which the employer would have been entitled had he paid the lump sum himself. However, where it appears to the Minister that the employer's refusal or failure to pay the sum was without reasonable excuse, the Minister may withhold the rebate in whole or in part and seek an increased sum from the employer.[202] In cases where the employer's failure to pay is attributable to its insolvency, the Minister may seek payment either from the bankruptcy arrangement, insolvent estate or winding up. Where the failure is due to the employer's death, the Minister may seek the lump sum from the estate.

TIME OFF

[15.98] During the two weeks of the redundancy notice period, an employee is entitled to reasonable, paid time off to look for new employment or to make arrangements for training for future employment.[203] The employer may request the employee to furnish him or her with evidence of arrangements made for these purposes and the employee must furnish such evidence provided it is not prejudicial to the employee's interest. In *Seldon v The Kendall Co (UK)*,[204] the Tribunal agreed that the employer's refusal to allow an employee time off to look for work was reasonable where the evidence showed that the employee had ignored job vacancies in his own area, and had chosen to travel further away to make speculative enquiries. The Tribunal also thought that it was relevant that he refused extra work offered to him by his present employer. As the employee had no specific lead to follow to justify travelling further afield, the employer's suspicion that his search for work was not genuine was held to be justified.

---

[198] Redundancy Payments Act, s 29(1). Pursuant to s 29(2), the Minister has the discretion to reduce the amount of the rebate payable to the employer by up to 20% where the employer fails to comply with the requirements regarding the notice of proposed dismissal.

[199] Redundancy Payments Act, s 32(2).

[200] Redundancy Payments Act, s 32(1).

[201] Redundancy Payments Act, s 32(4); Pursuant to s 43. all moneys due to the Social Insurance Fund are recoverable as debts due to the State and may be recovered by the Minister as a debt under statute in any court of competent jurisdiction.

[202] Redundancy Payments Act, s 32(4).

[203] Redundancy Payments Act, 1979, s 7.

[204] *Seldon v The Kendall Co (UK) Ltd* ET Case No 14442/85.

DISENTITLEMENT TO REDUNDANCY PAYMENT

(i) No redundancy situation

[15.99] In certain cases, an employee will not be entitled to a redundancy payment. For example an apprentice who is dismissed within one month after the end of the apprenticeship is not entitled to a redundancy payment.[205] Another obvious situation where this arises is where the employee is not in fact dismissed by the employer but chooses to resign, as the job continues to exist after the employee leaves.[206] In *Collins v Excel Property Services Ltd,*[207] the claimant resigned from her employment as a school cleaner. The company for which she had previously worked had lost the cleaning contract for that school and the claimant's employment had been transferred to the new contractor. The claimant resigned her position with the new contractor because she claimed that the cleaning equipment provided was of a lower quality than that provided by the respondent. She claimed a redundancy payment from her previous employer. The EAT held that the employee had transferred to the new contractor and, as a result, there was no case to answer against the respondent. Furthermore, the EAT stated that there was no redundancy situation as the position continued to exist in so far as the school still needed cleaning.

(ii) Unreasonable refusal of alternative employment

[15.100] An employee will also lose his entitlements where he unreasonably refuses an offer of alternative employment from his employer or an associated company.[208] Where the terms and conditions of the new contract are the same as those of the employee's previous contract, the renewal or re-engagement must take effect on or before the date of termination of the latter contract.[209] In cases where those terms and conditions are not the same, the offer must constitute an offer of suitable employment in relation to the employee.[210] Moreover, the renewal or re-engagement must take effect not later than four weeks after the date of termination of his earlier contract. The fact that an employee temporarily accepts an offer of alternative employment for not more than four weeks and then refuses the offer does not of itself constitute an unreasonable refusal.[211] According to the English EAT in *Cambridge & District Co-operative Society Ltd v Ruse,*[212] when considering similar wording in the equivalent English provision, the question of suitability may be determined objectively, whereas the reasonableness of the employee's refusal is subjective and must be considered from the employee's perspective. Thus the

---

[205] Redundancy Payment Acts, s (4); see *Cregan v Woods Electrical Ltd* RP 470/2006; see also *Murphy v Davenham Switchgear Ltd* RP 29/2008.
[206] See *Morton Sundour Fabrics Ltd v Shaw* [1966] ITR 327.
[207] *Collins v Excel Property Services Ltd* EAT, 31 December 1998.
[208] Redundancy Payments Acts, s 15.
[209] Redundancy Payments Acts, s 15(1).
[210] Redundancy Payments Acts, s 15(2).
[211] Redundancy Payments Acts, s 15(2B).
[212] *Cambridge & District Co-operative Society Ltd v Ruse* [1993] IRLR 156.

employee's subjective perception of the alternative job must be taken into account. In *Executors of Everest v Cox*[213] it was found that:

> The employee's behaviour must be judged from her point of view, on the basis of the facts as they appeared, or ought reasonably to have appeared, to her at the time the decision had to be made.

In *Hudson v George Harrison Ltd*,[214] the EAT held that the Tribunal was wrong in failing to take into account the employee's personal circumstances, including the fact that she had always lived and worked in the area, and she went home or swimming at lunch time or after work. The Tribunal had only focused on the small difference in time it would take the employee to travel to her new place of work and the provision of free transport.

(iii) Where payment is not agreed/paid within 52 weeks of termination

[15.101] An employee also loses his statutory redundancy payment entitlements where the payment is not agreed or paid and he fails to claim a redundancy payment within 52 weeks beginning on the date of dismissal or the date of termination of employment.[215] However, the Act provides for some degree of flexibility, as where the 52 week period has expired, the employee may apply to the EAT during the ensuing 52 weeks claiming the lump sum. The EAT may declare the employee entitled to such a sum if it is satisfied that the employee would have been entitled to the lump sum and the failure to claim was due to a reasonable cause.[216] While normally the entire period of 104 weeks begins to run on the date of dismissal or the date of termination of employment, the employee may apply to the EAT to commence the period on another date. When making such an application, the employee must satisfy the EAT that the failure to make the claim during that period was caused by his ignorance of his employer's identity and such ignorance arose out of, or was contributed to by, a breach of the employer's statutory duty to give the employee either notice of his proposed dismissal or a statutory redundancy certificate.[217] The EAT may determine that the time limit should run from any date it considers reasonable having regard to all the circumstances.

(iv) Dismissal for misconduct

[15.102] Employees dismissed for misconduct, for which the employer is entitled to terminate the employee's contract of employment without notice, are not entitled to a redundancy payment.[218] However, the Tribunal has taken a restrictive view of the type of conduct which gives rise to such an entitlement. What is required is '...very bad

---

[213] *Executors of Everest v Cox* [1980] ICR 415.

[214] *Hudson v George Harrison Ltd* EAT 0571/02; see also *Paton Calvert & Co Ltd v Waterside* [1979] IRLR 108; for a case where the employee's refusal was unreasonable see *Fuller v Stephanie Bowman (Sales) Ltd* [1977] IRLR 87.

[215] Redundancy Payments Acts, s 24; see *Dwyer v Monaghan Veterinary Laboratory Ltd* RP 250/2006.

[216] Redundancy Payments Acts, s 24(2A).

[217] Redundancy Payments Acts, s 24(3).

[218] Redundancy Payments Acts, s 14.

behaviour of such a kind that no reasonable employer could be expected to tolerate the continuance of the relationship for a minute longer.'[219]

[15.103] The misconduct must be genuine and proper disciplinary procedures followed. An employee may not be dismissed for misconduct after he or she has been issued with a notice of redundancy.[220] Moreover, in *Jenvey v Australian Broadcasting Corp,*[221] the Court implied a term into the employment contract that, once an employer had determined that an employee would be dismissed by reason of redundancy, the employer could not dismiss for another reason without good cause as this would deny the employee the benefits promised by the redundancy scheme.

[15.104] The fact that an employee's conduct led to the redundancy situation does not disentitle the employee to a redundancy payment. In *Sanders v Ernest A Neale Ltd*[222] the British National Industrial Relations Court dismissed the relevance of the employee's conduct in contributing to or creating the redundancy situation, when calculating his or her redundancy entitlements. In this respect, the Court observed that:

> Interruption of service due to industrial action can cause customers to look to competitors or to turn to substitute materials or services. This can lead to a diminution in the requirements of the business for employees to carry out work of a particular kind and to workers being dismissed. But the mere fact that the employees' action created the redundancy situation does not disentitle them to a redundancy payment. The entitlement depends upon the words of a statute and there is no room for any general consideration of whether it is equitable that the employee should receive a payment.

SEVERANCE PACKAGES

(i) *Ex gratia* payments

[15.105] An employer may also make an *ex gratia* payment over and above the statutory payment required under the Redundancy Payments Acts.[223] There are a number of reasons an employer may choose to make such a payment. Specifically, an *ex gratia* payment may minimise employee resistance to the proposed redundancies and decrease the likelihood of industrial relations disputes such as strikes and/or sit ins. Implementing redundancies needs the co-operation of employees and this may include winding down production and staggering the redundancies over a period of time. Incentivising employees to assist in an orderly close down is an important element in the process. In addition, where the redundancy only affects part of the company, *ex gratia* payments may decrease staff turnover in those sectors unaffected by the redundancy by providing

---

[219] *Lennon v Bredin* M160/178 see Madden and Kerr, *Unfair Dismissal: Cases and Commentary* (2nd edn, 1996).

[220] Redundancy Payments Acts, s 14(2).

[221] *Jenvey v Australian Broadcasting Corp* [2003] ICR 79; *Mallone v BPB Industries Ltd* [2002] ICR 1045.

[222] *Sanders v Ernest A Neale Ltd* [1974] IRLR 236 at 239; see also *Bates v Model Bakery Ltd* [1992] ELR 193 and *E & J Davis Transport Ltd v Chattaway* [1972] ITR 361 (NIRC).

[223] See Higgins, Colman, 'Severance Review' (2008) *IRN* 35 for overview of severance settlements in January to June 2008.

staff with the security of knowing that, even if their own position is affected at a later date, they are likely to be offered a similar redundancy package. Moreover, *ex gratia* payments are likely to have a positive impact on the employer's public reputation as being a responsible and caring employer.

[15.106] Typically *ex gratia* payments lie in the range of 3–6 weeks for every year of service in the particular employment, either in addition to, or inclusive of, the statutory lump sum entitlement. Payments differ somewhat depending on the circumstances, whether a total closure or a part rationalisation. However, in the case of long-service employees, a cap is sometimes placed on the maximum amount. Where the *ex gratia* payment is inclusive of the statutory entitlement, this should be expressly stated to ensure that employers are not exposed to additional costs.[224] The *ex gratia* element is usually calculated on the basis of actual pay (whether basic pay or total remuneration) rather than by applying the €600 per week limit under the statutory scheme. *Ex gratia* payments may also make provisions for other benefits such as health insurance or preferential loans being made available beyond the date of termination. Increasingly, employers make recruitment specialists available to advise employees on career options. No rebate is available in respect of the *ex gratia* element of any severance package.

[15.107] *Ex gratia* payments do not fall within the ambit of the Redundancy Payments Acts or the jurisdiction of the Tribunal.[225] A dispute as to the level of such a payment in any instance is a 'trade dispute' between the employer and employee under the Industrial Relations Acts 1946–2004, irrespective of the fact that the payment may meet or exceed all the basis minimum legal requirements. This leaves open the possibility of industrial action in the form of picketing, strikes, sit-ins and/or referral of disputes to the Labour Relations Commission and/or the Labour Court.

[15.108] In certain cases, the level of the *ex gratia* payment may become a well-established custom and practice, to such a degree that it is akin to a contractual entitlement. If an employer has, on a number of occasions made the same level of *ex gratia* payments available, this may be incorporated in a collective agreement, or be reduced to writing and become known as that company's established severance package. In the case of *Albion Automotive Ltd v Walker & Others*[226] it was held that the severance

---

[224] See *Minister for Labour v O'Connor* (1985) 4 JISLL which concerned a case were the employee was paid £500 by way of compensation for his dismissal for redundancy. His statutory redundancy entitlement was £132 and a dispute arose as to whether this was included in the amount paid. The employee had not been given his redundancy certificate. Kenny J held that, if an employer agrees to pay a larger sum than that to which the employee is statutorily entitled but does not get the certificate signed by the employee, the employee's statutory entitlement is not lost unless the employer establishes (i) the employee knew the amount of the statutory lump sum before or at the time of dismissal; and (ii) the employee agreed to accept the sum offered in discharge of the employer's statutory liability to pay the lump sum and of the claim which the employee believed he had against the employer for compensation for dismissal. See also *Talbot Ireland Ltd v the Minister for Labour and Others* 1983 No 407 SP; Madden, 'Compromising Statutory Entitlements-Redundancy' (1985) 3 ILT 18.

[225] *Hyde v Fr Kelleher* UD521/2001.

[226] *Albion Automotive Ltd v Walker & Others* [2002] EWCA Civ 946.

terms had become established custom and practice and formed part of the terms and conditions of employment. In that sense, the *ex gratia* elements are no longer discretionary but are rather a legal entitlement.

(ii) Compromise agreements

[15.109] Before paying an *ex gratia* redundancy package, it is advisable for employers to enter into compromise agreements with the relevant employees. In *Fowler v Hardward Distributors Dublin Ltd*,[227] the claimants both signed documents accepting the terms of the redundancy package and excluding the possibility of further action under any employment legislation. The EAT held that the agreement was in full and final settlement of any employment related claims the claimants may have had and that it had no jurisdiction to hear the claims. This decision and others have to be reconciled with the express provisions of the Redundancy Payments Acts and Unfair Dismissals Acts which provide that claims under these Acts cannot be waived or compromised. The basis of decisions upholding compromise agreements, which include in them express waivers of claims under these Acts, is that the agreement is a fully informed one and that the employee is fully aware of what rights and entitlements they have and what they are agreeing to, usually with the benefit of advice from a union representative or independent legal advice. In the UK, a separate certificate is affixed to the compromise agreement and signed by a solicitor of the employee verifying that advice has been given. The certificate system does not operate in Ireland but compromise agreements would usually confirm that the employee had the benefit of independent legal advice before entering into the agreement.

[15.110] Compromise agreements should include a clearly drafted waiver of the employee's right to challenge the redundancy and other potential claims in the future. In particular, the agreement should be clear as to the precise rights including those under employment protection legislation, which are the subject matter of the waiver. The employee should be advised as to the implications of signing the waiver and given the opportunity to obtain independent legal advice on the content and effect of the agreement.

[15.111] If there has been any history of illness, grievances, bullying, harassment or stress, both employer and employee must be clear as to whether the severance being paid on the occasion of the termination of employment on redundancy grounds is also in full and final settlement of any claims or liabilities arising out of any other issues or disputes. In the case of *Lane v MBNA (Bank of America)*,[228] it was found that an employee who had been made redundant had been victimised when the company

---

[227] *Fowler v Hardward Distributors Dublin Ltd* [1996] ELR 240; see also *Doyle & Ryan v Lithographic Plate Plan Ltd* UD 1049/2003. In *Fay v CR2 Ltd* UD 1233/2005, the Tribunal refused to accept that the claimant was estopped from taking the case in circumstances where she had been informed that the respondent would interpret her acceptance of the redundancy payment as being in full and final settlement of all claims arising out of her employment.

[228] *Heather Lane v MBNA* DEC – E2008-051.

declined to agree to exclude a discrimination claim from a proposed compromise agreement upon her redundancy.

[15.112] Moreover, the agreement should not be signed under duress. In *Shortt v Data Packaging Ltd,*[229] the EAT proceeded to hear a case in which the employee had signed a compromise agreement accepting the terms of the redundancy. The claimant claimed that the defendant's representative had suggested to him that he would not get his money unless he signed the document. The EAT held that this had essentially deprived the claimant of the exercise of his free will.

SEVERANCE SCHEMES/PROGRAMMES

[15.113] Employers seeking to reduce workforce numbers sometimes develop an organisation severance scheme. Such schemes may be voluntary or compulsory. The scheme can be voluntary and made available to all or to a certain segment of the organisation but again subject to the rules of the scheme and rather than an automatic entitlement.

Voluntary severance schemes

[15.114] In certain sectors, trade unions have, through either custom and practice or by collective agreement, secured the concession that redundancies can only be agreed by a voluntary process and that there can be no compulsory redundancies.[230] These schemes or programmes can be quite detailed and are introduced following a process of consultation and dialogue with employees and representatives. Details of the scheme will centre on eligibility, time frames for applying and details of the severance payments which may include:

(i)   statutory and *ex gratia* payments;

(ii)   health insurance and other benefits continued for a period of time; and/or

(iii)   possible added years for pension benefits.

[15.115] Applications are submitted to avail of the scheme and then the employer has to assess the response. On certain occasions there is an over-subscription of employees seeking to avail of the scheme. Difficulties arise where excess numbers apply for the scheme. The employer must then follow an objective process in determining those applications which it accepts and those it declines. In some cases, large employers have had to establish an adjudication process to deal with the grievances arising from a refusal. Voluntary schemes can therefore have a destabilising effect on an organisation, as expectations may have been raised for employees who have expressed a wish to avail of the package and have indicated a willingness to be made redundant. This can lead to disenchantment for employees. Moreover, while employers may achieve a desired cost reduction, they may find that the very people with skill sets it wishes to retain apply to avail of the scheme.

---

[229] *Shortt v Data Packaging Ltd* [1996] ELR 7.

[230] *Kaur v MG* [2004] EWCA Civ 1507.

Compulsory severance schemes/programmes

[15.116] As a result of some of the issues arising from implementing a voluntary scheme, employers frequently go straight to the compulsory process and in effect go through the consultation and selection process and determine the positions that are to be made redundant. For example, in a total closure situation clearly a compulsory scheme will apply.

[15.117] Information made available to employees being made redundant under a compulsory scheme will include vital information on timing, severance amount and a calculation for each employee.

[15.118] In both voluntary and compulsory schemes care needs to be taken to include all eligible employees including those on various types of leave: holidays, carers, maternity, adoptive, parental, sick or any other form of leave of absence. Also those employees on secondment from their employer need to be taken into account.

[15.119] It is also important that all employees are made fully aware of the impact of termination of their employment and this includes employees who may be in receipt of illness/incapacity income, a condition of which may require the individual to be in employment. This will not be the case once the employee is made redundant.

[15.120] Furthermore, outplacement services and counselling may also form part of both voluntary and compulsory severance schemes.

STATE SECTOR AND REDUNDANCY

[15.121] The permanent and pensionable nature of public sector employment represents a very valuable benefit to employees. The public sector employment ranges from the Government itself through its departments to a wide range of both commercial and non-commercial State bodies. Employment law relevant to public sector employment has developed a unique set of principles with protection against removal and dismissal. The Civil Service (Amendment) Act 2005, for the first time, brings certain civil servants under the provisions of the Unfair Dismissal Acts.

[15.122] Compulsory redundancies are unknown in the State sector to date. In many cases guarantees to that effect are incorporated in collective agreements or made a precondition to a particular State organisation or body either transferring to another State body or to the private sector.

[15.123] Voluntary early retirement schemes have been the traditional approach to achieving cost-cutting in the public sector. There have also been some voluntary severance programmes but most are allied to early retirement programmes. The Health Service Executive's (the HSE) proposals for a voluntary severance scheme indicate a change of approach to redundancies in the State sector albeit on a voluntary basis. A complicating cost factor in such schemes is the element of extensive pension entitlement.

EXCEPTIONAL COLLECTIVE REDUNDANCIES

[15.124] The Protection of Employment (Exceptional Collective Redundancies and Related Matters) Act 2007 (the 2007 Act) makes specific provisions for so-called exceptional collective redundancies. This legislation was introduced against the background of the replacement by Irish Ferries of about 500 existing permanent unionised staff with lower cost agency crews sourced in Eastern Europe by an agency in Cyprus. This replacement gave rise to serious concerns regarding the strategic use of redundancy and outsourcing as a means of job displacement.[231] The Social Partnership Agreement, *Towards 2016 – Ten Year Framework Social Partnership Agreement 2006–2016*, provided for the adoption of new tougher arrangements to deal with the effects of migration on collective bargaining and social relationships.[232]

[15.125] The essential objective of the 2007 Act is to increase the expense of exceptional collective redundancies for employers, thus rendering them a less attractive option. Pursuant to the provisions of the 2007 Act, the Minister may refuse to pay rebates to the employer in respect of the payment of a redundancy lump sum in the case of exceptional collective redundancies. In addition, if the Minister refuses to pay the rebate, the exemption from income tax in respect of the statutory element of lump sums paid to dismissed employees is lost. Furthermore, where employees are dismissed in the case of an exceptional collective redundancy situation, it is open to them to claim unfair dismissal. In those circumstances, an employee who has less than 20 years' continuous service may be compensated by up to 208 weeks' remuneration. For employees who have more than 20 years' continuous service, compensation may be up to 260 weeks' remuneration. This could result in substantial costs for an employer given that the collective nature of the redundancies would probably lead to a number of simultaneous claims being made to the EAT.

[15.126] Exceptional collective redundancies are essentially compulsory collective redundancies where the redundant employees are to be replaced within the State, either at the same location or elsewhere, by new employees carrying out similar functions with inferior terms and conditions of employment.[233] The new employees may either be directly employed by the employer or provide services to it through some other arrangement.

[15.127] The issue as to whether or not collective redundancies constitute exceptional collective redundancies is generally determined at first instance by the Redundancy Panel (the Panel) which is established under that 2007 Act and consists of three members.[234] One of the members is appointed by the National Implementation Body,

---

[231] See generally, Roche, 'Developments in Industrial Relations and Human Resource Management' (*ERSI Report*, Spring 2007).

[232] See Meenan, 'Exceptional Collective Redundancies' (2007) 4(3) *IELJ* 74; Kerr, Anthony 'Legislative Developments' (2007) 4(2) *IELJ* 63.

[233] Redundancy Payments Acts, s 7(2)(A) as inserted by s 16.

[234] Protection of Employment (Exceptional Collective Redundancies and Related Matters) Act 2007, s.5.

one by the Irish Congress of Trade Unions and one by the Irish Business and Employers Confederation.[235]

[15.128] Either an employer or the employee representatives may refer a proposal to create collective redundancies to the Panel, by written notice, in order to determine whether or not they would constitute exceptional collective redundancies.[236] The reference must be made during the 30 day consultation period set out under the Protection of Employment Acts.[237] In addition, the referring party must have sought to resolve the matter through local engagement and must have acted reasonably.[238] In particular, that party must not have acted in a manner which has frustrated the possibility of reaching agreement regarding restructuring or other changes necessary to secure the viability of the business of the employer. Moreover, the referring party must not have had recourse to 'industrial action' since the proposal was referred to the Panel. Where the referring party is the employee representatives, they must be acting with the approval of the majority of those whom they represent who are affected by the redundancy proposal.[239]

[15.129] Once the Panel receives a reference regarding a proposal to create collective redundancies, the Panel must inform the Minister of the fact and invite the affected parties to make submissions to it in relation to the proposal.[240] Where the Panel considers that the proposed collective redundancies are exceptional collective redundancies, it must, within seven working days of receipt of the reference, either request the Minister to seek an opinion from the Labour Court as to whether the proposal creates exceptional collective redundancies, or inform the Minister that the conditions for referring the proposal redundancies are not satisfied.[241]

[15.130] Where the Panel requests the Minister to refer the matter to the Labour Court, the Minister has seven days from receipt of the request to do so.[242] However, the Minister may make a request to the Labour Court on his own initiative if it appears to him that the proposed collective redundancies are exceptional collective redundancies and the

---

[235] Protection of Employment (Exceptional Collective Redundancies and Related Matters) Act 2007, s 5(2).

[236] Protection of Employment (Exceptional Collective Redundancies and Related Matters) Act 2007, s 6(1).

[237] Protection of Employment (Exceptional Collective Redundancies and Related Matters) Act 2007, s 6(1).

[238] Protection of Employment (Exceptional Collective Redundancies and Related Matters) Act 2007, s 6(3)(b).

[239] Protection of Employment (Exceptional Collective Redundancies and Related Matters) Act 2007, s 6(1)(a).

[240] Protection of Employment (Exceptional Collective Redundancies and Related Matters) Act 2007, s.6(2).

[241] Protection of Employment (Exceptional Collective Redundancies and Related Matters) Act 2007, ss 6(2) and (3).

[242] Protection of Employment (Exceptional Collective Redundancies and Related Matters) Act 2007, s 7(1).

relevant times limits have not expired.[243] This is so, even if no reference has been made to the Panel. In the latter case, the reference must be made during the 30 day consultation period set out in the Protection of Employment Acts.[244] However, where a reference has been made to the Panel and that Panel has not requested the Minister to make a reference, the Minister may still make a reference within a seven day period of receipt of the notice from the Panel.[245]

[15.131] The Labour Court has 16 days to hold a hearing in relation to a request from the Minister and issue an opinion to the Minister as to whether or not the proposed redundancies are exceptional collective redundancies.[246] However, the Labour Court may only issue such an opinion where it is satisfied that the same conditions as those applicable when referring the issue to the Panel are satisfied.[247] The Minister must notify the parties within seven working days of receiving the Labour Court's opinion.[248]

[15.132] Where the Labour Court concludes that the redundancies are exceptional collective redundancies and the employer nevertheless decides to proceed with them, the Minister has the option of refusing the employer the redundancy rebate from the Social Insurance Fund to which it would normally be entitled upon payment of a redundancy lump sum.[249]

[15.133] The 2007 Act also extends the time in which dismissals may not take place where a reference is made to the Panel or the Minister's request is lodged with the Labour Court. In the case of references to the Panel, the earliest a dismissal can take place is at the expiration of seven working days commencing on the date the Panel received the request. Where the Panel requests the Minister to refer the matter to the Labour Court, this period is extended by a further seven working days. Moreover, where the Minister lodges a request with the Labour Court, the period is again extended by 16 days, commencing on the date of the lodgment.[250]

---

[243] Protection of Employment (Exceptional Collective Redundancies and Related Matters) Act 2007, s 7(3).

[244] Protection of Employment (Exceptional Collective Redundancies and Related Matters) Act 2007, s 7(4)(a).

[245] Protection of Employment (Exceptional Collective Redundancies and Related Matters) Act 2007, s 7(4)(b).

[246] Protection of Employment (Exceptional Collective Redundancies and Related Matters) Act 2007, s 8(1).

[247] Protection of Employment (Exceptional Collective Redundancies and Related Matters) Act 2007, s 8(2).

[248] Protection of Employment (Exceptional Collective Redundancies and Related Matters) Act 2007, s 8(5).

[249] Protection of Employment (Exceptional Collective Redundancies and Related Matters) Act 2007, s 9.

[250] Protection of Employment (Exceptional Collective Redundancies and Related Matters) Act 2007, s 10(1).

[15.134] If an employer effects a dismissal in pursuance of a proposal for collective redundancies in breach of these time limits he may be guilty of an offence and liable to a fine up to €250,000.[251]

Conclusion

[15.135] Whatever its motivation, when the Redundancy Payment Act was adopted in 1967 it was a truly revolutionary piece of legislation in that it was one of the first to recognise that an employee has a certain proprietary interest in his employment.[252] At that time, there was little or no statutory protection for employees dismissed for reasons other than redundancy. Consequently in that initial period, it was in the employee's interests to prove that the dismissal was due to redundancy and in the employer's interest to disprove it. However, in the intervening years there has been a succession of Acts designed to protect the position of employees. In particular, the adoption of the Unfair Dismissals Acts has brought about a radical shift in that now, for the most part, a dismissed employee is more likely to bring a claim under the Unfair Dismissals Acts than the Redundancy Payments Acts and it is the employer who will seek to establish that the dismissal was due to redundancy.[253]

[15.136] As a result, it is advisable for all employers who are faced with a redundancy situation to bear in mind the possibility that a dismissed employee will institute proceedings for unfair dismissal. In the context of such an action, it will be for the employer to prove that the dismissal was due to redundancy. In this respect, the employer will have to establish both the existence of a redundancy situation and that the dismissal is attributable to that situation. In cases where the redundancy does not affect the entire workforce, employers should pay particular attention to ensuring the objectivity and reasonableness of the selection criteria used when selecting employees for redundancy and in determining the selection pool. Employers should engage in broad-based and informative consultations with individual employees and/or employees representatives regarding both the need for redundancy, including potential alternatives and the way in which employees are to be selected for redundancy. In this respect the more reasoned and transparent the procedure followed by the employer, the less likely the redundancy will be considered to be a cover for an unfair dismissal.

[15.137] While an employer is entitled to dismiss an employee due to redundancy, this does not release the employer from his or her obligations under contract and/or statute. In this respect, contractual notice periods and/or notice entitlements under the Minimum Notice and Terms of Employment Acts 1973–2001 are likely to be of particular relevance. In addition, employers should ensure that they comply with their consultation

---

[251] Protection of Employment (Exceptional Collective Redundancies and Related Matters) Act 2007, s 10(3).

[252] See *Wynes v Southrepps Hall Broiler Farm Ltd* (1968) 3 ITR 407; See also *Lloyd v Brassey* [1969] 2 QB 98.

[253] Where an employee successful challenges a purported redundancy on unfair dismissal grounds, any payment received by the employee in the context of redundancy will be off-set against any compensation awarded under the Unfair Dismissals Acts; see eg *Gammell v Pall Ireland* UD 1057/2007; *Cusack v Dejay Royal Alarms Ltd* UD 1159/2004.

requirements including those imposed pursuant to the Protection of Employment Acts, and the Employees (Provision of Information and Consultation) Act 2006. When determining selection procedures, employers should take into account the need to ensure equal treatment of part-time and fixed-term workers and avoid discrimination on the basis of any of the grounds set out in the Employment Equality Acts.

[15.138] Employees in Ireland find themselves competing with employees of the world in an open global economy. Outsourcing both in Ireland and overseas as well as dynamically-evolving technological advances has revolutionised all workplaces. Now the State sector, for many years a haven of security and stability, looks set for the first compulsory redundancies in the history of the Republic. Change, change management and innovation have led to a far more flexible and diverse Ireland with a well-educated workforce whose skill sets are well up to the challenges of the modern age. The degree to which employers and employees deploy those innovative traits will impact on Ireland's ability to attract and retain sustainable employment. Where it fails, inevitable consequences will include job losses and redundancies. The global economy and markets in a capitalist society will also continue to have an impact on employment. Redundancy law is the legal mechanism which gives effect to these consequences.

Part VII
Collective Aspects of the Employment Relationship

Chapter 16

Employee Involvement

Sinead Casey, Kevin Langford and Bairbre O'Neill

INTRODUCTION

[16.01] The purpose of this chapter is to examine the existing statutory and regulatory framework governing the scope of an employer's obligation to consult with, and furnish information to, its employees.

Before examining specific enactments, it is important to note that Ireland has historically maintained a *voluntarist* system of industrial relations. This means that while employees enjoy a constitutional right to form trade unions, employers are generally not required to recognise such trade unions as having the right to represent their members in dealings with the employer. On the other hand, the European Commission has long sought to establish procedures and mechanisms to enable workers to be informed and consulted about decisions likely to affect their interests. There is, therefore, some degree of tension between the traditional Irish voluntarist approach to employee participation in the workplace and European efforts to introduce institutionalised, and sometimes mandatory, employee participation in corporate decision-making.

It is not surprising, therefore, that the various statutes and statutory instruments considered in this chapter, are each transposed from European Directives. These are:

- Transnational Information and Consultation of Employees Act 1996;
- Employees (Provision of Information and Consultation) Act 2006;
- European Communities (Cross-Border Mergers) Regulations 2008;
- European Company Statute (as that term is defined below).

Consultation is a broad theme in employment law, which necessarily overlaps with certain topics dealt with individually elsewhere in this book. For example, more tailored consultation and information obligations are imposed on employers in specific contexts, most notably in the areas of collective redundancies and transfers of undertakings.[1] Where such topics are dealt with individually and comprehensively elsewhere in this book, it is not proposed to address them again here. However, the reader ought to be generally aware that distinct obligations to consult and to provide information are imposed on employers in those contexts.

---

[1] See the Protection of Employment Act 1977 (as amended), ss 9 and 10 and the European Communities (Protection of Employees on Transfer of Undertakings) Regulations 2003 (SI 131/2003), Reg 8. See also Ch 15, Redundancy and Ch 19, Transfer of Undertakings.

TRANSNATIONAL INFORMATION AND CONSULTATION OF EMPLOYEES ACT 1996

Introduction

[16.02] The Transnational Information and Consultation of Employees Act 1996 (the 1996 Act) came into effect on 22 September 1996. The Act transposes into Irish law Council Directive 1994/45/EC and sets forth procedures for consulting with and informing employees in Community-scale undertakings and Community-scale groups of undertakings. In particular, the Act provides for the establishment of European Works Councils (EWCs) in multinational companies. The Act applies to all companies with 1,000 or more workers, and at least 150 employees in each of two or more EU Member States.

The purpose of an EWC is to bring together employee representatives from the different European countries in which multinationals have operations. During EWC meetings, these representatives are informed and consulted by central management on transnational issues of concern to the company's employees. in so far as multinational companies develop strategies and production structures across borders, the meetings represent an important opportunity for local employee representatives to establish direct communication with central management and to cooperate with their colleagues representing employees from other countries.

According to the European Trade Union Confederation, of the estimated 2,264 companies covered by the legislation, some 828 (34%) have EWCs in operation, although the number of active EWCs is higher since some companies have set up more than one. Many of these firms are large multinationals, so the proportion of employees represented by EWCs is much higher: more than 64% or 14.5 million workers across Europe.[2] Thus, it is fair to say that the impact of this Directive has been significant.

Application – workforce thresholds

[16.03] The Act applies to Community-scale undertakings and Community-scale groups of undertakings. Both terms are defined in s 3 of the 1996 Act as requiring a minimum of 1000 employees with at least 150 employees in each of at least two Member States.

The number of employees in an undertaking is calculated as the average number of employees – including part-time employees – employed during the previous two years.[3] employee representatives are entitled to request details of the numbers employed, and upon receipt of such request, the employer is obliged to provide this information.

It is worth noting that the location of the headquarters of a multinational company or group of undertakings has no influence on the application of the EWC Directive. Even if the company's main HQ is outside the EU, as long as the company has 1,000 employees in the EU and at least 150 in two or more EU Member States the EWC Directive still applies. In fact, many companies registered for instance in the USA or Japan meet the above criteria and thus are covered by the EWC Directive.

---

[2]   Statistics as of May 2008. See http://www.etuc.org.
[3]   Transnational Information and Consultation of Employees Act 1996, s 4.

Exemptions – Article 13 agreements

[16.04] Article 13 of the EWC Directive provides that companies which established an EWC or a procedure for information and consultation before 22 September 1996 (the deadline for transposition into national legal systems and the operative date of the Act) are exempt from the regime of the EWC Directive. Such Art 13 agreements must cover the entire workforce. Under s 6 of the 1996 Act, such an agreement will not be valid unless it has been accepted by a majority of the workforce to which it applies.

By 22 September 1996, 27 Irish-based multinational operations had concluded such voluntary arrangements.[4]

General obligations under the 1996 Act

[16.05] Section 8 of the 1996 Act sets out the general obligation of community scale undertakings as regards the information and consultation of employees. The obligation is to establish either a 'European Works Council' or 'arrangements for the information and consultation of employees' or a 'European Employees' Forum.'

The composition, role and function of a special negotiating body

[16.06] The procedure by which these arrangements are put in place (absent the existence of an Art 13 Agreement) is by means of the special negotiating body (SNB) procedure set forth at s 10 of the 1996 Act.

An SNB may be established on the initiative of central management of the undertaking or on the written request of 100 employees or their representatives from at least two of the 30 countries now covered by the Directive. The function of an SNB is to negotiate with central management for the establishment of a European Employees' Forum or an information and consultation procedure.

The SNB must have a minimum of three members and may have a maximum number of members equal to the number of Member States in which the undertaking is active.

The functions of the SNB are set out in s 11 of the Act. The primary function of the SNB is to negotiate with central management, for a written agreement for the establishment of arrangements for the information and consultation of employees.

Section 11(7) stipulates that the reasonable expenses of an SNB shall be borne by the central management. An SNB can rely on the assistance of experts of its choice. However, the allowable costs are limited to one expert per meeting or equivalent.

Content of agreement

[16.07] The agreement reached between central management and the SNB may invoke the establishment of a European Employees' Forum or may opt for an alternative information and consultation procedure. In any event, the agreement shall specify:

(i)   The undertakings and/or establishments governed by its terms;

(ii)   The duration of the agreement and the procedure for its renegotiation; and

(iii) The method for transmitting information to employees.

---

4   Guinness, Aer Lingus, Bord na Mona, Texaco, Merck, Sharp & Dohme.

Where the agreement invokes the establishment of a European Employees' Forum, it shall also cover certain additional matters, including the composition and governance of that forum, the functions thereof, the venue and frequency of meetings.

Subsidiary requirements – the establishment of a European Works Council

[16.08] Section 13 of the 1996 Act provides that an agreement between the SNB and central management may also establish a European Works Council (as distinct from a European Employees' Forum), invoking the rules and procedures set forth in the second schedule to the Act. Such a council may also be established by default where either:

(i) The central management refuses to commence negotiations within six months of a request under s 10; or,

(ii) Where, after three years have elapsed from the date of the request, the parties are unable to conclude an agreement.

Protection of employee representatives

[16.09] The Act affords a degree of protection to employee representatives. Section 17 contains a general prohibition that such employees must not suffer any unfair treatment or other action prejudicial to their employment because of their status or reasonable activities as employee representatives.

Proposals for reform of EWC Directive

[16.10] At present there is a proposal to amend the EWC Directive by:[5]

(i) the introduction of general principles regarding the arrangements for transnational information and consultation of employees, the introduction of a definition of information, and making the definition of consultation more precise;

(ii) the limitation of the competence of European Works Councils to issues of a transnational nature and the introduction of a link, defined as a priority by agreement within the undertaking, between the national and transnational levels of information and consultation of employees;

(iii) clarification of the role of employee representatives and of the opportunity to benefit from training, as well as recognition of the role of trade union organisations in relation to employee representatives;

(iv) clarification of the responsibilities regarding the provision of information enabling the commencement of negotiations and rules on negotiating agreements to set up new European Works Councils;

(v) adaptation of the subsidiary requirements applicable in the absence of an agreement to developing needs;

---

5 Proposal for a Directive of the European Parliament and Council on the establishment of a European Works Council or a procedure in Community-scale undertakings and Community-scale groups of undertakings for the purposes of informing and consulting employees (recast) COM(2008) 419 of 2 July 2008.

(vi) introduction of an adaptation clause applicable to agreements governing European Works Councils if the structure of the undertaking or group of undertakings changes and, unless the adaptation clause is applied, continuation of the agreements in force.

It remains to be seen whether these amendments will be made to the Directive and whether they will practically strengthen the existing framework for information and consultation of employees in Community-scale undertakings.

EMPLOYEES (PROVISION OF INFORMATION AND CONSULTATION) ACT 2006

Introduction

[16.11] The Employees (Provision of Information and Consultation) Act 2006 (the 2006 Act) came into effect on 24 July 2006. The 2006 Act, which implements EU Directive 2002/14/EC, provides a general framework for the provision of information to, and consultation with, employees.

'Information' is defined as the transmission by the employer to employees and/or their representatives of data in order to enable them to acquaint themselves with the subject matter and to examine it. 'Consultation' means the exchange of views and establishment of dialogue between the employer and employees or their representatives.

The Act is significant in so far as it introduces, for the first time, a general obligation on employers to establish arrangements for informing and consulting their employees. At the outset, it is important to note that the Act does not confer an automatic or absolute right on employees to be consulted or informed. Rather, as discussed below, the Act is limited to undertakings above a certain size and the provisions do not apply automatically but must be triggered by a request made to the employer by a quota of employees.

According to the then-Minister of State at the Department of Enterprise Trade and Employment[6] the 2006 Act:

> respects Ireland's voluntarist tradition of industrial relations and allows maximum flexibility to employers and employees to implement new procedures or continue with existing customised information and consultation arrangements.

Interaction with other legislation providing for information and consultation

[16.12] The rights and obligations contained in the Act are expressly without prejudice to antecedent information and/or consultation procedures contained in other legislation, namely:

(i) the Protection of Employment Act 1977, as amended, dealing with collective redundancies;

(ii) the European Communities (Protection of Employees on Transfer of Undertakings) Regulations 2003 dealing with transfer of undertakings;

---

6   610 Dáil Debates Col 84.

(iii)   the Transnational Information and Consultation of Employees Act 1996 dealing with information and consultation procedures in Community-wide undertakings (considered above); and

(iv)   other legislation which includes provisions on information and consultation.

Application – undertakings of 50 or more employees

[16.13] Section 3(1) of the 2006 Act sets forth a general entitlement to information and consultation, as follows: 'Subject to the provisions of this Act, an employee employed in an undertaking employing 50 or more employees has a right to information and consultation.'

As is clear from the foregoing, the Act applies only to 'undertakings' employing a threshold number of 50 or more employees. An undertaking is defined as a public or private undertaking carrying on an economic activity, whether or not operating for gain.

Phased application – workforce thresholds

[16.14] Directive 2002/14/EC[7] allowed for a phased introduction of its provisions and the Irish implementing legislation availed of that concession to the fullest extent possible. Section 4 of the 2006 Act provided that the Act applied from the following dates depending on the numbers employed by an undertaking:

Number of Employees	Date of Application
At least 150	4 September 2006
At least 100	23 March 2007
At least 50	23 March 2008

The number of employees in an undertaking is calculated as the average number employed during the previous two years.[8] Employees are entitled to request details of the numbers employed, and upon receipt of such request, the employer is obliged to provide this information within a four week period.

If the number of employees falls below the workforce threshold of 50 referred to above and remains below that threshold for a period of 12 months, any information and consultation arrangement established under the Act may be dissolved upon the request of the employer or a majority of employees.

Employee representatives

[16.15] Section 6 of the 2006 Act provides for the election or appointment of employee representatives who are employed by the undertaking concerned. However, if it is the practice of an employer to conduct collective bargaining negotiations with a trade union or an 'excepted body'[9] representing at least 10% of employees, then the employees are entitled to elect or appoint representatives from amongst the members of the trade union or excepted body on a pro rata basis by reference to the total number of employee representatives who are elected or appointed.

---

[7]   Directive 2002/14/EC, Art 10.

[8]   Employees (Provision of Information and Consultation) Act 2006, s 5.

[9]   As defined in the Trade Union Act 1941, s 6(3).

Process for establishing information and consultation arrangements

[16.16] Section 7 of the 2006 Act provides that the process for establishing information and consultation arrangements can be triggered either at the initiative of the employer or the employee.

Employer initiative

An employer may of its own initiative enter into negotiations with employees and/or their representatives to establish information and consultation arrangements.

Employee initiative

Alternatively, an employer must, at the written request of at least 10% of employees, enter into negotiations to establish information and consultation arrangements. The written request can be made either directly to the employer or can be made to the Labour Court. 10% of employees means the lesser of:

 (i) 10% of the employees in the undertaking, or

 (ii) 100 employees,

but, in any event, cannot be less than 15 employees.

If, at the time of making a request, the employee threshold is not met, then the employees are barred from making another request for negotiations for two years. The parties have six months from commencing negotiations (or a longer period if agreed between them) to establish an information and consultation arrangement or forum either by means of a 'negotiated agreement' or by adopting the Standard Rules on Information and Consultation contained in the Act either by agreement or by default.

Negotiated agreements

Requirements

[16.17] An agreement establishing an information and consultation arrangement may be negotiated by the employer and the employees/their representatives. In order to be valid, s 8 provides that a negotiated agreement must be:

 (i) in writing and dated;

 (ii) signed by the employer;

 (iii) approved by the employees;

 (iv) applicable to all employees; and

 (v) available for inspection by employees at the place agreed between the parties.

There may be more than one negotiated agreement covering different parts of the workforce.

Conditions for approval

[16.18] A negotiated agreement will be regarded as having been approved by the employees where either:

(i)   the employees vote in favour of the agreement by a majority ballot; or

(ii)   a majority of employee representatives elected or appointed under the Act approve the agreement; or

(iii)   the result of any other agreed procedure discloses that it has been so approved.

The balloting procedure referred to must be confidential and capable of independent verification and of being used by all employees.

Content of negotiated agreement

[16.19] According to s 8 of the 2006 Act a negotiated agreement must include reference to the following matters:

(i)   the duration of the agreement and the procedure, if any, for its re-negotiation;

(ii)   the subjects for information and consultation;

(iii)   the method and time frame by which information has to be provided/ consultation is to be conducted; and

(iv)   the procedure for dealing with confidential information.

A negotiated agreement can be renewed either before it expires or within six months after the expiry date.

Pre-existing agreements

[16.20] Before the operative date on which the Act applies to an undertaking as set out above, an employer and employees could enter into an agreement providing for information and consultation arrangements. Such agreements, which are referred to as a 'pre-existing agreement[s]', had the advantage that they could be tailored to suit the individual circumstances of the employer concerned.

Requirements

[16.21] These are set out in s 9 of the 2006 Act and are the same as in the case of negotiated agreements set out above at para **[16.17]**.

Conditions for approval

[16.22] A pre-existing agreement will be regarded as having been approved by the employees where either:

(i)   the employees vote in favour of the agreement by a majority ballot; or

(ii)   the result of any other agreed procedure discloses that it has been so approved.

Content of pre-existing agreement

[16.23] A negotiated agreement must include reference to the following matters:

(i)   the duration of the agreement and the procedure, if any, for its review;

(ii)   the subjects for information and consultation; and

(iii)   the method and time frame by which information has to be provided/ consultation is to be conducted.

A pre-existing agreement is deemed to remain in force for the period provided for in the agreement. In the case of an open-ended agreement, it remains in force until brought to an end in accordance with the terms of the agreement or by agreement of the parties. Where a pre-existing agreement is not in force for six months then the process for establishing information and consultation arrangements provided for in s 7 will apply.

Standard rules on information and consultation

[16.24] Section 9 of the 2006 Act contains a default mechanism whereby Standard Rules on Information and Consultation (the standard rules) will apply in a number of circumstances, namely:

(i) by agreement between the employer and its employees; or

(ii) by default where an employer refuses to enter into negotiations to establish an information and consultation arrangement within three months of receipt of a written request from employees or from the Labour Court; or

(iii) by default where the employer/employees fail to conclude a negotiated agreement within the period of six months from commencing negotiations (or such longer period as had been agreed).

If the employer and employees/their representatives reach a negotiated agreement, which is not approved by the employees, then the Standard Rules will not apply for a period of two years. Also, if a negotiated agreement is entered into and approved during the two-year period then the Standard Rules will not apply.

Summary of standard rules

[16.25] The Standard Rules are set out in Sch 1 to the 2006 Act and provide, *inter alia*, for the establishment of an Information and Consultation Forum (the Forum). The key provisions of the Standard Rules are as follows:

(i) The Forum set up under the Standard Rules must be composed of employee representatives who are employees of the undertaking.

(ii) The employee representatives must be elected or appointed in a manner agreed between the employer and the employees.

(iii) The Forum must have between three and 30 members and may agree its own internal structures.

(iv) The Forum must adopt its own rules of procedure subject to certain minimum requirements set out in the Act.

(v) For the purpose of the Standard Rules, 'Information and Consultation' includes:

   (a) information on the recent and probable development of the undertaking's activities and economic situation;

   (b) information and consultation on the situation, structure and probable development of employment within the undertaking and any anticipatory measures envisaged, in particular where there is a threat to employment; and

(c)   information and consultation on decisions likely to lead to substantial changes in work organisation or in contractual relations including those covered by legislation on transfer of undertakings and collective redundancies.

(vi)   The employer must provide the Forum with information at the time and in the fashion and with the content appropriate to enable the Forum to conduct an adequate study and where necessary prepare for consultation.

(vii)   Consultation must take place in a certain manner expressly set out in the Act.

(viii)   The operational expenses of the Forum must be borne by the employer who must provide the members of the Forum with any financial resources necessary and reasonable to enable them to perform their duties.

(ix)   The Act contains detailed provisions with regard to how employee representatives are to be elected.

Direct/indirect involvement

[16.26] In relation to negotiated agreements and pre-existing agreements, employees have a choice under s 11 of the 2006 Act to exercise their right to information and consultation either directly or through the elected or appointed representatives.

Where a system of direct involvement is in place either in whole or in part, employees for whom the direct involvement system operates may seek to be represented by the employee representatives elected or appointed under the Act. In order to do this at least 10% of employees for whom the direct involvement system operates must make a written request either to the employer or to the Labour Court. Also, the request must be approved by a majority of employees to whom the direct involvement system applies following a secret ballot.

Cooperation

[16.27] The Act imposes a general obligation on the parties to 'work in a spirit of cooperation having due regard to their reciprocal rights and duties, and taking into account the interest both of the undertaking and of its employees.'[10]

Protection of employee representatives

[16.28] The Act affords a degree of protection to employee representatives. Section 13 contains a general prohibition that an employer must not penalise employee representatives for performing their functions under the Act. Penalisation means dismissal, unfavourable changes in conditions of employment, unfair treatment (including selection for redundancy) or any other action prejudicial to the employee. Complaints with regard to penalisation may be made to the Rights Commissioner service. Where a complaint of penalisation is upheld, a Rights Commissioner can require an employer to take a specified course of action and may award compensation of up to two years' remuneration.

---

[10]   Employees (Provision of Information and Consultation) Act 2006, s 12.

Employee representatives are entitled to reasonable facilities, including paid time off, in order to enable them to carry out their functions promptly and efficiently having regard to the needs, size and capability of the undertaking and in a manner that does not impair the efficient operation of the undertaking.

Confidential information

[16.29] Employee representatives, employee participants in an information and consultation arrangement, members of a Forum set up under the Standard Rules and experts providing assistance are under a duty not to disclose to employees or to third parties any information which in the legitimate interest of the undertaking has been expressly provided in confidence.

However, an individual may disclose information which has been provided in confidence to either employees or third parties where those employees or third parties are themselves subject to a duty of confidentiality under the Act. The duty of confidentiality applies after termination of employment or the expiry of the person's term of office. An employer may refuse to communicate information or to undertake consultation where by reference to objective criteria this would either seriously harm the functioning of the undertaking or be prejudicial to it.

Members and staff of the Labour Court as well as experts or mediators appointed by the Labour Court under the Act, are also under an obligation not to disclose information obtained in confidence.

Dispute resolution

[16.30] Under s 15 of the 2006 Act the Labour Court is empowered to investigate disputes between employers and employees/representatives concerning various sections of the Act and to make recommendations. Such disputes may only be referred to the Labour Court after referral of the matter through internal dispute resolution procedures and to the Labour Relations Commission. Where, following the making of a recommendation by the Labour Court, the dispute still has not been resolved, the Labour Court is empowered to make a determination, which is legally binding.

Disputes relating to the certain matters can be referred directly to the Labour Court for determination:

(i)   where the employer refuses to communicate information or undertake consultation because it would seriously harm the functioning of the undertaking, be prejudicial to the undertaking or it is prohibited by legislation;

(ii) where the employer discloses information to an individual subject to the condition that information is not to be disclosed to a third party due to its confidential nature; or

(iii) where an individual discloses confidential information, which in the legitimate interest of the undertaking has been expressly provided in confidence.

A party to any dispute under s 15 of the Act may appeal from a determination of the Labour Court to the High Court, but only on a point of law.[11] There has, to date, been only one reported recommendation by the Labour Court under s 15.[12]

Inspectors

[16.31] The 2006 Act provides for the appointment of inspectors who have extensive investigatory powers. Such inspectors are entitled to enter a place of work at a reasonable time to carry out examinations or enquiries and to require employers to produce records, which the employer is obliged to keep by law.

Offences

[16.32] A breach of several of the Act's provisions amounts to a criminal offence. On summary conviction for an offence under the Act, a person can be subject to a fine of up to €3,000 and/or a term of six months imprisonment. If the offence is tried on indictment, the person may be subject to a fine of up to €30,000 and/or a term of imprisonment of up to three years.

Provisions dealing with information on transfer of undertakings

[16.33] The Act also contains an amendment to the European Communities (Protection of Employees on Transfer of Undertakings) Regulations 2003 (the 2003 Regulations). The effect of this amendment is that for the first time the transferor is obliged to provide full information to the transferee in relation to terms and conditions of employment of the staff being transferred. This is an important new obligation on the employer and it applies to any information, about which the transferor knows or ought to have known.

If the transferor fails to comply with this obligation and the transferee is obliged to pay compensation to employees pursuant to a complaint brought under the Regulations, then the transferee may recover from the transferor a proportion of the amount of compensation awarded which is attributable to the failure of the transferor to provide the required information or documents.

This will be of particular importance where there is no contractual or other business relationship between the transferor and transferee, eg where one service provider takes over a contract from another.

EUROPEAN COMMUNITIES (CROSS-BORDER MERGERS) REGULATIONS 2008

Introduction

[16.34] The European Communities (Cross-Border Mergers) Regulations 2008[13] (the 2008 Regulations) were signed into law on 27 May 2008 with immediate effect. The Regulations transpose into Irish law Council Directive 2005/56/EC on cross-border mergers. The Regulations set out a framework for cross-border mergers including

---

[11] On the procedure for such an appeal, see Ch 22, Practice and Procedure in Employment Law.

[12] *Health Service Executive v Health Service Staff Panel* RIC 1/2008 (Labour Court).

[13] European Communities (Cross-Border Mergers) Regulations 2008 (SI 157/2008).

categories and processes by which such mergers can be effected. Prior to the introduction of this new legislation the sole means by which Irish limited liability companies could carry on mergers was by acquisition. The Regulations provide for a new pan-European procedure and will apply to a merger between an Irish company eligible to merge under Irish law and at least one company formed and registered in an EEA State other than Ireland, where the merger occurs by way of:

(i)   merger by acquisition (where an existing company acquires all the assets and liabilities of another company);

(ii)   merger by absorption (where an existing company acquires all the assets and liabilities of its wholly-owned subsidiary); or

(iii)   merger by transformation (where the new company acquires the assets and liabilities of two or more existing companies).

The 2008 Regulations refer to the 'transferor company' and the 'successor company'. Under the Interpretation section of the Regulations these terms are defined as follows:

> Transferor company in relation to a cross-border merger, means a company, whether an Irish company or an EEA company, the assets and liabilities of which are to be, or have been, transferred by way of that cross-border merger.

> Successor company in relation to a cross-border merger, means the Irish company or EEA company to which assets and liabilities are to be, or have been, transferred from the transferor companies by way of that cross-border merger.

The implementation of the legislation allows intra-group and post-acquisition restructurings to be made on a cross-border basis. However, there are strict requirements to be adhered to under the 2008 Regulations in order for the merger to receive the requisite shareholder and court approvals. It remains to be seen whether the protection of employee participation rights under the Regulations will act as a deterrent for using the scheme where the successor company is an Irish entity.

Requirements or pre-merger criteria

[16.35] Under the 2008 Regulations where an Irish company is involved, in addition to the Irish company being capable of merging under Irish national law, certain pre-merger criteria must be satisfied. These requirements include:

(i)   the preparation of draft common terms adopted by the board of directors of each Irish merging company setting out the details of the merger including specific information about the merging companies and the proposed transaction;

(ii)   the drafting of a Directors' explanatory report explaining the implications of the cross-border merger for members, creditors and employees of the company and stating the legal and economic grounds for the draft terms of the merger;

(iii)   subject to certain exceptions, the drafting of an expert report for the shareholders of the company on the draft common terms stating the legal and economic grounds for the common draft terms and the implications of the cross-border merger for the company's members, creditors and employees;

(iv)   the submission of a notice along with a copy of the common draft terms to the Registrar of Companies to be published in the CRO Gazette and the separate publication of a notice in two national daily newspapers;

(v)   the passing of appropriate shareholder resolutions at a general meeting of each Irish merging company; and

(vi)   where employee participation is already a feature of one or more of the companies involved in the merger, provision should be made regarding employee participation in the new company, subject to certain exceptions. This requirement is discussed in detail below.

The effect of carrying out a merger

[16.36] The net effect of carrying out a merger is that the transferor companies will transfer all of their assets, liabilities, proceedings, rights, obligations, contracts, agreements, instruments etc. to the successor company and then it will be dissolved without the need for liquidation. After completion, the applicable company law is the law in the State in which the surviving company resulting from the merger has its registered office.

Employee participation rights

[16.37] One of the key aspects of the 2008 Regulations is the protection of employee participation rights which is dealt with under Part 3 of the Regulations. Employee participation is the practice of mandatory representation of employees on the board of companies of a certain size and includes the right of employees to elect or object to a nomination of the board. The 2008 Regulations require that where the employees in a transferor company have employee participation rights, these must be protected. The concepts of employee information and consultation procedures are already a feature of Irish law, eg under the Employees (Provision of Information and Consultation) Act 2006, but Ireland does not have any equivalent legislation in relation to employee participation. The Regulations do not, however, create new rights where employee participation rights do not already exist but simply provide that where employee participation is already a feature of one or more of the companies involved in the merger, provision should be made regarding employee participation in the new company In such instances, the companies may either negotiate a new agreement with employees on their participation rights or alternatively they can adopt the default position of the standard rules.

(a) Application

[16.38] Regulation 23(3) provides that the rules in force concerning employee participation in the State (if any), shall not apply where at least one of the merging companies has, in the six months before the publication of the common draft terms, an average number of employees that exceeds 500 and is operating under an employee participation scheme. Furthermore the rules in force concerning employee participation in the State (if any), shall not apply where there is no provision in any enactment for at least the same level of employee participation as operated in the relevant merging companies or where there is no provision in any enactment for employees of the successor company that are situated in other EEA States of the same entitlement to exercise employee participation rights as is enjoyed by those employees employed in the State.

(b) *Negotiations with employees and agreement*

[16.39] The management or administrative organ of each merging company must take the necessary steps to start negotiations with the representatives of their employees on arrangements for the involvement of those employees in the successor company.[14] Negotiations must be started as soon as possible after the publication of the draft terms of the cross-border merger. Before commencing negotiations the merging company must provide information to employee representatives (or to the employees where there are no such representatives) on the identity of the merging companies, the number of employees in each and the number of such employees covered by the employee participation scheme.

The management or administrative organs of the merging companies must establish a special negotiating body that is representative of the employees of the merging companies.[15] Seats on the negotiating body must be distributed in proportion to the number of workers employed in each EEA State. There must be at least one member representing each transferor company.

In order for an employee to be eligible to stand as a candidate in the election of members of the special negotiating body the employee must have been employed in the State by one of the merging companies for at least one year or be a trade union official or be an official of an excepted body.[16] The candidate must also be nominated by a trade union or excepted body already recognised by the relevant merging companies for collective bargaining or information and consultation purposes or by at least two employees.[17] The 2008 Regulations set out detailed rules on the conduct of elections.

Once elected, the special negotiating body and the management or administrative organs of the merging companies shall negotiate and determine, by written agreement, arrangements for the involvement of employees within the successor company. In order to facilitate this agreement, the management or administrative organs of the merging companies must inform the special negotiating body of the plan, the expected time-frame, and the actual process of carrying out the cross-border merger.[18] For the purposes of the negotiations, the special negotiating body may engage experts of its choice to assist with its work. Negotiations should be commenced as soon as the special negotiating body is established and the negotiations may continue for up to six months (or up to 12 months by joint agreement) from the establishment of that body.[19]

The agreement reached by the special negotiating body must specify the scope of the agreement, the substance of any arrangements for employee participation and the date of

---

[14] SI 157/2008, Reg 24.

[15] SI 157/2008, Reg 25.

[16] SI 157/2008, Reg 26(8).

[17] SI 157/2008, Reg 26(8).

[18] SI 157/2008, Reg 28(2).

[19] SI 157/2008, Reg 34.

entry into force of the agreement, its duration, the circumstances requiring renegotiation of the agreement and the procedure for its renegotiation.[20]

Once an agreement is reached it is binding on the entire group of companies within the company resulting from the cross-border merger, irrespective of the EEA State in which it was signed and the location of those companies.[21] Decisions taken by the special negotiating body must be by both an absolute majority of its members, with each member having one vote, and an absolute majority of the employees represented by those members.

Under Reg 37, where the successor company is operating under an employee participation system, that company must ensure that employees' participation rights are protected in the event of subsequent domestic mergers for a period of three years after the cross-border merger has taken effect.

(c)   The standard rules

[16.40] The 2008 Regulations contain a default mechanism whereby Standard Rules on employee participation will apply. Under Reg 35, if an agreement has not been concluded within the 6 month (or 12 month) period, the Standard Rules set out under Sch 1 of the 2008 Regulations apply in certain circumstances:

(i)   if the management or administrative organs of the merging companies decide to accept the application of the Standard Rules in relation to the successor company and, on that basis, to continue with the merger and the special negotiating body has not made a decision; or

(ii)   if the parties agree at the outset to the application of the Standard Rules.

Under the Standard Rules members of the representative body are elected in proportion to the number of employees employed in each EEA State by the merging companies. The election procedure must be agreed on by the special negotiating body. The representative body has the right to be informed and consulted and, for that purpose, to meet with the competent organ of the successor company at least once a year, on t he basis of regular reports drawn up by the competent organ, on the progress of the business of the successor company. The meeting shall relate in particular to the structure, economic and financial situation, the probable development of the business and of production and sales, the situation and probable trend of employment, investments and substantial changes concerning the organisation, introduction of new working methods or production processes, transfers of production, mergers, cut-backs or closures of undertakings, establishments or important parts thereof, and collective redundancies. Where there are exceptional circumstances affecting the employees' interests to a considerable extent, particularly in the event of relocations, transfers, the closure of establishments or undertakings or collective redundancies, the representative body has the right to be informed. The representative body has the right to meet at its request the competent organ of the successor company, or any more appropriate level of management within the successor company, so as to be informed and consulted on

---

[20]   SI 157/2008, Reg 33(2).
[21]   SI 157/2008, Reg 28(4).

measures significantly affecting employees' interests. The members of the representative body shall inform the employees of the successor company or their representatives of both the content and outcome of the information and consultation procedures.

The employees of the successor company and their representative body have the right to elect, appoint, recommend or oppose the appointment of a number of members of the administrative or supervisory body of that company equal to the highest proportion in force in the merging companies concerned before registration of the successor company.

(d) Confidential information

[16.41] Employees, members of the special negotiating body, members of the representative body, employee representatives and experts engaged to provide assistance are under a duty not to reveal any information which in the legitimate interest of the company has been expressly provided in confidence. The duty of confidentiality applies after termination of employment or the expiry of the person's term of office.

A company may refuse to communicate information to a special negotiating body where by reference to objective criteria this would either seriously harm the functioning of the company or be prejudicial to it.

(e) Dispute resolution

[16.42] Under Reg 40 a dispute between a company and its employees or their representatives within the scope of the Regulations may only be referred to the courts after recourse to the internal dispute resolution procedure (if any) in place in the relevant company concerned has failed to resolve the dispute, and the dispute has been referred to the Labour Relations Commission and, having made available such of its services as are appropriate for the purpose of resolving the dispute, the Commission provides a certificate to the Court stating that the Commission is satisfied that no further efforts on its part will advance the resolution of the dispute.

(f) Protection of employee representatives

[16.43] Protection from penalisation is afforded to members of the special negotiating body, representative body and employee representatives under Reg 39. Penalisation is defined as including dismissal, selection for redundancy, unfavourable changes to conditions of employment and any other action prejudicial to employment. Under Sch 2 of the 2008 Regulations a complaint may be made to the Rights Commissioner service that a company has contravened Reg 39. The Rights Commissioner may declare that the complaint was or was not well founded. As a result the Rights Commissioner may require the company to take a specified course of action or require the company to pay compensation of such amount (if any) as is just and equitable having regard to all the circumstances but not exceeding two years' remuneration in respect of the person's employment.

Members of the special negotiating body and employee representatives must be afforded reasonable facilities, including time off, to enable him or her to perform his or her functions promptly and efficiently.[22] However, this is subject to the needs, size and

---

[22] SI 157/2008, Reg 39.

capabilities of the relevant company and the proviso that it must not operate to impair the efficient operation of that company.

EUROPEAN COMPANY STATUTE

Introduction

[16.44] The European Company Statute is established by two pieces of legislation, namely Regulation EC 2157/2001 which is directly applicable in Member States and which establishes the company law rules and Directive 2001/86/EC on worker involvement (the 2001 Directive).

The European Company Statute is given effect in Ireland by the European Communities (European Public Limited-Liability Company) Regulations 2007[23] and the European Communities (European Public Limited-Liability Company) (Forms) Regulations 2007[24].

The European Company Statute gives companies with commercial interests in more than one Member State the option of forming a European Company, known formally by its Latin name of 'Societas Europeae' (SE), the objective of which is to make it easier for such companies to operate across the EU. An SE will be able to operate on a European-wide basis and be governed by Community law directly applicable in all Member States. An SE will be able to operate throughout the EU with one set of rules and a unified management and reporting system rather than the different national laws of each Member State where they have subsidiaries.

An SE can be created in several ways:

(i)   by the merger of at least two existing public limited companies from at least two different EEA countries- companies taking part in the merger can be part of a group, eg parent company and its subsidiary or subsidiaries of a common parent company;

(ii) by the formation of a holding company promoted by public or private limited companies from at least 2 different EEA countries;

(iii) by the formation of a subsidiary by companies from at least two different EEA countries by subscription of its shares- the SE must be wholly owned by these two companies but there is no requirement for an equal shareholding;

(iv) by the transformation of a public limited company which has, for at least two years, had a subsidiary in another EEA company.

The Statute also regulates matters such as minimum capital, management structures and general meetings, but in other areas such as accounting, auditing and winding up defers to the national law applicable to public limited companies, subject to appropriate modifications. An SE can, in most cases, choose the EEA country in which it will be registered and have its registered office. The European Company Statute aims to

---

[23]   European Communities (European Public Limited-Liability Company) Regulations 2007 (SI 21/2007).

[24]   European Communities (European Public Limited-Liability Company) (Forms) Regulations 2007 (SI 22/2007).

encourage more companies to exploit cross-border opportunities and strives to make the Internal Market a practical reality for business, thereby boosting Europe's competitiveness. Use of the European Company Statute framework is optional.

For companies active across the internal market the European Company Statute offers the opportunity to operate on a pan-European basis, enabling companies to expand and restructure without the costly and time consuming legal and corporate requirements of setting up a network of subsidiaries. However, employers must be mindful of the requirements under the Regulations and the need to negotiate with employees and their representatives to reach agreement on the arrangements for the involvement of employees in the SE.

Employee involvement

[16.45] The employee involvement aspects of the Statute are set out in the European Communities (European Public Limited-Liability Company) (Employee Involvement) Regulations 2006[25] (the 2006 Regulations) which transpose the 2001 Directive and came into effect on 14 December 2006.

The 2006 Regulations define consultation, information and involvement of employees as follows:

> 'consultation' means the establishment of dialogue and exchange of views between the representative body or the employee representatives (or both) and the competent organ of the SE at a time, in a manner and with a content which allows the employee representatives, on the basis of the information provided, to express an opinion on measures envisaged by the competent organ which may be taken into account in the decision making process within the SE.

> 'information' means the informing of the representative body or the employee representatives (or both) by the competent organ of the SE on questions which concern the SE itself and any of its subsidiaries or establishments situated in another Member State or which exceeds the powers of the decision-making organs in a single Member State at a time, in a manner and with a content which allows the employee representatives to undertake an in-depth assessment of the possible impact and, where appropriate, prepare consultations with the competent organ of the SE.

> 'involvement of employees' means any mechanism including information, consultation and participation, through which employee representatives may exercise an influence on decisions to be taken within the company.

(a) Negotiations with employees

[16.46] Regulation 4 outlines the requirement to begin negotiations with employees and provides that where the competent organs of companies draw up a plan for the establishment of an SE they must take the necessary steps to start negotiations with the representatives of the companies' employees on arrangements for the involvement of employees in the SE. Negotiations should be started as soon as possible. The timing of negotiations will differ depending on the way that the SE will be created. In the case of

---

[25] European Communities (European Public Limited-Liability Company) (Employee Involvement) Regulations 2006 (SI 623/2006).

an SE to be created by merger or by the creation of a holding company, negotiations should begin after the publication of the draft terms. In the case of an SE to be created by the formation of a subsidiary, negotiations should begin after the agreement of a plan to form a subsidiary. In the case of an SE to be created by transformation, negotiations should commence after the agreement of a plan to transform. Before commencing negotiations, information should be provided to employee representatives (or where there are no such representatives, to the employees themselves) about the identity of the participating companies, concerned subsidiaries and establishments, the number of employees in each, identified according to the country in which they are located, and the number of such employees covered by a participation system.

Seats on the negotiating body are distributed in proportion to the number of workers employed by the companies and their subsidiaries in each Member State by allocating one seat per portion of employees in each Member State which equals 10%, or a fraction thereof, of the number of employees employed by the companies and the subsidiaries in all relevant Member States taken together. In the case of an SE established by merger further additional members may be given seats.[26] The Regulations set out the rules on the conduct of the election, the constitution and the voting procedure of the special negotiating body.

The remit of the special negotiating body is to negotiate and determine by written agreement with the competent organs of the companies arrangements for the involvement of employees within the SE. In order to reach written agreement, the competent organs of the companies must convene a meeting with the special negotiating body and inform it of the plan, the expected timetable and the actual process of establishing the SE.[27] For the purposes of its negotiations, the special negotiating body may engage experts of its choice to assist with its work. Decisions taken by the special negotiating body must be taken by an absolute majority of its members, with each member having one vote, provided that such a majority also represents an absolute majority of the employees.[28] Once the agreement is signed, the special negotiating body must take the necessary steps for it to be communicated to the employees of the SE. The agreement reached is binding on the entire group of companies within the SE, irrespective of the Member State in which it was signed and the location of those companies.[29]

Regulation 13 provides that an agreement reached by the special negotiating body with the competent organs of the companies should specify:

(i)   the scope of the agreement;

(ii)   the composition of seats on the representative body which will be the discussion partner of the SE in connection with arrangements for information and consultation;

---

[26]   SI 623/2006, Reg 5.
[27]   SI 623/2006, Reg 8(2).
[28]   SI 623/2006, Reg 9.
[29]   SI 623/2006, Reg 8(3).

(iii) the functions and procedure for the information and consultation of the representative body;

(iv) the financial and material resources to be allocated by the SE to the representative body;

(v) if, during negotiations, the parties decide to establish one or more information and consultation procedures instead of a representative body, the arrangements for implementing those procedures;

(vi) if, during the negotiations, the parties decide to establish arrangements for participation, the substance of those arrangements; and

(vii) the date of entry into force of the agreement, its duration, the circumstances requiring renegotiation of the agreement and the procedure for its renegotiation.

Negotiations should commence as soon as the special negotiating body is established and may continue for up to six months from the establishment of that body, or up to 12 months if decided by joint agreement.[30] If no agreement has been concluded within this timeframe and the parties decide to accept the application of the Standard Rules then the Standard Rules will apply. The Standard Rules may also apply if the parties agree to this at the outset.

Under Reg 11 the special negotiating body may decide not to open negotiations with the competent organs of the companies or to terminate negotiations already opened, and to rely on the rules on information and consultation of employees in force in each of the Member States where the SE has its employees.

(b) Protection of employee representatives

[16.47] Regulation 19 provides protection from penalisation for the performance of functions in accordance with the Regulations for members of the special negotiating body, members of the representative body and employee representatives. Penalisation is defined as including dismissal or unfavourable changes to conditions of employment, selection for redundancy and any other action prejudicial to employment. Members of the special negotiating body and employee representatives must be afforded reasonable facilities, including time off, to enable him or her to perform his or her functions promptly and efficiently. However, this is subject to the needs, size and capabilities of the relevant company and the proviso that it must not operate to impair the efficient operation of that company. A complaint of penalisation may be brought to the Rights Commissioner service. The Rights Commissioner may declare that the complaint was or was not well founded. As a result, the Rights Commissioner may require the company to take a specified course of action or require the company to pay compensation of such amount (if any) as is just and equitable having regard to all the circumstances but not exceeding two years' remuneration in respect of the person's employment.

---

[30] SI 623/2006, Reg 14.

(c) Confidential Information

[16.48] Employees, members of the special negotiating body, members of the representative body, employee representatives and experts engaged to provide assistance are under a duty not to reveal any information which in the legitimate interest of the company has been expressly provided in confidence. The duty of confidentiality applies after termination of employment or the expiry of the person's term of office.

A company may refuse to communicate information to a special negotiating body where by reference to objective criteria this would either seriously harm the functioning of the company or be prejudicial to it.

(d) Dispute resolution

[16.49] Under Reg 20 a dispute between a company and its employees or their representatives within the scope of the Regulations may only be referred to the courts after recourse to the internal dispute resolution procedure (if any) in place in the relevant company concerned has failed to resolve the dispute, and the dispute has been referred to the Labour Relations Commission and, having made available such of its services as are appropriate for the purpose of resolving the dispute, the Commission provides a certificate to the Court stating that the Commission is satisfied that no further efforts on its part will advance the resolution of the dispute.

(e) The standard rules

[16.50] The Regulations include a default mechanism whereby Standard Rules on consultation and information will apply. Under Reg 15 where an agreement has not been reached within the prescribed timeframe and the competent organs of each of the companies decide to accept the application of the Standard Rules, the Standard Rules will apply. The Standard Rules may also apply where the parties agree to their application at the outset.

Under the Standard Rules members of the representative body are elected in proportion to the number of employees employed in each EEA State by the companies. The election procedure must be agreed on by the special negotiating body. The representative body has the right to be informed and consulted and, for that purpose, to meet with the competent organ of the companies at least once a year, on the basis of regular reports drawn up by the competent organ, on the progress of the business. The meeting shall relate in particular to the structure, economic and financial situation, the probable development of the business and of production and sales, the situation and probable trend of employment, investments and substantial changes concerning the organisation, introduction of new working methods or production processes, transfers of production, mergers, cut-backs or closures of undertakings, establishments or important parts thereof, and collective redundancies. Where there are exceptional circumstances affecting the employees' interests to a considerable extent, particularly in the event of relocations, transfers, the closure of establishments or undertakings or collective redundancies, the representative body has the right to be informed. The representative body has the right to meet at its request the competent organs of the companies, or any more appropriate level of management, so as to be informed and consulted on measures significantly affecting employees' interests. The members of the representative body shall inform the employees or their representatives of both the content and outcome of the information and consultation procedures.

The employees of the successor company and their representative body have the right to elect, appoint, recommend or oppose the appointment of a number of members of the administrative or supervisory body of that company equal to the highest proportion in force in the merging companies concerned before registration of the successor company.

Chapter 17

Trade Unions

Cathy Maguire BCL LLM BL

TRADE UNIONS AND THE CONSTITUTION

[17.01] Bunreacht na hÉireann 1937, Art 40.6.1° provides:

> The State guarantees liberty for the exercise of the following rights, subject to public order and morality:–
>
> (i)   [...]
>
> (ii) [...]
>
> (iii) The right of the citizens to form associations and unions. Laws, however, may be enacted for the regulation and control in the public interest of the exercise of the foregoing right.

Freedom to form trade unions/choose between trade unions

[17.02] Article 40.6.1° of the Constitution has been interpreted by the courts to mean that the State may not unduly restrict the freedom to form or join trade unions, or the freedom to choose between trade unions, as demonstrated by *NUR v Sullivan*.[1] Part III of the Trade Union Act 1941 was designed to prevent the proliferation of trade unions, and to streamline the collective bargaining process. It provided that a particular trade union or two or more specified trade unions might be granted the sole right to organize workers of a particular class. No other union should have the right to accept members of the class affected.

[17.03] The ITGWU applied for a determination that it be granted the sole right to organise workers in the road passenger service of CIE. The NUR, a rival trade union, and certain workers who were affected, issued High Court proceedings claiming that Pt III of the Act of 1941 was invalid having regard to Art 40.6 of the Constitution. The plaintiffs failed in the High Court on the ground, *inter alia*, that the power of the legislature to regulate the freedom of association encompassed the power to deny that freedom entirely. The Supreme Court reversed the High Court and held, *per* Murnaghan J, that Pt III of the Act of 1941 was unconstitutional:

> The Trade Union Act 1941, ... does not prohibit all association, but it purports to limit the right of the citizen to join one or more prescribed associations, ie the Union or Unions in respect of which a determination has been made. Any such limitation does undoubtedly deprive the citizen of a free choice of the persons with whom he shall associate. Both logically and practically, to deprive a person of the choice of the persons with whom he

---

[1]   *NUR v Sullivan* [1947] IR 77.

will associate is not a control of the exercise of the right of association, but a denial of the right altogether.[2]

[17.04] The State may, however, limit the activities in which trade unions may legitimately engage, as shown by *Aughey v Ireland*.[3] In *Aughey v Ireland,* the plaintiffs challenged the validity of the Garda Síochána Act 1977 which limits the number of associations which may seek to control or influence the pay, pensions or conditions of service of members of the Garda Síochána. *NUR v Sullivan* was distinguished on the basis that the challenged provision did not prohibit membership of a trade union, but merely limited the activities in which such a trade union could legitimately engage. Although the legislature cannot eliminate the freedom to choose between trade unions the freedom has been limited by trade unions themselves. Indeed, such limitation is vital to the trade union movement to prevent the proliferation of unions and promote harmonious inter-union relationships. The transfer of members between trade unions is regulated by a voluntary code contained in para 46 of the constitution of the ICTU. It provides that affiliated unions may not accept an applicant for membership who is a member or ex-member of another union without that other union's consent. An affiliated trade union which ignores this rule risks expulsion from Congress. This rule does not conflict with Art 40.6.1° of Bunreacht na hÉireann: *Murphy v Stewart*.[4] The limitation on the freedom to choose between trade unions does not infringe the Constitution since the limitation is imposed by trade unions themselves. If the existing members of a trade union were forced to accept a new member against their will, their freedom of association would be subverted.

No right to join

[17.05] In the ordinary course, there is no right to join a particular union. However, in extreme circumstances, the right to earn a livelihood may entitle a citizen to insist upon membership of a particular union. In *Tierney v Amalgamated Society of Woodworkers*[5] the plaintiff had been refused membership of the defendant union on the grounds that he was not a genuine carpenter. He sought a declaration that he was qualified to join the union, and an order directing the union to accept his application for membership. The constitutional right of freedom of association was not expressly mentioned. Instead, the plaintiff relied, *inter alia*, upon the right to work. The plaintiff's arguments were rejected by the Supreme Court. It was held that the right to work does not entitle the citizen to work in any particular capacity; if he cannot work in one trade or profession he must work in some other trade or profession. On this interpretation, the right to work is virtually incapable of grounding judicial intervention into union admissions.

[17.06] The reasoning in *Tierney's case* was expanded upon in *Murphy v Stewart*[6] when para 46 of the constitution of the ICTU came under judicial scrutiny. The plaintiff was a member of the National Union of Vehicle Builders (NUVB). Despite the objection of the

---

[2]   [1947] IR 77 at 102.
[3]   *Aughey v Ireland* [1989] ILRM 87.
[4]   *Murphy v Stewart* [1973] IR 97.
[5]   *Tierney v Amalgamated Society of Woodworkers* [1959] IR 254.

NUVB, the ITGWU accepted him into membership. The matter came before the Disputes Committee of the Irish Congress of Trade Unions which ruled that the plaintiff be restored to membership of the NUVB. The ITGWU complied with this ruling. Subsequently, the ITGWU once more requested the NUVB to consent to the transfer of the plaintiff's transfer of membership. Consent was refused, and the ITGWU informed the plaintiff that it would no longer consider his application for membership. The plaintiff responded by challenging the decision of the NUVB to refuse the ITGWU permission to accept his application for membership. He succeeded in the High Court where it was held that the challenged decision constituted an infringement of his constitutional right to join the union of his choice. The Supreme Court reversed this decision on appeal. In exercising its right to refuse to give the required consent, the union had not infringed any constitutional right of the plaintiff:

> In the ordinary sense, there is no constitutional right to join the union of one's choice. The consititutional guarantee is the guarantee to form associations or unions, but in ordinary circumstances before a person can join an existing union or association he must be entitled to do so either by law, or by the rules of that association or union, or by the consent of its members.[7]

[17.07] It is noteworthy that Walsh J went on to state *obiter* that the right to work might, in extreme circumstances, entitle a citizen to the membership of a particular trade union:

> This is, broadly speaking, the effect of the decision in *Tierney v Amalgamated Society of Woodworkers*; but it is not a completely unqualified statement of the constitutional position. It has been submitted in this Court on behalf of the plaintiff, and not really contested by the defendants, that among the unspecified personal rights guaranteed by the Constitution is the right to work; I accept that proposition. The question of whether that right is being infringed or not must depend upon the particular circumstances of any given case; if the right to work was reserved exclusively to members of a trade union which held a monopoly in this field and the trade union was abusing the monopoly in such a way as to effectively prevent the exercise of a person's constitutional right to work, the question of compelling that union to accept the person concerned into membership (or, indeed, of breaking the monopoly) would fall to be considered for the purpose of vindicating the right to work.[8]

Trade unions may not discriminate against applicants for membership on the basis of nationality where the applicant is a national of a Member State of the European Union.[9] Nor may they discriminate on the grounds of gender, marital status, family status, sexual

---

[6]   [1973] IR 97 at 116. Note also *Walsh v Irish Red Cross* (3 February 1995, unreported) HC (Geoghegan J), (7 March 1997, unreported) SC, where it was held that, having regard to the statutory provisions creating the association, and the association's rules, the relationship between the association and its members was non-consensual. The association had no right to refuse an applicant for membership who was eligible and who paid the appropriate fee. The significance of this ruling would seem to be confined to associations created by statute.

[7]   [1973] IR 97 at 117.

[8]   [1973] IR 97 at 117.

[9]   Council Reg 1612/68.

orientation, religious belief, age, disability, race and membership of the travelling community, pursuant to the Employment Equality Acts 1998–2008.[10]

Right to dissociate

[17.08] Article 40.6.1°(iii) of Bunreacht na hÉireann has been interpreted as guaranteeing the right of the citizen not to join an association against his or her will.[11] The right to dissociate was first recognised in *Educational Co of Ireland v Fitzpatrick (No 2)*.[12] The plaintiff in *Educational Co of Ireland v Fitzpatrick (No 2)* obtained an injunction to restrain the defendants from picketing its premises with the intention of compelling the plaintiff to coerce other employees into union membership. Both the High Court and the Supreme Court held that picketing is an activity which is inherently unlawful. The Trade Disputes Act 1906 granted immunity from that illegality when certain conditions were fulfilled. However, the Act of 1906 was subject to the Constitution, and it was void as being repugnant to the Constitution to the extent to which it granted legality to an act designed to frustrate the right of free dissociation of the employees.[13]

[17.09] In *Meskell v CIE*[14] the Supreme Court endorsed the decision in *Educational Company of Ireland v Fitzpatrick*. In *Meskell* the defendant company and four trade unions had agreed that the company would employ only trade union members. In order to give effect to this agreement, the defendant lawfully dismissed all employees with an offer of instant re-employment on condition that the workers became members of one of the four trade unions which were parties to the agreement. The plaintiff objected on principle to being forced to join a trade union and refused to accept re-employment on the terms offered. He brought an action in which he claimed compensation for violation of his constitutional rights. Although the plaintiff failed at first instance, his action succeeded in the Supreme Court where it was held that the defendants were party to a conspiracy to deprive the plaintiff of his right not to be coerced into joining a union. It was held that the common-law right of dismissal had been exercised in order to coerce the plaintiff into abandoning his constitutional right of dissociation. The common-law right was thereby abused and the Constitution must prevail.

Right to participate in the democratic process of the union

[17.10] The Irish courts have recognised a constitutional right of trade union members to participate in the democratic processes of their union: *Rodgers v ITGWU*.[15] The right has perhaps been better stated to be a right which trade union members enjoy to fair

---

[10] Employment Equality Act 1998, s 13 as amended.

[11] Note that the European Convention on Human Rights, Art 11 has been interpreted to include a right of dissociation: *Young, James and Webster v United Kingdom* [1981] IRLR 408; *Sigurjónsson v Iceland* (1993) 16 EHRR 462 (ECtHR).

[12] *Educational Co of Ireland v Fitzpatrick (No 2)* [1961] IR 345.

[13] See also *Sorensen and Rasmussen v Denmark* [2008] 46 EHRR 572 (ECtHR).

[14] *Meskell v CIE* [1973] IR 121.

[15] [1978] ILRM 51.

procedures when their union takes a decision which materially affects their interests: *Doyle v Croke*.[16]

[17.11] In *Rodgers v ITGWU* the defendant union introduced a scheme of compulsory retirement for members reaching the age of 65. Adoption of the scheme was by vote of the members. No notice of the proposed scheme was given to the plaintiff and he failed to participate in the meeting. On his objection, a further meeting was held and the matter reconsidered. On this occasion, the plaintiff was aware that compulsory retirement would be discussed, but nonetheless he failed to attend the meeting. He subsequently challenged the union's resolution adopting the retirement scheme on the grounds, *inter alia*, of failure to observe fair procedures. The plaintiff argued that the union's resolution imposed a penalty on him, that the proceedings at the meeting were quasi-judicial, and that he was therefore entitled to fair procedures in the conduct of the meeting. This argument was rejected. The plaintiff's right to fair procedures was, however, held to be grounded in Art 40.6.1°(iii). Finlay P held that it was:

> [a] necessary corollary to the right to join and become a member of a trade union that the right must extend to taking part in the democratic processes provided by it and in particular to taking part in the decision-making processes within the rules of the trade union.[17]

[17.12] On this formula, the right is dependent on the union rule book and may be excluded by its terms. Furthermore, Finlay P's assertion of a right to join and become a member of a trade union contradicts the opinion of the Supreme Court on the matter: the cases of *Tierney v Amalgamated Society of Woodworkers*[18] and *Murphy v Stewart*[19] demonstrate that there exists no such right, save possibly where a particular employment depends on membership.

[17.13] *Doyle v Croke*[20] concerned a dispute as to who should share in a sum paid to the ITGWU in settlement of a dispute for additional redundancy payments. The plaintiffs contended that the union held the amount in trust for all members who were employed at the factory; the union claimed that by virtue of decisions taken by union members prior to the settlement, the money was held in trust for only 150 members of the union. Costello J scrutinised the procedure adopted at and prior to the members' meetings laying down the criteria to be satisfied by those who would share in the settlement; he also examined the decision whereby the union drew up a list of those who satisfied the criteria and were entitled to share in the settlement. Each was tainted by failure to observe fair procedures: the first by a failure to give adequate notice, the second by the presence of bias in the decision makers. Costello J held that the right to fair procedures was grounded in Art 40.6.1°, Art 40.3 (which guarantees the personal rights of the Citizen) and the common law. With regard to Art 40.6.1° he remarked as follows:[21]

---

[16] *Doyle v Croke* (6 May 1988, unreported) HC (Costello J); (1988) 7 JISLL 150.

[17] [1978] ILRM 51 at 58.

[18] *Tierney v Amalgamated Society of Woodworkers* [1959] IR 254.

[19] [1973] IR 97 at 116.

[20] *Doyle v Croke* (6 May 1988, unreported) HC (Costello J); (1988) 7 JISLL 150.

[21] (1988) 7 JISLL 150 at 159.

[I]t seems to me that if the constitutional right of citizens to form associations and unions is to be effective the Article in which it is to be found should not be construed restrictively as the right would be of limited value if it did not protect individual members against procedures which might be unfair to them.

[17.14] Note that decisions which are democratic in nature may not attract the rules of natural justice: *McEvoy v Prison Officers' Association.*[22] This case stands at the borderline of disciplinary and governmental affairs. The plaintiff was president of the defendant union, an honorary position. He was removed by way of a vote of no confidence, proposed on foot of rule 62 of the union's constitution:

If the National Executive Council decides by a two-thirds majority of its members present and entitled to vote to pass a vote of no confidence in any member of the Administrative Council, that member shall cease to be a member of the Administrative Council and of the National Executive Council forthwith and shall not be entitled to attend any subsequent meetings of the Administrative Council or of the National Executive Council.

The plaintiff challenged his removal on the grounds that the defendant union had not observed fair procedures in removing him from his position. He succeeded in the High Court, where he was awarded £10,000 damages. On appeal, the Supreme Court reversed the High Court decision, holding that the defendant was not obliged to comply with fair procedures in passing the motion of no confidence. O'Flaherty J contrasted the procedure laid down by the constitution for the motion of no confidence with that for the discipline of members. He held that in passing the motion of no confidence the defendant was not obliged to observe fair procedures. It was sufficient that it observe the terms of the constitution and that it act *bona fide*.

No right to recognition

[17.15] The Constitution does not oblige an employer to recognise the association or trade union which seeks to represent employees' interests. This was demonstrated by *Association of General Practitioners & Ors v Minister for Health.*[23] The first plaintiff was a company having as one of its objects the promotion of the interests of general medical practitioners. The remaining plaintiffs were medical doctors and members of the company. The defendant had negotiated with a rival body, the Irish Medical Organisation (IMO), and had settled terms upon which health boards would contract with general medical practitioners for the provision of free medical services. The plaintiffs sought to compel the defendant to negotiate with them in setting the terms and conditions of employment by the health boards. They contended that they had a constitutional right to be represented by the association of their choice when their terms and conditions of employment were being decided. They argued that their right to dissociate had been compromised. They did not wish to be represented by the IMO in negotiations with the Minister, but wished to be represented by the first named plaintiff instead.

---

[22] *McEvoy v Prison Officers' Association* [1999] ELR.

[23] *Association of General Practitioners & Ors v Minister for Health* [1995] 2 ILRM 481.

[17.16] O'Hanlon J rejected the plaintiffs' contention:[24]

> I do not consider that there is any obligation imposed by ordinary law or by the Constitution on an employer to consult with or negotiate with an organisation representing his employees or some of them when the conditions of employment are to be settled or reviewed.
>
> The employer is left with freedom of choice as to whether he will negotiate with any organisation or consult with them on such matters and is also free to give a right of audience to one representative body and refuse it to another, if he chooses to do so.

A FRAMEWORK FOR BARGAINING

[17.17] Until the close of the 19th century, trade unionism in the UK and Ireland was characterised by the hostile attitude of the law. As trade union activity became acceptable, a legal framework regulating trade unions was constructed. It has been refined and expanded over time. Unions must come within this framework if they are to obtain the benefits of the Trade Union and Industrial Relations Acts.

What is a trade union? The statutory definition

[17.18] The legal definition of trade unions which is now in force was first laid down by the Trade Union Act 1871, and refined by the Trade Union Act Amendment Act 1876 and the Trade Union Act 1913. The resultant definition may be stated as follows:

> The expression 'trade union', for the purpose of the Trade Union Acts means any combination, whether temporary or permanent, the principal objects of which are under its constitution the regulation of the relations between workmen and masters, or between workmen and workmen, or between masters and masters, or the imposing of restrictive conditions on the conduct of any trade or business, and also the provision of benefits to members.

[17.19] The Acts, however, do not affect the following agreements:

   (i)   any agreement between partners as to their own business;

   (ii)   any agreement between an employer and those employed by him as to such employment, or

   (iii) any agreement in consideration of the sale of the goodwill of a business or of instruction in any profession, trade or handicraft.

This definition encompasses many bodies other than those usually thought of as trade unions. An employer's association might constitute a trade union within the terms of this definition. Generally, a body which falls within the definition of a trade union does not thereby obtain any benefits under the Acts. In order to obtain those benefits, it must seek certification or registration and authorisation. However, certain provisions of the code apply to trade unions merely by virtue of the fact that they fulfil the definition of what a union is and what its principles are. In *National Union of Journalists and Irish Print Union v Sisk*[25] the Supreme Court held that the National Union of Journalists, although

---

[24] *Association of General Practitioners & Ors v Minister for Health* [1995] 2 ILRM 481 at 489.
[25] *National Union of Journalists and Irish Print Union v Sisk* [1990] ELR 177.

not a certified union or a registered union in Irish law, fulfilled the definition of trade union and was therefore entitled to receive a transfer of engagements from the Irish Print Union under the Trade Union Act 1975.

Certified trade unions

[17.20] Under the Trade Union Act 1913, s 2(3), a trade union which is not a registered trade union may apply to the Registrar of Friendly Societies for a certificate that it is a trade union within the meaning of the Trade Union and Industrial Relations Acts 1871–1990. Certification does not confer any benefits, save that such a body need not prove its status in litigation.

Registered trade unions

[17.21] The system of registration operates under the Trade Union Act 1871. The principle advantages conferred by registration are as follows:

  (i)   it facilitates the trade union in dealing with property;

  (ii)   it enables the officers of the union to bring or defend an action at law to protect its property, and

  (iii)   it assists the union in protecting its funds against fraud.

Registration also entails a number of obligations. Among these are the duty to make annual returns to the Registrar of Friendly Societies showing assets and liabilities at the time of return, together with receipts and expenditure during the preceding year. Moreover, registered trade unions may be sued in their registered names.

Excepted bodies – authorised trade unions – negotiation licences

[17.22] Under the Trade Union Act 1941, if a trade union wishes to engage in collective bargaining, it must either be,

  (i)   an excepted body; or

  (ii)   an authorised trade union which holds a negotiation licence.

Excepted bodies

[17.23] Excepted bodies are defined by s 6(3) of the Trade Union Act 1941 as amended as:[26]

  (i)   employers who negotiate with their own employees;

  (ii)   civil service staff associations recognised by the Minister for Finance;

  (iii)   teachers' organisations recognised by the Minster for Education;

  (iv)   joint labour committees, ie committees established pursuant to statute for the regulation of rates of pay and terms and conditions of employment of particular employment sectors;

  (v)   a body granted the status of an excepted body by the Minister for Enterprise, Trade and Employment; and

---

[26] See Kerr, The Trade Union and Industrial Relations Act (3rd edn, Roundhall) pp 62–65.

(vi)   a 'house union', ie a body which consists of employees all of whom are employed by the same employer and which negotiates on behalf of those employees and no others. *Iarnród Éireann v Holbrooke*[27] makes it clear that a body cannot be said to be an 'excepted body' within this definition if the employer refuses to negotiate with it.

Authorised trade unions — negotiation licences

[17.24] Authorised trade unions are those trade unions which hold a negotiation licence.[28] Certain restrictions are placed upon the granting and retention of negotiation licences with a view to limiting the number of unions. The precise requirements which a trade union must fulfil in order to obtain or retain a negotiation licence vary depending on whether the union is Irish or foreign based, and whether it made its first application for a negotiation licence prior to or after the Trade Union Act 1971. The requirements may be broadly stated as follows:

(i)   Irish unions must be registered; foreign unions must have a controlling authority within the State;

(ii)   unions which first applied for a negotiation licence after 1971 must show that, at a date not less than 18 months prior to the application, and at the date of the application, that they had not less than 1000 members resident in the State. They must also fulfil certain notification requirements;

(iii)   every category of union must keep a certain sum of money deposited with the High Court.

[17.25] The advantages which are enjoyed by an authorised union holding a negotiation licence are:

(i)   it may carry out collective bargaining;[29]

(ii)   it obtains the benefits of Pt II of the Industrial Relations Act 1990;[30]

(iii)   it may invoke the Industrial Relations (Amendment) Act 2001;[31]

(iv)   Its members and officials obtain the benefits of ss 11, 12 and 13 of the Industrial Relations Act 1990; and

(v)   Its members obtain certain benefits under employment protection legislation, eg under the Unfair Dismissals Acts, a dismissal for membership of an authorised trade union holding a negotiation licence or an excepted body constitutes an unfair dismissal.[32]

---

[27] *Iarnród Éireann v Holbrooke* [2001] 1IR 237.

[28] See the Trade Union Act 1941, ss 5 and 7.

[29] Trade Union Act 1941, s 5.

[30] Industrial Relations Act 1990, ss 8 and 9.

[31] The Industrial Relations (Amendment) Act 2001, s 13(2) provides that the Act shall be construed as one with the Industrial Acts 1946–2001. The Industrial Relations Act 1946, s 3 provides that the expression 'trade union' means a trade union which is the holder of a negotiation licence.

[32] Unfair Dismissals Act 1977, ss 1 and 6(2)(a).

Status of trade unions: unregistered trade unions

[17.26] Unregistered trade unions have no legal personality separate from that of their members – the nearest equivalent is a social club. Any legal action taken by or against such a union must be taken by way of representative action.

Status of trade unions: registered trade unions

[17.27] However, registered trade unions are said to be quasi-corporations: although not corporations, they possess many of the attributes of corporations.[33]

The significance of quasi-corporate status is that:

(i)   the union can sue and be sued in its own name;

(ii) the union's funds are liable to damages for wrongs carried out by the union, or for wrongs carried out by the union's officials or employees for which the union is vicariously liable; and[34]

(iii) the courts will not, as a general rule, entertain litigation arising out of some irregularity by the union which may be ratified by the general meeting. Note, however, that the many exceptions to this rule (known as the rule in *Foss v Harbottle*) have robbed it of much of its practical impact.[35]

TRADE UNIONS IN THE WORK PLACE

Collective bargaining

[17.28] When employers and trade unions negotiate with each other to fix wages and other conditions of employment, they are engaged in collective bargaining. Indeed, in the eyes of the law, they may be engaged in collective bargaining if they merely 'sit around a table ... with a view to reaching agreement if possible'.[36]

Who may engage in collective bargaining?

[17.29] Every employer may engage in collective bargaining, but if a trade union wishes to engage in collective bargaining, it must either be an excepted body, or an authorised trade union which holds a negotiation licence.[37] If a trade union breaches the Trade Union Acts, it may be removed from the register,[38] in which case it will lose its authorised status and its negotiation licence, or simply have its negotiation licence withdrawn.[39] Since the very purpose of a trade union is to engage in collective

---

[33] See further *R (Irish Union of Distributive Workers and Clerks) v Rathmines Urban District Council* [1928] IR 260.

[34] *R (Irish Union of Distributive Workers and Clarks) v Rathmines Urban District Council* [1928] IR 260 and Kerr and Whyte, *Irish Trade Union Law* (Thomson Roundhall, 1985) pp 48–50.

[35] *Cotter v National Union of Seamen* [1929] 2 Ch 58.

[36] *Ryanair v Labour Court* (1 February 2007, unreported) SC, [2007] IESC 6.

[37] See above paras **[17.18]–[17.28]**.

[38] Trade Union Act Amendment Act 1876, s 8.

[39] Industrial Relations Act 1990, s 16(5).

bargaining on behalf of its members, if it loses its negotiation licence it may no longer act effectively as a trade union.

Closed shop

[17.30] A closed shop is an agreement between an employer and a union that all employees, or employees of a particular class or grade, will be or become union members. A pre-entry closed shop requires that a worker be a union member before he is engaged. It may be unlawful if the trade union has an effective monopoly in a particular area of work.[40] It may also be unlawful if it operates to exclude a category of persons from employment who are protected by employment law, unless the reason for the closed shop can be shown to be objectively justified by reference to reasons other than discriminatory reasons which are prohibited. The latter proposition is demonstrated by *Nathan v Bailey Gibson*.[41] Ms Nathan was an employee of Baily Gibson Ltd who wished to apply for a different position within the company. However, there was a pre-entry closed shop agreement between Bailey Gibson Ltd and the Irish Print Union (IPU) that members of the IPU would have first refusal on that position. The membership of the IPU was principally composed of men because it organised in an area of employment which was traditionally male. Ms Nathan was not a member of the IPU (she was in fact a member of another union) and therefore did not have access to the position. Ms Nathan claimed that since the membership of the IPU was predominantly male, the pre-entry closed shop operated to discriminate against her on the grounds of sex and was therefore in breach of the Employment Equality Act 1977. Although successful before the equality officer, Ms Nathan's claim was rejected by the Labour Court. The Labour Court impliedly accepted that the pre-entry closed shop had a disproportionate impact on women, but because this was due to historical reasons, it determined that discrimination on the grounds of sex had not been made out.

[17.31] The Supreme Court allowed Ms Nathan's appeal. It held that once a practice was shown to have a disproportionate impact on one sex, the employer was then obliged to show that the practice was objectively justified by reasons unconnected with sex. It is noteworthy that when the case was remitted to the Labour Court for its consideration, it determined that in fact the practice did not have a disproportionate impact on members of Ms Nathan's sex. If the closed shop were not in being, the job would have been offered to employees in Bailey Gibson Ltd. Therefore, the class of persons affected by the pre-entry closed shop were employees of Bailey Gibson Ltd who were not members of the IPU. Since this class was predominantly male, Ms Nathan failed to establish a *prima facie* case of discrimination against her on the grounds of sex. A post-entry closed shop permits the employer to recruit a non-member, but when employment commences, the employee must join the union. It is unlawful to enforce the post-entry closed shop. Citizens have a constitutional right not to belong to a trade union and they cannot be

---

[40] *Murphy v Stewart* [1973] IR 97 at 116.
[41] *Nathan v Bailey Gibson* (7 October 1992, unreported) HC (Murphy J), [1996] ELR 114 (SC), [1998] ELR 51 (Labour Court).

forced to give up that right, either by dismissal carried out by the employer[42] or by industrial action carried out by the trade union.[43]

Collective agreements

[17.32] If collective bargaining is successful, it will result in a collective agreement, ie an agreement between the employer and the trade union. The agreement may deal with the employer/employee relationship by setting wages or terms and conditions of employment. On the other hand, it may deal with the employer/trade union relationship, for example by laying down the procedures to be followed should a dispute arise between them.[44]

Recruitment and trade union membership

[17.33] There is no statutory provision which prohibits an employer from discriminating against an applicant for employment because he is a trade union member. However, such a tactic might well be challenged in the courts.

An employer who declines to engage a worker because he is not a trade union member, or because he is not a member of a particular union, risks having that action overturned by the courts, particularly where the person in question belongs to a category which is under-represented in the union in question and that category is protected by legislation.

Dismissal and trade union membership

[17.34] An employer may not dismiss an employee because he is or proposes to become a member of a trade union or an excepted body. Nor may he dismiss an employee for activities carried out on behalf of a trade union or excepted body where the employee engages in the activity outside work hours, or during times agreed under his contract of employment. The trade union in question must be an authorised trade union holding a negotiation licence. Dismissals for these reasons are automatically unfair.[45] An employer may not dismiss an employee who declines to become a trade union member. This prohibition arises from the citizen's constitutional right to dissociate.

Remedies for the individual dismissed for membership

[17.35] The dismissed employee may make a complaint to a Rights Commissioner or the Employment Appeals Tribunal.[46] If a dismissal results wholly or mainly from trade union membership or activity, a claimant who might otherwise be excluded from the

---

[42] *Meskell v CIE* [1973] IR 121.

[43] *Educational Company of Ireland v Fitzpatrick* [1961] IR 345.

[44] On the legal status of collective agreements, see Ch 18, Industrial Relations, paras **[18.04]**–**[18.32]**.

[45] Unfair Dismissals Act 1977, s 6(2)(a).

[46] Unfair Dismissals Act 1977, s 8.

ambit of the Acts will be able to seek redress under the Acs.[47] For example, an employee who has been in the job for less than one year (the usual qualifying period) will be able to claim, as will an employee dismissed during probation, training or apprenticeship.

The burden lies on the employee to show that the dismissal resulted wholly or mainly from trade union membership or activities.[48] The employer must then seek to rebut the charge. The employee, if successful, may be awarded compensation, re-instatement (ie the same job) or re-engagement (ie a different job)[49]

Remedies for the individual dismissed for refusal to join

[17.36] An existing employee who is dismissed for refusal to join a trade union may also make a complaint to a Rights Commissioner or the Employment Appeals Tribunal. While such a dismissal is not deemed automatically unfair by the Unfair Dismissals Acts 1977–2007, a dismissal for such a reason could not be deemed fair in all the circumstances given that it constitutes a breach of the constitutional right to dissociate. In order to invoke the Acts, he or she must come within their ambit. All of the usual exclusions apply, in contrast to the situation where an employee is dismissed for trade union membership or activity. For example, he or she must have fulfilled the one year qualifying period. The burden lies on the employer to show that in all the circumstances the dismissal was fair. The employee, if successful, may be awarded compensation, re-instatement or re-engagement. An employee with less than one year's service, or who is otherwise excluded from the ambit of the Unfair Dismissals Acts, who is dismissed for refusal to join a trade union may apply to the courts for relief for breach of a constitutional right, ie the right not to join a trade union. Possible remedies include injunction, declaration and damages.

Shop stewards' entitlements

[17.37] Shop stewards have no statutory rights, save the right enjoyed by all trade union members not to be dismissed for trade union membership or activities, where he or she engages in the activity outside work hours, or during times agreed under his contract of employment. However, under the Industrial Relations Act 1990, Code of Practice on Employee Representatives,[50] it may be prudent for employers to grant shop stewards certain rights. Breach of the Code does not of itself render the employer liable to any proceedings. However, the code is admissible in evidence before a court, the Labour Court, the Labour Relations Commission and the Employment Appeals Tribunal, and may be taken into account by them.[51] The Code defines employee representatives for the

---

[47] Unfair Dismissals (Amendment) Act 1993, s 14:
   Unfair Dismissals Act 1977, ss 2(1), 3 and 4 and subsections (1) and (6) of the Principal Act [Unfair Dismissals Act 1977] shall not apply to a person referred to in paragraph (a) or (b) of the said section 2(1) or the said ss 3 or 4 who is dismissed if the dismissal results wholly or mainly from one or more of the matters referred to in sub-s (2)(a) of the said s 6.

[48] Unfair Dismissals (Amendment) Act 1993, s 14.

[49] Unfair Dismissals Act 1977, s 7.

[50] SI 169/1993.

[51] Industrial Relations Act 1990, s 42.

purposes of the Code as employees who have been so designated by a trade union and who participate in the negotiation of terms and conditions of employment and the settlement of disputes or grievances which may arise within the employment. It enumerates some of the principal duties and responsibilities of employee representatives. It then provides for the protection of employee representatives from adverse treatment without prior consultation between the employer and the relevant trade union. Finally, it covers the facilities which should be afforded to employee representatives. These include the following:

1. **Time off**

    Time off when carrying out their representative functions, and for trade union meetings and training courses which relate to their activities as employee representatives. The question of payment of wages in respect of time off should be the subject of discussion in advance at the level of the establishment.

2. **Access to workplaces**

    Reasonable access to all workplaces where they represent trade union members and where such access is necessary to enable them to carry out their representative functions.

3. **Access to management**

    Employee representatives should have access, without undue delay, to management at the appropriate level on matters relating to their representative functions and responsibilities.

4. **Collecting union dues**

    In the absence of a check off agreement (whereby union dues are automatically deducted from wages), an employee representative should be permitted to collect union dues regularly at the place of employment.

5. **Distributing documents**

    Employers and trade unions should agree arrangements whereby employee representatives, acting on behalf of their trade union, may post notices in the workplace. Employee representatives should be permitted to distribute documents relating to trade union activities in the workplace.

Industrial action

[17.38] In the normal course, those engaging in industrial action commit a host of torts and common law crimes, eg criminal conspiracy, the tort of conspiracy and inducing breach of contract.[52] There is a view that picketing is *per se* unlawful. In any event it may involve other torts, eg nuisance, watching and besetting, trespass to the subsoil and indirect inducement of breach of contract.[53] Furthermore, a registered trade union may be sued for the unlawful acts of its officials, on the basis that the trade union is a principal and the officials are its agents.[54] The most commonly litigated torts are those of

---

[52] *Lumley v Gye* (1853) 2 E&B 216, 118 ER 749; *Temperton v Hughes* [1893] 1 QB 715.

[53] *Sherriff v McMullen* [1952] IR 236.

[54] *Taafe Vale Railway v Amalgamated Society of Railway Servants* [1901] AC 426.

direct inducement of breach of contract and indirect inducement of breach of contract. Direct inducement of breach of contract occurs where A intentionally persuades B to act in breach of his or her contractual obligations to C. C may sue A for direct inducement of breach of contract. The tort originated in the case of *Lumley v Gye*.[55] The defendant in that case ran a music hall. He persuaded a singer, Miss Wagner, to breach her agreement to play at the plaintiff's concert rooms and to play for him instead. The English High Court, Queen's Bench Division held that a cause of action lay for the intentional and malicious inducement of breach of contract for personal service.

[17.39] The tort was extended to the arena of industrial action with *Temperton v Hughes*.[56] The plaintiff, a builders' supplier, was in a dispute with a trade union. The defendants, officials of the trade union, persuaded builders to refuse to take further supplies from the plaintiff in breach of their contracts with him. It was held that the tort of direct inducement of breach of contract did not apply merely to contracts of personal service. It has been held subsequently that it is unnecessary to prove malice.[57]

Industrial Relations Act 1990: introduction

[17.40] Industrial action would therefore be impossible unless trade unions and their members were allowed some protection from the common law. These were first granted by the Trade Disputes Act 1906, which has been replaced by the Industrial Relations Act 1990:

> Clearly the legislature sought to achieve a greater degree of responsibility by unions and their members in pursuing industrial action; additional protections for trade unions which acted with that sense of responsibility and a degree of discipline within the trade union movement which would ensure that settlements negotiated with employers would be observed by all trade unionists.[58]

The immunities

[17.41] The Industrial Relations Act 1990[59] (the 1990 Act) confers immunities from the common law for certain acts. They are contained in ss 10, 11, 12 and 13 of the 1990 Act. The operation of the immunities will be examined in the following way:

(i)   Preliminary requirements.

(ii)   What are the immunities?

(iii)   How can the immunities be lost?

---

[55] *Lumley v Gye* (1853) 2 E&B 216, 118 ER 749.

[56] *Temperton v Hughes* [1893] 1 QB 715.

[57] *South Wales Miners' Federation v Glamorgan Coal Co* [1905] AC 239.

[58] *Per* Murphy J, *Nolan Transport (Oaklands) Ltd v Halligan* [1998] ELR 177 at 194–195.

[59] Replacing the Trade Disputes Act 1906 and the Trade Disputes (Amendment) Act 1982. Many of the key phrases are repeated in the 1990 Act. The caselaw under the previous legislation is therefore relevant.

Immunities: Preliminary requirements

Who benefits?

[17.42] Under s 9 of the 1990 Act, ss 11, 12 and 13, discussed below, apply only to trade unions which hold a negotiation licence, their members and officials. The benefit of s 10 is not contingent on this status.

Which acts benefit?

[17.43] Only acts carried out 'in contemplation or furtherance of a trade dispute' are covered by ss 10, 11, 12 and 13 of the 1990 Act. This phrase lays down the boundaries of lawful industrial action. A trade dispute is defined as 'any dispute between employers and workers which is connected with the employment or non-employment, or the terms or conditions of or affecting the employment, of any person'.[60] It therefore excludes such matters as demarcation disputes between employees or industrial action in pursuit of a political aim. Note also that a dispute which aims to deprive others of their constitutional rights does not constitute a legitimate trade dispute within the meaning of the Act.[61] A trade dispute need not be in existence in order for the immunities to apply; the word contemplation indicates that they also apply when the dispute is imminent.[62] However, mere anticipation of a dispute is insufficient.[63] An act may be said to be in furtherance of a trade dispute when the person acting believes *bona fide* that the act will further the trade dispute.[64]

One man disputes: procedures must be exhausted

[17.44] Under s 9 of the 1990 Act, where the dispute in question relates to the terms or conditions of or affecting the employment of an individual worker, and there are agreed procedures for the resolution of individual grievances, ss 11, 12 and 13 apply only where those procedures have been exhausted. Section 10 is unaffected.

What are the immunities?

Individuals' immunities: conspiracy

[17.45] Section 10 confers immunity upon those acting in contemplation or furtherance of a trade dispute in respect of criminal conspiracy if the act in question committed by one person would not be punishable as a crime. It similarly confers immunity in respect of tortious conspiracy where the act would not be actionable if done by one person alone. In contrast to the immunities conferred by ss 11, 12 and 13, this immunity is available to those who are neither members nor officials of authorised trade unions.[65] Where

---

[60]   Industrial Relations Act 1990, s 8.
[61]   *Educational Company of Ireland v Fitzpatrick* [1961] IR 323.
[62]   *Crazy Prices (Northern Ireland) Ltd v Hewitt* [1980] NI 150.
[63]   *Esplanade Pharmacy v Larkin* [1957] IR 285.
[64]   *Express Newspapers v McShane* [1980] AC 672.
[65]   See the Industrial Relations Act 1990, s 9.

industrial action is carried out in disregard of or contrary to the outcome of a secret ballot, the benefit of s 10 is lost.[66]

Individuals' immunities: picketing

[17.46] Section 11 provides immunity in respect of peaceful picketing. Section 11(1) provides that picketing shall be lawful where carried out in contemplation or furtherance of a trade dispute merely for the purpose of peacefully obtaining or communicating information or of peacefully persuading any person to work or abstain from working. It is crucial to distinguish between peaceful and non-peaceful persuasion. The use of abusive language will render a picket non-peaceful, as will excessive numbers.[67] Picketers may only attend at or, where that is not practicable, at the approaches to, a place where their employer works or carries on business.[68]

[17.47] Section 11(2) provides that it shall be lawful to picket an employer who is not a party to the trade dispute. This is known as secondary picketing. As with primary picketing, it may only be carried out in a peaceful manner, for the purpose of obtaining or communicating information or of peacefully persuading any person to work or abstain from working, and at, or or, where that is not practicable, at the approaches to, a place where that employer works or carries on business. Where it differs from primary picketing is that it may only be carried out if it is reasonable for those picketing to believe that that employer has directly assisted their employer who is a party to the trade dispute for the purpose of frustrating the strike or other industrial action. It seems from the wording of section 11(2) itself that reasonable belief of an intention to frustrate the strike must be proven in order to invoke the protection of s 11(2). Where industrial action is carried out in disregard of or contrary to the outcome of a secret ballot, the benefit of s 11 is lost.[69]

Individual immunities: various

[17.48] Section 12 confers immunity for inducement of breach of contract of employment, a threat to induce breach of contract of employment and unlawful interference with trade or business. Where industrial action is carried out in disregard of or contrary to the outcome of a secret ballot, the benefit of s 12 is lost.[70]

Trade union immunity

[17.49] Section 13 confers immunity upon authorised trade unions from actions in tort for acts carried out in contemplation or furtherance of a trade dispute.

---

[66] Industrial Relations Act 1990, s 17.

[67] *EI Co Ltd v Kennedy* [1968] IR 69. What is permissible is a question of degree: *Brendan Dunne Ltd v Fitzpatrick* [1958] IR 29.

[68] See *Westman Holdings v McCormack* [1992] 1 IR 151; *G&T Crampton Ltd v Building and Allied Trades Union* [1998] ELR 4 and *Chieftan Construction Ltd v Ryan* (1 May 2008, unreported) HC (Edwards J), [2008] IEHC 147.

[69] Industrial Relations Act 1990, s 17.

[70] Industrial Relations Act 1990, s 17.

How can the immunities be lost?

Acts in contravention or disregard of a secret ballot

[17.50] Unions are required to insert balloting rules into their rule books. If the union holds a ballot for industrial action, and the action is carried out in contravention or disregard of the result, the benefit of ss 10, 11 and 12 of the 1990 Act are lost. Section 13 is unaffected.

Ballots

[17.51] Section 14(1) of the 1990 Act requires that the rule book of every trade union which holds a negotiation licence must contain provisions as to balloting members in respect of strikes or other industrial action. Section 14(2) states in considerable detail the content of such rules:

The rules of every trade union shall contain a provision that—

(a) the union shall not organise, participate in, sanction or support a strike or other industrial action without a secret ballot, entitlement to vote in which shall be accorded equally to all members whom it is reasonable at the time to believe will be called upon to engage in the strike or other industrial action;

(b) the union shall take reasonable steps to ensure that every member entitled to vote in the ballot votes without interference from, or constraint imposed by, the union or any of its members, officials or employees and, so far as is reasonably possible, that such members shall be given a fair opportunity of voting;

(c) the committee of management or other controlling authority of a trade union shall have full discretion in relation to organising, participating in, sanctioning or supporting a strike or other industrial action notwithstanding that the majority of those voting in the ballot, including an aggregate ballot referred to in paragraph (d), favour such strike or other industrial action;

(d) the committee of management or other controlling authority of a trade union shall no organise, participate in, sanction or support a strike or other industrial action against the wishes of a majority of its members voitng in a secret ballot, except where, in the case of ballots by more than one trade union, an aggregate majority of all the votes cast, favours such strike or other industrial action;

(e) where the outcome of a secret ballot conducted by a trade union which is affiliated to the Irish Congress of Trade Unions or, in the case of ballots by more than one such trade union, an aggregate majority of all the votes cast, is in favour of supporting a strike organised by another trade union, a decision to take such supportive action shall not be implemented unless the action has been sanctioned by the Irish Congress of Trade Unions;

(f) as soon as practicable after the conduct of a secret ballot the trade union shall take reasonable steps to make known to its members entitled to vote in the ballot:

    (i) the number of ballot papers issued;

    (ii) the number of votes cast;

    (iii) the number of votes in favour of the proposal;

    (iv) the number of votes against the proposal, and,

    (v) the number of spoilt votes.'

The rights created by the rules are declared by s 14(3) to be for the benefit of union members only.

Ballots: advantages of compliance

Section 19

[17.52] Section 19 of the 1990 Act provides extensive protection to trade unions against injunctions, on the fulfilment of certain conditions.

Injunctions

[17.53] Prior to the enactment of the 1990 Act, interlocutory injunctions in particular posed a difficulty for trade unions. It was relatively easy for employers to obtain interlocutory injunctions restraining industrial action. The Courts applied the ordinary principles laid down in *American Cyanamid v Ethicon*[71] and endorsed by *Campus Oil v Minister for Industry and Energy*.[72] The test was as follows:

1. Is there a serious question to be tried?
2. Does the balance of convenience favour the granting of the injunction?

The particular difficulty faced by a trade union as respondent to such an application was that while the employer/applicant could show monetary loss if the injunction were refused, the worker/respondent who would lose an industrial relations advantage, would be unable to quantify his loss.

[17.54] This difficulty was well illustrated by *Bayzana Ltd v Galligan*.[73] Workers employed by Irish Meat Producers Ltd (IMP) were dismissed on the grounds of redundancy. IMP refused to pay the workers the redundancy payment which they sought. The workers picketed the IMP premises where they had been employed, consisting of a factory and a farm. IMP then sold the premises to the plaintiff. The plaintiff sought to harvest silage from the land, return cattle on the land to third parties who owned the cattle and to dispose of a large quantity of frozen meat stored on the premises belonging to a third party by selling it into intervention. Despite the pickets, the plaintiff succeeded in harvesting the silage and in returning the cattle to their owners. However, the plaintiff failed to dispose of the frozen meat because Department of Agriculture Officials refused to pass the pickets to certify the meat. The meat was worth approximately £5,000,000. However, if the meat were not sold by a particular date, its value would drop to £1,000,000. During this time, two IMP employees worked on the premises maintaining the cold storage and IMP managers occasionally visited the premises.

[17.55] The High Court granted an injunction restricting the number of pickets to two at any one entrance at any time. The plaintiff appealed to the Supreme Court. The Court applied the principles in *American Cyanamid*[74] (which had been applied in Ireland in

---

71 *American Cyanamid v Ethicon* [1975] 1 All ER 504.
72 *Campus Oil v Minister for Industry and Energy* [1983] IR 88.
73 *Bayzana Ltd v Galligan* [1987] IR 238.
74 *American Cyanamid Co v Ethicon Ltd* [1975] AC 396, [1975] 2 WLR 316, [1975] 1 All ER 504.

Campus Oil[75] and *Elm Motors*[76]). It appears that in reply to questions by the Chief Justice, counsel for the defendants conceded that there was a fair question to be tried as to whether the actions of the defendants were in furtherance of a trade dispute because the plaintiff did not concede any connection between it and IMP and asserted a total incapacity to influence IMP in regard to the trade dispute. It therefore remained for the Court to consider the balance of convenience. The Court also laid stress upon the fact that the intervention grants available to the owners of the meat would be lost within a matter of weeks without any real material benefit to the plaintiffs. The Court considered the merits of the various options open to the defendants and concluded that while they would lose a major weapon in their industrial action, they could nonetheless picket other IMP premises and, if successful at the trial of the action, could resume the picket and prevent the development of the premises. Accordingly, the Court granted the injunction sought.

[17.56] The case is most interesting for its dissenting judgment, delivered by McCarthy J. Notwithstanding the concession made by counsel for the defendants, he was of the view that there was no fair question to be tried as to whether the defendants were acting in furtherance of a trade dispute. He was of the view that the picketing of the premises where the defendants were formerly employed, where two IMP employees were regularly working for the maintenance of the cold store in which a large quantity of meat was authorised to be put by IMP is on its face in furtherance of the trade dispute being so closely connected with the dispute. He was also of the view that the balance of convenience favoured the granting of the injunction:

> It is notorious that in actions of this kind, the resolution of the interlocutory motion is, effectively, the resolution of the action. This does not mean that the plaintiff has established his right to win, but that the plaintiff wins if he can get an interlocutory injunction. This should not be the case but it is. In the course of argument, I asked Mr Salafia to refer to any case in the last decade or two in which an injunction had been granted restraining picketing, where there had been a subsequent trial, irrespective of the result. He was unable to do so. The reason is a very practical one, quite apart from the natural reluctance to endanger union funds in respect of law costs. If an interlocutory injunction is granted, either at first instance or on appeal, by the time the trial takes place, however relatively short the interval may be, the bloom has gone off the steel of industrial action; men give up – seek other jobs – go elsewhere for that purpose – emigrate. Worst of all, they may well settle for less than what are their true rights because they think, however mistakenly, that the dice are loaded against them in the law courts... We have not been referred to any case in which an attempt was made to pursue a claim for damages by a trade union or its members pursuant to an undertaking to that effect given by an employer of other party seeking and obtaining an interlocutory injunction. Such an undertaking is very appropriate to may types of interlocutory injunction but, as I asked Mr White and Mr Salafia during the hearing, how do defendants in a case such as the present prove any loss, if they win the case, if a trial does take place. Any attempt to prove by parole testimony that, in the view of the trade union, they would have got a better settlement if they hadn't been stopped carrying out their industrial action would hardly stand cross-examination of

---

[75] *Campus Oil v Minister for Industry (No 2)* [1983] IR 88, [1984] ILRM 45.
[76] *Irish Shell v Elm Motors* [1984] IR 200, [1984] ILRM 595.

any competence, if it wasn't already bedevilled by the natural reluctance of a trade union official to admit that he not get the best possible settlement. In my judgment there is no reality whatever in the undertaking as to damages proffered on the part of the plaintiff here; I do not doubt that it is well able to pay damages but that is not the point.

[17.57] Section 19 of the 1990 Act attempted to resolve this difficulty. It provides extensive protection to trade unions against injunctions, on the fulfilment of certain conditions. These provisions do not apply to proceedings relating to unlawful entry onto damage to the property of another, or in respect of proceedings arising out of or relating to any action resulting or likely to result in death or personal injury.

Under s 19(1), if a trade union fulfils certain conditions, an employer may not obtain an injunction *ex parte*, ie without notifying the union or employees against whom it is directed. Those conditions are as follows:

1. A secret ballot has been held in accordance with the rules of the trade union as provided for in s 14 of the Act;
2. The outcome of the ballot favours the strike or other industrial action; and
3. The trade union before engaging in the strike or other industrial trade union gives notice of not less than one week of its intention to do so.

Under s 19(2) no injunction, either interlocutory or final, may issue where these three conditions are satisfied, and the respondent fulfils a fourth:

4. The respondent establishes a fair case that he was acting in contemplation or furtherance of a trade dispute.

The requirements constitute consecutive hurdles that the respondent who seeks to rely on s 19 must vault.

If the respondent to an injunction application fails to satisfy each of the requirements of s 19, the application will fall to be determined on the ordinary principles.

Ballots: penalties for non-compliance

What if a trade union has no balloting rules in its rule book?

[17.58] A trade union which fails to incorporate balloting rules into its rule book as required by s 14 is not entitled to hold a negotiation licence.[77]

What if a trade union disregards its balloting rules?

[17.59]

1. **Discipline by Registrar**

    A trade union which persistently disregards any requirement of its balloting rules inserted pursuant to section 14 may be disciplined by the Registrar of Friendly Societies. The ultimate penalty is revocation of the negotiation licence.[78]

---

[77] Industrial Relations Act 1990, s 16.
[78] Industrial Relations Act 1990, s 16.

2. **Action by Members**

Industrial action taken contrary to the result of a ballot, or without holding a ballot, is *ultra vires* the union. This means that the union may be restrained by the members from calling such action,[79] using union funds to further such action, or invoking the union's disciplinary machinery to punish those who refuse to take part.[80]

3. **Loss of Immunities under s 17**

Under s 17, industrial action carried out contrary to the result of a ballot cannot claim the benefit of ss 10, 11 and 12. Note that the benefit of section 13 is not lost. Furthermore, industrial action carried out without a ballot is not so penalised and may still claim the benefit of ss 10, 11, 12 and 13.[81]

4. **Loss of Benefits under s 19**

Industrial action carried out in accordance with a ballot, provided other conditions are fulfilled, obtains the benefit of s 19, which gives trade unions certain protections against injunctive relief.[82]

When may an employer complain of a breach of the balloting provisions?

[17.60] Since the 1990 Act confers certain protections upon trade unions which are lost when the industrial action is carried out in disregard or in contravention of the result of a ballot, or without a ballot, (under ss 17 and 19) an employer may complain of a breach of the balloting provisions when seeking an injunction to restrain the industrial action and/or damages in respect of the industrial action.

Ballots: the case law

Nolan Transport v Halligan

[17.61] The Supreme Court decision in *Nolan Transport v Halligan*[83] has done much to clarify the circumstances in which an employer engaged in an industrial dispute may make complaints regarding a secret ballot. The plaintiff employed the first and second defendants who were members of the fourth defendant trade union. An incident occurred which led the first and second defendant to believe themselves dismissed and industrial action ensued. The plaintiff initiated proceedings, seeking injunctive relief and damages against the defendants. Keane J granted the plaintiff an interlocutory injunction restraining picketing in so far as it was otherwise than peaceful.[84] Following a full hearing in the High Court, Barron J held that there was no bona fide trade dispute: the issue of dismissals was no more than an event which the union used to its advantage. The union's true purpose was an unlawful one, ie to compel the plaintiff's employees into

---

[79] *Taylor and Foulstone v NUM* [1984] IRLR 445.

[80] *Porter v NUJ* [1979] IRLR 404 (CA), [1980] IRLR 404 (HL).

[81] Industrial Relations Act 1990, s 17.

[82] See paras **[17.68]** above and paras **[17.71]**–**[17.82]** below.

[83] *Nolan Transport v Halligan* [1995] ELR 1 (HC), [1998] ELR 177 (SC).

[84] (22 March 1994, unreported) HC (Keane J).

union membership. Furthermore, the declared result of the ballot preceding industrial action did not reflect the votes actually cast and was deliberately false. Accordingly he awarded extensive damages against the defendants and a permanent injunction restraining industrial action against the plaintiff. The Supreme Court did not overturn any primary findings of fact made by the trial judge, although it did overturn a number of inferences made by him. It accepted that there had been a bona fide trade dispute, and held that the irregularities in the ballot did not operate to deprive either the individuals involved in the industrial action or the trade union itself of the benefit of the immunities conferred by the 1990 Act.

[17.62] The Supreme Court did not consider it appropriate to determine the motivation or ultimate ambitions of those engaged in industrial action in order to establish whether the dispute was bona fide. Instead, it enquired whether there were facts which would justify the belief of the individual defendants and their union that they had been wrongfully dismissed. It concluded that there were, and that the dispute was therefore bona fide and furthermore that the dispute was genuine in that it represented the immediate quarrel between the parties. It overturned Barron J's inference that the union had acted with the intention of compelling the plaintiff's employees to join the union. Since the dispute was bona fide, the defendants would enjoy the immunities conferred by the 1990 Act save in so far as they were removed or restricted by the 1990 Act. The Supreme Court did not disturb Barron J's finding that the declared result of the ballot did not reflect the votes actually cast and was deliberately false. However, this finding did not act to deprive the defendants of the immunities conferred by the 1990 Act. Section 17 of the 1990 Act provides that individuals lose the immunities when they act in disregard of or contrary to the outcome of a secret ballot.

[17.63] On the facts before the Court, the individual defendants did not lose the benefit of the immunities pursuant to s 17: either no secret ballot had been held or the secret ballot 'in its outcome' favoured industrial action. In other words, the individual defendants could not be fixed with liability for any irregularities in the ballot. They had acted in accordance with its declared result and therefore enjoyed the benefit of the immunities. Nor did the union itself lose the immunity from actions in tort conferred by s 13 since that immunity is not made conditional upon a secret ballot.

[17.64] This decision is to be welcomed in particular for its elucidation of the scheme of the 1990 Act, and in particular, the role of secret ballots. As pointed out by Murphy J, s 14 of the 1990 Act does not itself require that industrial action be authorised by a secret ballot. Instead it requires that trade unions insert rules into their rule books requiring such ballots and stipulates sanctions for the failure to have such rules or to observe them. A union which authorises industrial action without the sanction of the membership in a secret ballot which has been properly conducted risks the loss of its negotiation licence under the Act, or a claim for breach of contract by union members. The Court was unanimous in its observation that secret ballots are primarily a matter of internal union management. However, there appeared to be a divergence between Murphy J and O'Flaherty J as to the circumstances in which secret ballots are no longer an internal matter. According to Murphy J, this occurs where the 1990 Act confers rights and duties upon 'outsiders' by reference to the holding of a secret ballot, eg by ss 17 and

19. By contrast, O'Flaherty J maintained that when a flaw is exposed in the balloting procedure, it is no longer an internal matter. He dismissed the question of privity of contract saying simply that:

> the duty to observe the law devolves on everyone ... simply because the obligation comes through the rules rather than directly from the legislation is of no great importance ... there is a serious obligation on union management to give proper example to the rest of the people by ensuring that the requirements concerning the holding of a proper secret ballot are always observed.

G&T Crampton Ltd v BATU

[17.65] *G&T Crampton Ltd v Building and Allied Trades Union*[85] concerned the application of s 19 of the 1990 Act. Laffoy J granted an interlocutory injunction restraining the defendants from picketing at the plaintiff's site. She applied the test specified by s 19 of the Act. Since there was no evidence before the court as to the result of the secret ballot, or that the secret ballot favoured picketing the plaintiff's site, the defendants were not entitled to rely on section 19. The plaintiff's application therefore fell to be decided upon the ordinary principles and was allowed. On appeal, the Supreme Court considered whether s 19 had been satisfied, using the ordinary principles. It was held that a fair question had been raised as to whether ss 19 and 14 had been fulfilled and that Laffoy J was entitled to conclude that the conditions precedent to the implementation of s 19 had not been established. It is arguable, however, that the ordinary principles should not be used to determine whether s 19 has been satisfied since the very purpose of section 19 was to avoid the application of this test. The question of the fulfilment of ss 19 and 14 should be determined in a more definitive way at the interlocutory stage.

[17.66] This problem was adverted to by Murphy J in *Nolan Transport (Oaklands) Ltd v Halligan*:[86]

> In the circumstances it may be said that there has not been a definitive interpretation of s 19(2) of the 1990 Act but I would find it difficult to escape the conclusion reached by Keane J [in *Nolan Transport (Oaklands) Ltd v Halligan*] and accepted by Laffoy J [in *G&T Crampton Ltd v BATU*] that the onus lies upon the party resisting an application for an interlocutory injunction to show that a secret ballot as envisaged by s 14 has been held. Moreover it could hardly be sufficient to establish the existence of a stateable case in relation to the compliance with the rules required to be adopted by a union pursuant to s 14 aforesaid. The decision of a court on an interlocutory application as to whether or not the particular immunity granted by s 19(2) is available is itself a final decision and determines finally whether that statutory benefit is available to the trade union. Concern must exist, as to how decisions of that nature could be made in practice. There may be serious difficulty, and even a degree of unreality, in requiring the court to make an actual determination on the balance of probabilities as to whether all of the requirements of the secret ballot have been complied with when the substantive issue itself is dealt with at that stage on the basis of a 'serious issue to be tried'. The demands which such a requirement

---

[85] *G&T Crampton Ltd v Building and Allied Trades Union* [1998] ELR 4.
[86] *Nolan Transport (Oaklands) Ltd v Halligan* [1998] ELR 177 at 199–200.

could impose are illustrated by the urgency with which the interlocutory proceedings in the *Crampton* case were dealt with in both the High Court and this Court and to which the Chief Justice drew attention in his judgment.

Malincross Ltd v BATU

[17.67] The plaintiff in *Malincross Ltd v BATU*[87] held a licence to develop and build an estate of houses on a site in Balbriggan, County Dublin. The plaintiff sub-contracted the building works to another company, BP O'Sullivan (Leinster) Ltd. A trade dispute arose between BP O'Sullivan (Leinster) Ltd and its employees who were members of the defendant trade union. The defendant trade union conducted a ballot and the defendant trade union, together with the second, third, fourth and fifth defendants, placed a picket on the site in furtherance of the trade dispute. The plaintiff then terminated the sub-contract and BP O'Sullivan (Leinster) Ltd vacated the site. The picket continued at the site and the plaintiff applied to the High Court for an injunction restraining the picket. Counsel on behalf of the defendants argued that the picket was lawful. He relied on s 11(1)(a) of the 1990 Act which permits peaceful picketing by employees at 'a place where their employer works or carries on business'. He relied on the Dáil debates in arguing that this expression permitted picketing at a place where an employee works or carried on work in the past. McCracken J held that there was a fair case to be tried as to the construction of s 11(1)(a) in this regard.

[17.68] Counsel further argued that the Court was prohibited from granting an injunction restraining the picket and relied on s 19(2) of the 1990 Act in making this argument. McCracken J held that the defendant trade union held a secret ballot in accordance with its rules, that those rules were as provided for in s 14 of the 1990 Act and that the defendant trade union had given the requisite notice to BP O'Sullivan (Leinster) Ltd of its intention to take industrial action. It further held that the defendant trade union established a fair case that it was acting in contemplation or furtherance of a trade dispute at the time the ballot was held.

[17.69] However, McCracken J then turned to the terms of the proposal balloted upon. The ballot paper read as follows:

> SUBJECT – to engage in industrial action with BP O'Sullivan (Leinster) Ltd, including the placing of pickets on company site at Naul Road, Balbriggan.

McCracken J addressed the issue whether this ballot authorised the placing of pickets at the site when it ceased to be the site of BP O'Sullivan (Leinster) Ltd. He noted:

> The sufficiency of the secret ballot is clearly a condition precedent to the right of the defendants to resist an interlocutory injunction under section 19(2). While the members of the union clearly authorized strike action at the employer's premises, and therefore direct strike action against the employer, I think there is a serious issue as to whether that in itself is sufficient to justify strike action in relation to what were once the employer's premises but no longer remain so. The purpose of the Act would appear to be to ensure that, if the union is entitled to the protection of section 19(2), then it must have the clear support of its members. I think there is a serious issue to be tried, but no more, as to whether the

---

87   *Malincross Ltd v BATU* [2002] ELR 78.

picketing of the plaintiff's premises once the defendant has left those premises is authorized by the ballot and until that question has been determined, in my view the condition precedent to section 19(2) has not been established by the defendants.

McCracken J went on to consider the last submission on behalf of the defendant trade union. It was argued that there was a transfer of undertaking from BP O'Sullivan (Leinster) Ltd to the plaintiff such that the plaintiff now employed the second, third, fourth and fifth defendants. McCracken J commented that this was a complex matter which would require a great deal more evidence than was before him, and held that it was a matter for the ultimate hearing of the action. He continued:

> [A]s I have determined that there is a bona fide dispute as to whether the preconditions of section 19(2) have been complied with, the defendant is not entitled to rely upon the subsection (2) to prevent the grant of an interlocutory injunction. In those circumstances, I then have to apply the ordinary principles as laid down by the Supreme Court in *Campus Oil Ltd v Minister for Industry and Energy* [1983] IR 88.

McCracken J applied those principles. He concluded that the balance of convenience favoured the plaintiff and granted the injunction.

Daru Blocklaying Ltd v BATU

[17.70] The plaintiff in *Daru Blocklaying Ltd v BATU*[88] was a block laying sub-contractor carrying out works on a site in Swords, Co Dublin. It carried out its business by engaging blocklayers as independent subcontractors. A dispute arose between the plaintiff and the defendant trade union as to the employment status of certain blocklayers who had been engaged by the plaintiff. The defendant trade union conducted a ballot and placed a picket on the site in Swords. The plaintiff applied to the High Court and sought an injunction restraining the picketing. Kelly J granted the injunction sought.

[17.71] In the course of his judgment, Kelly J held that a number of serious issues arose for determination at trial: first, whether the picketing was peaceful or carried out for the purposes permitted by the 1990 Act; secondly, whether the registered employment agreement for the construction industry was binding on the defendant trade union such that it was in breach of contract by the industrial action which was undertaken; and thirdly, whether the individual defendants fell within the protection afforded by s 11(1) of the 1990 Act given the plaintiff's contention that they had never been in the employment of the plaintiff and fourth, whether there was a bona fide trade dispute.

[17.72] Kelly J considered the adequacy of damages and the balance of convenience and concluded that the balance of convenience lay in favour of the granting of an injunction. Kelly J then considered whether he was precluded from granting an injunction by the terms of s 19(2) of the 1990 Act. He noted that a trade union official attached to the defendant trade union had averred that he had conducted a ballot in accordance with the rules of the union and the terms of the 1990 Act. His affidavit exhibited the ballot papers cast by the three members balloted. He averred that the outcome of the ballot was unanimously in favour of industrial action and he gave the requisite notice of the

---

[88] *Daru Blocklaying Ltd v BATU* (12 July 2002, unreported) HC (Kelly J).

industrial action. Kelly J noted that while only three persons were balloted, a far greater number picketed the premises. He stated that the union was obliged to ensure that all members whom it was reasonable at the time of the ballot for the union concerned to believe will be called upon to engage in the strike or other industrial action be balloted. There was nothing on affidavit to suggest that that exercise had been carried out. Moreover, there was no evidence at all of compliance with s 14(f) of the 1990 Act which requires unions to give their members certain information regarding the ballot following the ballot. Kelly J concluded:

> In my opinion the onus is upon the defendants to satisy the court as to compliance with the provisions of section 14. That onus is not discharged in this case by a bald assertion that the ballot has been carried out in accordance with the rules of the union and the provisions of the Act. Evidence of sufficient weight must be given of such compliance.

P Elliot & Co v BATU

[17.73] The plaintiff in *P Elliot & Co v BATU*[89] was a construction company with sites in Dublin and Limerick. The defendant trade union represented the plaintiff's workers. The plaintiff and its workers were covered by a registered employment agreement setting minimum rates of pay and conditions of employment. That agreement also provided procedures for dispute resolution and provided that no strike or lock out should take place until the procedures had been completed and the Labour Court has issued a recommendation. The company had entered into collective bargaining with the defendant trade union and had concluded an agreement conferring more favourable rates of pay and conditions of employment upon its workers in Dublin. However, that agreement did not extend to workers in Limerick.

[17.74] The defendant trade union raised a dispute with the plaintiff, seeking an extension of the agreement to cover workers in Limerick, and invoked the dispute resolution procedures specified by the registered employment agreement. Meanwhile, the agreement between the plaintiff and the defendant trade union relating to the Dublin workers was to expire. The defendant trade union sought renewal of the agreement and the plaintiff refused to renew the agreement. The defendant trade union again invoked the dispute resolution procedures in the registered employment agreement. Those procedures were not yet exhausted.

[17.75] The Labour Court issued a recommendation rejecting the union's first claim, relating to the Limerick workers. The trade union balloted its members in Dublin and Limerick who rejected the Labour Court recommendation. The trade union then balloted its members in Dublin and Limerick for industrial action 'up to and including the placing of pickets'. The members voted in favour of industrial action and pickets were placed on the plaintiff's sites in Dublin and Limerick. The plaintiff instituted proceedings and applied to the High Court seeking an interlocutory injunction restraining the defendants from maintaining the pickets on their sites. Crucially, the plaintiff argued that the defendants could not rely upon s 19 of the 1990 Act in resisting

---

[89] *P Elliot & Co v BATU* (20 October 2006, unreported) HC (Clarke J).

an interlocutory injunction. However, for the first time, the defendants successfully relied upon s 19.

[17.76] Clarke J noted that prior to the enactment of the 1990 Act, the normal outcome of an interlocutory hearing, if there was a fair case to be tried, was that the balance of convenience was taken to favour the employer and an injunction imposed. Clearly s 19(2) was designed to alter that situation. Clarke J considered that he had to determine whether section 19(2) applied based on the evidence available. The defendant trade union put forward comprehensive evidence of the secret ballot, including a schedule with the signatures of all those who had voted in the ballot, and the ballot papers themselves. The first ballot asked the voters to 'accept or reject Labour Court Recommendation No 18588 dated 31 May 2006'. The second ballot, approximately two weeks later, asked the voters to vote for or against the following proposition: 'to engage in industrial action with P Elliott & Company Limited up to and including the placing of pickets on company premises.' The plaintiff argued that the second ballot was flawed in that it did not state that the industrial action was in support of the dispute arising from the rejection of the Labour Court Recommendation. In addition, it argued that the ballot should have identified the specific form of industrial action contemplated, rather than simply referring to 'industrial action ... up to and including the placing of pickets'. It also argued that only the Limerick workers should have been balloted on the issue as the dispute concerned the rates of pay and conditions of work of the Limerick workers.

[17.77] Clarke J stated that a practical approach should be adopted in reading the ballot paper. The test was whether a reasonable member of the trade union concerned would know what they were voting for or against. The text should not be parsed or analysed as if it were a formal legal instrument. Given that the second ballot was conducted just two weeks after the rejection of the first ballot, no reasonable member of the trade union could have been under any misapprehension that the second ballot was concerned with the same dispute. Furthermore, the policy of the 1990 Act was that the managing body of a trade union should retain control over the precise way in which industrial action is pursued. Therefore, it was wholly consistent with the 1990 Act that the trade union should seek authority from its members to engage in a range of industrial action, leaving it up to the managing body of the union to determine precisely what action should be carried out from time to time, provided that the industrial action actually taken can be said to be fairly within the parameters of that authorised by the ballot.

[17.78] Finally, Clarke J considered whether it was appropriate to include the Dublin workers in the ballot. Section 14(2)(a) requires a ballot of all members 'whom it is reasonable at the time of the ballot for the union concerned to believe will be called upon to engage in the strike or other industrial action'. The Dublin and Limerick workers were all employees of the one employer. All were members of the same trade union. If it was desired that all should participate in industrial action in furtherance of a dispute which only affected some, then all required to be balloted. Far from it being inappropriate to ballot the Dublin workers, s 14 required that they be included in the ballot given that they would also be expected to engage in the industrial action following the ballot.

How may a union demonstrate compliance with its balloting provisions?

[17.79] Trade union rule books tend to reproduce the terms of s 14(2) of the 1990 Act. A union engaging in industrial action should be in a position to comfortably demonstrate compliance with its rules. A bald assertion that the ballot has been carried out in accordance with the rules of the union and s 14 will not suffice. The following general points may be made:[90]

1. The ballot papers should set the issue forth clearly.

2. The ballot papers should state exactly the form of industrial action contemplated; it may be inadequate simply to state 'ballot for strike or other industrial action'.

3. An independent person should supervise the whole operation, adopting much the same role as a returning office in a Dáil Éireann election. He or she should be impartial, and seen as such, strict in seeing that the rules or observed and clear in the rulings he or she makes.

4. The union should be in a position to demonstrate that it balloted all members whom it was reasonable at the time of the ballot for the union to believe would be called upon to engage in the strike or other industrial action to be balloted.

5. The union should be in a position to confirm compliance with the terms of section 14(2)(f) and set out the information which was required to be given to the electorate under that paragraph.

6. If circumstances change, so that the industrial action is no longer the industrial action contemplated by the ballot paper, the union should halt the industrial action, re-ballot its members and give the requisite notice before commencing industrial action once more.

Injunction to restrain industrial action: recent development

[17.80] *Chieftan Construction Ltd v Ryan*[91] concerned an application by the plaintiff for an interlocutory injunction to restrain unofficial picketing by the defendants. The plaintiff dismissed the defendants from its employment on the grounds of redundancy. The defendants, members of Services Industrial Professional Technical Union, believed that they were to be replaced by agency workers. They placed an unauthorised picket the plaintiff's premises. The plaintiff sought an interlocutory injunction. The plaintiff argued that the picketing did not fall within s 11(1). That sub-section authorises peaceful picketing by workers where 'their employer works or carries on business'. The plaintiff argued that it was not to be regarded as the defendants' employer because the phrase *'where their employer works or carries on business'* is couched in the present tense and only embraces current employment as of the time of picketing. Edwards J analysed the jurisprudence on the relevant test. He concluded as follows:[92]

---

[90] These points are derived from the judgments in *G&T Crampton Ltd v Building and Allied Trades Union* [1998] ELR 4 and *Nolan Transport (Oaklands) Ltd v Halligan* [1998] ELR 177.

[91] *Chieftan Construction Ltd v Ryan* (1 May 2008, unreported) HC (Edwards J), [2008] IEHC 147.

[92] (1 May 2008, unreported) HC, at 16–17.

It is clear from the foregoing review of the authorities that Irish law precludes a judge in most cases from having regard to the strength of the case after it has been decided that the plaintiff has raised a fair or substantial or serious issue to be tried. However, I can divine no clear guidance from the judgments in *Campus Oil* as to whether or not regard can be had to the strength of the case in considering whether the plaintiff has in fact raised a fair or substantial or serious issue to be tried. The very looseness of the language used and the interchangeability of the adjectives employed suggests strongly to me that what is required is a consideration of the 'substance' of the point raised in the broad sense that I have spoken about rather than in the narrow sense. In addition I find support for my view in the following statement of Diplock J in the *American Cyanamid* case (part of the larger quotation approved by the Supreme Court in *Campus Oil):*

> '... unless the material available to the court at the hearing of the application for an interlocutory injunction fails to disclose that the plaintiff has *any real prospect* (my emphasis) of succeeding in his claim for a permanent injunction at the trial, the court should go on to consider whether the balance of convenience lies in favour of granting or refusing the interlocutory relief that is sought.'

It seems to me that any evaluation of a plaintiff's prospects of success must necessarily involve a consideration of both the utility and the strength of the point in question. Moreover, the use of the adjective 'real' imports a need to evaluate the 'reality' of the prospects of success and that requires an examination, if it be possible, of the strength of a plaintiff's case.'

[17.81] Edwards J considered the strength of the plaintiff's case:[93]

The only point in the case is what is the correct interpretation of section 11(1) of the Industrial Relations Act 1990. I am satisfied that the point raised by the plaintiffs has the requisite utility in that, if their interpretation is upheld, the plaintiff would be entitled to succeed at the trial. However, following a careful consideration of Industrial Relations Act 1990 as a whole, and in particular Part II thereof, and with due regard to the canons for the construction of statutes generally, and section 5(1) of the Interpretation Act 2005 in particular, I regard the plaintiffs' prospects of success as remote. I am not to be taken as deciding the issue, that will be a matter for the Court of trial, but in considering the question as to whether or not the plaintiff has established a fair or substantial or serious issue to be tried I feel bound to take into account my view that the plaintiffs' case, though arguable, is weak. In all the circumstances of the case I am not satisfied that the plaintiffs' point has sufficient substance, in the broad sense, to persuade me that there is a fair or substantial or serious issue to be tried.

Edwards J therefore refused the injunction. This case stands as authority that a plaintiff seeking an interlocutory injunction to restrain industrial action will be required to demonstrate a prospect of success at trial in order to obtain that injunction. This suggests that those engaging in industrial action even without a ballot will have greater success in resisting interlocutory injunctions than in the past.

The fallout from industrial action

[17.82] On the fall out from industrial action, see Ch 18, Industrial Relations at paras **[18.49]–[18.73]**.

---

[93] (1 May 2008, unreported) HC, at 18–19.

Chapter 18

Industrial Relations Law

Anthony Kerr

INTRODUCTION

[18.01] Industrial Relations in Ireland have to a large extent been characterised by a commitment to legal abstention sometimes referred to as 'voluntarism'.[1] The system in the main is a voluntary one, in the sense that trade unions and employers are free to agree or not to agree on the substantive principles which are to govern their mutual rights and obligations, and to regulate their behaviour, without the intervention of the State. The role of the State has been, historically, one of facilitating the relationship between trade unions and employers by providing both the legislative framework within which trade unions can operate[2] and the machinery to assist the parties to resolve disputes that may arise between them.[3] Accordingly, the relevant legislation confers no positive rights on workers or the trade unions of which they are members, whether to strike or picket, merely immunities against certain common law doctrines.[4]

[18.02] The extent to which the State has now intervened in the relationship between employers and their employees, and has conferred valuable rights on employees relating to virtually all aspects of the employment relationship, has raised doubts as to whether the labour relations process in Ireland can still be regarded as 'voluntarist'.[5] It remains the case, however, that neither employers nor trade unions, or their members, are legally required to avail of the machinery provided by the State prior to engaging in any form of

---

[1] Wallace, Gunnigle and McMahon, *Industrial Relations in Ireland* (3rd edn, Gill & McMillan, 2004) pp 71 and 73.

[2] See the Trade Union Act 1871 and the Trade Union Amendment Act 1876. More recent legislation includes the Trade Union Acts 1941, 1971 and 1975 and Part II of the Industrial Relations Act 1990.

[3] Principally the Labour Court established by the Industrial Relations Act 1946, the Rights Commissioners established by the Industrial Relations Act 1969 and the Labour Relations Commission established by the Industrial Relations Act 1990.

[4] See the Trade Union Act 1871, ss 2 and 3 which provide that the purposes of any trade union shall not, by reason merely that they are in restraint of trade, be deemed to be unlawful so as to render any member of such trade union liable to criminal prosecution for conspiracy or so as to render void or voidable any agreement or trust. See also Industrial Relations Act 1990, ss 10, 11, 12 and 13 (replacing the equivalent provisions of the Conspiracy and Protection of Property Act 1875 and the Trade Disputes Act 1906).

[5] See Gibbs, 'Beyond voluntarism in collective labour law' (2005) 2 *IELJ* 3; Doherty, 'It's Good to Talk ... Isn't It? Legislating for Information and Consultation in the Irish Workplace' (2008) 30 *DULJ* (ns) 120, 123 citing Teague 'New Developments in Employment Disputes Resolution' (2005) 4 *LRC Rev* 5.

industrial action.[6] Moreover, if the parties do avail of that machinery, they are not legally bound by any recommendation that might be issued.[7] Nor is there any general legal obligation on employers to bargain collectively with or recognise the trade union of which their employees, or some of them, are members.[8] Where an employer does recognise a trade union, any agreement entered into between them is not generally regarded as being a legally binding contract.[9]

[18.03] Accordingly this chapter confines itself to three discrete areas where law and industrial relations intersect; namely Collective Bargaining, the Industrial Relations (Amendment) Act 2001, and Industrial Action and the Contract of Employment.

COLLECTIVE BARGAINING AND THE LAW

[18.04] The Trade Union Act 1941 recognises that the principal function of a trade union is to engage in the carrying on of negotiations for fixing wages and other terms and conditions of employment.[10] The carrying on of such negotiations is usually referred to as 'collective bargaining' and the outcome of such negotiations is usually referred to as a 'collective agreement'.

[18.05] The nature of collective bargaining is a topic on which industrial relations theorists are divided. For the Webbs, collective bargaining was merely the collective equivalent of individual bargaining:

> instead of an employer making a series of separate contracts with isolated workmen he meets with a collective will and settles in a single agreement the principles upon which, for the time being, all workers of a particular class, group or grade will be engaged.[11]

For Flanders, this analysis was deficient in that an individual contract of employment provides for an exchange of work for wages and for the conditions of that exchange whereas collective bargaining is 'essentially a rule making process and this is a feature which has no proper counterpart in individual bargaining'.[12] This explains why Kahn

---

[6] The only situation in which the immunities contained in ss 10, 11 and 12 of the 1990 Act are not available is where there are agreed procedures for the resolution of individual disputes and those procedures have not been resorted to or exhausted: see s 9(2) of the Industrial Relations Act 1990.

[7] See *State (St Stephen's Green Club) v Labour Court* [1961] IR 85.

[8] *Association of General Practitioners v Minister for Health* [1995] 1 IR 382. Although note s 16(2) of the Postal and Telecommunications Services Act 1983 which requires that the articles of association of An Post and what is now Eircom Ltd must provide that the company 'shall in consultation and agreement with recognised trade unions and staff associations, set up machinery for the purposes of negotiation concerned with the pay and conditions of service of the staff'.

[9] *Ford Motor Co Ltd v Amalgamated Union of Engineering and Foundry Workers* [1969] 2 QB 303.

[10] The long title to the 1941 Act provides, in relevant part, that the Act is to provide for 'the licensing of bodies carrying on negotiations for fixing wages or other conditions of employment'. See also Ewing, 'The Function of Trade Unions' (2005) 34 *ILJ* 1.

[11] Webb and Webb, *Industrial Democracy* (1897), p 178.

[12] 'Collective Bargaining: a theoretical analysis' (1969) 6 *BJIR* 1, 4.

Freund defined a collective agreement as both 'an industrial peace treaty and at the same time a source of rules for terms and conditions of employment'.[13] Fox, however, argued that individual bargaining also defines the rules which will be observed by both parties if the contract is entered into.[14] As Wallace, Gunnigle and McMahon observe in *Industrial Relations in Ireland*,[15] the practical implications of this debate are 'limited' but it is useful in drawing attention to the 'multifaceted nature of the process'.

The terms 'collective bargaining negotiations' and 'collective agreement' are referred to in a number of statutes, only some of which expressly define such terms. For instance, the term 'collective bargaining negotiations' is used both in the Worker Participation (State Enterprises) Act 1977 and the Industrial Relations (Amendment) Act 2001 but it is only defined for the purposes of the former. Similarly the term 'collective agreement' is used in the Terms of Employment (Information) Act 1994, the Protection of Young Persons (Employment) Act 1996, the Organisation of Working Time Act 1997, the Employment Equality Act 1998, the Protection of Employees (Part-Time Work) Act 2001 and the Protection of Employees (Fixed Term Work) Act 2003 but it is not defined in the 1994 Act and is defined differently in the other statutes.

Definitions

[18.06] Section 1 of the Worker Participation (State Enterprises) Act 1977 defines 'collective bargaining negotiations' as meaning

> [n]egotiations between any employer, employers' organisation or other body or persons representative of employers on the one hand and any organisation or other body of persons representative of employees on the other hand, being negotiations which are concerned with remuneration or other terms or conditions of employment, or the working conditions of employees.

As the expression is not defined in the Industrial Relations (Amendment) Act 2001, the Labour Court initially took the view that it should be assigned 'the meaning which it would normally bear in an industrial relations context'.[16] Collective bargaining, the Court said, comprehended more than mere negotiation or consultation on individual employment related issues. An 'essential characteristic' was that it was conducted 'between parties of equal standing who are independent in the sense that one is not controlled by the other'.[17] In *Ryanair Ltd v Labour Court*,[18] however, the Supreme Court said that the Labour Court were incorrect. In their view the term should be given 'an ordinary dictionary meaning' and that 'collective bargaining negotiations', in what the Supreme Court described as a 'non unionised company', did not have to take the same form and adopt the same procedures as would apply in collective bargaining with a trade union.[19]

---

13 *Labour and the Law* (1977), p 124.

14 'Collective bargaining, Flanders and the Webbs' (1975) 13 *BJIR* 151, 155.

15 'Collective bargaining, Flanders and the Webbs' (1975) 13 *BJIR* 151 at pp 242–243.

16 See *Ashford Castle Ltd v SIPTU* [2004] ELR 214 at 217.

17 As to the degree of independence the Court required, see *MI North Link Ltd v SIPTU* LCR 18307 and *Green Isle Foods v SIPTU* LCR 18431.

18 *Ryanair Ltd v Labour Court* [2007] 4 IR 199.

[18.07] Section 1(1) of the Protection of Young Persons (Employment) Act 1996 defines a 'collective agreement' as meaning:

an agreement by or on behalf of an employer on the one hand, and by or on behalf of a trade union or trade unions representative of the employees to whom the agreement relates on the other hand.

[18.08] Section 2(1) of the Organisation of Working Time Act 1997 defines a 'collective agreement' as meaning:

an agreement by or on behalf of an employer on the one hand and by or on behalf of a body or bodies representative of the employees to whom the agreement relates on the other hand.[20]

Section 2(1) of the Employment Equality Act 1998 defines a 'collective agreement' as meaning:

an agreement between an employer and a body or bodies representative of the employees to which the agreement relates.[21]

Legal enforceability

[18.09] The question as to whether a collective agreement, howsoever defined, is legally enforceable has yet to be definitively considered in this jurisdiction. The dominant view is that both parties to a collective agreement, generally speaking, do not intend to create legal relations. This is clear from the decision of Barrington J in *O'Rourke v Talbot Ireland Ltd*.[22]

The plaintiffs had been made redundant in 1980 and in their proceedings they claimed a declaration that the defendant company was bound by an agreement made in 1979 whereby they alleged that the company gave them a guarantee of security of tenure until at least 1984. The evidence before the High Court was that management were anxious to secure the agreement of the plaintiffs (who were all foremen employed at the company's plant in Santry) to certain redeployment proposals. A meeting took place and the foremen, acting through a three-man committee, agreed to co-operate in return for a guarantee that there would be no compulsory redundancies amongst the foremen for the next five years. This guarantee was given in writing on company note paper. The branch secretary of the plaintiffs' trade union acknowledged that most collective agreements were binding in honour only but stated that the agreement which the plaintiffs had secured was unique in his experience as a trade union official in that he regarded it as giving 'cast iron and personal guarantees to each of the men concerned'.[23]

---

[19] [2007] 4 IR 199 at 218, *per* Geoghegan J. It is unclear as to which dictionary the Supreme Court were referring, as the term 'collective bargaining' is defined in the *Oxford English Dictionary* as 'negotiation of wages etc by an organised body of employees' and in the *Chambers Dictionary* as 'talks between a trade union and a company's management to negotiate on pay and working conditions'.

[20] An identical definition is contained in the Protection of Employees (Part-Time Work) Act 2001, s 3(1) and the Protection of Employees (Fixed-Term Work) Act 2003, s 2(1).

[21] The definition was inserted by the Equality Act 2004, s 3.

[22] *O'Rourke v Talbot Ireland Ltd* [1984] ILRM 587.

[23] [1984] ILRM 587 at 592.

[18.10] The company submitted that the agreement was not legally enforceable and Barrington J accepted that 'generally speaking' such agreements did not contemplate legal relations and, further, accepted management's evidence that they had not intended to enter into legal relations. He pointed out, however, that this was never expressed or communicated to the plaintiffs who had made it clear that they were not looking for 'some pious aspiration or commitment in honour'.[24]

[18.11] Barrington J did not feel it necessary to determine whether the agreement itself was legally enforceable for three reasons:

> Firstly, we are not here dealing with a trade union or a group of trade unions negotiating on behalf of all the men employed in a vast concern or a particular industry but with three foremen negotiating on behalf of not more than seventeen of their peers and referring back to their peers and getting authority from time to time. Secondly, a productivity agreement which might not be legally enforceable in all its terms can still amend particular provisions in a worker's contract of employment eg his rate of pay. In the present case I have no doubt that the foremen made quite clear that they were looking for an alteration in their terms of employment. Finally, the plaintiffs in the present case carried out their side of the bargain and are standing over the authority of the agents who negotiated the agreement on their behalf.[25]

Incorporation

[18.12] It follows that the individual contract of employment is the main point of contact between the collective bargaining process and any legal process. From a legal perspective the collective agreement is primarily a source from which individual terms or conditions may be derived. As Kilner Brown J once said:

> Collective agreements are not by themselves of any legal significance unless they are translated into a contractual relationship between employer and employee.[26]

It would appear that collectively agreed terms are not automatically to be treated as having been incorporated into individual contracts of employment.[27] So, in *Reilly v Drogheda Borough Council*,[28] the plaintiff commenced employment as a retained fire-fighter in 1980, at which time the retirement age was 65. In 2002, the trade union of which he was a member entered into a collective agreement with the local authorities including the defendant, which set the retirement age at 55. Laffoy J held that the plaintiff's contractual retirement age could only be varied by consensus and she

---

[24] *O'Rourke v Talbot Ireland Ltd* [1984] ILRM 587 at 594. See also *King v Aer Lingus plc* [2005] 4 IR 310, where the parties to a collective agreement had agreed to 'commission lawyers to convert the existing paperwork containing the guarantees into a legally binding irrevocable agreement form'.

[25] [1984] ILRM 587 at 594.

[26] *Land v West Yorkshire Metropolitan County Council* [1979] ICR 452 at 458. See also *Alexander v Standard Telephones and Cables Ltd (No 2)* [1991] IRLR 286.

[27] See O'Higgins CJ and Kenny J in *Gouldings Chemicals Ltd v Bolger* [1977] IR 211 at 231 and 237 respectively.

[28] *Reilly v Drogheda Borough Council* [2009] ELR 1.

concluded that there was no evidence before her suggesting that he had acquiesced in the change of retirement age brought about by the collective agreement.

[18.13] The position is different where an employee's contract of employment expressly provides that his or her terms and conditions of employment will be determined by collective agreements made from time to time with any recognised trade union representing employees within the undertaking.[29]

[18.14] Occasionally, statutes may provide that the provisions of a collective agreement are to be incorporated into an employee's contract of employment. An example is contained in the Postal and Telecommunications Services Act 1983 which provided for the formation of two limited companies – An Post and what is now known as Eircom Ltd – and the transfer of responsibilities to them from the Department of Posts and Telegraphs. Section 45(2) of the 1983 Act provides:

> Save in accordance with a collective agreement negotiated with any recognised trade union or staff association concerned, a member of the staff of the Department of Posts and Telegraphs who is transferred on the vesting day to either company shall not, while in the service of the company, receive a lesser scale of pay or be brought to less beneficial conditions of service than the scale of pay to which he was entitled and the conditions of service to which he was subject immediately before the vesting day.[30]

[18.15] In *Ó Cearbhaill v Bord Telecom Éireann*,[31] the plaintiffs (who were all members of the Communications Workers Union) objected to the implementation of a restructuring agreement negotiated between the union and the company because they feared it would negatively impact on their prospects of promotion. In the Supreme Court, Blayney J said that the opening words of s 45(2), namely 'save in accordance with a collective agreement negotiated with a recognised trade union or staff association concerned', meant that the plaintiffs had to accept, by reason of a collective agreement of the type indicated, less beneficial conditions of service than those to which they were previously entitled.[32]

[18.16] Even where there is express, or perhaps implied, provision for the incorporation of collectively agreed terms, such terms can only be incorporated into individual contracts of employment where they are apt or suitable for inclusion. So in *Kaur v MG Rover Group Ltd*,[33] for example, the English Court of Appeal held that a commitment in a collective agreement that there would be no 'compulsory redundancy' was neither

---

[29] See, for instance, the Terms of Employment (Information) Act 1994, s 3(3) which permits reference to a collective agreement governing, *inter alia,* the rate or method of calculation of the employee's remuneration and the hours of work in any written statement provided to an employee pursuant to s 3(1) of the 1994 Act.

[30] Equivalent provisions include the Transport (Re-organisation of Córas Iompair Éireann) Act 1986, s 14(5), the Marine Protection Act 1991, s 8(7), the Environmental Protection Agency Act 1992, s 31(2) and the Irish Aviation Authority Act 1993, s 40(2).

[31] *Ó Cearbhaill v Bord Telecom Éireann* [1994] ELR 54.

[32] [1994] ELR 54 at 57.

[33] *Kaur v MG Rover Group Ltd* [2005] IRLR 40.

intended to be incorporated into individual contracts of employment nor apt for such incorporation.[34]

Registered employment agreements

[18.17] One way for a collective agreement to be given legal effect is for the parties to apply to the Labour Court, pursuant to the Industrial Relations Act 1946, to have the agreement registered. The effect of registration is that the agreement will apply to every worker of the class, type or group to which it is expressed to apply and to his or her employer, notwithstanding that such worker or employer is not a party to the agreement and would not otherwise be bound thereby, and its provisions can be legally enforced.[35]

[18.18] Section 27(1) of the 1946 Act provides that any party to an 'employment agreement' may apply to the Labour Court to register the agreement in the Register of Employment Agreements which the Court is required to maintain under s 26. The expression 'employment agreement' is defined in s 25 as:

> an agreement relating to the remuneration or the conditions of employment of workers of any class, type or group made between a trade union of workers and an employer or trade union of employers or made, at a meeting of a registered joint industrial council, between members of the council representative of workers and members of the council representative of employers.

Where an application is duly made to the Labour Court to register the agreement, s 27(3) provides that the Court shall register the agreement if it is satisfied:

(i)   that, in the case of an agreement to which there are two parties only, both parties consent to its registration and, in the case of an agreement to which there are more than two parties, there is substantial agreement amongst the parties representing the interests of workers and employers, respectively, that it should be registered;

(ii)   that the agreement is expressed to apply to all workers of a particular class, type or group and their employers where the Court is satisfied that it is a normal and desirable practice or that it is expedient to have a separate agreement for that class, type or group;

(iii)   that the parties to the agreement are substantially representative of such workers and employers;

(iv)   that the agreement is not intended to restrict unduly employment generally or the employment of workers of a particular class, type or group or to ensure or

---

[34]   [2005] IRLR 40 at 45, *per* Keene LJ. See also *British Leyland UK Ltd v McQuilken* [1978] IRLR 245. See, further, Twomey 'Castles in the air: Collective agreements, compulsory redundancies and *Kaur v MG Rover*' (2006) 3 *IELJ* 77.

[35]   The relevant provisions, which are contained in Part III of the 1946 Act, replaced and improved those contained in the Conditions of Employment Act 1936, s 50. At the end of 2007 there were 46 employment agreements on the Register (Labour Court *Annual Report 2007* p 23). For an assessment of the registration system see Horgan 'The Failure of Legal Enforcement – A Review of the Registration of Agreements in the Labour Court' (1985) 4 *JISLL* 28.

protect the retention in use of inefficient or unduly costly machinery or methods of working;

(v)   that the agreement provides that if a trade dispute occurs between workers to whom the agreement relates and their employers a strike or lock-out shall not take place until the dispute has been submitted for settlement by negotiation in the manner specified in the agreement; and

(vi)   that the agreement is in a form suitable for registration.

Such agreements are particularly apt in labour intensive sectors where labour costs are a high proportion of overall costs and where employers compete against each other for available work through competitive tender.

[18.19] In *National Union of Security Employers v Labour Court*,[36] Flood J held that the Labour Court had to approach the question of 'satisfaction', for the purposes of s 27(3), in the light of:

(a)   the fact that the overall purpose of the agreement is to create harmony within the industry as a whole,

(b)   the agreement is intended to bind all persons in the industry,

(c)   that sanctions will flow from the breach of the agreement by firms in the industry,

(d)   that the parties to the agreement are substantially representative of employers in the industry, and workers in the industry.

In this case, Flood J granted a declaration that the purported registration of an agreement for the security industry was invalid and of no effect. He was satisfied that the Labour Court had 'simply rubber-stamped' a request to register an agreement and that the Court, in so doing, had not followed fair procedures.

[18.20] If a registered employment agreement provides for its variation, s 28 of the 1946 Act provides that any party to the agreement may apply to the Labour Court to vary the agreement 'in its application to any worker or workers to whom it applies'. Where such an application is made the Court is required to consider the application and to 'hear all persons appearing to the Court to be interested and desiring to be heard'. After such consideration the Court may, as it thinks fit, refuse the application or make an order varying the agreement 'in such manner as it thinks proper'.

[18.21] In *Serco Services Ireland Ltd v Labour Court*,[37] Carroll J struck down an order made by the Labour Court varying the Registered Employment Agreement for the Electrical Contracting Industry because the variation order purported to extend the scope of the agreement so as to apply its provisions to workers to whom it did not previously apply. This, she said, was something which the Labour Court had no power to do under s 28.

[18.22] Section 29(1) of the 1946 Act provides that the registration of an employment agreement may be cancelled by the Labour Court on the joint application of all parties

---

[36] *National Union of Security Employers v Labour Court* (1994) 10 JISLL 97.
[37] *Serco Services Ireland Ltd v Labour Court* [2002] ELR 1.

thereto 'if the Court is satisfied that the consent of all such parties to its cancellation has been given voluntarily'. Section 29(2) goes on to provide that the Labour Court may cancel the registration of an employment agreement if it is satisfied that there has been 'such substantial change in the circumstances of the trade or business to which it relates since the registration of the agreement that it is undesirable to maintain registration'. Accordingly, the Labour Court must be satisfied of three matters. First, the Court must be satisfied that there have been changes in the circumstances of the trade or business since registration. Secondly, the Court must be satisfied that any such changes are substantial as opposed to ordinary or ongoing. Thirdly, the Court must be satisfied that any such substantial changes make it undesirable to maintain registration of the agreement. In *National Electrical Contractors of Ireland v Technical Engineering and Electrical Union*,[38] the Labour Court ruled that the burden of proof in respect of all three matters falls on the party or parties seeking cancellation. In respect of the third matter, the Court noted that the subsection was expressed in negative terms and said that there must be 'evidence of some weight to indicate that, because of changed circumstances, the overall or dominant effect of the agreement has become deleterious to the interests of all parties in the sector or that some other compelling reason exists as to why registration of the agreement should be cancelled'. The Court also held that a person who was not a party to the agreement, but who was affected by it, could apply to have it cancelled.

[18.23] As noted above, s 30(1) of the 1946 Act provides that a registered employment agreement, as long as it continues to be registered, shall apply to every worker of the class, type or group to which it is expressed to apply and to his or her employer, notwithstanding that such worker or employer is not a party to the agreement. Section 30(2) and (3) go on to provide that, if a contract between such a worker and his or her employer provides for payment of remuneration at a rate less than the rate provided by the agreement, or for conditions of employment less favourable than those fixed by the agreement, the contract shall have effect as if the agreement rate or the agreement conditions were substituted for the contract rate or the contract conditions as the case may be.

[18.24] In the event that an employer does not pay a worker the rate of remuneration provided for by a registered employment agreement, the worker would have the right to institute civil proceedings to recover same. In addition s 54(1) of the Industrial Relations Act 1990 provides that an inspector may institute, on behalf of the worker, civil proceedings for the recovery of any monies due.[39]

[18.25] Apart from any individual enforcement of the provisions of a registered employment agreement, s 32(1) of the 1946 Act and s 10 of the Industrial Relations Act 1969 provide for a procedure whereby a trade union representative of workers affected by such an agreement, or an employer or a trade union representative of employers

---

[38] *National Electrical Contractors of Ireland v Technical Engineering and Electrical Union* REP1/2009.

[39] The subsection also empowers the inspector to institute civil proceedings to enforce a condition of a registered employment agreement. Note also the role of the Pensions Board in the enforcement of pension entitlements: Pensions Act 1990, s 87.

affected by such an agreement, may complain to the Labour Court that an employer affected by the agreement has failed or neglected to comply with same. Where such complaint is made, the Court must consider the complaint and hear all persons appearing to the Court to be interested and desiring to be heard. If, after such consideration, the Court is satisfied that the complaint is well founded, the Court may by order direct the said employer to do such things as will in the opinion of the Court result in the agreement being complied with by the said employer. Failure to comply with such order is a criminal offence but the District Court is not empowered to order the employer to pay to the worker the difference between the agreement rate and the rate actually paid.

[18.26] Section 32(2) of the 1946 Act provides a procedure whereby an employer, or a trade union representative of employers, affected by a registered employment agreement can complain to the Labour Court that a trade union representative of workers affected by the agreement is 'promoting or assisting out of its funds in the maintenance of a strike which to the knowledge of the general committee of management of the trade union of workers is in contravention of the agreement and which has for its object the enforcement of a demand on the employer to grant to a worker remuneration or conditions other than those fixed by the agreement'.

[18.27] Where such complaint is made, the Labour Court must consider the complaint and hear all persons appearing to the Court to be interested and desiring to be heard.[40] If, after such consideration, the Court is satisfied that the complaint is well founded, the Court may by order direct the trade union to refrain from assisting out of its funds in the maintenance of the said strike or the Court may cancel the registration of the agreement.[41] Failure to comply with such order is a criminal offence.[42]

[18.28] The Labour Court has confirmed that s 32(2) imposes two conditions, both of which have to be satisfied before it can exercise the jurisdiction conferred thereby. Not only did the strike have to be for terms and conditions over above those set by the agreement, it also had to be in contravention of the agreement itself.[43]

[18.29] Section 33(1) of the 1946 Act provides that the Labour Court, on the application of 'any person', may give its decision on any question as to the interpretation of a registered employment agreement or its application to a particular person. The approach the Labour Court will adopt when exercising its jurisdiction under this section was outlined in *Mythen Brothers Ltd v Building and Allied Trades Union*.[44] The Court said that, because such an agreement was 'an industrial relations instrument' drafted by 'industrial relations practitioners', its interpretation should not be approached 'as if it were a statute or the product of legal draftmanship'. Its terms should be construed 'by

---

[40]   Industrial Relations Act 1946, s 32(2)(a).

[41]   Industrial Relations Act 1946, s 32(2)(b).

[42]   Industrial Relations Act 1946, s 32(4) which, as amended by the Industrial Relations (Miscellaneous Provisions) Act 2004, s 14, provides for penalties of up to €3,000 and up to a further €1,000 for every day that the offence is continued.

[43]   *See P Elliott Construction v Building and Allied Trades Union* REA 105/2006.

[44]   *Mythen Brothers Ltd v Building and Allied Trades Union* [2006] ELR 237.

applying to them a meaning which they would normally bear in the conduct of industrial relations so as to achieve the result envisaged by the parties to the agreement'.

Approval of collective agreements

[18.30] The Labour Court also has an important role in approving collective agreements which derogate, *inter alia*, from the four or six month reference periods prescribed by s 15 of the Organisation of Working Time Act 1997.[45]

[18.31] Section 24(2) of the 1997 Act provides that, on an application being made by any of the parties thereto, the Labour Court may 'approve of' a collective agreement. On receipt of such application, the Court is required to consult 'such representatives of employees and employers as it considers to have an interest in the matters to which the collective agreement, the subject of the application, relates'.[46]

[18.32] Section 24(4) of the 1997 Act provides that the Court shall not approve of a collective agreement unless the following conditions are fulfilled, namely:

   (i)   the Court is satisfied that it is appropriate to approve of the agreement having regard to the provisions of the Council Directive permitting the entry into collective agreements for the purposes concerned;

   (ii)   the agreement has been concluded in a manner usually employed in determining the pay or other conditions of employment of employees in the employment concerned;

   (iii) the body which negotiated the agreement on behalf of the employees concerned is the holder of a negotiation licence under the Trade Union Act 1941, or is an excepted body within the meaning of that Act which is sufficiently representative of the employees concerned;[47] and

   (iv) the agreement is in such form as appears to the Labour Court to be suitable for the purposes of the agreement being approved of under s 24.[48]

INDUSTRIAL RELATIONS (AMENDMENT) ACT 2001

[18.33] As noted above, there is no general right at common law or under the Constitution to be represented by an organisation of an employee's choice in the negotiation of terms and conditions of employment. The High Court has ruled that there is no obligation on an employer 'to consult with or negotiate with any organisation representing his employees or some of them, when the conditions of employment are to be settled or reviewed'. An employer is left with 'freedom of choice as to whether he will negotiate with any organisation or consult with them on such matters, and is also

---

[45] Some agreements contain exemptions from the rest period provisions set out in ss 11, 12 and 13 of the 1997 Act: see s 4(5) of the 1997 Act.

[46] Organisation of Working Time Act 1997, s 24(3).

[47] *Quaere* whether the requirement to be 'sufficiently representative' of the employees concerned applies only to an excepted body. The punctuation would suggest that this is the case.

[48] At the end of 2007, the Labour Court had approved 202 collective agreements which were expressed to apply to some 114,287 workers.

free to give a right of audience to one representative body and refuse it to another, if he chooses to do so'.[49]

[18.34] It is the case, however, that a dispute between an employer and its employees (or some of them), as to whether their trade union should be recognised for collective bargaining purposes, is a trade dispute for the purposes both of the Industrial Relations Act 1946 and of Part II of the Industrial Relations Act 1990. Such a dispute can thus be referred to the Labour Court under s 20(1) of the Industrial Relations Act 1969.[50]

[18.35] Nevertheless, following some high profile recognition disputes,[51] the trade unions began to seek a process whereby their members' terms and conditions of employment could be improved where no union was recognised for collective bargaining purposes. This culminated in the submission by the Irish Congress of Trade Unions of proposals on union recognition and the right to bargain to the social partnership negotiations which produced the agreement known as *Partnership 2000*.

[18.36] It was decided that a High Level Group consisting of representatives of the social partners, the development agencies and various government departments be established to consider these proposals. The Group issued its final report in March 1999 which reflected the agreement of all parties that the 'voluntarist approach' to dispute resolution was to be preferred and that the issues raised were best resolved, not by providing for a statutory right to trade union recognition, but rather by providing an incentive for employers to agree on a collective bargaining arrangement.[52] This incentive was to be provided by giving the Labour Court the power to regulate by binding decision the pay and other terms and conditions of employment in employments where there was an absence of collective bargaining.[53]

---

[49] *Per* O'Hanlon J in *Association of General Practitioners v Minister for Health* [1995] 1 IR 382 at 391. The Labour Court has always accepted that employers are under no legal obligation to enter into negotiations over pay and conditions of employment: see *Cork Milling Co v ATGWU* LCR 358 and *Caltex (Ireland) Ltd v ITGWU* LCR 500.

[50] The invariable practice of the Labour Court is to recommend that the employer should recognise the trade union for the purpose of collective bargaining and that the parties should meet at an early date for the purpose of agreeing a framework within which normal industrial relations matters can be dealt with cooperatively: see, even after the enactment of the 2001 Act, *Sabrewatch Ltd v SIPTU* LCR 17443; *Greenstar Materials Recovery Ltd v SIPTU* LCR 17490; *Cairborne Trading Ltd v SIPTU* LCR 17578; *Fruit of the Loom v SIPTU* LCR 17600; *Pirannah Freight Ltd v SIPTU* LCR 17654; *Irish Estates v TEEU* LCR 17694; *Shannon Environmental Services Ltd v SIPTU* LCR 17716; *Fujitsu Siemens v TEEU* LCR 19203; *Electronic Data Systems v IBOA* LCR 19306. See also *Becton Dickinson & Co Ltd v Lee* [1973] IR 1 at 24–25 where Walsh J ruled that a recognition dispute was a trade dispute for the purposes of the Trade Disputes Act 1906.

[51] Principally in Ryanair, Nolan Transport and Pat the Baker.

[52] The report is reproduced in *Industrial Relations News* (IRN11, 18 March 1999).

[53] This approach is in marked contrast to that adopted in the United Kingdom where a statutory recognition procedure, as contained in the Trade Union and Labour Relations (Consolidation) Act 1992, Sch A1 (inserted by the Employment Relations Act 1999 and amended by the Employment Relations Act 2004), came into force in June 2000. (contd.../)

[18.37] There were two components to the mechanism proposed by the Group. The first was a voluntary option whereby both parties agreed to use the services of the Labour Relations Commission in an attempt over a six week period to resolve the issues in dispute. The framework for the voluntary processing of recognition disputes is now set out in the Commission's Enhanced Code of Practice on Voluntary Dispute Resolution which was declared in 2004 by the Minister to be a Code of Practice for the purposes of the Industrial Relations Act 1990.[54]

[18.38] Where the employer refused or failed to avail of the voluntary option, or, having availed of the option, the issues remained unresolved, the Group recommended a 'fall back' procedure whereby the Labour Court would be given new powers. It is this second component which is given effect by the Industrial Relations (Amendment) Act 2001.[55]

[18.39] The Labour Court has recognised that it is 'abundantly clear' from the 2001 Act's legislative history and its terms that it cannot be used to force employers to engage in collective bargaining.[56] Notwithstanding trade union criticism of the Act (even as amended in 2004), following the decision of the Supreme Court in *Ryanair Ltd v Labour Court*,[57] it is clear that the Act does provide 'a measure of protection to employees where pay and conditions are not freely determined by collective bargaining'.[58]

[18.40] The 2001 Act (as amended) provides that a trade union or an excepted body can refer a 'trade dispute' to the Labour Court where the following circumstances[59] pertain:

(a) it is not the practice of the employer to engage in collective bargaining negotiations in respect of the grade, group or category or workers who are party to the trade dispute and the internal dispute resolution procedures (if any) normally used by the parties concerned have failed to resolve the dispute;

(b) either the employer has failed to observe a provision of the relevant Code of Practice on Voluntary Dispute Resolution specifying the period of time for the doing of anything or, the dispute having been referred to the Commission, the Commission is unable to advance resolution;

(c) the trade union or the excepted body or the employees have not acted in a manner that has frustrated the employer in observing a provision of the Code of Practice; and

(d) the trade union or the excepted body or the employees have not had recourse to industrial action after the dispute in question was referred to the Labour

---

53 (\....contd) The procedure is thoroughly analysed by Dukes 'The Statutory Recognition Procedure 1999: No Bias in Favour of Recognition?' (2008) 37 *ILJ* 236.

54 SI 76/2004. This replaces the Industrial Relations Act 1990 (Code of Practice on Voluntary Disputes Resolution) (Declaration) Order 2000 (SI 145/2000).

55 The 2001 was substantially amended by the Industrial Relations (Miscellaneous Provisions) Act 2004.

56 See, for instance, *IMPACT v Ryanair Ltd* [2005] ELR 99, 105.

57 *Ryanair Ltd v Labour Court* [2007] 4 IR 199.

58 *Per* the Labour Court (chaired by Kevin Duffy) in *IMPACT v Ryanair Ltd* [2005] ELR 99, 105.

59 As set out in s 2(1) as amended by s 2 of the 2004 Act.

Relations Commission in accordance with the provisions of the Code of Practice.

[18.41] The Labour Court, having investigated the dispute, is empowered to issue a non-binding recommendation which can cover terms and conditions of employment and dispute resolution and disciplinary procedures in the employment concerned but which cannot provide for the establishment of collective bargaining arrangements.[60] If this recommendation does not resolve the dispute, then the trade union or excepted body can apply to the Labour Court for a determination in similar terms.[61] If that determination is not implemented, the trade union or excepted body can apply to the Circuit Court for an Order implementing the determination.[62]

[18.42] The term 'trade dispute' is not defined in the 2001 Act but s 13 provides that that Act is to be construed together with the Industrial Relations Act 1946. Consequently the Labour Court has held[63] that the appropriate definition for the purposes of the 2001 Act is that set out in s 3 of the 1946 Act, namely:

> 'any dispute or difference between employers and workers or between workers and workers connected with the employment or non-employment, or the terms of the employment, or with the conditions of employment, of any person'.[64]

Nor is the term 'collective bargaining negotiations' defined in either the 1946 Act or the 2001 Act. Its meaning was considered by the Labour Court in *Ashford Castle Ltd v SIPTU*[65] where the Labour Court held that, in the absence of any statutory definition, it must be assigned 'the meaning which it would normally bear in an industrial relations context'. The Court added that 'collective bargaining' comprehended more than mere negotiation or consultation on individual employment related issues and that an essential characteristic was that it was conducted 'between parties of equal standing who are independent in the sense that one is not controlled by the other'. In *Ryanair Ltd v Labour Court*,[66] however, the Supreme Court held that the Labour Court's approach was incorrect. Speaking for a unanimous Supreme Court, Geoghegan J said that the term should be given 'an ordinary dictionary meaning'. He was of the opinion that the Labour

---

[60] Industrial Relations (Amendment) Act 2001, s 5.

[61] Industrial Relations (Amendment) Act 2001, s 6.

[62] Industrial Relations (Amendment) Act 2001, s 10 as substituted by s 4 of the 2004 Act. The procedure governing applications for enforcement is set out in the Circuit Court Rules (Industrial Relations Acts) 2007 (SI 12/2007) which provide that all applications under this section should be made by way of Motion on Notice.

[63] See, for instance, *IMPACT v Ryanair Ltd* [2005] ELR 99; *United Airlines v Communications Workers Union* [2006] ELR 188; *Johnston, Mooney & O'Brien v SIPTU* LCR 18454; and *Galway Clinic v SIPTU* LCR 18815.

[64] This definition differs somewhat from that contained in s 8 of the Industrial Relations Act 1990 in that it includes a dispute between workers and workers and in that it includes a 'difference' as well as a 'dispute'. In *Ryanair Ltd v Labour Court* [2007] 4 IR 199 at 216 the Supreme Court indicated, however, that it did not follow, despite the use of the two words, that 'difference' meant something distinct from a 'dispute'.

[65] *Ashford Castle Ltd v SIPTU* [2004] ELR 214.

[66] *Ryanair Ltd v Labour Court* [2007] 4 IR 199.

Court had implicitly taken the view that 'collective bargaining' in what he described as a non-unionised company, such as Ryanair, had to take 'the same form and adopt the same procedures as would apply in collective bargaining with a trade union'. He continued:

> If there is a machinery in Ryanair whereby the pilots may have their own independent representatives who sit around the table with representatives of Ryanair with a view to reaching agreement if possible, that would seem to be 'collective bargaining' within an ordinary dictionary meaning. It would seem strange if definitions peculiar to trade union negotiations were to be imposed on non-unionised companies.[67]

[18.43] The issue of whether the employer has been frustrated in observing a provision of the Code of Practice has been considered in a number of cases. In *United Airlines v Communications Workers Union*,[68] the Labour Court indicated that the relevant provisions of the 2001 Act contemplated 'conduct which frustrates an employer in seeking to comply with the provisions of the Code of Practice in relation to such matters as time limits'. It did not refer 'to the negotiating stance taken by the parties in their engagement under the code'. In *Kildare Hotel and Golf Club v AMICUS*,[69] the Labour Court said that the employer had to show that the conduct of the union was such as to prevent it from complying with a relevant provision of the Code of Practice. This could arise where a trade union failed to make itself available for meetings within the specified time frame or where the union refused 'to specify its claims with sufficient particularity so as to allow the employer to meaningfully respond'.

[18.44] Section 5 of the 2001 Act empowers the Labour Court to make a non-binding recommendation regarding the action which should be taken having regard to terms and conditions of employment, and to dispute resolution and disciplinary procedures in the employment concerned. The Court is specifically precluded from including in any such recommendation any provision for arrangements for collective bargaining.[70]

[18.45] The Labour Court has commented, in *Bank of Ireland v Irish Bank Officials Association*,[71] that the powers given to it by this section are a 'far reaching departure from the normal approach to the resolution of industrial disputes'. They provide in effect that the Court may arbitrate in a dispute on the unilateral application of one party and in circumstances where the employer may not consent to the process. Accordingly the Court's intervention was only appropriate 'where it is necessary in order to provide protection to workers whose terms and conditions of employment, when viewed in their totality, are significantly out of line with appropriate standards'. It follows that the

---

[67] [2007] 4 IR 199 at 218. See, subsequently, *Bell Security v TEEU* LCR 19188 where the Labour Court declined jurisdiction because it was satisfied that it was the practice of the employer to engage in collective bargaining negotiations (within the *Ryanair* formulation) notwithstanding 'the inherent and manifest inequality of negotiating capacity between the employee and management representatives'. See also the text at fn 19 above.

[68] *United Airlines v Communications Workers Union* [2006] ELR 188.

[69] *Kildare Hotel and Golf Club v AMICUS* LCR 18672.

[70] See s 5(2).

[71] *Bank of Ireland v Irish Bank Officials Association* LCR 17745.

Court's approach is formulating recommendations under this section should be to consider the likely pay levels and other conditions which might apply had collective bargaining taken place.[72]

[18.46] Although the Court cannot recommend that the parties engage in, or make arrangements for, collective bargaining, it can make provision for a grievance and/or disciplinary procedure. Consequently the Court is not precluded from making a recommendation for the representation of individuals in matters of dispute or difference with their employer not involving collective bargaining. In most cases, the Court has required the introduction of such a procedure which conforms to the general provisions of the Commission's Code of Practice on Grievance and Disciplinary Procedures, which specifically allows for a trade union official in his or her professional capacity to represent an employee in processing individual grievances and disciplinary matters where the employee wishes to avail of such representation, even if the grievance relates to remuneration.[73]

[18.47] Section 6 of the 2001 Act empowers the Labour Court, where it is satisfied that a dispute that is the subject of a recommendation under s 5 has not been resolved, to make a determination in the same terms as the recommendation. Again the Labour Court is specifically precluded from including in any such determination any provision for arrangements for collective bargaining.[74] It is clear that, before it can issue a determination, the Labour Court must first form the opinion that the dispute which was the subject of the recommendation has not been resolved. In *Dunnes Stores v MANDATE*,[75] the Court said that an issue in dispute could only be regarded as resolved when both parties were satisfied that it was resolved. The Court added that, normally, a dispute was resolved when the recommendation was accepted by both parties and was either implemented or a timeframe agreed for its implementation.

[18.48] Section 10(1) of the 2001 Act provides that, where an employer fails to comply with the terms of a determination under s 6, a trade union or excepted body may make an application to the Circuit Court for an enforcement order. Section 10(2) makes it clear that the Circuit Court, on application being made to it, must make an order directing the employer to carry out the determination in accordance with its terms 'without hearing the employer or any evidence (other than in relation to the matters referred to in subsection (1))'.

---

[72] See, for example, *Moquette Ltd v MANDATE* LCR 17607; *Clearstream Technologies Ltd v SIPTU* LCR 17897; *GE Healthcare v SIPTU* LCR 18013; *Quinn Cement v SIPTU* LCR 18151; and *Kildare Hotel and Golf Club v AMICUS* LCR 18672.

[73] See, for instance, *Analog Services v SIPTU* LCR 18137 and *Genesis Group v AMICUS* DIR 11/2005. The Commission's Code of Practice is contained in the Sch to SI 146/2000.

[74] Industrial Relations (Amendment) Act 2001, s 6(2).

[75] *Dunnes Stores v MANDATE* DIR 4/2006.

INDUSTRIAL ACTION AND THE CONTRACT OF EMPLOYMENT

Introduction

[18.49] When workers go on strike or engage in more limited forms of industrial action, a number of legal issues arise. These include, but are not limited to, whether the worker, in so doing, is acting in breach of his or her contract of employment and whether the employer is entitled to dismiss or take other retaliatory action. In addition, when workers go on strike consideration has to be given as to the impact that may have on their continuity of service.

Definitions

[18.50] The most obvious and well documented form of industrial action is the strike.[76] It is defined in s 6 of the Redundancy Payments Act 1967 and s 1 of the Minimum Notice and Terms of Employment Act 1973, for the purposes of that legislation, as meaning:

> the cessation of work by a body of persons employed acting in combination, or a concerted refusal or a refusal under a common understanding of any number of persons employed to continue to work for an employer in consequence of a dispute, done as a means of compelling their employer or any person or body of persons employed, or to aid other employees in compelling their employer or any person or body of persons employed, to accept or not to accept terms or conditions of or affecting employment.

An almost identical definition is contained in s 1(1) of the Unfair Dismissals Act 1977.

[18.51] The definition contained in s 8 of the Industrial Relations Act 1990 (which applies also to the Payment of Wages Act 1991) is slightly different, namely:

> a cessation of work by any number or body of workers acting in combination or a concerted refusal or a refusal under a common understanding of any number of workers to continue to work for their employer done as a means of compelling their employer, or to aid other workers in compelling their employer, to accept or not to accept terms or conditions of or affecting employment.

These definitions all contain two essential elements: a cessation of work and concerted action. They are also defined in terms of ends, based on a purpose of compelling employers or others to accept or not to accept terms or conditions of employment. A concerted cessation of work in protest at the Government's policy on asylum seekers, therefore, would not be a strike for the purpose of the above mentioned legislation.

[18.52] Industrial action, however, is a much broader concept than the concerted withdrawal of labour and includes such action as a go-slow, a work-to-rule, an overtime ban or a refusal to perform certain duties. Because employers tend to discontinue the payment of wages or salary to those of their employees who go on strike (and strikers

---

[76] See, for instance, Brannick, Doyle and Kelly 'Industrial Conflict' in Murphy and Roche eds, *Irish Industrial Relations in Practice* (2nd edn, 1997) pp 299–325 and Wallace, Gunnigle and McMahon, *Industrial Relations in Ireland* (3rd edn, 2004) pp. 213–237.

are disentitled to unemployment benefit or assistance[77]), resort to other forms of industrial action is becoming increasingly common.

[18.53] The term 'industrial action' is defined in s 8 of the Industrial Relations Act 1990 (and also for the purposes of the Payment of Wages Act 1991) as meaning:

> any action which affects, or is likely to affect, the terms or conditions, whether express or implied, of a contract and which is taken by any number or body of workers acting in combination or under a common understanding as a means of compelling their employer, or to aid other workers in compelling their employer, to accept or not to accept terms or conditions of or affecting employment.

The term 'industrial action' is also defined in s 1(1) of the Unfair Dismissals Act 1977 in similar terms, subject to a crucial distinction, namely:

> *lawful* action taken by any number or body of employees acting in combination or under a common understanding, in consequence of a dispute, as a means of compelling their employer or any employee or body of employees, or to aid other employees in compelling their employer or any employee or body of employees, to accept or not to accept terms or conditions of or affecting employment (emphasis added).

Continuity

[18.54] As far as the effect on continuity of employment is concerned, this is now governed by the provisions of the First Sch to the Minimum Notice and Terms of Employment Act 1973. Paragraph 1 thereof provides that the service of an employee in his or her employment shall be deemed to be continuous unless that service is terminated either by dismissal or by the employee 'voluntarily leaving' his or her employment. Paragraph 4 then provides that a strike by an employee shall not amount to that employee's 'voluntarily leaving' his or her employment. Paragraph 11 provides that if, in any week or part of a week, an employee is absent from his or her employment because he or she was 'taking part in a strike in relation to the trade or business in which he [or she] is employed' that week shall not count as a period of service. If an employee is absent from his or her employment 'by reason of a strike or lock-out in a trade or business other than that in which he [or she] is employed', paragraph 13 provides that that week *shall* count as a period of service.

---

[77] See Social Welfare (Consolidation) Act 2005, ss 68 and 147 which provide that a person who has lost employment by reason of 'a stoppage of work' due to a trade dispute at his or her place of employment is disqualified from receiving certain social welfare payments. An application, however, can be made to the Social Welfare Tribunal (the Tribunal) which is empowered to consider, *inter alia*, whether a person was deprived of employment 'through some act or omission on the part of the employer concerned which amounted to unfair or unjust treatment': see ss 331–333 of the 2005 Act. The role of the Tribunal, which was first established in 1982 following the High Court decision in *State (Kearns) v Minister for Social Welfare* (10 February 1982, unreported), was recently considered by Murphy J in *Iarnród Éireann v Social Welfare Tribunal* (30 November 2007, unreported). See also Clark 'Towards the 'Just' Strike? Social Welfare Payments for Persons Affected by a Trade Dispute in the Republic of Ireland' (1985) 48 *MLR* 659.

Effect of strike on contract of employment

[18.55] The attitude of the common law was very straightforward. Workers who participated in a strike had either broken or terminated their contracts of employment depending on whether notice of the appropriate length had been given. If the former, it was regarded as repudiation entitling the employer to summarily dismiss.[78] It also had the consequence of exposing both the participants and organisers of the strike to civil liability for the torts of conspiracy, intimidation and inducement of breach of contract.

[18.56] The issue of whether participation in a strike necessarily involved the worker terminating or breaking his or her contract of employment came before the English Court of Appeal in *Morgan v Fry*.[79] Lord Denning MR put forward the novel proposition that, if a strike takes place preceded by due and adequate notice, the contract of employment was neither broken nor terminated; it was suspended and was revived when the strike was over.[80] Neither of his two colleagues agreed. Davies LJ held that strike notice amounted to notice to terminate the existing contract.[81] Russell LJ held that, since a strike was a breach of contract, strike notice amounted to a threatened breach.[82]

[18.57] When the issue subsequently came before the English Employment Appeal Tribunal in *Simmons v Hoover Ltd*,[83] Phillips J reiterated what he considered to be the traditional view, namely that participation in a strike was a repudiatory breach of the contract of employment and that strike notice was merely notice to the employer that the workers were going to break their contracts by going on strike.[84]

Lord Denning's 'suspension' theory was approved, however, by a majority of the Supreme Court in *Becton Dickinson & Co Ltd v Lee*.[85] Walsh J, with whom Ó Dálaigh CJ and Butler J agreed, asserted that there was:

> to be read into every contract of employment an implied term that the service of a strike notice of a length not shorter than would be required for notice to terminate the contract would not in itself amount to notice to terminate the contract and would not in itself constitute a breach of the contract and that to take action on foot of the strike notice would likewise not be a breach of the contract.[86]

[18.58] Walsh J agreed with Lord Denning that it was to be implied into every contract of employment that if a strike takes place, after due notice, the contract is suspended.

---

[78] See, for instance, *Bowes & Partners v Press* [1894] 2 QB 202.

[79] *Morgan v Fry* [1968] 2 QB 710.

[80] [1968] 2 QB 710 at 728.

[81] [1968] 2 QB 710 at 731.

[82] [1968] 2 QB 710 at 734.

[83] *Simmons v Hoover Ltd* [1977] ICR 83.

[84] See also *Boxfoldia Ltd v National Graphical Association* [1988] IRLR 283, where Saville J ruled that, in calling a strike of its members, the union had induced the workers in question wrongfully to repudiate their contracts of employment, even though 14 days' notice had been given.

[85] *Becton Dickinson & Co Ltd v Lee* [1973] IR 1. This decision was subsequently confirmed by a unanimous Supreme Court in *Bates v Model Bakery Ltd* [1993] 1 IR 359.

[86] [1973] IR 1 at 35.

Walsh J observed that such an implied term would not be read into a contract where there was an express provision to the contrary or where by necessary implication a provision to the contrary must be read into the contract. He added however:

> An express no-strike clause in a contract is itself such an unusual feature of the contract of employment and is such an apparent departure from the long-established right to strike that a court would be slow to imply it where it is not expressly included in the contract or where it is not a necessary implication; a court would probably only do so in cases where there was some particular provision for machinery to deal with disputes, the provision being so phrased as to give rise to the implication that it had been agreed between the parties that no other course would be adopted during the currency of the contract.[87]

Dismissal

[18.59] As regards the dismissal of those workers who take part in a strike (as defined) or lawful industrial action, the fairness of same is regulated by s 5(2) of the Unfair Dismissals Act 1977 (the 1977 Act), as amended by s 4 of the Unfair Dismissals (Amendment) Act 1993. That subsection (as amended) provides:

> The dismissal of an employee for taking part in a strike or other industrial action shall be deemed for the purposes of this Act to be an unfair dismissal if –
>
> (a) one of more employees of the same employer who took part in the strike or other industrial action were not dismissed for so taking part, or
>
> (b) one or more of such employees who were dismissed for so taking part were subsequently permitted to resume their employment on terms and conditions at least as favourable to the employees as those specified in paragraph (a) or (b) of subsection (1) of section 7 of this Act and the employee was not.

[18.60] Section 5(2A) of the 1977 Act[88] provides that, without prejudice to the applicability of any of the provisions of s 6 of the 1977 Act, where an employee is dismissed for taking part in a strike or other industrial action, and none of those who took part in the strike or industrial action were re-engaged, in determining whether the dismissal is an unfair dismissal regard should be had to:

(i) the reasonableness or otherwise of the conduct (whether by act or omission) of the employer or employee in relation to the dismissal;

(ii) the extent (if any) of the compliance or failure to comply by the employer with any dismissals procedure;

(iii) the extent (if any) of the compliance or failure to comply by the employer with any ministerially approved Code of Practice; and

---

[87] *Becton Dickinson & Co Ltd v Lee* [1973] IR 1 at 38.

[88] Inserted by the Protection of Employment (Exceptional Collective Redundancies and Related Matters) Act 2007, s 26.

(iv)   whether the parties have adhered to any agreed grievance procedures applicable to the employment in question at the time of the strike or industrial action.

These subsections effect a conclusive presumption that selective dismissals for taking part in a strike or lawful industrial action are unfair.[89] Moreover non-selective dismissals and dismissals for taking part in unlawful industrial action are subject to the general presumption of unfairness established by s 6 of the 1977 Act.[90]

Participation

[18.61] The meaning of the phrase 'taking part in a strike' has not been considered in this jurisdiction but has given rise to some disagreement amongst the English judiciary. In *McCormick v Horsepower Ltd*,[91] Lawton and Templeman LJJ stressed the element of common purpose or concerted interest. Mere refusal to pass a picket line was not enough to prove participation in a strike. In *Coates v Modern Methods and Material Ltd*,[92] Stephenson and Kerr LJJ were of a contrary opinion with the former saying that participation in a strike had to be judged 'by what the employee does and not by what he thinks or why he does it'.[93] Stephenson LJ went on to say that 'in the field of industrial action those who are not openly against it are presumably for it'.

Obligation to pay wages

[18.62] A series of English cases are authority for the proposition that, where a worker is engaged in industrial action which amounts to a breach of his or her contract of employment, the employer is not obliged to pay the worker his or her wages or salary or any part thereof.

[18.63] In *Miles v Wakefield Metropolitan District Council*,[94] the plaintiff was a superintendent registrar of births, deaths and marriages. His normal working week consisted of 37 hours, including three hours on Saturday morning. In August 1981 the plaintiff's trade union instructed all superintendent registrars to take industrial action involving the refusal to conduct weddings on Saturdays. The plaintiff complied with that instruction. He remained willing to work a 37 hour week and to attend to his office on Saturdays to do other work but the MDC made it clear that, if registrars were not prepared to undertake the full range of their duties on Saturdays, they were not required to attend for work on Saturdays and, accordingly, would not be paid. The dispute ended in October 1982.

---

89   See *Tuke v Coilte Teo* [1998] ELR 324.
90   See *Power v National Corrugated Products* UD336/1980.
91   *McCormick v Horsepower Ltd* [1981] ICR 535.
92   *Coates v Modern Methods and Material Ltd* [1982] ICR 763.
93   [1982] ICR 763 at 777.
94   *Miles v Wakefield Metropolitan District Council* [1987] AC 529.

[18.64] Between August 1981 and October 1982 the MDC deducted 3/37ths of the plaintiff's salary representing the three hours pertaining to Saturdays, totalling £774, notwithstanding his attendance to other work on those days. The plaintiff's action to recover the sum was dismissed. The House of Lords held that a worker's right to remuneration depended on his or her doing, or being willing to do, the work that he or she was employed to do and, if he or she declined to do that work, the employer need not pay him or her. The rationale was stated (by Lord Brightman) as being that such workers could not recover their wages or salary because they could not prove that they had performed or intended to perform their contractual obligations. In other words, wages and work are interdependent. A plaintiff in an action for remuneration under a contract of employment must assume the initial burden of proving his or her readiness and willingness to render the services required by the contract (subject to any express or implied term exonerating the employee from inability to perform due, for instance, to illness).

[18.65] In *Wiluszynski v Tower Hamlets London Borough Council,*[95] the plaintiff was employed by the defendant Council as an estate officer with duties including the answering of councillors' inquiries. In response to a union instruction calling on the Council's estate officers not to answer such inquiries during an industrial dispute, the Council notified the officers that, unless they were prepared to answer the inquiries, they would be neither required to attend for work nor paid. If they did attend, such attendance would be regarded as voluntary. For the period 14 August to 17 September 1985, when he carried on his duties on the Council's premises other than answering the councillors' inquiries, the plaintiff was not paid any part of his salary, for which he brought an action to recover. The plaintiff's action was dismissed by the Court of Appeal. Since the plaintiff was in breach of his contract of employment by not performing all of his duties and the Council had made it clear that, if he was not prepared to comply with his contract, he was not required to work and would not be paid, the plaintiff was not entitled to sue for remuneration in the absence of evidence that he performed any part of his duties at the direction or request of the Council.

[18.66] The Court of Appeal specifically rejected the argument that, because the plaintiff had substantially performed his duties and the Council knowingly took the benefit of the work actually done, only a deduction of no more than 5% was permissible.[96]

[18.67] The views expressed in *Miles* and *Wiluszynski*, that an employer is entitled to refuse to accept any partial performance of a contract of employment, were adopted by Judge Ballagh and Judge Smithwick (both of the District Court) in *Loftus v Ulster*

---

95 *Wiluszynski v Tower Hamlets London Borough Council* [1989] ICR 493.
96 See Fox LJ at 500. See, to similar effect, *Ticehurst v British Telecommunications plc* [1992] IRLR 219 but note the decision of Fullager J in *Wellbourne v Australian Postal Commission* [1984] VR 257 and that of Rogers J in *Csomore v Public Service Board of New South Wales* (1987) 10 NSWLR 687.

Bank,[97] *Maher v Allied Irish Banks,*[98] and *O'Donovan v Allied Irish Banks,*[99] although in each of these decisions the plaintiffs succeeded on the particular facts of their case.

[18.68] More recently the issue has been revisited in *Spackman v London Metropolitan University.*[100] The plaintiff was employed by the University as a lecturer. In consequence of a dispute between the University and her trade union, she took part in periods of non-strike industrial action between May and July 2005 in that she and her colleagues, although attending for work, boycotted certain specified activities (principally all quality assurance procedures and processes). The University responded by instituting arrangements whereby a reduction in salary of 30% was made for those staff known to be participating in the industrial action. The plaintiff sought full reimbursement. In the alternative, she argued that the 30% reduction was not commensurate with the actual work undertaken and it was suggested that a deduction of no more than 10% was warranted. An issue also arose as to whether it was possible to make a *quantum meruit* claim in respect of less than full service under a contract of employment.

[18.69] Recorder Luba QC ruled that the University was entitled to make the 30% deduction from the plaintiff's salary in respect of periods of time when she had only given partial performance of her contract of employment. An employee engaging in collective industrial action takes the risk that, even if he or she presents for work and undertakes some or the most part of his or her ordinary duties, the employer may pay him or her nothing at all. If the employee gets anything it would be more than he or she was legally entitled to expect.

[18.70] Recorder Luba QC also ruled that the notion of *quantum meruit* could not realistically apply in the context of collective industrial action short of a strike.

[18.71] In *Cooper v Isle of Wight College,*[101] the claimants took part in industrial action consisting of a one day strike. The College responded by making a deduction from the claimants' salaries. It was not in dispute between the parties that the employer was entitled to make some deduction, having regard to the decision in *Miles*, but the issue raised was the *quantum* of deduction.

Blake J summarised the contending positions as follows:

> Mr White QC for the claimants submits that what *Miles* establishes is that the maximum deduction that can be made in such circumstances is the value of the day's pay that otherwise would be paid to the claimants. Ms Tether for the defendants disputes this and submits that what can be deducted is the loss to the employer of the withdrawal of the

---

[97] *Loftus v Ulster Bank* (1995) 10 JISLL 47. The action was brought in the District Court because the Payment of Wages Act 1991, s 5(5) provides that the relevant provisions of that Act do not apply to a deduction made by an employer from the wages of an employee 'where the employee has taken part in a strike or other industrial action and the deduction is made ...on account of the employee's having taken part in that strike or other industrial action'.

[98] *Maher v Allied Irish Banks* [1998] ELR 204.

[99] *O'Donovan v Allied Irish Banks* [1998] ELR 209.

[100] *Spackman v London Metropolitan University* [2007] IRLR 744.

[101] *Cooper v Isle of Wight College* [2008] IRLR 124.

services of the day of the strike, and that this sum is necessarily greater than the amount the employee would receive by way of pay.[102]

The difference between the two bases for the deduction was explicable by the fact that, under their contracts, the claimants were entitled to receive their normal remuneration for all 'bank and public holidays' and to a further 25 working days in each holiday year. The claimants contended that this produced a formula for calculating a day's pay of 1/260 achieved by deducting the 104 weekend and non-working days from the 365 days in a normal calendar year and discounting the odd day. The defendants submitted that the formula should be 1/228 which discounted the paid holidays to which the claimants were entitled.

[18.72] Before adjudicating on the parties' respective submissions, Blake J considered whether the deduction should instead be calculated as 1/365 but he concluded that, where there was a definition of a 'normal working week' in the contract and a contractual entitlement to holiday pay, then the salary payable should be apportioned over the days of the normal working week throughout the year.

[18.73] Having examined the 'applicable reasoning' in *Miles*, Blake J. concluded that the correct test was to determine 'whether the employee could sue for the withheld wages rather than focusing on what the overall losses to the employer were by reason of the partial non-performance'. Consequently Blake J. was satisfied that the wage that was payable on the day of the strike was '1/260 rather than 1/228 of the annual wage payable'.[103]

---

[102] *Cooper v Isle of Wight College* [2008] IRLR 124 at 125.
[103] [2008] IRLR 124 at 127.

Part VIII
Transfer of Undertakings

Chapter 19

Transfer of Undertakings

Gary Byrne

INTRODUCTION

[19.01] Ireland's common law system bases the employment relationship between employer and employee on their contractual relationship. That contractual relationship is examined in detail in Ch 2, The Contract and Relationship of Employment. As noted in Ch 3, The Terms of the Employment Contract, the employment relationship is significantly supplemented by the addition of implied terms at common law and the overlay of a large amount of statute law forming a significant web of rights and obligations applicable to both parties. One area where significant difficulty arose in the past for employees was the transfer of the business in which they were employed to a new employer. Where there is a change of shareholder in a company, the company itself, which is the party contracting with the employee does not change and continues to own and operate the business in which the employee is employed. There is, therefore, no change in the contract between the employing entity and the employee.

Difficulties can arise, however, where the employer ceases to own or operate the business such as in an asset sale. In an asset sale, the employing company sells the tangible and intangible assets of the business it owns and operates. The assets are taken over by another legal entity which continues or resumes the operation of the business, whether in an identical or an altered fashion.

Under the law of contract, if someone takes over the shareholding in a company they take all the liabilities of that company, which would include contracts of employment and, therefore, the workforce of that company. If, however, it simply purchases assets from the first legal entity it becomes the owner of those assets only and it does not automatically follow that anything else transfers such as debts, liabilities, employees, collective agreements etc. It was therefore possible to purchase the assets of a business and leave the employees behind. The assets could then be used to carry on a similar or identical business with new employees. The employees of the former owner/operator of the business would remain contracted to that employer who may have no further need for them and they became redundant.

[19.02] Until 1977, there was no protection available in law in Ireland for employees whose employer sold on the business in an asset sale, other than some statutory provisions that preserved continuity and other statutory benefits but only if the employees transferred to the new employer which in turn could only be done by agreement. Even where the new employer was to take employees of the former business into its employment it had no obligation to do so on any particular terms and could offer transferring employees terms and conditions significantly less beneficial than they enjoyed with the previous owner of the business. There was therefore a need for protection for employees where their employer sold on the business activity, but not the employing entity, what Dr John McMullen describes as a 'statutory bridge' between the old and new employments to allow employees the right to remain in employment with the new employer.[1] This was addressed by what was then the EEC in enacting a Directive on the transfer of undertakings known as the Acquired Rights Directive 1977. That Directive was succeeded by two further Directives.

HISTORY AND BACKGROUND TO THE ACQUIRED RIGHTS DIRECTIVES

[19.03] In the early 1970s, a proposal was put to the European Parliament that a Directive be enacted to confer rights on employees to transfer in the event of the business in which they were employed changing hands and to provide for the harmonisation of the relevant legislation of Member States. Various reports, proposals and draft Directives were worked on through 1974 and 1975 with the final draft Directive being completed in 1976. The Acquired Rights Directive 1977 was ultimately adopted by the Council of the European Union on 14 February 1977. This first Acquired Rights Directive gave rise to considerable legal debate in particular on its applicability to a myriad of day to day situations that arose in relation to the transfer of businesses in Europe. The case law of the European Court of Justice (ECJ) pointed up significant flaws and problems with the original Directive which led to a proposal in 1994 that an amending or replacing Directive be enacted.

[19.04] On 29 June 1988, the Council adopted a new Directive 98/50/EC. The case law of the ECJ continued to throw up difficulties of interpretation and a large body of case law grew up around the area of transfers of undertakings. It was hoped that the second Directive would address certain problems that had arisen with the operation of the first Directive, most notably the lack of clarity on how contracting out of services by an employer should be treated[2] the difficulties that had arisen regarding information and consultation with employees and the very significant problem of the original Directive apparently having taken away from both employers and employees the right to agree new terms and conditions consequent on or subsequent to a transfer of an undertaking. Directive 98/50 also sought to refine the definition of a transfer which had proven to be surprisingly problematic. This was sought to be achieved in Art 1(3) of Directive 98/50. The new Directive did not definitively address the question of joint and several liability of a transferor and a transferee which was a practical requirement that was much needed and provided for in the original draft of the Directive but left that issue to Member States. The Directive also relaxed certain of the rules regarding insolvency and tidied up the information and consultation requirements. Unfortunately however the Directive proved to be something of a sticking plaster solution which brought about very little change and left many situations where there was still considerable confusion as to the

---

[1] See Dr McMullen's detailed and comprehensive work on the law in relation to transfer of undertakings, *Business Transfers and Employee Rights* (LexisNexis Butterworths, looseleaf, update December 2008). The discussion of the 'statutory bridge' is contained in the Introduction, section C.

[2] See, as examples, Case C-392/92 *Schmidt* [1994] ECR I-1311 and Case C-13/95 *Süzen* [1997] ECR I-1259.

precise legal requirements of the law on transfer of undertakings, Directive 98/50 amended Directive 77/187 rather than repealing and replacing it. It quickly became apparent that a proper codification of the law on transfer of undertakings was required.

[19.05] Council Directive No 2001/23/EC of 12 March 2001 (the Acquired Rights Directive) is the third Directive on the approximation of the laws of the Member States relating to the safeguarding of employees' rights in the event of transfers of undertakings, businesses or parts of undertakings or businesses. The Directive adds to, and consolidates, the 1977 and 1998 Directives. The Directive provides in its preamble:

> Whereas
>
> (1) Council Directive 77/187/EEC of 14 February 1977 on the approximation of the laws of the Member States relating to the safeguarding of employees' rights in the event of transfers of undertakings, businesses or parts of undertakings or businesses has been substantially amended. In the interests of clarity and rationality, it should therefore be codified...
>
> (3) It is necessary to provide for the protection of employees in the event of a change of employer, in particular, to ensure that their rights are safeguarded.
>
> (4) Differences still remain in the Member States as regards the extent of the protection of employees in this respect and these differences should be reduced.

The aim of the 2001 Directive was to reduce the differences then existing in Member States on the protection of employees in situations where the ownership of the undertaking in which they worked, changed to a new employer.

The Irish Regulations

[19.06] The Irish Government decided to effectively adopt the wording of the Directive verbatim by way of Statutory Instrument and on 11 April 2003 the Minister for Enterprise, Trade and Employment signed into law the European Communities (Protection of Employees on Transfer of Undertakings) Regulations 2003 (the Regulations).[3] The Regulations revoke and repeal the previous legislation on the transfers of undertakings.[4] The Regulations also effect compliance with the Acquired Rights Directive.

Between February 1977, when the first Directive was enacted, and March 2001 when the Acquired Rights Directive was enacted, Courts and Tribunals throughout the European Union and in particular the ECJ heard many cases and applied the law to the particular facts of those cases thereby giving guidance as the interpretation of the wording of the Acquired Rights Directive 1977. The Directive and the Regulations therefore allowed the opportunity for the legislature to clarify a number of interpretations that were less than clear and some that appeared to be contradictory. In the main that opportunity was not taken and some areas such as outsourcing/change of contractors remain problematic.

---

[3] SI 131/2003.
[4] SI 306/1980 and SI 487/2000.

SCOPE OF DIRECTIVE AND REGULATIONS

[19.07] 'Employee' is defined under the Regulations as a person of any age, who has entered into or works under (or, where the employment has ceased, entered into or worked under) a contract of employment. Other persons deemed to be employees for the purpose of the Regulations are:

(a) A person holding office under, or in the service of, the State;

(b) A civil servant within the meaning of the Civil Service Regulation Act 1956 (No. 46 of 1956) shall be deemed to be an employee employed by the State or Government; and

(c) An officer or servant of a harbour authority, health board or vocational education committee shall be deemed to be an employee employed by the authority, board or committee.

Persons employed on seagoing vessels are not covered by the Regulations as seagoing vessels are specifically excluded from the scope of the Directive and Regulations.

The Regulations do not apply to a share sale because there must be a change of employer.[5]

Where the Directive and/or Regulations are breached, liability in the main falls on the transferee. If an employer ceases to trade by reason of insolvency and the business is subsequently transferred the provisions of the Directive and Regulations will not apply. Regulation 6 excludes the transfer of an undertaking, business or part of an undertaking or business where the transferor is the subject of bankruptcy or insolvency proceedings. However, if the sole or main reason for the institution of bankruptcy or insolvency proceedings in respect of a transfer is the evasion of an employer's legal obligation under the Regulations, the Regulations will apply to the transfer.

The Regulations apply to public and private undertakings engaged in economic activities whether or not they are operating for gain.[6] The administrative reorganisation of public administrative authorities or the transfer of administrative functions between public administrative authorities is not a transfer for the purposes of the Regulations, as held by the ECJ in *Henke v Gemeinde Schierke and Verwaltungsgemeinschaft 'Brocken'*.[7]

Undertaking

[19.08] Article 1(a) of the Acquired Rights Directive provides:

> This Directive shall apply to any transfer of an undertaking, business or part of an undertaking or business to another employer as a result of a legal transfer or merger.

The term 'undertaking' is not defined by the Directive or the Regulations. Regulation 3(2) defines 'transfer' as 'the transfer of an economic entity which retains its identity'.

---

[5] EC (Protection of Employees on Transfer of Undertakings) Regulations 2003, Reg 3(1). See ECJ decision in *Allen v Amalgamated Construction Co Ltd* [2000] IRLR 119.

[6] SI 131/2003, Reg 3(3).

[7] Case C-298/94 *Henke v Gemeinde Schierke and Verwaltungsgemeinschaft Brocken* [1996] IRLR 701.

'Economic entity' is defined in Reg 3(2) as:

> an organised grouping of resources which has the objective of pursuing an economic activity whether or not that activity is for profit or whether it is ancillary to another economic or administrative entity.

Economic entity/undertaking

[19.09] The way in which the ECJ has approached the concept of an economic entity indicates that the term 'economic entity' is interchangeable with the term 'undertaking'. In *Süzen v Zehnacker Gebaudereinigung GmbH Krankenhausservice*[8] the ECJ observed:

> The aim of the Directive is to ensure continuity of employment relationships within an economic entity ... The decisive criterion for establishing the existence of a transfer within the meaning of the Directive is whether the entity in question retains its identity as indicated *inter alia* by the fact that its operation is actually continued or resumed. For the Directive to be applicable the transfer must relate to a stable economic entity whose activity is not limited to performing one specific works contract. The term economic entity thus refers to an organised grouping of persons and assets facilitating the exercise of an economic activity which pursues a specific objective.

In the UK case of *Isles of Scilly Council v Brintel Helicopters Ltd and Ellis* the EAT stated:[9]

> An economic entity may well just comprise activities and employees. In the service industry tangible assets may be unimportant or possibly non-existent. Thus for example the economic entity may consist of the provision of services where the real asset may be goodwill or possibly just the right to provide the service in question.

Transfer

[19.10] The Regulations apply to any transfer of an undertaking, business, or part of an undertaking or business from one employer to another employer as a result of a legal transfer (including the assignment or forfeiture of a lease) or merger.[10]

'Transfer' is defined as 'the transfer of an economic entity which retains its identity'.[11]

[19.11] *Spijkers*[12] was one of the earliest decisions of the ECJ interpreting the terms of the Directive, and one which continues to maintain seminal importance in the law relating to the transfer of undertakings. Mr Spijkers worked for a company known as Colaris at their slaughterhouse located in the inappropriately-named Ubach über

---

8 Case C-13/95 *Süzen* [1997] ECR I-1259.

9 *Isles of Scilly Council v Brintel Helicopters Ltd and Ellis* [1995] IRLR 6.

10 EC (Protection of Employees on Transfer of Undertakings) Regulations 2003, Reg 3(1). This gives effect to Case C-324/84 *Foreningen Af Arbejdsledere i Danmark v Daddy's Dance Hall A/S* [1988] ECR 739 in which the ECJ decided these transactions were covered by the Directive.

11 EC (Protection of Employees on Transfer of Undertakings) Regulations 2003, Reg 3(2). This gives effect to the ECJ case of Case C-24/85 *Spijkers v Gebroeders Benedik Abbatoir CV* [1986] ECR 1119.

12 Case C-24/85 *Spijkers v Gebroeders Benedik Abbatoir CV* [1986] ECR 1119.

Worms. Colaris agreed to sell the slaughterhouse together with offices, land and specified equipment to Benedik CV on 27 December 1982. From that date Colaris ceased trading. No trading was carried out until Benedik commenced trading on 7 February 1983. There was, therefore, no goodwill in the business at the time Benedik commenced trading. Benedik did not commence the identical trade as Colaris but carried on a similar type of trade using all of the Colaris employees, whom it re-employed under contracts agreed with those employees, with the exception of Mr Spijkers and one other employee who was too ill to work. Mr Spijkers claimed that there had been a transfer of an undertaking and that Benedik should pay him from 27 December 1982 and provide him with work. Advocate General Slynn made the following observations in his opinion:[13]

> It is clear that the overriding objective of the Directive is to protect workers in a business which is transferred. In deciding whether there has been a transfer ... all the circumstances have to be looked at. Technical rules are to be avoided ... the substance matters more than the form. The essential question is whether the transferee has obtained a business or an undertaking (or a part thereof) which he can continue to operate. That at the time of transfer the business is still active, that machinery is being used, customers supplied, workers employed and that all the physical assets and goodwill are sold are strong indications that a transfer ... has taken place. But these are not all necessary pre-requisites of a transfer in every case ... the fact that at the date of transfer trading has ceased or has been substantially reduced does not prevent there being a transfer of a business if the wherewithal to carry on the business such as plant, building and employees are available and are transferred. Nor is the fact that goodwill or existing contracts are not transferred conclusive against there being a transfer.[14]

The Court followed that line of reasoning and held that in order for a business activity to come within the definition of the transfer of an undertaking 'the business in question ... [must] ... retain its identity'. The Court held that there did not need to be a transfer of goodwill and that there could be cessation and resumption of the same or similar economic activities and stated:[15]

> Consequently it cannot be said that there is a transfer of an enterprise, business or part of a business on the sole ground that its assets have been sold. On the contrary, in a case like the present, it is necessary to determine whether what has been sold is an economic entity which is still in existence and this will be apparent from the fact that its operation is actually being continued or has been taken over by the new employer, with the same economic or similar activities.

The Court then set out the factors that must be considered in ascertaining if a transfer has taken place:

> To decide whether these conditions are fulfilled it is necessary to take account of all the factual circumstances of the transaction in question including the type of undertaking or business in question, the transfer or otherwise of tangible assets such as buildings and stocks, the value of intangible assets at the date of transfer, whether the majority of the

---

[13]   Case C-24/85 *Spijkers v Gebroeders Benedik Abbatoir CV* [1986] ECR 1119.
[14]   Case C-24/85 *Spijkers v Gebroeders Benedik Abbatoir CV* [1986] ECR 1119.
[15]   Case C-24/85 *Spijkers v Gebroeders Benedik Abbatoir CV* [1986] ECR 1119.

staff are taken over by the new employer, the transfer or otherwise of the circle of customers and the degree of similarity between activities before and after the transfer, and the duration of any interruption in those activities. It should remain clear however that each of these factors is only a part of the overall assessment which is required and therefore they cannot be examined independently of each other.

The *Spijkers* tests for identifying the existence of a transfer have survived the passage of time and are still relevant. It must be kept in mind, however, that each of the tests is in itself merely guidance and when each test has been answered the totality has to be assessed to see whether or not it adds up to there being a transfer.

Cessation and later resumption

[19.12] The fact that a transferor ceases the business entirely and there is then a lapse of time before the transferee resumes the business does not prevent there being a transfer of the undertaking or business concerned. Advocate General Slynn went on to observe in *Spijkers*:[16]

> That after the sale there is a gap before trading is resumed is a relevant fact but it is not conclusive against there being a transfer within the meaning of the Directive. The transferee may well want to spend time reorganising or renovating the premises or equipment ... the fact that the business is carried on in a different way is not conclusive against there being a transfer – new methods, new machinery, new types of customer are relevant factors but they do not of themselves prevent there being in reality a transfer of a business or undertaking. Though it is plain that a sale may take place simply of the physical assets or part of them with no intention in any real sense that the business should thereafter be carried on care must be taken to ensure that such a sale is not a disguise to avoid obligations to the workers.

In the High Court case of *Sheehy v Ryan & Moriarty*[17] the plaintiff had been employed as diocesan secretary by Bishop Lennon. Bishop Lennon was succeeded by the first defendant Bishop Ryan who served notice of termination of employment on the plaintiff on 22 July 2002. Bishop Moriarty succeeded Bishop Ryan with effect from 31 August 2002. The plaintiff's notice expired on 19 September 2002. As part of a number of claims the plaintiff claimed that the change of Bishop between the two defendants constituted the transfer of an undertaking. The High Court rejected this argument stating that the diocese did not change its identity on the appointment of a new Bishop and that a change of Bishop was more akin to a change in managing director and could not be construed as a transfer of an undertaking.

Change of ownership

[19.13] *Spijkers* is a straightforward case of a business changing hands. It was understood initially that the Directive only applied on a change of ownership. However, the decision in *Daddy's Dance Hall*[18] showed that the Directive could apply where there

---

[16] C-24/85 *Spijkers v Gebroeders Benedik Abbatoir CV* [1986] ECR 1119.
[17] *Sheehy v Ryan & Moriarty* [2004] 4 ELR 87.
[18] Case 324/84 *Foreningen af Arbejdsledere i Danmark v Daddy's Dance Hall A/S* [1988] ECR 739.

was no change in the legal owner of a business but rather a change in the person or body responsible for the management or day-to-day operation of the business.

Irma Catering, a company, leased restaurants and bars from another company, Palads Teatret. The lease was determined on 28 January 1983 with effect from 25 February 1983. Mr Tellerup was an employee of the business operated by Irma Catering and was dismissed on notice to expire on 30 April 1983. On 25 February 1983, a new lease was granted by Palads Teatret to a different company, Daddy's Dance Hall. Mr Tellerup was re-engaged by Daddy's Dance Hall. He was later dismissed by Daddy's Dance Hall on 26 April 1983. A dispute arose about the terms of Mr Tellerup's employment at the date of termination and the length of notice to which he was entitled from Daddy's Dance Hall. It was held that Daddy's Dance Hall must carry the liabilities of Irma Catering. The ECJ held that the Directive applies to a situation where, after the termination of a lease, the owner of the undertaking leases it to a new lessee who continues to run the business and held, 'It is of no importance to know whether the ownership of the undertaking has been transferred'. It should be noted that there was no contract between Irma Catering and Daddy's Dance Hall. The Court held:[19]

> The Directive therefore applies as soon as there is a change, resulting from a conventional sale or from a merger, of the natural or legal person responsible for operating the undertaking who consequently enters into obligations as an employer towards the employees working in the undertaking and it is of no importance to know whether the ownership of the undertaking has been transferred.

> It follows that when the lessee who has the capacity of proprietor of the undertaking at the termination of the lease loses this capacity and a third person acquires it under a new lease concluded with the owner the resulting operation is capable of falling within the scope of application of the Directive as defined in Article 1(1). The fact that in such case the transfer takes place in two phases in the sense that as a first step the undertaking is transferred back from the original lessee to the owner who then transfers it to the new lessee, does not exclude the applicability of the Directive as long as the economic unit retains its identity. This is the case in particular when as in the instant case the business continues to be run without interruption from the new lessee with the same staff that was employed in the undertaking before the transfer.

[19.14] A similar line of reasoning to the *Daddy's Dance Hall* decision was followed in *Landsorganisationen i Danmark v Ny Mølle Kro*[20] and in *Berg and Busschers v Besselsen*[21]

[19.15] This approach was followed by the Employment Appeals Tribunal in *Guidon v Hugh Farrington and Ushers Island Petrol Station*[22] the claimant worked with Local Stores (Trading) Ltd trading as Seven-Eleven. Seven-Eleven had a branch in the Ushers Island Petrol Station which was owned by Mr Farrington. Seven-Eleven went into receivership and its lease at Ushers Island was surrendered on 14 June 1991, which was

---

[19] Case 324/84 *Foreningen af Arbejdsledere i Danmark v Daddy's Dance Hall A/S* [1988] ECR 739, at paras 9 and 10.

[20] Case 287/86 *Landsorganisationen i Danmark v Ny Mølle Kro* [1987] ECR 5465.

[21] Joined Cases 144 and 145/87 *Berg and Busschers v Besselsen* [1988] ECR 2559.

[22] *Guidon v Hugh Farrington and Ushers Island Petrol Station* [1993] ELR 98.

a Friday and a normal day of work for the claimant. The claimant returned to work at Ushers Island on 17 June 1991 and was advised that her employment had terminated. She claimed to have been unfairly dismissed by the respondent and claimed that the respondent was a transferee within the meaning of the Directive and Regulations, the lease having been surrendered and the business reverting to him. The EAT had regard to the ECJ decisions in *Ny Mølle Kro* and *Berg v Besselsen* and held that there had been a transfer of the undertaking of the Seven-Eleven shop to the respondent Mr Farrington. The dismissal of the claimant on the grounds of transfer was prohibited by the Directive and Regulations and in the circumstances was deemed to be unfair.

Contractual relationship between transferor and transferee

[19.16] The *Daddy's Dance Hall*,[23] *Ny Mølle Kro*[24] and *Berg*[25] cases illustrate how a transfer may result even where there is no contract between the transferor and the transferee. This was made very clear in *Redmond Stichting v Bartol*.[26] The Dr Sophie Redmond Foundation provided assistance to drug addicts, including those of a particular ethnic origin, in the Netherlands. The foundation was funded by grants from the Groningen local authority. The local authority terminated the grants to the Redmond Foundation and instead funded another foundation, the Sigma Foundation, which provided general assistance to those who had problems with drug dependency on condition that that foundation would be accessible to drug addicts. The clients/patients of the Redmond Foundation were transferred to the Sigma Foundation. The local authority had been leasing a building to the Redmond Foundation which they transferred to Sigma. Some of the Redmond employees transferred to the Sigma Foundation on foot of offers of new contracts of employment from Sigma.

Some of those employees not transferred to the Sigma Foundation who had been employed by the Redmond Foundation claimed that there had been a transfer of an undertaking within the meaning of the Directive and that their employment should transfer also. The ECJ held that the Directive applied.[27] The main points to note from the judgment are:

(i)   There is a transfer where a public body terminates a subsidy paid to one legal entity as a result of which the activities of that entity are terminated and transferred to another legal entity with similar aims.

---

23 Case 324/84 *Foreningen af Arbejdsledere i Danmark v Daddy's Dance Hall A/S* [1988] ECR 739.
24 Case 287/86 *Landsorganisationen i Danmark v Ny Mølle Kro* [1987] ECR 5465.
25 Joined Cases 144 and 145/87 *Berg and Busschers v Besselsen* [1988] ECR 2559.
26 Case C-29/91 *Redmond (Dr Sophie) Stichting v Bartol* [1992] ECR I-3189.
27 See also Case C-172/94 *Merckx and Neuhuys v Ford Motor Co Belgium SA* [1996] ECR I-1253 where the ECJ held that the Directive applied where an undertaking holding a motor vehicle dealership for a particular territory discontinued its business and the dealership is then transferred to another undertaking which takes on part of its staff and is recommended to customers, without any transfer of assets.

(ii)   The Directive does not exclude non-profit-making bodies such as charities or foundations. The Directive applies to all employees who are covered by a protection against dismissal under national law even if it is limited.

(iii) The fact that the termination of the subsidy to the Redmond Foundation was a unilateral act of the local authority did not affect the determination as to whether or not there had been a transfer.

(iv)   The decisive criterion for establishing whether there is a transfer of an undertaking is whether the unit in question retains its identity after the transfer. In order to ascertain whether or not there is a transfer it is necessary to determine whether the functions performed are in fact carried out or resumed by the new legal entity with the same or similar activities.

The decision makes clear that privatisations of hitherto publicly provided services may come within the scope of the Directive and Regulations.

Transfer of part of an undertaking

[19.17] The Regulations provide that they apply not just to the transfer of an undertaking or business but also to the transfer of part of an undertaking or business. It has been seen that where part of a business is an economic entity in itself that part may be easily identifiable as the subject matter of a transfer of part of a business. Difficulties may arise where the part sold off or transferred was not a readily identifiable economic entity prior to the transfer as it depended for its existence on being part of a larger economic entity.

[19.18] The issue, in particular, can be what employees are transferred with the part of the business. The question of how to identify the employees to be so transferred was considered by the ECJ in *Botzen v Rotterdamsche Droogdok Maatschappij*.[28] Mr Botzen and his seven co-plaintiffs were assigned to parts of a business which were not the subject matter of transfer. One of the questions addressed to the Court was:

> Does the scope of the Directive also extend to the rights conferred upon and the obligations imposed upon the transferor by contracts of employment which exist at the date of transfer and which are made with employees whose duties are not performed exclusively with the aid of assets which belong to the transferred part of the undertaking?

Advocate General Slynn dealt with the issue as follows:

> I do not consider that it is necessary or desirable in this case to seek to define comprehensively what is 'part of' a business. That is largely a question of fact though it will usually involve the transfer of a department or factory or facet of the business. It may perhaps also involve the sale of a fraction of a single unit of business. Once it is decided as a fact that part of the business is transferred then those workers who during their working hours are wholly engaged in that part are entitled to rely on the terms of the Directive. It will of course cover the full-time and part-time workers. A basic working test, it seems to me, is to ask whether, if that part of the business had been separately owned before the transfer the worker would have been employed by the owners of that part over the owners of the remaining part. The only exception I would admit to the requirement that an employee must be 'wholly' engaged in that part of the business would be where an

---

[28]   Case C-186/83 *Botzen v Rotterdamsche Droogdok Maatschappij* [1985] ECR 519.

employee was required to perform other duties to an extent which could fairly be described as *de minimis*. On the other hand if a worker in fact is engaged in the activities of the whole business or in several parts then he cannot be regarded for the purpose of the Directive as an employee 'of' the part of the business transferred.

The decision of the full court in *Botzen* is not particularly helpful in that the Court held that the test to be applied was whether or not there had been a transfer of the part of the business for which the employee was assigned and which formed the organisational framework within which their employment relationship took effect. The Advocate General's guidance remains useful.

Part of an undertaking or a mere activity

[19.19] The subject matter of a transfer is not always easily distinguishable as being part of the undertaking from which it is transferred. The question may arise as to whether or not it is an integral part of the economic entity constituting the undertaking or, alternatively, whether it is merely an activity of the undertaking which activity in itself is not an economic activity capable of being the subject matter of a transfer within the meaning of the Directive. The ECJ gave guidance on this issue in *Schmidt*.[29] The bank which employed Ms Schmidt, which of itself was clearly an 'undertaking', decided that it no longer wished to employ Ms Schmidt to carry out daily cleaning work of the bank and decided to contract out the work to a contract cleaning company. The question arose, however, as to whether or not the cleaning work constituted part of the undertaking of the bank. The bank contended that the performance of the cleaning operations was neither the main function nor an ancillary function of the undertaking. Therefore, the bank claimed, the contract did not involve the transfer of an economic unit and did not come within the scope of the Directive. In its submissions to the Court, the Commission took the view that if the cleaning was carried out by staff of the undertaking it was a service which the undertaking itself performed and the fact that such work was merely an ancillary activity not necessarily connected with the main objects of the undertaking could not have the effect of excluding the transfer from the scope of the Directive. The Court held:[30]

> The fact that the activity in question was performed prior to the transfer, by a single employee [is not sufficient] to preclude the application of the Directive.

> The decisive criterion for establishing whether there is a transfer ... is whether the business in question retains its identity. ... the retention of that identity is indicated *inter alia* by the actual continuation or resumption by the new employer of the same or similar activities.

TRANSFER OF CONTRACT RIGHTS AND OBLIGATIONS

[19.20] One of the main effects of a transfer coming within the scope of the Directive and Regulations is provided in Reg 4(1):

---

[29] Case C-392/92 *Schmidt Spar und Leibkasse der Fruheren amter Bordesholm* [1994] ECR I-1311.
[30] Case C-392/92 *Schmidt Spar und Leibkasse der Fruheren amter Bordesholm* [1994] ECR I-1311 at paras 15 and 17.

The transferor's rights and obligations arising from a contract of employment existing on the date of a transfer shall, by reason of such transfer, be transferred to the transferee.

[19.21] In *Astley v Celtec Ltd,*[31] the ECJ provided guidance as to the meaning of the term 'date of a transfer':

[t]he date of a transfer within the meaning of that provision is the date on which responsibility as employer for carrying on the business of the unit transferred moves from the transferor to the transferee. That date is a particular point in time, which cannot be postponed to another date at the will of the transferor or transferee.

[19.22] The ECJ held in *Berg and Busschers v Besselsen*[32] that, in circumstances where Member States have not determined that the transferor and the transferee shall be severally liable after the transfer, Art 3(1) must be interpreted as meaning that, after the date of a transfer, the transferor is, by virtue of the transfer alone, discharged from liability. In *Rotsart de Hertaing v J Benoidt SA (in liquidation)*[33] the ECJ held:

Article 3(1) of the Directive is to be interpreted as meaning that the contracts of employment and employment relationships existing on the date of the transfer of an undertaking, between the transferor and the workers employed in the under- taking transferred, are automatically transferred from the transferor to the transferee by the mere fact of the transfer of the undertaking, despite the contrary intention of the transferor or transferee and despite the latter's refusal to fulfil his obligations.

The right to object

[19.23] The transfer of the employee from transferor to transferee is automatic irrespective of the wishes of either party. This is subject only to the right of the employee to object to a transfer of his or her employment relationship. The ECJ held in *Katsikas v Konstantinidis*[34] that employees were entitled to object to the transfer of their employment contract. The legal effect of this objection is a matter for each Member State to determine. In England, in the event that an employee objects to the transfer the employee will be treated as having resigned from employment with the transferor. The British Transfer of Undertakings Regulations provide that where an employee objects to a transfer, his contract with the transferor is at an end but he will not be treated as having been dismissed by the transferor. The Irish Regulations do not deal with this issue. However, in *Leddy v Symantec,*[35] the EAT ruled that an employee who objects to working with a new employer may prevent the transfer of the employment relationship to the transferee and may also claim a redundancy payment from the transferor.[36]

Agreement to change

[19.24] It may be desirable from a commercial and industrial relations point of view that the parties to an employment relationship should remain free to agree changes in terms

---

[31] Case C-478/03 *Astley v Celtec Ltd* [2005] IRLR 647.

[32] Joined Cases 144 and 145/87 *Berg and Busschers v Besselsen* [1988] ECR 2559.

[33] Case C-305/94 *Rotsart de Hertaing v J Benoidt SA (in liquidation)* [1996] ECR I-52927.

[34] Cases C-132, 138, 139/91 *Katsikas v Konstantinidis* [1993] ECR I-6577.

[35] *Leddy v Symantec* RP200/2007 (EAT).

[36] This case is considered in McMullen, *Business Transfers and Employee Rights* (LexisNexis Butterworths, looseleaf, update December 2008), Ch 15, para 43.3.

and conditions of employment regardless of whether or not a transfer is or has taken place within the meaning of the Directive. Regulation 9 provides that any provision in an agreement which excludes or limits the application of any provision of the Regulations shall be void. If a provision in an agreement is or becomes less favourable to an employee than a similar entitlement conferred by the Regulations, then the agreement is deemed to be 'modified so as not to be less favourable'. Regulation 9 clarifies that nothing in the Regulations shall be construed as prohibiting the inclusion in an agreement of a provision more favourable to an employee than any provision of the Regulations. As the Regulations specifically transfer the then existing contractual rights as of the date of a transfer, this provision has to be read as allowing employees to agree more favourable terms.

The rights and obligations that transfer

[19.25] The rights of employees which become subject to transfer and the obligations of the transferee consequent on the transfer depend on the rights and obligations that were in existence as of the date of transfer. To ascertain the full extent of such rights and obligations the existence of a contract of employment or employment relationship as of the date of transfer must be established. The terms and conditions applying as between the parties must then be analysed to ascertain what exactly transfers.

[19.26] The extent of potential liabilities that may be the subject of a transfer is considerable and includes all contractual liabilities such as remuneration, holidays and other benefits including benefits-in-kind. The contractual liabilities that transfer may include rights to 'golden parachutes' that may, for example, be contained in senior executive service agreements and which may be triggered by the transfer; and contractual rights to enhanced redundancy payments.

One of the main problems for a transferee is where the contractual matters that transfer were particularly tailored to the transferor's identity. The transferee may simply not be in a position to replicate these contractual benefits even if the transferee wished to do so.

Disciplinary procedures, grievance procedures and other internal procedures geared toward one organisation theoretically transfer. Liability for breach of contract may arise if they are not replicated, which may then compel the transferee to compensate the transferring employee. For example, commission schemes may be related to the transferor's performance as opposed to the individual's performance. It simply would not be feasible for the transferee to honour such a scheme. Whatever the problems, the contractual obligation transfers and the transferee should implement a scheme similar to that of the transferor providing for similar remuneration or rewards as a way of reducing damages which could flow in a breach of contract claim.[37]

---

[37] See *Mitie Managed Services Ltd v French* [2002] ICR 1395 where the UK EAT held, in relation to a claim that a profit sharing scheme must transfer, that the entitlement of the transferred employee in such a case is to participation in a scheme of substantial equivalence.

Collective agreements

[19.27] As all rights and entitlements of employees who transfer must be honoured by the transferee, benefits under collective agreements also transfer. If the collective agreement is applicable only to the transferor company then the collective agreement is likely to transfer in full to the transferee. There are, however, collective agreements that might apply generally to a group of employers, perhaps in the State sector or in a particular industry, and the transferee may not be part of that group. The collective agreement may not then apply to the transferee after the transfer.

Transfer of restrictive covenants

[19.28] While practitioners tend to focus on the *obligations* that pass to the transferee, the *rights* of the transferor vis-à-vis its employees also pass to the transferee. Given that the Regulations are clear that the rights of a transferor arising from a contract of employment or from an employment relationship transfer to the transferee then it is to be expected that if restrictive covenants are otherwise effective in law the benefit of those restrictive covenants and contractual obligations must pass to the transferee. This is a comparatively rare situation, in which an employer may seek to invoke the terms of the Regulations in its favour.[38]

Pension entitlements

[19.29] Regulation 4(3) deals with rights under or in connection with occupational pension schemes, and is in marked contrast to the provision in Reg 4(1) that a transferor's rights and obligations arising from a contract of employment existing on the date of a transfer shall, by reason of the transfer, be transferred to the transferee. Regulation 4(3) makes a significant qualification to this general requirement in stating that the general obligation to honour all the terms and conditions of a contract of employment does not 'apply in relation to employees' rights to old-age or survivors' benefits under supplementary or inter-company pension schemes' falling outside the Social Welfare Acts.[39] However, Reg 4(4)(b) provides for an obligation on the part of a transferee to ensure that the interests of employees and of persons no longer employed in the transferor's business are protected in respect of rights conferring on them immediate or prospective entitlement to old age benefits including survivors' benefits.

INFORMATION AND CONSULTATION

[19.30] The parties to a transfer have obligations to notify, inform and possibly to consult employees and their representatives before the transfer takes effect. Given the importance to employees of a change in their employer, it is essential in order for employees to protect their own interests that they get advance notice of any proposed change and the Directive and Regulations make specific and wide-ranging provisions in this regard. These provisions are particularly important to anyone entering into negotiations for the purchase or transfer of a business.

---

[38] See *Morris Angel & Son Ltd v Hollande* [1993] IRLR 169.
[39] This carve-out is provided in Art 3(4)(a) of the Directive.

[19.31] Article 7 of the Acquired Rights Directive confers joint obligations on the transferor and the transferee to inform employee representatives of the reasons for the transfer, the legal, economic and social implications of the transfer for the employees, and of any measures envisaged in relation to the employees. This information is to be given in good time before the transfer is carried out and, in any event, before the employees are directly affected by the transfer 'as regards their conditions of work and employment'.

[19.32] This Article is mirrored by Reg 8 of the Regulations which provides:

(1) The transferor and transferee concerned in a transfer shall inform their respective employees' representatives affected by the transfer of—

(a)   the date or proposed date of the transfer;

(b)   the reasons for the transfer;

(c)   the legal implications of the transfer for the employees and a summary of any relevant economic and social implications of the transfer for them; and

(d)   any measures envisaged in relation to the employees.

(2) The transferor shall give the information in paragraph (1) to the employees' representatives, where reasonably practicable, not later than 30 days before the transfer is carried out and, in any event, in good time before the transfer is carried out.

(3) The transferee shall give the information in paragraph (1) to the employees' representatives, where reasonably practicable, not later than 30 days before the transfer is carried out and, in any event, in good time before the employees are directly affected by the transfer as regards their conditions of work and employment.

(4) Where the transferor or the transferee envisages any measures in relation to employees, he or she shall consult the representatives of the employees, where reasonably practicable, not later than 30 days before the transfer is carried out and, in any event, in good time before the transfer is carried out, in relation to any such measures with a view to reaching an agreement.

(5) Where there are no employees' representatives in the undertaking or business of the transferor or, as the case may be, in the undertaking or business of the transferee, the transferor or the transferee, as may be appropriate, shall put in place a procedure whereby the employees may choose from among their number a person or persons to represent them (including by means of an election) for the purposes of this Regulation.

(6) Where, notwithstanding paragraph (5), there are still no representatives of the employees in an undertaking or business concerned (through no fault of the employees), each of the employees concerned must be informed in writing, where reasonably practicable, not later than 30 days before the transfer and, in any event, in good time before the transfer, of the following:

(a)   the date or proposed date of the transfer;

(b)   the reasons for the transfer;

(c)   the legal implications of the transfer for the employee and a summary of any relevant economic and social implications for that employee; and

(d)   any measures envisaged in relation to the employees.

(7) The obligations specified in this Regulation shall apply irrespective of whether the decision resulting in the transfer is taken by the employer or an undertaking controlling the employer and the fact that the information concerned was not provided to the employer by the undertaking controlling the employer shall not release the employer from those obligations.

Employee representatives

[19.33] The Regulations define employee representative as a trade union, staff association or excepted body with which it has been a practice of the employees employer to conduct collective bargaining negotiations, or, in their absence, a person or persons chosen by such employees under an arrangement put in place by the employer to represent them in negotiations with the employer.[40] As to how the arrangement to appoint employee representatives could be put in place, the UK Department for Business, Enterprise and Regulatory Reform Guide on the UK Regulations[41] provides useful guidance which is useful in the Irish context also:

> The legislation does not specify how many representatives must be elected or the process by which they are to be chosen. An employment tribunal may wish to consider, in determining a claim that the employer has not informed or consulted in accordance with the requirements, whether the arrangements were such that the purpose of the legislation could not be met. An employer will therefore need to consider such matters as whether:
>
> • the arrangements adequately cover all categories of employees who may be affected by the transfer and provide a reasonable balance between the interest of the different groups;
>
> • the employees have sufficient time to nominate and consider candidates;
>
> • the employees (including any who are absent from work for any reason) can freely choose who to vote for;
>
> • there is any normal company custom and practice for similar elections and if so whether they are good reasons for departing from it.

[19.34] As to when the obligation to inform and consult arises, the UK High Court provided logical guidance in *Griffin v South West Water Services Ltd*.[42] The Court considered the EC Collective Redundancies Directive[43] (as amended). Article 2 of that Directive provides:

> Where an employer is contemplating collective redundancies, he shall begin consultations with the workers' representatives in good time with a view to reaching an agreement.

The Court, when considering the obligation to consult with workers' representatives, in that context, stated:

---

[40] EC (Protection of Employees on Transfer of Undertakings) Regulations 2003, reg 2(1).

[41] Department for Business, Enterprise and Regulatory Reform, *Employment Rights on the Transfer of an Undertaking, A guide to the 2006 TUPE Regulations for employees, employers and representatives* (March 2007).

[42] *Griffin v South West Water Services Ltd* [1995] IRLR 15.

[43] 75/129/EEC.

The obligation to consult only arises when the employer's contemplation of redundancies has reached the point where he is able to identify the workers likely to be affected and can supply the information which the Article requires him to supply. Provided he does this in sufficient time to enable consultation to take place with the workers' representatives 'with a view to reaching an agreement' (or, as it is put in the amended Article, 'in good time with a view to reaching an agreement') I cannot see that the Article requires the employer to embark upon the process of consultation at any particular moment, much less as soon as he can be said to have in mind that collective redundancies may occur. The essential point, to my mind, is that the consultation must be one where, if they wish to do so, the workers' representatives can make constructive proposals and have time in which to do so before the relevant dismissal notices are sent out.

A breach of the obligations to inform and consult, along with constituting a breach of the Regulations, may also ground a claim for unfair constructive dismissal and/or a referral of the claim as a trade dispute under the Industrial Relations Acts 1969–2004.

TRANSFER-RELATED DISMISSALS

[19.35] Article 4 of the Directive allows for dismissals to take place for economic, technical or organisational reasons entailing changes in the workforce. No guidance is given as to what is meant by any of the terms 'economic', 'technical' or 'organisational', nor is there any guidance given as to the extent of 'changes in the workforce' which may or must result following on such dismissals.

Regulation 5 provides:

(1) The transfer of an undertaking, business or part of an undertaking or business shall not in itself constitute grounds for dismissal by the transferor or the transferee and such a dismissal, the grounds for which are such a transfer, by a transferor or a transferee is prohibited.

(2) Nothing in this Regulation shall be construed as prohibiting dismissals for economic, technical or organisational reasons entailing changes in the work force.

(3) If a contract of employment is terminated because the transfer involves a substantial change in working conditions to the detriment of the employee concerned, the employer concerned shall be regarded as having been responsible for termination of the contract of employment.

Dismissal for economic, technical or organisational reasons – the 'ETO defence'

[19.36] Only the transferee can rely on the 'permission' provided by Reg 5(2) to dismiss employees for economic, technical or organisational reasons entailing changes in the workforce. It might be very clear prior to a transfer taking effect that the transferee will not require an employee or employees post transfer, but, as the reason for not requiring them is that of the transferee it must take the employee or employees into its employment and then seek to rely on Reg 5(2). Because of the requirement that only a transferee can rely on the ETO defence, employers have found it difficult to justify making changes prior to a transfer in order to make their business more saleable or more attractive.[44]

If, after a transfer, employees are surplus to the transferee's requirements and could in a non-transfer situation be properly regarded as redundant, then the ETO defence will apply. The Irish cases, particularly decisions of the EAT, have tended to equate the ETO defence with the concept of redundancy. In *Morris v Smart Brothers Ltd*[45] the EAT examined a situation where Smart Brothers had operated eight retail clothing outlets in Dublin together with a head office, warehouse and wholesale business. When the company ran into trading difficulties it was broken up and various shops were sold off, some to co-respondents of Smart Brothers in this particular case. The EAT had to consider the position of employees in some of the stores which had changed hands and continued to operate. The EAT held that there had been transfer of an undertaking in the sale of shops by Smart Brothers to some of the respondent companies. The EAT held:

(i) The employment of all of the staff ended by reason of redundancy when Smart Brothers ceased to carry on business. There was therefore no claim of unfair dismissal against Smart Brothers as redundancy is a substantial ground justifying dismissal under unfair dismissals legislation.

(ii) Individual shops which had been subsidiaries of Smart Brothers continued operating as clothing shops under various new owners. The EAT held that, notwithstanding the application of the Directive and Regulations, in those circumstances no liability for staff remained with Smart Brothers in respect of the failure of transferees to engage staff who previously had worked at those locations. The dismissal of the employees by Smart Brothers was not grounded in the transfer 'in itself' but arose because that company ceased trading, leading to the redundancy of its employees. That is an economic reason as permitted by the Directive.

(iii) While one of the shops retained its identity it retained a greatly reduced workforce and moved from being 100 per cent retail to 50 per cent retail, 50 per cent wholesale. Two people remained employed in the business; one was the owner and the other was an individual moved from another branch because of his experience of the wholesale trade. The EAT held that the reduction in staff numbers on the retail side and the introduction of wholesale business amounted to 'economic, technical or organisational reasons entailing changes in the workforce'.

(iv) In respect of one of the shops that retained its identity with the same trade as had been carried on by Smart Brothers, an employee succeeded in his claim of unfair dismissal when he was not engaged by the transferee whom the EAT held had failed to show an economic, technical or organisational reason to justify the non- employment of the individual concerned.

Changes in the workforce

[19.37] Economic, technical or organisational reasons must entail 'changes in the workforce'. This normally requires a change in the numbers of people employed to

---

[44] See *Wheeler v Patel* [1987] IRLR 211; *Gateway Hotels Ltd v Stewart* [1988] IRLR 287 and *Ibex Trading Co Ltd v Walton* [1994] IRLR 594.

[45] *Morris v Smart Brothers Ltd* UD 688/93.

perform particular functions, not merely a change in their terms and conditions.[46] Where a transferee purchases a business or part of a business to add to a pre-existing business, difficulties may arise where attempts are made to harmonise terms and conditions as between the two groups of employees. There appears to be very little scope for employers other than to improve all terms and conditions to the best available or, at the very least, to '*red circle*' the less attractive terms and conditions in so far as they apply to some employees within the total workforce.

SERVICE PROVIDERS[47]

[19.38] The outsourcing or contracting out of the provision of a service may constitute a transfer under the Regulations.[48] The ECJ made this clear in *Rask and Christensen v ISS Kantineservice A/S*.[49] The Court held in *Rask*:[50]

> Thus, where one businessman entrusts, by means of an agreement, responsibility for running a facility of his undertaking, such as a canteen, to another businessman who thereby assumes the obligations of employer vis-à-vis the employees assigned to that facility, the resulting transaction may fall within the scope of the Directive, as defined in Article 1(1). The fact that in such a case the activity transferred is merely an ancillary activity for the transferor without a necessary connection with its company objects cannot have the effect of excluding that transaction from the scope of the Directive. Nor does the fact that the agreement between the transferor and the transferee relates to provision of services exclusively for the benefit of the transferor in return for a fee, details of which are laid down by the agreement, preclude the applicability of the Directive.

The replacement by an undertaking of a contractor providing services to it may also constitute a transfer under the Regulations.[51] The crucial point in determining if the replacement constitutes a 'transfer' is that the identity of the entity transferred is maintained.[52]

---

[46] See *Berriman v Delabole Slate Ltd* [1985] IRLR 305.

[47] For detailed analysis of the, at times complex, issues raised by the outsourcing of services in the context of the Acquired Rights Directive, see McMullen, *Business Transfers and Employee Rights* (LexisNexis Butterworths, looseleaf, update December 2008), Ch 5, paras 162–220.

[48] Such a transfer is often referred to as a 'first generation transfer'.

[49] Case C-209/91 *Rask and Christensen v ISS Kantineservice A/S* [1992] ECR 5755.

[50] Case C-209/91 [1992] ECR 5755 at para 17.

[51] Case C-13/95 *Süzen* [1997] ECR I 1259; Case C-48/94 *Rygaard* [1995] ECR I 2745. Such a transfer is often referred to as a 'second generation transfer.'

[52] Case C-13/95 *Süzen* [1997] ECR I 1259. This approach has been adopted in a number of decisions of the EAT: *Cannon v Noonan Cleaning Ltd and CPS Cleaning Services Ltd* [1998] ELR 153; *Shiels v Noonan Cleaning Ltd and ISS Contract Cleaners Ltd* UD 461/1997; *Bruton v Knights Cleaning Services Ltd* UD 803/97; *Collins v Excel Property Services Ltd* RP 27/98; *Digan v Sheehan Security Corporation Ltd* UD 235/2003; and *Power v St Paul's Nursing Home and T & M Cleaning Ltd* [1998] ELR 212. These cases are considered in McMullen, *Business Transfers and Employee Rights* (LexisNexis Butterworths, looseleaf, update December 2008), Ch 15, paras 24–28.

BREACH OF REGULATIONS – COMPLAINTS

[19.39] The 2003 Regulations confer jurisdiction on Rights Commissioners, with appeal to the Employment Appeals Tribunal, and from there to the High Court on a point of law in relation to any complaints about breach of the Regulations, as provided for in Regs 12 to 14 inclusive.[53] A complaint can be brought that an employer has contravened any of the Regulations other than Reg 4(4)(a) which deals with pension issues and Reg 13 which deals with procedural requirements of the Employment Appeals Tribunal in hearing appeals under the Regulations themselves. Unlike under unfair dismissals legislation, where a claim can be brought to the Rights Commissioner or directly to the EAT at the claimant's election, the Regulations provide that the complaint must initially go to the Rights Commissioner who will hold a hearing and do one or more of the following:

(i)   Declare that the complaint is or is not well founded.

(ii)   Require the employer to comply with the Regulations and set out a specified course of action in that regard.

(iii). Require the employer to pay compensation which in the case of Regulation 8 (the information and consultation provisions) shall not exceed four weeks' remuneration and in the case of contravention of any other Regulation compensation not exceeding two years' remuneration.

The remedies remain the same if the matter progresses on appeal to the EAT and/or the High Court on a point of law only.

EXTRA-TERRITORIAL TRANSFERS

Off shoring – out sourcing – transferring to another jurisdiction

[19.40] Businesses may look to other jurisdictions for cheaper services or production costs or businesses may be sold, involving the transfer of the business or parts of the business outside of Ireland.

If a transfer is made within the EU or the European Economic Area (EEA) (where the Acquired Rights Directive applies) then the Directive and Regulations will apply. Irish employees may have a practical difficulty in enforcing their rights. The Brussels Regulations[54] will apply which allow judgments of Courts or Tribunals in Member States covered by the Regulations be recognised and enforced in other Member States without new proceedings having to be brought. The application of the Rome Convention will determine the applicable law whether in Ireland or elsewhere and the Regulations, will apply to confer rights on the employees concerned.

The transfer of a business outside of the EU/EEA was raised in the case of *Holis Metal Industries Ltd v GMB.*[55] In *Holis* the transfer of part of the undertaking was to

---

[53] On the practice and procedure for the purposes of these regulations, see Ch 22, Practice and Procedure in Employment Law.

[54] 44/2001/EC.

[55] *Holis Metal Industries Ltd v GMB* [2008] IRLR 187 (UK EAT).

Israel. The employees had the option to move to Israel but chose not to do so. After the transfer the transferor declared them redundant. The complaint to the UK EAT was of an alleged breach of the duty to consult both under the transfer regulations and the collective redundancy regulations. The EAT had to decide whether the Transfer of Undertaking Regulations applied to the transfer of a business outside of the EEA. The Tribunal held that the UK Regulations have the potential to apply to a transfer of a business from the UK (which is a stipulation of the UK Regulations) to a non-EU State. The Tribunal noted that the Directive and Regulations clearly have an international element and, given that the legislation is concerned with protecting employees where there is a change of employer, the Regulations will apply even if the transfer takes place across borders within or outside the EU.

There is no Irish decision on the question of whether the Regulations apply to transfers to a non EEA/EU State. However, the reasoning of the EAT in *Holis* is logical and it would seem, though it is not beyond question, that the Regulations would apply to such a transfer.[56]

---

[56] See further European Commission report on the Acquired Rights Directive, COM (2007) 334 final, published on 4 July 2007. The report was made as a result of the Commission's obligations under Art 10 of the Acquired Rights Directive to submit an analysis of the effects of the Directive to the Council. The report noted (at p 10) that 'the absence of explicit treatment of cross-border transfers in the Directive, which nevertheless applies to transfers in which the undertaking being transferred falls within the territorial scope of the Treaty, can cause uncertainty on the part of employers and employees.'

Part IX
Immigration and International Employment

Chapter 20

Immigration and International Employment

Niall Buckley, Ger Connolly and Bryan Dunne

IMMIGRATION

Niall Buckley and Ger Connolly

INTRODUCTION

General

[20.01] Immigration represents a relatively new phenomenon in Ireland. From a very low base in the mid-1990s, non-Irish nationals accounted for an estimated 15 per cent of the Irish population by 2007. The economic growth which prompted this migration flow was not wholly anticipated by the Irish Government, and a comprehensive immigration policy was slow to evolve to match the significant influx of non-nationals seeking work.[1]

[20.02] Once legally working in Ireland, migrant workers in principle enjoy the same statutory employment protections as their Irish counterparts. Despite this uncontroversial statement of principle, the practical reality is more complex. The intersection of immigration and employment law raises a range of problematic issues.

[20.03] Part I of this chapter looks at some of the regular issues which may arise in relation to foreign workers and how such individuals may legally enter Ireland and take up employment here. At the outset, it is important to stress that fundamentally different criteria apply as between nationals of the European Economic Area (EEA) and Switzerland, and migrant workers from other non-EEA countries.

Immigration legislation and policy

[20.04] Immigration policy has developed over the past number of years on a somewhat *ad hoc* basis under a less than satisfactory legislative framework. While a substantial overhaul of the immigration process is proposed in the Immigration, Residence and Protection Bill 2008, the principal legislation in this area at the time of writing remains the Immigration Acts 1999–2004, the Aliens Act 1935 and the Refugee Act 1996 (as amended). This entire sphere remains very substantially subject to administrative discretion, and has been criticised by certain commentators as inaccessible and subject to ill-defined policy rules and practices heavily dependent on ministerial discretion.[2] The Department of Justice's own discussion document of April 2005 on Immigration and

---

[1] In 1999, 6,000 work permits were issued. By 2003, this figure increased to 48,000. In all, a total of 110,000 non-EEA nationals entered employment the State in from 2002–2006.

[2] Paper delivered by Aisling Ryan, Solicitor at a Law Society Conference on Migrant Workers and Human Rights Law, 15 October 2005.

Residence in Ireland concedes that many of the recently introduced provisions have been 'stop-gap measures ... to address specific aspects of immigration that needed an urgent legislative response.'[3]

Entry and registration requirements

[20.05] All non-EEA[4] (and non-Swiss) citizens are required to report to immigration control on their arrival in Ireland although under the Immigration Act 2004 (Visas) (No 2) Order 2006, citizens of a number of countries do not require visas for entry.[5] All non-EEA nationals who wish to remain in the State for longer than 90 days are required to register with their local Garda Registration Office. If a person is from a country not requiring a visa and intends to stay for more than three months he/she must register with the Garda Síochána (Garda National Immigration Bureau in Dublin) and apply for permission from the Minister for Justice, Equality and Law Reform to remain. If an individual is from a country requiring a visa for entry, there are a range of categories of visas granted, including tourist, business, work and study visas, and these are divided between short stay visa (C – up to 90 days) and long-stay visas (D).[6] Persons availing of long stay visas must register with the Garda National Immigration Bureau within 90

---

[3] Department of Justice, Equality and Law Reform, *Immigration and Residence in Ireland – Outline Policy Proposals for an Immigration and Residence Bill* – Discussion Document, April 2005.

[4] References to European Economic Area (EEA) citizens includes Swiss citizens, where referred to throughout Part I, unless expressly stated.

[5] Citizens of the following countries do not require an entry visa for Ireland: Andorra; Antigua And Barbuda; Argentina; Australia; Austria; Bahamas; Barbados; Belgium; Belize; Bolivia; Botswana; Brazil; Brunei; Bulgaria; Canada; Chile; Costa Rica; Croatia; Cyprus; Czech Republic; Denmark; Dominica; El Salvador; Estonia; Fiji; Finland; France; Germany; Greece; Grenada; Guatemala; Guyana; Honduras; Hong Kong (Special Administrative Region) (*See Further ; information Below).; Hungary; Iceland; Israel; Italy; Japan; Kiribati; Latvia; Lesotho; Liechtenstein; Lithuania; Luxembourg; Macau (Special Administrative Region); Malawi; Malaysia; Maldives; Malta; Mauritius; Mexico; Monaco; Nauru; Netherlands; New Zealand; Nicaragua; Norway; Panama; Paraguay; Poland; Portugal; Romania; Saint Kitts & Nevis; Saint Lucia; Saint Vincent & The Grenadines; Samoa; San Marino; Seychelles; Singapore; Slovak Republic; Slovenia; Solomon Islands; South Africa; South Korea; Spain; Swaziland; Sweden; Switzerland; Tonga; Trinidad & Tobago; Tuvalu; United Kingdom & Dependent Territories (Noted Below); United States of America; Uruguay; Vanuatu; Vatican City; Venezuela. Citizens of the following British Dependent territories do not require a visa either: Anguilla; Bermuda; British Antarctic Territory (South Georgia, South Sandwich Islands); British Indian Ocean Territories (Chagos Archipelago, Peros Banos, Diego Garcia, Danger Island); Cayman Islands; Falkland Islands And Dependencies; Gibraltar; Montserrat; Pitcairn (Henderson, Ducie and Oneno Islands); St. Helena And Dependicies (Ascension Island, Tristan Da Cunha); The Soverign Base Areas of Akrotiri And Dhekila; Turks And Caicos Island; British Virgin Islands.

[6] The Irish Naturalisation and Immigration Service identifies the following as the main categories of visa: Visits/Holidays; Business; Business Permission; Conference; Performances; Training; Exam; Fully Registered Doctor; Temporary Registered Doctor; Researchers; Vander Elst; Employment; Join Spouse/Parent on Work Permit; Family Member of Irish National; Family Member of EU/EEA/Swiss National; Family Reunification for Refugees; Medical Treatment.

days of arriving in Ireland. Persons who have entered the State on C visit visas cannot have their permission to remain in the State extended. Upon expiry of the visa, they must leave and reapply from outside the State should they wish to return.

Immigration stamps

[20.06] A range of immigration stamps are issued by the immigration authorities as evidence of the terms of a person's permission to be in the State. At present, these include Stamps 1–4. Stamp 1 permits a person to remain in Ireland for a limited period on condition that the holder does not engage in business without the permission of the Minister for Justice or enter employment unless his/her employer has obtained a work permit. It typically may apply to non-EEA nationals issued with a work permit; non-EEA nationals issued with a Green Card Permit; non-EEA nationals who have been granted permission to operate a business in the State; and Working Holiday Authorisation holders. Stamp 1A permits a person to remain in Ireland until a specified time for the purpose of full-time training with a named body and does not permit employment.[7] Stamp 2 permits a person to remain in Ireland for a limited period to pursue a course of study on condition that they do not engage in work other than casual employment (20 hours per week during school term and 40 hours per week during holidays). This stamp usually applies to non-EEA students. Stamp 2A permits a person to remain in Ireland to pursue a course of studies on condition that the holder does not enter employment, does not engage in any business or profession, has no recourse to public funds and does not remain later than a specified date.[8] Stamp 3 does not allow holders to engage in any work, business or profession and would typically be granted to non-EEA visitors, retired persons of independent means, members of religious orders and/or dependents of work permit holders. Stamp 4 permits persons to remain in Ireland until a specified date without limiting their right to work. It may be granted to non-EEA family members of EEA citizens; non-EEA spouses of Irish citizens; refugees; and persons granted family reunification rights and non-EEA parents of Irish-born children.

Residency and citizenship

[20.07] After a continuous period of legitimate residence in the State, individuals become entitled to apply for long-term residency rights. Somewhat different provisions apply in relation to the acquisition of long-term residency rights as between EEA and non-EEA nationals. Foreign workers may also seek to apply for Irish citizenship through naturalisation. The law relating to naturalisation and citizenship is governed by the Nationality and Citizenship Acts 1956–2004. Persons may apply for citizenship if they have been living in Ireland continuously for one year immediately prior to making the application and have been living in Ireland for a period of four of the preceding eight years. The Minister for Justice, Equality and Law Reform may grant citizenship applications at 'his absolute discretion' if he is satisfied that the applicant: (i) is over 18; (ii) is of good character; (iii) intends to reside in the State after naturalisation; and (iv)

---

[7] This category is typically applied to non-EEA accountancy students.

[8] This stamp governs non-EEA nationals attending courses of study not recognised by the Department of Education and Science.

has made a declaration of loyalty to the State.[9] The entitlement to citizenship through marriage has been substantially repealed via the 2004 Act and married persons must now apply through the naturalisation process. The acquisition of Irish citizenship does not require renunciation of other citizenships, and thus people can maintain dual or multiple nationalities.

EUROPEAN UNION AND EUROPEAN ECONOMIC AREA NATIONALS[10]

[20.08] Nationals of the Member States of the EEA do not require leave to enter the Republic of Ireland and are free, with some exceptions discussed below in relation to: (i) recent accession states; and (ii) certain categories of work on grounds of public policy, security and health, to take up employment in the Republic of Ireland. With Ireland's accession to the EEC on 1 January 1973, the provisions of the Treaty of Rome came into effect, guaranteeing the free movement of workers amongst all the Member States. The territorial scope of these free movement provisions have been progressively expanded with the accession of further Member States, and their application to EEA countries. The EEA now encompasses the EU Member States (Austria, Belgium, Bulgaria, Cyprus, the Czech Republic, Denmark, Estonia, Finland, France, Germany, Greece, Hungary, Ireland, Italy, Latvia, Lithuania, Luxembourg, Malta, Netherlands, Poland, Portugal, Romania, Slovakia, Slovenia, Spain, Sweden and the United Kingdom) as well as Iceland, Liechtenstein and Norway. In addition, Switzerland has bilateral accords with the European Union in relation to free movement of workers[11] and voted on 8 February 2009 to renew and extend them.

[20.09] Article 39 (formerly Art 48 until renumbered by the Treaty of Amsterdam) provides:

1. Freedom of movement for workers shall be secured within the Community.

2. Such freedom of movement shall entail the abolition of any discrimination based on nationality between workers of the Member States as regards employment, remuneration and other conditions of work and employment.

3. It shall entail the right, subject to limitations justified on grounds of public policy, public security or public health:

    (a) to accept offers of employment actually made;

    (b) to move freely within the territory of Member States for this purpose;

    (c) to stay in a Member State for the purpose of employment in accordance with the provisions governing the employment of nationals of that State laid down by law, regulation or administrative action;

---

[9] Irish Nationality and Citizenship Acts 1956–2004, s 15.

[10] For further discussion in context of European Union Law generally, see Wyatt and Dashwood, *European Union Law* (5th edn, Sweet & Maxwell, 2006), Ch 18; Craig and De Búrca, *EU Law: Texts Cases and Materials* (4th edn, Oxford University Press, 2007), Ch 21; Steiner, Woods & Twigg Flesner, *EU Law* (9th edn, Oxford University Press, 2006), Ch 20.

[11] The Agreement on the Free Movement of Persons (21 June 1999) entered into force on 1 June 2002. The Protocol on the extension of the Agreement on the Free Movement of Persons to the 10 new EU Member States (26 October 2004) entered into force on 1 April 2006.

(d) to remain in the territory of a Member State after having been employed in that State, subject to conditions which shall be embodied in implementing regulations to be drawn up by the Commission.

4. The provisions of this article shall not apply to employment in the public service.

[20.10] The European Court of Justice (ECJ) has stated that the provisions of the Treaty relating to freedom of movement for workers are intended to facilitate the pursuit by Community nationals of occupational activities of all kinds throughout the Community and preclude national legislation which might place Community nationals at a disadvantage when they wish to extend their activities beyond the territory of a single Member State.[12] There are thus two aspects to the evolution of the case law and legislation in this sphere: the removal of discriminatory obstacles and the conferral of substantive rights on EU workers.

[20.11] Article 40 empowers the Council to legislate for the measures required to bring about freedom of movement for workers and to abolish restrictions. Under this power, the Council issued Directive 68/360 on the abolition of restrictions on movement and residence within the Community for workers of Member States and their families. This has since been repealed[13] and replaced by Directive 2004/38 on the right of citizens of the Union and their family members to move and reside freely within the territory of the Member States. Regulation 1612/68, meanwhile, was passed to implement the 'abolition of any discrimination based on nationality between workers of the Member States as regards employment, remuneration and other conditions of work and employment'. Divided into several parts, Part I entitled 'Employment and workers' families' is of most substantive importance. It deals with access to employment and equality of treatment in relation to work and social advantages. Thus, Directive 2004/38, along with Regulation 1612/68 which it significantly amends, are the legislative mainstays in this area.

Direct effect

[20.12] Article 39 of the EC Treaty has direct effect, not just vertical effect vis-à-vis public authorities, but also extends to rules regulating employment imposed by governing bodies and associations and/or through collective bargaining.[14] The ECJ has made that clear in *Walrave and Koch*[15] and the celebrated *Bosman*[16] case where it stated that the provision applies not only 'to the action of public authorities but extends also to rules of any other nature aimed at regulating gainful employment in a collective manner'. The Court further stated that the abolition of obstacles to freedom of

---

[12] Case C-443/93 *Ioannis Vougioukas* [1995] ECR I-4033 para 39. See also Case 143/87 *Stanton v INASTI* [1988] ECR 3877, para 13.

[13] Along with Directives 64/221 68/360/EEC, 72/194/EEC, 73/148/EEC, 75/34/EEC, 75/35/EEC, 90/364/EEC, 90/365/EEC and 93/96/EEC.

[14] C-341/05 *Laval un Partneri Ltd v Svenska Byggnadsarbetareförbundet (Laval)* [2007] ECR I-11767; [2008] 2 CMLR 9; See C-438/05 *ITWF v Viking Line ABP (Viking)* [2007] ECR I-10779; [2008] 1 CMLR 51.

[15] Case 36/74 *Walrave and Koch v Association Union Cyclisted Internationale* [1974] ECR 1405.

[16] Case C-415/93 *Union Royale Belge des Sociétés de Football Association and others v Bosman* [1995] ECR I-4921.

movement 'would be compromised if the abolition of State barriers could be neutralized by obstacles' imposed by 'associations or organizations not governed by public law'.[17] The extent of Art 39's horizontal effect was considered in *Angonese*.[18] The case concerned a dispute over an Italian bank's requirement that job applicants possess a certificate of bilingualism (Italian and German) issued by the local authority in which the Bank was situated. The Cassa di Riparmio bank was permitted, but not mandated, to impose this language requirement by virtue of a collective agreement between national savings banks in Italy. Angonese was an Italian national whose mother tongue was German. Although he was perfectly bilingual, he was not in possession of the requisite certificate, which would only be issued by the Bolzano local authority to persons who had sat an exam in Bolzano. Angonese argued that this illegitimately discriminated against persons from other Member States applying for the post. The ECJ held that the Treaty's prohibition on discrimination 'must be regarded as applying to private persons as well,'[19] and thus did bind private employers. The Court further held that the Bank's refusal to accept other equivalent evidence of language competency constituted discrimination on grounds of nationality.

Employer/employee reciprocity

[20.13] Article 39 can be relied upon by worker and employer alike. Thus, the ECJ remarked in *Clean Car Autoservice*:

> While those rights are undoubtedly enjoyed by those directly referred to – namely, workers – there is nothing in the wording of article 48 [now 39] to indicate that they may not be relied upon by others, in particular employers.[20]

An employer can therefore legitimately invoke the Treaty provision where its freedom to employ a national of another Member State is curtailed.

Territorial scope

[20.14] The protections afforded under Art 39 extend to work done outside the European Union, providing the employment relationship was entered into within the Community.[21] In *Boukhalfa*, a case concerning a Belgian national working in the German embassy in Algiers, the Court extended this principle to all aspects of the employment relationship which are governed by the legislation of the employing Member State even where the contract of employment was entered into and is primarily performed in a non-member country.[22] The requirement of a Community element can lead to reverse discrimination

---

[17] Case C-415/93, *Union Royale Belge des Sociétés de Football Association and others v Bosman* [1995] ECR I-4921at paras 82-83. See further *Merida* [2004] ECR I-8471.

[18] Case C-281/98 *Roman Angonese v Cassa di Riparmio di Bolzano SpA* [2000] ECR I-4139. See note: Doherty, (2000) 7(7) CLP 173.

[19] C-281/98 *Roman Angonese v Cassa di Riparmio di Bolzano SpA* [2000] ECR I-4139 at para 36.

[20] Case C-350/96 *Clean Car Autoservice* [1998] ECR I-2521.

[21] Case C-36/74 *Walrave and Koch v Asociation Union Cyclisted Internationale* [1974] ECR 1405 at para 28.

[22] Case C-214/95 *Boukhalfa v BRD* [1996] ECR I-2253.

where there are wholly internal restrictions imposed or regional based differences in the treatment of nationals.[23]

Meaning of worker

[20.15] Treaty rights and protections are conferred on workers and the community legislation refers to employed persons, however the term 'worker' and 'employed person' are not expressly defined in Art 39 of the EC Treaty or Art 1 of Regulation 1612/68, respectively. In a series of cases, the ECJ has interpreted the concepts broadly, having regard to the Treaty objectives.[24] The Court considers the term 'worker' to be a Community concept rather than a matter for national law, and draws upon the economic and social dimensions of the Community in elaborating its scope. In *Hoekstra*, the Court opined that if the definition of the term were a matter for national law, it would be possible for each Member State to modify the meaning of migrant worker so as to eliminate at will the protections afforded by the Treaty.[25]

[20.16] While a person's status as an employee or self-employed person is frequently crucial for availing of domestic employment legislation remedies, the distinction does not have the same decisive implications in a community law context. Wyatt and Dashwood write that the definition of worker in the Community sense 'rarely causes difficulty because if an economically active migrant is not a worker, he/she is as like as not to be self-employed in which case either Art 43 of the EC Treaty or Art 49 of the EC Treaty will apply.'[26] Thus for many years, the crucial distinction for the invocation of full Community law protections was between economically and non-economically active migrants. Commencing, with the advent of EU citizenship under the Maastricht Treaty, the cardinal importance of this distinction has gradually diminished but it remains important and economically active migrants continue to enjoy significant advantages under EU law.[27]

Economic value threshold

[20.17] The economic value of labour has been a factor in the determination of whether someone is a worker, but the threshold is not an onerous one. In *Lawrie Blum*,[28] the Court was asked to consider whether someone undergoing the final stage of professional teacher training was in employment. It was held that the essential feature of a worker is that the person performs a service of some economic value for and under the direction of

---

[23] Case C-175/78 *R v Saunders* [1979] ECR 1129. Nic Shuibhne queries whether it is time to abandon the 'wholly internal rule', Nic Shuibhne, 'Free Movement of Persons and the Wholly Internal Rule: Time to Move On' [2002] CMLR 731.

[24] For example Case C-75/63 *Hoekstra v BBDA* [1964] ECR 177; Case C-53/81 *Levin v Staatssecretaris van Justitie* [1982] ECR 1035; Case 66/85 *Lawrie Blum v Land Baden-Württemberg* [1986] ECR 2121.

[25] Case C-75/63 *Hoekstra v BBDA* [1964] ECR 177 at para 184.

[26] Wyatt and Dashwood, *European Union Law* (5th edn, Sweet & Maxwell, 2006) at 18.008.

[27] See further Ch. 17 and 18, Wyatt and Dashwood *European Union Law* (5th edn, Sweet & Maxwell, 2006); Ch 23 Craig and De Búrca, *EU Law: Texts Cases and Materials* (4th edn, Oxford University Press, 2007).

[28] Case 66/85 *Lawrie Blum v Land Baden-Württemberg* [1986] ECR 2121.

another for remuneration. Initially, prior to the introduction of Union citizenship, full free movement rights were linked to one's ability to independently sustain oneself in another Member State as an economically active migrant. For this reason, issues arose as to whether part-time workers enjoyed the protections afforded by Art 39. The court addressed this issue squarely in *Levin v Staatssecretaris van Justitie*.[29] Levin was a British citizen, living in the Netherlands and married to a non-EC national. Her application for a residence permit was rejected. She worked part-time as a chambermaid and the Dutch authorities considered that as her earnings fell below the minimum wage, her employment did not provide sufficient financial support to qualify her as an EC worker.

[20.18] The ECJ interpreted the term 'worker' to encompass part-time and seasonal employment, providing it involved the pursuit of effective and genuine activities, and not on so small a scale as to be marginal and ancillary. The court set down a number of important principles. First, the rules on free movement of persons must be inclusively interpreted. Secondly, part-time employment provided an important means by which persons could realise an important community goal of raising their living standards. Thirdly, the motive of a worker in seeking to avail of Art 39 was largely irrelevant, provided they were engaging in genuine economic activity. This issue was more closely examined in *Kempf*[30] where a German national teaching twelve piano lessons a week in the Netherlands sought to claim welfare to supplement his work income and then sought further benefits when he had to give up work for health reasons. The Dutch government sought to argue that where the person's income was below the minimum level of subsistence such that they were applying for benefit while working, the person could not be regarded as engaging in genuine and effective work. The Court again held that Mr Kempf's work was not on such a small scale as to be purely a marginal and ancillary activity.

[20.19] In *Steymann*[31] the Court embraced an even broader definition of economic activity. Steymann was in paid employment as a plumber for a short time in the Netherlands. He then joined a religious community (the Bhagwan Community) and provided plumbing services on its premises, which included a commercial bar, discotheque and laundrette. His application for a residence permit was refused on the ground that he was not pursuing economic activity as an employed person. Notwithstanding that the work was unpaid (although he did receive pocket money and had accommodation provided), the Court held that work rendered by persons in such communal living circumstances could come within the ambit of Art 39.

Purpose of employment

[20.20] Generally speaking, the reason why a person seeks work in another Member State is immaterial to their classification as a worker, provided it is genuine and not

---

[29] Case C-53/81 *Levin v Staatssecretaris van Justitie* [1982] ECR 1035.
[30] Case 139/85 *Kempf v Staatsecrataris van Justitie* [1986] ECR 1741.
[31] Case 196/87 *Steymann v Staatsecretaris*.

marginal economic activity.[32] This is so even where it appears that a person has only taken up employment in another Member State as a deliberate ploy to trigger EU rights.[33] Somewhat contrastingly, in *Bettray*[34] the Court did inquire where the primary purpose of the work was part of a drug rehabilitation programme rather than a genuine contribution to economic activity. In *Trojani*,[35] a French National was working in a Salvation Army work reintegration programme in Belgium. The ECJ left it open to the national court to decide whether the work in question was genuine and/or effective but made clear that the mere fact that the job's principal purpose was social reintegration did not in itself disqualify it from being regarded as genuine economic activity.

Job-seekers

[20.21] In order to ensure that the aim of a free labour market is advanced, the ECJ has engaged in a purposive interpretation of Art 39 to encompass the right to enter another Member State 'to look for or pursue an occupation.'[36] The Court consolidated this approach in *Antonissen*[37] where a Belgian national had moved to England in 1984. He had sought work unsuccessfully and in 1987 was sentenced to imprisonment for possession of cocaine. On his release, the Secretary of State sought to deport him. The Court recognised that a narrow interpretation of the free movement provision, conditional on an offer of employment having been already made, could render the provision substantially ineffective and stymie the free flow of workers. The Court declared that the article:

> [...] must be interpreted as enumerating, in a non-exhaustive way, certain rights benefiting nationals of Member States in the context of the free movement of workers and that that freedom also entails the right for nationals of Member States to move freely within the territory of the other Member States and to stay there for the purposes of seeking employment.[38]

The Court made clear that a job-seeker's status was not equivalent to that of an employed person and a Member State could reserve the right to deport a person who had not found work within a 'reasonable period' and could not demonstrate a 'genuine chance' of being engaged.

[20.22] Initially, the ECJ restrictively interpreted the right of job-seekers to avail equally of social welfare and tax advantages in other Member States, as secured for workers in Reg 1612/68. This jurisprudence, elaborated in *Lebon*[39] and *Commission v Belgium*[40]

---

[32] Case C-53/81 *Levin v Staatssecretaris van Justitie* [1982] ECR 1035.
[33] Case C-109/01 *Akrich* [2003] ECR I-9067; [2004] 2 WLR 871. The appellant moved from the K to work in Ireland and shortly after sought to return to the United Kingdom in order to circumvent a prior UK deportation order.
[34] Case 344/87 *Bettray v Staatssecretaris van Justitie* [1989] ECR 1621.
[35] Case C-456/02 *Trojani v CPAS* [2004] ECR I-7573.
[36] Case 48/75 *Royer* [1976] ECR 497.
[37] C-292/89 *Antonissen* [1991] ECR I-745.
[38] C-292/89 *Antonissen* [1991] ECR I-745 at para 13.
[39] Case 316/85 *Lebon* [1987] ECR 281.
[40] Case C-278/94 *Commission v Belgium* [1996] ECR I-4307.

was designed to combat any phenomenon of welfare tourism. The *Collins*[41] case represented a new direction in the Court's approach, taking account of the advent of Union Citizenship. Mr Collins was an Irish citizen who studied for a time in the United Kingdom in 1978 and worked there briefly in 1981. He returned there in 1998 and sought jobseeker's allowance. He was refused benefit as he was not habitually resident in the United Kingdom. The ECJ held that he was entitled to equal treatment in relation to financial benefits 'intended to facilitate access to employment.' This was consolidated in *Ioannidis*[42] where a Greek citizen having completed a degree in Belgium sought to avail of a 'tideover allowance,' a Belgian government benefit available to young persons seeking first employment or person who had already worked but not for a sufficient period to qualify for full unemployment benefit. The Court held that it was not acceptable that Ioannidis should be refused this benefit solely on the basis that he had not completed his secondary education in Belgium.

Equality, discrimination and justification

[20.23] Article 39(2) envisages the abolition of any discrimination amongst workers based on nationality, and Arts 7–9 of Regulation 1612/68 endeavour to put flesh on the bones of what constitutes equal treatment for workers of EU Member States. Art 24 of Directive 2004/68, discussed below, expressly extends this equal treatment principle to all EU citizens and their families, subject to the existing exceptions enumerated in the Treaty and secondary legislation.

Discrimination

[20.24] Discrimination necessarily entails different treatment to comparable situations or the same treatment to different situations.[43] Direct discrimination, typically discrimination provided for in law, will clearly be caught unless it comes within one of the exceptions set out in Arts 39(3) or 39(4).[44] In such instances, a strong burden of justification will be placed on the Member State. In *Commission v French Republic*,[45] provisions of the French Maritime Code which required a certain proportion of ship crew members to be French nationals was successfully impugned. The Court held that Art 39 rendered inapplicable provisions of domestic law which contravened the Treaty provision. In addition to legislative measures, the prohibition applies to discriminatory treatment on nationality grounds by public bodies such as universities.[46]

[20.25] Indirect discrimination constitutes a more regular source of controversy. This involves ostensibly neutral rules whose application intrinsically favours nationals over migrant workers. Craig and de Búrca cite benefits conditional on residence or place of origin requirements as a frequent example of such provisions.[47] In *Ugliola*,[48] an Italian

---

41 Case C-138/02 *Collins* [2004] ECR I-2703.
42 Case C-258/04 *Ioannidis* [2005] ECR I-8275.
43 Case C-391/97 *Frans Gschwind v Finanzamt Aachen-Aussenstadt* [1999] ECR I-5451 at para 21.
44 Case 15/69 *Marsman* [1969] ECR 363.
45 Case 167/63 *Commission v French Republic* [1974] ECR 359.
46 Case C-212/99 *Commission v Italy* [2001] ECR I-4923.

challenged a provision under which periods in German military service were reckonable in establishing seniority of service and job security. No corresponding provision existed for military service in other Member States. The Court held that the German provision unjustifiably introduced indirect discrimination in favour of its own nationals. *Sotgiu*[49] was an Italian working for the German postal service whose family resided in Italy. He received a daily separation allowance. The Government introduced an increase for those workers residing in Germany but continued the old rate for workers residing abroad, of whatever nationality. The Court made clear that the prohibition applied not only to 'overt discrimination by reason of nationality but also all covert forms of discrimination which, by the application of other criteria of differentiation, lead in fact to the same result'. In the instant circumstances, however, the increase was a temporary one and conditional on workers agreeing to transfer to a new location. Language requirements have also been at the centre of a number of cases. In *Groener*,[50] a Dutch national working part-time in Ireland as an art teacher was rejected for a full-time post, as she did not pass the Irish language oral examination. Although recognising that the instruction was likely to be entirely through English, the Court accepted that a language requirement could be a legitimate public policy to preserve the use of Irish, provided it was not applied in a disproportionate fashion.[51] Issues also frequently arise in relation to recognition of qualifications from the worker's home state. These are sometimes referred to as double-burden regulatory requirements and were rejected in *Commission v Portugal*.[52]

[20.26] It is increasingly apparent from the recent ECJ case law that it is not strictly necessary that a measure be overtly discriminatory to constitute a restriction on free movement of persons, services or capital. Snell describes the progressive abandonment of the discriminatory requirement when scrutinising barriers to free movement.[53] The ECJ ruled in *Bosman* that such measures are contrary to the free movement of workers, if they represent significant obstacles to free movement, notwithstanding that they are not essentially discriminatory. Bosman challenged the Belgian football association's rules which required a club seeking to sign an out-of-contract player to pay a compensatory sum to his former club for 'training'. He wished to move on a free transfer to a French club. Although the system applied equally internally as between all Belgian clubs and a player's nationality was not a consideration, the Court held that it fell foul of Art 39. Despite its non-discriminatory application, the ECJ held that it directly affected 'players' access to the employment market in other Member States' and thus impeded the free movement of workers.

---

[47] Craig and De Búrca, *EU Law: Texts Cases and Materials* (4th edn, Oxford University Press, 2007) at 759.

[48] Case 15/69 *Württembergische Milchverwertung-Südmilch AG v Salvatore Ugliola* [1970] ECR 363.

[49] Case 152/73 *Sotgiu v Deutsche Bundespost* [1974] ECR 153.

[50] Case C-379/87 *Groener v Minister for Education* [1989] ECR 3967.

[51] Case C-281/98 *Roman Angonese v Cassa di Risparmio di Bolzano SpA* [2000] ECR I-4139.

[52] Case C-171/02 *Commission v Portugal* [2004] ECR I-5464.

[53] Snell, 'Non-Discriminatory Tax Obstacles in Community Law' (2007) 56 *ICLQ* 339.

[20.27] Restrictions leading to indirect discrimination can be saved if there is an objective justification for them and the measures are proportionate to this aim. In the case of *Bachmann*,[54] pension contributions were tax deductible provided they were made in Belgium but not to pensions schemes based in other Member States. The Belgian government argued that the differential treatment was necessary to preserve the cohesion of the Belgian taxation system and that any apparent unfairness was offset by the ultimate taxation of the pensions payable by the insurers. In other cases, such as *Baars*[55] and *Verkooijen*[56] the ECJ has been less receptive to taxation cohesion arguments. Snell contends that the 'obstacles-oriented' focus has not been fully applied to the area of tax and that discrimination rationales still explain the outcomes in most of the cases.[57] The Court will not readily yield to arguments of objective justification and as the case law of *Terhoeve*[58] and *Rockler*[59] demonstrates, justification arguments will be subject to close scrutiny.

Public service exception

[20.28] 'Employment in the public service' is excluded from the scope of Art 39 but the ECJ has sought to strictly limit the exception to the purposes for which the Court considers it is included in the Treaty. Craig and de Búrca describe the battle over the scope of this exception as 'hard fought' with Member States forcefully asserting sovereignty arguments in the face of the Court's restrictive, purposive reading of the provision's ambit.[60] In *Sotgiu*, it was argued that as the contractual relationship between a German post office worker and his employer was one governed by public law, it was within the public service. The Court made clear that it would adjudge whether the public service proviso applied, declaring that the designation of the legal relationship between employee and the employing administration 'can be varied at the whim of the national legislature and cannot therefore provide a criterion for interpretation appropriate to the requirements of Community law.'[61] Article 39(4) could limit the admission of foreign nationals to 'certain activities' in the public service, but could not justify discrimination once they were already employed.

[20.29] The parameters of the ECJ's test were more clearly elaborated in *Commission v Belgium*[62] where the Commission challenged nationality requirements in Belgian law for

---

54 *Bachmann* [1992] ECR I-305.
55 Case C-251/98 *Baars* [2000] ECR I-2787.
56 Case C-35/98 *Verkooijen* [2000] ECR I-4071.
57 Snell, (2007) 56 *ICLQ* 339.
58 Case C-18/95 *FC Terhoeve v Inspecteur van de Belastingdienst Particulieren/ Ondernemingen Buitenland* [1999] ECR I-345, para 39.
59 Case C-137/04 *Rockler v Försäkringskassan* [2006] ECR I-1441.
60 Craig and De Búrca, *EU Law: Texts Cases and Materials* (4th edn, Oxford University Press, 2007) at 764. See also Mancini, 'Free Movement of Workers in the Case Law of the ECJ' and O'Keefe Judicial Interpretation of the Public Service Exception to the Free Movement of Workers in Curtin, O'Keeffe (eds) *Constitutional Adjudication in European Community and National Law* (Butterworths, 1992).
61 Case 152/73 *Sotgiu v Deutsche Bundespost* [1974] ECR 153 at para 5.
62 Case 149/79 *Commission v Belgium* [1980] ECR 3881.

a wide range of posts in the 'public service' including railway workers, nurses, plumbers, carpenters and architects. The French and Belgian governments argued for an *institutional* concept based on the entity employing the workers. The ECJ rejected this, deeming that the Art 39(4) exclusion was directed at posts involving:

(i)   the exercise of powers conferred by public law; and

(ii) duties designed to 'safeguard the general interests of the State'.

Such posts involved a 'special relationship of allegiance to the State' which might be presumed to flow from nationality.[63] Thus, the Court elaborated a functional concept of public service based on the 'exercise of official authority.'[64] The fact that the higher grades of some positions might involve such responsibilities did not justify similar exclusionary treatment of more junior positions. The Court identified two functions which might come within the exception in *Commission v Italy*[65]: posts involving the management of a public body and posts advising the State on scientific and technical questions. In *Commission v France* (Re French Nurses),[66] French legislation limiting appointment of nurses in public hospitals to French nurses was successfully impugned by the Commission. Despite the elaboration of a twin limb test, there remains much room for disagreement regarding the appropriate ambit of the exception and it continues to be an issue which pits the Commission against Member States. Craig and De Búrca observe that the issue is still 'fraught with ideological tensions'.[67]

Entry and residence rights of workers and their families: Directive 2004/38/EC

[20.30] Directive 2004/38 on the right of citizens of the European Union and their family members to move and reside freely within the territory of the EU replaces Directive 68/360. It was enacted to facilitate realisation of the Treaty rights in relation to free movement and standardise the formal requirements with travel and residence. Articles 2 and 3 define the scope of family member as including a spouse; a registered partner (if partnerships are recognised in the home State); children under age 21 or otherwise dependent on the worker/spouse; and dependant relatives in the ascending line. Furthermore, Member States are required to facilitate the admission, and justify refusal, of any other family member not within this definition if that member is dependent on the worker in the country from which they have come, or are members of the household in the worker's home state. The same criteria apply to partners with whom the EU citizen has a durable relationship and family members whose serious health condition requires personal care by the EU citizen.[68] Articles 4 and 5 deal

---

[63] Case 149/79 [1980] ECR 3881 at para 10.

[64] Case 149/79 [1980] ECR 3881 at para 6.

[65] Case C-225/85 *Commission v Italy.*

[66] Case C-307/84 *Commission v France* [1986] ECR 1725.

[67] Craig and De Búrca, *EU Law: Texts Cases and Materials* (4th edn, Oxford University Press, 2007) at p 768.

[68] Directive 2004/38, Art 3(2)(a).

respectively with the entitlement to exit and enter Member States on production of a valid passport or appropriate identification and prohibits any visa requirements.[69]

Residency

[20.31] Article 6 provides for a basic right of up to three months' residence in any Member State for European Union citizens and for family members accompanying them. Article 7 entitles persons (and family members) to longer rights of residence provided they are economically active[70] (whether workers or self-employed), economically self sufficient or students. Article 7(3) elaborates specific criteria in relation to job-seekers, which draw on the ECJ's existing jurisprudence on this issue. While a person will not lose a right of residence if he/she becomes incapable of work through illness or accident or involuntary unemployment, by implication Art 7(3)(b) suggests the right may be lost if a worker is *voluntarily* unemployed having been working for less than one year.

[20.32] Permanent Residence rights are provided for under Arts 16–18 and accrue to EU citizens and their families (whether EU nationals or not) after five years of lawful residence.[71] While temporary absences of under six months per year will not affect the running of time, this right may be lost if a person is absent from the State for a period of two consecutive years.[72] In certain circumstances, such as retirement, incapacity or death, Art 17 provides for the acquisition of permanent residency within lesser periods. Having satisfied the residency requirements, EU citizens and their families are entitled to certification of permanent residence.

Equal treatment of non-EU family members

[20.33] Article 24 declares that migrant EU citizens 'shall enjoy equal treatment' to Member State nationals,[73] and specifically extends this protection to third country national family members. The second paragraph of the article provides a derogation on the equal treatment entitlement in relation to a person's first three months of residence or where they have the status of job-seeker. In so excluding job-seekers from the full benefit of provisions on non-discrimination, *Golynker*[74] suggests that the Directive lags behind the judgment in *Collins*. Article 23 provides:

---

[69] Directive 2004/38, Art 5(2) permits limited visa requirements for family members who are third country nationals in accordance with Regulation 539/2001.

[70] As discussed at para **[20.17]** this has been defined by the ECJ as engaging in genuine economic activity which is not marginal or ancillary

[71] Directive 2004/38, Art 16 deals with EU citizens, Art 18 with non-EU family members of EU citizens.

[72] Directive 2004/38, Art 16 (3) and (4).

[73] This is obviously subject to the enumerated exceptions discussed above and set out in the Treaties and secondary legislation.

[74] Golynker, 'Job seekers' rights in the European Union: Challenges of Changing the Paradigm of Social Solidarity' (2005) 30 *EL Rev* 111.

Irrespective of nationality, the family members of a Union citizen who have the right of residence or the right of permanent residence in a Member State shall be entitled to take up employment or self-employment there.

Thus in *Diatta*[75] the Court held that a spouse's right (then governed by Art 11 of Regulation 1612/68) encompassed the right to live elsewhere in the State apart from her husband for the purpose of exercising her right to work. In *Metock*[76] the ECJ ruled that Irish legislation requiring that an EU national have previously resided in another EU state with their third country national spouse prior to coming to Ireland was in breach of the Directive. The Court ruled that the spouse benefited from the provisions of Art 3(2) 'irrespective of when and where their marriage took place.' Scope for anomalies remain and it is not clear whether non-economically active EU family members will always be entitled to the same range of benefits which the comparable third country national family members would be, claiming through their worker relation.

Public policy, security and health derogations[77]

[20.34] Member States are entitled, under Art 39(3), to derogate from the free movement guarantees on grounds of public policy, public security or public health. Articles 27–33 of Directive 2004/38 detail some of the factors governing the exercise of this derogation by Member States and the necessary procedural formalities. Invocation of the derogation to serve economic ends is expressly prohibited. Proportionality is a cardinal principle for the application of measures on any of the three grounds and where individuals are the subject of restrictions on public policy or security grounds, it must be based exclusively on his/her personal conduct of the individual. Article 28 might be regarded as an express elaboration of the manner in which the proportionality principle must be applied requiring the State to have regard to how long the individual concerned has resided, his/her age, state of health, family and economic situation, social and cultural integration into the host Member State and the extent of his/her links with the country of origin. It introduces a three-tiered level of protection against expulsion of EU citizens from the territory of Member States, distinguishing between:

(i) a base level of protection for all persons governed by EU law;

(ii) enhanced protection for persons who have a right of permanent residence in a Member State; and

(iii) further heightened protection for minors or persons who have resided in a Member State for upwards of ten years. It should be stressed that this derogation is extremely limited and there are exceedingly few instances in four decades of ECJ jurisprudence where it has been successfully invoked by a Member State.[78]

---

[75] Case C-267/83 *Diatta*.

[76] Case C-127/08 *Metock*.

[77] See Ch 23, Steiner, Woods, Twigg-Flesner, *EU Law* (9th edn, OUP, 2006), Wyatt and Dashwood, *European Union Law* (5th edn, Sweet & Maxwell, 2006) at 17-023 for a comprehensive treatment of this area.

[78] A public policy derogation was successfully invoked against a member of the Church of Scientology in Case C-41/74 *Van Duyn* [1975] ECR 1337.

[20.35] In *Bouchereau*,[79] the Court restricted the circumstances in which a prior criminal conviction could be taken into account to circumstances where it evidenced a 'genuine, present and sufficiently serious threat affecting one of the fundamental interests of society'. General preventative measures based on the mere fact of a criminal record, rather than the particular conduct of an individual are not legitimate. In *Adoui and Cornuaille*, the Belgian Government's decision to order the expulsion of the applicants based on suspected prostitution was not a legitimate derogation, where such conduct was not prohibited by law when attributable to its own nationals. The conduct relied upon must be the subject of serious domestic sanction. Internal restrictions on movement within the territory of the Member State can only be applied to EU nationals to an equivalent extent that they exist for Member State nationals,[80] save where the conduct could have legitimately prompted an expulsion order against the EU national.[81]

[20.36] Article 29 deals with the public health exception and permits restrictions in relation to diseases of epidemic potential (as defined by the World Health Organisation) and such other infections and contagious and parasitic diseases as are the subject of protection provisions applying to nationals of the host Member State. The health derogation may only be invoked during the first three months of a person's stay.

Social and tax advantages

[20.37] Article 7(2) of Reg 1612/68 has been described as packing the 'largest punch of all EC secondary legislation.'[82] It secures the same social and tax advantages for EU workers as national workers. Initially in *Michel S*,[83] the ECJ had interpreted a scope for this provision limited to benefits connected with employment but a broader ambit was soon fastened upon in *Christini v SNCF*.[84] An Italian widow of an Italian worker who had been living and working in France applied for a special fare reduction for parents of large families. She was refused on the grounds that she was not a French National. The French government sought to argue before the ECJ that the Article only extended to benefits available within the ambit of one's employment. The Court took a different view and ruled that the Article extended to all social and tax advantages and continued after the death of the worker in question. This was consolidated by a formula elaborated in *Even*,[85] where the Court declared that Art 7(2) covers those advantages which

---

[79] Case C-30/77 *Bouchereau* [1977] ECR 1999. See further Case C-67/74 *Bonsignore* [1975] ECR 297 and Case C-116/81 *Adoui and Cornuaille* [1982] ECR 1665.

[80] Case C-36/75 *Rutili v Ministre de l'Intérieur* [1975] ECR 1219.

[81] Case C-100/01 *Ministre de l'Intérieur v Oteiza Olazabal* [2002] ECR I-10981.

[82] Steiner, Woods, Twigg-Flesner, *EU Law* (9th ed, OUP, 2006) at 426. See further Moore, 'Freedom of Movement and Migrant Workers' Social Security: An Overview of the Case Law of the Court of Justice 1997–2001' (2001) 39 *CML Rev* 807; 'Freedom of Movement and Migrant Workers' Social Security: An Overview of the Case Law of the Court of Justice 1992-1997' (1998) 35 *CML Rev* 409.

[83] Case C-76/72 *Michel S v Fonds National de Reclassement Handicapés* [1973] ECR 457.

[84] Case C-32/75 *Christini v SNCF* [1975] ECR 1085.

[85] Case C-207/78 *Ministère Public v Even and Office National des Pensions pour Travailleurs Salariés* [1980] 2 CMLR 71.

'whether or not linked to a contract of employment, are generally granted to national workers primarily because of their objective status as workers or by virtue of the mere fact of their residence on national territory.'[86] Not all State support falls within the remit of Art 7(2) however. In *Baldinger*,[87] former prisoners of war were paid an allowance, provided they were Austrian nationals. The ECJ accepted that the rationale of the allowance was to compensate persons for the hardships they had endured for their country and was not because of their status as worker or because of their residence. In *Lebon*[88] the Court also distinguished between the range of benefit rights available to those workers who had 'settled' in the host country and those who are seeking work but have not yet worked. We have also seen in *Bachmann* that the ECJ may tolerate differential tax treatment where it is necessary to preserve the cohesion of the taxation system but any distinctions must be clearly justified.

[20.38] Article 7(3) deals with educational rights and provides that EC workers shall have 'access to training in vocational schools and retraining centres' under the same conditions as national workers. In *Lair*[89] this was interpreted restrictively to exclude universities. This restrictive reading may be explained as attempting to prevent the use of the broad definition of worker as a vehicle to disingenuously gain access to educational benefits. In *Ninni-Orasche*,[90] however, the ECJ dismissed the suggestion that a person could 'abusively ... create a situation enabling her to claim the status of a worker' in order to acquire advantages linked to that status. There, the applicant had been living in the State for two and a half years and taken up employment as a waitress for just a couple of months, prior to enrolling in university. Under Art 12, workers' children enjoy rights of access to education.

Accession Member States

[20.39] The 2003 Accession Treaty provided for the existing 15 Member States to make transitional arrangements for access to their labour markets by nationals of eight of the Member States that joined the EU on 1 May 2004 (Czech Republic, Estonia, Hungary, Latvia, Lithuania, Poland, Slovakia and Slovenia).[91] Ireland elected not to impose any restriction on the workers of these accession States to access Irish labour markets and so no permit regime applies and they enjoy full free movement rights. In general, full free movement provisions will apply throughout the European Union to these 2004 accession Member States from 1 May 2009, although a Member State may request the Commission to permit continued restrictions for a further two years if it is experiencing serious disturbances in its labour market.

---

[86] Case C-207/78 *Ministère Public v Even and Office National des Pensions pour Travailleurs Salariés* [1980] 2 CMLR 71 at para 3.

[87] Case C-386/02 *Baldinger v Pensionsversicherungsanstalt der Arbeiter* [2004] ECR I-8411.

[88] Case C-316/85 *Centre public d'Aide Sociale de Courcelles v Lebon*.

[89] Case C-39/86 *Lair* [1988] ECR 316.

[90] Case C-413/01 *Ninni-Orasche*.

[91] See Adinolfi, 'Free Movement and Access to Work of Citizens of the New Member States: The Transitional Measures' (2005) 42 *CML Rev* 469 for a fuller analysis of the transitional measures.

Bulgaria and Romania

[20.40] Bulgaria and Romania joined the Union on 1 January 2007. Notwithstanding this, they are subject to transitional arrangements in relation to free movement of workers should existing Member States wish to apply them. Ireland has imposed these transitional arrangements on Bulgarian and Romanian nationals by insisting that they continue to require an employment permit to take up employment and that the job will continue to be subject to the current requirement of a labour market test. However, these employment permit requirements apply only to the first continuous 12 months of employment in the State. At the end of this twelve month period a Bulgarian or Romanian national will be free to work in Ireland without any further need for an employment permit. Nationals of Bulgaria and Romania who have been lawfully working in Ireland for a continuous period of 12 months prior to 31 December 2006 or who already have existing residence status do not require work permits.

[20.41] On 17 December 2008, the Government announced that from 1 January 2009, it would continue to restrict access to the Irish labour market for nationals of Bulgaria and Romania.[92] The Government stated that this decision will be kept under on-going review and will be assessed comprehensively before the end of 2011.

EEA Nationals [Iceland, Liechtenstein and Norway]

[20.42] The European Economic Area Agreement (the EEA Agreement), signed in Oporto on 2 May 1992, extends the application of the four fundamental freedoms of the internal market, the free movement of goods, services, capital and persons, so that they apply within the EEA in the same way as in the European Community. It applies to three of the four European Free Trade Area (EFTA) countries, namely Iceland, Liechtenstein and Norway. Thus, the same provisions apply in relation to employment of citizens of these states as to citizens of all the Member States of the European as discussed in paragraphs **[20.08]** to **[20.38]**. The EFTA Surveillance Authority and the EFTA Court Monitor are responsible for enforcement on the part of EFTA states. Article 6 of the EEA provides that in so far as provisions of the Agreement are 'identical in substance to the corresponding rules of the Treaty' they shall be interpreted in conformity with the relevant rulings of the ECJ given prior to the date of signature of the EEA Agreement. In relation to rulings of the ECJ which post-date the EEA Agreement, Article 3(2) of the European Surveillance Authority/Court Agreement provides that the Authority and the Court shall pay due account to the principles laid down by the relevant rulings of the ECJ.

Switzerland

[20.43] The European Communities and Swiss Confederation Act 2001 was passed to give effect to the Agreement on Free Movement of Persons between the EC and the Swiss Confederation signed on 21 June 1999. This Act extends the full effect of the European Community free movement of workers provisions to Swiss nationals with effect from 1 June 2002. A Protocol extending the Agreement to the 10 new EU

---

[92] www.entemp.ie/labour/workpermits/bulgariaromania.htm.

Member States (26 October 2004) entered into force on 1 April 2006 with certain immigration restrictions in relation to the eight Eastern European states. A second Protocol deals with Bulgarian and Romanian Nationals. On 8 February 2009, Switzerland voted to renew and extend the free movement of workers agreements.

NON-EEA NATIONALS

[20.44] Where a prospective employee is not automatically entitled to work in Ireland, they must obtain permission to do so through the employment permit system. Employment permit schemes for non-EEA nationals are established under the Employment Permits Acts 2003 and 2006 (the 'Employment Permits Acts'). The Acts confer powers upon the Minister for Enterprise, Trade and Employment to establish employment permit regimes.[93]

[20.45] A non-EEA national may not enter the services of an employer in the State or be in employment in the State, except in accordance with an employment permit granted by the Minister for Enterprise, Trade and Employment.[94] Non-EEA nationals (or their employers on their behalf) must therefore make an application for the appropriate employment permit to the Department of Enterprise, Trade and Employment. The original permit is issued to the employee directly and contains a statement of employment rights. There are four main types of employment permit:

  (i)   Green Card Permits;

  (ii)   Work Permits;

  (iii) Intra Company Transfer Permits; and

  (iv)   Work permits for spouses and dependents of employment permits holders.

[20.46] Regardless of the type of employment permit being sought, a standard application form must be completed for each permit. Section 6 of the Employment Permits Acts sets out the information which must be included on each application form. This includes:

  (i)   a full and accurate description of the employment in respect of which the application is made (the 'employment concerned'), the terms and conditions, including the hours of work in each week of the employment, and the duration of the employment;

  (ii)   information in respect of the qualifications, skills or experience that are required for the employment concerned;

  (iii) information and where appropriate, any relevant documents in respect of the qualifications, skills or experience of the foreign national;

  (iv)   specify the place at or in which the employment concerned is to be carried out;

---

[93] These regimes, in general, are designed to respond to labour market needs. As they are subject to frequent change, the Department of Enterprise, Trade and Employment (www.entemp.ie) should be consulted when details of the up-to-date policy/regime is required.

[94] Employment Permits Acts, s 2.

(v) specify the remuneration and any deductions, where agreed, for board and accommodation, or either of them, in respect of the employment concerned;

(vi) in respect of the foreign national concerned:

- specify whether or not he or she has sought permission to land in the State on a previous occasion; or

- has been in the State on a previous occasion without permission to land;

(vii) whether he or she is in the State at the time of the application;

(viii) provide information and documents relating to the permission granted to him or her to land in the State; and

(ix) provide such other information as may be prescribed, or which the Minister may request and which, in the Minister's opinion, might materially assist in the making of a decision on the application.

Green Card permits

[20.47] Under the Employment Permits Act 2006, a Green Card permit scheme was introduced for the first time for occupations which the Government considers to be of high strategic importance and where it is of the opinion that skill shortages exist. This new Green Card scheme replaced the previous work visa/work authorisation scheme.[95]

[20.48] Green Card permits apply to two categories of occupation which are based on salary level. Where the annual salary (excluding bonuses) is to be €60,000 or more, a Green Card permit is available for all occupations other than those which are contrary to the public interest. Where the annual salary is between €30,000 and €59,999 (excluding bonuses) a Green Card permit is available for a restricted number of strategically important occupations which are specified by the Department of Enterprise, Trade and Employment. These include information technology professionals, healthcare professionals, engineers, construction professionals, researchers, and various financial and business professionals. The key advantage of satisfying these monetary thresholds is that no prior advertisement of the position is necessary nor must any labour market needs test be complied with.

Applying for a Green Card

[20.49] In addition to completing the Green Card application form and satisfying the relevant monetary thresholds, the proposed employee must possess the relevant qualifications, skills or experience required for the position. A copy of such qualifications must be submitted with the application form.

[20.50] The issuing of a Green Card permit is also contingent on a job offer from a *bona fide* employer, trading in Ireland, and registered with the Companies Registration Office and the Revenue Commissioners. The Department of Enterprise, Trade and

---

[95] During the late 1990s, to facilitate the recruitment of suitably qualified people from non-EEA countries for designated sectors of the employment market where skill shortages were particularly acute, a working visa and work authorisation scheme was introduced. This fast-track visa was particularly prevalent in the medical and information technology sectors.

Employment guidance note states that to qualify as 'trading in Ireland', the potential employer must have a base in Ireland rather than have merely a representative presence.[96] Newly incorporated companies registered in the State for the first time must provide evidence of these registrations by submitting confirmation of their tax number from the Revenue Commissioners and providing the Company Registration Number on the application form itself.

[20.51] The employee concerned must be employed by the Irish company and be paid in Ireland. Applications from recruitment agencies, agents, intermediaries or companies who intend to outsource or subcontract the employee to work in another company will not be accepted under this scheme.

Job offer

[20.52] Green Card applications must be accompanied by a job offer. The job offer must be on company headed paper, dated within the previous 60 days, must be of two years or more duration and must specify the following:

    (i)   a full description of the proposed employment;

    (ii)   starting date;

    (iii)   the proposed employee's salary excluding bonuses; and

    (iv)   information in respect of the qualifications, skills or experience that are required for the employment.

[20.53] As the current guidelines require job offers to be of two years' or more duration, it at present impossible to offer an employee a contract of employment of a lesser duration. Over the last number of years, the use of a one year fixed term contract of employment has become popular in Ireland. However, such an offer will not satisfy the criteria for a Green Card. It is important to note, however, that while the job offer must be of two years' duration or more, this does not in any way guarantee the person two years continuous employment. The individual's employment may be terminated upon the giving of the appropriate notice contain in the person's contract of employment or in accordance with the Minimum Notice and Terms of Employment Act 1973.[97] In doing so, caution should be exercised as the employment permit holder is entitled to the same statutory protections as their Irish counterparts such as protection from dismissal, discrimination etc.

Ratio of EEA/ Non-EEA nationals

[20.54] A Green Card will not be granted to companies where a consequence of granting the employment permit would be that more than 50% of employees in the firm would be non-EEA nationals.[98] This rule does not apply where the employee makes the

---

[96] Department of Enterprise Trade and Employment, *Employment Permits Arrangements: Guide to Green Card Permits* (November 2008).

[97] See Ch 3, *The Terms of the Employment Contract* at para **[3.44]**.

[98] Minimum Notice and Terms of Employment Act 1973, s 10(1).

application themselves. There is no difference between the employment permit granted on foot of an employer or employee application.

Fee and Duration

[20.55] Once issued, a Green Card permits the employee to work in the State with that particular employer in the occupation specified on the permit. It is issued for an initial period of two years and can be renewed for a further three years. After five years, the work permit can be renewed indefinitely. A fee of €1,000 is payable for a two-year work permit and €1,500 for a three-year work permit. It is expected that when a work permit is issued in the State the employee will stay with the initial employer for a period of 12 months but then may move employer, provided a new application for a Green Card is made. Once the individual is legally resident in the State, they are entitled to bring their family to Ireland.

Renewal of Green Card

[20.56] Green Card permit holders whose permit and immigration registration card (GNIB card) is due to expire in 2009 will not be required to apply for a new permit through the Department of Enterprise, Trade and Employment.[99] Instead Green Card permit holders must present themselves at the Garda National Immigration Bureau with their existing Green Card permit, a copy of their P60 from their employer for the previous year and their preceeding three months' pay slips. Provided they have complied with their previous employment permit conditions and are of good character, a Stamp 4 shall be place in their passport for one year's duration which will entitle them to continuing working. If the Immigration, Residence Protection Bill 2008 is enacted, Green Card holders will be able to apply under that legislation for long-term residency. The granting of the Stamp 4 is an interim status that simply exempts the person from requiring a new Green Card. It does not convey long-term residency status and does not confer the full benefits of Irish citizenship. The Green Card permit holder will still need to make an application for long-term residency where the necessary legislation application process is put in place.

Work permits

[20.57] A Work Permit may be granted for those occupations with a salary of €30,000 (excluding bonuses) or more and, in very limited circumstances, in a salary range below €30,000 (excluding bonuses). There are certain job categories which are ineligible for a work permit and this list is published by the Department of Enterprise Trade and Employment.[100] These include categories such as clerical and administration positions, general operatives/labour, all sales staff etc as it is the Government's view that such staff can be sourced within the EEA.

---

[99] http://www.entemp.ie/labour/workpermits/greencardrenewal.htm.

Labour market needs test

[20.58] Unlike the Green Card scheme, the employer must satisfy a labour market needs test prior to submitting an application for a Work Permit. In practice, this test requires the employer to advertise the position on the FÁS/EURES employment network for a period of at least four weeks and also in a national newspaper for at least three days to ensure that, in the first instance, an EEA national cannot be sourced to fill the vacancy or in the second instance, a national of Bulgaria or Romania. Evidence that this requirement is complied with must be included with the application. There is no requirement to submit a job offer as required by a Green Card application. A completed application form in itself is sufficient.

Ratio of EEA/non-EEA nationals

[20.59] A Work Permit will not be granted to companies where a consequence of granting the employment permit would be that more than 50% of employees in the firm would be non-EEA nationals.[101] This rule does not apply where the employee makes the application themselves. There is no difference between the employment permit granted on foot of an employer or employee application.

Fees and Duration

[20.60] Once issued, a Work Permit entitles the employee to work in the State with that particular employer in the occupation specified on the permit. It is issued for an initial period of two years and can be renewed for a further three years. After five years, the Work Permit can be renewed indefinitely. A fee of €1,000 is payable for a two-year Work Permit and €1,500 for a three-year Work Permit. It is expected that when a Work Permit is issued in the State the employee is expected to stay with the initial employer for a period of 12 months but then may move employer, provided a new application for a Work Permit is made. Once the individual is legally resident in the State they are entitled to bring their family to Ireland.

Policy on unlimited Work Permits

[20.61] An unlimited Work Permit is issued at the fifth renewal stage or after five years' continuous service if an employee has been employed by the same employer.[102] An unlimited permit has a start date but no expiry date and it entitles the employee to work

---

[100] Ineligible Job Categories include all Clerical and Administrative Positions, all General Operatives/Labourers, all Operator and Production Staff, all retail sales vacancies, sales representatives, Supervisory/ Specialist, all drivers (excluding HGV); Nursery/ Crèche Workers, Child Minder/ Nanny; all staff except chefs; Bookbinder, Bricklayer, Cabinet Maker, Carpenter / Joiner, Carton Maker, Fitter – Construction Plant, Electrician, Instrumentation Craftsperson, Fitter, Tiler – Floor / Wall, Mechanic – Heavy Vehicles, Instrumentation Craftsperson, Metal Fabricator, Mechanic – Motor, Originator, Painter And Decorator, Plumber, Printer, Engineer – Refrigeration, Sheet Metal Worker, Tool Maker, Vehicle Body Repairer, Machinist – Wood, Plasterers and Welders.

[101] Employment Permits Acts, s 10(1).

[102] http://www.entemp.ie/labour/workpermits/elements/unlimited.htm.

for a specified employer for an unlimited period without the need to renew their permit yearly. In the event that the employee changes employment then a new permit application must be made on their behalf. If an employee qualifies for an unlimited work permit, this should be specified when submitting the application form. There is no charge for an unlimited Work Permit.

Intra-Company Transfer Permit Scheme

[20.62] Intra-Company transferees can be senior management, key personnel or those undergoing a training program. Guidance has been given by the Department of Enterprise Trade and Employment on what each of these terms means.[103]

Senior management

[20.63] For an employee to be considered senior management, they must be primarily involved in the management of the organisation and must supervise or control the work of other professional and managerial employees or manage an essential function within the organisation. The individual must have authority to hire and fire or recommend these courses of action, as well as other personnel functions. Their functions must be exercised at a senior level within the organisation's hierarchy or with respect to the function managed and the person must exercise discretion over the day to day operations of the activity or function over which the employee has authority.

Key personnel

[20.64] Key personnel are defined as persons working within an organisation who possess specialist knowledge essential to the establishment of the service, research equipment, techniques or management. In assessing such knowledge, account will be taken of whether or not the person has a high level of qualification or experience relating to the type of work or trade requiring specific technical knowledge, including membership of an accredited profession.

Personnel participating in a training programme

[20.65] Applications for permits in respect of inter-company events may be considered provided it has been demonstrated that a detailed training programme will be undertaken.

Monetary thresholds and prior service

[20.66] In addition to being considered senior management, key personnel or those undergoing a training program, monetary thresholds are also imposed on Intra-Company Transfers. The transferees must be earning a minimum annual salary of €40,000 (excluding bonuses) and have at least 12 months' service with the foreign employer prior to the transfer. As evidence of this, the employee must submit their previous 12 months' payslips. Unlike all other employment permits, the transferee may continue to be paid outside of Ireland. Given the significant amount of foreign businesses with operations in Ireland, this scheme has proven to be extremely popular.

---

[103] http://www.entemp.ie/publications/labour/2007/guideict.pdf.

Links between companies

[20.67] The Irish company must have a direct link with the overseas company by common ownership, either one company must be owned by the other or both companies must be part of the same group controlled by the same parent company. Documentary evidence of this link is required.

Ratio of EEA/ Non-EEA nationals

[20.68] Normally, the number of inter-company transferees should not exceed 5% of the total Irish workforce in a firm, although in exceptional circumstances such as small firms or start up companies, a higher percentage may be permitted on a strictly temporary basis with an absolute limit of 50% of non-EEA staff.[104] No guidance has been provided as to when this temporary exemption is to apply. As with Green Cards and Work Permits, this ratio percentage does not apply to applications made by employees.

Fees and duration

[20.69] The duration of an Intra Company Transfer Permit is for a defined period up to maximum of 24 months in the first instance, and may be extended upon application to a maximum stay of five years. The fee for a permit of up to six months duration is €500, for a 6 – 24 month period, €1,000 and for up to 36 months, €1,500. A foreign national availing of the permit will be required to leave the State at the end of this period of time. The individual cannot work for any other employer other than that named in the permit. Once the individual is legally resident in the State they are entitled to bring their family to Ireland.

Spouses and dependents of employment permit holders

[20.70] Spouses and dependents of employment permit holders may also apply for work permits.[105] Spouses and dependents of employment permit holders may apply for a work permit in respect of all occupations. Therefore, the list of ineligible job categories does not apply to spouses or dependents. The proposed employer is not required to undertake a labour market test.

[20.71] In order to apply for such a permit, the employment permit holder must have a valid:

   (i)   Green Card; or

   (ii)   Work Permit; or

   (iii)   Working Visa; or

   (iv)   Work Authorisation; or

   (v)   Inter-Company transfer.

[20.72] The employment permit holder must be working within the terms of their employment permit. A work permit issued under the scheme will normally be issued for

---

[104] Employment Permits Acts, s 10(2).
[105] http://www.entemp.ie/publications/labour/2007/guidespousals.pdf.

a period up to the expiry date of the permit of the existing employment permit holder. In order to apply for this scheme, the foreign national in question must be legally resident in the State with their spouse and/or dependent. Where the application is being made for an employment permit holder for a spouse or dependent residing outside the State, this will be subject to the normal employment permit procedures. In addition to making an employment permit application, the individual must include a copy of their marriage certificate in respect of an application for a spouse or a birth certificate in respect of an application for a dependent, the relevant passport pages of the existing permit holder which shows their most recent immigration stamp, their employment permit and most recent visa (where appropriate).

Individual arrangements

[20.73] For certain categories of workers, the Department of Enterprise, Trade and Employment applies individual arrangements.

Nurses and doctors

[20.74] Special rules apply for employment permit holders for doctors and nurses.[106] For a nurse or doctor, an employment permit will be issued for a period of up to two years on foot of an application where an employment relationship already exists. For a nurse, this will mean that the applicant will have to submit supporting documentation from An Bord Altranais, together with a copy of the employment contract. Doctors must be either interns or fully registered doctors with the Irish Medical Council. The type of permit granted will depend on the duration of the job offer and the starting salary. No labour market needs test will apply to employment permit applications in respect of nurses and doctors.

Sports professionals

[20.75] The requirement to have a valid employment permit extends to sport professionals. Such applications must be supported by the appropriate sporting body. While the usual criteria applies to such applications, where supported by the appropriate sporting body, the Department of Enterprise Trade and Employment will grant work permits where the person is earning a salary of less than €30,000.[107]

Employees who hold an employment permit from another EU country

[20.76] In *Vander Elst v Office des Migrations Internationales*[108] the ECJ extended the benefits of free-movement principles under Art 49 of the Treaty to non-EU nationals provided they are entitled to lawfully work in another Member State, and certain other criteria are met. Vander Elst was a Belgian employer operating a demolition business which employed Moroccan nationals in Belgium. All were legally entitled to live and work there. The employer undertook to provide services to a client in Reims in France. He obtained short stay (one month) entry visas for the Moroccan employees from the French Consulate and dispatched his Moroccan workers to France to carry out the work.

---

[106] http://www.entemp.ie/labour/workpermits/doctorsandnurses.htm.

[107] http://www.entemp.ie/labour/workpermits/sportsprofessionals.htm.

[108] Case C-43/93 *Vander Elst v Office des Migrations Internationales* [1994] ECR I-3803.

Following a site inspection, the French authorities claimed that the employees did not hold valid French work permits. Vander Elst was fined and ordered to pay a sum to the International Migration Office. He appealed, and the case was eventually referred to the ECJ. The ECJ supported Vander Elst and laid down guidelines to be followed by any company intending to send third country nationals to fulfil a service contract in another EU country. Provided the non-EEA national is lawfully resident in the same Member State as his employer (who must also be lawfully established there) and the employee was lawfully employed by an employer who is providing a cross-border service of a temporary nature, the non-EEA person can work in that country without an employment permit.

[20.77] Had the *Vander Elst* ruling been applied uniformly by Member States, one imagines it would have greatly facilitated cross-border service provision. The reality is rather different. States such as Greece and Luxemburg have disregarded the *Vander Elst* ruling. While the principle is acknowledged in Denmark and Austria, these countries maintain a requirement for a work permit, contrary to the ECJ holding. Meanwhile, the Dutch authorities describe the work permit application as a mere administrative formality to ensure the necessary elements of the *Vander Elst* principle are satisfied.

[20.78] The principle is recognised by Ireland. Non-EEA nationals who fall within the *Vander Elst* exemption do not have to obtain an employment permit. However such individuals must still register with the immigration authorities and provide evidence of the contract which they are here to service. The maximum duration which an individual can stay in Ireland is usually up to one year. When making an application the following documentation is required:

(i)　fully completed and signed application form;

(ii)　the employee's passport;

(iii)　evidence of the employee's right to reside and work in the EU Member State the employee is coming from, and evidence that he/she has permission to return there following the termination of the contract in Ireland; and

(iv)　declaration from the employer confirming that the employee is lawfully employed by the employer, that he/she is coming to Ireland to provide services on the employer's behalf, the name and contact details for the employer in Ireland, and that he/she will be returning to work in the other EU Member State following completion of the project in Ireland.[109]

Policy on redundancy

[20.79] The Department of Enterprise, Trade and Employment has a stated policy whereby it will look favourably on applications in respect of foreign nationals who have been made redundant within the last three months and who have valid employment permits.[110] Provided the employee can prove that they have been made redundant by their previous employer and where they have found new employment, no ineligible job

---

[109] See Irish Naturalisation and Immigration Service website for guidelines.
[110] http://www.entemp.ie/labour/workpermits/redundant.htm.

categories will apply to this person and no labour market needs test will apply. The Department of Enterprise Trade and Employment states that such applications will be given priority.

Students

[20.80] Citizens of non-EEA countries, for which visas are required, who wish to pursue a course of study in Ireland, can apply for a student visa to enter Ireland. Once in the State and registered with the immigration authorities, they have the right to take up casual employment without an employment permit. These visas will be granted to non-EEA nationals who have enrolled in a recognised full-time course of education for a period of at least one year for at least fifteen hours study per week.[111] Those students who are registered as full-time students with An Garda Síochána are permitted to work part-time in Ireland up to a maximum of 20 hours a week and full-time during vacation periods to support themselves. The right to work ceases on completion of the course.

Graduate scheme

[20.81] The Minister for Enterprise Trade and Employment introduced a new policy in relation to third level graduates in April 2007. Essentially, the graduate is granted a period of six months from the date of their results within which to obtain a Green Card or Work Permit, or permission to remain in the State by some other means. During this six month period the graduate must be genuinely seeking employment after education. They are allowed to work for up to 40 hours without an employment permit. However, the graduate must obtain permission to remain from the GNIB or their local Garda registration office if residing outside of Dublin. Once this six month period has expired, the graduate is expected either to have obtained an employment permit or is expected to leave the State. Under the Graduate Scheme, the Department of Enterprise Trade and Employment will consider work permit applications for graduates with a starting salary lower than €30,000, if it can be shown that this is the industry norm for the relevant graduate occupation.[112]

Business permission

[20.82] Where non-EEA individuals wish to relocate to Ireland for business purposes in a capacity other than as an employee, they must obtain business permission from the Minster for Justice, Equality and Law Reform.[113] This applies to all non-EEA nationals who are self-employed or who are shareholding directors. A permission from the Minister entitles a person to establish and engage in business for a particular period of time. There are certain requirements which attach to Business Permission. The non-EEA national must be willing to invest at least €300,000 in a business in the State. Certain exceptions apply to this capital requirement, such as, for example, where the non-EEA national is an artist, and in such circumstances, the Business Permission may issue without the necessity to invest such a large amount of capital. However, these

---

[111] http://www.inis.gov.ie/en/INIS/Pages/Student_Visa_Guidelines.

[112] http://www.entemp.ie/labour/workpermits/graduatescheme.htm.

[113] http://www.inis.gov.ie/en/INIS/BUSINESS.pdf/Files/BUSINESS.pdf.

applications can take six months to a year to process. The conditions generally applying to a business permission are as follows:

(i)   the person must have at least €300,000 available for investment in Ireland;

(ii) the proposed venture must result in the employment of at least two EEA nationals;

(iii) the proposed business must enhance a commercial activity and the general competitiveness of the State;

(iv) the proposed business must be a viable trading concern and provide the applicant with sufficient income to support himself/herself and any dependants without resorting to social assistance or paid employment for which a work permit would be required; and

(v)   the applicant must be in possession of a valid passport and be of good character.

[20.83] Applicants who are successful in applying for Business Permission will be granted permission to operate their business for an initial period of 12 months, with the possibility of extension by applying to the Minister. Extensions will generally be granted as long as the conditions of the Business Permission continue to be met. Audited accounts, business plans and evidence of compliance with taxation requirements may also be required.

Business visitors

[20.84] Non-EEA nationals coming to Ireland for a business trip/business meeting or conference can, of course, do so. However, if the non-EEA national requires a visa in order to enter Ireland, he or she must submit the appropriate visa application together with the accompanying documentation to their local Irish embassy or consulate, prior to entering Ireland.[114] If the individual is coming to Ireland for the purposes of a business conference or meeting, they should carry with them a letter from the conference host outlining the nature and duration of the proposed stay in Ireland or the letter of invitation to the meeting. Non-EEA national business visitors who are not visa-required should carry with them a similar letter of invitation from the Irish company or from the conference host setting out where they intend to stay during the visit, for how long and who will be responsible for their expenses, accommodation etc in order to present to the immigration officials at the port of entry.

Illegal workers and irregular status

Generally

[20.85] The Employment Permit Acts provide for a range of offences in relation to illegal workers and employment permit abuses. It is illegal to take up employment or to

---

[114] In order to speed up this process, the Department of Foreign Affairs are currently implementing a new computerised visa system, which includes an online facility. This system will be introduced to all Irish Embassies/Consulates/Visa Offices on a phased basis during 2008/09. For a list of the countries whose residents can currently apply using the AVATS online facility see http://www.inis.gov.ie/en/INIS/Pages/Supported_Countries.

employ a person without a valid work permit where one is required. A number of problems arise in relation to access to justice for illegal workers or workers whose legal status has lapsed for one reason or another and some of these issues are addressed in this section.

Offences

[20.86] Section 2(3) of the Employment Permits Acs provides that it is an offence to employ non-nationals or for non-nationals to be in employment, save in accordance with a work permit. Section 2(10) and s 3 of the Acts enumerate the exceptions namely, EEA nationals, refugees and other persons whose permission to remain in the State allows them to work without requiring an employment permit.[115] Section 34 of the Employment Permits Act 2006 introduces presumptive burdens regarding employment. Evidence by a Garda, an immigration officer or other authorised officer to the effect that a person was doing an act consistent with being employed shall raise a presumption that the person was employed. It is a full defence for an employer to show that he/she took all reasonable steps to ensure compliance.

[20.87] Section 18 of the Acts prohibits forgery, fraudulent alteration or use of employment permits. Section 19 prohibits employers from transferring permits between persons and/or using permits for work other than that for which it was granted. Section 23 prohibits employers from making any deductions from a worker's employment for obtaining/renewing a work permit, or for the cost of his/her recruitment, or travel expenses previously paid to the worker. Employers are also prohibited from retaining personal documents belonging to permit holders. It is an offence to knowingly provide false or misleading information in an application.[116]

[20.88] There are a number of exclusively summary offences. Obstruction of an officer authorised by the Minister under the Employment Permits Acts in the course of his duty, failure to comply with a requirement under s 22 of the Acts without reasonable excuse and provision of false or misleading information are all summary offences.[117] Where a person's employment is terminated, the employee and the employer are obliged to surrender the original and copy permit to the Minister within four weeks. Failure to do so constitutes a summary offence.[118] Where a permit has been granted, s 27 requires employers to retain records of the employment, the duration of the employment and particulars of the permit for a period of five years or such greater time as the person remains in employment. Failure to retain such records also constitutes a summary offence. Section 32(4) provides that summary proceedings may be instituted within 24 months of the date of the offence.[119]

---

[115] This has been amended in relation to nationals of Bulgarian and Romania by Employment Permits Act 2006, s 3.

[116] Employment Permits Acts, s 25.

[117] Employment Permits Acts, s 22(10).

[118] Employment Permits Acts, s 24(2).

[119] Employment Permits Acts, s 32(4).

Corporate liability

[20.89] Section 33 of the Acts provides that where an offence has been committed by a body corporate and is proven to be committed with the consent of, or is attributable to the neglect of, a director or other officer of the company, that person can be proceeded against for the same offence and punished accordingly.

Penalties

[20.90] Any person in breach of ss 2(1), 2(2) or 2B of the Employment Permits Acts is liable on summary conviction to a fine not exceeding €3,000 or imprisonment of up to 12 months, or both. In the event of a conviction on indictment, a person is liable to a fine of up to €250,000 or up to 10 years' imprisonment or both.[120] Convictions for offences under ss 18(2), 19(3), 23(4) or 25 carry a maximum fine of €5,000 and/or up to 12 months' imprisonment on summary conviction and a maximum fine of €50,000 and/or up to five years' imprisonment on indictment.[121] Persons guilty of offence under ss 22(10), 24(2) or 27(6) are liable on summary conviction to a maximum fine of €5,000 and/or up to 12 months' imprisonment.[122]

Irregular status

[20.91] Large numbers of workers lapse into irregular status, whether through redundancy, dismissal, change of employment without acquisition of a new work permit or expiry of the initial permit. While the Department of Enterprise, Trade and Employment has a stated policy[123] of favourably considering permit applications in respect of foreign nationals who have been made redundant within the last three months and who are valid employment permit holders, there is no express policy in relation to persons who have been unfairly dismissed.

[20.92] Persons working without valid employment permits may find any labour law action severely compromised by the illegality of their employment contract. As evidenced by the EAT decision in *Lewis v Squash Ireland*,[124] the courts will typically refuse to enforce contracts of employment which are tainted with illegality.[125] The Unfair Dismissals (Amendment) Act 1993 alleviated some of the harsher effects of this doctrine on employees by providing that an individual could continue to sustain an unfair dismissal action notwithstanding a contravention of the Income Tax or Social

---

[120] Employment Permits Acts, s 2(3).

[121] Employment Permits Acts, s 32(1).

[122] Employment Permits Acts, s 32(2).

[123] http://www.entemp.ie/labour/workpermits/redundant.htm. This policy is noted above at para **[20.79]**.

[124] *Lewis v Squash Ireland* [1983] ILRM 363.

[125] However, see the UK EAT decision in *Blue Chip Trading Ltd v Helbawi* [2009] IRLR 128, where the EAT considered that the parts of the performance of an employment contract which were illegal, as the employee did not have a valid work permit at those times, could be severed for the purposes of a claim for minimum wage under the relevant legislation. The claim for minimum wage could proceed in respect of the part of the performance of the contract which was legal.

Welfare Acts in the employment contract.[126] No statutory saver exists for illegal workers in breach of the Employment Permit Acts, however.

[20.93] The EAT decision of *Dubyna v Hourican Hygiene Services*[127] suggests the emergence of a more lenient approach, at least where workers are unaware that they had no valid work permit. In that case, a Ukrainian employee was dismissed after her employer failed to obtain a work permit for her. Her original employer (the holder of the permit) had let her go due to lack of work. The respondent initially employed her on a part-time basis from August 2002 and then took her on full-time in January 2003, repeatedly assuring her that it was familiar with work permit procedures and would process an application on her behalf. Despite assurances, an application for a permit was delayed and eventually withdrawn from the Department of Enterprise, Trade and Employment by the new employer. The claimant made a number of inquiries in relation to the permit and was assured that her employer was taking care of it. In October the employer informed the claimant there were problems in relation to her permit and requested she reduce her hours to 20 hours per week and register as a student. Her employment was terminated in November 2003 due to a lack of work permit. The EAT considered that it was an implied term of one's contract that an employer would process an application for a work permit in a proper and diligent manner, as the employer was the only person who could obtain a work permit. The Tribunal distinguished between a contract for an illegal purpose and the instant circumstances in this case where the claimant was not aware of any illegality. She was awarded €32,800. Similarly in *Nafieza McWhite v Supermacs Ireland Ltd,*[128] the EAT stated that 'if the employment is terminated as a result of no permit having been applied for then, on the facts of it, any consequential dismissal is unfair'. Potentially this approach may be affected by the introduction of the Employment Permits Act 2006, as workers themselves can now apply for work permits directly. However, the approach is still of relevance as employees still need the employer to sign the application.

[20.94] The rights of illegal workers remain uncertain in the absence of further guiding authority. It is unlikely workers who knowingly work without a valid permit will enjoy statutory employment protections. It is arguably unfair, however, that they should be barred from any right of action against their employer. As a matter of practice, the consequences of disclosing illegal work practices before a court or employment forum are typically far graver for an employer and for this reason they will frequently prefer to settle the claim, rather than argue that the contract is void for illegality.

Access to justice and employment contingent status

[20.95] Migrant workers' permission to remain in the State is frequently contingent on their employment status. The decision whether to invoke employment law rights and risk provoking termination of employment or simply 'suffer in silence,' therefore constitutes a frequent dilemma. While anti-penalisation/victimisation provisions exist to

---

[126] Unfair Dismissal (Amendment) Act 1993, s 7(11).
[127] *Dubyna v Hourican Hygiene Services* UD 781/2004.
[128] *Nafieza McWhite v Supermacs Ireland Ltd* UD928/2005.

protect most persons relying on employment protection legislation,[129] these may not in practice prevent the breakdown of the employment relationship. If a person's work environment deteriorates severely or they are actually dismissed as a consequence of making a claim, they may realistically only have recourse to financial compensation. Clearly, pending long-term residency applications may be jeopardised by the absence of ongoing employment. This necessarily gives migrant workers pause for thought when contemplating claims for minimum wage, holiday pay, discriminatory treatment or other statutory rights. While the Department of Justice, Equality and Law Reform invariably seeks to treat persons who have been the victim of labour exploitation favourably, given the breadth of administrative discretion, employment permit holders remain justifiably anxious about the potential knock-on effect of litigating employment rights issues on their status in the country.

National Employment Rights Authority

[20.96] The National Employment Rights Authority (NERA) was established on an interim basis by the Government in February 2007.[130] It is intended that NERA will be established on a statutory basis upon the enactment of the Employment Compliance Bill 2008. During the Second Stage debate on the Bill in Dáil Éireann,[131] the Minister of State stated:

> At its heart [the Bill] is the intention that all employees, but particularly low-paid and other vulnerable groups, can have their rights and entitlements pursued and vindicated by a dedicated State labour inspectorate.

[20.97] The primary aim of NERA is to increase the level of monitoring and ensure compliance with employment rights legislation in Ireland. As part of its overall functions NERA will manage the labour inspectorate and employment rights sections of the Department of Enterprise Trade and Employment. Under the proposed Bill, NERA will be empowered to carry out investigations relating to the employment status of all workers. Acting on a non-statutory basis, NERA was responsible for recovery of over €3m in wages owed to employees in 2008.[132] The annual figures also showed that during 2008, NERA's inspectors carried out a total of 27,900 calls, interviews and inspections, an increase of 96% on 2007. Given that 74% of all employment permits relate to areas of work in the so-called 'low skills' category, it is hoped that NERA will ensure that non-EEA workers will have their employment rights recognised.[133]

---

[129] For example, the National Minimum Wage Act 2000; Employment Equality Acts 1998–2008; Safety, Health and Welfare at Work Act 2005; Carer's Leave Act 2001; Protection of Employees (Part-Time Work) Act 2001; Protection of Employees (Fixed-Term Work) Act 2003.

[130] On NERA's origin and functions, see Ch 1, Sources and Institutions, at paras **[1.25]–[1.27]**.

[131] Dáil Debates, Vol 673 No 4 (5 February 2009) at p 671.

[132] NERA's Annual Review, published 10 February 2009.

[133] Figures submitted by the Migrant Rights Centre Ireland in their Submission to the National Action Plan for Social Inclusion Introduction.

FUTURE DEVELOPMENTS

[20.98] The geo-political agenda which has pre-dominated in the wake of the '9/11' terrorist attacks has led to greater emphasis on security-related immigration measures at the expense of hindering travel access for non-EEA nationals. This has had the effect of impeding one of the European Commission's stated goals of achieving a broad equivalence between the rights and entitlements of EU citizens and of third-country nationals legally resident in the EU.[134] However, during France's presidency of the European Union in the second half of 2008, new attempts were made to push for the 27 Member States to introduce a charter on immigration that would create a more uniform approach to the different immigration policies of Member States. Although Ireland remains opposed to complete harmonisation of immigration policy at a European level, as new EU policy draws closers towards implementation, the domestic regime is likely to be affected.

Immigration, Residence and Protection Bill 2008

[20.99] The Immigration, Residence and Protection Bill 2008 (the 2008 Bill) was published on 24 January 2008. While it was envisaged that it would be passed by Government in late 2008, it is now more likely that it will be passed sometime in 2009. In a press release explaining the rationale behind the 2008 Bill,[135] the then Minister for Justice, Equality and Law Reform stated that one of the aims of the Bill is to regulate 'regular migration' into the State and to provide for a long-term residence status to certain categories of migrants. The 2008 Bill in particular provides that foreign nationals legally resident in the State will have to carry a credit card-sized permit containing biometric information. The permit will be required as a means of verifying whether a foreign national is lawfully present in the State. This has caused some debate and may be subject to further change.

[20.100] The 2008 Bill contains provision for foreign nationals to obtain long-term residence permits. The holders will be given rights in the State similar in most respects to those of Irish citizens. This status will make Ireland a more attractive place for those non-EEA nationals, who are highly skilled and who possess experience in specific industries, to come and take up employment here. Where standard eligibility requirements are met, this permit is granted for a period of five years and is renewable thereafter on satisfying certain conditions. The requirements include:

(i)   lawful presence in the State for five out of the previous six years;

(ii)   being of good character;

---

[134] Council Directive 2003/109/EC came into force on 12 February 2004. This Directive concerns the status of third-country nationals who are long-term residents in the European Union. It is based on the broad agreement reached by Member StateMember States at the European Council meeting held in Tampere, Finland between 15–16 October 1999, where each Member State emphasised the need to give equitable treatment to Non-EU member country nationals legally resident in the EU.

[135] Address by the Minister for Justice, Equality and Law Reform at the launch of the Immigration, Residence and Protection Bill 2008 on 29 January 2008.

(iii)   the demonstration of a reasonable competency of the Irish or English language;

(iv)   satisfying the Minister for Justice, Equality and Law Reform (the Minister) that reasonable efforts have been made to integrate into Irish society; and

(v)   evidence that the candidate has supported himself during his presence in the State.

[20.101] Under the 2008 Bill, certain foreign nationals or classes of foreign nationals can be classified as exempt from the requirement to obtain a visa by the Government. 'Visa-exempt foreign nationals' can be designated as such by Order of the Minister using specified criteria, which include occupation. Therefore, there is scope to provide speedier entry to Ireland for skilled occupations.

[20.102] In summary, the 2008 Bill aims to encourage those with experience, skills or qualifications that are in short supply to come and work in Ireland. The Government has also indicated that it may accelerate applications for residence permits for those highly skilled individuals who have been working under the Green Card permit scheme and who meet the criteria. According to the Department of Justice, Equality and Law Reform, those who do not qualify for legal status will be liable to be removed summarily and detained if necessary to ensure removal. This particular aspect has come under criticism from some human rights advocates.

The European Union Blue Card

[20.103] While the idea for an EU-wide policy on skilled immigration was first canvassed in 1999, it was only in October 2007 that the concept of the EU Blue Card emerged following a Commision proposal for a Council Directive.[136] Inspired by the United States Green Card, the proposal seeks to establish more attractive entry and residence conditions for third-country nationals to take up highly qualified employment in EU Member States. Conceived in response to perceived skills shortages in certain sectors and an ageing European labour force, the EU Blue Card would provide a common fast-track procedure to allow skilled migrants from outside the EEA and Switzerland to live and work in an EU Member State and to facilitate movement for work to another Member State.

[20.104] Under the proposed scheme, common criteria would apply requiring a work contract, professional qualifications and a minimum salary level. Additionally, workers would enjoy a series of socio-economic rights and favourable conditions for family reunification.

[20.105] The proposed Blue Card scheme has faced opposition from some EU countries, however. Germany, Austria and the Netherlands have expressed reluctance to relinquish further control over their labour markets. Recent accession states, meanwhile, are keen to see work restrictions that are imposed on their own citizens by older Member States phased out first. Under the provisions of the Protocol to the Treaty of Amsterdam, Ireland, Denmark and the United Kingdom only participate in such harmonised immigration measures on an opt-in basis. Despite favourable consideration from the

---

[136] COM (2007) 637 of 23 October 2007.

Joint Oireachtas Committee on European Scrutiny,[137] the Government did not opt-in within three months of the proposal. It remains open to Ireland to adopt any Directive which ultimately results.

[20.106] On 20 November 2008, the EU Parliament broadly endorsed the Blue Card proposal, adopting by clear majority a consultative report seeking to clarify aspects of the scheme.[138] The scheme is not expected to be implemented until at least 2011, when existing work restrictions are lifted for citizens of Eastern European Member States. It is expected that the Blue Card system will be voted upon in the European Council in late 2009.

Schengen Visa

[20.107] The Schengen Agreement was originally created independently of the European Union, in part due to the lack of consensus amongst EU members, and in part because those ready to implement the idea did not wish to wait for others to be ready to join. The Schengen Agreement was signed in Schengen, Luxembourg, on 15 June 1985, by Germany, France, Belgium, the Netherlands and Luxembourg and now forms part of the Treaty of Amsterdam. The Schengen zone now includes most of Western Europe, including Iceland and Norway. At present, the only EU countries left out of the Schengen zone are Ireland, United Kingdom, Cyprus, Bulgaria, and Romania.

[20.108] Once a person obtains a Schengen Visa, they can travel to any (or all) member countries using one single visa, thus avoiding the expense of obtaining individual visas for each country. This is particularly beneficial for persons who wish to visit several European countries on the same trip. The Schengen visa is a 'visitor visa'. It is issued to citizens of countries who are required to obtain a visa before entering the EU. The purpose of the visit must be leisure, tourism, or business and allows the holder to travel freely within the Schengen countries for a maximum stay of up to 90 days in a six-month period.

[20.109] Although Ireland continues to opt out of the Schengen Agreement, Ireland's position is now seen as increasingly anomalous. The European Parliament has urged Ireland and Britain to fully participate in Schengen, and acceptance of the Schengen principle is a prior condition of entry for new applicant States. Ireland continues to argue that it should control its own policy on the movement of persons across its frontiers. It therefore continues to insist upon the necessity for it retain its own border checks, making it impossible for it to fully to sign up to Schengen.[139]

---

[137] Joint Oireachtas Committee, EU Scrutiny Report No. 12 (8 April 2008).

[138] European Parliament legislative resolution of 20 November 2008 on the proposal for a Council directive on the conditions of entry and residence of third-country nationals for the purposes of highly qualified employment.

[139] Paper delivered by Piaras Mac Éinrí, Irish Centre for Migration Studies, NUI Cork on 'The Implications for Ireland and the UK arising from the Development of Recent EU Policy on Migration'.

English proficiency requirement

[20.110] Under plans being discussed within the Irish Government, foreign workers wishing to renew their work permits may have to prove that they can speak an adequate level of English. The Minister for Integration stated that he wanted to 'link' English language standards into the employment permits system. While the Minister said that it would be 'prescriptive' and 'unfair' to attach an English language element to those seeking an initial employment permit, he said that it could be introduced 'for the purposes of renewal' of an employment permit, adding, 'It is my firm belief that, from an integration perspective, we do need to build language skills into the Green Card system and the Work Permit system'.[140]

[20.111] Should some level of English proficiency be added to the criteria for obtaining an employment permit, the issues which arose in *58 Named Complainants v Goode Concrete Ltd*[141] may cease to be relevant. In this case, the Equality Tribunal held that employers should put in place clear procedures for ensuring that non-national employees understand their terms and conditions of employment as well as health and safety documentation.

[20.112] Goode Concrete had an extremely diverse workforce. Fifty-eight employees, representing six different nationalities, brought discrimination claims on race grounds. In most instances, the discriminatory treatment alleged was the company's failure to provide each employee with a contract of employment and safety documentation in their own language. The Equality Tribunal upheld the complaints. Each complainant was awarded €5,000 for the effects of this discrimination. The cumulative award against Goode Concrete amounted to €327,000. Furthermore, the Equality Officer ordered the employer to implement clear procedures to ensure that non-national employees understand their terms and conditions of employment and all safety documentation.

[20.113] The Equality Officer noted that other company documentation had been translated into Russian, and accepted that it could be considered reasonable for an employer to provide contracts in an alternative of the two languages where the employees understood Russian in addition to their native tongue. Alternatively, if an employer is not in a position to provide contracts of employment in different languages to its employees, the Equality Officer suggested it should have the English language version explained to all employees, using a translator acting on behalf of the employer. It was not appropriate for the translator to be another employee. All employees should then be asked to sign a document confirming that the contract of employment has been explained to them.[142]

INTERNATIONAL EMPLOYMENT

---

[140] Speech given by the Minister for Integration, Conor Lenihan at the Launch of 'On Speaking Terms: Introductory and Language Programmes for Migrants in Ireland', 11 September 2007.

[141] *58 Named Complainants v Goode Concrete Ltd* DEC-E2008-020.

[142] This case has been appealed to the Labour Court.

Bryan Dunne

INTRODUCTION

[20.114] As international employment and cross-border secondment becomes increasingly common, employees may now operate across several jurisdictions and legal systems. While this is a necessary part of international commerce, it may present particular legal issues for employers and employees. The most immediate of these may be determining who the actual employer is and the law that shall govern the employment relationship on a day to day basis. For some time now, framework rules have been in place between a number of jurisdictions to help determine the law that shall govern an employment contract in such circumstances,[143] and where the matter should be litigated in the event of a dispute.[144] However, the answers to these questions depend in each instance on the particular arrangement. The infinite variations on the nature of cross-border employment have seen this become an, at times complex area of practice.[145]

[20.115] The actual position of the employee in international and secondment arrangements will depend on the degree to which the employer and employee have properly planned the arrangement. The employer and employee often enter into these type of arrangements without much forethought for formalities such as identifying the correct employing entity, governing law or appropriate jurisdiction or even more immediate operational issues such as which party should be responsible for paying salary, what currency it will be paid in or taxed, and whether the employee should be entitled to return to the original job on termination of the foreign placement.

[20.116] The complexity of international and secondment arrangements arises from the following:

(i)   the arrangement does not usually operate on the traditional direct employer and employee relationship basis. Instead, it involves an employee being placed or seconded by his original employer to a third party, be it a subsidiary of the same group, a client or some other entity; and

(ii)   a second or possibly even a number of different jurisdictions' laws may be relevant to the employment relationship.[146]

---

[143] The Rome Convention on the Law Applicable to Contractual Obligations 1980, see paras **[20.154]–[20.164]** below.

[144] The Brussels Convention on Jurisdiction and the Enforcement of Judgments in Civil and Commercial Matters 1968 (The Brussels Convention); see para **[20.143]–[20.150]** below.

[145] See *Saggar v The Ministry of Defence* [2005] IRLR 618; per Mummerly LJ: 'unfortunately it has not proved possible, (and it probably never will be possible) to achieve legal certainty in this area, either by legislation or by the judicial interpretation of it. The practical difficulty in framing the legislation and in judicial generalisations about its effect, is that employment relationships are increasingly complex, flexible and dynamic; they can endure for varying amounts of time and during the course of the relationship, places, patterns, and countries of employment can change'.

[146] See Sabirau Perez, 'Changes of the Law Applicable to an International Contract of Employment', *International Labour Review*, Volume 139 (2000) No 3.

[20.117] Part II of this chapter considers (i) the nature of international employment and secondment; (ii) the various models that can be used and the matters that should be addressed in such arrangements to ensure legal certainty and operational efficiency and limit the risks of dispute between the parties; (iii) international frameworks in place to determine governing law and appropriate jurisdiction; (iv) the Posted Workers Directive;[147] and (v) the extra-territorial application of Irish employment legislation.

THE NATURE OF INTERNATIONAL EMPLOYMENT AND SECONDMENT

[20.118] In its most simple form, secondment is an arrangement whereby one employer 'loans' an employee to a second employer. The employee, often also referred to as a 'secondee', remains employed by the original employer at all times, but performs duties for the benefit of the second employer on a day to day basis. It typically also involves the employee being relocated to the second employer's premises for the duration of the agreed period. Secondment is often also referred to as a placement, posting or external assignment. It can involve a variety of different forms. The crucial difference between employment and secondment is that the employee is not actually employed by the second employer, even though the relationship may, on the face of it, appear almost identical.

[20.119] Dr Mary Redmond, in *Dismissal Law in Ireland*, notes that although two employers may determine legal responsibilities, the contractual relationship between the employer and the employee cannot be affected without the employee's express agreement.[148] An employer cannot therefore require an employee to go on secondment or to transfer his employment without the employee's agreement. That said, relationships can change significantly over the passage of time without the parties expressly agreeing on a change of status, such that an employee can become the second employer's employee without being aware of it.[149]

[20.120] In a typical employment relationship, an employee is retained directly by an employer to perform certain duties. Even where this involves a period of employment abroad, the employee is still clear as to who his employer is. In a secondment arrangement the employee is *'loaned out'* by his original employer to a second employer, and performs duties for the second employer over the period of secondment. Secondment or placement does not necessarily involve cross-border employment. However, where an employee is sent overseas by his employer for a given period of time, it usually involves some element of secondment or assignment with the overseas employer. In the area of international secondment and placement, employers can use any number of different structures to set up the arrangement. Indeed, many employers end up proceeding with a particular model by default by simply not giving any consideration to the structure of the arrangement.

---

[147] Directive 96/71/EC of the European Parliament and of the Council of 16 December 1996 concerning the posting of workers in the framework of the provision of services.

[148] Redmond, *Dismissal Law in Ireland* (2nd edn, Tottel Publishing, 2007) at 478.

[149] See *Walsh v Oliver Freaney & Co and Dunnes Stores Ltd* [1995] ELR 209.

INTERNATIONAL EMPLOYMENT AND SECONDMENT – WORKING MODELS

[20.121] A number of different models may be used to effect a secondment or to introduce an international element to an employment relationship. The most common working models are as follows:

Direct Foreign Employment: In this model, an employer hires an employee either in the home country or the local labour market to work for it. While issues such as the place of work, the currency in which the employee will be paid, where the employee is taxed etc will be different from a normal employment relationship, the relationship is traditional in every other sense. There is no secondment or placement since the employee will perform his duties for the entity that hired him;

Foreign Secondment: In this case, the original or home employer employs the employee and seconds him to a host employer for a particular period of time in whatever location the host is based. The employee remains employed by the home employer at all times, even though he performs duties for the host employer. For the duration of the secondment period, the employee remains the ultimate responsibility of the home employer in terms of overall performance management and liability, save to the extent otherwise agreed. This type of arrangement is often referred to as foreign placement or assignment;

Parallel or Second Contract Secondment: This model is similar to Foreign Secondment, with one significant difference. In this scenario, the home employer suspends its contract of employment with the employee and the employee in turn enters into a parallel or contemporaneous contract of employment with the host employer for the agreed period. In reality, the contract is not so much suspended as an agreement reached between the home employer and the employee that the particular terms that would otherwise require performance during the period will be put on hold, on the premise that the employee will return to the original role at the end of the secondment.[150] Strictly speaking the employee is not being seconded to the host employer but actually employed by it; and

Replacement Foreign Contract: In some cases, the home employer and the employee will terminate the original contract of employment, and the employee will then enter into a subsequent and exclusive contract with the host employer. This is quite similar to the Parallel or Second Contract Secondment arrangement, save that the original contract does not run at the same time. It will be a matter of agreement in each case as to whether or not the employee will be entitled to return to the original role on termination of the new contract. Again, it is not a secondment, since the employee is directly employed by the host employer.

[20.122] Once the parties have decided what model to use, both a carefully-planned structure on the ground and a properly documented contractual relationship between all

---

[150] See *Pugliese v Finmeccanica Spa* [2004] AII ER (EC) 154, which recognised the legal validity of an employee having two concurrent contracts of employment.

relevant parties are important to ensure that the model holds up. While all of the above models can be used in domestic employment or secondment, the focus of this chapter is on the use of these models on a cross-border basis. In each case it is necessary to look at the actual workings of the arrangement to identify which model is actually being used. The increasing practice of referring to any such model as a secondment irrespective of whether it actually involves a technical secondment can make this more complex. Employers can also recruit in the local labour market and employ an individual through a local subsidiary, though in such circumstances, it would not be a foreign assignment or employment for either the employee or the employer.

[20.123] The starting point for any employer or employee in foreign secondment should therefore be to decide which model to use. More often than not, there are broader corporate and income tax issues at play which will determine which model the parties decide on.[151] Failure to properly plan the arrangement can lead to ongoing confusion and dispute between the parties not only on the identity of the employer but also on operational matters such as which party is responsible for income tax and national insurance, employer pension obligations, reporting lines, liability in the event of a dispute over termination or workplace injury, etc.

[20.124] The Terms of Employment (Information) Act 1994 will also require the employer to provide the employee with a revised statement of terms and conditions, detailing such changes that arise as a result of the foreign secondment, eg change in workplace, change in employer, change in annual leave, remuneration.[152]

International employment and secondment – who is the employer

[20.125] The concern for any second employer in a secondment arrangement is that it could be deemed to be the secondee's employer as a matter of law, even if it is intended and agreed between the parties that the employee shall remain employed by the original employer. Where the parties do not address the matter, regard must be had to both the contract and the conduct of the parties in how the relationship operates, to determine the employer.

[20.126] A seconded employee may, over the passage of time and due to the conduct of the parties, become an employee of the second employer. In *Lynch v Palgrave Murphy Ltd*,[153] the Supreme Court considered the circumstances in which an employee on temporary assignment from the permanent employer to another employer could be considered to have become the employee of the second employer so as to make the second employer vicariously liable for the employee's negligence. The Court stated that there is 'abundant authority for stating that, while such matters as payment and power of dismissal may be taken into consideration, the decisive factor in deciding whether a

---

[151] The employer may also be anxious to avoid creating a taxable presence in the host country and similarly the employee will want to either maintain the original tax status in the home country or establish a new tax status in the host country.

[152] Terms of Employment (Information) Acts 1994–2001, s 5.

[153] *Lynch v Palgrave Murphy Ltd* [1962] IR 150.

person doing work for another is or is not the servant of that other is whether the latter has complete control as to how the particular work shall be done'.[154]

[20.127] The EAT decision in *Walsh v Oliver Freaney & Co and Dunnes Stores Ltd*[155] provides a useful analysis of who the employer is in the circumstances of a rather unclear secondment arrangement. The claimant in that case, commenced work with Oliver Freaney in 1977 as a qualified accountant. He was seconded to Dunnes Stores in 1982, but continued to be paid by Oliver Freaney, who in turn invoiced Dunnes Stores. The claimant received a P60 annually from Oliver Freaney. From 1982 on, he was based exclusively in Dunnes Stores' offices and remained in the role up to the termination of his employment. While he initially continued to report to Oliver Freaney, he subsequently reported directly to Dunnes Stores senior management.

[20.128] Difficulties arose between Mr Walsh and Dunnes Stores over financial information he had disclosed internally in October 1993. Around the same time he was asked to prepare a detailed profitability report, but was refused access to his normal workplace to prepare the report, and was told that he would only be given financial information after consideration by the company. He was also told that he no longer had an office. He was advised that if he did not complete the report on time, he would be dismissed, and later that evening heard on the radio that his employment had actually been terminated. The dismissal was confirmed in a letter dated 27 October 1993 from Dunnes Stores personnel department. The form P45 and the claimant's final payment were in the name of Oliver Freaney.

[20.129] Before giving judgment, the EAT had to firstly determine which of the two closely connected parties was Mr Freaney's actual employer. It noted the reasoning in *Lynch v Palgrave Murphy*.[156] However, in its view, the main test to be used here was the control test. The EAT focused on the following factors in identifying the employer:

(i) where the claimant worked: the claimant had worked exclusively on Dunne Stores' premises from 1982 up to his dismissal in 1993;

(ii) who paid the claimant: the claimant had received certain payments from Oliver Freaney & Co. However, additional payments and benefits in kind, including a credit card allowance, an annual cash bonus and the use of a company car had been provided directly by Dunnes Stores;

(iii) who gave the claimant his instructions: since 1982 the claimant was given his instructions by, and reported exclusively to, Dunnes Stores and was solely accountable to them during this period;

(iv) who had to perform the contract: the claimant, rather than Oliver Freaney, or any other of its employees, had to personally perform the duties for Dunnes Stores; and

(v) who dismissed the claimant: the claimant was dismissed by Dunnes Stores.

---

[154] [1962] IR 150 at 161 (Walsh J). On the various tests which may be used to determine employment status, see Ch 2.

[155] *Walsh v Oliver Freaney & Co and Dunnes Stores Ltd* [1995] ELR 209.

[156] *Lynch v Palgrave Murphy* [1964] IR 150.

[20.130] On balance, the EAT thus found that over time, Mr Walsh had reached a point where he had only a tenuous connection with Oliver Freaney, which was used essentially as a paying agent by Dunnes Stores, and so found as a matter of fact and law that he was employed by Dunnes Stores.

[20.131] A number of cases illustrate that the construction of the secondment agreement and the contract of employment are important factors in determining whether an employee remains an employee of the original employer.

[20.132] In *Royal Bank of Scotland PLC v Bannerman Johnstone Maclay*,[157] the Court found that an important, though not necessarily conclusive source of evidence, on the question of whether an employee on secondment was in the employment of the temporary employer, was the contract or agreement that regulated the employee's secondment between the parties. The Court also considered whether the employee remained under the 'general direction and control of the defendant and within their general employment'.[158] The Court noted that a heavy burden of proof lies on the general employer who pleads that an employee was transferred to the employment of another. That question is sensitive to the facts and circumstances of the case.

[20.133] In *Denham v Midland Employers Mutual Assurance Ltd*,[159] Denning LJ, in considering whether the general employer had completely relinquished his right to control and transferred that right to the temporary employer, stated as follows:

> [s]uch a transfer rarely takes place, if ever, when a man is lent with a machine, such as a crane or lorry: nor when a skilled man is lent so as to exercise his skill for the temporary employer. In such a case the parties do not contemplate that the temporary employer shall tell the man how to manipulate his machine or to exercise his skill. But a transfer does sometimes take place in the case when an unskilled man is lent to help with labouring work. The temporary employer can then no doubt tell the labourer how he is to do the job. The labourer becomes so much part of the organisation to which he is seconded that the temporary employer is responsible for him and to him.[160]

Form of contract

[20.134] The form of contract to be used in an international or secondment arrangement will depend on the particular model. There are, however, certain minimum requirements which should be addressed to ensure clarity.

Individual contract of employment

[20.135] In all arrangements, the main purpose of the documentation should be to confirm who the employer is, and to provide for any other operational changes to the existing relationship as a result of the foreign assignment, unless the employee is a new hire. Assuming the employee has already received a written statement of terms and

---

[157] *Royal Bank of Scotland PLC v Bannerman Johnstone Maclay* [2005] Scot Court of Session CSIH 39 (26 May 2005).
[158] [2005] CSIH 39 at para 66.
[159] *Denham v Midland Employers Mutual Assurance Ltd* [1955] 2 QB 437.
[160] [1955] 2 QB 437 at 444.

conditions as required under the Terms of Employment (Information) Act 1994, a new or revised contract of employment should be put in place between the original employer and the employee which, at a minimum, addresses the following legal and practical matters:

Identity of employer – the contract should make it quite clear which party, be it the home employer or the host employer, will be the employer. If it is to be a secondment arrangement, the contract should provide that the home employer is the employer. If considered necessary, the contract should provide for the employer's discretion to transfer the contract of employment on a subsequent occasion to any other third party. If agreed between the parties, set out clearly in the written terms, and exercised reasonably, this should be in order;

Remuneration – there are a number of issues to be covered on this front, including the currency in which salary will be paid, where and how the salary will be paid, be it in Ireland or the foreign jurisdiction and also the jurisdiction in which income tax and national insurance will be deducted. If it is to be a genuine secondment, the home employer should continue to pay the employee directly, and seek reimbursement from the host employer on a full costs basis. This will depend on the individual circumstances as to whether the parties are better off taxing the remuneration in the home or host country, and of course the extent to which this can legally be achieved. Professional tax planning will be required, which may also impact on the form of documentation used. The contract may also refer to tax equalisation;

Benefits – presuming the employee receives certain additional benefits such as employer pension contributions, performance, bonus, share options, health cover etc, the contract should confirm which of these benefits will continue and whether there are any additional benefits that he will receive as a consequence of the assignment;

Responsibilities and position – Disputes can often arise over what the employee's actual role and responsibility will be. The scope of the role should be detailed from the outset so that there is no confusion amongst the parties as to the extent and scope of the new role;

Reporting lines – The employee will also need to know who he will be reporting to during the secondment, be it to a local management or home employer management as before. This can also become quite relevant in determining governing law and jurisdiction, as well as identifying the correct employer. In the case of a secondment, the employee should maintain ultimate reporting responsibility to the home employer, to satisfy the control test;

Confidentiality and data protection – While the law on confidentiality and data protection will be that of the relevant jurisdiction, the contract should provide for the confidentiality of any sensitive information to which the employee will have access in the foreign employment, particularly if working for a client or other third party. The clause should also provide for any necessary consent to the transfer of employee data to the host employer as relevant under the Data Protection Acts 1988–2003;

Governing law and exclusive jurisdiction – As addressed further below, the contract should expressly set out what law shall govern the contract (subject to local mandatory legal requirements) and also where the appropriate jurisdiction for the hearing of any dispute will be. It is standard to provide for the same governing law and jurisdiction;

Location and relocation – The contract should specify the place of work. Depending on the circumstances, the employer may want to include the right to relocate the employee to a third location for the purposes of the secondment;

Immigration Depending on the jurisdiction, the employee may require an appropriate work permit or visa. If so, the contract should make this a pre-condition to working in that jurisdiction and provide that the employee must maintain the authorisation for the duration of the secondment;

Termination – This can require significant planning by both the employer and employee to ensure that all issues are addressed, as it tends to be the issue that most frequently leads to dispute.[161] The documentation should advise whether termination of the secondment constitutes termination of the overall employment, or whether the employee is entitled to return to the original position and on what basis. Dr Redmond notes that termination of the secondment agreement by the host employer will not result in liability under the Unfair Dismissals Acts 1977–2007 as the employee's contract is not terminated. The secondment agreement, will, however, be terminated.[162] Each element should be considered in the particular context. For example, it is not uncommon for the notice period to correspond with the end of the school term in order to avoid taking children out of school mid-term. From an employee perspective, the parties should consider the minimum period of time that would be required to properly relocate back to the home jurisdiction.

Restrictive Covenants – The employee's original contract of employment may only contain post termination protection in relation to the original employer, if at all. The revised contract should therefore expressly include the host employer since, depending on the jurisdiction, there may be additional formalities to be addressed in the wording to ensure it will be enforceable. For example, it is becoming increasingly common in continental Europe for an employer to have to pay some form of compensation during the period of the restrictive covenant, as seen in both Italy and France;[163]

Duration – If the role is for a specific purpose, this purpose should be identified. If appropriate, the clause should contain a provision for reducing or extending the period of secondment, or to otherwise terminate the period of secondment on an agreed period of notice during its term. In the absence of an agreed notice period or right to terminate during the term, there is no implied right to terminate such a secondment.[164]

---

[161] See *Cronin v Eircom* [2006] IEHC 380 (25 October 2006), and also *Evans v SDL International* [1999] EAT 879/99.

[162] Redmond, *Dismissal Law in Ireland* (2nd edn, Tottel Publishing, 2007) at 478.

[163] The Italian Civil Code, s 2125. See also Algazy, 'The International Scope of Restrictive Covenants in Contracts of Employment', ELA Briefing Vol 7 (5 April 2000).

[20.136] The above are just a number of matters which should be addressed in any such contract. Whether all of the above, or indeed any additional terms, should be included will depend on the circumstances in each case. These are also matters which should be addressed exclusively between the home employer and the employee. In certain instances, parties will try to address all matters in the one agreement, with the revised contract becoming a tri-partite agreement between the home employer, the employee and the host employer. Quite apart from the practical difficulties in drafting and interpreting such a document, it invites unnecessary issues as to whether the host employer is substituting itself for the home employer in the overall relationship. The safest approach is for the revised contract to be between the home employer and employee only.

Individual employee issues

[20.137] As a foreign placement will often involve an employee either leaving behind or relocating a family, otherwise standard features of the employment relationship can take on a more personal significance for the employee. For this reason, it is quite common for an employee on foreign assignment to be given expatriate benefits which are intended to firstly ensure that the employee is personally and financially no worse off in terms of the level of remuneration, standard of living and protection for family, or to otherwise address any personal concerns the employee may have about the foreign posting. The type of issues that would typically be provided for are as follows:

Tax equalisation and planning – In most cases, the foreign relocation is at the employer's request, so the employee should not suffer a tax disadvantage as a result of this. In such circumstances, employers will often provide for tax equalisation, whereby the employer makes up any shortfall in net salary which the employee suffers as a result of a change in tax status. At a minimum, employers will usually cover the cost of any necessary tax advice and planning to minimise any additional tax risk to the employee;

Cost of living allowance – Depending on the location which the employee is being relocated to, a cost of living allowance may be payable.[165] Cost of living allowances are typically linked to the cost of living in the relevant jurisdiction, consumer price index or other such indices;

Housing allowance – The normal arrangement is for employees in such situations to either be provided with paid housing by the employer or a contribution towards rented accommodation, either for the secondment period or while looking for a house. This may also cover any stamp duty or similar local authority charges involved in purchasing a new home. This will ultimately depend on the duration of the posting;

Relocation allowance – Relocating from one jurisdiction to another will also involve significant personal cost. It may also require storage costs for a period of time while searching for new accommodation. This cost would usually be covered by the employer on a reasonable and vouched basis for a set period of time. The employer should be clear

---

[164] *Cronin v Eircom* [2006] IEHC 380 (25 October 2006).

[165] See *Croft v Vita Ltd* [2006] IRLR 289, a House of Lords decision where Cathay Pacific air stewards received a cost of living allowance if based in Hong Kong, but not in London.

as to the amount it will cover, the procedure for reclaiming the expense, and the period which it will be payable for. It would also be standard in such an arrangement for the employer to provide a claw-back, such that if the employee leaves the position within a specific period of time, he will liable to repay some, if not all, of the costs. Indeed, this is usually applied to all relocation costs incurred;[166]

Localisation –The contract may also provide for 'localisation'. Localisation occurs where an employee on foreign assignment or secondment stays beyond the initial agreed period at his request, but on the basis that he will be treated as if hired locally. This will usually involve a reduction in expatriate benefits otherwise available to the employee, and possible transfer onto a local contract;

Annual leave – An employer should be aware that, for personal reasons, annual leave will now be much more important to the seconded employee. This is particularly so if the employee is not relocating his family. The employer may therefore need to agree an increased period of annual leave or a guaranteed annual leave timetable, whereby the employee can take one week per quarter etc. Similarly, it would not be unusual for an employer to agree to cover the costs of family travel to the host country in such circumstances on a reasonable and vouched basis;

Healthcare and illness protection – Depending on the healthcare system in the host country, employers would be expected to cover the cost of providing at least an equivalent level of healthcare cover for the employee and possibly also spouse and children. From the employer's perspective, it should be made clear that in the event of long-term illness, the employer has the right to terminate the secondment and bring the employee back to the home jurisdiction as necessary, or to second a replacement in the interim; and

Family education – On the basis that many foreign assignments will involve family relocation, an employer may also be expected to contribute towards the cost of private education.[167] This is particularly relevant if in a non-English speaking jurisdiction the employee's children may need to attend private English speaking schools.

Home employer to host employer agreement

[20.138] The contractual arrangement between the home and host employer should be properly documented to reflect the particular model chosen, particularly if it is to be a secondment or if the host employer is a client or third party entity over which the home employer has no control, rather than a subsidiary of the same group.

---

[166] The actual amount repayable should reduce on a pro-rata basis for a period of twelve to twenty four months post payment, in order to avoid it being considered a penalty clause and thus unenforceable. See *Schiesser International (Ireland) Ltd v Gallagher* [1971] 106 ILTR 22, in which an obligation to repay all travelling and other expenses to the employer if the employee left within three years of commencing employment was set aside as the amount repayable remained the same over the course of the three years, as opposed to reducing on a *pro rata* basis during its term.

[167] See *Evans v SDL International* EAT 879/99, where a dispute over the level of private education contribution by the employer lead to the employee resigning and returning to the UK.

[20.139] Where the employee is being seconded on the basis that he will continue to be employed by the home employer but will perform duties for the host employer, this being the most frequent case, it is just as important to document that contractual relationship. This ensures that the model is properly structured, that each party is aware of their own responsibilities and obligations and that any potential liability in respect of the employee can be allocated. The type of matters that should be addressed in the contract between the home and host employer are as follows:

Status – In order to remain consistent with the employee's contract, it should explain that the employee will continue to be employed by the home employer, but will perform duties for the host employer for the duration of the secondment period. It should also contain an acknowledgement by the employee that he will not have any cause of action against the host employer as an employee or entitle him to any benefit or compensation from the host employer on termination of either the secondment or the home employer contract;

Remuneration – This should explain either that the salary will be paid directly by the home employer and that the host employer will reimburse it on a full cost basis, or alternatively that the host employer will pay the employee directly. As above, it is recommended that the employee continues to be paid directly by the home employer in order to support the secondment model, and avoid the host employer being deemed the actual employer as a matter of law;[168]

Taxation – The agreement should also record which of the two parties will be responsible for the deduction of tax and any consequent tax liability, though usually this will follow whichever party is responsible for the payment of salary. In some cases, the employee may pay income tax in one country and national insurance in another;[169]

Position and Responsibility – The contract should reflect what duties and responsibilities the employee will perform for the host employer and any necessary discretion on the part of either party to revise or vary the scope of duties to be performed;

Reporting Lines – On the basis that the party that is seen to control the employee is more likely to be considered the employer, it is important that the actual reporting relationship continues to show the home employer as the party having ultimate responsibility for the employee. In this regard, the employee's reporting line should ultimately be to his or her original manager in the home country. However, in order to address the obvious day to day operational issues that will arise during the secondment, the employee should also have a local manager within the host employer to whom he reports. The contract should clarify this arrangement and confirm that the home employer manager has overall management responsibility for the employee. The original employer will therefore also be responsible for any performance management, disciplinary action or other performance or salary reviews that are to be carried out with the employee. The host employer can participate in this process on a secondary basis, since on a practical level

---

[168] See *Walsh v Oliver Freaney & Co and Dunnes Stores Ltd* [1995] ELR 209.
[169] *Roche and others v Sealink Stena Line Ltd* UD 274/1992.

the original employer will most likely need the host employer's assistance in providing an update on the employee's performance etc for this purpose;

Duration and Termination – there are two separate issues that need to be addressed in the termination clause; namely termination of the employee's secondment and termination of the overall secondment arrangement. Ordinarily, both events would occur on the same date, as the employee completes the relevant project, returns to the home employer and the overall secondment arrangement ends. However, there are any number of circumstances that can arise during a secondment which can result in the employee's secondment period ending prematurely, while the secondment arrangement continues. For example, if the employee decides to resign during the assignment or the host employer decides the secondee is not performing well, the host employer may prefer to take on a replacement secondee. The termination clause should therefore give both parties the right to terminate not just the overall secondment arrangement, but also the right to terminate a particular employee's secondment and to require or provide a replacement. Given the time and effort which a home employer will put into arranging a secondment, and that there may not be a ready supply of replacement secondees, the host employer's right to request a replacement should be narrowly defined. Separately, and as with any commercial services agreement, both parties should have the right to terminate the overall arrangement on reasonable written notice in the ordinary course, which will automatically also terminate the employee's secondment. From the home employer's perspective, this notice should be somewhere equivalent to the period of time that it would take the employee to relocate. Again, bearing in mind the set up cost and effort, a secondment agreement may contain a fixed minimum period or an early termination penalty to cover the home employer's costs.

As the authority to terminate employment would be a strong indicator of who the employer is,[170] the documentation should make it quite clear that the host employer has no authority to terminate the secondee's employment. Equally, the clause should advise that the employee should have no cause of action against the host employer in the event of termination of employment, though this would be subject to local law in each case.

Right to Return to Home Employer – While it is more appropriately addressed in the employee's contract of employment, it can be of comfort for the host employer to have it confirmed that the employee will return to the home employer at the end of the secondment period;

Confidentiality and Intellectual Property (IP) – If the parties are subsidiaries within the same group, confidentiality or ownership of any new IP is not a particular concern. However, in cases where the host employer is a third party client, a joint venture entity or partner, confidentiality and IP protection will be crucial, and both sides will want reciprocal confidentiality and IP ownership arrangements in place, with the necessary carve out to allow the employee to provide the actual services and perform the duties required;

---

[170] See *Walsh v Oliver Freaney & Co. and Dunnes Stores Ltd* [1995] ELR 209.

Non-Solicitation – It is standard for such agreements to include a clause to the effect that the host employer will not seek to solicit the employee directly for an agreed period of time after the termination of the overall arrangement, or that if it does, it will pay a fixed sum to the home employer, if a third party client;

Indemnities and responsibility for liability – This can often be the most controversial part of negotiating such agreements and requires the parties to commercially agree who should be responsible for any loss or damage caused by the employee and any related liabilities. It would, at a minimum, require the host employer to take reasonable care in providing for the health and safety of the employee, as if it were its own employee, and comply with all relevant health and safety and anti-discrimination obligations.[171] Looking at the issue objectively, if the arrangement is implemented correctly, the employee will continue to be an employee of the home employer. As such, it will be vicariously liable for the employee's acts or omissions during this period. However, on a day to day basis, the employee is being managed by the host employer, such that any loss or damage caused by him is to a degree within its control, and beyond the home employer's control. This will depend very much on the circumstances, including the particular skill of the employee as to the degree to which they require operational control and management, and whether the loss or injury is directly caused by the host employer's instruction. As a matter of contract law, in the absence of any agreed indemnities, the home employer will for the most part be vicariously liable for any such loss or injury, which is in effect equivalent to an indemnity for the host employer. On a practical level, such matters are best addressed in the agreement.

Looking at the more specific employment law potential liabilities, such as compensation for unfair dismissal, sexual harassment, personal injuries, etc, the clause should generally provide that the home employer will be responsible under all relevant employment legislation, save where otherwise agreed or where any such liability is directly attributable to the host employer. As such, it would be typical for the home employer to bear responsibility for any claims for unfair or wrongful dismissal, redundancy payments, etc, unless the termination is at the host employer's request. However, matters which could be more relevant to the host employer such as personal injuries on its premises or harassment by one of its employees may be its responsibility.

Documentation

[20.140] When preparing the necessary documentation, practitioners should be conscious that the documentation will be persuasive in any subsequent analysis as to who the employer is, what law should govern the employment relationship, and where any dispute should be litigated. The parties should also make sure that having gone to time and effort of putting the correct form of legal structure and documentation in place that all parties are following it on the ground. While the contract will be persuasive, it will be no more than a starting point, if the manner in which the parties are

---

[171] Under the Employment Equality Acts 1998–2008, the home employer will still maintain responsibility for acts of harassment and/or sexual harassment by a third party, which would include a host employer or any of its employees.

implementing the relationship on the ground suggests it is something other than secondment.[172]

[20.141] It is also essential to ensure that the documentation is reviewed by a local lawyer in the host employer's jurisdiction to ensure that it is compliant with local law. This is a practical requirement where the Posted Workers Directive[173] applies and also on the basis that mandatory local law of the jurisdiction in which the employee is physically performing his duties will also apply under the Rome Convention and Regulations, irrespective of what governing law is chosen in the agreement.[174]

GOVERNING LAW AND JURISDICTION[175]

[20.142] Perhaps the most complex area of analysis in dealing with cross border employment once the structure is set up is in determining the governing law and jurisdiction. While there are framework rules in place to help with this analysis, the difficulty comes from the myriad of real life examples that modern employment relationships can present. A recent case in point is *O'Mahony v Accenture Ltd and Accenture LLP*.[176] The traditional model of foreign secondment, with an employee being employed in one country and placed on assignment in another country, has with the development of international trade become increasingly complex. It is not at all unusual for courts to now have to assess the governing law and appropriate jurisdiction in circumstances where an employee from one country is on foreign placement in a second country, but with responsibilities to perform duties in a number of jurisdictions across Europe or beyond on a day to day basis. This issue is examined below from two separate perspectives: firstly, within the EU, and secondly from Ireland to the US, which is more usual. However, as will be seen, the issue cannot be neatly addressed on an EU and non-EU basis, as the relevant rules of law apply beyond the EU in certain circumstances.

The Brussels Convention – determining jurisdiction

[20.143] The rules used to identify appropriate jurisdiction at European level were originally set out in the 1968 Brussels Convention.[177] The Brussels Convention has since been updated to reflect some of the more important decisions of the ECJ in this area since then and the various additions to the EU, by Council Regulation 44/2001 on jurisdiction and the recognition and enforcement of judgments in civil and commercial

---

[172] *Wilson v Maynard Ship Building Consulting* [1978] QB 665.

[173] Directive 96/71/EC of the European Parliament and of the Council of 16 December 1996 concerning the posting of workers in the framework of the provision of services.

[174] See paras **[20.154]**–**[20.164]** below.

[175] See generally Dicey and Morris, *The Conflicts of Law* (14th edn, Sweet and Maxwell) and Fawcett and Carruthers *Private International Law* (14th edn, Oxford University Press, 2008).

[176] See, for example, *O'Mahony v Accenture Ltd and Accenture LLP* [2006] US District Court Southern District of New York which concerned an Irish national working as a partner and employee of Accenture LLP, the US subsidiary of Accenture Limited, a Bermudan listed company on foreign assignment in Paris with Accenture SAS, Accenture's French subsidiary. The particular significance of this case was that US statutory employment protection for whistleblowers was deemed to apply to the employee while on secondment in France.

matters[178] (the Brussels Regulations).[179] The Brussels Regulations were transposed into Irish law by the European Communities (Civil and Commercial Judgments) Regulations 2002.[180] The Brussels Regulations apply to all proceedings instituted after its coming into effect on 1 March 2002.

[20.144] Article 1(1) of the Regulations provides that they shall 'apply in civil and commercial matters whatever the nature of the court or tribunal', subject to certain exceptions for social security, arbitration and other matters as identified in Art 1(2). They are not expressly limited to EU Member States only, though as a provision of EC law, they are only enforceable by courts within a Member State. Similarly, the Brussels Regulations apply irrespective of nationality,[181] so may be relied upon before a national court in any Member State by an individual, be they an EU national or otherwise.

[20.145] The general rule of jurisdiction under the Brussels Regulations is that a person should be sued in the courts of the State in which he or she is domiciled.[182] Domicile means ordinarily resident, and as such a person will be considered domiciled in a particular jurisdiction if he or she is ordinarily resident in that State. Similarly, the Brussels Regulations provide that a company or legal person is domiciled where it has its statutory seat, central administration or place of business.[183]

[20.146] While the general rule as set out above will apply in most cases, there are certain exceptions to this. These exceptions are for the most part designed to favour a plaintiff and to protect those seen as economically or socially vulnerable.[184] In the employment context, this means providing exceptional protection for employees. For example, it is considered unfair to put an employee to the expense and additional inconvenience of having to issue proceedings outside of his or her home jurisdiction. Article 19 of the Brussels Regulations therefore contains a specific exemption allowing an employee to issue proceedings in any of the following jurisdictions:

(i)   the country in which he or she is domiciled;

(ii)   the country in which the employee habitually carries out his or her work; or

---

[177] The Brussels Convention on Jurisdiction and the Enforcement of Judgments in Civil and Commercial Matters 1968 (the 'Brussels Convention'). The Convention was implemented into Irish domestic law by the Jurisdiction of Courts and Enforcement of Judgments Acts 1998. The Lugano Convention is an almost identical arrangement that regulates matters between EU and EFTA Member States (Norway, Iceland, Liechtenstein and Switzerland).

[178] 22 December 2000 OJ L 124/1.

[179] The Brussels Regulations are typically referred to as the Brussels Convention. For the purposes of clarity, they are referred to here as the Brussels Regulations.

[180] SI 52/2002.

[181] Brussels Regulations, Art 4(2).

[182] See Art 2(1).

[183] See Art 60(1).

[184] Brussels Regulations, Art 13 of the Preamble.

(iii)   if the employee does not or did not habitually carry out his or her work in any one country, the country in which the business which engaged the employee was or is now situated.

[20.147] Article 18 of the Brussels Regulations also indirectly address the situation most likely to apply to US and other non-EU employers. It states that if an employee enters into a contract of employment with an employer not domiciled in a Member State, but which has a branch, agency or other establishment in a Member State, the employer is deemed to be domiciled in that Member State.

[20.148] This formula is clearly drafted to cover the modern nature of international employment and secondment arrangements in that it envisages an employee having his or her workplace either in the same location as the employer, in a separate country, or in any number of additional countries. In contrast, under Art 20, employers may only issue proceedings against an employee in the Member State in which the employee is domiciled. In practical terms, this may not necessarily be the same State as the one in which the employer is domiciled.

[20.149] The issue may arise as to whether the Brussels Regulations apply to an employment relationship involving parties both in and outside the EU. This may arise where two parties are in dispute, one of the parties has issued proceedings and the defendant claims that the proceedings have been issued in the wrong jurisdiction, such that a judge has to decide whether: a) the Brussels Regulations apply to the conflict issue; and b) if so, where the matter should be litigated.

[20.150] In simple terms, if both potential jurisdictions are within the EU, then the matter is subject to the Brussels Regulations. If only one of the potential jurisdictions is within the EU, this is deemed sufficient for the Brussels Regulations to apply. This was confirmed by the ECJ in *Owusu v Jackson.*[185] Where the two jurisdictions in contention are both outside the EU, the Brussels Regulations do not apply. The only qualification on this last limb is where, by virtue of Art 18, the defendant has a branch, agency or other establishment within a Member State and so is deemed to be domiciled in a Member State, or a provision of local law in the relevant Member State would otherwise provide for jurisdiction, then the Regulations would apply.[186] In practical terms, the Brussels Regulations will therefore almost always apply when determining jurisdiction involving an Irish based or registered employer.[187]

Exclusive jurisdiction clauses

[20.151] Article 21 of the Brussels Regulations also support parties that wish to expressly agree in advance what jurisdiction will apply to the contract of employment. However, parties seeking to enforce the agreed jurisdiction clause must show that it was

---

[185] Case C-281/02 *Andrew Owusu v Jackson, trading as Villa Holidays Bal-In Villas* [2005] ECR I-1383.

[186] Brussels Regulations, Art 4(1) provides that if the defendant is not domiciled in the Member State, jurisdiction should be determined according to local law in each Member State. This is assuming that Art 18 does not apply,

[187] See also Cahill, Connery, Kennedy and Power *European Law* (Oxford University Press & Law Society of Ireland 2008).

entered into after the dispute had arisen or that it otherwise allows the employee to bring proceedings in court, other than those already available under Art 18. In reality, if the parties are in dispute, they may not always be able to agree a jurisdiction.

[20.152] Exclusive jurisdiction clauses should be in writing in order to ensure certainty and clarity, though surprisingly this is not a specific requirement of Art 21. However, if the parties can show that, even though not in writing, it is in accordance with established practice between the parties, it will be upheld. The Regulations also allow for recognition of clauses agreed by electronic communication.

[20.153] As a matter of HR best practice, and in order to avoid the difficulties that go with not having agreed jurisdiction, or even worse, the confusion that a clear governing law clause but silent jurisdiction clause can introduce, all contracts of employment should therefore contain an exclusive jurisdiction clause.

The Rome Convention – determining governing law

[20.154] The rules to identify governing law were originally set out under EU law in the Rome Convention.[188] Its purpose was to harmonise the various national rules on choice of law within the EU and in many regards can be seen as the necessary follow up to the rules on jurisdiction provided for in the Brussels Convention.

[20.155] The Rome Convention applies 'to contractual obligations in any situation involving a choice between the laws of different countries',[189] thus excluding tortious claims. The Convention is not expressly limited to contracting or Member States. Instead, it is intended to have universal application and as such, can apply equally to EU and non-EU contracts. However, as a provision of EU law, it is only enforceable by a court within the EU. There is no need for either party to the contract to be domiciled or resident in the EU. The universal application of the Convention avoids the need to distinguish between EU and non-EU choice of law rules or, perhaps even more complex, contracts involving an EU and a non-EU party.[190]

[20.156] As such, the Rome Convention applies to all conflict to contracts be they between two EU based parties, one EU and one non EU-based party and two non-EU based parties, if the dispute over governing law is being litigated before a court within the EU. If the parties are seeking to apply the rules under the Rome Convention before a court outside of the EU, then the Rome Convention shall not apply irrespective of whether or not the parties have any EU connection.

[20.157] One interesting aspect of this is that parties can therefore choose whatever law they wish to govern a contract, not just the law of an EU Member State. As such, an Irish court can be required to apply, for example French, Columbian or Australian law in a dispute before it. In so far as an Irish judge cannot be expected to be familiar with the

---

[188] The Rome Convention on the Law Applicable to Contractual Obligations 1980. The Convention was transposed into Irish law by the Contractual Obligations (Applicable Law) Act 1990.

[189] Brussels Regulaations, Art 1(1).

[190] See Fawcett and Carruthers *Private International Law* (14th edn, Oxford University Press, 2008) at 677.

particular foreign law, it will require the foreign law to be proved as a matter of expert evidence. This will fall to be addressed in accordance with the Rules of the Superior Courts.[191]

[20.158] The Rome Convention treats contracts of employment differently, so as to protect the weaker contracting party. The framework for determining governing law is contained in Art 6 of the Convention. The main provision in Art 6 is Art 6(2) which provides that in the absence of a choice of law, the governing law should be:

> the law of the place where the employee habitually carries out his work;

> if the employee does not habitually carry out his work in any one state, the law of the state in which the place of business for which he is engaged is situated; or

> if it appears from the circumstances as a whole that the contract is more closely connected with another state, the law of that state governs the contract.

[20.159] For example, if an Irish employer and a French employee based in France agreed that the contract should be subject to Dutch law, the contract will be governed by Dutch law. However, to the extent that any mandatory provisions of French law apply to the employee, and are more favourable than the equivalent Dutch provisions, they will over-ride the express intentions of the party to apply Dutch law. Mandatory rules are such entitlements and statutory protection that the parties cannot contract out of. This is typically limited to basic statutory protections, such as protection against unfair dismissal, minimum wage entitlements etc. In the same way that the Posted Workers Directive[192] was introduced to prevent social dumping, the application of mandatory local law prevented employers applying the lowest possible level of employee protection.

[20.160] The Rome Convention has been revised under the Rome I Regulations.[193] The Rome Regulations will apply to all contracts that come into effect after 17 December 2009, and have universal application.[194]

[20.161] The Rome Convention in Art 3 recognises parties' freedom to choose governing law. Article 11 of the Preamble to the Regulations also states that this freedom should be 'the corner stone of the system of conflict of law rules in matters of contractual obligations'. It provides that the proper law to govern a contract shall be the law as expressly chosen by the parties or that otherwise applies by implication. However, as before, this is subject to all applicable provisions of local law from which the parties cannot derogate (ie mandatory local law), which can be extremely important in the employment context.

---

[191] On the proof of foreign law in proceedings in the UK context, see Fawcett and Carruthers *Private International Law* (14th edn, Oxford University Press, 2008) pp 111 to 117.

[192] Directive 96/71/EC of the European Parliament and of the Council of 16 December 1996 concerning the posting of workers in the framework of the provision of services.

[193] Council Regulation 593/2008 on the law applicable to contractual obligations, due to come into effect on 17 December 2009.

[194] See also Lando and Nielsen, 'The Rome I Proposal' 3 *J Private International Law*, 29 (2007). Note also that while the UK and Denmark both originally chose not to opt into the Regulations, it is expected that they will both vote to accept them.

[20.162] Article 6 of the Convention and Art 8 of the Regulations provide that where the parties have not agreed a choice of law, the governing law shall be determined as follows:

(i)   the law of the country in which the employee habitually carries out his work;

(ii)   if not identifiable from (a), the country in which the business through which the employee was engaged is situated; or

(iii)   where it appears from the circumstances as a whole that the contract is more closely connected with a country other than that as indicated at (a) or (b) above, the law of that other country.

[20.163] In addition, Art 8(1) sof the Regulations pecifically protects the application of mandatory provisions of local law in whatever jurisdiction the employee is performing his duties, even where an express agreement exists on what law will otherwise apply.

[20.164] As the Rome Convention relates to contractual obligations only, any claims in regard to negligence or similar tort actions are to be considered under separate Regulations, EC 864/2007, known as the Rome II Regulations. The Rome II Regulations provide that any such claim should be subject to the law of the State in which the damage occurs, irrespective of the State in which the event giving rise to the damage took place. The Rome II Regulations came into effect on 11 January 2009 across the EU, excluding Denmark. However, for those circumstances in which the damage is clearly more connected with another State, the Regulations allow discretion to each Member State to deal with the matter appropriately. Choice of law will be allowed if it is clear from the circumstances that the parties intended that choice of law to apply to that situation also.

Relevant factors in determining jurisdiction and governing law – where is employee habitually carrying out work?

[20.165] Under both the Brussels Regulations and the Rome Regulations, one of the key determining considerations in multi-jurisdictional employment is where the employee habitually carries out his or her work. Various factors have been identified by the ECJ as being relevant to this analysis. They include where the employee actually lives, where the employee has his base or principle place of work from which he prepares for trips and returns after the performance of duties, where the employee pays tax and social security, the State in which the employee is paid his salary, the country where the employee or entity to whom he reports is based, or whether or not he is a director of other entities in other jurisdictions.

[20.166] The application of these rules to multi-jurisdictional issues is best illustrated in *Mulox IBC Ltd v Geels*,[195] a case concerning a Dutch national living in France, and employed by an English registered company as its International Marketing Director. The employee used his French home as an office and place of operations, making frequent trips throughout Europe. When in May 1990, his contract of employment was

---

[195] Case C-125/92 *Mulox IBC Ltd v Geels* [1993] ECR I-4075. The analysis in this case was supported also in Case C-383/95 *Rutten v Cross Medical Ltd* [1997] ECR I-57.

terminated, he challenged the decision before a French court. The French court accepted jurisdiction under the Brussels Convention and ordered the employer to pay damages for breach of contract. The employer appealed the decision on the grounds that the French courts had no jurisdiction since, *inter alia*, the place of performance of the contract was not exclusive to any one Member State.

[20.167] The court referred the point to the ECJ which ruled that the place where the obligation characterising the contract is normally performed is that where, or from which, the employee principally discharges his obligations to his employer. This particular wording and analysis is now reflected in the Rome Regulations. In order to determine the place of performance of a contractual obligation of this nature, the Court took into account the fact that the employee fulfilled his duties from an office situated in that contracting State, the employee had established his residence there, that it was the State from which he carried out his activities and to which he returned after each business trip. The Court further elaborated that in concluding that he habitually carried out his work in France, that it should take account of the need to ensure adequate protection for the employee as the weaker contracting party.

[20.168] In the more recent case of *Pugliese v Finmeccanica Spa*,[196] the ECJ extended the scope of this test, as it considered where an employee habitually carries out their work if employed in one location but immediately on commencement, is seconded to a separate location. Ms Pugliese was engaged by Aer Italia in January 1990 to work at its Turin plant. However, shortly prior to commencement, it was agreed that she would be seconded to work for Eurofighter GmbH, a joint venture between Aer Italia and Finmeccanica in Munich. It was agreed that her employment with Aer Italia would be suspended for a three-year period while on secondment to Eurofighter. Aer Italia agreed to cover her voluntary insurance contributions in Italy, return air fares for home visits and to recognise her period of time with Eurofighter as service on her original contract. It also undertook to pay a rent allowance or to bear the cost of rental accommodation in Munich for the three years. Eurofighter, however, was to pay her salary and certain other relevant allowances directly. She maintained her written contract with Aer Italia and entered into a second written contract with Eurofighter covering the seconded position, which was stated to be subject to German law and the exclusive jurisdiction of the Munich courts. Soon after, Aer Italia was acquired by the Finmeccanica Group, such that it subsequently became her direct employer.

[20.169] In early 1996, Finmeccanica informed Ms Pugliese that the secondment period would come to an end in February of that year and that she was to return to Aer Italia in Turin the next month. Her return date was extended while Aer Italia tried to find a position for her closer to Rome for family reasons. However, after a period of three months, Finmeccanica discontinued paying the rent on her accommodation in Munich, and all other previously paid expenses relating to the Munich secondment. When Ms Pugliese refused to report for the position in Turin, she was dismissed and subsequently issued proceedings in Munich. Aer Italia challenged the jurisdiction of the German court on the basis that as her contract of employment was with an Italian employer, it was a

---

[196] Case C-437/00 *Pugliese v Finmeccanica Spa* [2004] All ER (EC) 154.

matter for an Italian court. The matter was referred to the ECJ for its ruling under the then Brussels Convention.

[20.170] The question put to the ECJ was whether, in a dispute between an Italian national and an Italian employer relating to a contract of employment which identifies Turin as the place of work, can the employee be deemed to habitually carry out her work in Munich, considering that, from the commencement of employment, her contract was temporarily suspended while the employee carried out work under a separate contract of employment for a German company in Munich.

[20.171] The Court ruled that even though the employee was originally employed under an Italian contract of employment in Italy, she could be deemed to be habitually carrying out her work under the first contract of employment in Munich. However, this was on the basis that her first employer had a direct interest in the second contract being performed. The Court laid emphasis on the objectives of the Rome and Brussels Conventions to avoid multiplication of claims across different jurisdictions and also to protect an employee as the weaker party in an employment relationship.

[20.172] The Court considered the extent to which the Italian contract was connected to the German contract. The Court identified a number of relevant factors that it would look at in this regard, including the fact that the second contract was envisaged at the time the first contract was concluded, that the first contract was amended to allow for the second contract, the fact that there was an organisational link between the employers (which ultimately became even closer over the course of the secondment), that there was an agreed framework between the two employers providing for the co-existence of the two contracts, that the employer retained management powers in respect of the employee, and finally, the fact that the first employer was able to determine the duration of the secondment period. While the matter was remitted to the German Court, it would appear on the criteria identified by the ECJ that Aer Italia could be said to have had a direct interest in the performance of the German contract, such that Ms Pugliese was habitually employed in Munich and so Germany was therefore the correct jurisdiction.

[20.173] The more recent decision of *Weber v Universal Ogden Services Ltd*,[197] developed the theme further, in this case considering the position of an employee who, on a factual analysis, did not have any base. Mr Weber was employed with Universal in July 1987 until December 1993. Universal provided catering services onboard mining vessels and installations in and around the Dutch continental shelf. For the first six years of his employment, Mr Weber was working in different locations in Dutch waters, though he spent the three months up to the termination of his employment on a floating crane in Danish waters. Following termination of his employment in 1993, Mr Weber initiated proceedings before a Dutch Labour Court, claiming unlawful termination.

[20.174] The issue of jurisdiction came up and was ultimately referred to the ECJ to determine whether, for the purposes of Art 5(1) of the Brussels Convention (now Art 19(2) of the Brussels Regulations), the work done by Mr Weber on the Dutch continental shelf could be regarded as having been carried out in the Netherlands, and if

---

[197] *Weber v Universal Ogden Services Ltd* [2002] EU ECJ C-37/00.

so, whether he could be considered as having habitually worked in the Netherlands within the meaning of the Convention.

[20.175] The Court ruled that where an employee performs the contract of employment in several Member States, the place where he habitually works should be the place in which or where, taking into account all the circumstances, he performs the essential parts of his duties to the employer. In assessing a contract of employment that is performed in a number of Member States, it is necessary to look at the whole duration of the employment relationship in order to identify the place where the employee habitually works, unless otherwise clear that the employee has now a new permanent habitual place of work. In most cases, and failing any other criteria, that will be the place where the employee has worked the longest. On that basis, Mr Weber was deemed to be habitually working in the Netherlands.

Beyond the EU – conflict of laws

[20.176] Many Irish employers post employees outside of the EU, often to the US or Asia. This is a much less regulated area of practice in that the clear guidelines set out in the Brussels and Rome Regulations have no immediate equivalent. However, as seen, the Brussels and Rome Conventions and Regulations both have a quite far reaching effect. An employee of an Irish employer in a non-EU jurisdiction may be able to bring the dispute before an EU court.

[20.177] Where the circumstances are genuinely beyond the scope of the relevant Regulations, the issue of jurisdiction and governing law is determined by the relevant local provisions of private international law and common law.

POSTED WORKERS DIRECTIVE

[20.178] The purpose of the Posted Workers Directive.[198] is to ensure that employees who are sent on temporary foreign assignment within the EU will be covered by certain mandatory provisions of local employment law in the jurisdiction to which they are posted, irrespective of nationality or where ordinarily employed.

[20.179] A Communication from the Commission noted that, as of April 2006, approximately 0.4% of the European labour force or one million employees come within the scope of the Directive,[199] which in the context of the European labour market is not significant. However, it also noted that a posted worker can be on a temporary posting for an indefinite period of time, giving the example of the construction of a large building which can take several years but it is still of a temporary nature. As such, the

---

[198] Directive 96/71/EC of the European Parliament and of the Council of 16 December 1996 concerning the posting of workers in the framework of the provision of services.

[199] Communication from the Commission, Guidance on the posting of workers in the framework of the provision of services (SEC (2006) 439).

Directive is capable of covering a much broader group of cross-border employees than may be understood in the market place.[200]

Protection under the Directive

[20.180] The Directive arose out of the ECJ ruling in *Rush Portuguesa*.[201] In that case, a Portuguese-owned public works company, which had been sub contracted to build a railway line in France, arranged for its own Portuguese employees to come to France to carry out the work. The French National Immigration Board challenged the employer's right to do so and the matter went to the ECJ on a point of law relating to the freedom to provide services. The ECJ ruled that the Portuguese employer was entitled to use its own Portuguese employees in the provision of the service. However, it counterbalanced this by requiring the employer to apply all relevant French social and labour legislation to the Portuguese employees based in France during the period of the contract. The judgment was a significant landmark in both commercial equity and employee protection, in that it ensured that foreign competitors coming from jurisdictions where labour costs are lower cannot undercut local competitors. The Directive followed this ruling to avoid social dumping by employers across Member States by ensuring a minimum set of employment rights for employees posted by their employer to work in another country.

[20.181] The Directive applies to all employers within the EU, with certain limited exceptions for seagoing personnel, providing cross-border services where the employer:

(i) posts workers employed under contracts of employment with the home employer to any other Member State on behalf of the home employer and under its control, pursuant to a contract between the home employer and the party to whom the service will be provided in the Member State;

(ii) posts workers to an undertaking owned by the home employer in the second Member State, provided there is an employment contract between the home employer and the employer during this period; or

(iii) is a temporary employment undertaking or placement agency hiring out a worker to a user undertaking in a second Member State, provided there is a contract of employment between the home employer agency and the employee during the period.[202]

The Directive does not cover a non-EU employer posting employees to an EU location, though the Rome Regulations would apply local mandatory law at a minimum.

[20.182] A posted worker is defined in the Directive as 'a worker who for a limited period, carries out his work in the territory of a Member State, other than the State in which he normally works'.[203] A posted worker must therefore be an employee who is on

---

[200] The Commission also clarified that the proposed services Directive would not contain any provision in regard to the posting of foreign workers, such that there would be no cross over between both Directives.

[201] Case C-113/89 *Rush Portuguesa Lda v Office National D'Immigration* [1990] ECR I-1417.

[202] Directive 96/71/EC, Art 1(3).

a temporary assignment with the intention of returning to the home country or possibly moving to a third country once the project is concluded.[204]

[20.183] The Directive requires that posted workers shall enjoy the same terms and conditions of employment as provided by law, including by way of collective agreement or arbitration awards which have been declared universally applicable in the Member State, while posted there that apply to domestic employees. It specifically limits this, however, to terms and conditions in the area of:

(i)   maximum working periods and minimum rest periods;

(ii)   minimum paid annual leave;

(iii)   minimum rates of pay, including overtime, excluding occupational retirement pension schemes;

(iv)   conditions relating to hiring out employees, in particular temporary agency employees;

(v)   health, safety and hygiene at work;

(vi)   maternity protection;

(vii) protection in relation to employment of young people; and

(viii) gender equality and anti-discrimination protection.[205]

[20.184] Any employee on a foreign assignment within the scope of the Directive should therefore enjoy the same level of protection in the host country as a local employee. The obvious exception from the mandatory protection is the protection against dismissal. The most logical reason for excluding this must be that as a temporary assignment, the employee will most likely continue to enjoy the appropriate protection in the home country, so is not left without protection. To include it would only lead to an unnecessary multiplication of claims.

[20.185] In practical terms, Irish employers need only be conscious of the Directive when posting employees abroad, as opposed to taking employees into the Irish market, and even then it will only relate to those employees being posted abroad on a temporary basis. The only circumstances in which an Irish employer would need to be concerned with the Directive in Ireland would be where engaging a subcontractor from outside the jurisdiction who would be using posted workers on the relevant contract, to ensure that the subcontractor agrees to apply the minimum standards required. This is not so much a strict requirement of the Directive, but more from an industrial relations perspective to ensure that the Irish employer does not become involved in industrial action against the subcontractor on its premises. Irish employees will be more concerned with the implementation of the Directive in the relevant Member State as the applicable law. Employers will therefore need to take advice on local law in the relevant jurisdiction to

---

[203] Directive 96/71/EC, Art 2(1).

[204] The European Commission has provided useful guidance on the implementation of the Directive in Communication from the Commission, *Guidance on the posting of workers in the framework of the provision of services* (SEC (2006) 439).

[205] Directive 96/71/EC, Art 3(1).

ensure that they are providing the minimum protection required, not by the Irish legislation, but by the relevant Member State's implementation of the Directive. In reality, the Directive may not arise on a regular basis, as many such posting are so short that employees do not tend to raise the issue, even if eligible to do so, or involve any significant differences, due to the common minimum standards applied by various EU employment directives.

[20.186] The Directive was transposed into Irish law by s 20 of the Protection of Employees (Part-Time) Work Act 2001, by simply extending all Irish employment protection legislation to eligible posted workers. An employee posted to Ireland should therefore receive the full benefit of all Irish employment legislation as would apply to an Irish national or an employee permanently based in Ireland. In this respect, the legislation probably provides a greater level of protection to employees than that required by the Directive. However, the transposing legislation arguably falls short of ensuring posted workers get the full benefit of the Directive as it does not establish a specific avenue of redress for failure to apply the relevant law to posted workers. Instead, a posted worker has the same means of redress as a local employee. In many cases, the posted worker will have returned to their home country by the time the matter comes on for hearing, making it restrictively expensive to pursue.

[20.187] The scope and effect of the Directive was considered recently by the ECJ in *Laval Un Partneri Ltd v Svenska Byggnadsarbetareforbundet & Others*.[206] This case concerned a Latvian construction firm (Laval) working on a school building contract in Sweden. Laval had posted thirty five of its own Latvian employees to carry out the works, all of whom were employed on Latvian terms and conditions of employment, including local collective agreements. When Laval refused to pay local collective agreement rates, the trade unions picketed the site. As Swedish labour law did not have a system for declaring collective agreements universally applicable as envisaged by the Directive, the terms in the particular collective agreements were not therefore covered by or available to Laval's employees while in Sweden as posted workers.

[20.188] The dispute came before the ECJ. The question was whether or not Laval could be required to comply with the terms and conditions provided by the collective agreement that was not universally applicable. In its judgment, the ECJ agreed that the Directive does not preclude Member States from applying their own legislation or collective agreements under the categories of protection covered by the Directive to any employee posted to that territory. However, it does not allow Member States to introduce legislation in particular territories that would require a posting employer to go beyond the mandatory rules for minimum protection contained in the Directive. The Directive does not therefore protect a trade union pressurising a posting employer to honour a collective agreement by means of industrial action, that provides for minimum rates of pay that are more favourable than otherwise required under the Directive.

---

[206] Case C-341/05 *Laval Un Partneri Ltd v Svenska Byggnadsarbetareforbundet & Others* (18 December 2007).

[20.189] The decision was endorsed in *Ruffert v Land Niedersachsen*[207] where the ECJ ruled that requiring an employer to comply with terms and conditions contained in a collective agreement that was not of universal application but that only applied to a particular group of employees went beyond the purpose of the Directive.

EXTRA-TERRITORIAL APPLICATION OF IRISH EMPLOYMENT LEGISLATION

[20.190] The majority of Irish employment legislation is silent on the issue of extra-territorial application. Instead, it is presumed in all cases that the employee is ordinarily employed in Ireland.[208]

[20.191] However, s 25 of the Redundancy Payments Acts 1967–2007 provides a qualified entitlement to employees working overseas. In the first instance, it states that an employee will not be entitled to any redundancy payment if outside the State on the termination date, unless the employee otherwise ordinarily works in the State under his/her contract of employment. It also states that an employee working outside the State, but that was otherwise working in the State for at least two years 'immediately prior to the date of termination' will be entitled to redundancy in respect of all service with the relevant employer. The Acts provide that in calculating an employee's service for the purpose of statutory redundancy payment, the employer must recognise any service while outside of the State. The Acts recognise the possibility that an employee who ordinarily works outside the State may be entitled to a statutory redundancy payment if, prior to commencing the position outside the State, he/she was insurable under the Social Welfare Act 2005.

[20.192] Similarly, s 2(3) of the Unfair Dismissals Act 1977 provides that:

This Act shall not apply in relation to the dismissal of an employee who, under the relevant contract of employment, ordinarily worked outside the State, unless:

(i)   he was ordinarily resident in the State during the term of the contract; or

(ii)   he was domiciled in the State during the term of the contract and the employer;

    (I)   in case the employer was an individual, was ordinarily resident in the State, during the term of the contract, or

    (II)   in case the employer was a body corporate or an incorporated body of persons, had its principal place of business in the State during the term of the contract.

In this subsection 'term of the contract' means the whole of the period from the time of the commencement of work under the contract to the time of the relevant dismissal.

---

[207] Case C-346/06 *Ruffert v Land Niedersachsen* [2008] IRLR 647.

[208] This is in contrast to other jurisdictions where certain legislation is expressly stated to apply outside of the jurisdiction. For example, Title VII of the Americans with Disabilities Act 1990, and the Age Discrimination in Employment Acts 1967, cover all US citizens employed outside the US by a US employer, or a foreign company controlled by a US employer.

[20.193] This provision was considered by the EAT in *McIlwraith v Seitz Filtration (GB) Ltd*.[209] The Tribunal considered whether an employee, whose contract was for the most part connected with the UK, could be deemed to be ordinarily working in the State. While Mr McIlwraith's contract defined his work area as the Republic of Ireland and Northern Ireland, his employer was based in the UK and his contract contained an express UK governing law clause. Notwithstanding this, he sought to bring the matter before the Irish EAT claiming that Irish law was the correct governing law under Art 6 of the Rome Convention. This was on the basis that he habitually carried out his work in the performance of his contract in Ireland. On examination of the evidence, the EAT noted that, even though he was paid in sterling, he was paid into an Irish bank account, he paid Irish national insurance and received Irish Social Welfare benefits following termination, and he made self-assessment returns on his salary in Ireland.

[20.194] While there was little detail given on the extent to which he actually performed his duties in Ireland or the UK, or the amount of time actually spent in either jurisdiction, the EAT concluded that it was clear that he carried out his work in Ireland and thus was ordinarily working in Ireland. It further found that, notwithstanding the governing law clause in the contract, he was entitled to the benefit of the Unfair Dismissals Acts.

[20.195] The issue was also considered by the EAT in *Roche and Others v Sealink Stena Line Ltd*[210] in a case brought by a group of former employees following their selection for redundancy. The employer argued that they had no jurisdiction before the EAT as they could not be deemed to be ordinarily employed in the State as they were employed by a British registered company onboard ships subject to British law, that their base port was in the UK, their contracts were made in the UK, their salary was paid in sterling and they paid UK national insurance (though curiously income tax in Ireland) and finally that their statutory redundancy entitlements were paid by the UK authorities.

[20.196] The employees claimed that they all had private addresses in the State and that as Irish citizens were entitled to proceed in the jurisdiction. The Tribunal concluded that they were ordinarily resident in the State during the period of their employment for the purposes of the legislation. This judgment is not particularly useful as the Tribunal does not give much detail on its reasoning, and while it was noted that the respondent accepted the ruling without prejudice to its right to seek judicial review, the matter did not proceed any further. In *Davis v Sealink Stena Line Ltd*,[211] the EAT denied jurisdiction to an employee carrying out his duties abroad pursuant to a contract providing for a governing foreign law, even where the employee was ordinarily resident in the State during the term of employment.

---

[209] *McIlwraith v Seitz Filtration (GB) Ltd* UD 797–95.
[210] *Roche and Others v Sealink Stena Line Ltd* UD 274–1992.
[211] *Davis v Sealink Stena Line Ltd* UD 874/1993.

Conclusion

[20.197] By and large, Irish employment law will only apply within the confines of the jurisdiction, save where an employee is employed in a foreign jurisdiction on a contract stated to be subject to Irish law.'

Pensions and taxation

[20.198] On cross-border pensions, see Ch 11, Pay, Pensions and Benefits at para [11.196]–[11.212]. On the relevance of territoriality to taxation, see Ch 21, Taxation, para [21.02].

Part X
Taxation

Chapter 21

Taxation

Marie Griffin and Conor Hurley

TAXATION OF EMPLOYMENT INCOME[1]

Introduction

[21.01] Every person exercising an office or employment is (subject to available exemptions and reliefs) liable to income tax on all 'salaries, fees, wages, perquisites, or profits whatsoever therefrom'[2] (employment income). The principal charging section of Sch E[3] requires an individual to firstly exercise an office or employment, and secondly to derive employment income from that office or employment.[4] Income tax under Sch E is charged in respect of every public office or employment of profit, and in respect of every annuity, pension or stipend payable out of the public revenue of the State, (other than annuities charged under Sch C).[5] Income tax under Sch C is payable in relation to 'all profits arising from public revenue dividends payable in the State in any year of assessment'[6]). The term 'public revenue dividend' refers to dividends, annuities and interest payable out of the public revenue of any government.

Income tax under Sch E is also charged in respect of any Irish office, employment or pension. Non-Irish offices or employments are taxed under Sch D.[7] This chapter focuses on the taxation of employment income taxed by reference to Sch E (ie Irish employment income rather than foreign employment income). Reference is also made to payment of pay related social insurance (PRSI) in the context of an employment situation.

TERRITORIALITY

[21.02] Income from an office or employment which is exercised in Ireland, being Irish source income, is subject to Irish income tax under Sch E irrespective of the residence/domicile status of the individual entitled to the income. An individual is resident in Ireland for a tax year (ie 1 January to 31 December) if he is present in Ireland for at least 183 days or more in the year of assessment, or for at least 280 days in aggregate in the year of assessment and the preceding year combined. Periods of 30 days or less in a

---

1   This chapter summarises the taxation treatment of employment income. It does not provide a complex analysis of the issues as this goes beyond the scope of a summary chapter.
2   Taxes Consolidation Act 1997 (TCA 1997), s 112.
3   TCA 1997, s 19.
4   TCA 1997, s 112.
5   TCA 1997, s 19(1).
6   TCA 1997, s 17.
7   TCA 1997, s 18.

single year are ignored for the purposes of the '280 day' rule. Prior to Finance (No 2) Act 2008, an individual was regarded as present in Ireland for a particular day if they were present at midnight. This left considerable scope for the manipulation of the rules by individuals who did not want to be regarded as resident in Ireland for a particular year by ensuring they left the country before midnight on any particular day. Section 15 of Finance (No 2) Act 2008 now provides that an individual will be regarded as resident in Ireland for a particular day if they are present in Ireland at any time during a day. Where an individual is prevented from leaving the State on his or her intended day of departure because of extraordinary natural occurrences (for example, sudden and severe adverse weather conditions) or an exceptional third party failure or action (for example, the breakdown of an aircraft or a labour strike) – none of which could reasonably have been foreseen and avoided – the individual will not be regarded as being present in the State for tax residence purposes for the day after the intended day of departure provided the individual is unavoidably present in the State on that day due only to *'force majeure'* circumstances.

As a result of changes introduced in Finance Act 2006, if any of the duties of a foreign employment are exercised in Ireland, the individual is subject to Irish income tax under Sch E by reference to the proportion of the employment exercised in Ireland (irrespective of the residence/domicile status of the individual entitled to the income).[8] Prior to the change in legislation in 2006, a non Irish-domiciled individual was taxed on the remittance basis (ie only taxed on income remitted into Ireland) under Sch D Case III on income from a foreign employment, even if that individual was resident in Ireland. The amendments to the remittance basis introduced in 2006 (the 2006 rules) were relaxed in Finance (No 2) Act 2008. With effect from 2009, the remittance basis of taxation will apply to certain foreign domiciled individuals who are resident in Ireland and exercising employment duties in Ireland. The relief operates by way of a refund of income tax where the individual satisfies the conditions in the legislation. To qualify, the individual must be non Irish domiciled, but resident in Ireland for a period of at least three years. The relief can be claimed annually from the commencement of the period of residence.

Prior to arriving in Ireland, the individual must have been resident in a country with which Ireland has entered into a double taxation agreement (DTA country), but outside the European Economic Area (EEA). They must also be employed by a company established in a DTA country, but outside the EEA, and the individual's remuneration must be paid from abroad.

At the end of every tax year the individual can opt to be taxed on the greater of their remittances and €100,000 plus 50% of any emoluments in excess of €100,000. A refund of any excess tax paid will be made by the Revenue Commissioners on receipt of the appropriate claim from the individual.

Individuals who are ordinarily resident in Ireland, but not Irish resident, are taxed as Irish resident individuals (ie taxed on worldwide income) with the exception of income derived from an office or employment all of the duties of which are exercised outside Ireland.[9] In addition, duties which are performed in Ireland, which are 'merely

---

8   TCA 1997, s 18(2)(f).
9   TCA 1997, s 821.

incidental' to the performance of the duties of the employment outside Ireland are not taxable in Ireland. An individual is regarded as ordinarily resident in Ireland if they have been resident in Ireland for the preceding three tax years (ie they become ordinarily resident in the fourth tax year of residence). An individual ceases to be ordinarily resident after three successive tax years of being non Irish resident.

OFFICE OR EMPLOYMENT

Office

[21.03] There is no definition of what is regarded as an office, however there has been a substantial volume of case law on the subject of what constitutes an office. The statement of Rowlatt J in *Great Western Railway Company v Bater*,[10] still represents thinking on the subject, where he defined an office as:

> an office or employment which was a subsisting, permanent, substantive position, which had an existence independent of the person who filled it, and went on and was filled in succession by successive holders.

[21.04] In *Edwards v Clinch*[11] Buckley J reviewed the case law on the subject of what constituted an office and concluded than an office in his opinion was:

> a post which can be recognised as existing, whether it be occupied for the time being or vacant, and which if occupied, does not owe its existence in any way to the identity of the incumbent or his appointment to the post...It also follows, in my view that the office must have a sufficient degree of continuance to admit of its being held by successive incumbents; it need not be capable of permanent or prolonged or indefinite existence, but it cannot be limited to the tenure of one man, for if it were so, it would lack that independent existence which to my mind the word office imports.

The criteria of what constitutes a public office were set out in the leading UK case on the subject, *Mc Millan v Guest*.[12] The taxpayer was a director of an English company, but he had looked after the affairs of the company in North America where he lived. The court held that he had been correctly assessed to income tax by the Inland Revenue on remuneration received as a director of the English company. Sir Wilfred Greene MR attached great significance to the fact that as the company was situated and governed in England, every right enjoyed by and duty imposed on a director was to be exercised or discharged in that country and nowhere else. The office was essentially a complex of duties and rights that was bound up with the locality of the company itself. In Ireland it is accepted that an office will be regarded as a public office if it owes its existence to the laws of the State.[13] In practice there is no distinction between the income tax treatment of emoluments deriving from an office or a public office.

---

[10] *Great Western Railway Company v Bater* 8 TC 231.

[11] *Edwards v Clinch* [1981] STC 617.

[12] *Mc Millan v Guest* (1942) 24 TC 190.

[13] *Tipping v Jeancard* [1948] IR 233.A French resident individual, who was director of an Irish company held an Irish public office.

Employments

[21.05] If an Irish office exists, for example the office of a director (either public or private),the individual is charged to tax under Sch E. If there is no office, in order to be chargeable to income tax under Sch E, an individual must be engaged as an employee under a contract of service, as distinct from being engaged pursuant to a contract for services. The relationship of employer/employee is crucial. The question of whether an employer/employee relationship exists has been considered in Ch 2, The Contract and Relationship of Employment. The taxation treatment discussed in this chapter relates to the taxation of individuals engaged as employee and employed pursuant to a contract of service.

The Sch E system of taxation is administered through the pay as you earn (PAYE) system. For the purposes of PAYE, 'emoluments' means anything assessable to income tax under Sch E.[14] Any person paying emoluments is regarded as an employer, and an employee means any person in receipt of emoluments.[15] One must therefore be in receipt of emoluments from an employer in order to come within Sch E.

EMOLUMENTS

[21.06] Section 112 of the TCA 1997 provides that income tax is levied under Sch E on all 'salaries, fees, wages, perquisites, or profits' whatsoever derived from an office or employment. It is generally accepted that payments in the form of cash are regarded as taxable emoluments of an employment. In an employment situation it is generally straightforward to determine the emoluments which are subject to income tax. The determination becomes less clear cut when payment (in whole or in part) is made by non-cash methods or where it is not possible to determine if the payment being made in return for services related to the office or employment in question.

[21.07] A large volume of case law exists on the subject of what constitutes an emolument. In *Seymour v Reed*[16] Lord Cave stated:

> It must now (I think) be taken as settled that the words, 'salaries, fees, wages, perquisites or profits whatsoever' include all payments made to the holder of an office or employment as such, that is to say, by way of remuneration for his services, even though such payments may be voluntary, but they do not include a mere gift or present (such as a testimonial) which is made to him on personal grounds and not by way of payment for his services.

[21.08] In *Hochstrasser v Mayes*,[17] ICI, a pharmaceutical company operated a housing scheme for employees transferred from one part of the country to another. Two employees in the scheme were assessed on the compensation they received under the scheme for losses on the sale of their houses when transferred. The case came before Upjohn J who stated:

> Disregarding entirely contracts for full consideration in money or money's worth and personal presents, in my judgement not every payment made to the employee is necessarily made to him as a profit arising from his employment. Indeed, in my

---

14   TCA 1997, s 983.

15   TCA 1997, s 983.

16   *Seymour v Reed* 11 TC 625.

17   *Hochstrasser v Mayes* (1959) CH 22.

judgement, the authorities show that to be a profit arising from the employment the payment must be made in reference to the services the employee renders by virtue of his office, and it must be something in the nature of a reward for services past, present or future.

[21.09] The case was appealed to the House of Lords and the assessments were eventually discharged (ie the payments were not taxable as emoluments).

Per Lord Radcliffe:

The test to be applied is the same for all. It is contained in the statutory requirement that the payment if it is to be the subject of assessment must arise 'from' the office or employment. In the past several explanations have been offered by Judges of eminence as to the significance of from in this context. It has been said that the payment must have been made to the employee 'as such'. It has been said that it must have been made to him 'in his capacity as employee'. It has been said that it is assessable if paid 'by way of remuneration for his services' and further that this is what is meant by payment to him 'as such'. These are all glosses and they are all of value as illustrating the idea which is expressed by the words of the Statute. But it is perhaps worth observing that they do not displace those words. For my part I think that their meaning is adequately conveyed by saying that while it is not sufficient to render a payment assessable that an employee would not have received it unless he had been an employee, it is assessable if it had been paid to him in return for acting as or being an employee.

Here the payment was not paid as wages but paid to the employee in respect of his personal situation as a house owner. In order to be taxable the payment must be in return for services rendered to the employer or a reward for services past, present or future.

[21.10] In *Hamblett v Godfrey*[18] the right to belong to a trade union and certain other rights under the employment protection legislation was withdrawn from Civil Servants employed at the Government Communications Head Quarters (GCHQ) in the UK. The employees were offered the option of accepting the withdrawal of those rights or being transferred to another branch of the Civil Service. The staff who chose to remain at GCHQ of whom the taxpayer was one, were paid £1,000 each, expressed to be in recognition of the loss of rights previously enjoyed. They were assessed for income tax on the payment on the grounds that the payment constituted an emolument from their employment. The court held that in order to determine whether the £1,000 payment was an emolument arising from the taxpayers employment, it was necessary to consider the status of the payment and the context in which it was made.

[21.11] Having reviewed the earlier case law on the subject, Knox J was of the view that the question to be answered was whether the payment was received by the taxpayer from the employment? He believed the payment did derive from the employment and was therefore taxable as an emolument of the employment. His decision was upheld by the Court of Appeal. *Per* Purchas LJ:

The rights, the loss of which was being recognised, were rights under the employment protection legislation, and the right to join a union or other trade protection association. Both these rights, in my judgement, are directly connected with the fact of the taxpayer's

---

[18] *Hamblett v Godfrey* (1987) 1WLR 357.

employment. If the employment did not exist, there would be no need for the rights in the particular context in which the taxpayer found herself.

The findings and facts showed that the payment to the taxpayer was made in recognition of the loss of specified rights all of which were directly connected with her employment. It followed therefore, that the payment constituted an emolument from her employment and was accordingly taxable under Sch E.

To constitute an emolument therefore, the payment must be a payment made to an individual holding an office or employment as a reward for services provided to an employer.

Revenue guidance

[21.12] Given the complex nature of what constitutes pay for income tax purposes (the analysis of which is outside the scope of this chapter) guidance as to what constitutes a taxable emolument can be obtained from the 'Employers Guide to PAYE' issued by the Revenue Commissioners.[19]

'Pay for income tax purposes includes the following:

- Emoluments
- Restrictive covenants
- Remuneration
- Pay during illness
- Salary
- Holiday pay
- Wages
- 'Danger money'
- Fees
- 'Dirty money'
- Arrears of pay
- 'Tea money'
- Pension
- 'Height money'
- Bonuses
- 'Walking money'
- Overtime
- 'Site allowances'
- Commission
- 'Travelling time money'
- Christmas boxes
- Benefits-in-kind
- 'Tool money'
- Any non-cash benefits
- Non-cash emoluments

And other like allowances or payments'[20]

---

[19] www.revenue.ie /en/business/paye/guide/index/html (Updated 26 February 2008).

[20] Employers Guide to PAYE: htp://www.revenue.ie/en/business/paye/guide/index.html accessed on 11 February 2009.

Perquisites

[21.13] The concept of 'perquisites or profits' covers a wide range of payments and benefits provided to employees. In *Owen v Pook*,[21] Lord Pearse stated that the word 'perquisite' denotes something that benefits a man by going into his pocket. To be a perk, the benefit must be in the form of money or convertible to money. The amount assessed where an employee is given a benefit which can be converted into money is the amount which the employee can realise, ie the market value of the benefit, and not the cost to the employer of providing it.

Where non-monetary benefits are provided to employees the general rule is that such benefits are taxable under s 112 of the TCA 1997 if they can be turned to pecuniary account.[22] In *Tennant v Smith*, a bank required one of its bank managers to live at the bank house which included appropriate residential accommodation. It was held that the value of the house was not part of the emoluments or income of the manager. It was not money or monies worth in his hands and could not be turned into money. The court pointed out that in this case the bank wished the bank manager to live on the premises in order to be responsible for security. In order for something to be a perquisite what one received must be a benefit directly convertible into cash. Here the taxpayer could not sell the right to live in the premises. The case established a distinction between convertible and non-convertible benefits, with only the latter being tax-free. Specific legislation[23] was introduced to counter this and to tax non convertible benefits.

Benefits in kind

[21.14] Benefits that cannot readily be turned to pecuniary account are generally taxed (unless specifically exempted from tax) under s 118 of the TCA 1997. This section ensures that any employee in receipt of benefits in kind will be taxed on receipt of the benefit. Section 118 of the TCA 1997 is a very wide-ranging section and charges to income tax all benefits not otherwise within the charge to tax, which are granted to employees whose emoluments exceed €1,905 for the year of assessment. In the case of benefits granted to directors, the minimum remuneration threshold of €1,905 does not apply, and directors are taxed on benefits received irrespective of their level of remuneration.[24]

The charge to tax applies where an employer incurs an expense in the provision for it's directors or employees of the following benefits which are not other wise within the charge to income tax:[25]

    (i)   living or other accommodation;

    (ii)   entertainment;

    (iii)   domestic or other services;

    (iv)   other benefits or facilities of whatever nature.

---

[21]   *Owen v Pook* (1970) AC 244.
[22]   *Tennant v Smith* 3 TC 158.
[23]   TCA 1997, ss 117–119.
[24]   TCA 1997, s 116(3)(a).
[25]   TCA 1997, s 118.

Valuation of benefit in kind

[21.15] The valuation rules are contained in s 119 of the TCA 1997. The general rule for establishing the value of a taxable benefit (ie notional amount which will be liable to income tax, social insurance contributions and the health levy) is to take the higher of:

(i)   the expense incurred by the employer in connection with the provision of the benefit to the employee; or

(ii)   the value realisable by the employee for the benefit in money or money's worth

less any amount made good to the employer by the employee.[26]

[21.16] This general rule applies except if it is varied by the rules contained in s 119 of the TCA 1997. These rules provide:

(i)   where an asset remains the employer's property, then the expense of providing that asset is not directly assessable on any employee who has the use of the asset;[27]

(ii)   where the asset transferred to an employee has been used or has depreciated in value since it was acquired, the market value of the property and not the cost to the employer is to be taken into account for the purpose of assessing the employee to tax;[28]

(iii) where an asset (other than premises of the employer), is used by an employee and is subject to tax as a benefit in kind, the benefit assessable on the employee is equal to any current expenditure incurred by the employer in connection with the asset, and the annual value of the use of the asset, or any amount payable in respect of the rent or hire of the asset (whichever is the greater).[29]

In the case of premises provided to an employee, the annual value of the use of the asset is the 'annual letting value' ie the rent which might reasonably be expected to be obtained on a letting from year to year if the tenant undertook to pay all usual tenant's rates, and if the landlord undertook to bear the costs of the repairs and insurance, and the other expenses, if any, necessary for maintaining the premises in a state to command that rent.[30]

In the case of any other asset, the value of 5% of the market value of the asset at the time it was first provided by the employer is regarded as a benefit in kind.[31]

[21.17] In *Westcott v Bryan*,[32] a company provided a house for its managing director which was larger than he needed for his own use. The understanding was that he could

---

[26] Paragraph 3.5.2 Employers Guide to PAYE, www.revenue.ie /en/business/paye/guide/index/ html (Updated 26 February 2008).

[27] TCA 1997, s 119(1).

[28] TCA 1997, s 119(2).

[29] TCA 1997, s 119(3).

[30] TCA 1997, s 119(4)(a).

[31] TCA 1997, s 119(4)(b).

[32] *Westcott v Bryan* [1969] 3 ALL ER 564.

entertain clients overnight if necessary. He was assessed on the full amount of the annual value of the house and amounts paid by the company towards running it, less amounts reimbursed by him to the company towards the expenses. He contended that there should be an apportionment of the benefit in kind charge to exclude an amount referable to the availability of the house for company guests. The Inland Revenue attempted to contest this on the basis that no part of the house was set aside exclusively for company guests. The taxpayer succeeded and the assessment was fixed at three quarters of the company's expenditure less the whole of the taxpayers contribution. The principle of apportionment was accepted.

Exempt benefits

[21.18] Section 118 does provide for exemption from the charge to income tax in relation to certain benefits provided to an employee or director, for example:

(i)   the provision of any accommodation supplies or services provided for the director or employee himself and used by him solely in performing the duties of his employment, eg office furniture;

(ii)   the provision of living accommodation for an employee who is not a director who is required to live on the business premises provided either that such accommodation is necessary for employees of that class because of the nature of their employers trade, or that such accommodation has commonly been provided in trades of that kind since before 1948, eg bank managers, railway men;

(iii)   the provision of canteen meals which are provided for the staff generally;

(iv)   the provision of benefits accruing on the death or retirement of a director or employee;

(v)   a monthly or annual bus or train pass;

(vi)   a mobile telephone for business use, where private use of the mobile telephone is incidental;

(vii)   a high speed internet connection to the home of the employee or director;

(viii) computer equipment for business use where private use of the computer is incidental;

(iv)   annual membership fees of a professional body where membership is relevant to the employer's business;

(v)   a motor vehicle designed to carry goods and not commonly used as a private vehicle.

Childcare facilities

[21.19] There is also an exemption from the benefit in kind charge where an employer provides qualifying childcare services for a child of a director or employee.[33]

The childcare service (ie any form of childminding service or supervised activity to care for children) must be provided in a qualifying premises.

---

[33]   TCA 1997, s 120A.

A qualifying premises means premises which:

(i)   are made available solely by the employer, or by the employer jointly with other persons and the employer is wholly or partly responsible for financing and managing the provision of the childcare service;

(ii)   are made available by any other person(s) and the employer is wholly or partly responsible for financing and managing the provision of the childcare service; or

(iii) are made available by the employer jointly with other persons or are made available by any other person(s) and the employer is wholly or partly responsible for capital expenditure on the construction or refurbishment of the premises,

and in respect of which it can be shown that the requirements of Arts 9, 10 or 11, as appropriate, of the Child Care (Pre-School Services) Regulations 1996,[34] have been complied with.

If the employer is responsible for capital expenditure only, the exemption is restricted to the amount of the capital expenditure incurred on the construction or refurbishment of the premises.

Salary sacrifice agreements

[21.20] Salary sacrifice is an arrangement whereby an employee agrees to forgo part of their salary in return for provision by their employer of a benefit with a value corresponding to the amount forgone. The individual is however still subject to income tax on the gross salary without deduction for the amount forgone, as the Revenue Commissioners do not accept that salary sacrifice arrangements reduce an employee's taxable income.

In 2000 the Revenue did however state that in the specific context of the provision of bus or rail travel passes, that they would regard salary sacrifice as being effective for tax purposes so long as there was a bona fide and enforceable alteration to the terms and conditions of employment whereby the employee exercised a choice of benefit instead of salary, there was no entitlement to exchange the benefit for cash, and the choice exercised could not be made more frequently than once a year and then only with the consent of the employer.[35] These administrative practices in relation to travel passes was legislatively provided for in Finance Act 2008 and are reflected in s 118B of the TCA 1997.

It has been possible for many years to forgo salary in relation to the appropriation of shares to employees or directors under an approved profit sharing scheme.

Section 118B of the TCA 1997 affirms that these are the only two circumstances in which salary sacrifice is acceptable and effective for tax purposes.

The Revenue Commissioners will therefore not tax employees on the amount of salary sacrificed:[36]

---

[34] SI 398/1996.

[35] Tax Briefing, Issue 41 (September 2000).

[36] TCA 1997, s 118B.

(i) to acquire a travel pass issued by an approved transport provider, or

(ii) in relation to shares appropriated to employees or directors under an approved profit sharing scheme, such shares being exempt from a charge to tax under the legislation governing approved profit sharing schemes.[37]

Cycle to work scheme

[21.21] A cycle to work scheme was introduced in Budget 2009 with the details now contained in TCA 1997, s 118(5G).[38] The purpose of the scheme is that the provision of bicycles and associated safety equipment by employers to employees who agree to use the bicycles to travel to work will be regarded as a tax exempt benefit in kind. A limit of €1,000 will apply and the exemption can only be availed of once in any five year period. It will also be possible to avail of the scheme by means of salary sacrifice. In such circumstances, the salary sacrifice must be completed over a maximum period of 12 months.

Small benefits

[21.22] There is also an exemption from income tax for employees who receive a benefit with a value of €250 or less in the tax year from their employer:

Where an employer provides an employee with a small benefit (that is, a benefit with a value not exceeding €250) PAYE and PRSI need not be applied to that benefit. No more than one such benefit given to an employee in a tax year will qualify for such treatment. Where a benefit exceeds €250 in value the full value of the benefit is to be subjected to PAYE and PRSI. This concession does not apply to cash payments regardless of the amount.[39]

OTHER TAXABLE BENEFITS

Preferential loans

[21.23] Section 122 of the TCA 1997 deals specifically with loans provided by an employer to an employee where either no interest is payable or where interest is charged at a preferential interest rate. Where the employer is a company, a director of the company is regarded as an employee for the purposes of this section. A loan for the purposes of the charge to tax includes any form of credit, and references to a loan include references to any other loan applied directly or indirectly to replace another loan. An interest rate is regarded a preferential rate if it is below a rate specified by the Revenue Commissioners (specified rate). For 2009 the specified rates are 5.5% for preferential home loans and 15% for all other loans.[40]

---

[37] TCA 1997, s 510.

[38] Finance (No 2) Act 2008, s 7.

[39] Employers Guide to PAYE: www.revenue.ie/index.htm?/leaflets/employers-guide-to-paye/index.html.

[40] Finance (No 2) Act 2008, s 5.

The legislation is widely drafted and it includes loans given to the spouse of an employee and loans given to individuals before they commenced employment with the employer in question.

A loan will not be regarded a being a preferential loan if the loan is made by the employer to the employee at normal commercial interest rates (ie where interest is payable at a rate that is not less than the rate of interest at which the employer in the course of it's trade makes equivalent loans for similar purposes at arms length to persons other than employees or their spouses).[41]

Where in the year of assessment (or part of the year of assessment) any of the loan remains outstanding, the employee is taxed on the difference between the interest actually charged (if any) under the terms of the loan from the employer, and the interest chargeable at the specified rate.

Where any interest payable on a loan is released or written off by the employer, the employee is charged to tax on the value of the amount released or written off in the year in which the interest is released or written off. This applies equally to loans made to an individual by someone who becomes their employer after a loan has been made. The purpose of this anti-avoidance provision is to target loans made at a rate in excess of the specified rate of interest but which are in reality at a nil or lower rate as the interest is subsequently released or written off.

Notional loans

[21.24] If employees (including directors of a company) are permitted to acquire shares in a company (whether the employer company or not) by reason of their employment, either for no payment, or on payment of an amount which is less than the market value of the shares, the market value of the shares (where no payment is made) or the amount left outstanding, will be treated as a notional loan from the employer on which no interest is payable and will be subject to the benefit in kind rules in s 122A of the TCA 1997. If further payments are made for the shares, this will reduce the amount outstanding on the notional loan. Payment includes the giving of consideration in money or money's worth.

The notional loan is terminated when:

(i)   the amount outstanding on the shares is paid;

(ii) any obligation to pay the outstanding amount is released in such manner that the employee is no longer bound to account for the outstanding amount;

(iii) the shares are disposed of and the employee no longer has a beneficial interest in the shares;

(iv) the employee dies.

If the notional loan is terminated in circumstances outlined at (ii) or (iii), the amount of the notional loan outstanding at the time of termination will be regarded as having been released or written off and subject to income tax under the preferential loan provisions. No charge to income tax arises where the notional loan is terminated by reason of the death of the employee.

---

[41] TCA 1997, s 122(1).

[21.25] Where an employee acquires shares by reason of his employment (whether for full value or at an undervalue), and the shares are subsequently disposed of by surrender or otherwise, in circumstances where the employee or any person connected with the employee has a beneficial interest in the shares, for a consideration which exceeds the market value, the amount in excess of market value is regarded as an emolument of the individuals employment and charged to income tax accordingly. This would generally be at the individual's marginal rate of income tax for the tax year in question. The capital gains tax rules which normally apply on the disposal of assets and which would subject the proceeds to tax at 22% do not apply in these circumstances.

The notional loan rules also apply in circumstances where the employee acquires or disposes of an interest in shares which is less than the beneficial interest.

Company cars

[21.26] The provision of company cars is a benefit in kind which is outside the scope of s 118 of the TCA 1997 and is legislated for in s 121 of the TCA 1997.

Where a company car is made available to an employee, this is regarded as a benefit in kind for tax purposes. The benefit to the employee is the private use of a car provided by the employer. The value of the benefit is the amount by which what is known as the 'cash equivalent' of the benefit of the car for the tax year exceeds the aggregate of the amounts which the employee makes good to the employer in respect of the cost of providing or running the car.

[21.27] As a result of changes introduced in Finance Act (No 2) 2008, the cash equivalent of the benefit of a car will depend on the level of carbon emissions of the car and can be between 30% to 40% of the original market value of the car at the date of its first registration.[42] The original market value is the price which might reasonably be expected to be obtained for the car if sold in Ireland on the open market as a new car.

The cash equivalent can be reduced in the following ways:

(a)   any amount paid by the employee to reimburse the employer for use of the car can be from the deducted amount of the cash equivalent;

(b)   the benefit in kind charge is also reduced if the employee's annual business mileage rate is greater than 24,000 kilometres. The percentage reduction will depend on the number of business kilometres travelled.

Business Mileage Lower Limit	Business Mileage Upper Limit	Taxable Percentage of Original Market Value
Kilometres	*Kilometres*	*Per cent*
24,000	32,000	24
32,000	40,000	18
40,000	48,000	12
48,000		6

If the car is available for only part of the year, the cash equivalent is proportionally reduced.

---

42   TCA 1997, s 112(4B).

[21.28] An employee who does not clock up business mileage rates in excess of 24,000 kilometres can avail of a reduced benefit in kind charge if that individual spends at least 70% of their time away from their employment base performing the duties of their employment, and their annual business mileage exceeds 8,000 kilometres. In these circumstances the cash equivalent can be reduced by 20% (ie the benefit will equal 80% of the value of the benefit calculated by reference to the cash equivalent).

Prior to 1 January 2004, it was possible to reduce the benefit in kind charge by a maximum of 11.5% if the employee bore certain running costs, such as petrol, motor tax, motor insurance or the cost of repairs.

[21.29] The legislation imposes an obligation on the employee to deliver to the Revenue Commissioners, within 30 days of the end of the year of assessment, particulars of the car, its original market value, business mileage and private mileage for the year of assessment. If the employee fails to deliver these details or where the Revenue Commissioners are not satisfied with the details provided, an estimate of the original market value, private mileage and business mileage can be made by the inspector of taxes. In the absence of sufficient evidence to the contrary, the business mileage can be reduced by 5,000 miles and such mileage attributed to private use.

It has become more popular in recent years for car allowances to be given to employees instead of providing a company car. The allowance is regarded as an additional emolument of the employment and the employee is subject to income tax on the full value of the allowance.

Company vans

[21.30] The provision of a company van is also a benefit in kind which is outside the scope of the general benefit in kind charging section[43] and is legislated for in s 121A of the TCA 1997. Where a company van is provided to an employee and that van is available for the private use of the employee a benefit in kind charge will arise on the cash equivalent of the benefit less the amount which the employee makes good to the employer in respect of the cost of providing or running the van. The cash equivalent is calculated by reference to 5% of the original market value of the van.

The benefit in kind charge will not arise if the following conditions are satisfied:

(i)   the van is necessary for the employee's work;

(ii)   the employee is required by the employer to take the van home when not being used for work;

(iii)   private use of the van other than travel to and from work is prohibited and there is no other private us;, and

(iv)   the employee spends at least 80 per cent of his or her working time away from the premises of the employer to which the employee is attached.

The administrative provisions in relation to company cars apply equally to company vans.

---

[43]   TCA 1997, s 118.

Car park levy

[21.31] A car park levy of €200 per annum was announced in Budget 2009[44] for employees in the main urban areas who use car parking facilities provided by their employer. The levy will apply to private cars only. Disabled drivers are excluded from the charge. It is proposed that the levy will be collected in arrears via the payroll from employees.[45]

Expenses

[21.32] Section 117 of the TCA 1997 brings all expense allowances paid to employees within the charge to income tax under s 112 of the TCA 1997, whether paid periodically or as lump sum payments. Such expense payments (unless otherwise chargeable to tax) are regarded as a perquisite and taxable under the PAYE system of taxation. It is for the employee to claim a tax deduction for all expenses which have been wholly, exclusively and necessarily incurred in the performance of the duties of the office or employment.[46] This contrasts with the expenses deduction allowed for self-employed individuals, where expenses have to be wholly and exclusively incurred by the self employed individual for the purpose of their trade or profession.[47] The requirement that they be necessarily incurred does not arise.

In practice, where an employer directly reimburses an employee for actual expenses incurred wholly exclusively and necessarily in the performance of the duties of the employment, such expenses are not included as pay.[48] Clearly such reimbursement must not be disguised as remuneration. The employer must keep detailed records of the expenses paid, and if possible the relevant receipts, a description of the expenses, and any other relevant documentation to support the payment.

The Revenue Commissioners issued a Statement of Practice[49]in October 2007, the purpose of which was:

> to set out the tax treatment of the reimbursement of expenses of travel and subsistence to office holders (including directors) and employees with the view to having a consistent approach that takes into account the necessity of business travel for different categories of office holders and employees.[50]

Flat rate expenses

[21.33] It is also possible to pay expenses to employees by reference to a fixed scale of expenses.[51] The employee make a claim for subsistence and travel expenses which is usually based on the published Civil Service motor travel and subsistence rates.

---

44 Details contained in Finance (No 2) Act 2008, s 3.
45 TCA 1997, s 531O.
46 TCA 1997, s 114.
47 TCA 1997, s 81.
48 PAYE, Reg 10.
49 SP– IT/2/07 – Tax treatment of the reimbursement of Expenses of Travel and Subsistence to Office Holders and Employees. http://www.revenue.ie.
50 SP– IT/2/07 page 4, paragraph 1.1.
51 TCA 1997, s 115 provides the legislative basis for this practice.

Payments within the accepted Civil Services rates are not chargeable to income tax. If the expense actually incurred by the employee is higher than the published civil service rate the employee can recover the higher amount without deduction of income tax.

Records

[21.34] The employer must retain a record of all of the following:

(i)   the name and address of the director or employee;

(ii)   the date of the journey;

(iii) the reason for the journey;

(iv)   the starting point, destination and finishing point of the journey, number of kilometers travelled; and

(v)   the basis for the reimbursement of travel and subsistence expenses (eg an overnight stay away from an individual's normal place or work).

As regards the reimbursement of actual expenses vouched by receipts, the employer must retain such receipts, together with details of the travel and subsistence expenses incurred.

The period of retention of records is six years after the end of the tax year to which the records refer.[52]

Travel expenses

[21.35] To be considered a deductible expense, any travel expenses incurred by an employee must be necessarily incurred in the performance of the duties of the office or employment.[53] It is an established principle that travel to a place of employment is not an allowable deduction (ie from home to the normal place of work). This is regarded as expenditure incurred to put the employee in a position to carry out the duties of the office or employment. The normal place of work is the place where the employee normally performs the duties of the office or employment.

[21.36] In *Ricketts v Colquhoun*,[54] a barrister who lived and practiced in London was also the recorder of Portsmouth. The emoluments from his Portsmouth employment were assessed under Sch E. He claimed a deduction for his travelling expenses between London and Portsmouth, Portsmouth hotel expenses, and the cost of conveying his robes on attending the quarter sessions in Portsmouth. The Inland Revenue objected on the basis that the expenses were not necessarily incurred in the performance of his duties as recorder of Portsmouth. The deduction was refused on two counts:

(a)   the taxpayer travelled to get to his office and the travelling expenses were not incurred in order to perform his duties; and

(b)   the expenses were not necessarily incurred by the taxpayer in the performance of his duties.

---

[52]   TCA 1997, s 886.

[53]   TCA 1997, s 114.

[54]   *Ricketts v Colquhoun* [1926] AC 1.

Lord Blansborough said that the test of necessity was an objective one. Each and every incumbent of the office should have to incur the expense in order to make it necessary.

Relocation expenses

[21.37] Concessionally, no tax liability arises on the value of reasonable removal expenses including a temporary subsistence allowance borne by an employer on the occasion of a change of employment which requires an employee to change his place of residence.

Benefits in kind and the PAYE rules

[21.38] Since 1 January 2004, s 985A of the TCA 1997 treats the provision of benefits in kind (other than certain grants of shares and employer's contributions to a PRSA) as pay to which the PAYE system applies. For a grant of shares to qualify for the exemption from the application of the PAYE rules, the shares must be shares in the company in which the employee holds his/her office or employment, or a company which has control of that company.[55] The employer company will be controlled by another company if that other company possesses or is entitled to acquire:

(c)   the greater part of the share capital or issued share capital of the company or of the voting power in the company,

(d)   the greater part of the income of the company on distribution, if the whole of the income of the company were distributed, or

(e)   the greater part of the assets of the company which would be available for distribution on a winding up.[56]

Restrictive covenants

[21.39] Section 127 of the TCA 1997 provides for the taxation treatment of payments for restrictive covenants (ie a payment made in recognition of the restriction of an individuals right to work for a particular company or in a certain area). The legislation was introduced to counter the effect of the decision in *Beak v Robson*.[57] A sum paid to the taxpayer which was provided for in his contract of employment, to restrict his activities for a five year period was held not to be taxable. As a result of s 127 of the TCA 1997, any payment made in recognition of the restriction of an individuals activities is taxable and the payment is regarded as an emolument of the individuals employment.

Benefits in the form of shares

[21.40] The taxation treatment of shares granted to employees is provided for in various sections of the tax code, with the treatment varying depending on the manner in which the shares are granted. The taxation treatment of the more common of granting shares to employees is outlined.

---

55   TCA 1997, s 985A(1A).
56   TCA 1997, s 432(2).
57   *Beak v Robson* [1943] AC 352.

(a) Unapproved share option schemes

[21.41] Under a Share Option Scheme, employees are given the right, in exchange for a nominal payment, to acquire shares in the company at a price set at the date of grant. Normally, the Share Option Scheme will provide that options may only be exercised within a specified period from the date of grant. This is usually any date between the third and the tenth anniversary of the date of grant. The scheme may also provide that the options will only become exercisable on the achievement of certain performance targets by the company and/or the employee. The scheme may also provide that the options will lapse in certain circumstances such as termination of employment. Where an employee's employment is terminated involuntarily, the scheme will usually provide that the options will not lapse automatically on the termination of his employment but may be exercised for a limited period thereafter.

The Share Option Scheme will also provide what will happen in the event of a change of control in the company, or a reconstruction or alteration of its share capital. This is necessary in order to protect the rights of the shareholders.

[21.42] The general rule is that an income tax charge will arise on employees on the difference (the spread) between the option price and the market value of the shares at the date of exercise of the option. The spread is treated as a benefit which is part of the employees' employment income taxable under Sch E of the Irish income tax code. The current income tax rates are the standard rate of 20% and a higher rate of 41% (the marginal rate). Tax on the spread is charged at the marginal rate unless the individual applies in writing to the Revenue Commissioners to be taxed at the standard rate of 20%, and the Revenue Commissioners are satisfied that the individual is likely to be chargeable at the standard rate only for the year of assessment. A new income levy (introduced in Budget 2009[58]) of between 1% – 3% will also apply (the rate depending on the total amount of the income of the employee chargeable to income tax). The Revenue Commissioners reserve the right to tax an employee on the grant of any option which is capable of being exercised more than seven years after it is obtained.

The grant and exercise of the option by employees does not give rise to any other tax charge, nor is it subject to PRSI or the health levy. However, when the employee sells the shares he may be liable to capital gains tax (CGT) on any gain made on the sale of the shares (ie where the sale price exceeds the price paid for the shares).

[21.43] Income tax is payable within 30 days of the exercise of the right to acquire shares. Each payment must be accompanied by a return (Form RTSO1) containing details of the amount of the gain (ie spread between option price and market value of the shares at date of exercise of the option). If the tax is not paid by the due date, interest at a rate of 0.0322% per day or part of day is payable from the date payment is due until payment is made. It is not necessary for the Revenue Commissioners to issue an assessment in respect of the tax payable on any gain. Any income tax paid on the exercise of the option is credited against the individual's tax liability for the relevant tax year of assessment. However, any payment is not regarded as a payment on account of preliminary tax for the year in question.

---

58 Finance (No 2) Act 2008, s 2.

Employees are obliged to account for tax due on the exercise of options under the self assessment system, unless the employee has been exempted by an Inspector of Taxes from filing an income tax return under s 951(6) of the TCA 1997. If a person comes within the self assessment system, they are obliged to file a tax return by a specified date, and to pay any income tax due in respect of income subject to the self- assessment system (non-PAYE income) by a certain date. If the tax payer does not comply with this requirement, interest and penalties can be imposed. An income tax return must be filed by 31 October in the year following the relevant tax year of assessment and the balance of any income tax due must be paid on or before that date.

[21.44] Employers (or other relevant persons) are required to give notice of the following events to the Revenue Commissioners:

(i)   the grant of an option or other right which may become subject to tax;

(ii)   the allotment of any shares or transfer of any asset pursuant to such option or right;

(iii)   the giving of any consideration for the assignment or release of such option or right and

(iv)   the receipt of written notice of the assignment of any option or right.

The relevant date by which the requisite notice must be furnished to the Revenue commissioners is the 31 March in the year following the income tax year in which the option is granted. For example, if options were granted in the tax year ended the 31 December 2008 the relevant notification should be given by 31 March 2009.

International aspects

[21.45] Where a charge to income tax arises in respect of an option, such charge continues to exist even if the individual is no longer resident in Ireland for income tax purposes at the time the share option is exercised, assigned or released. Relief from double taxation under a double taxation treaty may be available if the gain is also chargeable in another jurisdiction. If no double taxation relief is available, the individual can deduct any foreign tax suffered (if applicable) from the gain and Irish tax is charged on the net sum.

[21.46] Prior to 5 April 2007, Revenue did not seek to impose an income tax charge where a share option was granted to an individual prior to that individual becoming resident in Ireland for tax purposes and the emoluments of his/her office or employment becoming chargeable to Irish tax, where at the time the share option was granted, such grant was not contingent on, or connected with, the duties of the office or employment being exercised in Ireland. However, since 5 April 2007, an Irish tax charge will apply where options are granted to individuals not resident in Ireland for tax purposes, and whose income is not within the charge to Irish tax, to any gains attributable to the period during which the duties of the office or employment are exercised in Ireland.

Dividend income on option shares acquired

[21.47] Any dividends earned on shares acquired by employees on exercise of options are regarded as part of that employee's total income for Irish income tax purposes if the employee is a person who is ordinarily resident and domiciled in Ireland. The employee should return details of the dividend to Revenue (under Sch D Case III (foreign income) if the stock held is in a foreign company or Sch F for dividends from Irish companies), and will be subject to Irish income tax at the appropriate rate (of 20%/41%). This income will also be subject to the income levy (1% or 2%), PRSI (4%) and the health levy (2% or 2.5%). Each shareholder should be provided with details of any withholding tax deducted from dividends as these may be available as a credit against the individual's Irish tax.

If the employee is resident in Ireland for tax purposes but not domiciled in this country or not ordinarily resident here, then any dividends earned on foreign shares which are not remitted to Ireland, will not be subject to Irish income tax.

Capital gains tax

[21.48] Employees resident and domiciled in Ireland are liable to Irish capital gains tax (CGT) on worldwide gains which would include any gains made on the sale of shares acquired under a share option scheme. Budget 2009 increased the rate of CGT from 20% to 22%[59] with effect from 15 October 2008. The liability will depend on how much the shares have appreciated in value since they were acquired. In computing the amount of the gain, the employee may deduct from the sale proceeds the option price plus any amount which was chargeable to income tax on the grant/exercise of the option. Each individual is entitled to receive a gain of €1,270 per annum free from CGT.

If the employee is resident in Ireland but not domiciled here, then he will not be liable to Irish capital gains tax on any gains made on the sale of foreign shares unless the sale proceeds are remitted to Ireland.

If the employee is not or has ceased to be resident in Ireland when the shares are sold, a liability to Irish capital gains tax will arise where the shares are in an unquoted company which derives the greater part of its value from its ownership of lands or minerals located in Ireland.

(b) Approved share option schemes

[21.49] The Taxes Acts provide for special tax treatment for share options granted under schemes approved by the Revenue Commissioners. In such cases there is to be no charge to income tax on the acquisition of an option. Furthermore, if a period of not less than three years elapses between the date of the grant of the option and the subsequent disposal by the employee of the shares, there is no income tax charge on the exercise of the option, as would be the case under an unapproved scheme. The employee will be subject to CGT at the rate of 22% on the amount of the gain realised on the disposal of the shares (ie the excess of proceeds of sale over the amount paid by the employee for the shares).

[21.50] The scheme must be open to all employees and full-time directors of the company and must provide that such employees are eligible to participate in the scheme on similar terms. Factors such as level of remuneration, length of service and similar

---

[59] Finance (No 2) Act 2008, s 44.

criteria may be used to vary the rights to be obtained by participants in the scheme. If the scheme contains a service requirement for eligibility, this cannot exceed three years. The scheme must not contain features which would discourage employees from participating, or have the effect of conferring benefits wholly or mainly on directors or higher paid employees of the company. The legislation permits the scheme to contain a 'key employee' element. As a result, options can be granted without the similar terms conditions applying in the case of key employees or directors. This is defined as meaning an employee or a full-time director of the company whose specialist skills, qualifications and relevant experience are vital to the future success of the company, and is so certified to the Revenue Commissioners by the company. In such a case, not more than 30% of the total number of shares over which rights are granted under the share scheme in any year can be allocated to key employees. Employees cannot acquire shares by reference to both criteria in the same year.

[21.51] The price at which scheme shares may be acquired is to be stated at the time the option is granted, and may not be less than the market value of the shares at that time or, if agreed with the Revenue Commissioners, at an earlier time. The legislation also lays down detailed requirements in relation to the scheme shares themselves. They must form part of the ordinary share capital of the company or of a company which has control of the company granting the shares (provided that in the latter case the shares are quoted on a recognised stock exchange). If the shares are not so quoted, the shares must be shares in a company not under the control of another company. The shares must be fully paid up, not redeemable and not subject to restrictions that do not apply to other shares of the same class. The memorandum and articles of association of the company may contain a restriction requiring the sale of the shares if the holder ceases to be an employee/director of the company.

[21.52] The scheme must not permit any person obtaining options to transfer those options, but it may provide that if a person dies before exercising an option, the option may be exercised within one year after the date of that person's death by his personal representatives, or the beneficiary of his estate.

Except in cases where a company establishes a trust or corporate structure to hold shares for the purposes of an employee share option scheme, any sum of money expended by a company in establishing a Revenue approved scheme is deductible. If approval for the scheme is given more than nine months after the end of the accounting period in which the expenditure was incurred, the deduction is given in the accounting period in which the approval was given.

(c) *Approved profit sharing schemes*

[21.53] An Approved Profit Sharing Scheme (APSS) is a mechanism whereby shares can be given to employees free of charge and free of tax up to a maximum value of €12,700 per employee per annum. The APSS must be established under a deed of trust which must be approved by the Revenue Commissioners. The employer contributes money to the trustees who use it to purchase shares and allocate these to the employees. The employer obtains a tax deduction for contributing the money to the trust fund, while the employees are not subject to income tax on the benefit received.

All employees in the company must be allowed to participate in the APSS on similar terms. This means that any employees who wish to participate in the scheme must be allocated shares on the same basis, though it is possible to distinguish between employees on the basis of objective criteria such as length of service. Any shares allocated to an employee under a APSS may not be sold within three years of the date of allocation, if the employee wishes to obtain the full exemption from tax. If the shares allocated to employees under the APSS are part of a special class of shares in the company, the majority of the shares in that class must not be held by employees.

An APSS may also include a facility for employees to either forgo salary in order to increase their entitlement under a scheme, or, to buy shares from their own resources in order to receive free shares under the scheme.

Contribution schemes

[21.54] The Revenue Commissioners place restrictions on the amount of any contribution as follows:

(i) the contributory amount must form only a subsidiary element of the overall scheme;

(ii) the maximum amount of shares purchased out of net salary cannot exceed 7.5% of basic salary;

(iii) where it is intended to include a minimum amount in respect of a participant's contribution, that minimum amount cannot exceed €127 or 1% of basic salary;

(iv) each participant must receive at least one free share for each share purchased;

(v) while the purchased shares do not form part of an approved profit sharing scheme, they must be retained for the employee by the trustees for a minimum period of two years.

Salary forgone

[21.55] Revenue have issued the following guidelines where an individual sacrifices salary to acquire additional shares:

(i) salary forgone must form only a subsidiary element of the overall scheme;

(ii) salary forgone must be optional for each participant;

(iii) the maximum amount of salary that may be forgone is 7½% of basic salary;

(iv) where it is intended to include a provision for a minimum amount of salary to be forgone, that minimum amount cannot exceed the lesser of €127 or 1% of basic salary;

(v) where varying percentages are included in a scheme the same choice must be given to all participants;

(vi) in respect of each participant there must be at least a 1:1 ratio between the shares appropriated in lieu of salary forgone and the shares funded by the other monies provided by the company.

For these purposes, shares funded by discretionary bonuses, will concessionally be regarded as part of the employer-funded element of a scheme so long as the bonuses are based on objective criteria and are payable to all employees and directors as a basis of entitlement under an approved scheme. The Revenue have announced that they will not approve new schemes which utilise non-discretionary (fixed) bonuses as a basis of entitlement nor permit existing schemes to incorporate fixed bonuses as a basis of entitlement.

Revenue has issued the above conditions as guidelines only and have emphasised that the granting of approval to salary sacrifice or contributory schemes is purely concessional and that each scheme must be considered according to its own rules. Thus while adherence to the guidelines should normally result in approval of a scheme, it is not a guarantee of approval.

(d) Convertible share schemes

[21.56] The UK case of *Weight v Salmon*[60] established the principle that an individual is taxed on the difference between the consideration paid for shares and the market value of the shares (ie the difference is a taxable perquisite). Prior to Finance Act 2008 it was possible to reward employees in a tax efficient manner by granting shares to employees on payment of a price which did not exceed the market value of the shares at the date of grant. The shares generally formed part of a special class of shares in the company which did not carry any voting or dividend rights but which could, in certain circumstances, be converted into ordinary shares in the company and which resulted in an increase in the value of the shares on conversion. Usually these conversion rights were triggered after an agreed period of time and, possibly also, after the achievement of certain performance targets. Given the limited nature of the rights attaching to such shares it was possible to attribute little or no value to the shares when granted such that no charge to income tax arose on the granting of the shares at market value, provided the employee paid such market value. Therefore, if an individual discharged full market value for the shares no taxable benefit arose. No charge to income tax arose on conversion of the shares, provided the conversion occurred automatically. The individual would have a liability to capital gains tax when the converted shares were ultimately disposed of which resulted in tax being levied at 20% on the disposal proceeds. This compared favourably to an income tax charge of 41% had income tax at the marginal rate being chargeable on the granting of the shares. Anti-avoidance legislation was introduced in Finance Act 2008 (contained in s 128C of the TCA 1997) to counter such convertible share schemes and to charge to income tax the granting of convertible securities.

Section 128C of the TCA 1997

[21.57] The legislation is designed to charge to income tax directors and employees who acquire convertible securities.

---

[60] *Weight v Salmon* 1935 TC 174.

'securities' are defined as including –

(a)   shares,

(b)   securities within the meaning of s 135 of the TCA 1997,

(c)   debentures, debenture stock, loan stock, bonds, certificates of deposit, and other instruments (including certificates and warrants) creating or acknowledging indebtedness, including certificates and other instruments providing for a share in the profits of a company,

(d)   options (other than options to acquire securities, except where such options are acquired under arrangements of which the main purpose or one of the main purposes is the avoidance of income tax, corporation tax or capital gains tax) and financial and commodity futures (within the meaning of the Investment Intermediaries Act 1995),

(e)   warrants and other instruments entitling their holders to subscribe for securities,

(f)   certificates and other instruments conferring rights in respect of securities held by persons other than persons on whom the rights are conferred and the transfer of which may be effected without the consent of those persons, and

(g)   units in a collective investment scheme,

but does not include cheques or other bills of exchange, bankers' drafts or letters of credit, statements showing balances in current, deposit or savings accounts, or leases and other dispositions of property[61];

[21.58] The securities will be convertible securities if:

(a)   they confer on the holder an entitlement (whether immediate or deferred and whether conditional or unconditional) to convert them into securities of a different description, or into money or money's worth, or

(b)   a contract, agreement, arrangement or condition authorises or requires the grant of an entitlement to convert them into securities of a different description, or into money or money's worth to the holder in certain circumstances, or provides for the conversion of the securities, otherwise than by the holder, into securities of a different description or into money or money's worth.[62]

Subject to certain exceptions, the acquisition of a beneficial interest in employment related securities by an employee or director is regarded as a chargeable event for income tax purposes and the employee or director is chargeable to income tax under Sch E in the year in which the chargeable event occurs, calculated by reference to formula set out in s 128C(8) of the TCA 1997.

[21.59] A chargeable event occurs if:

(a)   the securities (or the securities in which they are an interest) are converted into securities of a different description in circumstances in which the employee or director (or any other person who acquired the employment-related securities by reason of the director's or employee's office or employment) is beneficially entitled to the securities into which they have been converted;

---

61 TCA 1997, s 128C(1).
62 TCA 1997, s 128C(4).

(b)   the entitlement to convert the securities (or the securities in which they are an interest) into securities of a different description is released for consideration;

(c)   the employment related securities or any interest in them, are disposed of by the director or employee (or by any other person who acquired the employment-related securities by reason of the director's or employee's office or employment), for consideration at a time when the securities are still convertible securities; or

(d)   the employee or director (or any other person who acquired the employment-related securities by reason of the director's or employee's office or employment) receives a benefit in money or money's worth in connection with the entitlement to convert the securities.[63]

[21.60] The anti-avoidance legislation does not apply if:

(i)   the employment-related securities are shares in a company of a class all of which class are convertible securities;

(ii)   all the shares of the class are affected by an event similar to that which is a chargeable event in relation to the employment-related securities;

(iii)   the majority of the company's shares of the class are not employment-related securities; or

(iv)   if, at the time of the acquisition of the employment-related securities, the emoluments from the office or employment are not within the charge to tax under Sch E or Sch D.[64]

The formula for calculation of the chargeable amount will depend on the manner in which the chargeable event occurs, the effect of which is to charge the individual to income tax on the increase in value of the shares as a result of the chargeable event. The employee therefore suffers an increased income tax charge than that which would previously have arisen as the value of the shares on conversion did not fall within the charge to income tax prior to Finance Act 2008. Essentially the employee is taxed (at the marginal rate of tax) on the increase in value of the shares following the conversion event.

Tax avoidance

[21.61] Where convertible shares are acquired under an arrangement of which the main purpose or one of the main purposes is the avoidance of income tax, the income tax charge imposed on acquisition of the shares is to be calculated on the basis that the shares are immediately and fully convertible, unless the market value ignoring conversion is less than or equal the market value of the shares on conversion.

The acquisition of convertible securities brings an employee within the self assessment system, unless the employee has been exempted by an Inspector of Taxes from filing an income tax return under s 951(6) of the TCA 1997.[65] As outlined at para

---

[63]   TCA 1997, s 128C(7).
[64]   TCA 1997, s 128C(11).
[65]   TCA 1997, s 128C(13).

[21.43] above, if a person comes within the self assessment system, they are obliged to file a tax return by a specified date, and to pay any income tax due in respect of income subject to the self- assessment system (non-PAYE income) by a certain date. If the tax payer does not comply with this requirement, interest and penalties can be imposed. An income tax return must be filed by 31 October in the year following the relevant tax year of assessment and the balance of any income tax due must be paid on or before that date.

When computing the capital gains tax charge (if any) on the disposal of the employment related securities, the individual may deduct from the proceeds the amount of income tax charged on the acquisition of the securities. The income tax paid forms part of the consideration for the acquisition of the shares.[66]

Employers are required to give notice of the of the award of convertible securities or on the occurrence of a chargeable event to the Revenue Commissioners on or before the 31 March in the year following the income tax year in which the convertible securities are granted or the chargeable event occurs.[67]

(e) Partly paid share scheme

[21.62] In a partly paid share scheme employees subscribe for shares in the company on the basis that they need only pay to the company part of the nominal value of the shares when the shares are allotted to them. As the shares will not be fully paid following their allotment, both the terms of the scheme and the Articles of Association of the company will provide that the rights attaching to the shares will be restricted.

Since the shares are partly paid, any employees to whom such shares are allotted, will be liable to pay up the unpaid amount due on such shares in the event of the company going into liquidation. Accordingly, if the market value of the shares in the company appreciates quickly in the immediate future, the allotment of further shares under this scheme may become less attractive if employees are unsure as to whether the share price of the company will continue to perform thereafter. This is one advantage which a conventional share option scheme has over this type of scheme.

As outlined at para **[21.24]** there is a deemed benefit in kind charge under s 122A of the TCA 1997 in circumstances where employees are permitted to acquire shares by making a payment on account, such as par value only, with the balance of the subscription price left outstanding. (Revenue's practice is not to apply this charge in the case of shares acquired pursuant to approved profit sharing schemes).

(f) Save as you earn schemes

[21.63] Favourable tax treatment was introduced for save as you earn (SAYE) schemes in the Finance Act 1999, the rules of which are now contained in s 519A and Sch 12A of the TCA 1997. Under an SAYE scheme, an employee enters into a contract with the company whereby he agrees to save a portion of his salary each month. These savings are pooled with similar savings by other employees in a single deposit account thereby obtaining the maximum possible interest rate. At the time an employee enters into the

---

[66] TCA 1997, s 128C(14).
[67] TCA 1997, s 128C(15).

contract, he is also offered an option to subscribe for shares in the company at either the prevailing market price or a discount from the prevailing market price. After a period of years, normally between three to five, the savings of all the employees are released and the employees will then either keep the savings plus the interest earned or use it to exercise the options granted to them when they first began saving. The interest /bonus earned on the savings is exempt from income tax/Deposit Interest Retention Tax.

Where an individual obtains a right to acquire shares in accordance with a savings related share option scheme approved by the Revenue Commissioners, no tax will be chargeable in respect of the receipt or exercise of that right except in certain circumstances where the option is exercised within three years of the date on which it was granted. The employer company is granted a tax deduction for the costs of establishing the savings related share option scheme. The scheme must be open to all employees and full-time directors of the company. The price at which shares may be acquired must be settled at the date the option is granted and may be at a discount of up to 25% of the market value at that time.

The Minister for Finance has issued a specification outlining the requirements in relation to the operation of certified contractual savings schemes which must be used to fund the purchase of shares allocated to employees under the savings related share option scheme.

The maximum contribution is €500 per month, and the minimum is generally €12 per month.

(g) Share incentive schemes involving a clog

[21.64] These schemes (also known as restricted share schemes) involve the allocation of shares to an employee which are subject to contractual restrictions agreed between the company and the employee. These contractual restrictions usually prohibit the employee concerned from having the benefit of any rights (eg dividend or voting rights) attaching to the shares for a specified minimum period. In addition, the company and the employees may have agreed that the restrictions attaching to the shares will not be removed unless certain performance targets are met. The scheme may also provide that in certain circumstances, the employee can be required to sell his/her shares at a specified price. This price will depend on whether the restrictions have been lifted at the time of the sale. The specified circumstances will usually include a voluntary termination of employment by the employee concerned.

Usually, existing (not newly-issued shares) will be used in the scheme and this will require a trust to hold the shares so long as the restrictions continue to apply. This will be a discretionary employee benefit trust. The company will finance the trust (by loan or gift) to hedge all or part of the obligation to transfer shares to the executive at the end of the holding period. Usually the trust rather than the company makes the award of the shares to the executive.

In making the loan or gift to the trust the company will be availing of the exemption in s 60(13) of the Companies Act 1963 in respect of the provision of financial assistance for the purchase of shares in the company which are to be held for or on behalf of employees.

If employees receive shares under schemes which prohibit from them from disposing of the shares immediately, in practice the Revenue allow an abatement of the income tax charge depending on the clog (ie the number of years prohibiting disposal). This ranges from 10% discount for a one year clog to 55% discount for a clog in excess of five years. The charge to tax arises, and the abatement is allowed, in the year in which the shares are acquired.

For this treatment to apply, the prohibition on disposal must be an absolute one imposed for genuine commercial reasons (such as security law considerations as outlined above.) It will only apply to a grant of shares made in the employer company or the parent company.

(h) Share subscriptions

[21.65] Section 479 of the TCA 1997, allows for favourable tax treatment for employees who subscribe for new shares in a qualifying company. Under this relief, an employee is entitled to a once-off reduction in his/her taxable income equal to the amount of the subscription; presently subject to a maximum life-time deduction of €6,350. A qualifying company is a trading company (or a holding company whose business consists mainly or wholly of the holding of shares in trading companies which are at least 75% subsidiaries) incorporated or solely resident in the State at the time the shares are issued. No formal documentation is required. To qualify for tax relief, the employee merely subscribes for the shares and notifies his/her local tax inspector who grants the deduction for the tax year in which the shares are issued. The tax advantage to the employee is that because the cost of the shares is tax deductible, the net cost of the shares up to the relevant limit is considerably reduced.

Eligible shares are new fully paid-up ordinary shares which, for at least three years from the issue date carry no present or future preferential rights and are not subject to any restrictions not attached to all shares of the same class issued to or acquired by the eligible employees at not less than their market value at the issued date.

Tax relief is withdrawn in full if within three years of the date of subscription the shares are disposed of or the eligible employee receives any consideration in respect of the shares which is not income in his hands for income tax purposes. If the shares are held for over three years there is no withdrawal of the relief as previously allowed.

If a company were to make a bonus payment to an employee which is then used by the employee to subscribe for shares in the company up to a value of €6,350, the share subscription tax relief could be availed of with a net cost to the company equal to the PAYE deduction required to be made in respect of the bonus payment. The share subscription tax relief could also be availed of where a loan is made by the company to an employee which is then used to subscribe for shares in the company. A benefit in kind income tax charge would arise for the employee if the loan is subject to an interest charge below the rate specified from time to time by the Revenue Commissioner.

(i) Employee share ownership trust

[21.66] Employment Share Ownership Trust (ESOT) is a form of employee share scheme arrangement introduced in the Finance Act 1997.[68] ESOT provides for a

---

[68] Reflected in TCA 1997, s 519 and Sch 12.

mechanism whereby shares can be purchased out of money provided by the company and held in a trust for the ultimate benefit of the employee. The company establishing the ESOT will receive a tax deduction for any moneys contributed to the ESOT for the purchase of the shares. If the shares acquired by the ESOT are subsequently transferred to an APSS, no capital gains tax will be payable by the ESOT. In effect, an ESOT is merely a tax-efficient method of allowing a company to 'warehouse' a portion of its share capital in a trust which will ultimately benefit its employees. If the shares are transferred to the employees through an APSS they will not be subject to any income tax. Also the period during which shares were held in the ESOT count towards the three year holding period required by the APSS, provided the employee was a beneficiary throughout this time. If the shares are transferred to the employees by any other method they may be subject to income tax.

The trustees do not pay income tax on dividends declared on shares held by them.

Inducement payments

[21.67] Whether payments made to an individual on commencement of an office or employment or to encourage a person to take on a particular role are taxable as income in the hands of the individual will depend on the circumstances of the payment. Generally, such payments are once off in nature. For such a payment to be taxable as income the payment must be in the nature of a reward for future services.

[21.68] In *Pritchard v Arundale*,[69] a senior partner of a firm of accountants agreed to become Managing Director of a company for seven years from not later than 1 January 1963 if he was given 4,000 shares in the company by its principal shareholder. The shares were duly transferred to him in June 1962 and he commenced working for the company after retiring from his firm. He was assessed under Sch E on the value of the shares as emoluments of his office. The Commissioners discharged the assessment holding that the shares were not remuneration for future services. It was held by the court that the payment was made for giving up his position as partner in a stable and secure partnership and to take on a risky position in an emerging new company. The payment was of a capital nature and not in return for services rendered. The court regarded as important the fact that the transfer had been made by a third party (not his employer) and that the transfer was made six months before service started.

[21.69] In *Jarrould v Boustead*[70] a signing on fee to a football player to relinquish his amateur status on joining a rugby league club as a professional was held not to be assessable as the individual had given up his amateur status for life there was genuine relinquishment of a right or an advantage. This can be contrasted with the position in *Riley v Coglan*.[71] An amateur player received a signing on fee on joining a rugby league club as a professional, a proportion of which was returnable if he did not continue to serve the club for a period stipulated in the agreement. This provision was fatal to the case. The court held that it was an advance payment for future services. In the *Pritchard*

---

[69] *Pritchard v Arundale* (1972) Ch 229.
[70] *Jarrould v Boustead* (1964) 1 WLR 1357.
[71] *Riley v Coglan* (1967) 1 WLR 1300.

case the court considered it important that the transfer of shares to the accountancy partner was irrevocable and this indicated that the transfer of shares was not dependent on future services.

[21.70] This case of *Glantre Engineering Ltd v Goodhand*[72] involved a small company which was carrying on a small rapidly expanding engineering business. It needed a full time financial director and engaged individual in this capacity. He was a chartered accountant who at the time was employed full time by a leading international firm of accountants. The company paid him £10,000 on taking up the appointment and did not deduct tax from the payment under PAYE. The appeal was against a determination of tax payable by the employer under the PAYE regulations. The Special Commissioners dismissed the appeal rejecting the contention that the £10,000 was to compensate the individual for leaving his previous employment. Their decision was upheld. Following the decisions in *Jarrould v Boustead* and *Pritchard v Arundale*, whether a payment at the inception of an employment was an emolument was essentially a question of fact. It could not be said on the facts in this case that the only reasonable conclusion was that the payment of £10,000 to the individual was severable from his other benefits under his agreement with the company and not an inducement to him to change his job and take up employment with the company. Two important points emerged from the case:

(i)   on the facts no material advantage was surrendered and no substantial risk was taken by the individual. The payment was really a payment for services to be rendered;

The Appeal Commissioners decision on questions of fact was conclusive and the courts supported the finding of fact, ie that no advantage was surrendered.

(ii)   also, the payment was described as an inducement, which was fatal in the eyes of the court. The payment should be for a surrender of a previous advantage and described as such. Therefore, the description can be important.

Termination payments

[21.71] Certain payments made to employees on termination of their employment may not come within the general charging section of s 112 of the TCA 1997. Prior to the introduction of specific legislation addressing this point many payments made on termination of employment could be paid without deduction of income tax. A large volume of case law exists to support this treatment. For example, in *Mulvey v Coffey*,[73] the Governing body of UCD voted £1,000 to the retiring president after 31 years service in addition to maximum pensions. The phraseology used was unfortunate in that it stated that the payment was being made 'on account of a great number of services unrewarded as expressed in a labour of overtime work during the past seven or more years and the limited statutory pension to which he is entitled'. Gavan Duffy J decided that on a fair reading the money was paid not because the individual was the president but because a good man was giving up a good office and both deserved recognition and thanks. He therefore upheld the

---

[72]   *Glantre Engineering Ltd v Goodhand* (1983) 1 All ER 542.
[73]   *Mulvey v Coffey* (1942) IR 277.

decision of the Appeal Commissioners that the payment escaped tax as one fact for which there was evidence.

[21.72] As a result legislation was introduced to subject payments made on termination of employment to income tax. Section 123 of the TCA 1997 is the relevant charging section. Section 123 of the TCA 1997 applies to any payment (including payments in commutation of annual or periodical payments) which is not otherwise chargeable to income tax (ie not chargeable under the general charging provisions) which is paid directly or indirectly in relation to the termination of an office or employment, or in relation to a change in the functions or the emoluments of the office or employment. It is important to note that the treatment applies not only to termination situations but also to circumstances where there is a change in the functions of the employment. The provisions of s 123 of the TCA 1997 apply whether or not the payment is made in pursuance of a legal obligation. If the termination payment is paid as a result of any term in the employee's contract of employment or in the conditions of employment, it is generally taxable under Sch E as an emolument of the employment (for example, if the contract states that the employee will get one year's salary in the event of the termination of their employment, then that payment is a payment under their contract and is fully taxable). This rule applies also to payment in lieu of notice. If the payment in lieu of notice is provided for in the contract of service, then it will be fully taxable under Sch E as part of the individual's salary. If however payment in lieu of notice is not contractually provided for, it is generally treated as an ex-gratia payment and not regarded as part of salary. The payment is taxable as a termination payment (subject to available exemptions and reliefs described below). One area where termination payments were taxable (even apart from ss 123 and 201 of the TCA 1997) was where the employment contract provided for the termination payment in question. In *Dale v De Soissons*,[74] a taxpayer had been employed by a tobacco firm for many years. He entered into a new service agreement for a three year period to December 1947 with the right to the employer to terminate it at the end of 1945 or 1946 on payment of £10,000 or £6,000 respectively as compensation for loss of office. This provision was because of uncertainty in the tobacco industry at the time. The agreement was terminated on the 31 December 1945 and the £10,000 paid to him under the agreement was held to be assessable. As the employee was paid what he was entitled to receive under the contract it was taxable. It would not have been taxable if made ex gratia.

THE CHARGE TO TAX UNDER S 123 OF THE TCA 1997

[21.73] Subject to the reliefs and exemptions provided for in s 201 and Sch 3 of the TCA 1997, income tax is charged under Sch E in relation to any payment which is made to the holder or past holder of any office or employment (or to his executors or administrators). The charge to income tax applies whether the payment is made directly by the employer or by any other person.[75] The broad scope of this sub-section is designed to bring within the charge to income tax payments made by an entity other than the direct employer of the individual concerned, for example, where an associated company of the employer

---

[74] *Dale v De Soissons* (1950) 2 All ER 460.
[75] TCA 1997, s 123(2).

company makes a payment to the individual. Payments made to a spouse or dependent relative of the individual concerned, or payments made at the direction of that individual are regarded as payments to the individual who held the office or employment.[76] This is to ensure that the individual cannot avoid a liability to income tax by ensuring that the payment is made to someone else. Any valuable consideration other than money is treated as a payment of money equal to the value of the consideration at the date it is given.[77]

Where any payment is chargeable to income tax by virtue of s 123 of the TCA 1997, it is treated as income received by the employee on the following date:

(a) in the case of a payment in commutation of annual or other periodical payments, the date on which the commutation is effected;[78] and

(b) in the case of any other payment, the date of the termination or change in respect of which the payment is made.[79]

There are also provisions outlining the income tax treatment of payments where the individual who received the payment has died (or where that individual's estate receives the payment). If the payment would have been subject to income tax in the hands of the individual concerned, the income tax which would have been assessed on the individual is assessed and charged on his or her executors and is regarded as a debt due and payable out of the estate of the individual concerned.[80]

Reliefs and exemptions

[21.74] There is a complete exemption from the charge to income tax under s 123 of the TCA 1997 where a payment is made in connection with the termination of the holding of an office or employment by the death of the holder, or made on account of the injury to or disability of the holder of an office or employment[81]; The exemption from income tax in respect of payments made as a result of the injury to or disability of the employee will apply provided the nature of the disability is of a specific physical nature or a mental disorder as distinct from a decline of powers due to advance in age. In *O'Shea v Mulqueen,*[82] the employee was obliged to retire from Digital because of job-related stress. On accepting his resignation, the employer decided to make an *ex gratia* payment of £325,000 because of his ill health. It was held that this came within the exemption.

[21.75] Where a payment is made due to the death or the injury to or disability of the employee, the person making the payment must deliver the following particulars to the Revenue Commissioners within 46 days of the end of the tax year in which the payment is made:

---

[76] TCA 1997, s 123(3).
[77] TCA 1997, s 123(3).
[78] TCA 1997, s 123(4)(a).
[79] TCA 1997, s 123(4)(b).
[80] TCA 1997, s 123(5).
[81] TCA 1997, s 201(2)(a).
[82] *O'Shea v Mulqueen* [1995] 1 IR 504.

(a)   the name and address of the person to whom the payment is made;[83]

(b)   the personal public service (PPS) number of the individual who received the payment;[84]

(c)   the amount of the payment;[85] and

the basis on which the payment is not chargeable to tax under s 123 of the TCA 1997, indicating, in the case of a payment made on account of injury or disability, the extent of the injury or disability, as the case may be.[86]

An exemption also applies in relation to payments from certain retirement benefits scheme where the employee was charged to income tax in respect of sums paid or treated as paid by their employer, with a view to the provision of the benefit[87] and for payments paid by certain occupational pension schemes[88] Certain payments made to former members of the Oireachtas and public servants do not qualify for full exemption, but do qualify for the general exemptions provided for in s 201 and Sch 3 of the TCA 1997.[89]

[21.76] The statutory redundancy element of any termination payment received by an employee is exempt from tax.[90] If the payment to the employee exceeds the statutory redundancy amount, the termination payment is taxable (but may qualify for exemptions and reliefs set out below).

Basic exemption

* the first €10,160 plus €765 for each complete year of service is exempt from tax.[91]

Increased exemption

* the Basic Exemption may be increased provided (i) the employee has not, in the previous 10 tax years, claimed relief on a termination payment(s); and (ii) the amount of any tax free lump sum received or receivable in the future on the exercise of an option or a right to commute (in whole or in part) a pension in favour of a lump sum does not exceed €10,000. The Basic Exemption is increased by the amount by which €10,000 exceeds any such lump sum (the Increased Exemption).[92] For example, if the relevant tax free lump sum for the employee in question is €6,000 and the employee has not made a claim in the previous 10 years for tax relief on termination payments, the Basic Exemption may be increased by €4,000.

Standard Capital Superannuation Benefit

* relief from income tax may also be claimed under a formula known as the Standard Capital Superannuation Benefit (SCSB). The employee may take an amount equal to the SCSB tax free if that formula results in a higher tax free amount being available

---

[83] TCA 1997, s 201(2A)(a).

[84] TCA 1997, s 201(2A)(b).

[85] TCA 1997, s 201(2A)(c).

[86] TCA 1997, s 201(2A)(d).

[87] TCA 1997, s 201(2)(c).

[88] TCA 1997, s 201(2)(d).

[89] TCA 1997, s 201(3).

[90] TCA 1997, s 203.

[91] TCA 1997, s 201(1)(a).

[92] TCA 1997, Sch 3, Pt 2, para 8.

to the individual (i.e higher than the Basic and Increased Exemption amounts). This formula is generally more beneficial to longer serving employees.

The SCSB is calculated as follows:

$$\frac{A \times B}{15} - C$$

Where:

A = the average for 1 year of the employee's emoluments for the last three years of service;

B = the whole number of complete years of service in the office or employment; and

C = any tax free lump sum received or receivable under any approved pension scheme, statutory scheme or foreign government scheme in respect of the office or employment.–

An individual is entitled to choose the formula which gives the greatest measure of relief. Any amount received in excess of the exempt amount (calculated by reference to the Basic Exemption, or the Increased Exemption, or the SCSB) will be taxed at the employee's marginal rate of tax for the tax year in question. A termination payment is a lump sum paid in consideration for a number of years of service, assessed to income tax in a single year of assessment. Consequently in many cases the lump sum will be subject to the highest rate of income tax, and included as part of the individual's total income for a particular year. To counteract the inequality of this situation a system of top slicing relief is provided for in Sch 3 TCA. It is possible to have the rate of tax applied to the payment reduced by taxing the chargeable amount by reference to the employee's average rate of tax for the prior three tax years (rather than at his marginal rate in the year of receipt). The employee must apply for this relief to their tax district after the end of the year of assessment in which the payment has been received. If the employee's tax liability is less than that originally paid as a result of the top slicing relief, a refund of the excess tax paid will be made by the Revenue Commissioners to the employee.

Foreign service relief

- Relief is also available for employees where any element of the employee's period of service included foreign service. A period of employment would constitute foreign service if the earnings from the employment at that time were not subject to Irish tax.

If the employee's foreign service comprised either:

(i) three quarters of the whole period of service down to the date of termination of employment;

(ii) the whole of the last 10 years of service down to the date of termination of employment; or

(iii) any 10 of the last 20 years of service,

then the entire termination payment will be exempt from tax in Ireland (although there may be tax implications in the jurisdiction where the foreign service was carried out).

If the employee cannot qualify for entire exemption from tax under this foreign service rule, the employee may claim any relevant exemption (ie the exemption which affords the individual the greatest measure of relief) together with an additional relief calculated by reference to the proportion which the foreign service bears to the total service of the employee. This additional measure of relief is calculated by reference to the following formula:

$$P \times \frac{FS}{TS}$$

Where:

P = Payment (as reduced by the Basic Exemption, Increased Basic Exemption and/or SCSB)

FS = Period of foreign service

TS = Period of total service

- If the employee does not qualify for a complete exemption from income tax (after applying the various reliefs referred to above) the employer could consider paying part of the termination payment into a pension fund on behalf of the employee rather than paying the entire amount proposed as a termination payment.

Example

Joe Bloggs worked for Ireland Inc for 11 years and 5 months of which 3 years and 4 months were spent working abroad. He has been given a termination payment of €224,701.

JOE BLOGGS – Termination Payment SCSB Calculation

Employer	Ireland inc
Date of commencement of employment	1 June 1997
Date of termination of employment	31 October 2008
Length of service	11 years & 5 months
Length of foreign service	3 years & 4 months
Annual salary details	€
1 August 2005	136,440.00
1 August 2006	142,443.00
1 August 2007	148,141.00
1 August 2008	149,801.00
Last 36 months of service	1 November 2005 – 31 October 2008
1 November 2005 – 31 October 2006	139,941.75
1 November 2006 – 31 October 2007	145,766.83
1 November 2007 – 31 October 2008	149,109.33
Total	434,817.92
Average salary last 36 months	144,939.31

SCSB Calculation

$$\frac{€144,939.31 \times 11}{15} = €106.288.82$$

	€
Proposed termination payment	224,701.50
Statutory redundancy tax free amount	10,608.00
Balance	214,093.50
Exempt amount (Section 201 TCA 1997)	106,288.82
Amount subject to tax before foreign service relief	107,804.68
Foreign service relief	

$$\frac{€107,804.68 \times 40*}{137} = €31.475.82$$

*months

Taxable amount	76,328.86

TERMINATION PAYMENTS AND PRSI, THE INCOME LEVY AND THE HEALTH LEVY

[21.77] Termination payments are not 'reckonable earnings' for social insurance purposes and are therefore not liable to the social insurance contribution (PRSI) (currently 4% on income up to €52,000[93]). The health levy applies to the taxable element of the termination payment. The employee will be liable to the health levy of 2% or 2.5% on the taxable portion of the termination payment (not on the tax free element). In addition the income levy of 1% to 3% will also be payable on the taxable element of the termination payment. The employer must deduct these payments through the PAYE system and remit them to the Revenue Commissioners on the employee's behalf.

Employer's obligations

[21.78] The employer may pay a departing employee the Basic Exemption or the SCSB tax free without prior approval from the Revenue Commissioners. Advance approval should however be sought from the Revenue Commissioners before the Increased Basic Exemption is paid tax free. Employers are required to deliver particulars in writing to Revenue particulars of termination payments no later than 14 days after the end of the tax year in which they are made.

---

[93] Employee PRSI ceiling for 2009.

Retraining package

[21.79] Finance Act 2008 introduced an exemption from income tax on the first €5,000 of the cost of a retraining package for certain eligible employees who have been made redundant.[94] The employee must have had been in full time employment with the employer for a continuous period of two years, or be deemed to have at least two years' continuous service for the purposes of the law relating to redundancy. Retraining means a training course which is made available by the employer as part of a redundancy package, that is:

(i)   designed to impart or improve skills or knowledge relevant to, or intended to be used in, obtaining gainful employment or in the setting up of a business;

(ii)   primarily devoted to the teaching or practical application of such skills or knowledge; and

(iii)   completed within six months of the termination of the employment.[95]

A redundancy package for the purposes of this exemption means any scheme of compensation offered to the employee on termination of his or her employment.

[21.80] Income tax is not charged by virtue of s 123 of the TCA 1997 on the first €5,000 of the cost of retraining an eligible employee where the training forms part of the redundancy package and the employer makes retraining available for all eligible employees.[96]

This exemption does not apply to any retraining provided to the spouse or any dependent of the employer.[97] The exemption will also not apply in circumstances where there is an arrangement in place whereby the employee may receive the cost of retraining in money or moneys worth, wholly or partly, directly or indirectly, and the employee actually receives that cost.[98]

Taxation treatment of certain payments made by employers to employees arising from claims made under employment law

[21.81] An exemption from income tax was introduced in s 7 of the Finance Act 2004 (contained in s 192A of the TCA 1997) for certain payments made to employees as a result of claims made for infringement of an employee's rights or entitlements under employment legislation.

The exemption applies to the following payments:

[p]ayments arising out of claims made under a relevant Act following a formal hearing before a relevant authority (or through a mediation process) based on a recommendation, decision or determination by that relevant authority, and

in certain circumstances, payments arising out of claims made under a relevant Act made under an 'out of court' settlement (ie a settlement which has been agreed between an

---

94   TCA 1997, s 201(1A).
95   TCA 1997, s 201(1A)(a).
96   TCA 1997, s 201(1A)(b).
97   TCA 1997, s 201(1A)(c).
98   TCA 1997, s 201(1A)(d).

employee and his or her employer as an alternative to a formal hearing before, and a recommendation, decision or determination of, a relevant authority).

A 'relevant Act' means an enactment that contains provisions for the protection of employees' rights and entitlements or the obligations of employers towards employees. Examples of such legislation include:

Employment Equality Acts 1998–2008;

Maternity Protection Act 1994 and 2004;

Parental Leave Act 1998 and 2006;

Payment of Wages Act 1991;

Terms of Employment Information Acts 1994 and 2001;

Minimum Notice & Terms of Employment Acts 1973–2001;

Protection of Young Persons (Employment) Act 1996;

Protection of Employees (Part-Time Work) Act 2001;

Protection of Employees (Fixed-Term Work) Act 2003;

Redundancy Payments Acts 1967–2003;

Organisation of Working Time Act 1997;

Carer's Leave Act 2001.

Out of court settlements

[21.82] A payment made under such an agreement will also qualify for the exemption where all of the following conditions are met:

(i)   the agreement in settlement of a claim is evidenced in writing;

(ii)   the agreement is not between 'connected persons' (eg employer and relative, employer and director);

(iii)   the claim would have been a bona fide claim under a relevant Act had it been made to a relevant authority (eg sufficient grounds for the claim; claim is within the scope of one of the relevant acts; claim made within specified time limits, etc);

(iv)   the claim is likely to have been the subject of a recommendation, decision or determination by a relevant authority that a payment be made to the person making the claim; and

(v)   the payment does not exceed the maximum amount which could have been awarded under relevant legislation by the Rights Commissioner, Director of Equality Investigations, Employment Appeals Tribunal or Labour Court as appropriate.

Administration of the PAYE system

[21.83] The PAYE system is a collection system for income tax (including the new income levy introduced in Budget 2009), PRSI and the health levy. To facilitate collection of PRSI and the health levy, these are deducted at source from emoluments by the employer and remitted by the Collector General to the Department of Social and Family Affairs, which is the department responsible for their administration.

The employer's obligations are set out in Ch 4, Pt 42 of the TCA 1997, and the PAYE Regulations. Section 985 of the TCA 1997 obliges every employer to deduct income tax or make a repayment of income tax from any emoluments paid to an employee. The PAYE Regulations[99] provide for the detailed operation of the PAYE system and prescribe the manner in which the deduction of tax from salaries and wages under the PAYE system operates.

[21.84] The income tax year runs from January to December (ie the calendar year). Individuals are entitled to avail of the relevant tax credits and reliefs which their individual circumstances entitle them to for the particular year. At the beginning of each tax year the Revenue Commissioners determine the amount of tax credits to be given to an individual and furnish the individual with a certificate indicating the tax credits granted. The certificate will also indicate how much of the individuals income is subject to tax at the standard rate (standard rate cut off point). This determination is based on the information held by the Revenue Commissioners in relation to the individual. A copy of this certificate is provided to the individual's employer. An individual who is dissatisfied with the determination of tax credits/ standard rate cut off point can give notice in writing of his or her objection to the Inspector of Taxes within 21 days of the date of the date on which the determination was notified to him or her.[100] In practice however this procedure is generally not availed of as the certificate of tax credits will be amended by the Revenue Commissioners on receipt of any additional information relevant to the individual's circumstances which impact on the amount of tax credit or the standard rate cut off point.

For the 2009 tax year, a single individual is entitled to a tax credit of €1,830 and a married couple are entitled to a tax credit of €3,660. A PAYE tax credit of €1,830 is provided to all individuals in employment.

An individual's income tax charge for the tax year is reduced by the total of the income tax credit and the PAYE credit.

Income tax

[21.85] Income tax is levied at the standard rate (currently 20%) on all income up to the standard rate cut off point. Any income earned in excess of the standard rate cut off point is liable to income tax at the marginal rate (currently 41%). An income levy was introduced in Budget 2009. A levy of 1% applies on gross income up to €100,100. This income levy will increase to 2% on income between €100,101 and €250,120. Income in excess of €250,120 will suffer an income levy of 3%.[101] An exemption threshold of €18,304 applies relation to the income levy to ensure that persons on low income do not suffer the additional tax charge. There is however no relief for income marginally in excess of the exempt threshold, therefore if an individual earned €18,305 they would pay the income levy on that entire amount.

---

99 Income Tax (Employments) (Consolidated) Regulations 2001 (SI 559/2001) as amended by Income Tax (Employments) Regulations 2002 and Income Tax (Employments) Regulations 2003 (the PAYE Regulations).

100 PAYE, Reg 12.

101 Finance (No 2) Act 2008, s 2.

PRSI

[21.86] Contributions for PRSI purposes are determined by reference to the social insurance class of the employee, the class being determined by reference matters such as the type of employment and the level of income of the employee concerned. For PRSI purposes individuals engaged under a contract of service are regarded as employed contributors. Subject to certain exceptions, all employed contributors between the ages of 16 years and 66 years in insurable employment are compulsorily insured under the social insurance scheme. A detailed analysis of the social insurance system in Ireland is outside the scope of this chapter, and all references to PRSI are in relation to employees paying the full rate of PRSI (4%).

All employees paying the full rate of PRSI are exempt from paying PRSI on the first €127 of their weekly earnings. An annual ceiling of €52,000 applies for 2009 (ie earnings above €52,000 are not subject to PRSI). The health levy of 2% is applied on income up to €100,100 per annum, which is increased to €2.5% for earnings in excess of €100,101 annually. There is no ceiling in relation to the health levy.

The tables[102] below outline the tax credits, tax rates and tax bands available for the 2009 tax year.

Tax Credit	Amount
	€
Single Person	1,830
Married Person	3,660
PAYE Credit	1,830
Widowed Person (without dependent children)	2,430
One Parent Family Credit	1,830
Incapacitated Child Credit Max	3,660
Blind Tax Credit Single Person One Spouse Blind Both Spouses Blind	1,830 1,830 3,660
Widowed Parent Bereaved in 2008 2007 2006 2005 2004 2003	4,000 4,000 3,500 3,000 2,500 2,000
Age Tax Credit Single/Widowed Married	325 650
Dependent Relative	80
Home Carer	900

---

[102] Details provided by Budget Summary 2009 http://www.revenue.ie/.

Personal Circumstances	2009
	€
Single/Widowed without dependant children	36,400 @ 20%
	Balance @ 41%
Single/Widowed qualifying for One Parent Family Tax Credit	40,400 @ 20%
	Balance @ 41%
Married Couple one spouse with Income	45,400 @ 20%
	Balance @ 41%
Married Couple both spouses with Income	45,400 @ 20%
	with increase of
	27,400 max
	Balance @ 41%

Part XI
Practice and Procedure in Employment Law

Chapter 22

Practice and Procedure in Employment Law

Anthony Kerr and Cathal McGreal

INTRODUCTION

[22.01] Given the multiplicity of fora for the resolution of employment rights disputes and the disparate provisions of the relevant legislation, it is not possible to provide a consistent guide to practice and procedure in Employment Law. Depending on the nature of the claim, the forum may vary, the procedure may differ and the appeal process may diverge. Consequently, this chapter examines separately practice and procedure before:

  (i)   a rights commissioner;

  (ii)   the Employment Appeals Tribunal (EAT);

  (iii) the Equality Tribunal;

  (iv)   the Labour Court; and

  (v)   the Circuit Court.

In addition, consideration is given to the procedure regulating enforcement of and appeals from the decisions of the aforementioned and to certain specific issues such as extensions of time. Although some Regulations have been made prescribing the procedure to be adopted in particular cases, the various statutory employment rights bodies have, in the main, been left to devise their own procedures concerning the hearing of claims and appeals.

[22.02] Some points common to each of those bodies can be made at the outset. As statutory bodies deriving their jurisdiction from specific pieces of legislation, they have no inherent jurisdiction or any power to assume any jurisdiction which they have not been given.[1] The European Court of Justice, however, has ruled that such bodies are required by the Community law principles of equivalence and effectiveness to apply directly effective provisions of a relevant directive even though they have not been given express jurisdiction to do so under the provisions of domestic law transposing the directive.[2]

---

[1]   *Southern Health Board v Shuaib* EDA I/2003; *LW Associates Ltd v Lacey* HSD 5/2008. The Employments Appeals Tribunal, however, has claimed an inherent power to relist a case for hearing where there has been a manifest failure of natural justice: see *Hourigan v Curtin* M 309/1977 (reproduced in Madden and Kerr *Unfair Dismissal: Cases and Commentary* (2nd edn, IBEC, 1996), p 22.

[2]   Case C-268/08 *IMPACT v Minister for Agriculture and Food* [2008] 2 CMLR 1265.

[22.03] It is also clear that such bodies are not entitled to disregard the principles of fair procedure. Although the procedure before the first four of the aforementioned bodies is more informal than before the Circuit Court in that they may receive unsworn evidence, act on hearsay and depart from the strict rules of evidence, they are required to act fairly and in accordance with the principles of natural and constitutional justice.[3] In *Ryanair Ltd v IMPACT*,[4] the Supreme Court emphatically ruled that the Labour Court did not adopt fair procedures in not hearing evidence from 'at least one pilot who was an employee of Ryanair'. Although the decision concerned the Labour Court's jurisdiction under the Industrial Relations (Amendment) Act 2001, there is nothing in the judgment to suggest that the Supreme Court's observations do not apply with equal force to the other bodies and to the Labour Court when exercising its other jurisdictions. They are at all times obliged to act in accordance with basic fairness of procedures and to ensure evenness of treatment towards each side.

RIGHTS COMMISSIONERS

[22.04] The rights commissioners operate as a service of the Labour Relations Commission.[5] They were originally established pursuant to section 13 of the Industrial Relations Act 1969 but now enjoy jurisdiction under an extensive range of statutes and statutory instruments.[6] For present purposes that jurisdiction falls into three broad categories:

(i)   claims under the Industrial Relations Act 1969;

(ii) claims under the Unfair Dismissals Acts 1977–2007; and

(iii) claims under the employment rights and other legislation.

---

[3]   *Kiely v Minister for Social Welfare* [1977] IR 267 and *J&E Davy v Financial Services Ombudsman* [2008] 2 ILRM 507. This includes issues of potential bias on the part of the composition of the particular forum: see, for example: *Wexford Council of Trade Unions v Malone* [1997] ELR 235.

[4]   *Ryanair Ltd v IMPACT* [2007] 4 IR 199 at 225.

[5]   Industrial Relations Act 1990, s 35.

[6]   In addition to the legislation specifically considered in this chapter, rights commissioners are also entrusted with jurisdiction under the European Communities (Protection of Employment) Regulations 2000 (SI 488/2000); the European Communities (Protection of Employees on Transfer of Undertakings) Regulations 2003 (SI 131/2003); the Industrial Relations (Miscellaneous Provisions) Act 2004; the Safety, Health and Welfare at Work Act 2005; the Employees (Provision of Information and Consultation) Act 2006; the Employment Permits Act 2006; the European Communities (European Public Limited-Liability Company) (Employee Involvement) Regulations 2006 (SI 623/2006); the Consumer Protection Act 2007; the European Communities (European Co-Operative Society) (Employee Involvement) Regulations 2007 (SI 259/2007); and the European Communities (Cross-Border Mergers) Regulations 2008 (SI 157/2008).

[7]   See Industrial Relations Act 1969, s 13(8); Terms of Employment (Information) Act 1994, s 7(5); Maternity Protection Act 1994, s 31(3); Adoptive Leave Act 1995, s 34(2); Protection of Young Persons (Employment) Act 1996, s 18(6); (contd..../)

With one exception, Rights Commissioner investigations are held 'otherwise than in public'.[7] When exercising their jurisdiction under the Payment of Wages Act 1991, however, proceedings are required to be conducted in public 'unless, and to the extent that, the Commissioner, on application to him in that behalf by a party to the proceedings, decides otherwise'.

[22.05] The tendency in all cases, notwithstanding that the Rights Commissioner may not have been given express power so to do, is for an oral hearing to be convened at which the commissioner will put questions to the claimant and to the respondent and may request the production of documents in relation to the matters in dispute.[8] The Commissioner may also invite the parties to make submissions, either orally or in writing, in relation to the dispute.

[22.06] Rights commissioners have no power to take evidence on oath, nor can they compel the attendance of witnesses or require the production of documents. They have no power to award costs or expenses even where the commissioner considers that a party has acted frivolously or vexatiously.

Where a party fails or refuses to attend a hearing convened by a rights commissioner, the Commissioner may, once satisfied that he or she was notified of the hearing date, proceed with the hearing in that party's absence.[9]

Industrial relations claims

[22.07] Section 13(2) of the Industrial Relations Act 1969 provides that, where a trade dispute[10] (other than a dispute connected with rates of pay, hours or times of work or, or annual holidays of, a body of workers) exists or is apprehended and involves 'workers',[11] any party to the dispute may refer it to a rights commissioner. The Commissioner is required to 'investigate' the dispute, unless either the Labour Court has made a recommendation in relation to the dispute or a party to the dispute notifies the commissioner in writing, within 21 days after notice of reference has been sent to that party, that he or she objects to the dispute being investigated by a commissioner.[12] In either case, the Commissioner may not investigate the dispute. Nor can a commissioner investigate a dispute in relation to a dismissal in respect of which a recommendation has

---

[7] (\...contd) Organisation of Working Time Act 1997, s 27(8); Parental Leave Act 1998, s 18(6); National Minimum Wage Act 2000, s 24(7); Carer's Leave Act 2001, s 19(5); Protection of Employees (Part-Time Work) Act 2001, s 15(5); and Protection of Employees (Fixed Term Work) Act 2003, s 14(7).

[8] See Reg 8(1) and (2) of the Adoptive Leave (Referral of Disputes and Appeals) (Part V) Regulations 1995 (SI 195/1995) and Regs 5(1) and (2) of the Parental Leave (Disputes and Appeals) Regulations 1999 (SI 6/1999).

[9] See Reg 8 (3) of the Adoptive Leave (Referral of Disputes and Appeals) (Part V) Regulations 1995 (SI 195/1995) and Reg 5(3) of the Parental Leave (Disputes and Appeals) Regulations 1999 (SI 6/1999).

[10] Industrial Relations Act 1946, s 3 defines a trade dispute as 'any dispute or difference between employers and workers or between workers and workers connected with the employment or non-employment, or the terms of employment, or with the conditions of employment, of any person'.

been made by a rights commissioner under the Unfair Dismissals Act 1977 or a hearing by the Employment Appeals Tribunal under the 1977 Act has begun.[13]

Having investigated the dispute, the Commissioner is required to make a recommendation to the parties to the dispute 'setting forth his [or her] opinion on the merits of the dispute'.[14]

[22.08] Section 13(6) of the 1969 Act enables the Commissioner to provide for the regulation of proceedings before him or her in relation to an investigation under the section and empowers the commissioner to provide for the cases in which persons may appear before him or her by counsel or solicitor and, except as so provided, no person shall be entitled to appear by counsel or solicitor. Accordingly, good practice would suggest that the Labour Relations Commission be advised in advance of the hearing that the claimant or respondent, as the case may be, will be legally represented.

Unfair dismissal claims

[22.09] Section 8(1) of the Unfair Dismissals Act 1977 provides, in relevant part, that a claim for unfair dismissal may be brought by an employee before a rights commissioner and the commissioner 'shall hear the parties and any evidence relevant to the claim tendered by them'. Claims should be initiated by giving a notice in writing to the Labour Relations Commission within the period of six months beginning on the date of the relevant dismissal. If the commissioner is satisfied that 'exceptional circumstances' prevented the giving of the notice within that six month period, he or she may extend the time for up to a further six months.

[22.10] Section 8(2) goes on to require that the commissioner give a copy of the notice to the employer concerned 'as soon as may be after the receipt of the notice by the commissioner'.

The Rights Commissioner may not hear a claim for redress if:

---

[11] For the purposes of the 1969 Act, 'worker' is defined by Industrial Relations Act 1990, s 23(1) as 'any person aged 15 years or more who has entered into or works under a contract with an employer, whether the contract be for manual labour, clerical work or otherwise, whether it be expressed or implied, oral or in writing, and whether it be a contract of service or of apprenticeship or a contract personally to execute any work or labour'. The definition expressly excludes persons employed by or under the State, primary and secondary teachers and officers of vocational educational committees. The Labour Court has ruled that a retired employee does not fall within the definition: see, most recently, *University College Dublin v A Worker* LCR 19310; *University College Dublin v A Worker* LCR 19422 and *An Gaisce v A Named Claimant* LCR 19435.

[12] Industrial Relations Act 1969, s 13(3). The 21 day period was prescribed by the Industrial Relations Act 1990, s 36(1).

[13] Unfair Dismissals Act 1977, s 8(10)(a) as substituted by the Unfair Dismissals (Amendment) Act 1993, s 7(d).

[14] Industrial Relations Act 1969, s 13(3)(a)(i).

(a)   the Employment Appeals Tribunal has made a determination in relation to the claim, or

(b)   any party concerned notifies the Labour Relations Commission in writing within 21 days of the giving to the employer of the copy of the employee's initiating notice that he or she objects to the claim being heard by a rights commissioner.[15]

Where, in relation to a dismissal, a recommendation has been made by a rights commissioner under the Industrial Relations Act 1969 or a hearing by the Labour Court under the Industrial Relations Acts 1946–2004 has begun, a rights commissioner is not debarred from hearing an unfair dismissal claim but s 8(10)(b) of the Unfair Dismissals Act 1977 provides that the employee concerned 'shall not be entitled to redress under this Act in respect of the dismissal'.

[22.11] No regulations have been made prescribing the procedure to be followed regarding the bringing of claims before a rights commissioner or the procedure regarding the hearing of such claims. The Labour Relations Commission, however, has provided a form which can be used for the bringing of such claims.

Employment rights and other claims

[22.12] The other employment rights legislation typically provides that a complaint shall be initiated, presented or lodged by giving notice of it in writing to a rights commissioner within a specified period and that such notice should contain such particulars, and be in such form, as may be specified from time to time by the appropriate Minister.[16]

A dispute under the National Minimum Wage Act 2000 cannot be referred to or dealt with by a rights commissioner unless the employee has obtained a statement of his or her hourly rate of pay or, having requested the statement, has not been provided with it.[17]

[22.13] Once a complaint has been presented, the commissioner is required to give the parties an opportunity to be heard by him or her and to present or tender any evidence

---

[15]   Unfair Dismissals Act 1977, s 8(3). The practice of the Labour Relations Commission is to treat the date of receiving the notice by the employer as the date on which the 21 day period starts running: see *Charters v National Gallery of Ireland* r-052230-ud-07/JT. In the event of a valid objection, the claim will be heard by the Employment Appeals Tribunal.

[16]   Payment of Wages Act 1991, s 6(5)(a); Terms of Employment (Information) Act 1994, s 7(4)(a); Maternity Protection Act 1994, s 31(1); Adoptive Leave Act 1995, s 34(1); Protection of Young Persons (Employment) Act 1996, s 19(2)(a); Organisation of Working Time Act 1997, s 27(6); Parental Leave Act 1998, s 18(4); National Minimum Wage Act 2000, s 24(1); Carer's Leave Act 2001, s 19(3); Protection of Employees (Part-Time Work) Act 2001, s 16(5); Protection of Employees (Fixed Term Work) Act 2003, s 14(5). The Labour Relations Commission has provided forms (available on its website www.lrc.ie) which can be used for the bringing of such claims.

[17]   National Minimum Wage Act 2000, s 24(2)(a). The subsection also provides that a dispute cannot be referred to or dealt with by a rights commissioner where, in respect of the same alleged underpayment, the employer is or has been the subject of an investigation under s 33 or 34, or is or has been prosecuted for an offence under s 35 of the 2000 Act.

relevant to the complaint.[18] The complaint should be presented by the employee, but in some cases complaints may be presented by the employee's trade union[19] or, in the case of the Protection of Young Persons Employment Act 1996, by the young person's parent or guardian.[20] Employers may also lodge complaints under the Maternity Protection Act 1994, the Adoptive Leave Act 1995, the Parental Leave Act 1998 and the National Minimum Wage Act 2000.[21]

[22.14] The Payment of Wages 1991, the Maternity Protection Act 1994, the Adoptive Leave Act 1995 and the Protection of Young Persons (Employment) Act 1996 empower the Commissioner to extend the time for initiating complaints where there are 'exceptional circumstances'.[22] The Organisation of Working Time Act 1997, the Carer's Leave Act 2001, the Protection of Employees (Part-Time Work) Act 2001 and the Protection of Employees (Fixed Term Work) Act 2003 empower the commissioner to extend time for 'reasonable cause'.[23] The Parental Leave Act 1998 empowers the commissioner to extend time where it is 'reasonable' so to do.[24] The National Minimum Wage Act 2000 empowers the Commissioner to extend time *simpliciter*.[25] The Terms of Employment (Information) Act 1994, however, contains no provision for an extension of time.

[22.15] Successive Ministers for Enterprise, Trade and Employment have not seen it appropriate to make any regulations providing for any matters relating to proceedings under the employment rights legislation but the Minister for Justice, Equality and Law Reform has made regulations governing the procedure for maternity, adoptive leave and

---

[18] Payment of Wages Act 1991, s 6(1); Terms of Employment (Information) Act 1994, s 7.

[19] Organisation of Working Time Act 1997, s 27(2); Protection of Employees (Part-Time Work) Act 2001, s 16(1); and Protection of Employees (Fixed Term Work) Act 2003, s 14(1). In *Campbell Catering Ltd v SIPTU* DWT 35/2000, the Labour Court did not accept that the wording of s 27(2) of the 1997 Act restricted a trade union to making a complaint on behalf of a single employee affected by the subject matter of the complaint. The Court said that, although the subsection referred to 'an employee', this did not prevent a trade union from presenting more than one complaint, each identical in form and content, where the alleged infringement affected a multiplicity of employees.

[20] Protection of Young Persons (Employment) Act 1996, s 18(1).

[21] Maternity Protection Act 1994, s 30(4); Adoptive Leave Act 1995, s 32(2); Parental Leave Act 1998, s 18(2) and National Minimum Wage Act 2000, s 24(1).

[22] Payment of Wages 1991, s 6(4) of the 1991 Act; s 31(b) of the 1994 Act; s 34(1)(b) of the 1995 Act, and s 18(4) of the 1996 Act. The Rights Commissioner can only extend the time for up to a further six months from the expiry of the initial six-month period.

[23] Organisation of Working Time Act 1997, s 27(5); Carers Leave Act 2001, s 19(8); Part-Time Work Act 2001, s 16(4); and s 14(4) of the 2003 Act. The Rights Commissioner can only extend the time for up to a further six months in the case of the Carer's Leave Act 2001 and the Part-Time Work Act 2001 and for up to 12 months in the case of the 1997 and 2003 Acts.

[24] Parental Leave Act 1998, s 23(4). The commissioner can only extend time for a specified period not exceeding six weeks.

[25] National Minimum Wage Act 2000, s 24(2).

parental leave disputes. Unfortunately, these regulations confer different competencies on a rights commissioner.

(i) Maternity protection

[22.16] Regulation 3(1) of the Maternity Protection (Disputes and Appeals) Regulations 1995[26] requires that a 'notice of dispute' specify:

   (i)   the name and address of the party referring the dispute;

   (ii)   the name and address of the other party to the dispute; and

   (iii) particulars of the facts or contentions which the party referring the dispute will put forward at the hearing.

Regulation 3(4) provides, however, that 'a mistake of a formal nature shall not operate to invalidate a notice under this Regulation'.

[22.17] Section 31(2) of the 1994 Act provides that, as soon as may be after the Rights Commissioner has received such a notice, he or she must give a copy of the notice to the other party. The Regulations provide that that other party must, within 14 days of the receipt of that notice (or within such longer period as the commissioner may allow), indicate to the commissioner whether he or she intends to contest the dispute and, if so, specify the facts or contentions which he or she will put forward at the hearing.[27] A party who fails to so indicate will be treated as having given notice that he or she does not intend to contest the dispute.[28]

A notice required to be given to a rights commissioner is 'properly given' if sent by registered post to the Labour Relations Commission.[29]

[22.18] The Regulations do not expressly provide for the withdrawal of a notice of dispute. Nor do they expressly provide how the commissioner may regulate the hearing such as by inviting submissions. Nevertheless the practice is to allow withdrawals and for the commissioner to convene an oral hearing at which oral, if not written, submissions will be invited.

(ii) Adoptive leave

[22.19] The relevant regulations are the Adoptive Leave (Referral of Disputes and Appeals) (Part V) Regulations 1995,[30] Reg 3(1) of which requires that a 'notice of dispute' should contain the following particulars:

   (i)   the names, addresses and descriptions of the parties to the proceedings;

   (ii)   the grounds upon which the applicant's claim is based;

   (iii) the day of placement or, where there has been no placement, the date on which the employer received the first notification of the adopting parent's intention to

---

[26] SI 17/1995.

[27] SI 17/1995, Reg 3(2).

[28] SI 17/1995, Reg 3(3).

[29] SI 17/1995, Reg 12(1).

[30] SI 195/1995.

take adoptive leave, or, in the case of an adopting father, the date on which the adopting mother died;

(iv)   in case the notice was not given within the appropriate period, the reasons for the delay; and

(v)   the weekly remuneration of the adopting parent.

Regulation 7, however, provides that 'a mistake of a formal nature' shall not operate to invalidate a notice of dispute.

[22.20] Although s 34(1) of the 1995 Act provides that, as soon as may be after the Rights Commissioner has received such a notice, he or she must give a copy of the notice to the other party, the Regulations do not provide any period of time within which a respondent should indicate to the commissioner whether he or she intends to contest the dispute and, if so, the facts or contentions that would be put forward.

A notice required to be served on a rights commissioner should be sent to the Labour Relations Commission.[31]

[22.21] Regulation 4(1) expressly provides for the withdrawal by notice in writing to the Commissioner of a complaint.

Regulation 8(1) and (2) expressly provide that the Commissioner may:

(i)   request the parties to furnish him or her with particulars in relation to the dispute;

(ii)   invite the parties to make submissions, either orally or in writing, in relation to the dispute; and

(iii)   convene an oral hearing at which he or she may put questions to the parties and request the production of documents by them, in relation to the dispute.

Regulation 8(3) provides that, where a party fails or refuses, without just cause, to attend an oral hearing, the Commissioner may proceed with the hearing in that party's absence. Regulation 8(4) empowers the commissioner to draw such inferences, as to him or her seem proper, from a failure or refusal by a party to comply with a request to furnish particulars or to produce documents or from a failure or refusal by a party to answer a question put by the commissioner.

(iii) Parental leave

[22.22] The relevant Regulations are the Parental Leave (Dispute and Appeals) Regulations 1999,[32] Reg 3 of which requires that a 'notice of dispute' should contain the following particulars:

(a)   the name and address of the party referring the dispute;

(b)   the name and address of the other party to the dispute;

(c)   the nature of the dispute;

---

[31]   Unlike the Maternity and Parental Leave Regulations, these regulations do not stipulate that a notice is 'properly given' if sent by registered post.

[32]   SI 6/1999.

(d)   particulars of any facts or contentions which the party referring the dispute will put forward at the hearing.

If the dispute relates to parental leave, the notice should also specify:

(i)   the date on which the applicant for parental leave entered the employment in question;

(ii)   the name of the child to whom the parental leave relates;

(iii)   the date of the child's birth and, where appropriate, of the relevant adoption order;

(iv)   the period of parental leave sought or granted;

(v)   the date on which notice of parental leave was given;

(vi)   where appropriate, the date of the document confirming parental leave; and

(vii)   where appropriate, the date on which the parental leave terminated.

If the dispute relates to *force majeure* leave, the notice should also specify:

(i)   the name and address of the injured or ill person concerned;

(ii)   that person's relationship to the employee;

(iii)   the nature of the injury or illness; and

(iv)   the period of *force majeure* leave taken.

Regulation 18, however, provides that 'a mistake of a formal nature' shall not operate to invalidate a notice of dispute.

[22.23] Section 18(4) of the 1998 Act provides that the Rights Commissioner must give a copy of such a notice to the other party to the dispute. The regulations provide that that other party must, within 14 days of the receipt of that notice (or within such longer period as the Commissioner may allow), indicate to the commissioner whether he or she intends to contest the dispute and, if so, specify the facts or contentions which he or she will put forward at the hearing.[33]

A notice required to be given to a rights commissioner is 'properly given' if sent by registered post to the LRC.[34]

[22.24] Regulation 14(1) expressly provides for the withdrawal by notice in writing to the Commissioner of the reference.

Regulation 5(1) and (2) expressly provide that the Commissioner may:

(i)   request the parties to furnish him or her with particulars in relation to the dispute;

(ii)   invite the parties to make submissions, either orally or in writing, in relation to the dispute; and

(iii)   convene an oral hearing at which he or she may put questions to the parties, and request the production of documents by them, in relation to the dispute.

---

[33]   SI 6/1999, Reg 4(1).

[34]   SI 6/1999, Reg 19(1).

Regulation 5(3) provides that, where a party fails or refuses, without just cause, to attend an oral hearing the commissioner may proceed with the hearing in that party's absence. Regulation 5(4) empowers the commissioner to draw such inferences, as to him or her seem proper, from a failure or refusal by a party to comply with a request to furnish particulars or to produce documents or from a failure or refusal by a party to answer a question put by the Commissioner.

THE EMPLOYMENT APPEALS TRIBUNAL

[22.25] The Tribunal was originally established pursuant to s 39 of the Redundancy Payments Act 1967, and now enjoys jurisdiction under an extensive range of statutes and statutory instruments.[35] The Tribunal's jurisdiction is either first instance or appellate depending on the nature of the claim. In redundancy and minimum notice cases, it is the former. In maternity, adoptive leave, parental leave, carer's leave, terms of employment, payment of wages and young persons claims, it is the latter. In unfair dismissal cases it can be either. Each will be examined in turn.

[22.26] Tribunal hearings take place in public unless the Tribunal decides, at the request of either party, to hear the appeal in private.[36] The Maternity and Parental Leave Regulations, however, enable the Tribunal to hear part of the appeal in private.[37] The Tribunal has no power to make a restricted reporting order.

[22.27] On the hearing of a claim or appeal, the Tribunal is empowered to take evidence on oath and, for that purpose, may cause oaths to be administered to persons attending as witnesses.[38] The Tribunal is also empowered to require persons to attend the hearing to give evidence and to require persons to produce documents.[39] There is no rule limiting the time within which a summons may be sought but best practice which suggest that applications for a witness summons must be made to a sitting division of the Tribunal. Applications for a witness summons must be made to a sitting division of the Tribunal. There is no rule limiting the time within which a summons may be sought but best practice would suggest that applications should be made as soon as a party is notified of

---

[35] In addition to the legislation considered in this chapter, the Tribunal also has appellate jurisdiction from decisions of rights commissioners under the European Communities (Protection of Employment) Regulations 2000 (SI 488/2000) and the European Communities (Protection of Employees on Transfer of Undertakings) Regulations 2003 (SI 131/2003).

[36] Redundancy (Redundancy Appeals Tribunal) Regulations 1968 (SI 24/1968), Reg 11. The Tribunal's case law provides little guidance as to when it might be considered appropriate to hold a hearing *in camera*. Redmond, in *Dismissal Law in Ireland* (2nd edn, 2007), p 564 asserts that there must be 'strong grounds to oust the obligation to hold a public hearing'.

[37] Maternity Protection (Disputes and Appeals) Regulations 1995 (SI 17/1995), Reg 5(2); Parental Leave (Disputes and Appeals) Regulations 1999 (SI 6/1999), Reg 9(2).

[38] Redundancy Payments Act 1967, s 39(17)(a); Maternity Protection Act 1994, s 33(4); Adoptive Leave Act 1995, s 35(4)(a).

[39] Redundancy Payments Act 1967, s 39(17)(c); Maternity Protection Act 1994, s 33(6); Adoptive Leave Act 1995, s 35(4)(c). Failure to comply is a criminal offence.

the date of the hearing but, in any event, in good time so as to allow the witness reasonable opportunity to attend and, where required, to gather the documents.

The parties to a claim or an appeal 'may appear and be heard in person or may be represented by counsel or solicitor or by a representative of a trade union or of an employer's association or, with the leave of the Tribunal, by any other person'.[40]

[22.28] Various regulations have been made governing the procedure to be followed regarding the submission of claims and appeals to the Tribunal. The principal regulations are the Redundancy (Redundancy Appeals Tribunal) Regulations 1968.[41] Regulation 13 of these Regulations provides that a party may:

(a)   make an opening statement;

(b)   call witnesses;

(c)   cross examine any witnesses called by any other party;

(d)   give evidence on his or her own behalf; and

(e)   address the Tribunal at the close of evidence.[42]

Regulation 15 (which does not apply to minimum notice cases) permits the Tribunal to admit any duly authenticated written statement as *prima facie* evidence of any fact whenever it thinks it just and proper so to do.

[22.29] If, after notice of a hearing has been duly given, any of the parties fails to appear, the Tribunal may determine the question under appeal or may adjourn the hearing to a later date. If the Tribunal resolves to determine the question, it must consider all the evidence before it at the time of the hearing.[43]

The Tribunal's first instance jurisdiction

[22.30] Section 39(15) of the Redundancy Payments Act 1967 enables an employee who is dissatisfied with any decision of an employer under that Act (as amended) to appeal to the Tribunal against the decision. Regulations 3 and 4 of the Redundancy (Redundancy Appeals Tribunal) Regulations 1968[44] provide that the appeal should be in writing and

---

40   Redundancy (Redundancy Appeals Tribunal) Regulations 1968 (SI 24/1968), Reg 12; Maternity Protection (Disputes and Appeals) Regulations 1995 (SI 17/1995), Reg 5(3); Parental Leave (Disputes and Appeals) Regulations 1999 (SI 6/1999), Reg 9(3). The extent of the discretion to refuse leave to a representative was considered in *Robinson v Bent* UD 8/2006.

41   SI 24/1968 as amended by the Redundancy (Employment Appeals Tribunal) Regulations 1979 (SI 114/1979). The relevant regulations thereof are extended to most of the employment rights legislation: see Terms of Employment (Information) (Appeals and Complaints) Regulations 1994 (SI 244/1994), Reg 10 and Adoptive Leave (Referral of Disputes and Appeals) (Part V) Regulations 1995 (SI 195/1995), Reg 14.

42   See, to similar effect, Maternity Protection (Disputes and Appeals) Regulations 1995 (SI 17/1995), Reg 6 and Parental Leave (Disputes and Appeals) Regulations 1999 (SI 6/1999), Reg 10.

43   Redundancy (Redundancy Appeals Tribunal) Regulations 1968 (SI 24/1968), Reg 16; Maternity Protection (Disputes and Appeals) Regulations 1995 (SI 17/1995), Reg 6(4); Parental Leave (Disputes and Appeals) Regulations 1999 (SI 6/1999), Reg 19(3).

44   SI 24/1968.

should be accompanied by 'a statement of the facts and contentions' on which the appellant intends to rely.

[22.31] Section 11(1) of the Minimum Notice and Terms of Employment Act 1973 provides that any dispute arising on any matter under the Act should be referred to the Tribunal in the prescribed manner. The notice should be given in the form provided by the Minister for that purpose and should be accompanied by 'a statement of the facts and contentions' on which the appellant intends to rely.[45]

[22.32] Section 8(2) of the Unfair Dismissals Act 1977 provides that a claim for redress under the 1977 Act may be initiated by giving a notice in writing, containing such particulars (if any) as may be specified, to the Tribunal. Regulation 3 of the Unfair Dismissals (Claims and Appeals) Regulations 1977[46] provides that such a notice should specify:

(a)   the name and address of the person bringing the claim;

(b)   the name and address of the employer concerned;

(c)   the date of the commencement of the employment to which the notice relates;

(d)   the date of dismissal to which the notice relates; and

(e)   the amount claimed by the said person to be his or her weekly remuneration.

The notice should also indicate that the claimant objects to the claim being dealt with by a rights commissioner.

[22.33] A respondent has 14 days from receipt of the appeal or claim to enter an appearance by sending the Tribunal a statement indicating whether he or she intends to contest or oppose the claim and, if so, to what extent the facts and contentions advanced by the claimant are admitted or disputed and, in unfair dismissal claims, containing the facts and contentions on which he or she will ground such opposition.[47] The Regulations permit respondents to apply within the 14-day period for an extension of time in which to enter an appearance and provide that a respondent who has not entered an appearance 'shall not be entitled to take any part in the proceedings or to be represented thereat'.[48] Notwithstanding that the Tribunal does not have an express discretion to decide otherwise (except in unfair dismissal cases), the Supreme Court, in *Halal Meat Packers (Ballyhaunis) Ltd v Employment Appeals Tribunal*,[49] has made it clear that it will only be a rare case where the Tribunal would be justified in not hearing a respondent who had not entered an appearance.

---

[45]   Minimum Notice and Terms of Employment (Reference of Disputes) Regulations 1973 (SI 243/1973), Reg 4.

[46]   SI 286/1977.

[47]   Redundancy (Redundancy Appeals Tribunal) Regulations 1968 (SI 24/1968), Reg 9(1); Unfair Dismissals (Claims and Appeals) Regulations 1977 (SI 286/1977), Reg 5(1).

[48]   Redundancy (Redundancy Appeals Tribunal) Regulations 1968 (SI 24/1968), regulation 9(2); Unfair Dismissals (Claims and Appeals)Regulations 1977 (SI 286/1977), Reg 5(2) as amended by Maternity Protection (Disputes and Appeals) Regulations 1981 (SI 257/1981), Reg 15.

The Redundancy (Redundancy Appeals Tribunal) Regulations 1968 permit the withdrawal of an appeal or a claim by sending a notice of withdrawal to the Tribunal.[50]

The Tribunal may require any party to furnish in writing 'further particulars' with regard to the facts and contentions contained in either the notice of claim or the notice of appearance.[51]

The Tribunal's appellate jurisdiction

[22.34] The Tribunal has appellate jurisdiction from decisions of rights commissioners under the Unfair Dismissals Act 1977, the Payment of Wages Act 1991, the Terms of Employment (Information) Act 1994, the Maternity Protection Act 1994, the Adoptive Leave Act 1995, the Protection of Young Persons (Employment) Act 1996, the Parental Leave Act 1998 and the Carer's Leave Act 2001.

Once a party has appealed to the Tribunal, the Tribunal must hear the parties and any evidence relevant to the appeal or give them an opportunity to be heard and to present evidence relevant to the appeal.[52]

[22.35] Appeals are in the nature of a rehearing and are governed by procedures established pursuant to regulations made under the relevant statute. The Tribunal has no power to extend the time for appealing except in parental leave cases.[53] Nor has the Tribunal the power to remit a claim for further consideration by the rights commissioner.[54]

(i)   Unfair dismissal

[22.36] Section 9(1) of the Unfair Dismissals Act 1977 provides that 'a party concerned' may appeal to the Tribunal from a recommendation of a rights commissioner in relation to claim for redress under that Act. Any such appeal should be initiated by a party giving, 'within 6 weeks of the date on which the recommendation to which it relates was given to the parties concerned', a notice in writing containing such particulars (if any) as may be prescribed, and stating the intention of the party concerned to appeal against the recommendation.[55]

---

[49] *Halal Meat Packers (Ballyhaunis) Ltd v Employment Appeals Tribunal* [1990] ELR 49 at 60–64. Judge Sheridan has ruled that the 1977 Act dos not contain a mandatory provision for the entry of an appearance: *Coolmore (Castlehyde) and Associated Stud Farms v Lawrence* (16 August 1989) reproduced in Madden and Kerr, *Unfair Dismissal: Cases and Commentary* (2nd edn, IBEC, 1996), p 21.

[50] SI 24/1968, Reg 6 as substituted by the Redundancy (Employment Appeals Tribunal) Regulations 1979 (SI 144/1979).

[51] Redundancy (Redundancy Appeals Tribunal) Regulations 1968 (SI 24/1968), Reg 24.

[52] Unfair Dismissals Act 1977, s 9(1) of the 1977 Act; s 7(1) of the 1991 Act; Terms of Employment (Information) Act 1994, s 8(1); Maternity Protection Act 1994, s 33(1); s 35(1) of the 1995 Act; s 19(1) of the 1996 Act; s 19(1) of the 1998 Act; and s 20(1) of the 2001 Act.

[53] Parental Leave Act 1998, s 23(5). See also European Communities (Protection of Employees on Transfer of Undertakings) Regulations 2003 (SI 131/2003), Reg 11(2).

[54] *Southern Health Board v Mitchell* [2001] ELR 201; *Sunday World Newspapters Ltd v Kinsella* [2006] ELR 325; *Kirwan v Department of Justice, Equality and Law Reform* [2008] ELR 89; *Department of Health and Children v Rohan* DWT 92/2008.

[22.37] Regulation 3 of the Unfair Dismissals (Claims and Appeals) Regulations 1977[56] provides that a notice of appeal should specify:

(a)   the name and address of the person bringing the appeal;

(b)   the name and address of the employer or the employee, as the case may be, concerned;

(c)   the date of commencement of the employment to which the notice relates;

(d)   the date of dismissal to which the notice relates; and

(e)   the amount claimed to be the person's weekly remuneration.

An appeal may be withdrawn by sending a notification in writing signifying such withdrawal to the Tribunal.[57]

[22.38] It has been held by the Tribunal in *Geraghty v Moracrete Ltd*[58] that merely writing to the Rights Commissioner to advise him that the company rejected his findings and that it intends to appeal, does not constitute a valid appeal. On the other hand, writing to the Tribunal stating that the company intended appealing the recommendation and citing the reference number of the case in question was regarded as sufficient in *Complex Tooling and Moulding Ltd v Quigley*.[59] The Tribunal ruled that, although an appeal application form (Form TIB) was available, its use was not mandatory.

[22.39] Regulation 5 provides that the respondent, if he or she intends to oppose the appeal, should enter an appearance to the appeal by giving to the Tribunal, within 14 days of receipt of the notice of appeal, a notice in writing stating that he or she intends to oppose the appeal and containing the facts and contentions on which he or she will ground such opposition. The respondent may, before the expiration of the aforesaid 14 day period, apply for an extension of the period within which to enter an appearance.

[22.40] Regulation 5(2) provides that a respondent who does not enter such an appearance shall not be entitled to take part in or be present or represented at any proceedings before the Tribunal in relation to the appeal unless the Tribunal at its discretion otherwise decides. Given what the Supreme Court had to say in *Halal Meat Packers (Ballyhaunis) Ltd v Employment Appeals Tribunal*,[60] it seems unlikely that there would be many cases in which the Tribunal would be justified in not hearing a respondent who had not entered an appearance.

---

[55]   Unfair Dismissals Act 1977, s 9(2).

[56]   SI 286/1977.

[57]   SI 286/1977, Reg 4.

[58]   *Geraghty v Moracrete Ltd* UD335/1984.

[59]   *Complex Tooling and Moulding Ltd v Quigley* UD286/2000. See also *Corcoran v O'Brien* UD658/2002 and *Edwards v M & P Construction Ltd* UD 842/2004. However a differently-constituted Tribunal has ruled otherwise in *Coughlan v Cork Plastics Manufacturing Ltd* UD 649/2001.

[60]   *Halal Meat Packers (Ballyhaunis) Ltd v Employment Appeals Tribunal* [1990] ELR 49, 60–64. See also Judge Sheridan in *Coolmore (Castlehyde) and Associated Stud Farms v Lawrence* supra at fn 49.

Section 9(1) of the 1977 Act goes on to provide that, once a party has appealed to the Tribunal, the Tribunal 'shall hear the parties and any evidence relevant to the appeal tendered by them'.

The procedure at such hearings is governed by Regs 10–17 of the Redundancy (Redundancy Appeals Tribunal) Regulations 1968.[61]

(ii) Payment of wages

[22.41] Section 7(1) of the Payment of Wages Act 1991 provides that 'a party concerned' may appeal to the Tribunal from a decision of a rights commissioner under that Act. Any such appeal should be initiated by the party concerned giving 'within six weeks of the date in which the decision to which it relates was communicated to him' a notice in writing containing such particulars (if any) as may be prescribed and stating the intention of the party concerned to appeal the decision.

Regulation 3 of the Payment of Wages (Appeals) Regulations 1991[62] provides that such a notice should contain:

(a)   the names, addresses and descriptions of the parties;

(b)   the date of the decision to which the appeal relates and the name of the Rights Commissioner who made the decision; and

(c)   a brief outline of the grounds of the appeal.

Regulation 4 provides that an appeal may be withdrawn by giving a notification in writing signifying such withdrawal to the Tribunal.

[22.42] Unlike the provisions of the other employment rights legislation which require the Tribunal to give the notice of appeal to the other party, s 7(2)(b) of the 1991 Act requires the appellant to give to the respondent, within the six-week period, a copy of the notice. This provision has been strictly interpreted by different divisions of the Tribunal which have all ruled that the use of the word 'shall' requires a mandatory obligation of service on the respondent.[63] It would appear that this is so, even if the Tribunal has served the respondent with the notice within the six-week period.[64]

[22.43] Regulation 5(1) of the 1991 Regulations provides that the respondent to an appeal, if he or she intends to contest same, should enter an appearance to the appeal by giving a notice of appearance to the Tribunal within 14 days, or such longer period as the Tribunal may fix, from receipt of the copy of the notice of appeal. The notice of

---

61   SI 24/1968.
62   SI 351/1991.
63   See, for example, *Shahid Sultan v Nasem* [2001] ELR 302 and, more recently, *Gautam v Singh & Singh Ltd* PW91/2005. Where an appellant gives uncontested evidence of having effected service by ordinary post, the Tribunal has held that the onus is on the respondent to establish that it did not receive it: *Morris v Department of Justice, Equality and Law Reform* PW 24/2005.
64   See, for example, *Riehn v Royale* PW21/2005 and, more recently, *Tirnova v Vitra Ireland Ltd* PW72/2006.

appearance should be in a form specified by the Minister and should contain 'a brief outline of the grounds' on which the appeal will be contested.

The Regulations are silent as to the entitlement of a respondent who has not entered an appearance to take part in any proceedings before the Tribunal in relation to the appeal.

[22.44] Section 7(1) of the 1991 Act goes on to provide that, once a party has appealed to the Tribunal, the Tribunal 'shall give the parties an opportunity to be heard by it and to present to it any evidence relevant to the appeal'.

The procedure at such hearings is governed by Regs 10–17 of the Redundancy (Redundancy Appeals Tribunal) Regulations 1968.[65]

(iii) Other employment rights legislation

[22.45] The Terms of Employment (Information) Act 1994, the Maternity Protection Act 1994, the Adoptive Leave Act 1995, the Protection of Young Persons (Employment) Act 1996, the Parental Leave Act 1998 and the Carer's Leave Act 2001 all provide that 'a party concerned' may appeal to the Tribunal from a recommendation of a rights commissioner under the relevant Act.[66]

Any such appeal should be initiated by the party giving, within the prescribed period of the date on which the decision to which it relates was given to the parties concerned, a notice in writing to the Tribunal containing such particulars (if any) as may be prescribed and stating the intention of the party concerned to appeal against the recommendation.[67]

The prescribed period for appealing is six weeks in the case of the Terms of Employment (Information) Act 1994 and the Protection of Young Persons (Employment) Act 1996,[68] whereas, in the case of the Maternity Protection Act 1994, the Adoptive Leave Act 1995, the Parental Leave Act 1998 and the Carer's Leave Act 2001, the prescribed period is four weeks.[69]

With the exception of the Protection of Young Persons (Employment) Act 1996 and the Carer's Leave Act 2001, regulations have been made under the other employment rights legislation prescribing the procedure to be followed in any such appeal.

---

[65] SI 24/1968.

[66] Terms of Employment (Information) Act 1994, s 8(1); Maternity Protection Act 1994, s 33(1); Adoptive Leave Act 1995, s 35(1); Protection of Young Persons (Employment) Act 1996, s 19(1); Parental Leave Act 1998, s 19(1) and Carer's Leave Act 2001, s 20(1) respectively.

[67] Terms of Employment (Information) Act 1994, s 8(2); Maternity Protection Act 1994, s 33(2); Adoptive Leave Act 1995, s 35(2); Protection of Young Persons (Employment) Act 1996, s 19(2); Parental Leave Act 1998, s 19(2) and Carer's Leave Act 2001, s 20(2) respectively.

[68] Terms of Employment (Information) Act 1994, s 8(2)(a) and Protection of Young Persons (Employment) Act 1996, s 19(2)(a). A six-week period also applies to appeals under the European Communities (Protection of Employment) Regulations 2000 (SI 488/2000) and the European Communities (Protection of Employees on Transfer of Undertakings) Regulations 2003 (SI 131/2003).

[69] Maternity Protection Act 1994, s 33(2) of the 1994 Act; s 35(2) of the 1995 Act; s 19(2) of the 1998 Act; and s 20(2) of the 2001 Act.

[22.46] The Terms of Employment (Information) (Appeals and Complaints) Regulations 1994[70] require that a notice of appeal contain:

(a)   the names, addresses and descriptions of the parties to the proceedings to which the appeal relates;

(b)   the date of the recommendation to which the appeal relates and the name of the Rights Commissioner who made the recommendation; and

(c)   a brief outline of the grounds of the appeal.

[22.47] The Maternity Protection (Disputes and Appeals) Regulations 1995[71] require that a notice of appeal specify:

(a)   the name and address of the party bringing the appeal;

(b)   the name and address of the other party to the appeal;

(c)   particulars of the facts or contentions which the party bringing the appeal will put forward at the hearing.

[22.48] The Adoptive Leave (Referral of Disputes and Appeals) (Part V) Regulations 1995[72] require that a notice of appeal contain the following particulars:

(a)   the names, addresses and descriptions of the parties to the proceedings;

(b)   the grounds of appeal;

(c)   the weekly remuneration of the adopting parent; and

(d)   the date on which the decision to which the appeal relates was made and the name of the Rights Commissioner who made it.

[22.49] The Parental Leave (Disputes and Appeals) Regulations 1999[73] require that a notice of appeal specify:

(a)   the name and address of the party bringing the appeal;

(b)   the name and address of the other party to the appeal;

(c)   the date on which the decision to which the appeal relates was made and the name of the Rights Commissioner who made it; and

(d)   particulars of any facts or contentions which the party bringing the appeal will put forward at the hearing.

[22.50] All the regulations provide that a party to an appeal, if he or she intends to contest the appeal, shall enter an appearance within 14 days (or such longer period as the Tribunal may fix) of receipt of the notice of appeal.[74] The notice of appearance should

---

[70]   SI 244/1994.

[71]   SI 17/1995.

[72]   SI 195/1995.

[73]   SI 6/1999.

[74]   Terms of Employment (Information) (Appeals and Complaints) Regulations 1994 (SI 244/1994), Reg 5(1); Maternity Protection (Disputes and Appeals) Regulations 1995 (SI 17/1995), Reg 3(2); Adoptive Leave (Referral of Disputes and Appeals)(Part V) Regulations 1995 (SI 195/1995), Reg 5(1); Parental Leave (Disputes and Appeals) Regulations 1999 (SI 6/1999), Reg 4(1)(a).

contain either a brief outline of the grounds on which the appeal will be contested or the facts or contentions which the respondent will put forward.[75]

The regulations, other than the maternity protection regulations, provide that an appeal may be withdrawn by giving a notification in writing signifying such withdrawal to the Tribunal.[76]

[22.51] The relevant legislation provides that, once a party has appealed to the Tribunal, the Tribunal shall give the parties an opportunity to be heard by it and to present to it any evidence relevant to the appeal.[77]

The procedure at such hearings is governed by Regs 10–17 of the Redundancy (Redundancy Appeals Tribunal) Regulations 1968 or by specific provisions equivalent thereto.[78]

THE EQUALITY TRIBUNAL

[22.52] The Equality Tribunal was established pursuant to s 75 of the Employment Equality Act 1998 and enjoys jurisdiction under that Act (as amended) as well as under the Equal Status Act 2000 and Part VII of the Pensions Act 1990 (as amended).

[22.53] Any person who believes that he or she has experienced discrimination which is contrary to the 1998 Act (as amended) may seek redress by referring the case to the Equality Tribunal.[79] The Tribunal provides a complaint form (Form EEI.1) but this form is not a statutory form and is purely administrative in nature. Consequently the Tribunal has ruled that a complaint may be referred 'in any written format'.[80]

---

[75] Terms of Employment (Information) (Appeals and Complaints) Regulations 1994 (SI 244/1994), Reg 5(2); Maternity Protection (Disputes and Appeals) Regulations 1995 (SI 17/1995), Reg 3(1)(c); Adoptive Leave (Referral of Disputes and Appeals) (Part V) Regulations 1995 (SI 195/1995), Reg 5(2); Parental Leave (Disputes and Appeals) Regulations 1999 (SI 6/1999), Reg 4(1)(b).

[76] Terms of Employment (Information) (Appeals and Complaints) Regulations 1994 (SI 244/1994), Reg 4; Adoptive Leave (Referral of Disputes and Appeals) (Part V) Regulations 1995 (SI 195/1995), Reg 4(1); Parental Leave (Disputes and Appeals) Regulations 1999 (SI 6/1999), Reg 14(1).

[77] Terms of Employment (Information) Act 1994, s 8(1); Maternity Protection Act 1994, s 33(1); Adoptive Leave Act 1995, s 35(1); Protection of Young Persons (Employment) Act 1996, s 19(1); Parental Leave Act 1998, s 19(1); Carer's Leave Act 2001, s 20(1).

[78] SI 24/1968 which apply to Terms of Employment and Adoptive Leave cases by virtue of Terms of Employment (Information)(Appeals and Complaints) Regulations 1994 (SI 244/1994), Reg 10 and Adoptive Leave (Referral of Disputes and Appeals)(Part V) Regulations 1995 (SI 195/1995), Reg 14 respectively. For Maternity and Parental Leave cases see Maternity Protection (Disputes and Appeals) Regulations 1995 (SI 17/1995), Regs 6,7 and 9 and Parental Leave (Disputes and Appeals) Regulations 1999 (SI 6/1999), Regs 9–12.

[79] Employment Equality Act 1998, s 77(1) as substituted by Equality Act 2004, s 32. There is no 'class action' procedure: see *Verbatim Ltd v Duffy* (1994) 10 JISLL 172, 191 *per* Kinlen J.

[80] *A Female Employee v A Building Products Company* DEC-E2007-036.

Complaints must be referred to the Tribunal within six months of the date when the discrimination occurred or last occurred.[81] The Tribunal has power to extend the time up to 12 months where reasonable cause is shown.[82]

When a complaint is referred to the Tribunal, it will initially go to the Secretariat section whose staff acknowledge the complaint in writing. They will also carry out basic checks to make sure that the complaint appears to be within the terms of the legislation. If the complaint appears to be inadmissible, they will write to the complainant asking him or her to clarify the factual position. If the complaint still appears not be admissible, the case is closed. If it appears to be admissible, or if it is still unclear as to whether it is admissible, then the Secretariat will send a copy of the complaint to the respondent for its initial comments.

If the Director considers that the complaint could be resolved by mediation she will refer it to an equality mediation officer. If either party objects to mediation or the Director considers that it is not suitable, the case will go forward for investigation and will be assigned to an equality officer.

[22.54] Once an equality officer has been assigned, he or she will seek a detailed written submission from the complainant, if one has not already been provided. When the equality officer receives a complainant's submission, it will be copied to the respondent and a replying submission will be requested which should be provided within six weeks. If questions arise from the material submitted, the equality officer may make additional inquiries.

[22.55] The equality officer is conferred with extensive powers to require any person to produce any records, books or documents which are believed to contain relevant material; to inspect and copy relevant records; and to enter premises.[83] The Director may also require any person believed to possess relevant information to attend at a hearing in order to provide that information and to answer questions fully and truthfully.[84]

An equality officer has no power to administer the oath.[85] Investigations must be held 'in private'.[86]

[22.56] The procedure adopted is inquisitorial not adversarial, in that the equality officer will direct the hearing and will ask questions of each party and of any witnesses they bring, based on the material submitted. The equality officer will also give 'each party the opportunity to make any other points they wish, to ask witnesses their own questions and to comment on the points made by the other party'.[87] In its *Guide to Procedures* the

---

[81] Employment Equality Act 1998, s 77(5)(a) as substituted by Equality Act 2004, s 32.

[82] Employment Equality Act 1998, s 77(5)(b) as substituted by Equality Act 2004, s 32. Under the Employment Equality Act 1977, the relevant provision was s 19(5).

[83] Employment Equality Act 1998, s 94.

[84] Employment Equality Act 1998, s 95(3).

[85] Employment Equality Act 1998, s 95(3)(b), however, empowers the Director to request that persons required to attend, pursuant to subs (1)(b), sign a declaration of the truth of their answers to any questions put by the Director.

[86] Employment Equality Act 1998, s 79(2).

[87] Guide to Procedures in Employment Equality Cases (revised July 2005), s 10.

Equality Tribunal emphasises that the equality officer may also intervene 'to ensure that unrepresented complainants or respondents are not placed at a disadvantage'.[88]

[22.57] The witnesses may be allowed to remain throughout the hearing or may be asked to come in only for their own evidence. The equality officer will decide what is appropriate, taking into account factors 'such as the arrangements which will best support the effective and accurate giving of evidence, as well as practical considerations like the number of witnesses, and the space and facilities available'. The Equality Tribunal's *Guide to Procedures* makes it clear that each party, and their representatives, is responsible for the conduct of those accompanying them – whether they be witnesses or 'support persons'.[89] If the equality officer considers that any person is disrupting the effective conduct of the hearing, he or she may direct them to leave.

A complainant or respondent may represent themselves or they can be represented by 'any individual or body authorised by that party on their behalf'.[90]

Section 82(5) of the 1998 Act empowers an equality officer, in gender discrimination cases, to order the payment of Courts Act interest in respect of the whole or any part of the amount of compensation that he or she may award.

THE LABOUR COURT

[22.58] The Labour Court was established pursuant to s 10 of the Industrial Relations Act 1946. Apart from its function of investigating trade disputes and making recommendations in respect of same,[91] the Court hears appeals from decisions of rights commissioners under the Industrial Relations Act 1969,[92] the Organisation of Working Time Act 1997,[93] the National Minimum Wage Act 2000,[94] the Protection of Employees (Part-Time Work) Act 2001[95] and the Protection of Employees (Fixed Term Work) Act 2003.[96] The Court also hears appeals from decisions of the Equality Tribunal under the Employment Equality Acts 1998–2008.[97]

---

[88] Guide to Procedures in Employment Equality Cases (revised July 2005), s 10.

[89] Guide to Procedures in Employment Equality Cases (revised July 2005), s 10.

[90] Employment Equality Act 1998, s 77(1) as substituted by Equality Act 2004, s 32.

[91] Pursuant to s 68 of the 1946 Act. The Court has additional investigative functions under Industrial Relations Act 1969, s 20, Industrial Relations (Amendment) Act 2001 (as amended), s 2, Employees (Provision of Information and Consultation) Act, s 15, European Communities (European Public Limited-Liability Company) (Employee Involvement) Regulation 2006 (SI 623/2006), Reg 20, European Communities (European Cooperative Society) (Employee Involvement) Regulations 2007 (SI 259/2007), Reg 21 and European Communities (Cross-Border Mergers) Regulations 2008 (SI 157/2008), Reg 40.

[92] Industrial Relations Act 1969, s 13(9).

[93] Organisation of Working Time Act 1997, s 28(1).

[94] National Minimum Wage Act 2000, s 27(1).

[95] Protection of Employees (Part-Time Work) Act 2001, s 17(1).

[96] Protection of Employees (Fixed Term Work) Act 2003, 15(1). The Court also hears appeals from decisions of rights commissioners under the Industrial Relations (Miscellaneous Provisions) Act 2004, the Safety, Health and Welfare at Work Act 2005, the Employees (Provision of Information and Consultation) Act 2006, (contd.../)

[22.59] Although there is no statutory time limit for appealing under the 1969 Act, the other legislation requires that an appeal be initiated within six weeks of the date on which the decision was communicated to the party concerned.[98] The issue of when a decision could be considered as having been communicated to the party wishing to appeal was considered by the Labour Court in *Toscano v Mika*.[99] Here, the decision of the Rights Commissioner was dated 19 November 2007 and was sent by registered post the same day to the complainant's address in County Cork which was set out in her complaint form. This was returned, marked 'uncollected'. The LRC, however, were aware that, subsequent to lodgment of the complaint, the complainant had moved to County Clare. The complainant only received a copy of the decision on 7 February 2008, having repeatedly sought a copy of same, and appealed within 11 days of receipt of the decision.

The Labour Court was satisfied that all the evidence pointed to a position where the decision was not 'communicated' to the complainant until 7 February 2008 and, accordingly, the appeal was within the time prescribed.

[22.60] In the case of employment equality appeals, the period commences on the date of the decision.[100]

The Court has no power to extend the time for appealing, whether against the decision of the Equality Tribunal or a rights commissioner.[101]

The notice of appeal should contain such particulars as may be determined by the Labour Court. The Labour Court has provided a number of forms which can be used for the bringing of such appeals.

An appeal is in the nature of a re-hearing[102] and the Court has no inherent power to remit a claim for further consideration by the Equality Tribunal or the rights commissioner.[103]

---

[96] (\...contd) the Employment Permits Act 2006, the European Communities (European Public Limited-Liability Company) (Employee Involvement) Regulations 2006 (SI 623/2006), the Consumer Protection Act 2007, the European Communities (European Cooperative Society) (Employee Involvement) Regulations 2007 (SI 259/2007) and the European Communities (Cross-Border Mergers) Regulations 2008 (SI 157/2008).

[97] Employment Equality Act 1998, s 83(1).

[98] Organisation of Working Time Act 1997, s 28(2); Employment Equality Act 1998, s 83(1); National Minimum Wage Act 2000, s 27(1); Protection of Employees (Part-Time Work) Act 2001, s 17(2); Protection of Employees (Fixed Term Work) Act 2003, s 15(2).

[99] *Toscano v Mika* MWD 6/2008.

[100] See *Hegarty v Labour Court* [1999] 3 IR 603. The date of the decision is to be included in the calculation: see *Byrne v Minaguchi* EDA 4/2003 and *Dunnes Stores v Boylan* EDA 5/2003.

[101] See *Southern Health Board v Shuaib* EDA 1/2003 and *Toscano v Mika* MWD 6/2008.

[102] This is specifically provided for by National Minimum Wage Act 2000, s 27(3). In *HSE v Sheridan* EDA 20/2008, the Labour Court described its appllate role as one of 'considering anew all questions of fact and law arising in the case'.

[103] *Southern Health Board v Mitchell* [2001] ELR 201; *Sunday World Newspapers Ltd v Kinsella* [2006] ELR 325; *Kirwan v Department of Justice, Equality and Law Reform* [2008] ELR 89; *Department of Health and Children v Rohan* DWT 92/2008. (contd.../)

[22.61] The Court is empowered to take evidence on oath and for that purpose to cause to be administered oaths to persons attending as witnesses at the hearing.[104] The Court is also empowered to require the attendance of a person to give evidence or to produce documents.[105] The High Court has ruled that, since the legislation confers a discretion on the Labour Court to regulate its own procedures in respect of these matters, neither the parties nor the High Court could dictate as to the manner in which the Court should conduct its procedures 'once it exercises its powers in accordance with the statute from which it derives its authority to act'.[106] The High Court did comment, however, that the Labour Court should not allow itself to be deterred by considerations of difficulty or inconvenience from taking evidence on oath where it would otherwise be proper or desirable to do so.

[22.62] In *A Government Department v A Complainant*,[107] the Labour Court ruled that it would only exercise its power to compel the attendance of persons before it in circumstances where the Court was satisfied that the person concerned had 'relevant and admissible evidence to give in relation to facts at issue in the proceedings' and that that person was 'unable or unwilling to attend unless compelled to do so'.

[22.63] Section 83(2) of the Employment Equality Act 1998 provides that appeals under that Act shall be heard 'in private' unless, at the request of one of the parties, it determines to hold the appeal, or part thereof, in public. In *A Government Department v A Complainant*,[108] the Labour Court ruled that it would only embark upon a public hearing where there were 'special circumstances' relating to that particular case which made it desirable to do so. The onus lay on the party seeking to have the appeal conducted in public to establish that such special circumstances existed.

---

[103] (\...contd) Section 83(5), however, of the Employment Equality Act 1998 provides that, if the Labour Court's determination of an appeal against a decision of the Director on a preliminary issue under s 79(3) of the 1998 Act is in favour of the complainant, the case shall be referred back to the Director for an investigation of the substantive issue. Section 83(5), however, does not address the Labour Court's powers in relation to an appeal under s 79(3A). See also s 84 of the 1998 Act which empowers the Labour Court, where an appeal is brought under s 83, to refer all or any of the matters in issue on the appeal to the Director for further investigation or re-investigation. Section 84(4) also empowers the Labour Court, on an appeal under s 83, where it determines that the decision of the Director should be set aside, to refer the matters in issue back to the Director for a new investigation.

[104] Industrial Relations Act 1946, s 21(1)(a); Organisation of Working Time Act 1997, s 28(7); Employment Equality Act 1998, s 83(3); National Minimum Wage Act 2000, s 28(1); Protection of Employees (Part-Time Work) Act 2001, s 17(7); and Protection of Employees (Fixed Term) Work Act 2003, s 15(7).

[105] Industrial Relations Act 1946, s 21(1)(c); Organisation of Working Time Act 1997, s 28(7); Employment Equality Act 1998, s 83(3); National Minimum Wage Act 2000, s 28(3); Protection of Employees (Part-Time Work) Act 2001, s 17(7); and Protection of Employees (Fixed Term Work) Act 2003, s 15(7). The Labour Court also has extensive powers to obtain information under Employment Equality Act 1998, ss 94 and 95.

[106] *State (Casey) v Labour Court* (1984) 3 JISLL 135, 138 *per* O'Hanlon J.

[107] *A Government Department v A Complainant* EDA 15/2005.

[108] *A Government Department v A Complainant* EDA 15/2005.

[22.64] The Labour Court has ruled that it will not entertain an appeal which is moot.[109] The Labour Court has also ruled that its appellate functions can only be invoked, unless the relevant statute specifically provides otherwise, where there is 'a complete and final decision which determines whether or not there has been an infringement of the Act'.[110]

[22.65] The procedure adopted is more inquisitorial than adversarial in that the chair of the division of the Labour Court hearing the appeal will direct the hearing. The Court will have required the delivery of written submissions by both sides at least three working days prior to the hearing. The parties' representatives at the hearing then read those submissions into the Court's record. Any points on which clarification or elaboration is required is dealt with by way of questions from the members of the Court. The Court, however, does provide each party the opportunity to ask witnesses their own questions, whether by way of direct or cross-examination, and to comment on the points made by the other party.

[22.66] An appellant or respondent may represent themselves or they can be represented by counsel, solicitor, trade union, employers' association or other representative as appropriate. In employment equality cases, s 77(11) of the Employment Equality Act 1998 provides that a party may be represented by 'any individual or body authorised by that party on their behalf'. It should be noted that s 20(6) of the Industrial Relations Act 1946 provides that no person shall be entitled to appear by counsel or solicitor unless the rules made by the Court for the regulation of its proceedings so provide. Although no such rules have been made in the context of the employment rights or equality legislation, the Labour Court has always taken the view that the matters in issue in such cases are of such a nature that the parties should be represented by counsel or solicitor if they so wish.

THE CIRCUIT COURT

[22.67] The Circuit Court was originally established pursuant to the Courts of Justice Act 1924 but now derives its jurisdiction in civil matters from s 22 of the Courts (Supplemental Provisions) Act 1961. When exercising its ordinary civil jurisdiction, such as hearing an action for damages for wrongful dismissal, the Court is limited in the amount it can award.[111]

In the context of employment law, the Circuit Court has been conferred with three important jurisdictions in the areas of employment equality, unfair dismissal and enforcement. Its enforcement jurisdiction is dealt with separately below.

In proceedings before the Circuit Court, a plaintiff or defendant may represent himself or herself or be represented by solicitor and/or counsel. Trade union officials, representatives of an employers' association and other lay persons have no right of

---

[109] *Department of Education and Science v Skelly* EDA 13/2008.

[110] *Bus Éireann v SIPTU* PTD 8/2004.

[111] Unless the parties consent to the Circuit Court having unlimited jurisdiction, the current limit is €38,092.14.

audience. The normal rules as to costs apply, with the Circuit Court being specifically empowered to make such order as to costs as may be appropriate.[112]

In an employment equality claim or unfair dismissal appeal, the Circuit Court Judge may, if an application on that behalf is made by either party, refer, on such terms as to costs or otherwise as he or she thinks fit, any question of law arising in such matter to the Supreme Court by way of case stated for the determination of the Supreme Court.[113] If the Judge decides to so state a case, he or she may adjourn the pronouncement of his or her judgment or order in the matter pending the determination of such case stated.

The issue of whether a Circuit Court Judge may state a case before all of the evidence which might fall to be considered by him or her has concluded has resulted in a difference of judicial opinion. In *Corley v Gill*[114] the Supreme Court unanimously concluded that a case might only be stated at the conclusion of the evidence adduced before the Circuit Court Judge. In *Doyle v Hearne*,[115] however, the majority of the Supreme Court ruled that it was up to the Circuit Court judge to determine the time at which he or she would state a case to the Supreme Court.

[22.68] Notwithstanding that neither the Unfair Dismissals Acts 1977–2007 nor the Employment Equality Acts 1998–2008 expressly provide for an appeal from the Circuit Court, it has been held that such decisions are not 'final and conclusive' and may be appealed to the High Court under s 38 of the Courts of Justice Act 1936.[116]

Where the decision is made by a judge of the Circuit Court for the time being assigned to and sitting in the Dublin Circuit, the appeal shall lie to the High Court sitting in Dublin.[117] In every other case the appeal shall lie to the High Court on Circuit sitting in the appeal town for the county in which the action was heard and determined.[118]

Appeals shall be by notice of appeal served within 10 days from the date on which the judgment or order appealed was pronounced in open court.[119] An appeal does not operate as a stay of proceedings upon the judgment or order appealed from, unless the

---

[112] Rules of the Circuit Court 2001 (SI 510/2001), Ord 57 (as substituted by the Circuit Court Rules (General) 2007 (SI 312/2007), r 20), r 1(11) and Circuit Court Rules (Employment Equality Act 1998) 2004 (SI 880/2004), r 9. See also *McKenna v Pizza Express Restaurants Ltd* [2008] ELR 234, where Judge Flanagan held that the Circuit Court had a general jurisdiction to award costs in appeals from the Employment Appeals Tribunal.

[113] Courts of Justice Act 1947, s 16. The procedure is regulated by RSC 1986, Ord 59. An example is provided by *Central Bank of Ireland v Gildea* [1997] 1 IR 160, where, on the application of the employer, Judge Spain stated a case as to whether the employee was a person 'employed by or under the State' within the meaning of what was s 2(1)(h) of the Unfair Dismissals Act 1977 and required the employer to pay the employee's costs in the Supreme Court.

[114] *Corley v Gill* [1975] IR 313. See also *State (Harkin) v O'Malley* [1978] IR 219, 285–286 *per* Henchy J.

[115] *Doyle v Hearne* [1988] ILRM 318.

[116] See *McCabe v Lisney & Sons* [1981] ILRM 289; *Western Health Board v Quigley* [1982] ILRM 390; and *Commissioners of Irish Lights v Sugg* [1994] ELR 97.

[117] Courts of Justice Act 1936, s 38(1)(a).

[118] Courts of Justice Act 1936, s 38(1)(b).

[119] RSC 1986, Ord 61, r 2.

Circuit Court Judge or, upon appeal, the High Court shall so order and then only upon such terms as the relevant judge may fix.[120]

Section 38(2) of the 1936 Act provides that any such appeal shall be heard by way of a rehearing of the action. Section 38(3) empowers the Judge hearing the appeal to refer any question of law arising in such appeal to the Supreme Court by way of case stated.

Section 39 of the 1936 Act provides that the decision of the High Court or of the High Court on Circuit in such an appeal shall be final and conclusive and shall not be appealable to the Supreme Court.

Employment equality

[22.69] Section 77(3) of the Employment Equality Act 1998[121] provides that a claim for gender discrimination, instead of being referred to the Director of the Equality Tribunal, may be referred to the Circuit Court. Such claims are subject, however, to the same time limits as apply to claims to the Director. In so far as the Circuit Court is empowered to award compensation or arrears of remuneration, s 82(3) of the 1998 Act provides that 'no enactment relating to the jurisdiction of the Circuit Court shall be taken to limit the amount of compensation or remuneration which may be ordered by the Circuit Court'.[122]

The Circuit Court Rules (Employment Equality Act 1998) 2004[123] provide that claims for redress under the 1998 Act should be brought by way of an Employment Law Civil Bill in the form specified, which form requires the plaintiff to set out the details of his or her claim, including the basis upon which jurisdiction is claimed, in the Indorsement of Claim.

Applications should be brought and heard in the County where the defendant resides or ordinarily carries on any profession, business or occupation[124] and should be served in accordance with Ord 11 of the Rules of the Circuit Court 2001.[125] Applications for extension of time under s 77(6) of the 1998 Act are required to be made *ex parte* by way of *ex parte* docket grounded on affidavit prior to the issuing of the Civil Bill, which said affidavit should set out the reasonable cause which prevented the plaintiff from complying with the time limits set out in s 77(5) of the 1998 Act.[126]

[22.70] All Employment Law Civil Bills should be dated and should bear the name, address and description of the plaintiff. They should be signed by the plaintiff's

---

[120] RSC 1986, Ord 61, r 6.

[121] Inserted by s 32 of the Equality Act 2004, rule 6.

[122] So in *Atkinson v Carty* [2005] ELR 1, Judge Delahunt awarded damages of €137,000, less a finding of contributory negligence measured at 25%, and costs.

[123] SI 880/2004, r 6.

[124] Employment Equality Act 1998, s 80(2).

[125] Rules of the Circuit Court 2001 (RCC 2001), Ord 11 provides that, save where otherwise directed or permitted, service should be effected upon the defendant personally, wherever he or she is to be found within the jurisdiction, or at his or her residence within the jurisdiction personally upon the husband or wife of the defendant or upon some relative or employee of the defendant over the age of 16 years and apparently resident there.

[126] SI 880/2004, r 6(h).

solicitor, if any, or, if none, by himself or herself and should set out the redress sought by the plaintiff in accordance with s 82(3) of the 1998 Act.[127]

Rule 6(e) provides that, if the defendant wishes to dispute the plaintiff's claim either wholly or in part, he or she should 'within 10 days after service' of the Civil Bill enter an Appearance and within a further ten days thereafter deliver a Defence.

Upon application on notice of either party, the Circuit Court Judge may order any party to deliver full and better particulars of any matters stated in the application or to deliver copies of any documents referred therein.[128]

Save by special leave of the Court, all applications shall be heard on oral evidence.[129] Unlike claims before an Equality Officer, Circuit Court claims must be heard in public.

Section 80(4) of the Employment Equality Act 1998 enables the Circuit Court to request that the Director of the Equality Tribunal nominate an equality officer to investigate and prepare a report on any question specified by the Circuit Court. Where such a report is prepared, s 80(5) provides that the report should be furnished to the plaintiff and the defendant, and to any other person to whom it relates. The subsection further provides that the report shall be received as evidence in the proceedings and that the equality officer may be called as a witness to give evidence in the proceedings.

Unfair dismissal

[22.71] Section 11(1) of the Unfair Dismissals (Amendment) Act 1993 provides that a party concerned may appeal to the Circuit Court from a determination of the Employment Appeals Tribunal under the 1977 Act within six weeks from the date on which the determination is communicated to the parties. The appeal may be against the whole of the determination or only a part thereof.[130] The appeal is a full appeal on both fact and law and is in the nature of a rehearing.

The Supreme Court has confirmed that the Circuit Court has no jurisdiction to extend the time provided for appeal.[131] The High Court has also ruled that the essence of an appeal is not the issue or service of a notice of appeal as such, but the invoking of the Circuit Court's jurisdiction.[132] This was done by the issue of the originating document, in this case a notice of application to the Court in the form prescribed by the Rules of the Circuit Court. Time ceased to run when the proceedings were issued, not when they were served.[133]

The Rules of the Circuit Court 2001 provide that all appeals should be made by way of Motion on Notice which must set out the grounds upon which the appellant is relying for the reliefs sought.[134] The original letter or notice from the Tribunal communicating its determination, or a certified copy thereof, must be filed with the application.[135]

---

[127] SI 880/2004, r 6(d).
[128] SI 880/2004, r 6(f).
[129] SI 880/2004, r 6(g).
[130] RCC 2001, Ord 57, r 1(7).
[131] *McIlwraith v Fawsitt* [1990] 1 IR 343.
[132] *Morris v Power Supermarkets Ltd* [1990] 1 IR 296.
[133] *Morris v Power Supermarkets Ltd* [1990] 1 IR 296 *per* Barron J at 299.
[134] RCC 2001, Ord 57, r 1(2).
[135] RCC 2001, Ord 57, r 1(6)(i).

Applications should be brought and heard in the County where the employer concerned ordinarily resides or carries on any profession, business or occupation[136] and should be served no later than 10 days prior to the return date set out in the Motion either in accordance with Ord 11 or by being served upon the Solicitor on record before the Tribunal as acting for the defendant.[137]

All applications should be dated and should bear the name, address and description of the appellant and should be signed by his or her solicitor, if any, or, if none, by himself or herself.[138]

Upon application on notice of either party, the Circuit Court Judge may order any party to deliver full and better particulars of any matters stated in the application, or to deliver copies of any documents referred to therein.[139]

Save by special leave of the Court, or save as otherwise provided by the Unfair Dismissals Acts 1977–2007, all appeals shall be heard upon oral evidence.[140]

[22.72] Section 11(2)(a) of the 1993 Act provides that where, in proceedings under that section, the Circuit Court finds that an employee is entitled to redress, the Judge shall order the employer concerned to make to the employee 'the appropriate redress'. If the redress is an award of compensation, s 11(4)(a) of the 1993 Act empowers the Judge, if he or she considers it appropriate to do so, to direct the employer concerned to pay Courts Act interest on the compensation.

If an employer fails to comply with an order of the Circuit Court under s 11(2)(a) (here referred to as the former order), the Circuit Court shall, on application to it in that behalf by the employee, make such order for the enforcement of the former order as it considers appropriate having regard to all the circumstances.[141] If the former order directed the re-instatement or re-engagement of the employee concerned and the Court considers it appropriate to do so, having regard to all the circumstances, the Court may make an order directing the employer, in lieu of re-instating or re-engaging the employee, to pay compensation to him or her under s 7(1)(c) of the 1977 Act in respect of the loss of wages suffered by the employee and giving such directions for the enforcement of the latter order as it considers appropriate having regard to all the circumstances.[142]

The Rules of the Circuit Court provide that any such application should be made by way of Motion on Notice. A certified copy of the order made on the appeal and an affidavit or statutory declaration as to the service of that order must be filed with the application.[143]

---

[136] RCC 2001, Ord 57, r 1(3).

[137] RCC 2001, Ord 57, r 1(4).

[138] RCC 2001, Ord 57, r 1(8).

[139] RCC 2001, Ord 57, r 1(9).

[140] RCC 2001, Ord 57, r 1(10).

[141] Unfair Dismissals (Amendment) Act 1993, s 11(2)(b). If he or she considers it appropriate, having regard to all the circumstances, the Minister may make the application.

[142] Unfair Dismissals (Amendment) Act 1993, s 11(2)(b)(II).

[143] RCC 2001, Ord 57, r 2.

Upon application on notice of either party, the Circuit Court may order any party to deliver full and better particulars of any matters stated in the application or to deliver copies of any documents referred therein.[144]

EXTENSIONS OF TIME

[22.73] As noted above, the employment rights and equality legislation invariably provide that the time for lodging claims may be extended. In some cases, time may be extended if the appropriate body is satisfied that the failure to present the complaint within the specified time period was due to 'reasonable cause'. In other cases, however, time may only be extended if the appropriate body is satisfied that 'exceptional circumstances' prevented the presentation of the complaint within the specified time period. Where the body is satisfied that either 'reasonable cause' or 'exceptional circumstances' are present, the Employment Appeals Tribunal and the Labour Court have differed as to whether the extension of time is mandatory or discretionary. In *Cementation Skanska v Carroll*[145] the Labour Court said that, even where 'reasonable cause' was shown, it should still consider whether it was appropriate in the circumstances to grant an extension of time. On the other hand, the Employment Appeals Tribunal has held, in *Quinn v HSS Ltd*,[146] that where a claimant shows 'exceptional circumstances' the extension of time is mandatory but the length of the extension is discretionary, subject to the limits of the statute.

The cases demonstrate that the claimant must show not only that 'reasonable cause' or 'exceptional circumstances' were present but that they also prevented or inhibited the timely initiation of the claim. The cases also demonstrate that, in considering whether to grant an extension, the bar to be overcome is much lower when 'reasonable cause' rather than 'exceptional circumstances' is the test.

Reasonable cause

[22.74] The power to extend the time limit for reasonable cause was fully considered by the Labour Court in *Cementation Skanska v Carroll*,[147] a case under the Organisation of Working Time Act 1997. The Court said that, in considering whether reasonable cause exists, it was for the claimant to show that there were 'reasons which both explain the delay and afford an excuse for the delay'.[148] The Court went on to hold:

> The explanation must be reasonable, that is to say it must make sense, be agreeable to reason and not be irrational or absurd. In the context in which the expression 'reasonable cause' appears in statute it suggests an objective standard, but it must be applied to the

---

[144] RCC 2001, Ord 57, r 9.

[145] *Cementation Skanska v Carroll* DWT 38/2003.

[146] *Quinn v HSS Ltd* UD 1134/2005.

[147] *Cementation Skanska v Carroll* DWT 38/2003. See *Elephant Haulage Ltd v Juska* EET2/2008 and *HSE v Rauf* FTD 17/2008.

[148] Citing Costello J in *O'Donnell v Dun Laoghaire Corporation* [1991] ILRM 301, 315 (a case concerning whether there were 'good reasons' for extending time under RSC 1986, Ord 84, r 21).

facts and circumstances known to the claimant at the material time. The claimant's failure to present the claim within the six month time limit must have been due to the reasonable cause relied upon. Hence there must be a causal link between the circumstances cited and the delay and the claimant should satisfy the court, as a matter of probability, that had those circumstances not been present, he would have initiated the claim in time.

The Labour Court went on to say that the length of the delay should also be taken into account. A short delay might only require 'a slight explanation' whereas a long delay might require 'more cogent reasons'.

[22.75] This issue was also considered by the High Court in *Minister for Finance v Civil and Public Service Union.*[149] In this case, Laffoy J ruled that failure to pursue a claim which has crystallised until a legal precedent is in place which clarifies the law and indicates that the claim is likely to be successful, followed by prosecution of the claim when the precedent is publicised, did not constitute 'reasonable cause' within the meaning of s 19(5) of the Employment Equality Act 1977.

Exceptional circumstances

[22.76] The Employment Appeals Tribunal has ruled that 'exceptional circumstances' are 'strong words' and mean something 'out of the ordinary'.[150] At the very least, the circumstances must be 'unusual, probably quite unusual, but not necessarily highly unusual'.[151] The Labour Court has expressed itself in similar terms holding that, to be exceptional, a circumstance need not be unique or unprecedented or very rare 'but it cannot be one which is regular or routinely or normally encountered'.[152]

[22.77] In *Donaldson v South West Regional Tourism Authority Ltd,*[153] the time limit expired on 21 November 2004 and an unsigned RP51A was received by the Tribunal on 22 November 2004. The claimant submitted that the claim had in fact been lodged within the time limit and reliance was placed on two documents showing proof of attempts to transmit two emails to the Tribunal on 19 November 2004. On examining these documents, the Tribunal found that the address in both emails was incorrect in two material respects and consequently neither were 'received' by the Tribunal. The claimant submitted in the alternative that the circumstances surrounding the purported

---

[149] *Minister for Finance v Civil and Public Service Union* [2007] ELR 36.

[150] *Byrne v PJ Quigley Ltd* [1995] ELR 205.

[151] See also *Smyth v O'Kane Engineering Ltd* UD 890/1994; *Kiely v Preussag Fire Protection Ireland Ltd* UD 833/1996; *Casey v Committee of Sean Kelly Sports Centre* UD 63/1997; *Griffin v Canada Life Assurance Company* UD 146/1997; *Hickey v Schiesser International (Ireland) Ltd* UD 280/1997; *Leslie v Dawn International Ltd* UD 370/1997; *McDowell v Dolman Fashions Ltd* UD 580/1997; *Carolan v Stoneware and Fireclays Ltd* UD 608/1998; *Nangle v Aer Lingus* UD 942/1998; *Rathfarnham Delicatessen Ltd v Nolan* UD 295/2002; *McDonagh v Dell Computer Corporation* UD 348/2002.

[152] *Fitzsimons-Markey v Gaelscoil Thulach na nÓg* [2004] ELR 110. This case held that the failure of the complainant's Solicitor to lodge the claim within the initial six month period could amount to 'exceptional circumstances': see also *Gibbons v Viking Direct (Ireland) Ltd* UD356/2000.

[153] *Donaldson v South West Regional Tourism Authority Ltd* UD 1309/2004.

sending of the emails were sufficiently 'exceptional' to warrant an extension of time. The Tribunal decided that they were not and said that, with the advent of electronic mail, 'it behoves those lodging applications with the Tribunal to ensure that they have the correct email address and to seek confirmation of the receipt of the application or to otherwise confirm that the email has been read'.

PRELIMINARY POINTS

[22.78] Not infrequently, a complaint will involve consideration not only of the substantive issues raised, but also preliminary issues such as whether the complaint has been lodged in time, whether the complainant is entitled to bring the complaint (for example whether the person is an employee as defined) or whether the relevant forum has jurisdiction to entertain the complaint. The Employment Equality Act 1998 expressly confers a discretion on the Director of the Equality Tribunal to investigate certain issues as a preliminary issue.[154]

[22.79] The tendency of all first instance fora is to have the entirety of a case dealt with rather than having preliminary issues determined. This reflects the general principle that all issues arising in a case should be disposed of in a single set of proceedings and that litigation should not be fragmented. Nevertheless there will be cases in which a preliminary point should be determined separately from other issues arising in a case. In *Bus Eireann v SIPTU*,[155] the Labour Court indicated that this would normally be done 'where it could lead to considerable savings in both time and expense' and where the point was 'a question of pure law where no evidence was needed and where no further information is required'.

---

[154] Employment Equality Act 1998, s 79(3) provides that, in an equal pay case, the question of whether there are grounds other than gender etc for paying different rates of remuneration within the meaning of s 19(5) or s 29(5) may be investigated as a 'preliminary issue'. The Labour Court has held that this subsection should be construed strictly and did not empower the Equality Tribunal to determine issues arising under s 19(4) in a preliminary way: *The Courts Service v 28 Named Employees* EDA 19/2007. Section 79(3A), which was inserted by Equality Act 2004, s 35, also provides that, if an issue arises relating to the entitlement of any party to bring or contest proceedings under s 77 including:
    (a)   whether the complainant has complied with the statutory requirements relating to referrals,
    (b)   whether the discrimination occurred on or after 18 October 1999,
    (c)   whether the complainant is an employee, or
    (d)   any other related question of law or fact,
the Director may direct that the question be investigated as a preliminary issue.

[155] *Bus Éireann v SIPTU* PTD 8/2004, citing O'Higgins CJ in *Tara Exploration and Development Co Ltd v Minister for Industry and Commerce* [1975] IR 242 at 256. See also O'Flaherty J in *Duffy v News Group Newspapers Ltd (No 2)* [1994] 3 IR 63 at 77; Hardiman J in *RTF v Director of Public Prosecutions* [2005] 2 ILRM 367 at 372–373; and Denham J in *RN v Refugee Appeals Tribunal* [2008] 1 ILRM 289 at 293–295.

ADJOURNMENTS

[22.80] Once a hearing date has been set, good cause will be required for an adjournment. In the case of claims and appeals before the Employment Appeals Tribunal, Reg 13 of the Redundancy (Redundancy Appeals Tribunal) Regulations 1968[156] empowers the Tribunal to 'postpone or adjourn the hearing' from time to time.[157] Applications must be made to a sitting division of the Tribunal. There is no rule limiting the time within which adjournments should be sought but best practice would suggest that applications should be made within five working days of receipt of notification of the hearing or at the earliest opportunity thereafter. The party seeking the adjournment will be expected to seek and obtain the written consent of the other party. The party seeking the adjournment should have evidence of their endeavour to obtain the written consent of the other party if that other party is not at the hearing of the application. It should be noted that making an application within the five working days after receipt of notice of the hearing will not automatically secure an adjournment as the Tribunal still has to be satisfied that there is good cause for granting the adjournment. Unavailability of Counsel is never regarded as 'good cause'.

[22.81] In the case of the other employment rights bodies, applications for adjournments should be made in writing to the rights commissioner, the Chairman of the Labour Court or the Director of the Equality Tribunal as the case may be. In its *Guide to Procedures* the Equality Tribunal emphasises that any party who wants to request an adjournment of the date fixed for hearing will need to satisfy the Director 'that they have, at the least, a substantial reason, and have applied as soon as reasonably possible'. In cases involving rights commissioners, the practice is that requests for adjournments should detail the reasons for seeking the adjournment and must be received within 10 working days of the date of the letter informing the parties of the arrangements for the hearing.

BURDEN OF PROOF

[22.82] Generally speaking a complainant bears the legal burden of proving all facts essential to his or her claim. The standard of proof is on the balance of probabilities. This explains why in most employment cases the complainant is expected to present their case first, whether by way of submission or evidence or both. In some cases, however, statute has provided for an alteration in or a shifting of the burden of proof.

[22.83] In unfair dismissal cases, for example, the burden of proving the essential preliminary matters (such as the fact of dismissal) falls on the employee. Section 6(6) of the Unfair Dismissals Act 1977 provides, however, that in determining whether the

---

[156] SI 24/1968.

[157] In *Concannon v Geraghty* [1994] ELR 229, the Tribunal (chaired by Iarfhlaith Ó Néill SC) said that this regulation did not empower it to adjourn a case 'generally'. It could only adjourn 'from time to time', which was construed as meaning 'to adjourn to a definite time in the future'.

[158] The issue as to the burden of proof in alleged pregnancy related dismissals was fully considered by the Employment Appeals Tribunal in *Pedreschi v Burke* UD591/1999:

> The claimant must show the Tribunal that it has jurisdiction in the matter. Where the claimant successfully shows the Tribunal that her dismissal was, on the balance of probabilities, on the grounds of her pregnancy, or matters relating thereto, the Tribunal will then assume jurisdiction in the matter. (contd.../)

dismissal was unfair or not 'it shall be for the employer to show that the dismissal resulted wholly or mainly from one or more of the matters specified in subsection (4) of this section or that there were other substantial grounds justifying the dismissal.'[158]

[22.84] In employment equality cases, s 85A(1) of the Employment Equality Act 1998[159] provides that where 'facts are established by or on behalf of a complainant from which it may be presumed that there has been discrimination in relation to him or her, it shall be for the respondent to prove the contrary'. Section 33A(2) of the Maternity Protection Act 1994[160] provides to similar effect.

The extent of the evidential burden which a complainant must discharge was fully considered by the Labour Court in *Southern Health Board v Mitchell*:

> The first requirement is that the claimant must establish facts from which it may be presumed that the principle of equal treatment has not been applied to them. This indicates that a claimant must prove, on the balance of probabilities, the primary facts on which they rely in seeking to raise a presumption of unlawful discrimination. It is only if these primary facts are established to the satisfaction of the Court, and they are regarded by the Court as being of sufficient significance to raise a presumption of discrimination, that the onus shifts to the respondent to prove that there is no infringement of the principle of equal treatment.[161]

COSTS AND EXPENSES

[22.85] Although a rights commissioner has no power to award either party costs or expenses, statute does provide that, in certain circumstances, the Employment Appeals Tribunal, the Director of the Equality Tribunal and the Labour Court can award costs and expenses.

[22.86] Regulation 19(2) of the Redundancy (Redundancy Appeals Tribunal) Regulations 1968[162] provides that, where in the opinion of the Employment Appeals

---

[158] (\...contd)

In arriving at the decision as to whether a dismissal was on grounds of pregnancy or matters related thereto, the Tribunal will have regard to the evidence of the employer, who will seek to show that the dismissal was justified on substantial grounds, not related to the pregnancy of the employee.

[159] Inserted by Equality Act 2004, s 38. This section gives effect to Council Directive 97/80/EC (see now Art 19 of Parliament and Council Directive 2006/54/EC).

[160] Inserted by s 22 of the Maternity Protection (Amendment) Act 2004.

[161] [2001] ELR 201, 206. See, however, *ICTS (UK) Ltd v Ahmed* EDA 3/2004 where the Labour Court indicated that there would be situations where the *Mitchell* test would not be appropriate. The quality of evidence necessary to rebut a presumption of discrimination was considered in *Portroe Stevedores v Nevins* [2005] ELR 282.

[162] SI 24/1968. Minimum Notice and Terms of Employment (Reference of Disputes) Regulations 1973 (SI 243/1973), Reg 10 and Unfair Dismissals (Claims and Appeals) Regulations 1977 (SI 286/1977), Reg 10 apply Reg 19 to references to the Tribunal under the 1973 and 1977 Acts. See also Payment of Wages (Appeals) Regulations 1991 (SI 351/1991), Reg 10; Terms of Employment (Information) (Appeals and Complaints) Regulations 1994 (SI 244/1994), Reg 10; Maternity Protection (Disputes and Appeals) Regulations 1995 (SI 17/1995), Reg 10; Adoptive Leave (Referral of Disputes and Appeals) (Part V) Regulations 1995 (SI 195/1995), Reg 14; Parental Leave (Disputes and Appeals) Regulations 1999 (SI 6/1999), Reg 17.

Tribunal a party to the proceedings has acted 'frivolously or vexatiously', the Tribunal may make an order that that party shall pay to another party 'a specified amount in respect of travelling expenses and any other costs or expenses reasonably incurred by that other party in connection with the hearing'.[163] Regulation 19(3) goes on to provide, however, that 'costs shall not be awarded in respect of the costs or expenses in respect of the attendance of counsel, solicitor, officials of a trade union or of any employers' association appearing before the Tribunal in a representative capacity'.

Where the Tribunal makes an order under Reg 19(2), the amount referred to in the order is recoverable as a simple contract debt.[164]

[22.87] In *Ó Dulaing v Board of Management, Gaelscoil Thulach na nÓg*[165] the Tribunal, by majority decision, ruled that where a claimant withdrew his or her case prior to the commencement of the hearing and accordingly no *viva voce* evidence was given, it had no jurisdiction to award either costs or expenses.

[22.88] Regulation 20 empowers the Tribunal to award to a person appearing before it 'a sum in respect of travelling expenses and subsistence allowance' in accordance with the ministerally approved scale. Regulation 20A[166] empowers the Tribunal to award to a person appearing before it 'and whose attendance is deemed essential by the Tribunal' such sum in respect of expenses 'for loss of remunerative time' as the Tribunal considers reasonable.[167] Such sums are either paid out of the Social Insurance Fund or by the Minister.

[22.89] Section 21(4) of the Industrial Relations Act 1946 provides that, where a witness attends before the Labour Court in pursuance of a summons issued under that section, the Minister may, if he or she thinks fit, pay to him or her 'such sum in respect of expenses' incurred by him or her in connection with his or her attendance as the Minister may determine.

[22.90] Section 99A of the Employment Equality Act 1998[168] empowers the Director of the Equality Tribunal and the Labour Court, if they are of the opinion that a person is obstructing or impeding an investigation or appeal under that Act, to order that the person pay to another person 'a specified amount in respect of the travelling or other

---

[163] As to whether party has acted 'frivolously or vexatiously' see *Sherry v Panther Security Ltd* [1991] ELR 239; *Sheehan v M & M Keating & Sons Ltd* [1993] ELR 12 and *Skiba v McKenna* UD 520/2002.

[164] SI 24/1968, Reg 19(4).

[165] *Ó Dulaing v Board of Management, Gaelscoil Thulach na nÓg* UD 1028/2002. In *Annesley v Berry Bros & Rudd* UD 364/2007, however, the Tribunal awarded the employer witness expenses where the claimant had withdrawn her claim the day before the scheduled hearing but without informing the employer of same.

[166] Inserted by the Redundancy (Employment Appeals Tribunal) Regulations 1979 (SI 114/1979). Both Regs 20 and 20A apply to the other employment legislation.

[167] No such award can be made in respect of the attendance of appellants or respondents or their representatives: see Reg 20A(2).

[168] Inserted by Equality Act 2004, s 41.

expenses reasonably incurred by that other person' in connection with the investigation or appeal.[169]

The amount of any such expenses ordered to be paid may be recovered as a simple contract debt.[170]

ENFORCEMENT

[22.91] Where a decision of one of the employment rights bodies has neither been implemented nor appealed, the legislation provides a means whereby the decision can be enforced. This is because decisions of non-judicial tribunals are generally not self-executing. The precise mechanism, however, varies according to the statute under which the decision has been made.

[22.92] The legislation typically provides that, where a decision has not been carried out by the party concerned (usually the employer) in accordance with its terms, the time for bringing an appeal has expired and no such appeal has been brought, the other party (usually the employee) may bring the claim before a designated superior body (whether that be the Employment Appeals Tribunal, the Labour Court, the District Court or the Circuit Court) which *shall* 'without hearing the employer concerned or any evidence other than in relation to the matters aforesaid' make a decision to like effect to the original decision. These are mandatory provisions appearing to allow of no exceptions.

[22.93] In *Edwards v M & P Construction Ltd*,[171] the employee sought implementation of a rights commissioner's recommendation under the Unfair Dismissals Act 1977. The employer appeared before the Employment Appeals Tribunal and submitted that it had not received any notice from the Labour Relations Commission of the hearing and was not aware of the claim until it received a copy of the rights commissioner's recommendation. The Tribunal (chaired by Dermot MacCarthy SC) said that, although it was obliged to have regard to 'the strong words' used in s 8(4) of the 1977 Act, it was bound to act 'judicially' and to have regard to the principles of natural justice. In the Tribunal's opinion one of the 'matters aforesaid' that arose was whether the employer received notice of the Rights Commissioner hearing. The Tribunal was not satisfied, on the evidence, that the employer had received such notice and, accordingly, declined to make the order sought and, instead, treated the hearing as an appeal.

[22.94] Where an employee seeks to enforce a recommendation of a rights commissioner under the Unfair Dismissals Act 1977, the Terms of Employment (Information) Act 1994 or the Protection of Young Persons (Employment) Act 1996, the relevant provisions provide that the employee concerned may apply to the Employment Appeals Tribunal for a determination to the like effect as the recommendation.[172]

---

[169] Employment Equality Act 1998, s 99A(2) provides that expenses shall not be payable in respect of the attendance of any person representing a complainant or respondent.

[170] Employment Equality Act 1998, s 99A(3).

[171] *Edwards v M & P Construction Ltd* UD 842/2004.

[172] Unfair Dismissals Act 1977, s 8(4); s 8(6) of the 1994 Act; and s 19(6) of the 1996 Act. When hearing such an application, the Tribunal is not permitted to examine alternative remedies to that originally awarded: see *Davenport v Olympia Theatre Ltd* UD 374/1986 (reproduced in Madden and Kerr, *Unfair Dismissal: Cases and Commentary* (2nd edn, IBEC, 1996), p 21).

[22.95] The bringing of such an application should be effected by giving to the Tribunal a notice in writing containing such particulars as are prescribed in Reg 3 of the Unfair Dismissals (Claims and Appeals) Regulations 1977[173] and Reg 3 of the Terms of Employment (Information) (Appeals and Complaints) Regulations 1994[174] in respect of claims under those Acts. As no regulations have been made in respect of the 1996 Act, it is suggested that a suitably adapted notice be used in respect of claims under that Act.

[22.96] Where an employee seeks to enforce a decision of a rights commissioner under the Organisation of Working Time Act 1997, the National Minimum Wage Act 2000, the Protection of Employees (Part-Time Work) Act 2001, the Protection of Employees (Fixed Term Work) Act 2003, the relevant provisions provide that the party concerned may apply to the Labour Court for a determination to like effect as the decision.[175]

[22.97] The bringing of such an application should be effected by giving to the Labour Court a notice in writing containing such particulars (if any) as may be determined by the Labour Court. From the forms made available by the Labour Court, it would appear that the Court has determined that the following particulars are required:

  (i)   name, address and phone number of the employee;

  (ii)   name, address and phone number of the employee's representative (if any);

  (iii) name, address and phone number of employer;

  (iv)   name, address and phone number of employer's representative (if any);

  (v)   the reference number and date of the rights commissioner's decision; and

  (vi)   a brief summary of the grounds on which the complaint of non-implementation is being made.

[22.98] Section 28(8) of the 1997 Act requires that a complaint of non-implementation must be lodged at least six weeks after, but within 12 weeks of, the date on which the decision was communicated to the party.

[22.99] Where an employee seeks to enforce a decision of a rights commissioner or the EAT under the Payment of Wages Act 1991, s 8(1) of that Act provides that the decision may be enforced 'as if it were an order of the Circuit Court made in civil proceedings by the Judge of the Circuit Court for the place wherein the person in whose favour the decision or determination was made ordinarily resides'.

The enforcement of Circuit Court orders is governed in the main by Ord 36 of the Rules of the Circuit Court 2001.[176]

[22.100] Where a party seeks to enforce a decision of a rights commissioner or a determination of the Employment Appeals Tribunal under the Maternity Protection Act 1994, the Adoptive Leave Act 1995, the Parental Leave Act 1998 and the Carer's Leave Act 2001, the relevant provisions provide that the party concerned (or the Minister if he

---

[173] SI 286/1977.

[174] SI 244/1994.

[175] Unfair Dismissals Act 1977, s 28(8); s 31(1) of the 2000 Act; s 17(8) of the 2001 Act; and s 15(8) of the 2003 Act.

[176] SI 510/2001.

or she considers it appropriate) may apply to the Circuit Court for an order directing the party in default to carry out the decision or determination in accordance with its terms.[177]

[22.101] Section 22(2) of the 1998 Act and s 22 (2) of the 2001 Act, however, provide that, if the Circuit Court is satisfied that, owing to lapse of time, it would not be possible to comply with such an order, the Circuit Court shall make an order providing for 'such redress as it considers appropriate having regard to the provisions of this Act and all the circumstances'.

The Circuit Court is also empowered to award the payment of interest in respect of any compensation awarded by the commissioner or by the Tribunal.

The procedure governing such applications for enforcement is set out in Ord 57 of the Rules of the Circuit Court 2001.[178]

[22.102] Where an employee seeks to enforce a determination of the Employment Appeals Tribunal under the Terms of Employment (Information) Act 1994 or the Protection of Young Persons (Employment) Act 1996, s 9(1) of the 1994 Act and s 20(1) of the 1996 Act provide that the employee concerned (or his or her trade union or the Minister, if he or she considers it appropriate, or the young person's parent or guardian) may apply to the District Court for an order directing the employer to carry out the determination in accordance with its terms.

[22.103] The District Court is also empowered to award the payment of interest in respect of any compensation awarded by the Tribunal.

The procedure governing applications for enforcement is set out in the District Court (Terms of Employment) (Information)) Rules 2003.[179] No equivalent regulations have been promulgated for the 1996 Act, so it is suggested that a suitably adapted procedure be adopted in respect of applications under that Act.

---

[177] Maternity Protection Act 1994, s 37(3); s 39(2) of the 1995 Act; s 22(1) of the 1998 Act; and s 22(1) of the 2001 Act.

[178] SI 510/2001 as extended by the Circuit Court Rules (Carer's Leave Act 2001) 2005 (SI 387/2005). Applications should be made by way of Motion on Notice grounded upon Affidavit sworn by the party seeking enforcement, which Affidavit should exhibit:
    (a)   a certified copy of the decision or determination,
    (b)   a certified copy of the covering letter issued to the applicant,
    (c)   a copy Notice of Appeal, if applicable,
and should set out:
        all the facts relevant to the alleged failure to carry out the decision or determination,
        whether an appeal has been brought from the decision or determination and, if no such appeal has been brought, that the time for appeal has elapsed and, if such appeal has been brought, the date upon which Notice of Appeal was given and evidence of abandonment thereof.
    All such applications should be served no later than 10 days prior to the return date set out in the motion.

[179] SI 409/2003. Applications should be made by way of the prescribed Notice of Application and should be served on the respondent by prepaid registered post not later than seven days before the date of the sitting for which the application is returnable.

[22.104] Where an employee seeks to enforce a determination of the Employment Appeals Tribunal under the Unfair Dismissals Act 1977, s 11(3) of the Unfair Dismissals (Amendment) Act 1993 provides that an application can be made by the employee (or by the Minister, if he or she considers it appropriate having regard to all the circumstances) to the Circuit Court for an order directing the employer to carry out the determination in accordance with its terms. Such application cannot be made until after six weeks have elapsed from the date on which the determination was communicated to the parties.

If the determination directed the reinstatement or re-engagement of the employee concerned, s 11(3) of the 1993 Act empowers the Circuit Court, if it considers it appropriate so to do having regard to all the circumstances, to require the payment of compensation in lieu of reinstating or re-engaging the employee.

[22.105] Section 11(4) of the 1993 Act empowers the Circuit Court, if in all the circumstances it considers it appropriate so to do, to award interest on any compensation awarded (either by the Tribunal or by the Circuit Court).

The procedure governing applications for enforcement is set out in Ord 57 r 1 of the Rules of the Circuit Court 2001.[180] This rule provides that all applications for enforcement shall be made by way of Motion on Notice. Such applications must be brought in the County where the employer concerned ordinarily resides or carries on any profession, business or occupation. All applications must be served no later than 10 days prior to the return date set out in the motion. The following documents should be filed with the application:

(i)   a copy of the original notice of appeal to the Tribunal;

(ii)   a copy of the notice of appearance;

(iii)   a copy of the determination of the Tribunal;

(iv)   the original letter from the Tribunal notifying the making of communication of the said determination; and

(v)   a copy of any particulars provided by either party to the Tribunal.

Save by 'special leave' of the Circuit Court, the application will be heard upon oral evidence. The Circuit Court may make such order as to costs as may be appropriate including an order measuring costs.

[22.106] The amount of any compensation awarded by the Employment Appeals Tribunal under s 12(1) of the Minimum Notice and Terms of Employment Act 1973 is recoverable by the employee as 'a simple contract debt in a court of competent jurisdiction'. Any proceedings for the recovery of any sum due by way of compensation awarded by the Tribunal may be 'instituted and maintained on behalf of the employee' by the Minister or by the employee's trade union.[181]

[22.107] Where the EAT has made an award to an employee under the Redundancy Payments Act 1967 and the employee has taken 'all reasonable steps (other than legal proceedings)' to obtain payment, the employee may apply to the Minister for a payment

---

[180] SI 510/2001, as substituted by r 20 of the Circuit Court Rules (General) 2007 (SI 312/2007).

[181] Minimum Notice and Terms of Employment Act 1973, s 12(3).

under s 32 of the 1967 Act. This section authorises the Minister to pay the employee out of the Social Insurance Fund.

[22.108] Where an employee seeks to enforce a determination of the Labour Court under the Organisation of Working Time Act 1997, the National Minimum Wage Act 2000, the Protection of Employees (Part-Time Work) Act 2001 or the Protection of Employees (Fixed Term Work) Act 2003, the relevant provisions provide that the employee concerned (or his or her trade union or the Minister if he or she considers it appropriate) may apply to the Circuit Court for an order directing the employer to carry out the determination in accordance with its terms.[182]

[22.109] The procedure governing applications for enforcement is set out in Ord 57 of the Rules of the Circuit Court 2001.[183] The various rules provide that all applications shall be made by way of Motion on Notice. The motion should set out the grounds on which the Applicant relies for the relief sought and should have annexed thereto the original determination of the Labour Court or a certified copy of same. The motion should also state the date on which the determination of the Labour Court was communicated to the employee.

Such applications must be brought in the County where the employer concerned ordinarily resides or carries on any profession, business or occupation. All applications must be served no later than 10 days prior to the return date specified in the Notice of Motion. Save by 'special leave' of the Circuit Court, all applications must be heard upon oral evidence or as may be determined by the Court. The Circuit Court may make such order as to costs as may be appropriate including an order measuring costs.

[22.110] Where an employee seeks to enforce a 'final decision' of the Equality Tribunal or a 'final determination' of the Labour Court under Part VII of the Employment Equality Act 1998, s 91(1) of the 1998 Act provides that the employee concerned (or the Equality Authority) may apply to the Circuit Court for an order directing the employer, or any other person who is bound by the decision or determination, to carry it out in accordance with its terms.

[22.111] The Circuit Court is empowered to award the payment of interest in respect of any compensation awarded by the Equality Tribunal or by the Labour Court.

The procedure governing applications for enforcement is set out in the Circuit Court Rules (Employment Equality Act 1998) 2004.[184] All applications should be made by way of originating Notice of Motion. The motion should set out the grounds upon which the employee relies for the relief sought and must contain details of the failure by the employer (or other persons affected) to comply with the decision or determination. The

---

[182] Organisation of Working Time Act 1997, s 29(1); s 32(3) of the 2000 Act; s 18(1) of the 2001 Act; and s 16(1) of the 2003 Act. The Circuit Court also has jurisdiction under s 10 of the Industrial Relations (Amendment) Act 2001 to enforce a Labour Court determination made under s 6 of that Act. The procedure governing such applications is set out in the Circuit Court Rules (Industrial Relations Acts) 2007 (SI 12/2007) which provide that all such applications should be made by way of Motion on Notice.

[183] SI 510/2001, as substituted by rule 20 of the Circuit Court Rules (General) 2007 (SI 312/2007).

[184] SI 880/2004.

following documents should be filed: namely a certified copy of the decision and certified copies of all notices; pleadings; document; particulars or written submissions provided by either party and any other 'relevant documentation'. Any such application must be brought in the County where the employer ordinarily resides or carries on any profession, business or occupation. All applications must be served no later than 10 days prior to the return date set out in the motion. Save by 'special leave' of the Circuit Court, all applications shall be heard upon oral evidence.

APPEALS AND REFERENCES TO HIGH COURT

[22.112] Although s 17 of the Industrial Relations Act 1946 precludes an appeal to the High Court from a decision of the Labour Court under s 13(9) of the Industrial Relations Act 1969, all of the other employment legislation (with the exception of the Unfair Dismissals Acts) provides for an appeal on a point of law only to the High Court.[185] That legislation further provides that the Minister, at the request of the Employment Appeals Tribunal or the Labour Court (as the case may be), or the Employment Appeals Tribunal or the Labour Court itself may refer a question of law to the High Court.[186] In some cases the decision of the High Court is final and conclusive.[187]

---

[185] Redundancy Payments Act 1967, s 39(14); Minimum Notice and Terms of Employment Act 1973, s 11(2); Payment of Wages Act 1991, s 7(4)(b); Terms of Employment (Information) Act 1994, s 8(4)(b); Maternity Protection Act 1994, s 34(2); Adoptive Leave Act 1995, s 36(2); Protection of Young Persons (Employment) Act 1996, s 19(4)(b); Organisation of Working Time Act 1997, s 28(6); Parental Leave Act 1998, s 20(2); National Minimum Wage Act 2000, s 30(2); Carer's Leave Act 2001, s 23(2); Protection of Employees (Part-Time Work) Act 2001, s 17(6); Protection of Employees (Fixed Term Work) Act 2003, s 15(6). In equality cases, Employment Equality Act 1998, s 90(1) provides for an appeal on a point of law to the High Court from the Labour Court to the High Court but s 79(7) also provides for an appeal on a point of law in certain cases directly from decisions of the Equality Tribunal. In unfair dismissal cases Unfair Dismissals (Amendment) Act 1993, s 11(1) provides for a full appeal on both fact and law to the Circuit Court. Such appeals should be brought within six weeks from the date on which the determination is communicated to the parties. The Circuit Court has no jurisdiction to extend the time provided for appeal.: *McIlwraith v Fawsitt* [1990] 1 IR 343. It has also been decided that a further full appeal lies to the High Court: see *McCabe v Lisney & Sons* [1981] ILRM 289; *Western Health Board v Quigley* [1982] ILRM 390; and *Commissioners of Irish Lights v Sugg* [1994] ELR 97.

[186] Redundancy Payments Act 1967, s 40(1), Minimum Notice and Terms of Employment Act 1973, s 11(3), Payment of Wages Act 1991, s 7(4)(a), Terms of Employment (Information) Act 1994, s 8(4)(a) and Protection of Young Persons (Employment) Act 1996, s 19(4)(a) all empower the Minister, at the request of the Employment Appeals Tribunal, to refer a question of law to the High Court. Organisation of Working Time Act 1997, s 28(5), National Minimum Wage Act 2000, s 30(1), Protection of Employees (Part-Time Work) Act 2001, s 17(5) and Protection of Employees (Fixed Term Work) Act 2003, s 15(5) all empower the Minister, at the request of the Labour Court, to refer a question of law to the High Court. Maternity Protection Act 1994, s 34(1), Adoptive Leave Act 1995, s 36(1), Parental Leave Act 1998, s 20(1) and Carer's Leave Act 2001, s 23(1) all empower the Employment Appeals Tribunal to refer a question of law to the High Court. Employment Equality Act 1998, s 90(2), as substituted by Equality Act 2004, s 46, empowers the Labour Court to refer a point of law to the High Court.

[187] Payment of Wages Act 1991, s 7(4); (contd..../)

[22.113] In Redundancy and Minimum Notice cases the procedure is regulated by RSC 1986 Ord 105, r 1 of which provides that such appeals shall be brought by special summons. The summons should be issued within 21 days of the date on which notice of the decision of the Tribunal was given to the party appealing, provided that the time within which the summons may be issued may be extended on application *ex parte* at any time within six weeks from the date on which notice of the decision was given to the party making the appeal. Such appeals will appear in the High Court's Chancery list. RSC 1986 Order 105, r 6 specifically provides that no costs shall be allowed of any proceedings under Ord 105 'unless the Court shall by special order allow such costs'.

[22.114] In Employment Equality cases the procedure is regulated by RSC 1986 Order 106,[188] r 2 of which provides that such appeal shall be brought by originating notice of motion. That motion should be issued within 21 days of the date on which the decision or determination was given, provided that the time within which the motion may be issued may be extended on application *ex parte* or any time within six weeks from the date on which the decision or determination was given. Such appeals will appear in the High Court's Non-Jury list.

[22.115] In all other cases the procedure is regulated by RSC 1986 Ord 84C,[189] r 2 of which provides that such appeals should be brought by originating notice of motion. That motion should be issued within 21 days following the giving to the intending appellant of the decision or within such further period as the High Court may allow. The High Court, however, can only extend the time where it is satisfied 'that there is good and sufficient reason for extending the period and that the extension of the period would not result in an injustice being done'.[190] Such appeals will appear in the High Court's Non-Jury list. Any respondent intending to oppose the appeal must file and serve a statement of opposition together with a verifying affidavit *before* the return date of the notice of motion.[191] The appellant is then at liberty to file a further replying affidavit which must be served within 14 days of the service of the statement of opposition.[192] On the return date, the High Court must give such directions and make such order for the conduct of the proceedings 'as appears convenient for the determination of the proceedings in a manner which is just, expeditious and likely to minimise the costs of those proceedings'.[193]

---

[187] (\...contd) Terms of Employment (Information) Act 1994, s 8(4); Protection of Young Persons (Employment) Act 1996, s 19(4); Organisation of Working Time Act 1997, s 28(6); Protection of Employees (Part-Time Work) Act 2001, s 17(6); Protection of Employees (Fixed-Term Work) Act 2003, s 15(6). In all other cases a further appeal lies to the Supreme Court.

[188] As substituted by SI 293/2005.

[189] As inserted by SI 14/2007.

[190] RSC 1986, Ord 84C, r 2(5).

[191] RSC 1986, Ord 84C, r 5(1).

[192] RSC 1986, Ord 84C, r 5(2).

[193] RSC 1986, Ord 84C, r 7.

[22.116] In *Bates v Model Bakery Ltd*,[194] the Supreme Court set out the appropriate procedure for appealing cases under the Redundancy Payments Act 1967. The *dicta* of Finlay CJ,[195] however, are applicable to appeals under the other employment rights legislation.[196] The then Chief Justice said that the affidavit grounding the appeal should only exhibit the decision being appealed and any findings of fact or recital of evidence made by it and identifying the parties and the grounds on which the aggrieved party sought a determination on a question of law. He went on to say that there did not appear to be any room in the procedure for 'repeating and, in particular, for adding to or supplementing evidence which was given ... concerning the circumstances of the dispute'.[197]

---

[194] *Bates v Model Bakery Ltd* [1993] 1 IR 359.

[195] With whom Hederman, McCarthy and O'Flaherty JJ agreed.

[196] See Laffoy J in *B-Lex Ltd v Fields* [2008] ELR 210, 212 (a case under the Payment of Wages Act 1991).

[197] *Bates v Model Bakery Ltd* [1993] 1 IR 359, 365.

Appendices: Codes of Practice

Contents

Appendix A: Atypical Employees

Code of Practice for Determining Employment or Self-Employment Status of Individuals

This leaflet was prepared by the Employment Status Group set up under the Programme for Prosperity and Fairness. The group was set up because of a growing concern that there may be increasing numbers of individuals categorised as 'self employed' when the 'indicators' may be that 'employee' status would be more appropriate.

The leaflet has been updated in 2007 by the Hidden Economy Monitoring Group under Towards 2016 Social Partnership Agreement. The purpose of the document is to eliminate misconceptions and provide clarity. It is not meant to bring individuals who are genuinely self-employed into employment status. In most cases it will be clear whether an individual is employed or self-employed. However, it may not always be so obvious, which in turn can lead to misconceptions in relation to the employment status of individuals.

The criteria below should help in reaching a conclusion. It is important that the job as a whole is looked at, including working conditions and the reality of the relationship, when considering the guidelines. The overriding consideration or test will always be whether the person performing the work does so 'as a person in business on their own account.' Is the person a free agent with an economic independence of the person engaging the service? This economic test is paramount.

The Safety, Health and Welfare at Work Act, 2005 is the cornerstone of health and safety regulation in Ireland. Employers and Employees all have duties under the act. The legislation treats self-employed persons in a similar manner to employers. It places on them an onus to manage, plan and conduct all work activities to ensure the health and safety of all persons at a workplace. Generally speaking self-employed persons and contractors have a greater responsibility to manage health and safety issues than employees. However, regardless of a person's status, health and safety management and practice is essential in all work operations. More information is available from www.hsa.ie

Criteria on whether an individual is an employee

While all of the following factors may not apply, an individual would normally be an employee if he or she:

- Is under the control of another person who directs as to how, when and where the work is to be carried out.
- Supplies labour only.
- Receives a fixed hourly/weekly/monthly wage.

873

- Cannot sub-contract the work. If the work can be subcontracted and paid on by the person subcontracting the work, the employer/employee relationship may simply be transferred on.
- Does not supply materials for the job.
- Does not provide equipment other than the small tools of the trade. The provision of tools or equipment might not have a significant bearing on coming to a conclusion that employment status may be appropriate having regard to all the circumstances of a particular case.
- Is not exposed to personal financial risk in carrying out the work.
- Does not assume any responsibility for investment and management in the business.
- Does not have the opportunity to profit from sound management in the scheduling of engagements or in the performance of tasks arising from the engagements.
- Works set hours or a given number of hours per week or month.
- Works for one person or for one business.
- Receives expense payments to cover subsistence and/or travel expenses.
- Is entitled to extra pay or time off for overtime.

Additional factors to be considered:

- An individual could have considerable freedom and independence in carrying out work and still remain an employee.
- An employee with specialist knowledge may not be directed as to how the work is carried out.
- An individual who is paid by commission, by share, or by piecework, or in some other atypical fashion may still be regarded as an employee.
- Some employees work for more than one employer at the same time. Some employees do not work on the employer's premises.
- There are special PRSI rules for the employment of family members.
- Statements in contracts considered by the Supreme Court in the **'Denny'** case, such as 'You are deemed to be an independent contractor', 'It shall be your duty to pay and discharge such taxes and charges as may be payable out of such fees to the Revenue Commissioners or otherwise', 'It is agreed that the provisions of the Unfair Dismissals Act 1977 shall not apply etc', 'You will not be an employee of this company', 'You will be responsible for your own tax affairs' are not contractual terms and have little or no contractual validity. While they may express an opinion ofthe contacting parties, they are of minimal value in coming to a conclusion as to the work status of the person engaged.

Criteria on whether an individual is self-employed

While all of the following factors may not apply to the job, an individual would normally be self-employed if he or she:

- Owns his or her own business.

- Is exposed to financial risk, by having to bear the cost of making good faulty or substandard work carried out under the contract.
- Assumes responsibility for investment and management in the enterprise.
- Has the opportunity to profit from sound management in the scheduling and performance of engagements and tasks.
- Has control over what is done, how it is done, when and where it is done and whether he or she does it personally.
- Is free to hire other people, on his or her terms, to do the work which has been agreed to be undertaken.
- Can provide the same services to more than one person or business at the same time.
- Provides the materials for the job.
- Provides equipment and machinery necessary for the job, other than the small tools of the trade or equipment which in an overall context would not be an indicator of a person in business on their own account.
- Has a fixed place of business where materials equipment etc. can be stored.
- Costs and agrees a price for the job.
- Provides his or her own insurance cover e.g. public liability cover, etc.
- Controls the hours of work in fulfilling the job obligations.

Additional factors to be considered:

- Generally an individual should satisfy the self-employed guidelines above, otherwise he or she will normally be an employee.
- The fact that an individual has registered for self-assessment or VAT under the principles of self-assessment does not automatically mean that he or she is self-employed.
- An office holder, such as a company director, will be taxed under the PAYE system. However, the terms and conditions may have to be examined by the Scope Section of Department of Social and Family Affairs to decide on the appropriate PRSI Class.
- It should be noted that a person who is a self-employed contractor in one job is not necessarily self-employed in the next job. It is also possible to be employed and self-employed at the same time in different jobs.
- In the construction sector, for health and safety reasons, all individuals are under the direction of the site foreman/overseer. The self-employed individual controls the method to be employed in carrying out the work.

Consequences arising from the determination of an individual's status

The status as an employee or self-employed person will affect:

- The way in which tax and PRSI is payable to the Collector-General.
- An employee will have tax and PRSI deducted from his or her income.
- A self-employed person is obliged to pay preliminary tax and file income tax returns whether or not he or she is asked for them.

- Entitlement to a number of social welfare benefits, such as unemployment and disability benefits.
- An employee will be entitled to unemployment, disability and invalidity benefits, whereas a self-employed person will not have these entitlements.
- Other rights and entitlements, for example, under Employment Legislation.
- An employee will have rights in respect of working time, holidays, maternity / parental leave, protection from unfair dismissal etc.
- A self-employed person will not have these rights and protection.
- Public liability in respect of the work done.

Deciding status – getting assistance

Where there are difficulties in deciding the appropriate status of an individual or groups of individuals, the following organisations can provide assistance.

Tax and PRSI

- The Local Revenue Office or the Local Social Welfare Office.
- Scope Section in the Department of Social and Family Affairs.

For further details see [contact details at end of Code.]

If there is still doubt as to whether a person is employed or self-employed the Local Revenue Office or Scope Section of Department of Social and Family Affairs should be contacted for assistance. Having established all of the relevant facts, a written decision as to status will be issued. A decision by one Department will generally be accepted by the other, provided all relevant facts were given at the time and the circumstances remain the same and it is accepted that the correct legal principles have been applied to the facts established. However, because of the varied nature of circumstances that arise and the different statutory provisions, such a consensus may not be possible in every case.

The National Employment Rights Authority

The National Employment Rights Authority (NERA) was established on an interim basis in February 2007 in accordance with the commitment under Towards 2016, the Social Partnership Agreement for 2006–2015. Three units dealing with employment rights, which were formerly part of the Department of Enterprise, Trade and Employment have been subsumed into NERA: The Employment Rights Information Unit, the Labour Inspectorate and the Prosecution and Enforcement Unit. NERA's key objective is to achieve compliance with employment rights legislation. This will be achieved through provision of information, carrying out inspections and enforcement and prosecutions when necessary.

Relevant Contracts Tax – Form RCT 1

Relevant Contracts Tax (RCT) applies where a Subcontractor enters into a contract with a Principal Contractor (Principal) to carry out relevant operations (construction, forestry or meat processing operations). The Principal and Subcontractor must jointly complete Form RCT 1, declaring that the contract is a Relevant Contract (and not a contract of employment). Form RCT 1 has been revised to require further information from both Principal and Subcontractor as to why a proposed contract is considered to be a Relevant

Contract. An incorrect designation of the contract as a Relevant Contract will have consequences for both the Principal and the Subcontractor.

Further information is available from www.revenue.ie.

Employment which is not insurable

The 2003 and 2006 Employment Permits Acts provide for a large number of employer obligations and offences which include specifically the employment of non-EEA (non-European Economic Area) nationals except in accordance with an employment permit, where required. In this regard, a contract of employment between such a migrant worker and an employer which is not covered by a valid employment permit is an illegal contract and that employment is not consequently insurable under the Social Welfare Consolidation Act, 2005. Further information regarding Employment Permits legislation is available at www.entemp.ie/labour/workpermits or by calling LoCall 1890 201 606.

Useful contacts for information and leaflets:

The **Report of the Employment Status Group** is available for viewing on the websites of:

- Revenue Commissioners
- Department of Social & Family Affairs
- Department of Enterprise, Trade & Employment
- Irish Congress of Trade Unions
- Irish Business and Employers Confederation

Revenue Commissioners

See pages [of Code[1]] for list of Local Revenue Offices.

Department of Social and Family Affairs

Scope Section,
Department of Social and Family Affairs,
Oisin House,
Pearse Street,
Dublin 2.
(or any Social Welfare Local Office)

Phone No. (01) 673-2585
Email: scope@welfare.ie
Website: www.welfare.ie

Department of Enterprise, Trade and Employment

Davitt House,
65A Adelaide Rd,
Dublin 2.

---

[1] See www.revenue.ie for contact details.

LoCall 1890 220 222
Phone No. (01) 631-3131
Website: www.entemp.ie

National Employment Rights Authority (NERA)

Employment Rights Information Unit,
O'Brien Road,
Carlow.

LoCall 1890 808 090
Phone No. (059) 917-8990
E-mail: info@employmentrights.ie
Website: www.employmentrights.ie

Irish Congress of Trade Unions

31–32 Parnell Square,
Dublin 1.

Phone No. (01) 889-7777
Website: www.ictu.ie

Irish Business and Employers Confederation

Confederation House,
84/86 Lower Baggot Street,
Dublin 2.

Phone No. (01) 605-1500
Website: www.ibec.ie

Employment Appeals Tribunal

Davitt House,
65A Adelaide Road,
Dublin 2.

LoCall 1890 220 222
Phone No. (01) 631-3006/9
Website: www.eatribunal.ie

Health & Safety Authority

The Metropolitan Building,
James Joyce Street,
Dublin 1.

Locall 1890 289 389
Website: www.hsa.ie

Labour Court

Tom Johnson House,
Haddington Road,
Dublin 4.

LoCall 1890 220 228
Phone No. (01) 613-6666
Website www.labourcourt.ie

Labour Relations Commission & Rights Commissioners

Tom Johnson House,
Haddington Road,
Dublin 4.

LoCall 1890 220 227
Phone No. (01) 631-6700
Website www.lrc.ie

Construction Industry Federation

Construction House,
Canal Road,
Dublin 6.

Phone No. (01) 406-6000
Website www.cif.ie

Small Firms Association

Confederation House,
84-86 Lower Baggot Street,
Dublin 2.

Phone No. (01) 605-1668
Website: www.sfa.ie

Local Revenue Offices

[Code lists Revenue office contact details[2]]

Customers living in and businesses managed and controlled in the following
Updated December 2007
This leaflet has been compiled with the assistance of:

Department of Enterprise, Trade and Employment, National Employment Rights Authority, Department of Social and Family Affairs, Department of Finance, Irish Congress of Trade Unions, Irish Business and Employers Confederation, Small Firms Association, the Construction Industry Federation and Revenue Commissioners.

---

[2] See www.revenue.ie for contact details.

Industrial Relations Act 1990 (Code of Practice for Protecting Persons Employed in Other People's Homes) (Declaration) Order 2007

(SI 239/2007)[3]

WHEREAS the Labour Relations Commission has prepared under subsection (1) of section 42 of the Industrial Relations Act 1990 (No. 19 of 1990), a draft code of practice for protecting persons employed in other people's homes;

AND WHEREAS the Labour Relations Commission has complied with subsection (2) of that section and has submitted the draft code of practice to the Minister for Enterprise, Trade and Employment;

NOW THEREFORE I, Tony Killeen, Minister of State at the Department of Enterprise, Trade and Employment, in exercise of the powers conferred on me by subsection (3) of that section, the Labour (Transfer of Departmental Administration and Ministerial Functions) Order 1993 (S.I. No. 18 of 1993) (as adapted by the Enterprise and Employment (Alteration of Name of Department and Title of Minister) Order 1997 (S.I. No. 305 of 1997)), and the Enterprise, Trade and Employment (Delegation of Ministerial Functions) Order 2004 (S.I. No. 809 of 2004), hereby order as follows—

1. This Order may be cited as the Industrial Relations Act 1990 (Code of Practice for Protecting Persons Employed in Other People's Homes) (Declaration) Order 2007.

2. It is declared that the code of practice set out in the Schedule shall be a code of practice for the purposes of the Industrial Relations Act 1990 (No. 19 of 1990).

SCHEDULE
CODE OF PRACTICE FOR PROTECTING PERSONS EMPLOYED IN OTHER PEOPLE'S HOMES

1. Introduction

1.1 Section 42 of the Industrial Relations Act 1990 provides for the preparation of draft codes of practice by the Labour Relations Commission for submission to the Minister for Enterprise, Trade and Employment.

1.2 It was agreed in Section 23.2 of Part 2 of 'Towards 2016 — Ten Year Framework Social Partnership Agreement 2006 — 2015' that the Labour Relations Commission should be asked to develop a code of practice to set out the current employment rights and protections for persons employed in other people's homes and provide for—

- The obligation to provide a written statement of terms and conditions of employment as required under the Terms of Employment (Information) Acts 1994 and 2001, detailing hours, rates, duties, breaks/leave entitlements, treatment of travel time etc;

---

[3] Copyright Houses of the Oireachtas 2007.

- Provisions as regards the safeguarding of privacy;
- The employer will not keep any personal document belonging to an employee;
- The treatment of accommodation and making of any deductions;
- All additional duties will be by prior agreement only and out-of pocket expenses will be reimbursed promptly;
- The employer will facilitate the employee in the free exercise of personal pursuits; and
- The employer will not restrict the employee's right to trade union membership.

1.3 In preparing this code of practice, the Labour Relations Commission consulted with the representatives of the Social Partners, namely ICTU and IBEC, and, to the maximum extent possible, took account of their views.

2. Definition of 'employee'

In this code of practice, an 'employee' means a person who is employed in the home of another person, in accordance with the provisions of the Code of Practice for Determining Employment or Self-Employment Status of Individuals.

3. Purposes of the Code

The code seeks to:

- Set out certain employment rights and protections for persons employed in other people's homes; and
- Encourage good practice and compliance with the law concerning the employment of persons in other people's homes; and
- Increase awareness of the application of relevant legislation and codes of practice with regard to the sector to which this code applies.

4. General Principles

This code operates in accordance with the following principles:

- This code is applicable to all employees in other people's homes and to the employers of those employees;
- Employees in other people's homes have an equal entitlement to the employment rights and protections available to any other employee. Employers of those employees are entitled to all available statutory exemptions. (For example, section 3(2)(b) of the Organisation of Working Time Act 1997 excludes from the provisions of Part 2 of that Act, a person who is 'employed by a relative and is a member of that relative's household, and whose place of employment is a private dwelling house or a farm in or on which he or she and the relative reside'.); and
- This code encourages anti-discrimination practices by the employer and encourages employers to respect employees' entitlements under the Employment Equality Acts 1998 and 2004 and the Equal Status Acts 2000–2004.

5. Provisions of Code

5.1 The employer shall supply to the employee a written statement of terms and conditions of employment, as required under the Terms of Employment (Information) Acts 1994–2001, setting out clearly the following—

— Hours of work

— Rates of pay

— List of duties

— Periods of annual leave

— Place or places of work

— Commencement date

Details of rest breaks should be included in the written statement of terms and conditions of employment.

Notes

1. Rest breaks shall be given in accordance with the Organisation of Working Time Act 1997.
2. Hours of work shall be recorded in accordance with the Organisation of Working Time Act (Records) (Prescribed Form and Exemptions) Regulations 2001 (S.I. 473 of 2001).

5.2.1 The employer shall respect the dignity and privacy of the employee and shall take all steps necessary to safeguard the dignity and privacy of the employee working in the home. Where an employer intends to conduct surveillance of the workplace in the home, a statement to this effect must be included in the statement of terms and conditions of employment specified at point 5.1 above. Searches of the employee's personal belongings may only be conducted where such permission to search is provided for in the written statement of terms and conditions of employment. Such searches shall be exceptional and conducted in the employee's presence. The permission to search in accordance with the written statement of terms and conditions of employment does not extend to reading the employee's personal mail or listening in on personal phone calls.

5.2.2 In the event that the employee lives in the home, the employer shall provide a private secure room with a bed. If employees are required to share a bedroom with fellow employees, this should be clearly agreed in advance.

5.3 The employer will require the employee to carry out the duties specified in the written statement of terms and conditions of employment. Additional duties will only be carried out following clear agreement between the employer and employee, or as already provided for in the written statement of terms and conditions of employment.

5.4 Details regarding the place or places of work and travel to the place or places of work (e.g. to a holiday home of the employer, or in accompanying the employers family on holiday elsewhere, etc.) shall be included in the written statement of terms and conditions of employment. Where an employee accompanies an employer or members of the employers' family on holiday, working time will be calculated in accordance with the Organisation of Working Time Act 1997 and, in those circumstances, time worked and rest breaks/days taken in accordance with that Act shall not be treated as annual leave.

5.5 The employer shall supply to the employee detailed pay slips which set out—

— Payment intervals (weekly, fortnightly or monthly).

— Rate of pay per hour.

— Details of any overtime payments to be paid.

— Details of all PRSI/PAYE deductions.

— Details of any other deductions from pay (which will be made by prior agreement only and in accordance with the Payment of Wages Act 1991).

5.6 Employers should recognise that accidental breakages or damage will happen. Any deductions from the employee's wages shall only be made in accordance with the Payment of Wages Act 1991.

5.7 The employer may make deductions from wages where the employee is provided with meals and/or lives in the place of employment to amounts specified in the National Minimum Wage Act 2000, which are subject to amendment and currently are of the following amounts—

— Full board and lodging — €54.13 per week or €7.73 per day.

— Full board only — €32.14 per week or €4.60 per day.

— Lodgings only — €21.85 per week or €3.14 per day.

5.8 The employer shall not withhold any personal documentation belonging to the employee (e.g. passport, visa, identity cards, bank account documentation, etc). For the avoidance of doubt, the employer can retain copies of these documents where such copies are required to ensure compliance with other legislation.

5.9 The employer shall ensure that the employee is promptly reimbursed for all reasonable out-of-pocket expenses incurred during the course of his or her employment (e.g. travel fares, entrance charges, etc.) in connection with his or her employment.

5.10 The employer shall facilitate the employee in the free exercise of personal pursuits outside of the employee's working time as specified in the written statement of terms and conditions of employment.

5.11 The employer shall take all reasonable steps to ensure that the employee is aware of his or her statutory entitlements as an employee.

5.12 In accordance with Irish law, the employer shall not restrict the employee's right to trade union membership consistent with the employee's Constitutional right to join or not to join a trade union.

5.13 Both the employer and the employee will mutually respect each other and the employer will take all reasonable efforts to ensure that the employee's dignity in the workplace is respected and protected.

5.14 Both the employer and the employee should establish, where required by law, that relevant employment permits are held.

6. Further Information and Advice

6.1 For further information and advice on any aspect of this document please contact:

The Labour Relations Commission
Tom Johnson House, Haddington Road, Dublin 4
Tel: (01) 613 6700 Fax: (01) 613 6701
Web: www.lrc.ie
or
The Director of the National Employment Rights Authority
Davitt House, Adelaide Road, Dublin 2
Tel: (01) 631 3131 Fax: (01) 631 3329
Web: www.entemp.ie

6.2 For further information on the Employment Permits Acts 2003 and 2006 please contact:

Work Permits Section,
Department of Enterprise, Trade and Employment,
Davitt House, Adelaide Road, Dublin 2.
Tel: (01) 631 3333/631 3308 Fax: (01) 631 3268
Web: www.entemp.ie

6.3 For further information on the Employment Equality Acts 1998 and 2004 and the Equal Status Acts 2000–2004 please contact:

The Equality Authority,
2 Clonmel Street, Dublin 2.
Tel: (01) 417 3333 Lo Call: 1890 245 545
Web: www.equality.ie

Note: All legislation, both Acts and Statutory Instruments, cited in this Code of Practice are available from www.irishstatutebook.ie or www.entemp.ie

GIVEN under my hand, 18 May 2007

TONY KILLEEN
Minister of State at the Department of Enterprise, Trade and Employment.

EXPLANATORY NOTE

(This note is not part of the Instrument and does not purport to be a legal interpretation.)

The effect of this Order is to declare that the code of practice set out in the Schedule to this Order is a code of practice for the purposes of the Industrial Relations Act, 1990.

Appendix B: Working Time

Organisation of Working Time (Code of Practice on Compensatory Rest and Related Matters) (Declaration) Order 1998

(SI 44/1998)

WHEREAS the Labour Relations Commission may, by virtue of section 35 (2) of the Organisation of Working Time Act, 1997 (No. 20 of 1997), prepare a code of practice for the purposes of one or more sections of that Act (other than section 6(2)),

AND WHEREAS the Labour Relations Commission is required, by virtue of section 35(3) of the said Act, after consultation with the National Authority for Occupational Safety and Health, to prepare a code of practice for the purposes of section 6(2) of that Act,

AND WHEREAS the Labour Relations Commission, having consulted with the National Authority for Occupational Safety and Health and having complied with section 35(4) of the said Act, has prepared a code of practice for the purposes aforesaid and submitted a copy of it to the Minister for Labour, Trade and Consumer Affairs (being the Minister of State to whom functions in this matter have been delegated by the Order hereafter recited),

AND WHEREAS the Minister for Labour, Trade and Consumer Affairs may, by virtue of section 35(5)(b) of the said Act, make such modifications to a code of practice so submitted to him and declare, by order, the code as so modified to be a code of practice for the purposes of the section or sections concerned of that Act,

AND WHEREAS the Minister for Labour, Trade and Consumer Affairs has, by virtue of the said provision, made modifications that he considers appropriate to the code of practice so submitted to him for the purposes of declaring, pursuant to that provision, the code to be a code of practice for the purposes of the sections concerned of the said Act,

NOW, I Tom Kitt, Minister for Labour, Trade and Consumer Affairs, in exercise of the powers conferred on me by section 35(5)(b) of the Organisation of Working Time Act, 1997 (No. 20 of 1997), as adapted by the Enterprise and Employment (Alteration of Name of Department and Title of Minister) Order, 1997 (S.I. No. 305 of 1997), and the Enterprise, Trade and Employment (Delegation of Ministerial Functions) (No. 2) Order, 1997 (S.I. No. 330 of 1997), hereby order as follows:

1 Citation

This Order may be cited as the Organisation of Working Time (Code of Practice on Compensatory Rest and Related Matters) (Declaration) Order, 1998.

2 Code of Practice

The code of practice set out in the Schedule to this Order is hereby declared to be a code of practice for the purposes of section 6 of the Organisation of Working Time Act, 1997

(No. 20 of 1997), so much of the other provisions of Part I of that Act as relate to that section and so much of Parts II and IV of that Act as relate to that section.

SCHEDULE
ORGANISATION OF WORKING TIME ACT, 1997

CODE OF PRACTICE ON COMPENSATORY REST PERIODS AND RELATED MATTERS

Department of Enterprise, Trade and Employment, Dublin 2.

An Order (S.I. No. 44 of 1998) declaring this code to be a Code of Practice for the purposes of section 6 of the Organisation of Working Time Act, 1997 was made by Tom Kitt, Minister for Labour, Trade and Consumer Affairs on 24/2/1998.

Note: This Code of Practice is not a legal interpretation of the Act

1. LABOUR RELATIONS COMMISSION

1. The Labour Relations Commission has prepared this Code of Practice On Compensatory Rest in accordance with the provisions of section 35 of the Organisation of Working Time Act, 1997. When preparing the Code of Practice the Commission held meetings and consultations with the Irish Business and Employers Confederation, the Irish Congress of Trade Unions, the Labour Court, the Department of Enterprise, Trade and Employment and the Irish Co-Operative Organisation Society.

2. In accordance with section 35(3) of the Act the Commission has also consulted the National Authority of Occupational Safety and Health in the preparation of this Code.

3. The Commission has taken account of the views expressed by these organisations to the fullest extent possible in preparing this Code.

4. The Code is designed to assist employers, employees and their representatives in observing the 1997 Act generally as regards compensatory rest. It gives guidance, in particular, on arrangements that may be put in place to comply with the compensatory rest provisions which apply where, because of exemptions or collective agreements or emergencies or unforeseeable circumstances, employees cannot avail themselves of the rest or break periods provided for in sections 11, 12 or 13 of the Act.

5. While failure on the part of any person to observe the Code will not, in itself, render that person liable to civil or criminal proceedings, the Code shall be admissible in evidence before a Court, the Labour Court or a Rights Commissioner in proceedings under the Organisation of Working Time Act, 1997.

2. INTRODUCTION

NOTE

This section of the Code gives a general description of some of the provisions of the Organisation of Working Time Act, 1997 and is not a legal interpretation.

The Organisation of Working Time Act, 1997

1. The terms of the EU Directive on Working Time, (Council Directive 93/104/EC of 23 November, 1993), have been transposed into Irish law by means of the Organisation of Working Time Act, 1997 and Regulations made under the Safety, Health and Welfare at Work Act, 1989.

2. The Organisation of Working Time Act, 1997 became law on 7 May 1997. Section 35 of that Act provides for a Code of Practice that provides practical guidance as to the steps that may be taken for the purposes of complying with any section of the Act. The Commencement Order bringing the Act into operation, on a phased basis, was signed on 24 September 1997. Under the Commencement Order, section 35 of the Act, *inter alia*, came into operation on 30 September 1997. The provisions on rest and working hours are effective from 1 March 1998.

3. The Minister for Labour, Trade and Consumer Affairs, under section 35 of the 1997 Act, asked the Labour Relations Commission to prepare a Code of Practice for the purposes of section 6 of the Act. As section 35(3) of the Act provides that the Commission, after consultation with the National Authority for Occupational Safety and Health, shall prepare a Code of Practice for the purposes of section 6(2), this Code is prepared under section 35(2) for the purposes of section 6(1) and under section 35(3) for the purposes of section 6(2). Under the Commencement Order section 6 of the Act came into operation on 30 September, 1997.

4. The Organisation of Working Time Act, 1997, sets out statutory rights for employees in respect of rest, maximum working time and holidays. In summary, the key provisions of the Act on minimum rest and maximum working time are as follows:

- maximum average net weekly working time of 48 hours;
- a daily rest break of 11 consecutive hours;
- rest breaks while at work;
- a weekly rest break of 24 consecutive hours;
- maximum average night working of 8 hours;
- maximum hours of work for night workers engaged in work involving special hazards or a heavy physical or mental strain — an absolute limit of 8 hours in a 24 hour period.

5. The 48 hour working week comes into effect, generally, on 1 March, 1998. However, the Act contains transitional provisions. These provide that employees may work up to 60 hours per week from 1 March, 1998 to 28 February, 1999 and up to 55 hours per week from 1 March, 1999 to 29 February, 2000. The 48 hour week comes into effect in respect of all employees covered by the Act on 1 March, 2000. To work the maximum permitted hours during 1998 and 1999 an agreement must be reached between the parties which is approved of by the Labour Court. The Fifth Schedule to the Act details the procedures to be observed in implementing the transitional provisions (see also Guide to the Labour Court's Functions and Procedures for the purposes of the Act).

6. The specific provisions of the Act relating to rest times may be varied in certain circumstances —

- by Regulations,
- through legally binding collective agreements made under the Act and approved by the Labour Court,
- through registered employment agreements,
- through employment regulation orders, or
- as otherwise provided under the Act (e.g. emergencies, unforeseeable circumstances, certain shift changes, split shifts).

7. The circumstances in which the rest times and averaging periods for weekly working hours may be varied are as follows:—

   (I) SECTION 6(1) OF THE ACT PROVIDES FOR CIRCUMSTANCES:

- Where Regulations* exempt certain activities from the rest breaks, daily and weekly rest periods set out in sections 11, 12 and 13 of the 1997 Act.

* *See Annex to this Code — General Exemption Regulations (* S.I. No. 21 of 1998)

- Where collective agreements providing for a similar exemption have been concluded by the parties and approved by the Labour Court. (Registered Employment Agreements and Employment Regulation Orders may also provide for the variation of rest periods, but not of working time provisions.)

In every case at (I) above where statutory rest times are varied the employer concerned must ensure that equivalent compensatory rest is made available to the employee.

  (II) SECTION 6(2) OF THE ACT PROVIDES FOR CIRCUMSTANCES:

- Where shift workers who change shift and cannot avail themselves of the rest period are exempted (in respect of the daily and weekly rest periods).

- Where persons employed in activities consisting of periods of work spread out over the day are exempted (in respect of the daily and weekly rest periods).

- Where employers are exempted from the obligation to provide daily and weekly rest periods and rest breaks as provided for in sections 11, 12 and 13 of the Act due to exceptional circumstances or an emergency, including an accident or the imminent risk of an accident, or otherwise the occurrence of unusual and unforeseeable circumstances beyond the employer's control.

- Where statutory rest times are varied in any of the circumstances mentioned at (II) above the employer must ensure that the employee has available to himself or herself

    (i)   equivalent compensatory rest or

    (ii)   where this is not possible for objective reasons, appropriate protection.

Note

While circumstances relating to shift changeover come within the scope of the exemption included in the legislation, shift working is subject to the provisions in the Act providing for rest and maximum working time.

3. GENERAL PRINCIPLES OF AND ARRANGEMENTS FOR EQUIVALENT COMPENSATORY REST AND APPROPRIATE PROTECTION

General

1. Appropriate rest breaks from work are vital to the health and safety of workers and are of importance in the efficient and effective operation of the workplace. While the Organisation of Working Time Act, 1997 specifies minimum rest breaks employers may provide longer breaks.

Compensatory Rest Timescale (Section 6(1) and 6(2) of the Act)

2. Exempted employees who miss out on their statutory rest entitlements should receive equivalent compensatory rest as soon as possible after the statutory rest has been missed out on. It is most important for employers to make rest time available to employees to allow them to recuperate from long periods of work without adequate rest. The Organisation of Working Time Act, 1997 and the EU Directive on Working Time do not specify any timeframes within which compensatory rest must be made available. However, when determining when compensatory rest is to be given, an employer should always have regard to the circumstances pertaining in the individual place of employment and to the health and safety requirements for adequate rest. In this context, it is important that the compensatory rest for rest breaks at work and for daily rest breaks, in particular, be provided as soon as possible and, generally, in an adjacent time frame.

3. While it is not possible to provide extensive examples of the various situations that may arise in the many diverse employments, the following four examples may typify some work situations which may give rise to a need to grant compensatory rest.

Example 1

An exempted employee works Monday to Friday 9a.m. to 5.30p.m. He/she works in an industry which cannot be interrupted on technical grounds (an exempted activity). For 2 weeks per month that employee is 'on call' for maintenance work. On Wednesday night he/she is called out to perform emergency repair work. The call out commences at 8.30p.m. and finishes at 11.30p.m. The employee's entitlement to 11 hours consecutive rest is interrupted. Prior to the call out the employee had received 3 hours rest and after the call out he/she received 9.5 hours rest. In total the employee received 12.5 hours rest, therefore no further entitlement to rest arises as an exemption applies (see sections 2(7)(I) and 2(7)(II) of this Code).

If no exemption applied then the employee is entitled to the full 11 consecutive hours rest from the end of the call out.

*   *See Annex to this Code — General Exemptions Regulations (S.I. No. 21 of 1998)*

Example 2

Under an exemption provided for in a collective agreement approved of by the Labour Court an employee is permitted to work 14 consecutive 8 hour days. In those circumstances the employee, in respect of that period, has a minimum entitlement of 2 periods of 24 hours compensatory rest plus 2 periods of 11 consecutive hours daily rest. The employee is given 3 consecutive periods of 24 hours off immediately after the 14 consecutive working days. This goes beyond the requirement to give 2 periods of 24 hours compensatory rest preceded by the relevant daily rest requirement and is, therefore, acceptable.

Example 3

An employee is entitled to a break of at least 15 minutes after working for 4½ hours. If an exemption applies the taking of the break may be delayed but compensatory rest should be provided. In this circumstance the employee is given a later break of 15 minutes or breaks totalling 15 minutes by way of compensatory rest before the end of the day. No further compensatory rest is required.

Example 4

An exempted employee works a three cycle rotating shift pattern:

Week 1	8a.m.–4p.m.
Week 2	4p.m.–12a.m.
Week 3	12a.m.– 8a.m.

In a 5 over 7 day roster no changeover provides for less than 48 hours rest. Therefore, no entitlement to compensatory rest arises. In a 6 over 7 day roster, however, the changeover between week 2 and week 3 provides only for 24 hours rest. In this circumstance, the exempted employee is entitled to compensatory rest of 11 Consecutive hours.

General Comments on Compensatory Rest

The 11 consecutive hour interval between shifts is required for reasons of health and safety to ensure that employees have a minimum period of sleep. From a health and safety point of view, it is dangerous for employees to miss out on a minimum number of hours sleep and then report for work. Therefore, when any variation of the 11 consecutive hours statutory rest is permitted under the Act. the employer should ensure that the health and safely requirements for adequate compensatory rest are sufficient in the circumstances pertaining in that employment. This is equally applicable to the weekly rest provision. Consideration should also be given to such issues as distance from home and employment in order to ensure that adequate rest is obtained.

NOTE

Typically in industry call-out arrangements provide for 8 hours consecutive rest before returning to work. Such arrangements will, where an exemption is applicable, continue to be acceptable provided that the compensatory rest requirements are fulfilled.

Where variation of the weekly statutory rest periods is permitted under the 1997 Act the employer concerned should have regard to the circumstances pertaining in that employment and to the health and safety requirements for adequate rest for his/her employees.

Appropriate Protection

4. If for reasons that can be objectively justified, it is not possible for all employer to ensure that an employee has available to himself or herself the equivalent rest period or break set out in section 6(2) of the 1997 Act, the employer must make such arrangements as respects the employee's conditions of employment as will compensate the employee.

While neither 'arrangements as respects the employee's conditions of employment as will compensate the employee' nor 'appropriate protection' are defined in, respectively, the Act and the Directive the Act specifies that these concepts do not include:

   (i)   the granting of monetary compensation to the employee or

   (ii) the provision of any other material benefit to the employee, other than the provision of such a benefit as will improve the physical conditions under which the employee works or the amenities or services available to the employee while he or she is at work.

A common sense approach should be adopted by employers and employees in such situations which takes account of the circumstances existing in the employment and has regard to the safety, health and well being of employees. It would be desirable that employers and employees and/or their representatives agree appropriate protection measures as respects an employee's conditions of employment.

While it is not feasible to define such appropriate protection/conditions of employment measures, the concept might include measures which provide for, in addition to normal health and safety requirements:

   (i)   enhanced environmental conditions to accommodate regular long periods of attendance at work;

   (ii)   refreshment facilities, recreational and reading material;

   (iii) appropriate facilities/amenities such as television, radio and music;

   (iv)   alleviating monotonous work or isolation;

   (v)   transport to and from work where appropriate.

NOTE

The measures listed are not exhaustive and are for illustrative purposes only. Employers should consider other measures which might be more relevant to their circumstances.

4. COMPLAINTS PROCEDURE

1. The Organisation of Working Time Act, 1997 sets out a complaints procedure for dealing with the various complaints that may arise under the Act. While the procedure deals with general complaints concerning various entitlements, for the purposes of this Code the procedure concerns itself with complaints about the working hours, rest periods, compensatory rest and appropriate protection issues. For example, an employee may complain that he or she had not received an equivalent rest period or that he or she is not satisfied with the compensatory (or appropriate protection) arrangements provided.

Who can make a complaint?

2. An employee or any trade union of which the employee is a member, with the consent of the employee, may present a complaint. The Minister for Labour, Trade and Consumer Affairs may also present a complaint if it is apparent that an employer is not complying with a provision and where the employee/trade union has not done so and the Minister is of the opinion that the circumstances are such as to make it unreasonable to expect the employee/trade union to present such a complaint.

How is a complaint presented and processed?

3. Complaints arising under section 6 of the 1997 Act should be presented in the first instance to a Rights Commissioner. A complaint must be made within six months of the date of the alleged contravention by the employer. However, a complaint which is presented not later than twelve months after the six months time limit may be investigated if the Rights Commissioner is satisfied that the delay was due to reasonable cause. A complaint should be in writing and should contain the requisite particulars.

4. The Rights Commissioner must give the employer a copy of the complaint. The Rights Commissioner must hear the parties and allow relevant evidence to be presented. The investigation of a complaint will be held in private. The Rights Commissioner must furnish the Labour Court with a copy of each decision given under the 1997 Act.

5. The Rights Commissioner in making a decision shall do one or more of the following:

(a) declare that the complaint was, or, as the case may be, was not well founded,

(b) require the employer to comply with the relevant provisions,

(c) require the employer to pay compensation of such amount (if any) as is just and equitable having regard to all the circumstances, up to a maximum of two years' remuneration.

NOTE

Queries relating to complaints and procedures should be forwarded in writing to the Rights Commissioner Service, Labour Relations Commission, Tom Johnson House, Haddington Road, Dublin 4 – telephone (01) 6609662.

---

5. APPEALS

1. Either party may appeal a decision of a Rights Commissioner to the Labour Court. The appeal must be made within 6 weeks of the date on which the decision was communicated to the party. The notice of appeal should be submitted to the Labour Court on the relevant form, which is available from the Court.

2. The Labour Court must give a copy of the notice of appeal to the other party. The Labour Court shall give the parties an opportunity to be heard and to present relevant evidence to it. It will make a determination in writing affirming, varying or setting aside the decision. The Court must communicate that determination to the parties.

NOTE

The procedure on appeals is laid down by the Labour Court. Details of these procedures can be obtained from the Labour Court, Tom Johnson House, Haddington Road, Dublin 4 – (01) 6608444.

---

6. ENFORCEMENT OF DECISIONS OF THE RIGHTS COMMISSIONER/ DETERMINATIONS OF THE LABOUR COURT

1. An employee may bring a complaint to the Labour Court where an employer has not implemented a decision of the Rights Commissioner under the Act or has not appealed a decision within the requisite time. The Labour Court shall make a determination to the like effect as the original decision without hearing the employer concerned. The complaint must be brought by the employee not later than six weeks after the time limit for making an appeal has expired. Complaints of the non-implementation of Rights Commissioners' decisions under the Act should be submitted to the Labour Court on the relevant form, which is available from the Court. The Labour Court shall publish particulars of its determinations in such manner as it thinks fit.

2. The Minister, at the request of the Labour Court, may refer a question of law arising in proceedings before it, concerning appeals from the enforcement of recommendations of a Rights Commissioner, for determination by the High Court. The determination of the High Court shall be final and conclusive.

3. A party to proceedings may appeal to the High Court from a determination of the Labour Court on a point of law. The determination of the High Court shall be final and conclusive.

4. Where a determination of the Labour Court has not been implemented, within six weeks from the date on which the determination is communicated to the parties, the Circuit Court, on application to it by an employee, trade union or the Minister, shall, without hearing the employer or any evidence, make an order directing the employer to carry out the determination in accordance with its terms.

5. The Circuit Court, if it deems it appropriate to do so, may direct the employer to pay interest on the compensation in respect of any period commencing 6 weeks following

the communication of the Labour Court's determination to the parties and ending on the date of the order.

6. The application to the Circuit Court will be in the Circuit where the employer usually resides or carries out the business.

ANNEX
EXEMPTED ACTIVITIES

General Exemptions

The Organisation of Working Time (General Exemptions) Regulations, 1998 (S.I. No. 21 of 1998) prescribe, in accordance with Section 4(3) of the Organisation of Working Time Act, 1997, that persons employed in the following activities shall be exempt from the application of sections 11, 12 and 13 of the Act which deal respectively with daily rest, rests and intervals at work and weekly rest:

1. An activity in which the employee is regularly required by the employer to travel distances of significant length, either from his or her home to the workplace or from one workplace to another workplace.

2. An activity of a security or surveillance nature the purpose of which is to protect persons or property and which requires the continuous presence of the employee at a particular place or places, and, in particular, the activities of a security guard, caretaker or security firm.

3. An activity falling within a sector of the economy or in the public service—

    (a) in which it is foreseeable that the rate at which production or the provision of services, as the case may be, takes place will vary significantly from time to time, or

    (b) the nature of which is such that employees are directly involved in ensuring the continuity of production or the provision of services, as the case may be,

and, in particular, any of the following activities —

    (i) the provision of services relating to the reception, treatment or care of persons in a residential institution, hospital or similar establishment,

    (ii) the provision of services at a harbour or airport,

    (iii) production in the press, radio, television, cinematographic, postal or telecommunications industries,

    (iv) the provision of ambulance, fire and civil protection services,

    (v) the production, transmission or distribution of gas, water or electricity,

    (vi) the collection of household refuse or the operation of an incineration plant,

    (vii) any industrial activity in which work cannot, by reason of considerations of a technical nature, be interrupted,

    (viii) research and development,

    (ix) agriculture,

    (x) tourism.

NOTES —
EXCEPTIONS
Regulation 3 of the Regulations provides that the exemption shall not, as respects a particular employee, apply

(a) in relation to sections 11, 12 and 13 of the Act if the employee —

   (i) is not engaged wholly or mainly in carrying on or performing the duties of the activity concerned,

   (ii) is exempted from the application of that section by virtue of regulations under section 3(3) of the Act,

   or

   (iii) falls within a class of employee in relation to which a joint labour committee (within the meaning of the Industrial Relations Acts, 1946 to 1990) may perform functions under those Acts,

   or

(b) if and for so long as the employer does not comply with Regulation 5 of the Regulations in relation to him or her.

Compensatory rest periods

Regulation 4 of these Regulations provides that if an employee is not entitled, by reason of this exemption, to the rest period and break referred to in sections 11, 12 and 13 of the Act, the employer shall ensure that the employee has available to himself or herself a rest period and break that, in all the circumstances, can reasonably be regarded as equivalent to the first-mentioned rest period and break.

Duty of employer with respect to the health and safety of employee

Regulation 5 of the Regulations provides that:—

(1) an employer shall not require an employee to whom the exemption applies to work during a shift or other period of work (being a shift or other such period that is of more than 6 hours duration) without allowing him or her a break of such duration as the employer determines.

(2) in determining the duration of such a break, the employer shall have due regard to the need to protect and secure the health, safety and comfort of the employee and the general principle concerning the prevention and avoidance of risk in the workplace.

More Beneficial Arrangements

Regulation 6 of the Regulations provides that nothing in the Regulations shall prejudice a provision or provisions of a more beneficial kind to the employee concerned which is or are contained in —

(a) a collective agreement referred to in section 4(5) of the Act,

(b) a registered employment agreement, or

(c) an employment regulation order.

Exemption of Transport Activities

The Organisation of Working Time (Exemption of Transport Activities) Regulations, 1998 (S.I. No. 20 of 1998) prescribe, in accordance with Section 3 (3) of the Organisation of Working Time Act, 1997, that persons employed in a transport activity as follows shall be exempt from the application, *inter alia*, of sections 11, 12 and 13 of the Act dealing respectively with daily rest, rests and intervals at work and weekly rest:

1. An activity consisting of, or connected with, the operation of any vehicle, train, vessel, aircraft or other means of transport (whether of goods or persons) other than any activity of a person holding a position of an administrative, managerial or clerical nature that is not directly related to the operation of such a means of transport.

2. An activity that is carried on —

    (a) for the purpose of the transport timetable, that is to say an activity that is carried on for the purpose of ensuring the continuity or regularity of any service which provides a means of transport referred to in paragraph 1 above, or

    (b) for the purpose of ensuring the safety of such a means of transport,

other than any activity of a person holding a position of an administrative, managerial or clerical nature that is not directly related to the doing of the things required to be done for either such purpose.

3. In paragraph 1 'vessel' includes any vessel used to navigate inland waters (including any lake).

NOTE — Compensatory rest periods

It should be noted that an employer is not obliged to ensure that an employee engaged in these activities has available to himself or herself equivalent compensatory rest. However, Regulation 3 of these Regulations provides that the exemption shall not apply as respects a particular employee if he or she is not engaged wholly or mainly in carrying on or performing the duties of the activity concerned.

GIVEN under my hand this 24th day of February 1998.

TOM KITT, T.D.

Minister for Labour, Trade and Consumer Affairs.

EXPLANATORY NOTE

This Order declares the code of practice set out in the Schedule to the Order to be a code of practice on compensatory rest periods for the purposes of section 6 of the Organisation of Working Time Act, 1997 (No. 20 of 1997).

Organisation of Working Time (Code of Practice on Sunday Working in the Retail Trade and Related Matters) (Declaration) Order 1998

(SI 444/1998)

WHEREAS the Labour Relations Commission, by virtue of section 35(2) of the Organisation of Working Time Act, 1997 (No. 20 of 1997), may, and at the request of the Minister for Labour, Trade and Consumer Affairs (being the Minister of State to whom functions in this matter have been delegated by the Order hereafter recited), shall, prepare a code of practice for the purposes of one or more sections of that Act (other than section 6(2)) or, in the case of a request by the Minister for Labour, Trade and Consumer Affairs, a section of that Act (other than section 6(2)) specified in the request,

AND WHEREAS the Minister for Labour, Trade and Consumer Affairs has, pursuant to the said section 35(2), requested the Labour Relations Commission to prepare a code of practice for the purposes of section 14 of the said Act,

AND WHEREAS the Labour Relations Commission, in compliance with that request and with section 35(4) of the said Act, has prepared a code of practice for the purposes of section 14 of the said Act and submitted a copy of it to the Minister for Labour, Trade and Consumer Affairs,

NOW, I Tom Kitt, Minister for Labour, Trade and Consumer Affairs, in exercise of the powers conferred on me by section 35(5)(a) of the Organisation of Working Time Act, 1997 (No. 20 of 1997), as adapted by the Enterprise and Employment (Alteration of Name of Department and Title of Minister) Order, 1997 (S.I. No. 305 of 1997), and the Enterprise, Trade and Employment (Delegation of Ministerial Functions) (No. 2) Order, 1997 (S.I. No. 330 of 1997), hereby order as follows:

Citation

1. This Order may be cited as the Organisation of Working Time (Code of Practice on Sunday Working in the Retail Trade and Related Matters) (Declaration) Order, 1998.

Code of Practice

2. The code of practice set out in the Schedule to this Order is hereby declared to be a code of practice for the purposes of section 14 of the Organisation of Working Time Act, 1997 (No. 20 of 1997), and so much of Part IV of that Act as relates to that section.

SCHEDULE
ORGANISATION OF WORKING TIME ACT, 1997

CODE OF PRACTICE ON SUNDAY WORKING IN THE RETAIL TRADE

NOTE:— This Code of Practice is not a legal interpretation of the Act

1. INTRODUCTION

1. The Minister for Labour, Trade and Consumer Affairs, requested the Labour Relations Commission, pursuant to section 35(2) of the Organisation of Working Time Act, 1997 and in relation to the Sunday work supplemental provisions of section 14 of the Act, to prepare a Code of Practice on Sunday Working in the Retail Trade.

2. The Labour Relations Commission has prepared this Code of Practice on Sunday Working in the Retail Trade in accordance with the provisions of section 35(2) of the Organisation of Working Time Act, 1997. When preparing the Code of Practice the Commission sought submissions from the Irish Business and Employers Confederation, the Irish Congress of Trade Unions, the Union of Retail Bar and Administrative Workers (MANDATE) and the Services Industrial Professional Technical Union.

3. The Commission has taken account of the views expressed by these organisations to the fullest extent possible in preparing this Code.

4. The Code is designed to assist employers, employees and their representatives in observing the 1997 Act as regards Sunday working in the retail trade. It gives guidance, in particular, on arrangements that may be put in place to comply with the supplemental provisions of section 14 of the Act.

5. While failure on the part of any person to observe the Code will not, in itself, render that person liable to civil or criminal proceedings, the Code shall be admissible in evidence before a Court, the Labour Court or a Rights Commissioner in proceedings under the Organisation of Working Time Act, 1997.

2. SUPPLEMENTAL PROVISIONS OF SECTION 14 OF THE ORGANISATION OF WORKING TIME ACT, 1997 —SUNDAY WORK

NOTE

> This section of the code gives a general description of some of the supplemental provisions of section 14 of the Organisation of Working Time Act, 1997 and is not a legal interpretation.

1. The terms of the EU Directive on Working Time, (Council Directive 93/104/EC of 23 November 1993), were transposed into Irish law by means of the Organisation of Working Time Act, 1997 and Regulations made under the Safety, Health and Welfare at Work Act, 1989.

2. Section 14 of the Organisation of Working Time Act, 1997 sets out statutory rights for employees in respect of Sunday working. Any employee who is required to work on a Sunday and, his or her having to work on that day has not been taken account of in the determination of pay, shall be compensated as follows:

- by the payment to the employee of a reasonable allowance having regard to all the circumstances, or
- by increasing the employee's rate of pay by a reasonable amount having regard to all the circumstances, or

- by granting the employee reasonable paid time off from work having regard to all the circumstances, or
- by a combination of two or more of the above means.

3. General Principles of Compensatory Arrangements for Sunday Working in the Retail Trade

1. General

The retail trade consists of many varied groups of businesses such as drapery, grocery, hardware or fast food, operating in diverse business environments. The purpose of this Code is to ensure that best practices are operated by all employers for those employees who service that sector of industry through Sunday working. Sunday hours of work and rostering arrangements have a significant impact on the quality of life of workers as well as being important to the efficient operation of the enterprise. Therefore, they should be subject to discussion and consultation between the employer and the relevant trade union(s) representing employees or between the employer and the employees who are affected by Sunday trading, in circumstances where employees are not unionised.

2. The following is a general guide to all employers and their employees on the type of compensatory arrangements that should apply for Sunday working. While the compensatory arrangements listed are set out for general guidance only, employers may provide enhanced compensatory arrangements to suit particular business environments. Minimum compensatory requirements are set out at section 14 of the Organisation of Working Time Act, 1997.

3. Guidelines on Compensatory Arrangements for Sunday Working

3.1 Where a collective agreement of the type implied in section 14 of the Organisation of Working Time Act, 1997 exists between an employer and a trade union(s) representing employees or between an employer and employees who are not unionised, this should not be altered, except through the standard negotiating mechanisms.

3.2 In the absence of a collective agreement, best practice should be set by reference to compensation arrangements provided for in a collective agreement applying to comparable employees in the (retail) sector.

3.3 All new agreements being entered into should be negotiated between the employer and the relevant trade union(s) representing employees, based on a consensus approach. In circumstances where employees are not unionised the agreement should be negotiated between the employer and the employees who are affected by Sunday trading. Agreements should take account of the following:

- In accordance with provisions of the Organisation of Working Time Act, 1997 a premium payment will apply to Sunday working. Section 14 of the Act specifies the means by which the premium should be granted. The nature and value of this premium rate should be negotiated and agreed between the employer and the trade union(s) representing employees or between the employer and the employees who are affected by Sunday trading, in circumstances where employees are not unionised.

- Existing employees should have the option to volunteer to opt into working patterns, which include Sundays on a rota basis and form part of a regular working week (i.e. being required to work no more than 5 days out of 7).
- Newly recruited employees may be contracted to work Sundays as part of a regular rostered working pattern.
- Employees who have a minimum of two years' service on a Sunday working contract should have the opportunity to seek to opt out of Sunday working, for urgent family or personal reasons, giving adequate notice to the employer.
- Meal breaks on Sundays should be standardised in line with the other working days of the week.
- All employees should have the opportunity of volunteering to work on the peak Sunday trading days prior to Christmas, in addition to their normal working week. In these circumstances length of service will not be the overriding criterion for selection for Sunday working.

NOTE

The Labour Relations Commission will provide assistance to employers and trade union(s) representing employees and to employers and their employees who are not unionised, in the negotiation of collective agreements on compensatory arrangements of the kind specified in section 14 of the Organisation of Working Time Act, 1997. Requests for such assistance should be forwarded in writing to the Labour Relations Commission, Tom Johnson House, Haddington Road, Dublin 4—telephone 6609662 (01 area) and 1890 220227 (outside 01 area), fax (01) 6685069.

4. Complaints Procedure

1. The Organisation of Working Time Act, 1997 sets out a complaints procedure for dealing with the various complaints that may arise under the Act. While the procedure deals with general complaints concerning various entitlements, for the purposes of this Code the procedure concerns itself with complaints about Sunday working in the retail sector.

Who can make a complaint?

2. An employee or any trade union of which the employee is a member, with the consent of the employee, may present a complaint. The Minister for Labour, Trade and Consumer Affairs may also present a complaint if it is apparent that an employer is not complying with a provision and, where the employee/trade union has not done so and, the Minister is of the opinion that the circumstances are such as to make it unreasonable to expect the employee/trade union to present such a complaint.

How is a complaint presented and processed?

3. Complaints arising under section 14 of the 1997 Act, should be presented in the first instance to a Rights Commissioner. A complaint must be made within six months of the date of the alleged contravention by the employer. However, a complaint which is

presented not later than twelve months after the six months time limit may be investigated if the Rights Commissioner is satisfied that the delay was due to reasonable cause. A complaint should be in writing and should contain the requisite particulars.

4. The Rights Commissioner must give the employer a copy of the complaint. The Rights Commissioner must hear the parties and allow relevant evidence to be presented. The investigation of a complaint will be held in private. The Rights Commissioner must furnish the Labour Court with a copy of each decision given under the 1997 Act.

5. The Rights Commissioner in making a decision shall do one or more of the following:

(a) declare that the complaint was, or, as the case may be, was not well founded,

(b) require the employer to comply with the relevant provision(s),

(c) require the employer to pay compensation of such amount (if any) as is just and equitable having regard to all the circumstances, up to a maximum of two years' remuneration.

NOTE

Queries relating to complaints and procedures should be forwarded in writing to the Rights Commissioner Service, Labour Relations Commission, Tom Johnson House, Haddington Road, Dublin 4—telephone 6609662 (01 area) and 1890 220227 outside (01 area), fax (01) 6685069.

5. Appeals

1. Either party may appeal a decision of a Rights Commissioner to the Labour Court. The appeal must be made within 6 weeks of the date on which the decision was communicated to the party. The notice of appeal should be submitted to the Labour Court in writing.

2. The Labour Court must give a copy of the notice of appeal to the other party. The Labour Court shall give the parties an opportunity to be heard and to present relevant evidence to it. It will make a determination in writing affirming, varying or setting aside the decision. The Court must communicate that determination to the parties.

NOTE

The procedure on appeals is laid down by the Labour Court. Details of these procedures can be obtained from the Labour Court, Tom Johnson House, Haddington Road, Dublin 4— telephone 6608444 (01 area) and 1890 220228—(outside 01 area).

6. Enforcement of Decisions of the Rights Commissioner/Determinations of The Labour Court

1. An employee may bring a complaint to the Labour Court where an employer has not implemented a decision of the Rights Commissioner under the Act or has not appealed a

decision within the requisite time. The Labour Court shall make a determination to the like effect as the original decision without hearing the employer concerned. The complaint must be brought by the employee not later than six weeks after the time limit for making an appeal has expired. Complaints of the non-implementation of Rights Commissioners' decisions under the Act should be submitted to the Labour Court. The Labour Court shall publish particulars of its determinations in such manner as it thinks fit.

2. The Minister, at the request of the Labour Court, may refer a question of law arising in proceedings before it, concerning appeals from the enforcement of decisions of a Rights Commissioner, for determination by the High Court. The determination of the High Court shall be final and conclusive.

3. A party to proceedings may appeal to the High Court from a determination of the Labour Court on a point of law. The determination of the High Court shall be final and conclusive.

4. Where a determination of the Labour Court has not been implemented, within six weeks from the date on which the determination is communicated to the parties, the Circuit Court, on application to it, by an employee, trade union or the Minister, shall, without hearing the employer or any evidence, make an order directing the employer to carry out the determination in accordance with its terms.

5. The Circuit Court, if it deems it appropriate to do so, may direct the employer to pay interest on the compensation in respect of any period commencing 6 weeks following the communication of the Labour Court's determination to the parties and ending on the date of the order.

6. The application to the Circuit Court will be in the Circuit where the employer usually resides or carries out the business.

EXPLANATORY NOTE

This Order declares the code of practice set out in the Schedule to the Order to be a code of practice on Sunday working in the retail trade for the purposes of section 14 of the Organisation of Working Time Act, 1997 (No. 20 of 1997).

Appendix C: Bullying and Harassment

Industrial Relations Act 1990 (Code of Practice detailing Procedures for Addressing Bullying in the Workplace) (Declaration) Order 2002[4]

(SI 17/2002)

WHEREAS the Labour Relations Commission has prepared, under subsection (1) of section 42 of the Industrial Relations Act 1990 (No. 19 of 1990), a draft code of practice detailing procedures for addressing bullying in the workplace;

AND WHEREAS the Labour Relations Commission has complied with subsection (2) of that section and has submitted the draft code of practice to the Minister for Enterprise, Trade and Employment;

NOW THEREFORE, I, Mary Harney, Minister for Enterprise, Trade and Employment, in exercise of the powers conferred on me by subsection (3) of that section, the Labour (Transfer of Departmental Administration and Ministerial Functions) Order 1993 (SI No. 18 of 1993), and the Enterprise and Employment (Alteration of Name of Department and Title of Minister) Order 1997 (SI No 305 of 1997), hereby order as follows:

1. This Order may be cited as the Industrial Relations Act 1990 (Code of Practice detailing Procedures for Addressing Bullying in the Workplace) (Declaration) Order 2002.

2. It is hereby declared that the code of practice set out in the Schedule to this Order shall be a code of practice for the purposes of the Industrial Relations Act 1990 (No. 19 of 1990).

SCHEDULE
CODE OF PRACTICE DETAILING PROCEDURES FOR ADDRESSING BULLYING IN THE WORKPLACE

Introduction

1. Section 42 of the Industrial Relations Act 1990 provides, *inter alia*, for the preparation of draft Codes of Practice by the Labour Relations Commission for submission to the Minister and for the making by the Minister of an order declaring that the code received under Section 42 and scheduled to the order shall be a Code of Practice for the purposes of the said Act.

2. In September 1999, the Minister for Labour Affairs, Mr Tom Kitt T.D. established the Task Force on the Prevention of Workplace Bullying. In March 2001 the Task Force issued its report entitled 'Dignity at Work — the Challenge of Workplace Bullying'. In

---

4   Copyright Houses of the Oireachtas 2002

line with a recommendation of the report the Labour Relations Commission has prepared this code of Practice on Workplace Bullying.

3. In accordance with the provisions of the legislation, when preparing this Code of Practice the Commission consulted with representative organisations including the Irish Congress of Trade Unions, the Irish Business and Employers Confederation, Equality Authority, Employment Appeals Tribunal, Labour Court, Health and Safety Authority and a number of Government Departments. The Commission has taken account of the views expressed by these organisations to the maximum extent possible. The Commission has also consulted with the Implementation Advisory Committee on the Prevention of Workplace Bullying.

4. Other relevant Codes of Practice have been made under the Safety, Health and Welfare at Work Act 1989 and under the Employment Equality Act 1998.

Definition

5. For the purpose of this Code of Practice the definition of workplace bullying is as follows:

> 'Workplace Bullying is repeated inappropriate behaviour, direct or indirect, whether verbal, physical or otherwise, conducted by one or more persons against another or others, at the place of work and/or in the course of employment, which could reasonably be regarded as undermining the individual's right to dignity at work. An isolated incident of the behaviour described in this definition may be an affront to dignity at work but, as a once off incident, is not considered to be bullying.'[5]

General Provisions

6. The main purpose of this Code of Practice is to set out, for the guidance of employers, employees and their representatives, effective procedures for addressing allegations of workplace bullying. The Code sets out both an informal and formal procedure.

PROCEDURES

7. Informal Procedure

While in no way diminishing the issue or the effects on individuals, an informal approach can often resolve matters. As a general rule therefore, an attempt should be made to address an allegation of bullying as informally as possible by means of an agreed informal procedure. The objective of this approach is to resolve the difficulty with the minimum of conflict and stress for the individuals involved.

(a) Any employee who believes he or she is being bullied should explain clearly to the alleged perpetrator(s) that the behaviour in question is unacceptable. In circumstances where the complainant finds it difficult to approach the alleged perpetrator(s) directly, he or she should seek help and advice, on a strictly

---

[5] Recommended by the Report by the Task Force on the Prevention of Workplace Bullying — published by the Stationery Office, March 2001.

confidential basis, from a contact person. A contact person could, for example, be one of the following:

- a work colleague;
- a supervisor or line manager;
- any manager in the workplace;
- human resource/personnel officer;
- employee/trade union representative.

In this situation the contact person should listen patiently, be supportive and discuss the various options open to the employee concerned.

(b) Having consulted with the contact person, the complainant may request the assistance of the contact person in raising the issue with the alleged perpetrator(s). In this situation the approach of the contact person should be by way of a confidential, non-confrontational discussion with a view to resolving the issue in an informal low-key manner.

(c) A complainant may decide, for whatever reason, to bypass the informal procedure. Choosing not to use the informal procedure should not reflect negatively on a complainant in the formal procedure.

8. Formal Procedure

If an informal approach is inappropriate or if after the informal stage, the bullying persists, the following formal procedures should be invoked:-

a. The complainant should make a formal complaint in writing to his/her immediate supervisor, or if preferred, any member of management. The complaint should be confined to precise details of actual incidents of bullying.

b. The alleged perpetrator(s) should be notified in writing that an allegation of bullying has been made against them. They should be given a copy of the complainant's statement and advised that they shall be afforded a fair opportunity to respond to the allegation(s).

c. The complaint should be subject to an initial examination by a designated member of management, who can be considered impartial, with a view to determining an appropriate course of action. An appropriate course of action at this stage, for example, could be exploring a mediated solution or a view that the issue can be resolved informally. Should either of these approaches be deemed inappropriate or inconclusive, a formal investigation of the complaint should take place with a view to determining the facts and the credibility or otherwise of the allegation(s).

Investigation

d. The investigation should be conducted by either a designated member or members of management or, if deemed appropriate, an agreed third party. The investigation should be conducted thoroughly, objectively, with sensitivity, utmost confidentiality, and with due respect for the rights of both the complainant and the alleged perpetrator(s).

e. The investigation should be governed by terms of reference, preferably agreed between the parties in advance.

f. The investigator(s) should meet with the complainant and alleged perpetrator(s) and any witnesses or relevant persons on an individual confidential basis with a view to establishing the facts surrounding the allegation(s). Both the complainant and alleged perpetrator(s) may be accompanied by a work colleague or employee/trade union representative if so desired.

g. Every effort should be made to carry out and complete the investigation as quickly as possible and preferably within an agreed timeframe. On completion of the investigation, the investigator(s) should submit a written report to management containing the findings of the investigation.

h. Both parties should be given the opportunity to comment on the findings before any action is decided upon by management.

i. The complainant and the alleged perpetrator(s) should be informed in writing of the findings of the investigation.

Outcome

j. Should management decide that the complaint is well founded, the alleged perpetrator(s) should be given a formal interview to determine an appropriate course of action. Such action could, for example, involve counselling and/or monitoring or progressing the issue through the disciplinary and grievance procedure of the employment.[6]

k. If either party is unhappy with the outcome of the investigation, the issue may be processed through the normal industrial relations mechanisms.

Confidentiality

9. All individuals involved in the procedures referred to above should maintain absolute confidentiality on the subject.

Training/Awareness:

10. It is considered that all personnel who have a role in either the informal or formal procedure – e.g. designated members of management, worker representatives, union representatives etc — should be made aware of appropriate policies and procedures which should, if possible, include appropriate training.

EXPLANATORY NOTE

(This note is not part of the Instrument and does not purport to be a legal interpretation.)

The effect of this Order is to declare that the code of practice set out in the Schedule to this Order is a code of practice for the purposes of the Industrial Relations Act, 1990.

---

[6] See the Labour Relations Commission's Codes of Practice on – Grievance and Disciplinary Procedures and – Voluntary Dispute Resolution.

Employment Equality Act 1998 (Code of Practice) (Harassment) Order

(SI 78/2002)

This Code of Practice is useful as regards the nature and contents of policies on harassment and sexual harassment. However, this Code is out of date in the definition it provides of 'harassment' and 'sexual harassment' and must be used with care as the definitions of 'sexual harassment' and 'harassment' provided in the Employment Equality Act 1998 were amended by the Employment Equality Act 2004. On the changes made to the definitions, see Ch 14, Employment Equality.

WHEREAS the Equality Authority has prepared under sub-section (1) (as amended by paragraph (g) of the Schedule to the Equal Status Act 2000) of section 56 of the Employment Equality Act 1998 (No. 21 of 1998) a draft code of practice on sexual harassment and harassment at work;

AND WHEREAS the Equality Authority has complied with subsection (2) of that section and has submitted the draft code of practice to the Minister for Justice, Equality and Law Reform;

NOW THEREFORE, I, John O'Donoghue T.D., Minister for Justice, Equality and Law Reform, in exercise of the powers conferred on me by subsection (3) of that section, order as follows:

1. This Order may be cited as the Employment Equality Act 1998 (Code of Practice) (Harassment) Order 2002.

2. The draft code of practice submitted by the Equality Authority, the text of which is set out in the Schedule to this order, is declared to be an approved code of practice for the purposes of the Employment Equality Act, 1998.

SCHEDULE
CODE OF PRACTICE ON SEXUAL HARASSMENT AND HARASSMENT AT WORK

S39 EE Act. S39 ES Act

The functions of The Equality Authority under the Employment Equality Act 1998 (EE Act) and the Equal Status Act 2000 (ES Act) include:

— working towards the elimination of discrimination in employment and in relation to matters to which the ES Act applies

— the promotion of equality of opportunity

— the provision of information on the working of both Acts

— keeping under review the working of the EE Act and the ES Act and whenever necessary to make proposals to the Minister for Justice, Equality and Law Reform for the amendment of those Acts.

References in this code to the EE Act should be taken to mean the Employment Equality Act 1998.

References in this code to the ES Act should be taken to mean the Equal Status Act 2000.

References to the appropriate sections of these Acts are given in the margins.

S56 EE Act Paragraph (g) of the Schedule to the ES Act

Within these functions the Equality Authority may prepare codes of practice in furtherance of the elimination of discrimination and the promotion of equality of opportunity. Section 56(4) of the EE Act as amended by paragraph (g) of the Schedule to the ES Act provides that:

> 'An approved code of practice shall be admissible in evidence and, if any provision of the code appears to be relevant to any question arising in any criminal or other proceedings, it shall be taken into account in determining that question; and for this purpose 'proceedings' includes, in addition to proceedings before a court and under Part VII or under Part III of the Equal Status Act 2000, proceedings before the Labour Court, the Labour Relations Commission, the Employment Appeals Tribunal, the Director and a rights commissioner'.

What follows is a code of practice within the meaning of section 56(1) and (4) of the EE Act as amended by paragraph (g) of the Schedule to the ES Act.

(1) FOREWORD

Sexual harassment, and harassment on the eight discriminatory grounds, pollutes the working environment and can have a devastating effect upon the health, confidence, morale and performance of those affected by it. The anxiety and stress produced by sexual harassment and harassment may lead to those subjected to it taking time off work due to sickness and stress, being less efficient at work or leaving their job to seek work elsewhere. Employees often suffer the adverse consequences of the harassment itself and the short and long term damage to their employment prospects if they are forced to forego promotion or to change jobs. Sexual harassment and harassment may also have a damaging impact on employees not themselves the object of unwanted behaviour but who are witness to it or have a knowledge of the unwanted behaviour.

There are also adverse consequences arising from sexual harassment and harassment for employers. It has a direct impact on the profitability of the enterprise where staff take sick leave or resign their posts because of sexual harassment or harassment. It can also have an impact on the economic efficiency of the enterprise where employees' productivity is reduced by having to work in a climate in which the individual's integrity is not respected.

Some specific groups are particularly vulnerable to sexual harassment and harassment as there may be a link between the risk of sexual harassment or harassment and the recipient's perceived vulnerability — such as new entrants to the labour market, those with irregular or precarious employment contracts and employees in non-traditional jobs.

(2) INTRODUCTION

This code has been prepared by the Equality Authority with the approval of the Minister for Justice, Equality and Law Reform and after consultation with IBEC, ICTU and other relevant organisations representing equality interests.

Aim

This code aims to give practical guidance to employers, employers' organisations, trade unions and employees on:

— what is meant by sexual harassment and harassment in the workplace

— how it may be prevented

— what steps to take if it does occur to ensure that adequate procedures are readily available to deal with the problem and to prevent its recurrence.

Status

The code thus seeks to promote the development and implementation of policies and procedures which establish working environments free of sexual harassment and harassment and in which the dignity of everyone is respected.

The provisions of this code are admissible in evidence and if relevant may be taken into account in any criminal or other proceedings before a Court, under Part VII of the EE Act, proceedings before the Labour Court, the Labour Relations Commission, the Employment Appeals Tribunal, the Director of Equality Investigations and a rights commissioner.

This code does not impose any legal obligations in itself, nor is it an authoritative statement of the law — that can only be provided by the Office of the Director of Equality Investigations, the Labour Court and the Courts. It is the employer's responsibility to ensure compliance with the EE Act and European equality law.

Application and
Adaptation of the Code

The code is intended to be applicable to all employments, employment agencies and trade unions, employer bodies and professional bodies that are covered by the EE Act. Employers are encouraged to follow the recommendations in a way which is appropriate to the size and structure of their organisation. It may be relevant for small and medium sized enterprises to adapt some of the practical steps to their specific needs. Any adaptations that are made however, should be fully consistent with the code's general intention.

An employer shall be legally responsible for the sexual harassment and harassment suffered by employees in the course of their work unless the employer took reasonably practicable steps to prevent sexual harassment and harassment from occurring and to reverse the effects of it and to prevent its recurrence. Employers who take the steps that are set out in the code to prevent their employees from committing acts of unlawful sexual harassment or harassment or to reverse the effects of it and to prevent its recurrence, may avoid liability from such acts in any legal proceedings brought against them.

It is essential that employers have in place accessible and effective policies and procedures to deal with sexual harassment and harassment. These measures should be agreed by the employers with the relevant trade union or employee representatives. In so far as practicable, clients, customers and business contacts should also be consulted.

Equality of
Opportunity

A policy on sexual harassment and harassment at work is an integral part of equal opportunities strategies in the workplace. Such policies will be more effective when operated in conjunction with similar policies on equal opportunities and health and safety.

(3) EMPLOYMENT EQUALITY ACT 1998

The Law and
Employers'
Responsibilities. S8 EE
Act.

The EE Act prohibits discrimination on the nine specific grounds set out below in all aspects of a person's employment from:

— Access to employment
— Conditions of employment
— Training or experience
— Promotion or regarding
— Classification of posts
— Vocational training
— Equal Pay
— (It may also apply in certain circumstances when the relationship has ended for example to references).

The Act applies to employers, employment agencies, trade unions, employer bodies and professional and trade organisations.

An employer must not treat an employee *less favourably* due to their:

Discriminatory
Grounds

Gender — man, woman (this also includes transgender).

Marital Status — single, married, separated, divorced or widowed.

Family Status — responsibility as a parent or as a person *in loco parentis* in relation to a person under 18, or as a parent or the resident primary carer of a person over 18 with a disability which is of such a nature as to give rise to the need for care or support on a continuing, regular or frequent basis.

Sexual Orientation — heterosexual, bisexual or homosexual.

Disability — this is very broadly defined in the Act and will include the vast majority of disabilities.

'Disability' means—

(a) the total or partial absence of a person's bodily or mental functions, including the absence of a part of a person's body,

(b) the presence in the body of organisms causing, or likely to cause, chronic disease or illness,

(c) the malfunction, malformation or disfigurement of a part of a person's body,

(d) a condition or malfunction which results in a person learning differently from a person without the condition or malfunction, or

(e) a condition, disease or illness which affects a person's thought processes, perception of reality, emotions or judgment or which results in disturbed behaviour.

Age — between the ages of 18 and 65 (or from 15 in relation to vocational training).

Race — race, colour, nationality or ethnic or national origins.

Religious Belief — includes different religious background or outlook, (including absence of religious belief).

Membership of the Traveller Community — 'Traveller community' means the community of people who are commonly called Travellers and who are identified (both by themselves and others) as people with a shared history, culture and traditions including, historically, a nomadic way of life on the island of Ireland.

Reasonable Accommodation. S16 EE Act

Employers have additional obligations to reasonably accommodate employees with disabilities (to the extent that it does not cost more than nominal cost). This obligation should apply to the format and context of the policy, the procedures on sexual harassment and harassment and their implementation.

Victimisation. S74(2) EE Act

The EE Act protects employees who for example seek redress under the Act or give evidence in proceedings by prohibiting their being victimised by dismissal or other penalty for doing so.

Sexual Harassment and Harassment

The EE Act protects employees from employment related sexual harassment and harassment. There are different definitions and provisions in the EE Act. It distinguishes between sexual harassment (on the gender ground) and harassment that is based on one of the other grounds.

Sexual harassment and Discrimination. S23 (1) EE Act

Sexual harassment is a form of discrimination on the gender ground in relation to conditions of employment.

Harassment and Discrimination. S32 EE Act

Harassment that is based on the following grounds— marital status, family status, sexual orientation, religion, age, disability, race, or Traveller community ground— is a form of discrimination in relation to conditions of employment.

What is sexual harassment? S23 EE Act.

The definition of sexual harassment includes any:

— act of physical intimacy

— request for sexual favours

— other act or conduct including spoken words, gestures or the production, display or circulation of written words, pictures or other material that is *unwelcome and* could reasonably be regarded as *sexually offensive, humiliating or intimidating.*

Many forms of behaviour can constitute sexual harassment. It includes examples like those contained in the following list although it must be emphasised that the list is illustrative rather than exhaustive. A single incident may constitute sexual harassment.

Physical conduct of a sexual nature — This may include unwanted physical contact such as unnecessary touching, patting or pinching or brushing against another employee's body, assault and coercive sexual intercourse.

Verbal conduct of a sexual nature — This includes unwelcome sexual advances, propositions or pressure for sexual activity, continued suggestions for social activity outside the work place after it has been made clear that such suggestions are unwelcome, unwanted or offensive flirtations, suggestive remarks, innuendos or lewd comments.

Non-verbal conduct of a sexual nature — This may include the display of pornographic or sexually suggestive pictures, objects, written materials, emails, text-messages or faxes. It may also include leering, whistling or making sexually suggestive gestures.

Sex-based conduct — This would include conduct that denigrates or ridicules or is intimidatory or physically abusive of an employee because of his or her sex such as derogatory or degrading abuse or insults which are gender-related.

What is Harassment? S32(5) EE Act

The definition of harassment contained in section 32(5) of the EE Act is similar to that of sexual harassment but without the sexual element. The harassment has to be based on the relevant characteristic of the employee whether it be the employee's marital status, family status, sexual orientation, religious belief (or none), age, disability, race, colour, nationality or ethnic or national origin or membership of the Traveller community. Bullying that is not linked to one of the discriminatory grounds is not covered by the EE Act.

The protection of the Act extends to situations where the employee does not have the relevant characteristic but the harasser believes that he/she has that characteristic, for example, if the harasser thought the employee was gay and the employee wasn't.

Harassment is any act or conduct including spoken words, gestures or the production, display or circulation of written words, pictures or other material if the action or conduct is *unwelcome* to the employee and could reasonably be regarded as *offensive, humiliating or intimidating*.

Many forms of behaviour may constitute harassment including:

— Verbal harassment — jokes, comments, ridicule or songs
— Written harassment — including faxes, text messages, emails or notices
— Physical harassment — jostling, shoving or any form of assault
— Intimidatory harassment — gestures, posturing or threatening poses

913

— Visual displays such as posters, emblems or badges

— Isolation or exclusion from social activities

— Pressure to behave in a manner that the employee thinks is inappropriate, for example being required to dress in a manner unsuited to a person's ethnic or religious background.

Common element

The definitions of sexual harassment and harassment have several common concepts. There is an objective and subjective element to the different parts of the definition.

(a) Unwelcome conduct.

Act The EE Act does not prohibit all relations of a sexual or social nature at work. To constitute sexual harassment or harassment the behaviour complained of must firstly be *unwelcome*. It is up to each employee to decide (*a*) what behaviour is unwelcome, irrespective of the attitude of others to the matter and (*b*) from whom, if anybody, such behaviour is welcome or unwelcome, irrespective of the attitudes of others to the matter. The fact that an individual has previously agreed to the behaviour does not stop him/her from deciding that it has now become unwelcome. It is the unwanted nature of the conduct which distinguishes sexual harassment and harassment from friendly behaviour which is welcome and mutual.

(b) Sexually and/or otherwise offensive, humiliating or intimidating

In addition, to constitute sexual harassment or harassment under the EE Act the behaviour must also *be reasonably regarded as offensive, humiliating or intimidating to the employee.*

Intention

The intention of the perpetrator of the sexual harassment or harassment is irrelevant. The fact that the perpetrator has no intention of sexually harassing or harassing the employee is no defence. The effect of the behaviour on the employee is what is important.

Sexual harassment and harassment by employers, employees and non-employees. S23(1) S32(1) S23(4) S32(2) EE Act

The EE Act protects employees from sexual harassment and harassment by:

— the employer

— fellow employees

— clients

— customers

— other business contacts including any person with whom the employer might reasonably expect the employee to come into contact in the workplace. This may include those who supply or deliver goods/services to the employer, maintenance and other types of professional contractors as well as volunteers.

914

Non workplace sexual harassment and harassment	The scope of the sexual harassment and harassment provisions extend beyond the workplace for example to conferences and training that occur outside the workplace. It may also extend to work-related social events.
Different treatment because of acceptance of or rejection of sexual harassment or harassment. S 23(2)(b) S 32(2)(b) EE Act	The protection extends to where the employee is treated differently in the workplace because he/she has rejected or accepted the sexual harassment or harassment for example in relation to decisions concerning access to training, promotion or salary.
Employment Agencies and Vocational Training. S23(6) S32(7) EE Act	The provisions on sexual harassment and harassment also apply to employment agencies and vocational training.
Obligations on Employers	The EE Act requires employers to act in a *preventative* and *remedial* way.
Reasonably Practicable Steps	Employers are legally responsible for the sexual harassment and harassment directed at employees carried out by co-employees or clients, customers or other business contacts of the employer. It is a defence for the employer to prove that the employer took reasonably practicable steps to prevent:

— the employee from being harassed

— the employee from being treated differently in the workplace or in the course of employment and if and so far as any such treatment has occurred, to reverse the effects of it.

In order to rely on this defence employers would need to show that they have comprehensive, accessible, effective policies that focus on prevention and best practice and remedial action and an accessible effective complaints procedure. The steps taken to put the policies and procedures into practice will also be taken into account, as employers will not be able to rely on an excellent policy if it hasn't been effectively implemented. The core elements of a policy and complaints procedure will be dealt with below.

Time Limits and Remedies under the EE Act S74-93	A complaint of sexual harassment or harassment on any of the other grounds may be made to the Office of the Director of Equality Investigations who may refer the complaint to an Equality Officer or, with the parties agreement, for mediation.

All dismissal claims (including constructive dismissal) under the EE Act are heard by the Labour Court.

In sexual harassment claims (and all gender claims) the employee may bypass either of the above and refer the matter to the Circuit Court.

A complaint must be made within 6 months of the alleged incident of sexual harassment or harassment or the latest incident of such harassment. This may be extended to up to 12 months where exceptional circumstances prevented the making of the complaint within the 6 months.

The maximum that can be awarded by the Office of the Director of Equality Investigations and the Labour Court is 104 weeks pay. However, section 82(3) provides that no enactment relating to the jurisdiction of the Circuit Court shall be taken to limit the amount of compensation which may be awarded by the Circuit Court.

The Labour Court or the Circuit Court may order reinstatement or re-engagement.

S98 EE Act.

To dismiss an employee for making a complaint of sexual harassment or harassment under the EE Act in good faith, is an offence and an employer may also be subject to an order for re-instatement or re-engagement or the payment of compensation to the employee.

Right to seek information. S76 EE Act S81 EE Act

Prior to making a complaint under the EE Act an employee is entitled to seek material information' from an employer about alleged acts of sexual harassment or harassment or the employer's failure to deal with them or about the relevant procedures. There is no obligation on the employer to provide the information. However, the Circuit Court, the Director or the Labour Court in subsequent proceedings may draw such inferences as seem appropriate from the failure to supply the information.

(4) THE POLICY

Prevention

Prevention is the best way to minimise sexual harassment and harassment in the workplace. An effective policy, and a strong commitment to implementing it is required. The purpose of an effective policy is not simply to prevent unlawful behaviour but to encourage best practice and a safe and harmonious workplace where such behaviour is unlikely to occur. This policy is likely to be more effective when it is linked to a broader policy of promoting equality of opportunity.

Employers should adopt, implement and monitor a comprehensive, effective and accessible policy on sexual harassment and harassment.

Strategies to create and maintain a working environment in which the dignity of employees is respected are most likely to be effective when they are jointly agreed. In this way, employers and other parties to the employment relationship can create an anti-harassment culture and share a sense of responsibility for that culture.

The policy and complaints procedure should be adopted, where appropriate, in so far as is practicable with clients, customers and other business contacts after consultation or negotiation with trade union or employee representatives, where possible, over its content and implementation.

Simple direct language should be used in the policy. It should be accessible to those with literacy problems and those who may not speak fluent English.

(1) *The policy should begin by declaring*:

   (a) the organisation's commitment to ensuring that the workplace is free from sexual harassment and harassment

   (b) that all employees have the right to be treated with dignity and respect

   (c) that complaints by employees will be treated with fairness and sensitivity and in as confidential a manner as possible

   (d) that sexual harassment and harassment by employers, employees and non-employees such as clients, customers and business contacts will not be tolerated and could lead to disciplinary action (in the case of employees) and other sanctions for example the suspension of contracts or services or exclusions from premises (in the case of non-employees).

(2) *Definition*

   (a) the policy should set out definitions of sexual harassment and harassment which are simple, clear and practical;

   (b) a non-exhaustive list of examples should be provided;

   (c) the policy should state that the protection extends to:

      — sexual harassment and harassment by co-workers, clients, customers and other business contacts

      — beyond the workplace to conferences and training and may extend to work-related social events

      — different treatment of an employee because he/she has rejected or accepted the sexual harassment or harassment

      — employment agencies and vocational training;

(d) the policy should emphasise that it is up to the employee to decide what behaviour is unwelcome irrespective of the attitude of others to the matter;

(e) the policy should state that employees who make a complaint or who give evidence in proceedings etc. will not be victimised.

(3) *Allocation of responsibilities under the Act*

The policy should state that management and others in positions of authority have a particular responsibility to ensure that sexual harassment and harassment does not occur and that complaints are addressed speedily. The policy should state that in particular, management should:

— provide good example by treating all in the workplace with courtesy and respect

— promote awareness of the organisation's policy and complaints procedures

— be vigilant for signs of harassment and take action before a problem escalates

— respond sensitively to an employee who makes a complaint of harassment

— explain the procedures to be followed if a complaint of sexual harassment or harassment is made

— ensure that an employee making a complaint is not victimised for doing so

— monitor and follow up the situation after a complaint is made so that the sexual harassment or harassment does not recur.

(4) *Trade Unions*

The policy should address the contribution to be made by the trade union/s.

Trade unions can play a role in the prevention of sexual harassment and harassment in the workplace through their participation in the development and implementation of policies and procedures, through their information and training services, and through the collective bargaining process. Trade unions may also play a role in providing information, advice and representation to employees who have been sexually harassed or harassed, and to employees against whom allegations of sexual harassment and harassment have been made.

(5) *Employees*

The policy should make it clear that employees may contribute to achieving a sexual harassment and harassment free environment through co-operating with management and trade union strategies to eliminate sexual harassment and harassment and that sexual harassment and harassment by employees constitutes misconduct and may lead to disciplinary action.

(6) *Non-Employees*

The policy should point out that the sexual harassment and harassment by non-employees such as clients, customers and business contacts will not be tolerated and may lead to termination of contracts or suspension of services, or the exclusion from a premises or the imposition of other sanctions (as appropriate).

(7) *Communication of Policy*

The policy should include a commitment to effective communication of the policy. The policy should be communicated effectively to all those potentially affected by it including management, employees, customers, clients and other business contacts, including those who supply and receive goods and services. This effective means of communicating a policy could include for example, newsletters, training manuals, training courses, leaflets, websites, emails and notice boards.

To Employees

Employees, including those in management and all other positions of responsibility, should be made aware of the policy as part of any formal induction process whereby new employees become familiar with their job and their working environment and rules and regulations that apply such as health and safety.

Employers should consider a staff handbook where practicable to be distributed to all employees as part of the induction process. This handbook will need to be updated to reflect relevant changes.

To Non-Employees

There may be some practical difficulties in ensuring that the policy is effectively communicated to every relevant person particularly where there is no ongoing relationship. Summaries of policies should be prominently displayed. This may not be feasible for retail outlets or pubs. These should prominently display a short statement confirming the policy's existence and the organisation's commitment to it, making it clear that the complete policy is available.

The effective communication of the policy should be easier where there is an ongoing relationship with clients and customers. This can be achieved by way of a combination of means such as:

— leaflets summarising the policy being prominently displayed where members of the public, clients, and customers attend such as receptions and waiting rooms

— including a leaflet or short written statement summarising the policy in any of the company written material such as appropriate brochures etc.

— it may be appropriate for the contracts of the employer with clients, customers and other business contacts to provide that sexual harassment or harassment of employees of the employer will constitute a repudiation of the contract and may be a ground for the employer to treat the contract at an end.

(8) *Monitoring*

The policy should include a commitment to monitoring incidents of sexual harassment and harassment.

The only way an organisation can know whether its policy and procedures are working is to keep careful track of all complaints of sexual harassment and harassment and how they are resolved. This monitoring information should be used to evaluate the policy and procedures at regular intervals, with changes recommended when something is not working well.

(9) *Training*

The policy should include commitments to training staff on issues of sexual harassment and harassment.

An important means of ensuring that sexual harassment or harassment does not occur is through the provision of training for managers, supervisors and all staff. This should happen for staff at induction or through appropriate awareness raising initiatives. Such training should aim to identify the factors which contribute to a working environment free of sexual harassment and harassment and to familiarise participants with their responsibilities under the employer's policy and any problem they are likely to encounter.

This is considered especially important for those members of staff responsible for implementing the policy and processing complaints.

(10) *Complaints Procedure*

The policy should set out a complaints procedure.

It is essential for employers to attach to their policy a detailed complaints procedure that will be available to employees to process their complaint where they allege they have been subjected to sexual harassment or harassment.

Clients, customers and others who interact regularly with the organisation should be made aware of the employees' right to make a complaint and that they may be requested to participate in the process.

(11) *Reviews*

The policy should include a commitment to review on a regular basis in line with changes in the law, relevant case law or other developments.

A competent person should be designated to ensure that monitoring, training and reviews occur.

(5) THE COMPLAINTS PROCEDURE

The development of clear and precise procedures to deal with sexual harassment and harassment once it has occurred is of great importance. The procedure should ensure the resolution of problems in an effective and efficient manner. Practical guidance for employees on how to deal with sexual harassment and harassment when it occurs and with its aftermath, will make it more likely that it will be dealt with at an early stage.

The following are core elements which are relevant to any complaints procedure. They will need to be adapted and expanded upon to reflect the size and complexity of the employment.

(1) *Plain language*

Core Elements

The procedures should be set out clearly, step by step in plain language and in relevant languages and formats so that a person making a complaint knows what to do and who to approach.

(2) *Time limits*

Time limits should be set for every stage of the investigation.

(3) *Statutory rights*

The procedure should make it clear that using the complaints procedure will not affect the complainant's right to make a complaint under the EE Act and should point out the statutory time limits.

(4) *Victimisation*

The complaints procedure should make clear that an employee will not be victimised or subject to sanction for making a complaint in good faith, or for giving evidence in proceedings, or by giving notice of intention to do so.

The procedure should make clear that in the course of investigating the complaint the employer will make no assumptions about the guilt of the alleged harasser.

(5) *Sanctions*

Employees should be informed that in the event of the complaint being upheld that the disciplinary process will be invoked which may lead to disciplinary sanctions up to and including dismissal. Non-employees should be informed that in the event of the complaint being upheld that appropriate sanctions may be imposed which could in particular circumstances include termination of contract, suspension of service, exclusion from premises etc. as appropriate.

(6) *Confidentiality*

The procedure should make clear that confidentiality will be maintained throughout any investigation to the greatest effort consistent with the requirements of a fair investigation.

Resolving the Problem Informally

Most recipients of sexual harassment or harassment simply want the harassment to stop. The complaints procedure should provide for informal and formal methods of resolving problems.

The procedure should provide for a competent named person to be available to assist in the resolution of any problems through informal means and to provide information to both employees and non-employees on the procedure and on the policy in general.

The employee who is being sexually harassed or harassed should object to the conduct where this is possible and appropriate. The informal procedure should provide that employees should attempt to resolve the problem informally in the first instance. In some cases it may be possible and sufficient for the employee to explain clearly to the person engaging in the unwanted conduct that the behaviour in question is not welcome, that it offends them or makes them uncomfortable and that it interferes with their work.

In circumstances where it is too difficult for an individual to do this on his/her own, an alternative approach would be to seek support from, or for an initial approach to be made by, a sympathetic friend or designated person or trade union representative.

The informal process could provide for mediation.

Formal Complaints Procedure

The complaints procedure should provide for a formal complaints procedure where:

— the employee making the complaint wishes it to be treated formally or

— the alleged sexual harassment or harassment is too serious to be treated under the informal procedure or

— informal attempts at resolution have been unsatisfactory or

— the sexual harassment or harassment continues after the informal procedure has been followed.

Investigation of the complaint

The procedure should provide that investigation of any complaint will be handled with sensitivity and with due respect for the rights of both the complainant and the alleged harasser. The investigation should be, and be perceived to be, independent and objective. The purpose of the investigation is to investigate the allegations and will focus on the complaint.

Those carrying out the investigation should not be connected with the allegation in any way. It is preferable that at least two people should investigate a complaint but it is acknowledged that this may not always be practicable. Such an investigation team should have gender balance and ideally should seek to ensure diversity across the other eight grounds. All of those on the investigation team should have received appropriate training. Every effort should be made to resolve the complaint speedily.

The procedure should provide that both the complainant and alleged harasser should be informed of the following:

— what the formal procedure entails and the relevant time limits

— that both parties have the right to be accompanied and/or represented, by a representative, trade union representative or a friend or colleague

— that the complaint should be in writing and that the alleged harasser be given full details in writing of the nature of the complaint including written statements and any other documentation or evidence including witness statements, interview notes or records of meetings held with the witnesses

— that the alleged harasser be given time to consider the documentation and an opportunity to respond

— that confidentiality will be maintained throughout any investigation to the greatest extent consistent with the requirements of a fair investigation

— that a written record will be kept of all meetings and investigations

— that the investigation having considered all of the evidence before it and the representations made to it will produce a written report to both parties outlining its findings and the reasons for its final decision

— if the complaint is upheld against an employee the report will recommend whether the organisation's disciplinary procedure should be invoked

— if the complaint is upheld against a non-employee the report should recommend appropriate sanctions against the non-employee or his/her employer which could extend where appropriate in the circumstances to:

- exclusion of the individual from premises
- suspension or termination of service
- suspension or termination of a supply service or other contract

— the report may also, or as an alternative, recommend other actions such as the more effective promotion of the organisation's policy on sexual harassment and harassment or training

— if a right of appeal exists both parties should be informed of it and the time limits and procedures involved.

It is the responsibility of the employer to provide for proper notification of the complaint and fair determination of the complaint. What is required in any particular instance will depend on the circumstances and/or complexity of the case and may require the adaptation of the procedures.

Non-Employees

It is possible that if the person accused of sexual harassment or harassment is not an employee, he/she will not wish to participate in the formal procedure, and it will not be possible to secure their participation. Nonetheless a non-employee must be kept informed of all developments and given an opportunity to respond to them. The outcome of the investigation and any potential sanctions must also be explained to the non-employee and/or any person or company for whom he/she works.

(6) REASONABLE ACCOMMODATION

The context, form and implementation of the policy and procedures should be accessible to all with adjustments made and steps taken to ensure accessibility for people with disabilities and across the other grounds. Examples would include use of other languages in policy and procedure, availability of interpreters or signers and use of braille or large print formats etc.

(7) REVIEW OF THIS CODE

The EE Act has been in operation since October 1999. As case law emerges and as developments occur in the area of sexual harassment and harassment policies, it will be necessary to review and amend this code to reflect these changes.

(8) SOURCES FOR OTHER INFORMATION AND ADVICE

Equality Authority
Clonmel Street
Dublin 2
Tel: (01) 4173336; Lo-Call: 1890 245545;
e-mail: info@equality.ie; website: www.equality.ie

ICTU
31/32 Parnell Square
Dublin 1
Tel: (01) 8897777; website: www.ictu.ie

IBEC
84/86 Lwr. Baggot Street
Dublin 2
Tel: (01) 6601011; website: www.ibec.ie

Rape Crisis Centre
70 Lwr. Leeson Street
Dublin 2
Tel: (01) 6614911; (01) 6614564
(after 5.30 pm and weekends); Freefone: 1800 77 88 88

Labour Relations Commission
Tom Johnson House
Haddington Road
Dublin 4
Tel: (01) 6609662; website: www.lrc.ie

Health and Safety Authority
10 Hogan Place
Dublin 2
Tel: (01) 6147000; website: www.hsa.ie

The codes on bullying prepared by the Health and Safety Authority (Code of Practice on the Prevention of Workplace Bullying) and the Labour Relations Commission (S.I. No. 17 of 2002) may also be of assistance.

The Labour Court code of practice in relation to discipline should also be consulted (S.I. No. 321 of 1999).

APPENDIX I — EU DEVELOPMENTS

European Commission
Recommendation

The European Commission's code of practice annexed to its Recommendation of 27th November, 1991 on the protection of the dignity of women and men at work (92/131/EEC) provides the following definition:

> 'Sexual harassment means unwanted conduct of a sexual nature, or other conduct based on sex affecting the dignity of women and men at work'.

Future Development

It is likely that there will be a new Gender Employment Directive which will contain a definition of sexual harassment.

Framework Directive and 'Race' Directive Definitions

Council Directive 2000/78/EC of 27th November, 2000 establishing a general framework for equal treatment in employment and occupation and Council Directive 2000/43/EC of 29th June, 2000 implementing the principle of equal treatment between persons irrespective of racial or ethnic origin, contain definitions of harassment referable to religion or belief, disability, age or sexual orientation (Framework Directive) and racial or ethnic origin (Race Directive).

These Directives define harassment as follows:

> 'When unwanted conduct (related to membership of a particular group) (.....) takes place with the purpose or effect of violating the dignity of a person and of creating an intimidating, hostile, degrading, humiliating or offensive environment'.

Both Directives have to be implemented in Ireland by 2003 (Race Directive — 19 July, 2003; Employment Directive — 2 December, 2003 — however, in order to take account of particular conditions, Member States, may, if necessary, have an additional period of 3 years from 2 December, 2003, that is a total of 6 years to implement the provisions of the Directive on age and disability discrimination) and the definitions contained in the EE Act may require amendment.

Health and Safety Authority Code of Practice for Employers and Employees on the Prevention and Resolution of Bullying at Work[7]

Foreward

The Health and Safety Authority, at the request of, and with the consent of, the Minister for Labour Affairs, Tony Killeen, T.D. and following public consultation, including with the social partners, publishes this Code of Practice entitled 'Code of Practice for Employers and Employees on the Prevention and Resolution of Workplace Bullying', in accordance with section 60 of the Safety, Health and Welfare at Work Act 2005 (No. 10 of 2005), called the '2005 Act' after this.

This Code of Practice provides practical guidance for employers on identifying and preventing bullying at work arising from their duties under section 8(2)(b) of the 2005 Act as regards 'managing and conducting work activities in such a way as to prevent, so far as is reasonably practicable, any improper conduct or behaviour likely to put the safety, health and welfare at work of his or her employees at risk'. It also applies to employees in relation to their duties under section 13(1)(e) of the 2005 Act to 'not engage in improper conduct or behaviour that is likely to endanger his or her own safety, health and welfare at work or that of any other person'.

This Code of Practice comes into effect on 1st May 2007 and from that date it replaces the Code of Practice entitled 'Code of Practice on the Prevention of Workplace Bullying' which was issued by the Authority in March 2002 in accordance with the Safety, Health and Welfare at Work Act 1989. Notice of issue of this Code of Practice, and the withdrawal of the 2002 Code of Practice, was published in the Iris Oifigiúil of Friday, 30th March, 2007.

As regards the use of Codes of Practice in criminal proceedings, section 61 of the 2005 Act provides as follows—

(1) Where in proceedings for an offence under this Act relating to an alleged contravention of any requirement or prohibition imposed by or under a relevant statutory provision being a provision for which a code of practice had been published or approved by the Authority under section 60 at the time of the alleged contravention, subsection (2) shall have effect with respect to that code of practice in relation to those proceedings.

(2) (a) Where a code of practice referred to in subsection (1) appears to the court to give practical guidance as to the observance of the requirement or prohibition alleged to have been contravened, the code of practice shall be admissible in evidence.

(b) Where it is proved that any act or omission of the defendant alleged constitute the contravention:

(i) is a failure to observe a code of practice referred to in subsection (1), or

(ii) is a compliance with that code of practice,

then such failure or compliance is admissible in evidence.

---

[7] Published in March 2007 by the Health and Safety Authority, The Metropolitan Building, James Joyce Street, Dublin 1.© All rights reserved.

(3) A document bearing the seal of the Authority and purporting to be a code of practice or part of a code of practice published or approved of by the Authority under this section shall be admissible as evidence in any proceedings under this Act.'

M. O'Halloran

Assistant Chief Executive and Secretary to the Board

CODE OF PRACTICE FOR EMPLOYERS AND EMPLOYEES

on the Prevention and Resolution of Bullying at Work

1. INTRODUCTION

This Code of Practice, under the Safety, Health and Welfare at Work Act 2005, is aimed at preventing and dealing with bullying where it happens in Irish workplaces. It is a code for both employers and employees.

One in fourteen people reported having been bullied at work in a survey published in 2001 by the ESRI (O'Connell and Williams) for the Department of Enterprise, Trade and Employment. Survey Reports of Bullying Experiences in the Workplace (2007), conducted by the ESRI for the Department of Enterprise, Trade and Employment puts this incidence rate at almost one in thirteen with higher rates reported for female employees.

Bullying is a cost for both employers and employees. The cost can be both financial and human. If not sorted out internally, a serious case could bring an employer before a tribunal, the Labour Court and/or the civil courts. If destructive behaviour is tolerated and continues, it affects performance and general health and well-being of individuals and/or groups. The negative effects can last a long time.

Bullying can be carried out by supervisors, managers, subordinates, fellow employees, customers, business contacts or members of the public.

The Code explains what bullying means and deals with the responsibilities of employers and employees to prevent or resolve it. The Code reflects the legal requirement that employers carry out a risk assessment, and where bullying is identified as a hazard, they ensure that it is included in the safety statement.

The Code recommends dealing with cases internally through the following processes which are explained in the Code:

- informal resolution by a responsible person
- a formal complaints procedure.

Only if the internal processes fail, should it be necessary to get outside support.

Finally, the Code helps those involved to recognise the possible findings which result from the follow up and investigation of a bullying complaint where,

- the complaint is upheld as bullying behaviour
- the complaint is deemed to be unfounded as a bullying behaviour
- the complaint is deemed to be vexatious.

2. STATUS AND SCOPE OF THE CODE

This Code of Practice provides practical guidance for employers on identifying and preventing bullying at work arising from their duties under section 8(2)(b) of the 2005 Act as regards 'managing and conducting work activities in such a way as to prevent, so far as is reasonably practicable, any improper conduct or behaviour likely to put the safety, health and welfare at work of his or her employees at risk'. It also applies to employees in relation to their duties under section 13(1)(e) of the 2005 Act to 'not engage in improper conduct or behaviour that is likely to endanger his or her own safety, health and welfare at work or that of any other person'.

Extracts from the 2005 Act which are relevant are set out in Appendix 1:

- section 8. General duties of employer
- section 9. Information for employees
- section 10. Instruction, training and supervision of employees
- section 13. Duties of employee
- section 14. Interference, misuse, etc.
- section 19. Hazard identification and risk assessment
- section 20. Safety Statement
- section 60. Codes of practice
- section 61. Use of codes of practice in criminal proceedings
- Schedule 3. General Principles of Prevention.

This Code:

- outlines some of the more common behaviours associated with bullying at work
- identifies situations where bullying commonly occurs at work
- describes how to prepare a Bullying Prevention Policy
- sets out procedures for resolving bullying complaints at work.

Failure to follow this Code is not an offence but the Code is admissible in evidence in criminal proceedings under section 61 of the 2005 Act.

This Code applies to all employments in Ireland whether employees work at a fixed location, at home or are mobile.

3. BULLYING AT WORK

3.1. What is Bullying at Work?

Bullying at work has been defined as 'repeated inappropriate behaviour, direct or indirect, whether verbal, physical or otherwise, conducted by one or more persons against another or others, at the place of work and/or in the course of employment, which could reasonably be regarded as undermining the individual's right to dignity at work' [Report of the Task Force on the prevention of workplace bullying, 2001. Also used in the 2005 Report of the Expert Advisory Group on Workplace Bullying and in the Surveys conducted by the ESRI to determine the incidence of workplace bullying.]

An isolated incident of the behaviour in this definition may be an affront to dignity but as a once-off incident is not considered to be bullying.

Bullying puts at risk the safety, health and welfare of people at work.
A pattern of the following behaviours are examples of types of bullying:

- Exclusion with negative consequences
- Verbal abuse/insults
- Physical abuse*
- Being treated less favourably than colleagues
- Intrusion – pestering, spying or stalking
- Menacing behaviour
- Intimidation
- Aggression
- Undermining behaviour
- Excessive monitoring of work
- Humiliation
- Withholding work-related information
- Repeatedly manipulating a person's job content and targets
- Blame for things beyond the person's control.

This list is not exhaustive.

* *This Code does not aim to address physical assault at work. The Authority advises that where it may be a risk, employers have a dedicated policy on violence and assault with no tolerance of such behaviour.*

It is important to distinguish bullying from other inappropriate behaviours. For example, a once off incident of bullying behaviour may be an affront to dignity at work but is not considered to be bullying.

Harassment is closely related to bullying and while it is illegal and should not be tolerated in the workplace, it does not fit the definition. To assist in differentiating the two it is worth considering that harassment is governed by Equality legislation and is predicated on the person being a member of one of the nine categories specified within the anti-harassment legislation. Bullying is legally distinct from harassment as bullying behaviour is not predicated on membership of any distinct group.

Bullying at work does not include reasonable and essential discipline arising from the good management of the performance of an employee at work or actions taken which can be justified as regards the safety, health and welfare of the employees. For example, an employee whose performance is continuously signaled at a level below required targets may feel threatened and insecure in their work but this in itself does not indicate bullying.

Bullying at work can involve people in many different work situations and at all levels:

- manager/supervisor to employee
- employee to supervisor/manager
- one employee to another (or group to group)
- customer or business contact to employee
- employee/supervisor/manager to customer/business contact.

Factors which are known to signal a risk of bullying at work are:

- **High turnover of staff, high absenteeism or poor morale**;
- **Employment tenure** – a bully may regard new, casual or contract employees as easier targets than permanent employees;
- **Hierarchies** – hierarchies involving, for example, technical or non-professional employees working to professionally qualified employees which can sometimes present higher levels of bullying;
- **Changes in the workplace** – workplace changes which can increase the risk include change in ownership, new manager or supervisor, introduction of new work performance measures or of new technology or internal re-organisation;
- **Management of relationships in the workplace** – bullying may be more likely to happen in workplaces that do not have an effective management system which respects persons and monitors and supports work relationships;
- **Personality differences** – petty jealousies, personal biases, taking advantage of vulnerable or less 'street-wise' individuals can contribute to bullying;
- **Gender/age imbalance** – bullying may be more likely where there is an age or a gender imbalance in the workplace;
- **Other factors** include the composition of the workforce, interface with the public, history of tolerance of unacceptable behaviour, lack of or inadequate procedures or disregard of procedures for dealing with bullying.

3.2. Who bullies at work?

It is not possible to describe all bullies but persons who engage in bullying at work may have certain personal characteristics such as poor communication skills, difficulty in working with others, difficulty in delegating responsibility, poor organisational skills or low self-esteem. Good job design, training and supervision can help overcome these difficulties.

Bullying is recognised as being present in other walks of life such as in schools and in the home and bullying at work may be part of a wider cultural background.

3.3. Why deal with Bullying at Work?

Recent research suggests that almost one in every twelve people have reported being bullied at work. Bullying can have serious effects for both the person bullied and for the employer. Stress, ill health, loss of confidence and self esteem and career difficulties can result for a victim. For the employer, a dysfunctional workplace, reduced productivity, poor morale, lost time, industrial relations problems and litigation can follow.

3.4. Role of Employees – Prevention

Employees have rights and duties as regards safety, health and welfare at work under the 2005 Act.

Employees have rights to be treated with dignity and respect at work and not to have their safety, health or welfare put at risk through bullying by the employer, by other employees or other persons. They have a right to complain to the employer if bullied and not to be victimised for so doing. They have a right under safety and health laws to be represented in raising this with the employer.

Employees have duties to behave and conduct themselves so as to respect the right of employers and other employees to dignity, courtesy and respect at work and the right not to be placed at risk as regards to their safety, health and welfare from bullying at work. Employees should also cooperate by providing any relevant information when an allegation of bullying at work is being looked into whether in an informal or formal stage.

3.5. Role of Employer – Prevention

Every employer has a duty to manage and conduct work activities in such a way as to prevent any improper conduct or behaviour likely to put at risk employee's safety, health or welfare at work. The prevention of bullying must therefore be part of the management system.

Employers must prepare a Safety Statement under section 20 of the 2005 Act, based on an identification of the hazards to safety, health and welfare at the place of work, an assessment of the risks involved and setting down the preventive measures necessary to protect safety, health and welfare. Risk is the likelihood of a hazard causing harm and the extent of that harm.

The employer must consider if bullying at work is likely to be a hazard, the extent of risk involved and what preventive measures are necessary.

3.6. How to identify if bullying is a hazard at work

The following will help the employer to identify if bullying is a hazard at work:

- If unacceptable conduct or behaviour has been observed – see the examples under 3.1 above – **What is bullying at work?**
- If substantiated complaints of bullying at work have been made by employees or on their behalf;
- If the human resources unit, the company doctor, nurse, welfare officer or similar person reports bullying at work;
- If, perhaps taken with the above, there is sick leave above the norm, particularly with work related stress certified.

3.7. How to assess the risk?

The risk assessment should be based on:

- The factors listed above under 3.1- **What is bullying at work?** and any information from these factors which signal risks to safety, health and welfare if bullying exists;
- Information derived from organisational climate or work environment assessments or similar feedback mechanisms that may exist in the company;
- Views gathered from consulting with employees and their representatives.

3.8. What preventive measures are recommended?

Measures to prevent bullying at work include:

- Having in place a **Bullying Prevention Policy** which adequately addresses the risks that have been assessed. The policy should be clear in how it will measure implementation. (Where bullying has been identified as a risk, this policy must be referenced or included in the Safety Statement)

- Providing appropriate training and development at all levels but particularly for line manager roles;

- Ensuring clarity of individual and department goals, roles and accountabilities;

- Ensuring access to relevant competent and supportive structures both internal and external.

4. How to Prepare a Bullying Prevention Policy

Prevention is the best way to avoid the risk of bullying at work. An effective policy, and a strong commitment to implementing it is required. The purpose of an effective policy is not simply to prevent improper conduct and behaviour but also to encourage best practice and a safe and harmonious workplace where such behaviour is unlikely to occur.

Employers should therefore adopt, implement and monitor a comprehensive, effective and accessible policy on bullying at work.

4.1. Preparing the Policy

Strategies to create and maintain a working environment in which the dignity and respect of employees are appreciated and upheld are most likely to be effective when they are jointly agreed. In this way, employers and other parties to the employment relationship can create an anti-bullying culture and share a sense of responsibility for that culture. In very small businesses which may not have an employee representative structure, the policy and strategy should be advised to all employees.

The policy and complaints procedure should be adopted, where appropriate, in so far as is practicable with clients, customers and other business contacts after consultation or negotiation with trade union or employee representatives, on its content and implementation. Simple direct language should be used in the policy. Information given to employees should be in a form, manner and, as appropriate, language that is reasonably likely to be understood by the employees concerned.

The policy document should be written, dated and signed by a responsible person at senior management level and updated when appropriate, for example following a change that might impact the validity of the original risk assessment.

As required under safety and health laws and in keeping with normal industrial relations practice, there should be prior consultation, and participation where appropriate, regarding the policy and its implementation, with employees or their representatives, including the Safety Representative or the Safety Committee.

The policy should set out a complaints procedure as recommended within this Code.

It is prudent to keep a record of consultation actions in case of future requirement.

4.2. Core Elements and Implementation Steps

Employer's declaration

The **Bullying Prevention Policy** should declare:

- the employer's commitment to ensuring that the place of work is free from bullying at work and that the work environment is aimed at providing a high quality product or service in an atmosphere of respect, collaboration, openness, safety and equality;

- that all employees have the right to be treated with dignity and respect at work;

- that the risk of bullying has been assessed and preventive measures included, where necessary, in the **Safety Statement**;

- that consultation with employees or their representatives, including the **Safety Representative** and the **Safety Committee**, as appropriate, has taken place as regards the risk of bullying at work and preventative measures;

- that employees also have responsibility in creating and contributing to the maintenance of a work environment free from bullying or from conduct likely to contribute to bullying;

- that complaints by employees of bullying at work will be treated with fairness, sensitivity, respect and confidentiality for all parties concerned;

- that a person or persons alleged to have bullied will be afforded natural justice and treated with fairness, sensitivity and respecting the need for confidentiality with all parties concerned;

- that bullying at work by the employer, by employees and by non-employees, such as clients, customers, sub contractors and business contacts, will not be tolerated and the appropriate employing organisation should deal with the complaint in line with these procedures, which could lead to disciplinary procedures being applied;

- that a complaint of bullying which is found, following investigation, to be vexatious will be dealt with through the disciplinary procedure;

- that human resource management policies and practices will strive to prevent bullying at work;

- that the policy will be updated to reflect the company's experiences in implementing it, relevant changes in the workplace and any external factors that are relevant.

Scope

The **policy** should:

- describe what is meant by bullying at work as set out above under **What is bullying at work?**;

- include a non-exhaustive list of examples of bullying behavior relevant to the particular employment (see also **What is bullying at work?**);

- give the name or job title of the person who may be approached by a person wishing to complain of bullying at work;

- state that the protection extends to:
- bullying at work by management, fellow employees, subordinates, clients, customers and other business contacts;
- beyond the place of work to off-site and to work-related social events;
- state that all complaints of bullying will be taken seriously and will be followed through to resolution;
- employees who make a complaint will not be victimised.

4.3. Allocation of responsibilities as regards prevention of bullying at work

The policy should state that management, others in positions of authority and workplace representatives have a particular responsibility to ensure that bullying at work does not occur and that complaints are addressed speedily. The policy should state that in particular, management should:

- provide good example by treating all in the place of work wit courtesy and respect;
- promote awareness of the policy and complaints procedures;
- be vigilant for signs of bullying at work through observation and through seeking employee feedback and take action before a problem escalates;
- deal sensitively with employees involved in a bullying complaint whether as complainant or alleged bully;
- explain the procedures to be followed if a complaint of bullying at work is made;
- ensure that an employee making a complaint is not victimised for doing so;
- monitor and follow up the situation after a complaint is made so that the bullying at work does not recur.

Trade Unions

The policy should address the contribution to be made by the trade union/s, as appropriate, including as regards the prevention of bullying in the workplace through their participation in the development and implementation of policies and procedures, through their information and training services, and through the collective bargaining process. Trade unions may also play a role in providing information, advice and representation to employees who have been bullied at work, and to employees against whom allegations of bullying at work have been made.

Employees

The policy should indicate that employees can contribute to achieving a work environment which does not tolerate bullying at work. This could also include co-operating with preventive measures introduced by management, and also through trade union strategies to eliminate or avoid bullying at work. Employees should recognise that a finding of bullying at work will be dealt with through the disciplinary procedure. Equally a finding that the complaint was vexatious will be dealt with through the disciplinary procedure.

Non-Employees

The policy should indicate that bullying at work by non-employees such as clients, customers and business contacts is not tolerated and may lead to termination of contracts or suspension of services, or to exclusion from a premises or the imposition of other sanctions, as appropriate.

4.4 Communication of Policy

The policy should include a commitment to effective communication of the policy. It should be communicated effectively to all those potentially affected by it, including management, employees, customers, clients and other business contacts, such as those who supply and receive goods and services. Effective means of communicating a policy could include newsletters, training manuals, training courses, leaflets, websites, emails, toolbox talks and notice boards.

Communication to Employees

New employees, including those in management and all other positions of responsibility, should be made aware of the policy as part of any formal induction process to familiarise them with their job and their working environment and any rules and regulations that apply.

Where a staff handbook is distributed to employees as part of the induction process the Bullying Prevention Policy should be included.

Existing employees should receive updated and regular communication on the policy.

Communication to Non-Employees

A summary of the Bullying Prevention Policy should be prominently displayed where appropriate and as identified on the risk assessment, such as at places where members of the public, clients, and customers attend.

4.5 Monitoring

The policy should include a commitment to monitoring and recording incidents of bullying at work.

Statistics and information gathered from such monitoring should be recorded and used to assist the employer take corrective action or achieve continuous improvement in their bullying prevention policy and procedure.

4.6 Training and Supervision

Employees should be provided with such information, training, development and supervision as is necessary to ensure the prevention of employer bullying. This should include:

- making employees aware of the Bullying Prevention Policy;
- information on the appropriate behaviour to comply with the terms of the policy;
- training, if needed, in order to comply with the policy;

- assistance, if necessary, to overcome a bullying incident, as well as adequate and informed supervision of the work environment.

The policy should include commitments to staff training and supervision as identified in the risk assessment on issues related to bullying at work, including the provision of training for managers, supervisors and for all staff, at induction or through appropriate awareness raising initiatives. Such training should identify the factors which contribute to a working environment free of bullying and familiarise participants with their responsibilities under the policy and any problems they are likely to encounter.

Such training is especially important for those members of staff responsible for supervision and for implementing the policy and responding to complaints.

Best practice would ensure that records are kept by the employer of all such training.

4.7 Reviews

The policy should include a commitment to review on a regular basis in line with experience in the employment, changes in the law, relevant case law or other developments.

A responsible person should be named in the policy to ensure that monitoring, training and reviews take place.

5. OTHER PREVENTIVE MEASURES

5.1. Role clarity

As a matter of good practice, employers should define each employee's role and accountability as clearly as possible. This may include a written description of main duties and responsibilities and a clear line of supervision. This should be reviewed in a collaborative manner on an on-going basis and any changes in job content should be communicated clearly to the individual and those working alongside him/her.

5.2. Acknowledging responsibility – managers, supervisors and employees

Managers, and supervisors, have a responsibility to manage in such a way as to protect the safety, health and welfare of employees. This means accepting responsibility for preventing bullying at work and for resolving alleged cases of bullying at work.

Every employee is responsible for safeguarding his/her own safety and welfare, and that of his/her colleagues who may be affected by his/her actions, or omissions, while at work. Therefore each employee has a duty not to place the safety, health and welfare of colleagues at risk by engaging in bullying or, where in a position of authority, to take the appropriate steps to stop bullying if or when it occurs.

5.3. Access to 'contact person' and to competent advisory services

As part of the Bullying Prevention Policy employers should name a 'contact person' who can listen and advise about complaints of bullying at work and explain the procedures in place to resolve it. These individuals should receive appropriate training.

The Contact Person role is a voluntary role of facilitation to act as the first point of contact for someone who believes that he or she is being treated in a bullying manner. The Contact Person is nominated, through agreement with the employer. He/she has a listening brief and is a reference point for the complainant, and he/she could, for instance, provide the complainant with a copy of the policy, outline the routes available and explain the roles of personnel involved. The Contact Person does not get involved in any other way in the complaints procedure and is not an advocate for either party.

In smaller organisations, this role may be provided by an outside agency, such as a representative body or an advisory body.

Employers have a duty under safety and health laws to obtain the services of a competent person where necessary to help comply with such laws. There may be situations as regards bullying at work where an employer could benefit from expert assistance. This could be provided within the undertaking or sourced from outside. It could involve seeking help from an employer or other representative body which provides such advice or from relevant public bodies such as the Health and Safety Authority or the Labour Relations Commission. It could involve seeking the services of persons particularly qualified in mediation or counseling or training in this area.

6. RESOLVING BULLYING AT WORK

The following procedures, both informal and formal, should be outlined within the Bullying Prevention Policy and followed and implemented should a complaint be made.

6.1. Informal process

A problem-solving approach is promoted to ensure that the behaviour complained of, if established in fact, is eliminated and that working relationships are restored. An informal process should:

- Aim to assess the allegation and address it;
- Use agreed procedures;
- Be consistent, systematic, transparent and unbiased;
- Ideally have an intervention addressing the issue in place within three weeks or an agreed, indicative time frame;*
- Promote the restoration of harmony over the medium to long term.

On receipt of a complaint of alleged bullying, or a complaint that a bullying atmosphere or bullying type behaviours are occurring, an employer should try to have the matter resolved informally with the consent of the parties involved. For general non-specific issues, a proactive, non-judgmental intervention approach such as information sessions, clarifying what is acceptable interaction for a workplace and monitoring should be used.

Informal resolution of a specific bullying allegation could include for example, clarification of what bullying is, agreement to alter verbal style, agreement by the person complained of, if they accept that their behaviour was inappropriate, that the conduct will not be repeated, or an explanation to the complainant about what occurred from the point of view of the person complained of which dispels the complaint.

The first step in any informal resolution of a complaint should be to get the facts of the complaint, the specific issues complained of, when they occurred and to judge whether or not they fall within the definition of bullying, and thereafter to establish whether or not they are representative of the events complained of.

Generally, the employer or the person heading up the organisation is advised not to try personally to informally resolve the complaint but should instead refer the dispute for resolution to another senior manager, or such other person as may be agreed. This is to prevent any bias or perceived bias on the part of the employer, should the issue be referred to him/her at a later stage in the process.

In small and micro organisations, where internal structures are limited, if the complaint is made by or against a senior person within the organisation, it may be necessary to use the expertise of an independent professional body to access mediation or conciliation. Such bodies may include the Mediation Services of the **Labour Relations Commission**. Even in larger organisations, external assistance may be required in order to initiate an effective early resolution. In other cases in small and micro organisations, where there is no conflict of interest, the employer or organisation leader may try to resolve the matter informally in some circumstances provided objectivity is not compromised.

* *While it is crucially important for both the complainant and the person complained against that an effective process be put in place promptly upon a complaint being made, it is also very important that enough time be given to the process and to any mediation or monitoring that this involves. Therefore a time frame and speedy intervention is emphasised while not diminishing the fact that the intervention may carry on into the medium term in order to ensure it remedies the issues fully.*

KEY STEPS IN THE INFORMAL PROCESS ARE AS FOLLOWS:

6.1.a. A complainant alleges bullying

- Any employee who believes he or she is being bullied should, where possible, indicate directly to the person complained of that the behaviour in question is unacceptable. In circumstances where the complainant finds it difficult to approach the person complained of directly, he or she should seek help and advice, from a 'contact person' nominated by the employer under the Bullying Prevention Policy, or another colleague or trade union / staff representative.

- A 'contact person' is a person given authority by the employer to act as an initial facilitator where bullying is being alleged. See section 5.3 above which defines the role.

- The employer should designate a separate person who has had appropriate training and experience and who is familiar with the procedures involved to deal with the complaint on behalf of the organisation. This person should not be the 'contact person' and may be a supervisor/manager or someone in authority within the organisation. For each complaint that arises, a designated person should be assigned to deal with that specific case. This is a very important role and pivotal in altering bullying cultures and handling complaints effectively at informal stage. Effective guidance and training should be in place for those who are engaged at this level with the process.

- The complaint may be verbal or written. If verbal, a written note of what is complained of should be taken by the designated person and a copy given to the complainant.

- The designated person who is handling the complaint, should then establish the facts, the context and then the next course of action in dealing with the matter under the informal procedure.

- If the complaint concerns bullying as defined and includes concrete examples of inappropriate behaviour, the person complained against should be presented with the complaint and his/her response established.

- Thereafter a method should be agreed to progress the issue to resolution so that both parties can return to a harmonious working environment without bullying being a factor.

- If the behaviour complained of does not concern bullying as defined, an alternative approach should be put in place and a rationale recorded. If there are no concrete examples given, it must be deemed that there is no complaint to be answered by the person complained of as they have no recourse to repudiating an accusation that doesn't give any specifics.

- Line managers should be kept informed, as appropriate, about the process in train.

6.1.b. Intervention

The first step in the informal approach is to ascertain the facts of the accusation, and present them to the person complained of, where they are assessed to be validly made.

In following the informal process, steps to stop the bullying behaviour, where it has been identified, and monitor the situation along specified lines should be agreed with both parties. This may involve a direct or indirect approach and possible resolution through a programme to change behaviour. It may involve mediation* by an agreed mediator who is practiced in dealing with bullying at work.

Mediation is a voluntary and confidential process for resolving disputes wherein the parties agree to attempt to resolve the issues of the dispute without recourse to the judgment of others with the aid of a professional mediator.

Enough time needs to be allowed for the mediation or on-going monitoring process to be successful and behaviour change to be realistically achieved over the longer term. It may be necessary to consider if other working arrangements are required or feasible during this short-term phase. A proposal should be made, considered, and an action and time frame should be agreed, signed and dated, preferably by both parties.

- The designated person should keep **a record** of all stages; the complaint, the first meeting, action agreed and signed records of the final meeting. The purpose of the records, which do not include detail of discussions, is to provide evidence of the complaint having been met with an organizational response and attempt at resolution. Records should be kept in accordance with the Data Protection Act, specifically section 2(1) governing Retention, within an agreed HR filing system and be available only to those directly involved and within the confines of the obligations and duties of the Data Protection Act, 2003.

- Information disclosed in the course of mediation must remain within the mediation process and must not be given by the mediator to anyone or to an investigator if there is a subsequent investigation at formal stage.

- Confidentiality is crucial for this stage to be effective and breaches of confidentiality, where exposed, should be met with sanctions highlighted in advance.

6.1.c. Closure

- To obtain closure after a resolution is found through informal procedures both parties should be given support or periodical reviews, in so far as is reasonable, which, if necessary, could include counseling or other appropriate interventions or support services;
- Where a complaint has been assessed as vexatious, the matter should be progressed through the disciplinary procedures;
- In many situations, with the co-operation of all parties, the matter can rest here.

6.2. Formal process

If the issue is not or cannot be resolved through an informal process, or, if after that informal process the bullying persists, a formal process should be invoked. The process includes a formal complaint, and a formal investigation. The purpose of an investigation is to determine the facts and the credibility or otherwise of a complaint of bullying. Where an investigation is to be carried out, the procedures below should be followed.

KEY STEPS IN THE FORMAL INVESTIGATION PROCESS ARE AS FOLLOWS:

6.2.a. Formal complaint

The complainant should make a formal complaint, ideally in written form and signed and dated.

The complaint should be confined to precise details of alleged incidents of bullying, including their dates, and names of witnesses, where possible.

* Where this is not possible, a written record should be taken of the complaint by the designated person and signed by the complainant.

The complainant should be advised of the aims and objectives of the formal process, the procedures and time frame involved, and the possible outcomes. He/she should be assured of support as required throughout the process. He/she should again be given a copy of the Bullying Prevention Policy.

6.2.b. Information to the person complained against

The person complained against should be notified in writing that an allegation of bullying has been made against him/her. He or she should be assured of the organisation's presumption of his or her innocence of any wrongdoing at this juncture. He/she should be advised of the aims and objectives of the formal process and procedures and time frame involved and the possible outcomes. He/she should be assured of support as required throughout the process.

A meeting should be organised at which he/she is given a copy of the complaint in full and any relevant documents including the Bullying Prevention Policy.

6.2.c. Investigation

The investigation should be governed by terms of reference which should include the following:

- The investigation will be conducted in accordance with the employment's Bullying Prevention Policy which should reflect this Code of Practice.
- The likely time scale for its completion – an indicative time frame should be outlined and agreed and its rationale explained.
- The scope of the investigation, indicating that the investigator will consider whether the complaint falls within the definition of bullying at work and whether the complaint has been upheld.

Statements from all parties should be recorded in writing as the use of written statements tends to make matters clearer from the outset and maintains clarity throughout the investigation. Copies of the record of their statements should be given to and agreed with those who make statements to the investigator.

All parties should continue to work normally, if possible during the investigation.

The objective of an investigation is to ascertain whether or not, on the balance of probabilities, the behaviours complained of occurred. Evidence and witness statements are relied on for this purpose. The investigation should be conducted by either a designated member(s) of management (as outlined earlier in this Code) or, if necessary, (for example in the case of any possible conflict of interest) an agreed, external third party. In either case, the person nominated should have appropriate training and experience and be familiar with the procedures involved. The investigation should be conducted thoroughly, objectively, with sensitivity, utmost confidentiality, and with due respect for the rights of both the complainant and the person
complained of.

The investigator should meet with the complainant and the person complained of and any witnesses or relevant persons on an individual confidential basis with a view to establishing the facts. A work colleague or employee/trade union representative may accompany the complainant and the person complained of, if so desired.

The investigation should be completed as quickly as possible, preferably within an agreed timeframe. The investigator should submit the report to the employer which should include his or her conclusions. The complainant and the person complained of should be given a copy of the report as soon as possible by the employer and given an opportunity to comment, within a set deadline, before the employer decides on any action to take.

The employer should decide in the light of the investigator's report and the comments made, if any, what action is to be taken arising from the report. The employer should then in writing inform the complainant and the person complained against of the next steps. At the end of the process the documentation should be kept by the employer in line with the Retention guidance within the Data Protection Act, 2003 (already referred to in this Code) and made available only in compliance with that Act.

6.2.d. Action where the complaint is upheld

Where a complaint has been upheld, bullying has been identified as a behaviour which is a hazard in that organisation/department. Bullying behaviour is recognised as having potentially damaging effects to the health of the person bullied and damaging consequences for the organisation. Eliminating the hazardous behaviour and controlling the risks of it re-occurring is a requirement of the employer as part of his/her duty of care under Health and Safety legislation. Action should be taken to eliminate the risk of the bullying behaviour continuing or being repeated at a later date. A record of the interventions used for this purpose should be kept.

If a complaint is upheld the matter is now a disciplinary issue and the employer should follow the appropriate disciplinary procedures. An employer who does not have such procedures in place could refer to the Labour Relations Commission's Codes of Practice – Grievance and Disciplinary Procedures and Voluntary Dispute Resolution.

An employer should decide what further action as regards the complaint is necessary, including specific remedies to eliminate exposure to the hazard in future and to reduce the effects of the prior exposure for the complainant. The employer should keep the situation under review. It may be appropriate in some cases to provide for counseling for the complainant and also for the person complained against, or to decide on other steps such as better training or supervision, re-assignment or re-organisation of work.

6.2.e. Action where complaint is not upheld

It is important that employers, managers and supervisors monitor the situation to ensure that there is no victimisation or appearance of victimisation of a complainant following an investigation. It is crucial that situations are treated sympathetically where complaints are made in good faith but not upheld, and it should be noted that there are instances where this will be the case.

Where a complaint is not upheld, the employer has a duty to the person complained against. It should be made clear to both parties that the complaint is not upheld, and no wrongdoing has been found. Support and affirmation should be offered to the person against whom the complaint was made, and all efforts should be made to ensure that anyone with a prior knowledge of the complaint is made aware of the finding that it is not upheld.

Where, on the other hand, a complaint has been found to have been maliciously made, the employer's disciplinary procedure should apply.

6.3. Appeals

Within the formal system, an appeals process for both parties should be in place. The reason for the appeal should be outlined in writing to management if such an option is being taken. The appeal should be heard by another party, of at least the same level of seniority as – but preferably more senior than – the original investigator, and focus only on the aspect of the case cited by the appellant as being the subject of the appeal. The grounds of the appeal and any outcome and methodology employed should be appended to the investigation file.

Very small and micro organisations will need to consider at the outset of the formal process how they would manage a request for appeal and this may require outside independent support.

6.4. Closure and next steps

Both parties should be given appropriate support and periodical reviews, in so far as is reasonable, after a resolution is found so as to obtain closure. It must be accepted that investigations can result in very divisive relationships for individuals, teams and departments and some type of reconciliation or rehabilitative meetings, or team-working session would be advised to restore healthier working communication for the future. In many situations, with the cooperation of all parties, the matter can rest here.

7. IF INTERNAL PROCEDURES DO NOT RESOLVE A BULLYING COMPLAINT

If full utilisation of the range of available internal procedures has not resolved a bullying complaint, the services of a Rights Commissioner may be accessed directly by individuals involved.

Rights Commissioners can assess how procedures were applied in bullying cases and thereafter intervene in a range of ways, including, where appropriate, carrying out a new investigation. Application for a Rights Commissioner hearing must be made directly by the appellant, citing the Industrial Relations Acts 1969–2001. Application forms for such hearings are available on-line (www.lrc.ie) or by request from the Labour Relations Commission. Findings of Rights Commissioners, which are delivered in the form of a recommendation, can be appealed to the Labour Court.

Certain categories of worker, including gardai, teachers and civil servants are not governed by these IR Acts. Access to the machinery of the Rights Commissioner/LRC and Labour Court is confined to those defined as 'workers' – for more information, see section 23(1) of the Industrial Relations Act, 1990. This situation is not within the remit of this Code.

8. ROLE OF THE HEALTH AND SAFETY AUTHORITY

The role of the Health and Safety Authority in respect of bullying at work is to monitor if employers and employees are meeting their obligations and duty of care under the 2005 Act.

Where complaints of bullying at work are made to the Authority it can direct that the procedures in this Code be observed.

The Authority's role is to promote and to ensure compliance with this Code. The Authority can provide advice and support where necessary and use its powers of enforcement if bullying is a serious hazard which is not controlled and the safety, health and welfare of employees is at risk.

APPENDIX 1
EXTRACTS FROM THE SAFETY, HEALTH AND WELFARE AT WORK ACT 2005.

Section 8: General Duties of Employer

(1) Every employer shall ensure, so far as is reasonably practicable, the safety, health and welfare at work of his or her employees.

(2) Without prejudice to the generality of subsection (1), the employer's duty extends, in particular, to the following:

    (a)   managing and conducting work activities in such a way as to ensure, so far as is reasonably practicable, the safety, health and welfare at work of his or her employees;

(b) managing and conducting work activities in such a way as to prevent, so far as is reasonably practicable, any improper conduct or behaviour likely to put the safety, health or welfare at work of his or her employees at risk;

(c) as regards the place of work concerned, ensuring, so far as is reasonably practicable:

    (i) the design, provision and maintenance of it in a condition that is safe and without risk to health;

    (ii) the design, provision and maintenance of safe means of access to and egress from it; and

    (iii) the design, provision and maintenance of plant and machinery or any other articles that are safe and without risk to health;

(d) ensuring, so far as it is reasonably practicable, the safety and the prevention of risk to health at work of his or her employees relating to the use of any article or substance or the exposure to noise, vibration or ionising or other radiations or any other physical agent;

(e) providing systems of work that are planned, organised, performed, maintained and revised as appropriate so as to be, so far as is reasonably practicable, safe and without risk to health;

(f) providing and maintaining facilities and arrangements for the welfare of his or her employees at work;

(g) providing the information, instruction, training and supervision necessary to ensure, so far as is reasonably practicable, the safety, health, and welfare at work of his or her employees;

(h) determining and implementing the safety, health and welfare measures necessary for the protection of the safety, health and welfare of his or her employees when identifying hazards and carrying out a risk assessment under section 19 or when preparing a safety statement under section 20 and ensuring that the measures take account of changing circumstances and the general principles of prevention specified in Schedule 3;

(i) having regard to the general principles of prevention in Schedule 3, where risks cannot be eliminated or adequately controlled or in such circumstances as may be prescribed, providing and maintaining such suitable protective clothing and equipment as is necessary to ensure, so far as is reasonably practicable, the safety, health and welfare at work of his or her employees;

(j) preparing and revising, as appropriate, adequate plans and procedures to be followed and measures to be taken in the case of an emergency or serious and imminent danger;

(k) reporting accidents and dangerous occurrences, as may be prescribed, to the Authority or to a person prescribed under section 33, as appropriate; and

(l) obtaining, where necessary, the services of a competent person (whether under a contract of employment or otherwise) for the purpose of ensuring, so far as is reasonably practicable, the safety, health and welfare at work of his or her employees.

(3) Any duty imposed on an employer under the relevant statutory provisions in respect of any of his or her employees shall also apply in respect of the use by him or her of the services of a fixed term employee or a temporary employee.

(4) For the duration of the assignment of any fixed-term employee or temporary employee working in his or her undertaking, it shall be the duty of every employer to ensure that working conditions are such as will protect the safety, health and welfare at work of such an employee.

(5) Every employer shall ensure that any measures taken by him or her relating to safety, health and welfare at work do not involve financial cost to his or her employees.

Section 9: Information for employees

(1) Without prejudice to the generality of *section 8*, every employer shall, when providing information to his or her employees under that section on matters relating to their safety, health and welfare at work ensure that the information:

    (a)   is given in a form, manner and, as appropriate, language that is reasonably likely to be understood by the employees concerned, and

    (b)   includes the following information:

        (i)   the hazards to safety, health and welfare at work and the risks identified by the risk assessment;

        (ii)   the protective and preventive measures to be taken concerning safety, health and welfare at work under the relevant statutory provisions in respect of the place of work and each specific task to be performed at the place of work; and

        (iii)   the names of persons designated under section 11 and of safety representatives selected under section 25, if any.

(2) Where an employee of another undertaking is engaged in work activities in an employer's undertaking, that employer shall take measures to ensure that the employee's employer receives adequate information concerning the matters referred to in subsection (1).

(3) Every employer shall ensure that employees appointed under section 18 and safety representatives, if any, have access, for the purposes of performing their functions relating to the safety, health and welfare of employees, to:

    (a)   the risk assessment carried out under section 19;

    (b)   information relating to accidents and dangerous occurrences required to be reported to the Authority or a person prescribed under section 33 under the relevant statutory provisions; and

    (c)   any information arising from protective and preventive measures taken under the relevant statutory provisions or provided by the Authority, a person prescribed under section 33, or a person referred to in section 34(2).

(4) (a)   Where an employer proposes to use the services of a fixed term employee or a temporary employee, the employer shall, prior to commencement of employment, give information to the employee relating to:

        (i)   any potential risks to the safety, health and welfare of the employee at work;

        (ii)   health surveillance;

(iii) any special occupational qualifications or skills required in the place of work; and

(iv) any increased specific risks which the work may involve.

(b) Where an employer proposes to use the services of a temporary employee, the employer shall:

(i) specify to the temporary employment business concerned the occupational qualifications necessary for and the specific features of the work for which such an employee is required; and

(ii) ensure that the temporary employment business gives the information referred to in paragraph (a) to the employee.

(5) The temporary employment business referred to in subsection (4)(b) shall give to the employee the information referred to in subsection (4)(b)(i).

Section 10: Instruction, training and supervision of employees

(1) Without prejudice to the generality of section 8 and having regard to sections 25 and *26*, every employer shall, when providing instruction, training and supervision to his or her employees in relation to their safety, health and welfare at work, ensure that:

(a) instruction, training and supervision is provided in a form, manner and, as appropriate, language that is reasonably likely to be understood by the employee concerned;

(b) employees receive, during time off from their work, where appropriate, and without loss of remuneration, adequate safety, health and welfare training, including, in particular, information and instructions relating to the specific task to be performed by the employee and the measures to be taken in an emergency;

(c) in relation to any specific task assigned to an employee, that his or her capabilities in relation to safety, health and welfare are taken into account;

(d) in the case of:

(i) a class or classes of particularly sensitive employees to whom any of the relevant statutory provisions apply; or

(ii) any employee or group of employees exposed to risks expressly provided for under the relevant statutory provisions, the employees concerned are protected against the dangers that specifically affect them.

(2) Training under this section shall be adapted to take account of new or changed risks to safety, health and welfare at work and shall, as appropriate, be repeated periodically.

(3) Training under this section shall be provided to employees:

(a) on recruitment;

(b) in the event of the transfer of an employee or change of task assigned to an employee;

(c) on the introduction of new work equipment, systems of work or changes in existing work equipment or systems of work; and

(d) on the introduction of new technology.

(4) Where, in respect of any particular work, competency requirements are prescribed, the employer shall provide for the release of employees, during working hours, where

appropriate, and without loss of remuneration, for the purpose of attending training in matters relating to safety, health and welfare at work as regards the particular work.

(5) Every employer shall ensure that persons at work in the place of work concerned who are employees of another employer receive instructions relating to any risks to their safety, health and welfare in that place of work as necessary or appropriate.

(6) Every employer who uses the services of a fixed-term employee or a temporary employee shall ensure that the employee receives the training appropriate to the work which he or she is required to carry out having regard to his or her qualifications and experience.

Section 13: General Duties of Employee and Persons in Control of Places of Work

(1) An employee shall, while at work:

(a) comply with the relevant statutory provisions, as appropriate, and take reasonable care to protect his or her safety, health and welfare and the safety, health and welfare of any other person who may be affected by the employee's acts or omissions at work;

(b) ensure that he or she is not under the influence of an intoxicant to the extent that he or she is in such a state as to endanger his or her own safety, health or welfare at work or that of any other person;

(c) if reasonably required by his or her employer, submit to any appropriate, reasonable and proportionate tests for intoxicants by, or under the supervision of, a registered medical practitioner who is a competent person, as may be prescribed;

(d) co-operate with his or her employer or any other person so far as is necessary to enable his or her employer or the other person to comply with the relevant statutory provisions, as appropriate;

(e) not engage in improper conduct or other behaviour that is likely to endanger his or her own safety, health and welfare at work or that of any other person;

(f) attend such training and, as appropriate, undergo such assessment as may reasonably be required by his or her employer or as may be prescribed relating to safety, health and welfare at work or relating to the work carried out by the employee;

(g) having regard to his or her training and the instructions given by his or her employer, make correct use of any article or substance provided for use by the employee at work or for the protection of his or her safety, health and welfare at work, including protective clothing or equipment;

(h) report to his or her employer or to any other appropriate person, as soon as practicable:

(i) any work being carried on, or likely to be carried on, in a manner which may endanger the safety, health or welfare at work of the employee or that of any other person;

(ii) any defect in the place of work, the systems of work, any article or substance which might endanger the safety, health or welfare at work of the employee or that of any other person; or

(iii) any contravention of the relevant statutory provisions which may endanger the safety, health and welfare at work of the employee or that of any other person, of which he or she is aware.

(2) An employee shall not, on entering into a contract of employment, misrepresent himself or herself to an employer with regard to the level of training as may be prescribed under subsection (1)(f).

Section 14: Interference, misuse etc

A person shall not intentionally, recklessly or without reasonable cause:

(a) interfere with, misuse or damage anything provided under the relevant statutory provisions or otherwise for securing the safety, health and welfare of persons at work; or

(b) place at risk the safety, health or welfare of persons in connection with work activities.

Section 19: Hazard identification and risk assessment

(1) Every employer shall identify the hazards in the place of work under his or her control, assess the risks presented by those hazards and be in possession of a written assessment (to be known and referred to in this Act as a 'risk assessment') of the risks to the safety, health and welfare at work of his or her employees, including the safety, health and welfare of any single employee or group or groups of employees who may be exposed to any unusual or other risks under the relevant statutory provisions.

(2) For the purposes of carrying out a risk assessment under subsection (1), the employer shall, taking account of the work being carried on at the place of work, have regard to the duties imposed by the relevant statutory provisions.

(3) The risk assessment shall be reviewed by the employer where—

(a) there has been a significant change in the matters to which it relates; or

(b) there is another reason to believe that it is no longer valid, and, following the review, the employer shall amend the risk assessment as appropriate.

(4) In relation to the most recent risk assessment carried out by an employer, he or she shall take steps to implement any improvement considered necessary relating to the safety, health and welfare at work of employees and to ensure that any such improvement is implemented in respect of all activities and levels of the place of work.

(5) Every person to whom Sections 12 or 15 applies shall carry out a risk assessment in accordance with this section to the extent that his or her duties under those sections may apply to persons other than his or her employees.

Section 20: Safety statement

(1) Every employer shall prepare, or cause to be prepared, a written statement (to be known and referred to in this Act as a 'safety statement'), based on the identification of the hazards and the risk assessment carried out under section 19, specifying the manner in which the safety, health and welfare at work of his or her employees shall be secured and managed.

(2) Without prejudice to the generality of subsection (1), every employer shall ensure that the safety statement specifies:

(a)   the hazards identified and the risks assessed;

(b)   the protective and preventive measures taken and the resources provided for protecting safety, health and welfare at the place of work to which the safety statement relates;

(c)   the plans and procedures to be followed and the measures to be taken in the event of an emergency or serious and imminent danger, in compliance with sections 8 and 11;

(d)   the duties of his or her employees regarding safety, health and welfare at work, including cooperation with the employer and any persons who have responsibility under the relevant statutory provisions in matters relating to safety, health and welfare at work;

(e)   the names and, where applicable, the job title or position held of each person responsible for performing tasks assigned to him or her pursuant to the safety statement; and

(f)   the arrangements made regarding the appointment of safety representatives and consultation with, and participation by, employees and safety representatives, in compliance with sections 25 and 26, including the names of the safety representative and the members of the safety committee, if appointed.

(3) Every employer shall bring the safety statement, in a form, manner and, as appropriate, language that is reasonably likely to be understood, to the attention of:

(a)   his or her employees, at least annually and, at any other time, following its amendment in accordance with this section;

(b)   newly-recruited employees upon commencement of employment; and

(c)   other persons at the place of work who may be exposed to any specific risk to which the safety statement applies.

(4) Where there are specific tasks being performed at the place of work that pose a serious risk to safety, health or welfare, an employer shall bring to the attention of those affected by that risk relevant extracts of the safety statement setting out:

(a)   the risk identified;

(b)   the risk assessment; and

(c)   the protective and preventive measures taken in accordance with the relevant statutory provisions in relation to that risk.

(5) Every employer shall, taking into account the risk assessment carried out under section 19, review the safety statement where:

(a)   there has been a significant change in the matters to which it refers;

(b)   there is another reason to believe that the safety statement is no longer valid; or

(c)   an inspector in the course of an inspection, investigation, examination, inquiry under section 64 or otherwise directs that the safety statement be amended within 30 days of the giving of that direction;

and, following the review, the employer shall amend the safety statement as appropriate to co-operate.

(6) Every employer who is conducting activities, as may be prescribed in accordance with this subsection, who contracts with another employer for that employer to provide services

to him or her shall require that that employer is in possession of an up-to-date safety statement as required under this section.

(7) A copy of a safety statement, or relevant extract of it, shall be kept available for inspection at or near every place of work to which it relates while work is being carried out there.

(8) It shall be sufficient compliance with this section by an employer employing 3 or less employees to observe the terms of a code of practice, if any, relating to safety statements which applies to the class of employment covering the type of work activity carried on by the employer.

(9) Every person to whom section 12 or 15 applies shall prepare a safety statement in accordance with this section to the extent that his or her duties under those sections may apply to persons other than his or her employees.

Section 60: Codes of practice

(1) For the purpose of providing practical guidance to employers, employees and any other persons to whom this Act applies with respect to safety, health and welfare at work, or the requirements or prohibitions of any of the relevant statutory provisions, the Authority:

(a) may, and shall if so requested by the Minister, prepare and publish codes of practice; and

(b) may approve of a code of practice or any part of a code of practice made or published by any other body.

(2) Before publishing or approving of a code of practice or any part of a code of practice under this section, the Authority:

(a) shall obtain the consent of the Minister;

(b) may publish in such manner as the Authority considers appropriate a draft of the code of practice or sections of a draft code of practice and shall give persons one month from the date of publication of the draft code or sections within which to make written representations to the Authority in relation to the draft code or sections of the draft code, or such further period, not exceeding 28 days, as the Authority in its absolute discretion thinks fit; and

(c) following consultation and, where relevant, having considered the representations, if any, made, shall submit the draft code to the Minister for his or her consent to its publication or approval under this section, with or without modification.

(3) Where the Authority publishes or approves of a code of practice or approves of any part of a code of practice, it shall publish a notice of such publication or approval in *Iris Oifigiuil* and that notice shall:

(a) identify the code;

(b) specify the matters relating to safety, health and welfare at work or the relevant statutory provisions in respect of which the code is published or approved of; and

(c) specify the date on which the code shall come into operation.

(4) The Authority may with the consent of the Minister and following consultation with any other person or body that the Authority considers appropriate or as the Minister directs:

(a) amend or revoke any code of practice or part of any code of practice prepared and published by it under this section; or

(b)   withdraw its approval of any code of practice or part of any code of practice approved by it under this section.

(5) Where the Authority amends or revokes, or withdraws its approval of a code of practice or any part of a code of practice published or approved under this section, it shall publish notice of the amendment, revocation or withdrawal, as the case may be, in *Iris Oifigiuil.*

(6) The Authority shall make available for public inspection without charge at its principal office during normal working hours:

(a)   a copy of each code of practice published or approved by it; and

(b)   where a code of practice has been amended, a copy of the code as so amended.

(7) Notwithstanding the repeal of the Act of 1989 by section 4, a code of practice in operation immediately before the commencement of that section continues to be a code of practice as if prepared and published under this section.

Section 61: Use of codes of practice in criminal proceedings.

(1) Where in proceedings for an offence under this Act relating to an alleged contravention of any requirement or prohibition imposed by or under a relevant statutory provision being a provision for which a code of practice had been published or approved by the Authority under section 60 at the time of the alleged contravention, subsection (2) shall have effect with respect to that code of practice in relation to those proceedings.

(2) (a)   Where a code of practice referred to in *subsection (1)* appears to the court to give practical guidance as to the observance of the requirement or prohibition alleged to have been contravened, the code of practice shall be admissible in evidence.

(b)   Where it is proved that any act or omission of the defendant alleged to constitute the contravention:

(i)   is a failure to observe a code of practice referred to in *subsection (1)*; or

(ii)   is a compliance with that code of practice, then such failure or compliance is admissible in evidence.

(3) A document bearing the seal of the Authority and purporting to be a code of practice or part of a code of practice published or approved of by the Authority under this section shall be admissible as evidence in any proceedings under this Act.

Safety, Health and Welfare at Work Act 2005 (No. 10 of 2005)

SCHEDULE 3

SECTION 8

General Principles of Prevention

1.   The avoidance of risks.

2.   The evaluation of unavoidable risks.

3.   The combating of risks at source.

4.   The adaptation of work to the individual, especially as regards the design of places of work, the choice of work equipment and the choice of systems of work, with a view, in particular, to alleviating monotonous work and work at a predetermined work rate and to reducing the effect of this work on health.

5.   The adaptation of the place of work to technical progress.

6. The replacement of dangerous articles, substances or systems of work by safe or less dangerous articles, substances or systems of work.

7. The giving of priority to collective protective measures over individual protective measures.

8. The development of an adequate prevention policy in relation to safety, health and welfare at work, which takes account of technology, organisation of work, working conditions, social factors and the influence of factors related to the working environment.

9. The giving of appropriate training and instructions to employees.

APPENDIX 2
SOME RELEVANT ORGANISATIONS AND PUBLICATIONS

Health and Safety Authority (website: www.hsa.ie)

Guidelines on Risk Assessment and Safety Statements

Workplace Safety and Health Management

Labour Relations Commission (website: www.lrc.ie)

Procedures for Addressing Bullying in the Workplace Grievance and Disciplinary Procedures Voluntary Dispute Resolution SI 76 of 2004

Equality Authority (website: www.equality.ie)

Code of Practice on Sexual Harassment and Harassment at Work

Department of Enterprise, Trade and Employment (website: www.entemp.ie)

Bullying in the Workplace, Survey Reports, 2007

Appendix D: Part-Time Workers

Industrial Relations Act 1990 (Code of Practice on Access to Part-Time Working) (Declaration) Order 2006[8]

(SI 8/2006)

WHEREAS the Labour Relations Commission has prepared under subsection (1) of section 42 of the Industrial Relations Act 1990 (No. 19 of 1990), a draft code of practice on access to part-time working;

AND WHEREAS the Labour Relations Commission has complied with subsection (2) of that section and has submitted the draft code of practice to the Minister for Enterprise, Trade and Employment;

NOW THEREFORE, I, Tony Killeen, Minister of State at the Department of Enterprise, Trade and Employment, in exercise of the powers conferred on me by subsection (3) of that section, the Labour (Transfer of Departmental Administration and Ministerial Functions) Order 1993 (S.I. No. 18 of 1993) (as adapted by the Enterprise and Employment (Alteration of Name of Department and Title of Minister) Order 1997 (S.I. No. 305 of 1997)), and the Enterprise, Trade and Employment (Delegation of Ministerial Functions) Order 2004 (S.I. No. 809 of 2004), hereby order as follows: ·

1. This Order may be cited as the Industrial Relations Act 1990 (Code of Practice on Access to Part-Time Working) (Declaration) Order 2006.

2. It is declared that the code of practice set out in the Schedule to this Order shall be a code of practice for the purposes of the Industrial Relations Act 1990 (No. 19 of 1990).

SCHEDULE

Preamble – General Context

The importance of developing access to part-time work as a strategic response to growing demands for modern, flexible work-organisation, has been recognised and highlighted in economic and social policy development at international, EU and national levels. It is widely recognised that widening access to part-time work, in the context of encouraging and promoting the development of a flexible labour market, has positive economic and social benefits for employers and employees. In addition, widening access can have a role to play in facilitating further education and training, increasing participation of older people in the workplace, providing a meaningful option for many people with disabilities and providing work life balance work options generally.

---

[8] Copyright Houses of the Oireachtas 2006.

Benefits for the employer

- Retention of valued and experienced staff who might otherwise leave the organisation, thereby reducing training and recruitment costs;
- Availability of a wider range of candidates for vacancies, especially skilled and experienced people who might only be interested in working part-time;
- Flexibility to match work needs and staffing requirements more closely, for example flexibility in service delivery, hours worked and variations in workload;
- Improved productivity and reduced absenteeism;
- Increased employee commitment, morale and loyalty, which is associated with improved productivity.

Benefits for the employee

- Greater sense of responsibility, ownership and control of working life;
- Better relations with management;
- Improved job satisfaction generally;
- Better work life balance and reduced stress – employees are better able to balance work and non-work issues, for example caring responsibilities, commuting and pursuing further education.

1. Introduction

1.1 Section 42 of the Industrial Relations Act 1990 provides for the preparation of draft Codes of Practice by the Labour Relations Commission for submission to the Minister, and for the making by the Minister of an order declaring that a draft Code of Practice received under Section 42 and scheduled to the order shall be a Code of Practice for the purposes of the said Act.

Section 13 (5) of The Protection of Employees (Part-Time Work) Act 2001 provides that the Labour Relations Commission may prepare, in consultation with the social partners, a Code of Practice governing access to part- time work.

1.2 Clause 10.9 of Sustaining Progress (Social Partnership Agreement 2003 – 2005) provides as follows: 'The Government will request the Labour Relations Commission to develop a Code of Practice, in conjunction with the parties to the Pay Agreement, on access to part-time work in line with the provisions for consultation and evaluation as set out in Section 13 of the Protection of Employees (Part-Time Work) Act 2001.'

In March 2003 the Minister for Enterprise, Trade and Employment requested the Commission under Section 42 (1) of the Industrial Relations Act 1990 and Section 13 of the Protection of Employees (Part-Time Work) Act 2001, to prepare a Code of Practice on Access to Part-Time Work.

1.3 When preparing and agreeing this Code of Practice, the Commission consulted with relevant organisations and took account of the views expressed to the maximum extent possible.

1.4 For the purposes of this Code, 'part-time employee' means an employee whose normal hours of work are less than the normal hours.

2. Background

2.1 The rights of part-time employees to equal treatment in regard to their contractual terms and conditions of employment vis-à-vis full-time-employees are enshrined in The Protection of Employees (Part-Time-Work) Act 2001. In general terms, the Act provides that part-time employees must not be treated less favourably than comparable full-time employees unless there are objective grounds, and where a benefit is determined by the number of hours an employee works, it shall be on a pro-rata or proportionate basis to part-time employees. There is no provision in the Act, or elsewhere in Irish employment law, for a statutory entitlement to part-time work. Rather, the Act makes provision for the Labour Relations Commission to carry out studies for the purposes of identifying obstacles that may exist in particular industries or sectors to access to part-time work, and for the Commission, in consultation with the social partners, to prepare a Code of Practice which would be of practical benefit to employers and employees in addressing such obstacles.

2.2 The introduction of a Code of Practice on access to part-time working accords with the principle of minimising the potential for indirect discrimination in relation to part-time working and introduces positive measures to eliminate obstacles and barriers and encourage greater participation in employment on a number of grounds, as set down in the Employment Equality Acts 1998–2004.

3. Purpose of the Code

The Code seeks to:

- Encourage best practice and conformity with the provisions of the Employment Equality Acts 1998–2004 and the Protection of Employees (Part-Time Work) Act 2001;
- Promote the development of policies and procedures to assist employers, employees and their representatives, as appropriate, to improve access to part-time work for those employees who wish to work on a part-time basis;
- Promote discussion and encourage employers, employees and their representatives, as appropriate, to consider part-time work and to address any barriers that may exist;
- Stimulate employers – where consistent with business requirements – to provide wider access to part-time work options;
- Provide a framework and practical guidance on procedures for accessing part-time work;
- Inform those who are interested in part-time work.

4. General Principles

The Code operates from the basic principles that:

- The code is applicable to all employers and employees;
- Access to part-time work should, as far as possible, be available across different levels in the organisation;
- As far as possible, employers should give consideration to

- requests by employees to transfer from full-time to part-time work;
- requests by employees to transfer from part-time to full-time work-or to increase their working time should the opportunity arise.

- An employee moving to part-time work should suffer no diminution of status or employment rights generally, with the exception of pay, benefits as appropriate, etc (unless there are objective grounds);
- The pro-rata principle should apply where appropriate.

of work of an employee who is a comparable employee in the employment in relation to him or her.

5. Business Context

A key element in the consideration of improving access to part-time work – either introducing part-time working arrangements or enhancing existing arrangements – is the operational/business context of the organisation and the need to enhance economic competitiveness. The capacity of the organisation to facilitate part time working is dependant on business and operational factors, which may include:

- Concerns around increased costs – for example in administration, training and recruitment;
- Particular difficulties around the capacity of organisations with small numbers of employees to accommodate part-time working or to replace staff who are so facilitated;
- Concerns around day-to-day operations, for example impact on service delivery, implications for full time staff etc.

Essentially, consideration should be given to minimising potential constraints, for example administrative, financial or legal.

6. Reviewing and Developing Company/Organisational Policies and Practices

6.1 In general terms, providing for access to part-time work should be considered in the context of developing company/organisational policies and practices to respond to modern work environments, including mechanisms to promote flexible work organisation, equal opportunity and work life balance.

6.2 As best practice it is recommended that companies/organisations introduce, in consultation with their employees and representatives, as appropriate, new policies or review existing policies to facilitate effective access to and performance of part-time work and specify how part-time working arrangements will operate in the company or organisation.

6.3 Assessing/expanding scope of part-time working opportunities

Best practice recommends that employers assess within their own organisations the possibilities of either introducing part-time working or increasing the range/scope of existing part-time working arrangements. As best practice it is recommended that employers should explore, in consultation with their employees and representatives, as appropriate, the possibility of introducing part-time work opportunities and/or maximise the range of posts as suitable for part-time working at all levels in the organisation, including skilled and managerial positions. A range of objective criteria should be developed to determine the suitability or otherwise of positions for part-time working. Barriers to the introduction of part-time work, at all levels in the organisation, should be identified and considered when an application for part-time work is made or when a vacancy arises. In this regard possible measures on how best to overcome such barriers should be considered.

Factors to be taken into account in this regard may include:

- What demand is there, if any, for part-time working in the organisation?
- Where a demand is identified, can work be organised differently to facilitate part-time working?
- How does the organisation deal with/process a request for part-time working?
- What are the business implications of introducing or expanding part-time working, for example in terms of service delivery, covering absence, business continuity, administration and costs generally?
- Can part-time working – to a greater or limited extent, be accommodated having regard to both the business needs of the organisation and the needs of the employee(s)?
- Are there business benefits and opportunities to the organisation in widening access to part-time work?
- What posts – including managerial and skilled posts – are suitable (or unsuitable) for part-time working?
- Are there regulatory or licensing implications?
- Does an employee need to be present in a particular post during all hours of work and, if not, can the necessary work be done by a part-time worker?
- Implications of seniority/service as appropriate;
- If a request from an employee to work part-time is refused what are the implications? For example would the employee leave and, if so, what are the recruitment and training implications/costs of a replacement?
- Are there issues around demotivation/poor morale in not providing part-time working opportunities?
- Are there opportunities in the organisation for existing part-time workers to move around the organisation in the interests of job/career development?
- Are there Employment Equality Act implications? An application for part-time working should be considered on non-discrimination grounds in accordance with the legislation. What do the policies of the organisation provide for in terms of promoting equal opportunities and work life balance?
- What will be the impact of part-time working, if any, on existing employees and their workloads?
- Are there increased time demands on management?

The outcome of any assessment of part-time working possibilities should indicate the following:

- The relevant factors to be taken into account in evaluating/determining part-time working options for the organisation;
- The actual potential for part-time working to contribute to the success of the organisation;
- The barriers, where they exist, and what reasonable steps may be necessary to overcome such barriers;

Policies should be adapted, where possible.

A key element to be considered in introducing a successful part-time working policy, particularly in large organisations, is the necessity for the support and commitment of members of management at all levels of the organisation to such policies.

7. Recruitment

Where possible, when recruiting new employees, employers should consider the proposed content, status and positioning of vacant/new posts in the organisation to determine whether the posts being offered could be performed on a part-time basis.

8. Requests by employees to (a) transfer from full-time to part-time work and (b) transfer from part-time to full-time work or to increase their working time should the opportunity arise

The facility to change the existing hours of work of employees is a matter to be agreed between the employer and the employee, rather than a statutory entitlement. Best practice indicates that employers should treat such requests seriously and where possible explore with their employees if and how requests can be accommodated or how such transfers can be made.

In this regard employers should consider establishing a procedure allowing for (i) application, (ii) relevant consultation and discussion, (iii) decision and response, (iv) managing the outcome (implementation or refusal).

Recommended best practice indicates that such a procedure should provide for the following elements:

- An application from the applicant outlining the reasons for the request to transfer from full-time to part-time working, indicating whether the request is of a temporary or permanent nature.
- A reasonable timeframe to consider the request.
- In considering the application both the employer and employee should take account of all factors both relevant to the organisation and personal to the applicant. Relevant factors may include:
  - The personal and family needs of the applicant;
  - The number of employees already availing of part-time work;
  - Additional resources required to meet part-time cover and other business/operational needs of the organisation and implications of same;
  - The urgency of the request;
  - The period of time covered by the request;
  - The employee's legal rights and entitlements;

- The equal opportunities policy of the organisation;
- How the applicant's proposed revised hours will fit with the tasks of his/her job and how these tasks will be performed during the period of part-time work;
- The implications, if any, for the applicant's conditions of employment;
- The effect, if any, on the staffing needs of the organisation;
- Procedure for reviewing the arrangement.

- The employer should issue a decision to the applicant. If the application is successful, details of how the arrangement will work should be discussed with the applicant (and other work colleagues if appropriate) and agreed. It is useful to draw up an agreement, signed by the parties, detailing any changes to terms and conditions of employment, for example income, annual leave, pension entitlements etc.

- The consideration by an employer of a request for part-time work would have regard to the business needs of the organisation.

- If the application is refused (or deferred) the grounds for doing so should be made clear to the applicant.

- The applicant should have recourse to an appeals mechanism in the event that a mutually satisfactory solution is not reached, for example through the normal established grievance procedures in the organisation.

It should be noted that part-time working may not be appropriate to particular situations and an applicant should be prepared to accept a refusal, if there are good reasons for it. An employer may refuse a request for part-time working if it is satisfied that such arrangements would have an adverse effect on the operation of the business, lead to staffing difficulties or other relevant factors which might impact negatively on the business.

9. Training

Access to training can be an issue for part-time employees. Training courses in many organisations may be organised having regard to the availability of full-time employees. Part-time employees have less flexibility to attend training courses. For example it can be difficult for part-time employees to attend residential courses if they have other commitments, or other responsibilities prevent them from participating because of the inconvenient timing of training. As best practice it is recommended that employers should, where feasible, ensure that the needs of part-time employees are taken into account when the structure, time and location of training is being planned. Where necessary, part-time employees may have to complete training outside their normal hours of work.

10. Career Opportunities

The Code advocates an approach that aims to identify part-time working opportunities across different levels in an organisation. As best practice it is recommended that organisations review their training, performance appraisal, promotion/career development policies to ensure that there are no career development barriers, direct or indirect, to the progression of part-time workers in the organisation.

11. Information

Providing information to Employees

It is important that employees availing of part-time work are not disadvantaged with regard to access to information. As best practice it is recommended that employers should periodically review how individuals are provided with information on the availability of posts, both part-time and full-time.

Providing Information to Representative Bodies

Organisations may have arrangements in place for representing employees in discussions with management, for example collective bargaining arrangements, work councils or staff forums. It is important that representatives are kept informed about the organisation's policy and use of part-time working. The Labour Relations Commission will periodically monitor developments in this regard.

12. Review of Obstacles to the Performance of Part-Time Work

It is noted by the Labour Relations Commission that Section 13 of The Protection of Employees (Part-Time Work) Act 2001 provides that the Commission may, at the request of the Minister for Enterprise, Trade and Employment, study every sector of employment for the purposes of identifying obstacles that may exist in that industry or sector to persons being able to perform part-time work in that industry or sector and make recommendations as to how any such obstacles so identified could be eliminated.

13. Implementation of Code

The application of the Code relies on the full commitment of employers, employees and their representatives (as appropriate). All parties need to recognise that they have specific responsibilities in this regard including -

in the case of management, accepting that it has responsibility to:

- Have clear and objective criteria for identifying part-time work options and procedures for their adoption to meet employee needs;
- Consider the implications of part-time working for the organisation;
- Communicate the working arrangements to all staff;
- Monitor and review the new practices on a regular basis.

in the case of employees and their representatives (as appropriate), that they have responsibility to:

- Work within the policy guidelines agreed for part-time working;
- Consider the implications of part-time working for the individual employee, in consultation with relevant parties;
- Accept that not all positions may be suited to part-time working;
- Where part-time working is afforded, it is performed to the prescribed standard set by the organisation.

14. Application of the Code

In any proceedings before a Court, the Labour Court, the Labour Relations Commission, the Employment Appeals Tribunal, a Rights Commissioner or an Equality Officer, a code of practice shall be admissible in evidence and any provision of the code which appears to the court, body or officer concerned to be relevant to any question arising in the proceedings shall be taken into account in determining that question.

15. Review of Code

The Code will be subject to review after 3 years.

Given under my hand, 12 Jan. 2006

Tony Killeen

Minister of State at the Department of Enterprise, Trade and Employment.

Appendix E: Employee Involvement

Industrial Relations Act 1990 (Code of Practice on Information and Consultation) (Declaration) Order 2008[9]

(SI 132/2008)

1. Introduction

1.1 Section 42 of the Industrial Relations Act, 1990 provides for the preparation of draft Codes of Practice by the Labour Relations Commission for submission to the Minister, and for the making by the Minister of an order declaring that a draft Code of Practice received under Section 42 and scheduled to the order shall be a Code of Practice for the purposes of the said Act.

1.2 The Commission was requested by the Minister for Labour Affairs to prepare a Code of Practice to assist employers and employees in implementing the provisions of the Employees (Provision of Information and Consultation) Act, 2006.

2. Purpose

2.1 The purpose of this Code of Practice is to assist employers, employees and their representatives to develop effective arrangements for communications and consultation in accordance with the provisions of the Employees (Provision of Information and Consultation) Act, 2006. The Code draws on a number of sources:

- The Employees (Provision of Information and Consultation) Act, 2006;
- The experience of the Commission drawn from the delivery of its advisory, conciliation, dispute resolution and research services;
- Consultation with the Social Partners.

2.2 The Code seeks to provide a plain explanation of the legislation. While the thrust of the Code is about effective compliance with the legislation, organisations should look at effective communications and consultation as intrinsic elements to good employee/ employer industrial relations, having positive implications for performance and the workplace generally.

3. Employees (Provision of Information and Consultation) Act 2006

What is it?

3.1 Essentially, the Act is about giving employees the right to information and consultation about developments in their workplaces, about, for example, issues impacting on employment, in work organisation or in contractual relationships with employees.

---

[9] Copyright Houses of the Oireachtas 2008

Who does it apply to?

3.2 It applies to any business/organisation in the public or private sector (referred to as an 'undertaking' in the Act and defined as carrying out an economic activity, whether or not operating for gain) with the following minimum workforce thresholds:

- having at least 150 employees from 4 September 2006;
- having at least 100 employees from 23 March 2007;
- having at least 50 employees from 23 March 2008.

3.3 Simply put, the Act will apply, when it is fully in force by 23 March 2008, to any organisation in Ireland employing at least 50 employees.

How is the workforce threshold calculated?

3.4 The calculation is based during a two year period on an average of the number of employees employed in the organisation. Any employee (or a representative) can request data on the number of employees in the organisation. Employees may need information from their employer about the number of employees in the organisation – for example to find out whether the organisation comes within the scope of the legislation or to find out how many employees are required to make a valid employee request (see below). The employer is obliged to furnish this information within 4 weeks of date of receipt of the request (this can be extended by agreement).

3.5 If the number of employees falls below the workforce threshold referred to above and remains below it for 12 months, any Information and Consultation Forum established under the Act (see Section 3.3 re. Standard Rules Provisions) may be dissolved on the request of either the employer or employees.

4. Process for Establishing Information and Consultation Arrangements

How can an information and consultation arrangement be put in place?

4.1 It is important to note that the right to information and consultation does not operate automatically. Basically an employee request must be made by at least 10% of the employees in the organisation, subject to a minimum of 15 and a maximum of 100 employees. The Act provides that the request can be made either directly to the employer or to the Labour Court (or its nominee). Where a request is made to the Labour Court, it will then notify the employer, seek certain information that will allow it to verify the number and names of the employees who have made the request, and issue a notification confirming whether or not the request meets the employee threshold.

4.2 An employer may, at its own initiative, take steps to put in place an information and consultation arrangement. Obviously, an agreement put in place on foot of a freely entered into engagement process between employers and employees has positive benefits in terms of positive industrial relations generally including effectiveness, trust building and durability.

4.3 Where an employer is requested to put in place an information and consultation arrangement by at least 10% of its employees (see above), it is obliged to begin negotiations with the employees and or their representatives with a view to establishing arrangements. Once negotiations are entered into, there are two possible outcomes – either a negotiated agreement or the standard rules.

4.4 It is important to note that where employees make a written request for an arrangement but do not meet the minimum employee threshold, a further request cannot be made for 2 years.

What does an employee request look like?

4.5 A request should be in writing, give the names of those making it and state the date on which it is sent. It is important to note that the request needs the validation of the workforce as regards meeting the 'numbers' thresholds outlined above. Where there is a refusal to communicate information, an employee can refer a matter to the Labour Court, which may issue a determination on the matter.

How long can negotiations go on for?

4.6 Parties are given 6 months from the time of starting negotiations to agree an information and consultation arrangement. This period can be extended by agreement.

What happens if an employer does not respond to a valid employee request?

4.7 Where an employer refuses to enter into negotiations within 3 months of receiving a written request from employees (or the Labour Court), the Standard Rules provisions of the Act shall apply (see Section 3.3).

4.8 Overview – employee perspective

> *I'm an employee. How do I make a request under the Act to have an information and consultation arrangement put in place?*
>
> The process can be started by a group of employees – at least 10% of the workforce subject to a minimum of 15 employees or a maximum of 100 – making a request to the employer. However before any request is made you need to clarify that your organisation is covered by the new rules. Only if your organisation falls within the scope of the legislation and a sufficient number of you make a request, will your employer be obliged to do anything.
>
> *How do I know if my organisation falls within the scope of the legislation?*
>
> You need to know the numbers of people working in the organisation. You can request this information from your employer who is obliged to provide it no later than 4 weeks from date of request. The request should be made in writing and dated. The request can be made by a representative (must be employed in the organisation). If this is unsuccessful there is also the option of requesting the Labour Court to ask the employer for these details.
>
> *I've confirmed that my organisation falls within the scope of the legislation. What happens next?*
>
> A request to put in place an information and consultation arrangement must be made by at least 10% of the workforce subject to a minimum of 15 and a maximum of 100. You need to ensure therefore that you meet this threshold. You should be able to calculate this from the information provided by your employer. You should note that where a request is made but there are not sufficient numbers to do so, a further request cannot be made for 2 years. Assuming the employee threshold is met, a written request should be made to the employer. It is advisable that the request should be dated and signed to reduce any possibility of dispute.

Who are the representatives negotiating an information and consultation arrangement? Negotiating representatives are chosen by the employees to represent them in discussions with the employer to draw up an agreement. They can be elected in a ballot or simply appointed by the employees without election.

I am a union member. Will my union be my representative?

The legislation provides that where it is the practice of the employer to conduct collective bargaining negations with a union or excepted body, and a union or excepted body represents at least 10% of the employees, those employees are entitled to have their own representatives on a pro-rata basis to non-union representatives.

4.9 Overview – employer perspective

I don't have an information and consultation arrangement in place. What do I have to do?

One option is to do nothing and wait for a valid request from 10% of your workforce to negotiate new arrangements. The risk here of course is that by doing nothing you may get a valid request from 10% of your workforce essentially forcing you to negotiate on an arrangement.

You can take the initiative and negotiate on new information and consultation arrangements.

I already have an information and consultation arrangement in place. What do I have to do? The arrangement in place may not comply with the requirements under the Act, for example it may not be written down, cover all employees or have been approved by the employees. Basically you need to ensure that your arrangement meets the criteria in the Act (see Section 3.2)

5. Options under the Act for putting in place arrangements.

5.1 The Act provides that an information and consultation arrangement can be established either by means of a negotiated agreement, a pre-existing agreement or the Standard Rules.

6. Negotiated Agreements

What is a negotiated agreement?

6.1 Negotiated agreements are information and consultation agreements drawn up in negotiations between an employer and employees and/or their representatives. Employees who want a negotiated agreement must make a formal request under the legislation (see above). Employers can start the process themselves by notifying their employees that they will be doing so.

What is included in a negotiated agreement?

6.2 Parties are free to decide for themselves the subject matter of information and consultation along with methods and structures for delivery. Essentially parties can design an arrangement to suit their own particular requirements. Clearly, however, whatever arrangement is put in place should be workable, effective and enjoy the trust of the parties concerned.

What must a negotiated agreement look like?

6.3 Negotiated agreements must

- Identify the issues on which the organisation will inform and consult;
- Relate to all employees;
- Set out the method and timeframe by which information and consultation is to be provided, including whether it is to be provided directly to employees or indirectly through employees' representatives (address issues around number of representatives, how they will be appointed or elected, how they will serve, how they will be replaced etc)
- Set out the duration of the agreement and any renegotiation procedure;
- Be in writing and dated;
- Signed by the employer;
- Available for inspection as agreed between the parties;
- Set out the procedure for dealing with confidential information.

What issues need to be addressed at the pre-negotiation stage?

6.4 The following issues need to be addressed at the pre-negotiation stage:

- The appointment or election of negotiating representatives, ensuring that all employees are represented. The Act gives responsibility to the employer for arranging the appointment or election of employees' representatives. No limit is placed on the number of representatives. In organisations where it the practice of the employer to conduct collective bargaining with a trade union or excepted body and where the union or excepted body represents at least 10% of the workforce, the employees who are members of the union or excepted body are entitled to elect or appoint their own representatives; (see Section 5)
- Informing all employees in writing of the negotiating representatives;
- Timescales and extensions;
- Dispute resolution methods.

How can a negotiated agreement be approved by employees?

6.5 A negotiated agreement has to be approved by the employees. This can be done by either the majority of employees who cast a preference doing so in favour of the agreement (for example by voting in a ballot) or by approval of a majority of employees' representatives (elected or appointed for the purposes of negotiations in the context of the legislation). However, the parties are also free to agree another procedure to demonstrate approval. It is important that whatever approval process is adopted, that it is confidential, transparent and capable of independent verification. There may be associated costs with a plebiscite. In this regard it is suggested that the employer should carry any reasonable costs arising.

What happens if a negotiated agreement is rejected by employees?

6.6 Clearly, for a negotiated agreement to be put in place, the draft would have to be amended with a view to seeking approval later. A fully inclusive negotiation process at the drafting stage wherein the employees' representatives are fully engaged in the process will minimise the possibility of rejection.

6.7 An inability to agree an arrangement ultimately will result in the Standard Rules provisions applying (see Section 3.3)

7. Pre-Existing Agreements

What is a pre-existing agreement?

7.1 Some organisations have information and consultation arrangements already in place, which may be regarded by the parties as effective and suitable for their needs and in compliance with the legislation. The Act provides an opportunity for the parties to use such arrangements provided that these pre-existing agreements are in place by certain dates specified in the legislation. (It should be noted that after 23 March 2008 it will not be possible to put in place a pre-existing agreement)

What is included in a pre-existing agreement?

7.2 Again, as is the case with a negotiated agreement, parties are free to decide for themselves the subject matter of information and consultation along with methods and structures for delivery.

What must a pre-existing agreement look like?

7.3 The elements of a pre-existing agreement are similar to those that apply to a negotiated agreement.

How can a pre-existing agreement be approved by employees?

7.4 A pre-existing agreement has to be approved by the employees by means of the majority of employees who cast a preference doing so in favour of the agreement (there is no provision for approval by employees' representatives, as is the case with regard to a negotiated agreement). The parties are free to agree another procedure to demonstrate approval. It is important that whatever approval process is adopted, that it is confidential, transparent and capable of independent verification. There may be associated costs with a plebiscite. In this regard it is suggested that the employer should carry any reasonable costs arising.

What are the benefits of a pre-existing agreement?

7.5 It means that arrangements that are working well and have the support of employees can continue.

8. Agreements based on Standard Rules on Information and Consultation

What are Standard Rules?

8.1 The Standard Rules provisions are essentially a fall-back position. They only become relevant in the following circumstances:

- Where there is agreement on the part of both employees and employers to adopt them;
- Where the employer fails to initiate negotiations within 3 months of receiving a valid employee request;
- Where negotiations have failed to lead to an agreement within 6 months from start of negotiations.

How do Standard Rules Work?

8.2 Unlike negotiated agreements and pre-existing agreements where parties are free to devise and agree their own information and consultation arrangements (regarding for example content, methods and structure), arrangements based on the Standard Rules provisions are set out in the legislation. The key element in this is the establishment of an Information and Consultation Forum made up of employees' representatives. The Forum must be made of at least 3 but not more than 30 members. The structure of the Forum, rules of procedure, competence, expenses and practical arrangements for information and consultation are provided for. The arrangement that is set up must provide for employees' representatives i.e. it is not possible for an employer to inform and consult directly with employees.

How are information and consultation employees' representatives elected?

8.3 It is important to note that it is only in the Standard Rules provisions of the Act where the requirements regarding the election of employees' representatives, are detailed.

8.4 Employees' representatives must be elected in a ballot, according to the principle of proportional representation, in an agreed process organised by the employer, or in the absence of an election, appointed by the employees. The employer is responsible for associated costs.

9. Direct Channels

9.1 In relation to negotiated agreements and pre-existing agreements there are two core methods by which information and consultation can be carried out – either by the provision of information and consultation direct to employees or through employees' representatives. Essentially the Act provides that employers are free to continue with arrangements that deal with employees directly – as well as indirectly through employees' representatives. However it is important that the arrangement explicitly states which method is to be used. The Act also provides that employees must be free at a later stage to exercise their right to information and consultation through employees' representatives.

9.2 The Act prescribes a mechanism for processing a request by employees from a system of direct involvement to one involving representatives including a requirement that a minimum of 10% of employees for whom the direct involvement system operates must request the change, with the minimum requirement being subject to the approval of the majority of employees to whom the direct involvement system applies. Following approval of such a request there is an obligation on the employer to arrange for the election or appointment of representatives by the employees.

10. Employee Representation

10.1 Employers are responsible under the Act for arrangements providing for the election and appointment of employees' representatives. In this regard it should be noted that where it is the practice of the employer to conduct collective bargaining negotiations with a union or excepted body, and a union or excepted body represents at least 10% of the employees, those employees are entitled to have their own representatives on a pro-rata basis to other representatives.

10.2 The Act makes provision for information and consultation to be either provided directly to employees or through employees' representatives and for arrangements to be negotiated and approved by either employees or employees' representatives. This section focuses on issues arising where information and consultation is provided through employees' representatives, elected or appointed for the purposes of this Act.

10.3 With regard to employee representation, in practice there will be two main types of situation, depending on whether trade unions are recognised for the purposes of collective bargaining or not.

11. Employments where Collective Bargaining takes place

11.1 Under this heading there can be a variety of patterns of trade union recognition, ranging from situations where collective bargaining is in place for the entire workforce, to situations where the union/unions represents a minority/majority of the workforce. In some instances union representation and collective bargaining coverage may be limited to specific grades and/or professions within the overall workforce. Similarly many organisations will have developed their own customs, norms and practices that reflect their particular trade union and collective bargaining structures. Given the potential diversity of employment relations arrangements that can exist it is not considered possible/appropriate for the Code to cover every potential permutation. Rather the emphasis is on outlining some general principles of good practice that can assist in ensuring that negotiated information and consultation arrangements are viable, appropriate and genuinely representative of the whole workforce. A number of key issues of relevance include the following:

- **Pro-rata principle**:

  The Act states that where there is collective bargaining in place, and where the union or excepted body represents at least 10% of the employees in the organisation, the union will be entitled to appoint or elect representatives (on a pro-rata basis to other employees' representatives).

  Where the union represents the entire workforce, the union is entitled to elect or appoint all of the information and consultation representatives. Where the union represents less than the entire workforce (but at least 10% of the workforce) it is entitled to appoint representatives on a pro-rata basis to non-union representatives.

- **Multi-union workplaces**

  In multi-union workplaces, i.e. where collective bargaining arrangements are in place involving more than one union (and subject to the 10% threshold being met) it is open to the unions to agree arrangements between themselves with regard to the appointment of employees' representatives.

- **Scope**

  While the selection process of employees' representatives is likely to reflect existing union structures and collective bargaining arrangements, it is important that the representatives, elected or appointed for the purposes of this

Act are genuinely representative and should seek to reflect the make-up of the entire workforce. This would be particularly important, for example, in large organisations with diverse functions and/or working arrangements (for example shift patterns).

In practice an election should be held where the number of candidates exceeds the number of positions available. Where employees' representatives are to be chosen by election, an employee should be eligible to stand as a candidate provided he or she is nominated by at least two employees or a trade union.

It would be important that the design of the constituencies for the election of employees' representatives reflects both the existing trade union structures and collective bargaining arrangements and the overall employment relations culture within an organisation. Equally, where appropriate, such constituencies should also correlate with the aforementioned pro-rata principle for union / non-union representation. While the design of the actual constituencies for election/selection of employees' representatives is a key issue, it is also important to reiterate that the overall objective is to put in place information and consultation arrangements that ultimately will be appropriate, effective and representative of the workforce as a whole.

12. Other Employments

12.1 A variety of situations could apply ranging from organisations where there is no union recognition of any employee to organisations where the majority/minority of employees are recognised for collective bargaining purposes. A number of key issues include the following:

- **Scope**

  The number of representatives should reflect the make-up of the workforce. Essentially numbers would depend on the structure/size of the organisation, and the need to ensure all areas of the employment are represented. This would be particularly important in for example large organisations with diverse functions and those with shift arrangements.

- **Election/Appointment of Representatives**

  Representatives, whether elected or appointed, need to be genuinely representative of their constituency. Election arrangements need to be confidential and transparent. All employees in the employment should be invited to nominate either another employee with their consent or themselves for election. In practice an election should be held where the number of candidates exceeds the number of positions available. An election should be confidential, transparent and capable of independent verification. There may be costs associated with holding an election. It is suggested that the employer should carry any reasonable cost arising.

13. Reasonable Facilities

13.1 The Act provides that representatives should be reasonably facilitated in carrying out their roles as employees' representatives promptly and effectively. Typically this would include the following:

- Paid time off to prepare for and attend information and consultation meetings.
- Provision of telephone, photocopying and e-mail facilities including facilities to allow for informing and consulting with employees.
- Reasonable facilities, including paid time off, to attend training courses appropriate to functioning effectively as an information and consultation employee representative.

13.2 Due regard should be given to the capability of the organisation to meet these obligations.

14. Protection of Employees' Representatives

14.1 The Act provides that an employer should not penalise representatives for performing their functions under the Act (for example, by dismissal or other prejudicial treatment such as unfavourable changes in conditions of employment). The Act provides that a grievance arising in this regard can be referred to a Rights Commissioner and that a decision of a Rights Commissioner can be appealed to the Labour Court.

15. Responsibilities of Employees' Representatives

15.1 When negotiating, putting in place and participating in arrangements for information and consultation, representatives (and the employer) have a duty to work co-operatively and to take into account the best interests of both the employment and the employees.

16. Disputes around Information and Consultation in Arrangements

What happens if there is a dispute?

16.1 Differences may arise in relation to information and consultation arrangements. As best practice it is recommended that an arrangement should make a specific provision for dispute resolution. In this regard, in the interests of positive management/employee relationships and trust development, the emphasis should be on seeking to resolve the issue internally, i.e. directly between the parties (organisations with collective bargaining in place will have dispute resolution processes in place which could be adapted).

16.2 However, parties may not be able to reach agreement at local level. In these situations the Act makes extensive provision for third party dispute resolution in relation to different types of dispute arising from the various provisions of the Act. Specifically these relate to interpretation or operation of agreements or systems of direct involvement. It is important to note the first point of referral in this regard is the Conciliation Services of the Labour Relations Commission, which gives parties an opportunity to reach agreement on the matter in contention in an informal process under the chairmanship of an independent third party. If the dispute is not resolved, it is referred to the Labour Court for recommendation or determination. Ultimately a Labour Court determination can be enforced by the Circuit Court.

17. Confidentiality

17.1 The issue of confidentiality in the context of an information and consultation arrangement is significant. There can be sensitivities (or perception of sensitivities) on the part of organisations around concerns about disclosing information to employees on, for example, financial performance or strategy. The Act introduces a statutory basis for a duty of confidentiality as follows:

- Anyone who receives confidential information while participating in an information and consultation arrangement (e.g. a member of an Information and Consultation Forum, an employee representative or participant, an expert providing assistance) is bound by a duty of confidentiality not to reveal that information. Such a person may disclose information provided in confidence to employees and third parties where those in turn are subject to a duty of confidentiality under the Act.
- An employer may refuse to communicate information or undertake consultation with its employees provided it can show objectively that the information or consultation would seriously harm the functioning of the enterprise or be prejudicial to the enterprise.

What happens if there is a dispute around confidential information?

17.2 Disputes around, for example, breaching confidentiality, an employer refusing to communicate or consult on confidentiality grounds, may be referred directly, by an employer, employee or employees' representatives to the Labour Court for determination. The Labour Court may be assisted by a panel of experts to assist it in determining what is confidential information.

17.3 In general terms it is recommended that an information and consultation arrangement should address the issue of confidentiality in terms of clarifying relevant circumstances etc.

18. Staff Forums/Committees

18.1 The Act does not prescribe methods of delivery of communications and consultation (other than in regard to the Standard Rules provisions). Clearly an arrangement providing for information and consultation to be delivered through representatives will involve the establishment of an Information and Consultation Committee/Forum. As best practice it is recommended that the operating principles of the Committee/Forum should be agreed (e.g. in the form of a Charter). A number of matters have to be addressed in this regard including:

- The appointment or election of representatives/protection afforded them;
- The role/ purpose of the Forum i.e. to provide information and make provision for consultation and how this is to be provided;
- Operating procedures;
- Training of members (both employee and management representatives);
- Dealing with confidential information;
- Dispute Resolution;
- Role of experts.

19. Some Key Principles

- As can be seen, the Act offers parties flexibility to put in place an arrangement that best suits their needs in terms of subject matter and structure. Clearly, however, whatever arrangement is put in place should be, in the interests of a genuine communications and consultation strategy, in accordance with best practice, workable, effective and enjoy the trust of all concerned.

- Organisations should be proactive in putting in place arrangements, by looking at effective communications and consultation as intrinsic elements to good employee/employer industrial relations with positive implications for performance and the workplace generally.

- It is important to note that the Act does not prescribe any particular communications and consultation arrangements. That is entirely a matter for each organisation. An organisation has therefore the flexibility to design practical arrangements that suit its and its employees' needs.

- The importance of developing an arrangement openly, transparently and in full consultation with all parties i.e. management, employees and their representatives as appropriate, should not be underestimated. The joint development of an arrangement has major trust building benefits, will ensure a greater 'buy in' and result in a more robust arrangement in the long term.

- The provision of effective and relevant training in appropriate communication and consultation skills is essential. In particular joint management/employee training can have particular benefits in terms of mutual understanding and trust building.

- Effective communications and consultation are long term commitments, requiring time for trust to develop or improve and adapt/refine whatever arrangement is put in place. Essentially what is needed is belief from all concerned in the intrinsic value of good communications and consultation to all concerned parties.

20. Further Information and Advice

For further information and advice on any aspect of this document please contact:

The Labour Relations Commission
Tom Johnson House, Haddington Road, Dublin 4
Tel: (01) 613 6700 Fax: (01) 613 6701
Web: www.lrc.ie

For further information on the Information and Consultation Act 2006 please contact:

The Director of the National Employment Rights Authority
O'Brien Road, Carlow.
Tel: Lo Call 1890 80 80 90
Web: www.employmentrights.ie

Note: All legislation, both Acts and Statutory Instruments, cited in this Code of Practice are available from www.irishstatutebook.ie or www.entemp.ie

Appendix F: Dismissal

Industrial Relations Act, 1990 (Code of Practice on Grievance and Disciplinary Procedures) (Declaration) Order, 2000

(SI 146/2000)

WHEREAS the Labour Relations Commission has prepared under subsection (1) of section 42 of the Industrial Relations Act, 1990 (No. 19 of 1990), a draft code of practice on grievance and disciplinary procedures and which code is proposed to replace the code set out in the Schedule to the Industrial Relations Act, 1990, Code of Practice on Disciplinary Procedures (Declaration) Order, 1996 (S.I. No 117 of 1996);

AND WHEREAS the Labour Relations Commission has complied with subsection (2) of that section and has submitted the draft code of practice to the Minister for Enterprise, Trade and Employment;

NOW THEREFORE, I, Mary Harney, Minister for Enterprise, Trade and Employment, in exercise of the powers conferred on me by subsections (3) and (6) of that section, the Labour (Transfer of Departmental Administration and Ministerial Functions) Order, 1993 (S.I. No. 18 of 1993), and the Enterprise and Employment (Alteration of Name of Department and Title of Minister) Order, 1997 (S.I. No. 305 of 1997), and after consultation with the Commission, hereby order as follows:

1. This Order may be cited as the Industrial Relations Act, 1990 (Code of Practice on Grievance and Disciplinary Procedures) (Declaration) Order, 2000.

2. It is hereby declared that the code of practice set out in the Schedule to this Order shall be a code of practice for the purposes of the Industrial Relations Act, 1990 (No. 19 of 1990).

3. The code of practice set out in the Schedule to the Industrial Relations Act, 1990, Code of Practice on Disciplinary Procedures (Declaration) Order, 1996 (S.I. No 117 of 1996), is revoked.

SCHEDULE

1. Introduction

1. Section 42 of the Industrial Relations Act, 1990 provides for the preparation of draft Codes of Practice by the Labour Relations Commission for submission to the Minister, and for the making by him of an order declaring that a draft Code of Practice received by him under section 42 and scheduled to the order shall be a Code of Practice for the purposes of the said Act

2. In May 1999 the Minister for Enterprise, Trade and Employment requested the Commission under Section 42 of the Industrial Relations Act, 1990 to amend the Code of Practice on Disciplinary Procedures (S.I. No. 117 of 1996) to take account of the

recommendations on Individual Representation contained in the Report of the High Level Group on Trade Union Recognition. The High Level Group, involving the Departments of the Taoiseach, Finance and Enterprise, Trade and Employment, the Irish Congress of Trade Unions (ICTU), the Irish Business and Employers Confederation (IBEC) and IDA-Ireland, was established under paragraph 9.22 of *Partnership 2000 for Inclusion Employment and Competitiveness* to consider proposals submitted by ICTU on the Recognition of Unions and the Right to Bargain and to take account of European developments and the detailed position of IBEC on the impact of the ICTU proposals.

3. When preparing and agreeing this Code of Practice the Commission consulted with the Department of Enterprise, Trade and Employment, ICTU, IBEC, the Employment Appeals Tribunal and the Health and Safety Authority and took account of the views expressed to the maximum extent possible.

4. The main purpose of this Code of Practice is to provide guidance to employers, employees and their representatives on the general principles which apply in the operation of grievance and disciplinary procedures.

2. General

1. This Code of Practice contains general guidelines on the application of grievance and disciplinary procedures and the promotion of best practice in giving effect to such procedures. While the Code outlines the principles of fair procedures for employers and employees generally, it is of particular relevance to situations of individual representation.

2. While arrangements for handling discipline and grievance issues vary considerably from employment to employment depending on a wide variety of factors including the terms of contracts of employment, locally agreed procedures, industry agreements and whether trade unions are recognised for bargaining purposes, the principles and procedures of this Code of Practice should apply unless alternative agreed procedures exist in the workplace which conform to its general provisions for dealing with grievance and disciplinary issues.

3. Importance of Procedures

1. Procedures are necessary to ensure both that while discipline is maintained in the workplace by applying disciplinary measures in a fair and consistent manner, grievances are handled in accordance with the principles of natural justice and fairness. Apart from considerations of equity and natural justice, the maintenance of a good industrial relations atmosphere in the workplace requires that acceptable fair procedures are in place and observed.

2. Such procedures serve a dual purpose in that they provide a framework which enables management to maintain satisfactory standards and employees to have access to procedures whereby alleged failures to comply with these standards may be fairly and sensitively addressed. It is important that procedures of this kind exist and that the purpose, function and terms of such procedures are clearly understood by all concerned.

3. In the interest of good industrial relations, grievance and disciplinary procedures should be in writing and presented in a format and language that is easily understood.

Copies of the procedures should be given to all employees at the commencement of employment and should be included in employee programmes of induction and refresher training and, trade union programmes of employee representative training. All members of management, including supervisory personnel and all employee representatives should be fully aware of such procedures and adhere to their terms.

4. General Principles

1. The essential elements of any procedure for dealing with grievance and disciplinary issues are that they be rational and fair, that the basis for disciplinary action is clear, that the range of penalties that can be imposed is well-defined and that an internal appeal mechanism is available.

2. Procedures should be reviewed and up-dated periodically so that they are consistent with changed circumstances in the workplace, developments in employment legislation and case law, and good practice generally.

3. Good practice entails a number of stages in discipline and grievance handling. These include raising the issue with the immediate manager in the first instance. If not resolved, matters are then progressed through a number of steps involving more senior management, HR/IR staff, employee representation, as appropriate, and referral to a third party, either internal or external, in accordance with any locally agreed arrangements.

4. For the purposes of this Code of Practice, 'employee representative' includes a colleague of the employee's choice and a registered trade union but not any other person or body unconnected with the enterprise.

5. The basis of the representation of employees in matters affecting their rights has been addressed in legislation, including the Protection of Employment Act, 1977; the European Communities (Safeguarding of Employees Rights on Transfer of Undertakings) Regulations, 1980; Safety, Health and Welfare at Work Act, 1989; Transnational Information and Consultation of Employees Act, 1996; and the Organisation of Working Time Act, 1997. Together with the case law derived from the legislation governing unfair dismissals and other aspects of employment protection, this corpus of law sets out the proper standards to be applied to the handling of grievances, discipline and matters detrimental to the rights of individual employees.

6. The procedures for dealing with such issues reflecting the varying circumstances of enterprises/organisations, must comply with the general principles of natural justice and fair procedures which include:

- That employee grievances are fairly examined and processed;
- That details of any allegations or complaints are put to the employee concerned;
- That the employee concerned is given the opportunity to respond fully to any such allegations or complaints;
- That the employee concerned is given the opportunity to avail of the right to be represented during the procedure;
- That the employee concerned has the right to a fair and impartial determination of the issues concerned, taking into account any representations made by, or on

behalf of, the employee and any other relevant or appropriate evidence, factors or circumstances.

7. These principles may require that the allegations or complaints be set out in writing, that the source of the allegations or complaint be given or that the employee concerned be allowed to confront or question witnesses.

8. As a general rule, an attempt should be made to resolve grievance and disciplinary issues between the employee concerned and his or her immediate manager or supervisor. This could be done on an informal or private basis.

9. The consequences of a departure from the rules and employment requirements of the enterprise/organisation should be clearly set out in procedures, particularly in respect of breaches of discipline which if proved would warrant suspension or dismissal.

10. Disciplinary action may include:

- An oral warning
- A written warning
- A final written warning
- Suspension without pay
- Transfer to another task, or section of the enterprise
- Demotion
- Some other appropriate disciplinary action short of dismissal
- Dismissal

11. Generally, the steps in the procedure will be progressive, for example, an oral warning, a written warning, a final written warning, and dismissal. However, there may be instances where more serious action, including dismissal, is warranted at an earlier stage. In such instances the procedures set out at paragraph 6 hereof should be complied with.

12. An employee may be suspended on full pay pending the outcome of an investigation into an alleged breach of discipline.

13. Procedures should set out clearly the different levels in the enterprise or organisation at which the various stages of the procedures will be applied.

14. Warnings should be removed from an employee's record after a specified period and the employee advised accordingly.

15. The operation of a good grievance and disciplinary procedure requires the maintenance of adequate records. As already stated, it also requires that all members of management, including supervisory personnel and all employees and their representatives be familiar with and adhere to their terms.

EXPLANATORY NOTE

This note is not part of the Instrument and does not purport to be a legal interpretation.

The effect of this Order is to declare that the draft code of practice set out in the Schedule to this Order is a code of practice for the purposes of the Industrial Relations Act, 1990.

Appendix G: Trade Unions

Industrial Relations Act, 1990, Code of Practice on Employee Representatives (Declaration) Order, 1993

(SI 169/1993)

WHEREAS the Labour Relations Commission has prepared a draft code of practice on the duties and responsibilities of employee representatives and the protection and facilities to be afforded them by their employer;

AND WHEREAS the Labour Relations Commission has complied with subsection (2) of section 42 of the Industrial Relations Act, 1990 (No. 19 of 1990), and has submitted the draft code of practice to the Minister for Enterprise and Employment;

NOW THEREFORE, I, RUAIRÍ QUINN, Minister for Enterprise and Employment, in exercise of the powers conferred on me by subsection (3) of that section, hereby order as follows:

1. This Order may be cited as the Industrial Relations Act, 1990, Code of Practice on Employee Representatives (Declaration) Order, 1993.

2. It is hereby declared that the draft code of practice set out in the Schedule to this Order shall be a code of practice for the purposes of the Industrial Relations Act, 1990 (No. 19 of 1990).

SCHEDULE

DRAFT CODE OF PRACTICE ON THE DUTIES AND RESPONSIBILITIES OF EMPLOYEE REPRESENTATIVES AND THE PROTECTION AND FACILITIES TO BE AFFORDED THEM BY THEIR EMPLOYER

Introduction

Section 42 of the Industrial Relations Act, 1990 makes provision for the preparation of draft codes of practice by the Labour Relations Commission for submission to the Minister for Enterprise and Employment (Appendix).

The main purpose of this draft Code of Practice is to set out for the guidance of employers, employees and trade unions the duties and responsibilities of employee representatives (frequently referred to in trade union rule books and employer/trade union agreements as shop stewards) and the protection and facilities which should be afforded them in order to enable them to carry out their duties in an effective and constructive manner.

When preparing this draft Code of Practice the Commission held meetings and consultations with the Irish Congress of Trade Unions and the Irish Business and

Employers Confederation. It also consulted with the Departments of Enterprise and Employment and Finance. The Commission has taken account of the views expressed by these organisations to the maximum extent possible in preparing this draft Code. It has also had regard to the procedures and practices applied in undertakings and establishments which have pursued sound industrial relations policies and to the provisions of trade union rule books.

General

1. Employee representatives, for the purpose of this draft Code, are—

   (a) employees of an undertaking or establishment who have been formally designated employee representatives for that undertaking or establishment by a trade union in accordance with the rules of that trade union and any employer/ trade union agreement which relates to the appointment of such representatives in that undertaking or establishment and

   (b) who normally participate in negotiations about terms and conditions of employment for all or a section of the workforce and who are involved in the procedures for the settlement of any disputes or grievances which may arise in that undertaking or establishment.

Reference to trade unions throughout this draft Code includes reference to 'excepted bodies' under the Trade Union Acts, 1871-1990. An 'excepted body' is a body which may lawfully negotiate wages or other conditions of employment without holding a negotiation licence. 'Excepted body' is defined in section 6(3) of the Trade Union Act, 1941, as amended, and includes an association all the members of which are employed by the same employer.

2. The duties and responsibilities of employee representatives and the protection and facilities to be afforded them under this draft Code are indicative of the important position and role of such representatives in our system of industrial relations and in the resolution of disputes/grievances. The manner in which employee representatives discharge their duties and responsibilities significantly affects the quality of management/labour relations in the undertaking or establishment in which they work, its efficient operation and future development.

Duties and Responsibilities of Employee Representatives

3. The principal duties and responsibilities of employee representatives include—

   (a) representing members fairly and effectively in relation to matters arising within the undertaking or establishment in which they work and which concern employment and conditions of employment;

   (b) participating in negotiation and grievance procedures as provided for in employer/trade union agreements or in accordance with recognised custom and practice in the undertaking or establishment in which they work;

   (c) co-operating with the management of the undertaking or establishment in ensuring the proper implementation and observance of employer/trade union agreements, the use of agreed dispute and grievance procedures and the avoidance of any action, especially unofficial action, which would be contrary to such agreements or procedures and which would affect the continuity of operations or services;

(d) acting in accordance with existing laws and regulations, the rules of the union and good industrial relations practice; liaising with and seeking advice and assistance from the appropriate full-time trade union official;

(e) having regard at all times to the safe and efficient operation of the undertaking or establishment;

(f) subject to any other arrangements made between an employer and a trade union, employee representatives should conform to the same job performance standards, company rules, disciplinary conditions and other conditions of employment as comparable employees in the undertaking or establishment in which they work.

Election of Employee Representatives

4. Employee representatives should be elected/designated in accordance with the appropriate trade union rules and procedures and, where relevant, in accordance with employer/trade union agreements. These procedures and agreements should ensure that such representatives will be representative of the trade union members concerned. Such representatives should normally have a minimum of one year's service in the undertaking or establishment concerned; their appointment as employee representatives should be confirmed in writing by the union to the employer and the union should provide relevant information, advice and training to employee representatives on their principal functions and duties. Nothing in this draft Code precludes an employer from providing additional training.

5. The number of employee representatives should be reasonable having regard to the size of the undertaking or establishment concerned, the number of trade union members employed and the structure of trade union organisation within the undertaking or establishment.

6. Following notification of the appointment of an employee representative, the employer should provide the representative with relevant information about the normal procedures for communicating with the appropriate representatives of management.

Protection of Employee Representatives

7. Employee representatives who carry out their duties and responsibilities in accordance with paragraph 3 of this draft Code should not—

(a) be dismissed or suffer any unfavourable change in their conditions of employment or unfair treatment, including selection for redundancy, because of their status or activities as employee representatives, or

(b) suffer any action prejudicial to their employment because of their status or activities as employee representatives,

without prior consultation taking place between the management and the relevant trade union.

Where it is established that an employee representative has been dismissed in contravention of the provision at (*a*) above such representative should normally be reinstated.

8. Section 7 of this draft Code is without prejudice to the provisions of the Unfair Dismissals Acts, 1977 and 1991.

9. Where an employer considers that an employee representative has acted or is acting beyond the usual authority and functions of an employee representative as set out in paragraph 3 or in a manner which is damaging to the undertaking or establishment, the employer should, in the first instance, take the matter up with the employee representative concerned and failing satisfaction at that level with his/her trade union.

Facilities for Employee Representatives

10. For the purposes of effectively ensuring the provision of reasonable facilities for employee representatives in accordance with paragraph 11 below, employers and trade unions should enter into agreements at the level of the undertaking or establishment which would incorporate the following provisions suitably adapted to the circumstances of the particular undertaking or establishment as referred to in paragraph 12 below.

11. Employee representatives should be afforded such reasonable facilities as will enable them to carry out their functions as employee representatives promptly and efficiently and in accordance with paragraph 3.

12. The granting of such facilities should have regard to the provisions of paragraph 5 and especially to the needs, size and capabilities of the undertaking or establishment concerned and should not impair the efficient operation of the undertaking or establishment.

13. Employee representatives should be afforded necessary time off for carrying out their representative functions in the undertaking or establishment in which they work. In the absence of formal standing arrangements, employee representatives should obtain prior permission from an appropriate representative of management. Such permission should not be unreasonably withheld. Reasonable limits may be set on the amount of time off.

14. On the same basis as at paragraphs 10 and 12 above, employee representatives should be granted reasonable time off for trade union meetings and training courses which relate to their activities as employee representatives.

15. The question of payment of wages in respect of time off for any of the purposes set out at paragraphs 13 and 14 above should be the subject of discussion in advance at the level of the undertaking or establishment.

16. Employee representatives in the undertaking or establishment should be granted reasonable access to all workplaces where they represent trade union members and where such access is necessary to enable them to carry out their representative functions.

17. Employee representatives should have access, without undue delay, to management at the appropriate level on matters relating to their representative functions and responsibilities.

18. In the absence of check-off arrangements, employee representatives should, by agreement, be permitted to collect union dues regularly in the undertaking or establishment.

19. Employers and trade unions should agree arrangements whereby employee representatives, acting on behalf of their trade union, should be permitted to post notices relating to normal activities of the union in the undertaking or establishment in a place agreed with management to which employees have easy access.

20. Employee representatives, acting on behalf of their trade union, should be permitted to distribute non-political news sheets, pamphlets, publications and other documents relating to normal trade union activities amongst the members of the union in the undertaking or establishment.

21. The use of the facilities referred to in paragraphs 19 and 20 above should have regard to the orderly operation and tidiness of the undertaking or establishment.

22. Management and trade unions should agree on the particular information and facilities which should be made available to employee representatives to enable them to carry out their functions and responsibilities in accordance with this draft Code.

APPENDIX

Section 42 of the Industrial Relations Act, 1990 states:

(1) The Commission shall prepare draft codes of practice concerning industrial relations for submission to the Minister, either on its own initiative or at the request of the Minister.

(2) Before submitting a draft code of practice to the Minister, the Commission shall seek and consider the views of organisations representative of employers and organisations representative of workers, and such other bodies as the Commission considers appropriate.

(3) Where the Minister receives a draft code of practice from the Commission he may by order declare that the code, scheduled to the order, shall be a code of practice for the purposes of this Act.

(4) In any proceedings before a court, the Labour Court, the Commission, the Employment Appeals Tribunal, a Rights Commissioner or an equality officer, a code of practice shall be admissible in evidence and any provision of the code which appears to the court, body or officer concerned to be relevant to any question arising in the proceedings shall be taken into account in determining that question.

(5) A failure on the part of any person to observe any provision of a code of practice shall not of itself render him liable to any proceedings.

(6) The Minister may at the request of or after consultation with the Commission by order revoke or amend a code of practice.

(7) Every order made under this section shall be laid before each House of the Oireachtas as soon as may be after it is made and, if a resolution annulling the order is passed by either House within the next twenty-one days on which that House has sat after the order has been laid before it, the order shall be annulled

accordingly, but without prejudice to the validity of anything previously done thereunder.

GIVEN under my Official Seal, this 25th day of June 1993.

Ruairí Quinn

Minister for Enterprise and Employment.

EXPLANATORY NOTE

The effect of this Order is to declare that the draft code of practice set out in the schedule to this Order is a code of practice for the purposes of the Industrial Relations Act, 1990.

Appendix H: Industrial Relations

Industrial Relations Act 1990 (Enhanced Code of Practice on Voluntary Dispute Resolution) (Declaration) Order 2004[10]

(SI 76/2004)

WHEREAS the Labour Relations Commission has prepared under subsection (1) of section 42 of the Industrial Relations Act 1990 (No. 19 of 1990), a draft enhanced code of practice on voluntary dispute resolution where negotiation arrangements are not in place and where collective bargaining does not take place;

AND WHEREAS the Labour Relations Commission has complied with subsection (2) of that section and has submitted the draft enhanced code of practice to the Minister for Enterprise, Trade and Employment;

NOW THEREFORE, I, Frank Fahey, Minister of State at the Department of Enterprise, Trade and Employment, in exercise of the powers conferred on me by subsection (3) of that section, the Labour (Transfer of Departmental Administration and Ministerial Functions) Order 1993 (S.I. No. 18 of 1993) (as adapted by the Enterprise and Employment (Alteration of Name of Department and Title of Minister) Order 1997 (S.I. No. 305 of 1997)), and the Enterprise, Trade and Employment (Delegation of Ministerial Functions) Order 2003 (S.I. No. 156 of 2003), hereby order as follows:

1. This Order may be cited as the Industrial Relations Act 1990 (Enhanced Code of Practice on Voluntary Dispute Resolution) (Declaration) Order 2004.

2. It is declared that the enhanced code of practice set out in the Schedule to this Order shall be a code of practice for the purposes of the Industrial Relations Act 1990 (No. 19 of 1990).

3. The Industrial Relations Act 1990 (Code of Practice on Voluntary Dispute Resolution) (Declaration) Order 2000 (S.I. No. 145 of 2000) is revoked.

SCHEDULE

1 Introduction

1. Section 42 of the Industrial Relations Act 1990 provides for the preparation of draft Codes of Practice by the Labour Relations Commission for submission to the Minister, and for the making by him or her of an order declaring that a draft Code of Practice received by him or her under Section 42 and scheduled to the order shall be a Code of Practice for the purpose of the said Act.

2. Paragraph 9.22 of Partnership 2000 for Inclusion, Employment and Competitiveness established a High Level Group on Trade Union Recognition. The High Level Group,

---

involving the Departments of the Taoiseach, Finance and Enterprise, Trade and Employment, the Irish Congress of Trade Unions (ICTU), the Irish Business and Employers Confederation (IBEC) and IDA – Ireland, considered proposals submitted by the ICTU on the Recognition of Unions and the Right to Bargain and took account of European developments and the detailed position of IBEC on the impact of the ICTU proposals. As a result of these deliberations a set of procedures were put in place in the Code of Practice on Voluntary Dispute Resolution (S.I. No. 145 of 2000) and the Industrial Relations (Amendment) Act 2001.

3. Article 8.9 of Sustaining Progress Social Partnership Agreement 2003–2005 provides for the further development of employee representation. It was agreed by the trade union and employer organisations that there was a need to enhance the effectiveness of the existing procedures put in place in the Code of Practice on Voluntary Dispute Resolution and the Industrial Relations (Amendment) Act 2001.

4. The following measures were agreed for this purpose:

- the introduction of an indicative overall time-frame targeting 26 weeks – with provision for up to a maximum of 34 weeks where necessary – for the processing of cases under the Voluntary Dispute Resolution Code and the 2001 Act to the point of issuance of a determination, save when an extension is agreed by the parties;

- the amendment of Section 2 of the 2001 Act to provide that engagement by the Court could now take place on the basis of a breach of the time-frames within the Code, the exhaustion of the time-frames or the indication at any time by the Labour Relations Commission that it is unable to assist the parties; these provisions to be substituted for the existing Section 2(1)(b), while preserving the remainder of the Section;

- the amendment of Section 3 of the 2001 Act so as to allow the Court to combine both the preliminary and substantive hearings, where it considers this to be appropriate;

- the removal of the provision in the Act for the Labour Court to review a determination, prior to seeking enforcement of a determination by the Circuit Court, by deleting section 9 and amending section 10 to provide for an entitlement for the trade union or excepted body to apply to the Circuit Court for the enforcement of a determination immediately – or on expiry of whatever implementation period is provided for in the determination;

- the development of transitional provisions to allow for the processing of cases in current disputes where access to the Code of Practice on Dispute Resolution as at the date of agreement is not available;

- the introduction of a new Code of Practice setting out the different types of practice which would constitute victimisation arising from an employee's membership or activity on behalf of a trade union or a manager discharging his or her managerial functions, or other employees and the amendment of the Act to provide that the Labour Court should have regard to breaches of this Code and where appropriate should provide for redress when making its determination.

5. In April 2003 the Minister for Enterprise, Trade and Employment requested the Commission under section 42(1) of the Industrial Relations Act 1990 to prepare a draft Enhanced Code of Practice on Voluntary Dispute Resolution pursuant to the provisions of Article 8.9 of the Sustaining Progress Social Partnership Agreement 2003 – 2005.

6. In advance of the Minister's request the Department of Enterprise, Trade and Employment chaired discussions over a five-week period between trade union and employer organisations on the enhancement of the existing procedures (Article 8.11 of Sustaining Progress). The outcome of these discussions was communicated to the Labour Relations Commission in May 2003.

7. When preparing and agreeing this Enhanced Code of Practice, the Commission consulted with the Department of Enterprise, Trade and Employment, ICTU, IBEC, and the Labour Court and took account of the views expressed to the maximum extent possible.

8. The major objective of the Enhanced Code is to provide an improved framework that has the full support of all the parties for the processing of disputes arising in situations where negotiating arrangements are not in place and where collective bargaining fails to take place.

2 Procedures

Where negotiating arrangements are not in place and where collective bargaining fails to take place, the following process would be put in place with which management and unions should fully co-operate in seeking to resolve the issues in dispute effectively and expeditiously:

1. The procedure will last for a period of 6 weeks from the date of receipt by the other party of a written invitation from the Labour Relations Commission to participate in the procedure. The referring party may copy the original Labour Relations Commission referral to the other party at time of referral. The 6 weeks to include 2 weeks to arrange meetings and commence discussions on the issues in dispute and 4 weeks for substantive engagement on the issues in dispute. In the event that the parties are making substantial progress toward a resolution of the dispute this time frame can be extended by agreement (see paragraph 5 below).

2. In the first instance, the matter should be referred to the Labour Relations Commission in the prescribed format (see Appendix). An Advisory Officer will be appointed by the Commission to facilitate the procedure.

3. On receipt of the referral in the prescribed format the Advisory Officer will issue a written invitation (by registered post) to the other party to the dispute to participate in the voluntary dispute resolution procedure. Failure by the other party to indicate to the Advisory Officer (in writing) their willingness to participate in the procedure within 2 weeks (during which a reminder will issue) will be deemed to be a breach of the time frame. During this two-week period the Advisory Officer will seek to arrange a preliminary meeting with the other party.

4. On receipt of written confirmation (within 2 weeks) of the other party's willingness to participate in the procedure the Advisory Officer will work with the parties in an attempt to resolve the issues in dispute over a period of 4 weeks.

5. If progress is being made it may be agreed by the parties to extend the time frame. In this context the parties will seek the views of the Advisory Officer as to the likelihood of progress being made through the Labour Relations Commission intervention in the event of any such agreed extension. During any such extension an agreed cooling-off period can be put in place and the Advisory Officer will continue to work with the parties in an attempt to resolve any outstanding issues. The Labour Relations Commission may engage expert assistance throughout the procedure, including the involvement of ICTU and IBEC, should that prove helpful to the resolution of any differences.

6. If after the six-week period or following any agreed extension, including any agreed cooling-off period, all issues have been resolved, the Advisory Officer will disengage and the procedure will be deemed to be completed. Before disengaging, the Advisory Officer may make proposals to the parties for the peaceful resolution of any future grievances or disputes.

7. In the event of issues remaining unresolved the procedure will be deemed to have been exhausted and the Advisory Officer will then make an immediate written report to the Labour Court on the situation.

APPENDIX

Prescribed Format for Referrals to the Labour Relations Commission

The referring party must ensure that the following details are made available to the Labour Relations Commission at the time of referral and that all referrals are addressed to the **Director of the Advisory Service, Labour Relations Commission, Tom Johnson House, Haddington Road, Dublin 4.**

- Name and address of union official and contact number/fax/email address.
- Name and address of company, contact person, number/fax/e-mail address and details of any representative organisation where known (IBEC, CIF etc.)
- Category of members i.e. general operatives, admin., production, technical etc.
- A description of the issues in dispute.
- Any correspondence or dialogue entered into with other party by the initiating party.

Industrial Relations Act 1990 (Code of Practice on Victimisation) (Declaration) Order 2004[11]

(SI 139/2004)

WHEREAS the Labour Relations Commission has prepared under subsection (1) of section 42 of the Industrial Relations Act 1990 (No. 19 of 1990), a draft code of practice on victimisation arising from an employee's membership or activity on behalf of a trade union or a manager discharging his or her managerial functions, or other employees:

AND WHEREAS the Labour Relations Commission has complied with subsection (2) of that section and has submitted the draft code of practice to the Minister for Enterprise, Trade and Employment;

NOW THEREFORE, I, Frank Fahey, Minister of State at the Department of Enterprise, Trade and Employment, in exercise of the powers conferred on me by subsection (3) of that section, the Labour (Transfer of Departmental Administration and Ministerial Functions) Order 1993 (S.I. No. 18 of 1993), (as adapted by the Enterprise and Employment (Alteration of Name of Department and Title of Minister) Order 1997 (S.I. No. 305 of 1997)), and the Enterprise, Trade and Employment (Delegation of Ministerial Functions) Order 2003 (S.I. No. 156 of 2003), hereby order as follows:

1. This Order may be cited as the Industrial Relations Act 1990 (Code of Practice on Victimisation) (Declaration) Order 2004.

2. It is hereby declared that the code of practice set out in the Schedule to this Order shall be a code of practice for the purposes of the Industrial Relations Act 1990 (No. 19 of 1990).

SCHEDULE

1 Introduction

1. Section 42 of the Industrial Relations Act, 1990 provides for the preparation of draft Codes of Practice by the Labour Relations Commission for submission to the Minister, and for the making, by him/her of an order declaring that a draft Code of Practice received by him/her under section 42 and scheduled to the order shall be a Code of Practice for the purposes of the said Act.

2. Paragraph 9.22 of Partnership 2000 for Inclusion, Employment and Competitiveness established a High Level Group on Trade Union Recognition. The High Level Group, involving the Departments of the Taoiseach, Finance and Enterprise, Trade and Employment, the Irish Congress of Trade Unions (ICTU), the Irish Business and Employers Confederation (IBEC) and IDA-Ireland, considered proposals submitted by the ICTU on the Recognition of Unions and the Right to Bargain and took account of European developments and the detailed position of IBEC on the impact of the ICTU.

---

proposals. As a result of these deliberations a set of procedures were put in place in the Code of Practice on Voluntary Dispute Resolution (S.I. No. 145 of 2000) and the Industrial Relations (Amendment) Act 2001.

3. Article 8.9 of Sustaining Progress Social Partnership Agreement 2003–2005 provides for the further development of employee representation. It was agreed by the trade union and employer organisations that there was a need to enhance the effectiveness of the existing procedures put in place in the Code of Practice on Voluntary Dispute Resolution and the Industrial Relations (Amendment) Act 2001.

4. Among the measures agreed for this purpose was the introduction of a new Code of Practice setting out the different types of practice which would constitute victimisation arising from an employee's membership or activity on behalf of a trade union or a manager discharging his or her managerial functions, or other employees.

5. In April 2003 the Minister for Enterprise, Trade and Employment requested the Commission under section 42(1) of the Industrial Relations Act 1990 to prepare a draft Code of Practice on Victimisation pursuant to the provisions of Article 8.9 of Sustaining Progress Social Partnership Agreement 2003–2005.

6. When preparing and agreeing this Code of Practice, the Commission consulted with relevant organisations and took account of the views expressed to the maximum extent possible.

7. The major objective of the Code is the setting out of the different types of practice which would constitute victimisation arising from an employee's membership or activity on behalf of a trade union or a manager discharging his or her managerial functions, or other employees.

2. Purpose

1. The purpose of this Code of Practice is to outline, for the guidance of employers, employees and trade unions, the different types of practice which would constitute victimisation.

2. Victimisation in the context of this Code of Practice refers to victimisation arising from an employee's membership or non membership, activity or non-activity on behalf of a trade union or an excepted body, or a manager discharging his or her managerial functions, or any other employee in situations where negotiating arrangements are not in place and where collective bargaining fails to take place (and where the procedures under the Code of Practice on Voluntary Dispute Resolution have been invoked or steps have been taken to invoke such procedures).

3. Definitions

1. For the purposes of this Code, victimisation is defined in general terms as any adverse or unfavourable treatment that cannot be justified on objective grounds (objective grounds do not include membership of, or activity on behalf of, a trade union) in the context referred to at Clause 2 above. It shall not include any act constituting a dismissal of the employee within the meaning of the Unfair Dismissals Act 1977 to 2001, where there is a separate recourse available. For the avoidance of doubt, 'employee' in this

Code includes any person in the employment concerned, the duties of whom consist of or include managing the business or activity to which the employment relates.

For the purposes of this Code none of the following

    (a) the employer,

    (b) an employee, or

    (c) a trade union or an excepted body,

shall victimise an employee or (as the case may be) another employee in the employment concerned on account of

    i. the employee being or not being a member of a trade union or an excepted body, or

    ii. the employee engaging or not engaging in any activities on behalf of a trade union or an excepted body, or

    iii. the employee exercising his/her managerial duties, where applicable, to which the employment relates on behalf of the employer.

2. Examples of unfair or adverse treatment (whether acts of commission or omission) that cannot be justified on objective grounds may in the above contexts include an employee suffering any unfavourable change in his/her conditions of employment or acts that adversely affect the interest of the employee; action detrimental to the interest of an employee not wishing to engage in trade union activity or the impeding of a manager in the discharge of his/her managerial functions.

3. The legal definitions of employer, employee, contract of employment and trade unions shall be as set out in Part III of the Industrial Relations Act 1990. A trade union shall be taken to mean any authorised trade union as defined in the Trade Union Act 1941.

4. Avoidance

1. Where there is a dispute in an employment where collective bargaining fails to take place and where negotiating arrangements are not in place, no person, be they union representative, individual employee or manager, should be victimised or suffer disadvantage as a consequence of their legitimate actions or affiliation arising from that dispute. The positions and views of all concerned should be respected and all parties should commit themselves to resolve issues in dispute expeditiously and without personal rancour.

5. Procedure for Addressing Complaints of Vicimisation

1. A procedure for addressing complaints of victimisation is set out in the Industrial Relations (Miscellaneous Provisions) Act 2004. Section 9 of the Act provides that a complaint may be presented to a Rights Commissioner.

EXPLANATORY NOTE

This note is not part of the Instrument and does not purport to be a legal interpretation.

The effect of this Order is to declare that the draft Code of Practice set out in the Schedule to this Order is a Code of Practice for the purposes of the Industrial Relations Act 1990.

Index

All references are to *paragraph* numbers

Data protection (contd)
statistical research or other scientific purposes, 6.30
subject access rights
    exceptions, 6.44–6.45
    generally, 6.42–6.43
tax collection, and, 6.23
terminology, 6.15–6.18
Death
maternity leave, and, 5.13
Deductions from wages
pensions, and, 11.45–11.46
Defence forces
race discrimination, and, 13.133
unfair dismissal, and, 14.75
Deferred payments
remuneration, and, 11.02
Department of Enterprise, Trade and Employment
generally, 1.31
Different treatment
fixed-term workers, and 10.27
Direct discrimination
And see DISCRIMINATION
age discrimination, 13.155–13.160
generally, 13.09
Direct effect
fixed-term workers, and
    broader implications, 10.23
    generally, 10.14–10.22
Directors
employment status, and, 2.66
Disability discrimination
'appropriate measures', 13.194
comparator, 13.199
'disability', 13.190–13.191
dismissal, and, 13.206–13.208
educational qualification, and, 13.209–13.210
exceptions, 13.209–13.210
generally, 13.190–13.195
harassment, and, 13.21
occupation qualification, and, 13.209–13.210
pensions, and, 11.130–11.132

pre-employment medical, 13.200
'reasonable accommodation', 13.192–13.193, 13.201–13.205
redress
    available orders, 13.211
    compensation awards, 13.212–13.216
    introduction, 13.211
    order that person take a specified course of action, 13.217–13.219
remuneration rate, 13.195
scope of disability, 13.196–13.198
Disciplinary procedure
standard contract terms, and, 3.28–3.29
Discovery orders
bullying, harassment and stress at work, and, 7.94–7.96
Discrimination
access to employment, 13.05
age discrimination
    burden of proof, 13.169–13.171
    collective agreements, and, 13.154
    costs, 13.168
    direct discrimination, 13.155–13.160
    ethos and approach, 13.166–13.167
    exceptions, 13.153–13.154
    generally, 13.147–13.149
    harassment, and, 13.21
    indirect discrimination, 13.161–13.168
    interview process, 13.172–13.173
    legislative framework, 13.150–13.152
    mandatory retirement age, and, 13.154
    occupational benefit schemes, and, 13.154
    pensions, and, 13.185–13.189
    post-qualification experience, 13.165
    promotions, 13.162–13.164
    recruitment, and, 13.154
    redundancy packages, 13.174–13.176
    retirement, and, 13.177–13.184
    scope of probation, 13.155–13.168
    seniority, and, 13.154
    severance packages, 13.174–13.176
association, by, 13.10